Readings in
Computer Architecture

Readings in Computer Architecture

Mark D. Hill
University of Wisconsin-Madison

Norman P. Jouppi
Compaq Western Research Laboratory

Gurindar S. Sohi
University of Wisconsin-Madison

MORGAN KAUFMANN PUBLISHERS

AN IMPRINT OF ACADEMIC PRESS
A Harcourt Science and Technology Company
SAN FRANCISCO   SAN DIEGO   NEW YORK   BOSTON
LONDON   SYDNEY   TOKYO

Senior Editor Denise E. M. Penrose
Director of Production and Manufacturing Yonie Overton
Production Editor Sarah Burgundy
Production Assistant Claire Montaut
Assistant Editor Marilyn Uffner Alan
Editorial Coordinator Meghan Keeffe
Cover Design Eileen Wagner
Text Design, Composition, and Pasteup Susan M. Sheldrake, ShelDragon Graphic Design
Copyeditor Kathy Finch
Indexer Steve Rath
Printer Victor Graphics

Designations used by companies to distinguish their products are often claimed as trademarks or registered trademarks. In all instances where Morgan Kaufmann Publishers is aware of a claim, the product names appear in initial capital or all capital letters. Readers, however, should contact the appropriate companies for more complete information regarding trademarks and registration.

Advice, Praise, and Errors: Any correspondence related to this publication or intended for the authors should be addressed to the Editorial and Sales Office of Morgan Kaufmann Publishers, Dept. CAR APE. Information regarding errors found in the original material is encouraged; electronic mail can be sent to carbugs@mkp.com. Please check the errata page at *http://www.mkp.com/architecture-readings* to see if the bug has already been reported.

ACADEMIC PRESS
A Harcourt Science and Technology Company
525 B Street, Suite 1900, San Diego, CA 92101-4495, USA
http://www.academicpress.com

Academic Press
Harcourt Place, 32 Jamestown Road, London, NW1 7BY, United Kingdom
http://www.academicpress.com

Morgan Kaufmann Publishers
340 Pine Street, Sixth Floor, San Francisco, CA 94104-3205, USA
http://www.mkp.com

04 03 02 01   5 4 3 2

Library of Congress Cataloging-in-Publication Data
Hill, Mark D. (Mark Donald)
    Readings in computer architecture / Mark D. Hill, Norman P. Jouppi, Gurindar Sohi.
        p.   cm.
    Includes bibliographical references (p.
    ISBN 1-55860-539-8
    1. Computer architecture. I. Jouppi, Norman P. (Norman Paul) II. Sohi, Gurindar. III. Title
QA76.9.A73H55 2000
004.2'2—dc21
                                                                99-44480
                                                                CIP

To Sue, Nicole, and Gregory
To Lili, Mark, and Matthew
To Marilyn and Jacinth

Contents

Preface

In theory, theory and practice are the same.
In practice, they're different.
—Attribution unknown

We are pleased to present you with this collection of readings in computer architecture. Computer architecture can be considered the science and art of selecting and interconnecting hardware components to create a computer that meets functional, performance, and cost goals. Computer architecture has a rich history of practice whose mastery aids those interested in moving the field forward.

Computer architecture continues to flourish in a dynamic environment. One can think of it as an interface with hardware implementation technologies below and application and system software above. From below, exponential semiconductor advances continue to provide a greater number of faster transistors, while at the same time altering tradeoffs both on and between chips (e.g., on-chip wires can exceed gate delays). Architects use the additional transistors in new ways to make the compound growth of a computer system's capacity exceed the rate at which transistors are getting faster.

From above, the applications that use architectures change. Classic applications have evolved, while new application domains emerge as advances make computing cost-effective to new areas. Application areas include scientific computing (e.g., quantum dynamics to vehicle crash simulation), business data processing (e.g., accounting to data mining), personal productivity tools (e.g., word processing and spreadsheets), global connectivity (e.g., electronic mail to telecommuting), and emerging applications (e.g., personal digital assistants to virtual reality).

It is to the students, researchers, and practitioners of this dynamic field of computer architecture that we offer this new collection of readings. The rest of this preface discusses why we are introducing this reader now, how we select and introduce papers, and how one might use this reader.

Why Have a Computer Architecture Reader Now?

Why a reader now, when the last widely successful readers are decades old, there are good textbooks in the field, and the Web is expanding as a source for technical information? In our view, the last widely successful collection of readings in computer architecture was from Bell and Newell in 1971 [2] updated by Siewiorek in 1982 [6]. These readers were excellent, but much has happened since they were published, and they are currently out of print.

Another reader that complements this one is the recently published collection of selected papers from the first twenty-five years of the *International Symposium on Computer Architecture* (ISCA) edited by Sohi in 1998 [8]. Our reader differs from the ISCA reader in two important ways. First, we have drawn papers from many sources, not just from the ISCA. Second, we have contributed introductory material that puts multiple papers in context. In contrast, the ISCA reader has an introduction by each of the original author groups that describes how their paper came about, and, sometimes, their view on its future impact. We find these insights valuable and recommend the ISCA reader to you as well.

Why have a reader when there are good textbooks in the field? The answer to this question has deep roots in the history of science. A *primary source* is a work written by the people who did the work (discovery, invention, etc.) and when they did it. A *secondary source* is a work written after the primary source and usually by different authors. Textbooks are the vehicle usually used to introduce people to scientific or engineering disciplines. Textbooks are secondary sources designed for teaching. They summarize, synthesize, and interpret work in the intellectual model (*paradigm*) that prevails when they are written. They are indispensable for giving people a reasonably recent snapshot of the state of the art. Noteworthy textbooks in computer architecture include Almasi and Gottlieb [1], Culler, Singh, and Gupta [3], Hennessy and Patterson [4], and Stone [9].

Students and professionals who wish to contribute to advancing a field, however, must eventually move beyond textbooks to primary sources. New primary sources provide the most recent thinking that will not appear in textbooks for one or more years. In computer architecture, the pressure on "bleeding-edge" primary sources is so great that conference papers have more impact on intellectual progress than do journal papers (which have a longer delay between submission and appearance).

This reader contains many old primary sources. We see three reasons why people should read both old and new primary sources. First, the experience of reading old primary sources trains people to read new ones. Second, it makes them aware of the process of discovering. Primary sources over time give a "motion picture" rather than a "snapshot," enabling people to see how the movie progresses and how they might continue moving the movie forward. Finally, it allows people to see ideas in the context of multiple paradigms instead of just within the current paradigm. Students in the early 1980s, for example, could take whole courses on computer architecture with no mention of out-of-order execution, which was previously invented but out of vogue. We encourage readers interested in how science advances to read the landmark primary source by Thomas Kuhn [5].

Why have a reader when people can just use the Web? The primary value of this reader is our editorial judgment for selecting papers (discussed in the following section) and background we provide in introducing them and placing them in context. This value is not diminished by the existence of the World Wide Web.

A secondary value of a reader is the coalescing into one hard copy the hard copies of many papers that are time consuming to obtain. This value remains present for the many pre-Web papers we have selected (and is enhanced as post-Web researchers are more reluctant to do the leg work to obtain hard copies the traditional way). This value is significantly diminished, however, for post-Web papers.

Our approach is to turn the Web into an advantage. This hard copy reader is supplemented with a Web component at URL:

http://www.mkp.com/architecture-readings.

This Web page is modeled after this hard copy reader. Its ten sections follow the ten chapters of this reader. Each section contains pointers to recent papers and some text to introduce them and put them in con-

text. In particular, the papers represent the best of the state of the art (e.g., a new microprocessor paper). Furthermore, our Web component will be updated, at least, annually to make this reader a living document that responds more rapidly than is possible with hard copy editions. Thus, the Web allows us to dynamically extend the value of our editorial judgment in a way not practical before the Web.

What's in this Reader and Why?

This reader focuses on what we believe are and will continue to be the critical issues facing computer architects. These include issues in *technology, evaluation methods, instruction set design, instruction level parallelism, dataflow/multithreading, memory systems, input/output systems, single-instruction multiple data parallelism,* and *multiple-instruction multiple data parallelism.* The down side of our focus, however, is that many important areas of inquiry are not covered (e.g., computer-aided design and computer arithmetic).

After limiting our focus, we were still left with the challenging task of selecting fifty-odd papers to fill a single bound volume from thousands of computer architecture papers that have been published. (For this reason, we hope that you do not judge us too harshly if we left out a few of your favorite papers.) We have used several guidelines for selecting papers. We looked for papers that:

- are primary sources
- have lasting impact
- are readable
- are an illustrative case study
- contribute insight to the modern reader

We did not apply these guidelines rigidly, in part, because they can contradict one another (e.g., some primary sources are inscrutable to the modern reader). One consequence of our emphasis on primary sources is that we exclude most survey papers, including influential ones (e.g., Smith's cache survey [7]).

Furthermore, the papers selected (and our original material) underwent two rounds of thoughtful review and discussion with a dozen researchers from academia and industry. They—see the acknowledgments at the end of this preface—helped to refine the selected papers to even better reflect what the community considers important as well as what students should know. We, the editors, resolved conflicts in the advice we received and accept all responsibility for the final version.

We have organized this reader into ten chapters. Each chapter is introduced by some original material that places the papers in context, introducing each and, in many cases, providing additional content pertinent to the chapter topic but beyond the scope of the included papers.

Chapter 1, Classic Machines: Technology, Implementation, and Economics; examines the foundation of computer architecture. This chapter begins a discussion of classic machines from the ENIAC to Cray's machines with an emphasis on how implementation technologies influenced architecture. It then discusses Gordon Moore's amazing technology predictions from the 1960s (e.g., Moore's Law) and how they lead to microprocessor-based computers. Included papers discuss IBM 360, CDC 6600, Cray 1, Moore's predictions, and early Intel microprocessors.

Chapter 2, Methods, is not about computer architecture, per se, but about some of the methods used to evaluate and refine architectures. Without these methods, the progress we have come to expect would not be possible. This chapter discusses the scientific method and the three major classes of methods that computer architects use: analytic modeling, simulation, and system monitoring. Techniques are illustrated with case studies from memory hierarchy evaluation. Included papers present Amdahl's Law, a system-monitoring study of the VAX-11/780, and trace-driven simulation algorithms of evaluating alternative caches.

Chapter 3, Instruction Sets, discusses the interface between software and hardware that is so critical, in that it enables software to run on multiple generations of hardware. This chapter examines how changes in implementation technology and compiler technology have changed instruction set tradeoffs, including putting the complex instruction set computer (CISC) versus reduced instruction set computer (RISC) debate of the 1980s into perspective. Included papers discuss instruction sets as compiler targets, RISC, CISC, the most widely used instruction set (Intel 80386), and ideas on predication pertinent to emerging instruction sets such as IA-64.

Chapter 4, Instruction Level Parallelism (ILP), examines issues critical to accelerating processor execution rates beyond the increases provided by faster transistors and bit-level parallelism. This chapter examines issues for executing multiple instructions in parallel, which include hazards, precise exceptions, speculative execution, branch prediction, and explicitly parallel architectures, such as very long instruction word (VLIW). Included papers discuss the IBM

360/91, IBM RS/6000, MIPS R10000, branch prediction, precise exceptions, out-of-order execution, and a survey of instruction level parallelism issues.

Chapter 5, Dataflow and Multithreading, discusses these two approaches to increasing parallelism and tolerating latency. Dataflow has had considerable intellectual impact, and multithreading appears poised to significantly impact practice. This chapter explains how classic dataflow pushes limits by eliminating the program counter, whereas multithreading more conventionally (and more practically) uses multiple program counters. Included papers discuss foundational dataflow work, the tagged-token dataflow approach, an early multithreaded computer (HEP), and recent simultaneous multithreading ideas.

Chapter 6, Memory Systems, examines caches and virtual memory, two critical aspects of the memory hierarchy that can largely determine sustained computer performance. Because textbooks cover both concepts in detail, both discussions begin with early concepts and then examine selected more-recent concepts that are illustrated in the papers. Included are cache papers that discuss the first data cache proposals (Wilkes), the first commercial cache (IBM 380/85), nonblocking caches, snooping cache coherence, and victim caches/stream buffers. Included virtual memory papers present the first virtual memory system (Atlas), a 1980s virtual memory system from VAX-11/780, and a case study of some of the interactions between caches and virtual memory.

Chapter 7, I/O: Storage, Networks, and Graphics, examines systems needed to make computers interact with the outside world. In particular, this chapter discusses Input/Output (I/O) economics, presents a case study of personal computer (PC) I/O systems options, and introduces included papers. Included papers discuss historical I/O systems, disk modeling, redundant arrays of inexpensive disks (RAID), Ethernet local area network, routing in interconnection networks, and a case study of graphics support.

Chapter 8, Single Instruction Multiple Data (SIMD) Parallelism, discusses an approach to parallel computing where a single thread of control directs the manipulation of multiple data operations. SIMD's perceived utility has waxed and waned several times over the past decades. Even though interest in SIMD has currently waned, readers should be familiar with it because it is likely to wax again in the future. This chapter introduces basic SIMD concepts and included papers. Included papers discuss the original SIMD/MIMD taxonomy, a SIMD machine that issued dependent operations (BSP), and massive processing in memory.

Chapter 9, Multiprocessors and Multicomputers, discusses computing systems in which multiple processors can operate independently. This is called *multiple instruction multiple data* (MIMD) parallelism. Such systems have long been the "future" of computing, but now they have finally earned substantial commercial success. This chapter discusses parallel software, shared-memory multiprocessors (processors joined via the memory system), multicomputers (processors joined via the I/O system), and selected future trends. Included shared-memory multiprocessor papers discuss an early prototype machine (CMU C.mmp), memory consistency models, cache coherence, a recent scalable example (Stanford DASH), and a *cache-only memory architecture* (COMA). Multicomputer papers discuss an early multicomputer (Caltech Cosmic Cube) and shared memory on multicomputers.

Finally, Chapter 10, Recent Implementations and Future Prospects, revisits some of the issues for modern machines that Chapter 1 raised for classic machines. Included papers discuss Intel Pentium, Intel Pentium Pro, and future microprocessor trends.

How to Use this Book

We have prepared this book with the hope that it will be valuable to both professionals and students. Both groups can read these primary sources and our original commentary to learn more about the rich history of computer architecture and to better see how to move the field forward.

For instructors, we see three beneficial ways to use our reader. First, it can be used as a supplement to a primary textbook. At the University of Wisconsin, for example, we have a primary graduate architecture course that focuses on uniprocessors. Most recent instructors have used Hennessy and Patterson [4] and a custom reader of papers. We anticipate some instructors will use this reader and some recent papers from the Web (at this reader's Web site and elsewhere) to replace their current custom reader. Wisconsin also has a secondary graduate architecture course that focuses on parallel processing. It has recently used Culler, Singh, and Gupta [3] and a custom reader. As above, one could replace the custom reader with this reader and supplementary Web papers.

A second approach fits schools having a first course that uses a textbook and a second course whose orientation toward projects or case studies favors a custom reader. Once again, this reader and Web papers could replace the custom reader.

A third model is for graduate courses that eschew textbooks and just use readers (as occurs for some offerings of Wisconsin's courses). This approach requires considerable skill and effort from faculty to tie together disjoint ideas. Using this reader and selected other papers, possibly Web only, will ease the instructor's burden, because we make considerable effort to tie our included papers together.

Acknowledgments

We wish to thank the many people that have contributed ideas, comments, and criticism to this reader, especially Arvind, MIT; Douglas Clark, Princeton; Matthew Farrens, UC-Davis; Josh Fisher, Hewlett-Packard; Kourosh Gharachoraloo, Compaq; James Goodman, University of Wisconsin-Madison; John Hennessy, Stanford; Wen-Mei Hwu, University of Illinois at Champaign-Urbana; Dave Nagle, Carnegie Mellon; Rishiyur Nikhil, Compaq; Yale Patt, University of Michigan; Constantine Polychronopoulos, University of Illinois at Champaign-Urbana; Todd Rockoff, Advantest; Balaram Sinharoy, IBM T. J. Watson Research Center; Jim Smith, University of Wisconsin-Madison; Mike Smith, Harvard; Mark Smotherman, Clemson; Dan Sorin, University of Wisconsin-Madison; Mateo Valero, Universitat Politcnica de Catalunya; David Wood, University of Wisconsin-Madison; and Cheng-Zhong Xu, Wayne State. Of course, all responsibility for what is said or included in this reader falls on us.

We also want thank the wonderful staff at Morgan Kaufmann for their talents, efforts, and encouragement, especially Denise Penrose, Marilyn Alan, Sarah Burgundy, and Meghan Keeffe.

References

[1] G. S. Almasi and A. Gottlieb. *Highly Parallel Computing.* Menlo Park, CA: Benjamin/Cummings, 1994.

[2] C. G. Bell and A. Newell. *Computer Structures: Readings and Examples.* New York: McGraw-Hill, 1971.

[3] D. Culler, J. P. Singh, and A. Gupta. *Parallel Computer Architecture: A Hardware/Software Approach,* San Francisco, CA: Morgan Kaufmann, 1998.

[4] J. L. Hennessy and D. A. Patterson. *Computer Architecture: A Quantitative Approach,* 2nd ed. San Francisco, CA: Morgan Kaufmann, 1996.

[5] T. S. Kuhn. *The Structure of Scientific Revolutions*, 2nd ed. Chicago, IL: Univ. of Chicago Press, 1970.

[6] D. P. Siewiorek, C. G. Bell, and A. Newell. *Computer Structures: Principles and Examples.* New York: McGraw-Hill, 1982.

[7] A. J. Smith. Cache Memories. *ACM Computing Surveys*, 14(3):473–530, 1982.

[8] G. S. Sohi. *25 Years of the International Symposia on Computer Architecture: Selected Papers.* New York, NY: ACM Press, 1998.

[9] H. S. Stone. *High-Performance Computer Architecture*, 3rd ed. Reading, MA: Addison-Wesley, 1993.

Included Papers

Chapter 1: Classic Machines: Technology, Implementation, and Economics

G. M. Amdahl, G. A. Blaauw, and F. P. Brooks, Jr., "Architecture of the IBM System/360," *IBM Journal of Research and Development*, Apr. 1964.

J. E. Thornton, "Parallel operation in the Control Data 6600," *Fall Joint Computers Conference*, vol. 26, pp. 33–40, 1961.

R. M. Russell, "The CRAY-1 computer system," *Communications of the ACM*, 21(1):63–72, 1978.

J. S. Kolodzey, "CRAY-1 computer technology," *IEEE Transactions on Components, Hybrids, and Manufacturing Technology*, CHMT-4(2), pp. 181–187, June 1981.

G. E. Moore, "Cramming more components onto integrated circuits," *Electronics*, pp. 114–117, Apr. 1965.

S. Mazor, "The history of the microcomputer—Invention and evolution," *Proceedings of the IEEE*, pp. 1601–1607, Dec. 1995.

Chapter 2: Methods

G. M. Amdahl, "Validity of the single processor approach to achieving large scale computing capabilities," *AFIPS Conference Proceedings*, pp. 483–485, Apr. 1967.

M. D. Hill and A. J. Smith, "Evaluating associativity in CPU caches," *IEEE Transactions on Computers*, C-38(12):1612–1630, 1989.

J. S. Emer and D. W. Clark, "A characterization of processor performance in the VAX-11/780," *Proceedings of the Eleventh International Symposium on Computer Architecture*, Ann Arbor, MI, pp. 301–310, June 1984.

Chapter 3: Instruction Sets

W. A. Wulf, "Compilers and computer architecture," *IEEE Computer*, 14(7):41–48, 1981.

G. Radin, "The 801 minicomputer," *Proceedings of the Symposium on Architectural Support for Programming Languages and Operating Systems*, pp. 39–47, Mar. 1982.

D. A. Patterson and D. R. Ditzel, "The case for the reduced instruction set computer," *ACM Computer Architecture News*, 8(6):25–33, 15 Oct. 1980.

R. P. Colwell, C. Y. Hitchcock III, E. D. Jensen, H. M. Brinkley Sprunt, and C. P. Kollar, "Instruction Sets and Beyond: Computers, complexity, and controversy," *IEEE Computer*, 18(9), 1985.

J. Crawford, "Architecture of the Intel 80386," *Proceedings of the ICCD*, pp. 155–160, Oct. 1986.

S. A. Mahlke, R. E. Hank, J. E. McCormick, D. I. August, and W. W. Hwu, "A comparison of full and partial predicated execution support for ILP processors," *Proceedings of the 22nd Annual Symposium on Computer Architecture* pp. 138–150, June 1995.

Chapter 4: Instruction Level Parallelism (ILP)

D. W. Anderson, F. J. Sparacio, and R. M. Tomasulo, "The IBM System/360 model 91: Machine philosophy and instruction-handling," *IBM Journal of Research and Development*, Jan. 1967.

J. E. Smith and A. R. Pleszkun, "Implementing precise interrupts in pipelined processors," *IEEE Transactions on Computers*, C-37(5):562–573, May 1988.

J. E. Smith, "A study of branch prediction strategies," *Proceedings of the Eighth Annual Symposium on Computer Architecture*, pp. 135–148, May 1981.

T.-Y. Yeh and Y. N. Patt, "Two-level adaptive training branch prediction," *Proceedings of the 24th Annual Workshop on Microprogramming (MICRO-24)*, Albuquerque, NM, pp. 55–60, Dec. 1991.

Y. N. Patt, W. W. Hwu, and M. Shebanow, "HPS, a new microarchitecture: Introduction and rationale," *Proceedings of the 18th Annual Workshop on Microprogramming*, Pacific Grove, CA, pp. 103–108, Dec. 1985.

G. S. Sohi and S. Vajapeyam, "Instruction issue logic for high-performance, interruptable pipelined processors," *Proceedings of the 14th Annual Symposium on Computer Architecture* pp. 27–34, June 1987.

G. F. Grohoski, "Machine organization of the IBM RISC System/6000 processor," *IBM Journal of Research and Development*, 34(1):37–58, 1990.

K. C. Yeager "The Mips R10000 superscalar microprocessor," *IEEE Micro*, 16(2):28–40, 1996.

B. R. Rau and J. A. Fisher, "Instruction-level parallel processing: History, overview, and perspective," *The Journal of Supercomputing*, 7(1):9–50, 1993. Reprinted in Rau and Fisher (eds.), *Instruction-Level Parallelism*, Norwell, MA: Kluwer, 1993.

Chapter 5: Dataflow and Multithreading

J. B. Dennis and D. P. Misunas, "A preliminary architecture for a basic data-flow processor," *Proceedings of the 2nd Annual Symposium on Computer Architecture, Computer Architecture News*, 3(4):126–132, 1974.

Arvind and R. S. Nikhil, "Executing a program on the MIT tagged-token dataflow architecture," *IEEE Transactions on Computers*, 39(3):300–318, 1990.

B. J. Smith, "Architecture and applications of the HEP multiprocessor computer system," *Proceedings of the International Society for Optical Engineering*, 241–248, 1981.

D. M. Tullsen, S. J. Eggers, J. S. Emer, H. M. Levy, J. L. Lo, and R. L. Stamm, "Exploiting choice: Instruction fetch and issue on an implementable simultaneous multithreading processor," *Proceedings of the 23rd Annual Symposium on Computer Architecture*, pp. 191–202, May 1996.

Chapter 6: Memory Systems

M. V. Wilkes, "Slave memories and dynamic storage allocation," *IEEE Transactions on Electronic Computers*, EC-14(2):270–271, 1965.

J. S. Liptay, "Structural aspects of the System/360 model 85, part II: The cache," *IBM Systems Journal*, 7(1):15–21, 1968.

D. Kroft, "Lockup-free instruction fetch/prefetch cache organization," *Proceedings of the Eighth Symposium on Computer Architecture* pp. 81–87, May 1981.

J. R. Goodman, "Using cache memory to reduce processor-memory traffic," *Proceedings of the Tenth International Symposium on Computer Architecture*, Stockholm, Sweden, pp. 124–131, June 1983.

N. P. Jouppi, "Improving direct-mapped cache performance by the addition of a small fully-associative cache and prefetch buffers," *Proceedings of the 17th Annual Symposium on Computer Architecture, Computer Architecture News*, 18(2):364–373, 1990

T. Kilburn, D. B. G. Edwards, M. J. Lanigan, and F. H. Sumner, "One-level storage system," *IRE Transactions*, EC-11(2):223–235, 1962.

D. W. Clark and J. S. Emer, "Performance of the VAX-11/780 translation buffer: Simulation and measurement," *ACM Transactions on Computer Systems*, 3(1):31–62, 1985.

W.-H. Wang, J.-L. Baer, and H. M. Levy, "Organization and performance of a two-level virtual-real cache hierarchy," *Proceedings of the 16th Annual International Symposium on Computer Architecture*, Jerusalem, pp. 140–148, June 1989.

Chapter 7: I/O: Storage Systems, Networks, and Graphics

M. Smotherman, "A sequencing-based taxonomy of I/O systems and review of historical machines," *ACM Computer Architecture News* 17(5):5–15, Sept. 1989.

Storage Systems
C. Ruemmler and J. Wilkes, "An introduction to disk drive modeling," *IEEE Computer* 27(3):17–28, 1994.

D. A. Patterson, G. Gibson, and R. H. Katz, "A case for redundant arrays of inexpensive disks (RAID)," *Proceedings of the ACM SIGMOD Conference*, Chicago, IL, June 1988.

Networks
R. M. Metcalfe and D. R. Boggs, "Ethernet: Distributed packet switching for local computer networks." *Communications of the ACM*, 19(7):395–404.

L. M. Ni and P. K. McKinley, "A survey of wormhole routing techniques in direct networks," *IEEE Computer*, 26(2):62–76, 1993.

Graphics
K. Akeley, "Reality engine graphics," *SIGGRAPH '93 Proceedings*, pp. 109–116.

Chapter 8: Single-Instruction Multiple Data (SIMD) Parallelism

M. J. Flynn, " Very high-speed computing systems," *Proceedings of the IEEE* , vol. 54, no. 12, Dec. 1966.

D. J. Kuck and R. A. Stokes, "The Burroughs scientific processor (BSP)," *IEEE Transactions on Computers*, C-31(5):363–376, 1982.

M. Gokhale, B. Holmes, and K. Iobst, "Processing in memory: The Terasys massively parallel PIM array," *IEEE Computer*, 28(4):23–31, 1995.

Chapter 9: Multiprocessors and Multicomputers

W. A. Wulf and S. P. Harbison, "Reflections in a pool of processors/An experience report on C.mmp/Hydra," *Proceedings of the National Computer Conference (AFIPS)*, June 1978.

L. Lamport, "How to make a multiprocessor computer that correctly executes multiprocess programs," *IEEE Transactions on Computers*, C-28(9):690–691, 1979.

L. M. Censier and P. Feautrier, "A new solution to coherence problems in multicache systems," *IEEE Transactions on Computers*, C-27(12):1112–1118, 1978.

D. Lenoski, J. Laudon, K. Gharachorloo, W.-D. Weber, A. Gupta, J. Hennessy, M. Horowitz, and M. Lam, "The Stanford Dash multiprocessor," *IEEE Computer*, 25(3):63–79, 1992.

E. Hagersten, A. Landin, and S. Haridi "DDM—A cache-only memory architecture," *IEEE Computer*, 25(9):44–54, 1992.

C. L. Seitz, "The cosmic cube," *Communications of the ACM*, pp. 22–33, Jan. 1985.

K. Li and P. Hudak, "Memory coherence in shared virtual memory systems," *ACM Transactions on Computer Systems*, 7(4):321–359, 1989.

Chapter 10: Recent Implementations and Future Prospects

D. Alpert and D. Avnon, "Architecture of the Pentium microprocessor," *IEEE Micro*, 13(3):11–21, 1993.

D. Papworth, "Tuning the Pentium Pro microarchitecture," *IEEE Micro*, 16(2):8–15, 1996.

M. Slater, "The microprocessor today," *IEEE Micro*, 16(6):32–44, 1996.

A. Yu, "The future of microprocessors," *IEEE Micro*, 16(6):46–53, 1996.

CHAPTER 1

Classic Machines: Technology, Implementation, and Economics

1.1 Introduction

The technology for implementation of computing systems has varied widely over the last one hundred years. Computers and their architecture at any point in time have been a consequence of the capabilities and limitations of the technology of their day. In this section, we illustrate this principle with a brief tour of computer history from a technological standpoint. It is essential to have a good understanding of technology, the trend of its advancement, and its limitations in order to have a good understanding of future developments in computers and their architecture.

1.2 Early Computer Technology

During the first third of the twentieth century, technology was limited to mechanical and electromechanical calculators.[1] During the 1930s, several experimenters began building electronic calculating machines with vacuum tubes. From 1937 through 1942, Atanasoff and Berry at Iowa State University constructed a computer (the ABC) using binary circuits built with vacuum tubes and a capacitive drum memory. This machine had almost become fully operational when the demands of World War II caused its development to stop. The next significant vacuum-tube computer development was the ENIAC, which became operational in 1945 at the Moore School of Electrical Engineering of the University of Pennsylvania.

1.2.1 ENIAC Computer Technology

The ENIAC had over 18,000 vacuum tubes. Vacuum tubes require a heater element in order to displace electrons from their cathodes. This requires a significant amount of power. The heater element also has a tendency to burn out after a period of operation. Thus, based on the total power consumed by all the tubes and the expected time between tube failures, there is a maximum practical size of a vacuum tube computer. At the time of ENIAC, many vacuum tubes had lifetimes of only a few thousand hours. Worse yet, tube failures were spread over the lifetime of the tube as described by probability distributions. Given these handicaps, one would think it would be impossible to build a computer with 18,000 tubes given these characteristics.

---

[1]Information about these early calculators and computers up until 1965 can be found in the excellent reference of Williams [26].

ENIAC: Courtesy of the Hagley Museum and Library

Fig. 1.1. A close-up view of the ENIAC with Pres Eckert. The large panel of rotary switches mounted on wheels is one of the three constant tables. Programs were entered using the banks of switches below waist level.

J. Presper Eckert solved the tube reliability problem with a number of techniques:

- Tube failures were bimodal, with more failures near the start of operation as well as after many hours and less during the middle operating hours. In order to achieve better reliability, he used tubes that had already been burnt-in and had not suffered from "infant mortality." Also, the machine was not turned off at nights because power cycling was a source of increased failures.

- Components were run at only one half of their rated capacity, reducing the stress and degradation of the tube and significantly increasing their operating lifetime.

- Binary circuits were used, so tubes that were becoming weak or leaky would not cause an immediate failure, as they would in an analog computer.

- The machine was built from circuit modules whose failure was easy to ascertain and that could be quickly replaced with identical modules.

As a result of this excellent engineering, ENIAC was able to run for as long as a day or two without a failure! ENIAC was capable of computing 5,000 operations per second. It took up 2,400 cubic feet of circuitry, weighed 30 tons, and consumed 140 kW of power.

The architecture of ENIAC was like an electronic version of a collection of mechanical adding machines. It had no main memory as we think of it today but only had a collection of 20 ten-digit accumulators. The digits in the accumulators were stored in rings consisting of ten flip-flops, with a digit being signified by the corresponding flip-flop being set and all of the others in the ring being clear. A ten-digit accumulator required a total of 550 vacuum tubes! Programs were entered on plugboard panels and numerical constants could be entered into three function tables consisting of cabinets of rotary switches (see Fig. 1.1).

Toward the end of the ENIAC project, Eckert, John Mauchly, John von Neumann, and others working on the project developed the idea of the stored-program computer. This was published in a report titled, "First

Draft of a Report on the EDVAC" [24] in June 1945, with von Neumann listed as the only author. Later, in the summer of 1946, a special summer institute was held at the Moore School. This institute was widely attended by researchers from around the world and led to a burst of computer construction at many places.

As can be imagined, the primary limitation of the ENIAC was its lack of a memory (especially for implementing a stored program). Even if a more-efficient binary representation was used for the memory, tube flip-flop circuits would be too expensive and unreliable to be used to build a stored program computer. What was needed was a reliable, inexpensive, and fast technology for memory. In the late 1940s and early 1950s researchers experimented with several different technologies for implementing computer memories. These included electrostatic memories (such as the Williams tube) and various types of acoustic delay lines (such as mercury delay lines).

1.2.2 EDSAC Computer Technology

Maurice Wilkes attended the 1946 summer institute at the Moore School and immediately returned to Cambridge University and embarked on implementing

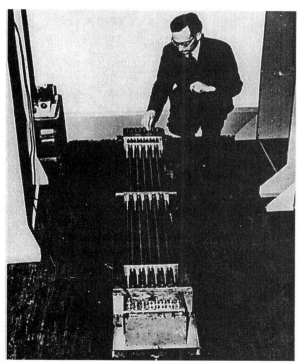

Courtesy of The Computer Museum of Boston

Fig. 1.2. Maurice Wilkes looking at the first set of mercury delay line memories for EDSAC. This set contained 16 tubes, of which the top row of five can be seen [25].

a stored-program computer. First, Wilkes attacked the problem of providing a memory for the computer. By early 1947, he had designed and built the first working mercury acoustic delay memory (see Fig. 1.2). It consisted of 16 steel tubes, each capable of storing 32 words of 17 bits each (16 bits plus a sign) for a total of 512 words (roughly 1 Kbytes). Now that a suitable memory technology had been demonstrated, design and construction of the machine could proceed. Because the mercury acoustic delay lines were a bit-serial memory technology, this dictated a bit-serial machine organization.

Wilkes was more interested in having a machine he could program than pushing the state of the art in hardware technology. As a result of this conservative hardware design, he settled on a machine cycle time (500 kHz) that was slower by a factor of two than other machines being discussed at the time. Partly as a result of this conservative hardware design and early success with practical memory technology, Electronic Delay Storage Automatic Calculator (EDSAC) became the first large-scale operational stored program computer in May of 1949. This lead to the project leading the way in many software innovations. One crucial innovation from the early experience of the EDSAC project was a subroutine call instruction that saved the calling address for later use as a return address. At the time, this was called the Wheeler jump, after David J. Wheeler who invented it while he was working on the project as a graduate student. Another innovation from Wheeler was the world's first relocating program loader.

Because of the clock cycle time of the machine and the bit-serial machine organization, simple commands took 1.5 ms. However, a bigger limitation was the speed of the I/O devices. EDSAC used paper tape readers and teleprinters for I/O devices. The teleprinters could print 10 characters per second, whereas an optical paper tape reader could read 50 characters per second (each character consisting of only 6 bits)!

1.2.3 Manchester/Ferranti Mark I Computer Technology

The University of Manchester was an early leader in the implementation of stored-program computers. A simple testbed machine with only five instructions and 32 words of memory ran the first stored program on June 21, 1948. Because of this early success, they decided to build a full-scale computer. The design work for this machine was contracted out to the Ferranti Corporation. The machine used Williams tubes invented at Manchester by Frederic C. Williams and Tom Kilburn for electrostatic main memory. But because the Williams tube only stored 32 words of 32 bits, there was a need for a larger storage device.

Andrew D. Booth at Birkbeck College in London was an early innovator of storage devices. He developed thermal memories, mechanical memories, delay lines, and rotating magnetic memories. After early experiments with disk memories failed, he developed the first drum memory with help from his father, a mechanical engineer.

The Manchester team decided to build a storage hierarchy with Williams tubes and a magnetic drum. By using eight upgraded Williams tubes, they provided a total of 256 forty-bit words of main memory in the Ferranti Mark I of 1951. This was backed up by a drum containing 16,384 words of storage. The Mark I only took 0.03 seconds to transfer a subroutine from the drum to main memory. (In comparison, EDSAC could only read 1.5 characters from a paper tape in this amount of time.) The Mark I was also the first computer with index registers. Their early experience with transferring blocks of memory from primary to secondary storage and expertise in addressing led to the Manchester team's invention of virtual memory in the Atlas machine in the late 1950s.

The Mark I was still a bit-serial machine (as dictated by the bit-serial access of the Williams tubes), so its operation was again rather slow compared to its cycle time. A typical operation such as addition required 1.2 ms. In order to further improve computer performance, a large-scale reliable main memory with reasonable cost and parallel access was needed so that a bit-parallel computer could be built.

1.2.4 Whirlwind Computer Technology

The Whirlwind machine was designed and built in the late 1940s and early 1950s at MIT [18]. It was intended to be a bit-parallel machine and so much faster than previous machines (hence its name). In addition, it was designed for a much faster maximum 5-MHz clock frequency. Initially it was designed using a rank of sixteen Williams tubes, making for a 16-bit parallel memory. However, the Williams tube memories were a limitation in terms of operating speed, reliability, and cost.

To solve this problem, Jay W. Forrester and others developed magnetic core memories. When the electrostatic memory was replaced with a primitive core memory, the operating speed of Whirlwind doubled, and the maintenance time on the machine fell from four hours per day to two hours per week, and the

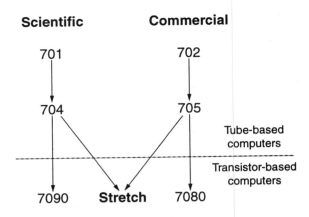

Fig. 1.3. The IBM Stretch's relations.

mean time between memory failures rose from two hours to two weeks! Core memory technology was crucial in enabling Whirlwind to perform 50,000 operations per second in 1952 and to operate reliably for relatively long periods of time.

Now that a good memory technology had been found, the tube circuits used for arithmetic and control became the major limitation.

1.2.5 Germanium Transistor-Based Computers: The IBM Stretch

By 1955, quite a few manufacturers were building computers based on vacuum tubes and magnetic core memories. Because the number of components available for design of the CPU's was limited by the reliability and cost of vacuum tubes, computers tended to be quite specialized in their targeted market segments. For example, a machine targeted toward scientific users could not afford to have circuitry for packed-decimal arithmetic for accounting; similarly, machines targeted for commercial users could not afford to support floating point. Moreover, machines targeted at high-performance users tended to have larger word lengths, which lower performance and lower cost machines could not afford. Coupled with programming in assembly language, this led to considerable development costs for all of the different models as well as incompatible software bases.

IBM had a scientific and a commercial tube-based computer line, starting with the 701 and 702 models, respectively. These models were significantly redesigned and improved and sold as the 704 and 705. In 1955, IBM initiated a research project to produce a computer one hundred times faster than both the 704 or the 705 models and incorporating both scientific and commercial functionality. This machine was

Stretch (IBM 7030): Photograph courtesy of IBM

Fig. 1.4. An overall view of Stretch, which was first shipped to customers in 1961.

formally called the 7030, but most people knew it by its project name "Stretch" [2, 5, 6]. Its place in the IBM product line is shown in Fig. 1.3. A photograph of Stretch is shown in Fig. 1.4.

By switching to early germanium transistor technology, the circuitry in Stretch ran ten times faster. Also, by using a high-speed core memory, memory access became about six times faster than the core memory in the 704. However, the project goals of two orders of magnitude speed improvement went far beyond the speedups obtainable from new technologies. This would require many architectural innovations which would, in turn, require many more circuits than previous computers, but this was made possible by the increased reliability, smaller size, and lower cost of transistors compared with vacuum tubes. This resulted in a theme that is still being exploited today: using additional circuits provided by technology to exploit instruction-level parallelism.

With Stretch, the exploitation of instruction-level parallelism took many novel forms. First, the processing of instructions was pipelined (this was called "overlapped" or "lookahead" then), so that six instructions were in some

phase of execution at any point in time. Second, in order to provide higher bandwidth to memory, memory was split into multiple banks. Because successive words were stored in different banks, new data could often be fetched every 0.2 μs even though the core memory had a 2-μs latency. Third, an autonomous transfer engine was provided to transfer data between the memory and peripheral devices (e.g., DMA or a primitive channel).

The designers realized that improving the performance of the CPU without improving the performance of the I/O devices would result in low overall system speedup. Thus, as part of the Stretch project the first disk drives with multiple read/write arms were developed. Their capacity (2 Mbytes) and transfer speed were far in excess of anything else available at the time and resulted in the abandonment of drums for secondary storage.

Although Stretch did not fully meet its goal of 100 times increase in performance (especially on commercial codes, which had byte-serial data storage—see Table 1.1), it resulted in many major advances in architecture and technology. Moreover, in combining both scientific and commercial capabilities, it was a precursor to the IBM System 360 architecture.

	Time in Microseconds		
Operation	**IBM 704**	**IBM 705**	**Stretch**
Floating add	84	–	1.0
Floating multiply	204	–	1.8
Floating divide	216	–	7.0
Five-digit add	–	119	3.5
Five-digit multiply	–	799	40.0
Five-digit divide	–	4828	65.0

Table 1.1. Key Operation Latencies in the IBM 704, 705, and Stretch

1.2.6 Large-Scale Planar Silicon Transistor Computers

There is a striking chronological relationship between the appearance of the silicon planar transistor and the Control Data 6600. —J. E. Thornton, *Design of a Computer: The Control Data 6600* [21], p. 19. See also Fig. 1.5, reprinted from p. 21 of Thornton [21].

Stretch was designed with germanium transistors. By the early 1960s, planar (double-diffused) silicon transistors had been developed, with significantly improved reliability and performance characteristics over germanium transistors. "Planar" refers to the fact that those transistors were made by diffusing impurities into a flat wafer of silicon to form the base and emitter.

The main benefits of silicon planar transistors over germanium are:

- higher junction temperatures allowed (and hence higher reliability at lower temperatures)
- higher current and power levels available
- higher speed (by using a n-p-n configuration instead of p-n-p)
- lower cost

The combination of all these advantages was a key enabler of a generation of machines in the mid 1960s with greatly improved performance, reliability, and cost. These machines included the CDC-6600 and the IBM 360 family.

1.3 The Rise and Fall of Supercomputers

Until the late 1990s, high-end CPUs were a breed apart. Historically, high-end computers were made using bipolar transistors. This is in contrast to the MOS transistors used in microprocessors today. Bipolar transistors in the

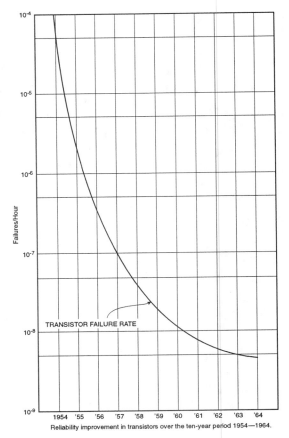

Transistor reliability graph from page 21 of Design of a Computer: The CDC 6600 *by Jim Thornton.*

Fig. 1.5. Reliability improvement in transistors over the 10-year period from 1954 to 1964.

1960s were relatively easy to make, because their active portion consisted of two p-n junctions that could be grown by diffusion processes. They were also more than ten times faster than early MOS transistors, which were not produced in practical numbers until the late 1960s.

Because bipolar transistors were relatively fast, much of the delay in an 1960s- or 1970s-era high-end computer resulted from the time required to send signals through the wires of the computer. Some high-end computers (such as the CDC Cyber 205 series) used coaxial wiring that allowed transmission of signals at 70% of the speed of light. However, the Cray machines used slightly slower twisted-pair wiring but relied on denser packaging and circuitry to reduce the size of the machine, hence reducing the delays caused by communicating from one part of the machine to another.

There were many models of supercomputers built by different manufacturers. In this section, we focus primarily on computers designed by Seymour Cray for three reasons. First, most of them were the highest

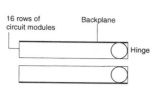

Fig. 1.6. A 1604 logic "book."

performance computers of their day. Second, they introduced a number of important architectural and implementation features. Third, by concentrating on a single lineage of computers, the underlying trends in technology become clearer.

The shape of machines built by Seymour Cray is an interesting study in itself. Seymour Cray was the champion of computer packaging and computational bandwidth. His first large scale machine, the CDC 1604, used a single "book" configuration. Two backplanes stuffed with sixteen rows of small circuit modules were flexibly mounted to the rest of the machine by hinges. This allowed the boards to be spread apart during construction or testing, like the pages in a young child's board book (see Fig. 1.6).

1.3.1 The CDC 6600

The CDC 6600 combined four books of four pages each with their spines facing the center of the machine. This formed an plus-shaped "+" center of the machine, as shown in Fig. 1.7. This configuration was later widely used by large mainframes and Japanese supercomputers. For photographs of the 6600 and other Cray machines, see the Web companion to this book for links to online photographs.

1.3.2 The CDC 7600

A major advance in the 7600 over the 6600 was the introduction of fully pipelined units. This gave it a peak performance around seven times faster than the 6600, even though the clock was not quite four times faster (27.5 ns). It also reduced the need to keep the components in such close proximity to each other. Instead of large blocks of unpipelined logic which had to be close to each other, pipelining the functional units allowed each individual functional unit pipestage to be smaller physically and faster even though the whole pipelined functional unit was larger. Fig. 1.8 shows the machine was constructed in the shape of a

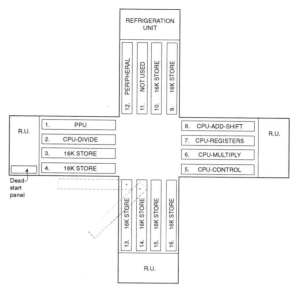

Figure 26 from page 35 of Thornton's Design of a Computer

Fig. 1.7. The classic 6600 plus-shaped machine configuration, widely used in later supercomputers by other makers. In the 6600, each page of the four books consisted of up to 756 "cordwood" logic modules.

large "C", with four panels on three sides and two panels and an opening on the fourth side.

The complete pipelining enabled the use of a large "C"-shaped chassis, but may have also required it. Because the machine was fully pipelined, the bandwidth required between units was greater than in the 6600. The restriction of edge-only access to each page in a book would provide much lower bandwidth than if the complete face of every page were accessible for

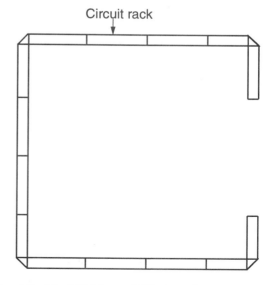

Fig. 1.8. The 7600 large "C"-shaped chasis configuration.

wiring. Whatever the case, the 7600 was certainly much easier to wire than the confined space between the spines of the four 6600 books. And as a final benefit, when seen from above the machine is the first letter of Seymour Cray's last name. Later machines at Control Data Corporation (CDC) under Jim Thornton elongated the classic plus-sign shape into a "t" shape.

Another major improvement in the 7600 over the 6600 was a significantly upgraded I/O system. Unlike the 6600, which implemented ten virtual peripheral processor units (PPUs) on a single physical PPU by time multiplexing, the 7600 had up to fifteen physical PPUs. This provided much higher performance I/O capabilities.

Once the functional units were completely pipelined, the limited number of registers provided in the 6600 architecture (of which the 7600 was back-wardly compatible) would be a major limit. Moreover, the 7600 was limited to issuing one instruction per cycle, a factor of nine less peak-instruction bandwidth than that provided by the fully pipelined functional units. Both these limitations were overcome by the addition of vector registers and operations in the Cray-1.

The 7600 had a 100×100 Linpak performance of 7X the 6600. It first shipped in 1969, five years after the 6600. This was an annualized performance improvement of 48%. For comparison, note that the annual scaling of device count from Moore's Law is 59%, and the annual scaling in MOS device speed from scaling theory [7] is 26%. The maximum potential performance increase for MOS devices would be given by the product of the device count and the device speed growth rates.

1.3.3 The 8600 Program

After the 7600, Seymour Cray moved back to his home town in Wisconsin with a group of engineers to work on the 8600. The 8600 tried out tightly coupled multiprocessors (it had four processors accessing a common memory), while a team in Minnesota under Thornton tried out vectors. The 8600 implemented an architecture similar to the 7600 but it was a bold packaging departure. The machine was much smaller and more of a true circular shape than the 7600. But the most challenging aspect of the 8600 was that its boards were full of tiny discrete components (e.g., transistors covered only by a drop of epoxy 2.5 mm in diameter instead of the relatively large metal cans of the day) that were to be tightly interconnected in truly 3-dimensional (3-D) bricks. This provided many more wires in the vertical direction between parallel board faces than that available only on the board edges. This

can be seen as the next logical step from the progression of the 6600 and 7600:

- The 6600 had modules in racks, with wiring between racks only at the rack edges.
- The 7600 had modules in racks, with wiring from the parallel face of the racks but only from the edges of the modules.
- The 8600 was to have wiring between the faces of the modules themselves.

The dense packaging would allow the machine to have a 8-ns cycle time.

Unfortunately, there were three problems with the 8600 program. First, the tight stacking of boards and components generated a lot of heat, which was difficult to remove from the board stack, resulting in overheating. Second, the 3-D connections between boards (and there were a lot of them) were very small, and they were difficult to test and assemble. This resulted in poor manufacturing yield and unreliability. But the third problem was that before these issues could be resolved, financial difficulties at CDC mandated the canceling of the 8600 project. As a result, Seymour Cray and a small team left CDC to form Cray Research, but they did get initial funding from CDC.

1.3.4 The Cray-1

At Cray research, the initial emphasis was to quickly develop a risk-free supercomputer to begin providing income for operations of the company. So, instead of attacking the relatively hard problems facing the 8600, a less-aggressive approach was called for. The result was the Cray-1 [19], which physically resembled the 8600 but was much larger, because it only used communication between module edges instead of module faces. This also made it easier to cool by using cold plates at the edge of each module (with racks placed side by side in 270° of a circle).

The Cray-1 was a more-conservative design than the 8600 in terms of clock rate and packaging. Also, the vector architecture was an extension of the full pipelining of the 7600, with the addition of more registers (eight 64-element vector registers plus the 64 register B and T banks behind the A and S registers). Vector registers were "architectural firsts" that led to much-improved performance.

The Cray-1 also contained a number of technology firsts. It used the first commercial emitter coupled logic (ECL) integrated circuits that compensated for changes in temperature, supply voltage, and process. Machines before the Cray-1 used bipolar transistors as a switch (like in transistor-transistor logic, or TTL), which resulted in the transistors going into saturation and making them relatively slow to switch. In contrast, the ECL circuits in the Cray-1 were built from high-speed differential amplifiers whose transistors never enter saturation. Besides being fast, because ECL gates are differential amplifiers, they produce both true and complement outputs. This allows them to provide more logical functions per gate stage than other circuit technologies. ECL gates also have high fan-outs and allow construction of OR gates merely by connecting emitter-follower outputs together (wire-ORs). The high gate functionality of ECL helped enable a logic design for the Cray-1 using only eight gate delays per cycle. Combined with the high gate speed of ECL, the Cray-1 achieved a cycle time much faster than any other computer of its time. Its 12.5-ns cycle time was not surpassed by commodity CMOS microprocessors until two decades after the first Cray-1 shipped in 1976. Even IBM mainframes using a variant of bipolar TTL logic and expensive multichip modules did not surpass the Cray-1's cycle time for fifteen years. One lesson here is that the speed of a "bipolar" machine greatly depends on the circuit technology.

From a business standpoint, the Cray-1 was relatively easy to manufacture and had a significant performance lead over all other supercomputers. This headroom allowed Cray research to create several direct derivatives of the Cray-1, the Cray-1S and the Cray-1M. Around sixty-five of the family were sold. This is in contrast to a more typical number of twenty to fifty units for an economically successful multimillion-dollar supercomputer and a much lower typical number for failures.

The Cray-1 clock cycle time was one third that of the 7600. With the addition of vectors, it achieved a 100 x 100 Linpak performance of 27 MFLOPS, which was about eight times faster than the 7600. Shipping seven years after the 7600, this represented a performance growth rate of about 35% per year. This was below the 48% growth rate from the 6600 to the 7600 and significantly below MOS microprocessor performance growth rates of close to 60% [9].

1.3.5 The Cray-2

Now that the foundation of the company was assured, Seymour Cray returned to more of a research style (befitting the name of the company). Furthermore, a

line of derivative machines in improved technologies (the letter series X-MP, Y-MP, etc., designed under Steve Chen) continued to support the company.[2] The next machine Seymour Cray would build was remarkably like an updated version of the 8600: the Cray-2.

Initially, to get a significant clock speed increase over the Cray-1, Seymour Cray wanted to use gallium arsenide in the Cray-2. This direction towards GaAs can be seen at the end of the Cray-1 technology paper [11]. But gallium arsenide technology was not mature enough yet to be useful, so after some delay the Cray-2 ended up being built out of 16-gate bipolar ECL gate arrays. The Cray-2 was a four-way multiprocessor (like the 8600 but with the addition of vectors), and it solved the 3-D circuit stack problem. A more reliable board-interconnection technology was found that allowed many more connections between the parallel faces of boards than from their edges. The heat problem was solved by immersing the whole machine in Fluorinert. Although Fluorinert was originally developed as an artificial blood substitute, it was not used medically. However, being a liquid, it had better heat capacity than air and was electrically and materially inert. This Cray-2 had a 4.1-ns clock cycle time (3X faster than the Cray-1 but only two times faster than the proposed 8600) and up to four processors. The vector architecture was almost the same as the Cray-1 but it did not allow chaining. The Cray-2 used DRAMs for main memory (in contrast to SRAMs in the Cray-1 and X-MP), so it had much longer memory latencies and had to be highly banked (128-way) [10]. As a result of the slower memory, the performance per processor was skewed toward long vector codes and did not scale by the clock frequency. The machine was a four-processor multiprocessor. This improved performance on parallel applications but did not increase uniprocessor performance. Combined with the project delays and the implementation of more-flexible chaining in the letter series along with multiple memory ports (the Cray-1 and Cray-2 only had one memory port per processor), this resulted in less success for the Cray-2. But it still sold thirty copies, mainly to customers needing its larger main memory capacity.

Now supercomputer development was falling significantly behind the volume MOS technology scaling curve driven by lithography. The Cray-2 came out in 1985, nine years after the Cray-1, but its clock cycle time was only 3X faster. This was only a compound annual growth rate of 13% per year.

---

[2]Over two hundred X-MPs were sold!

1.3.6 The Cray-3 and the Death of Traditional Supercomputers

After the Cray-2, Seymour Cray resumed work on GaAs. His next machine would remove the last vestige of two-dimensionality from his designs: the signature "C" shape. The "C" is two-dimensional (2-D) in that signals traveling from one part of the "C" to another must travel in a (curved) 2-D space of board stacks and stacked racks. The Cray-3 would be a cubic shape, with a base that was 1 foot on each side. This was an extremely aggressive undertaking, for reasons of difficulty of testing and manufacturing such a machine. Internal parts of the machine would not be accessible for testing, and the small size of the interconnections would require robotic assembly using tiny wires and precision laser welding.

Again, Seymour's parent company did not have the resources to continue development of the existing profitable line of computers and Seymour's risky new venture. This led Seymour Cray to spin off his project again as part of a new company in 1989. Because the name Cray Research was already in use, Seymour Cray called his new company Cray Computer. This is ironic since Cray Research was in the business of producing computers and Cray Computer was more of a research venture.

The Cray-3 was announced in 1993. Although the machine was supposed to have sixteen processors, only one processor was ever delivered for evaluation. It had a 2-ns cycle time. This was eight years after the Cray-2 but was only faster by a factor of two. The uniprocessor performance growth had decreased to an annual rate of only 9%, but at the same time the technology was getting much more difficult to manufacture and test. This was not economically sustainable as a business, even compared with the more traditional letter line of computers from Cray Research. The Cray Research T90, announced in 1994, used bipolar standard cells and had a clock cycle time of 2.2 ns. But it also had dual vector pipes, support for chaining, a scalar cache, and had up to thirty-two processors. This gave it an aggregate peak performance 8X more than a full Cray-3. It may be that a 3-D computer will never be economically or even technologically justifiable.

By the time of the Cray-3 announcement in 1993, scaling of volume CMOS process technology had resulted in clock speeds of up to 200 MHz, as evidenced by the DEC Alpha 21064 microprocessor [14]. This chip was limited in performance by its I/O interface, which only consisted of pins along the edge of the chip. More recently, volume microprocessor chips have adopted bump technology, which allows interconnections over the entire face of a die instead of just at the edges. Thus, in a sense, they are following in Seymour Cray's footsteps technologically but in a fashion that must remain profitable.

1.4 The Rise of MOS Microprocessor-Based Computers

The primary reason why non-saturating bipolar technologies such as ECL were so much faster than MOS in the 1970s was that they had very narrow base widths that could be carefully controlled by diffusion (and later ion implantation) to be much smaller than the lithographic line widths of their day. For example, the transistors used in the IBM 360/91 in 1967 had a base width of 0.5 µm [12], whereas production lithographic feature sizes were around 20 µm [9]. However, there are certain limits to how narrow bipolar bases can be made, and these limits are close to what MOS transistors are achieving with advanced lithography today. For example, recent high-performance bipolar gate-array processes have base widths of around 0.08 µm, giving a compound annual rate of change of only 6.3% per year since 1967.[3] Thus, as Moore's Law [16] advanced, the performance gap between nonsaturating bipolar technologies and MOS technologies closed.

Differences in production volumes of different technologies leads to different levels of sustainable technology investment. The bipolar technology used in supercomputers was a very high-end technology, and shipped in relatively low volumes. This meant that much less money was available for investment in bipolar technology. As a result, both lithographic and device development of bipolar technology started lagging that of MOS technology by the late 1980s. This reduced even further the relative performance advantage of bipolar technologies versus volume MOS technologies, leading to even smaller relative volumes. This is obviously a bad spiral to be on. As a result, by 1998, supercomputers and mainframes being built in the United States use multiple copies of microprocessors made with volume CMOS technology.

If a computer ships in low volumes, the design cost of the machine must be amortized over a small number

[3]Obviously, there are many other important parameters that determine the performance of transistors that we have ignored for the purpose of this discussion.

of machines. This also limits the resources that are economically available for their design. As a result, supercomputers and mainframes have always been built with standardized building blocks. An extreme example of that was the Cray-1, which was built using only four different integrated circuits. How much more performance would have been achievable if full-custom techniques were used instead? As an example, multiplexors built solely from AND/NAND gates require two levels of logic, whereas in a custom multiplexor gate, the delay from the data inputs to the data outputs is reduced to one gate delay. Similarly, if a logic function really requires six inputs, a whole extra logic level will be required if only 5/4 input gates are available.

In contrast, the initial microprocessors were developed with volume markets in mind. They also had very meager device budgets. This led to a full-custom approach and innovative circuit designs that have persisted until this day in high-performance MOS microprocessors. The combination of full-custom design with aggressive circuit design probably accounts for a factor of three in system performance over a processor built from a large MOS standard-cell library.

Many young engineers believe the "best product" will win in the marketplace. Unfortunately, the marketplace is much more complicated than this. One example of this is microprocessor instruction-set architectures. One might expect the cleanest, most powerful architecture with the highest performance implementations to be the most successful. (An example with these characteristics is Compaq's Alpha, which currently has a market share of less than 0.1%.) Instead, one would expect the arguably most irregular and lowest performance instruction-set architecture (with such "bad" features as only a few registers, nonorthogonality, a single condition code register, and a segmented address space, just to name a few) not to be very successful at all. However, evolution in instruction-set architecture does not involve survival of the fittest in the biological sense, because the strength of an ISA greatly depends on the size of the installed software base. The 8008 was the first high-performance microprocessor architecture (compared to the 4004, the first microprocessor architecture). Because it was the first, it was the most successful when it started. In order to preserve its customer base, the most successful architecture at a given point in time will be extended with new features necessitated by the current technology. This will ensure that the commercially most successful architecture continues

to be successful. After many generations of adding new features onto an existing instruction-set architecture that was not designed with expandability in mind, you can imagine the creature that results. Thus, in instruction-set architecture evolution, the surviving architecture will therefore be among the "least fit." This does not preclude its implementations from being among the "most fit," however, as we shall explain in the last chapter of this reader.

1.5 Discussion of Included Papers

In this section we introduce papers that describe the technology, implementation, and economics of classic machines.

1.5.1 Amdahl, Blaauw, and Brooks's "Architecture of the IBM System/360" [1]

In November 1961, IBM formed a group known as the SPREAD committee, which was chartered to set IBM's design goals for the next decade and to create an engineering and marketing plan to unify the efforts of the three IBM computer divisions. At the end of December 1961, the report of the group was released. It advocated production of a family of compatible machines ranging from the smallest commercial machines of the day to scientific computers even more powerful than Stretch. After much engineering effort, on April 7, 1964 IBM announced the 360 architecture with over 150 new products, services, and devices [17]. The family name 360 was chosen by IBM to say that it excelled at all "360 degrees of data processing."

At the same time as the announcement, an excellent paper giving the design rationale for the 360 architecture appeared in IBM's *Journal of Research and Development* [1]. Not only does it describe the architecture in detail, but it describes the tradeoffs that were evaluated leading up to the architecture. It is worthy of study by all computer architects and is included in this reader.

1.5.2 Thornton's "Parallel Operation in the Control Data 6600" [22]

> Last week Control Data . . . announced the 6600 system. I understand that in the laboratory developing the system there are only 34 people including the janitor. Of these, 14 are engineers and 4 are programmers. . . . Contrasting this modest effort with our vast development activities, I fail to understand why we have lost our industry leadership position by letting someone

else offer the world's most powerful computer."
—*Thomas Watson, IBM CEO 8/28/63*

It seems like Mr. Watson has answered his own question. —*Seymour Cray's response to Thomas Watson*

As the two quotes above show, the CDC 6600 was developed by a small team of focused, excellent designers. They had a narrow target market (scientific computing), and hence the machine could be specialized for that market. One example of this is the 60-bit native word length (very long for those years), and that it only supported two data operand types: 60-bit floating-point values and 60-bit integers. Another was that it was the first machine to have independent floating-point functional units (which required a large percentage of the machine's resources). The use of specialized functional units resulted in much lower operation latencies than the microcoded adder/shifter data paths that were common at the time in other implementations. For example, the latency of a 60-bit precision floating-point addition was only 400 ns! This is in contrast to IBM 360 implementations, which had to implement decimal and string data types and were generally built around smaller data busses. (The IBM 360/91, which was not shipped until November 1967, was an exception, because it omitted hardware support for decimal arithmetic.) The IBM 360 architecture was also limited to four 64-bit floating-point registers, which limited the potential overlap between floating-point instructions and necessitated the invention of the Tomasulo algorithm (a form of register renaming) for the 360/91 [23].

Because of the small size of the 6600 design team, the machine out of necessity was built around straight-forward but elegant principles. This made it an early example of a reduced instruction set computer (RISC) architecture. Also, by having a small flexible design team, the design process could move more quickly.

The 6600 introduced a number of architectural innovations that impacted computer architecture for many years. First, the machine had ten "peripheral processors" to handle I/O functions. However, they were implemented by cycle-interleaving on a single physical CPU (i.e., a barrel or multithreaded processor). Ten virtual processors were implemented because the memory read/write cycle time was ten cycles, so that each virtual processor had the appearance of having single-cycle access to main memory.

Second, the 6600 introduced a form of dynamic scheduling called a "scoreboard." The scoreboard allowed instructions to issue out of order and took advantage of the parallelism afforded by the machine's ten independent functional units. Because the machine did not have condition codes (as did the IBM 360), it was much easier to reorder the execution of instructions. The machine had eight operand registers, which could be used for either floating-point or fixed-point data values, and eight address registers. Writing a result to address registers 1–5 had the side effect of loading the contents of the memory address specified by that result into an operand register. Writing a result to address registers 6 or 7 had the side effect of writing the contents of the corresponding operand register to main memory. Having explicit registers for the result of memory address calculations led to natural forms of autoincrementing and autodecrementing loads and stores.

This book is dedicated to A6 & A7, without which none of the results in this book could have been saved. —*Ralph Grishman's book dedication for* Assembly Language Programming for the Control Data 6000 Series and the Cyber 70 Series *[8]*

The 6600 was also a excellent technical implementation. It was heavily pipelined for its day (integer addition had a three cycle latency). Because it could issue an instruction per cycle in the best case, the deeper pipeline helped it to exploit instruction-level parallelism. To support the computational bandwidth of the functional units, the main memory of the machine was banked thirty-two ways!

Jim Thornton wrote a classic book on the design of the 6600 [21], which unfortunately is out of print. A condensation of the material in the book appeared at the Fall Joint Computers Conference in 1964, which we have included [22].

1.5.3 Russell's "The Cray-1 Computer System" [19]

Russell's paper provides an excellent introduction to the architecture and implementation of the Cray-1. One of the notable innovations discussed in the paper are the Cray-1's vector registers. (Previous vector machines only had memory-to-memory operations, which had long start-up times and hence required long vectors before a significant performance improvement would be gained.) Besides being the first machine with vector registers, the Cray-1 also supported chaining of operations through the registers. This allowed the result elements of one vector operation (including vector loads and stores) to be consumed by a second operation before the whole first vector was computed, greatly reducing the latency of a computation. The Cray-1 architecture was also notable for its introduction of a second level of programmer-controlled register files, the B and T registers. See section 1.3.4 of this chapter for more highlights of this paper.

1.5.4 Kolodzey's "Cray-1 Computer Technology" [11]

Kolodzey's paper effectively explains how the Cray-1 was built in seven pages. One of the most interesting figures is the chassis layout of the machine. This shows how the machine architecture is implemented. In this figure, one can see the flow of the long reciprocal unit pipeline away from the core of the machine where more critical control functions lie. The paper also gives lots of implementation information, from components to interconnection, power, and cooling. For example, one chip type constitutes 95% of the IC's in the machine, and the whole machine dissipated 130 kW! Note that the combination of a 16 x 4-bit register part with 4-input AND/NAND gates naturally led to register files with 64 entries for each of the eight vector registers, the B, T, and the four instruction buffers.

The Cray-1 used latches instead of flip-flops because they have lower latency. However, in a latch-based design, the fastest circuit paths must be slower than one half the machine cycle time, otherwise signals may advance through more than one state device in a cycle. For this reason, the Cray-1 had to pad circuit paths that were significantly faster than the clock cycle time with extra wire and/or gate delay.

1.5.5 Moore's "Cramming More Components onto Integrated Circuits" [16]

Continuous improvements in base technology have made computer architecture a dynamic field. If our implementation technology was still the same as in 1965, very little work in computer architecture would have been needed over the last thirty-five years. Most of the improvements in technology have resulted from lithography and semiconductor technology. The pace and benefits of advances in lithography and semiconductor technology were envisioned by Gordon Moore twenty-five years ago and summarized in a short article in the premier trade magazine of the time.

This article defines Moore's Law, which states that the number of transistors per chip doubles every year. One corollary of that law is that the price per transistor decreases by a factor of two each year. Three

other corollaries are that the power of a function as well as delay decreases with scaling, and the reliability of a function increases with scaling.

One aspect often overlooked when referencing Moore's Law is that for the last 30 years semiconductor technology has been roughly quadrupling every three years. This gives an exponential base of about 1.59 instead of the base of 2 proposed in Gordon Moore's original paper. Given that Moore was extrapolating from only four nonzero data points spread over four years, a lack of precision in the exponent base is not unexpected. In equation form, a more accurate formula for Moore's Law is:

$$N_{devices\ on\ chip} = 1.59^{(year-1959)}$$

In other words, the number of transistors on a chip increases by 59% each year. The formula can be remembered by taking the offset year in the exponent and replacing the first "9" in the year by a decimal point to give the base or vice versa.

More important than the precision of the exponent base are all the implications of technology scaling that are presented in the paper. It is for this reason that we consider this short paper the most amazing of all the papers included in this reader. Much of the paper reads as if it were written yesterday, not over thirty years ago. The contrast with other papers of the time and since is startling. For contrast, consider the "Amdahl's Law" paper presented in Chapter 2, where "Amdahl's Law" isn't even formally stated. Other predictive papers over the last forty years have typically made a handful of predictions and are lucky if one or two of them come true. (Remember predictions of maglev trains, bubble memories, nuclear power too cheap to meter, common-place space travel, and computerized natural language translation by 1970?) In contrast, the Moore's Law paper makes over twenty-five predictions, and *all* of them have come true. There are twelve predictions alone in the introduction that have been fulfilled. It makes you wonder whether Gordon Moore didn't invent a time travel machine first before writing his paper.

Besides introducing Moore's Law and its corollaries, the paper points out other implications of scaling on technology. Here are some of the more important predictions:

■ Proliferation of electronics, pushing this science into many new areas. (Try to envision what the world was like in 1965: electromechanical pulse-dial phone switches, consumer electronics limited to AM radios containing a few transistors, large television sets built with vacuum tubes.)

- Home computers. (Computers were mainframes—although DEC would introduce the PDP-8 minicomputer in 1965.)
- Automatic controls for automobiles (a very large market today).
- Personal portable communications equipment (e.g., cell phones).
- Electronic wristwatches—a market that Gordon Moore would later get into at Intel, until the economics didn't pay because it became a commodity market.
- Increasing reliability with integration. (Too bad this doesn't apply to software!)
- Limited role for gallium arsenide.
- Integration density with minimum cost per component.
- Power dissipation of each component decreases with integration, making further integration possible without meltdown.
- Product limits resulting from size of market and increasing engineering costs.
- Building large systems out of standard functions. (In the 1970s this meant TTL, today it means commodity processors.)
- Integration of linear circuits limited by poor properties of integrated passive components; switch to use of digital filters instead (e.g., DSP's now found in everything from cell phones to PC sound cards).
- Lumped parameter circuit design made possible at lower microwave frequencies.
- Phased array radars enabled.

The effects of Moore's Law on device and circuit characteristics was developed into classical scaling theory by Denard et al. [7] in the early 1970s. This was later simplified and popularized in Mead-Conway [15] VLSI classes at the beginning of the 1980s.

As long as Moore's Law continues, lots of good and exciting things will happen. The technology scaling of integrated circuits has been the driver for much of the economic productivity improvements over last twenty years, resulting in significantly increased standards of living. Even the modern-day Internet would not be possible without highly integrated electronics for inexpensive PC's and affordable network routers. Finally, the success of the semiconductor industry over the last four decades in following Moore's Law has kept computer architecture a dynamic field of study.

1.5.6. Mazor's "The History of the Microcomputer— Invention and Evolution" [13]

The Mazor paper explains how the Intel 4004, 8008, 8080, and 8086 came to be. Most amazing about the 8080 design was that it was implemented with only 4,500 transistors. This paper points out that the 8080 architecture was designed for low-cost embedded applications, and this accounts for many of its limitations. This paper has many insights into the cost considerations, markets, and design process of the first microprocessors. Surprisingly, power dissipation, pin counts, packaging, and tooling costs were as crucial then as they are today.

1.6 References

A number of books contain a wealth of information on computers from the 1940s through the 1970s. Noteworthy examples include books by Bell and Newell [4], Siewiorek, Bell, and Newell [20], and Bell, Mudge, and McNamara [3].

[1]   G. M. Amdahl, G. A. Blaauw, and Frederick P. Brooks Jr.; "Architecture of the IBM System/360," *IBM Journal of Research and Development*, pp. 87–101, Apr. 1964.

[2]   C. Bashe, L. Johnson, J. Palmer, and E. Pugh, *IBM's Early Computers*, Cambridge, MA: MIT Press, 1986.

[3]   G. Bell, C. Mudge, and J. McNamara, *Computer Engineering: A DEC View of Hardware Systems Design.* Bedford, MA: Digital Press, 1978.

[4]   G. Bell and A. Newell, *Computer Structures: Readings and Examples.* New York: McGraw-Hill, 1971.

[5]   G. A. Blaauw and F. P. Brooks Jr., *Computer Architecture: Concepts and Evolution.* Reading, MA: Addison Wesley Longman, 1997.

[6]   W. Bucholz (Ed.), *Planning a Computer System.* New York: McGraw-Hill 1962. (IBM Stretch (7030)).

[7]   R. H. Denard, F. H. Gaensslen, H.-N. Yu, V. L. Rideout, E. Bassous, and A. R. LeBlanc, "Design of ion-implanted MOSFETs with very small physical dimensions," *IEEE Journal of Solid-State Circuits*, SC(9):256–268, 1974.

[8]   R. Grishman. *Assembly Languages Programming for the Control Data 6000 Series and the Cyber 70 Series.* New York: Alogrithmics Press, 1974.

[9]   J. L. Hennessy and N. P. Jouppi, "Computer technology and architecture: An evolving interaction," *IEEE Computer*, 24(9):18–29, 1991.

[10] R. W. Hockney and C. R. Jesshope, *Parallel Computers 2.* Bristol, England: Adam Hilger, 1988.

[11] J. S. Kolodzey, "Cray-1 computer technology," *IEEE*

Transactions on Component Hybrids, and Manufacturing Technology, CHMT-4(2):181–186, 1981.

[12] J. Langdon and E.J. Van Derveer, "Design of a high-speed transistor for the ASLT current switch," *IBM Journal of Research and Development,* 11(1):69–73, 1967.

[13] S. Mazor, "The history of the microcomputer—Invention and evolution," *Proceedings of the IEEE,* 83(12):1601–1608, 1995.

[14] E. McLellan, "The Alpha AXP architecture and 21064 processor," *IEEE Micro,* 13(3):36–47, 1993.

[15] C. Mead and L. Conway, *Introduction to VLSI.* Reading, MA: Addison-Wesley, 1980.

[16] G. E. Moore, "Cramming more components onto integrated circuits," *Electronics,* pp. 114–117, Apr. 1965.

[17] E. Pugh, L. Johnson, and J. Palmer, *IBM's 360 and Early 370 Systems.* Cambridge, MA: MIT Press.

[18] K. C. Redmond and T. M. Smith, *Project Whirlwind: The History of a Pioneer Computer.* Bedford, MA: Digital Press, 1980.

[19] R. M. Russell, "The Cray-1 computer system," *Communications of the ACM,* 21(31):63–72, 1978.

[20] D. Siewiorek, G. Bell, and A. Newell, *Computer Structures: Principles and Examples.* New York: McGraw-Hill, 1982.

[21] J. E. Thornton, *Design of a Computer: The Control Data 6600.* Glenview, IL: Scott Foresman, 1970.

[22] J. E. Thornton, "Parallel operation in the Control Data 6600," *Proceedings of the Fall Joint Computers Conference,* vol. 26, pp. 33–40, 1964.

[23] R. M. Tomasulo, "A efficient algorithm for exploiting multiple arithmetic units," *IBM Journal of Research and Development,* 11(1):25–33, 1967.

[24] J. von Neumann, First Draft of a Report on the EDVAC. Tech. Rep. Philadelphia: University of Pennsylvania Moore School, 1945.

[25] M. V. Wilkes, *Computing Perspectives.* San Francisco, CA: Morgan Kaufmann, 1995.

[26] M. R. Williams, *A History of Computing Technology,* 2nd ed. Los Alamitos, CA: IEEE Press, 1997.

G. M. Amdahl
G. A. Blaauw
F. P. Brooks, Jr.

Architecture of the IBM System/360

Abstract: The architecture* of the newly announced IBM System/360 features four innovations:

1. An approach to storage which permits and exploits very large capacities, hierarchies of speeds, read-only storage for microprogram control, flexible storage protection, and simple program relocation.

2. An input/output system offering new degrees of concurrent operation, compatible channel operation, data rates approaching 5,000,000 characters/second, integrated design of hardware and software, a new low-cost, multiple-channel package sharing main-frame hardware, new provisions for device status information, and a standard channel interface between central processing unit and input/output devices.

3. A truly general-purpose machine organization offering new supervisory facilities, powerful logical processing operations, and a wide variety of data formats.

4. Strict upward and downward machine-language compatibility over a line of six models having a performance range factor of 50.

This paper discusses in detail the objectives of the design and the rationale for the main features of the architecture. Emphasis is given to the problems raised by the need for compatibility among central processing units of various size and by the conflicting demands of commercial, scientific, real-time, and logical information processing. A tabular summary of the architecture is shown in the Appendices.

Introduction

The design philosophies of the new general-purpose machine organization for the IBM System/360 are discussed in this paper.† In addition to showing the architecture* of the new family of data processing systems, we point out the various engineering problems encountered in attempts to make the system design compatible, at the program bit level, for large and small models. The compatibility was to extend not only to models of any size but also to their various applications—scientific, commercial, real-time, and so on.

---

* The term *architecture* is used here to describe the attributes of a system as seen by the programmer, i.e., the conceptual structure and functional behavior, as distinct from the organization of the data flow and controls, the logical design, and the physical implementation.

† Additional details concerning the architecture, engineering design, programming, and application of the IBM System/360 will appear in a series of articles in the *IBM Systems Journal*.

The section that follows describes the objectives of the new system design, i.e., that it serve as a base for new technologies and applications, that it be general-purpose, efficient, and strictly program compatible in all models. The remainder of the paper is devoted to the design problems faced, the alternatives considered, and the decisions made for data format, data and instruction codes, storage assignments, and input/output controls.

Design objectives

The new architecture builds upon but differs from the designs that have gradually evolved since 1950. The evolution of the computer had included, besides major technological improvements, several important systems concepts and developments:

1. Adaptation to business data processing.

2. Growing importance of the total system, especially the input/output aspects.

3. Universal use of assembly programs, compilers, and other metaprograms.

4. Development of magnetic recording on tapes, drums, and disks.

5. Hundred-fold expansion of storage capacities.

6. Adaptation for real-time systems.

During this period most new computer models, from the point of view of their logical structure, were improved, enlarged, or technologically recast versions of the machines developed in the early 1950's. IBM products are not atypical; the evolution has gone from IBM 701 to 7094, 650 to 7074, from 702 to 7080, and from 1401 to 7010.

The system characteristics to be described here, however, are a new approach to logical structure and function, designed for the needs of the next decade as a coordinated set of data processing systems.

• *Advanced concepts*

It was recognized from the start that the design had to embody recent conceptual advances, and hence, if necessary, be incompatible with existing products. To this end, the following premises were considered:

1. Since computers develop into families, any proposed design would have to lend itself to growth and to successor machines.

2. Input/output (I/O) devices make systems specifically useful for given applications. A general method was needed for using I/O devices differing in data rate, access, and function.

3. The real value of an information system is properly measured by answers-per-month, not bits-per-microsecond. The former criterion required specific advances to increase throughput for a given internal speed, to shorten turn-around time for a given throughput, and to make the whole complex of machines and programming systems easier to use.

4. The functions of the central processing unit (CPU) proper are specific to its application only a minor fraction of the time. The functions required by the system for its own operation, e.g., compiling, input/output management, and the addressing of and within complex data structures, use a major share of time. These functions had to be made efficient, and need not be different in machines designed for different applications.

5. The input/output channel and the input/output control program had to be designed for each other.

6. Machine systems had to be capable of supervising themselves, without manual intervention, for both real-time and multiprogrammed, or time-shared, applications. To realize this capability requires: a comprehensive interruption system, tamper-proof storage protection, a protected supervisor program, supervisor-controlled program switching, supervisor control of all input/output (including unit assignment), nonstop operation (no HALT), easy program relocation, simple writing of read-only or unmodified programs, a timer, and interpretive consoles.

7. It must be possible and straightforward to assemble systems with redundant I/O, storages, and CPU's so that the system can operate when modules fail.

8. Storage capacities of more than the commonly available 32,000 words would be required.

9. Certain types of problems require floating-point word length of more than 36 bits.

10. As CPU's become increasingly reliable, built-in thorough checking against hardware malfunction is imperative for all systems, regardless of application.

11. Since the largest servicing problem is diagnosis of malfunction, built-in hardware fault-locating aids are essential to reduce down-times. Furthermore, identification of individual malfunctions and of individual invalidities in program syntax would have to be provided.

• *Open-ended design*

The new design had to provide a dependable base for a decade of customer planning and customer programming, and continuing laboratory developments, whether in technology, application and programming techniques, system configuration, or special requirements.

The various circuit, storage, and input/output technologies used in a system change at different times, causing corresponding changes in their *relative* speeds and costs. To take advantage of these changes, it is desirable that the design permit asynchronous operation of these components with respect to each other.

Changing application and programming techniques would require open-endedness in function. Current trends had to be extrapolated and their consequences anticipated. This anticipation could be achieved by direct provision, e.g., by increasing storage capacities and by using multiple-CPU systems, various new I/O devices, and time sharing. Anticipation might also take the form of generalization of function, as in code-independent scan and translation facilities, or it might consist of judiciously reserving spare bits, operation codes, and blocks of operation codes, for new modes, operations, or sets of operations.

Changing requirements for system configuration would demand not only such approaches as a standard interface between I/O devices and control unit, but also capabilities for a machine to directly sense, control, and respond to other equipment modules via paths outside the normal data routes. These capabilities permit the construction of supersystems that can be dynamically reconfigured under program control, to adapt more precisely to specialized functions or to give graceful degradation.

In many particular applications, some special (and often minor) modification enhances the utility of the system. These modifications (RPQ's), which may correct some shortsightedness of the original design, often embody operations not fully anticipated. In any event, a good general design would obviate certain modifications and accommodate others.

• *General-purpose function*

The machine design would have to provide individual system configurations for large and small, separate and mixed applications as found in commercial, scientific, real-time, data-reduction, communications, language, and logical data processing. The CPU design would have to be facile for each of these applications. Special facilities such as decimal or floating-point arithmetic might be required only for one or another application class and would be offered as options, but they would have to be integral, from the viewpoint of logical structure, with the design.

In particular, the general-purpose objective dictated that:

1. Logical power of great generality would have to be provided, so that all combinations of bits in data entities would be allowed and might be manipulated with operations whose power and utility depend upon the general nature of representations rather than upon any specific selection of them.

2. Operations would have to be code-independent except, of course, where code definition is essential to operation, as in arithmetic. In particular, all bit combinations should be acceptable as data; no combination should exert any control function when it appears in a data stream.

3. The individual bit would have to be separately manipulatable.

4. The general addressing system would have to be able to refer to small units of bits, preferably the unit used for characters.

Further, the implications of general-purpose CPU design for communications-oriented systems indicated a radical departure from current systems philosophy. The conventional CPU, for example, is augmented by an independent stored-program unit (such as the IBM 7750 or 7740) to handle all communications functions. Since the new CPU would easily perform such *logical* functions as code translation and message assembly, communications lines would be attached directly to the I/O channel via a control unit that would perform only character assembly and the electrical line-handling functions.

• *Efficient performance*

The basic measure of a good design is high performance in comparison to other designs having the same cost. This measure cannot be ignored in designing a compatible line. Hence each individual model and systems configuration in the line would have to be competitive with systems that are specialized in function, performance level or both. That this goal is feasible in spite of handicaps introduced by the compatibility requirement was due to the especially important cost savings that would be realized due to compatibility.

• *Intermodel compatibility*

The design had to yield a range of models with internal performance varying from approximately that of the IBM 1401 to well beyond that of the IBM 7030 (STRETCH). As already mentioned, all models would have to be strictly program compatible, upward and downward, at the program bit level.

The phrase "strictly program compatible" requires a more technically precise definition. Here it means that a valid program, whose logic will not depend implicitly upon time of execution and which runs upon configuration **A**, will also run on configuration **B** if the latter includes at least the required storage, at least the required I/O devices, and at least the required optional features. Invalid programs, i.e., those which violate the programming manual, are not constrained to yield the same results on all models. The manual identifies not only the results of all dependable operations, but also those results of exceptional and/or invalid operations that are not dependable. Programs dependent on execution-time will operate compatibly if the dependence is explicit, and, for example, if completion of an I/O operation or the timer are tested.

Compatibility would ensure that the user's expanding needs be easily accommodated by any model. Compatibility would also ensure maximum utility of programming support prepared by the manufacturer, maximum sharing of programs generated by the user, ability to use small systems to back up large ones, and exceptional freedom in configuring systems for particular applications.

It required a new concept and mode of thought to make the compatibility objective even conceivable. In the last few years, many computer architects had realized, usually implicitly, that logical structure (as seen by the programmer) and physical structure (as seen by the engineer) are quite different. Thus each may see registers, counters, etc., that to the other are not at all real entities. This was not so in the computers of the 1950's. The *explicit* recognition of the duality of structure opened the way for the compatibility within System/360. The compatibility requirement dictated that the basic architecture had to embrace different technologies, different storage-circuit speed ratios, different data path widths, and different data-flow complexities. The basic machine structure and implementation at the various performance levels are shown in Fig. 1.

The design decisions

Certain decisions for the architectural design became mileposts, because they (a) established prominent characteristics of the System/360, (b) resolved problems concerning the compatibility objective, thus illuminating the essential differences between small models and large, or (c) resolved problems concerning the general-purpose objective, thus illuminating the essential differences among applications. The sections that follow discuss these de-

Figure 1 **Machine structure and implementation.**

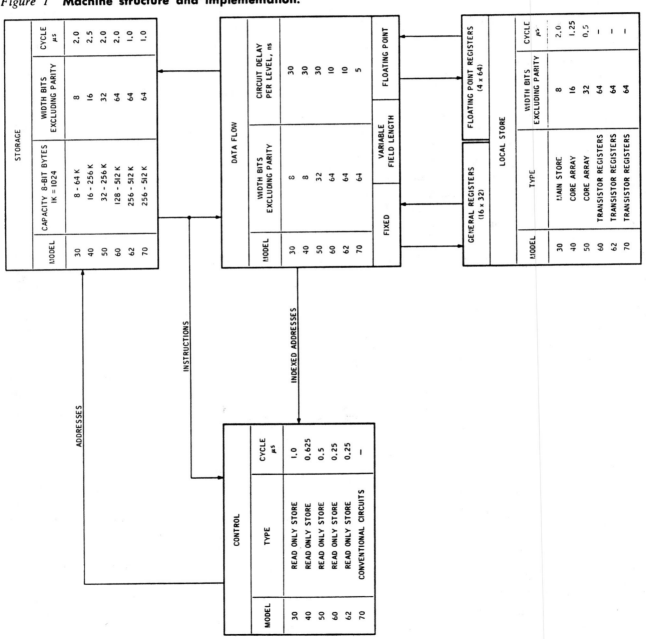

cisions, the problems faced, the alternatives considered, and the reasons for the outcome.

• *Data format*

The decision on basic format (which affected character size, word size, instruction field, number of index registers, input-output implementation, instruction set layout, storage capacity, character code, etc.) was whether data length modules should go as 2^n or 3.2^n. Even though many matters of format were considered in the basic choice, we will for convenience treat the major components of the decision as if they were independent.

Character size, 6 vs 4/8. In character size, the fundamental problem is that decimal digits require 4 bits, the alphanumeric characters require 6 bits. Three obvious alternatives were considered — 6 bits for all, with 2 bits wasted on numeric data; 4 bits for digits, 8 for alphanumeric, with 2 bits wasted on alphanumeric; and 4 bits for digits, 6 for alphanumeric, which would require adoption of a 12-bit module as the minimum addressable element. The 7-bit character, which incorporated a binary recoding of decimal digit pairs, was also briefly examined.

The 4/6 approach was rejected because (a) it was desired to have the versatility and power of manipulating character streams and addressing individual characters, even in models where decimal arithmetic is not used, (b) limiting the alphabetic character to 6 bits seemed short-sighted, and (c) the engineering complexities of this approach might well cost more than the wasted bits in the character.

The straight-6 approach, used in the IBM 702–7080 and 1401–7010 families, as well as in other manufacturers' systems, had the advantages of familiar usage, existing I/O equipment, simple specification of field structure, and commensurability with a 48-bit floating-point word and a 24-bit instruction field.

The 4/8 approach, used in the IBM 650–7074 family and elsewhere, had greater coding efficiency, spare bits in the alphabetic set (allowing the set to grow), and commensurability with a 32/64-bit floating-point word and a 16-bit instruction field. Most important of these factors was coding efficiency, which arises from the fact that the use of numeric data in business records is more than twice as frequent as alphanumeric. This efficiency implies, for a given hardware investment, better use of core storage, faster tapes, and more capacious disks.

Floating-point word length, 48 vs 32/64. For large models addition time goes up slowly with word length, and multiplication time rises almost linearly. For small, serial models, addition time rises linearly and multiplication as the square of word length. Input/output time for data files rises linearly. Large machines more often require high precision; small machines more urgently require short operands. For this aspect of the basic format problem, then, definite conflicts arose because of compatibility.

Good data were unavailable on the distribution of required precision by the number of problems or running time. Indeed, accurate measures could not be acquired on such coarse parameters as frequency of double-precision operation on 36-bit and 48-bit machines. The question became whether to force all problems to the longer 48-bit word, or whether to provide 64 to take care of precision-sensitive problems adequately, and either 32 or 36 to give faster speed and better coding efficiency for the rest. The choice was made for the IBM System/360 to have both 64- and 32-bit length floating point. This choice offers the user the option of making the speed/space vs precision trade-off to best suit his requirements. The user of the large models is expected to employ 64-bit words most of the time. The user of the smaller models will find the 32-bit length advantageous in most of his work. All floating-point models have both lengths and operate identically.

Hexadecimal floating-point radix. With no conflcts in questions of large vs small machines, base 16 was selected for floating point. Studies by Sweeney[1] show that the frequency of pre-shift, overflow, and precision-loss post-shift on floating-point addition are substantially reduced by this choice. He has shown that, compared with base 2, the percentage frequency of occurrence of overflow is 5 versus 20, pre-shift is 43 versus 58, and precision-loss post-shift is 11 versus 18. Thus speed is noticeably enhanced. Also, simpler shifting paths, with fewer logic levels, will accomplish a higher proportion of all required pre-shifting in a single pass. For example, circuits shifting 0, 1, 2, 3, or 4 binary places cover 82% of the base 2 pre-shifts. Substantially simpler circuits shifting 0, 1, or 2 hexadecimal places cover 93% of all base 16 pre-shifts. This simplification yields higher speed for the large models and lower cost for the small ones.

The most substantial disadvantage of adopting base 16 is the shift in bit usage from exponent to fraction. Thus, for a given range and a given *minimum* precision, base 16 requires 2 fewer exponent bits and 3 more fraction bits than does base 2. Alternatively and equivalently, rounding and truncation effects are 8 times as large for a given fraction length. For the 64-bit length, this is no problem. For the 32-bit length, with its 24-bit fraction, the minimum precision is reduced to the equivalent of 21 bits. Because the 64-bit length was available for problems where the minimum precision cramped the user, the greater speed and simplicity of base 16 was chosen.

Significance arithmetic. Many schemes yielding an estimate of the significance of computed results have been proposed. One such scheme, a modified form of unnormalized arithmetic, was for a time incorporated in the design. The scheme was finally discarded when simulation runs showed this mode of operation to cost about one hexadecimal digit of actual significance developed, as compared with normalized operation. Furthermore, the significance estimate yielded for a given problem varied substantially with the test data used.

Sign representations. For the fixed-point arithmetic system, which is binary, the two's complement representation for negative numbers was selected. The well-known virtues of this system are the unique representation of zero and the absence of recomplementation. These substantial advantages are augmented by several properties especially useful in address arithmetic, particularly in the large models, where address arithmetic has its own hardware. With two's complement notation, this indexing hardware requires no true/complement gates and thus works faster. In the smaller, serial models, the fact that high-order bits of address arithmetic can be elided without changing the low-order bits also permits a gain in speed. The same truncation property simplifies double-precision calculations. Furthermore, for table calculation, rounding or truncation to an integer changes all variables in the same direction, thus giving a more acceptable distribution than does an absolute-value-plus-sign representation.

The established commercial rounding convention made the use of complement notation awkward for decimal data; therefore, absolute-value-plus-sign is used here. In floating point, the engineering virtues of normalizing only high-order zeros, and of having all zeros represent the smallest possible number, decided the choice in favor of absolute-value-plus-sign.

Variable- versus fixed-length decimal fields. Since the fields of business records vary substantially in length, coding efficiency (and hence tape speed, file capacity, CPU speed, etc.) can be gained by operating directly on variable-length fields. This is easy for serial-by-byte machines, and the IBM 1401–7010 and 702–7080 families are among those so designed. A less flexible structure is more appropriate for a more parallel machine, and the IBM 650–7074 family is among those designed with fixed-word-length decimal arithmetic.

As one would expect, the storage efficiency advantage of the variable data format is diminished by the extra instruction information required for length specification. While the fixed format is preferable for the larger machines, the variable format was adopted because (a) the small commercial users are numerous and only recently trained in variable-format concepts, and (b) the large commercial system is usually I/O limited; hence the internal performance disadvantage of the variable format is more than compensated by the gain in effective tape rate.

Decimal accumulators versus storage-storage operation. A closely related question involving large/small models concerned the use of an accumulator as one of the operands on decimal arithmetic, versus the use of storage locations for all operands and results. This issue is pertinent even after a decision has been made for variable-

length fields in storage; for example, it distinguishes IBM 702–7080 arithmetic from that of the IBM 1401–7010 family.

The large models readily afford registers or local stores and get a speed enhancement from using these as accumulators. For the small model, using core storage for logical registers, addition to an accumulator is no faster than addition to a programmer-specified location. Addition of two arbitrary operands and storage of the result becomes LOAD, ADD, STORE, however, and this operation is substantially slower for the small models than the MOVE, ADD sequence appropriate to storage-storage operation. Business arithmetic operations (as hand coded and especially as compiled from COBOL) often take this latter form and rarely occur in strings where intermediate results are profitably held in accumulators. In address arithmetic and floating-point arithmetic, quite the opposite is true.

Field specification: word-marks versus length. Variable-length fields can be specified in the data via delimiter characters or word-marks, or in the instruction via specification of field length or start-finish limits. For business *data*, the word-mark has some slight advantage in storage efficiency: one extra bit per 8-bit character would cost less than 4 extra length bits per 16-bit address. Furthermore, instructions, and hence addresses, usually occupy most core storage space in business computers. However, the word-mark approach implies the use of word-marks on instructions, too, and here the cost is without compensating function. The same is true of all fixed-field data, an important consideration in a general-purpose design. On balance, storage efficiency is about equal; the field specification was put in the instruction to allow all data combinations to be valid and to give easier and more direct programming, particularly since it provides convenient addressing of parts of fields. Length was chosen over limit specification to simplify program relocation and instruction modification.

ASCII vs BCD codes. The selection of the 8-bit character size in 1961 proved wise by 1963, when the American Standards Association adopted a 7-bit standard character code for information interchange (ASCII). This 7-bit code is now under final consideration by the International Standards Organization for adoption as an international standards recommendation. The question became "Why not adopt ASCII as the *only* internal code for System/360?"

The reasons against such exclusive adoption was the widespread use of the BCD code derived from and easily translated to the IBM card code. To facilitate use of both codes, the central processing units are designed with a high degree of code independence, with generalized code translation facilities, and with program-selectable BCD or ASCII modes for code-dependent instructions. Neverthe-

Figure 2a **Extended binary-coded-decimal (BCD) interchange code.**

Bit Positions → 01

4567	00·00	00·01	00·10	00·11	01·00	01·01	01·10	01·11	10·00	10·01	10·10	10·11	11·00	11·01	11·10	11·11
0000	NULL				BLANK	&	–						>	<	‡	0
0001							/		a	j			A	J		1
0010									b	k	s		B	K	S	2
0011									c	l	t		C	L	T	3
0100	PF	RES	BYP	PN					d	m	u		D	M	U	4
0101	HT	NL	LF	RS					e	n	v		E	N	V	5
0110	LC	BS	EOB	UC					f	o	w		F	O	W	6
0111	DEL	IDL	PRE	EOT					g	p	x		G	P	X	7
1000									h	q	y		H	Q	Y	8
1001					.		,	"	i	r	z		I	R	Z	9
1010					?	!		:								
1011					.	$	,	#								
1100					←	*	%	@								
1101					(	)	⁀	'								
1110					+	;	_	=								
1111					‡	¢	$\pm$	√								

Column group headers: 01 = 00, 01, 10, 11; within each, 23 = 00, 01, 10, 11.

Figure 2b **8-bit representation of the 7-bit American Standard Code for Information Interchange (ASCII).**

Bit Positions → 76

4321	00·00	00·01	00·10	00·11	01·00	01·01	01·10	01·11	10·00	10·01	10·10	10·11	11·00	11·01	11·10	11·11
0000	NULL	DC_0			BLANK	0					@	P				p
0001	SOM	DC_1			!	1					A	Q			a	q
0010	EOA	DC_2			"	2					B	R			b	r
0011	EOM	DC_3			#	3					C	S			c	s
0100	EQT	DC_4 STOP			$	4					D	T			d	t
0101	WRU	ERR			%	5					E	U			e	u
0110	RU	SYNC			&	6					F	V			f	v
0111	BELL	LEM			'	7					G	W			g	w
1000	BKSP	S_0			(	8					H	X			h	x
1001	HT	S_1			)	9					I	Y			i	y
1010	LF	S_2			*	:					J	Z			j	z
1011	VT	S_3			+	;					K	[			k	
1100	FF	S_4			,	<					L	\			l	
1101	CR	S_5			–	=					M	]			m	
1110	SO	S_6			.	>					N	↑			n	ESC
1111	SI	S_7			/	?					O	←			o	DEL

Column group headers: 76 = 00, 01, 10, 11; within each, X5 = 00, 01, 10, 11.

less, a choice had to be made for the code-sensitive I/O devices and for the programming support, and the solution was to offer both codes, fully supported, as a user option. Systems with either option will, of course, easily read or write I/O media with the other code. The extended BCD interchange code and an 8-bit representation of the 7-bit ASCII are shown in Fig. 2.

Boundary alignment. A major compatibility problem concerned alignment of field boundaries. Different models were to have different widths of storage and data flow, and therefore each model had a different set of preferences. For the 8-bit wide model the characters might have been aligned on character boundaries, with no further constraints. In the 64-bit wide model it might have been preferred to have no fields split between different 64-bit double-words. The general rule adopted (Fig. 3) was that each fixed field must begin at a multiple of its field length, and variable-length decimal and character fields are unconstrained and are processed serially in all models. All models must insure that programmers will adhere to these rules. This policing is essential to prevent the use of technically invalid programs that might work beautifully on small models but not on large ones. Such an outcome would undermine compatibility. The general rule, which has very few and very minor exceptions, is that invalidities defined in the manual are detected in the hardware and cause an interruption. This type of interruption is distinct from an interruption caused by machine malfunctions.

• *Instruction decisions*

Pushdown stack vs addressed registers. Serious consideration was given to a design based on a pushdown accumulator or stack.[2] This plan was abandoned in favor of several registers, each explicitly addressed. Since the advantages of the pushdown organization are discussed in the literature,[3] it suffices here to enumerate the disadvantages which prompted the decision to use an addressed-register organization:

1. The performance advantage of a pushdown stack organization is derived principally from the presence of several fast registers, not from the way they are used or specified.

2. The fraction of "surfacings" of data in the stack which are "profitable," i.e., what was needed next, is about one-half in general use, because of the occurrence of repeated operands (both constants and common factors). This suggests the use of operations such as TOP and SWAP, which respectively copy submerged data to the active positions and assist in clearing submerged data when the information is no longer needed.

3. With TOP's and SWAP's counted, the substantial instruction density gained by the widespread use of implicit addresses is about equalled by that of the same instruc-

tions with explicit, but truncated, addresses which specify only the fast registers.

4. In any practical implementation, the depth of the stack has a limit. The register housekeeping eliminated by the pushdown organization reappears as management of a finite-depth stack and as specification of locations of submerged data for TOP's and SWAP's. Further, when part of a full stack must be dumped to make room for new data, it is the *bottom* part, not the active part, which should be dumped.

5. Subroutine transparency, i.e., the ability to use a subroutine recursively, is one of the apparent advantages of the stack. However, the *disadvantage* is that the transparency does not materialize unless additional independent stacks are introduced for addressing purposes.

6. Fitting variable-length fields into a fixed-width stack is awkward.

In the final analysis, the stack organization would have been about break-even for a system intended principally for scientific computing. Here the general-purpose objective weighed heavily in favor of the more flexible addressed-register organization.

Full vs truncated addresses. From the beginning, the major challenge of compatibility lay in storage addressing. It was clear that large models would require storage capacities in the millions of characters. Small (serial) models would require short addresses to conserve precious core space and instruction fetch time. Some help was given by the decision to use register addressing, which reduces address appearances in the instruction stream by a factor approaching 2.

An early decision had dictated that all addresses had to be indexable, and that a mechanism had to be provided for making all programs easily relocatable. The indexing technique had fully proved its worth in current systems.[4] This technique suggested that abundant address size could be attained through a full-sized index register, used as a base. This approach, coupled with a truncated address in the instruction, gives consequent gains in instruction density. The *base-register* approach was adopted, and then augmented, for some instructions, with a second level of indexing.

Now the question was: How much capacity was to be made directly addressable, and how much addressable only via base registers? Some early uses of base register techniques had been fairly unsuccessful, principally because of awkward transitions between direct and base addressing. It was decided to commit the system completely to a base-register technique; the direct part of the address, the *displacement*, was made so small (12 bits, or 4096 characters) that direct addressing is a practical programming technique only on very small models. This

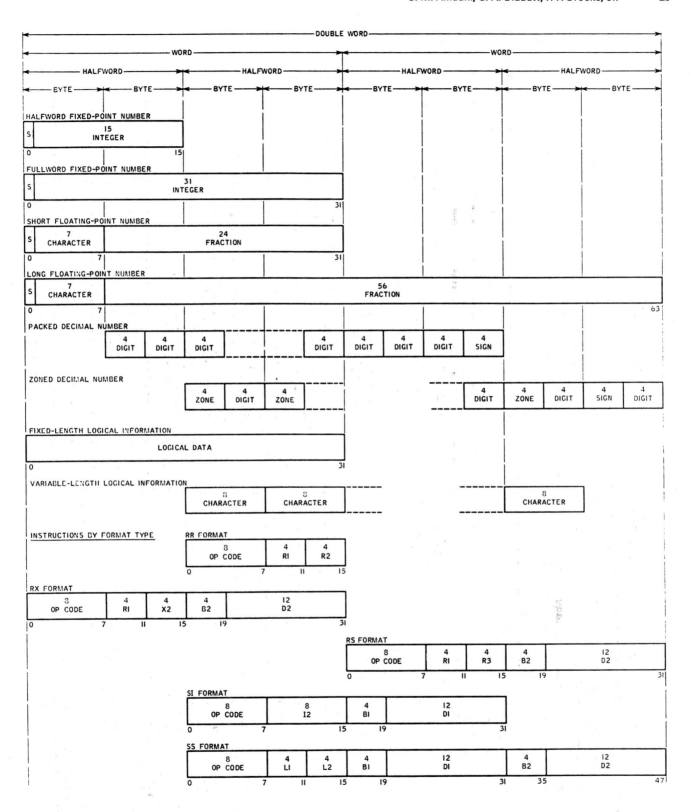

Figure 3 **Boundary alignment of formats.**

commitment implies that all programs are location-independent, except for constants used to load the base registers. Thus, all programs can easily be relocated. This commitment also implies that the programming support effectively and efficiently handles the mechanics of base-register use. The assembler automatically constructs and assigns base-plus-displacement addresses as it constructs the symbol table. The compilers not only do this, but also allocate base registers to give efficient programs.

Decimal vs binary addressing. It was decided to use binary rather than decimal addressing, because (a) assembly programs remove the user one level from the address, thus reducing the importance of familiar usage, (b) binary addressing is more efficient in the ratio 3.32/4.00, and (c) table exploitation is easier and more general because any datum can be made into or added to a binary address, yielding a valid address. This decision, however, represented some conflict with past approaches. Machines for purely business applications had often used decimal addressing (in the ancestral machine of the family). Most business computers now have binary addressing or have evolved to mixed-radix addressing.

Multiple accumulators. An extrapolation of technological trends indicated the probable availability of small, high-speed storage. Consequently, the design uses a substantial number of logically identifiable registers, which are physically realized in core storage, local high-speed storage, or transistors, according to the model. There are sixteen 32-bit general-purpose registers and four 64-bit floating-point registers in the logical design, with room for expansion to eight floating-point registers. Surprisingly enough, the multiple-register decision was not a large-small conflict. Each model has an appropriate (and different) mechanization of the same logical design.

Storage hierarchies. Technology promises to yield a continuing spectrum of storage systems whose speed varies inversely with capacity for equal cost-per-bit. Of equal significance, problem requirements naturally follow a matching pattern — small quantities of data are used with great frequency, medium quantities with medium frequency, and very large quantities with low frequency. These facts promise substantial performance/cost advantages if storage hierarchies can be effectively used.

It was decided to accept the engineering, architectural, and programming disciplines required for storage-hierarchy use. The engineer must accommodate in one system several storage technologies, with separate speeds, circuits, power requirements, busing needs, etc., all requiring asynchronous operation of all storage with respect to the CPU. The system programmer must contend with awkward boundaries within total storage capacity and must allocate usage. He must devise addressing for very large capacities, block transfers, and means of handling, indexing across and providing protection across

gaps in the addressing sequence.

Separate vs universal accumulators. There are several advantages of having fixed- and floating-point arithmetic use the same logical (as opposed to physical) registers. There are some less obvious disadvantages which weighed in favor of separate accumulator sets. First, in a given register specification (4 bits, in our case) the use of separate sets permits more registers to be specified because of the information implications of the operation code. Second, in the large models instruction execution and the preparation of later instructions are done concurrently in separate units. To use a single register set would couple these closely, and reduce the asynchronous concurrency that can be attained. Historically, index registers have been separated from fixed-point registers, limiting analysis of register allocation to index quantities only. Integration of these facilities brings the full power of the fixed-point arithmetic operation set to bear upon indexing computations. The advantages of the integration appear throughout program execution (even compiler and assembly execution), whereas the register allocation burdens only compilation and assembly.

- *Input/output system*

The method of input/output control would have been a major compatibility problem were it not for the recognition of the distinction between logical and physical structures. Small machines use CPU hardware for I/O functions; large machines demand several independent channels, capable of operating concurrently with the CPU and with each other. Such large-machine channels often each contain more components than an entire small system.

Channel instructions. The logical design considers the channel as an independently operating entity. The CPU program starts the channel operation by specifying the beginning of a channel program and the unit to be used. The channel instructions, specialized for the I/O function, specify storage blocks to be read or written, unit operations, conditional and unconditional branches within the channel program, etc. When the channel program ends, the CPU program is interrupted, and complete channel and device status information are available.

An especially valuable feature is *command chaining*, the ability of successive channel instructions to give a sequence of different operations to the unit, such as SEARCH, READ, WRITE, READ FOR CHECK. This feature permits devices to be reinstructed in very short times, thus substantially enhancing effective speed.

Standard interface. The generalization of the communication between the central processing unit and an input/output device has yielded a channel which presents a standard interface to the device control unit. This interface was achieved by making the channel design transparent, passing not only data, but also control and status information between storage and device. All functions peculiar to the device are placed in the control unit. The interface requires a total of 29 lines and is made independent of time through the use of interlocking signals.

Implementation. In small models, the flow of data and control information is time-shared between the CPU and the channel function. When a byte of data appears from an I/O device, the CPU is seized, dumped, used and restored. Although the maximum data rate handled is lower (and the interference with CPU computation higher) than with separate hardware, the function is identical.

Once the channel becomes a conceptual entity, using time-shared hardware, one may have a large number of channels at virtually no cost save the core storage space for the governing control words. This kind of *multiplex channel* embodies up to 256 conceptual channels, all of which may be concurrently operating, when the total data rate is within acceptable limits. The multiplexing constitutes a major advance for communications-based systems.

Conclusion

This paper has shown how the design features were chosen for the logical structure of the six models that comprise the IBM System/360. The rationale has been given for the adoption of the data formats, the instruction set, and the input/output controls. The main features of the new machine organization are its general-purpose utility for many types of data processing, the new approaches

to large-capacity storage, and the machine-language compatibility among the six models.

The contributions discussed in this paper may be summarized as follows:

1. The relative independence of logical structure and physical realization permits efficient implementation at various levels of performance.

2. Tasks that are common to operating a system for most applications require a complement of instructions and system functions that may serve as a base for the addition of application-oriented functions.

3. The formats, instructions, register assignment, and over-all functions such as protection and interruption of a computer can be so defined that they apply to many levels of performance and that they permit diverse specialization for particular applications.

It is hoped that the discussions of these design features will shed some light on the present and future needs of data processing system organization.

Appendices

The design resulting from the decision process sketched above is tabulated in five appendices showing formats, data and instruction codes, storage assignments and interruption action. (*Appendices 1 through 5 appear on the following four pages.*)

Acknowledgments

The implementation of System/360 depends upon diverse developments by many colleagues. The most important of these developments were glass-encapsulated semi-integrated semiconductor components, printed circuit backpanels and interconnections, new memories, read-only storages and microprogram techniques, new I/O devices, and a new level and approach to software support.

The scope of the compatibility objective and of the whole System/360 undertaking was largely due to B. O. Evans, Data Systems Division Vice-President—Development.

References

1. D. W. Sweeney, "An Analysis of Floating-Point Addition and Shifting," to be published in the *IBM Systems Journal*.
2. See, for example, R. S. Barton, "A New Approach to the Functional Design of a Digital Computer," *Proc. WJCC* 19, 393–396 (1961).
3. F. P. Brooks, Jr., "Recent Developments in Computer Organization," *Advances in Electronics* 18, 45–64 (1963).
4. G. A. Blaauw, "Indexing," in *Planning a Computer System*, W. Buchholz, ed., McGraw-Hill Book Company Inc., 1962, pp. 150–178.

Received January 21, 1964

Appendix 2 continued

from addressable registers and storage. The PSW is stored upon interruption. The Channel Command Word controls input/output operation and sequencing. The commands which may be given to the channel are listed as part of the table. The Channel Address Word is used to initiate input/output sequencing. The Channel Status Word indicates the channel status at the completion of an input/output operation or, when specified, during an I/O operation.

CONTROL WORD FORMATS

Base and Index Registers

```
r-0-0-0-0-0-0-0-0-1-1-1-1-1-1-1-1-2-2-2-2-2-2-2-2-3-...
                  BASE ADDRESS OR INDEX
 0-1-2-3-4-5-6-7-8-9-0-1-2-3-4-5-6-7-8-9-0-1-2-3-4-5-6-7-8-9-0-1

 0 -  7  Ignored
 8 - 31  Base address or index
```

Program Status Word

```
r-0-0-0-0-0-0-0-0-1-1-1-1-1-1-1-1-2-2-2-2-2-2-2-2-3-3-
| SYSTEM MASK |  KEY  | A M W P |   INTERRUPTION CODE
 0-1-2-3-4-5-6-7-8-9-0-1-2-3-4-5-6-7-8-9-0-1-2-3-4-5-6-7-8-9-0-1

 3-3-3-3-3-3-3-4-4-4-4-4-4-4-4-4-5-5-5-5-5-5-5-5-6-6-6-6-
|ILC|CC|PROGRAM|        INSTRUCTION ADDRESS
       | MASK |
 2-3-4-5-6-7-8-9-0-1-2-3-4-5-6-7-8-9-0-1-2-3
```

```
 0 -  7  System mask
      0    Multiplexor channel mask
      1    Selector channel 1 mask
      2    Selector channel 2 mask
      3    Selector channel 3 mask
      4    Selector channel 4 mask
      5    Selector channel 5 mask
      6    Selector channel 6 mask
      7    External mask
 8 - 11  Protection key
12       ASCII mode (A)
13       Machine check mask (M)
14       Wait state (W)
15       Problem state (P)
16 - 31  Interruption code
32 - 33  Instruction length code (ILC)
34 - 35  Condition code (CC)
36 - 39  Program mask
     36   Fixed-point overflow mask
     37   Decimal overflow mask
     38   Exponent underflow mask
     39   Significance mask
40 - 63  Instruction address
```

Appendix 1 All operation codes are shown in the following table. The 8-bit codes are grouped by the main classes, such as fixed-point arithmetic, floating-point arithmetic and logical operations. The codes are furthermore grouped according to the five main instruction formats RR (register-register), RX (register-indexed storage location), RS (register-storage), SI (storage-immediate information) and SS (storage-storage).

OPERATION CODES

FORMAT	RR	RR	RR	RR
CLASS	BRANCHING AND STATUS SWITCHING	FIXED-POINT FULLWORD, AND LOGICAL	FLOATING-POINT LONG	FLOATING-POINT SHORT
xxxx	0000xxxx	0001xxxx	0010xxxx	0011xxxx
0000		LOAD POSITIVE	LOAD POSITIVE	LOAD POSITIVE
0001		LOAD NEGATIVE	LOAD NEGATIVE	LOAD NEGATIVE
0010		LOAD AND TEST	LOAD AND TEST	LOAD AND TEST
0011		LOAD COMPLEMENT	LOAD COMPLEMENT	LOAD COMPLEMENT
0100	SET PROGRAM MASK	AND	HALVE	HALVE
0101	BRANCH AND LINK	COMPARE LOGICAL		
0110	BRANCH ON COUNT	OR		
0111	BRANCH/CONDITION	EXCLUSIVE OR		
1000	SET KEY	LOAD	LOAD	LOAD
1001	INSERT KEY	COMPARE	COMPARE	COMPARE
1010	SUPERVISOR CALL	ADD	ADD N	ADD N
1011		SUBTRACT	SUBTRACT N	SUBTRACT N
1100		MULTIPLY	MULTIPLY	MULTIPLY
1101		DIVIDE	DIVIDE	DIVIDE
1110		ADD LOGICAL	ADD U	ADD U
1111		SUBTRACT LOGICAL	SUBTRACT U	SUBTRACT U

FORMAT	RX	RX	RX	RX
CLASS	FIXED-POINT HALFWORD AND BRANCHING	FIXED-POINT FULLWORD AND LOGICAL	FLOATING-POINT LONG	FLOATING-POINT SHORT
xxxx	0100xxxx	0101xxxx	0110xxxx	0111xxxx
0000	STORE	STORE	STORE	STORE
0001	LOAD ADDRESS			
0010	STORE CHARACTER			
0011	INSERT CHARACTER			
0100	EXECUTE	AND		
0101	BRANCH AND LINK	COMPARE LOGICAL		
0110	BRANCH ON COUNT	OR		
0111	BRANCH/CONDITION	EXCLUSIVE OR		
1000	LOAD	LOAD	LOAD	LOAD
1001	COMPARE	COMPARE	COMPARE	COMPARE
1010	ADD	ADD	ADD N	ADD N
1011	SUBTRACT	SUBTRACT	SUBTRACT N	SUBTRACT N
1100	MULTIPLY	MULTIPLY	MULTIPLY	MULTIPLY
1101		DIVIDE	DIVIDE	DIVIDE
1110	CONVERT-DECIMAL	ADD LOGICAL	ADD U	ADD U
1111	CONVERT-BINARY	SUBTRACT LOGICAL	SUBTRACT U	SUBTRACT U

Appendix 1 continued

FORMAT CLASS	RS,SI BRANCHING, STATUS SWITCHING AND SHIFTING	RS,SI FIXED-POINT, LOGICAL, AND INPUT/OUTPUT		
xxxx	1000xxxx	1001xxxx	1010xxxx	1011xxxx
0000	SET SYSTEM MASK	STORE MULTIPLE		
0001		TEST UNDER MASK		
0010	LOAD PSW	MOVE		
0011	DIAGNOSE			
0100	WRITE DIRECT	AND		
0101	READ DIRECT	COMPARE LOGICAL		
0110	BRANCH/HIGH	OR		
0111	BRANCH/LOW-EQUAL	EXCLUSIVE OR		
1000	SHIFT RIGHT SL	LOAD MULTIPLE		
1001	SHIFT LEFT SL			
1010	SHIFT RIGHT S			
1011	SHIFT LEFT S			
1100	SHIFT RIGHT DL	START I/O		
1101	SHIFT LEFT DL	TEST I/O		
1110	SHIFT RIGHT D	HALT I/O		
1111	SHIFT LEFT D	TEST CHANNEL		

FORMAT CLASS		SS LOGICAL		SS DECIMAL
xxxx	1100xxxx	1101xxxx	1110xxxx	1111xxxx
0000		MOVE NUMERIC		
0001		MOVE		MOVE W OFFSET
0010		MOVE ZONE		PACK
0011		AND		UNPACK
0100		COMPARE LOGICAL		
0101		OR		
0110		EXCLUSIVE OR		
0111				
1000				ZERO AND ADD
1001				COMPARE
1010				ADD
1011				SUBTRACT
1100		TRANSLATE		MULTIPLY
1101		TRANSLATE AND TEST		DIVIDE
1110		EDIT		
1111		EDIT AND MARK		

Legend
```
N  = Normalized         U = Unnormalized
SL = Single logical     S = Single
DL = Double logical     D = Double
```

Appendix 2 continued

Channel Command Word
```
 0-0-0-0-0-0-0-0-1-1-1-1-1-1-1-1-2-2-2-2-2-2-2-2-3-3
 0-1-2-3-4-5-6-7-8-9-0-1-2-3-4-5-6-7-8-9-0-1-2-3-4-5-6-7-8-9-0-1
| COMMAND CODE |            DATA ADDRESS               |

 3-3-3-3-3-3-4-4-4-4-4-4-4-4-4-5-5-5-5-5-5-5-5-5-6-6
 2-3-4-5-6-7-8-9-0-1-2-3-4-5-6-7-8-9-0-1-2-3-4-5-6-7-8-9-0-1-2-3
| FLAGS |0 0 0|  *  |            COUNT                |
```

```
 0  -  7   Command code
 8  - 31   Data address
32  - 36   Command flags
      32     Chain data flag
      33     Chain command flag
      34     Suppress-length indication flag
      35     Skip flag
      36     Program-controlled interruption flag
37  - 39   Zero
40  - 47   Ignored
48  - 63   Count
```

Channel Address Word
```
 0-0-0-0-0-0-0-0-1-1-1-1-1-1-1-1-2-2-2-2-2-2-2-2-3-3
 0-1-2-3-4-5-6-7-8-9-0-1-2-3-4-5-6-7-8-9-0-1-2-3-4-5-6-7-8-9-0-1
| KEY |0 0 0 0|           COMMAND ADDRESS             |
```

```
 0  -  3   Protection key
 4  -  7   Zero
 8  - 31   Command address
```

Channel Status Word
```
 0-0-0-0-0-0-0-0-1-1-1-1-1-1-1-1-2-2-2-2-2-2-2-2-3-3
 0-1-2-3-4-5-6-7-8-9-0-1-2-3-4-5-6-7-8-9-0-1-2-3-4-5-6-7-8-9-0-1
| KEY |0 0 0 0|           COMMAND ADDRESS             |

 3-3-3-3-3-3-4-4-4-4-4-4-4-4-4-5-5-5-5-5-5-5-5-5-6-6
 2-3-4-5-6-7-8-9-0-1-2-3-4-5-6-7-8-9-0-1-2-3-4-5-6-7-8-9-0-1-2-3
|            STATUS            |            COUNT      |
```

```
 0  -  3   Protection key
 4  -  7   Zero
 8  - 31   Command address
32  - 47   Status
      32     Attention
      33     Status modifier
      34     Control unit end
      35     Busy
      36     Channel end
      37     Device end
      38     Unit check
      39     Unit exception
      40     Program-controlled interruption
```

(continued overleaf)

Appendix 2 **The formats of all control words required for CPU and channel operation are shown in the following table. The base and index registers provide 24 bits of address and are specified by the B and X fields of instructions. The Program Status Word controls instruction sequencing and indicates the complete CPU status apart**

Appendix 2 continued

```
41      Incorrect length
42      Program check
43      Protection check
44      Channel data check
45      Channel control check
46      Interface control check
47      Chaining check
48 - 63 Count
```

Appendix 3 All permanently assigned storage locations are shown in this table. These locations are addressed by the CPU and I/O channels during initial program loading, during interruptions and in order to update the timer. During initial program loading 24 bytes are read from a specified input device into locations 0 to 23. This information is subsequently used as CCW's to specify the locations of further input information and as a PSW to control CPU operation after the loading operation is completed. During an interruption the current PSW is stored in the "old" location and the PSW from the "new" location is obtained as the next PSW. The timer is counted down and provides an interrupt when zero is passed. All permanently assigned locations may also be addressed by the program.

PERMANENT STORAGE ASSIGNMENT

ADDRESS	LENGTH	PURPOSE
0 0000 0000	double word	Initial program loading PSW
8 0000 1000	double word	Initial program loading CCW1
16 0001 0000	double word	Initial program loading CCW2
24 0001 1000	double word	External old PSW
32 0010 0000	double word	Supervisor call old PSW
40 0010 1000	double word	Program old PSW
48 0011 0000	double word	Machine old PSW
56 0011 1000	double word	Input/output old PSW
64 0100 0000	double word	Channel status word
72 0100 1000	word	Channel address word
76 0100 1100	word	Unused
80 0101 0000	word	Timer
84 0101 0100	word	Unused
88 0101 1000	double word	External new PSW
96 0110 0000	double word	Supervisor call new PSW
104 0110 1000	double word	Program new PSW
112 0111 0000	double word	Machine new PSW
120 0111 1000	double word	Input/output new PSW
128 1000 0000	double word	Diagnostic scan-out area*

---

* The size of the diagnostic scan-out area depends upon the particular model and I/O channels.

Appendix 4 continued

<u>Legend</u>

available	Unit and channel available
busy	Unit or channel busy
carry	A carry out of the sign position occurs
complete	Last result byte nonzero
CSW ready	Channel status word ready for test or interruption
CSW stored	Channel status word stored
equal	Operands compare equal
F	Fullword
g zero	Result is greater than zero
H	Halfword
halted	Data transmission stopped. Unit in halt-reset mode
high	First operand compares high
incomplete	Nonzero result byte; not last
L	Long precision
l zero	Result is less than zero
low	First operand compares low
mixed	Selected bits are both zero and one
not oper	Unit or channel not operational
not working	Unit or channel not working
not zero	Result is not all zero
one	Selected bits are one
overflow	Result overflows
S	Short precision
stopped	Data transmission stopped
working	Unit or channel working
zero	Result or selected bits are zero

<u>Note</u>

The condition code also may be changed by LOAD PSW, SET SYSTEM MASK, DIAGNOSE, and by an interruption.

Appendix 5 All interruptions which may occur are shown in the following table. Indicated here are the code in the old PSW which identifies the source of the interruption, the mask bits which may be used to prevent an interruption, and the manner in which instruction execution is affected. The instruction to be performed next if the interruption had not occurred is indicated in the instruction address field of the old PSW. The length of the preceding instructions, if available, is shown in the instruction length code, ILC, as is further detailed in the table.

INTERRUPTION ACTION

INTERRUPTION SOURCE IDENTIFICATION	INTERRUPTION CODE PSW BITS 16-31	MASK BITS SET	ILC	INSTRUCTION EXECUTION
Input/Output (old PSW 56, new PSW 120, priority 4)				
Multiplexor channel	00000000 aaaaaaaa	0	x	complete
Selector channel 1	00000001 aaaaaaaa	1	x	complete
Selector channel 2	00000010 aaaaaaaa	2	x	complete
```
```

Appendix 5 continued

Selector channel 3	00000011 aaaaaaaa	3	x	complete
Selector channel 4	00000100 aaaaaaaa	4	x	complete
Selector channel 5	00000101 aaaaaaaa	5	x	complete
Selector channel 6	00000110 aaaaaaaa	6	x	complete

Program (old PSW 40, new PSW 104, priority 2)

Operation	00000000 00000001	1,2,3	suppress
Privileged operation	00000000 00000010	1,2	suppress
Execute	00000000 00000011	2	suppress
Protection	00000000 00000100	0,2,3	suppress/terminate
Addressing	00000000 00000101	0,1,2,3	suppress/terminate
Specification	00000000 00000110	1,2,3	suppress
Data	00000000 00000111	2,3	terminate
Fixed-point overflow	00000000 00001000	36	complete
Fixed-point divide	00000000 00001001	1,2	suppress/complete
Decimal overflow	00000000 00001010	37	complete
Decimal divide	00000000 00001011	3	suppress
Exponent overflow	00000000 00001100	1,2	terminate
Exponent underflow	00000000 00001101	38	complete
Significance *	00000000 00001110	1,2	complete
Floating-point divide	00000000 00001111	1,2	suppress

Supervisor Call (old PSW 32, new PSW 96, priority 2)

Instruction bits	00000000 rrrrrrrr	1	complete

External (old PSW 24, new PSW 88, priority 3)

External signal 1	00000000 xxxxxxx1	7	x	complete
External signal 2	00000000 xxxxxx1x	7	x	complete
External signal 3	00000000 xxxxx1xx	7	x	complete
External signal 4	00000000 xxxx1xxx	7	x	complete
External signal 5	00000000 xxx1xxxx	7	x	complete
External signal 6	00000000 xx1xxxxx	7	x	complete
Interrupt key	00000000 x1xxxxxx	7	x	complete
Timer	00000000 1xxxxxxx	7	x	complete

Machine Check (old PSW 48, new PSW 112, priority 1)

Machine malfunction	00000000 00000000	13	x	terminate

Legend

a   Device address bits
r   Bits of R1 and R2 field of SUPERVISOR CALL
x   Unpredictable

INSTRUCTION LENGTH RECORDING

INSTRUCTION LENGTH CODE	PSW BITS 32-33	INSTRUCTION BITS 0-1	INSTRUCTION LENGTH	INSTRUCTION FORMAT
0	00	00	Not available	Not available
1	01	01	One halfword	RR
2	10	10	Two halfwords	RX
2	10	10	Two halfwords	RS or SI
3	11	11	Three halfwords	SS

Appendix 4

Appendix 4 All instructions which set the condition code (bits 32 and 33 of the PSW) are listed in the following table. All other instructions leave the condition code unchanged. The condition code determines the outcome of a BRANCH ON CONDITION instruction. The four-bit mask contained in this instruction specifies which code settings will cause the branch to be taken.

	CONDITION CODE SETTING			
	0	1	2	3
Fixed-Point Arithmetic				
ADD H/F	zero	l zero	g zero	overflow
ADD LOGICAL	zero	not zero	zero,carry	carry
COMPARE H/F	equal	low	high	--
LOAD AND TEST	zero	l zero	g zero	--
LOAD COMPLEMENT	zero	l zero	g zero	overflow
LOAD NEGATIVE	zero	l zero	--	--
LOAD POSITIVE	zero	--	g zero	overflow
SHIFT LEFT DOUBLE	zero	l zero	g zero	overflow
SHIFT LEFT SINGLE	zero	l zero	g zero	overflow
SHIFT RIGHT DOUBLE	zero	l zero	g zero	--
SHIFT RIGHT SINGLE	zero	l zero	g zero	--
SUBTRACT H/F	zero	l zero	g zero	overflow
SUBTRACT LOGICAL	--	not zero	zero,carry	carry
Decimal Arithmetic				
ADD DECIMAL	zero	l zero	g zero	overflow
COMPARE DECIMAL	equal	low	high	--
SUBTRACT DECIMAL	zero	l zero	g zero	overflow
ZERO AND ADD	zero	l zero	g zero	overflow
Floating-Point Arithmetic				
ADD NORMALIZED S/L	zero	l zero	g zero	overflow
ADD UNNORMALIZED S/L	zero	l zero	g zero	overflow
COMPARE S/L	equal	low	high	--
LOAD AND TEST S/L	zero	l zero	g zero	--
LOAD COMPLEMENT S/L	zero	l zero	g zero	--
LOAD NEGATIVE S/L	zero	l zero	--	--
LOAD POSITIVE S/L	zero	--	g zero	--
SUBTRACT NORMALIZED S/L	zero	l zero	g zero	overflow
SUBTRACT UNNORMALIZED S/L	zero	l zero	g zero	overflow
Logical Operations				
AND	zero	not zero	--	--
COMPARE LOGICAL	equal	low	high	--
EDIT	zero	l zero	g zero	--
EDIT AND MARK	zero	l zero	g zero	--
EXCLUSIVE OR	zero	not zero	--	--
OR	zero	not zero	--	--
TEST UNDER MASK	zero	mixed	--	one
TRANSLATE AND TEST	zero	incomplete	complete	--
Input-Output Operations				
HALT I/O	not working	halted	stopped	not oper
START I/O	available	CSW stored	busy	not oper
TEST CHANNEL	not working	CSW ready	working	not oper
TEST I/O	available	CSW stored	working	not oper

PARALLEL OPERATION IN THE CONTROL DATA 6600

James E. Thornton
Control Data Corporation
Minneapolis, Minnesota

HISTORY

About four years ago, in the summer of 1960, Control Data began a project which culminated last month in the delivery of the first 6600 Computer. In 1960 it was apparent that brute force circuit performance and parallel operation were the two main approaches to any advanced computer.

This paper presents some of the considerations having to do with the parallel operations in the 6600. A most important and fortunate event coincided with the beginning of the 6600 project. This was the appearance of the high-speed silicon transistor, which survived early difficulties to become the basis for a nice jump in circuit performance.

SYSTEM ORGANIZATION

The computing system envisioned in that project, and now called the 6600, paid special attention to two kinds of use, the very large scientific problem and the time sharing of smaller problems. For the large problem, a high-speed floating point central processor with access to a large central memory was obvious. Not so obvious, but important to the 6600 system idea, was the isolation of this central arithmetic from any peripheral activity.

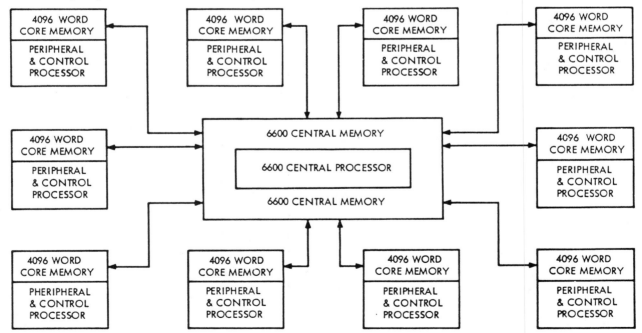

Figure 1.   Control Data 6600.

It was from this general line of reasoning that the idea of a multiplicity of peripheral processors was formed (Fig. 1). Ten such peripheral processors have access to the central memory on one side and the peripheral channels on the other. The executive control of the system is always in one of these peripheral processors, with the others operating on assigned peripheral or control tasks. All ten processors have access to twelve input-output channels and may "change hands," monitor channel activity, and perform other related jobs. These processors have access to central memory, and may pursue independent transfers to and from this memory.

Each of the ten peripheral processors contains its own memory for program and buffer areas, thereby isolating and protecting the more critical system control operations in the separate processors. The central processor operates from the central memory with relocating register and file protection for each program in central memory.

PERIPHERAL AND CONTROL PROCESSORS

The peripheral and control processors are housed in one chassis of the main frame. Each processor contains 4096 memory words of 12 bits length. There are 12- and 24-bit

instruction formats to provide for direct, indirect, and relative addressing. Instructions provide logical, addition, subtraction, shift, and conditional branching. Instructions also provide single word or block transfers to and from any of twelve peripheral channels, and single word or block transfers to and from central memory. Central memory words of 60 bits length are assembled from five consecutive peripheral words. Each processor has instructions to interrupt the central processor and to monitor the central program address.

To get this much processing power with reasonable economy and space, a time-sharing design was adopted (Fig. 2). This design contains a register "barrel" around which is moving the dynamic information for all ten processors. Such things as program address, accumulator contents, and other pieces of information totalling 52 bits are shifted around the barrel. Each complete trip around requires one major cycle or one thousand nanoseconds. A "slot" in the barrel contains adders, assembly networks, distribution network, and interconnections to perform one step of any peripheral instruction. The time to perform this step or, in other words, the time through the slot, is one minor cycle or one hundred nanoseconds. Each of the ten processors, therefore, is allowed

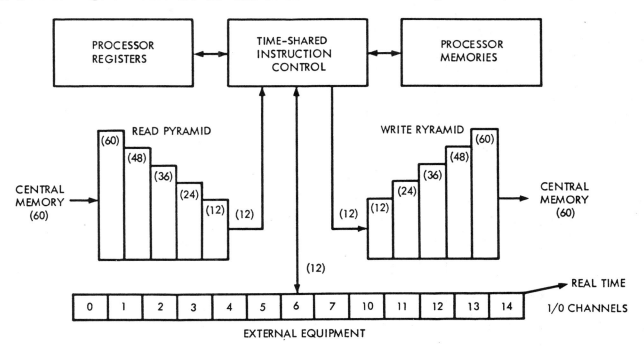

Figure 2. 6600 Peripheral and Control Processors.

one minor cycle of every ten to perform one of its steps. A peripheral instruction may require one or more of these steps, depending on the kind of instruction.

In effect, the single arithmetic and the single distribution and assembly network are made to appear as ten. Only the memories are kept truly independent. Incidentally, the memory read-write cycle time is equal to one complete trip around the barrel, or one thousand nanoseconds.

Input-output channels are bi-directional, 12-bit·paths. One 12-bit word may move in one direction every major cycle, or 1000 nanoseconds, on each channel. Therefore, a maximum burst rate of 120 million bits per second is possible using all ten peripheral processors. A sustained rate of about 50 million bits per second can be maintained in a practical operating system. Each channel may service several peripheral devices and may interface to other systems, such as satellite computers.

Peripheral and control processors access central memory through an assembly network and a dis-assembly network. Since five peripheral memory references are required to make up one central memory word, a natural assembly network of five levels is used. This allows

five references to be "nested" in each network during any major cycle. The central memory is organized in independent banks with the ability to transfer central words every minor cycle. The peripheral processors, therefore, introduce at most about 2% interference at the central memory address control.

A single real time clock, continuously running, is available to all peripheral processors.

CENTRAL PROCESSOR

The 6600 central processor may be considered the high-speed arithmetic unit of the system (Fig. 3). Its program, operands, and results are held in the central memory. It has no connection to the peripheral processors except through memory and except for two single controls. These are the exchange jump, which starts or interrupts the central processor from a peripheral processor, and the central program address which can be monitored by a peripheral processor.

A key description of the 6600 central processor, as you will see in later discussion, is "parallel by function." This means that a number of arithmetic functions may be performed

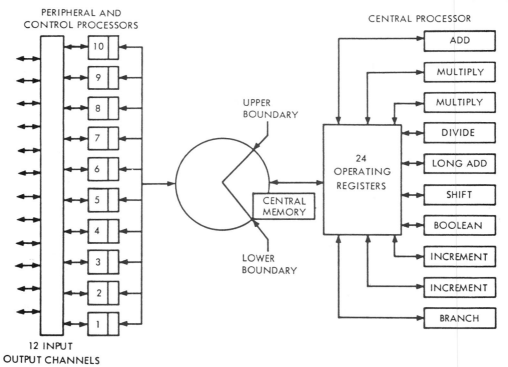

Figure 3. Block Diagram of 6600.

concurrently. To this end, there are ten functional units within the central processor. These are the two increment units, floating add unit, fixed add unit, shift unit, two multiply units, divide unit, boolean unit, and branch unit. In a general way, each of these units is a three address unit. As an example, the floating add unit obtains two 60-bit operands from the central registers and produces a 60-bit result which is returned to a register. Information to and from these units is held in the central registers, of which there are twenty-four. Eight of these are considered index registers, are of 18 bits length, and one of which always contains zero. Eight are considered address registers, are of 18 bits length, and serve to address the five read central memory trunks and the two store central memory trunks. Eight are considered floating point registers, are of 60 bits length, and are the only central registers to access central memory during a central program.

In a sense, just as the whole central processor is hidden behind central memory from the peripheral processors, so, too, the ten functional units are hidden behind the central registers from central memory. As a consequence, a considerable instruction efficiency is obtained and an interesting form of concurrency is feasible and practical. The fact that a small number of bits can give meaningful definition to any function makes it possible to develop forms of operand and unit reservations needed for a general scheme of concurrent arithmetic.

Instructions are organized in two formats, a 15-bit format and a 30-bit format, and may be mixed in an instruction word (Fig. 4).

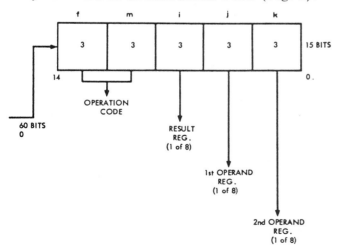

Figure 4. 15-Bit Instruction Format

As an example, a 15-bit instruction may call for an ADD, designated by the f and m octal digits, from registers designated by the j and k octal digits, the result going to the register designated by the i octal digit. In this example, the addresses of the three-address, floating add unit are only three bits in length, each address referring to one of the eight floating point registers. The 30-bit format follows this same form but substitutes for the k octal digit an 18-bit constant K which serves as one of the input operands. These two formats provide a highly efficient control of concurrent operations.

As a background, consider the essential difference between a general purpose device and a special device in which high speeds are required. The designer of the special device can generally improve on the traditional general purpose device by introducing some form of concurrency. For example, some activities of a housekeeping nature may be performed separate from the main sequence of operations in separate hardware. The total time to complete a job is then optimized to the main sequence and excludes the housekeeping. The two categories operate concurrently.

It would be, of course, most attractive to provide in a general purpose device some generalized scheme to do the same kind of thing. The organization of the 6600 central processor provides just this kind of scheme. With a multiplicity of functional units, and of operand registers and with a simple and highly efficient addressing system, a generalized queue and reservation scheme is practical. This is called the *scoreboard*.

The scoreboard maintains a running file of each central register, of each functional unit, and of each of the three operand trunks to and from each unit. Typically, the scoreboard file is made up of two-, three-, and four-bit quantities identifying the nature of register and unit usage. As each new instruction is brought up, the conditions at the instant of issuance are set into the scoreboard. A snapshot is taken, so to speak, of the pertinent conditions. If no waiting is required, the execution of the instruction is begun immediately under control of the unit itself. If waiting is required (for example, an input operand may not yet be available in the central registers), the scoreboard controls the delay, and when released, allows the unit to begin its execution. Most important, this activity is accomplished in the scoreboard and the functional unit, and does not necessarily limit later instructions from being brought up and issued.

In this manner, it is possible to issue a series of instructions, some related, some not, until no functional units are left free or until a specific register is to be assigned more than one result. With just those two restrictions on issuing (unit free and no double result), several independent chains of instructions may proceed concurrently. Instructions may issue every minor cycle in the absence of the two restraints. The instruction executions, in comparison, range from three minor cycles for fixed add, 10 minor cycles for floating multiply, to 29 minor cycles for floating divide.

To provide a relatively continuous source of instructions, one buffer register of 60 bits is located at the bottom of an instruction stack capable of holding 32 instructions (Fig. 5). Instruction words from memory enter the bottom register of the stack pushing up the old instruction words. In straight line programs, only the bottom two registers are in use, the bottom being refilled as quickly as memory conflicts allow. In programs which branch back to an instruction in the upper stack registers, no refills are allowed after the branch, thereby holding the program loop completely in the stack. As a result, memory access or memory

conflicts are no longer involved, and a considerable speed increase can be had.

Five memory trunks are provided from memory into the central processor to five of the floating point registers (Fig. 6). One address register is assigned to each trunk (and therefore to the floating point register). Any instruction calling for address register result implicitly initiates a memory reference on that trunk. These instructions are handled through the scoreboard and therefore tend to overlap memory access with arithmetic. For example, a new memory word to be loaded in a floating point register can be brought in from memory but may not enter the register until all previous uses of that register are completed. The central registers, therefore, provide all of the data to the ten functional units, and receive all of the unit results. No storage is maintained in any unit.

Central memory is organized in 32 banks of 4096 words. Consecutive addresses call for a different bank; therefore, adjacent addresses in one bank are in reality separated by 32. Addresses may be issued every 100 nanoseconds. A typical central memory information transfer rate is about 250 million bits per second.

As mentioned before, the functional units are hidden behind the registers. Although the units might appear to increase hardware duplication, a pleasant fact emerges from this design. Each unit may be trimmed to perform its func-

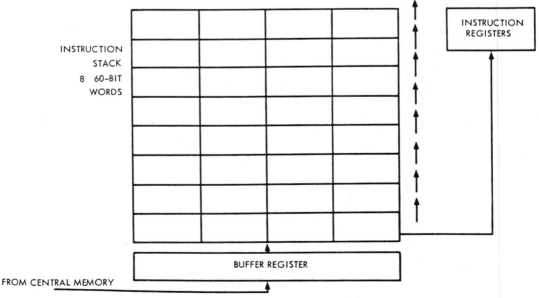

Figure 5.   6600 Instruction Stack Operation.

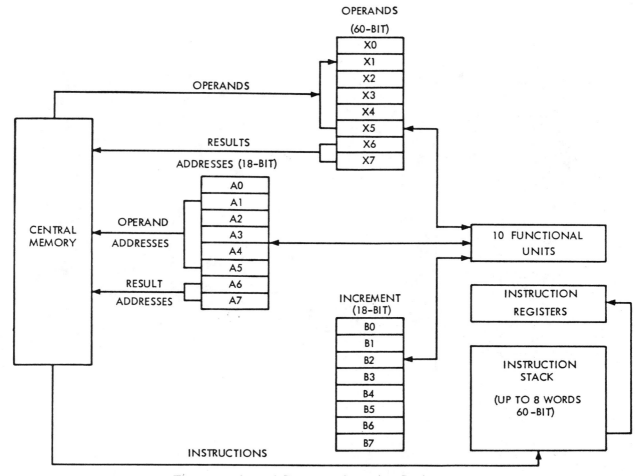

Figure 6. Central Processor Operating Registers.

tion without regard to others. Speed increases are had from this simplified design.

As an example of special functional unit design, the floating multiply accomplishes the coefficient multiplication in nine minor cycles plus one minor cycle to put away the result for a total of 10 minor cycles, or 1000 nanoseconds. The multiply uses layers of carry save adders grouped in two halves. Each half concurrently forms a partial product, and the two partial products finally merge while the long carries propagate. Although this is a fairly large complex of circuits, the resulting device was sufficiently smaller than originally planned to allow two multiply units to be included in the final design.

To sum up the characteristics of the central processor, remember that the broadbrush description is "concurrent operation." In other words, any program operating within the central processor utilizes some of the available concurrency. The program need not be written in a particular way, although certainly some optimization can be done. The specific method of accomplishing this concurrency involves *issuing* as many instructions as possible while handling most of the conflicts during *execution*. Some of the essential requirements for such a scheme include:

1. Many functional units
2. Units with three address properties
3. Many transient registers with many trunks to and from the units
4. A simple and efficient instruction set

CONSTRUCTION

Circuits in the 6600 computing system use all-transistor logic (Fig. 7). The silicon transistor operates in saturation when switched "on" and averages about five nanoseconds of stage delay. Logic circuits are constructed in

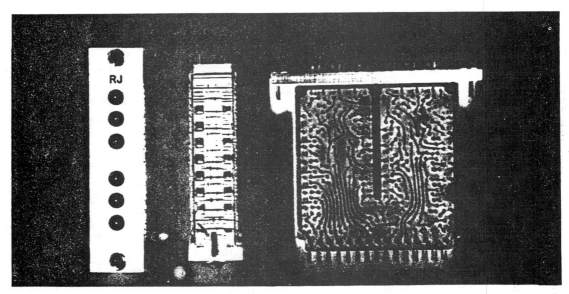

Figure 7.   6600 Printed Circuit Module.

a cordwood plug-in module of about 2½ inches by 2½ inches by 0.8 inch. An average of about 50 transistors are contained in these modules.

Memory circuits are constructed in a plug-in module of about six inches by six inches by 2½ inches (Fig. 8). Each memory module contains a coincident current memory of 4096 12-bit words. All read-write drive circuits and

Figure 8.   6600 Memory Module.

bit drive circuits plus address translation are contained in the module. One such module is used for each peripheral processor, and five modules make up one bank of central memory.

Logic modules and memory modules are held in upright hinged chassis in an X shaped cabinet (Fig. 9). Interconnections between modules on the chassis are made with twisted pair transmission lines. Interconnections between chassis are made with coaxial cables.

Both maintenance and operation are accomplished at a programmed display console (Fig. 10). More than one of these consoles may be included in a system if desired. Dead start facilities bring the ten peripheral processors to a condition which allows information to enter from any chosen peripheral device. Such loads normally bring in an operating system which provides a highly sophisticated capability for multiple users, maintenance, and so on.

The 6600 Computer has taken advantage of certain technology advances, but more particularly, logic organization advances which now appear to be quite successful. Control Data is exploring advances in technology upward within the same compatible structure, and identical technology downward, also within the same compatible structure.

Figure 9.   6600 Main Frame Section.

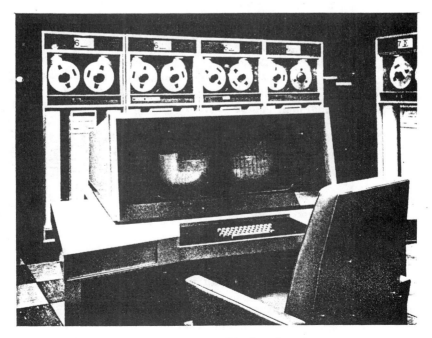

Figure 10.   6600 Display Console.

| Computer | G. Bell, S. H. Fuller, and |
| Systems | D. Siewiorek, Editors |

The CRAY-1
Computer System

Richard M. Russell
Cray Research, Inc.

This paper describes the CRAY-1, discusses the evolution of its architecture, and gives an account of some of the problems that were overcome during its manufacture.

The CRAY-1 is the only computer to have been built to date that satisfies ERDA's Class VI requirement (a computer capable of processing from 20 to 60 million floating point operations per second) [1].

The CRAY-1's Fortran compiler (CFT) is designed to give the scientific user immediate access to the benefits of the CRAY-1's vector processing architecture. An optimizing compiler, CFT, "vectorizes" innermost DO loops. Compatible with the ANSI 1966 Fortran Standard and with many commonly supported Fortran extensions, CFT does not require any source program modifications or the use of additional nonstandard Fortran statements to achieve vectorization. Thus the user's investment of hundreds of man months of effort to develop Fortran programs for other contemporary computers is protected.

Key Words and Phrases: architecture, computer systems

CR Categories: 1.2, 6.2, 6.3

Introduction

Vector processors are not yet commonplace machines in the larger-scale computer market. At the time of this writing we know of only 12 non-CRAY-1 vector processor installations worldwide. Of these 12, the most powerful processor is the ILLIAC IV (1 installation), the most populous is the Texas Instruments Advanced Scientific Computer (7 installations) and the most publicized is Control Data's STAR 100

(4 installations). In its report on the CRAY-1, Auerbach Computer Technology Reports published a comparison of the CRAY-1, the ASC, and the STAR 100 [2]. The CRAY-1 is shown to be a more powerful computer than any of its main competitors and is estimated to be the equivalent of five IBM 370/195s.

Independent benchmark studies have shown the CRAY-1 fully capable of supporting computational rates of 138 million floating-point operations per second (MFLOPS) for sustained periods and even higher rates of 250 MFLOPS in short bursts [3, 4]. Such comparatively high performance results from the CRAY-1 internal architecture, which is designed to accommodate the computational needs of carrying out many calculations in discrete steps, with each step producing interim results used in subsequent steps. Through a technique called "chaining," the CRAY-1 vector functional units, in combination with scalar and vector registers, generate interim results and use them again immediately without additional memory references, which slow down the computational process in other contemporary computer systems.

Other features enhancing the CRAY-1's computational capabilities are: its small size, which reduces distances electrical signals must travel within the computer's framework and allows a 12.5 nanosecond clock period (the CRAY-1 is the world's fastest scalar processor); a one million word semiconductor memory equipped with error detection and correction logic (SECDED); its 64-bit word size; and its optimizing Fortran compiler.

Architecture

The CRAY-1 has been called "the world's most expensive love-seat" [5]. Certainly, most people's first reaction to the CRAY-1 is that it is so small. But in computer design it is a truism that smaller means faster. The greater the separation of components, the longer the time taken for a signal to pass between them. A cylindrical shape was chosen for the CRAY-1 in order to keep wiring distances small.

Figure 1 shows the physical dimensions of the machine. The mainframe is composed of 12 wedge-like columns arranged in a 270° arc. This leaves room for a reasonably trim individual to gain access to the interior of the machine. Note that the love-seat disguises the power supplies and some plumbing for the Freon cooling system. The photographs (Figure 2 and 3) show the interior of a working CRAY-1 and an exterior view of a column with one module in place. Figure 4 is a photograph of the interior of a single module.

An Analysis of the Architecture

Table I details important characteristics of the CRAY-1 Computer System. The CRAY-1 is equipped with 12 i/o channels, 16 memory banks, 12 functional

Fig. 1. Physical organization of mainframe.

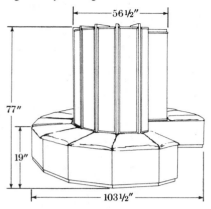

- Dimensions
  Base—103¾ inches diameter by 19 inches high
  Columns—56½ inches diameter by 77 inches high including height of base
- 24 chassis
- 1662 modules; 113 module types
- Each module contains up to 288 IC packages per module
- Power consumption approximately 115 kw input for maximum memory size
- Freon cooled with Freon/water heat exchange
- Three memory options
- Weight 10,500 lbs (maximum memory size)
- Three basic chip types
  5/4 NAND gates
  Memory chips
  Register chips

units, and more than 4k bytes of register storage. Access to memory is shared by the i/o channels and high-speed registers. The most striking features of the CRAY-1 are: only four chip types, main memory speed, cooling system, and computation section.

Four Chip Types

Only four chip types are used to build the CRAY-1. These are 16 × 4 bit bipolar register chips (6 nanosecond cycle time), 1024 × 1 bit bipolar memory chips (50 nanosecond cycle time), and bipolar logic chips with subnanosecond propagation times. The logic chips are all simple low- or high-speed gates with both a 5 wide and a 4 wide gate (5/4 NAND). Emitter-coupled logic circuit (ECL) technology is used throughout the CRAY-1.

The printed circuit board used in the CRAY-1 is a 5-layer board with the two outer surfaces used for signal runs and the three inner layers for −5.2V, −2.0V, and ground power supplies. The boards are six inches wide, 8 inches long, and fit into the chassis as shown in Figure 3.

All integrated circuit devices used in the CRAY-1 are packaged in 16-pin hermetically sealed flat packs supplied by both Fairchild and Motorola. This type of package was chosen for its reliability and compactness. Compactness is of special importance; as many as 288 packages may be added to a board to fabricate a module (there are 113 module types), and as many as 72 modules may be inserted into a 28-inch-high chassis.

Fig. 2. The CRAY-1 Computer.

Fig. 3. CRAY-1 modules in place.

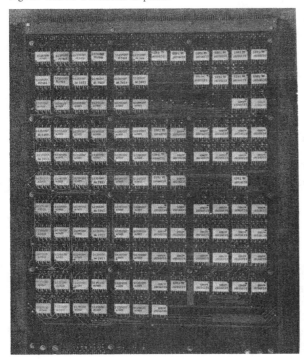

Fig. 4. A single module.

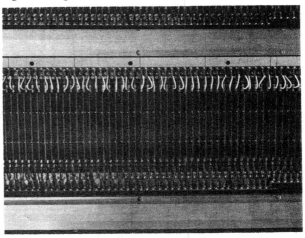

Table I. CRAY-1 CPU characteristics summary

Computation Section
   Scalar and vector processing modes
   12.5 nanosecond clock period operation
   64-bit word size
   Integer and floating-point arithmetic
   Twelve fully segmented functional units
   Eight 24-bit address (A) registers
   Sixty-four 24-bit intermediate address (B) registers
   Eight 64-bit scalar (S) registers
   Sixty-four 64-bit intermediate scalar (T) registers
   Eight 64-element vector (V) registers (64-bits per element)
   Vector length and vector mask registers
   One 64-bit real time clock (RT) register
   Four instruction buffers of sixty-four 16-bit parcels each
   128 basic instructions
   Prioritized interrupt control
Memory Section
   1,048,576 64-bit words (plus 8 check bits per word)
   16 independent banks of 65,536 words each
   4 clock period bank cycle time
   1 word per clock period transfer rate for B, T, and V registers
   1 word per 2 clock periods transfer rate for A and S registers
   4 words per clock period transfer rate to instruction buffers (up to
     16 instructions per clock period)
i/o Section
   24 i/o channels organized into four 6-channel groups
   Each channel group contains either 6 input or 6 output channels
   Each channel group served by memory every 4 clock periods
   Channel priority within each channel group
   16 data bits, 3 control bits per channel, and 4 parity bits
   Maximum channel rate of one 64-bit word every 100 nanoseconds
   Maximum data streaming rate of 500,000 64-bit words/second
   Channel error detection

Such component densities evitably lead to a mammoth cooling problem (to be described).

Main Memory Speed

CRAY-1 memory is organized in 16 banks, 72 modules per bank. Each module contributes 1 bit to a 64-bit word. The other 8 bits are used to store an 8-bit check byte required for single-bit error correction, double-bit error detection (SECDED). Data words are stored in 1-bank increments throughout memory. This organization allows 16-way interleaving of memory accesses and prevents bank conflicts except in the case of memory accesses that step through memory with either an 8 or 16-word increment.

Cooling System

The CRAY-1 generates about four times as much heat per cubic inch as the 7600. To cool the CRAY-1 a new cooling technology was developed, also based on Freon, but employing available metal conductors in a new way. Within each chassis vertical aluminum/stainless steel cooling bars line each column wall. The

Fig. 5. Block diagram of registers.

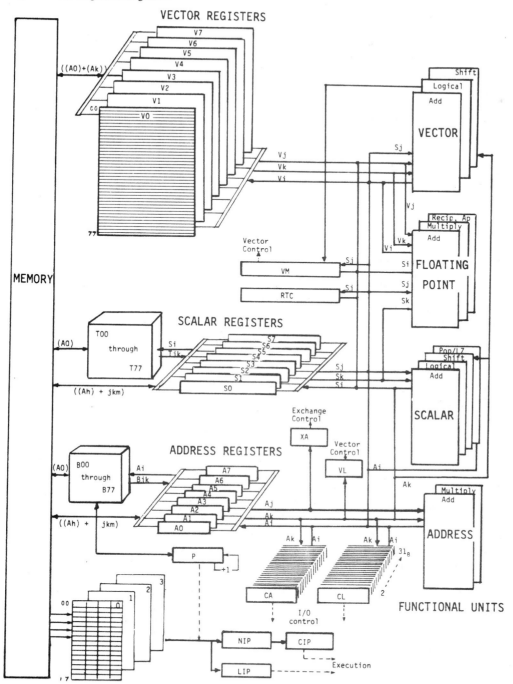

VECTOR REGISTERS

MEMORY

SCALAR REGISTERS

ADDRESS REGISTERS

INSTRUCTION BUFFERS

FUNCTIONAL UNITS

Freon refrigerant is passed through a stainless steel tube within the aluminum casing. When modules are in place, heat is dissipated through the inner copper heat transfer plate in the module to the column walls and thence into the cooling bars. The modules are mated with the cold bar by using stainless steel pins to pinch the copper plate against the aluminum outer casing of the bar.

To assure component reliability, the cooling system was designed to provide a maximum case temperature of 130°F (54°C). To meet this goal, the following temperature differentials are observed:

Temperature at center of module	130°F (54°C)
Temperature at edge of module	118°F (48°C)
Cold plate temperature at wedge	78°F (25°C)
Cold bar temperature	70°F (21°C)
Refrigerant tube temperature	70°F (21°C)

Functional Units

There are 12 functional units, organized in four groups: address, scalar, vector, and floating point. Each functional unit is pipelined into single clock segments. Functional unit time is shown in Table II. Note that all of the functional units can operate concurrently so that in addition to the benefits of pipelining (each functional unit can be driven at a result rate of 1 per clock period) we also have parallelism across the units too. Note the absence of a divide unit in the CRAY-1. In order to have a completely segmented divide operation the CRAY-1 performs floating-point division by the method of reciprocal approximation. This technique has been used before (e.g. IBM System/360 Model 91).

Registers

Figure 5 shows the CRAY-1 registers in relationship to the functional units, instruction buffers, i/o channel control registers, and memory. The basic set of programmable registers are as follows:

8 24-bit address (A) registers
64 24-bit address-save (B) registers
8 64-bit scalar (S) registers
64 64-bit scalar-save (T) registers
8 64-word (4096-bit) vector (V) registers

Expressed in 8-bit bytes rather than 64-bit words, that's a total of 4,888 bytes of high-speed (6ns) register storage.

The functional units take input operands from and store result operands only to A, S, and V registers. Thus the large amount of register storage is a crucial factor in the CRAY-1's architecture. Chaining could not take place if vector register space were not available for the storage of final or intermediate results. The B and T registers greatly assist scalar performance. Temporary scalar values can be stored from and reloaded to the A and S register in two clock periods. Figure 5 shows the CRAY-1's register paths in detail. The speed of the CFT Fortran IV compiler would be seriously impaired if it were unable to keep the many Pass 1 and Pass 2 tables it needs in register space. Without the register storage provided by the B, T, and V registers, the CRAY-1's bandwidth of only 80 million words/second would be a serious impediment to performance.

Instruction Formats

Instructions are expressed in either one or two 16-bit parcels. Below is the general form of a CRAY-1 instruction. Two-parcel instructions may overlap memory-word boundaries, as follows:

Fields	g	h	i	j	k	m
	0–3	4–6	7–9	10–12	13–15	16–31
Bit positions	(4)	(3)	(3)	(3)	(3)	(16)
			Parcel 1			Parcel 2

The computation section processes instructions at a maximum rate of one parcel per clock period.

Table II. CRAY-1 functional units

	Register usage	Functional unit time (clock periods)
Address function units		
address add unit	A	2
address multiply unit	A	6
Scalar functional units		
scalar add unit	S	3
scalar shift unit	S	2 or 3 if double-word shift
scalar logical unit	S	1
population/leading zero count unit	S	3
Vector functional units		
vector add unit	V	3
vector shift unit	V	4
vector logical unit	V	2
Floating-point functional units		
floating-point add unit	S and V	6
floating-point multiply unit	S and V	7
reciprocal approximation unit	S and V	14

For arithmetic and logical instructions, a 7-bit operation code (gh) is followed by three 3-bit register designators. The first field, i, designates the result register. The j and k fields designate the two operand registers or are combined to designate a B or T register.

The shift and mask instructions consist of a 7-bit operation code (gh) followed by a 3-bit i field and a 6-bit jk field. The i field designates the operand register. The jk combined field specifies a shift or mask count.

Immediate operand, read and store memory, and branch instructions require the two-parcel instruction word format. The immediate operand and the read and store memory instructions combine the j, k, and m fields to define a 22-bit quantity or memory address. In addition, the read and store memory instructions use the h field to specify an operating register for indexing. The branch instructions combine the i, j, k, and m fields into a 24-bit memory address field. This allows branching to any one of the four parcel positions in any 64-bit word, whether in memory or in an instruction buffer.

Operating Registers

Five types of registers—three primary (A, S, and V) and two intermediate (B and T)—are provided in the CRAY-1.

A *registers*—eight 24-bit A registers serve a variety of applications. They are primarily used as address registers for memory references and as index registers, but also are used to provide values for shift counts, loop control, and channel i/o operations. In address applications, they are used to index the base address for scalar memory references and for providing both a base address and an index address for vector memory references.

The 24-bit integer functional units modify values

(such as program addresses) by adding, subtracting, and multiplying A register quantities. The results of these operations are returned to A registers.

Data can be transferred directly from memory to A registers or can be placed in B registers as an intermediate step. This allows buffering of the data between A registers and memory. Data can also be transferred between A and S registers and from an A register to the vector length registers. The eight A registers are individually designated by the symbols A0, A1, A2, A3, A4, A5, A6, and A7.

B *registers* — there are sixty-four 24-bit B registers, which are used as auxiliary storage for the A registers. The transfer of an operand between an A and a B register requires only one clock period. Typically, B registers contain addresses and counters that are referenced over a longer period than would permit their being retained in A registers. A block of data in B registers may be transferred to or from memory at the rate of one clock period per register. Thus, it is feasible to store the contents of these registers in memory prior to calling a subroutine requiring their use. The sixty-four B registers are individually designated by the symbols B0, B1, B2, . . . , and B77$_8$.

S *registers* — eight 64-bit S registers are the principle data handling registers for scalar operations. The S registers serve as both source and destination registers for scalar arithmetic and logical instructions. Scalar quantities involved in vector operations are held in S registers. Logical, shift, fixed-point, and floating-point operations may be performed on S register data. The eight S registers are individually designated by the symbols S0, S1, S2, S3, S4, S5, S6, and S7.

T *registers* — sixty-four 64-bit T registers are used as auxiliary storage for the S registers. The transfer of an operand between S and T registers requires one clock period. Typically, T registers contain operands that are referenced over a longer period than would permit their being retained in S registers. T registers allow intermediate results of complex computations to be held in intermediate access storage rather than in memory. A block of data in T registers may be transferred to or from memory at the rate of one word per clock period. The sixty-four T registers are individually designated by the symbols T0, T1, T2, . . . , and T77$_8$.

V *registers* — eight 64-element V registers provide operands to and receive results from the functional units at a one clock period rate. Each element of a V register holds a 64-bit quantity. When associated data is grouped into successive elements of a V register, the register may be considered to contain a vector. Examples of vector quantities are rows and columns of a matrix, or similarly related elements of a table. Computational efficiency is achieved by processing each element of the vector identically. Vector merge and test instructions are provided in the CRAY-1 to allow operations to be performed on individual elements designated by the content of the vector mask (VM)

register. The number of vector register elements to be processed is contained in the vector length (VL) register. The eight V registers are individually designated by the symbols V0, V1, V2, V3, V4, V5, B6, and V7.

Supporting Registers

The CPU contains a variety of additional registers that support the control of program execution. These are the vector length (VL) and vector mask (VM) registers, the program counter (P), the base address (BA) and limit address (LA) registers, the exchange address (XA) register, the flag (F) register, and the mode (M) register.

VL *register* — the 64-bit vector mask (VM) register controls vector element designation in vector merge and test instructions. Each bit of the VM register corresponds to a vector register element. In the vector test instruction, the VM register content is defined by testing each element of a V register for a specific condition.

P *register* — the 24-bit P register specifies the memory register parcel address of the current program instruction. The high order 22 bits specify a memory address and the low order two bits indicate a parcel number. This parcel address is advanced by one as each instruction parcel in a nonbranching sequence is executed and is replaced whenever program branching occurs.

BA *registers* — the 18-bit base address (BA) register contains the upper 18 bits of a 22-bit memory address. The lower four bits of this address are considered zeros. Just prior to initial or continued execution of a program, a process known as the "exchange sequence" stores into the BA register the upper 18 bits of the lowest memory address to be referenced during program execution. As the program executes, the address portion of each instruction referencing memory has its content added to that of the BA register. The sum then serves as the absolute address used for the memory reference and ensures that memory addresses lower than the contents of the BA register are not accessed. Programs must, therefore, have all instructions referencing memory do so with their address portions containing relative addresses. This process supports program loading and memory protection operations and does not, in producing an absolute address, affect the content of the instruction buffer, BA, or memory.

LA *register* — the 18-bit limit address (LA) register contains the upper 18 bits of a 22-bit memory address. The lower 4 bits of this address are considered zeros. Just prior to initial or continued execution of a program, the "exchange sequence" process stores into the LA register the upper 18 bits of that absolute address one greater than allowed to be referenced by the program. When program execution begins, each instruction referencing a memory location has the absolute address for that reference (determined by summing its address portion with the BA register contents) checked against the LA register content. If the absolute address equals or exceeds the LA register content, an out-of-range error condition is flagged and program execution terminates. This process supports the memory protection operation.

XA *register* — the 8-bit exchange address (XA) register contains the upper eight bits of a 12-bit memory address. The lower four bits of the address are considered zeros. Because only twelve bits are used, with the lower four bits always being zeros, exchange addresses can reference only every 16th memory address beginning with address 0000 and concluding with address 4080. Each of these addresses designates the first word of a 16-word set. Thus, 256 sets (of 16 memory words each) can be specified. Prior to initiation or continuation of a program's execution, the XA register contains the first memory address of a particular 16-word set or exchange package. The exchange package contains certain operating and support registers' contents as required for operations following an interrupt. The XA register supports the exchange sequence operation and the contents of XA are stored in an exchange package whenever an exchange sequence occurs.

F *register* — the 9-bit F register contains flags that, whenever set, indicate interrupt conditions causing initiation of an exchange sequence. The interrupt conditions are: normal exit, error exit, i/o interrupt, uncorrected memory error, program range error, operand range error, floating-point overflow, real-time clock interrupt, and console interrupt.

M *register* — the M (mode) register is a three-bit register that contains part of the exchange package for a currently active program. The three bits are selectively set during an exchange sequence. Bit 37, the floating-point error mode flag, can be set or cleared during the execution interval for a program through use of the 0021 and 0022 instructions. The other two bits (bits 38 and 39) are not altered during the execution interval for the exchange package and can only be altered when the exchange package is inactive in storage. Bits are assigned as follows in word two of the exchange package.

Bit 37 — Floating-point error mode flag. When this bit is set, interrupts on floating-point errors are enabled.

Bit 38 — Uncorrectable memory error mode flag. When this bit is set, interrupts on uncorrectable memory parity errors are enabled.

Bit 39 — Monitor mode flag. When this bit is set, all interrupts other than parity errors are inhibited.

Integer Arithmetic

All integer arithmetic is performed in 24-bit or 64-bit 2's complement form.

Floating-Point Arithmetic

Floating-point numbers are represented in signed magnitude form. The format is a packed signed binary fraction and a biased binary integer exponent. The fraction is a 49-bit signed magnitude value. The exponent is 15-bit biased. The unbiased exponent range is:

$$2^{-20000_8} \text{ to } 2^{+17777_8},$$

or approximately

$$10^{-2500} \text{ to } 10^{+2500}$$

An exponent equal to or greater than 2^{+20000_8} is recognized by the floating-point functional units as an overflow condition, and causes an interrupt if floating point interrupts are enabled.

Chaining

The chaining technique takes advantage of the parallel operation of functional units. Parallel vector operations may be processed in two ways: (a) using different functional units and V registers, and (b) chaining; that is, using the result stream to one vector register simultaneously as the operand set for another operation in a different functional unit.

Parallel operations on vectors allow the generation of two or more results per clock period. A vector operation either uses two vector registers as sources of operands or uses one scalar register and one vector register as sources of operands. Vectors exceeding 64 elements are processed in 64-element segments.

Basically, chaining is a phenomenon that occurs when results issuing from one functional unit (at a rate of one/clock period) are immediately fed into another functional unit and so on. In other words, intermediate results do not have to be stored to memory and can be used even before the vector operation that created them runs to completion.

Chaining has been compared to the technique of "data forwarding" used in the IBM 360/195. Like data forwarding, chaining takes place automatically. Data forwarding consists of hardware facilities within the 195 floating-point processor communicating automatically by transferring "name tags," or internal codes between themselves [6]. Unlike the CRAY-1, the user has no access to the 195's data-forwarding buffers. And, of course, the 195 can only forward scalar values, not entire vectors.

Interrupts and Exchange Sequence

Interrupts are handled cleanly by the CRAY-1 hardware. Instruction issue is terminated by the hardware upon detection of an interrupt condition. All memory bank activity is allowed to complete as are any vector instructions that are in execution, and then an exchange sequence is activated. The Cray Operating System (COS) is always one partner of any exchange sequence. The cause of an interrupt is analyzed during an exchange sequence and all interrupts are processed until none remain.

Only the address and scalar registers are maintained in a program's exchange package (Fig. 6). The user's B, T, and V registers are saved by the operating system in the user's Job Table Area.

Fig. 6. Exchange package.

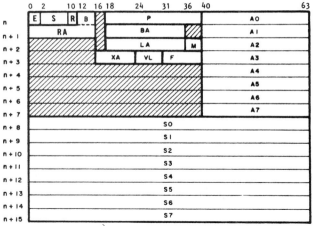

M - Modes[+]

36	Interrupt on correctable memory error
37	Interrupt on floating point
38	Interrupt on uncorrectable memory error
39	Monitor mode

F - Flags[+]

31	Console interrupt
32	RTC interrupt
33	Floating point error
34	Operand range
35	Program range
36	Memory error
37	I/O interrupt
38	Error exit
39	Normal exit

Registers

S	Syndrome bits
RAB	Read address for error (where B is bank)
P	Program address
BA	Base address
LA	Limit address
XA	Exchange address
VL	Vector length

E - Error type (bits 0,1)

| 10 | Uncorrectable memory |
| 01 | Correctable memory |

R - Read mode (bits 10,11)

00	Scalar
01	I/O
10	Vector
11	Fetch

[+]Bit position from left of word

The CRAY-1's exchange sequence will be familiar to those who have had experience with the CDC 7600 and Cyber machines. One major benefit of the exchange sequence is the ease with which user jobs can be relocated in memory by the operating system. On the CRAY-1, dynamic relocation of a user job is facilitated by a base register that is transparent to the user.

Evolution of the CRAY-1

The CRAY-1 stems from a highly successful line of computers which S. Cray either designed or was associated with. Mr. Cray was one of the founders of Control Data Corporation. While at CDC, Mr. Cray was the principal architect of the CDC 1604, 6600, and 7600 computer systems. While there are many similarities with these earlier machines, two things stand out about the CRAY-1; first it is a vector machine, secondly, it utilizes semiconductor memories and integrated circuits rather than magnetic cores and discrete components. We classify the CRAY-1 as a second generation vector processor. The CDC STAR 100A and the Texas Instruments ASC are first-generation vector processors.

Both the STAR 100 and the ASC are designed to handle long vectors. Because of the startup time associated with data streaming, vector length is of critical importance. Vectors have to be long if the STAR 100 and the ASC vector processors are to be at all competitive with a scalar processor [3]. Another disadvantage of the STAR 100 architecture is that elements of a "vector" are required to be in consecutive addresses.

In contrast with these earlier designs, the CRAY-1 can be termed a short vector machine. Whereas the others require vector lengths of a 100 or more to be competitive with scalar processors, the cross-over point between choosing scalar rather than vector mode on the CRAY-1 is between 2 and 4 elements. This is demonstrated by a comparison of scalar/vector timings for some mathematical library routines shown in Figure 1 [7].

Also, the CRAY-1's addressing scheme allows complete flexibility. When accessing a vector, the user simply specifies the starting location and an increment. Arrays can be accessed by column, row, or diagonal; they can be stepped through with nonunary increments; and, there are no restrictions on addressing, except that the increment must be a constant.

Vector Startup Times

To be efficient at processing short vectors, vector startup times must be small. On the CRAY-1, vector instructions may issue at a rate of one instruction parcel per clock period. All vector instructions are one parcel instructions (parcel size = 16 bits). Vector instructions place a reservation on whichever functional unit they use, including memory, and on the input operand registers. In some cases, issue of a vector instruction may be delayed by a time (in clock periods) equal to vector length of the preceding vector operation + 4.

Functional unit times are shown in Table II. Vector operations that depend on the result of a previous vector operation can usually "chain" with them and are delayed for a maximum "chain slot" time in clock periods of functional unit time + 2.

Once issued, a vector instruction produces its first result after a delay in clock periods equal to functional unit time. Subsequent results continue to be produced at a rate of 1 per clock period. Results must be stored in a vector register. A separate instruction is required to store the final result vector to memory. Vector register capacity is 64-elements. Vectors longer than 64 are processed in 64-element segments.

Some sample timings for both scalar and vector are shown in Table III [8]. Note that there is no vector ASIN routine and so a reference to ASIN within a vectorized loop generates repetitive calls to the scalar ASIN routine. This involves a performance degradation but does allow the rest of the loop to vectorize (in a case where there are more statements than in this example). Simple loops 14, 15, and 16 show the

Table III.

Execution time in clock periods per result for various simple DO loops of the form

DO 10 I = 1,N

10 A(I) = B(I)

Loop Body	$N = 1$	10	100	1000	1000 Scalar
1. $A(I) = 1.$	41.0	5.5	2.6	2.5	22.5
2. $A(I) = B(I)$	44.0	5.8	2.7	2.5	31.0
3. $A(I) = B(I) + 10.$	55.0	6.9	2.9	2.6	37.0
4. $A(I) = B(I) + C(I)$	59.0	8.2	3.9	3.7	41.0
5. $A(I) = B(I)*10.$	56.0	7.0	2.9	2.6	38.0
6. $A(I) = B(I)*C(I)$	60.0	8.3	4.0	3.7	42.0
7. $A(I) = B(I)/10.$	94.0	10.8	4.1	3.7	52.0
8. $A(I) = B(I)/C(I)$	89.0	13.3	7.6	7.2	60.0
9. $A(I) = SIN(B(I))$	462.0	61.0	33.3	31.4	198.1
10. $A(I) = ASIN(B(I))$	430.0	209.5	189.5	188.3	169.1
11. $A(I) = ABS(B(I))$	61.0	7.5	2.9	2.6	
12. $A(I) = AMAX1(B(I), C(I))$	80.0	11.2	5.2	4.8	
13. $\begin{cases} C(I) = A(I) \\ A(I) = B(I) \\ B(I) = CCI \end{cases}$	90.0	12.7	6.3	5.8	47.0
14. $A(I) = B(I)*C(I) + D(I)*E(I))$	110.0	16.0	7.7	7.1	57.0
15. $A(I) = B(I)*C(I) + (D(I)*E(I))$	113.0	14.7	6.6	6.0	63.0
16. $A(I) = B(I)*C(I) + D(I)$	95.0	12.7	5.5	5.0	52.0

Fig. 7. Scalar/vector timing.

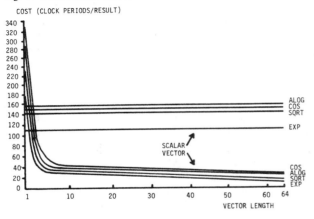

influence of chaining. For a long vector, the number of clock periods per result is approximately the number of memory references + 1. In loop 14, an extra clock period is consumed because the present CFT compiler will load all four operands before doing computation. This problem is overcome in loop 15 by helping the compiler with an extra set of parentheses.

Software

At the time of this writing, first releases of the CRAY Operating System (COS) and CRAY Fortran Compiler (CFT) have been delivered to user sites. COS is a batch operating system capable of supporting up to 63 jobs in a multiprogramming environment. COS is designed to be the recipient of job requests and data files from front-end computers. Output from jobs is normally staged back to the front-ends upon job completion.

CFT is an optimizing Fortran compiler designed to compile ANSI 66 Fortran IV to take best advantage of the CRAY-1's vector processing architecture. In its present form, CFT will not attempt to vectorize certain

Fig. 8. Front-end system interface.

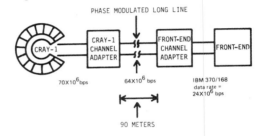

loops which, due to dependence conditions, appear at first sight, unvectorizable.

However, future versions of CFT will be designed to eliminate as many dependency conditions as possible increasing the amount of vectorizable code. Basically, to be vectorizable, a DO loop should manipulate arrays and store the results of computations in arrays. Loops that contain branches such as GO TO's, IF's, or CALL statements are not currently vectorized. Loops may contain function references if the function is known to the compiler to have a vector version. Most of the mathematical functions in the CRAY library are vectorizable. By using the vector mask and vector merge features of the CRAY-1, future versions of the compiler will be able to vectorize loops containing IF and GO TO statements.

Early experience with CFT has shown that most Fortran loops will not run as fast as optimally hand-coded machine language equivalents. Future versions of CFT will show improved loop timings due mainly to improved instruction scheduling.

Other CRAY-1 software includes Cray Assembler Language (CAL) which is a powerful macro assembler, an overlay loader, a full range of utilities including a text editor, and some debug aids.

Front-End Computer Interface

The CRAY-1 was not designed for stand-alone operation. At the very minimum a minicomputer is required to act as a conduit between the CRAY-1 and the everyday world. Cray Research software development is currently being done using a Data General Eclipse computer in this category. The Cray Research "A" processor, a 16-bit, 80 MIPS minicomputer is scheduled to replace the Eclipse in early 1978. Front-end computers can be attached to any of the CRAY-1's 12 i/o channels.

The physical connection between a front-end computer and the CRAY-1 is shown in Figure 8. In this example an IBM 370/168 is assumed in the front-end role. Note that each computer requires a channel adapter between its own channel and a Cray Research phase-modulated long line. The link can only be driven at the speed of its slowest component. In this example it is the IBM block multiplexer channel speed of 3 megabytes/second. The discipline of the link is governed by the Cray Link Interface Protocol.

CRAY-1 Development Problems

Two of the most significant problems [9] encountered on the way to the CRAY-1 were building the first cold bar and designing circuits with a completely balanced dynamic load.

Building the Cold Bar

It took a year and a half of trial and error before the first good cold bar was built. The work was done by a small Minnesota company. A major problem was the discovery, quite early, that aluminum castings are porous. If there is a crack in the stainless steel tubing at the bond between the tubing and the elbow then the Freon leaks through the aluminum casing. The loss of the Freon is not itself a problem, but mixed with the Freon is a little oil, and the oil can cause problems if it is deposited on the modules. Aluminum also tends to get bubbles in it when it is cast, requiring a long process of temperature cycling, preheating of the stainless steel tube, and so on.

Designing the Circuits

CRAY-1 modules are 6 inches wide. The distance across the board is about a nanosecond which is just about the edge time of the electrical signals. Unless due precautions are taken, when electric signals run around a board, standing waves can be induced in the ground plane. Part of the solution is to make all signal paths in the machine the same length. This is done by padding out paths with foil runs and integrated circuit packages. All told, between 10 and 20 per cent of the IC packages in the machine are there simply to pad out a signal line. The other part of the solution was to use only simple gates and make sure that both sides of every gate are always terminated. This means that there is no dynamic component presented to the power supply. This is the principal reason why simple gates are used in the CRAY-1. If a more complex integrated circuit package is used, it is impossible to terminate both sides of every gate. So all of the CRAY-1's circuits are perfectly balanced. Five layer boards have one ground layer, two voltage layers, and then the two logic layers on the outside. Twisted pairs which interconnect the modules are balanced and there are equal and opposite signals on both sides of the pairs. The final result is that there is just a purely resistive load to the power supply!

Summary

The design of the CRAY-1 stems from user experience with first generation vector processors and is to some extent, evolved from the 7600 [2]. The CRAY-1 is particularly effective at processing short vectors. Its architecture exhibits a balanced approach to both scalar and vector processing. In [1], the conclusion is drawn that the CRAY-1 in scalar mode is more than twice as fast as the CDC 7600. Such good scalar performance is required in what is often an unvectorizable world.

At the time of this writing, Cray Research has shipped CRAY-1 systems to three customers (Los Alamos Scientific Laboratory, National Center for Atmospheric Research, and the European Center for Medium Range Weather Forecasts) and has contracts to supply three more systems, two to the Department of Defense, and one to United Computing Systems (UCS). Production plans already anticipate shipping one CRAY-1 per quarter. As the population of CRAY-1 computers expands, it will become clear that the CRAY-1 has made a significant step on the way to the general-purpose computers in the future.

Received February 1977; revised September 1977.

Acknowledgments. Acknowledgments are due to my colleagues at Cray Research. G. Grenander, R. Hendrickson, M. Huber, C. Jewett, P. Johnson, A. La Bounty, and J. Robidoux, without whose contributions, this paper could not have been written.

References
1. CRAY-1 Final Evaluation by T. W. Keller, LASL, LA-6456-MS.
2. CRAY-1 Report, Auerbach Computer Technology Report, Auerbach Publisher's, 6560 North Park Drive, Pennsauken, N. J. 08109.
3. Preliminary Report on Results of Matrix Benchmarks on Vector Processors: Calahan, Joy, Orbits, System Engineering Laboratory, University of Michigan, Ann Arbor, Michigan 48109.
4. Computer Architecture Issues in Large-Scale Systems, 9th Asilomar Conference, Naval Postgraduate School, Monterey, California.
5. Computer World, August 1976.
6. The IBM 360/195 by Jesse O'Murphy and Robert M. Wade, Datamation, April 1970.
7. Work done by Paul Johnson, Cray Research.
8. Work done by Richard Hendrickson, Cray Research.
9. The section on CRAY-1 development problems is based on remarks made by Seymour Cray in a speech to prospective CRAY-1 users in 1975.

CRAY-1 Computer Technology

JAMES S. KOLODZEY, MEMBER, IEEE

Abstract—Hardware and packaging technology which provide the high performance of the CRAY-1 computer are reviewed. A brief overview of the computer is given, followed by a description of the computer circuits, packaging, power distribution, and cooling system.

I. INTRODUCTION

SINCE ITS introduction in 1976, the CRAY-1 has developed a reputation as a fast and reliable scientific processor. The CRAY-1S, announced in 1979, offers enhanced input/output (I/O) capability and an increase of the maximum memory size from one million to four million words. A photo of the CRAY-1S is shown in Fig. 1, where the large section at the left contains the central processing unit (CPU) and memory, and the smaller section at the right contains the I/O processor. Fig. 2 shows the CPU chassis layout and circuit module locations. Data and control signal paths are given in Fig. 3. Applications for the CRAY-1 include large-scale calculations of the type required in weather forecasting, petroleum and earthquake seismology, structural analysis, nuclear engineering, and particle physics.

The CRAY-1 characteristic of combined high performance and reliability results from simple hardware design. One chip type is used predominantly in the CPU, and one memory chip type is used in the memory banks. Each arithmetic operation has a dedicated hardware functional unit, and the logic and circuit design is governed by straightforward ground rules. The power supplies are simple rectifier/filter types and the cooling system is a standard refrigeration unit. Whenever possible problems were solved with existing technology. This paper reviews the CRAY-1 hardware in detail.

II. SYSTEM OVERVIEW

Table I is a listing of some CRAY-1S performance characteristics. The logic gates in the CPU are mostly emitter-coupled logic (ECL) dual NAND integrated circuits (IC's). Gate counts of the hardware functional units are given in Table II. Additional gates are used for control and storage functions which tie the hardware functions together. A full memory CRAY-1S contains four million words of high speed ECL random access memory (RAM). The 4K × 1 bit random access memory (RAM) chips are arranged to give a word length of 64 bits plus 8 bits for single error correction, double error detection (SECDED). The SECDED is an implementation of a Hamming code. A total of 73 728 RAM chips are used.

The CRAY-1 is a vector processor with the ability to operate iteratively on strings of up to 64 (vector length) operands

Fig. 1.   CRAY–1S mainframe.

or operand pairs. By contrast, scalar processors perform one iteration on one or a pair of operands. Each operand has a word length of 64 bits, which for floating point operations comprises a 49-bit signed coefficient and a 15-bit exponent. The CRAY-1 has the ability to operate efficiently even with short vector lengths [1], and it is also a fast scalar processor.

Machine performance is expressed in millions of floating point operations per second (megaflops) because a single vector instruction is equivalent to a loop of several scalar instructions. The CRAY-1 has been shown capable of a sustained rate of 138 Mflops and to achieve 250 Mflops in short bursts [2]. System reliability is excellent, with an availability greater than 98 percent. Mean time between interruption (MTBI) is more than 100 h, and mean time to repair (MTTR) is about 1 h [3].

III. CIRCUIT COMPONENTS

One chip type comprises about 95 percent of the IC's in the CPU. The chip is a negative logic, five and four input dual NAND gate (5/4 gate) with complementary outputs. A logic diagram is shown in Fig. 4. The 5/4 gate is an ECL circuit with 750 ps propagation delay and 60 mW per gate power dissipation (120 mW per package). The 0.036 in square silicon die is packaged in a hermetically sealed 16-pin ceramic flatpack. Package dimensions are 3/8 × 1/4 × 1/12 in with leads on 50 mil centers as shown along with the smaller resistor package (described below) in Fig. 5. The ceramic flatpack is used for reliability, small size, and speed.

Other chips are a dual D flip flop, a 16 × 4 bit register with a 6 ns access time, and the 4K × 1 bit RAM with 25 ns access time packaged in an 18-pin ceramic flatpack.

In addition to the IC's the only other circuit component on the printed circuit (PC) board is the transmission line termina-

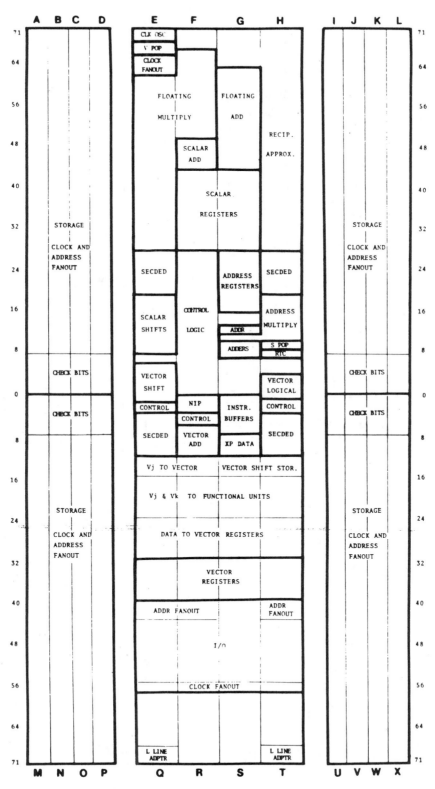

Fig. 2.   General chassis layout.

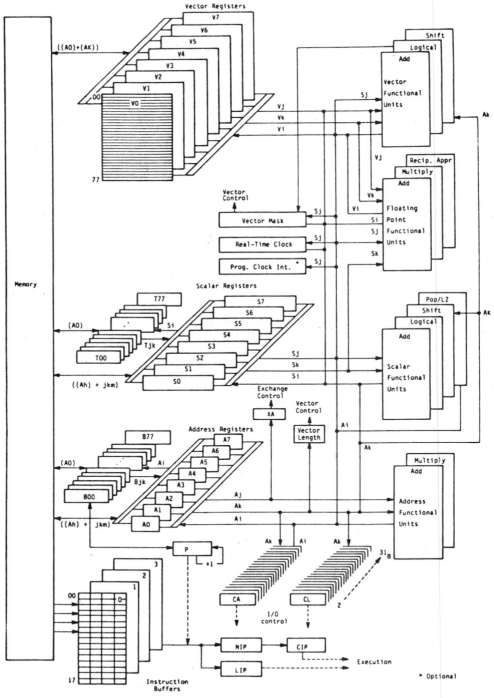

Fig. 3.   Computation section.

TABLE I
CRAY-1S SPECIFICATIONS

CPU:	230 000 gates
Memory:	4 million words
Clock:	12.5 ns
Power:	130 kW
Operations:	138 Mflops
	250 Mflops burst
Availability:	98 percent
MTBI:	100 h

TABLE II
CRAY-1S GATE COUNTS

Functional Unit	Gate Count	Percentage of Total
Address adder	1952	2.59
Address multiply	4009	5.33
Scalar add	2968	3.94
Scalar single shift	1452	1.93
Scalar double shift	2976	3.95
Constant to Si	482	0.64
Pop and zero count to Ai	403	0.54
Vector integer add	2216	2.94
Vector logical	1984	2.64
Vector shift	3460	4.60
Vector pop count	490	0.65
Floating add	8247	11.0
Floating multiply	23116	30.7
Reciprocal	21504	28.6
Total	75259	100.05

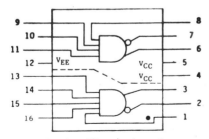

Fig. 4. 5/4 gate schematic.

Fig. 5. 5/4 gate and resistor package.

tion resistor. Two 60-Ω tantalum nitride thin film resistors are packaged in a ceramic T package with a common termination voltage lead. The 1300 W/in^2 power handling capability of the thin film material allows for a very small size resistor. Peak power dissipation is approximately 20 mW per resistor,

resulting in about 1.5 W/in^2 for the resistor film. A total of 495 934 resistor packages are used in the CRAY-1.

IV. CIRCUIT INTERCONNECTION

The field replaceable units in the CRAY-1 are modules of the type shown in Fig. 6. Visible here is a 6×8 in multilayer printed circuit board which can accomodate up to 144 IC packages in a 12×12 array. The PC boards are five-layer structures with the following layer assignments: components and signal traces; ground (V_{CC}); $-2V(V_{TT})$; $-5.2V(V_{EE})$; and a second-signal layer. The board material is G10 glass-epoxy with 1 oz copper conductor layers. Via and component holes are plated through with a 0.022-in inside diameter.

With signal rise times (10 percent–90 percent) of 750 ps, open line stub lengths must be less than 0.5 in to hold reflections under 35 percent overshoot and under 12 percent undershoot. Larger reflections can saturate gate inputs and reduce noice immunity. Longer signal runs must use transmission lines terminated in the line characteristic impedance. The CRAY-1 boards have 7-mil wide lines and 7-mil spaces. The 7-mil height above a ground (or power) plane results in a 60-Ω microstrip line with a delay of 0.15 ns/in. Gate loads appear as open stubs on the line as shown in Fig. 7. Fan out is limited to four on board or three off board to reduce ac loading problems.

Signal propagation between gates is governed by strict timing rules as shown in Fig. 8. The 12.5 ns clock is divided into eight "gate times" of about 1.5 ns each. Roughly half the gate time is due to circuit propagation delay, and half is due to board-foil delay. Unused gates can be dropped from the path by adding 3 in of foil conductor.

A CRAY-1 module consists of two PC boards sandwiching a 0.08-in thick copper cooling plate that is also the ground bus. Signal communication between boards is performed differentially over 120-Ω twisted pair in the backplane as shown schematically in Fig. 9. The 120-Ω twisted pair is matched to two 60-Ω board traces in series. This differential method permits a low cross talk communication path and provides both the signal and its complement for use on the receiving module. An inverter gate (and gate delay) is therefore saved if the signal complement is needed. The twisted pair attaches to the module by a 96-pin pair connector with pins on 0.05 in centers. The board side of the connector pair is visible in Fig. 6 at the top.

Interconnection ground rules restrict twisted pair lengths to multiples of gate times, or multiples of 1 ft to a maximum of 4 ft. These circuit rules prevent timing problems or race conditions from happening anywhere in the machine. The CRAY-1 backplane contains 67 mi of twisted pair wire. The first machine was completed with no wiring errors.

V. SYSTEM POWER

Voltage requirements for the PC board are $-5.2V(V_{EE})$ for the IC's and $-2V(V_{TT})$ for the termination resistors. No bypass capacitors are used on the PC board. A benefit of using the 5/4 gate IC is that it provides a balanced load to the supply. When one output turns on, another turns off, and the power supply loading is purely resistive and constant. Any ripple which occurs during the transitions is filtered out by

Fig. 6. CRAY-1 module.

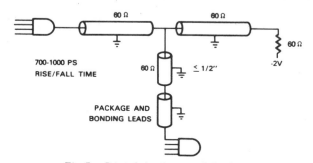

Fig. 7. Printed circuit transmission lines.

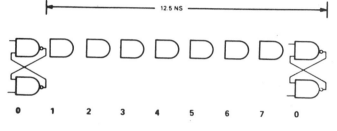

6 NS GATE DELAY
6.5 NS WIRING DELAY

Fig. 8. CRAY-1 gate timing.

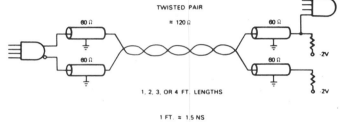

Fig. 9. Intermodule communication.

the 16-nF capacitor formed by the power and ground plane in the PC board.

A CPU module (two boards) can dissipate up to 36 W (7 A) from V_{EE} and about 1.2 W (0.6 A) from V_{TT}. There are 576 CPU modules. Taking an average of 25 W per module, the CPU dissipates a total of 14.4 kW. Each memory module contains 64 of the 4K × 1 bit ECL RAM chips which dissipate about 1 W each, and some interface logic chips. The power dissipation of the memory module is about 70 W. A full four million word CRAY-1S contains 1152 memory modules with a total memory power dissipation of 81 kW. Total power dissipation for the computer is 95 kW. Approximately 130 kW is supplied to the entire machine including power supply losses.

The computer modules receive V_{EE} and V_{TT} power from power supplies located under the seats around the periphery of the computer. These power supplies are simple linear rectifier-filter types which receive 400 Hz ac voltage from 36 variable transformers on a power distribution unit (PDU). The PDU receives 208 Vac at 400 Hz from a motor generator (MG) set which converts 480 V at 60 Hz to 208 V at 400 Hz. Each installation has two MG sets with one available for backup.

VI. SYSTEM COOLING

The CRAY-1S cooling system is designed to limit the IC die temperature to a maximum of 65°C. This provides a reliability margin from the 150°C absolute maximum IC junction temperature. The IC package case is maintained at 54°C. Heat generated in the silicon die flows through the IC package to the PC board ground plane and then to the 0.08-in thick copper cold plate. The cold plate conducts the board heat to its edges, which are held to 25°C by contact with a cast aluminum cold bar. The aluminum cold bars form the twelve vertical columns in the computer mainframe into which the modules slide horizontally on 0.4-in spacings. A refrigerant, Freon 22, flows through stainless steel tubes embedded in the cold bars. The development of the composite aluminum/stainless steel cold bars represents a solution to one of the more difficult design problems of the CRAY-1. Cast aluminum is actually porous and oil mixed in with the Freon can cause reliability problems if it leaks onto the modules. A method to bond stainless steel tubing into cast aluminum had to be invented in order to make the cold bars practical.

The refrigerant is maintained at 18.5°C by an evaporative refrigeration system. Freon 22, which boils −41°C (at atmospheric pressure), absorbs heat from the cold bar and changes to the gas phase. It passes through a compressor and condenses back to a liquid by releasing heat to a cold water supply which flows at 40 gal/min. The maximum heat load of this system is 580 000 B/h.

VII. FUTURE TECHNOLOGY

Key hardware problems in designing high-speed computers are heat removal, circuit interconnection, IC packaging, circuit density, and device speed. Improvements in these areas can directly improve computer performance.

Many factors contribute to the cooling problem. A given circuit technology is power-delay product limited. Short gate propagation delays require a high gate power dissipation. Large numbers of gates per chip as in LSI will cause total chip power to be well over 1 W, and the requirement for dense packaging for short wire delays will cause a heat density problem. Furthermore, cooler circuits run more reliably. All this creates demand for a high performance cooling system.

Until the day when a whole mainframe is on a chip, inter-chip wire propagation delays will slow down system speed. This delay is minimized by using low dielectric PC board materials such as Teflon ($e_r = 2.4$) and polymide ($e_r = 3.5$) rather than glass-epoxy ($e_r = 4.5$). Using surface microstrip lines rather than buried stripline also decreases wire delay. Fine signal line widths and spacings help shrink chip-chip spacings, especially with large numbers of leads per package. Present CRAY-1 boards use 7 mil lines and spaces. Four to five mil lines may be the limit for subtractively etched PC boards, so new techniques will be needed.

Smaller IC packages help both mechanically with reduced PC board real-estate and electrically with reduced lead inductance and capacitance. Table III lists some properties of packaging materials. Improved designs such as ceramic chip carriers permit a higher board density and a more uniform wire length from external lead to IC die. A rough rule of thumb for wire inductance is 12 nh/in. With subnanosecond signal edge speeds, bond wire lengths of more than a few hundred mils can cause severe delay and waveform degration. A package can add 1 pF or more to the gate input capacitance. This can add to signal delay by a factor of 30 ps/pF.

Improved circuit technology gives a direct benefit to computer speed. Table IV gives some rough numbers of circuit performance for comparison purposes. Silicon ECL may reach a delay limit in the low hundreds of picoseconds, and a power-delay limit in the low picojoule range. Significant improvement is gained by switching to high mobility materials such as gallium arsenide or indium phosphide. Technical problems need to be solved, however. Processing of these materials is still in the early stages. Gates have been fabricated using GaAs transistors, but problems exist with device threshold voltage uniformity and limited current drive due to input saturation as compared to silicon bipolar or MOS devices. An insulated gate structure would alleviate the current drive

TABLE III
SOME MATERIAL PARAMETERS

	Signal Line Width	Dielectric Constant	Thermal Conductivity
Glass-Epoxy	0.004 in	4.5	0.0024 $\frac{W}{CM\text{-}^\circ C}$
Alumina	0.003 in	8.9	0.28 $\frac{W}{CM\text{-}^\circ C}$
Beryllia	0.003 in	6.8	1.68 $\frac{W}{CM\text{-}^\circ C}$
Silicon	2 um	11.7	1.50 $\frac{W}{CM\text{-}^\circ C}$

TABLE IV
CIRCUIT TECHNOLOGY GATE PROPAGATION DELAYS AND POWER DELAY PRODUCTS

	T_{pd}	$P_d \times T_{pd}$
Silicon	400 ps	4.5 pJ
Gallium arsenide	80 ps	0.1 pJ
Josephson junctions	15 ps	1.0 fJ

limitation and permit a high performance memory circuit. Further speed increase from these materials occurs by operating at liquid nitrogen temperatures (77 K) [4]. At low temperatures, device mobility increases and delays of 20 ps and power-delays of 10 FJ may be possible [5]. The lowest power technology would use Josephson Junctions (JJ's), but the necessity of liquid helium (4°K) cooling may make JJ's less attractive than cooled GaAs.

VIII. CONCLUSION

This paper has provided a review of the CRAY-1 computer hardware. It has been shown that high performance components, clever packaging, and systems design have made the CRAY-1 system practical [6].

ACKNOWLEDGMENT

The author wishes to thank all the Cray personnel whose efforts and contributions made the CRAY-1, and therefore this paper, possible.

REFERENCES

[1] P. M. Johnson, "An introduction to vector processing," *Comput. Design*, pp. 89–97, Feb. 1978.
[2] R. M. Russell, "The CRAY-1 Computer System," *Commun. Assoc. Comput. Machinery*, vol. 21, no. 1, pp. 63–72, Jan. 1978.
[3] Cray Research Inc. field engineering statistics.
[4] M. S. Shur and L. F. Eastman, "Ballistic and near ballistic transport in GaAs," *IEEE Trans. Electron Devices*, vol. ED-1, no. 8, pp. 147–148, Aug. 1980.
[5] W. Twaddell, "IC's and semiconductors," *EDN*, pp. 37–50, Dec. 15, 1979.
[6] *CRAY-1S Series Hardware Reference Manual*, CRAY-1 Computer Systems, HR-0808, Cray Research Inc., 1980.

Cramming More Components onto Integrated Circuits

GORDON E. MOORE, LIFE FELLOW, IEEE

With unit cost falling as the number of components per circuit rises, by 1975 economics may dictate squeezing as many as 65 000 components on a single silicon chip.

The future of integrated electronics is the future of electronics itself. The advantages of integration will bring about a proliferation of electronics, pushing this science into many new areas.

Integrated circuits will lead to such wonders as home computers—or at least terminals connected to a central computer—automatic controls for automobiles, and personal portable communications equipment. The electronic wristwatch needs only a display to be feasible today.

But the biggest potential lies in the production of large systems. In telephone communications, integrated circuits in digital filters will separate channels on multiplex equipment. Integrated circuits will also switch telephone circuits and perform data processing.

Computers will be more powerful, and will be organized in completely different ways. For example, memories built of integrated electronics may be distributed throughout the machine instead of being concentrated in a central unit. In addition, the improved reliability made possible by integrated circuits will allow the construction of larger processing units. Machines similar to those in existence today will be built at lower costs and with faster turnaround.

I. PRESENT AND FUTURE

By integrated electronics, I mean all the various technologies which are referred to as microelectronics today as well as any additional ones that result in electronics functions supplied to the user as irreducible units. These technologies were first investigated in the late 1950's. The object was to miniaturize electronics equipment to include increasingly complex electronic functions in limited space with minimum weight. Several approaches evolved, including microassembly techniques for individual components, thin-film structures, and semiconductor integrated circuits.

Each approach evolved rapidly and converged so that each borrowed techniques from another. Many researchers believe the way of the future to be a combination of the various approaches.

The advocates of semiconductor integrated circuitry are already using the improved characteristics of thin-film resistors by applying such films directly to an active semiconductor substrate. Those advocating a technology based upon films are developing sophisticated techniques for the attachment of active semiconductor devices to the passive film arrays.

Both approaches have worked well and are being used in equipment today.

II. THE ESTABLISHMENT

Integrated electronics is established today. Its techniques are almost mandatory for new military systems, since the reliability, size, and weight required by some of them is achievable only with integration. Such programs as Apollo, for manned moon flight, have demonstrated the reliability of integrated electronics by showing that complete circuit functions are as free from failure as the best individual transistors.

Most companies in the commercial computer field have machines in design or in early production employing integrated electronics. These machines cost less and perform better than those which use "conventional" electronics.

Instruments of various sorts, especially the rapidly increasing numbers employing digital techniques, are starting to use integration because it cuts costs of both manufacture and design.

The use of linear integrated circuitry is still restricted primarily to the military. Such integrated functions are expensive and not available in the variety required to satisfy a major fraction of linear electronics. But the first applications are beginning to appear in commercial electronics, particularly in equipment which needs low-frequency amplifiers of small size.

III. RELIABILITY COUNTS

In almost every case, integrated electronics has demonstrated high reliability. Even at the present level of production—low compared to that of discrete components—it offers reduced systems cost, and in many systems improved performance has been realized.

Integrated electronics will make electronic techniques more generally available throughout all of society, performing many functions that presently are done inadequately by other techniques or not done at all. The principal advantages will be lower costs and greatly simplified design—payoffs from a ready supply of low-cost functional packages.

For most applications, semiconductor integrated circuits will predominate. Semiconductor devices are the only reasonable candidates presently in existence for the active elements of integrated circuits. Passive semiconductor elements look attractive too, because of their potential for low cost and high reliability, but they can be used only if precision is not a prime requisite.

Silicon is likely to remain the basic material, although others will be of use in specific applications. For example, gallium arsenide will be important in integrated microwave functions. But silicon will predominate at lower frequencies because of the technology which has already evolved around it and its oxide, and because it is an abundant and relatively inexpensive starting material.

IV. COSTS AND CURVES

Reduced cost is one of the big attractions of integrated electronics, and the cost advantage continues to increase as the technology evolves toward the production of larger and larger circuit functions on a single semiconductor substrate. For simple circuits, the cost per component is nearly inversely proportional to the number of components, the result of the equivalent piece of semiconductor in the equivalent package containing more components. But as components are added, decreased yields more than compensate for the increased complexity, tending to raise the cost per component. Thus there is a minimum cost at any given time in the evolution of the technology. At present, it is reached when 50 components are used per circuit. But the minimum is rising rapidly while the entire cost curve is falling (see graph). If we look ahead five years, a plot of costs suggests that the minimum cost per component might be expected in circuits with about 1000 components per circuit (providing such circuit functions can be produced in moderate quantities). In 1970, the manufacturing cost per component can be expected to be only a tenth of the present cost.

The complexity for minimum component costs has increased at a rate of roughly a factor of two per year (see graph). Certainly over the short term this rate can be expected to continue, if not to increase. Over the longer term, the rate of increase is a bit more uncertain, although there is no reason to believe it will not remain nearly constant for at least ten years. That means by 1975, the number of components per integrated circuit for minimum cost will be 65 000.

I believe that such a large circuit can be built on a single wafer.

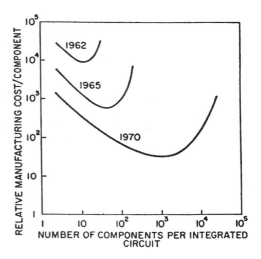

Fig. 1.

V. TWO-MIL SQUARES

With the dimensional tolerances already being employed in integrated circuits, isolated high-performance transistors can be built on centers two-thousandths of an inch apart. Such a two-mil square can also contain several kilohms of resistance or a few diodes. This allows at least 500 components per linear inch or a quarter million per square inch. Thus, 65 000 components need occupy only about one-fourth a square inch.

On the silicon wafer currently used, usually an inch or more in diameter, there is ample room for such a structure if the components can be closely packed with no space wasted for interconnection patterns. This is realistic, since efforts to achieve a level of complexity above the presently available integrated circuits are already under way using multilayer metallization patterns separated by dielectric films. Such a density of components can be achieved by present optical techniques and does not require the more exotic techniques, such as electron beam operations, which are being studied to make even smaller structures.

VI. INCREASING THE YIELD

There is no fundamental obstacle to achieving device yields of 100%. At present, packaging costs so far exceed the cost of the semiconductor structure itself that there is no incentive to improve yields, but they can be raised as high as is economically justified. No barrier exists comparable to the thermodynamic equilibrium considerations that often limit yields in chemical reactions; it is not even necessary to do any fundamental research or to replace present processes. Only the engineering effort is needed.

In the early days of integrated circuitry, when yields were extremely low, there was such incentive. Today ordinary integrated circuits are made with yields comparable with those obtained for individual semiconductor devices. The same pattern will make larger arrays economical, if other considerations make such arrays desirable.

Fig. 2.

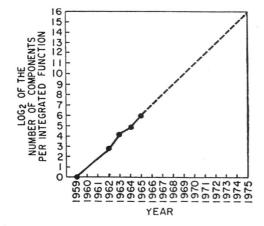

Fig. 3.

VII. HEAT PROBLEM

Will it be possible to remove the heat generated by tens of thousands of components in a single silicon chip?

If we could shrink the volume of a standard high-speed digital computer to that required for the components themselves, we would expect it to glow brightly with present power dissipation. But it won't happen with integrated circuits. Since integrated electronic structures are two dimensional, they have a surface available for cooling close to each center of heat generation. In addition, power is needed primarily to drive the various lines and capacitances associated with the system. As long as a function is confined to a small area on a wafer, the amount of capacitance which must be driven is distinctly limited. In fact, shrinking dimensions on an integrated structure makes it possible to operate the structure at higher speed for the same power per unit area.

VIII. DAY OF RECKONING

Clearly, we will be able to build such component-crammed equipment. Next, we ask under what circumstances we should do it. The total cost of making a particular system function must be minimized. To do so, we could amortize the engineering over several identical items, or evolve flexible techniques for the engineering of large functions so that no disproportionate expense need be borne by a particular array. Perhaps newly devised design automation procedures could translate from logic diagram to technological realization without any special engineering.

It may prove to be more economical to build large systems out of smaller functions, which are separately packaged and interconnected. The availability of large functions, combined with functional design and construction, should allow the manufacturer of large systems to design and construct a considerable variety of equipment both rapidly and economically.

IX. LINEAR CIRCUITRY

Integration will not change linear systems as radically as digital systems. Still, a considerable degree of integration will be achieved with linear circuits. The lack of large-value capacitors and inductors is the greatest fundamental limitation to integrated electronics in the linear area.

By their very nature, such elements require the storage of energy in a volume. For high Q it is necessary that the volume be large. The incompatibility of large volume and integrated electronics is obvious from the terms themselves. Certain resonance phenomena, such as those in piezoelectric crystals, can be expected to have some applications for tuning functions, but inductors and capacitors will be with us for some time.

The integrated RF amplifier of the future might well consist of integrated stages of gain, giving high performance at minimum cost, interspersed with relatively large tuning elements.

Other linear functions will be changed considerably. The matching and tracking of similar components in integrated structures will allow the design of differential amplifiers of greatly improved performance. The use of thermal feedback effects to stabilize integrated structures to a small fraction of a degree will allow the construction of oscillators with crystal stability.

Even in the microwave area, structures included in the definition of integrated electronics will become increasingly important. The ability to make and assemble components small compared with the wavelengths involved will allow the use of lumped parameter design, at least at the lower frequencies. It is difficult to predict at the present time just how extensive the invasion of the microwave area by integrated electronics will be. The successful realization of such items as phased-array antennas, for example, using a multiplicity of integrated microwave power sources, could completely revolutionize radar.

G. E. Moore is one of the new breed of electronic engineers, schooled in the physical sciences rather than in electronics. He earned a B.S. degree in chemistry from the University of California and a Ph.D. degree in physical chemistry from the California Institute of Technology. He was one of the founders of Fairchild Semiconductor and has been Director of the research and development laboratories since 1959.

The History of the Microcomputer—Invention and Evolution

STANLEY MAZOR, SENIOR MEMBER, IEEE

Invited Paper

Intel's founder, Robert Noyce, chartered Ted Hoff's Applications Research Department in 1969 to find new applications for silicon technology—the microcomputer was the result. Hoff thought it would be neat to use MOS LSI technology to produce a computer. Because of the ever growing density of large scale integrated (LSI) circuits a "computer on a chip" was inevitable. But in 1970 we could only get about 2000 transistors on a chip, and a conventional CPU would need about 10 times that number. We developed two "microcomputers" 10 years ahead of "schedule," by scaling down the requirements and using a few other "tricks" described in this paper.

I. Introduction

Intel's first microcomputer ad appeared in November 1971:

"Announcing a new era in integrated electronics."

Intel delivered two different microcomputers five months apart: the MCS-4, emphasizing low cost, in November 1971, and the MCS-8, for versatility in April 1972. "The MCS-4 and MCS-8 CPU chip sell in quantity for less than $100 each, and are powerful alternatives to random logic" [1]. These two Micro Computer Systems (MCS) were aimed at two very different markets. One would eventually lead to the under $1 controller, the other would be the engine for a versatile personal computer (PC). By analogy it was like creating the "motorbike" and the "station wagon" at the same time. The advertised prophecy of "a new era" became fulfilled over the subsequent 20 year period.

A. Automobile Analogy

Our challenge was how to scale down a general purpose computer to fit on to a chip. Imagine that the only passenger vehicle in existence is an eight-passenger van costing $50 000. At first it would be difficult to imagine a $1000 version of this vehicle. The specifications would need to be drastically reduced to meet the price goal. Some ideas to consider:

1) reducing capacity by 75%
2) reducing speed by 90%
3) reducing range by 75%.

The golf cart might be the result. However, if golf carts are unknown at the time, it is not easy to envision how to scale down a van.

What features of a computer can be scaled down? That depends on what it will be used for. Fortunately for us, our first customer's application was for a desktop calculator; we scaled down the computer's speed and memory size to meet the needs of this particular application. As computers go, the microcomputer was not very capable; some would say that we set the computer industry back 10 years. We thought we were moving the LSI world ahead by 10 years [2]. I will share some of my recollections of the early days of Intel microprocessors.

II. Intel MCS-4 4-b Chip Set

Although Intel began as a memory chip company [3], in 1969 we took on a project for Busicom of Japan to design eight custom LSI chips for a desktop calculator. Each custom chip had a specialized function—keyboard, printer, display, serial arithmetic, control, etc. With only two designers, Intel didn't have the manpower to do that many custom chips. We needed to solve their problem with fewer chip designs. Ted Hoff chose a programmed computer solution using only one complex logic chip (CPU) and two memory chips; memory chips are repetitive and easier to design. Intel was a memory chip company, so we found a way to solve our problem using memory chips!

In 1970 Intel designers implemented a 4-b computer on three LSI chips (CPU, ROM, RAM) housed in 16-pin packages [4]. Reducing the data word to 4-b (for a BCD digit) was a compromise between 1-b serial calculator chips and conventional 16-b computers. The scaled down 4-b word size made the CPU chip size practical ($\sim$ 2200 transistors). We used the 16-pin package, because it was the *only one* available in our company. This limited pin count forced us to time multiplex a 4-b bus. This small bus simplified the printed circuit board (PCB), as it used fewer connections. However, the multiplexing logic increased chip area of the specialized ROM/RAM memory chips, which then had to have built-in address registers. Increasing the transistor count to save chip connections was a novel idea. In school we learned to minimize logic, not interconnections! Later, LSI "philosophers" would preach "logic is free" [5].

1) MCS-4 Features [6], [7]:

256 × 8 Read Only Memory (2 kb ROM)
 with 4-b I/O port
80 × 4 Random Access Memory (320 b RAM)
 with 4-b output port
4-b CPU chip with:
 16 × 4-b index registers
 45 1 and 2 byte instructions
 4-level Subroutine Address Stack
 12-b Program Counter (4 k addresses).

A. ROM Chip (4001)

Conventional calculators utilized specialized custom chips for keyboard, display, and printer control. With the MCS-4 all control logic is done in firmware, program stored in ROM [8]. A single ROM chip design is customized (with a mask during chip manufacturing) for a customer's particular program. The CPU's 12-b Program Counter addresses up to 16 ROM chips. Simple applications use only one ROM chip; the desktop calculator used four. The same chip mask also configured each ROM port bit as an input or output.

Additionally, the ROM chip had an integrated address register, an output data register, multiplexors, and control and timing logic. The specialized RAM chip had similar resources.

B. RAM Chip (4002)

Calculators need to hold several 16-digit decimal floating point numbers. We organized the RAM accordingly, and ended up with a 20-digit word (80 b):

16 digits for the fraction
2 digits for the exponent
2 digits for signs and control
20 digits × 4 b/digit

The RAM chip stored four 80-b numbers and additionally the chip had an output port. The use of three-transistor dynamic memory cells made the RAM chip feasible [9]. A built-in refresh counter was used to maintain data integrity. Refresh took place during instruction fetch cycles, when the RAM data was not being accessed. Dynamic RAM memory cells were also used inside the CPU for the 64-b index register array and 48-b Program counter/stack array. Intel expertise in dynamic memory was an enabling factor for the MCS-4!

C. Input/Output Ports

To conserve chip count and to utilize existing power/clock pins, the 16-pin ROM and RAM chips also had integrated 4-b ports for direct connection of I/O devices. To activate an output, a program selected a particular RAM/ROM chip (using an index register) and sent 4-b of Accumulator data from the CPU to the selected output port. In the desk calculator application, the display, keyboard, and printer were connected to these ports. Keyboard scanning, decoding, and debouncing [10] were all done under program control of the I/O ports; all printer and display refresh was done in firmware [11]. A small shift register (4003) was used for output port expansion. External transistors and diodes were used for amplification and isolation.

D. Microprocesor—CPU Chip (4004)

In the calculator application, each user key stroke caused thousands of CPU instructions to be executed from ROM. We wrote many subroutines which operated on 16-digit numbers stored in RAM. As an example, a 10-byte loop for digit serial addition took about 80 μs/digit (similar speed as IBM 1620 computer sold in 1960 for $100 000). In this add routine a CPU index register would address each of the 16 digits stored in the RAM memory. The program would bring in one digit at a time into the CPU's accumulator register to do arithmetic. A Decrement and Jump instruction was used to index to the next RAM location.

One major difference compared to most computers, was the MCS-4's separate program and data memories. Conventional computers ran programs from RAM (core) memory. However, our application firmware needed to be permanently stored in ROM. A major change was needed for subroutine linkage. Normally, as part of a minicomputer [12] subroutine call instruction execution (PDP-8, HP 2114) the calling program's return address would be saved at the top of the subroutine in RAM. Since MCS-4 routines were in ROM (can't write into it) we could not use this method. Instead, we used a push down stack inside the CPU for saving up to three return addresses. This was not a new idea. Stacks had been used in Burrough's computers and the IBM 1620, which Ted Hoff and I had programmed—we used our experience with large scale computers. Ultimately this limited depth of four levels (which was all we could squeeze on to this small chip) was frustrating for programmers and succeeding generations went to eight or more levels (8008, 4040, 8048). Today's computers have stacks of many megabytes; but their usage is very similar to their use in the 4004.

E. Distributed Logic Architecture

The time division multiplexing of the 4-b bus, the on-chip dynamic RAM memories, and the CPU's address stack are the highlights of the MCS-4 architecture. However, there is another interesting feature—distributed decoding of instructions. The ROM/RAM chips watched the bus, and locally decoded port instructions, as they were sent from the ROM. This eliminated the need for the CPU to have separate signal lines to the I/O ports, and also saved CPU logic. This is not a feature used in conventional computers.

F. MCS-4 Applications

The smallest system would contain two chips—a CPU and a ROM. A typical calculator had 4 ROM's and a RAM chip—with five I/O ports, (20) wires for connecting peripheral devices. A fully loaded system could have 16 ROM and 16 RAM chips, and obviously a plethora of I/O ports. Typical applications included:

digital scales	taxi meters
gas pumps	traffic light
elevator control	vending machines
medical instruments	

Busicom of Japan produced several calculator models using the MCS-4 chip set. Ted Hoff and I made the original proposal for the MCS-4 and did the feasibility study for the first calculator. Federico Faggin did all of the logic and circuit design and implemented the layout; Busicom's M. Shima wrote most of Busicom's firmware. (Later Shima joined Intel as the 8080 designer.) The Intel patent on the MCS-4 (Hoff, Faggin, Mazor) has 17 claims, but the single chip processor is not claimed as an invention.

Intel supported the MCS-4 with a Cross assembler and later with a stand alone development system, the Intellec "blue" box. Intel's marketing efforts of H. Smith, R. Graham, and Ed Gelbach gained attention.

The MCS-4 evolved into the single chip microcomputers 8048/8051 [13]. These chips emphasized small size and low cost. These, along with a variety of other manufacturer's parts have evolved into the under $1 computer on a chip used in toys, automobiles, and appliances [14]. These chips are very pervasive—almost invisible.

III. INTEL 8008 MICROPROCESSOR

Intel made a custom 512-b shift register memory chip [15] for use in (their customer) Datapoint's low cost bit-serial computer. This 8-b CPU, implemented with TTL MSI, had around 50 data processing instructions. In response to their inquiry about an 8×16 stack chip, and based upon our progress with the MCS-4, I proposed an 8-b parallel single chip CPU in 12/69 [16]. This custom chip design was never used by Datapoint, and it became a standard Intel product, which marketing dubbed the 8008 (twice 4004!).

Although the arithmetic unit and registers were twice as large as in the MCS-4, we expected that the control logic could be about the same if we deleted a few Datapoint defined instructions. Unlike the MCS4's two memory address space, the 8008 had one memory address space for program and data [17]. The symmetric and regular instruction set was attractive. However, the only memory addressing was indirect through the High-Low (HL) register pair. Today's computers have huge amounts of memory, and a plethora of memory addressing instructions.

The 8008 CPU had six 8-b general purpose registers (B,C,D,E,H,L) and an 8-b accumulator. The push down program counter stack had 8-levels. Both of these register arrays were implemented with dynamic memory cells and the CPU had built-in "hidden" refresh during instruction fetch cycles, similar to the MCS-4.

We decided that the 8008 would utilize standard memory components (not custom ROM's and RAM's as in the MCS-4). This increased the parts count on a minimum system because separate address registers, multiplexors and I/O latch chips would need to be added to make the system work; in practice about 40 additional small chips were needed. But standard memories were available in high volume at low cost, and in a larger system the extra chip overhead could be tolerated. Using memory chips with different access times requires a synchronizer scheme, and therefore ready/wait signal pins were provided to perform a handshake function. These interface signals are more sophisticated in today's processors, but the 8008 demonstrated the idea.

The availability of Electrically Programmed ROM's (EPROM) was significant in allowing customers to experiment with their software. A product synergy evolved between Intel's memory component business and the microprocessor.

Intel had an 18-pin package in volume production for the 1k dynamic RAM chip (1103); this gave two more pins for the 8008 than we had on the MCS-4, but we still had to time-multiplex an 8-b bus. By reducing the Program Counter width to 14-b we saved two package pins. The jump instruction contained a 16-b address, but two of the bits were ignored. The 8008 could have 16 k bytes of memory, and at the time, this seemed enormous. (Today, users want 16 meg.)

A. Little Endian

Some have wondered why the addresses in the 8008 were stored "backward" with the little end first, e.g., the low order byte of a two byte address is stored in the lower addressed memory location. I (regrettably) specified this ordering as part of the JUMP instruction format in the spirit of compatibility with the Datapoint 2200. Recall that their original processor was bit serial; the addresses would be stored low to high bit in the machine code (bit-backward). Other computer makers organize the addresses with the "big end" first. The lack of standardization has been a problem in the industry.

B. Applications

One of the first users of the 8008 was Seiko in Japan for a sophisticated scientific calculator. Other uses included business machines and a variety of general purpose computers.

Most of the 8008 instruction set was defined by Datapoint's H. Pyle and V. Poor [16]. Hoff and I wrote the specification for the 8008 single chip CPU. Hal Feeney did all of the chip design under Faggin's supervision. I did the logic simulation for Feeney. Les Vasdasz [18] was our overall manager. Sandy Goldstein wrote a cross assembler; Gary Kildall (Digital Research) created PLM-8 and then CP/M. This operating system is famous and helped lead to the development of Microsoft's DOS.

Intel did not apply for a patent on the 8008. Datapoint contracted with Texas Instruments in 1970 to get a second source for this chip. TI patented their design, but never got into production [19].

After about one year of experience with programming the 8008 CPU chip [20], we had a number of requested enhancements from our users. We proposed to build the 8080 as a follow on chip; this chip was very popular and led to the microcomputer revolution and the Personal Computer. It is ironic that Datapoint ultimately competed in the marketplace with PC products based upon *their own*, Datapoint defined, architecture!

IV.   8080—MORE AND NO MORE

A. *More*

Based upon Intel's success with their new microcomputer product line Faggin convinced Vasdasz in 1972 to fund a project to convert the P-MOS 8008 into the newer N-MOS technology. This technology offered about a 2× speedup without making logic changes. After a short study, it was determined that a new mask set was needed because of the incompatibility of transistor size ratios. Faggin reckoned that since a new mask set was needed, he would fix some of the 8008's shortcomings [21].

We evolved the 8080 specification [22] to improve performance 10×. We used the greater density to put in more logic (~4500 transistors) and do more in parallel; the on chip control logic grew by 50%. We put the stack in memory, did 16-b operations, and improved memory addressing. Now 40-pin plastic packages were available, and the address bus and data bus could be brought out in parallel. This design also simplified the external circuitry and TTL voltage compatible signals were provided.

Deleting the on-chip stack saved chip area, but was a net advantage to the user—now the stack had unlimited size. I defined the stack as growing downward from the high end of memory; this facilitated indexing into the stack and simplified displaying the stack. This was abandoned on the 8086.

In the 8080, the registers were arranged as pairs of 8 b, to provide 16-b data handling. The three register pairs were designated as: BC, DE, HL—The High/Low register pair was the only way to address memory in the older 8008. This was limiting to programmers, so in the 8080 direct memory addressing instructions were added, as well as several specialized instructions for the HL register pair. One instruction XTHL provided for exchanging the top of stack with HL; another instruction, XHLD swapped the contents of HL with the DE register pair. As these special instructions were not very symmetric, applying only to HL, we optimized their logic implementation. One of Ted Hoff's tricks was the use of an *exchange flip/flop* for

DE/HL This flip flop designated one of the pairs as HL and the other register pair as DE. Simply toggling this flip/flop affected an apparent exchange! This saved a lot of logic; but by mistake, the reset pin had been connected to this flip/flop. An early 8080 user manual stated: "after reset, the HL/DE register contents may be exchanged" (later the reset connection was cut). The lack of instruction set symmetry was a nuisance to programmers and later CPU's instruction sets were considerably more regular; of course there were more transistors "to burn."

B. *No More*

M. Shima [21] was the 8080 project manager under Faggin. My specification used all 256 operation codes, and 12th from the bottom of my list was an obscure instruction (XTHL) for exchanging the top of stack with the HL register pair. This instruction required five memory cycles to execute, and would be used to pass arguments to subroutines. I carefully explained each instruction to Shima, whose patience was tested as I detailed the XTHL operation. He drew a line under this instruction, and declared:

"No more."

This is why the last 12 instructions were never implemented and why there was room in the instructions set for the 8085 microprocessor's added instructions [23].

The 8080 was very successful in the market. Meanwhile, competition blossomed and a variety of great processors developed [24] including the Motorola 6800 and the MOS Technology 6502. Shima and Faggin (with R. Ungerman) formed Zilog, and competed with an enhanced processor, the Z-80 [25]. The 8080 CPU chip was patented by Intel (Faggin, Shima, Mazor) and has three claims [26].

C. *8085*

To meet competition in 1976, Intel decided to develop a more integrated version of the 8080. This chip contained ~6500 transistors. The new N-MOS was more TTL compatible and this chip needed few external parts. There were 12 unused operation codes in the 8080 which provided room to expand the CPU's function. At Intel, a committee studied, argued, and finally decided after many months which instructions to add [27]. Although, all of these new codes were utilized by the 8085 designers, by the time this product got to market it was almost obsolete. To reduce compatibility requirements with the 8086 which was in design, 10 of the new 12 instructions were never announced in the data sheet. They have only been an interesting historical anomaly and a lesson about design by committee.

D. *8086*

In 1978, Intel's W. Davidow, vice president of the microcomputer group, rushed to staff a 16 b microcomputer development project. It was to have around 30 000 transistors [28], 12 times more than the 4004. This new computer had multiplication and division and a host of other new features [29]. However, it was constrained to be upwardly compatible with the 8080 (and 8008). Accordingly, the

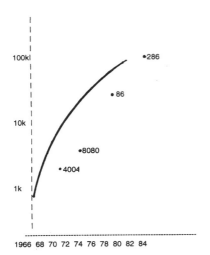

Fig. 1. MOS transistor per chip—1966 forecast (solid line) and actual (dots).

designers decided to keep the 16 b basic addresses and to use segment registers to get extended 20 b addresses. Two versions were created—the 8088 had an 8-b data bus for compatibility with 8-b memory systems, and the 16 b 8086 [30].[1] With 1 megabyte of memory addressing, this processor was a serious contender in the computer market place. This chip density required to match the 16-b minicomputers was "arriving" as had been predicted [31].

The decision by IBM to use the 8088 in a word processor and personal computer created enormous market momentum for Intel. The 186, 286, 386, 486 followed over the next 15 years, with some shadow of 8008 features still apparent. These components would be "truly pervasive" [32].

V. HISTORICAL PERSPECTIVE

A. Technology Predictions

The promises of high density solid state circuitry were becoming apparent in the 1950's. In 1959, Holland contemplated large scale computers built with densities of 10^8 components per cubic foot [34]. The integrated circuit was developed in parallel at both TI and Intel. Technology forecasts were made by Fairchild's Gordon Moore and Robert Noyce in the mid-1960's—the density of IC's was doubling every year [35]. "Entire subsystems on a chip" were predicted if a high volume standard chip could be defined. By 1966 Petritz of TI was forecasting about 10 k transistors per chip for 1970 and 100 k (optimistically) by 1976 [31]. See Fig. 1 for a 1966 forecast of chip complexity. It was then estimated that abut 10 k–20 k gates would fit on a chip and that a good portion of a CPU would therefore be on one chip.

In 1966, Hobbs forecasted the reduced cost of arrays, predicting that the CPU cost would become "negligible" [5]. Practical people recognized that the issues were the

[1] The 8086 had a large staff. If a few names are to be mentioned they are S. Morse, W. Pohlman, B. Ravenel, J. McKevitt, J. Bayliss, and in Marketing, D. Gellatly [33].

"number of unique part numbers and the production volume" after all only a few thousand computers were made each year [36].

B. SSI, MSI, LSI Chips

By 1968 16-b minicomputers utilized a single printed circuit board CPU containing around 200 chips. These were medium scale integrated circuits (MSI) with ~ 100 transistors per chip, and small scale IC's (SSI). Obviously, the more transistors that could be put on a chip, the fewer chips needed on a PCB. Since manufacturers were trying to reduce costs, there was a constant battle to reduce the number of chips used—could a CPU be built, with 150, 80, or 25 chips?

By 1970 there were a few projects to build a 16 b minicomputer CPU using multiple LSI chips. A 1000 transistor chip would be called large scale (LSI). These projects were being done with military sponsorship at Raytheon and RCA. The air force was especially interested in light weight airborne minicomputers. These were full 16-b minicomputers and did not have a scaled down specification (like the MCS-4), except for their physical size [37], [38]. They utilized 4-b or 8-b arithmetic and register "slices"; a minimum CPU would require 8–12 LSI chips with about 6–8 different part numbers. These were R&D projects [39], [40].

C. LSI Economics

The use of custom LSI in an application required very high production volume to commercially justify the significant tooling costs. One would need to produce around 100 000 systems for commercial feasibility. The only high volume commercial applications in the early 1970's were calculators; almost every calculator manufacturer was designing custom LSI chips. These chips were invariably very specialized for arithmetic, printers, and keyboards—(Busicom's original request).

Besides tooling costs, another problem is to get an economic die size. If a die is too small it does not contain enough circuitry to justify a fair price. If a die is too ambitious and large, the manufacturing yield will be too low and the chip will be too expensive [41]. See Fig. 2 for an illustration of complexity, cost, and yield. Worst of all, at the beginning of a complex chip project it is not easy to accurately forecast the final die size. Defining standard high volume LSI chips is challenging [36], [42].

Consequently, in 1970, no one had defined general purpose LSI building blocks that were usable in a variety of applications. The only LSI building blocks available were memory chips. Honeywell tried to get multiple sources for a 64-b bipolar LSI memory chip, but that was on the leading edge of bipolar technology, and not many vendors could make them [43]. Metal gate MOS ROM's and 200-b shift registers were available from a few sources: AMI, Electronic Arrays, MOS Technology, and General Instruments. See Table 1 for 1965 LSI chip examples. Although these chips had around 1000 transistors, they were

Table 1 MOS Chip Availability in 1965

Manufacturer	Type	Transistors	Power, mW	Pads
GME	100-b shift register	600	200	12
GI	21-b static shift register	160	150	11
TI	Binary-to-digital decoder	150	25	26

very regular in structure and easy to design. Because their internal wiring was minimal, they were $2x - 5x$ more dense than "random logic" chips.

D. Partitioning into Packages

One difficulty implementing any system on a set of LSI chips is partitioning [44] into pieces with a reasonable number of I/O pins on each. It was very expensive to get more than 20 pins. Around 1970 there were very few commercially available low cost packages. The most common had only 14-pins and sold for around $1. Cost sensitive applications such as desk calculators could not afford 48-pin packages which were then selling for around $10.

Optimization consists of maximizing the number of gates inside compared to the number of pins outside—the *gate to pin ratio*. Memory chips with 1 kb in an 18-pin package gave an excellent gate/pin ratio of about 100:1. Each time the technology allowed a doubling of bits on a chip, only one more address pin was needed. A shift register was even better, because regardless of the number of bits added, the input/output pin count stayed constant.

If a CPU were to be built of LSI chips it was not obvious how to break it into pieces with a small number of I/O pin connections and a high gate/pin ratio. Simply put, if you cut an ordinary CPU into two pieces you would have hundreds of signals which would need to cross the chip boundaries.

Each package pin also required a lot of MOS chip "real estate" for amplifiers to drive the heavy off chip capacitive loads and for the wire bonding pads which go from the chip to the package. Besides the cost, placing more pins on an LSI chip also lowered the reliability. Hence, most commercial LSI applications were constrained by the few leads available on IC packages. This is why the early microprocessors were in 16 and 18 pin packages.

E. Semiconductor Technology

On-chip interconnections are also a major problem. A CPU chip contains "random logic" requiring many interconnection wires. Prior to 1980 most semiconductor chips had only one layer of metal. This metal was used for global connections such as power, ground, clocks, and major busses. Local connections were made using poorer quality, higher resistance, lines of poly-silicon or diffusion.

The silicon gate process [18], developed originally at Fairchild Semiconductor in around 1967, provided slightly better local interconnections and crossovers. This technology also offered lower capacitance, smaller size (self-

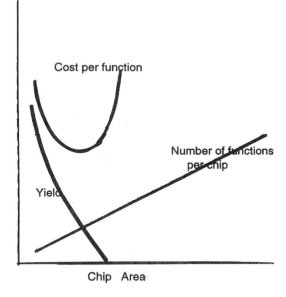

Illustration of: Complexity, Cost, Yield

Fig. 2. Relationships of complexity, cost, and yield to chip area.

aligned structures) and lower voltage operation. This was a key technology enabler for microprocessor development at Intel. The 8008 chip for Datapoint was implemented using silicon gate technology. In contrast, TI, was at that time, using metal gate MOS technology and used about twice the amount of silicon area for a similar chip.

Silicon gate P-MOS needed a 14 V supply, and was often biased between +5 V and −9 V to give pseudo-TTL compatibility. This relatively high voltage aggravated the severe power budget facing the circuit designer. Small IC packages cannot dissipate more than 1/2 W of power in normal air cooled systems. The compromise was to use dynamic logic operating at low duty cycles to reduce heat. In 1995, power dissipation is still a major design factor in commercial system design. It has been one of the driving factors toward 1.5–2.5 V technology; battery operation is another factor.

F. Circuit Factors

The P-MOS transistors in 1970 required 14 V to operate. To reduce the overall power dissipation most of the circuits were operated dynamically in a two phase operation. First a circuit was precharged using an on-chip amplifier, and then the circuit was conditionally discharged, based upon logic decisions. Previously, "bootstrap" amplifiers were built using the gate "overlap capacitance" as part of the circuit. However, silicon gate self-aligned geometry eliminated this capacitor. F. Faggin innovated a new and efficient bootstrap amplifier as part of his early circuit design of Intel's chips.

Another element which made micro's feasible was the dynamic RAM cell. The memory storage is obtained by storing a charge on a small capacitor. This capacitor is usually integrated into a three-transistor memory cell. However, the memory starts to fade after about 5 ms, so that an external "refresh" circuit needs to read, test, and restore the charge on a periodic basis. Static memory cells required twice the chip area and used much more power; they were impractical for use inside the CPU. Recall that Intel was only a memory company in 1970. Hoff had done research on memory cell design and, proposed to use dynamic RAM inside the CPU for index registers and stack. Hoff's insight was essential for enabling the first microprocessor chip.

G. CAD Tools

Since the mid-1960's computer makers had been doing circuit analysis using "home grown" tools. Hoff and I developed a transient analysis program (PULS) to help with MOS circuit design. Intel's Dov Frohman, who invented the EPROM (he didn't call it a FROM), provided the transistor model. Intel's designers used PULS to help them achieve the desired ac/dc performance. Hoff wrote our first logic simulator for the PDP-8; later I used a commercial (Applicon) tool for the PDP-10. I abused the DEC macro assembler to get the first MCS-4 code assembled and into the 4001 ROM bit map. We developed the early calculator firmware with this assembler. The availability of these CAD tools allowed our designers to catch design errors early and were essential to Intel's success. A few Silicon Valley CAD companies were spawned from these in house CAD groups.

H. The Microcomputer Name

In the mid-1960's midicomputers and minicomputers were selling in the marketplace. Some computers used a microprogram, stored in ROM; the inner part of such a computer was called an "engine" or "microengine" or "microprocessor." In 1970, a microcomputer was normally interpreted as a computer considerably smaller than a minicomputer, possibly using ROM for program storage. By extension, the terms "nano-computer" and "pico-computer" have also been used by computer engineers indicating relative size and performance of computers.

In the late 1960's Fairchild had a logic family called μ-logic, so the prefix was also used for "micrologic" in IC's. (Since most of the Intel guys had come from Fairchild we avoided references to their product line; Intel did not use the Greek letter).

Lo [45] mentions "the computer on a chip" in 1968, and *Scientific American* also featured "Computer on a Chip," with 400 gates in 1970 [2]. IBM looked for ways of simplifying computers. In 1968, Hitt proposed a 4-b computer with no arithmetic unit and no registers (CADET—can't add doesn't even try). But this very simple computer was not built with LSI and was still called a minicomputer [11].

The single chip central processor unit (CPU) has been commonly called a microprocessor. With off chip memory, it is usually called a microcomputer. Single chip computers are often called microcontrollers. The 4004 specification was for a microcomputer.

VI. SUMMARY

Integrated circuit technology has been evolving in a predictable manner for the past 30 years. Although a computer on a chip was eventually realizable, it was problematical how to use LSI chips which had fewer than 20 000 transistors. Most of the work focused on partitioning 16-b computers into multiple chips, but few of these projects were successful. Early Intel microprocessors succeeded because they were scaled down computers. Like a golf cart, they were very limited, "but got across the green." When the densities reached 200 k+ transistors per chip, microprocessors became the dominant computer technology.

REFERENCES

[1] "The alternative," Intel Corp. brochure, 1971.
[2] F. G. Heath, "Large scale integration in electronics," *Scientif. Amer.*, p. 22, Feb. 1970.
[3] G. Blynsky, "Little chips invade the memory market," *Fortune Mag.*, pp. 100–104, Apr. 1971.
[4] M. E. Hoff, S. Mazor, and F. Faggin, "Memory system for a multi-chip digital computer," US Patent #3,821,715, Intel Corp., June 1974.
[5] L. C. Hobbs, "Effects of large arrays on machine organization and hardware/software tradeoffs," *1966 FJCC*, vol. 29, p. 89.
[6] "MCS-4 micro computer set," data sheet #7144, Intel Corp., 1971.
[7] F. Faggin *et al.*, "The MCS-4—An LSI micro computer system," *IEEE Region 6 Conf. 1972*, pp. 8–11.
[8] H. Smith, "Impact of LSI on microcomputer and calculator chips," *IEEE NEREM '72 Rec.*
[9] J. Karp, A. Regitz, and S. Chou, "A 4096-bit dynamic MOS RAM," *ISSCC Dig. Papers*, pp. 10–11, Feb. 1972.
[10] S. Mazor and D. Hall, "Microprocessor software debounces input switches," *Design News*, vol. 34, pp. 109–114, June 1978.
[11] D. C. Hitt *et al.*, "The mini-computer—A new approach to computer design," *IEEE 1968 FJCC*, IBM Corp., pp. 655–662.
[12] R. Hooper, "The minicomputer, a programming challenge," *1968 FJCC*, pp. 649–654.
[13] S. Mazor and L. Goss, "A new single chip microcomputer for control applications," *IECI 77*, pp. 109–112, Mar. 1977.
[14] S. Mazor and J. Haynes, "Blood analyzer with one-chip micro-computer," *Medical Electron.*, vol. 10, no. 5, pp. 49–51, Oct. 1979.
[15] M. Hoff and S. Mazor, "Operation and application of shift registers," *Comput. Design*, pp. 57–62, Feb. 1971.
[16] V. Poor, "Letters," Datapoint, *Fortune Mag.*, p. 94, Jan. 1976.
[17] M. Hoff, "The new LSI components," *6th Annu. IEEE Comput. Soc. Int. Conf.*, 1972.
[18] L. Vasdasz, A. Grove, G. Moore, and T. Rowe, "Silicon gate technology," *IEEE Spectrum*, pp. 27–35, Oct. 1969.
[19] G. Boone, "Computing system CPU," US Patent #3,757,306, Texas Instrum., Sept. 1973.
[20] *Intel MCS-8 User Manual*, 1972.
[21] M. Shima, F. Faggin, and S. Mazor, "An N-channel 8-bit single chip microprocessor," *IEEE ISSCC*, pp. 56–57, Feb. 1974.
[22] *Intel MCS-80 User Manual*, 1974.
[23] M. Shima, *The Birth of the Microcomputer: My Recollections.* Tokyo: Iwanami Shoten, 190 pp.
[24] G. Bylinsky, "Here comes the second computer revolution," *Fortune Mag.*, Nov. 1975.
[25] F. Faggin, "Letters," Zilog, *Fortune Mag.*, p. 94, Jan. 1976.
[26] F. Faggin, M. Shima, and S. Mazor, "Single chip CPU," US Patent #4,010,449, Intel Corp.
[27] *Intel MCS-85 Users Manual*, Mar. 1977.
[28] S. Morse, W. Pohlman, and B. Ravenel, "The Intel 8086 microprocessor," *Comput.*, pp. 18–27, June 1978.
[29] S. Mazor, "Programming the 8086," *Comput. Design*, Dec. 1980 to Feb. 1981 (3 parts).

[30] *Intel MCS-86/88 Users Manual*, July 1978.
[31] R. Petritz, "Large-scale integrated electronics," in *Proc. FJCC*, 1966, pp. 65–87.
[32] P. E. Haggerty, "Integrated electronics—A perspective," *Proc. IEEE*, vol. PROC–52, pp. 1400–1405, Dec. 1964.
[33] S. Morse, B. Ravenel, S. Mazor, and W. Pohlman, "Intel microprocessors 8008 to 8086," *Comput.*, pp. 42–60, Oct. 1980.
[34] J. Holland, "A universal computer capable of executing an arbitrary number of sub-programs simultaneously," in *Proc. 1959 EJCC*.
[35] R. Noyce, "A look at future costs of large integrated arrays," in *Proc. 1966 FJCC*, pp. 111–115.
[36] M. E. Conway and L. M. Spandorfer, "A computer designer's view of large scale integration," *1968 FJCC*, p. 835.
[37] R. K. Booher, "MOS GP computer," *1968 FJCC*, vol. 33, pp. 877–886.
[38] J. J. Pariser and H. E. Maurer, "Implementation of the NASA modular computer with functional characters," *1969 FJCC*, p. 231.
[39] F. D. Erwin and J. F. McKevitt, "Characters—Universal architecture for LSI," *1969 FJCC*, vol. 35, p. 69.
[40] A. Alaspa and A. Dingwall, "COS/MOS parallel processor array," *IEEE J. Solid-State Circ.*, vol. SC-5, Oct. 1970.
[41] Philco Ford, "Large scale integrated circuit arrays," TR# AFAL-TR-69-23, Air Force Avionics Labs, June 1969.
[42] H. G. Rudenberg, "Large scale integration: Promises versus accomplishments—The dilemma of our industry," *1969 FJCC*, vol. 35, p. 359.
[43] Intel 3101 64-bit Static RAM Data Sheet, 1970.
[44] N. Cserhalmi *et al.*, "Efficient partitioning for the batch-fabricated fourth generation computer," *1968 FJCC*, vol. 33, pp. 857–866.
[45] A. W. Lo, "High-speed logic and memory—past, present, and future," *1968 FJCC*, vol. 33, pp. 1459–1465.
[46] R. Noyce and M. Hoff, "A history of microprocessor development at Intel," *IEEE Micro*, vol. 1, no. 1, pp. 8–21, Feb. 1981.
[47] S. Mazor, "Programming and/or logic design," *IEEE Comput. Group Conf.*, June 1968, pp. 69–71.
[48] M. E. Hoff and S. Mazor, "Standard LSI for a micropro-grammed processor," in *NEREM '70 Proc.*, Nov. 1970, pp. 92–93.

[49] S. Mazor, "A new single chip CPU," *Compcon*, pp. 177–180, Feb. 1974.
[50] "Intel advertisement," *Electron. News*, Nov. 1971.
[51] S. Mazor, "VLSI computer architecture issues," *Process. and Devices Symp.*, Electron Devices Group, Santa Clara Valley, CA, Apr. 1981.
[52] S. Mazor and S. Wharton, "Compact code—IAPX 432 addressing techniques," *Comput. Design*, p. 249, May 1982.
[53] L. Jack and S. Mazor, "Rapid VHSIC insertion through the application of silicon compiler technology," in *Dig. 1985 GOMAC Conf.*, Nov. 1985, p. 117.
[54] S. Mazor and P. Langstraat, *A Guide to VHDL*. New York: Kluwer, 1994.
[55] G. Hyatt, "Single chip integrated circuit computer architecture," US Patent #4,942,516, July 1990.

Stanley Mazor (Senior Member, IEEE) studied mathematics at San Francisco State College.

In 1964 he joined Fairchild Semiconductor R&D, where he helped specify and implement the Symbol high-level language computer. From 1969 to 1984 he was with Intel Corporation, where he worked on the specification of the early Intel microprocessors. He also supervised Intel's microcomputer training development group. He also spent two years in Brussels as an Applications Engineer supporting European customers. From 1984 to 1988 he was the Director of Customer Engineering Services at Silicon Compiler Systems (SCS), where he developed application-specific IC's. In 1988 he joined Synopsys, where he was Technical Training Manager. He is presently Director of Technical Services at C·ATS, Palo Alto, CA. He also taught courses at the University of Santa Clara and Stanford University, and has been a Guest Professor in China, Finland, and Sweden. He has published over 45 articles and papers on the design and application of VLSI, including signal processing, instrumentation, security, and optimization.

Mr. Mazor received the Best Paper Award for his GOMAC contribution on VHSIC insertion in 1986. He is active in the COMPCON program committee and the Asilomar Microcomputer Workshop.

CHAPTER 2

Methods

2.1 Introduction

This chapter is not about computer architecture, per se, but about the methods used to evaluate alternative architectures. We include this introduction to methods because disciplined methods are essential for the advancement of computer architecture, as they are for all branches of science and engineering.

The chapter begins with a review of the scientific method and calls for its increased use in practice. It then discusses the three major classes of methods that computer architects use: analytic modeling, simulation, and system monitoring. Each section includes case studies to illustrate concepts. The chapter concludes with a discussion comparing methods and introductions to the included papers.

2.2 The Scientific Method

One model of innovation is that a person should come up with an idea (inspiration) and then argue orally or in writing for the idea. This approach works well in some fields, for example, philosophy and literary criticism. However, it works less well in science and engineering. In science and engineering, more progress has been made by subjecting new ideas to reality to see if they are better than existing ideas.

Francis Bacon crystallized this approach as the two-part *scientific method* in *Novum Organum* (1620). In the first part, the scientist comes up with a wild new idea with a flash of inspiration after years of delving into a problem. This idea is called a *hypothesis*. In the second part, the scientist puts the new idea to experimental tests to see whether it is actually better than existing alternatives. A hypothesis that has

withstood the scrutiny of many experiments is called a *theory*. It is this second part that separates the scientific method from other methods of inquiry.

Applying the scientific method to engineering problems, such as in computer architecture, involves an additional degree of freedom. Principally, scientists seek to discover the phenomenon that is "out there," while engineers design new phenomenon. Technologies change, workloads change, and architectural ideas change. Thus, we can never do experiments to identify the best cache ever.

Nevertheless, architects are often lax in applying the scientific method. All too often, people develop an idea and then write some simulations to support the idea in one or more papers.

A more proactive application of the scientific method was presented by Platt [14]. Consider Platt's method applied to the problem of determining why a multiprocessor program runs so slowly:

- *Develop alternative hypotheses.* Hypothesis 1: The program has synchronization bottlenecks. Hypothesis 2: The program is taking too many cache misses. Having multiple hypotheses gives parallelism to the following steps and helps keep us from getting too attached to one hypothesis.
- *Develop one or more experiments that can exclude or corroborate an alternative hypothesis.* Experiment 1: Add code in every critical section that stalls for time T and counts how often it is executed. Can you develop experiments for Hypothesis 2?
- *Predict experimental results before running the experiment.* If Hypothesis 1 is true, a P-processor program that executes S stalls should slow by much

more than $T \times S/P$. If not, Hypothesis 1 is excluded.

- *Run experiments.* If the program runs only $T \times S/P$ slower, then Hypothesis 1 is excluded. We can continue with experiments for our alternatives or return to the first step and develop new hypotheses. If the program does run much more slowly, then Hypothesis 1 is corroborated. We should develop refined hypotheses (e.g., the synchronization bottleneck is for data structure A or B) and return to the first step.

Most computer architects agree in principle that using the scientific method is a good idea. Nevertheless, the literature is replete with examples in which authors see an effect, speculate about its cause, and move on without conducting an experiment to corroborate their speculation.

2.3 Analytic Modeling

Computer architects study computer systems with three basic methods: analytic models, simulation, and system monitoring. We now discuss each in turn.

Analytic models are an important—and currently underutilized—tool for understanding computer systems (and avoiding being drowned in data). Analytical models are mathematical expressions that approximate some behaviors of a system by capturing some system features and omitting others [10–12]. An accurate model predicts system behavior close to actual behavior. An insightful model omits irrelevant system aspects so that what remains captures the essence of what is important. Ideally, one prefers accurate, insightful models, but it is often worth trading some accuracy for much greater simplicity.

The rest of this subsection seeks to whet your appetite for analytic models by introducing some simple ones, hinting at more powerful techniques, and give three cache modeling case studies.

2.3.1 Three Simple but Useful Models

Analytic models vary from simple to complex. Three useful simple ones are Little's Law, simple queues, and Amdahl's Law.

Little's Law. This law applies to any stable (i.e., the number customers in the system does not go to infinity) system that can be modeled as a queue (i.e., customers arrive, wait for service, are serviced, and leave) [10, 12]. Little's Law says:

```
Average number of customers in the system =
    Average rate customers leave ×
    Average time a customer spends in the system.
```

Consider an application of Little's Law to a nonblocking cache. How many outstanding requests K should be supported to process a miss every 50 ns to a memory whose average latency (with contention) is 200 ns? The answer given by Little's Law is four requests = (one request/50 ns) × (200 ns). In many cases, however, one would want more than four to handle "bursts" of requests. Simple queues provide a way to model burstiness.

Simple queues. Consider a model of a queue to a single server, where the queue size does not grow to infinity (i.e., the queue is stable) and customers arrive at a time independent of the current time (stationary) as well as independent of the number of customers already enqueued (open) [10, 12]. Let *throughput* be the rate customers leave this queue and *utilization* the fraction of time the server is busy. Then, for this so-called G/G/1 queue:

```
Throughput =                    1
               ────────────────────────────────────
               Average time between customer arrivals
Utilization = Average time to service a customer
              ──────────────────────────────────────
              Average time between customer arrivals.
```

Often, we can further assume that customers arrive at a time independent of past arrivals (Poisson or Markovian arrivals) and service times are distributed exponentially (Markovian service times).[1] These additional assumptions create an M/M/1 queue and allow us to estimate *average latency*—the time from when a customer arrives to when it leaves—with a simple equation:

```
Average latency = Average time to service a customer
                  ──────────────────────────────────
                          1−Utilization.
```

To see the utility of an M/M/1 queue, consider designing a simple nonpipelined bus where requests will arrive "at random" about every 50 ns, and you are supposed to service them with a latency of no more than 55 ns. If you pretend that requests come in at precisely

---

[1]An exponential service time distribution means that the probability that a particular service time is less than x is $1 - e^{-x/s}$, where s is the average service time. In practice it is not critical that service times be distributed exactly exponentially. It is only important that many service times are not much larger than others. In particular, the following result is only slightly pessimistic approximation of a system where all service times are exactly equal (deterministic).

50-ns intervals, designing a bus with a service time of 49 ns seems sufficient. If you do this and requests come in at random, bursts will cause the actual latency to be about 2450 ns (49/[1 − 49/50]). To handle bursts, the M/M/1 queue predicts you should instead "over"-design the bus by a factor of two, because a service time of 25 ns yields an average latency of 50 ns (25/[1 − 25/50]).

An important corollary of M/M/1 queues is that one can design for high utilization or low latency but not both, as long as arrivals come at random. A queue with 90% utilization has a latency 10X worse than the average time to service a customer, whereas a queue whose latency is 10% worse than the average time to service a customer has a utilization of 9%. Improving utilization and latency together requires that arrivals not be random (e.g., by using schedules).

Amdahl's Law. Amdahl's Law is so well known that people sometimes forget how widely applicable it is [2]. Consider a system that originally spends F fraction of time, $0 \leq F \leq 1$, doing function X. Consider an enhancement that speeds up function X by:

$$S_X = \frac{\text{Time to do } X \text{ originally}}{\text{Time to do } X \text{ with enhancement}}$$

If the new system performs X at the same frequency, then Amdahl's Law predicts:

$$\text{Overall speedup} = \frac{1}{([1-F] + F / S_X)}.$$

For example, let's calculate the overall speedups for (1) a factor of ten improvement in a function used 5% of the original time and (2) a 10% improvement of something that operates 95% of the time. Plugging values into Amdahl's Law reveals speedups of 1.047 for (1) and 1.094 for (2). Therefore, attack the common case first. Furthermore, by taking the limit as S_X goes to infinity, we get:

$$\text{Overall speedup} \leq \frac{1}{1 - F}$$

Thus, the improvement because of (a) is bounded by 1.052.

2.3.2 More Powerful Modeling Techniques

The academic literature is replete with examples of more powerful modeling techniques. These techniques can model effects that are very subtle but that often require more mathematical sophistication to develop and use. If you are a student, you may benefit from taking a few courses in probability, statistics, renewal theory, Markov chains, and queuing theory.

We do not have the space here to introduce complex modeling techniques at a level of detail that would allow the reader to use them. Instead, we will whet your appetite for two modeling techniques, Markov chains and queueing networks, and one solution technique, customized mean value analysis.

A Markov chain describes a system with n states where the probability that the next state is j given that the current state is i is p_{ij} regardless of all previous states [10–12]. Markov chains permit simple analysis: for example, to determine the steady-state probability of being in state i. Consider a cache coherence protocol (with states invalid, shared, and exclusive) where we have measured the state transition frequencies. If we further assume that one spends about the same amount of time in each state, a Markov chain can be used to determine the steady-state probability of being in each state.

Queuing networks are a very powerful model technique [10–12]. They are constructed by interconnecting service centers. Each service center has one or more servers (one, k, infinite) that serve customers with some time distribution (exponential, deterministic) after some queuing discipline (first-come-first-serve, last-come-first-serve). A center with one server using exponential service time after a first-come-first-serve queue, for example, would be like the server in an M/M/1 queue. Unlike an M/M/1 queue, however, arrivals are not likely to be Markovian but are instead determined by the rest of the queuing network.[2] One can use a queuing network to model a symmetric multiprocessor memory system as follows: Have a service center for each processor, each cache, each snoop, the bus, and the memory. Have cache misses leave the cache, arbitrate for the bus, use snoops and memory, and so forth. Probabilities can be assigned based on the type of bus request and where it finds the data.

Once one has a queuing network, the next step is to "solve" it to answer questions like, "What is the average memory latency?" This can be done analytically for a restricted class of networks called product-form or separable networks. Alternatively, one can always simulate the network. In many cases in computer

---

[2]There are, however, a useful class of queuing networks—product form networks—whose structure lets one treat arrivals as Markovian to greatly simplify solving for many important properties.

architecture, customized mean value analysis provides the most attractive solution method.

Customized mean value analysis (CMVA) works for a large class of queuing networks but can only provide mean values [12]. Thus, it can yield the average memory latency, but not the distribution of memory latencies. The basic idea is a write a set of custom equations that describe what a customer must endure. A cache miss, for example, must go to the bus and may go to other processors and memory. At each center, the customer endures some mean queuing delay and some mean service latency. Mean service latency is easy to calculate. Mean queuing delay is calculated by assuming customers arrive "at random" when they are able to arrive. Sometimes these equations can be solved in closed form, even though most commonly simple iterative methods suffice. CMVA has been successfully applied to many systems. For a recent example, please see Sorin et al. [20].

2.3.3 A Case Study: Three Cache Models

We next present three cache models to illustrate how modeling can be productively employed at various levels of detail to provide varying levels of insight and accuracy.

Hill's 3C model of cache behavior is an example of a very simple model [6]. The 3C model partitions cache misses into *compulsory misses* (that must occur in any cache), *capacity misses* (because of a cache's finite size), and *conflict misses* (from restricted associativity). The model defines miss type operationally. The conflict miss ratio, for example, is the miss ratio of a cache less the miss ratio of a cache of the same size and block size that is fully associative and uses least recently used (LRU) replacement.

The 3C model is simple. It provides some insight even without numbers. Jouppi, for example, credits it for helping him come up with victim caches and stream buffers [8]. On the other hand, the 3C model does not provide much accuracy or predictive power. Measuring the 3Cs for a direct-mapped cache, for example, will not let you predict the miss ratio for a two-way set-associative cache.

Smith's set-associative model is less simple but has more predictive power than the 3C model [6,19]. This model asks:

Why do set-associative cache perform worse than fully associative ones? Is it that real workloads have pathological conflicts? Or is it just

that if you uniformly distribute references among C sets of small size A, by random chance some sets will get too many references?

Smith's model examines these hypotheses. He uses Bayes' rule to translate fully-associative miss ratios for caches of every size into set-associative miss ratios, assuming misses map independently and uniformly to all sets. Fully associative simulation data is fed into the model so that it can make set-associative predictions. These predictions are then compared with set-associative simulation data. The results are an excellent fit. Thus, the experiment corroborates the hypothesis that "random" behavior is sufficient to explain the difference between set-associative and fully associate miss ratios.

Smith's model has predictive power and can be accurate, but it is limited to matters of associativity. It would be nice to have a model that was comprehensive. Arguably the most successful comprehensive cache model is by Agarwal, Horowitz, and Hennessy [1]. This model has components for start-up effects, non-stationary behavior, intraprogram interactions, and interprogram interactions. Within these, intuitive equations model such things as set-conflicts and spatial locality. Parameters for the model are gathered from simulation data. Then the model is validated against other simulated configurations. The model achieves good accuracy and excellent relative accuracy across variations in cache size, associativity, block size, and multiprogramming degree.

In our opinion, these results make this model the most successful comprehensive cache model ever. Why then isn't every cache designer required to learn it? The problem is that this model is too complex to provide insight to a large audience, and it has too many inputs to be practical for specific predictions. In particular, gathering all the input parameter values requires a simulation infrastructure capable of gathering all the results. A lesson for model designers is that one should consider both insight and accuracy.

2.4 Simulation

Simulation is arguably the preferred methodological tool of computer architects. With *simulation*, a computer program—called the simulator—running on a *host* computer is used to mimic the functionality, and usually some performance metrics, of a *target* computer system.

2.4.1 Alternative Levels of Abstraction

Simulations can be performed at many levels of abstraction. At a very high level, one can simulate an analytic model to solve it. This level blurs the distinction between analytic modeling and simulation and, perhaps, is best considered a solution technique for analytic models.

Functional. A *functional* (or *architectural*) *simulator* mimics at least the application binary interface (ABI) of the target computer system. Complete functional simulators will also mimic how the hardware appears to the target operating system, whereas less-complete ones will only approximate a subset of the ABI. In any case, the goal is to be able to run target software correctly as it reads target inputs and produces target outputs. Functional simulators also often produce workload metrics, such as number or instructions or floating-point multiplies executed. Functional simulators operate on a workload consisting of one or more target programs with associated target inputs. This type of simulation is called *execution-driven*, because the workload executes during simulation and can be affected by simulation. In a multiprocessor simulation, for example, changing the cache size can affect which thread wins the race to a lock.

A simulator's *slowdown* is the time is takes to execute a simulation of some target software on a host of comparable power to the target divided by the time it would take to run the target software on the target. Smaller slowdowns are good and a slowdown of 1 is ideal. Functional simulators have slowdowns between 1 and 10.

Microarchitectural. The next level down in simulation is *microarchitectural simulation*, the bread-and-butter technique of computer architects. A microarchitectural simulation mimics the behavior of microarchitectural features, such as caches, memory banks, branch prediction tables, pipeline bypass stalls, and reservation stations. It produces performance metrics, such as cycles to execute a program and cache miss ratio. Microarchitectural simulations can be execution driven (i.e., present an ABI to target software) or trace driven. A trace is a log of relevant workload activity (e.g., a series of dynamic memory references). Trace generation is performed prior to simulation, for example: by system monitoring. *Trace-driven simulation* consumes the trace as it executes. Traces allow trace generation and simulation to be decoupled but preclude the simulation from affecting the traced workload.

Microarchitectural simulations may model aspects of computer system microarchitecturally, functionally, or not at all. An execution-driven simulation concentrating on cache behavior, for example, could accurately model cache microarchitecture but just mimic the function of the rest of the processor. A trace-driven cache simulator might omit the rest of the processor altogether. Depending on the level of detail, microarchitectural simulators suffer slowdowns of 10–10,000.

Arguably, the most powerful current microarchitectural simulator is Stanford's SimOS [17]. SimOS can simulate SGI Challenge-like multiprocessors with functional fidelity sufficient to boot a commercial operating system and run a commercial database. SimOS supports alternative modules that enable different aspects of a system to be modeled at different levels of detail at different times. One can, for example, use fast functional simulation to boot the operating system and initialize applications.

Gate-level. A gate-level simulator is one that is sufficiently detailed to model the actual structure of hardware. Is a barrel shifter implemented with multiplexors or pass transistors? How large are control program logic arrays? Gate-level simulation of a complete computer system for even a few cycles is very hard, and operation on a sensible workload is usually impractical. Instead, architects and implementors use gate level simulation for a few aspects of a system while modeling other aspects functionally or not at all. When many aspects of a system are not modeled, a challenge is providing workload inputs to a gate-level simulation. This problem is often called *test vector generation*.

Circuit simulation and below. Even lower down are analog circuit simulations, such as SPICE. These simulators are typically applied to isolated aspects of computer systems, such as adder carry chains, register cells, and long-line drivers. At an even lower level, one can simulate based on device physics, which is becoming increasingly necessary for dynamic memory design.

Summary. In practice, many simulations combine components from different levels. High-level components are used when simulation speed is important, detailed aspects have not yet been designed, or this aspect of the design is not the current focus of activity. Low-level components are used otherwise. Multiple level of the same component can also be run in parallel to provide evidence that the lower level implementation matches the higher level specification.

2.4.2 Case Study: Microarchitectural Simulation of Memory Hierarchies

Memory systems have long been the focus of microarchitectural simulations, because those simulations have been so effective at improving memory hierarchies. We can learn about simulation challenges by considering how memory system simulation has evolved from the first cache paper by Wilkes [22] that had no numbers to recent multiprogramming multiprocessor memory system evaluations [16, 17].

Trace-driven memory system simulation was the method of choice through at least Smith's classic survey [18]. These simulations omit all aspects of a computer system but its cache. They model the workload as a trace that exists prior to simulation. A *trace* is a long sequence of tuples (e.g., a million or more) representing the dynamic memory references of a workload. Each tuple contained an address (virtual or physical), type (read, write, instruction fetch), and sometimes length (e.g., 4 bytes). Traces are large and stored on tape or disk. Trace-driven cache simulators model the state and tags of a cache and nothing else. In particular, the processor, cache data, or memory does not have to be modeled.

Nevertheless, trace-driven cache simulations are exceedingly time consuming, especially because one typically wants to evaluate the performance of many alternative caches. Mattson et al. [13] attack this problem in a seminal paper that finds ways to evaluate multiple alternative caches in one pass through an address trace. This work is summarized in this reader in Hill and Smith [6] in a way we think is more accessible than the original work. The basic idea can be illustrated by considering alternative fully associative caches that use LRU replacement (and have the same block size and do no prefetching). The state of all the alternative caches can be modeled with a single linked list, where the head points to most recently used (MRU) block and the i MRU block points to the $i + 1$ MRU block. For example (from Fig. 6 [6]):

$$6 \rightarrow 5 \rightarrow 3 \rightarrow 4 \rightarrow 0 \rightarrow 7 \rightarrow 2 \rightarrow 8.$$

If the next reference is to block 2, this technique—called *stack simulation*—finds the block at *distance* 7 and updates the list to make 2 most recently used:

$$2 \rightarrow 6 \rightarrow 5 \rightarrow 3 \rightarrow 4 \rightarrow 0 \rightarrow 7 \rightarrow 8.$$

Caches of size 7 and larger hit, whereas caches smaller than 7 miss.

Stack simulation can easily be extended to simultaneously simulate alternative caches with any fixed number of sets and to so-called *stack replacement algorithms*, which include random and Belady's optimal,

but not first-come-first-serve. Hill and Smith extend stack simulation with *all-associativity simulation*. A single all-associativity simulation run can evaluate alternative caches of all sizes and associativities with LRU replacement, some restrictions on set-mapping functions, and a fixed block size. Thus, a designer can evaluate all caches about a design point with one simulation per block size of interest!

At this point, it might look like memory hierarchy simulation research could stop. But, as always, designs move forward and whittle away at the effectiveness of methods. First, single caches were replaced with two levels of caches. Fortunately, Przybylski [15] showed that caches whose size differs by a factor of eight or more could be simulated independently. This result is practical, because level-two caches are almost always at least 8X larger than level-one caches. Second, level-two caches became very large (e.g., ≥ 1 Mbytes) and could be evaluated only with very large traces (e.g., giga-references per program). This has led researchers to considered sampling in time and space (cache sets) to reduce trace size [9]. Third, caches began to employ more timing-dependent behavior, such as prefetching and nonblocking support. Evaluating the effectiveness of these features requires the modeling of timing both in the incoming workload and in the memory system. Fourth, caches are increasingly integrated with speculative out-of-order processing engines, further obscuring the relationship between miss ratio and program execution time. These trends are encouraging the elimination of traces in favor of execution-driven simulation that models both the cache and processor. The desire for results of higher and higher fidelity is forcing both the cache and processor to be modeled at a detailed microarchitectural level. Finally, increased interest in P-processor multiprocessors has multiplied simulation requirements by P and added tricky interaction cases [17].

In summary, new designs will require new methods. Understanding how past methods have evolved in present methods facilitates developing new methods from existing ones.

2.5 System Monitoring

George Santayana said, "Those who cannot remember the past are condemned to repeat it." System monitoring is the technique that computer architects use to learn from the present (soon-to-be past). With *system monitoring* (often called *hardware monitoring*), one records information about the behavior of a running system. Examples of system monitoring include using an oscilloscope to record bus transactions, reading hardware performance counters, and modifying an executable to output information at procedure call sites.

Even though system monitoring can take many forms, its practice shares several unifying features. Most important is that the system to be monitored must exist. Thus, system monitoring can give us incredible detail about current hardware and software, but extrapolation to systems must be done with other methods. Nevertheless, most new systems use evolutionary hardware extensions to run evolutionarily new software. In these situations, system monitoring can provide valuable information on what to do. Equally importantly, system monitoring can tell us what not to do. An optimization may sound good, but system monitoring can reveal that the optimized situation does not occur often enough to be bothered with (remember Amdahl's Law).

2.5.1 Monitoring Mechanisms

System monitoring requires monitoring mechanisms. *Monitoring mechanisms* reveal system information to the monitor. The classic monitoring mechanism is the oscilloscope probe. In the days of medium-scale integration, such probes could access most of a system's architectural and microarchitectural state. Today, one can typically access only level-one cache misses (with great difficulty because of high frequencies) and system bus transactions. Tomorrow, probe access will likely be even more limited. Recognizing these limitations, hardware designers are now adding explicit monitoring mechanisms. Current examples include register- and memory-mapped cycle counters, cache miss counters, and bus-transactions-of-type-X counters. Future machines are likely to include an even richer array of monitoring mechanisms as performance optimization becomes more important and die area less precious. Finally, system monitoring mechanisms can be software only. On one hand, this can take the form of small changes to existing software to record activity (e.g., augmenting a software TLB handler to log TLB misses). On the other hand, it can mean a wholesale rewriting of executables to augment them with monitoring functions (e.g., as can be done with ATOM [21]).

2.5.2 Perturbation, Repeatability, Representativeness, and Sampling

Three important concerns of system monitoring are perturbation, repeatability, and representativeness. *Perturbation* occurs whenever the behavior of the system being monitored is not statically identical to an unmonitored system. A program-counter trace of an executable augmented by ATOM, for example, is not the same as the program-counter trace from an unmodified executable. On the other hand, reading a cycle-count register before and after a long-running application will cause negligible perturbation. In many cases, one can mitigate the effects of perturbation by compensating. The augmented executable, for example, can easily be modified to emit the program counters of the unmodified executable. Other cases are not as trivial. If executable editing slows applications by a factor of two, for example, then disk accesses and clock interrupts will appear twice as fast. One can compensate by delaying disk accesses and clock interrupts, but is this enough? The bottom line is that the careful system monitor hypothesizes that he or she is perturbing the system and tries to gather evidence to contradict this hypothesis.

System monitors must also be concerned with *repeatability*. Real systems may not run the same way twice because of different initial conditions or different concurrent activity. The number of conflict misses an application suffers in a physically-index level-two cache, for example, can be affected by what physical page frames are on the free list. There are two tools for dealing with repeatability. First, one can minimize potential causes of variation. Most commonly, this is done by rebooting the system and disallowing concurrent activity. Second, one can perform multiple runs of the "same" case. In some cases, one can informally verify that the variation between runs of the "same" case are much smaller than the variation between runs of different cases. In other cases, one should turn to the statistical technique developed for this issue: *analysis of variance* [7]. The careful system monitor hypothesizes that the effects he or she is measuring result from random variation and then tries to gather evidence that they are instead due to systematic effects.

Finally, the data gathered with system monitoring should be *representative* of the *population* of all possible data. Because the full data is typically exceedingly large, one is forced to collect some number of *observations* to form a *sample* of the population. The process, called *sampling*, can be implicit or explicit. When one selects twelve programs to be monitored, one effectively takes a sample from the population of relevant programs and implicitly assumes that these programs are representative of a much larger population of programs. Common sense must be applied here. Is SPEC95 representative of the population of programs my machine will run? If the answer is "no," all the other wonderful work in a system monitoring experiment is worthless.

On the other hand, sampling is explicit when we repeatedly collect bursts of cache miss addresses. Statistics allows us to make very powerful inferences from unbiased random samples to the population in general (e.g., the mean of a sample tends to the mean of the population with some expected variation). An observation within a sample is unbiased if it accurately captures the system feature being measured. A snapshot of consecutive level-one cache miss addresses, for example, will not exactly yield the level-two cache miss ratio for the snapshot, because the level-two cache state at the beginning of the snapshot is unknown. This effect is mitigated with a snapshot using set sampling that takes the same number of cache misses from fewer sets. Whereas care must be taken to corroborate that the sampled sets are representative of all sets, set sampling has proven very effective for studying large caches [9].

2.5.3 Analysis

The final step of system monitoring is analysis of the data obtained from the monitoring mechanisms. This data is often low level (e.g., program counter virtual addresses) and voluminous. The goal of analysis is to transform the data into insight. Analysis should make data more high-level (e.g., by mapping program counters to procedure names). It should also reduce volume by transforming raw data into averages, histograms, or distributions. Care must be taken to mitigate the chance that analysis destroys evidence of effects. Procedure names may obscure an effect related to an address level-two cache set. Averaging can hide bimodal distributions. Once again, careful application of analysis requires that one assume he or she might be obscuring effects and that he or she gather evidence that this is not the case.

2.5.4 Case Study

For an excellent case study of system monitoring, please see Emer and Clark's "A characterization of processor performance in the VAX-11/780" [4]. This paper is included in this reader and introduced in section 2.7.3.

2.6 Discussion

Next we compare methods and touch upon selected areas not covered in this chapter.

2.6.1 A Comparison of Methods

Analytic modeling, simulation, and system monitoring are complementary tools for computer architects. Analytic models can provide insight long before a system exists. Simple models are useful by anyone. More-complex models require expertise to construct, but can be built and solved rapidly. Analytic models, however, cannot model all details of a system. Thus, other methods are needed to examine more-detailed effects and verify when analytic models are sufficiently accurate.

Simulation is the principal tool of computer architects. Simulations can model any system to any required level of detail. Simulators, however, require much more work to construct than do analytic models. In our view, computer architects currently put too much faith in simulation. Simulations are believed without much scrutiny as to whether the simulation code has bugs or just plain assumes away important effects. Whereas analytic models make assumptions explicit, simulator assumptions are often buried deep in proprietary code. We recommend that computer architects put less faith in simulators that have not survived the scrutiny of some verification.

Finally, system monitoring is the backward-looking method. It requires the system to exist, can rarely vary the system in many ways, and is usually hard to do. Nevertheless, it provides a wealth of data that is true for at least one real system and is useful to similar systems.

2.6.2 Important Aspects Not Included

Any short introduction and three papers on methods must omit important aspects. A few of these are discussed here.

Experimental design. Designing an experiment is harder than this chapter's discussion implies. For example, one must learn to control random error, make sure all important factors are considered, and isolate the effects and interactions of factors. We refer the reader to Jain [7, pt. IV].

Benchmark selection. As eluded to earlier, benchmark selection is critical to avoid "garbage-in-garbage-out." Good discussions of benchmark selection can be found in Hennessy and Patterson [5] and Culler, Singh, and Gupta [3].

Sizing and scaling. What do results mean if an application's input size is scaled down to permit simulation to complete in reasonable time? Can we scale down cache sizes to compensate? If this program were run on really fast systems, would users want the same answer faster or a more detailed answer in similar time? To answer these and related questions, we direct the reader to Culler, Singh, and Gupta [3].

Computer-aided design (CAD) and testing/verification. Finally, this chapter ignores the many issues that surround the design, verification, and testing of computer systems.

2.7 Discussion of Included Papers

We have selected three sample papers to illustrate models, simulation, and monitoring.

2.7.1 Amdahl's "Validity of the Single-Processor Approach to Achieving Large Scale Computing Capabilities" [2]

Amdahl's three-page paper presents what is now called "Amdahl's Law." Amdahl's Law appears in the prose and not as an explicit equation. It is part of an argument defending why uniprocessors will survive the current (in 1967) threat from multiprocessors. Amdahl was right—uniprocessors did survive.

2.7.2 Hill and Smith's "Evaluating Associativity in CPU Caches" [6]

This paper includes ideas for modeling caches and evaluating them with trace-driven simulation. Some of the important ideas (as viewed from 1998) are as follows: Section IIA reviews Mattson's *stack simulation*, which allows the simultaneous trace-driven simulation of alternative caches with the same number of sets. Section IVA formally presents *inclusion* and *set-refinement*, two useful properties for simultaneously simulating alternative caches. Section IVC presents *all-associativity simulation*, which enables the simultaneous simulation of alternative caches of all sizes and associativities (provided they use LRU replacement, have the same block size, and do no prefetching). Section VA presents the *3C model* and gives example data from an all-associativity simulation. Finally, Section VB reviews Smith's set-associative model and provides simulation data to support the hypothesis that set-associative caches miss more often than do fully associative ones because, due to random chance, some sets receive more active blocks than others.

2.7.3 Emer and Clark's "A Characterization of Processor Performance in the VAX-11/780" [4]

Even though the VAX-11/780 and the associated data are not current, Emer and Clark's paper illustrates an excellent example of how to perform system monitoring experiments and how the data obtained can be surprising and valuable. The VAX-11 architecture is a *complex instruction set computer* (CISC) with 32-bit virtual addresses, 16 general-purpose registers, no separate floating-point registers, and variable-length memory-to-memory instructions. Each instruction consists of a 1-byte opcode (that specifies the operation and number of operands) followed by 0–6 operand specifiers. Each specifier uses one of twenty-six methods to specify how to obtain an operand (e.g., register, various sizes of immediates, base plus displacement, indexed, and several more complex memory-referencing schemes). Specifiers also are of variable size with the *i + 1-st* specifier beginning after the *i-th* specifier ends. Thus, VAX-11 decoding is logically sequential both within and between instructions.

The paper begins by summarizing the VAX-11/780's implementation of the VAX-11 architecture (see Fig. 1). Control is specified with a microprogram and the microprogram program counter (uPC) that is exposed. The system monitoring data presented in this paper is obtained by attaching a probe to the uPC that records the number of times each uPC value was visited for up to 2 hours of execution time. The authors then use knowledge of the microprogram to translate uPCs into architectural events (that would happen on any VAX-11) and implementation events (VAX-11/780-specific). Experiments are run with two live nonrepeatable workloads (in vivo) and three synthetic repeatable ones (in vitro).

Architectural results show many things that are now widely known, in part, because of this paper. Simple instructions are common (84% of dynamic instructions). Branches are common (19%). Loop branches are usually taken (91%), whereas other conditional branches are less predictable (41% taken). Register operands are most common (41% of specifiers), whereas complex memory addressing modes are rare (7%). Average instruction size is 3.8 bytes. Instructions do 0.8 data reads and 0.4 data writes. (RISCs do fewer data memory operations because of more registers and better register allocation.)

Implementation also provided a wealth of information. The biggest surprise was that the VAX-11/780, widely known as a 1-million-instruction-per-second (MIPS) machine took 10.6 200-ns cycles to execute an average instruction. Thus, it was actually a 0.5 MIPS machine. Other data show that one half of execution time is spent decoding instructions, simple instructions use 10% of execution time (remember they are 84% of all instructions), and memory stalls waste 2.1 cycles per instruction (a small fraction of the VAX-11/780's 10.6 cycles per instruction, but a big deal for future RISCs that eliminated much of the VAX-11 decode overhead).

2.8 References

[1] A. Agarwal, M. Horowitz, and J. Hennessy, "An analytical cache model," *ACM Transactions on Computer Systems*, 7(2):184–215, 1989.

[2] G. M. Amdahl, "Validity of the single-processor approach to achieving large scale computing capabilities," In *AFIPS Conference Proceedings*, pp. 483–485, Apr. 1967.

[3] D. Culler, J. P. Singh, and A. Gupta, *Parallel Computer Architecture: A Hardware/Software Approach*. San Francisco, CA: Morgan Kaufmann, 1998.

[4] J. S. Emer and D. W. Clark, "A characterization of processor performance in the VAX-11/780," *Proceedings 11th International Symposium on Computer Architecture*, pp. 301–310, June 1984.

[5] J. L. Hennessy and D. A. Patterson, *Computer Architecture: A Quantitative Approach*, 2nd ed. San Francisco, CA: Morgan Kaufmann, 1996.

[6] M. D. Hill and A. J. Smith, "Evaluating associativity in CPU caches," *IEEE Transactions on Computers*, C-38(12):1612–1630, 1989.

[7] R. Jain, *The Art of Computer Systems Performance Analysis: Techniques for Experimental Design, Measurement, Simulation, and Modeling*. New York: Wiley, 1991.

[8] N. P. Jouppi, "Improving direct-mapped cache performance by the addition of a small fully-associative cache and prefetch buffers," *The 17th Annual International Symposium on Computer Architecture*, pp. 364–373, May 1990.

[9] R. E. Kessler, M. D. Hill, and D. A. Wood, "A comparison of trace-sampling techniques for multi-megabyte caches," *IEEE Transactions on Computers*, 43(6):664–675, 1994.

[10] L. Kleinrock. *Queuing Systems Volume I: Theory*. New York: Wiley, 1975.

[11] L. Kleinrock. *Queuing Systems Volume II: Computer Applications*. New York: Wiley, 1976.

[12] E. D. Lazowska, J. Zahorjan, G. S. Graham, and K. C. Sevcik, *Quantitative System Performance: Computer System Analysis Using Queueing Network Models*. Englewood Cliffs, N.J.: Prentice Hall, 1984.

[13] R. L. Mattson, J. Gecsei, D. R. Slutz, and I. L. Traiger, "Evaluation techniques for storage hierarchies," *IBM Systems Journal*, 9(2):78–117, 1970.

[14] J. R. Platt, "Strong inference," *Science*, 146(3642):347–353, 1964.

[15] S. Przybylski, M. Horowitz, and J. Hennessy, "Characteristics of performance-optimal multi-level cache hierarchies," *Proceedings 16th Annual International Symposium on Computer Architecture*, pp. 114–121, June 1989.

[16] P. Ranganathan, V. S. Pai, H. Abdel-Shafi, and S. V. Adve, "The interaction of software prefetching with ILP processors in shared-memory systems," *Proceedings of the 24th Annual International Symposium on Computer Architecture*, pp. 144–156, June 1997.

[17] M. Rosenblum, E. Bugnion, S. Devine, and S. Herrod, "Using the SimOS machine simulator to study complex computer systems," *ACM Transactions on Modeling and Computer Simulation*, 7(1):78–103, 1997.

[18] A. J. Smith, "Cache memories" *ACM Computing Surveys*, 14(3):473–530, 1982.

[19] A. J. Smith, "A comparative study of set associative memory mapping algorithms and their use for cache and main memory," *IEEE Transactions on Software Engineering*, SE-4(2):121–130, 1978.

[20] D. J. Sorin, V. S. Pai, S. V. Adve, M. K. Vernon, and D. A. Wood, "Analytic evaluation of shared-memory systems with ILP processors," *Proceedings of the 25th Annual International Symposium on Computer Architecture*, pp. 380–391, June 1998.

[21] A. Srivastava and A. Eustace, "ATOM: A system for building customized program analysis tools," *SIGPLAN Notices*, 29(6):196–205, June 1994. *Proceedings of the ACM SIGPLAN '94 Conference on Programming Language Design and Implementation*.

[22] M. V. Wilkes, "Slave memories and dynamic storage allocation," *IEEE Transactions on Electronic Computers*, EC-14(2):270–271, 1965.

Validity of the single processor approach to achieving large scale computing capabilities

by DR. GENE M. AMDAHL
International Business Machines Corporation
Sunnyvale, California

INTRODUCTION

For over a decade prophets have voiced the contention that the organization of a single computer has reached its limits and that truly significant advances can be made only by interconnection of a multiplicity of computers in such a manner as to permit cooperative solution. Variously the proper direction has been pointed out as general purpose computers with a generalized interconnection of memories, or as specialized computers with geometrically related memory interconnections and controlled by one or more instruction streams.

Demonstration is made of the continued validity of the single processor approach and of the weaknesses of the multiple processor approach in terms of application to real problems and their attendant irregularities.

The arguments presented are based on statistical characteristics of computation on computers over the last decade and upon the operational requirements within problems of physical interest. An additional reference will be one of the most thorough analyses of relative computer capabilities currently published— "Changes in Computer Performance," *Datamation*, September 1966, Professor Kenneth E. Knight, Stanford School of Business Administration.

The first characteristic of interest is the fraction of the computational load which is associated with data management housekeeping. This fraction has been very nearly constant for about ten years, and accounts for 40% of the executed instructions in production runs. In an entirely dedicated special purpose environment this might be reduced by a factor of two, but it is highly improbably that it could be reduced by a factor of three. The nature of this overhead appears to be sequential so that it is unlikely to be amenable to parallel processing techniques. Overhead alone would then place an upper limit on throughput of five to seven times the sequential processing rate, even if the housekeeping were done in a separate processor. The non-housekeeping part of the problem could exploit at most a processor of performance three to four times the performance of the housekeeping processor. A fairly obvious conclusion which can be drawn at this point is that the effort expended on achieving high parallel processing rates is wasted unless it is accompanied by achievements in sequential processing rates of very nearly the same magnitude.

Data management housekeeping is not the only problem to plague oversimplified approaches to high speed computation. The physical problems which are of practical interest tend to have rather significant complications. Examples of these complications are as follows: boundaries are likely to be irregular; interiors are likely to be inhomogeneous; computations required may be dependent on the states of the variables at each point; propagation rates of different physical effects may be quite different; the rate of convergence, or convergence at all, may be strongly dependent on sweeping through the array along different axes on succeeding passes; etc. The effect of each of these complications is very severe on any computer organization based on geometrically related processors in a paralleled processing system. Even the existence of regular rectangular boundaries has the interesting property that for spatial dimension of N there are 3^N different point geometries to be dealt with in a nearest neighbor computation. If the second nearest neighbor were also involved, there would be 5^N different point geometries to contend with. An irregular boundary compounds this problem as does an inhomogeneous interior. Computations which are dependent on the states of variables would require the processing at each point to consume approximately the same computational time as the sum of computations of all physical effects within a large region. Differences or changes in propagation rates may affect the mesh point relationships.

Ideally the computation of the action of the neighboring points upon the point under consideration involves their values at a previous time proportional to the mesh spacing and inversely proportional to the propagation rate. Since the time step is normally kept constant, a faster propagation rate for some effects would imply interactions with more distant points. Finally the fairly common practice of sweeping through the mesh along different axes on succeeding passes poses problems of data management which affects all processors, however it affects geometrically related processors more severely by requiring transposing all points in storage in addition to the revised input-output scheduling. A realistic assessment of the effect of these irregularities on the actual performance of a parallel processing device, compared to its performance on a simplified and regularized abstraction of the problem, yields a degradation in the vicinity of one-half to one order of magnitude.

To sum up the effects of data management housekeeping and of problem irregularities, the author has compared three different machine organizations involving approximately equal amounts of hardware. Machine A has thirty two arithmetic execution units controlled by a single instruction stream. Machine B has pipelined arithmetic execution units with up to three overlapped operations on vectors of eight elements. Machine C has the same pipelined execution units, but initiation of individual operations at the same rate as Machine B permitted vector element operations. The performance of these three machines are plotted in Figure 1 as a function of the fraction of the number of instructions which permit parallelism. The probable region of operation is centered around a point corresponding to 25% data management overhead and 10% of the problem operations forced to be sequential.

The historic performance versus cost of computers has been explored very thoroughly by Professor Knight. The carefully analyzed data he presents reflects not just execution times for arithmetic operations and cost of minimum of recommended configurations. He includes memory capacity effects, input-output overlap experienced, and special functional capabilities. The best statistical fit obtained corresponds to a performance proportional to the square of the cost at any technological level. This result very effectively supports the often invoked "Grosch's Law." Utilizing this analysis, one can argue that if twice the amount of hardware were exploited in a single system, one could expect to obtain four times the performance. The only difficulty is involved in knowing how to exploit this additional hardware. At any point in time it is difficult to foresee how the previous bottlenecks in a sequential computer will be effectively overcome. If it were easy they would not have been left as bottlenecks. It is true by historical example that the successive obstacles have been hurdled, so it is appropriate to quote the Rev. Adam Clayton Powell—"Keep the faith, baby!" If alternatively one decided to improve the performance by putting two processors side by side with shared memory, one would find approximately 2.2 times as much hardware. The additional two tenths in hardware accomplishes the crossbar switching for the sharing. The resulting performance achieved would be about 1.8. The latter figure is derived from the assumption of each processor utilizing half of the memories about half of the time. The resulting memory conflicts in the shared system would extend the execution of one of two operations by one quarter of the execution time. The net result is a price performance degradation to 0.8 rather than an improvement to 2.0 for the single larger processor.

Comparative analysis with associative processors is far less easy and obvious. Under certain conditions of regular formats there is a fairly direct approach. Consider an associative processor designed for pattern recognition, in which decisions within individual elements are forwarded to some set of other elements. In the associative processor design the receiving elements would have a set of source addresses which recognize by associative techniques whether or not it was to receive the decision of the currently declaring element. To make a corresponding special purpose non-associative processor one would consider a receiving element and its source addresses as an instruction, with binary decisions maintained in registers. Considering the use of thin film memory, an associative cycle would be longer than a non-destructive read cycle. In such a tech-

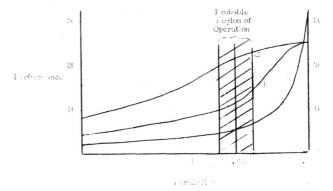

Figure 1

nology the special purpose non-associative processor can be expected to take about one-fourth as many memory cycles as the associative version and only about one-sixth of the time. These figures were computed on the full recognition task, with somewhat differing ratios in each phase. No blanket claim is intended here, but rather that each requirement should be investigated from both approaches.

(This figure corresponds to Figure 1 from Amdahl's paper and has been redrawn to improve its readability).

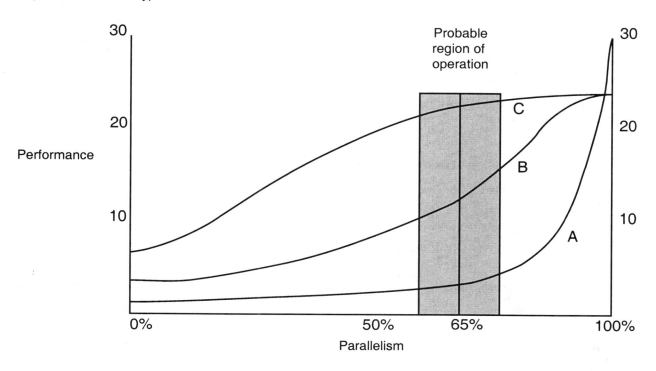

Evaluating Associativity in CPU Caches

MARK D. HILL, MEMBER, IEEE, AND ALAN JAY SMITH, FELLOW, IEEE

Abstract—Because of the infeasibility or expense of large fully-associative caches, cache memories are usually designed to be set-associative or direct-mapped. This paper presents 1) new and efficient algorithms for simulating alternative direct-mapped and set associative caches, and 2) uses those algorithms to quantify the effect of limited associativity on the cache miss ratio.

We introduce a new algorithm, *forest simulation*, for simulating alternative direct-mapped caches and generalize one, which we call *all-associativity simulation*, for simulating alternative direct-mapped, set-associative, and fully-associative caches. We find that while all-associativity simulation is theoretically less efficient than forest simulation or stack simulation (a commonly used simulation algorithm); in practice, it is not much slower and allows the simulation of many more caches with a single pass through an address trace.

We also provide data and insight into how varying associativity affects the miss ratio. We show: 1) how to use simulations of alternative caches to isolate the cause of misses; 2) that the principal reason why set-associative miss ratios are larger than fully-associative ones is (as one might expect) that too many active blocks map to a fraction of the sets even when blocks map to sets in a uniform random manner; and 3) that reducing associativity from eight-way to four-way, from four-way to two-way, and from two-way to direct-mapped causes relative miss ratio increases in our data of respectively about 5, 10, and 30 percent, consistently over a wide range of cache sizes and a range of line sizes.

Index Terms—Associativity, buffer, cache memory, computer architecture, direct-mapped, memory systems, performance evaluation, set-associative and trace-driven simulation algorithms.

I. INTRODUCTION

THREE important CPU cache parameters are cache size, block (line) size, and associativity [27]. Cache size (buffer size, capacity) is so important that it is a part of almost all cache studies (for a partial bibliography see [29]). Block size (line size) has recently been examined in detail in [30]. Here we concentrate on associativity (degree of associativity, set size) which is the number of places in a cache where a block can reside.

Selecting optimal associativity is important, because changing associativity has a significant impact on cache performance and cost. Increasing associativity improves the likelihood that a block is resident by decreasing the probability that too many recently-referenced blocks map to the same place and by allowing more blocks to be considered for replacement. The effect of associativity on cache miss ratio has never been isolated and quantified, and that is one of the major goals of this paper. Conversely, increasing associativity often increases cache cost and access time, since more blocks (frames) must be searched in parallel to find a reference [16].

Fig. 1 illustrates set-associativity. A set-associative cache uses a *set-mapping function f* to partition all *blocks* (data in an aligned, fixed-sized region of memory) into a number of equivalence classes. Some number of *block frames* in the cache are assigned to hold recently-referenced blocks from each equivalence class. Each group of block frames is called a *set*. The number of such groups, equal to the number of equivalence classes, is called the *number of sets (s)*. The number of block frames in each set is called the *associativity* (degree of associativity, set size, n). The number of block frames in the cache (c) always equals the associativity times the number of sets ($c = n \cdot s$). A cache is *fully-associative* if it contains only one set ($n = c, s = 1$), is *direct-mapped* if each set contains one block frame ($n = 1, s = c$), and is *n-way set-associative* otherwise (where n is the associativity, $s = c/n$).

On a reference to block x, the set-mapping function f feeds the "set decoder" with $f(x)$ to select one set (one row), and then each block frame in the set is searched until x is found (a cache hit) or the set is exhausted (a cache miss). On a cache miss, one block in set $f(x)$ is replaced with the block x obtained from memory. Finally, the word requested from block x is returned to the processor. Here for conceptual simplicity we show the word within the block selected last (in the box "compare block number with tags and select data word"). Many implementations, however, select the word within the block while selecting the set to reduce the number of bits that must be read; i.e., only words are gated into the multiplexer, not full lines. The most commonly used set-mapping function is the block number modulo the number of sets, where the number of sets is a power of two. This set mapping function is called *bit selection* since the set number is just the number given by the low-order bits of the block address. For 256 sets, for example, $f(x) = x$ mod 256 or $f(x) = x$ AND 0xff, where mod is remainder and AND is bitwise AND.

The method we use for examining associativity in CPU caches is *trace-driven simulation*. It uses one or more (ad-

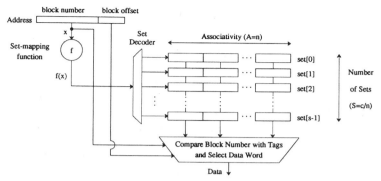

Fig. 1.   Set-associative mapping.

dress) *traces* and a (cache) *simulator*. A trace is the log of a dynamic series of memory references, recorded during the execution of a program or workload. The information recorded for each reference must include the address of the reference and may include the reference's type (instruction fetch, data read, or data write), length, and other information. A *simulator* is a program that accepts a trace and parameters that describe one or more caches, mimics the behavior of those caches in response to the trace, and computes performance metrics (e.g., miss ratio) for each cache.

We analyze associativity in caches with trace-driven simulation for the same reasons as are discussed in [28]. The principal advantage of trace-driven simulation over random number driven simulation or analytical modeling is that there exists no generally-accepted model for program behavior (at the cache level) with demonstrated validity and predictive power. The major disadvantage is that workload samples must be relatively short, due to disk space and simulation time limits.

The CPU time required to simulate many alternative caches with many traces can be enormous. Mattson *et al.* [19] addressed a similar problem for virtual memory simulation by developing a technique we call *stack* simulation, which allows miss ratios for all memory sizes to be computed simultaneously, during one pass through the address trace, subject to several constraints including a fixed page size. While stack simulation can be applied to caches, each cache configuration with a different number of sets requires a separate simulation. For this reason, this paper first examines better algorithms for simulating alternative direct-mapped and set-associative caches, and then uses those algorithms to study associativity in caches.

The rest of this paper is organized as follows. Section II reviews previous work on cache simulation algorithms and associativity in caches. In Section III, we explain our methods in more detail and describe our traces. Section IV discusses cache simulation algorithms, including properties that facilitate rapid simulation, a new algorithm for simulating alternative direct-mapped caches, and an extension to an algorithm for simulating alternative caches with arbitrary set-mapping functions. Section V examines the effect of associativity on miss ratio, including categorizing the cause of misses in set-associative caches, relating set-associative miss ratios to fully-associative ones, comparing miss ratios from similar

set-associative caches, and extending the *design target miss ratios* from [28] and [30] to caches with reduced associativity.

Readers interested in the effect of associativity on miss ratio but not in cache simulation algorithms may skip Section IV, as Section V is written to stand alone.

II. RELATED WORK

A. Simulation Algorithms

The original paper on memory hierarchy simulation is by Mattson *et al.* [19]. They introduce *inclusion*, show when inclusion holds, and develop *stack simulation*, which uses inclusion to rapidly simulate alternative caches. *Inclusion* is the property that after any series of references, larger alternative caches always contain a superset of the blocks in smaller alternative caches.[1] Mattson *et al.* show inclusion holds between alternative caches that have the same block size, do no prefetching, use the same set-mapping function (and therefore have the same number of sets), and use replacement algorithms that before each reference induce a total priority ordering on all previously referenced blocks (that map to each set) and use only this priority ordering to make the next replacement decision. Replacement algorithms which meet the above condition, called *stack algorithms*, include LRU, OPTIMUM, and (if properly defined) RANDOM [6]. FIFO does not qualify since cache capacity affects a block's replacement priority. In Section IV-A, we will prove when inclusion holds for caches that use arbitrary set-mapping functions and LRU replacement.

Mattson *et al.* develop *stack simulation* to simulate alternative caches that have the same block size, do no prefetching, use the same set-mapping function, and use a stack replacement algorithm. Since inclusion holds, a single list per set, called a *stack*, can be used to represent caches of all associatives, with the first *n* elements of each stack representing the blocks in an *n*-way set-associative cache. For each reference, stack simulation performs three operations: 1) locate the reference in the stack, 2) update one or more metrics to indicate which caches contained the reference, and 3) update the stack to reflect the contents of the caches after the reference. We

---

[1] *Inclusion* is different from *multilevel inclusion* defined by Baer and Wang [5]. While inclusion is a property relating alternative caches, multilevel inclusion relates caches in the same cache hierarchy.

call these three operations FIND, METRIC, and UPDATE, and will show that the algorithms discussed in later in Sections IV-B and IV-C use the same steps.

The most straightforward implementation of stack simulation is to implement each stack with a linked list and record hits to position n by incrementing a counter *distance[n]*. After N references have been processed, the miss ratio of an n-way set-associative cache is simply $1 - \sum_{i=1}^{n} distance[i]/N$. Since performance with a linked list will be poor if many elements of a stack must for searched on each reference, other researchers have developed more complex implementations of stack simulation, using hash tables, m-ary trees, and AVL trees [8], [21], [33]. While these algorithms are useful for some memory hierarchy simulations, Thompson [33] concludes that linked list stack simulation is near optimal for most CPU cache simulations. Linked list stack simulation is fast when few links are traversed to find a reference. On average, this is the case in CPU cache simulations since 1) CPU references exhibit a high degree of locality, and 2) CPU caches usually have a large number of sets and limited associativity, dividing active blocks among many stacks and bounding maximum stack size; different results are found for file system and database traces. For this reason, we consider only linked list stack simulation further, and use *stack simulation* to refer to linked list stack simulation.

Mattson *et al.* also briefly mention a way of simulating caches with different numbers of sets (and therefore different set-mapping functions). In two technical reports, Traiger and Slutz extend the algorithms to simulate alternative caches with different numbers of sets and block sizes [34], and with different numbers of sets, block sizes, and subblock sizes (sector and block sizes, address and transfer block sizes) [24]. They require that all alternative caches use LRU replacement, bit-selection for set mapping, and have block and subblock sizes that are powers of two. (Bit selection uses some of the bits of the block address as a binary number to specify the set.) In Section IV-C, we generalize to arbitrary set-mapping functions their algorithm for simulating alternative caches that use bit selection.

The speed of stack simulation can also be improved by deleting references (trace entries) that will hit and not affect replacement decisions in the caches to be simulated [25]. Puzak [23] shows that if all caches simulated use bit selection and LRU replacement, references that hit the most recently used element of a set can be deleted without affecting the total number of misses. We will show that this result trivially follows from properties we define in Section IV-A, allowing such references to be deleted from traces before using any of our simulation algorithms. (The total number of memory references in the original trace must be retained, in order to compute the miss ratio.)

B. Associativity

Previous work on associativity can be broken into the following three categories: 1) papers that discuss associativity as part of a more general analysis of 32 kbyte and smaller caches, among the more notable of which are [18], [17], [7], [32], [27],[2] and [11], and [13]; 2) papers that discuss associativity and other aspects of cache design for larger caches ([4], [2], and [22]); and 3) those that discuss only associativity ([26] and [16]). Since caches have been getting larger, papers in category 1) can also be characterized as older, while those in category 2) are more recent.

Papers in category 1) provide varying quantities of data regarding the effect of changing associativity in small caches. The qualitative trend they support is that changing associativity from direct-mapped to two-way set-associative improves miss ratio, doubling associativity to four-way produces a smaller improvement, doubling again to eight-way yields an even smaller improvement, and subsequent doublings yield no significant improvement. Our quantitative results are consistent with results in these papers. We extend their results by examining relative miss ratio changes to isolate the effect of associativity from other cache aspects, and by examining some larger caches.

Alexander *et al.* use trace-driven simulation to study small and large caches [4]. Unfortunately, the miss ratios they give are much lower than those that have been measured with hardware monitors and real workloads; see [28] for reports of real measurements.

Agarwal *et al.* use traces gathered by modifying the microcode of the VAX 8200 to study large caches and to try to separate operating system and multiprogramming effects [2]. They briefly examine associativity, where they find that associativity in large caches impacts multiprogramming workloads more strongly than uniprocessor workloads. They find for one workload that decreasing associativity from two-way to direct-mapped increases the multiprogramming miss ratio by 100 percent and the uniprogramming miss ratio by 43 percent. These numbers are much larger than the average miss ratio change we find (30 percent).

Przybylski *et al.* [22] examine cache implementation trade-offs. They find that reducing associativity from two-way to direct-mapped increases miss ratio 25 percent, regardless of cache size, which is consistent with our results. One contribution of that paper is a method of translating the architectural impact of a proposed design change into time by computing the cache hit time increase that will exactly offset the benefit of the proposed change. A change improves performance only if the additional delay required to implement the change is less than the above increase. Przybylski *et al.* find that the architectural impact times for increasing associativity are often small, especially for large caches, calling into question the benefit of wide associativity.

The first paper to concentrate exclusively on associativity is [26]. That paper presents a model that allows miss ratios for set associative caches to be accurately derived from the fully associative miss ratio. In Section V-B, we further validate those results by showing that the model accurately relates the miss ratios of many caches, including large direct-mapped caches, to LRU distance probabilities.

The second paper to concentrate on associativity is [16], based on parts of [15]. It shows that many large single-level

---

[2] This survey includes results for some large caches with wide associativity (e.g., 32-way set-associative 64 kbyte caches).

caches in uniprocessors should be direct-mapped, since the drawbacks of direct-mapped caches (e.g., worse miss ratios and more-common worst case behavior) have small significance for large caches with small miss ratios, while the benefits of direct-mapped caches (lower cost and faster access time) do not diminish with increasing cache size. Here we examine miss ratio in more detail, but do not discuss implementation considerations.

III. METHODS AND TRACES

In this section, we discuss the use of the miss ratio as a suitable metric (among others), describe the traces that we use, show how we estimate average steady-state miss ratios, and show that our traces yield results consistent with those observed from running systems.

To first order, the effective access time of a cache can be modeled as $t_{cache} + miss\_ratio \cdot t_{memory}$. (Additional factors which affect access time including the overhead of write backs, extra time for line crossers, page crossers, and TLB misses, and the fact that writes may be slower than reads. These latter delays are much less significant than those given in the expression.) The *miss ratio* is the number of cache misses divided by the number of memory references, t_{memory} is the time for a cache miss, and t_{cache} is the time to access the cache on a hit. The two latter parameters are implementation dependent, and in [15] there is a discussion of their effect on cache performance. As noted earlier, increases in associativity, while generally improving the miss ratio, can increase access time, and thus degrade overall performance. Here, we concentrate on miss ratio because it is easy to define, interpret, compute, and is implementation independent. This independence facilitates cache performance comparisons between caches not yet implemented and those implemented with different technologies and in different kinds of systems.

Results in this paper are based on two partially overlapping groups of traces, called the *five-trace* and *23-trace* groups, respectively. Table I presents data on the traces. The first column gives the name of each trace sample. The second gives the fraction of all references that are instruction references. In these simulations, we do not distinguish between data reads and writes. The third column gives the length of the address traces in 1000's of references. The final column gives the number of distinct bytes referenced by the trace, where any reference in an aligned 32-byte block is considered to have touched each byte in the block.

Each of the trace samples in the five-trace group comes from the second 500 000 references of a longer trace. The first three samples are user and system VAX-11 traces gathered with ATUM [1]. Trace *mul2_2nd500k* contains a circuit simulator and a microcode address allocator running concurrently under VMS. Trace *mul8_2nd500k* is an eight-job multiprogrammed workload under VMS: spice, alloc, a Fortran compile, a Pascal compile, an assembler, a string search in a file, jacobi (a numerical benchmark) and an octal dump. Trace *ue_2nd500k* consists of several copies of a program that simulates interactive users running under Ultrix. The other two samples in the trace group, *mvs1_2nd500k* and *mvs2_2nd500k*, are collections of IBM 370 references from

TABLE I
DATA ON TRACES

Five-Trace Group			
Trace Sample Name	Instruction References (%)	Length (1000's of references)	Dynamic Size (K-bytes)
mul2_2nd500K	53	500	218
mul8_2nd500K	51	500	292
ue_2nd500K	55	500	277
mvs1_2nd500K	52	500	163
mvs2_2nd500K	55	500	201

23-Trace Group			
Trace Name	Instruction References (%)	Length (1000's of references)	Dynamic Size (K-bytes)
dec0	50	362	120
	50	353	125
fora	52	388	144
forf	52	401	128
	53	387	152
	53	414	105
	52	368	205
fsxzz	51	239	104
ivex	60	342	210
macr	55	343	199
memxx	49	445	139
mul2	52	386	204
	53	383	169
	56	367	165
mul8	51	408	218
	54	390	196
	46	429	194
null	58	170	55
savec	50	432	94
	61	228	54
ue	56	358	205
	57	372	191
	55	364	221

system calls invoked in two Amdahl standard MVS workloads [28].

The second trace group contains 23 samples of various workloads gathered on a VAX-11 with ATUM [1]. Trace samples that exhibit unstable behavior (e.g., a particular doubling of cache size or associativity alters the miss ratio observed by many factors of two) have been excluded from both groups.

We estimate the steady-state miss ratios for a trace sample using the miss ratio for a trace after the cache is *warm* (the *warm-start miss ratio*). A cache is *warm* if its future miss ratio is not significantly affected by the cache recently being empty [2]. We compute warm-start miss ratios using the second 250K references of each 500K-reference trace sample. We found that most caches with our traces are warm by 250K references by locating the knee in the graph of the cumulative misses to empty block frames versus references, a method of determining when caches are warm proposed in Agarwal *et al.* [2]. Furthermore, results for these multiprogrammed traces properly include cold-start effects whenever a process resumes execution.

Fig. 2(a) and (b) displays miss ratio data for unified caches (mixed, i.e., cache data and instructions together) with 32-byte blocks. Solid lines show the average warm-start miss ratios with different associativities (1, 2, 4, and 8). The average warm-start miss ratio is the arithmetic average of warm-start miss ratios for each of the five traces in the five-trace group. The arithmetic mean is used because it represents the miss ratio of a workload consisting of an equal number of references from each of the traces. Previous experiments (as were done for [31] and [15]) showed that little difference was observed when other averaging methods were used. The dashed line (labeled "inf") gives the warm-start miss ratio of an infi-

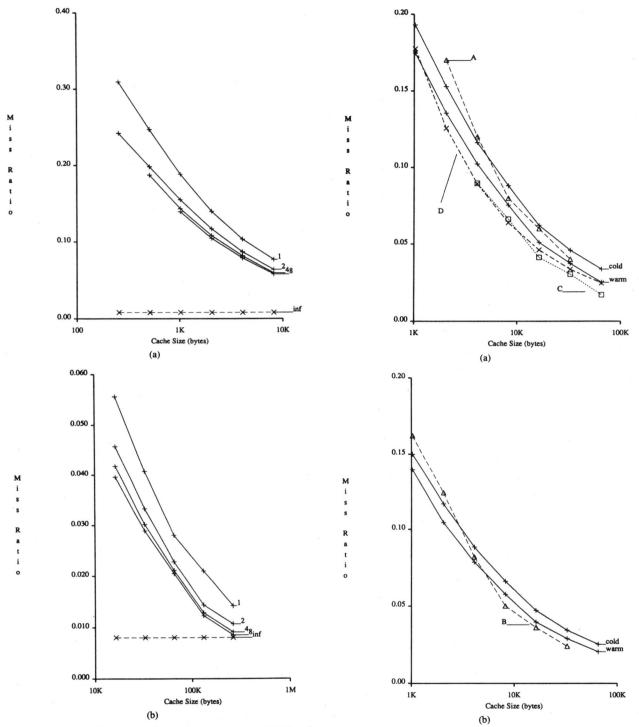

Fig. 2.   Miss ratios for five-trace workload with caches of associativities of 1, 2, 4, and 8. The dashed line shows the miss ratio for an infinite cache. (a) Smaller caches. (b) Larger caches.

Fig. 3.   Comparison of our miss ratio data (solid lines) with other published data (*A*, *B*, *C*, *D*). (a) 16-byte blocks. (b) 32-byte blocks.

nite cache, a cache so large that it never replaces any blocks. Measurements for the 23-trace group are similar.

Fig. 3 compares miss ratios for the five-trace group in eight-way set-associative unified caches, having 16-byte and 32-byte blocks, to miss ratios from other sources. Line "cold" measures miss ratios from an empty cache, while line "warm"

does not count misses until after 250K references. Since the trace samples include multiprogramming effect, both contain some cold-start misses [12]. Lines labeled *A* and *B* show the design target miss ratios for fully-associative caches from [28] and [30]. The line labeled *C* from [2] shows four-way set-associative miss ratio results from Fig. 17 in that paper. Finally, the line labeled D from [27] shows four-, six- and eight-way set-associative miss ratios taken from hardware monitor measurements on an Amdahl 470 (Fig. 33 of that paper, assuming 50 percent supervisor execution). Fig. 3 demonstrates that the miss ratios of the five-trace group are consistent with those measured and/or proposed for actual operating environments.

Despite the similarities with previously published data, miss ratio data for large caches (greater than 64K bytes) are subject to greater error, since only a few thousand misses may occur during a trace sample. To reduce sensitivity to such error, results in Section V concentrate on the relationship between the miss ratios of alternative caches rather than on the miss ratio values themselves.

IV. Simulation Techniques for Alternative Direct-Mapped and Set-Associative Caches

In this section we first discuss two properties, *set refinement* and *inclusion*, that facilitate the rapid simulation of alternative caches. We then develop a new algorithm that uses both set-refinement and inclusion to rapidly simulate alternative direct-mapped caches. Next we generalize an algorithm that simulates alternative set-associative caches using bit selection [34] to one that allows arbitrary set-mapping functions. Finally we compare implementations of the algorithms.

A. Properties that Facilitate Rapid Simulation

Two properties useful for simulating alternative direct-mapped and set-associative caches are *set-refinement*[3] (introduced below) and *inclusion* (introduced in Mattson *et al.* [19]). Here we discuss these properties with respect to caches that have the same block size, do no prefetching, use LRU replacement, have arbitrary associativities, and can use arbitrary set-mapping functions. Let $C_1(A = n_1, F = f_1)$ and $C_2(A = n_2, F = f_2)$ be two such caches, where cache C_i has associativity n_i and set-mapping function f_i, $i = 1, 2$.

Definition 1: Set-refinement: Set-mapping function f_2 *refines* set-mapping function f_1 if $f_2(x) = f_2(y)$ implies $f_1(x) = f_1(y)$, for all blocks x and y.

Furthermore, cache $C_2(A = n_2, F = f_2)$ is said to *refine* an alternative cache $C_1(A = n_1, F = f_1)$ if set-mapping function f_2 *refines* set-mapping function f_1. *Refines* is so named because f_2 *refines* f_1 implies set-mapping function f_2 induces a *finer* partition on all blocks than does f_1. Since set refinement is clearly transitive, if f_{i+1} refines f_i for each $i = 1, L - 1$ then f_j refines f_i for all $j > i$, implying a hierarchy of sets. We will use set refinement to facilitate the rapid simulation of alternative direct-mapped caches (Section IV-B) and set-associative caches (Section IV-C).

Definition 2: Inclusion: Cache $C_2(A = n_2, F = f_2)$ *includes* an alternative cache $C_1(A = n_1, F = f_1)$ if, for any block x after any series of references, x is resident in C_1 implies x is resident in C_2.

Thus, when cache C_2 includes cache C_1, C_2 always contains a superset of the blocks in C_1. Inclusion facilitates rapid simulation of alternative caches by allowing hits in larger caches

to be inferred from hits detected in smaller ones. Mattson *et al.* [19] show when inclusion holds for alternative caches that use the same set-mapping function (and hence the same number of sets). Next we show when it holds with LRU replacement and arbitrary set-mapping functions.

Theorem 1: Given the same block size, no prefetching and LRU replacement, cache $C_2(A = n_2, F = f_2)$ includes cache $C_1(A = n_1, F = f_1)$ if and only if set-mapping function f_2 refines f_1 (set-refinement) and associativity $n_2 \geq n_1$ (nondecreasing associativity).

Proof: Suppose cache C_2 includes cache C_1. Suppose further that a large number of blocks map to each set in both caches, as is trivially true for practical set-mapping functions (e.g., bit selection). To demonstrate that inclusion implies both set-refinement and nondecreasing associativity, we show that a block can be replaced in cache C_1 and still remain in cache C_2, violating inclusion, if either 1) set-refinement does not hold or 2) set-refinement holds but the larger cache has the smaller associativity.

1) If cache C_2 does not refine cache C_1, then there exists at least one pair of blocks x and y such that $f_2(x) = f_2(y)$ and $f_1(x) \neq f_1(y)$. Since we assume many blocks map to each set, there exist many blocks z_i for which $f_2(z_i) = f_2(x) = f_2(y)$. Since $f_1(x) \neq f_1(y)$, either $f_1(z_i) \neq f_1(x)$ or $f_1(z_i) \neq f_1(y)$ (or both), implying set-refinement is violated many times. Without loss of generality, assume that many z_i's map to different f_1 sets than x (otherwise, many map to a different f_1 sets than y). Let n_2 of these be denoted by $w_1, \cdots, w_{n_2}$.[4] Consider references to $x, w_1, \cdots, w_{n_2}$. Inclusion is now violated since x is in cache C_1, but not in cache C_2. It is in cache C_1, because blocks $w_1, \cdots, w_{n_2}$ mapped to other sets than x and could not force its replacement; x is replaced in n_2-way set-associative cache C_2, since LRU replacement is used and the n_2 other blocks mapped to its set are more recently referenced.

2) Let $x_0, \cdots, x_{n_2}$ be a collection of blocks that map to the same f_2 set. Since we are assuming f_2 refines f_1, they also map the same f_1 set. Consider references to $x_0, x_1, \cdots, x_{n_2}$. Inclusion is now violated since x_0 is in n_1-way set-associative cache C_1, but not in n_2-way set-associative cache $C_2(n_1 > n_2$ implies $n_1 \geq n_2 + 1)$.

Suppose cache C_2 refines cache C_1 and $n_2 \geq n_1$. Initially both caches are empty and inclusion holds, because everything (nothing) in cache C_1 is also in cache C_2. Consider the first time inclusion is violated, i.e., some block is in cache C_1 that is not in cache C_2. This can only occur when some block x_0 is replaced from cache C_2, but not from cache C_1. A block x_0 can only be replaced from cache C_2 if n_2 blocks, x_1 through x_{n_2}, all mapping to $f_2(x_0)$, are referenced after it. By set-refinement, $f_1(x_0) = f_1(x_1) = \cdots = f_1(x_{n_2})$. Since $n_2 \geq n_1$, x_0 must also be replaced in cache C_1.   □

Several corollaries, used to develop the cache simulation algorithms in the next two sections, follow directly from the above definitions and theorem.

1) If cache C_2 refines cache C_1 and their set-mapping functions f_2 and f_1 are different (partition blocks differently), then cache C_2 has more sets than cache C_1. The number of sets

---

[3] *Set-refinement* is called *set-hierarchy* in [15].

[4] Blocks $w_1, \cdots, w_{n_2}$ exist if at least $2n_2$ blocks map to set $f_2(x)$.

in a cache is equal to the number of classes in the partition induced by its set-mapping function. If f_2 has fewer classes than f_1 and at least one block maps to every f_1 class, set-refinement is violated since some pair of those blocks must map to the same f_2 class. If f_2 has the same number of classes as f_1 and at least one block maps to every f_1 class, then there exists a one-to-one correspondence between f_2 classes and f_1 classes, implying both functions induce the same partition.

2) If bit selection is used, a cache with 2^i sets refines one with 2^j ones, for all $i \geq j$. That is, set-mapping function x mod 2^i refines x mod 2^j, $i \geq j$. For all blocks x and y (x mod $2^i = y$ mod 2^i) implies (x mod $2^j = y$ mod 2^j), because 2^i can be factored into positive integers 2^{i-j} and 2^j, and (x mod $ab = y$ mod ab) implies (x mod $b = y$ mod b), for all positive integers a and b.

3) Cache C_2 must be strictly larger than a *different* cache C_1 to include it. Two caches are different if they can contain different blocks (after some series of references). If cache C_2 is smaller than cache C_1, inclusion is violated whenever C_1 is full. If C_2 and C_1 are the same size, different, and both full, then inclusion will be violated whenever they hold different blocks.

4) Set refinement implies inclusion in direct-mapped caches. By Theorem 1, inclusion requires set-refinement and nondecreasing associativity. Since all direct-mapped caches have associativity one, only set-refinement is necessary.

5) Inclusion holds between direct-mapped caches using bit selection. Implied by corollaries 2) and 4).

6) Inclusion does not hold between many pairs of different set-associative caches. It does not hold a) between two different set-associative caches of the same size [by corollary 3)], b) if the larger cache has smaller associativity (Theorem 1), and c) if set-refinement is violated (also Theorem 1). Set-refinement can be violated even when bit selection is used (e.g., the larger cache is twice as big but has four times the associativity of the smaller cache).

7) The *includes* relation is a partial ordering of the set of caches. The proof of this, omitted here, need only show that *includes* is reflexive, antisymmetric, and transitive; see [15].

8) Similarly, the *refines* relation is a partial ordering of the set of caches.

9) The *refines* relation can speed the simulation of alternative caches that use LRU replacement. Let these caches be denoted by C_i, $i = 1, 2, \cdots$. Construct a direct-mapped cache $C_0(A = 1, F = f_0)$ such that all caches C_i refine C_0. For arbitrary set-mapping functions, $f_0(x) = 0$ can be used; if all caches C_i use bit selection and have 2^m or more sets, $f_0(x) = x$ mod 2^m should be used. In any case, simulation speed can be improved by deleting all references (trace entries) that hit in cache C_0 and recording the deleted references as hits in all caches simulated. Such deletion is possible when caches C_i include cache C_0 and the deleted references would not have affected any replacement decisions [25]. Since each cache C_i refines cache C_0 and C_0 is direct-mapped, all caches C_i include cache C_0 by Theorem 1. All deleted references do not affect LRU replacement decisions since they are all to the most-recently-referenced (MRU) block in each set. To see why this is true for a cache $C_i(A = n_i, F = f_i)$, consider the

direct-mapped cache $C_i'(A = 1, F = f_i)$ that always contains the MRU blocks from cache C_i. Cache C_i' refines cache C_0, since cache C_i' has the same set-mapping function as cache C_i and cache C_i refines cache C_0. Since *refines* implies *includes* in direct-mapped caches, all deleted references are in cache C_i' (and therefore to cache C_i's MRU blocks). Puzak shows this result for bit-selection [23].

B. Simulating Direct-Mapped Caches

This section develops a new algorithm, called *forest simulation*, for simulating alternative direct-mapped caches. Forest simulation requires that the set-mapping functions of all caches obey set-refinement. Since typical alternative designs for direct-mapped caches use numbers of sets which are powers of two, with the set selected via bit selection, this algorithm is applicable to the common case.

In the last section, we showed set-refinement implies inclusion in direct-mapped caches. Forest simulation takes advantage of inclusion, as does stack simulation, by searching for a block from the smallest to largest cache. When a block is found, a hit is implicitly recorded for all larger caches.

The data structure used by forest simulation to store cache blocks is a forest (a set of disjoint trees) where the number of levels equals the number of caches simulated, and the number of nodes in level i equals the number of blocks frames in the ith smallest cache. If bit selection is used by all caches, the forest can be stored in an array that contains twice as many elements as the largest cache, since the $i - 1$st smallest cache is at most half the size of the ith smallest cache.

Fig. 4(a) displays a forest for direct-mapped caches of size 1, 2, 4, and 8 block frames. The forest contains only one tree, because the smallest cache has only one block frame, and is binary, because each cache in this example is twice as large as the next smaller cache. We assume here that blocks are mapped to block frames with bit selection. Each node holds the information for one block frame in a direct-mapped cache. Nodes are labeled with the tag values which they could contain if bit selection is used for all caches. The node at the root of the tree has no block number bits constrained, because a one-block direct-mapped cache can hold any block. This is illustrated with a t representing arbitrary high-order bits of the block number and three x's representing DON'T CARES for the three low-order bits. The tags $txx0$ and $txx1$ in the nodes of level two indicate that the blocks can reside in these nodes are constrained to have even and odd block numbers, respectively. Similar rules with more bits constrained apply to the rest of the levels.

For each reference, the key idea in forest simulation is to begin at level 1 and proceed downward in the forest until the reference is found or the forest exhausted. At each level, the location of the search is guided by the set-mapping function for that level. At each level traversed, the node examined is changed to contain the reference. If the node is found at level i, *distance*[i] is incremented. After N references have been processed, the miss ratio of the ith smallest direct-mapped cache is $1 - \sum_{j=1}^{i} distance[j]/N$.

Consider the example shown in Fig. 4(b) and (c). Fig. 4(b) depicts the forest of Fig. 4(a) after a series of references.

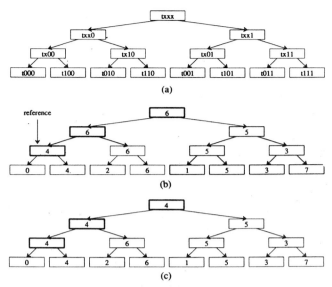

Fig. 4. Forest simulation example: the effect of referencing block 4 on directed-mapped caches of 1, 2, 4, and 8 block frames. (a) A forest with bit selection. (b) Before reference to block 4. (c) After the reference.

Information in the tree tells us that block 6 is in a cache of size one block frame; blocks 6 and 5 are in a direct-mapped cache of size two; blocks 4, 6, 5, and 3 are in a direct-mapped cache of size four; and blocks 0 through 7 are in a direct-mapped cache of size eight. Let the next reference be to block 4. A path from the root to a leaf is determined using the set-mapping function for each cache. A search begins at the root and stops when block 4 is found. All nodes encountered in the search that do not contain block 4 are modified to do so. The nodes in bold are examined to find block 4. Since block 4 is located at level 3, caches at levels 1 and 2 miss and caches at levels 3 and 4 hit. Fig. 4(c) shows the tree after this reference has been processed. The nodes in bold now contain the referenced block.

Fig. 5 shows pseudocode for the algorithm. We will analyze the performance of forest simulation in Section IV-D.

The principal limitation of forest simulation is that it only works for direct-mapped caches. Extending the algorithm to set-associative caches is possible, but complex, since a forest gives only a partial ordering of recently-referenced blocks and set-refinement does not imply inclusion in set-associative caches. Consider using the forest of Fig. 4(b) to simulate a two-block fully-associative cache that uses LRU replacement. It is not possible to tell whether the reference to block 4 hits in such a cache, since any of blocks 2, 4, or 5 could be second-most-recently referenced.

Forest simulation can be extended to simulate n-way set associativity by replacing each node in the forest by an n-element LRU stack. At each reference, rather than just replacing the element at a node with the newest reference, the stack at that node is updated in the normal LRU manner; the descent in the tree stops as soon as the target block is found at level one in the stack at the current node. This is because, by reasoning similar to that used to show corollary 9), the reference will also be at distance one in all further levels. As should

be evident, forest simulation (for direct-mapped caches) is a special case of this general algorithm, with the "n-element" stack consisting of only one element.

We do not develop this algorithm further, because the discussion of the next section presents two forms of an algorithm for simulating alternative set-associative caches that is more general (set-refinement is not required) or faster.

C. Simulating Set-Associative Caches

This section develops an algorithm, called *all-associativity simulation*, for simulating alternative direct-mapped and set-associative caches that have the same block size, do no prefetching, and use LRU replacement. All-associativity works for caches with arbitrary set-mapping functions, but works more efficiently if set-refinement holds. All-associativity simulation does not try to take advantage of inclusion, since inclusion does not hold between many pairs of set-associative caches (see Section IV-A). This work generalizes to arbitrary set-mapping functions an algorithm developed for caches using bit selection only [19], [34]. The algorithms discussed in this section can also be extended to handle multiple-block sizes and sector sizes [24], [34].

In theory, the storage required for all-associativity simulation is $O(N_{\text{unique}})$, where N_{unique} is the number of unique blocks referenced in an address trace. Our experience is that the storage required in practice, however, is usually much smaller than the size of modern main memories. Simulation of a one-million-address trace having an infinite cache miss ratio of one percent, for example, requires storage for 10 000 blocks. Since blocks can be stored in two words (a tag plus a pointer), less than 100K bytes are needed. Future simula-

---

```
integer L  /* number of direct-mapped caches */
/* set-mapping functions that obey set-refinement */
/* i.e., f_{i+1} refines f_i for i=1, ..., L-1. */
function f_1(x), ..., f_L(x)

integer c_1, ..., c_L  /* cache sizes (in blocks); let C_i be Σ_{j=1}^{i} c_j and C_0 = 0 */

integer N  /* counts the number of references */
/* distance counts so that miss_ratio(A=1, F=f_i) = 1 - Σ_{j=1}^{i} distance[i]/N */
integer distance[1:L]
integer forest[1:C_L]  /* the forest */
define map(x, i) = ( f_i(x) + C_{i-1} )  /* maps the forest into an array */


For each reference x {
        read(var x)
        N++

        /* FIND */
        found = FALSE
        for i=1 to L or found {
                y = forest[map(x, i)]

                if (x==y)
                        found = TRUE
                        /* METRIC */
                        distance[i]++
                else
                        /* UPDATE */
                        forest[map(x, i)] = x
        }
}
```

Fig. 5. Forest simulation.

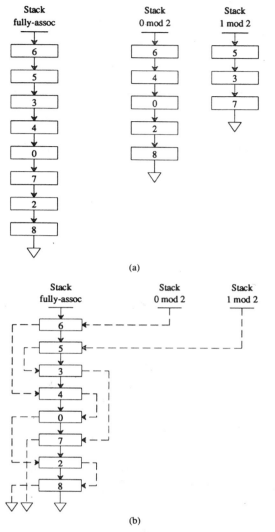

(a)

(b)

Fig. 6. Concurrent stack simulation with one (fully-associative) and two sets (even and odd blocks partitioned). (a) Separate storage. (b) Shared storage.

tions of multiple-megabyte caches may require tens of billions of references to be processed, potentially resulting in excess storage use. Storage for simulations of finite caches can be periodically (e.g., every 100 million references) reclaimed by discarding blocks not in the superset of the caches of interest; this latter approach is used in most other simulation algorithms as well. The algorithms below neglect storage reclamation.

Figs. 9 and 10 at the end of this section present pseudocode for all-associativity simulation not using and using set-refinement. The rest of this section provides insight into how all-associativity simulation works by developing it from stack simulation. A reader who understands the operation of the algorithms from Figs. 9 and 10 may skip to the next section.

If we wish to simulate caches that have one, two, and four sets selected by bit selection (set-mapping functions $x \mod 1$, $x \mod 2$, and $x \mod 4$) we can run three concurrent stack simulations (one with one stack, another with two and a third with four.) Fig. 6(a) illustrates the first two stack simulations.

Due to locality, blocks that reside in one alternative cache will tend to reside in the other caches. Thus, as illustrated in Fig. 6(b), we can save storage by allocating storage for a block once and using multiple links to insert it into the multiple stacks. For LRU replacement, however, the order of two blocks in all stacks is always the same (the more-recently-referenced one is nearer the top) and is unaffected by what other blocks are members of a particular stack.[5] This implies that all links must point down, and therefore can be inferred instead of stored.

Instead of following the links of each stack and counting the blocks traversed, a block's stack distance for each set-mapping function can be calculated by traversing the fully-associative stack until the reference is found or the stack exhausted. For each stack node y before the reference x is found or the stack exhausted, we determine whether $f_i(y) = f_i(x)$ with each set-mapping function f_i. Whenever the equality holds, we increment *stack_count[i]*. If the reference is found, all *stack_count[i]*'s are incremented. After the reference is found or the stack exhausted, each *distance[i, stack_count[i]]* is incremented to indicate a hit to distance *stack_count[i]* with set-mapping function f_i. Fig. 7 illustrates that this method, which we call *all-associativity* simulation, on a reference to block 2.

The above method works for arbitrary set-mapping functions. A faster algorithm is possible if $f_{i+1}(x)$ refines $f_i(x)$, for $i = 1$ to $L-1$. All-associativity simulation can take advantage of set-refinement two ways. First, if f_1 implies multiple sets (not fully-associative), the algorithm can operate on the number of stacks induced by f_1 instead of simulating with one long fully-associative stack. The information lost by not maintaining one stack is the relative order of blocks in different f_1 sets. This information is not needed since the contrapositive of the implication used to define *refines* is $f_i(x) \neq f_i(y)$ implies $f_{i+1}(x) \neq f_{i+1}(y)$. Thus, two blocks in different f_1 sets will never be compared. Simulating with multiple stacks is faster than simulating with one, because the average number of active blocks the algorithm must look through to find a block is smaller, since active blocks are spread across many stacks (e.g., 512 stacks for simulating the VAX-11/780's cache [11]).

Second, the examination of "$f_i(x) = f_i(y)$ for $i = L$ down to 1" can be terminated the first time $f_i(x)$ equals $f_i(y)$, since the set-refinement forces the equality to hold for all smaller i. Furthermore, instead of incrementing *stack_count[i]* for each i where the equality holds, we need only increment *stack_partial_count[i]* for the maximum i for which it holds. When the processing for a reference terminates, we can compute *stack_count[i]* as $\sum_{j=i}^{L} stack\_partial\_count[j]$ and increment *distance[i, stack_count[i]]*, for $i = 1, L$. Thus, using

---

[5] In RANDOM replacement, on the other hand, two blocks can be reordered in one group of stacks and not another if the current reference maps below them in one set of stacks and to another stack in another group of stacks. Consider blocks 0, 1, and 2 and a fully-associative stack and a pair of stacks for even and odd blocks. Reference 1, 0, and 2. The fully-associative stack holds (2 0 1), while the even and odd stacks hold (2 0) and (1). Now rereference block 1. RANDOM replacement requires that there is a 50 percent chance that the fully-associative stack changes to (1 0 2). Since the even stack is unaffected by a reference to an odd block, it remains as (2 0) and blocks 0 and 2 are now in a different order in different stacks.

Stack fully-assoc	Block 2 found?	Fully-Assoc f(x) = 0		Two Sets f(x) = x mod 2		Four Sets f(x) = x mod 4	
		Same set?	stack_count[1]	Same set?	stack_count[2]	Same set?	stack_count[3]
6	no	yes	1	yes	1	yes	1
5	no	yes	2	no	1	no	1
3	no	yes	3	no	1	no	1
4	no	yes	4	yes	2	no	1
0	no	yes	5	yes	3	no	1
7	no	yes	6	no	3	no	1
2	yes	yes	7	yes	4	yes	2
8							
	Stack Distance:		= 7		= 4		= 2

Fig. 7. All-associativity simulation example: referencing block 2 in caches with 1, 2, and 4 sets.

Stack fully-assoc	Number of LSB matched	stack_partial _count[0]	stack_partial _count[1]	stack_partial _count[2]
6	2	0	0	1
5	0	1	0	1
3	0	2	0	1
4	1	2	1	1
0	1	2	2	1
7	0	3	2	1
2	found	3	2	2
8	—			
Stack Distance:		3+2+2 = 7	2+2 = 4	2 = 2

Fig. 8. All-associativity simulation with set-refinement example: referencing block 2 in caches with 1, 2, and 4 sets.

set-refinement reduces the inner loop of all-associativity simulation with L set-mapping functions from L compares and 0 to L increments, to 1 to L compares and 0 or 1 increments. Since the expected number of compares in the improved algorithm can be as small as two,[6] this can result in nontrivial savings if L is large. Fig. 8 illustrates this optimization on reference to block 2.

D. Implementation and Comparison of Simulation Algorithms

To study the performance of stack, forest, and all-associativity simulation and to study CPU caches per se, we implemented these algorithms in C under UNIX 4.3 BSD. Stack and forest simulation were added to a general cache simulator that originally contained 1250 C statements[7] [14]. Adding stack simulation increased total code size by 150 statements, and adding forest simulation, 220 statements. Stack simulation is implemented using linked lists. The forest sim-

---

[6] Assume sets are selected with bit selection and the least-significant address bits of nodes in a stack are uniformly distributed. The probability that exactly i least significant bits match is $1/2^{i+1}$. The number of iterations given an i-bit match is $i + 1$, with the final iteration used to detect the first mismatch. The expected number of iterations does not exceed two, since $\sum_{i=1}^{\infty} (i+1)/2^{i+1} = 2$.

[7] Measured by the number of source lines containing a semicolon or closing brace.

TABLE II
SIMULATION TIMES

Cache Size (bytes)	Associativity	Run-time in sec/1M-references (normalized)					
		Stack		Forest		All-Associativity	
<trivial trace>		304.3	(0.984)	304.7	(0.985)	294.6	(0.952)
16K	1-way	309.3	(1.000)	307.6	(0.994)	300.8	(0.972)
16K	4-way	312.5	(1.010)	--	--	309.2	(1.000)
1K to 8K	1-way	1234.4 [8]	(4.0)	326.1	(1.054)	402.9	(1.303)
16K to 128K	1-way	1234.4 [8]	(4.0)	321.0	(1.038)	332.3	(1.074)
16K to 128K	1-, 2- & 4-way	1806.6 [8]	(6.0)	--	--	366.6	(1.185)

[8] Instead of determining the time for each stack simulation, we optimistically approximate the time required as the time for a fast stack simulation (128 kbyte direct-mapped cache) times the number of runs required.

```
integer L   /* number of set-mapping functions */
function f₁(x), ..., f_L(x)  /* arbitrary set-mapping functions */
integer N   /* counter for the number of references */
integer max_assoc  /* maximum associativity for metrics */
```

/* distance counts so that $miss\_ratio(A=k, F=f_i) = 1 - \sum_{j=1}^{k} distance[i,j]/N$ */

```
integer distance[1:L, 1:max_assoc]
integer stack_count[1:L]  /*stack distance counters; reset for each reference. */

define stacknode_type {
        integer block_number
        stacknode_type *next
}
stacknode_type *stack  /* top of stack pointer */
/* Let N_unique be the number of unique blocks referenced. */
stacknode_type stacknodes[1:O(N_unique)]  /* dynamically allocated pool of stacknodes. */

For each reference x {
        for i=1 to L { stack_count[i] = 0 }
        read(var x)
        N++

        /* FIND */
        found = FALSE
        previous_node_pointer = NULL
        node_pointer = stack
        while ((NOT found) AND (node_pointer!=NULL)) {
                y = node_pointer->block_number
                if (x==y) {
                        found = TRUE
                        for i=1 to L { stack_count[i]++ }
                }
                else {
                        for i=1 to L {
                                if (f_i(x)==f_i(y))  stack_count[i]++
                        }
                        previous_node_pointer = node_pointer
                        node_pointer = node_pointer->next
                }
        }
        /* METRIC */
        if (found) {
                for i=1 to L {
                        /*Record hits to distances ≤ max_assoc. */
                        if (stack_count[i] ≤ max_assoc) distance[i, stack_count[i]]++
                }
        }
        /* If found, move the stack node of x to the top of the stack. */
        /* Otherwise, store x in a new stacknode and move it to the top of the stack. */
        UPDATE(x, found, previous_node_pointer, node_pointer)
}
```

Fig. 9.   All-associativity simulation.

ulation implementation restricts the set-mapping functions to be the block number modulo the cache size in block frames, a slight generalization of bit selection. We implemented all-associativity simulation in a separate program containing 800 C statements and having far fewer options than the simula-

tor above, and with the set-mapping function restricted to bit selection.

Table II lists simulation times for C language implementations of stack, forest, and all-associativity simulation. All caches simulated have 32-byte blocks, do no prefetching, use

```
integer L  /* number of set-mapping functions */
/* set-mapping functions that obey set-refinement, */
/* i.e., f_{i+1} refines f_i for i=1, ..., L-1. */
function f_1(x), ..., f_L(x)
integer number_of_stacks  /* number of sets induced by f_1(x) */
integer N  /* number of references */
integer max_assoc  /* maximum associativity for metrics */
/* distance counts so that miss_ratio(C(A=k, F=f_i)) = 1 - Σ_{j=1}^{k} distance[i,j]/N */
integer distance[1:L, 1:max_assoc]
integer stack_partial_count[1:L]  /* stack distance counters; reset for each reference. */

define stacknode_type {
        integer block_number
        stacknode_type *next
}
stacknode_type *stack[0:number of stacks-1]  /* top of stack pointers */
/* Let N_{unique} be the number of unique blocks referenced. */
stacknode_type stacknodes[1:O(N_{unique})]  /* dynamically allocated pool of stacknodes. */




For each reference x {
        for i=1 to L { stack_partial_count[i] = 0 }
        read(var x)
        N++
        stack_number = f_1(x)
        /* FIND */
        found = FALSE
        previous_node_pointer = NULL
        node_pointer = stack[stack_number]
        while ((NOT found) AND (node_pointer!=NULL)) {
                y = node_pointer->block_number
                if (x==y) {
                        found = TRUE
                        stack_partial_count[L]++
                }
                else {
                        match = FALSE
                        for i=L down to 1 OR match {
                                if (f_i(x)==f_i(y)) {
                                        match = TRUE
                                        stack_partial_count[i]++
                                }
                        }
                        previous_node_pointer = node_pointer
                        node_pointer = node_pointer->next
                }
        }
        /* METRIC */
        if (found) {
                stack_count = 0
                for i=L down to 1 {
                        stack_count = stack_count + stack_partial_count[i]
                        /* Record hits to distances ≤ max_assoc. */
                        if (stack_count ≤ max_assoc) distance[i, stack_count]++
                }
        }
        /* If found, move the stack node of x to the top of its stack. */
        /* Otherwise, store x in a new stacknode and move it to the top of the stack. */
        UPDATE(x, stack_number, found, previous_node_pointer, node_pointer)
```

Fig. 10.   All-associativity simulation with set-refinement.

LRU replacement, are unified (data and instructions cached together) and use bit selection. Results in the first row ("trivial trace") are for a trace consisting of one million copies of the same address, yielding one miss and 999 999 hits. All other results presented here are for a trace of one million memory references from system calls generated by an Amdahl standard MVS workload [28]. We also examined traces from three other architectures [15]. We omit these results here, since they are similar to those with the MVS trace. Results not in parentheses are the elapsed virtual times in seconds for simulation runs on an otherwise unloaded Sun-3/75 with 8M of memory, no local disk, and trace data read from a file server via an ethernet. Results in parentheses are normalized to the time for stack simulation to simulate a single 16 kbyte direct-mapped (1-way) cache with the MVS trace.

We compare these algorithms using only memory trace data, as opposed to data from other caching systems, because set-associativity is rarely used outside of CPU caches. Readers interested in simulation performance times for fully-associative caches, driven by traces of memory and disk references, should consult [33].

The simulation times in Table II allow us to answer the following three questions regarding how these implementations perform.

1) Are the implementations comparable?

Yes. We determine that implementations are comparable by simulating single caches, which, in theory, require the same simulation time. For a synthetic trace and a real trace and for two associativities, we found the virtual times (CPU times) for implementations of stack and forest simulation differed by less than 0.5 percent, while the implementation of all-associativity simulation is 1–3 percent faster (see Table II). That all-associative simulation is slightly faster is not surprising, since it was implemented in a separate program, while stack and forest simulation are part of a more powerful cache simulator.

2) What algorithm is fastest for simulating a collection of direct-mapped caches of similar size?

Forest simulation. However, forest simulation is not significantly faster than all-associativity simulation if caches are large. Both forest and all-associativity simulation are much faster than stack simulation since they require only one run, whereas stack simulation needs one run per cache size.

3) What algorithm is fastest for simulating a collection of direct-mapped and set-associative caches of similar size?

All-associativity simulation. All-associativity simulation requires only one run, which is not much slower than a single, simple simulation run. Forest simulation is not able to simulate nondirect-mapped caches. Stack simulation requires one run per unique number of sets. Simulating caches of c, $2c$, $4c$ through $2^s c$ block frames with associativities 1, 2, 4 through 2^a requires $s + a - 1$ stack simulations. One with $c/2^a$ sets, a second with $c/2^{a-1}$ sets, $\cdots$, another with c sets, another with $2c$ sets, $\cdots$, and finally one with $2^s c$ sets. The simulation in the final row of Table II, for example, required six stack simulations, using 128, 256, $\cdots$ and 4K stacks, respectively.

The speedups illustrated here for trace lengths of one million references (30 min down to 6 min) are impressive, but not critical. Traces to exercise multiple-megabyte caches, however, will be much longer. All-associativity simulation will allow billion-reference traces to be processed in a few days rather than a few weeks. Furthermore, simulating a wide variety of caches in one pass as a trace is generated facilitates simulations with traces too large to store.

V. THE RELATIONSHIP BETWEEN ASSOCIATIVITY AND MISS RATIO

In this section, we analyze how changes in associativity alter cache miss ratio. We find empirically that some simple relationships exist between the miss ratios of direct-mapped, set-associative, and fully-associative caches, largely independently of cache size. We concentrate on the relationship between miss ratios of alternative caches, rather than the absolute size of miss ratio, because our traces samples are short, never exceeding 500K references. We assume throughout that caches have a fixed block size, use LRU replacement, do no prefetching and pick the set of a reference with bit selection.

A. Categorizing Set-Associative Misses

The simulation algorithms described earlier facilitate computing the miss ratios for many alternative cache sizes and associativities. These data can be used to increase our understanding of a single cache's miss ratio. We do this by subdividing the observed misses into three categories: (set-)conflict misses (due to too many active blocks mapping to a fraction of the sets), capacity misses (due to fixed cache size), and compulsory misses (necessary in any case[9]).

The size of these components can be calculated as follows. First, the conflict miss ratio is the cache's miss ratio less the miss ratio for a fully-associative cache of the same size. Second, the capacity miss ratio is the fully-associative cache's miss ratio less the miss ratio for an infinite cache (one so large it never replaces a block). Finally, the compulsory miss ratio is the infinite cache's miss ratio, which is not zero since initial references to blocks still miss. This categorization is easy to compute, since it can be derived from average miss ratios and does not require a detailed manipulation of simulation programs (as does the model in [3]).

Table III illustrates this miss ratio categorization "ue," a trace of VAX-11 interactive users under Ultrix (see Table I). All miss ratios are warm-start and for a unified cache with 32-byte blocks. Under each miss ratio component, the first number is the component's absolute size, while the second is its relative contribution to the overall miss ratio. The reader should concentrate on trends rather than miss ratio values, since this table only gives results for three short trace samples of one workload. Compulsory miss ratios and results for larger caches are subject to more error. (That one conflict miss ratio is negative (eight-way set-associative 1 kbyte cache) is unimportant, since 1) the magnitude is very small (−0.0006), indicating that cache has approximately the same miss ratio as fully-associative cache, and 2) the behavior is possible [31].)

For this trace, we see 1) the absolute size of the conflict miss ratios for set-associative caches (not direct-mapped) are small,

[9] That is, necessary without violating our assumptions of a fixed block size, LRU replacement, no prefetching, and bit selection.

TABLE III
THREE MISS RATIO COMPONENTS

Cache Size (bytes)	Degree of Associativity	Miss Ratio	Miss Ratio Components (Relative Percent)					
			Conflict		Capacity		Compulsory	
1K	1-way	0.1913	0.0419	22%	0.1405	73%	0.0090	5%
1K	2-way	0.1609	0.0115	7%	0.1405	87%	0.0090	6%
1K	4-way	0.1523	0.0029	2%	0.1405	92%	0.0090	6%
1K	8-way	0.1488	-0.0006	-0%	0.1405	94%	0.0090	6%
2K	1-way	0.1482	0.0361	24%	0.1032	70%	0.0090	6%
2K	2-way	0.1223	0.0102	8%	0.1032	84%	0.0090	7%
2K	4-way	0.1148	0.0027	2%	0.1032	90%	0.0090	8%
2K	8-way	0.1128	0.0006	1%	0.1032	91%	0.0090	8%
4K	1-way	0.1089	0.0270	25%	0.0730	67%	0.0090	8%
4K	2-way	0.0948	0.0129	14%	0.0730	77%	0.0090	9%
4K	4-way	0.0868	0.0049	6%	0.0730	84%	0.0090	10%
4K	8-way	0.0842	0.0022	3%	0.0730	87%	0.0090	11%
8K	1-way	0.0868	0.0257	30%	0.0521	60%	0.0090	10%
8K	2-way	0.0693	0.0082	12%	0.0521	75%	0.0090	13%
8K	4-way	0.0650	0.0040	6%	0.0521	80%	0.0090	14%
8K	8-way	0.0629	0.0018	3%	0.0521	83%	0.0090	14%
16K	1-way	0.0658	0.0194	29%	0.0375	57%	0.0090	14%
16K	2-way	0.0535	0.0070	13%	0.0375	70%	0.0090	17%
16K	4-way	0.0494	0.0029	6%	0.0375	76%	0.0090	18%
16K	8-way	0.0478	0.0014	3%	0.0375	78%	0.0090	19%
32K	1-way	0.0503	0.0134	27%	0.0279	55%	0.0090	18%
32K	2-way	0.0412	0.0043	11%	0.0279	68%	0.0090	22%
32K	4-way	0.0383	0.0014	4%	0.0279	73%	0.0090	23%
32K	8-way	0.0377	0.0008	2%	0.0279	74%	0.0090	24%

making further increases in associativity of limited benefit, 2) the absolute size of conflict miss ratios for direct-mapped caches gets smaller with increasing cache size, making increasing associativity less important, and 3) the compulsory miss ratio is fixed but gets relatively more important with increasing cache size, limiting the potential benefit of further cache size increases. One deficiency of this categorization is that the magnitude of the capacity miss ratio does not bound the miss ratio reduction that increasing cache size can yield. This is because increasing cache size also increases the number of sets, reducing the conflict miss ratio.

B. How Set-Associative Miss Ratios Relate to Fully-Associative Ones

It has been previously shown [26] that set-associative miss ratios can be closely estimated from fully-associative ones; this observation was validated for several traces for 16 and 64 sets. We review that calculation in this section, and validate the results over a larger range of cache sizes and number of sets.

The model derives LRU distance probabilities with s sets, $p_i(s)$, from fully-associative LRU distance probabilities, q_i. $p_i(s)$ is the probability a reference is made to the ith most-recently-referenced block in one of s sets, while q_i is the probability a reference is made to the ith most-recently-referenced block in any set. Consequently, $q_i = p_i(1)$. LRU distance probabilities are equivalent to the miss ratios of caches using LRU replacement. The miss ratio for an n-way set-associative cache with s sets is $1 - \sum_{i=1}^{n} p_i(s)$, while the miss ratio for an n-block fully-associative cache is $1 - \sum_{i=1}^{n} q_i$.

Bayes rule[10] allows us to express a set-associative LRU distance probability in terms of fully-associative LRU distance probabilities:

$$p_n(s) = \sum_{i=1}^{\infty} \text{Prob}(\text{LRU distance } n \text{ with } s \text{ sets}$$
$$| \text{LRU distance } i \text{ with } 1 \text{ set}) \cdot q_i.$$

[10] For some event A and a set of mutually exclusive and exhaustive events B_i, Bayes' rule states that $\text{Prob}(A) = \Sigma \, \text{Prob}(A|B_i) \cdot \text{Prob}(B_i)$.

The above equation can be used to estimate set-associative LRU distance probabilities from fully-associative LRU distance probabilities, or equivalently set-associative miss ratios from fully-associative miss ratios, using a simple approximation for Prob(LRU distance n with s sets | LRU distance i with 1 set). The approximation is based on the assumption that the probability that two blocks map the same set is $1/s$ and independent of where other blocks map. A reference to set-associative distance n occurs if exactly $n - 1$ more-recently-referenced blocks map to the reference's set, while a reference to fully-associative distance i implies $i - 1$ blocks are more-recently-referenced. By the above assumption, the probability that exactly $n - 1$ of the $i - 1$ more-recently-referenced blocks map to the set of the reference is 0 for $n > i$ and approximately

$$\binom{i-1}{n-1} \left[\frac{1}{s}\right]^{n-1} \left[\frac{s-1}{s}\right]^{i-n}, \qquad \text{for } n \leq i.$$

Substitution yields

$$p_n(s) \approx \sum_{i=n}^{\infty} \binom{i-1}{n-1} \left[\frac{1}{s}\right]^{n-1} \left[\frac{s-1}{s}\right]^{i-n} \cdot q_i.$$

Fig. 11 shows actual miss ratios (solid lines) and miss ratios predicted with the above equation (dashed lines) for associativities 1, 2, 4, and 8. Data are based on using trace "mul2" to drive a unified cache with 32-byte blocks. Results here and for several other traces [15] yield three conclusions.

1) The predictions are quite accurate. In most cases, the relative error is less than 5 percent; only rarely is it greater than 10 percent.

2) Predictions are usually more pessimistic than the actual miss ratios. The cause of this phenomenon is that blocks selected with bit selection collide slightly less often than blocks whose set is selected at random (as the above approximation assumes), due to spatial locality [26].

3) The relative error gets smaller with increasing associativity, which is expected since many-way set-associative caches have miss ratios nearly identical to fully-associative caches.

That this method is accurate is not important for deriving set-associative miss ratios, since all-associativity simulation allows exact values to be calculated efficiently. Rather, it is important in that it provides insight into the difference between set-associative and fully-associative miss ratios, showing that the actual increase in miss ratio is nearly identical to the increase that results from assuming that active blocks map to sets with independent and equal probability.

C. How Set-Associative Miss Ratios Relate to Each Other

Empirically we see that miss ratio is affected by changes in cache size, block size, and associativity. We would like to find some simple rules that can be used to quantify changes in associativity on cache miss ratios; we do that in this section.

We find that by examining relative miss ratio differences rather than absolute miss ratio differences one can almost eliminate the effect of cache size. Consider an n-way set-associative cache and a $2n$-way set-associative cache, hav-

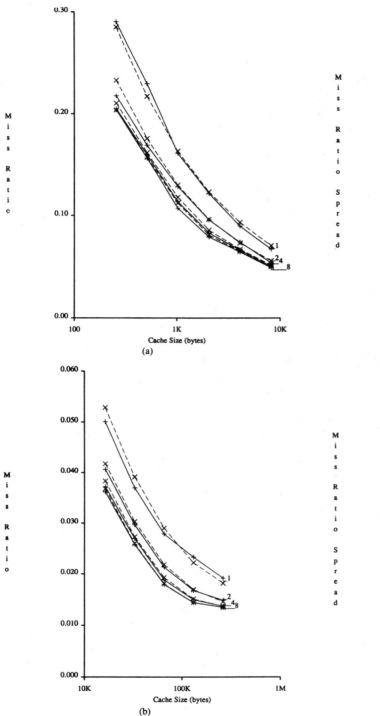

Fig. 11. Predicted (dashed) and actual (solid) miss ratios for trace "mul2" with caches of associativity 1, 2, 4, and 8. (a) Smaller caches. (b) Larger caches.

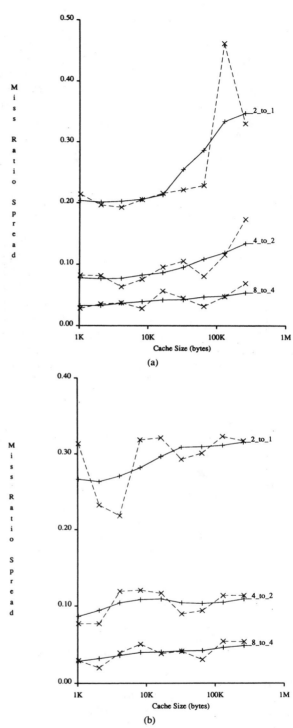

Fig. 12. Unified cache miss ratio spreads (solid lines are smoothed data). A line labeled "$2n\_to\_n$" displays $[m(A = n) - m(A = 2n)]/m(A = 2n)$ where $m(A = n)$ is the miss ratio of an n-way set-associative cache. (a) Five-trace group. (b) 23-trace group.

ing the same capacity, the same block size, and miss ratios $m(A = n)$ and $m(A = 2n)$. Let the *miss ratio spread* be the ratio of the miss ratios, less one:

$$\frac{m(A = n)}{m(A = 2n)} - 1 = \frac{m(A = n) - m(A = 2n)}{m(A = 2n)}.$$

Figs. 12 and 13 and Table IV present data from trace-driven simulation. As discussed in Section III, data for larger caches are subject to more error than data for smaller caches, and measurements for caches larger than 64K should be treated with considerable caution. Fig. 12 shows some miss ratio

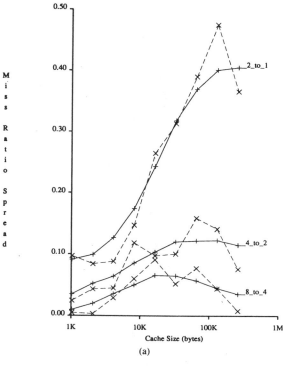

(a)

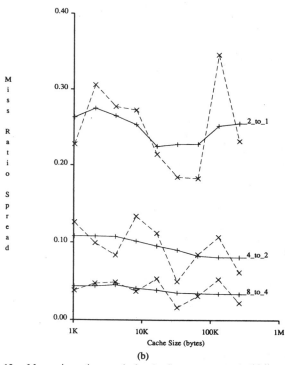

(b)

Fig. 13.   More miss ratio spreads for the five-trace group (solid lines are smoothed data). (a) Instruction caches. (b) Data caches.

TABLE IV
SMOOTHED MISS RATIO SPREADS

Smoothed Miss Ratio Spreads for Unified Caches

Cache	Block Size 16 Bytes			Block Size 32 Bytes			Block Size 64 Bytes		
Size	8-to-4	4-to-2	2-to-1	8-to-4	4-to-2	2-to-1	8-to-4	4-to-2	2-to-1
1K	4%	9%	20%	5%	10%	30%	5%	12%	41%
2K	5%	10%	22%	5%	12%	29%	6%	13%	38%
4K	5%	11%	23%	6%	12%	29%	7%	14%	38%
8K	5%	10%	25%	6%	12%	29%	7%	14%	37%
16K	5%	10%	26%	5%	12%	31%	7%	13%	38%
32K	5%	10%	28%	5%	11%	32%	6%	13%	38%
64K	4%	10%	28%	5%	11%	33%	5%	12%	39%
128K	5%	10%	28%	5%	11%	33%	5%	12%	40%
256K	4%	10%	28%	5%	12%	34%	6%	13%	40%
AVG	5%	10%	25%	5%	11%	31%	6%	13%	39%

Smoothed Miss Ratio Spreads for Instruction Caches

Cache	Block Size 16 Bytes			Block Size 32 Bytes			Block Size 64 Bytes		
Size	8-to-4	4-to-2	2-to-1	8-to-4	4-to-2	2-to-1	8-to-4	4-to-2	2-to-1
1K	5%	11%	16%	4%	11%	16%	6%	10%	16%
2K	6%	13%	18%	5%	14%	17%	6%	13%	18%
4K	6%	13%	20%	6%	15%	20%	7%	15%	20%
8K	7%	13%	22%	7%	15%	23%	7%	15%	24%
16K	7%	13%	26%	7%	14%	28%	7%	15%	29%
32K	6%	12%	28%	7%	14%	30%	7%	15%	32%
64K	5%	11%	30%	6%	12%	32%	6%	13%	35%
128K	4%	11%	29%	5%	12%	32%	5%	14%	35%
256K	3%	8%	28%	4%	10%	31%	4%	12%	36%
AVG	6%	12%	24%	6%	13%	25%	6%	14%	27%

Smoothed Miss Ratio Spreads for Data Caches

Cache	Block Size 16 Bytes			Block Size 32 Bytes			Block Size 64 Bytes		
Size	8-to-4	4-to-2	2-to-1	8-to-4	4-to-2	2-to-1	8-to-4	4-to-2	2-to-1
1K	6%	13%	27%	6%	14%	30%	7%	14%	33%
2K	6%	12%	28%	7%	13%	31%	8%	14%	35%
4K	6%	11%	26%	7%	13%	29%	8%	14%	34%
8K	5%	10%	26%	6%	11%	30%	7%	13%	36%
16K	4%	9%	24%	5%	10%	28%	6%	12%	35%
32K	3%	8%	24%	4%	9%	29%	5%	11%	36%
64K	3%	8%	23%	3%	9%	28%	4%	11%	35%
128K	3%	7%	22%	4%	9%	29%	4%	11%	36%
256K	3%	7%	20%	4%	9%	27%	5%	12%	35%
AVG	4%	9%	24%	5%	11%	29%	6%	12%	35%

spreads (recommended in [9]). We selected the weights to reduce variation between adjacent spreads, without suppressing larger trends. We assigned a weight of 0.20 to both adjacent spreads and 0.15 to spreads two sizes away, leaving a weight of 0.30 for the spread being smoothed.

Table IV shows similar results from an alternative computation, taking the geometric average of the miss ratio spreads of individual traces. This method yields slightly larger spreads than those calculated using the ratio of average miss ratios (as in Fig. 12). Miss ratio spreads in rows labeled "AVG" are calculated by taking the geometric mean of the ratio of miss ratios for cache sizes from 1K to 256K bytes.

These results together with more data in [15] exhibit the following trends.

1) Miss ratio spreads for caches with more restricted associativity are larger, implying, for example, that direct-mapped and two-way set-associative miss ratios are further apart than two-way and four-way set-associative miss ratios. This result corroborates the previous work of many others.

2) Except for small instruction caches, miss ratio spreads do not vary rapidly with changing cache size, even though the miss ratios in their numerators and denominators vary by over an order of magnitude. The miss ratio spreads between small direct-mapped and two-way set-associative instruction caches are smaller than many other spreads due to the sequential behavior of instruction reference streams, which minimizes the usefulness of increasing associativity in small instruction

spreads of unified caches with 32-byte blocks for the five- and 23-trace groups. Fig. 13 examines miss ratio spreads for instruction and data cache with the five-trace group. The average miss ratio spread is computed using the ratio of the average miss ratios. Dashed lines present raw data, while solid lines are smoothed using a weighted average of adjacent

caches [31]. This sequentiality is much less of a factor for large instruction caches, and for such large instruction caches, the miss ratio spreads are similar to those for data and unified caches. The only major exception to these observations is the miss ratio spread between direct-mapped and two-way set-associative 128 kbyte caches with the five-trace group. We believe that the cause of this aberration lies in the particular traces and trace lengths used, not in some property of 128 kbyte caches.

3) Miss ratio spreads are positively correlated with block size. While the difference is not important with wide associativity, the miss ratio spread between direct-mapped and two-way set-associative unified caches with the 23-trace group increases from 25 to 31 to 39 percent as block size goes from 16 to 32 to 64 bytes. The reason for this is that for a given cache size, as the blocks become larger, the number of sets decreases, and the probability that two active blocks map into the same set increases (i.e., bigger blocks are more likely to "bump into each other".)

4) Miss ratio spreads between unified and data caches are similar. Instruction cache spreads are similar or smaller (see also [10]). Miss ratio spreads between direct-mapped and two-way set-associative instruction caches are significantly smaller than other spreads, as has been observed elsewhere [31].

Since the miss ratio spreads do not vary greatly with cache size, we can provide insight into the relationship between miss ratio and associativity by computing miss ratio spreads averaged over many cache sizes, as is done in Table IV. To one significant figure, halving associativity with these traces from eight-way to four-way to two-way to direct-mapped causes miss ratio spreads of 5, 10, and 30 percent regardless of cache size, cache type, or block size. Equivalently, one can look at set-associative miss ratios relative to direct-mapped or fully-associative ones, as depicted in Table V. Relative to direct-mapped, the miss ratios for eight-, four- and two-way set-associative are, respectively, about 34, 30, and 22 percent lower. Assuming that eight-way set-associative is effectively fully-associative, the miss ratio increases by 5 percent for four-way, 17 percent for two-way, and 52 percent for direct-mapped.

Our examination of miss ratios for caches with different associativities has shown that the miss ratio spread does not change significantly over a wide range of cache sizes, with exception of small instruction caches, for which the spread is unusually small. Consequently, the absolute miss ratio difference decreases as caches get larger, since absolute miss ratios get smaller. When the absolute miss ratio difference becomes sufficiently small, an interesting change occurs: the effective access time of a direct-mapped cache can be smaller than that of a set-associative cache of the same size, even though the direct-mapped cache has the larger miss ratio. This change occurs when implementation differences, that have previously been ignored, become more important than absolute miss ratio differences. This topic is considered in some detail in [16] and [22].

D. Extending Design Target Miss Ratios

In [28], it was noted that absolute miss ratios computed from trace-driven simulations were often optimistic. That pa-

TABLE V
RELATIVE MISS RATIO CHANGE

Relative Miss Ratio Change for the Five-Trace Group							
Cache Type	Block Size	From Direct-Mapped To			From Eight-Way To		
		8-way	4-way	2-way	4-way	2-way	1-way
Unified	16	-31%	-27%	-20%	5%	17%	47%
	32	-33%	-30%	-22%	5%	18%	52%
	64	-38%	-34%	-26%	6%	21%	63%
Instruction	16	-31%	-27%	-20%	5%	17%	48%
	32	-32%	-28%	-21%	6%	18%	51%
	64	-33%	-30%	-22%	6%	18%	54%
Data	16	-32%	-29%	-21%	5%	16%	48%
	32	-34%	-31%	-23%	5%	17%	52%
	64	-39%	-35%	-26%	6%	20%	64%

Relative Miss Ratio Change for the 23-Trace Group							
Cache Type	Block Size	From Direct-Mapped To			From Eight-Way To		
		8-way	4-way	2-way	4-way	2-way	1-way
Unified	16	-30%	-27%	-20%	5%	15%	44%
	32	-35%	-32%	-24%	5%	17%	54%
	64	-40%	-36%	-28%	6%	20%	67%
Instruction	16	-31%	-27%	-19%	6%	17%	45%
	32	-32%	-28%	-20%	6%	19%	49%
	64	-34%	-30%	-21%	6%	20%	53%
Data	16	-29%	-26%	-19%	4%	14%	42%
	32	-33%	-30%	-22%	5%	16%	50%
	64	-38%	-34%	-26%	6%	19%	61%

per then presented *design target miss ratios* which were miss ratios derived from hardware monitor measurements, personal experience, and trace-driven simulations using realistic workloads; those miss ratios were intended to represent realistic figures for real systems under real workloads. The data in [28] presented miss ratios for fully associative caches with 16-byte blocks, broken down into figures for unified, instruction, and data caches. In another paper [30], the design target miss ratios were extended to block sizes ranging from 4 to 128 bytes. This was done by finding the relative change in miss ratio as the block size changed (by taking "ratios of miss ratios" for a variety of traces) and propagating the design target miss ratios for 16-byte block to other block sizes.

We use the same method in Table VI to extend the design target miss ratios to caches of limited associativity. We assume that eight-way set-associative miss ratios are equal to the fully-associative design target miss ratios, and compute other set-associative miss ratios using the smoothed *ratios of miss ratios* shown in Table IV. We do not extend the design target miss ratios to caches larger than 32 kbytes, because the original design target miss ratios in [28] and [30] are limited to caches of 32 kbytes or less, and the methodology for extending them to larger cache sizes is beyond the scope of this paper; note, however, that data in [27] suggest that as a rough rule of thumb, the miss ratio drops as the square root of the cache size.

VI. CONCLUSIONS

We have examined properties and algorithms for simulating alternative caches and have examined the relationship between associativity and miss ratio. We find that both *inclusion* (that larger caches contain a superset of the blocks in smaller caches [19]) and *set-refinement* (that blocks mapping to the same set in larger caches map to the same set in smaller caches) can be used by *forest simulation*, a new algorithm for rapidly simulating alternative direct-mapped caches. We show that inclusion is not useful, but set-refinement can be useful for *all-associativity simulation*, an algorithm for rapidly simulating alternative direct-mapped, set-associative, and fully-

TABLE VI
DESIGN TARGET MISS RATIOS

Design Target Miss Ratios for Unified Caches

Cache Size	Block Size 16 Bytes				Block Size 32 Bytes				Block Size 64 Bytes			
	8-way	4-way	2-way	1-way	8-way	4-way	2-way	1-way	8-way	4-way	2-way	1-way
1K	0.210	0.219	0.239	0.288	0.162	0.170	0.188	0.244	0.137	0.144	0.162	0.229
2K	0.170	0.179	0.197	0.240	0.124	0.130	0.146	0.188	0.098	0.104	0.118	0.163
4K	0.120	0.126	0.140	0.172	0.082	0.087	0.097	0.126	0.059	0.063	0.072	0.099
8K	0.080	0.084	0.093	0.116	0.050	0.053	0.059	0.077	0.033	0.035	0.040	0.055
16K	0.060	0.063	0.069	0.088	0.036	0.038	0.042	0.055	0.023	0.025	0.028	0.038
32K	0.040	0.042	0.046	0.059	0.024	0.025	0.028	0.037	0.014	0.015	0.017	0.023

Design Target Miss Ratios for Instruction Caches

Cache Size	Block Size 16 Bytes				Block Size 32 Bytes				Block Size 64 Bytes			
	8-way	4-way	2-way	1-way	8-way	4-way	2-way	1-way	8-way	4-way	2-way	1-way
1K	0.200	0.211	0.234	0.271	0.134	0.140	0.155	0.179	0.098	0.104	0.115	0.133
2K	0.150	0.159	0.179	0.210	0.098	0.103	0.117	0.138	0.068	0.072	0.082	0.097
4K	0.100	0.106	0.120	0.143	0.063	0.067	0.076	0.091	0.043	0.046	0.053	0.063
8K	0.060	0.064	0.072	0.089	0.037	0.039	0.045	0.056	0.023	0.025	0.028	0.035
16K	0.050	0.053	0.060	0.076	0.029	0.031	0.035	0.045	0.018	0.019	0.022	0.029
32K	0.030	0.032	0.036	0.046	0.017	0.018	0.021	0.027	0.010	0.011	0.012	0.016

Design Target Miss Ratios for Data Caches

Cache Size	Block Size 16 Bytes				Block Size 32 Bytes				Block Size 64 Bytes			
	8-way	4-way	2-way	1-way	8-way	4-way	2-way	1-way	8-way	4-way	2-way	1-way
1K	0.160	0.170	0.192	0.244	0.138	0.146	0.166	0.216	0.140	0.150	0.170	0.227
2K	0.120	0.127	0.143	0.183	0.094	0.101	0.114	0.149	0.083	0.089	0.102	0.138
4K	0.100	0.106	0.117	0.148	0.070	0.075	0.084	0.109	0.054	0.058	0.067	0.090
8K	0.080	0.084	0.092	0.116	0.053	0.056	0.062	0.081	0.039	0.042	0.047	0.064
16K	0.060	0.062	0.068	0.084	0.039	0.041	0.045	0.058	0.026	0.028	0.031	0.042
32K	0.040	0.041	0.045	0.055	0.025	0.026	0.028	0.037	0.017	0.018	0.020	0.027

associative caches. Our algorithm is a generalization of an earlier algorithm [19], [34]. We find all-associativity simulation is tremendously effective, allowing dozens of caches to be evaluated in time that is within a small constant factor of the time needed to simulate one cache with wide associativity.

Our empirical examination of associativity and miss ratio provides data and insight into how miss ratio is affected by changes in associativity. In particular:

• We show how to divide cache misses into *conflict, capacity*, and *compulsory* misses, using only average miss ratios from alternative caches. Increasing associativity but not cache size can only reduce conflict misses. Increasing cache size but not associativity increases the number of sets, and therefore may decrease conflict and capacity misses. Compulsory misses cannot be reduced without increasing block size or prefetching.

• By applying a model from [26] to a wide variety of caches, we show that the difference between set-associative and fully-associative miss ratios (the rate of conflict misses) can be predicted by assuming blocks map to sets uniformly and independently, resulting in too many active blocks mapping to a fraction of the sets.

• We find empirically that *miss ratio spread*, the relative change in miss ratio caused by reducing associativity, is relatively invariant for caches of significantly different size and miss ratio. Our data show that reducing associativity from eight-way to four-way, from four-way to two-way, and from two-way to direct-mapped causes relative miss ratio increases of about 5, 10, and 30 percent, respectively. We also use miss ratio spreads to provide design target miss ratios for caches with limited associativity.

ACKNOWLEDGMENT

We would like to thank R. Katz, D. Patterson, and other members of the SPUR project for their many suggestions that improved the quality of our research, H. Stone for comments on [15], and S. Dentinger, G. Gibson, and V. Madan for reading and improving drafts of this paper.

REFERENCES

[1] A. Agarwal, R. L. Sites, and M. Horowitz, "ATUM: A new technique for capturing address traces using microcode," in *Proc. 13th Int. Symp. Comput. Architecture*, June 1986, pp. 119–129.

[2] A. Agarwal, M. Horowitz, and J. Hennessy, "Cache performance of operating systems and multiprogramming workloads," *ACM Trans. Comput. Syst.*, vol. 6, no. 4, pp. 393–431, Nov. 1988.

[3] ——, "An analytical cache model," *ACM Trans. Comput. Syst.*, vol. 7, no. 2, pp. 184–215, May 1989.

[4] C. Alexander, W. Keshlear, F. Cooper, and F. Briggs, "Cache memory performance in a UNIX environment," *Comput. Architecture News*, vol. 14, no. 3, pp. 14–70, June 1986.

[5] J. Baer and W. Wang, "On the inclusion properties for multi-level cache hierarchies," in *Proc. 15th Annu. Int. Symp. Comput. Architecture*, Honolulu, HI, June 1988, pp. 73–80.

[6] L. A. Belady, "A study of replacement algorithms for a virtual-storage computer," *IBM Syst. J.*, vol. 5, no. 2, pp. 78–101, 1966.

[7] J. Bell, D. Casasent, and C. G. Bell, "An investigation of alternative cache organizations," *IEEE Trans. Comput.*, vol. C-23, no. 4, pp. 346–351, Apr. 1974.

[8] B. T. Bennett and V. J. Kruskal, "LRU stack processing," *IBM J. Res. Develop.*, pp. 353–357, July 1975.

[9] J. M. Chambers, W. S. Cleveland, B. Kleiner, and P. A. Tukey, *Graphical Methods for Data Analysis*. Boston, MA: Duxbury, 1983.

[10] J. Cho, A. J. Smith, and H. Sachs, "The memory architecture and the cache and memory management unit for the Fairchild CLIPPER Processor," Comput. Sci. Div. Tech. Rep. UCB/Comput. Sci. Dep. 86/289, Univ. of California, Berkeley, Apr. 1986.

[11] D. W. Clark, "Cache performance in the VAX-11/780," *ACM Trans. Comput. Syst.*, vol. 1, no. 1, pp. 24–37, Feb. 1983.

[12] M. C. Easton and R. Fagin, "Cold-start versus warm-start miss ratios," *Commun. ACM*, vol. 21, no. 10, pp. 866–872, Oct. 1978.

[13] I. J. Haikala and P. H. Kutvonen, "Split cache organizations," CS Rep. C-1984-40., Univ. of Helsinki, Aug. 1984.

[14] M. D. Hill, DineroIII Documentation, Unpublished Unix-style Man Page, Univ. of California, Berkeley, October 1985.

[15] ——, "Aspects of cache memory and instruction buffer performance," Ph.D. dissertation, Comput. Sci. Div. Tech. Rep. UCB/Comput. Sci. Dep. 87/381, Univ. of California, Berkeley, Nov. 1987.

[16] ——, "A case for direct-mapped caches," *IEEE Comput. Mag.*, vol. 21, pp. 25–40, Dec. 1988.

[17] K. R. Kaplan and R. O. Winder, "Cache-based computer systems," *IEEE Comput. Mag.*, vol. 6, pp. 30–36, Mar. 1973.

[18] J. S. Liptay, "Structural aspects of the System/360 Model 85, Part II: The cache," *IBM Syst. J.*, vol. 7, no. 1, pp. 15–21, 1968.

[19] R. L. Mattson, J. Gecsei, D. R. Slutz, and I. L. Traiger, "Evaluation techniques for storage hierarchies," *IBM Syst. J.*, vol. 9, no. 2, pp. 78–117, 1970.

[20] R. L. Mattson, "Evaluation of multilevel memories," *IEEE Trans. Magn.*, vol. MAG-7, no. 4, pp. 814–819, Dec. 1971.

[21] F. Olken, "Efficient methods for calculating the success function of fixed space replacement policies," Masters Report, Lawrence Berkeley Laboratory LBL-12370, Univ. of California, Berkeley, May 1981.

[22] S. Przybylski, M. Horowitz, and J. Hennessy, "Performance tradeoffs in cache design," in *Proc. 15th Annu. Int. Symp. Comput. Architecture*, Honolulu, HI, June 1988, pp. 290–298.

[23] T. R. Puzak, "Analysis of cache replacement algorithms," unpublished Ph.D. dissertation, Dep. Elec. Comput. Eng., Univ. of Massachusetts, Feb. 1985.

[24] D. R. Slutz and I. L. Traiger, "Evaluation techniques for cache memory hierarchies," IBM Tech. Rep. RJ 1045 (#17547), May 1972.

[25] A. J. Smith, "Two methods for the efficient analysis of memory address trace data," *IEEE Trans. Software Eng.*, vol. SE-3, no. 1, pp. 94–101, Jan. 1977.

[26] ——, "A comparative study of set associative memory mapping algorithms and their use for cache and main memory," *IEEE Trans. Software Eng.*, vol. SE-4, pp. 121–130, Mar. 1978.

[27] ——, "Cache memories," *Comput. Surveys*, vol. 14, no. 3, pp. 473–530, Sept. 1982.

[28] A. J. Smith, "Cache evaluation and the impact of workload choice," in *Proc. 12th Int. Symp. Comput. Architecture*, June 1985, pp. 63–73.

[29] ——, "Bibliography and readings on CPU cache memories and related topics," *Comput. Architecture News*, Jan. 1986, pp. 22–42.

[30] ——, "Line (block) size choice for CPU caches," *IEEE Trans. Comput.*, vol. C-36, no. 9, pp. 1063–1075, Sept. 1987.

[31] J. E. Smith and J. R. Goodman, "Instruction cache replacement policies and organizations," *IEEE Trans. Comput.*, vol. C-34, pp. 234–241, Mar. 1985.

[32] W. D. Strecker, "Cache memories for PDP-11 family computers," in *Proc. 3rd Int. Symp. Comput. Architecture*, Jan. 1976, pp. 155–158.

[33] J. G. Thompson, "Efficient analysis of caching systems," Comput. Sci. Div. Tech. Rep. UCB/Comput. Sci. Dept. 87/374, Univ. of California, Berkeley, Oct. 1987.

[34] I. L. Traiger and D. R. Slutz, "One-pass techniques for the evaluation of memory hierarchies," IBM Tech. Rep. RJ 892 (#15563), July 1971.

Mark D. Hill (S'81–M'87) received the B.S.E. degree in computer engineering from the University of Michigan, Ann Arbor, in 1981, and the M.S. and Ph.D. degrees in computer science from the University of California, Berkeley, in 1983 and 1987, respectively.

He is currently an Assistant Professor in the Computer Sciences Department at the University of Wisconsin, Madison. While at U.C. Berkeley, he was a principal contributor to SPUR, a project that built a shared-bus multiprocessor. His research interests center on computer architecture, with an emphasis on performance considerations and implementation factors in memory systems.

Dr. Hill is a member of ACM and a 1989 recipient of the National Science Foundation's Presidential Young Investigator award.

Alan Jay Smith (S'73–M'74–SM'83–F'89) was born in New Rochelle, NY. He received the B.S. degree in electrical engineering from the Massachusetts Institute of Technology, Cambridge, and the M.S. and Ph.D. degrees in computer science from Stanford University, Stanford, CA, the latter in 1974.

He is currently a Professor in the Computer Science Division of the Department of Electrical Engineering and Computer Sciences, University of California, Berkeley, where he has been on the faculty since 1974, and was Vice Chairman of the EECS department from July 1982 to June 1984. His research interests include the analysis and modeling of computer systems and devices, computer architecture, and operating systems. He has published a large number of research papers, including one which won the IEEE Best Paper Award for the best paper in the IEEE TRANSACTIONS ON COMPUTERS in 1979. He also consults widely with computer and electronics companies.

Dr. Smith is a member of the Association for Computing Machinery, the Society for Industrial and Applied Mathematics, the Computer Measurement Group, Eta Kappa Nu, Tau Beta Pi, and Sigma Xi. He was chairman of the ACM Special Interest Group on Operating Systems (SIGOPS) from 1983 to 1987, was on the board of directors of the ACM Special Interst Group on Measurement and Evaluation (SIGMETRICS) from 1985 to 1989, was an ACM National Lecturer (1985–1986) and an IEEE Distinguished Visitor (1986–1987), is an Associate Editor of the *ACM Transactions on Computer Systems* (TOCS), a subject area editor of the *Journal of Parallel and Distributed Computing* and is on the editorial board of the *Journal of Microprocessors and Microsystems*. He was program chairman for the Sigmetrics '89/Performance '89 Conference.

A Characterization of Processor Performance in the VAX-11/780

Joel S. Emer

Digital Equipment Corp.
77 Reed Road
Hudson, MA 01749

Douglas W. Clark

Digital Equipment Corp.
295 Foster Street
Littleton, MA 01460

ABSTRACT

This paper reports the results of a study of VAX-11/780 processor performance using a novel hardware monitoring technique. A micro-PC histogram monitor was built for these measurements. It keeps a count of the number of microcode cycles executed at each microcode location. Measurement experiments were performed on live timesharing workloads as well as on synthetic workloads of several types. The histogram counts allow the calculation of the frequency of various architectural events, such as the frequency of different types of opcodes and operand specifiers, as well as the frequency of some implementation-specific events, such as translation buffer misses. The measurement technique also yields the amount of processing time spent in various activities, such as ordinary microcode computation, memory management, and processor stalls of different kinds. This paper reports in detail the amount of time the "average" VAX instruction spends in these activities.

1. INTRODUCTION

Processor performance is often assessed by benchmark speed, and sometimes by trace-driven studies of instruction execution; neither method can give the details of instruction timing, and neither can be applied to operating systems or to multiprocessing workloads. From the hardware designer's or the computer architect's point of view, these are serious limitations. A lack of detailed timing information impairs efforts to improve processor performance, and a dependence on user program behavior ignores the substantial contribution to system performance made by operating systems and by multi-processing effects.

In this paper we use a novel method to characterize VAX-11/780 processor performance under real timesharing workloads [13]. Our main goal is to attribute the time spent in instruction execution to the various activities a VAX instruction may engage in, such as operand fetching, waiting for cache and translation buffer misses, and unimpeded microcode execution. Another goal is to establish the frequency of occurrence of events important to performance, such as cache misses, branch instruction success, and memory operations. Throughout this paper we will report most results in frequency or time *per VAX instruction*. This provides a good characterization of the overall performance

effect of many architectural and implementation features.

Prior related work includes studies of opcode frequency and other features of instruction-processing [10, 11, 15, 16]; some studies report timing information as well [1, 4, 12].

After describing our methods and workloads in Section 2, we will report the frequencies of various processor events in Sections 3 and 4. Section 5 presents the complete, detailed timing results, and Section 6 concludes the paper.

2. DEFINITIONS AND METHODS

2.1 VAX-11/780 Structure

The 11/780 processor is composed of two major subsystems: the CPU pipeline, and the memory subsystem. These subsystems and their constituent components are illustrated in Figure 1. The CPU pipeline is responsible for most of the actual instruction execution, and as is shown, consists of three stages. The operation of the CPU pipeline may be most easily understood by noting that VAX instructions are composed of an opcode followed by zero to six *operand specifiers*, which describe the data operands required by the instruction. The 11/780 implementation of the VAX architecture breaks the execution of an instruction into a sequence of operations that correspond to the accessing of the data operands of the instruction and then its execution. In general these operations correspond to the tasks that flow down the CPU pipeline.

The individual stages of the CPU pipeline are: the *I-Fetch* stage, which sequentially fetches the instruction stream into the Instruction Buffer or IB; the *I-Decode* stage, which takes instruction bytes from the IB and decodes an opcode and/or specifier, determines a microcode dispatch address for the EBOX, and extracts additional specifier information that is used by the EBOX; and the *EBOX* stage, which is a microcoded function unit that does most of the actual work associated with fetching operands and executing instructions. In fact, the EBOX and the I-Decode stages are very tightly coupled, so that I-Decode operations only take place under specific control of the EBOX. The first I-Decode for an instruction cannot occur until the previous instruction has been competed, so the EBOX

FIGURE 1

VAX-11/780 Block Diagram

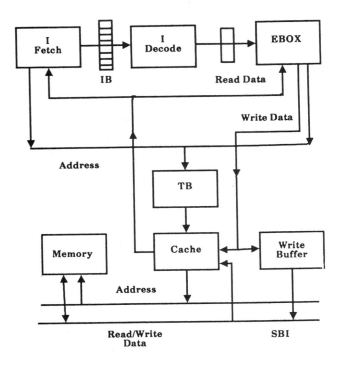

experiences a single non-overlapped I-Decode operation cycle for each instruction.

The EBOX can perform a number of autonomous operations, such as arithmetic and boolean computations; it can command the I-Fetch unit to start fetching at the target of a branch instruction; it can command reads and writes of memory data; and as a stage of the CPU pipeline, it can branch to a microinstruction location determined by the I-Decode stage. In this final instance it may have to wait as a result of a pipeline delay if the I-Decode stage has not yet been able to compute the desired location. We will call this delay an *IB stall*.

As the EBOX contains the microcode and does the majority of the instruction computation, we will be focusing mainly on its activity. We use the EBOX microinstruction time of 200 nanoseconds as the definition of a *cycle*.

In the process of instruction execution by the CPU pipeline, both the I-Fetch and EBOX stages may make references to memory. In order to support the virtual memory of the VAX these references must first pass through a *translation buffer*, or *TB*, where the virtual address generated by the CPU is translated into a physical address. A successful translation is called a TB *hit*, and conversely a failed translation is called a TB *miss*. In the event of a TB miss for an EBOX reference, a microcode interrupt is asserted and a microcode routine is invoked which inserts the desired translation into the TB. In the event of a TB miss for an I-Fetch reference, a flag is

set; when the EBOX finds insufficient data bytes in the IB to do a desired decode, it recognizes that the flag is set and again goes about the task of putting the appropriate translation into the TB.

After successful translation by the TB, the physical address that was generated is used to access the *data cache*. Just as with the TB, we can have cache hits and misses. In the case of a read hit, data is simply passed back to the requesting unit. In the case of a read miss, a reference is made over the backplane bus, called the *SBI* for *Synchronous Backplane Interconnect*, to fetch the data from memory into the cache and to forward it to the requesting unit. During the time the data is being read from memory on behalf of an EBOX request the EBOX itself is *read stalled* waiting for the data, while during I-Fetch requests the EBOX is free to run unimpeded unless it too needs data from memory. A read operation which results in a hit in both the TB and cache consumes one cycle.

Only the EBOX is capable of doing data writes, and the 11/780 implements a *write-through* memory scheme in which all data writes are passed through to the memory via the SBI. Just as with reads, the TB is used to generate a physical address for the reference. In order to avoid waiting for the write to complete in memory the 11/780 provides a 4-byte *write buffer*. Thus it takes one cycle for the EBOX to initiate a write and then it continues microcode execution, which will be held up in the future only if another write request is made before the last one completed. The delay caused when a write encounters another write in progress is called a *write stall*. In addition, during a data write, the cache is accessed to update its contents with the data being written. Note, however, that if the write access misses, the cache is not updated.

2.2 Methods: Micro-PC Histogram Technique

Our measurements were collected with a special purpose hardware monitor that enabled us to create histograms of microcode execution in the 11/780 processor. This uPC monitor consists of a general purpose histogram count board, which has 16,000 addressable count locations (or histogram buckets), and is capable of incrementing the count in a selected location at the microcode execution rate of the 780. A processor-specific interface board was also required. It provided the address of a histogram count bucket and control lines to signal when a count should be made. For these experiments the interface board addressed a distinct histogram bucket for each microcode location in the processor's control store, and a count was taken for each microinstruction executed.

The histogram collection board was designed as a Unibus device, and Unibus commands can be used to start and stop data collection, as well as to clear and read the histogram count buckets. Coincidentally, since the 11/780 has a Unibus, the histogram collection monitor could be installed directly on the system being measured, obviating the cost and nuisance of using a second machine for the hardware monitor. This was a further convenience as the data collected was immediately available on a machine of sufficient capacity to do the data reduction. Note, however, that while actually monitoring microcode execution, the data collection hardware is totally passive, causing no Unibus activity and having no effect on the execution of programs on the system. Thus this technique yields measurements of *all system activity at full speed.*

The capacity of the counters on the histogram collection board were sufficient to collect data for 1 to 2 hours of heavy processing on the CPU.

Since much of the activity in the 11/780 processor is under the direct command of microcode functions, the frequency of many events can be determined through examination of the relative execution counts of various microinstructions.The uPC histogram data is especially useful, since it forms a general resource from which the answers to many questions concerning the operation of the 11/780 running the same workload can be obtained simply by doing additional interpretation of the raw histogram data.

One disadvantage of this method of hardware monitoring lies in the fact that certain hardware events are not visible to the microcode. For example, the counts of instruction stream memory references are not available, because they are made by a distinct portion of the processor not under direct control of the microcode. Another is that to save microcode space, the microprogrammers frequently shared microinstructions; in such cases we cannot usually distinguish the sharers. A third disadvantage of this measurement technique is that the analysis produces only average behavior characterizations of the processor over the measurement interval, since no measures of the variation of the statistics during the measurement are collected.

The uPC histogram measurements were taken in two different experimental settings: live timesharing, and synthetic workloads. The live timesharing measurements were taken from two different machines within Digital engineering. The first machine belonged to the research group, and was used for general timesharing and some performance data analysis. Its workload consisted of such things as text-editing, program development, and electronic mail. It was relatively lightly loaded during the measurement interval, with approximately 15 users logged in.

The second timesharing measurements were taken from a machine being used by a group in the initial stages of development of a VAX CPU. The load on this machine consisted of the same type of general purpose timesharing as in the first experiment, with the addition of some circuit simulation and microcode development. This machine had a heavier load with approximately 30 users logged in during the measurement interval.

Although realistic, these live timesharing workloads are difficult to characterize and are not repeatable, since the computational load varies greatly over time. A second experimental setting addressed this problem. In it, a Remote Terminal Emulator or RTE [7, 14] provided a real-time

simulation of a number of timesharing users connected to the VAX. The RTE is a PDP-11 with many asynchronous terminal interfaces; output characters generated by the RTE from canned user scripts are seen as terminal input characters by the VAX, and vice versa. Three RTE-generated workloads were measured: an educational environment, with 40 simulated users doing program development in various languages and some file manipulation; a scientific/engineering environment, with 40 simulated users doing scientific computation and program development; and a commercial transaction-processing environment, with 32 simulated users doing transactional database inquiries and updates.

All five experiments lasted about one hour. In this paper we will report results for the *composite* of all five, that is, the sum of the five uPC histograms.

The VMS operating system (version 2) [5, 9] was used in all our experiments. The VMS Null process, which runs when the system is idle, was excluded from measurement because its trivial code structure (branch to self, awaiting an interrupt) would bias all per-instruction statistics in proportion to the idleness of the system.

All of the VAXes had Floating Point Accelerators, and all had 8 Megabytes of memory.

3. ARCHITECTURAL EVENTS

An *architectural event* is an event that would occur in any implementation of the VAX architecture; an *implementation event* is one whose occurrence depends on the particular implementation of that architecture. Thus, for example, a data-stream memory read is usually an architectural event, but a consequent cache miss is an implementation event. We discuss the former here, and the latter in Section 4.

We will need to make certain assumptions about all VAX implementations for this distinction to be valid. We assume, for the purposes of our discussion, that:

o   All VAX implementations have 32-bit data paths to the closest level of the memory hierarchy (usually the cache). Since the VAX is a 32-bit architecture, this is a very minor restriction. This allows us to count architectural memory references by measuring hardware references in the 11/780 implementation.

o   All VAX implementations experience the same rate of operating system events. This allows us to treat instruction frequency as an architectural concern, ignoring the fact that an increased rate of, say, page faults would increase the frequency of instructions in the page fault routine.

3.1 Opcodes

VAX opcode frequency has been reported and discussed in other papers [4, 15]. The uPC method cannot distinguish all opcodes in the 11/780. The predominant reason for this is that hardware is used for the implementation of some opcode-specific functions. For example, integer add and subtract instructions use the same microcode, with the ALU control field determined by hardware that looks at the opcode.

We can, however, report the frequency of *groups* of opcodes. Table 1 shows this for our composite workload. The following observation about this table is by now almost a cliché: moves, branches, and simple instructions account for most instruction executions. It will turn out, however, that some of the rarer, more complex instructions are responsible for a great deal of the memory references and processing time; this point has also been made before [12]. Note that VAX *subroutine* linkage is quite simple, involving only a push or pop of the PC together with a jump; *procedure* linkage is more complex, involving considerable state saving and restoring on the stack [6, 13].

A particularly interesting opcode-oriented performance measure is the frequency of PC-changing instructions and the proportion of conditional branches that actually do branch. In Table 2 below we show these figures for the composite workload. The upper section of the table consists of members of the SIMPLE group of Table 1. Because of microcode-sharing, two unconditional branches (BRB and BRW) are grouped with simple conditional branches. We believe from other measurements that these are about 2 percent of all instructions, leaving about 17 percent due to true conditional branches. The remaining rows are the PC-changing instructions from the FIELD, CALL/RET and SYSTEM instruction groups.

PC-changing instructions are quite common, accounting for almost 40 percent of all instructions executed in the composite workload. Furthermore, the proportion of these that actually change the PC is also quite high. Both properties are in line with other measurements of such instructions, both in the VAX and other architectures. Note that about 9 out of 10 loop branches actually branched. Therefore the average number of iterations of all loops that used these instructions was about 10.

3.2 Operand Specifiers

VAX instructions specify the location of their data through one or more encoded *operand specifiers* that follow the opcode in the I-stream. These indicate, for example, whether a read operand is to be found in a register, or in memory addressed by a register, or with a variety of other addressing modes [6, 13]. The *data type* (byte, longword, floating-point, etc.) and *access mode* (read, modify, write, etc.) of an operand specifier are defined by the instruction that uses it. Branch displacements are considered separately.

In the 11/780 microcode, all access to scalar data, and to the addresses of non-scalar data, are done by specifier microcode. We thus consider the reading and writing of scalar data, and the address

TABLE 1

Opcode Group Frequency

Group name	Constituents	Frequency (Percent)
SIMPLE	Move instructions Simple arith. operations Boolean operations Simple and loop branches Subroutine call and return	83.60
FIELD	Bit field operations	6.92
FLOAT	Floating point Integer multiply/divide	3.62
CALL/RET	Procedure call and return Multi-register push and pop	3.22
SYSTEM	Privileged operations Context switch instructions Sys. serv. requests and return Queue manipulation Protection probe instructions	2.11
CHARACTER	Char. string instructions	0.43
DECIMAL	Decimal instructions	0.03

TABLE 2

PC-Changing Instructions

Branch Type	Percent of Inst.	Percent that branch	Act. branch as percent of all inst.
Simple cond., plus BRB, BRW	19.3	56	10.9
Loop branches	4.1	91	3.7
Low-bit tests	2.0	41	0.8
Subroutine call and return	4.5	100	4.5
Unconditional (JMP)	0.3	100	0.3
Case branch (CASEx)	0.9	100	0.9
Bit branches	4.3	44	1.9
Procedure call and return	2.4	100	2.4
System branches (CHMx, REI)	0.4	100	0.4
TOTAL	38.5	67	25.7

calculation of non-scalar data, to be associated with operand specifier processing and not with the instruction itself. A simple integer Move, for example, is accomplished entirely by specifier microcode: first a read, then a write.

The 11/780 specifier-processing microcode allows us to distinguish first specifiers, called *SPEC1* (those that directly follow the opcode) from all other specifiers, called *SPEC2-6*. It also lets us count PC-relative *branch displacements*, which appear in the last specifier position of certain PC-changing instructions. Not all PC-changing instructions use branch displacements: some determine their targets with ordinary operand specifiers (e.g., JMP, CALLS), while others determine their targets implicitly (e.g., RSB, RET, REI).

Table 3 shows the number of specifiers and branch displacements per average VAX instruction.

Table 4 shows the frequency of operand specifier types. Because of microcode-sharing, we are able to report the individual frequencies of the various types of memory-referencing specifiers only in the total column. Memory-referencing specifiers can optionally be indexed: the percentage of all specifiers that are indexed is shown in the bottom line of the table.

Register mode is the most common addressing mode, especially in specifiers after the first. Since the last specifier is generally the destination of the instruction's result (if not a branch), this probably reflects a tendency to store results in registers. The encoded short literal, in which a single byte is expanded to one of a small number of values whose data type is instruction-dependent, is also quite common, particularly as the first specifier. We note the scarcity of *immediate* data ((PC)+), the other method of supplying I-stream constants to the instruction. Short literals apparently do this job fairly well.

The most common memory specifier is displacement off a register. Other results [15] suggest that the displacement is most often a byte, less often a 4-byte longword, and least often a word. Index mode is surprisingly common; 6.3 percent of all specifiers were indexed.

The average number of specifiers per instruction in the composite workload is 1.48 (remember that this does not include branch displacements).

3.3 Memory Operations

3.3.1 Data

Operand-specifier processing accounts for a majority of the D-stream memory operations performed on the VAX. Most other reads and writes are due to the manipulation of non-scalar data such

TABLE 3

Specifiers and Branch Displacements per Average Instruction

First specifiers	0.726
Other specifiers	0.758
Branch displacements	0.312

TABLE 4

Operand specifier distribution (percent)

		SPEC1	SPEC2-6	Total
Register	R	28.7	52.6	41.0
Short Literal	#n	21.1	10.8	15.8
Immediate	(PC)+	3.2	1.7	2.4
Displacement	D(R)			25.0
Reg. Deferred	(R)			9.2
Auto-inc.	(R)+			2.1
Disp. Deferred	@D(R)	47.0	34.9	2.7
Absolute	@(PC)+			0.6
Auto-inc.def.	@(R)+			0.3
Auto-dec.	-(R)			0.9
Percent Indexed	[R]	8.5	4.2	6.3

as character strings and stack frames. Table 5 reports the frequency of read and write operations per average instruction, broken down by the source of the operation. After specifiers, procedure call and return instructions, which push and pop registers on and off the stack, account for the greatest portion of reads and writes.

Because the results are in terms of events *per average instruction*, the number of reads reported for the CALL/RET group, for example, is *not* the average number of reads executed by the average CALL/RET instruction. Rather, it is the number of CALL/RET reads averaged over *all* instruction executions. Put another way, it is the number of CALL/RET reads weighted by the frequency of occurence of instructions in the CALL/RET group. This way of looking at the data directly measures the contribution of the various instruction groups to overall performance.

Overall, the ratio of reads to writes is about two to one. Some of these references are to 32-bit longwords that are *unaligned* with respect to the physical organization of the cache, and that therefore require two physical references. The frequency of

TABLE 5

D-stream Reads and Writes per Average Instruction

	Reads	Writes
Spec1	.306	.000
Spec2-6	.148	.161
Simple	.029	.033
Field	.049	.007
Float	.000	.008
Call/Ret	.133	.130
System	.015	.014
Character	.039	.046
Decimal	.002	.001
Other	.062	.008
TOTAL	.783	.409

TABLE 6

Estimated Size of Average Instruction

Object	Number per inst	Est. Size	Est. Size per inst.
Opcode	1.00	1.00	1.00
Specifiers	1.48	1.68	2.49
Branch disp.	0.31	1.00	0.31
TOTAL			3.8

TABLE 7

Interrupt and Context-Switch Headway

Event	Instruction headway
Software Interrupt Requests	2539
Hardware and Software Interrupts	637
Context Switches	6418

unaligned D-stream references is very low: 0.016 per instruction in the composite workload.

3.3.2 Instructions

Many memory reads are due to instruction fetching, but it is difficult to characterize this in a strictly architectural way. Different organizations of the I-stream prefetching hardware can have very different streams of references to memory. The only truly architectural feature of the I-stream references is the *size* of the instructions. The average size of an operand specifier can be calculated from Table 3, together with displacement figures (byte, word, longword) from [15], and is 1.68 bytes. The average instruction has one byte of opcode, some number of specifiers, and some fractional number of branch displacements. Table 6 puts all of this together to show that the average size of a VAX instruction in our workload was 3.8 bytes.

3.4 Other Events

Two other interesting architectural events are interrupts and context switches. The latter are accomplished by the save-process-context and load-process-context instructions (SVPCTX and LDPCTX). In VMS these are used only for a switch from one user process to another; interrupts, in particular, do not cause context switches. The frequency of these events is shown in Table 7. For ease of understanding we invert our usual metric and report these in terms of the average instruction *headway* between events. VMS sometimes services hardware interrupts by chaining together several successively lower-priority software interrupts. Table 7 includes the headway between requests for software interrupts.

The context-switch figure is useful in setting the "flush" interval in cache and translation buffer simulations. The impact of context switching on VAX Translation Buffer performance is discussed in [3].

4. IMPLEMENTATION EVENTS

By an implementation event we mean an event whose occurrence depends on the particular implementation of the VAX architecture. A cache miss is an example; whether a memory reference hits or misses in the cache depends on the size and configuration--indeed, even the *presence*--of the cache in a particular implementation of the architecture.

4.1 I-stream References

The 11/780's Instruction Buffer or IB makes its I-stream referencing behavior implementation-specific. The 8-byte IB makes a cache reference whenever one or more bytes are empty. When the requested longword arrives possibly much later, if there was a cache miss the IB accepts as many bytes as it has room for then. Thus the IB can make repeated references (as many as four) to the same longword, but this is clearly not a requirement of the architecture.

Because the IB is controlled by hardware, the uPC histogram technique cannot count IB references. But in our earlier cache study [2] we found that the average number of cache references by the IB per VAX instruction was around 2.2, for three day-long measurements of live timesharing workloads.

Since the average VAX instruction is 3.8 bytes long (Table 6), we conclude that those 2.2 references yielded on average 3.8 bytes, for an average delivery *per reference* of 1.7 bytes.

4.2 Cache And Translation Buffer Misses

The 11/780 cache is controlled by hardware, so the frequency of cache misses is not measurable with the uPC technique. Our earlier cache study, however, found that in live timesharing workloads the number of cache read misses per instruction was 0.28, with 0.18 due to the I-stream and 0.10 due to the D-stream. The performance cost of these misses is microcode *stalls*, which are discussed below.

The virtual-to-physical address Translation Buffer, on the other hand, is controlled by microcode, and is therefore directly visible with the uPC technique. A TB miss results in a microcode trap to a miss service micro-routine. Entries to this routine indicate occurrences of TB misses, and a count of all cycles within the routine yields the time spent handling TB misses.

The TB miss rate for the composite workload was 0.029 misses per instruction, 0.020 from the D-stream and 0.009 from the I-stream. The average number of cycles used to service a miss was 21.6, of which 3.5 were read stalls due to the requested page-table entry not being in the cache. See [3] for more information on the performance of the VAX-11/780 TB.

4.3 Stalls

A *stall* occurs when a microcode request cannot yet be satisfied by the hardware. The result is one or more cycles of suspended execution until the reason for the stall goes away. As described in Section 2.1, there are three types of stall in the VAX-11/780: read stall, write stall, and IB stall.

A read stall occurs when there is a cache miss on a D-stream read. The requesting microinstruction simply waits for the data to arrive. In the simplest case (no concurrent memory activity of other types) this takes 6 cycles on the 11/780. Cache hits cause no stalls.

A write will stall if attempted less than 6 cycles after the previous write (in the simplest case). VAX instructions that do many writes, such as character-string moves, are sometimes microprogrammed to reduce write stalls by writing only in every sixth cycle.

The last type of stall, IB stall, occurs when the IB does not contain enough bytes to satisfy the microcode's request. This can occur at any point in I-stream processing, including the initial decode of the opcode, specifier decodes, and requests for literal or immediate data. Note that IB stall does not occur in direct response to an IB cache miss; only when the empty byte is actually needed by the microcode can stall occur, and by then the cache miss may have finished.

The occurrence and duration of all three types of stalls are implementation-specific characteristics of the VAX-11/780. The duration, but not the frequency of occurrence of all three can be measured with the uPC technique. The histogram board actually contains two sets of counts, one for non-stalled microinstructions, and one for read- or write-stalled microinstructions. If the microinstruction at address X does a cache read, then the non-stalled count at location X will contain the actual number of successful reads done by that microinstruction, while the stalled count at location X will contain the total number of cycles in which that microinstruction was stalled. Write stalls and read stalls are differentiated by whether the microinstruction does a read or a write (it cannot do both).

IB stalls are handled in a slightly different way. Requests for bytes from the IB result in microcode dispatches; decoding hardware maps the IB contents into various dispatch microaddresses, one of which indicates that there were insufficient bytes in the IB. The number of executions of the microinstruction at that microaddress is the number of cycles with IB stall.

5. TIME: CYCLES PER INSTRUCTION

The great strength of the uPC histogram technique is its ability to classify every processor cycle and thus to establish the durations of processor events. Table 8 shows the number of cycles per average instruction, arranged in two orthogonal dimensions. The first dimension (rows) represents the stages of an instruction's execution: its initial Decode; then its operand specifier and branch displacement processing; then its execute phase; and finally several *overhead* activities.

Instruction decode, as discussed in Section 2.1 above, takes exactly one EBOX cycle, but may stall if there are insufficient bytes in the IB.

Operand specifier processing consists of address calculation for memory specifiers, and the actual read and/or write of data for both memory and register specifiers, provided the data is scalar. Branch displacement processing consists of the calculation of the branch target address, which requires one cycle. An additional cycle is consumed in the execute phase of the instruction to redirect the IB to fetch down the target stream.

The execute phase of an instruction consists of those microcycles associated with an instruction's actual computation. Table 8 reports these results by opcode group as defined in Table 1.

The overhead activities are not associated with any particular instruction. They include interrupts and exceptions (Int/Except), memory management and alignment microcode (Mem Mgmt), and abort cycles (one for each microcode trap and one for each microcode patch).

The second dimension of Table 8 (columns) classifies microinstruction execution into one of six

TABLE 8

Average VAX Instruction Timing (Cycles per Instruction)

	Compute	Read	R-Stall	Write	W-Stall	IB-Stall	Total
Decode	1.000					0.613	1.613
Spec1	0.895	0.306	0.364				1.565
Spec2-6	1.052	0.148	0.116	0.161	0.192	0.102	1.771
B-Disp	0.221					0.005	0.226
Simple	0.870	0.029	0.017	0.033	0.027		0.977
Field	0.482	0.049	0.058	0.007	0.002		0.600
Float	0.292	0.000	0.000	0.008	0.001		0.302
Call/Ret	0.937	0.133	0.074	0.130	0.184		1.458
System	0.434	0.015	0.031	0.014	0.028		0.522
Character	0.318	0.039	0.099	0.046	0.004		0.506
Decimal	0.026	0.002	0.000	0.001	0.002		0.031
Int/Except	0.055	0.002	0.005	0.004	0.006		0.071
Mem Mngmt	0.555	0.061	0.200	0.004	0.003		0.824
Abort	0.127						0.127
TOTAL	7.267	0.783	0.964	0.409	0.450	0.720	10.593

categories. The "Compute" category represents autonomous EBOX operations, that is, microinstructions that do no memory references. The other categories are memory references and the various types of stall. On the 11/780 the six categories are mutually exclusive, so times in the individual categories can be summed, yielding the TOTAL column of Table 8.

With some minor exceptions† every microcycle in 11/780 execution falls into exactly one row and exactly one column. The numbers reported in Table 8 are the numbers of cycles spent at each row/column intersection, divided by the number of VAX instructions executed. They are therefore the numbers of cycles per average instruction for each category. The row and column totals allow analysis of a single dimension: for example, in the average instruction of 10.6 cycles, a (column) total of 0.96 cycles were lost in read stall, and a (row) total of 0.30 cycles were spent in floating-point execution.

Table 8 shows where 11/780 performance may be improved, and where it may not be improved. For example, saving the non-overlapped Decode cycle could save one cycle on each non-PC-changing instruction. (The later VAX model 11/750 did this.)

----

†Two remarks on the operand-specifier portion of Table 8 are necessary. First, the 11/780 has special hardware to optimize the execution of certain instructions with literal or register operands. In these cases the first cycle of execution is combined with the last cycle of specifier processing. We report such cycles in the specifier rows of Table 8; they amounted to 0.15 cycles per instruction for the SIMPLE group and 0.01 cycles per instruction for the FIELD group. The second remark concerns the treatment of first specifiers that are indexed. Microcode sharing forces use to report the calculation of the base address in the SPEC2-6 category. We extimate that this causes about 0.06 cycles per instruction belonging to SPEC1 to be reported in SPEC2-6.

On the other hand, optimizing FIELD memory writes will have a payoff of at most 0.007 cycles per instruction, or only about 0.07 percent of total performance.

A number of other observations can be made based on Table 8:

o   The average VAX instruction in this composite workload takes a little more than 10 cycles. This makes the numbers in Table 8 easily intepretable as percentages of the total time per instruction.

o   The TOTAL column shows that almost half of all the time went into decode and specifier processing, counting their stalls.

o   The opcode group with the greatest contribution is the CALL/RET group, despite its low frequency (see Table 1).

o   The execution phase of the SIMPLE instructions, which constitute 84 percent of all instruction executions (Table 1), accounts for only about 10 percent of the time in the composite workload.

o   System and Character instructions, though rare (Table 1), also make noticeable contributions to performance.

o   Most IB stalls occur on the initial specifier decode, rather than on subsequent specifier decodes. Although there are more bytes in the initial decode then the subsequent decodes, we interpret this to mean that most IB stall is incurred on cache misses at the target reference of a branch.

o   We note that there are fewer cycles of compute in B-DISP than there are branch displacements (see Table 3), because the branch displacement need

TABLE 9

Cycles per instruction Within Each Group

	Compute	Read	R-Stall	Write	W-Stall	Total
Simple	1.04	0.03	0.02	0.04	0.03	1.17
Field	6.97	0.71	0.85	0.11	0.04	8.67
Float	8.07	0.00	0.00	0.23	0.03	8.33
Call/Ret	29.08	4.14	2.29	4.03	5.71	45.25
System	20.59	0.71	1.47	0.67	1.30	24.74
Character	73.51	8.97	22.83	10.76	0.97	117.04
Decimal	84.37	5.64	1.59	3.94	5.24	100.77

not be computed when the instruction does not branch.

A comparison of the Read and Read-Stall columns of Table 8 yields another set of observations:

o Stalled cycles are half the number of operation cycles in the CALL/RET group, but more than twice the number of operation cycles in the Character group. This is presumably due to the good cache locality of the stack and the relatively poor locality of character strings.

o Memory management has more than 3 times as many read-stalled cycles as reads. This largely reflects the tendency of references to Page Table Entries to miss in the cache.

Comparing Write and Write-stall columns yields several more observations:

o The CALL/RET group generates a large amount of write stalls. This is due to the write-through cache and the one-longword write butter, which force the CALL instruction to stall while pushing the caller's state onto the stack.

o Character instructions have little write stall, because as mentioned earlier, the microcode was explictly written to avoid write stalls.

Table 9 shows the number of cycles per average instruction *within each group*, exclusive of specifier decode and processing, and *not* weighted by frequency of occurence. For example, the average instruction in the Decimal group did 84 cycles of Compute and took 101 cycles overall.

Table 9 illustrates a number of interesting properties:

o The computation associated with the average simple instruction is quite simple: a little over one cycle is all that it needs.

o However, the range of cycle time requirements of average representatives of these groups covers two orders of magnitude.

o With around 4 reads and writes per average CALL/RET or PUSHR/POPR instruction we conclude that about 8 registers are being pushed and popped.

o The average character instruction reads and writes 9 to 11 longwords, so the average size of a character string is 36-44 characters.

6. CONCLUSION

We have presented detailed instruction timing results for the VAX-11/780, evaluated under a timesharing workload. These results are, of course, dependent on the characteristics of that workload.

The uPC histogram method has provided a great deal of useful data, showing precisely the impact of architectural and implementation characteristics on average processor performance. The generation of a uPC histogram provides the analyst with a database from which many performance characteristics can be determined. These analyses are particularly useful because they are all derived from the same workload.

ACKNOWLEDGMENTS

We would like to thank Garth Wiebe and Jean Hsiao for their assistance with the uPC histogram monitor development.

REFERENCES

[1]   Alpert, D. Carberry, D., Yamamura, M.,Chow, Y., and Mak, P32-bit Processor Chip Integrates Major System Functions. *Electronics 56*, 14 (July 14, 1983), pp. 113-119.

[2]   Clark, D.W. Cache Performance in the VAX-11/780. *ACM TOCS 1*, 1 (Feb. 1983), pp. 24-37.

[3]   Clark, D.W. and Emer, J.S. Performance of the VAX-11/780 Translation Buffer: Simulation and Measurement. Submitted for publication, Nov. 1983.

[4]   Clark, D.W. and Levy, H.M., Measurement and Analysis of Instruction Use in the VAX-11/780. *Proc. 9th Annual Symp. on Comp. Arch.*, Austin, April 1982, pp. 9-17.

[5]   Digital Equipment Corp. VAX/VMS Internals and Data Structures. Document No. AA-K785A-TE, Digital Equipment Corp., Maynard, MA.

[6]   Digital Equipment Corp. *VAX-11 Architecture Reference Manual*. Document No. EK-VAXAR-RM-001, Digital Euipment Corp., Maynard, MA, May 1982.

[7]   Greenbaum, H.J. A Simulator of Multiple Interactive Users to Drive a Time-Shared Computer System. M.S. Thesis, MIT Project MAC report MAR-TR-54, Oct.1968.

[8]   Huck, J.C. *Comparative Analysis of Computer Architectures*. Ph.D. thesis, TR No. 83-243, Computer Systems Lab., Stanford, May 1983.

[9]   Levy, H.M., and Eckhouse, R.H. Computer Programming and Architecture: The VAX-11. Digital Press, Bedford, MA, 1980.

[10]   Lunde, A. Empirical Evaluation of Some Features of Instruction Set Processor Architectures. *CACM 20*, 3 (March 1977), 143-153.

[11]   McDaniel, G. An Analysis of a Mesa Instruction Set Using Dynamic Instruction Frequencies. *Symposium on Architectural Support for Programming Languages and Operating Systems*, Palo Alto, CA, March 1982, pp. 167-176.

[12]   Peuto, B.L., and Shustek, L.J. An Instruction Timing Model of CPU Performance. *Proc. 4th Annual Symp. on Computer Architecture*, 1977, pp. 165-178.

[13]   Strecker, W.D., VAX-11/780--A Virtual Address Extension for the PDP-11 Family Computers. *Proc. NCC*, AFIPS Press, Montvale, N.J., 1978.

[14]   Watkins, S.W., and Abrams, M.D. Survey of Remote Terminal Emulators. NBS Special Publication 500-4, April 1977.

[15]   Wiecek, C.A. A Case Study of VAX-11 Instruction Set Usage for Compiler Execution. *Symposium on Architectural Support for Programming Languages and Operating Systems*, Palo Alto, CA, March 1982, pp. 177-184.

[16]   Winder,. R.O. A Data Base for Computer Performance Evaluation. IEEE Computer 6, 3. (March 1973), pp. 25-29.

Instruction Sets

3.1 Introduction

The instruction set has long enjoyed a prominent role in computer architecture. Being the interface between hardware and software, the design of an instruction set is influenced by both hardware and software issues and is at the center of most hardware versus software debates. Perhaps more than any other aspect of computer architecture, issues in the design of an instruction set have gone through cycles as hardware and software have evolved. And the temptation to solve the "problem of the day" using the instruction set has always been strong.

The instruction set defines the *architecture* of the computer, that is, its functionality. This includes the operations it performs, the storage (registers and memory) it can address, and how the operations are specified and encoded. This functionality is then *implemented* in a given technology. The same functionality can be implemented in a variety of ways and in a variety of technologies, with different cost/performance attributes, and at different times.

To be successful, an architecture must live across several implementations that all maintain the same functionality; otherwise, every new generation will require new software. This becomes even more important as the installed base increases and becomes more diverse. The challenge for a computer architect is to define a functionality that can span multiple implementation generations yet solve current problems in an efficient manner. This is a difficult task, because defining functionality for future generations requires knowledge about future implementation techniques (especially future microarchitectures), which are unknown. The natural tendency is to focus on more short-term problems (i.e., current problems and problems on the horizon). More often than not, architects have used the instruction set to solve the problem of the day, only to have the solution return as a problem in a later generation.

3.2 Historical Evolution

The evolution of instruction sets is closely tied to the evolution of technology used to implement them. In the early days of computers, implementation resources were at a premium, and it was not practical to spend too many resources on control. Control was hardwired, and this implied instruction sets that could easily be implemented with hardwired control—other issues were secondary.

The 1960s saw the widespread adoption of micro-programming as a means for implementing control. Before microprogrammed control, the complexity and hardware cost of a machine were intimately tied to the semantics of the instruction set. With microprogrammed control, the complexity of implementing the control hardware was somewhat divorced from the specifics of an instruction set: The same basic control hardware could be used to interpret and control different instruction sets with changes required perhaps only in the control microprogram. Alternately, the same instruction set could be implemented with different microarchitectures with varying cost-performance criteria, allowing for families of machines with different cost/performance, all running the same instruction set.

The use of microprogrammed control became pervasive in the 1960s and 1970s—only a few high-end machines, such as the machines built by Control Data Corporation (CDC), used hardwired control. With implementation complexity of an instruction set essentially removed from the picture (with microprogrammed control, the implementation complexity of significantly different instructions sets was not significantly different), architects turned to other parameters that influenced the design of instruction sets. Two of the other important parameters were ease of programming in a given instruction set and memory requirements.

In the 1960s and 1970s, compilers were still in their infancy, and the instruction set was viewed as a target for a human programmer, not for a compiler. It was natural to design instruction sets that were considered easier to program in. One measure of "ease" considered important by some architects was the "proximity" of an instruction set to a high-level language (HLL),—the rationale being that this proximity would facilitate translation from a HLL to assembly language (either manually or automatically) [9]. There was also a sentiment that different HLLs required different instruction set support. And the ease with which microprogrammable control allowed new instructions to be added to a machine architecture did little to discourage this sentiment.

Another issue that greatly influenced instruction set design was the memory requirements of a program and the processor-memory traffic generated when executing a program. Memory sizes were quite small (tens to hundreds of kilobytes), and caches were not in widespread use. Small memory sizes meant that programs should be small, and this meant that instructions sets should be highly encoded—specifying a sequence of operations with one instruction might result in a smaller program than specifying the same sequence of operations with multiple instructions. Furthermore, without caches (or with very small caches), instructions would need to be fetched from memory, and the rate at which this transfer of information could take place would limit the rate at which instruction processing could be carried out. Because processor-memory bandwidth was at a premium, the solution was to have highly encoded instructions that would minimize the required processor-memory bandwidth.

The above parameters led to the development of highly encoded instruction sets that were intended to be interpreted by microcoded engines; these instruction sets are commonly referred to as complex (or CISC) instruction sets today. Technological advancements in the late 1970s and early 1980s again changed the landscape for instruction sets. Two important technological changes were advances in compilers and the advent of very large scale integration (VLSI).

With advances in compilers, instruction sets started to become a target for compilers and not for assembly language programmers. This shifted the balance toward "elemental" instructions, that is, instructions that were composed of simple operations and provided primitives from which solutions could be built. More complex instructions, consisting of a collection of operations, that may have been easier for humans to program in, weren't necessarily easy for a compiler to use; this required the compiler to recognize situations that matched the exact pattern of operations in a complex instruction. Because it was easier for a compiler to generate code for a desired task as a sequence of primitive operations rather than use a complex instruction that matched the specific situation (see a discussion of this in [15]), compilers routinely avoided using the more complex instructions when they compiled programs. Evidence mounted that the more complex instructions in an architecture that provided them were not being used. (This evidence was later quantified by several experimental studies, such as [2,14].) And if a complex instruction wasn't going to be used in programs, what was the point of having it?

In the early 1980s, VLSI technology allowed sufficient hardware resources for an integer processor (with reasonably straightforward hardwired control) to be built as a single chip. On-chip processing could be carried out reasonably efficiently, but going off-chip incurred a significant penalty (the processor-memory bandwidth problem of previous generation now manifested as an on-chip-off-chip bandwidth problem). The question then was, How to design a processor (and an instruction set) in such a technology?

Along with compiler advances and VLSI, there

were other parameters that influenced instruction set design in the early 1980s. An important consideration was to improve the instruction processing rate (via the use of pipelining). Other issues were a large number of registers (to facilitate register allocation of frequently used variables), and the need for more address bits (see [1] for a discussion of this issue). These issues led to the development of RISC instruction sets, which generally had the following features: fixed-length instructions (to facilitate pipelining), elemental instructions that were easy to implement with a limited amount of hardware control and were easy for compilers to generate, and a load/store architecture (a consequence of elemental instructions). To accommodate 32 registers and have fixed-length instructions, instructions were typically 32 bits each (versus varying instruction sizes in earlier architectures). Of course, the larger instruction size resulted in larger programs, but memory sizes had increased, accommodating larger program sizes. And because on-chip resources were not needed for microprogrammed control, they could be used for on-chip caches (especially instruction caches). These caches would obviate the off-chip bandwidth demands that might result from the larger instruction size.

Despite being motivated by the philosophy of providing primitives and not solutions, the temptation to solve the "problem of the day" could not be avoided by architects of some of the RISC instruction sets: For example, delayed branches were used to alleviate the branch penalty in a 5-stage instruction processing pipeline, and register windows were proposed to reduce procedure-calling overhead [6,11,12].

In the 1980s, there was a lot of debate about the superiority of RISC instruction sets. RISC proponents argued that RISC instruction sets were technically superior to CISC instruction sets in a fundamental way, whereas CISC proponents argued that the reasons were not fundamental (i.e., potential drawbacks could be overcome if sufficient hardware resources were expended). Lost in this technical discussion was the business model—when there is a large installed base of application software, the reason to alter the instruction set (as opposed to enhancing it in a backward compatible fashion) has to be very compelling.

Semiconductor technology of the late 1980s and early 1990s allowed more than a million transistors to be integrated on one microprocessor chip. This allowed implementors of CISC instruction sets to expend hardware resources on more sophisticated (parallel) decoders (to overcome impediments to

pipelining caused by variable-length instructions), combinations of hardwired/microprogrammed control, and so forth, narrowing the performance gap that implementations of RISC instruction sets enjoyed because they did not require such hardware. In the RISC case, these additional resources were typically used for more on-chip cache. Because the incremental performance benefits of more cache for the RISC processors were not as great, overall performance gap between RISC and CISC processors narrowed.

In the 1990s, the emphasis in processor design shifted to *instruction-level parallelism* (ILP) as the quest for more performance continued. The need to process more than one instruction at a time was felt— even implementations of RISC instruction sets had to resort to relatively sophisticated parallel decoders. And with the desire to overcome performance impediments using dynamic scheduling (see the discussion of ILP in chapter 4), a significant amount of hardware was devoted to an out-of-order execution engine (e.g., branch predictors, physical registers, reorder buffers). The relative difference in the amount of hardware required to implement RISC and CISC instruction sets narrowed, even more so when the amount of hardware expended on the caches was taken into consideration.

With an increased instruction processing rate, the need to have an uninterrupted supply of instructions became acute. Because (conditional) branch instructions created uncertainty in the instruction supply, dealing with branches became one of the most important problems facing processor architects. As expected, many architects resorted to the instruction set for a solution: The use of *predicated execution* became popular. However, because full-fledged predicated execution was not practical to add to an existing instruction set (it required an entirely new instruction set), architects made use of a limited form of predicated execution— *conditional move* instructions [13]. An architecture that had the luxury of starting out with a clean slate— the 64-bit architecture jointly developed by Hewlett-Packard and Intel (IA-64) adopted full predication [7]. And just like other problems before, in cases where the instruction set could not be used to solve the branch problem, architects had to resort to other microarchitectural techniques to solve the problem; for example, better branch predictors and other means to reduce the penalty of squashing instructions on a branch misprediction.

In the late 1990s, the increasing disparity between logic and memory speeds and increased instruction processing rates meant that memory latencies, as measured in instruction processing opportunities, increased greatly. This called for solution that allowed data values to be prefetched from memory, that is, fetched before they were actually needed. Whereas some architects searched for microarchitectural mechanisms for data prefetching, others resorted to the instruction set. Special varieties of load instructions were introduced that were meant to be placed in the code sufficiently ahead of program instructions that actually operated on the data values. Long memory latencies and relatively small basic block sizes meant that these special load instructions had to be hoisted past previous branch instructions; that is, they had to be executed in a speculative fashion. Speculatively executed loads might cause traps that would not have occurred had they not been scheduled aggressively and executed speculatively. This called for special instruction set support for nontrapping versions of speculatively executed loads as well as for recognizing exceptions where they would have occurred had the load instructions not been scheduled aggressively [8].

For the most part, the debate about instruction sets has assumed that performance was the ultimate objective, and cost and other issues (e.g., power dissipation) were a secondary concern. The quest for higher performance has driven the architecture of processors intended for mainframes and supercomputers in the 1960s–1980s as well as for servers, desktops and personal computers in the 1980s and 1990s. And the instruction set has played a prominent role in debate about how best to meet the performance objectives. The late 1990s have also witnessed the emergence of new markets for processing power: cellular phones, PDAs, embedded controllers, and so forth. In these markets, performance can be a secondary objective, with other objectives, such as cost, being more important. As is to be expected, the instruction set is again at the center of the debate: Although program size was not considered to be an important parameter in the desktop environment, it is becoming an important parameter in these markets, because such systems do not have the luxury of having reasonably large amounts of memory. And rather than design an entirely new architecture for such markets, existing microprocessor manufacturers are tempted to see how their existing architecture(s) could be enhanced to better suit the applications. At least one RISC architecture, MIPS, has responded by defining multiple instruction sizes in an attempt to reduce the program size.

3.3 Discussion of Included Papers

Next we present a brief discussion of the papers.

3.3.1 Wulf's "Compilers and Computer Architecture" [15]

This paper contains a compiler writer's view on machine architecture and instruction sets. Recognizing that instruction sets are a target for a compiler and not for human programmers, the paper lists several principles that should be kept in mind by both machine designers and compiler writers.

The paper starts out by commenting on a statement that many believed to be true: The quality of code generated by a compiler was not very important, because both machine speeds and memory sizes were going to increase greatly, easily accommodating inefficiencies in compiled code. Today, when machines are 500–1000 times faster than when the paper was written (1981), and memory sizes are 50–100 times larger, very few question the need for compilers to generate high-quality, optimized code! One reason why performance (and the quality of code) has continued to be important is that newer applications have evolved. A more important reason is a nontechnical one: Manufacturers will continue to strive for higher performance as long as there are (or there is a threat of) competitive products with higher performance.

The paper argues that instruction sets should be designed so that they are regular, orthogonal, and composable. These features allow the compiler to use a divide-and-conquer approach to reduce the number of cases that have to be analyzed. Of other principles mentioned in the paper, perhaps the two most important which apply to instruction set design as well as many other aspects of computer system design are "One versus All" and "Provide primitives, not solutions." With these principles, the author cautions instruction set designers not to provide some subset of all possible solutions, as it complicates the decision making for the compiler significantly. And the author cautions designers not to look for (instruction set) solutions to a given problem, because a special-purpose solution is applicable only to a particular situation, and the onus is on the compiler to determine if the situation matches the (provided) solution. If the match is only approximate, building a solution using primitives may actually be more efficient than the special-case solution.

3.3.2 Radin's "The IBM 801 Minicomputer" [12]

The paper by Radin presents the philosophy of the IBM 801 project. The 801 project was a pioneering project that espoused the codesign of compilers and instruction set architectures. It started the philosophy of basing the ISA design on what a compiler needs versus the other philosophies of ISA design that were prevalent at that time; for example, making the ISA easier for the assembly language programmer, making the ISA so that processor-memory bandwidth demands are minimized, and so forth. The 801 ideas influenced the Berkeley RISC [11] and the Stanford MIPS [6] projects. However, unlike those projects, the 801 was not driven by constraints of single-chip VLSI implementations.

3.3.3 Patterson and Ditzel's "The Case for the Reduced Instruction Set Computer" [10]

The paper by Patterson and Ditzel was the first published paper arguing for the RISC approach for general-purpose processor design. Observing that: (1) VLSI technology allowed an entire integer processor to be put on a single chip (if the control for such a processor did not require too many chip resources), (2) integrating functionality on to a single chip provided significant performance advantages, (3) pipelining was a key technology to improve the instruction processing rate, and (4) most programs contained only a few instructions from the elaborate repertoire of instructions available in instruction sets, the authors proposed a reduced instruction set computer (RISC).

The idea of a RISC computer was to have an instruction set that was "reduced" or simple enough so that it could be implemented without sacrificing some basic tenets of high-performance implementations. An important contribution of this paper was to bring some basic tenets of high-performance processor design (e.g., pipelining) into the mainstream. Even though high-end machines such as the CDC 6600 used these principles, they were not used by designers of microprocessors and minicomputers.

This and others papers written by the RISC researchers started a debate about RISC versus CISC and the merits of instruction sets that continued throughout the 1980s. This debate died down in the 1990s when semiconductor technology provided sufficient on-chip resources to allow implementations of CISC architectures to employ more-sophisticated techniques for instruction processing (e.g., out-of-order superscalar).

3.3.4 Colwell et al.'s "Instruction Sets and Beyond: Computers, Complexity, and Controversy" [3]

This article, written as a rejoinder to a series of articles arguing for RISC instructions sets, is an excellent example of a paper that tries to get to the bottom of things. It raises several issues that any computer designer should keep in mind when deciding on a path to pursue.

First, it observes that technical elegance alone does not drive computer design. Many nontechnical (especially non-ISA-related) reasons influence the design of a computer. These include the need to support an installed software base (upward compatibility) and the benefits of "familiarity", that is, benefits gained from prior experience of building similar systems. And it emphasizes the need to have a well-defined and stable interface that hardware designers can design to.

Second, it observes that computer design does not follow an all-or-none approach, and that proposals for different approaches need not be segmented: one side might easily be able to adopt parts of what appears to be an entirely different proposal. Therefore, the potential benefits of different parts of a proposal need to be isolated. The example used in this paper is that of multiple register sets, which were proposed for the Berkeley RISC I processor but could easily be adopted into a CISC processor if there was a compelling need for it.

A sidebar in this paper also mentions the Military Computer Families (MCF) study [5], which proposed measures with which to assess the "quality" of a computer architecture, including the program size and the memory bus traffic.

3.3.5 Crawford's "Architecture of the Intel 80386" [4]

The paper by Crawford describes the instruction set as well as other aspects of the architecture (e.g., memory management and protection) of the Intel 80386. The Intel architecture, commonly referred to as the x86 architecture, provides a classic example of the nontechnical issues that computer architects must deal with. Starting out with an 8-bit architecture in the 8080, it was expanded to a 16-bit architecture in the 8086 and to a 32-bit architecture (IA-32) with the 80386.

Nontechnical reasons heavily influenced the decision to expand the architecture and instruction set in an incremental fashion, rather than start out with a clean slate at every major transition (e.g., 16 bits to 32 bits). First, software providers have little reason to stay with a microprocessor vendor if they have to recompile their programs for a new instruction set. Second, consumers do not like the idea of having to upgrade all their software every time they desire to upgrade their hardware.

Crawford's paper describes how Intel transitioned from a 16-bit architecture to a 32-bit architecture in an upward-compatible manner. The problems that had to be dealt with included instruction encodings for both 16- and 32-bit operations. The paper describes the solution that they adopted: When faced with real-world constraints that include many non-technical parameters, the ideal solutions may not necessarily be the most elegant ones from a technical viewpoint.

3.3.6 Mahlke et al.'s "A Comparison of Full and Partial Predicated Execution Support for ILP Processors" [7]

The paper by Mahlke, Hank, McCormick, August, and Hwu, discusses predicated execution instruction, set and complier support for predicated execution. It distinguishes between two options for predicated execution: full predication, in which a new instruction set is required, and partial predication, which can be incorporated into more traditional instruction sets in a fairly straightforward manner. The paper discusses how compilers can make use of predicated execution and what optimizations might be possible. It then evaluates the potential benefits of predicated execution for a variety of configurations of statically scheduled ILP processors, observing that partial predication could result in a 30% performance benefit when compared to no predication, and full predication could result in an additional 30% performance benefit for the chosen processor configurations.

The results of this paper were used by Hewlett-Packard and Intel to justify their support for predicated execution in the IA-64 instruction set when it was introduced at the Microprocessor Forum in October 1997.

3.4 Lessons to Be Learned

Looking back, we see that instruction set architecture has been the subject of extensive discussion and debate among computer architects over the years, attracting more attention than many other aspects of computer architecture. The instruction set provides a convenient means of solving the problem of the day, and consequently there have been countless debates over the virtues of different flavors of instructions when considering solutions to particular problems. Without a doubt, these debates will continue into the future. Unfortunately, these debates typically center on a subset of the technical parameters that are relevant at a given point in time. One must be cautious, however,

and understand that (1) instruction set issues are heavily influenced, perhaps more so than any other aspect of computer architecture, by nontechnical issues whose importance can easily subsume technical issues, and (2) rapidly advancing technology is likely to provide solutions to problems without having to use the instruction set.

Computer architects need to anticipate likely solutions to problems without immediately resorting to the instruction set for a solution. On the other side of the coin, architects need to anticipate the possible problems that a solution chosen for a current-generation problem might cause for future-generation implementations, especially if the solution involves the instruction set. Unfortunately, this is easier said than done.

3.5 References

[1]   G. Bell and W. D. Strecker, "Computer structures: What have we learned from the PDP-11?" *Proceedings of the 3rd Annual Symposium on Computer Architecture*, pp. 1–14, Jan. 1976.

[2]   D. W. Clark and H. M. Levy, "Measurement and analysis of instruction use in the VAX-11/780," *Proceedings of the 9th International Symposium on Computer Architecture*, pp. 9–17, April 1982.

[3]   R. P. Colwell, C. Y. Hitchcock III, E. D. Jensen, H. M. Brinkley Sprunt, and C.P. Kollar, "Instruction sets and beyond: Computers, complexity and controversy," *IEEE Computer*, vol. 18(9) pp. 8–19, 1986.

[4]   J. Crawford, "Architecture of the Intel 80386," *Proceedings of the International Conference on Computer Design (ICCD)*, pp. 155–160, Oct. 1986.

[5]   S. H. Fuller and W. E. Burr, "Measurement and evaluation of the alternative computer architectures," *IEEE Computer*, 10(10):24–35, Oct. 1977.

[6]   J. Hennessy, N. Jouppi, F. Baskett, T. Gross, and J. Gill, "Hardware/software tradeoffs for increased performance," *Proceedings of the International Symposium on Architectural Support for Programming Languages and Operating Systems*, pp. 2–11, Mar. 1982.

[7]   S. Mahlke, R. Hank, J. McCormick, D. August, and W.-M. Hwu, "A comparison of full and partial predicated execution support for ILP processors," *Proceedings of the 22nd Annual International Symposium on Computer Architecture*, pp. 138–150, June 1995.

[8]   S. A. Mahlke, W. Y. Chen, W.-M Hwu, B. Ramakrishna Rau, and M. S. Schlansker, "Sentinel scheduling for VLIW and superscalar processors," *Proceedings of the 5th International Conference on*

Architectural Support for Programming Languages and Operating Systems, pp. 238–247, Oct. 1992.

[9] G. J. Myers, *Advances in Computer Architecture.* New York: Wiley, 1981.

[10] D. A. Patterson and D. R. Ditzel, "The case for the reduced instruction set computer," *ACM SIGARCH Computer Architecture News*, vol. 8, pp. 25–33, Oct. 1980.

[11] D. A. Patterson and C. H. Sequin, "RISC 1: A reduced instruction set VLSI computer," *Proceedings of the 8th Annual International Symposium on Computer Architecture*, pp. 443–459, May 1981.

[12] G. Radin, "The 801 Minicomputer," *Proceedings of the International Symposium on Architectural Support for Programming Languages and Operating Systems*, pp. 39–47, Mar. 1982.

[13] R. L. Sites, "Alpha AXP Architecture," *Communications of the ACM*, vol. 36, pp. 43–47, Feb. 1993.

[14] C. A. Wiecek, "A Case Study of VAX-11 Instruction Set Usage for Compiler Execution," *Proceedings of the International Symposium on Architectural Support for Programming Languages and Operating Systems*, pp. 177–184, Mar. 1982.

[15] W. A. Wulf, "Compilers and computer architecture," *IEEE Computer*, 14 (8):41–47, 1981.

An examination of the relation between architecture and compiler design leads to several principles which can simplify compilers and improve the object code they produce.

Compilers and Computer Architecture

William A. Wulf
Carnegie-Mellon University

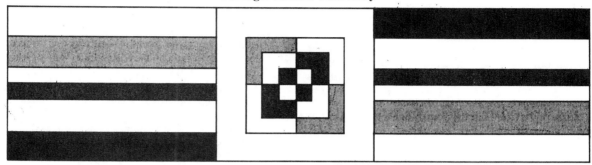

The interactions between the design of a computer's instruction set and the design of compilers that generate code for that computer have serious implications for overall computational cost and efficiency. This article, which investigates those interactions, should ideally be based on comprehensive data; unfortunately, there is a paucity of such information. And while there is data on the use of instruction sets, the relation of this data to compiler design is lacking. This is, therefore, a frankly personal statement, but one which is based on extensive experience.

My colleagues and I are in the midst of a research effort aimed at automating the construction of production-quality compilers. (To limit the scope of what is already an ambitious project, we have considered only algebraic languages and conventional computers.) In brief, unlike many compiler-compiler efforts of the past, ours involves automatically generating all of the phases of a compiler—including the optimization and code generation phases found in optimizing compilers. The only input to this generation process is a formal definition of the source language and target computer. The formulation of compilation algorithms that, with suitable parameters, are effective across a broad class of computer architectures has been fundamental to this research. In turn, finding these algorithms has led us to critically examine many architectures and the problems they pose. Much of the opinion that follows is based on our experiences in trying to do this, with notes on the difficulties we encountered.

Articles of this sort commonly begin by observing that the cost of hardware is falling rapidly while the cost of software is rising. The inevitable conclusion is that we ought to find ways for the hardware to simplify the software task. One area in which this might be done is in the design of instruction sets that better reflect the needs of high-level languages. Better instruction sets would both simplify compilers and improve the size and speed of the programs they generate. This observation and conclusion are absolutely correct. Treated too simplistically, however, they lead to mistaken inferences. For instance, many people have concluded that efficiency of the object code from a compiler is no longer important—or, at least, that it will not be in the near future. This is patently false. To suggest why I believe it is false and to lay the groundwork for much of what follows, let me illustrate with an example. Today I use a timesharing system that is five times faster than the one I used a decade ago; it also has eight times the primary memory and vastly more secondary storage. Yet, it supports about the same number of people, and response is worse. The reason for this anomaly is simply that our aspirations have grown much faster than technology has been able to satisfy them. It now takes more cycles, more memory, more disk—more everything—to do what a typical user wants and expects. I believe this is a good thing; despite its degraded performance, the system is more responsive to my overall needs—it's more humane. Nonetheless, there is a premium on the efficiency of the programs it executes.

The past is always our safest predictor of the future, at least if we interpret it properly. Although hardware costs will continue to fall dramatically and machine speeds will increase equally dramatically, we must assume that our aspirations will rise even more. Because of this we are not about to face either a cycle or memory surplus. For the near-term future, the dominant effect will not be machine cost or speed alone, but rather a continuing attempt to increase the return from a finite resource—that is, a particular computer at our disposal. This isn't a simple matter of "yankee thrift." Given any system, people will want to improve it and make it more responsive to human needs; inefficiencies that thwart those aspirations will not be tolerated.

The cost equation

Before discussing the mutual impact of compilers and target-machine architectures, we need to clarify the objectives of the exercise. A number of costs, and conversely benefits, are involved. They include

- designing (writing) compilers,
- designing the hardware architecture,
- designing the hardware implementation of that architecture,
- manufacturing the hardware (i.e., replicating the implementation),
- executing the compiler, and
- executing the compiled programs.

The relative importance of these costs is, of course, installation- and application-dependent—one cannot make statements about their relative importance without more specific information. Nonetheless, there are some general observations that bear on what follows.

First, note that only the fourth item, the cost of the replication of hardware, has decreased dramatically. While standardized MSI and LSI chips have worked to decrease the cost of hardware design, the engineering of complete processors on a single chip has worked to increase it again. Designing irregular structures at the chip level is *very* expensive.

Designing irregular structures at the chip level is *very* expensive.

Second, all of the design activities (compilers, architectures, and implementations) are one-time costs. From the customer's perspective, they are amortized over the number of units sold. Thus, it makes sense to design an architecture more responsive to compilation problems only if the reduction in the cost of writing the compiler, executing it, or executing the code generated by it, offsets the increase in the cost of design. Often this is easily done, as will be discussed later. However, we must remember that it is still more expensive to design hardware than to design software that does the same job, unless the job is very simple. This explains why it doesn't make sense, for example, to move the entire compiler into hardware.

Third, both software and architectures have a life substantially longer than that of the hardware technology for which they are initially implemented. Despite the predictable decline in hardware costs, too often architectures have been designed to cater to the anomalies of the technology prevalent at the time they were designed. In effect, there has been a confusion between the second and third costs listed above.

Finally, the last two items—the costs of compiling and executing programs—are not strictly comparable to those preceding them. Dollar costs can be assigned to these, of course. Often, however, the correct measure is not in terms of dollars but in terms of things that cannot be done as a consequence of compilation or execution inefficiencies. A typical installation can only occasionally acquire a new computer (and suffer the trauma of doing so). Be-

tween acquisitions the available computer is a fixed and finite resource. Hence inefficiencies in compilation and execution manifest themselves as decreased productivity, unavailable functionality, and similar costs. Although difficult to measure, these costs are the first-order effects noticed by users once a machine has been acquired.

Some general principles

Principles that would improve the impedance match between compilers and a target computer have been followed in many contemporary architectures:

- *Regularity.* If something is done in one way in one place, it ought to be done the same way everywhere. This principle has also been called the "law of least astonishment" in the language design community.
- *Orthogonality.* It should be possible to divide the machine definition (or language definition) into a set of separate concerns and define each in isolation from the others. For example, it ought to be possible to discuss data types, addressing, and instruction sets independently.
- *Composability.* If the principles of regularity and orthogonality have been followed, then it should also be possible to compose the orthogonal, regular notions in arbitrary ways. It ought to be possible, for example, to use every addressing mode with every operator and every data type.

However, these principles have not been completely followed, and the deviations from them present the compiler writer with some of his worst problems.

I will have a few more principles to suggest below. Before doing so, however, let me comment on the preceding ones.

Although many compiler optimizations are cast in terms of esoteric-sounding operations such as flow analysis and algebraic simplification—in fact these techniques are simply aimed at performing an enormous case analysis. The objective is to determine the best object code for a given source program. Because the case analysis is so enormous, the various optimization algorithms attempt to glean information and/or shape the intermediate form(s) of the program in a manner that allows the final case analysis and code selection to be done rapidly and thoroughly.

Viewing a compiler's task as a large case analysis helps to explain why regularity, orthogonality, and composability are so important to simplifying the task. Every deviation from these principles manifests itself as an ad hoc case to be considered. And, alas, the consideration of a special case is not limited to the code selection process; because every preparatory phase requires certain information intermediate representations, the manifestations of the anomaly creep back through nearly all of them. I will try to illustrate this with more examples in the next section. For the moment, however, consider the genre of general-register machines. The name suggests that the registers are all "general"—i.e., that they can be used for any of the purposes to which registers are put on the machine. In fact, however, almost no machine actually treats all the registers uniformly—multiplicands must be in "even" registers, or double precision operands must be in even-odd pairs, or a zero in an indexing field of an instruction denotes no indexing (and hence the zeroth register cannot be used for indexing), or some operations can be performed only between registers while others can be performed only between a register and memory, or any of many other variations. Each of these distinctions is a violation of one or more of the principles above and results in additional complexity.

Some additional, more specific principles are

- *One vs. all.* There should be precisely one way to do something, or all ways should be possible.
- *Provide primitives, not solutions.* It is far better to provide good primitives from which solutions to code generation problems can be synthesized than to provide the solutions themselves.

Both of these also relate to the simplicity (or complexity) of the compiler's case analysis. Consider the "one-vs.-all" principle. Either of these extreme positions implies that the compiler need not do any case analysis. If, for example, the only conditional branching instructions are ones that test for EQUALITY and LESS THAN, there is only one way to generate code for each of the six relations. Alternatively, if there is a direct implementation of all six relations, there is an obvious coding for each. Difficulties arise, however, if only three or four of the six are provided. For example, the compiler must decide whether, by commuting operands, there is a cheaper implementation of some of the remaining relations. Unfortunately, this is not a simple decision—it may imply determining whether side-effect semantics are violated, whether there is an interaction with register allocation, and so on.

Now consider the "provide primitives, not solutions" principle. In what I believe to be an honest attempt to help compiler writers, some modern architectures have provided direct implementations of high-level concepts such as FOR and CASE statements and PROCEDURE calls. In many, if not most cases, these turn out to be more trouble than they are worth. Invariably they either support only one language well, or are so general that they are inefficient for special cases—thus forcing the compiler to perform even more analysis to discover the common cases where a more efficient implementation is possible. The problem arises from a "semantic clash" between the language and high-level instructions; by giving too much semantic content to the instruction, the machine designer has made it possible to use the instruction only in limited contexts. Again, I will try to illustrate the problem in the following section.

The last three principles are even more blatantly my opinion than those listed earlier:

- *Addressing.* Address computations are paths! Addressing is not limited to simple array and record accesses! The addressing modes of a machine should be designed to recognize these facts.
- *Environment support.* All modern architectures support arithmetic and logical computations reasonably well. They do not do nearly as well in supporting the run-time environments for programs—stack frames, displays or static/dynamic links, exceptions, pro-

cesses, and so on. The writer should provide such run-time support.
- *Deviations.* The writer should deviate from these principles only in ways that are implementation-independent.

The first two of these principles, addressing and environment support, are among the most difficult to deal with—and among the most likely to run afoul of the earlier "primitives, not solutions" principle. The conscientious designer must remember that different languages impose different constraints on the notions of procedures, tasks, and exceptions. Even things as mundane as case and iteration statements and array representations are dictated by the semantics of the language and may differ from one language to another.

I will have more to say about these points later, but let me illustrate some of the issues with the problem of addressing. In my experience, effective use of implicit addressing is the most important aspect of generating good code. It is often the most difficult to achieve. In general, accessing a datum from a data structure involves following a path whose length is arbitrary (but is known at compile time). Each step along the path is an addition (indexing into arrays or records) or an indirection (through pointers of various sorts). Typical computers supply a fixed and finite menu—a collection of special cases—of such path

---

Some architectures have provided direct implementations of high-level concepts. In many cases these turn out to be more trouble than they are worth.

---

steps. The compiler's problem is how to choose effectively from among this menu; I know of no technique for doing this except exhaustive special-case analysis. Even when the target computer's addressing modes are well-suited to the most common cases, its compiler remains complex since it must be ready to handle the general case.

The last principle is, I suppose, more in the nature of a plea. At any time there are technological anomalies that can be exploited to make a machine faster or cheaper. It is tempting to allow these factors to influence the architecture—many examples abound. It takes the greatest restraint to look beyond the current state of technology, to realize that the architecture will outlive that state, and to design for the future. I think that most of the violations of notions like orthogonality and regularity can be traced to a shortsighted view of costs. Adhering to the principles presented here has a measurable hardware cost to be sure, but one which decreases exponentially as technology changes.

Kudos and gripes

From the compiler writer's perspective, various machines have both good and bad features which illustrate—or violate—the principles discussed above. This is not meant to be an exhaustive list of such features, nor is it intended to criticize particular computers or manufacturers.

On regularity. As a compiler writer, I must applaud the trend in many recent machines to allow each instruction operand to be specified by any of the addressing modes. The ability of the compiler to treat registers and memory as well as source and destination symmetrically is an excellent example of the benefits of regularity. The compiler is simpler and the object code is better.

Not all aspects of modern machines have been designed regularly, however. Most machines support several data types (including fixed and floating-point forms), several types of words (essentially boolean vectors), and several types of addresses—often with several sizes of each and sometimes with variations such as signed and unsigned and normalized or unnormalized. It is rare for the operators on these types to be defined regularly, even when it would make sense for them to be. A compiler, for example, would like to represent small integers as addresses or bytes. Yet, one machine provides a complete set of byte

---

The familiar arithmetic shift instructions are another example of irregularity.

---

operations that are symmetric with word (integer) operations except that the ADD and SUB bytes are missing, and another defines the setting of condition codes slightly differently for byte operations than for full-word operations. Such differences prevent simple compilers from using the obvious byte representations. In more ambitious compilers, substantial analysis must be done to determine whether the differences matter in the particular program being compiled.

The familiar arithmetic shift instructions are another example of irregularity. I trust everyone realizes that arithmetic-right-shift is *not* a division by a power of two on most machines.

A particularly annoying violation of regularity arises from the instructions of machines that make special provision for "immediate mode" arithmetic. We know from analysis of source programs that certain constants, notably 0, ±1, and the number of bytes per word, appear frequently. It makes good sense to provide special handling for them in an instruction set. Yet it seems that many machine designers feel that such instructions are useful only in forming addresses—or at least that they need not have effects identical to their more expensive equivalents. Manifestations include

- condition codes that are not set in the same way,

- carries that do not propagate beyond the size of an "address," and

- operations that are restricted to operate on a selected set of "index registers."

In practice, of course, $i = i + 1$ (and its implicit counterpart in iteration statements) is one of the most common

source program statements. Irregularities such as those above preclude simple compilers from using immediate mode arithmetic for these common cases and add substantial complexity to more ambitious compilers.

Similar remarks apply to the floating-point instructions of many machines. In addition to providing an even more restricted set of operations, these machines often fail to support the abstraction of "real" numbers intended by many higher-level languages. (Someone once observed that the best characterization of the floating-point hardware of most machines is as "unreal" numbers!) Most language designers and programmers want to think of real numbers as an abstraction of real arithmetic (except for their finite precision)—they would like, for example, for them to be commutative and associative. Floating-point representation is often neither, and hence the compiler writer is constrained from exploiting some obvious optimizations. The cost is both increased compiler complexity and slower programs—and the sad thing is that the cases where the optimizations are illegal are rare in practice.

On orthogonality. By orthogonality I mean the ability to define separate concerns—such as addressing, operations, and data types—separately. This property is closely allied with regularity and composability. The failure of general-register machines to treat all their registers alike could be characterized as a failure of any of these properties. Several machines contain both long and short forms of branch instructions, for example, in which the short form is taken as a constant displacement relative to the program counter and is an addressing mode not available in any other kind of instruction. Some machines include instructions whose effect depends on the addressing mode used. For example, on some machines sign extension is (or is not) done depending on the destination location. Some other machines create long or short forms of the result of a multiplication, depending on the even-oddness of the destination register. Some of the most popular machines contain different instruction sets for register-to-register, memory-to-register, and memory-to-memory operations (and worse, these instruction sets partially—but not completely—overlap).

It should be clear that the compiler should perform a separate analysis for each of these cases. And unlike some of my previous examples, this requirement should apply to simple as well as ambitious compilers.

On composability. From the compiler writer's perspective, the ideal machine would, among other things, make available the full cross-product of operations and addressing modes on similar data types. The ADD instruction should have identical effects whether it adds literals, bytes, or words, for example. Moreover, any addressing mode available in one variant should be available in the others.

More germane to the present point is the notion of conversion. Many machines fail badly in this respect. For example, most only provide relational operators (i.e., conditional branch instructions) that affect control flow, while source languages generally allow relational expressions to appear in contexts where a boolean value must be made manifest (e.g., allow them to be stored into a user's boolean variable). In addition, many machines do not provide for conversion between data types such as integer and floating point, nor do they provide a conversion that differs from that specified in source languages.

The root of the problem lies in the fact that programming languages view type as a property of data (or variables), while machines view type as a property of operators. Because the number of machine data types is moderately large, the number of operation codes needed to implement a full cross-product is unreasonable. For example, it is usually impossible to add a byte to a word without first converting the byte to full-word form. The need for such explicit conversions makes it difficult to determine when overall cost is reduced by choosing a particular representation. Admittedly, where the conversion is a significant one (as in converting integer to floating-point representation) this doesn't feel so bad—but it adds complexity to the compiler as well as slowing both compilation and execution in trivial cases.

I will end this discussion with an example of the complexity imposed on a compiler by the lack of regularity, orthogonality, and composability. Consider a simple statement such as A := B*C and suppose we are compiling for a machine on which the operand of a multiply must be in an odd register. A simple compiler generally allocates registers "on the fly" as it generates code. In this example, such a strategy appears to work well enough; the allocator requires only minor complexity to know about even/odd registers, and the code generator must specify its needs on each request. But in a trivially more complex expression such as A := (B + D)*C, the strategy breaks down. Addition can be done in either an even or odd register; a simple "on the fly" allocation is as likely to get an even register as an odd one for B + D—and, of course, the choice of an even one will necessitate an extra data move to implement the multiplication by C. More ambitious compilers must therefore analyze a complete expression tree before making any allocations. In trees involving conflicting requirements, an assignment must be found that minimizes data movements.

Ambitious compilers can even have a problem with the simple assignment A :+ B*C. Such compilers often employ a technique called "load/store motion" in which they attempt to move variables accessed frequently in a program region into registers over that region; this tends to eliminate loads and stores. The simple assignment above suggests that it would be good to have A allocated to an odd register, since the entire right-hand side could then be evaluated in A and another data move eliminated. Whether this is desirable, however, depends on all the other uses of A in the program region under the register in which A resides. This involves more complex analysis than that for single expressions and, again, may require trade-offs in the number of data moves needed.

Note that such complexities arise in other contexts besides even/odd register pairs. At least one machine has distinct accumulators and index registers plus a few elements that can be used as either. Precisely the same sort of compiler difficulties arise in deciding where the result of an arithmetic expression or user variable should go; the compiler must examine all uses to determine whether the result is used in an indexing context, an arithmetic context, or both.

On one vs. all. I am sure most readers who are familiar with a number of machines can supply examples of violations of this principle. My favorite can be found in one of the newest machines—one with a generally excellent instruction set. This set includes reasonably complete boolean operations, but does not provide AND, instead providing only AND NOT. AND is commutative and associative, but AND NOT is not, so it requires a truly bewildering analysis to determine which operand to complement and when to apply DeMorgan's law in order to generate an optimal code sequence.

On primitives vs. solutions. Most people would agree that Pascal is more powerful than Fortran. The precise meaning of "more powerful" may be a bit unclear, but certainly any *algorithm* than can be coded in Fortran can also be coded in Pascal—but not conversely. However, this does not mean that it is easy, or even possible, to translate Fortran *programs* into Pascal. Features such as

---

A machine that attempts to support all implementation requirements will probably fail to support any of them efficiently.

COMMON and EQUIVALENCE are not present in Pascal—and some uses of them are even prohibited by that language. There is a "semantic clash" between the languages.

The same phenomenon can be observed in machine designs. Among the common higher-level languages one finds many different views of essentially similar concepts. The detailed semantics associated with parameter passing, FOR statements, type conversions, and so on are often quite different. These differences can lead to significantly different implementation requirements. A machine that builds-in instructions satisfying one set of these requirements cannot support other languages. A machine that attempts to support all the requirements will probably fail to support any of them efficiently—and hence will provoke additional special-case analysis in the compiler. Examples of the misplaced enthusiasm of machine designers include

- subroutine call instructions that support, for example, only some parameter passing mechanisms,

- looping instructions that support only certain models of initialization, test and increment, and recomputation,

- addressing modes that presume certain stack frame layouts—or even presume particular representations of arrays,

- case instructions that only do or don't implicitly test the boundary conditions of the case index and only do or don't assume such bounds are static at compile time,

- instructions that support high-level data structures (such as queues) and make assumptions that differ from some common implementations of these structures, and
- elaborate string manipulation.

In many of these cases, the high-level instructions are synthesized from more primitive operations which, if the compiler writer could access them, could be recomposed to more closely model the features actually needed. An ideal solution to this problem would provide a modest amount of writable microstore for use by the run-time system. The compiler writer could then tailor the instruction set to the needs of a particular language.

On addressing. Modern programming languages permit the definition of data structures that are arbitrary compositions of scalars, arrays, records, and pointers. At least in principle it is possible to define an array of records, a component of which is a pointer to a record containing an array of arrays of yet another kind of record. Accessing a component at the bottom level of this structure involves a lengthy sequence of operations. Further, because of the interactions among block structure, recursive procedures, and ''by reference'' parameter passing, finding the base address of such a structure can be equally complex—possibly involving indexing through the ''display,'' various sorts of ''dope'' (descriptor) information, and several levels of indirection through reference parameter values. In practice, of course, data structures are seldom this complex, and most variables accessed are either local to the current procedure or global to the entire program—but the compiler must be prepared to handle the general case. And, surprisingly, even relatively simple constructs such as accessing an element of an array in the current stack frame can give rise to much of this complexity.

The algorithm to access an element of a data structure can be viewed as walking a path from the current invocation record to the element; the initial portion of the path locates the base address of the structure via the display, etc., and the final portion is defined by the structure itself. Each step of the path involves indirection (following a pointer), computing a record element displacement, or indexing (by an array subscript)—all of which may involve multiplication of a subscript by the size (in address units) of the array component. For many languages, constraint checks on array subscripts and nil pointers must also be performed along the path.

It is clearly advantageous to use the target computer's effective address computations to implicitly perform as many of the path steps as possible. Unfortunately, most contemporary machines were designed with a simpler data structure model in mind. Rather than supporting steps along a general path, these machines generally provide an ad hoc collection of indexing and indirection that can be used for only a subset of such steps—there is no notion of their composition. For example,

- one of the most popular machines has no indirection at all, thus forcing an explicit instruction each time a pointer must be followed;

- most machines that provide both indexing and indirection define a fixed order—e.g., first do the indexing, then the indirection, although the opposite order is just as common in practice;
- some modern machines provide implicit multiplication of one operand of an indexing operation, but only by the size of scalars (whereas in general the element of an array may not be a scalar); and
- many machines limit the size of the literal value in an indexing mode, thus forcing contorted code for larger displacements or for cases where the displacement isn't known until link time.

The addressing modes are useful for some, but never all, of these cases. Worse, sometimes more than one mode can be used and the compiler must make a nontrivial choice. Again, the compiler must be made more complex to exploit the hardware. It would be far better (and probably simpler in the hardware as well) to have a more general and consistent model.

On environments. I believe that most people now appreciate hardware support for recursive procedure invocation, dynamic storage allocation, and synchronization and communication processes. I won't comment on this except to note the danger of providing such support at too high a level and hence introducing a semantic clash with some languages. Instead, I will point out some neglected areas of the support environment that induce significant overheads in the implementation of at least some languages. These include:

- *Uninitialized variables.* Many languages define a program to be erroneous if the value of a variable is fetched before being set. The code and data structures to support this are expensive. Yet at least one old machine provided a way to check these ''for free'' by setting bad parity on uninitialized variables.

- *Constraint checks.* Many languages specify that certain properties of a value be checked before use. Subscript range checking is a particular instance of this, but there are many other cases as well. Generally, machines provide no direct implementation of this, thus forcing explicit tests in the code and often eliminating clever uses of the effective address hardware.

- *Exceptions.* Exceptions (analogous to PL/I's ON conditions) are a part of many languages. Yet few machines support them, and an efficient software implementation of them often violates the hardware assumptions of the support provided for procedures.

- *Debugging support.* If most programming is to be done in high-level languages, then it is axiomatic that debugging should be at the same level. Because most machines do not support this, however, the designer of the debugging system is usually faced with two choices, both unpalatable. The first is to force the user to debug at a low level. The second is to create a special debugging mode in which extra code provides the run-time debugger with the necessary information—this in turn makes it difficult to debug the production version of a system.

A note on stacks. A common belief is that all compiler writers prefer a stack machine. I am an exception to that belief—at least insofar as stacks for expression evaluation are concerned. (Stacks to support environments are a different matter.) It is certainly true that there is a trivial mapping from parse trees to postfix, and hence simple compilers can be made even simpler if their target has an expression stack. For more ambitious compilers, however, stack machines pose almost all the same optimization problems as register machines. A common subexpression is still a common subexpression. A loop invariant expression is still invariant. Expression reordering, done on a register machine to minimize the number of registers used, also reduces the depth of the evaluation stack—thus increasing the likelihood that the entire computation can be held in the fast top-of-stack registers. Even register allocation has a counterpart—i.e., allocating variables to the stack frame so that the most frequently accessed ones can utilize short addressing forms on machines that provide such a feature. Moreover, deciding whether an optimization is desirable can be more difficult on a stack machine. On a register machine, for example, it is almost always desirable to save the value of a common subexpression, while on a stack machine it is necessary to determine whether the added cost of storing and retrieving the value is offset by that value's uses. Thus, while expression stacks are nice for simple compilers, they are in no sense a solution.

A note on interpreters and writable microcode. An increasingly popular approach, especially in the microprocessor domain, is to microprogram a special-purpose interpreter for a given source language. This has been done extensively for Pascal, for example. As noted above, in general I prefer "primitives, not solutions" (especially the wrong solutions); tailoring the instruction set through microprogramming is one way to achieve that.

There are problems with this approach, however. It implies that we must find ways to ensure that user-written microcode cannot subvert operating system protection. Similarly, we must provide a means for dynamically associating the right interpreter with a given process, and this may imply substantial context-swap overheads unless one is very careful. (I am making an assumption here. Namely, I believe that multiprogramming, multiprocessing, and protection will all become common in the microprocessor world—essentially in forms evolved from what we see in current large systems. I also believe that single-language systems are not a solution; we must assume a multilanguage environment. The rationale for my beliefs is not appropriate to this article, but the most recent announcements from several chip manufacturers corroborate my views.)

Above all, the approach is not a panacea! In at least one case I have examined, the code produced for such an interpreter is roughly two times slower and larger than it needs to be. In another case, a sophisticated optimizing compiler had to be built just to get reasonable performance.

Both the compiler writer and the machine designer have multiple objectives. The machine designer should certainly attend to the concerns of high-level-language implementation—since most programs will be written in one—but he must also attend to cost, reliability, compatibility, customer acceptance, and so on. The compiler writer must faithfully implement the semantics of the source language, must provide a friendly interface to the user, and must try to reach a reasonable compromise between the speed of compilation and the quality of the resulting object code. Being realistic, both designer and writer know that they can affect only a subset of these objectives on each side. However, they also know that they can still do a great deal to improve the impedance match between languages and machines and so reduce total costs. ■

Acknowledgments

This research was sponsored by the Defense Advanced Research Projects Agency and monitored by the Air Force Avionics Laboratory. The views and conclusions contained in this article are those of the author and should not be interpreted as representing the official policies, either expressed or implied, of the Defense Advanced Research Projects Agency or the US government.

 **William A. Wulf** is a professor of computer science at Carnegie-Mellon University. Prior to joining CMU in 1968, he was an instructor of applied mathematics and computer science at the University of Virginia. His research interests span the fields traditionally called "programming systems" and "computer architecture." He is especially interested in the construction of large systems, notably compilers and operating systems, and in the way the construction of these systems interacts with the architecture of the machine on which they run. Wulf's research activities have included the design and implementation of the Bliss system implementation language, participation in the PDP-11 design, construction of C.mmp—a sixteen-processor multiprocessor computer, the design and implementation of the Hydra operating system for C.mmp, the design of the Alphard programming language, and participation in the development of Ada, the DoD language for embedded computer applications.

Wulf holds the BS in physics and the MSEE from the University of Illinois and the PhD from the University of Virginia.

THE 801 MINICOMPUTER

George Radin, IBM Fellow
IBM Thomas J. Watson Research Center
P. O. Box 218
Yorktown Heights, New York 10598

Abstract

This paper provides an overview of an experimental system developed at the IBM T. J. Watson Research Center. It consists of a running hardware prototype, a control program and an optimizing compiler. The basic concepts underlying the system are discussed as are the performance characteristics of the prototype. In particular, three principles are examined:
- system orientation towards the pervasive use of high level language programming and a sophisticated compiler,
- a primitive instruction set which can be completely hard-wired,
- storage hierarchy and I/O organization to enable the CPU to execute an instruction at almost every cycle.

Introduction

In October, 1975, a group of about twenty researchers at the IBM T. J. Watson Research Center began the design of a minicomputer, a compiler, and a control program whose goal was to achieve significantly better cost/performance for high level language programs than that attainable by existing systems. The name 801 was chosen because it was the IBM number of the building in which the project resided. (The twenty creative researchers were singularly uninspired namers.)

In addition to a running research prototype the project resulted in an understanding of many design mistakes and thus has spawned a second generation research activity which is currently being pursued. This paper is a description of the basic design principles and the resulting system components (hardware and software).

Basic Concepts

Single Cycle Implementation

Probably the major distinguishing characteristic of the 801 architecture is that its instructions are constrained to execute in a single, straightforward, rather primitive machine cycle. A similar general approach has been pursued by a group at the University of California [1].

Complex, high-function instructions, which require several cycles to execute, are conventionally realized by some combination of random logic and microcode. It is often true that implementing a complex function in random logic will result in its execution being significantly faster than if the function were programmed as a sequence of primitive instructions. Examples are floating point arithmetic and fixed point multiply. We have no objection to this strategy, provided the frequency of use justifies the cost and, more important, provided these complex instructions in no way slow down the primitive instructions.

But it is just this pernicious effect on the primitive instructions that has made us suspicious. Most instruction frequency studies show a sharp skew in favor of high usage of primitive instructions (such as Load, Store, Branch, Compare, Add). If the presence of a more complex set adds just one logic level to a 10 level basic machine cycle (e.g. to fetch a micro instruction from ROS), the CPU has been slowed down by 10%. The frequency and performance improvement of the complex functions must first overcome this 10% degradation, and then justify the additional cost. If the presence of complex functions results in the CPU exceeding a packaging constraint on some level (e.g. a chip, a board), the performance degradation can be even more substantial.

Often, however, a minicomputer that boasts of a rich set of complex instructions has not spent additional hardware at all, but has simply microprogrammed the functions. These microinstructions are designed to execute in a single cycle and, in that cycle, to set controls most useful for the functions desired. This however, is exactly the design goal of the 801 primitive instruction set. We question, therefore, the need for a separate set of instructions.

In fact, for "vertical microcode", the benefits claimed are generally not due to the power of the instructions as much as to their residence in a high-speed control store. This amounts to a hardware architect attempting to guess which subroutines, or macros, are most frequently used and assigning high speed memory to them. It has resulted, for instance, in functions like Extended-Precision Floating Point Divide and Translate-and-Test on S/370's residing in high speed storage, while procedure prologues and the First-Level-Interrupt-Handler are in main storage. The 801 CPU gets its instructions from an "instruction cache" which is managed by LRU information. Thus all frequently used functions are very likely to be found in this high-speed storage, exhibiting the performance characteristics of vertical microcode.

Programming complex functions as software procedures or macros rather than in microcode has three advantages:

First, the CPU is interruptible at "microcode" boundaries, hence more responsive. Architectures with complex instructions either restrict interrupts to instruction boundaries, or (as in, for instance, the Move Characters Long instruction on the S/370) define specific interruptible points. If the instruction must be atomic, the implementation must ensure that it can successfully complete before any observable state is saved. Thus, in the S/370 Move Character instruction, before starting the move all pages are pretouched (and locked, in an MP system) to guard against a page fault interrupt occurring after the move has begun. If interruptible points are architected, the state must be such that the instruction is restartable.

The second advantage of programming these functions is that an optimizing compiler can often separate their components, moving some parts out of a loop, commoning others, etc.

Thirdly, it is often possible for parts of a complex instruction to be computed at compile time. Consider, for instance, the S/370 Move Character instruction once again. Each execution of this instruction must determine the optimal move strategy by examining the lengths of the source and target strings, whether (and in what direction) they overlap, and what their alignment characteristics are. But, for most programming languages, these may all be known at compile time. Consider also a multiply instruction. If one of the operands is a constant, known at compile time, the compiler can often produce more efficient "shift/add" sequences than the general multiply microcode subroutine.

The major disadvantage to using procedures instead of microcode to implement complex functions occurs when the micro instruction set is defined to permit its operands to be indirectly named by the register name fields in the instruction which is being interpreted. Since, in the 801 and in most conventional architectures, the register numbers are bound into the instructions a compiler must adopt some specific register usage convention for the procedure operands, and move the operands to these registers when necessary.

A computer whose instructions all execute very efficiently, however, is attractive only if the number of such instructions required to perform a task is not commensurately larger than that required of a more complex instruction set. The 801 project was concerned only with the execution of programs compiled by our optimizing compiler. Therefore, within the constraints of a primitive data flow, we left the actual definition of the instructions to the compiler writers. The results will be discussed later, but generally show pathlengths (that is, number of instructions executed) about equivalent to those on a S/370 for systems code, and up to 50% longer for commercial and scientific applications (given no hardware floating point).

Overlapped Storage Access

801 instruction mixes show that about 30% of instructions go to storage to send or receive data, and between 10% and 20% of instructions are taken branches. Moreover, for many applications, a significant portion of the memory bandwidth is used by I/O. If the CPU is forced to wait many cycles for storage access its internal performance will be wasted.

The second major design goal of the 801 project, therefore, was to organize the storage hierarchy and develop a system architecture to minimize CPU idle time due to storage access. First, it was clear that a cache was required whose access time was consistent with the machine cycle of the CPU. Secondly we chose a "store-in-cache" strategy (instead of "storing through" to the backing store) so that the 10% of expected store instructions would not degrade the performance severely. (For instance, if the time to store a word through to the backing store is ten cycles, and 10% of instructions are stores, this will add up to one cycle to each instruction on average depending on the amount of execution overlap.)

But a CPU organization that needs a new instruction at every cycle as well as accessing data every third cycle will still be degraded by a single conventional cache that delivers a word every cycle. Thus we decided to split the cache into a part containing data and a part containing instructions. In this way we effectively doubled the bandwidth to the cache and allowed asynchronous fetching of instructions and data at the backing store.

Most conventional architectures make this decision difficult because every store of data can be a modification of an instruction, perhaps even the one following the store. Thus the hardware must ensure that the two caches are properly synchronized, a job that is either expensive or degrading, or both. Even instruction prefetch mechanisms are complex since the effective address of a store must be compared to the Instruction Address Register.

Historically, as soon as index registers were introduced into computers the frequency of instruction modification fell dramatically until, today, instructions are almost never modified. Therefore the 801 architecture does not require this hazard detection. Instead it exposes the existence of the split cache to software and provides instructions by which software can synchronize the caches when required. In our system the only program that modifies instructions is the one that loads programs into memory.

Similarly, in conventional systems in which the existence of a cache is unobservable to the software, I/O must (logically) go through the cache. This is often accomplished in less expensive systems by sending the I/O physically through the cache. The result is that the CPU is idle while the I/O proceeds, and that after an I/O burst the contents of the cache no longer reflect the working set of the process being executed, forcing it back into transient mode. Even in more expensive systems a broadcasting or directory-duplication strategy may result in some performance degradation.

We observed that responsibility for the initiation of I/O in current systems was evolving towards paging supervisors, system I/O managers using fixed block transfers, and, for low speed devices, a buffer strategy which moves data between subsystem buffers and user areas. This results in the I/O manager knowing the location and extent of the storage being accessed, and knowing when an I/O transfer is in process. Thus this software can properly synchronize the caches, and the I/O hardware can transmit directly to and from the backing store. The result of this system approach in our prototype is that even when half of the memory bandwidth is being used for I/O the CPU is virtually undegraded.

Notice that in the preceding discussions (and in the earlier discussion of complex instructions) an underlying strategy is being pervasively applied. Namely, wherever there is a system function that is expensive or slow in all its generality, but where software can recognize a frequently occurring degenerate case (or can move the entire function from run time to compile time) that function is moved from hardware to software, resulting in lower cost *and* improved performance.

An interesting example of the application of this strategy concerns managing the cache itself. In the 801 the cache line is 32 bytes and the largest unit of a store is four bytes. In such a cache, whose line size is larger than the unit of a store and in which a "store in cache" approach is taken, a store directed at a word which is not in the cache must initiate a fetch of the entire line from the backing store into the cache. This is because, as far as the cache can tell, a load of another word from this line might be requested subsequently. Frequently, however, the store is simply the first store into what to the program is newly acquired space. It could be a new activation on a process stack just pushed on procedure call (e.g. PL/I Automatic); it could be an area obtained by a request to the operating system; or it could be a register save area used by the First Level Interrupt Handler. In all of these cases the hardware does not know that no old values from that line will be needed, while to the compiler and supervisor this situation is quite clear. We have defined explicit instructions in the 801 for cache management so that software can reduce these unnecessary loads and stores of cache lines.

One other 801 system strategy leads to more effective use of the cache. Conventional software assumes that its memory is randomly addressable. Because of this assumption each service program in the supervisor and subsystems has its own local temporary storage. Thus an application program requesting these services will cause references to many different addresses. In a high-level-language-based system like the 801, control program services are CALL'ed just like a user's subroutines. The result is that all these service programs get their temporary areas from the same stack, resulting in much reuse of cache lines and, therefore, higher cache hit ratios.

So far we have discussed 801 features that result in overlapped access to the cache between instructions and data, overlapped backing store access among the caches and I/O, less hardware synchronizing among the caches and I/O, and techniques to improve the cache hit ratios. One other aspect of the 801 CPU design and architecture should be described to complete the picture.

Even if almost all instruction and data references are found in the cache, and the cache and backing store are always available to the CPU, a conventional CPU will still often be idle while waiting for a load to complete or for the target of a branch to be fetched. Sophisticated CPU's often keep branch-taken histories or fetch ahead on both paths in order to overcome this idle time. In the 801 project we observed that, with a small number of hardware primitives, software (i.e. the compiler) could reorder programs so that the semantics remained unchanged but the hardware could easily overlap this idle time with useful work.

On load instructions the register that is to be the target of the load is locked by the CPU. The CPU then continues execution of the instruction stream until it reaches an instruction that requires this register, at which time it idles until the load is completed. Thus, if the compiler can find a useful instruction to put after the load that does not require the result of the load, the CPU will not be idle at all while the data cache fetches the requested word. (And if the compiler can find several such instructions to put after the load, execution of these will even overlap cache miss.)

Similarly for branches, the 801 architecture defines, for every type of branch instruction, an alternate form called Branch with Execute. (This is similar to the delayed branch in the RISC computer [1].) These instructions have exactly the same semantics as their corresponding branch instructions, except that while the instruction cache is fetching the branch target the CPU executes the instruction that has been placed immediately after the Branch with Execute instruction. For instance, in the sequence:

    LOAD R1, A
    BNZ L

the CPU would be idle while the instruction cache was fetching L, if the branch was taken. Changing the BRANCH-NON-ZERO to a BRANCH NON-ZERO WITH EXECUTE, and moving the LOAD instruction results in:

    BNZX L
    LOAD R1,A

which has exactly the same semantics but allows the CPU to execute the LOAD while the instruction cache is fetching the instruction at L. The 801 compiler is able, generally, to convert about 60% of the branches in a program into the execute form.

A Compiler-Based System

So far we have discussed two major ideas which pervade the 801 system. First, build a CPU that can execute its instructions quickly (i.e. in one relatively short machine cycle), and define these instructions to be a good target for compilation so that resulting pathlengths are generally commensurate with those for the same functions on more complex instruction sets (e.g. S/370). Second, define the storage hierarchy architecture, the CPU instructions, the I/O architecture and the software so that the CPU will generally not have to wait for storage access. The third major idea centers about the 801 compiler. A fundamental decision of the 801 project was to base the entire system on its pervasive use. This has resulted in the following system characteristics:

Instruction sets for conventional CPU's have been defined with an implicit assumption that many programmers will use assembly language. This assumption has motivated the definition of complex instructions (such as Edit and Mark, Translate and Test) almost as much as has the notion of a fast control store. But, increasingly, programmers do not use assembly language except where optimal performance is essential or machine functions are required that are not reflected in the source language.

The compiler for the 801 has demonstrated that it can produce object code that is close enough to best hand code generally so that assembly language programming is almost never needed for performance. The operating system has isolated those machine-dependent functions not reflected in the language (such as Disable, Start I/O, Dispatch) and developed efficient procedures which provide these functions with minimal linkage overhead.

The result is a system in which less than a thousand lines of supervisor code (and some of the "microcode" subroutine implementations of the complex functions) are written in Assembly language. This has relieved the 801 architecture of the burden of being easy to program directly. Virtually the only programmers who are concerned with the nature of the architecture are the compiler writers, and the "core" supervisor writers. All others see the system only through a high level language. Because of this, the 801 architects were able to base their decisions solely on the needs of these few programmers, and on cost/performance considerations.

Thus the 801 architecture was defined as that set of run-time operations which:
- could not be moved to compile time,
- could not be more efficiently executed by object code produced by a compiler which understood the high level intent of the program,
- was to be implemented in random logic more effectively than the equivalent sequence of software instructions.

It might at first seem surprising that compiler writers would not want powerful high level instructions. But in fact these instructions are often hard to use since the compiler must find those cases which exactly fit the architected construct. Code selection becomes not just finding the fewest instructions, but the right instructions. And when these instructions name operands in storage instead of in registers, code selection will depend upon the results of register allocation.

The 801 approach to protection is strongly based upon this compiler intermediary between users and the hardware. Conventional systems expect application programmers, and certainly subsystem programmers, to use assembly language or other languages in which it is possible to subvert the system (either deliberately or accidentally). Thus hardware facilities are required to properly isolate these users. The most popular examples of these facilities are storage protect keys, multiple virtual address spaces, and supervisor state. These facilities are often costly and sometimes degrade performance. But what is more important is that they are often inadequate. Since even 16 different keys are insufficient to assign uniquely, for instance, different users are sometimes given the same key or the system limits the number of active users. Also, because the key disciplines are only two level, many subsystems are forced to run with full addressing capability.

If, however, users are constrained to a properly defined source language, and their programs are processed by an intelligent compiler and run on an operating system that understands the addressing strategies of the compiler, it is possible to provide better protection at less cost. The 801 system, therefore, is based upon the assumption that certain critical components of the compiler are correct, and that all programs executing on the system (except for a small supervisor core) have been compiled by this compiler. The system will guarantee:

• that all references to data (scalars, arrays, structures, areas) really do point to that data, and that the extents of the references are included in the extents of the data,

• that a reference to dynamically allocated-and-freed data is made only between an allocation and a free,

• that all branches are to labels, and all calls are to proper entry points in procedures,

• that the extents of all arguments to a procedure match the extents of their corresponding parameters, so that the protection persists across calls,

• that all declarations of global (external) variables in separately compiled procedures have consistent extents.

This checking is often done at compile time, link edit time, or program fetch time, but, when necessary, trap instructions are introduced into the object code to check at run time. The resulting increase in pathlength due to this run time checking is generally less than 10% because this code is optimized along with the rest of the program [5].

Notice that this is not a "strongly typed" approach to checking. Overlays of one data type on another are permitted, provided the domains are not exceeded. But our experience in running code conventionally on the S/370 and then on the 801 with this checking has shown that many program bugs are discovered and that, more importantly, they tend to be the kinds of bugs that elude normal component test procedures.

It was noted earlier that, because the operating system was also written in the 801's high level language and compiled by the 801 compiler, its service programs were simply CALL'ed like any external procedure, resulting in better cache behavior. An even more important consequence of this design, however, is that the checking of matches between arguments and parameters is performed at the time a program is loaded into memory and linked to the supervisor. This results in efficient calls to supervisor services, especially when compared to conventional overhead. It means, also, that the compiler-generated "traceback" mechanism continues into the operating system, so that when an error occurs the entire symbolic call chain can be displayed.

The linkage between procedures on the 801 is another example of a consistent machine design based on a system used solely via a high level language. We wanted applications on the 801 to be programmed using good programming style. This implies a large number of procedures and many calls. In particular it implies that very short procedures can be freely written and invoked. Thus, for these short procedures, the linkage must be minimal.

The 801 procedure linkage attempts to keep arguments in registers where possible. It also expects some register values to be destroyed across a CALL. The result is that a procedure call can be as cheap as a Branch and Link instruction when the called procedure can execute entirely out of available registers. As more complex functions are required they increase the overhead for linkage incrementally.

Finally, the pervasive use of a high level language and compiler has given the project great freedom to change. The architecture has undergone several drastic changes, and countless minor ones. The linkage conventions, storage mapping strategies, and run time library have similarly been changed as experience provided new insights. In almost every case the cost of the change was limited to recompilations.

This ability to preserve source code, thus limiting the impact of change, can have significant long range impact on systems. New technologies (and packaging) often offer great performance and cost benefits if they can be exploited with architecture changes.

System Components

The Programming Language

The source language for the 801 system is called PL.8. It was defined to be an appropriate language for writing systems programs and to produce optimized code with the checking described above.

PL.8 began as an almost-compatible subset of PL/I, so that the PL.8 compiler was initially compiled by the PL/I Optimizer. It contains, for instance, the PL/I storage classes, functions, floating point variables, varying character strings, arrays with adjustable extents, the structured control primitives of PL/I, the string-handling built-in-functions, etc. It differs from PL/I in its interpretation of bit strings as binary numbers, in its binary arithmetic (which simply reflects the arithmetic of the 801 hardware) and in some language additions borrowed from Pascal. It does not contain full PL/I ON conditions, multiple entry points, or the ability to develop absolute pointers to Automatic or Static storage. Relative pointers, called Offsets, can be developed only to Areas. This discipline has several advantages:

- All program and data areas can be moved freely by the system, since absolute addresses are never stored in user-addressable data structures.

- Any arithmetic data type can be used as an offset (relative pointer) and all arithmetic operations can be freely performed, since the extent checks will be made on every use.

- A store, using a computed offset, can only affect other data in that particular area. Thus, the locations whose values could have been changed by this store are significantly limited. This enhances the power of the optimization algorithms.

- It leads to better structured, more easily readable programs.

The Optimizing Compiler

There have been about seven programmers in the compiler group since the project began. A running compiler was completed after about two years. Since then the group has been involved with language extensions, new optimization techniques, debugging, and useability aids. It should be noted, however, that the Computer Sciences department at Yorktown Heights has been working on compiler algorithms for about twenty years, many of which were simply incorporated into this compiler.

The PL.8 compiler adopts two strategies which lead to its excellent object code. The first is a strategy which translates in the most straightforward, inefficient (but correct) manner from PL.8 source language to an intermediate language (IL). This translation has as its only objective the production of semantically correct object code. It seeks almost no special cases, so that it is relatively easy to debug. Moreover the intermediate language which is its target is at a very low level, almost the real 801 machine.

The next phase of the compiler develops flow graphs of the program as described in [2], and, using these graphs, performs a series of conventional optimization algorithms, such as:

- common sub-expression elimination,
- moving code out of loops,
- eliminating dead code,
- strength reduction.

Each of these algorithms transforms an IL program into a semantically equivalent, but more efficient, IL program. Thus these procedures can be (and are) called repetitively and in any order. While these procedures are quite sophisticated, since each of them acts on the entire program and on all programs, a bug in one of them is very easily observed.

The power of this approach is not only in the optimizing power of the algorithms but in the fact that they are applied to such a low level IL. Conventional global optimizing compilers perform their transformations at a much higher level of text, primarily because they were designed to run in relatively small size memory. Thus they can often not do much more than convert one program to another which could have been written by a more careful programmer. The PL.8 compiler, on the other hand, applies its optimization algorithms to addressing code, domain checking code, procedure linkage code, etc.

The second compiler strategy which is different from conventional compilers is our approach to register allocation [3,4]. The IL, like that of most compilers, assumes an arbitrarily large number of registers. In fact the result of each different computation in the program is assigned a different (symbolic) register. The job for register allocation is simply to assign real registers to these symbolic registers. Conventional approaches use some subset of the real registers for special purposes (e.g. pointers to the stack, to the code, to the parameter list). The remaining set is assigned locally within a statement, or at best a basic block (e.g. a loop). Between these assignments results which are to be preserved are temporarily stored, and variables are redundantly loaded.

The 801 approach observes that the register assignment problem is equivalent to the graph coloring problem, where each symbolic register is a node and the real registers are different colors. If two symbolic registers have the property that there is at least one point in the program where both their values must be retained, we model that property on the graph as a vertex between the two nodes. Thus the register allocation problem is equivalent to the problem of coloring the graph so that no two nodes connected by a vertex are colored with the same crayon.

This global approach has proven very effective. Surprisingly many procedures "color" so that no store/load sequences are necessary to keep results in storage temporarily. (At present the compiler "colors" only computations. There is, however, no technical reason why local variables could not also be "colored" and we intend to do this eventually.) When it does fail, other algorithms which use this graph information are employed to decide what to store. Because of this ability of the compiler to effectively utilize a large number of registers, we decided to implement 32 general purpose registers in the hardware.

The compiler will also accept Pascal programs, producing compatible object code so that PL.8 and Pascal procedures can freely call one another. It will also produce efficient object code for the S/370, thus providing source code portability.

Instructions and Operands

Instruction formats and data representations are areas which saw significant change as the project evolved. This section describes the current version of the architecture. The kind of instruction and operand set requested by the compiler developers turned out, fortunately, to be precisely one which made hardware implementation easier. The overriding theme was regularity. For instance:

- All operands must be aligned on boundaries consistent with their size (i.e. halfwords on halfword boundaries, words on word boundaries). All instructions are fullwords on fullword boundaries. (This results in an increase in program size over two-and-four byte formats, but the larger format allows us to define more powerful instructions resulting in shorter pathlengths.) Since the 801 was designed for a cache/main store/hard disk hierarchy, and virtual memory addressing, the consequence of larger programs is limited to more disk space and larger working sets (i.e., penalties in cache-hit-ratio and page-fault frequency).

With this alignment constraint the hardware is greatly simplified. Each data or instruction access can cause at most one cache miss or one page fault. The caches will have to access at most one aligned word. Instruction prefetch mechanisms can easily find op codes if they are searching for branches. Instruction alignment and data alignment are unnecessary. Instruction Length Count fields (as in the S/370 PSW) are unnecessary and software can always backtrack instructions. Moreover, for data, traces show that misaligned operands rarely appear and when they do are often the result of poor programming style.

- Given four byte instructions, other benefits accrue. Register fields in instructions are made five bits long so that the 801 can name 32 registers. (This aspect of 801 architecture makes it feasible to use the 801 to emulate other architectures which have 16 GPR's, since 16 801 registers are still available for emulator use.)

Four byte instructions also allow the target register of every instruction to be named explicitly so that the input operands need not be destroyed. This facility is applied pervasively, as in "Shift Reg A Left by contents of Reg B and Store Result in Reg C". This feature of the architecture simplifies register allocation and, eliminates many Move Register instructions.

- The 801 is a true 32 bit architecture, not a 16 bit architecture with extended registers. Addresses are 32 bits long; arithmetic is 32 bit two's complement; logical and shift instructions deal with 32 bit words (and can shift distances up to 32). A useful way to reduce pathlength (and cache misses) is to define a rich set of immediate fields, but of course it is impossible to encode a general 32 bit constant to fit into an immediate field in a four byte instruction. The 801 defines the following subsets of such constants which meet most requirements:

• A 16 bit immediate field for arithmetic and address calculation (D field) which is interpreted as a two's complement signed integer. (Thus the constants $\pm 2^{15}$ can be represented immediately.)

• A 16 bit logical constant. Each logical operation has two immediate forms - upper and lower, so that in at most two instructions (cycles) logical operations can be performed using a 32 bit logical constant.

• An 11 bit encoding of a Mask (i.e. a substring of ones surrounded by zeros or zeros surrounded by ones). Thus for shift, insert, and isolate operations the substring can be defined immediately.

• A 16 bit immediate field for branch target calculation (D-field) which is interpreted as a signed two's complement offset from the address of the current instruction. (Thus a relative branch to and from anywhere within a 32K byte procedure can be specified immediately.)

• A 26 bit immediate field specifying an offset from the address of the current instruction or an absolute address, so that branches between procedures, to supervisor services, or to "microcode subroutines" can be specified without having to establish addressability.

- Load and Store instructions are available in every combination of the following options:

• Load or Store,
• character, halfword, sign-extended halfword, fullword,
• Base + Index, or Base + Displacement effective address calculation. (Usage statistics for S/370 show low use for the full B+X+D form. Thus a three input adder did not seem warranted.)
• Store the effective address back into the base register (i.e. "autoincrement") or not.

- Branches are available with the following branch target specifications

• absolute 26 bit address,
• Instruction Address Register + Displacement (signed 16 or 26 bit word offset),
• Register + Register,

Branch and Link forms are defined normally. But conditional branches are defined not only based upon the state of the Condition Register but on the presence or absence of a one in any bit position in any register. (This allows the Test Under Mask - Branch Condition sequence in S/370 to be executed in one machine cycle (and no storage references) if the bit is already in a register. Again the power of global register allocation makes this more probable.)

- There are Compare and Trap instructions defined which allow the S/370 Compare - Branch Condition sequence to be executed in one machine cycle for those cases where the test is for an infrequently-encountered exception condition. These instructions are used to implement the run-time extent checking discussed earlier.

- Arithmetic is 32 bit two's complement. There are special instructions defined to allow MAX, MIN, and decimal add and subtract to be coded efficiently. There are also two instructions defined (Multiply Step and Divide Step) to allow two 32 bit words to be multiplied in 16 cycles (yielding a 64 bit product) and a 64 bit dividend to be divided by a 32 bit divisor in 32 cycles (yielding a 32 bit quotient and a 32 bit remainder).

- The 801 has a rich set of shift and insert instructions. These were developed to make device controller "microcode", emulator "microcode" and systems code very efficient. The functions, all available in one machine cycle, are:

• ring shift a register up to 31 positions (specified in another register or in an immediate field),
• using a mask (in another register or in an immediate field) merge this shifted word with all zeros (i.e. isolate the field) or with any other register (i.e. merge), or with the result of the previous shift (i.e. long shift),
• store this back into any other register or into storage (i.e. move character string).

(This last facility allows misaligned source and target character string moves to execute as fast as two characters/cycle.)

Interrupts and I/O

I/O in the 801 prototype is controlled by a set of adapters which attach to the CPU and memory by two buses. The External Bus attaches the adapters to the CPU. It is used by software to send commands and receive status, by means of synchronous Read and Write instructions. Data is transmitted between the adapters and the 801 backing store through the MIO (Memory-I/O) bus. (As described above it is the responsibility of the software to synchronize the caches.)

Rather than support integrated and complex (multi-level) interrupt hardware, the 801 again moves to software functions that can be performed more efficiently by programming. Software on systems that provide, say, eight interrupt levels often find this number inadequate as a distinguisher of interrupt handlers. Thus a software first level interrupt handler is programmed on top of the hardware, increasing the real time to respond. Moreover the requirement to support eight sets of registers results in these being stored in some fast memory rather than in logic on-chip. This results in a slower machine cycle. If the real time responsiveness of a system is measured realistically it must include not only the time to get to an interrupt handler but the time to process the interrupt, which clearly depends on the length of the machine cycle. Thus in a practical sense the 801 is a good real-time system.

Interrupt determination and priority handling is packaged outboard of the CPU chips in a special unit called the External Interrupt controller (along with the system clocks, timers, and adapter locks). (This packaging decision allows other versions of 801 systems to choose different interrupt strategies without impacting the CPU design.) In this controller there are (logically) two bit vectors. The first, the Interrupt Request Vector (IRV) contains a bit for each device which may wish to interrupt the CPU (plus one each for the clocks, timers, and the CPU itself for simulating external interrupts). These bits are tied by lines to the devices.

The second vector, called the Interrupt Mask Vector (IMV) contains a bit corresponding to each bit in the IRV. The IMV is loaded by software in the CPU. It dynamically establishes the priority levels of the interrupt requesters. If there is a one in a position in the IRV corresponding to a one in the corresponding position of the IMV, and the 801 CPU is enabled for interrupt, the CPU is interrupted.

On interrupt the CPU becomes disabled and unrelocated, and begins executing the First Level Interrupt Handler (FLIH) in lower memory. The FLIH stores the interrupted state, reads the IRV and determines the requester. Using this position number, it sends a new IMV (reflecting the priority of the requester) and branches to the interrupt handler for that requester, which executes enabled and relocated. Pathlengths for the FLIH are less than 100 instructions (and can be reduced for a subclass of fast-response interrupts), and less than 150 instructions for the dispatcher (when the interrupt handler completes).

Internal Bus

We have, so far, described a CPU that must have the following (logical) buses to storage:

- a command bus to describe the function requested,
- an address bus,
- a source data bus for Stores,
- a target data bus for Loads.

We observed that other functions might be implemented outboard of the CPU and could attach to the CPU via these same buses (e.g. floating point). Therefore we exposed these buses in an 801 instruction, called Internal Bus Operation. This instruction has operands to name the following:

- the bus unit being requested,
- the command,
- the two operands (B,D, or B,X) which will be added
   to produce the output on the address bus,
- the source register,
- the target register, if needed,

and three flags:
- privileged command or not,
- target register required or not,
- address bus sent back to Base register, or not.

Having defined this generic instruction we gave bus unit names to the instruction and data caches, the external interrupt controller, the timer, and the relocate controller, and assigned the IBO op code to all instructions directed to these units.

Prototype Hardware

A hardware prototype has been built for an early version of the 801 architecture, out of MECL 10K DIP's. It runs at 1.1 cycles per instruction. (This number must be taken as an out-of-cache performance figure because the applications which currently run show hit ratios at close to 100% after the initial cache load.) We do not yet have multiple-user measurements.

The register file is capable of reading out any three and writing back any two registers within a single cycle. Thus the CPU is pipelined as follows:

- The first level of the pipeline decodes the instruction, reads two registers into the ALU, executes the ALU, and either latches the result or, for Load or Store instructions, sends the computed address to the cache. On a store instruction, the data word is also fetched from the register file and sent to the cache.

- The second level of the pipeline sends the latched result through the shifter, sets the condition register bits, and stores the result back into a register. During this cycle also, if a word has been received from the cache as the result of a load instruction it is loaded into the register.

(The hardware monitors register names to bypass the load when the result is being immediately used.)

The cache is designed so that on a miss the requested word is sent directly to the CPU, thus reducing lockout while the cache line is being filled.

Performance Comparisons

Figures 1 and 2 show some early performance comparisons. Since the compiler will produce object code for the S/370 as well as the 801, these comparisons are possible for the same source programs and the same compiler. We use the number of cycles in the inner loops, and the number of storage references in the inner loops to approximate dynamic performance.

Figure 1 shows results for an in-memory sort procedure. Figure 2 shows the results for randomly selected modules from the compiler itself. Note that as the modules get larger the power of global register allocation results in fewer storage references. Note also that, in spite of the fact that the 801 contains no complex instructions, the 801 modules contain fewer instructions and fewer instruction executions. This is because the complex instructions are generally very infrequent whereas the 801 has a more powerful set of primitive instructions.

Figure 1

Performance Comparisons

Program: <u>Heap Sort programmed in PL.8</u>

| | | | In Inner Loop | | |
CPU	Code Size (Bytes)	No. of Instructions	Data Ref's	Cycles	Cycles/Inst.
S/370-168	236	33	8	56	1.7
801	240	28	6	31	1.1

Figure 2

Programs: <u>Randomly Selected Modules in PL.8 Compiler</u>

Module	Code Size (Bytes)	Dynamic Comparisons	
		Instructions Executed	Data Storage References
(In increasing size order	801/S/370	801/S/370	801/370
FIND	1.02	.91	.60
SEARCHV	.93	.83	.38
LOAD S	.83	.91	.43
P2_EXTS	1.00	1.00	.57
SORT_S1	.86	.78	.59
PM_ADD1	.86	.96	.63
ELMISS	.87	.86	.69
PM_GKV	.92	.76	.46
P5DBG	.98	.81	.52
DESCRPT	.86	.75	.42
ENTADD	.79	.76	.42
Total	.90	.80	.50

Conclusions

While we do not have nearly enough measurements to draw hard conclusions, the 801 group has developed a set of intuitive principles which seem to hold consistently:

- At least in the low-to-mid range of processor complexity, a general purpose, register-oriented instruction set can be at least as good as any special vertical microcode set. Thus there should be only one hard-wired instruction set, and it should be directly available to the compiler.

- A good global register allocator can effectively use a large number of general purpose registers. Therefore all the registers which the CPU can afford to build in hardware should be directly and simultaneously addressable. Stack machines, machines that hide some of the registers to improve CALL performance, multiple-interrupt level machines, all seem to make poorer use of the available registers.

- Protection is far more effectively provided at a level where the source language program is understood.

- It is easy to design and build a fast, cheap CPU, and will be more so as VLSI evolves. The harder problem is to develop software, architecture and hardware which does not keep the CPU idling due to storage access.

Acknowledgments

The seminal idea for the 801 and many subsequent concepts are due to John Cocke.

In six years, the list of contributors has grown too large to list here. The following people have been with the project from beginning until the present and are responsible for most of the design and implementation.

Hardware: Frank Carrubba, manager. Paul Stuckert, Norman Kreitzer, Richard Freitas, Kenneth Case

Software: Marc Auslander, manager
Compiler: Martin Hopkins, manager. Richard Goldberg, Peter Oden, Philip Owens, Peter Markstein, Gregory Chaitin.
Control Program: Richard Oehler, manager. Albert Chang.

Joel Birnbaum was the first manager of the project and later a constant supporter. Bill Worley also contributed significantly through the years.

References

[1] Patterson, David A. and Séquin, Carlo H., "RISC-I: A Reduced Instruction Set VLSI Computer," Eighth Annual Symposium in Computer Architecture, May, 1981.

[2] Cocke, John and Markstein, Peter W., "Measurement of Program Improvement Algorithms," Information Processing 80, North-Holland Publishing Co., 1980.

[3] Chaitin, Gregory J. et al, "Register Allocation via Coloring," Computer Languages, Vol. 6, pp. 47-57, 1981, Great Britain.

[4] Chaitin, Gregory J., "Register Allocation and Spilling via Coloring," IBM Research Report RC9124, 1981.

[5] Markstein, V., Cocke, J., and P. Markstein, "Optimization of Range Checking," IBM Research Report RC8456, 1980.

The Case for the
Reduced Instruction Set Computer

David A. Patterson

Computer Science Division
University of California
Berkeley, California 94720

David R. Ditzel

Bell Laboratories
Computing Science Research Center
Murray Hill, New Jersey 07974

INTRODUCTION

One of the primary goals of computer architects is to design computers that are more cost-effective than their predecessors. Cost-effectiveness includes the cost of hardware to manufacture the machine, the cost of programming, and costs incurred related to the architecture in debugging both the initial hardware and subsequent programs. If we review the history of computer families we find that the most common architectural change is the trend toward ever more complex machines. Presumably this additional complexity has a positive tradeoff with regard to the cost-effectiveness of newer models. In this paper we propose that this trend is not always cost-effective, and in fact, may even do more harm than good. We shall examine the case for a Reduced Instruction Set Computer (RISC) being as cost-effective as a Complex Instruction Set Computer (CISC). This paper will argue that the next generation of VLSI computers may be more effectively implemented as RISC's than CISC's.

As examples of this increase in complexity, consider the transitions from IBM System/3 to the System/38 [Utley78] and from the DEC PDP-11 to the VAX11. The complexity is indicated quantitatively by the size of the control store; for DEC the size has grown from 256 x 56 in the PDP 11/40 to 5120 x 96 in the VAX 11/780.

REASONS FOR INCREASED COMPLEXITY

Why have computers become more complex? We can think of several reasons:

Speed of Memory vs. Speed of CPU. John Cocke says that the complexity began with the transition from the 701 to the 709 [Cocke80]. The 701 CPU was about ten times as fast as the core main memory; this made any primitives that were implemented as subroutines much slower than primitives that were instructions. Thus the floating point subroutines became part of the 709 architecture with dramatic gains. Making the 709 more complex resulted in an advance that made it more cost-effective than the 701. Since then, many "higher-level" instructions have been added to machines in an attempt to improve performance. Note that this trend began because of the imbalance in speeds; it is not clear that architects have asked themselves whether this imbalance still holds for their designs.

Microcode and LSI Technology. Microprogrammed control allows the implementation of complex architectures more cost-effectively than hardwired control [Husson70]. Advances in integrated circuit memories made in the late 60's and early 70's have caused microprogrammed control to be the more cost-effective approach in almost every case. Once the decision is made to use microprogrammed control, the cost to expand an instruction set is very small; only a few more words of control store. Since the sizes of control memories are often powers of 2, sometimes the instruction set can be made more complex at no extra hardware cost by expanding the microprogram to completely fill the control memory. Thus the advances in implementation technology resulted in cost-effective implementation of architectures that essentially moved traditional subroutines into the architecture. Examples of such instructions are string editing, integer-to-floating conversion, and mathematical operations such as polynomial evaluation.

Code Density. With early computers, memory was very expensive. It was therefore cost effective to have very compact programs. Complex instruction sets are often heralded for their "supposed" code compaction. Attempting to obtain code density by increasing the complexity of the instruction set is often a double-edged sword however, as more instructions and addressing modes require more bits to represent them. Evidence suggests that code compaction can be as easily achieved merely by cleaning up the original instruction set. While code compaction is important, the cost of 10% more memory is often far cheaper than the cost of squeezing 10% out of the CPU by architectural "innovations." Cost for a large scale cpu is in additional circuit packages needed while cost for a single chip cpu is more likely to be in slowing down performance due to larger (hence slower) control PLA's.

Marketing Strategy. Unfortunately, the primary goal of a computer company is not to design the most cost-effective computer; the primary goal of a computer company is to make the most money by selling computers. In order to sell computers manufacturers must convince customers that their design is superior to their competitor's. Complex instruction sets are certainly primary "marketing" evidence of a better computer. In order to keep their jobs, architects must keep selling new and better designs to their internal management. The number of instructions and their "power" is often used to promote an architecture, regardless of the actual use or cost-effectiveness of the complex instruction set. In some sense the manufacturers and designers cannot be blamed for this as long as buyers of computers do not question the issue of complexity vs. cost-effectiveness. For the case of silicon houses, a fancy microprocessor is often used as a draw card, as the real profit comes from luring customers into buying large amounts of memory to go with their relatively inexpensive cpu.

Upward Compatibility. Coincident with marketing strategy is the perceived need for upward compatibility. Upward compatibility means that the primary way to improve a design is to add new, and usually more complex, features. Seldom are instructions or addressing modes removed from an architecture, resulting in a gradual increase in both the number and complexity of instructions over a series of computers. New architectures tend to have a habit of including all instructions found in the machines of successful competitors, perhaps because architects and customers have no real grasp over what defines a "good" instruction set.

Support for High Level Languages. As the use of high level languages becomes increasingly popular, manufacturers have become eager to provide more powerful instructions to support them. Unfortunately there is little evidence to suggest that any of the more complicated instruction sets have actually provided such support. On the contrary, we shall argue that in many cases the complex instruction sets are more detrimental than useful. The effort to support high-level languages is laudable, but we feel that often the focus has been on the wrong issues.

Use of Multiprogramming. The rise of timesharing required that computers be able to respond to interrupts with the ability to halt an executing process and restart it at a later time. Memory management and paging additionally required that instructions could be halted before completion and later restarted. Though neither of these had a large effect on the design of instruction sets themselves, they had a direct effect on the implementation. Complex instructions and addressing modes increase the state that has to be saved on any interrupt. Saving this state often involves the use of shadow registers and a large increase in the complexity of the microcode. This complexity largely disappears on a machine without complicated instructions or addressing modes with side effects.

HOW HAVE CISC'S BEEN USED?

One of the interesting results of rising software costs is the increasing reliance on high-level languages. One consequence is that the compiler writer is replacing the assembly-language programmer in deciding which instructions the machine will execute. Compilers are often unable to utilize complex instructions, nor do they use the insidious tricks in which assembly language programmers delight. Compilers and assembly language programmers also rightfully ignore parts of the instruction set which are not useful under the given time-space tradeoffs. The result is that often only a fairly small part of the architecture is being used.

For example, measurements of a particular IBM 360 compiler found that 10 instructions accounted for 80% of all instructions executed, 16 for 90%, 21 for 95%, and 30 for 99% [Alexander75]. Another study of various compilers and assembly language programs concluded that "little flexibility would be lost if the set of instructions on the CDC-3600 were reduced to ½ or ¼ of the instructions now available."[Foster71] Shustek points out for the IBM 370 that "as has been observed many times, very few opcodes account for most of a program's execution. The COBOL program, for example, executes 84 of the available 183 instructions, but 48 represent 99.08 % of all instructions executed, and 26 represent 90.28 %."[Shustek78] Similar statistics are found when examining the use of addressing modes.

CONSEQUENCES OF CISC IMPLEMENTATIONS

Rapid changes in technology and the difficulties in implementing CISCs have resulted in several interesting effects.

Faster memory. The advances in semiconductor memory have made several changes to the assumptions about the relative difference in speed between the CPU and main memory. Semiconductor memories are both fast and relatively inexpensive. The recent use of cache memories in many systems further reduces the difference between CPU and memory speeds.

Irrational Implementations. Perhaps the most unusual aspect of the implementation of a complex architecture is that it is difficult to have "rational" implementations. By this we mean that special purpose instructions are not always faster than a sequence of simple instructions. One example was discovered by Peuto and Shustek for the IBM 370 [Peuto,Shustek77]; they found that a sequence of load instructions is faster than a load multiple instruction for fewer than 4 registers. This case covers 40% of the load multiple instructions in typical programs. Another comes from the VAX-11/780. The INDEX instruction is used to calculate the address of an array element while at the same time checking to see that the index fits in the array bounds. This is clearly an important function to accurately detect errors in high-level languages statements. We found that for the VAX 11/780, replacing this single "high level" instruction by several simple instructions (COMPARE, JUMP LESS UNSIGNED, ADD, MULTIPLY) that we could perform the same function 45%

faster! Furthermore, if the compiler took advantage of the case where the lower bound was zero, the simple instruction sequence was 60% faster. Clearly smaller code does not always imply faster code, nor do "higher-level" instructions imply faster code.

Lengthened Design Time. One of the costs that is sometimes ignored is the time to develop a new architecture. Even though the replication costs of a CISC may be low, the design time is greatly expanded. It took DEC only 6 months to design and begin delivery of the PDP-1, but it now takes at least three years to go through the same cycle for a machine like the VAX.[1] This long design-time can have a major effect on the quality of the resulting implementation; the machine is either announced with a three year old technology or the designers must try to forecast a good implementation technology and attempt to pioneer that technology while building the machine. It is clear that reduced design time would have very positive benefits on the resulting machine.

Increased Design Errors. One of the major problems of complex instruction sets is debugging the design; this usually means removing errors from the microprogram control. Although difficult to document, it is likely that these corrections were a major problem with the IBM 360 family, as almost every member of the family used read only control store. The 370 line uses alterable control store exclusively, due perhaps to decreased hardware costs, but more likely from the bad experience with errors on the 360. The control store is loaded from a floppy disk allowing microcode to be maintained similarly to operating systems; bugs are repaired and new floppies with updated versions of the microcode are released to the field. The VAX 11/780 design team realized the potential for microcode errors. Their solution was to use a Field Programmable Logic Array and 1024 words of Writable Control Store (WCS) to patch microcode errors. Fortunately DEC is more open about their experiences so we know that more than 50 patches have been made. Few believe that the last error has been found.[2]

RISC AND VLSI

The design of single chip VLSI computers makes the above problems with CISC's even more critical than with their multi-chip SSI implementations. Several factors indicate a Reduced Instruction Set Computer as a reasonable design alternative.

Implementation Feasibility. A great deal depends on being able to fit an entire CPU design on a single chip. A complex architecture has less of a chance of being realized in a given technology than does a less complicated architecture. A good example of this is DEC's VAX series of computers. Though the high end models may seem impressive, the complexity of the architecture makes its implementation on a single chip extremely difficult with current design rules, if not totally impossible. Improvement in VLSI technology will eventually make a single chip version feasible, but only after less complex but equally functional 32-bit architectures can be realized. RISC computers therefore benefit from being realizable at an earlier date.

---

[1] Some have offered other explanations. Everything takes longer now (software, mail, nuclear power plants), so why shouldn't computers? It was also mentioned that a young, hungry company would probably take less time than an established company. Although these observations may partially explain DEC's experiences, we believe that, regardless of the circumstances, the complexity of the architecture will affect the design cycle.

[2] Each patch means several microinstructions must be put into WCS, so the 50 patches require 252 microinstructions. Since there was a good chance of errors in the complex VAX instructions, some of these were implemented only in WCS so the patches and the existing instructions use a substantial portion of the 1024 words.

Design Time. Design difficulty is a crucial factor in the success of VLSI computer. If VLSI technology continues to at least double chip density roughly every two years, a design that takes only two years to design and debug can potentially use a much superior technology and hence be more effective than a design that takes four years to design and debug. Since the turnaround time for a new mask is generally measured in months, each batch of errors delays product delivery another quarter; common examples are the 1-2 year delays in the Z8000 and MC68000.

Speed. The ultimate test for cost-effectiveness is the speed at which an implementation executes a given algorithm. Better use of chip area and availability of newer technology through reduced debugging time contribute to the speed of the chip. A RISC potentially gains in speed merely from a simpler design. Taking out a single address mode or instruction may lead to a less complicated control structure. This in turn can lead to smaller control PLA's, smaller microcode memories, fewer gates in the critical path of the machine; all of these can lead to a faster minor cycle time. If leaving out an instruction or address mode causes the machine to speed up the minor cycle by 10%, then the addition would have to speed up the machine by more than 10% to be cost-effective. So far, we have seen little hard evidence that complicated instruction sets are cost-effective in this manner.[3]

Better use of chip area. If you have the area, why not implement the CISC? For a given chip area there are many tradeoffs for what can be realized. We feel that the area gained back by designing a RISC architecture rather than a CISC architecture can be used to make the RISC even more attractive than the CISC. For example, we feel that the entire system performance might improve more if silicon area were instead used for on-chip caches [Patterson,Séquin80], larger and faster transistors, or even pipelining. As VLSI technology improves, the RISC architecture can always stay one step ahead of the comparable CISC. When the CISC becomes realizable on a single chip, the RISC will have the silicon area to use pipelining techniques; when the CISC gets pipelining the RISC will have on chip caches, etc. The CISC also suffers by the fact that its intrinsic complexity often makes advanced techniques even harder to implement.

SUPPORTING A HIGH-LEVEL LANGUAGE COMPUTER SYSTEM

Some would argue that simplifying an architecture is a backwards step in the support of high-level languages. A recent paper [Ditzel,Patterson80] points out that a "high level" architecture is not necessarily the most important aspect in achieving a High-Level Language Computer System. A High-Level Language Computer System has been defined as having the following characteristics:

(1) *Uses high-level languages for all programming, debugging and other user/system interactions.*

(2) *Discovers and reports syntax and execution time errors in terms of the high-level language source program.*

(3) *Does not have any outward appearance of transformations from the user programming language to any internal languages.*

Thus the only important characteristic is that a combination of hardware and software assures that the programmer is always interacting with the computer in terms of a high-level language. At no time need the programmer be aware of any lower levels in the writing or the debugging of a program. As long as this requirement is met, then the goal is achieved. Thus it makes no difference in

---

[3] In fact, there is evidence to the contrary. Harvey Cragon, chief architect of the TI ASC, said that this machine implemented a complex mechanism to improve performance of indexed reference inside of loops. Although they succeeded in making these operations run faster, he felt it made the ASC slower in other situations. The impact was to make the ASC slower than simpler computers designed by Cray [Cragon 80].

a High-Level Language Computer System whether it is implemented with a CISC that maps one-to-one with the tokens of the language, or if the same function is provided with a very fast but simple machine.

The experience we have from compilers suggests that the burden on compiler writers is eased when the instruction set is simple and uniform. Complex instructions that supposedly support high level functions are often impossible to generate from compilers.[4] Complex instructions are increasingly prone to implementing the "wrong" function as the level of the instruction increases. This is because the function becomes so specialized that it becomes useless for other operations.[5] Complex instructions can generally be replaced with a small number of lower level instructions, often with little or no loss in performance.[6] The time to generate a compiler for a CISC is additionally increased because bugs are more likely to occur in generating code for complex instructions.[7]

There is a fair amount of evidence that more complicated instructions designed to make compilers easier to write often do not accomplish their goal. Several reasons account for this. First, because of the plethora of instructions there are many ways to accomplish a given elementary operation, a situation confusing for both the compiler and compiler writer. Second, many compiler writers assume that they are dealing with a rational implementation when in fact they are not. The result is that the "appropriate" instruction often turns out to be the wrong choice. For example, pushing a register on the stack with **PUSHL R0** is slower than pushing it with the move instruction **MOVL R0,-(SP)** on the VAX 11/780. We can think of a dozen more examples offhand, for this and almost every other complicated machine. One has to take special care not to use an instruction "because its there." These problems cannot be "fixed" by different models of the same architecture without totally destroying either program portability or the reputation of a good compiler writer as a change in the relative instruction timings would require a new code generator to retain optimal code generation.

The desire to support high level languages encompasses both the achievement of a HLLCS and reducing compiler complexity. We see few cases where a RISC is substantially worse off than a CISC, leading us to conclude that a properly designed RISC seems as reasonable an architecture for supporting high level languages as a CISC.

---

[4] Evidence for and against comes from DEC. The complex MARK instruction was added to the PDP-11 in order improve the performance of subroutine calls; because this instruction did not do exactly what the programmers wanted it is almost never used. The damaging evidence comes from the VAX; it is rumored that the VMS FORTRAN compiler apparently produces a very large fraction (.8?) of the potential VAX instructions.

[5] We would not be surprised if FORTRAN and BLISS were used as models for several occurrences of this type of instruction on the VAX. Consider the **branch if lower bit set** and **branch if lower bit clear** instructions, which precisely implement conditional branching for BLISS, but are useless for the more common branch if zero and if not zero found in many other languages; this common occurrence requires two instructions. Similar instructions and addressing modes exist which appeal to FORTRAN.

[6] Peuto and Shustek observed that the complex decimal and character instructions of the IBM and Amdahl computers generally resulted in relatively poor performance in the high end models. They suggest that simpler instructions may lead to increased performance [Peuto,Shustek77]. They also measured the dynamic occurrence of pairs of instructions; significant results here would support the CISC philosophy. Their conclusion:
"An examination of the frequent opcode pairs fails to uncover any pair which occurs frequently enough to suggest creating additional instructions to replace it."

[7] In porting the C compiler to the VAX, over half of the bugs and about a third of the complexity resulted from the complicated INDEXED MODE.

WORK ON RISC ARCHITECTURES

At Berkeley. Investigation of a RISC architecture has gone on for several months now under the supervision of D.A. Patterson and C.H. Séquin. By a judicious choice of the proper instruction set and the design of a corresponding architecture, we feel that it should be possible to have a very simple instruction set that can be very fast. This may lead to a substantial net gain in overall program execution speed. This is the concept of the Reduced Instruction Set Computer. The implementations of RISC's will almost certainly be less costly than the implementations of CISC's. If we can show that simple architectures are just as effective to the high-level language programmer as CISC's such as VAX or the IBM S/38, we can claim to have made an effective design.

At Bell Labs. A project to design computers based upon measurements of the C programming language has been under investigation by a small number of individuals at Bell Laboratories Computing Science Research Center for a number of years. A prototype 16-bit machine was designed and constructed by A.G. Fraser. 32-bit architectures have been investigated by S.R. Bourne, D.R. Ditzel, and S.C. Johnson. Johnson used an iterative technique of proposing a machine, writing a compiler, measuring the results to propose a better machine, and then repeating the cycle over a dozen times. Though the initial intent was not specifically to come up with a simple design, the result was a RISC-like 32-bit architecture whose code density was as compact as the PDP-11 and VAX [Johnson79].

At IBM. Undoubtedly the best example RISC is the 801 minicomputer, developed by IBM Research in Yorktown Heights, N.Y.[Electronics76] [Datamation79]. This project is several years old and has had a large design team exploring the use of a RISC architecture in combination with very advanced compiler technology. Though many details are lacking their early results seem quite extraordinary. They are able to benchmark programs in a subset of PL/I that runs about five times the performance of an IBM S/370 model 168. We are certainly looking forward to more detailed information.

CONCLUSION

There are undoubtedly many examples where particular "unique" instructions can greatly improve the speed of a program. Rarely have we seen examples where the same benefits apply to the system as a whole. For a wide variety of computing environments we feel that careful pruning of an instruction set leads to a cost-effective implementation. Computer architects ought to ask themselves the following questions when designing a new instruction set. If this instruction occurs infrequently, is it justifiable on the grounds that it is necessary and unsynthesizable, for example, a Supervisor Call instruction. If the instruction occurs infrequently and is synthesizable, can it be justified on the grounds that it is a heavily time consuming operation, for example, floating point operations. If the instruction is synthesizable from a small number of more basic instructions, what is the overall impact on program size and speed if the instruction is left out? Is the instruction obtainable for free, for example, by utilizing unused control store or by using an operation already provided by the ALU? If it is obtainable for "free", what will be the cost in debugging, documentation, and the cost in future implementations? Is it likely that a compiler will be able to generate the instruction easily?

We have assumed that it is worthwhile to minimize the "complexity" (perhaps measured in design time and gates) and maximize "performance" (perhaps using average execution time expressed in gate delays as a technology-independent time unit) while meeting the definition of a High-Level Language Computer System. In particular, we feel that VLSI computers will benefit the most from the RISC concepts. Too often, the rapid advancements in VLSI technology have been used as a panacea to promote architectural complexity. We see each transistor as being precious for at least the next ten years. While the trend towards architectural complexity may be one path towards improved computers, this paper proposes another path, the Reduced Instruction Set Computer.

ACKNOWLEDGEMENTS

For their prompt and constructive comments on this paper, the authors wish to express thanks to A.V. Aho, D. Bhandarkar, R. Campbell, G. Corcoran, G. Chesson, R. Cmelik, A.G. Fraser, S.L. Graham, S.C. Johnson, P. Kessler, T. London, J. Ousterhout, D. Poplawski, M. Powell, J. Reiser, L. Rowe, B. Rowland, J. Swensen, A.S. Tanenbaum, C. Séquin, Y. Tamir, G. Taylor, and J. Wakerly. Those students at Berkeley who have participated in the RISC project are acknowledged for their excellent work. RISC research at Berkeley was sponsored in part by the Defense Advance Research Projects Agency (DoD), ARPA Order No. 3803, and monitored by Naval Electronic System Command under Contract No. N00039-78-G-0013-0004.

REFERENCES

[Alexander75] W.C. Alexander and D.B. Wortman, "Static and Dynamic characteristics of XPL Programs," *Computer,* pp. 41-46, November 1975, Vol. 8, No. 11.

[Cocke80] J. Cocke, *private communication,* February, 1980.

[Cragon80] H.A. Cragon, in his talk presenting the paper "The Case Against High-Level Language Computers," at the International Workshop on High-Level Language Computer Architecture, May 1980.

[Datamation79] *Datamation,* "IBM Mini a Radical Departure," October 1979, pp. 53-55.

[Ditzel,Patterson80] "Retrospective on High-Level Language Computer Architecture," *Seventh Annual International Symposium on Computer Architecture,* May 6-8, 1980, La Baule, France.

[Electronics76] *Electronics Magazine,* "Altering Computer Architecture is Way to Raise Throughput, Suggests IBM Researchers," December 23, 1976, pp. 30-31.

[Foster71] C.C. Foster, R.H. Gonter and E.M. Riseman, "Measures of Op-Code Utilization," *IEEE Transactions on Computers,* May, 1971, pp. 582-584.

[Husson70] S.S. Husson, *Microprogramming: Principles and Practices,* Prentice-Hall, Engelwood, N.J., pp. 109-112, 1970.

[Johnson79] S.C. Johnson, "A 32-bit Processor Design," Computer Science Technical Report # 80, Bell Labs, Murray Hill, New Jersey, April 2, 1979.

[Patterson,Séquin80] D.A. Patterson and C.H. Séquin, "Design Considerations for Single-Chip Computers of the Future," *IEEE Journal of Solid-State Circuits, IEEE Transactions on Computers,* Joint Special Issue on Microprocessors and Microcomputers, Vol. C-29, no. 2, pp. 108-116, February 1980.

[Peuto,Shustek77] B.L. Peuto and L.J. Shustek, "An Instruction Timing Model of CPU Performance," *Conference Proc., Fourth Annual Symposium on Computer Architecture,* March 1977.

[Shustek78] L.J. Shustek, "Analysis and Performance of Computer Instruction Sets," Stanford Linear Accelerator Center Report 205, Stanford University, May, 1978, pp. 56.

[Utley78] B.G. Utley *et al,* "IBM System/38 Technical Developments," IBM GS80-0237, 1978.

ERRATA

The footnote at the bottom of page 29 in "The Case for
the Reduced Instruction Set Computer" contains an error.
Harvey Cragon was speaking on reducing the semantic gap by
making computers more complicated. The most appropriate
slide is quoted directly below:

"... When doing vector operations the performance was
approximately the same on these two machines (the CDC
7600 and the TI ASC). Memory bandwidth was approximately equal. The buffering of the hardware DO LOOP
accomplished the same memory bandwidth reduction as did
the buffering of the normal instruction stream on the
7600. After the proper macros had been written for the
7600, and the calling procedure incorporated into the
compiler, equal access to the vector capability was
provided from FORTRAN. Due in large measure to the
complexity introduced by the vector hardware, scalar
performance on the ASC is less than the 7600. The
last, and most telling argument, is that more hardware
was needed on the ASC than was required on the 7600.
The additional hardware for building the rather elaborate DO LOOP operations did not have the pay-off that
we had anticipated.

The experience with the ASC, and other experiences,
have led me to question all the glowing promises which
are made if we will only close the semantic gap. The
promised benefits do not materialize, generality is
lost."

Clearly the relative speeds of the two depend upon the mix
of scalar and vector operations in a given application.

We also inadvertently changed Harvey's middle initial:
he is Harvey G. Cragon.

                    Dave Patterson
                    Dave Ditzel

Instruction Sets and Beyond:

Computers, Complexity, and Controversy

**Robert P. Colwell, Charles Y. Hitchcock III,
E. Douglas Jensen, H. M. Brinkley Sprunt,
and Charles P. Kollar**

Carnegie-Mellon University

Computer design should focus on the assignment of system functionality to implementation levels within an architecture, and not be guided by whether it is a RISC or CISC design.

The avalanche of publicity received by the reduced instruction set computer has swept away objectivity in the technical communities and obscured many important issues. RISC design seriously challenges some implicit assumptions that have guided computer design for years. A study of its principles should yield a deeper understanding of hardware/software tradeoffs, computer performance, the influence of VLSI on processor design, and many other topics. Articles on RISC research, however, often fail to explore these topics properly and can be misleading. Further, the few papers that present comparisons with complex instruction set computer design often do not address the same issues. As a result, even careful study of the literature is likely to give a distorted view of this area of research. This article offers a useful perspective of RISC/Complex Instruction Set Computer research, one that is supported by recent work at Carnegie-Mellon University.

Much RISC literature is devoted to discussions of the size and complexity of computer instruction sets. These discussions are extremely misleading.

Instruction set design is important, but it should not be driven solely by adherence to convictions about design style, RISC or CISC. The focus of discussion should be on the more general question of the assignment of system functionality to implementation levels within an architecture. This point of view encompasses the instruction set—CISCs tend to install functionality at lower system levels than RISCs—but also takes into account other design features such as register sets, coprocessors, and caches.

While the implications of RISC research extend beyond the instruction set, even within the instruction set domain, there are limitations that have not been identified. Typical RISC papers give few clues about where the RISC approach might break down. Claims are made for faster machines that are cheaper and easier to design and that "map" particularly well onto VLSI technology. It has been said, however, that "Every complex problem has a simple solution...and it is wrong." RISC ideas are not "wrong," but a simple-minded view of them would be. RISC theory has many implications that are not obvious. Research in this area has helped focus attention on some important issues in computer architecture whose resolutions have too often been determined by defaults; yet RISC proponents often fail to discuss the application, architecture, and implementation contexts in which their assertions seem justified.

While RISC advocates have been vocal concerning their design methods and theories, CISC advocates have been disturbingly mute. This is not a healthy state of affairs. Without substantive, reported CISC research, many RISC arguments are left uncountered and, hence, out of perspective. The lack of such reports is due partially to the proprietary nature of most commercial CISC designs and partially to the fact that industry designers do not generally publish as much as academics. Also, the CISC design style has no coherent statement of design principles, and CISC designers do not appear to be actively working on one. This lack of a manifesto differentiates the CISC and RISC design styles and is the result of their different historical developments.

Towards defining a RISC

Since the earliest digital electronic computers, instruction sets have tended to grow larger and more complex. The 1948 MARK-1 had only seven instructions of minimal complexity, such as adds and simple jumps, but a contemporary machine like the VAX has hundreds of instructions. Furthermore, its instructions can be rather complicated, like atomically inserting an element into a doubly linked list or evaluating a floating point polynomial of arbitrary degree. Any high performance implementation of the VAX, as a result, has to rely on complex implementation techniques such as pipelining, prefetching, and multi-cycle instruction execution.

This progression from small and simple to large and complex instruction sets is striking in the development of single-chip processors within the past decade. Motorola's 68020, for example, carries 11 more addressing modes than the 6800, more than twice as many instructions, and support for an instruction cache and coprocessors. Again, not only has the number of addressing modes and instructions increased, but so has their complexity.

This general trend toward CISC machines was fueled by many things, including the following:

- New models are often required to be upward-compatible with existing models in the same computer family, resulting in the supersetting and proliferation of features.

- Many computer designers tried to reduce the "semantic gap" between programs and computer instruction sets. By adding instructions semantically closer to those used by programmers, these designers hoped to reduce software costs by creating a more easily programmed machine. Such instructions tend to be more complex because of their higher semantic level. (It is often the case, however, that instructions with high semantic content do not exactly match those required for the language at hand.)

- In striving to develop faster machines, designers constantly moved functions from software to microcode and from microcode to hardware, often without concern for the adverse effects that an added architectural feature can have on an implementation. For example, addition of an instruction requiring an extra level of decoding logic can slow a machine's entire instruction set. (This is called the "$n + 1$" phenomenon.[1])

- Tools and methodologies aid designers in handling the inherent

complexity of large architectures. Current CAD tools and microcoding support programs are examples.

Microcode is an interesting example of a technique that encourages complex designs in two ways. First, it provides a structured means of effectively creating and altering the algorithms that control execution of numerous operations and complex instructions in a computer. Second, the proliferation of CISC features is encouraged by the quantum nature of microcode memories; it is relatively easy to add another addressing mode or obscure instruction to a machine which has not yet used all of its microcode space.

Instruction traces from CISC machines consistently show that few of the available instructions are used in most computing environments. This situation led IBM's John Cocke, in the early 70's, to contemplate a departure from traditional computer styles. The result was a research project based on an ECL machine that used a very advanced compiler, creatively named "801" for the research group's building number. Little has been published about that project, but what has been released speaks for a principled and coherent research effort.

The 801's instruction set was based on three design principles. According to Radin,[2] the instruction set was to be that set of run-time operations that

- could not be moved to compile time,
- could not be more efficiently executed by object code produced by a compiler that understood the high-level intent of the program, and
- could be implemented in random logic more effectively than the equivalent sequence of software instructions.

The machine relied on a compiler that used many optimization strategies for much of its effectiveness, including a powerful scheme of register allocation. The hardware implementation was guided by a desire for leanness and featured hardwired control and single-cycle instruction execution. The architecture was a 32-bit load/store machine (only load and store instructions accessed memory) with 32 registers and single-cycle instructions. It had separate instruction and data caches to allow simultaneous access to code and operands.

Some of the basic ideas from the 801 research reached the West Coast in the mid 70's. At the University of California at Berkeley, these ideas grew into a series of graduate courses that produced the RISC I* (followed later by the RISC II) and the numerous CAD tools that facilitated its design. These courses laid the foundation for related research efforts in performance evaluation, computer-aided design, and computer implementation.

The RISC I processor,[3] like the 801, is a load/store machine that executes most of its instructions in a single cycle. It has only 31 instructions, each of which fits in a single 32-bit word and uses practically the same encoding format. A special feature of the RISC I is its large number of registers, well over a hundred, which are used to form a series of overlapping register sets. This feature makes procedure calls on the RISC I less expensive in terms of processor-memory bus traffic.

Soon after the first RISC I project at Berkeley, a processor named MIPS (Microprocessor without Interlocked Pipe Stages) took shape at Stanford. MIPS[1] is a pipelined, single-chip processor that relies on innovative software to ensure that its pipeline resources are properly managed. (In machines such as the IBM System/360 Model 91, pipeline interstage interlocking is per-formed at run-time by special hardware). By trading hardware for compile-time software, the Stanford researchers were able to expose and use the inherent internal parallelism of their fast computing engine.

These three machines, the 801, RISC I, and MIPS, form the core of RISC research machines, and share a set of common features. We propose the following elements as a working definition of a RISC:

(1) *Single-cycle operation* facilitates the rapid execution of simple functions that dominate a computer's instruction stream and promotes a low interpretive overhead.
(2) *Load/store design* follows from a desire for single-cycle operation.
(3) *Hardwired control* provides for the fastest possible single-cycle operation. Microcode leads to slower control paths and adds to interpretive overhead.
(4) *Relatively few instructions and addressing modes* facilitate a fast, simple interpretation by the control engine.
(5) *Fixed instruction format* with consistent use, eases the hardwired decoding of instructions, which again speeds control paths.
(6) *More compile-time effort* offers an opportunity to explicitly move static run-time complexity into the compiler. A good example of this is the software pipeline reorganizer used by MIPS.[1]

A consideration of the two companies that claim to have created the first commercial "RISC" computer, Ridge Computers and Pyramid Technology, illustrates why a definition is needed. Machines of each firm have restricted instruction formats, a feature they share with RISC machines. Pyramid's machine is not a load/store computer, however, and both Ridge and Pyramid machines have variable length instructions and use multiple-cycle interpretation and microcoded control engines. Further, while their instruction counts might seem reduced when compared to a VAX, the Pyramid has almost 90 instructions and the Ridge has over 100. The use of microcoding in these machines is for price and performance reasons. The Pyramid machine also has a system of multiple register sets derived from the Berkeley RISC I, but this feature is orthogonal to RISC theory. These may be successful machines, from both technological and marketing standpoints, but they are not RISCs.

The six RISC features enumerated above can be used to weed out misleading claims and provide a springboard for points of debate. Although some aspects of this list may be arguable, it is useful as a working definition.

Points of attention and contention

There are two prevalent misconceptions about RISC and CISC. The first is due to the RISC and CISC acronyms, which seem to imply that the domain for discussion should be restricted to selecting candidates for a machine's instruction set. Although specification format and number of instructions are the primary issues in most RISC literature, the best generalization of RISC theory goes well beyond them. It connotes a willingness to make design tradeoffs freely and consciously across architecture/implementation, hardware/software, and compile-time/run-time boundaries in order to maximize performance as measured in some specific context.

The RISC and CISC acronyms also seem to imply that any machine can be classified as one or the other and that

---

* Please note that the term "RISC" is used throughout this article to refer to all research efforts concerning Reduced Instruction Set Computers, while the term "RISC I" refers specifically to the Berkeley research project.

the primary task confronting an architect is to choose the most appropriate design style for a particular application. But the classification is not a dichotomy. RISCs and CISCs are at different corners of a continous multidimensional design space. The need is not for an algorithm by which one can be chosen: rather, the goal should be the formulation of a set of techniques, drawn from CISC experiences and RISC tenets, which can be used by a designer in creating new systems. [4-6]

One consequence of the us-or-them attitude evinced by most RISC publications is that the reported performance of a particular machine (e.g., RISC I) can be hard to interpret if the contributions made by the various design decisions are not presented individually. A designer faced with a large array of choices needs guidance more specific than a monolithic, all-or-nothing performance measurement.

An example of how the issue of scope can be confused is found in a recent article. [7] By creating a machine with only one instruction, its authors claim to have delimited the RISC design space to their machine at one end of the space and the RISC I (with 31 instructions) at the other end. This model is far too simplistic to be useful; an absolute number of instructions cannot be the sole criterion for categorizing an architecture as to RISC or CISC. It ignores aspects of addressing modes and their associated complexity, fails to deal with compiler/architecture coupling, and provides no way to evaluate the implementation of other non-instruction set design decisions such as register files, caches, memory management, floating point operations, and co-processors.

Another fallacy is that the total system is composed of hardware, software, and application code. This leaves out the operating system, and the overhead and the needs of the operating system cannot be ignored in most systems. This area has received

far too little attention from RISC research efforts, in contrast to the CISC efforts focused on this area. [8,9]

An early argument in favor of RISC design was that simpler designs could be realized more quickly, giving them a performance advantage over complex machines. In addition to the economic advantages of getting to market first, the simple design was supposed to

---

The insinuation that the Micro-VAX-32 follows in a RISC tradition is unreasonable. It does not follow our definition of a RISC; it violates all six RISC criteria.

---

avoid the performance disadvantages of introducing a new machine based on relatively old implementation technology. In light of these arguments, DEC's MicroVAX-32 [10] is especially interesting.

The VAX easily qualifies as a CISC. According to published reports, the MicroVAX-32, a VLSI implementation of the preponderance of the VAX instruction set, was designed, realized, and tested in a period of several months. One might speculate that this very short gestation period was made possible in large part by DEC's considerable expertise in implementing the VAX architecture (existing products included the 11/780, 11/750, 11/730, and VLSI-VAX). This shortened design time would not have been possible had DEC had not first created a standard instruction set. Standardization at this level, however, is precisely what RISC theory argues against. Such standards constrain the unconventional RISC hardware/software tradeoffs. From a commercial standpoint, it is significant that the MicroVAX-32 was born into a world where compatible assemblers, compilers, and operating systems abound, something that would certainly not be the case for a RISC design.

Such problems with RISC system designs may encourage commercial RISC designers to define a new level of standardization in order to achieve some of the advantages of multiple implementations supporting one standard interface. A possible choice for such an interface would be to define an intermediate language as the target for all compilation. The intermediate language would then be translated into optimal machine code for each implementation. This translation process would simply be performing resource scheduling at a very low level (e.g., pipeline management and register allocation).

It should be noted that the Micro-VAX-32 does not directly implement all VAX architecture. The suggestion has been made that this implementation somehow supports the RISC inclination toward emulating complex functions in software. In a recent publication, David Patterson observed:

Although I doubt DEC is calling them RISCs, I certainly found it interesting that DEC's single chip VAXs do not implement the whole VAX instruction set. A MicroVAX traps when it tries to execute some infrequent but complicated operations, and invokes transparent software routines that simulate those complicated instructions. [11]

The insinuation that the Micro-VAX-32 follows in a RISC tradition is unreasonable. It does not come close to fitting our definition of a RISC; it violates all six RISC criteria. To begin with, any VAX by definition has a variable-length instruction format and is not a load/store machine. Further, the MicroVAX-32 has multicycle instruction execution, relies on a microcoded control engine, and interprets the whole array of VAX addressing modes. Finally, the MicroVAX-32 executes 175 instructions on-chip, hardly a reduced number.

A better perspective in the Micro VAX-32 shows that there are indeed cost/performance ranges where microcoded implementation of certain functions is inappropriate and software emulation is better. The importance of carefully making this assignment of function to implementation level—software, microcode, or hardware—has been amply demonstrated in many RISC papers. Yet this basic concern is also evidenced in many CISC machines. In the case of the MicroVAX-32, floating point instructions are migrated either to a coprocessor chip or to software emulation routines. The numerous floating-point chips currently available attest to the market reception for this partitioning. Also migrated to emulation are the console, decimal, and string instructions. Since many of these instructions are infrequent, not time-critical, or are not generated by many compilers, it

would be difficult to fault this approach to the design of an inexpensive VAX. The MicroVAX-32 also shows that it is still possible for intelligent, competent computer designers who understand the notion of correct function-to-level mapping to find microcoding a valuable technique. Published RISC work, however, does not accommodate this possibility.

The application environment is also of crucial importance in system design. The RISC I instruction set was designed specifically to run the C language efficiently, and it appears reasonably successful. The RISC I researchers have also investigated the Smalltalk-80 computing environment. [12] Rather than evaluate RISC I as a Smalltalk engine, however, the RISC I researchers designed a new RISC and report encouraging performance results from simulations. Still, designing a processor to run a single

language well is different from creating a single machine such as the VAX that must exhibit at least acceptable performance for a wide range of languages. While RISC research offers valuable insights on a per-language basis, more emphasis on cross-language anomalies, commonalities, and tradeoffs is badly needed.

Especially misleading are RISC claims concerning the amount of design time saved by creating a simple machine instead of a complex one. Such claims sound reasonable. Nevertheless, there are substantial differences in the design environments for an academic one-of-a-kind project (such as MIPS or RISC I) and a machine with lifetime measured in years that will require substantial software and support investments. As was pointed out in a recent *Electronics Week* article, R. D. Lowry, market development manager for Denelcor,

Risc II and the MCF evaluation

In the mid 70's, a committee was created by the Department of Defense to "evaluate the efficiency of several computer architectures independently of their implementations." [1,2] This committee developed the Military Computer Family studies based on the premise that the "architectural efficiency" of a computer corresponds to its life-cycle cost, given some standard of implementation technology. The MCF committee developed a means of evaluating architectural efficiency that consisted of two parts: (1) an initial screening to determine the "reasonableness" of an architecture based on several qualitative and quantitative factors (described later) and (2) a methodical application of benchmarks for machines that successfully passed this screening.

The MCF evaluations have been considered by many to be an important milestone in the systematic evaluation of computer architec-

tures. The published evaluations of RISC machines have indicated performance advantages large enough to merit attention and analysis. To learn about RISC architecture and the usefulness of the MCF evaluation procedure, we applied the complete MCF evaluation to the Berkeley RISC II since it posed the fewest obstacles.

The MCF program evaluates architectures standardized at the instruction set level, since, according to Burr, it "is the only [way to ensure] complete software transportability across a wide range of computer implementations." [1] This view is contrary to a fundamental RISC tenet that one should zealously pursue unconventional tradeoffs across the architecture/implementation boundary that can produce higher performance.

In addition, the architecture that was judged the best by the MCF evaluation criteria was the VAX, a particularly intriguing judgement considering the uniformly bad reviews

given the VAX in RISC performance studies. Furthermore many of these RISC performance studies used variations and carefully chosen subsets of the MCF benchmarks. [3] Evaluating the RISC II with a full MCF analysis sheds new light on this seeming discrepancy.

MCF evaluation criteria. The first part of the MCF evaluation is an initial screening to ensure that the candidate architecture contains features deemed essential to a successful military computer: virtual memory, protection, floating point, interrupts and traps, subsetability, multiprocessor support, I/O controllability, extensibility, and the ability to execute out of read-only memory. Current RISC II systems have not provided many of these features, but most of these requirements could be met with additional resources.

The initial screening also analyzes quantitative factors. Since this

noted that "commercial-product development teams generally start off a project by weighing the profit and loss impacts of design decisions."[13] Lowry is quoted as saying, "A university doesn't have to worry about that, so there are often many built-in deadends in projects. This is not to say the value of their research is diminished. It does, however, make it very difficult for someone to reinvent the system to make it a commercial product." For a product to remain viable, a great deal of documentation, user training, coordination with fabrication or production facilities, and future upgrades must all be provided. It is not known how these factors might skew a design-time comparison, so all such comparisons should be viewed with suspicion.

Even performance claims, perhaps the most interesting of all RISC assertions, are ambiguous. Performance as measured by narrowly compute-bound, low-level benchmarks that have been used by RISC researchers (e.g., calculating a Fibonacci series recursively) is not the only metric in a computer system. In some, it is not even one of the most interesting. For many current computers, the only useful performance index is the number of transactions per second, which has no direct or simple correlation to the time it takes to calculate Ackermann's function. While millions of instructions per second might be a meaningful metric in some computing environments, reliability, availability, and response time are of much more concern in others, such as *space* and *aviation* computing. The extensive error checking incorporated into these machines at every level may slow the basic clock time and substantially diminish performance. Reduced performance is tolerable; but downtime may not be. In the extreme, naive application of the RISC rules for designing an instruction set might result in a missile guidance computer optimized for running its most common task—diagnostics. In terms of instruction frequencies, of course, flight control applications constitute a trivial special case and would not be given much attention. It is worth emphasizing that in efforts to quantify performance and apply those measurements to system design, one must pay attention not just to instruction execution frequencies, but also to cycles consumed per instruction execution. Levy and Clark make this point regarding the VAX instruction set,[14] but it has yet to appear in any papers on RISC.

When performance, such as throughput or transactions per second, is a first-order concern, one is faced with the task of quantifying it. The Berkeley RISC I efforts to establish the machine's throughput are laudable, but

---

screening includes such practicalities as the manufacturer's current customer base and the amount of existing software, the RISC II would compare unfavorably to the VAX in this part of the evaluation. While these factors were important in military computer standards, they are clearly irrelevant here.

After the initial screening, a series of test programs was executed on a simulator of the candidate architecture. To avoid compiler ambiguities, the benchmarks were programmed in the assembly language of the test system. The MCF committee was interested solely in compiled code performance, yet the members recognized that varying levels of compiler technology should not be allowed to affect the outcome of the study; compiler sophistication has nothing to do with inherent "architectural efficiency." At the time of the MCF evaluations, it was believed that even the best compilers would be unlikely to generate better code than expert programmers. Sixteen benchmark programs were developed: they were representative of the tasks performed by military computers and were small enough for humans to write in a highly optimized form.

None of the sixteen benchmarks tests methods of subroutine linkage (although one of the benchmarks considered, but rejected, for the MCF study was the highly recursive Ackermann's function). Failure to test call efficiency was not an oversight by the MCF committee; two measures of subroutine efficiency are included in the quantitative factors section of the initial screening.

Rather than rely on combined architecture/implementation measurements such as execution throughput, the MCF measures of computer architecture efficiency were defined to be program size (S), memory bus traffic (M), and canonical processor cycles (R). The S measure includes the local data and stack space used by the benchmark, as well as its program space. (The benchmarks reflect a circa-1970 assumption that code and data each occupy about half of the available memory space.) The M measure for a benchmark is the number of bytes that the processor reads and writes to memory (no transparent caching scheme is used). To compute the R measure, the architecture being evaluated is emulated on a canonical processor. The R measure is the sum of the internal data register-to-register transfers required by the canonical processor. Thus, this measure is supposed to model the data traffic of the processor's internal activities during benchmark execution. To evaluate different architectures, these measures are used as dimensions of comparison.

RISC theory asserts that simple instructions can be made to execute very quickly if their implementations are unencumbered by the large con-

before sweeping conclusions are drawn one must carefully examine the benchmark programs used. As Patterson noted:

> The performance predictions for [RISC I and RISC II] were based on small programs. This small size was dictated by the reliability of the simulator and compiler, the available simulation time, and the inability of the first simulators to handle UNIX system calls. [11]

Some of these "small" programs actually execute millions of instructions, yet they are very narrow programs in terms of the scope of function. For example, the Towers of Hanoi program, when executing on the 68000, spends over 90 percent of its memory accesses in procedure calls and returns. The RISC I and II researchers recently reported results from a large benchmark, [11] but the importance of large, heterogenous benchmarks in performance measurement is still lost on many commercial and academic computer evaluators who have succumbed to the misconception that "microbenchmarks" represent a useful measurement in isolation.

Multiple register sets

Probably the most publicized RISC-style processor is the Berkeley RISC I. The best-known feature of this chip is its large register file, organized as a series of overlapping register sets. This is ironic, since the register file is a performance feature independent of any RISC (as defined earlier) aspect of the processor. Multiple register sets could be included in any general-purpose register machine.

It is easy to believe that MRSs can yield performance benefits, since procedure-based, high-level languages typically use registers for information specific to a procedure. When a procedure call is performed, the information must be saved, usually on a memory stack, and restored on a procedure return. These operations are typically very time consuming due to the intrinsic data transfer requirements. RISC I uses its multiple register sets to reduce the frequency of this register saving and restoring. It also takes advantage of an overlap between register sets for parameter passing, reducing even further the memory reads and writes necessary. [15]

RISC I has a register file of 138 32-bit registers organized into eight overlapping "windows." In each window, six registers overlap the next window (for outgoing parameters and incoming results). During any procedure, only one of these windows is actually accessible. A procedure call changes the current window to the next

---

trol engine normally required for complex instructions. Consequently, since the MCF evaluation avoids measuring implementation features, any performance gains realized by such simplified control engines are ignored, while penalties, such as the increased processor-memory traffic of these load/store machines, are still taken into account. This effect has been noted before in applying the MCF evaluation to real machines. [4]

Results and interpretation. The RISC II architecture was evaluated by simulating assembly language versions of the 16 benchmarks. To gauge the results, its performance was compared to that of the VAX, rated "best" by the MCF measures. The VAX had a significantly lower S measure (memory space requirements) in 14 of the 16 benchmarks, requiring an average of three and a half times less memory than RISC II. This result seems inconsistent with published RISC reports which found that the RISC I took an average of only 50 percent more memory. This difference is dramatic. Much of it may be due to the fact that previous studies used a compiler that produces reasonable code for the RISC II, but produces suboptimal code for the VAX (since it may not have been sophisticated enough to exploit the available complex instructions as a human would). If the latest compilers were used for both machines, the space difference between the machines would likely be reduced to that of handcoding in assembly language, which we used.

The RISC II had a much higher M (memory traffic measure) for 11 of the benchmarks, averaging over two and a half times more processor-memory traffic than the VAX. This MCF criterion shows the large penalty paid by RISC II because of its load/store architecture. It is accentuated by the generic RISC need to fetch more instructions per program, since RISC instructions have low semantic content.

The VAX also had a lower (better) R measure for 10 of the benchmarks, and it was substantially lower on five of them. Again, much of this difference was due to the increased number of instruction fetches required by RISCs. One of the ten benchmarks modelled the cost of a context swap, which is high on RISC II because of the amount of state information in the register file. On average, about half of the register file (approximately 64 registers) must be saved and restored in each process swap.

These benchmarks showed the RISC II to disadvantage on floating point, [5] integer multiplication, bit test and set operations, variable-sized block moves, and character string searches—operations for which RISC II has no primitive instructions. As a result, numerous instructions are required to emulate on a RISC

window by incrementing a pointer, and the six outgoing parameter registers become the incoming parameters of the called procedure. Similarly, a procedure return changes the current window to the previous window, and the outgoing result registers become the incoming result registers of the calling procedure. If we assume that six 32-bit registers are enough to contain the parameters, a procedure call involves no actual movement of information (only the window pointer is adjusted). The finite on-chip resources limit the actual savings due to register window overflows and underflows. [3]

It has been claimed that the small control area needed to implement the simple instruction set of a VLSI RISC leaves enough chip area for the large register file. [3] The relatively small amount of control logic used by a RISC does free resources for other uses, but a large register file is not the

only way to use them, nor even necessarily the best. For example, designers of the 801 and MIPS chose other ways to use their available hardware; these RISCs have only a single, conventionally sized register set. Caches, floating-point hardware, and interprocess communication support are a few of the many possible uses for those resources "freed" by a RISC's simple instruction set. Moreover, as chip technology improves, the tradeoffs between instruction set complexity and architecture/implementation features become less constrained. Computer designers will always have to decide how to best use available resources and, in doing so, should realize which relations are intrinsic and which are not.

The Berkeley papers describing the RISC I and RISC II processors claimed their resource decisions produced large performance improvements, two to four times over CISC machines like

the VAX and the 68000. [3,11] There are many problems with these results and the methods used to obtain them. Foremost, the performance effects of the reduced instruction set were not decoupled from those of the overlapped register windows. Consequently, these reports shed little light on the RISC-related performance of the machine, as shown below.

Some performance comparisons between different machines, especially early ones, were based on simulated benchmark execution times. While absolute speed is always interesting, other metrics less implementation-dependent can provide design information more useful to computer architects, such as data concerning the processor-memory traffic necessary to execute a series of benchmarks. It is difficult to draw firm conclusions from comparisons of vastly different machines unless some effort has been

what other machines provide in their instruction set; the MCF study provides a quantitative evaluation of this effect. The RISC II was comparable to the VAX on benchmarks that involved simple arithmetic and one-level array indexing.

Conclusions. Although the VAX achieves a better score on every aspect of the MCF evaluation than does the RISC II, it would be dangerous to conclude that the VAX is a "better" machine. The MCF study characterizes the life-cycle costs of various architectures based on a set of weighting factors culled from the military environment. The VAX can be said to be better only in the sense that the MCF life-cycle cost models clearly favor it.

Since RISC research explicitly gives up the possible benefits of the traditional architecture/implementation dichotomy to increase execution throughput, the most basic MCF

tenet does not hold for RISCs. The MCF life-cycle cost models did not include execution throughput, so the RISC II performance-related features were ignored, yet the price paid for these features is clear.

The MCF study's S, M, and R measures of architectural efficiency are open to question. For example, the R measure of internal processor overhead is of dubious utility when the architectures being compared are dissimilar. It is hard to see what canonical processor could be devised to serve as a common implementation of the RISC II and the Intel 432, for example.

The MCF study remains, however, the only large-scale evaluation of computer systems that includes as a primary figure of merit system life-cycle costs instead of easy throughput comparisons based on many arbitrary and implicit assumptions. The care taken by MCF in factoring out the myriad interrelated elements of a

computer system leaves it an excellent model for future evaluation efforts.

References

1. W.E. Burr, A.H. Coleman, and W.R. Smith, "Overview of the Military Computer Family Architecture Selection," *NCC Conference Proceedings* AFIPS, Montvale, N.J., 1977, pp. 131-137.
2. S.H. Fuller and W.E. Burr, "Measurement and Evaluation of Alternative Computer Architectures," *Computer*, Vol.10, No.10, Oct. 1977, pp. 24-35.
3. David A. Patterson, Richard S. Piepho, "RISC Assessment: A High-Level Language Experiment," *Proc. Ninth Ann. Symp. Computer Architecture*, 1982, pp. 3-8.
4. J.B. Mountain and P.H. Enslow Jr., "Application of the Military Computer Family Architecture Selection Criteria to the PRIME P400," *Computer Architecture News*, Vol. 6, No.6, Feb. 1978.
5. D. Patterson, "RISC Watch," *Computer Architecture News*, Vol. 12, No.1, Mar. 1984, pp. 11-19.

made to factor out implementation-dependent features not being compared (e.g., caches and floating point accelerators).

Experiments structured to accommodate these reservations were conducted at CMU to test the hypothesis that the effects of multiple register sets are orthogonal to instruction set complexity.[16] Specifically, the goal was to see if the performance effects of MRSs were comparable for RISCs and CISCs. Simulators were written for two CISCs (the VAX and the 68000) without MRSs, with non-overlapping MRSs and with overlapping MRSs. Simulators were also written for the RISC I, RISC I with non-overlapping register sets, and RISC I with only a single register set. In each of the simulators, care was taken not to change the initial architectures any more than absolutely necessary to add or remove MRSs. Instead of simulating execution time, the total amount of processor-memory traffic (bytes read and written) for each benchmark was recorded for comparison. To use this data fairly, only different register set versions of the same architecture were compared so the ambiguities that arise from comparing different architectures like the RISC I and the VAX were avoided. The benchmarks used were the same ones originally used to evaluate RISC I. A summary of the experiments and their results are presented by Hitchcock and Sprunt.[17]

As expected, the results show a substantial difference in processor-memory traffic for an architecture with and without MRSs. The MRS versions of both the VAX and 68000 show marked decreases in processor-memory traffic for procedure-intensive benchmarks, shown in Figures 1 and 2. Similarly, the single register set version of RISC I requires many more memory reads and writes than RISC I with overlapped register sets (Figure 3). This result is due in part to the method used for

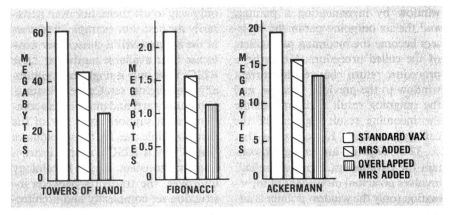

Figure 1. Total processor-memory traffic for benchmarks on the standard VAX and two modified VAX computers, one with multiple register sets and one with overlapped multiple register sets.

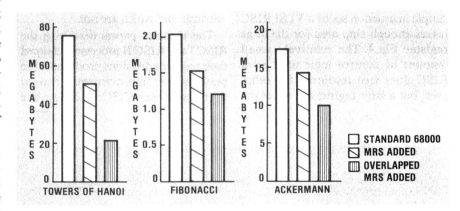

Figure 2. Total processor-memory traffic for benchmarks on the standard 68000 and two modified 68000s, one with multiple register sets and one with overlapped multiple register sets.

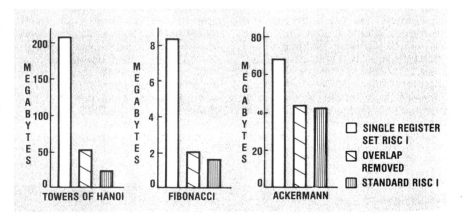

Figure 3. Total processor-memory traffic for benchmarks on the standard RISC I and two modified RISC I's, one with no overlap between register sets and one with only one register set.

handling register set overflow and underflow, which was kept the same for all three variations. With a more intelligent scheme, the single register set RISC I actually required fewer bytes of memory traffic on Ackermann's function than its multiple register set counterparts. For benchmarks with very few procedure calls (e.g., the sieve of Eratosthenes), the single register set version has the same amount of processor-memory traffic as the MRS version of the same architecture. [17]

Clearly, MRSs can affect the amount of processor-memory traffic necessary to execute a program. A significant amount of the performance of RISC I for procedure-intensive environments has been shown to be attributable to its scheme of overlapped register sets, a feature independent of instruction-set complexity. Thus, any performance claims for reduced instruction set computers that do not remove effects due to multiple register sets are inconclusive, at best.

These CMU experiments used benchmarks drawn from other RISC research efforts for the sake of continuity and consistency. Some of the benchmarks, such as Ackermann, Fibonacci, and Hanoi, actually spend most of their time performing procedure calls. The percentage of the total processor-memory traffic due to "C" procedure calls for these three benchmarks on the single register set version of the 68000 ranges from 66 to 92 percent. As was expected, RISC I, with its overlapped register structure that allows procedure calls to be almost free in terms of processor-memory bus traffic, did extremely well on these highly recursive benchmarks when compared to machines with only a single register set. It has not been established, however, that these benchmarks are representative of any computing environment.

The 432

The Intel 432 is a classic example of a CISC. It is an object-oriented VLSI microprocessor chip-set designed expressly to provide a productive Ada programming environment for large scale, multiple-process, multiple-processor systems. Its architecture supports object orientation such that every object is protected uniformly without regard to traditional distinctions such as "supervisor/user mode" or "system/user data structures." The 432 has a very complex instruction set. Its instructions are bit-encoded and range in length from six to 321 bits. The 432 incorporates a significant degree of functional migration from software to on-chip microcode. The interprocess communication SEND primitive is a 432 machine instruction, for instance.

Published studies of the performance of the Intel 432 on low-level benchmarks (e.g., towers of Hanoi[18]) show that it is very slow, taking 10 to 20 times as long as the VAX 11/780. Such a design, then, invites scrutiny in the RISC/CISC controversy.

One is tempted to blame the machine's object-oriented runtime environment for imposing too much overhead. Every memory reference is checked to ensure that it lies within the boundaries of the referenced object, and the read/write protocols of the executing context are verified. RISC proponents argue that the complexity of the 432 architecture, and the additional decoding required for a bit-encoded instruction stream contribute to its poor performance. To address these and other issues, a detailed study of the 432 was undertaken to evaluate the effectiveness of the architectural mechanisms provided in support of its intended runtime environment. The study concentrated on one of the central differences in the RISC and CISC design styles: RISC designs avoid hardware/microcode structures in-

tended to support the runtime environment, attempting instead to place equivalent functionality into the compiler or software. This is contrary to the mainstream of instruction set design, which reflects a steady migration of such functionality from higher levels (software) to lower ones (microcode or hardware) in the expectation of improved performance.

This investigation should include an analysis of the 432's efficiency in executing large-system code, since executing such code well was the primary design goal of the 432. Investigators used the Intel 432 microsimulator, which yields cycle-by-cycle traces of the machine's execution. While this microsimulator is well-suited to simulating small programs, it is quite unwieldy for large ones. As a result, the concentration here is on the low-level benchmarks that first pointed out the poor 432 performance.

Simulations of these benchmarks revealed several performance problems with the 432 and its compiler:

(1) The 432's Ada compiler performs almost no optimization. The machine is frequently forced to make unnecessary changes to its complex addressing environment, and it often recomputes costly, redundant subexpressions. This recomputation seriously skews many results from benchmark comparisons. Such benchmarks reflect the performance of the present version of the 432 but show very little about the efficacy of the architectural tradeoffs made in that machine.

(2) The bandwidth of 432 memory is limited by several factors. The 432 has no on-chip data caching, no instruction stream literals, and no local data registers. Consequently, it makes far more memory references than it would otherwise have to. These reference requirements also make the code size much larger, since many more bits are required to reference data within an object than within a local register.

And because of pin limitations, the 432 must multiplex both data and address information over only 16 pins. Also, the standard Intel 432/600 development system, which supports shared-memory multiprocessing, uses a slow asynchronous bus that was designed more for reliability than throughput. These implementation factors combine to make wait states consume 25 to 40 percent of the processor's time on the benchmarks.

(3) On highly recursive benchmarks, the object-oriented overhead in the 432 does indeed appear in the form of a slow procedure call. Even here, though, the performance problems should not be attributed to object orientation or to the machine's intrinsic complexity. Designers of the 432 made a decision to provide a new, protected context for every procedure call; the user has no option in this respect. If an unprotected call mechanism were used where appropriate, the Dhrystone benchmark [19] would run 20 percent faster.

(4) Instructions are bit-aligned, so the 432 must almost of necessity decode the various fields of an instruction sequentially. Since such decoding often overlaps with instruction execution, the 432 stalls three percent of the time while waiting for the instruction decoder. This percentage will get worse, however, once other problems above are eliminated.

Colwell provides a detailed treatment of this experiment and its results.[20]

This 432 experiment is evidence that RISC's renewed emphasis on the importance of fast instruction decoding and fast local storage (such as caches or registers) is substantiated, at least for low-level compute-bound benchmarks. Still, the 432 does not provide compelling evidence that large-scale migration of function to microcode and hardware is ineffective. On the contrary, Cox et al.[21] demonstrated

that the 432 microcode implementation of interprocess communication is much faster than an equivalent software version. On these low-level benchmarks, the 432 could have much higher performance with only a better compiler and minor changes to its implementation. Thus, it is wrong to conclude that the 432 supports the general RISC point of view.

In spite of—and sometimes because of—the wide publicity given to current RISC and CISC research, it is not easy to gain a thorough appreciation of the important issues. Articles on RISC research are often oversimplified, overstated, and misleading, and papers on CISC design offer no coherent design principles for comparison. RISC/CISC issues are best considered in light of their function-to-implementation level assignment. Strictly limiting the focus to instruction counts or other oversimplifications can be misleading or meaningless.

Some of the more subtle issues have not been brought out in current literature. Many of these are design considerations that do not lend themselves to the benchmark level analysis used in RISC research. Nor are they always properly evaluated by CISC designers, guided so frequently by tradition and corporate economics.

RISC/CISC research has a great deal to offer computer designers. These contributions must not be lost due to an illusory and artificial dichotomy. Lessons learned studying RISC machines are not incompatible with or mutually exclusive of the rich tradition of computer design that preceded them. Treating RISC ideas as perspectives and techniques rather than dogma and understanding their domains of applicability can add important new tools to a computer designer's repertoire. □

Acknowledgements

We would like to thank the innumerable individuals, from industry and academia, who have shared their thoughts on this matter with us and stimulated many of our ideas. In particular, we are grateful to George Cox and Konrad Lai of Intel for their help with the 432 microsimulator.

This research was sponsored in part by the Department of the Army under contract DAA B07-82-C-J164.

References

1. J. Hennessy et al., "Hardware/Software Tradeoffs for Increased Performance," *Proc. Symp. Architectural Support for Programming Languages and Operating Systems*, 1982, pp. 2-11.
2. G. Radin, "The 801 Minicomputer," *Proc. Symp. Architectural Support for Programming Languages and Operating Systems*, 1982, pp. 39-47.
3. D. A. Patterson and C. H. Sequin, "A VLSI RISC," *Computer*, Vol. 15, No. 9, Sept. 1982, pp. 8-21.
4. R. P. Colwell, C. Y. Hitchcock III, and E. D. Jensen, "A Perspective on the Processor Complexity Controversy," *Proc. Int. Conf. Computer Design: VLSI in Computers*, 1983, pp. 613-616.
5. D. Hammerstrom, "Tutorial: The Migration of Function into Silicon," *10th Ann. Int'l Symp. Computer Architecture*, 1983.
6. J. C. Browne, "Understanding Execution Behavior of Software Systems," *Computer*, Vol. 17, No. 7, July 1984, pp. 83-87.
7. H. Azaria and D. Tabak, "The MODHEL Microcomputer for RISCs Study", *Microprocessing and Microprogramming*, Vol. 12, No. 3-4, Oct.-Nov. 1983, pp. 199-206.
8. G. C. Barton "Sentry: A Novel Hardware Implementation of Classic Operating System Mechanisms," *Proc. Ninth Ann. Int'l Symp. Computer Architecture*, 1982, pp. 140-147.
9. A. D. Berenbaum, M. W. Condry, and P. M. Lu, "The Operating System and Language Support Features of the BELLMAC-32 Microprocessor,"

Proc. Symp. Architectural Support for Programming Languages and Operating Systems, 1982, pp. 30-38.

10. J. Hennessy, "VLSI Processor Architecture," *IEEE Transactions on Computers*, Vol. C-33, No. 12, Dec. 1984, pp. 1221-1246.

11. D. Patterson, "RISC Watch," *Computer Architecture News*, Vol. 12, No. 1, Mar. 1984, pp. 11-19.

12. David Ungar et al., "Architecture of SOAR: Smalltalk on a RISC," *11th Ann. Int'l Symp. Computer Architecture,* 1984, pp. 188-197.

13. W. R. Iversen, "Money Starting to Flow As Parallel Processing Gets Hot," *Electronics Week,* Apr. 22, 1985, pp. 36-38.

14. H. M. Levy and D. W. Clark, "On the Use of Benchmarks for Measuring System Performance" *Computer Architecture News,* Vol. 10, No. 6, 1982, pp. 5-8.

15. D. C. Halbert and P. B. Kessler, "Windows of Overlapping Register Frames", CS292R Final Reports, University of California, Berkeley, June 9, 1980.

16. R. P. Colwell, C. Y. Hitchcock III, and E. D. Jensen, "Peering Through the RISC/CISC Fog: An Outline of Research," *Computer Architecture News,* Vol. 11, No. 1, Mar. 1983, pp. 44-50.

17. C. Y. Hitchcock III and H. M. B. Sprunt, "Analyzing Multiple Register Sets," *12th Ann. Int'l Symp. Computer Architecture*, 1985, in press.

18. P. M. Hansen et al., "A Performance Evaluation of the Intel iAPX 432," *Computer Architecture News*, Vol. 10, No. 4, June 1982, pp. 17-27.

19. R. P. Weicker, "Dhrystone: A Synthetic Systems Programming Benchmark," *Comm. ACM*, Vol. 27, No. 10, Oct. 1984, pp. 1013-1030.

20. R. P. Colwell, "The Performance Effects of Functional Migration and Architectural Complexity in Object—Oriented Systems," PhD. thesis, Carnegie-Mellon University, Pittsburgh, PA. Expected completion in June, 1985.

21. G. W. Cox et al., "Interprocess Communication and Processor Dispatching on the Intel 432," *ACM Trans. Computer Systems*, Vol. 1, No. 1, Feb. 1983, pp. 45-66.

Robert P. Colwell recently completed his doctoral dissertation on the performance effects of migrating functions into silicon, using the Intel 432 as a case study. His industrial experience includes design of a color graphics workstation for Perq Systems, and work on Bell Labs' microprocessors. He received the PhD and MSEE degrees from Carnegie-Mellon University in 1985 and 1978, and the BSEE degree from the University of Pittsburgh in 1977. He is a member of the IEEE and ACM.

Charles Y. Hitchcock III is a doctoral candidate in Carnegie-Mellon University's Department of Electrical and Computer Engineering. He is currently pursuing research in computer architecture and is a member of the IEEE and ACM. He graduated with honors in 1981 from Princeton University with a BSE in electrical engineering and computer science. His MSEE from CMU in 1983 followed research he did in design automation.

E. Douglas Jensen has been on the faculties of both the Computer Science and Electrical and Computer Engineering Departments of Carnegie-Mellon University for six years. For the previous 14 years he performed industrial R/D on computer systems, hardware, and software. He consults and lectures extensively throughout the world and has participated widely in professional society activities.

H. M. Brinkley Sprunt is a doctoral candidate in the Department of Electrical and Computer Engineering of Carnegie-Mellon University. He received a BSEE degree in electrical engineering from Rice University in 1983. His research interests include computer architecture evaluation and design. He is a member of the IEEE and ACM.

Charles P. Kollar is a senior research staff member in Carnegie-Mellon University's computer Science Department. He is currently pursuing research in decentralized asynchronous computing systems. He has been associated with the MCF and NEBULA project at Carnegie-Mellon University since 1978. Previous research has been in the area of computer architecture validation and computer architecture description languages. He holds a BS in computer science from the University of Pittsburgh.

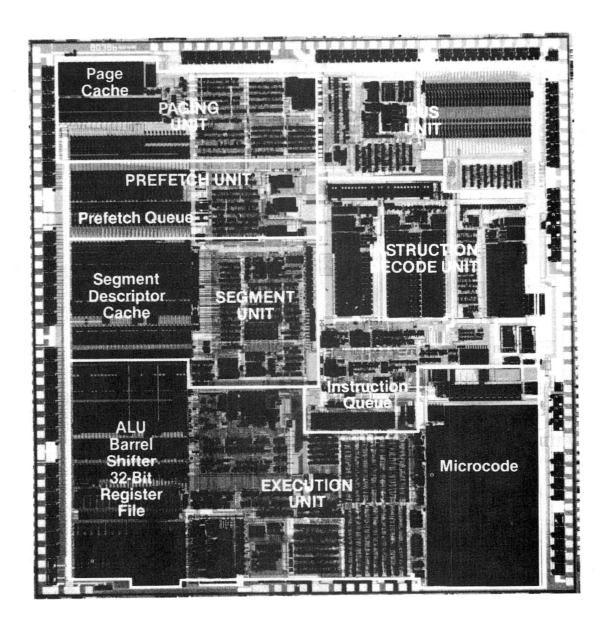

Architecture of the Intel 80386

John Crawford

Intel Corporation, SC4-59
2525 Walsh Ave.
Santa Clara, Ca. 95051

ABSTRACT

Intel's 80386 32-bit microprocessor[1,2,3] is the newest member of the 86 Family of microprocessors. It features a full 32-bit architecture implemented in a 1.5μ CMOS technology[6], supports an average instruction rate of 3 to 4 million instructions per second, and is fully software compatible with the 8086, 8088, 80186, 80188, and 80286 microprocessors. Memory management is fully supported with on-chip paging underneath segmentation.

Introduction

The 386 offers a full 32-bit architecture to the programmer, featuring 32-bit registers, 32-bit address formation, and a full set of 32-bit instructions. At the same time, the 386 is object code compatible with the 16 bit members of Intel's 86 family of processors. A complete segmented/paged Memory Management and Protection mechanism supports segments up to 4 Gigabytes in size, and uses a standard two-level paging mechanism underneath segmentation to support physical memory management of these large segments.

Segmentation and Paging are fully supported on-chip with a high-speed address translation pipeline which caches segmentation and paging mapping information on-chip. Address translation is fully pipelined with other CPU operations so that a memory Load instruction, including segment and page address translation, requires just 4 clock cycles (250 ns at 16 Mhz) and a Store instruction requires just 2 clock cycles (125 ns at 16 Mhz).

Basic Architecture

General Registers

Eight 32-bit general registers shown in figure 1 are named EAX, EBX, ECX, EDX, ESP, EBP, ESI, and EDI, and provide high-speed storage for integer data and addresses. The low order 16 bits of these registers contain the 16-bit 8086/80286 registers AX, BX, CX, DX, SP, BP, SI, and DI. Eight 8-bit registers AH, AL, BH, BL, CH, CL, DH, and DL provide direct access to the upper and lower 8 bits of the AX, BX, CX, and DX

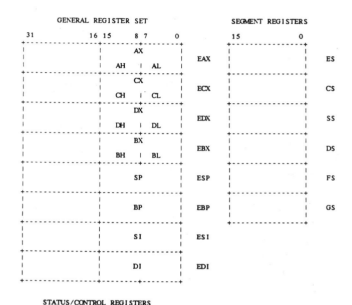

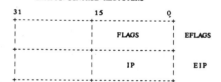

Figure 1 – General Registers

registers. When accessed as 8 or 16-bit registers, the other bits of the 32-bit registers are undisturbed.

Two additional 32-bit registers, also shown in figure 1, support processor control. The 32-bit EIP register is the *Instruction Pointer* register, and points to the next instruction the processor is to execute. The 32-bit EFLAGS register provides a number of status and control bits. Status bits are set after most arithmetic operations to indicate carry, overflow, sign, and zero result. Control bits are provided to mask interrupts, provide single-step execution, and control a number of execution modes. The lower 16 bits of EIP and EFLAGS contain the 8086/80286 IP and FLAGS registers.

Three additional sets of registers provide specialized functions for processor control. One set of registers controls the operation of the memory management hardware and provides base addresses for the memory mapping tables. A second set of registers provides access to the hardware to simplify production testing.[4] A third set of registers support effective software debugging. Four address registers and two status/control registers provide the ability to set up to four code or data breakpoints at arbitrary addresses, and to break program execution when a breakpoint is encountered.

Memory Addressing

Segmentation. In order to manage its large virtual memory space, the 386 uses a segmented, or two-dimensional, addressing mechanism. Segments divide main memory into multiple linear address spaces, which correspond to the logical units viewed by the programmer. Within a segment, data is addressed by giving a simple byte offset. Because they divide memory into multiple linear address spaces, segments greatly simplify the relocation, sharing, and protection of multiple logical units. Up to 16K (2^{14}) segments can be defined in each task, and each segment can be up to 4 Gigabytes (2^{32}) in size, so the virtual address space is 64 Tera-bytes (2^{46}) per task.

Segment Regsisters. Due to the use of segmentation, main memory addresses consist of two parts: a segment part and and offset within that segment. 6 Segment registers, shown in figure 1, are provided to hold the segment parts of addresses. In order to address data within a segment, a 16-bit selector which identifies that segment must be loaded into one of these 6 segment registers. 14 bits of the selector provide an index into a protected segment descriptor table where the processor reads the base address, limit, and access attributes of the segment, as described in a later section. Two of the segment registers are dedicated to holding selectors for the current code segment (CS) and stack segment (SS). The remaining four segment registers are available to allow up to 4 data segments to be referenced at any point in time.

Addressing Modes. 32-bit offsets within segments are generated by adding together up to 3 components: a 32-bit base register, a 32-bit index register scaled by 1,2,4, or 8, and an 8 or 32-bit displacement. Any of the 8 general registers can supply the base or index parts of a memory address. Table 2 summarizes the 32-bit address mode choices available on the 80386. For compatibility with previous processors, the full set of 16-bit address modes are also supported on the 80386, but are not illustrated here.

Immediate Operands. The simplest way to supply an instruction operand is to include it directly within the instruction. These *immediate* operands can be 8, 16, or 32-bits in size. Full size constants of 8, 16, or 32 bits

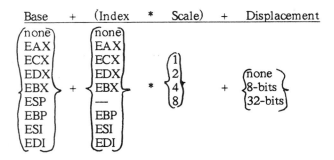

Table 2 - 80386 Addressing Modes

can be supplied for instructions which operate on byte, word, or double-word data. A 16 or 32-bit immediate operand can be given as a sign-extended 8-bit immediate in order to conserve code space in the frequent case of a small number of significant digits in the immediate operand.

Data Types

On the 386, as well as all other members of the 86 family of processors, main memory is byte addressable, so each 8-bit byte in memory has an address. If more than 8 bits are required to represent the values in a data type, multiple sequential bytes are used, with the low order bytes stored at lower addresses, and with the address of the datum given by the address of the low order byte. As with the other 86 family members, a *word* is 16-bits wide, and a *double-word, or dword,* is 32 bits wide. Floating point numbers are stored in 32, 64, and 80 bit formats, which occupy 4, 8, and 10 consecutive bytes, respectively.

Data Type and Instruction Summary	
8, 16, *32-bit* Integer	Add, Subtract, Multiply, Divide
	Add w/Carry, Sub w/Borrow
	Increment, Decrement, Negate
8, 16, *32-bit* Ordinal	And, Or, Xor, Not,
	Move, Push, Pop, Exchange
	Move with Sign/Zero Extend
	Shift, Rotate, *Double Shift*
	Compare, Test
packed BCD	Add, Subtract, Multiply, Divide
unpacked BCD	
16, 32, 64-bit Integer	Add, Subtract, Multiply, Divide
32, 64, 80-bit Real	Compare, Remainder, Round
80-bit BCD	Move, Exchange, Convert, Scale
	log, exponential, square root
	tangent, *sine, cosine,* arctan
BYTE string	Move, Compare
WORD string	Fill, Scan, Translate
DWORD string	
(*1..4G* bytes length)	
bit array (1.4G bits)	*Test, Set, Clear, Complement*

Table 3 - Data Types and Instruction Summary

Table 3 summarizes the data types directly supported by the 80386 and its companion floating point coprocessor, and lists the most important instructions supplied for each type. New data types and instructions are printed in italics.

Instruction Forms

The 80386 provides a rich set of instructions which can be broken into data manipulation instructions (e.g. add, move), and control transfer instructions (e.g. jump, call). Instructions can have no operands, one operand, or two operands, where the operands can be in a processor register, main memory, or directly in the instruction as an immediate operand. Representative data manipulation instructions are listed in table 3, with new instructions in italics.

Data Manipulation Instructions. One operand instructions can take their operands either from memory or from a register. These instructions generally use this single operand both as a source and a destination. Two operand instructions are available in the forms listed in table 4. Note the presence of instruction forms with memory destinations. These operate directly on data located in memory without the need to first load the data into a register.

Two Operand Instruction Forms	
Destination	Source
Register	Register
Register	Immediate
Register	Memory
Memory	Register
Memory	Immediate

Table 4 - Two Operand Instruction Forms

A powerful set of efficient string instructions is provided for operating on strings with BYTE, WORD, or DWORD elements. A string move instruction operates at the maximum bus bandwidth for rapidly moving blocks of data in memory. Two strings can be compared. A string can be filled with a fixed value, can be scanned for the first occurance of a given value, or can be translated using a character translation table. A set of string moves is provided to transfer data rapidly between memory and I/O space to support fast device access such as to hard disks or network controllers.

Control Transfer Instructions. A set of conditional jumps conditions changes in program flow on the settings of the status bits in the EFLAGS register (e.g. carry, sign, greater/less than, equal). Two sets of unconditional Call, Jump, and Return instructions are provided to transfer either within a segment, or between two segments. Intra-segment transfers change only the contents of the EIP register. Inter-segment transfers change both the EIP register and the CS segment register to begin execution in a different segment.

The CALL and RETURN instructions use the program stack contained in the segment addressed by the SS register, and whose top is marked by the ESP register. Parameter passing and local variable allocation on this program stack are supported directly in the instruction set. Parameters can be placed on the stack before executing a CALL instruction with PUSH instructions, and can be accessed within the called procedure at a small displacement from the ESP or EBP registers. ESP can be used for simple languages which do not require the maintenence of a subprogram display. EBP is useful as a pointer to the activation record for the current subroutine in languages which require the ability to address local variables of outer procedures, and to maintain the necessary static and dynamic links. Two instructions, ENTER and LEAVE, support procedure entry and exit. ENTER will build the display for a new procedure and allocate space for local variables on the stack. LEAVE will deallocate the display and local variables just before returning. The RETURN instruction can adjust the ESP register to remove parameters pushed before the matching CALL by subtracting from ESP after the return pointer is popped off the stack.

Instruction Encoding. In order to support binary compatibility with the previous 16-bit members of the 86 family, the 80386 instruction encoding includes all of the 8 and 16-bit instructions from the 80286. The 32-bit instructions were added by using the same instruction set encoding, but simply interpreting the 16-bit instructions as 32-bit instructions by use of an operand size indication. The operand size can be set to 16 or 32 for all the instructions in a code segment with an attribute bit in the code segment descriptor. Or, the operand size can be set for a single instruction by prepending an instruction prefix byte to that instruction. The code segment attribute provides an efficient method to type entire code segments as one size or the other. The prefix provides the flexibility to operate on 16-bit data in a 32 bit code segment, and vice-versa.

A similar sizing mechanism is used to select between 32-bit addressing and 16-bit addressing. The code segment attribute indicates the default address size for an entire code segment, and an instruction prefix indicates that a different address size should be used for a single instruction.

A number of new instructions were added to the 386 and 387 in addition to the 32-bit extensions described above. Representative operations are listed in table 3 in italics.

Memory management and Protection

The memory management mechanism combines both segmentation and paging for a flexible, complete mapping and protection mechanism.[5] Segmentation is the top, logical level of the memory management model. It supports the definition of protected regions of memory that correspond directly to constructs used by the programmer (e.g. code procedures, data structures, stacks). Four levels of protection are provided with the segment model: at a given time the processor can be executing at one of four privilege levels from 0 (most privileged) to 3 (least privileged). If executing at privilege level n the processor can only access segments at level n or levels of lesser privilege (numerically greater levels).

Paging underneath segmentation provides an efficient mechanism for the management of physical memory, both in the processor's main memory and the paging disk on virtual memory systems.

Figure 5 illustrates the two stages of address translation. First a two part virtual address is translated by segmentation to a 32-bit linear address, that is then passed through the page translation mechanism to obtain the physical address. The page translation step can be disabled by setting a processor control bit. In this case, the address put out by the segment address translation process is the physical address. This provides support for systems that do not need paging, and also provides compatiblity with the 80286, which did not support paging.

The segmented protection model is a superset of that provided for the 80286, in order to support binary compatibility even at the OS level. The model was extended to support 32-bit segment base addresses and 4 gigabyte segment sizes for the 80386, but the concepts and mechanisms were carried forward from the 80286.

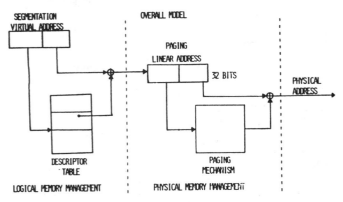

Figure 5 - Overall Address Translation

Segmentation

Memory is addressed with a two part address, a segment part and an offset within a segment. Segments are identified by user programs by use of a 16-bit *selector* which contains a 14-bit index into protected *descriptor* tables maintained by OS software. The descriptor associated with a selector contains the base address, size, and access attributes for the segment. To address data within a given segment, the base address is added to the offset part of the two part address to obtain a 32-bit *linear* address that is the output of the segment address relocation process. A fault is reported

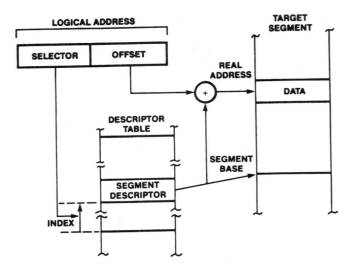

Figure 6 - Segment Address Translation

if the offset is larger than the segment size, or if the type of the access is not permitted by the access attributes in the descriptor. Rather than access the descriptor table for every memory access, descriptors are "cached" into shadow registers every time a selector is loaded into a segment register. Once cached, all references to the segment are relocated and validated by the processor before accessing physical memory. The segment address translation process is illustrated in fig. 6.

Paging

A standard 2 level page table is used, with 4K pages, as illustrated in figure 7. A processor register points to the base of the first level table. Table entries at both levels are 4 bytes wide, and each table contains 1K entries, so the page tables themselves exactly fit into 4K pages to simplify allocation and swapping of page tables.

The 32-bit address from the segment translation process is divided into 3 parts for page mapping. The upper 10 bits select an entry in the first level table which points to a second level table. The middle 10 bits select an entry in this second level table which contains the upper 20 bits of the physical address of the desired

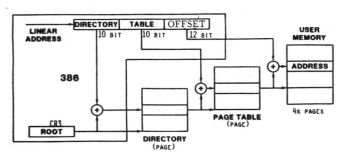

Figure 7 - Page Address Translation

page. The lower 12 bits of the input address, which do not participate in the page translation process, are concatenated with these upper 20 bits to form the output physical address.

This page translation process requires two memory accesses to the page table map for every memory access. A page translation cache, sometimes called a translation look-aside buffer (TLB), is used to cache the 32 most recent virtual to physical address translations to avoid referencing the memory-resident page tables.

Full support for virtual memory is provided, including full restartability of all instructions, and provision of page usage statistics with Dirty and Accessed bits per page. Instruction restart is supported to ease the burden on operating system software in recovering from page faults. After a missing page is retrieved from the disk, the faulting program is simply restarted by returning to the instruction which caused the page fault.

Protection

The segmented memory model provides protection between tasks, and between user programs and the operating system. Each task can have its own address space, supported by its own set of segment and page tables, to provide protection between tasks. To efficiently support an address space per task, two segment descriptor tables are used. One, the Global Descriptor Table (GDT), is shared by all tasks in the system, and generally holds descriptors for OS code and data. The second table, the Local Descriptor Table (LDT), is unique to each task in the system.

Within a task, four privilege levels are defined to partition the segments defined by a task between system access and user access. As illustrated in figure 8, the processor executes at one of four privilege levels and has access to segments at that level or higher (less privileged) levels. Attempts to access segments at

lower (more privileged) levels cause protection traps. This permits user and system segments to reside in a common address space, and still protects system segments from unrestricted user access.

Changes in privilege levels are controlled by Gates. Gates are special segment descriptor types that indirect access to a fixed entry point in another segment. This provides a restricted transfer of control from higher levels (less privileged) to specific entry points in lower levels using the standard inter-segment CALL instruction. To avoid protection holes inherent in the use of a single stack, each privilege level has its own program stack. During level transitions through gates, the progam stack of the new level is made the active stack by reloading the SS and ESP registers. Parameter passing is supported during the gate transition by the ability to copy data from the caller's stack to the callee's stack. Through the use of gates, the user program, while completely restricted from access to system level segments, can be allowed to call OS service routines directly with the same inter-level CALL, and the same parameter passing conventions used to transfer control to other user-level routines.

Tasks

Another dimension of the Operating System support incorporated into the 80386 is the direct support of the task concept, to provide efficient context switching in multi-tasking environments. A special segment type, a Task State Segment (TSS), is provided to store the machine state for a dormant process. This segment contains the general registers, EFLAGS, EIP, segment registers, and pointers to the Local Descriptor Table and Page Table for the task.

The 80386 will perform a complete task switch if an inter-segment CALL or JUMP instruction, or an interrupt indicates a transfer to a TSS. A task switch operation involves storing the current processor state in the current TSS, making the new TSS the current TSS, and then loading the processor state from this new TSS. A task switch initiated by a CALL instruction or interrupt will also store the selector for the old TSS into a link field in the new TSS to permit the old task to be resumed upon "return" from the new task.

I/O Space

A 64K I/O address space, totally separate from the main memory space, is provided for a clean interface to device registers in peripheral contollers. A set of instructions provide data movement between the I/O space and the AL, AX, or EAX registers. String instructions provide a high-bandwidth transfer between I/O space and a block of main memory.

This I/O space is protected from arbitrary access through two mechanisms. The 2-bit IOPL field in the EFLAGS register defines the highest privilege level for which unrestricted I/O access is permitted. A variable length I/O permission bitmap located in the current

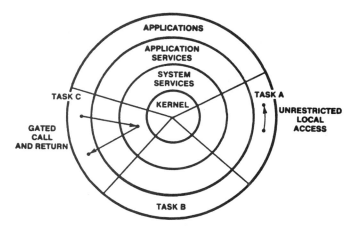

—A HIERARCHY OF TRUST—

Figure 8 - 4 Rings of Privilege

TSS contains a bit for every I/O address. A program executing at a higher (less privileged) level than IOPL will consult this I/O permission bitmap if it attempts to execute an I/O instruction. If the bitmap indicates that the task has permission to access the given I/O address, the I/O instruction will execute normally. Otherwise, the I/O instruction is aborted, and a protection fault is generated.

Virtual 8086 Mode

A special processor mode, named *Virtual 8086 Mode*, was added to support multitasking of 8086 (8088, 80186, 80188) tasks within the segmented/paged protected environment. This mode allows a 386 OS to provide a complete virtual 8086 machine to execute even "dirty" PC applications, each with its own copy of an 8086 operating system. Within this environment, segment registers are loaded as in the 8086, and relocate 16-bit addresses within the 1 Megabyte space supported by the 8086. This 1 megabyte address space is mapped by paging to allow protection and swapping of virtual 8086 programs. I/O instructions use the I/O permission bitmap described above to give "dirty" applications direct access to a restricted set of I/O devices, to support fast I/O interfacing. Interrupts and exceptions which occur when the processor is executing in Virtual 8086 mode cause a mode switch back to protected mode where the interrupt is handled by the protected mode OS. This OS must emulate certain privileged instructions that may be executed by the Virtual 8086 program, and can choose to handle interrupts itself, or reflect them back to the Virtual 8086 program.

Interrupts

The 80386 supports a vectored interrupt mechanism to signal asynchronous external events and to report error or exceptional conditions that occur as part of instruction execution. Interrupts are vectored through a 256 entry Interrupt Descriptor Table. Interrupts can be handled by interrupt procedures within the current task, or can cause a task switch to a new task. Entries in the IDT are gates which identify the entry points of interrupt handling procedures, or identify the TSS for an interrupt handling task.

Conclusion

The 80386 combines a full 32-bit architecture with full object code compatibility with the previous 16-bit members of the 86 family. A flexible and powerful memory management model combining both segmentation and paging is fully supported with on-chip hardware to minimize cost and maximize performance. Virtual 8086 mode, combined with the I/O permission bitmap, provides an environment for efficient execution of even "dirty" PC programs within the protected, paged, multi-tasked environment supported by the 80386. Thanks to these key architectural features, the 80386 provides access to a vast amount of industry standard software, while at the same time delivering state of the art performance in a 32-bit CPU.

References

[1] "80386 Programmer's Reference Manual", Intel Corp., Santa Clara, CA, 1986.

[2] "80386 Hardware Reference Manual", Intel Corp., Santa Clara, CA, 1986.

[3] "80386 System Software Writer's Guide" Intel Corp., Santa Clara, CA, 1986.

[4] P. Gelsinger, "Built-in Self Test for the 80386", Proceedings, ICCD Conference, Oct. 1986.

[5] P. J. Denning, "Virtual Memory", *Computing Surveys*, *Vol. 2, No. 3*, pp. 153-189.

[6] J. Prak, "High Performance Technology, Circuits, and Packaging for the 80386", Proceedings, ICCD Conference, Oct. 1986.

A Comparison of Full and Partial Predicated Execution Support for ILP Processors

Scott A. Mahlke*   Richard E. Hank   James E. McCormick   David I. August   Wen-mei W. Hwu

Center for Reliable and High-Performance Computing
University of Illinois
Urbana-Champaign, IL 61801

Abstract

One can effectively utilize predicated execution to improve branch handling in instruction-level parallel processors. Although the potential benefits of predicated execution are high, the tradeoffs involved in the design of an instruction set to support predicated execution can be difficult. On one end of the design spectrum, architectural support for full predicated execution requires increasing the number of source operands for all instructions. Full predicate support provides for the most flexibility and the largest potential performance improvements. On the other end, partial predicated execution support, such as conditional moves, requires very little change to existing architectures. This paper presents a preliminary study to qualitatively and quantitatively address the benefit of full and partial predicated execution support. With our current compiler technology, we show that the compiler can use both partial and full predication to achieve speedup in large control-intensive programs. Some details of the code generation techniques are shown to provide insight into the benefit of going from partial to full predication. Preliminary experimental results are very encouraging: partial predication provides an average of 33% performance improvement for an 8-issue processor with no predicate support while full predication provides an additional 30% improvement.

1 Introduction

Branch instructions are recognized as a major impediment to exploiting instruction-level parallelism (ILP). ILP is limited by branches in two principle ways. First, branches impose control dependences which restrict the number of independent instructions available each cycle. Branch prediction

---

* Scott Mahlke is now with Hewlett Packard Laboratories, Palo Alto, CA.

in conjunction with speculative execution is typically utilized by the compiler and/or hardware to remove control dependences and expose ILP in superscalar and VLIW processors [1] [2] [3]. However, misprediction of these branches can result in severe performance penalties. Recent studies have reported a performance reduction of two to more than ten when realistic instead of perfect branch prediction is utilized [4] [5] [6]. The second limitation is that processor resources to handle branches are often restricted. As a result, for control intensive applications, an artificial upper bound on performance will be imposed by the branch resource constraints. For example, in an instruction stream consisting of 40% branches, a four issue processor capable of processing only one branch per cycle is bounded to a maximum of 2.5 sustained instructions per cycle.

Predicated execution support provides an effective means to eliminate branches from an instruction stream. Predicated or guarded execution refers to the conditional execution of an instruction based on the value of a boolean source operand, referred to as the predicate [7] [8]. This architectural support allows the compiler to employ an *if-conversion* algorithm to convert conditional branches into predicate defining instructions, and instructions along alternative paths of each branch into predicated instructions [9] [10] [11]. Predicated instructions are fetched regardless of their predicate value. Instructions whose predicate is true are executed normally. Conversely, instructions whose predicate is false are nullified, and thus are prevented from modifying the processor state.

Predicated execution provides the opportunity to significantly improve branch handling in ILP processors. The most obvious benefit is that decreasing the number of branches reduces the need to sustain multiple branches per cycle. Therefore, the artificial performance bounds imposed by limited branch resources can be alleviated. Eliminating frequently mispredicted branches also leads to a substantial reduction in branch prediction misses [12]. As a result, the performance penalties associated with mispredictions of the eliminated branches are removed. Finally, predicated execution provides an efficient interface for the compiler to expose multiple execution paths to the hardware. Without compiler support, the cost of maintaining multiple execution paths in hardware grows exponentially.

Predicated execution may be supported by a range of architectural extensions. The most complete approach is full predicate support. With this technique, all instructions are provided with an additional source operand to hold a predicate specifier. In this manner, every instruction may be a predicated. Additionally, a set of predicate defining opcodes are added to efficiently manipulate predicate values. This approach was most notably utilized in the Cydra 5 minisupercomputer [8] [13]. Full predicate execution support provides the most flexibility and the largest potential performance improvements. The other approach is to provide partial predicate support. With partial predicate support, a small number of instructions are provided which conditionally execute, such as a conditional move. As a result, partial predicate support minimizes the required changes to existing instruction set architectures (ISA's) and data paths. This approach is most attractive for designers extending current ISA's in an upward compatible manner.

In this paper, the tradeoffs involved in supporting full and partial predicated execution are investigated. Using the compilation techniques proposed in this paper, partial predicate support enables the compiler to perform full if-conversion to eliminate branches and expose ILP. Therefore, the compiler may remove as many branches with partial predicate support as with full predicate support. By removing a large portion of the branches, branch handling is significantly improved for ILP processors with partial predicate support. The relatively few changes needed to add partial predicate support into an architecture make this approach extremely attractive for designers.

However, there are several fundamental performance limitations of partial predicate support that are overcome with full predicate support. These difficulties include representing unsupported predicated instructions, manipulating predicate values, and relying extensively on speculative execution. In the first case, for an architecture with only partial predicate support, predicated operations must be performed using an equivalent sequence of instructions. Generation of these sequences results in an increase in the number of instructions executed and requires a larger number of registers to hold intermediate values for the partial predicate architecture. In the second case, the computation of predicate values is highly efficient and parallel with full predicate support. However, this same computation with partial predicate support requires a chain of sequentially dependent instructions, that can frequently increase the critical path length. Finally, the performance of partial predicate support is extensively dependent on the use of speculative execution. Conditional computations are typically represented by first performing the computation unconditionally (speculative) and storing the result(s) in some temporary locations. Then, if the condition is true, the processor state is updated, using one or more conditional moves for example. With full predicate support, speculation is not required since all instructions may have a predicate specifier. Thus, speculation may be selectively employed where it improves performance rather than always being utilized.

The issues discussed in the paper are intended for both designers of new ISA's, as well as those extending existing ISA's. With a new instruction set, the issue of supporting full or partial predicate support is clearly a choice that is available. Varying levels of partial predicate support provide

options for extending an existing ISA. For example, introducing *guard* instructions which hold the predicate specifiers of subsequent instructions may be utilized [14].

2   ISA Extensions

In this section, a set of extensions to the instruction set architecture for both full and partial predicate support are presented. The baseline architecture assumed is generic ILP processor (either VLIW or superscalar) with in-order issue and register interlocking. A generic load/store ISA is further assumed as the baseline ISA.

2.1   Extensions for Full Predication

The essence of predicated execution is the ability to suppress the modification of the processor state based upon some condition. There must be a way to express this condition and a way to express when the condition should affect execution. Full predication cleanly supports this through a combination of instruction set and micro-architecture extensions. These extensions can be classified as support for suppression of execution and expression of condition.

Suppression of Execution. The result of the condition which determines if an instruction should modify state is stored in a set of 1-bit registers. These registers are collectively referred to as the predicate register file. The setting of these registers is discussed later in this section. The values in the predicate register file are associated with each instruction in the extended instruction set through the use of an additional source operand. This operand specifies which predicate register will determine whether the operation should modify processor state. If the value in the specified predicate register is 1, or true, the instruction is executed normally; if the value is 0, or false, the instruction is suppressed.

One way to perform the suppression of an instruction in hardware is to allow the instruction to execute and to disallow any change of processor state in the write-back stage of the pipeline. This method is useful since it reduces the latency between an instruction that modifies the value of the predicate register and a subsequent instruction which is conditioned based on that predicate register. This reduced latency enables more compact schedules to be generated for predicated code. A drawback to this method is that regardless of whether an instruction is suppressed, it still ties up an execution unit. This method may also increase the complexity of the register bypass logic and force exception signalling to be delayed until the last pipeline stage.

An instruction can also be suppressed during the decode/issue stage. Thus, an instruction whose corresponding predicate register is false is simply not issued. This has the advantage of allowing the execution unit to be allocated to other operations. Since the value of the predicate register referenced must be available during decode/issue, the predicate register must at least be set in the previous cycle. This dependence distance may also be larger for deeper pipelines or if bypass is not available for predicate registers. Increasing the dependence distance between definitions and uses of predicates may adversely affect execution time by lengthening the schedule for predicated code. An example of this

P_{in}	Comparison	U	$\overline{U}$	OR	$\overline{OR}$	AND	$\overline{AND}$
0	0	0	0	-	-	-	-
0	1	0	0	-	-	-	-
1	0	0	1	-	1	0	-
1	1	1	0	1	-	-	0

(The top of the table is labeled P_{out} spanning the U, $\overline{U}$, OR, $\overline{OR}$, AND, $\overline{AND}$ columns.)

Table 1: Predicate definition truth table.

suppression model is the predicate support provided by the Cydra 5 [8]. Suppression at the decode/issue stage is also assumed in our simulation model.

Expression of Condition. A set of new instructions is needed to set the predicate registers based upon conditional expressions. These instructions can be classified as those that define, clear, set, load, or store predicate registers.

Predicate register values may be set using predicate define instructions. The predicate define semantics used are those of the HPL Playdoh architecture [15]. There is a predicate define instruction for each comparison opcode in the original instruction set. The major difference with conventional comparison instructions is that these predicate defines have up to two destination registers and that their destination registers are predicate registers. The instruction format of a predicate define is shown below.

pred_<*cmp*> Pout1<*type*>, Pout2<*type*>, src1, src2 (P_{in})

This instruction assigns values to *Pout1* and *Pout2* according to a comparison of *src1* and *src2* specified by <*cmp*>. The comparison <*cmp*> can be: equal (eq), not equal (ne), greater than (gt), etc. A predicate <*type*> is specified for each destination predicate. Predicate defining instructions are also predicated, as specified by P_{in}.

The predicate <*type*> determines the value written to the destination predicate register based upon the result of the comparison and of the input predicate, P_{in}. For each combination of comparison result and P_{in}, one of three actions may be performed on the destination predicate. It can write 1, write 0, or leave it unchanged. A total of $3^4 = 81$ possible types exist.

There are six predicate types which are particularly useful, the unconditional (U), OR, and AND type predicates and their complements. Table 1 contains the truth table for these predicate types.

Unconditional destination predicate registers are always defined, regardless of the value of P_{in} and the result of the comparison. If the value of P_{in} is 1, the result of the comparison is placed in the predicate register (or its compliment for $\overline{U}$). Otherwise, a 0 is written to the predicate register. Unconditional predicates are utilized for blocks which are executed based on a single condition, i.e., they have a single control dependence.

The OR type predicates are useful when execution of a block can be enabled by multiple conditions, such as logical AND (&&) and OR (||) constructs in C. OR type destination predicate registers are set if P_{in} is 1 and the result of the comparison is 1 (0 for $\overline{OR}$), otherwise the destination predicate register is unchanged. Note that OR type predicates must be explicitly initialized to 0 before they are defined and used. However, after they are initialized multiple OR type predicate defines may be issued simultaneously and in any

```
if (a&&b)        beq   a,0,L1       pred_clear
  j = j + 1;     beq   b,0,L1       pred_eq p1_OR,p2_U̅,a,0
else             add   j,j,1        pred_eq p1_OR,p3_U̅,b,0 (p2)
  if (c)         jump  L3           add     j,j,1 (p3)
    k = k + 1;  L1:                 pred_ne p4_U,p5_U̅,c,0 (p1)
  else           bne   c,0,L2       add     k,k,1 (p4)
    k = k - 1;   add   k,k,1        sub     k,k,1 (p5)
i = i + 1;       jump  L3           add     i,i,1
                L2:
                 sub   k,k,1
                L3:
                 add   i,i,1

   (a)              (b)                (c)
```

Figure 1: Example of predication, (a) source code, (b) assembly code, (c) assembly code after if-conversion.

order on the same predicate register. This is true since the OR type predicate either writes a 1 or leaves the register unchanged which allows implementation as a wired logical OR condition. This property can be utilized to compute an execution condition with zero dependence height using multiple predicate define instructions.

AND type predicates, are analogous to the OR type predicate. AND type destination predicate registers are cleared if P_{in} is 1 and the result of the comparison is 0 (1 for $\overline{AND}$), otherwise the destination predicate register is unchanged. The AND type predicate is particularly useful for transformations such as control height reduction [16].

Although it is possible to individually set each predicate register to zero or one through the use of the aforementioned predicate define instructions, in some cases individually setting each predicate can be costly. Therefore, two instructions, *pred_clear* and *pred_set*, are defined to provide a method of setting the entire predicate register file to 0 or 1 in one cycle.

Code Example. Figure 1 contains a simple example illustrating the concept of predicated execution. The source code in Figure 1(a) is compiled into the code shown in Figure 1(b). Using if-conversion [10], the code is then transformed into the code shown in Figure 1(c). The use of predicate registers is initiated by a *pred_clear* in order to insure that all predicate registers are cleared. The first two conditional branches in (b) are translated into two *pred_eq* instructions. Predicate register *p1* is OR type since either condition can be true for *p1* to be true. If *p2* in the first *pred_eq* is false the second *pred_eq* is not executed. This is consistent with short circuit boolean evaluation. *p3* is true only if the entire expression is true. The "then" part of the outer if statement is predicated on *p3* for this reason. The *pred_ne* simply decides whether the addition or subtraction instruction is performed. Notice that both *p4* and *p5* remain at zero if the *pred_ne* is not executed. This is consistent with the "else" part of the outer if statement. Finally, the increment of *i* is performed unconditionally.

2.2 Extensions for Partial Predication

Enhancing an existing ISA to support only partial predication in the form of conditional move or select instructions trades off the flexibility and efficiency provided by full pred-ication in order to minimize the impact to the ISA. Several existing architectures provide instruction set features that reflect this point of view.

Conditional Move. The conditional move instruction provides a natural way to add partial support for predicated execution to an existing ISA. A conditional move instruction has two source operands and one destination operand, which fits well into current 3 operand ISA's. The semantics of a conditional move instruction, shown below, are similar to that of a predicated move instruction.

$$cmov\ dest,src,cond$$
$$if\ (\ cond\ )\ dest = src$$

As with a predicated move, the contents of the source register are copied to the destination register if the condi-tion is true. Also, the conditional modification of the target register in a conditional move instruction allows simultane-ous issue of conditional move instructions having the same target register and opposite conditions on an in-order pro-cessor. The principal difference between a conditional move instruction and a predicated move instruction is that a reg-ister from the integer or floating-point register file is used to hold the condition, rather than a special predicate register file. When conditional moves are available, we also assume conditional move complement instructions ($cmov\_com$) are present. These are analogous in operation to conditional moves, except they perform the move when *cond* is false, as opposed to when *cond* is true.

The Sparc V9 instruction set specification and the DEC Alpha provide conditional move instructions for both inte-ger and floating point registers. The HP Precision Architec-ture [17] provides all branch, arithmetic, and logic instruc-tions the capability to conditionally nullify the subsequent instruction. Currently the generation of conditional move instructions is very limited in most compilers. One excep-tion is the DEC GEM compiler that can efficiently generate conditional moves for simple control constructs [18].

Select. The select instruction provides more flexibil-ity than the conditional move instruction at the expense of pipeline implementation. The added flexibility and in-creased difficulty of implementation is caused by the addi-tion of a third source operand. The semantics of the select instruction are shown below.

$$select\ dest,src1,src2,cond$$
$$dest = (\ (cond)\ ?\ src1\ :\ src2\ )$$

Unlike the conditional move instruction, the destination register is always modified with a select. If the condition is true, the contents of **src1** are copied to the destination, otherwise the contents of **src2** are copied to the destination register. The ability to choose one of two values to place in the destination register allows the compiler to effectively choose between computations from "then" and "else" paths of conditionals based upon the result of the appropriate com-parison. As a result, select instructions enable more efficient transformations by the compiler. This will be discussed in more detail in the next section. The Multiflow Trace 300 series machines supported partial predicated execution with select instructions [19].

3   Compiler Support

The compiler eliminates branch instructions by introducing conditional instructions. The basic transformation is known as if-conversion [9] [10]. In our approach, full predicate sup-port is assumed in the intermediate representation (IR) re-gardless of the the actual architectural support in the tar-get processor. A set of compilation techniques based on the hyperblock structure are employed to effectively exploit predicate support in the IR [11]. For target processors that only have partial predicate support, unsupported predicated instructions are broken down into sequences of equivalent in-structions that are representable. Since the transformation may introduce inefficiencies, a comprehensive set of peephole optimizations is applied to code both before and after con-version. This approach of compiling for processors with par-tial predicate support differs from conventional code genera-tion techniques. Conventional compilers typically transform simple control flow structures or identify special patterns that can utilize conditional moves or selects. Conversely, the approach utilized in this paper enables full if-conversion to be applied with partial predicate support to eliminate control flow.

In this section, the hyperblock compilation techniques for full predicate support are first summarized. Then, the trans-formation techniques to generate partial predicate code from a full predicate IR are described. Finally, two examples from the benchmark programs studied are presented to compare and contrast the effectiveness of full and partial predicate support using the these compilation techniques.

3.1   Compiler Support for Full Predication

The compilation techniques utilized in this paper to exploit predicated execution are based on a structure called a *hy-perblock* [11]. A hyperblock is a collection of connected basic blocks in which control may only enter at the first block, des-ignated as the entry block. Control flow may leave from one or more blocks in the hyperblock. All control flow between basic blocks in a hyperblock is eliminated via if-conversion. The goal of hyperblocks is to intelligently group basic blocks from many different control flow paths into a single block for compiler optimization and scheduling.

Basic blocks are systematically included in a hyperblock based on two, possibly conflicting, high level goals. First, performance is maximized when the hyperblock captures a large fraction of the likely control flow paths. Thus, any blocks to which control is likely to flow are desirable to add to the hyperblock. Second, resource (fetch bandwidth and function units) are limited; therefore, including too many blocks may over saturate the processor causing an overall performance loss. Also, including a block which has a com-paratively large dependence height or contains a hazardous instruction (e.g., a subroutine call) is likely to result in per-formance loss. The final hyperblock consists of a linear se-quence of predicated instructions. Additionally, there are ex-plicit exit branch instructions (possibly predicated) to any blocks not selected for inclusion in the hyperblock. These branch instructions represent the control flow that was iden-tified as unprofitable to eliminate with predicated execution support.

	fully predicated code		partially predicated code	
before promotion	load mul add	temp1,addrx,offx (Pin) temp2,temp1,2 (Pin) y,temp2,3 (Pin)	load cmov mul cmov add cmov	temp3,addrx,offx temp1,temp3,Pin temp4,temp1,2 temp2,temp4,Pin temp5,temp2,3 y,temp5,Pin
after promotion	load mul add	temp1,addrx,offx temp2,temp1,2 y,temp,2,3 (Pin)	load mul add cmov	temp1,addr,offx temp2,temp1,2 temp3,temp2,3 y,temp3,Pin

operation: load x
            y = 2x+3

Note: non-excepting instructions
      assumed.

Figure 2: Example of predicate promotion.

3.2   Compiler Support for Partial Predication

Generating partially predicated code from fully predicated code involves removing predicates from all instructions which are not allowed to have a predicate specifier. The only instruction set remnants of predication in the partially predicated code are conditional move or select instructions. Transforming fully predicated code to partially predicated code is essentially accomplished by converting predicated instructions into speculative instructions which write to some temporary location. Then, conditional move or select instructions are inserted to conditionally update the processor state based on the value of the predicate. Since all predicated instructions are converted to speculative instructions, the efficiency of the partially predicated code is heavily dependent on the underlying support for speculation provided by the processor. In this section, the code generation procedure chosen to implement the full to partial predication transformation is described. The procedure is divided into 3 steps, predicate promotion, basic conversion, and peephole optimization.

Predicate Promotion. The conversion of predicated instructions into an equivalent set of instructions that only utilize conditional moves or selects introduces a significant amount of code expansion. This code expansion is obviously reduced if there are fewer predicated instructions that must be converted. Predicate promotion refers to removing the predicate from a predicated instruction [11]. As a result, the instruction is unconditionally executed. By performing predicate promotion, fewer predicated instructions remain in the IR that must be converted.

An example to illustrate the effectiveness of predicate promotion is presented in Figure 2. The code sequence in the upper left box is the original fully predicated IR. Straightforward conversion to conditional move code, as will be discussed in the next subsection, yields the code in the upper right box. Each predicated instruction is expanded into two instructions for the partial predicate architecture. All the conditional moves in this sequence, except for the last, are unnecessary if the original destination registers of the predicated instructions are temporary registers. In this case, the predicate of the first two instructions can be promoted, as shown in the lower left box of Figure 2. The *add* instruc-

tion is the only remaining predicated instruction. Finally, conversion to conditional move code after promotion yields the code sequence in the bottom right box of Figure 2. In all, the number of instructions is reduced from 6 to 4 in this example with predicate promotion.

It should be noted that predicate promotion is also effective for architectures with full predicate support. Predicate promotion enables speculative execution by allowing predicated instructions to execute before their predicate is calculated. In this manner, the dependence between the predicate definition and the predicated instruction is eliminated. The hyperblock optimizer and scheduler utilize predicate promotion when the predicate calculation occurs along a critical dependence chain to reduce this dependence length.

Basic Conversions. In the second step of the transformation from fully predicated code to partially predicated code, a set of simple transformations, referred to as basic conversions, are applied to each remaining predicated instruction independently. The purpose of the basic conversions is to replace each predicated instruction by a sequence of instructions with equivalent functionality. The sequence is limited to contain conditional moves as the only conditional instructions. As a result, most instructions in the sequence must be executed without a predicate. These instructions thus become speculative. When generating speculative instructions, the compiler must ensure they only modify temporary registers or memory locations. Furthermore, the compiler must ensure the speculative instructions will not cause any program terminating exceptions when the condition turns out to be false. Program terminating exceptions include illegal memory address, divide-by-zero, overflow, or underflow.

The basic conversions that may be applied are greatly simplified if the underlying processor has support full support for speculative execution. In particular, non-excepting or silent, instructions allow for the most efficient transformations. For such an architecture, the basic conversions for the main classes of instructions are summarized in Figure 3. The simplest conversion is used for predicated arithmetic and logic instructions and also for memory loads. The conversion, as can be seen in Figure 3, is to rename the destination of the predicated instruction, remove the predicate, and then conditionally move the result into the original destination based on the result of the predicate.

The basic conversions for memory store instructions are similar. Since the destination of a store instruction is a memory location instead of a register, a different technique must be used to insure that the an invalid value is not written to the original destination of the store. Figure 3 shows that the address of the store is calculated separately. Then a conditional move is used to replace the address of the store with $safe_addr$ when the predicate of the store is false. The macro $safe_addr$ refers to a reserved location on the stack.

The conversions for predicate definition instructions are the most complicated because predicate definitions have rather complicated logic capabilities. The conversions for two representative predicate definition instructions are shown in Figure 3. The predicate definition instructions are identical except for the type on the destination predicate register. The transformation for the *OR* type predicate

Fully Predicated Code	**Basic Conversions, Non-excepting Instructions**	
predicate definition instructions		
pred_lt Pout$_{OR}$,src1,src2 (Pin)	lt and or	temp,src1,src2 temp,Pin,temp Pout,Pout,temp
pred_lt_f Pout$_U$,src1,src2 (Pin)	lt_f and	temp,src1,src2 Pout,Pin,temp
arithmetic & logic instructions		
add dest,src1,src2 (Pin)	add cmov	temp,src1,src2 dest,temp,Pin
div_f dest,src1,src2 (Pin)	div_f cmov	temp_dest,src1,src2 dest,temp_dest,Pin
memory instructions		
store addr,off,src (Pin)	add cmov_com store	temp_addr,addr,off temp_addr,$safe_addr,Pin temp_addr,0,src
load dest,addr,off (Pin)	load cmov	temp_dest,addr,off dest,temp_dest,Pin
branch instructions		
jump label (Pin)	bne	Pin,0,label
blt src1,src2,label (Pin)	ge blt	temp,src1,src2 temp,Pin,label
jsr label (Pin)	beq jsr NEXT:	Pin,0,NEXT label

Figure 3: Basic conversions assuming non-excepting instructions available in the architecture.

Fully Predicated Code	**Basic Conversions, Excepting Instructions**	
predicate definition instructions		
pred_lt_f Pout$_U$,src1,src2 (Pin)	mov cmov_com lt_f and	temp_src,src2 temp_src,$safe_val,Pi temp_dest,src1,temp_src Pout,temp_dest,Pin
arithmetic & logic instructions		
div_f dest,src1,src2 (Pin)	mov cmov_com div_f cmov	temp_src,src2 temp_src,$safe_val,Pin temp_dest,src1,temp_src dest,temp_dest,Pin
memory instructions		
load dest,addr,off (Pin)	add cmov_com load cmov	temp_addr,addr,off temp_addr,$safe_addr,Pin temp_dest,temp_addr,0 dest,temp_dest,Pin

Figure 4: Basic conversions without non-excepting instructions available in the architecture.

produces three instructions. The first instruction performs the *lt* comparison of *src1* and *src2*, placing the result in a temporary register. Each predicate definition transformation generates such a comparison instruction. The second instruction performs a logical *AND* which clears the temporary register if the predicate *Pin* is false. This clearing instruction is generated only if the predicate definition instruction is predicated. The third instruction performs a logical *OR* of the value in the temporary register with the previous value of the *OR* type predicate *Pout* and deposits the result t in *Pout*. For an *AND* type predicate, the result would be stored with a logical *AND*. For an unconditional predicate, a separate depositing instruction is not necessary.

The basic conversions for branches are relatively straight forward and are left to the reader. Predicated subroutine calls are handled by branching around them when the predicate is false since conditional calls were not assumed in the architecture.

Conversions are also possible if no speculation support is provided. However, in addition to insuring that registers or memory locations are not illegally modified, the basic conversions must also prevent exceptions when the original predicate is false. Figure 4 shows three typical conversions. The non-excepting versions of these appeared in Figure 3. Note that the excepting versions produce more instructions than the corresponding conversions for non-excepting instructions. For predicate definition, arithmetic, and logic instructions, the only difference in the conversions is that a value that is known to prevent an exception is conditionally moved into one of the source operands of the previously predicated instruction. These values, which depend on the type of instruction, are referred to as *$safe_val* in the fig-

ure. The conversions for floating point conditional branch instructions are similar. Conversion for load instructions is also similar, only an address known not to cause an illegal memory access is moved into the address source of the load.

Peephole Optimizations. The basic transformations of the previous section introduce some inefficiencies since each instruction is considered independently. Many of these inefficiencies can be removed by applying a set of peephole optimizations after the basic transformation. The goal of these optimizations is to reduce the instruction count and dependence height of the partial predicate code. The optimizations find opportunities for improving code efficiency by investigating the interactions of the various transformations, exploiting special cases, and utilizing the additional functionality of the *select* instruction over the conditional move. Some of the optimizations in this section rely on the existence of complementary *AND* and *OR* instructions (*and_not* and *or_not*). These instructions are simply logical instructions in which the second source operand is complemented. The existence of these instructions is assumed in the base instruction set.

Basic conversions of predicate defines introduce redundant comparison and logic instructions. For predicates which only differ in predicate type (*U*, *OR*, *AND*), the comparisons are obviously redundant. Applying common subexpression elimination, copy propagation, and dead code removal after conversion effectively eliminates these redundancies. In some cases, the transformations of similar predicate definitions result in opposite comparisons. If one of these comparisons can be inverted, then one of the comparisons may be eliminated. A comparison can be inverted when each use of the result of this comparison can be inverted without the addition of an instruction. The result of a comparison in a predicate definition instruction used only by *and*, *and_not*, *or*, *or_not*, *cmov*, *cmov_com*, *select*, or a conditional branch may be inverted. The only two non-invertible sources which might contain the result of a predicate definition conversion are the non-inverted inputs of *and_not* and *or_not*. Therefore, in most cases, one of two complementary comparisons resulting from similar predicate definitions can be eliminated.

The use of OR type predicates is extremely efficient for architectures with full predicate support. Sequences of OR type predicate definitions which all write to the same destination predicate may be simultaneously executed. However, with partial support, these sequences of OR type predicate definitions result in a sequential chain of dependent instructions. These strict sequential dependences may be overcome using associativity rules to reduce the height of the dependence chain. The dependence height of the resulting code is $log_2(n)$, where n is the number of OR type predicate definitions. An example of OR-Tree optimization is presented in Section 3.3.

Some additional optimizations are possible if a *select* instruction is available. The functionality of the *select* instruction is described in Section 2.2. Through the use of a *select* instruction, one instruction from the sequences used for excepting arithmetic and memory instructions shown in Figure 4 can be eliminated. The detailed use of selects is not discussed in this paper due to space considerations.

3.3 Benchmark Examples

In order to more clearly understand the effectiveness of predicated execution support and the performance tradeoffs of full versus partial support, two examples from the set of benchmarks are presented. The first example is from *wc* and the second is from *grep*. These benchmarks were chosen because they are relatively small, yet they are very control-intensive so they clearly illustrate the effectiveness of full and partial predicate support.

Example Loop from Wc. Figure 5(a) shows the control flow graph for the most important loop segment from the benchmark *wc*. The control flow graph is augmented with the execution frequencies of each control transfer for the measured run of the program. This loop is characterized by small basic blocks and a large percentage of branches. The loop segment contains 13 basic blocks with a total of 34 instructions, 14 of which are branches. The performance of an 8-issue ILP processor without predicated execution support is limited by this high frequency of branches. Overall, a speedup of 2.3 is achieved for an 8-issue processor over a 1-issue processor (see Figure 8).

The assembly code after hyperblock formation for the loop segment with full and partial predicate support is shown in Figures 5(b) and (c), respectively. The issue cycle is given to the right of each assembly code instruction. Note that the assembly code is not reordered based on the issue cycle for ease of understanding. The schedule assumes a 4-issue processor which can issue 4 instructions of any type except branches, which are limited to 1 per cycle. With both full and partial predicate support, all of the branches except three are eliminated using hyperblock formation. The three remaining branches, conditional branch to block C, conditional branch to EXIT, and the loop backedge, are highly predictable. Therefore, virtually all the mispredictions are eliminated with both full and partial predicate support in this loop. The resulting performance is increased by 17% with partial predicate support and an additional 88% with full predicate support (see Figure 8).

The performance difference between full and partial predicate support comes from the extra instructions required to represent predicate defines and predicated instructions. As a result, the issue resources of the processor are over saturated with partial predicate support. In the example in Figure 5, the number of instructions is increased from 18 with full predicate support to 31 with partial predicate support. This results in an increase in execution time from 8 to 10 cycles. For the entire benchmark execution, a similar trend is observed. The number of instructions is increased from 1526K with full predicate support to 2999K with partial predicate support, resulting in a speedup increase of 2.7 with partial support to 5.1 with full support (see Figure 8 and Table 2).

Example Loop from Grep. Figure 6 shows the assembly code for the most important loop segment from the benchmark *grep*. The base processor model, which does not support any predicated execution, employs speculative execution in conjunction with superblock ILP compilation techniques to achieve the schedule shown in Figure 6(a) [20]. Each of the conditional branches in the figure are very infrequently taken, thus the sequence of instructions iterates very frequently. Overall, *grep* is dominated by an extremely high frequency of branches. This high frequency of branches is the performance bottleneck of this loop since only 1 branch resource is available. However, the branches are highly predictable. Thus, hyperblock compilation techniques focus on reducing this branch bottleneck for processors with limited branch resources.

With full predicate support, the compiler is able to combine the branches into a single exit branch using OR type predicate definitions. Since OR type predicate definitions can be issued simultaneously, an extremely tight schedule can be achieved. The execution time is dramatically reduced from 14 to 6 cycles with full predicate support. With partial predicate support, the same transformations are applied. Therefore, the same number of branches are eliminated. However, the representation of OR type predicates is less efficient with partial predicate support. In particular, the logical OR instructions cannot be simultaneously issued. The or-tree optimization discussed previously in Section 3.2 is applied to reduce the dependence height of the sequence and improve performance. In the example, partial predicate support improves performance from 14 to 10 cycles. Overall for the final benchmark performance, partial predicate support improves performance by 46% over the base code and full predicate support further improves performance by 31%.

4 Experimental Evaluation

4.1 Methodology

The predication techniques presented in this paper are evaluated through emulation-driven simulation. The benchmarks studied consist of *008.espresso, 022.li, 023.eqntott, 026.compress, 052.alvinn, 056.ear, and 072.sc* from SPEC-92, and the Unix utilities *cccp, cmp, eqn, grep, lex, qsort, wc, and yacc*. The benchmark programs are initially compiled to produce intermediate code, which is essentially the instruc-

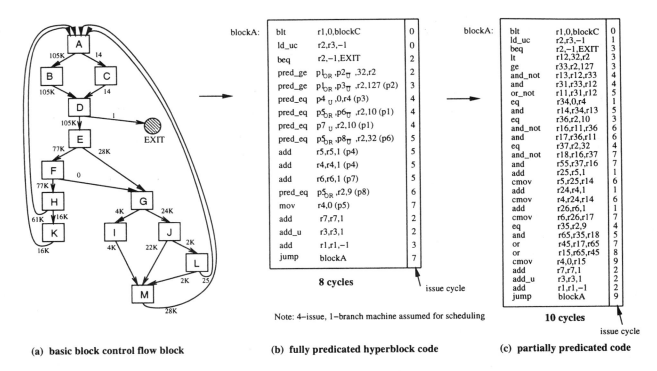

<table>
<tr><td colspan="3">blockA:</td><td></td></tr>
</table>

blockA:	blt	r1,0,blockC	0
	ld_uc	r2,r3,−1	0
	beq	r2,−1,EXIT	2
	pred_ge	p1$_{OR}$,p2$_U$,32,r2	2
	pred_ge	p1$_{OR}$,p3$_U$,r2,127 (p2)	3
	pred_eq	p4 $_U$,0,r4 (p3)	4
	pred_eq	p5$_{OR}$,p6$_U$,r2,10 (p1)	4
	pred_eq	p7 $_U$,r2,10 (p1)	4
	pred_eq	p5$_{OR}$,p8$_U$,r2,32 (p6)	5
	add	r5,r5,1 (p4)	5
	add	r4,r4,1 (p4)	5
	add	r6,r6,1 (p7)	5
	pred_eq	p5$_{OR}$,r2,9 (p8)	6
	mov	r4,0 (p5)	7
	add	r7,r7,1	2
	add_u	r3,r3,1	2
	add	r1,r1,−1	3
	jump	blockA	7

8 cycles

← issue cycle

Note: 4–issue, 1–branch machine assumed for scheduling

blockA:	blt	r1,0,blockC	0
	ld_uc	r2,r3,−1	1
	beq	r2,−1,EXIT	3
	lt	r12,32,r2	3
	ge	r33,r2,127	3
	and_not	r13,r12,r33	4
	and	r31,r33,r12	4
	or_not	r11,r31,r12	5
	eq	r34,0,r4	1
	and	r14,r34,r13	5
	eq	r36,r2,10	3
	and_not	r16,r11,r36	6
	and	r17,r36,r11	6
	eq	r37,r2,32	4
	and_not	r18,r16,r37	7
	and	r55,r37,r16	7
	add	r25,r5,1	1
	cmov	r5,r25,r14	6
	add	r24,r4,1	1
	cmov	r4,r24,r14	6
	add	r26,r6,1	1
	cmov	r6,r26,r17	7
	eq	r35,r2,9	4
	and	r65,r35,r18	5
	or	r45,r17,r65	6
	or	r15,r65,r45	8
	cmov	r4,0,r15	9
	add	r7,r7,1	2
	add_u	r3,r3,1	2
	add	r1,r1,−1	2
	jump	blockA	9

10 cycles

issue cycle

(a) basic block control flow block   **(b) fully predicated hyperblock code**   **(c) partially predicated code**

Figure 5: Example loop segment from *wc*.

tion set of an architecture with varying levels of support for predicated execution. Register allocation and code scheduling are performed in order to produce code that could be executed by a target architecture with such support. To allow emulation of the code on the host HP PA-RISC processor, the code must be modified to remove predication, while providing accurate emulation of predicated instructions.

Emulation ensures that the optimized code generated for each configuration executes correctly. Execution of the benchmark with emulation also generates an instruction trace containing memory address information, predicate register contents, and branch directions. This trace is fed to a simulator for performance analysis of the particular architectural model being studied. We refer to this technique as emulation-driven simulation. The simulator models, in detail, the architecture's prefetch and issue unit, instruction and data caches, branch target buffer, and hardware interlocks, providing an accurate measure of performance.

Predicate Emulation. Emulation is achieved by performing a second phase of register allocation and generating PA-RISC assembly code. The emulation of the varying levels of predicate support, as well as speculation of load instructions is done using the bit manipulation and conditional nullification capabilities of the PA-RISC instruction set [17]. Predicates are emulated by reserving n of the callee-saved registers and accessing them as $32 \times n$ 1-bit registers.

The instruction sequence required to emulate a predicate define instruction is dependent upon the predicate types of the destination predicate registers. As an example, consider the predicated predicate define instruction (1) in Figure 7. In this example, predicate registers $p1$, $p2$, and $p3$ have been assigned bits 1,2, and 3 of general register $\%r3$, respectively. Instruction (1) is defining predicate register $p1$ as OR type

and $p3$ as unconditional complement. The first instruction in the five instruction assembly code sequence, places a 0 in bit 3 of register $\%r3$, unconditionally setting $p3$ to 0. The second instruction will branch around the remaining instructions if the predicate $p2$ is 0. If $p2$ is 1 the third instruction then performs the comparison, and using the conditional nullification capabilities of that instruction, determines which of the next two instructions will be executed. If the contents of $\%r24$ is 0, then only the fifth instruction will be executed, writing a 1 to bit 1 of $\%r3$, setting $p1$ to 1. Otherwise, only the fourth instruction will be executed, writing a 1 to bit 3 of $\%r3$, setting $p3$ to 1.

Predicated instructions are emulated by extracting the bit from one of the reserved registers that corresponds to the predicate for that instruction. The value of that bit is used to conditionally execute the predicated instruction. For example, instruction (2) in Figure 7 is predicated on $p3$. Thus, bit 3 is extracted from $\%r3$ and is used to conditionally nullify the increment of $\%r25$.

Conditional Move Emulation. The emulation of conditional move and select instructions is done in a similar fashion. Instruction (3) in Figure 7 is a conditional move of $r6$ into $r5$ if the contents of $r8$ is non-zero. Emulation requires two instructions. The first performs the comparison and nullifies the subsequent copy of 6 into 5 if $r8$ is zero. Instruction (4) in Figure 7 is a select instruction. As with the conditional move instruction, the first instruction performs a comparison to determine the contents of $r8$. If $r8$ is zero, $r7$ will be copied into $r5$, otherwise $r6$ is copied into $r5$ as described in Section 2.2.

Processor Models. Three processor models are evaluated this paper. The baseline processor is a k-issue processor, with no limitation placed on the combination of instruc-

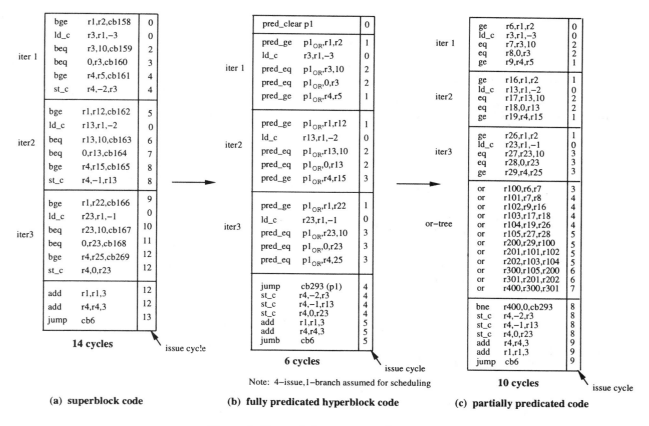

(a) superblock code   **(b) fully predicated hyperblock code**   **(c) partially predicated code**

Note: 4–issue,1–branch assumed for scheduling

Figure 6: Example loop segment from *grep*.

tions which may be issued each cycle, except for branches. The memory system is specified as either perfect or consists of a 64K directed mapped instruction cache and a 64K direct mapped, blocking data cache; both with 64 byte blocks. The data cache is write-through with no write allocate and has a miss penalty of 12 cycles. The dynamic branch prediction strategy employed is a 1K entry BTB with 2 bit counter with a 2 cycle misprediction penalty. The instruction latencies assumed are those of the HP PA-RISC 7100. Lastly, the baseline processor is assumed to have an infinite number of registers. The baseline processor does not support any form of predicated execution. However, it includes non-excepting or silent versions of all instructions to fully support speculative execution. Superblock ILP compilation techniques are utilized to support the baseline processor [20]. The baseline processor is referred to as *Superblock* in all graphs and tables.

For partial predicate support, the baseline processor is extended to support conditional move instructions. Note that since non-excepting versions of all instructions are available, the more efficient conversions are applied by the compiler for partial predication (Section 3.2). The partial predicate support processor is referred to as *Conditional Move*. The final model is the baseline processor extended to support full predication as described in Section 2.1. This model is referred to as *Full Predication*. For this model, hyperblock compilation techniques are applied. Performance of the 3 models is compared by reporting the speedup of the particular processor model versus the baseline processor. In

(1)	pred_eq	$p1_{OR}$, $p3_{\overline{U}}$,r24,0 (p2)	DEPI	0,3,1,%r3
			BB,>=,N	%r3,2,$pred_0
			COMCLR,=	%r0,%r24,%r0
			DEPI,TR	1,3,1,%r3
			DEPI	1,1,1,%r3
			$pred_0	
(2)	add	r25,r25,1 (p3)	EXTRU,EV	%r3,3,1,%r0
			ADDI	1,%r25,%r25
(3)	cmov	r5,r6,r8	COMCLR,=	%r8,%r0,%r0
			COPY	%r6,%r5
(4)	select	r5,r6,r7,r8	COMCLR,=	%r8,%r0,%r0
			OR,TR	%r6,%r5
			COPY	%r7,%r5

Figure 7: HP PA-RISC emulation of predicate support.

particular, speedup is calculated by dividing the cycle count for a 1-issue baseline processor by the cycle count of a k-issue processor of the specified model.

4.2   Results

Figure 8 shows the relative performance achieved by superblock, conditional move, and full predication for an issue-8, 1-branch processor. Full predication performed the best in every benchmark with an average speedup of 63% over superblock.[1] Speedup with conditional move code fell between superblock and full predication for all benchmarks except *072.sc* which performed slightly below superblock

---

[1] Averages reported refer to the arithmetic mean.

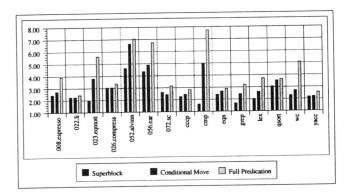

Figure 8: Effectiveness of full and partial predicate support for an 8-issue, 1-branch processor with perfect caches.

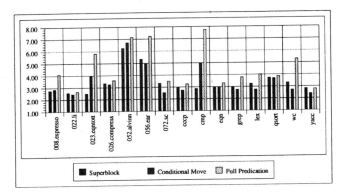

Figure 9: Effectiveness of full and partial predicate support for an 8-issue, 2-branch processor with perfect caches.

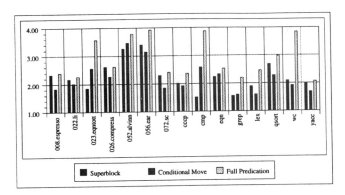

Figure 10: Effectiveness of full and partial predicate support for an 4-issue, 1-branch processor with perfect caches.

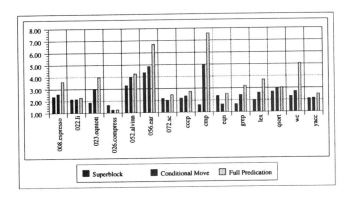

Figure 11: Effectiveness of full and partial predicate support for an 8-issue, 1-branch processor with 64K instruction and data caches.

code's performance. The unusual behavior of *072.sc* was primarily due to increased dependence chain lengths caused by the conditional move transformations. On average, though, conditional move code had a speedup of 33% over superblock. The speedup for conditional move code is very substantial. Most researchers and product developers have reported small gains except for certain special cases with conditional moves. However, utilizing the hyperblock techniques in conjunction with the conditional move transformations yields consistent performance improvements.

Full predication also achieved performance gain on top of the conditional move model. This illustrates that there is significant performance gain possible provided by the ISA changes to support full predication. In particular, the efficiency of representing predicated instructions, the reduced dependence heights to represent predicated instructions, and the ability to simultaneously execute *OR* type predicate defines provided full predicate support with the additional performance improvement. On average, a gain of 30% over the conditional move model was observed.

Increasing the branch issue rate from 1 to 2 branches per cycle provides interesting insight into the effectiveness of predicated execution. Figure 9 shows the performance result of an 8-issue processor that can execute 2 branches per cycle. The performance improvement of conditional move code and full predicate against superblock code is reduced. This is attributal to improving the performance of superblock. The

conditional move and full predication code has had many of the branches removed with hyperblock formation. Therefore, increasing the number of branches does not noticeably improve the performance of conditional move and full predication code. On average, conditional move performed only 3% faster than superblock while full predication performed 35% faster than superblock.

Figure 10 shows performance of the benchmarks on a 4 issue processor that can issue 1 branch per cycle. The most noticeable trend across these benchmarks is that while full predication consistently beats superblock code, conditional move code performs worse than superblock in the majority of benchmarks. Since support for predication in the condition move code is limited, the compiler must compensate by creating many more instructions than it would with full predicate support. These extra instructions are absorbed by the 8 issue machine, but saturate the 4 issue machine creating poor results. These results indicate a more conservative hyperblock formation algorithm needs to be employed for the conditional move model with a 4-issue processor. For full predication, substantial performance gain is still possible for the 4-issue processor, with an average of 33% speedup over superblock.

To evaluate the cache effects associated with predicated execution, Figure 11 is presented. As expected all three methods were affected by a realistic cache model. However,

Benchmark	Superblk	Cond. Move	Full Pred.
008.espresso	489M	812M (1.66)	626M (1.28)
022.li	31M	38M (1.23)	32M (1.04)
023.eqntott	1030M	1230M (1.19)	885M (0.86)
026.compress	90M	128M (1.41)	108M (1.20)
052.alvinn	3574M	4003M (1.12)	3603M (1.01)
056.ear	11225M	13838M (1.23)	11073M (0.99)
072.sc	91M	85M (0.93)	75M (0.83)
cccp	3701K	5077K (1.37)	3855K (1.04)
cmp	932K	1422K (1.53)	922K (0.99)
eqn	44M	49M (1.11)	44M (0.99)
grep	1282K	2467K (1.92)	1647K (1.28)
lex	36M	75M (2.10)	46M (1.29)
qsort	44M	70M (1.61)	49M (1.11)
wc	1493K	2999K (2.01)	1526K (1.02)
yacc	43M	66M (1.53)	50M (1.16)

Table 2: Dynamic instruction count comparison.

two benchmarks stand out. The real cache significantly reduced the performance of *026.compress* in all three models. Conditional move and full predication code increased data memory traffic more by performing speculative execution using predicate promotion. Since these promoted instructions often caused cache misses, the performance of conditional move and full predication code dropped significantly. *Eqn* also exhibited an interesting result. Conditional move performed poorly while full predication and superblock remained proportionally the same. This is a side effect of the increased instruction cache miss rate due to conditional move's larger instruction count. This is evidenced by the dynamic instruction count of *eqn* in Table 2. On average predicated code still yielded good results over superblock with full predication performing 54% faster than superblock and conditional moves performing 24% faster than superblock.

The dynamic instruction count of all benchmarks with respect to a processor model is shown in Table 2. Full predication code can increase dynamic instruction count over superblock as is executes both paths of an *if-then-else* construct. Superblock code can increase dynamic instruction count over full predication by unnecessary speculated instructions into frequently executed paths. Therefore the overall relation in instruction count between full predication and superblock can vary as the results indicate. Conditional move code's dynamic instruction count is hit hardest; however, since it suffers from executing code normally hidden by branches combined with the inefficiencies associated with not having full predicate support. Conditional move code had an average of 46% more dynamic instructions than superblock, while full predication had only 7% dynamic instruction.

Finally, as shown in Table 3, the number of branches in partially and fully predicated code is substantially less than in the superblock code. Much of the speedup of full and partial predication comes from the elimination of branches. Mispredicted branches incur a significant performance penalty. With fewer branches in the code, there are fewer mispredictions. Also, in many architectures, because of the high cost of branch prediction, the issue rate for branches is less than the issue rate for other instructions. Therefore, fewer branches in the code can greatly increase the available ILP. Partially and fully predicated code have very close to the same number of branches, with fully predicated code often

having just a few less. The small difference in the number of branches is a result of adding branches around predicated subroutine calls in partially predicated code. The differences in the misprediction ratios for partially and fully predicated code is also a result of predicated subroutine calls.

An odd behavior is observed for *grep* in Table 3. The number of mispredictions for the conditional move and full predication models are larger than that of the superblock model. This is caused by a branch combining transformation employed for hyperblocks by the compiler which is heavily applied for *grep*. With this transformation, unlikely taken branches are combined to a single branch. The goal of the transformation is to reduce the number of dynamic branches. However, the combined branch typically causes more mispredictions than the sum of the mispredictions caused by the original branches. As a result, the total number of mispredictions may be increased with this technique.

5 Concluding Remarks

The code generation strategy presented in this paper illustrates the qualitative benefit of both partial and full predication. In general, both allow the compiler to remove a substantial number of branches from the instruction stream. However, full predication allows more efficient predicate evaluation, less reliance on speculative execution, and fewer instructions executed. As shown in our quantitative results, these benefits enable full predication to provide more robust performance gain in a variety of processor configurations.

For an eight issue processor that executes up to one branch per cycle, we show that conditional move allows about 30% performance gain over an aggressive base ILP processor with no predication support. This speedup is very encouraging and shows that a relatively small architectural extension can provided significant performance gain. Full predication offers another 30% gain over conditional move. The performance gains of full and partial predication support illustrate the importance of improving branch handling in ILP processors using predicated execution.

Results based on a four issue processor illustrate the advantage of full predication support. Full predication support remains substantially superior even in the presence of a low issue rate. This is due to its efficient predicate evaluation and low instruction overhead. This contrasts with conditional move support where the extra dynamic instructions over utilize the processor issue resources and result in a sizable performance degradation for the majority of the benchmarks. Nevertheless, the substantial performance gain for two of the benchmarks suggests that conditional move could be a valuable feature even in a low issue rate processor. However, this does indicate that a compiler must be extremely intelligent when exploiting conditional move on low issue rate processors.

All of the results presented in this paper are based on a 2-cycle branch prediction miss penalty. This was chosen to show conservative performance gains for predicated execution. For machines with larger branch prediction miss penalties, we expect the benefits of both full and partial prediction to be much more pronounced. Furthermore, when more advanced compiler optimization techniques become available,

Benchmark	Superblock			Conditional Move			Full Predication		
	BR	MP	MPR	BR	MP	MPR	BR	MP	MPR
008.espresso	75M	3402K	4.55%	38M	2066K	5.38%	33M	1039K	3.15%
022.li	7457K	774K	10.38%	6169K	694K	11.25%	6110K	702K	11.5%
023.eqntott	315M	42M	13.47%	53M	6732K	12.66%	51M	6931K	13.57%
026.compress	12M	1344K	10.9%	9269K	864K	9.32%	9240K	867K	9.38%
052.alvinn	463M	1091K	0.24%	74M	896K	1.23%	74M	1032K	1.38%
056.ear	1539M	66M	4.3%	443M	16M	3.52%	442M	15M	3.4%
072.sc	22M	1232K	5.49%	11M	1044K	9.19%	11M	934K	8.26%
cccp	921K	66K	7.19%	537K	65K	12.17%	534K	65K	12.15%
cmp	530K	4395	0.83%	26K	31	0.12%	26K	31	0.12%
eqn	7470K	1612K	8.2%	4506K	514K	11.4%	4495K	511K	11.37%
grep	663K	9660	1.46%	171K	20K	11.7%	171K	20K	11.73%
lex	14M	232K	1.65%	3070K	201K	6.55%	3030K	196K	6.46%
qsort	8847K	1332K	15.06%	6092K	597K	9.79%	6066K	610K	10.06%
wc	478K	33K	6.85%	224K	57	.025%	224K	57	.025%
yacc	12M	517K	4.31%	5944K	445K	7.48%	5900K	431K	7.31%

Table 3: Comparison of branch statistics: number of branches (BR), mispredictions (MP), and miss prediction rate (MPR).

we expect the performance gain of both partial and full predication to increase. We also feel it would be interesting to explore the range of predication support between conditional move and full predication support.

Acknowledgements

The authors would like to thank Roger Bringmann and Dan Lavery for their effort in helping put this paper together. We also wish to extend thanks to Mike Schlansker and Vinod Kathail at HP Labs for their insightful discussions of the Playdoh model of predicated execution. Finally, we would like to thank Robert Cohn and Geoff Lowney at DEC, and John Ruttenberg at SGI for their discussions on the use of conditional moves and selects. This research has been supported by the National Science Foundation (NSF) under grant MIP-9308013, Intel Corporation, Advanced Micro Devces, Hewlett-Packard, SUN Microsystems and AT&T GIS.

References

[1] J. E. Smith, "A study of branch prediction strategies," in *Proceedings of the 8th International Symposium on Computer Architecture*, pp. 135–148, May 1981.

[2] J. Lee and A. J. Smith, "Branch prediction strategies and branch target buffer design," *IEEE Computer*, pp. 6–22, January 1984.

[3] T. Y. Yeh and Y. N. Patt, "A comparison of dynamic branch predictors that use two levels of branch history," in *Proceedings of the 20th Annual International Symposium on Computer Architecture*, pp. 257–266, May 1993.

[4] M. D. Smith, M. Johnson, and M. A. Horowitz, "Limits on multiple instruction issue," in *Proceedings of the 3rd International Conference on Architectural Support for Programming Languages and Operating Systems*, pp. 290–302, April 1989.

[5] D. W. Wall, "Limits of instruction-level parallelism," in *Proceedings of the 4th International Conference on Architectural Support for Programming Languages and Operating Systems*, pp. 176–188, April 1991.

[6] M. Butler, T. Yeh, Y. Patt, M. Alsup, H. Scales, and M. Shebanow, "Single instruction stream parallelism is greater than two," in *Proceedings of the 18th International Symposium on Computer Architecture*, pp. 276–286, May 1991.

[7] P. Y. Hsu and E. S. Davidson, "Highly concurrent scalar processing," in *Proceedings of the 13th International Symposium on Computer Architecture*, pp. 386–395, June 1986.

[8] B. R. Rau, D. W. L. Yen, W. Yen, and R. A. Towle, "The Cydra 5 departmental supercomputer," *IEEE Computer*, vol. 22, pp. 12–35, January 1989.

[9] J. R. Allen, K. Kennedy, C. Porterfield, and J. Warren, "Conversion of control dependence to data dependence," in *Proceedings of the 10th ACM Symposium on Principles of Programming Languages*, pp. 177–189, January 1983.

[10] J. C. Park and M. S. Schlansker, "On predicated execution," Tech. Rep. HPL-91-58, Hewlett Packard Laboratories, Palo Alto, CA, May 1991.

[11] S. A. Mahlke, D. C. Lin, W. Y. Chen, R. E. Hank, and R. A. Bringmann, "Effective compiler support for predicated execution using the hyperblock," in *Proceedings of the 25th International Symposium on Microarchitecture*, pp. 45–54, December 1992.

[12] S. A. Mahlke, R. E. Hank, R. A. Bringmann, J. C. Gyllenhaal, D. M. Gallagher, and W. W. Hwu, "Characterizing the impact of predicated execution on branch prediction," in *Proceedings of the 27th International Symposium on Microarchitecture*, pp. 217–227, December 1994.

[13] G. R. Beck, D. W. Yen, and T. L. Anderson, "The Cydra 5 minisupercomputer: Architecture and implementation," *The Journal of Supercomputing*, vol. 7, pp. 143–180, January 1993.

[14] D. N. Pnevmatikatos and G. S. Sohi, "Guarded execution and branch prediction in dynamic ILP processors," in *Proceedings of the 21st International Symposium on Computer Architecture*, pp. 120–129, April 1994.

[15] V. Kathail, M. S. Schlansker, and B. R. Rau, "HPL playdoh architecture specification: Version 1.0," Tech. Rep. HPL-93-80, Hewlett-Packard Laboratories, Palo Alto, CA 94303, February 1994.

[16] M. Schlansker, V. Kathail, and S. Anik, "Height reduction of control recurrences for ILP processors," in *Proceedings of the 27th International Symposium on Microarchitecture*, pp. 40–51, December 1994.

[17] Hewlett-Packard Company, Cupertino, CA, *PA-RISC 1.1 Architecture and Instruction Set Reference Manual*, 1990.

[18] D. S. Blickstein *et al.*, "The GEM optimizing compiler system," *Digital Technical Journal*, vol. 4, pp. 121–136, 1992.

[19] P. G. Lowney *et al.*, "The Multiflow trace scheduling compiler," *The Journal of Supercomputing*, vol. 7, pp. 51–142, January 1993.

[20] W. W. Hwu *et al.*, "The Superblock: An effective technique for VLIW and superscalar compilation," *The Journal of Supercomputing*, vol. 7, pp. 229–248, January 1993.

Instruction-Level Parallelism (ILP)

4. 1 Introduction

Instruction-level parallel (ILP) processing deals with issues related to exploiting parallelism at the instruction level. At the heart of ILP processing is the *instruction processing schedule*, that is, the schedule in which instructions are processed. Instructions in a processing schedule obey some ordering constraints (e.g., instructions are processed in the order that they are fetched, or instructions are processed in an order that does not violate write-after-write dependences, or instructions are processed in an order that does not violate read-after-write dependences). To facilitate a more parallel processing schedule, it can be beneficial to resort to techniques that can alleviate some of the ordering constraints.

ILP processing encompasses the set of techniques that are needed to achieve a desired rate of instruction processing, that is, a desired instruction processing schedule. In order to understand what these techniques

are, and the context for their evolution, it is instructive to revisit the actions involved in instruction processing. In the von Neumann model of stored program computers, a processor is given a program stored in memory; the processor has to fetch instructions of the program, decode them, and execute them. Historically, programs have been created assuming *serial* execution semantics, that is, the creator of a program can assume that the processing of an instruction is complete before the processing of the next instruction begins. An alternative is to have more parallel semantics inherent in the instructions. For example, a program could consist of parcels of instructions, with the parcels having serial processing semantics but no processing order semantics present among the instructions in a parcel. Most instruction sets fall in the former category and have serial execution semantics. An example of the latter category are *long instruction word* (LIW) instruction sets [2, 4, 17].

Once defined, the instruction set serves as the interface between the hardware and the software, and, for a variety of reasons, the instruction set has been chosen as the level for maintaining software compatibility. That is, different generations of ILP processors can process instructions of a program at different rates and with different execution orders and processing schedules, but they must do so in a manner that ensures that the semantics of the program are not violated. In particular, if an instruction set has the notion of serial execution, then in order to allow a program to be interrupted and restarted later (e.g., in case of a page fault or other exception condition), a *precise machine state* needs to be captured. At the time of an exception, a precise state is the state of the machine (architecturally visible registers and memory) that would result if: (1) all instructions prior to the offending instruction have executed and updated the state, and (2) no instructions succeeding the offending instruction, including the offending instruction, have updated the state. An ILP processor is said to have *precise interrupts* or *precise exceptions* if a precise state can be recovered at any time.

In the ideal case, the only ordering constraints that govern the execution of the instructions of a program are *read after write* (RAW) or true dependences, as we discuss in Chapter 5.[1] However, serial-program semantics imposes other ordering constraints on the instructions of the program, most of which are artificial. That is, even operations that are known to be independent and could execute in parallel appear to be dependent because of the sequential semantics of the program. The role of an ILP processor is to take a serial program—a specification of operations to execute—remove much of the nonessential sequentiality in this specification so that the program can be processed in parallel, and turn it into a parallel (i.e., higher performance) version. However, this "transformation" must occur transparently; the creator of the program must still view the execution of the program as serial, one instruction at a time. An ILP processor that executes a serial program in parallel is called a *superscalar* processor. (More accurately, superscalar implies the processing, i.e., fetching, decoding, execution, etc., of multiple instructions per cycle.) Sections 4.2–4.5 provide the background for the papers that developed techniques to allow ILP processing of a serial program, and section 4.6 discusses ILP processing when the instruction set has LIW instructions.

4.2 Instruction Processing

The first step toward improving the instruction processing rate is the idea of pipelining. Here, instruction processing is divided into several stages, and the processing of different instructions can be overlapped. By proper organization of the pipeline stages, the instructions can be made to flow through the pipeline in the serial program order, and it is quite straightforward to maintain a precise state: Updates to program state are made only toward the end of the pipeline and only when it is known that such an update is valid [7]. However, simple serial pipelining alone does not allow efficient execution schedules to be achieved in all cases. In some cases, better processing schedules can be achieved if fast instructions are allowed to pass slower ones. Allowing such out-of-order execution of instructions, however can result in a violation of *write after write* (WAW) dependences. A WAW dependence occurs when multiple instructions update the same storage element (register); it must appear that these updates occur in proper sequence. A WAW dependence is an artificial dependence that is a result of a limited storage name space. If out-of-order execution of instructions is to be permitted, mechanisms to overcome WAW hazards are needed.

The IBM 360/91, a pioneering machine built in the 1960s, made several key contributions to high-performance instruction processing [1]. Among other things, the designers of this machine realized the importance of overcoming artificial scheduling constraints imposed by WAW hazards. In this machine, there were four floating-point registers, and the machine had no cache: It took 12 cycles to service a load operation from the memory. To tolerate this long memory latency, the load operation had to be overlapped with other instructions (e.g., instructions from other loop iterations). With the small number of available registers, this meant possible overlap with other instructions that wrote into the same destination register as the load instruction. An important contribution of the 360/91 was a mechanism for overcoming WAW hazards in instruction processing [24]. This mechanism, which is commonly referred to as *Tomasulo's algorithm*, converts the sequential program representation into a *dataflow* representation and then processes the instructions as per the ordering constraints in the dataflow representation rather than in the specified program order. WAW hazards, an artifact of a limited number of register names, are overcome with a process

---

[1]Recent work suggests that even these ordering constraints can be removed with speculative techniques such as *value prediction* [11].

known as *register renaming*: There are more physical storage elements that hold the results of instructions (reservation stations in the 360/91) than there are architectural registers. The architectural register names in an instruction are used to obtain a name (i.e., a tag) for a physical storage element, and physical storage element names, rather than architectural register names, are used for instruction execution.

Though the process of register renaming in the 360/91 was developed for the purpose of overcoming WAW hazards resulting from a small number of registers, the applicability of the concept is much more general. This process becomes even more important when instructions are executed speculatively, regardless of the number of architectural registers. There, physical registers will be needed to hold the outcomes of instructions executed speculatively, and a renaming process is needed to match the source operands of an instruction to the correct instruction that creates the source operand value.

The IBM 360/91 also recognized the importance of maintaining an uninterrupted supply of instructions for overall performance. To avoid a disruption when a branch instruction was encountered, it fetched (but did not execute) instructions from both paths of a branch. It also had a loop buffer (a small instruction cache) that supplied instructions in a "loop mode."

4.3 Precise Exceptions

High-performance instruction processing typically implies an instruction processing order that is different from program order. In particular, the dataflow-like processing of instructions in the 360/91 allowed instructions to be executed out of program order. Moreover, the conventional wisdom of the time was that the state of the machine (e.g., registers) are to be updated when an instruction completes execution. If instructions are allowed to complete execution and update machine state out of program order, a precise state cannot be guaranteed: The state of the registers at a given point depends on a variety of run time conditions, which may differ from one run of the program to another.

In the 360/91, interrupts (more accurately, exceptions) were *imprecise*, because maintaining a precise state would require additional hardware, and there seemed to be no compelling reasons that would improve machine utility. The most compelling reason for precise interrupts is to allow transparent exception handling: pinpointing an instruction that causes the exception and transferring control to an exception handler.

The 360/91 did not support virtual memory, where transparent handling of page fault exceptions is required, and therefore did not have one of the most important reasons for precise exceptions. The major remaining cause of exceptions was arithmetic exceptions (overflow, divide by zero, etc.), and such exceptions could be considered to be "programming errors." In such cases, the designers of the machine deemed it sufficient to inform the user that an exception had occurred, and it was up to the (sophisticated) user to infer where the error was. The lack of precise exceptions had an important consequence: The machine was hard to debug, because errors were not always reproducible.

An important idea first commercialized in the late 1960s was the idea of virtual memory: the transparent appearance of an addressable memory larger than what was physically present in the machine [3]. This appearance is given by a layer of software that is responsible for moving pages between a virtual store and a physical store when a desired page is not present in the physical store (i.e., a page fault exception occurs). These software layers assume sequential program execution, so to support transparent virtual memory, a precise machine state needed to be recovered at any point in the program at which a page fault could occur (essentially any point in the program).

Many machines that employed high-performance instruction processing techniques shied away from supporting virtual memory because of the likely overhead of maintaining a precise state. The CDC Cyber 180 series of machines decided to support virtual memory and employ high-performance instruction processing techniques. Therefore, they needed to develop methods to implement precise interrupts. The Smith and Pleszkun paper describes three schemes to implement precise interrupts, one of which was originally developed for the CDC Cyber 180 [20]. The three methods are: (1) a history buffer method, where a history buffer contains old values of registers, while the main register file is updated out of program order; (2) a reorder buffer method where instructions write into a reorder buffer when they complete execution, from which they are written into a register file in program order; and (3) a future file method, where there are two register files, an architecturally precise file that is updated in program order and an imprecise, or future, file that is updated out of program order.

In the reorder buffer method, the state of the machine is not updated as soon as an instruction has completed execution. Though not made until later, this simple observation has powerful implications: A processor can do whatever it wants with instruction processing in order to achieve a desired level of performance, as long as the appearance of sequential execution is maintained (i.e., as long as the machine state is updated in program order). The decoupling between the completion of an instruction and the update of the register file also introduced a new phase in the processing of an instruction: the *commit* or *retire* phase. As we discuss next, this simple observation had a significant impact on the design of 1990s' superscalar processors.

4.4 Processor Models for Speculative Execution

To further improve the instruction processing rate for a serial program, we need to develop a more-parallel processing schedule, and this requires more parallelism. However, branch instructions constrain the parallelism, because it is not known which instructions are to be executed until the outcome of the branch is known. Given that every fifth or sixth instruction is a branch in many codes, techniques to overcome the impediments caused by branches were needed. One important technique is *speculative execution*: The outcome of a branch is predicted, and instructions from the predicted path are executed speculatively. The overall operation of an ILP processor supporting speculative execution is the following: process instructions until a branch is encountered, predict the outcome of the branch and speculatively process the instructions following the branch, develop an execution schedule that (possibly) consists of both speculative and non-speculative instructions, and take corrective action in case of an incorrect speculation. Though the above has historically been called speculative execution, it is more apt to call it *control speculative execution*, because we are speculating the outcome of a branch instruction. As we discuss later, other forms of speculation can be used to overcome other constraints to instruction processing, and such techniques are likely to be used in future ILP processors.

4.4.1 Branch Prediction

An important component of a speculative execution processor is a *branch predictor*. Arguably, this is the most important component of such a processor, because the accuracy of the branch predictor determines the fidelity of the instructions being processed: The more accurate the predictor, the larger the number of "useful" instructions in the processing schedule. Quite naturally, the branch predictor has been the focus of much study in ILP processors.

The Smith paper on branch prediction was the first paper to describe and evaluate a family of dynamic branch prediction schemes [19]. One of the more accurate predictors described in this paper is the two bit counter. Branch prediction saw limited use in the 1980s, as processors of that era did not make much use of instruction level parallelism, and for the level of parallelism they were trying to exploit—simple pipelines—other solutions existed to the branch problem (e.g., delayed branches and early resolution of branches) [7]. A typical use of branch prediction was to determine which instructions to fetch and decode; instructions were typically not executed speculatively.

The processors of the 1990s felt the need to exploit more ILP, and to do this they had to rely on speculative execution. This increased the importance of branch prediction, which became a heavily investigated subject. The paper by Yeh and Patt introduced a different way of looking at the problem of branch prediction [26]. Whereas the Smith paper proposes schemes that predict the outcome of a branch based on the previous history of a branch in isolation (more accurately, the history of branches that map onto the same prediction table entry), the Yeh and Patt paper proposes prediction schemes that track patterns of branch outcomes and use this information, along with a history of branch outcomes for a given pattern, to make predictions. In other words, the outcome of a branch is determined not only by the past history of the branch, but also by the outcomes of (some) other branches. This observation was also made independently by Pan, So, and Rahmeh [15]. This new way of looking at the branch prediction problem inspired an entire body of research in branch prediction in the 1990s.

A complementary approach to control speculation is to eliminate branches using *conditional* (or *guarded* or *predicated*) execution [12]. Here, control dependences are converted to data dependences. These two approaches are not mutually exclusive: Both can be applied simultaneously. In superscalar processors, control speculation has been the more popular approach to date, especially because it requires no modification to an instruction set. In implementations of future instruction sets that support predicated execution, such as the Hewlett Packard/Intel IA-64 [2], one can expect to see the use of both techniques.

4.4.2 Mechanisms to Support Speculative Execution

To support speculative execution, mechanisms are needed to process both speculative and nonspeculative instructions simultaneously yet give the appearance of serial processing. That is the subject of the Patt, Hwu, and Shebanow [16] and the Sohi and Vajapeyam [21] papers, which describe instruction processing models for executing both speculative and nonspeculative instructions out of program order—basic technologies to support the parallel execution of a serial program. A key observation in these papers is that a mis-speculation can be treated like an exception condition, albeit one that occurs quite frequently (every few tens or hundreds of instructions). Mechanisms to recover a precise state in case of an exception, similar to those developed to support virtual memory, could be used to support control speculation.

In addition to precise state recovery mechanisms, supporting speculation also requires mechanisms to store the results of speculative instructions and the accompanying mechanisms to match instructions that produce values with instructions that consume them. Storage for speculative values is provided by a set of physical storage elements (i.e., physical registers) and a register-renaming mechanism used to link up the dependent instructions. The above mechanisms could be considered independently or collectively in a given design. When considered collectively, a choice made for one mechanism could impact the choices for another.

The Patt, Hwu, and Shebanow and the Sohi and Vajapeyam papers take somewhat different approaches to the problem(s), the basic difference being the starting point for the mechanism used to recover a precise state. The high performance substrate (HPS) model, described in the paper by Patt, Hwu and Shebanow, uses a checkpoint repair mechanism (similar to a history buffer for maintaining precise interrupts) [8], whereas the register update unit (RUU) model described by Sohi and Vajapeyam uses a reorder buffer mechanism [20]. Along with a checkpoint repair mechanism, the HPS paper proposes the use of *node tables* (or reservation stations) to provide physical storage and a Tomasulo-like register-renaming scheme. The model is one of a "restricted dataflow" machine, that is, dataflow execution with a subset of the dynamic instruction stream. The HPS paper also introduced the notion of an "active window," that is, the scope of dataflow execution—this is commonly referred to as the "instruction window" today. The RUU paper made the observation that the reorder buffer mechanism to support precise interrupts and the mechanisms to support out-of-order and speculative execution were synergistic: the reorder buffer could be

used for physical register storage, register renaming, and supporting speculative execution with only minor modification to the basic precise-interrupt mechanism.

4.5 Examples of ILP Processors

Though high-performance instruction processing techniques were routinely used in high-end processors, the golden age of ILP processors did not start until the late 1980s. The ILP era first started with multiple instruction issue and quickly expanded to include speculative execution.

One of the earliest commercially successful superscalar processor was the IBM RS/6000, which is described in the paper by Grohoski [5]. It borrowed heavily from its ancestor, the IBM 360/91, and other IBM research projects (notably the ACS and the 801 projects) and was the first commercially successful processor to use register renaming (it had 40 physical registers and 32 architectural registers).

A big debate that has divided ILP processors has been static versus dynamic scheduling, that is, at what point (compile-time or run-time) to schedule instructions so that they can efficiently execute in parallel. An important parameter in this debate is the business model: Can one assume that applications can (and will) be recompiled for a new processor implementation when the processor is being designed? The RS/6000 did not have to run any legacy software; it was a new instruction set and programs had to be compiled to run on it. Therefore, it could assume that the compiler had complete freedom to schedule code to optimize performance, and accordingly there was little benefit in expending hardware resources to do the same. Moreover, the complexities of building hardware to support dynamic scheduling, precise interrupts, and speculative execution were unknown (a previous experiment at dynamic scheduling, the IBM 360/91 was notoriously difficult to debug because it lacked precise exceptions), and requiring functionality from software appeared to be simpler (and easier to rectify) than requiring functionality from hardware. Accordingly, the RS/6000 did not have hardware support for dynamic scheduling (as we understand it today) and speculative execution. Another important superscalar processor of the early 1990s, the Digital Alpha 21064 [13], made the same assumption, and it did not support speculative execution and dynamic scheduling. It also had the luxury of starting out with a clean slate, with a new instruction set (although the instruction set was designed so that it would be an easy target for translation of VAX code). Later implementations of the Alpha architecture, for example, the Alpha 21264 [9], as well as follow-ons to the RS/6000 (implementations of the PowerPC architecture) moved toward speculative execution and dynamic scheduling as they were constrained by the requirements of binary compatibility and felt the need to achieve higher performance with changing technology parameters.

Many architectures that had been designed in the mid-1980s (e.g., MIPS, Motorola 88K) and earlier (e.g., Intel X86 and Motorola 68K) did not have the luxury of requiring recompilation, because they had a large application base that relied on binary compatibility. Engineers working on implementations of these instruction sets started developing techniques to achieve performance via dynamic scheduling and speculative execution while maintaining precise exceptions, using prior academic work as a starting point. This resulted in a series of machines that implemented these concepts, albeit in somewhat different ways, depending on circumstances unique to their respective situations: the Motorola 88110 (and the 88120, which was abandoned when Motorola decided to drop the 88K architecture in favor of the PowerPC), the MIPS R10000, the AMD K5, the Intel P6, the IBM PowerPC 604, and others. The paper by Yeager [25] describes the microarchitecture of the MIPS R10000, which epitomizes this class of machines, which are commonly referred to as dynamically scheduled, or out-of-order (OOO) superscalar processors today.

Any new design has a long learning curve: It takes longer to design machinery whose design has not been attempted before and therefore is not understood. And first attempts tend to be conservative: It is natural to emphasize correctness over aggressiveness in a new design. The first dynamically scheduled superscalar processors were no different. Many of them chose to optimize instructions per cycle over clock speed, and this led several people to argue that dynamically scheduled processors have an inherent handicap in clock speed; that is, with all the extra hardware required, it was not possible to achieve high clock speeds. This concern has not entirely been borne out. In 1999, most microprocessor manufacturers support OOO execution in their high-end microprocessors, including vendors like Digital, which started out with statically scheduled superscalar processors when they had a clean slate and when the complexities of building OOO superscalar processors were not understood. And such processors do not appear to have a major handicap in clock speed when compared with contemporary statically scheduled superscalar processors.

4.6 Explicitly Parallel ILP Processors

Superscalar processors try to parallelize the execution of a sequential program, a program which has been created assuming that its instructions will execute one by one. An alternative approach is to have *explicitly parallel* instructions and create a program with such instructions. An explicitly parallel instruction consists of several sub-instructions (each of which would be similar to a single instruction in a sequential instruction set) that can all execute in parallel.

LIWs are intimately tied to the instruction scheduling process. The rationale is as follows: The compiler can develop a schedule of execution statically, that is, determine which instructions can be executed in parallel in a given time step. This schedule of execution can then be recreated dynamically in the following manner: (1) pack all the instructions in a given time step of the schedule into an LIW and (2) have the hardware sequence through each LIW sequentially. When the hardware processes one such long instruction, it processes multiple smaller instructions and proceeds through one step of the execution schedule. Of course, the compiler creates the execution with certain assumptions (e.g., the execution latencies of an operation). If these assumptions are going to be violated at run time, appropriate measure are needed to ensure that the specified execution order will generate correct results. For example, if a schedule has been created assuming that a given load operation hits in a cache, a cache miss would require that instruction processing be stalled.

An extreme case of an LIW is the very long instruction word (VLIW) approach [4]. Here, the constituent instructions of an LIW directly specify the work to be carried out by each functional units in that instruction step (i.e., step of the execution schedule).

Advocates of LIW architectures argue that by packing multiple independent instructions in a long word, the hardware can be simplified, because it does not have to decode the multiple instructions and determine their dependence status. By virtue of being packed together in the same instruction word, the (independence) status of instructions is known. And even though the software needed to create a parallel schedule is more complex, it is a one-time cost. Moreover, because the compiler has already scheduled instructions, there is no need for complex hardware to do scheduling dynamically; simple serial processing of instructions should suffice.

To build a parallel execution schedule, the compiler must extract and expose parallelism and allow it to be conveyed to the hardware via LIWs. In the situation where there are regular loops (especially without branches within an iteration) with lots of parallelism, techniques such as loop unrolling and software pipelining allow independent operations from multiple iterations to be packed into the same LIW instruction. But many program situations do not have regular branch-free loops, many do not have loops, and many have code with lots of branches. To overcome impediments to parallelism created by branches, there are two options. The first option is to eliminate branches using predicated execution. Here, control dependences are converted to data dependences, and the resulting (predicated) code can be scheduled just like ordinary branch-free code. This implies that instructions from both the taken and nontaken paths of a branch will be executed, regardless of the value of the control variable (which determines branch outcome). A second option is to use control-speculative execution, similar to what was done in hardware for superscalar processors, but in software. Both options require special instruction set support.

A consequence of the serial processing assumption typically made for LIW architectures is that long-latency operations must be placed "early" in the schedule. These operations can only be executed when instruction sequencing reaches them, and this can happen early enough only if they are placed earlier in the schedule. Load operations can be long-latency operations, especially if they miss in the first-level cache. Accordingly, these operations must be scheduled for execution early, possibly before branches that determine their execution (i.e., in a control speculative manner) and before other store instructions on which they *may* be dependent (i.e., in a *data-speculative* manner).[2] Because such loads may cause exceptions that might not have occurred had they been executed in true program order (i.e., in a noncontrol speculative manner), special support is required to suppress exceptions and only recognize them at the point they would have occurred in a sequential execution. And special support is also required to check to see that the data dependence speculation was correct and to take corrective action if it was not.

The paper by Fisher and Rau [18] surveys and provides a historical context for several techniques that underly the design of statically scheduled LIW processors. These include software pipelining, predicated execution, speculation, and LIWs.

Even though LIW architectures can be viewed as an artifact of static scheduling, it is important to note that the construction of an LIW instruction, and the process used to schedule it, are independent. Once constructed, an LIW instruction can be viewed as a single instruction in a serial program (albeit one with several suboperations), and any of the plethora of techniques developed to improved the scheduling and execution of instructions of a serial program can be used. This is especially true as technology changes allow (and require) more parallel execution, but business reasons preclude instruction set changes and/or recompilation for different processor generations.

Recently Intel and Hewlett-Packard announced the IA-64 architecture, which they term an explicitly parallel instruction computer (EPIC) architecture [2]. From what has been made public to date, it appears to be a wide instruction set architecture, with three instructions per 128-bit instruction parcel. It supports predicated execution and speculative execution. Initial implementations of IA-64 are likely to be statically scheduled. As the IA-64 architecture becomes more widely adopted, and if business reasons preclude recompilation (either static or dynamic) for future implementations, one can expect to see implementations employing dynamic scheduling techniques in addition to static scheduling techniques.

4.7 Future ILP Processing Techniques

As technology improvements continue to allow more hardware resources and as the demand for more performance continues, innovative microarchitectural techniques will continue to be developed. These techniques will rely on speculation to overcome barriers that constrain the processing of instructions. An important point to keep in mind is that once a technique to handle one form of speculation exists (e.g., a technique to handle control speculation), the same technique or other, related techniques can be used to handle other forms of speculation as well. Recently, there has been work on *data dependence speculation* to overcome artificial constraints on the scheduling of memory

---

[2]Note that even though this form of speculation is frequently referred to as *data speculation*, a better term is *data dependence speculation*, because the speculation is that the load is not dependent on the (ambiguous) store. More recently, other forms of data speculation, that is, *data value speculation*, have been proposed, where the speculation is on the outcome of an operation.

operations—mechanisms to support this form of speculation are no different from those required to support control speculation [14]. To overcome true dependence constraints, *data value speculation* has been proposed [10]. These speculative execution techniques allow unconstrained execution of instructions once they have been fetched into the machine, but instruction fetch still continues to be a serial process, that is, a potential bottleneck. Another step toward increasing instruction processing flexibility is the development of a more "parallel" and "out-of-order" instruction fetch process. One way to accomplish this is to view the instruction sequencing process as a hierarchical (two-step) process, a step that sequences through a program in large or "task-sized" steps (for example, steps of several blocks of instructions) and another process that is a collection of multiple sequencers, each sequencing through and fetching the individual instructions of a given task [22]. In this case, the instruction fetch process can be viewed as another operation whose latency can then be tolerated in a variety of ways.

Techniques to allow flexibility in instruction processing, however, cannot be developed independent of an implementation. Even though this statement has always been true, its importance will increase in the future. With increasing clock frequencies, and the commensurate importance of wire delays vis-à-vis logic delays, the need to have decentralized structures will increase. The Digital 21264 is an example of this trend—it divides the instruction scheduling logic into two parts in order to achieve a high clock frequency. Other considerations, such as complexity of design and verification, will tilt the balance toward designs that are composed of multiple, replicated components. Such designs will have distributed instruction fetching, distributed instruction processing, distributed storage structures (both for memory and registers), and so forth. The parallelism that is being exploited among the different entities of such a microarchitecture is at a level of groups of instructions, or at a thread level (in addition to the parallelism within a group of instructions that each individual entity might exploit). Such microarchitectures can also be considered to be thread-level speculative processors. Several proposals for such processors were being investigated at the time this book was written [6, 22, 23].

4.8 References

[1] D. W. Anderson, F. J. Sparacio, and R. M. Tomasulo, "The IBM System/360 Model 91: Machine philosophy and instruction-handling," *IBM Journal of Research and Development*, pp.8–24, Jan. 1967.

[2] J. Crawford and J. Huck, "Motivations and design approach for the IA-64 64-Bit instruction set architecture" *Microprocessor Forum*, San Jose, CA, 14 Oct. 1997

[3] P. J. Denning, "Virtual Memory," *ACM Computing Surveys*, vol. 2, pp. 153–189, Sept. 1970.

[4] J. A. Fisher, "Very long instruction word architectures and the ELI-512," *Proceedings of the 10th Annual International Symposium on Computer Architecture*, pp.140–150, June 1983.

[5] G. F. Grohoski, "Machine organization of the IBM RISC System/6000 processor," *IBM Journal of Research and Development*, vol. 34, pp. 37–58, Jan. 1990.

[6] L. Hammond, M. Willey, and K. Olukotun, "Data speculation support for a chip multiprocessor," *Proceedings of the 8th International Conference on Architectural Support for Programming Languages and Operating Systems,* pp. 58–69, Oct. 1998.

[7] J. L. Hennessy and D. A. Patterson, *Computer Architecture: A Quantitative Approach*. San Francisco, CA: Morgan Kaufmann, 1996.

[8] W. W. Hwu and Y. N. Patt, "Checkpoint repair for high-performance out-of-order execution machines," *IEEE Transactions on Computers*, C-36(12): 1496–1514, 1987.

[9] J. Keller, *The 21264: A superscalar Alpha processor with out-of-order execution*. Hudson, MA: Digital Equipment Corp., Oct. 1996.

[10] M. H. Lipasti, C. B. Wilkerson, and J. P. Shen, "Value locality and load value prediction," *Proceedings of the 7th International Conference on Architectural Support for Programming Languages and Operating Systems*, pp. 138–147, 1996.

[11] M. H. Lipasti and J. P. Shen, "Exceeding the dataflow limit via value prediction," *Proceedings of the 29th Annual International Symposium on Microarchitecture*, pp. 226–237, Dec. 1996.

[12] S. A. Mahlke, R. E. Hank, J. E. McCormick, D. I. August, and W. W. Hwu, "A comparison of full and partial predicted execution support for ILP processors," *Proceedings of the 22nd Annual International Symposium on Computer Architecture*, pp. 138–150, June 1995.

[13] E. McLellan, "The Alpha AXP architecture and 21064 processor," *IEEE Micro*, pp. 36–47, June 1993.

[14] A. Moshovos, S. E. Breach, T. N. Vijaykumar, and G. S. Sohi, "Dynamic speculation and synchronization of data dependences," *Proceedings of the 24th Annual International Symposium on Computer Architecture*, pp. 181–193, June 1997.

[15] S.-T. Pan, K. So, and J. T. Rahmeh, "Improving the accuracy of dynamic branch prediction using branch correlation," *Proceedings of the 5th International Conference on Architectural Support for Programming Languages and Operating Systems*, pp. 76–84, Oct. 1992.

[16] Y. N. Patt, W. W. Hwu, and M. Shebanow, "HPS, a new microarchitecture: Rationale and introduction," *Proceedings of the 18th Annual Workshop on Microprogramming,* Pacific Grove, CA, pp. 103–108, Dec. 1985.

[17] B. R. Rau, D. W. L. Yen, W. Yen, and R. Towle, "The Cydra 5 departmental supercomputer: Design philosophies, decisions, and trade-offs," *IEEE Computer*, 22(1):12–35, 1989.

[18] B. R. Rau and J. A. Fisher, "Instruction-level parallel processing: History, overview, and perspective," *The Journal of Supercomputing*, vol. 7, 1993.

[19] J. E. Smith, "A study of branch prediction strategies," *Proceedings of the 8th International Symposium on Computer Architecture*, pp. 135–148, May 1981.

[20] J. E. Smith and A. R. Pleszkun, "Implementation of precise interrupts in pipelined processors," *Proceedings of the 12th Annual International Symposium on Computer Architecture*, pp. 36–44, June 1985.

[21] G. S. Sohi and S. Vajapeyam, "Instruction issue logic for high-performance, interruptable pipelined processors," *Proceedings of the 14th Annual International Symposium on Computer Architecture*, pp. 27–31, June 1987.

[22] G. S. Sohi, S. E. Breach, and T. N. Vijaykumar, "Multiscalar processors," *Proceedings of the 22nd Annual International Symposium on Computer Architecture*, pp. 414–425, June 1995.

[23] J. G. Steffan and T. C. Mowry., "The potential for using thread-level data speculation to facilitate automatic parallelization," *Proceedings of the 4th International Symposium on High-Performance Computer Architecture*, Feb. 1998.

[24] R. M. Tomasulo, "An efficient algorithm for exploiting multiple arithmetic units," *IBM Journal of Research and Development*, pp. 25–33, Jan. 1967.

[25] K. C. Yeager, "The MIPS R10000 superscalar microprocessor," *IEEE Micro*, 16(2): 28–40, Apr. 1996.

[26] T.-Y. Yeh and Y. N. Patt, "Two-level adaptive training branch prediction," *Proceedings of the 24th Annual International Symposium on Microarchitecture*, pp. 51–61, Nov. 1991.

D. W. Anderson
F. J. Sparacio
R. M. Tomasulo

The IBM System/360 Model 91: Machine Philosophy and Instruction-Handling

Abstract: The System/360 Model 91 central processing unit provides internal computational performance one to two orders of magnitude greater than that of the IBM 7090 Data Processing System through a combination of advancements in machine organization, circuit design, and hardware packaging. The circuits employed will switch at speeds of less than 3 nsec, and the circuit environment is such that delay is approximately 5 nsec per circuit level. Organizationally, primary emphasis is placed on (1) alleviating the disparity between storage time and circuit speed, and (2) the development of high speed floating-point arithmetic algorithms.
This paper deals mainly with item (1) of the organization. A design is described which improves the ratio of storage bandwidth and access time to cycle time through the use of storage interleaving and CPU buffer registers. It is shown that history recording (the retention of complete instruction loops in the CPU) reduces the need to exercise storage, and that sophisticated employment of buffering techniques has reduced the effective access time. The system is organized so that execution hardware is separated from the instruction unit; the resulting smaller, semiautonomous "packages" improve intra-area communication.

Introduction

This paper presents the organizational philosophy utilized in IBM's highest performance computer, the System/360[1] Model 91. The first section of the paper deals with the development of the assembly-line processing approach adopted for the Model 91. The organizational techniques of storage interleaving, buffering, and arithmetic execution concurrency required to support the approach are discussed. The final topic of this section deals with design refinements which have been added to the basic organization. Special attention is given to minimizing the time lost

due to conditional branches, and the basic interrupt problem is covered.

The second section is comprised of a treatment of the instruction unit of the Model 91. It is in this unit that the basic control is exercised which leads to attainment of the performance objectives. The first topic is the fetching of instructions from storage. Branching and interrupting are discussed next. Special handling of branching, such that storage accessing by instructions is sometimes eliminated, is also treated. The final section discusses the interlocks required among instructions as they are issued to the execution units, the initiation of operand fetches from storage, status switching operations, and I/O handling.

CPU organization

The objective of the Model 91 is to attain a performance greater by one to two orders of magnitude than that of the IBM 7090. Technology (that is, circuitry and hardware) advances* alone provide only a fourfold performance increase, so it is necessary to turn to organizational techniques for the remaining improvement. The appropriate

Figure 1 Typical instruction function time sequence.

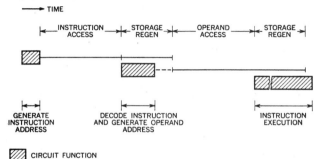

---

* Circuits employed are from the IBM ASLT family and provide an in-environment switching time in the 5 nsec range.

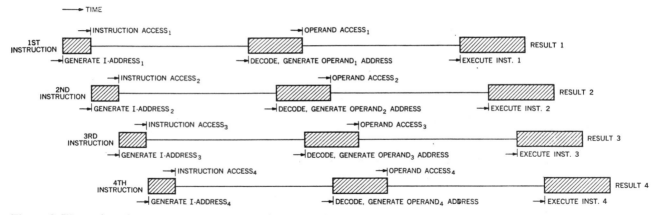

Figure 2 Illustration of concurrency among successive instructions.

selection of existing techniques and the development of new organizational approaches were the objectives of the Model 91 CPU design.

The primary organizational objective for a high performance CPU is concurrency—the parallel execution of different instructions. A consideration of the sequence of functions involved in handling a typical processor instruction makes the need for this approach evident. This sequence—instruction fetching, instruction decoding, operand address generating, operand fetching, and instruction execution—is illustrated in Fig. 1. Clearly, a primary goal of the organization must be to avoid the conventional concatenation of the illustrated functions for successive instructions. Parallelism accomplishes this, and, short of simultaneously performing identical tasks for adjacent instructions, it is desired to "overlay" the separate instruction functions to the greatest possible degree. Doing this requires separation of the CPU into loosely coupled sets of hardware, much like an assembly line, so that each hardware set, similar to its assembly line station counterpart, performs a single specific task. It then becomes possible to enter instructions into the hardware sets at shortly spaced time intervals. Then, following the delay caused by the initial filling of the line, the execution results will begin emerging at a rate of one for each time interval. Figure 2 illustrates the objective of the technique.

Defining the time interval (basic CPU clock rate) around which the hardware sets will be designed requires the resolution of a number of conflicting requirements. At first glance it might appear that the shorter the time interval (i.e., the time allocated to successive assembly line stations), the faster the execution rate will be for a series of instructions. Upon investigation, however, several parameters become apparent which frustrate this seemingly simple pattern for high performance design. The parameters of most importance are:

1. An assembly-line station platform (hardware "trigger") is necessary within each time interval, and it generally adds a circuit level to the time interval. The platform "overhead" can add appreciably to the total execution time of any one instruction since a shorter interval implies more stations for any pre-specified function. A longer instruction time is significant when sequential instructions are logically dependent. That is, instruction n cannot proceed until instruction $n + 1$ is completed. The dependency factor, therefore, indicates that the execution time of any individual instruction should not be penalized unnecessarily by overhead time delay.

2. The amount of control hardware—and control complexity—required to handle architectural and machine organization interlocks increases enormously as the number of assembly line stations is increased. This can lead to a situation for which the control paths determining the gating between stations contain more circuit levels than the data paths being controlled.

Parameters of less importance which influence the determination of the basic clock rate include:

1. The number of levels needed to implement certain basic data paths, e.g., address adders, instruction decoders, etc.

2. Effective storage access time, especially when this time is relatively short. Unless the station-to-station time interval of the CPU is a sub-multiple of storage access time the synchronization of storage and CPU functions will involve overhead time.

Judgment, rather than algorithms, gave the method by which the relative weights of the above parameters were evaluated to determine the basic station-to-station time

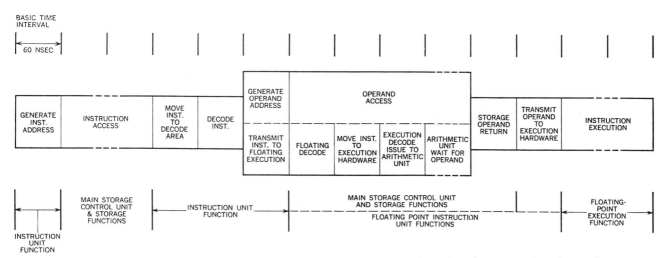

Figure 3 CPU "assembly-line stations required to accommodate a typical floating-point storage-to-register instruction.

interval.* The interval selected led to a splitting of the instruction handling functions as illustrated in Fig. 3.†

It can be seen in Fig. 3 that the basic time interval accommodates the assembly line handling of most of the basic hardware functions. However, the storage and many execution operations require a number of basic intervals. In order to exploit the assembly line processing approach despite these time disparities, the organizational techniques of storage interleaving,² arithmetic execution concurrency, and buffering are utilized.

Storage interleaving increases the storage bandwidth by enabling multiple accesses to proceed concurrently, which in turn enhances the assembly line handling of the storage function. Briefly, interleaving involves the splitting of storage into independent modules (each containing address decoding, core driving, data read-out sense hardware, and a data register) and arranging the address structure so that adjacent words—or small groups of adjacent words—reside in different modules. Figure 4 illustrates the technique.

The depth of interleaving required to support a desired concurrency level is a function of the storage cycle time, the CPU storage request rate, and the desired effective access time. The effective access time is defined as the sum of the actual storage access time, the average time spent waiting for an available storage, and the communication time between the processor and storage.*

Execution concurrency is facilitated first by the division of this function into separate units for fixed-point execution and floating-point execution. This permits instructions of the two classes to be executed in parallel; in fact, as long as no cross-unit dependencies exist, the execution does not necessarily follow the sequence in which the instructions are programmed.

Within the fixed-point unit, processing proceeds serially, one instruction at a time. However, many of the operations

---

* Effective access times ranging from 180–600 nsec are anticipated, although the design of the Model 91 is optimized around 360 nsec. Interleaving 400 nsec/cycle storage modules to a depth of 16 satisfies the 360 nsec effective access design point.

Figure 4 Arrangement of addresses in n storage modules of m words per module.

ADDRESS 0	1	-----------	$n-1$
n	$n+1$	-----------	$2n-1$
$2n$	$2n+1$	-----------	$3n-1$

$(m-2)n$	$(m-2)n+1$	-----------	$(m-1)n-1$
$(m-1)n$	$(m-1)n+1$	-----------	$mn-1$

---

* The design objective calls for a 60 nsec basic machine clock interval. The judgment exercised in this selection was tempered by a careful analysis of the number of circuit levels, fan in, fan out, and wiring lengths required to perform some of the basic data path and control functions. The analysis indicated that 11 or 12 circuit levels of 5–6 nsec delay per level were required for the worst-case situations.

† Figure 3 also illustrates that the hardware sets are grouped into larger units—instruction unit, main storage control element, fixed-point execution unit, floating-point execution unit. The grouping is primarily caused by packaging restrictions, but a secondary objective is to provide separately designable entities having minimum interfacing. The total hardware required to implement the required CPU functions demands three physical frames, each having dimensions 66" L × 15" D × 78" H. The units are allocated to the frames in such a way as to minimize the effects of interframe transmission delays.

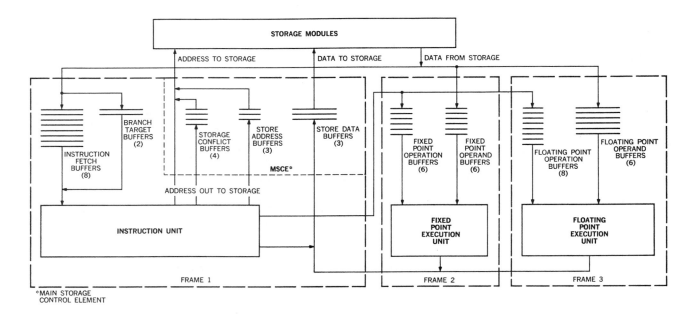

Figure 5 Buffer allocation and function separation.

require only one basic time interval to execute, and special emphasis is placed on the storage-to-storage instructions to speed up their execution. These instructions (storage-to-storage) enable the Model 91 to achieve a performance rate of up to 7 times that of the System/360 Model 75 for the "translate-and-test" instruction. A number of new concepts and sequences[3] were developed to achieve this performance for normally storage access-dependent instructions.

The floating-point unit is given particular emphasis to provide additional concurrency. Multiple arithmetic execution units, employing fast algorithms for the multiply and divide operations and carry look-ahead adders, are utilized.[4] An internal bus has been designed[5] to link the multiple floating-point execution units. The bus control correctly sequences dependent "strings" of instructions, but permits those which are independent to be executed out of order.

The organizational techniques described above provide balance between the number of instructions that can be prepared for arithmetic execution and those that can actually be executed in a given period, thereby preventing the arithmetic execution function from creating a "bottleneck" in the assembly line process.

Buffering of various types plays a major role in the Model 91 organization. Some types are required to implement the assembly line concept, while others are, in light of the performance objectives, architecturally imposed. In all cases the buffers provide queueing which smooths the total instruction flow by allowing the initiating assem-

bly line stations to proceed despite unpredictable delays down the line. Instruction fetch, operand fetch, operand store, operation, and address buffering are utilized among the major CPU units as illustrated in Fig. 5.*

Instruction fetch buffering provides return data "sinks" for previously initiated instruction storage requests. This prefetching hides the instruction access time for straight-line (no branching) programs, thereby providing a steady flow of instructions to the decoding hardware. The buffering is expanded beyond this need to provide the capacity to hold program loops of meaningful size. Upon encountering a loop which fits, the buffer locks onto the loop and subsequent branching requires less time, since it is to the buffers rather than to storage. The discussion of branching given later in this paper gives a detailed treatment of the loop action.

Operand fetch buffers effectively provide a queue into which storage can "dump" operands and from which execution units can obtain operands. The queue allows the isolation of operand fetching from operand usage for the storage-to-register and storage-to-storage instruction types. The required depth† of the queue is a function of the number of basic time intervals required for storage

---

* Eight 64-bit double words comprise the array of instruction buffers. Six 32-bit operand buffers are provided in the fixed-point execution unit, while six 64-bit buffers reside in the floating-point execution unit. Three 64-bit store operand buffers along with three store address and four conflict address buffers are provided in the main storage control element. Also, there are six fixed-point and eight floating-point operand buffers.

† To show precise algorithms defining these and other buffering requirements is impractical, since different program environments have different needs. The factors considered in selecting specific numbers are cited instead.

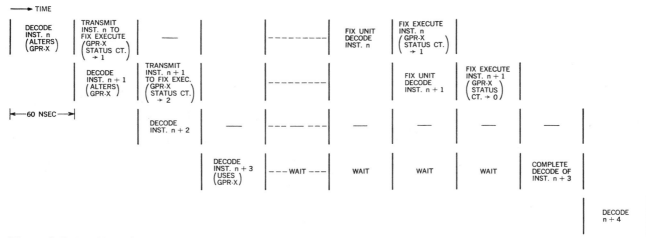

Figure 6 GPR address interlock.

accessing, the instruction "mix" of the operating program, and the relative time and frequency of execution bottlenecks. Operand store buffering provides the same function as fetch buffering, except that the roles of storage and execution are reversed. The number of store buffers required is a function of the average waiting time encountered when the desired storage module is busy and the time required for the storage, when available, to utilize the operand.

Operation buffers in the fixed-point and floating-point execution units allow the instruction unit to proceed with its decoding and storage-initiating functions while the execution units wait for storage operands or execution hardware. The depth of the operation buffering is related to the amount of operand buffering provided and the "mix" of register-to-register and storage-to-register instruction types.

Address buffering is used to queue addresses to busy storage modules and to contain store addresses during the interval between decoding and execution of store instructions. The instruction unit is thereby allowed to proceed to subsequent instructions despite storage conflicts or the encountering of store operations. These buffers have comparators associated with them to establish logical precedence when conflicting program references arise. The number of necessary store address buffers is a function of the average delay between decode and execution, while the depth of the queue caused by storage conflicts is related to the probable length of time a request will be held up by a busy storage module.[6]

• *Concurrency limitations*

The assembly line processing approach, using the techniques of storage interleaving, arithmetic concurrency, and buffering, provides a solid high-performance base.

The orientation is toward smooth-flowing instruction streams for which the assembly line can be kept full. That is, as long as station n need only communicate with station $n + 1$ of the line, highest performance is achieved. For example, floating-point problems which fit this criterion can be executed internally on the Model 91 at up to 100 times the internal speed of the 7090.[7]

There are, however, cases where simple communication between adjacent assembly line stations is inadequate, e.g., list processing applications, branching, and interrupts. The storage access time and the execution time are necessarily sequential between adjacent instructions. The organization cannot completely circumvent component delay in such instances, and the internal performance gain diminishes to about one order of magnitude greater than that of the 7090.

The list processing application is exemplified by sequentialism in addressing, which produces a major interlock situation in the Model 91. The architecturally specified usage of the general purpose registers (GPR's) for both address quantities and fixed-point data, coupled with the assembly line delay between address generation and fixed-point execution, leads to the performance slowdown. Figure 6 illustrates the interlock and the resulting delay. Instructions n and $n + 1$ set up the interlock on GPR X since they will alter the contents of X. The decode of $n + 3$ finds that the contents of X are to be used as an address parameter, and since the proper contents are not available $n + 3$ must wait until $n + 1$ is executed. The interlock technique involves assigning the decode area a status count for each GPR. A zero status count indicates availability. As fixed-point instructions pass through the decode, they increment the appropriate counter(s). A decode requiring an unavailable (non-zero status count) GPR cannot be completed. As the fixed-point execution unit

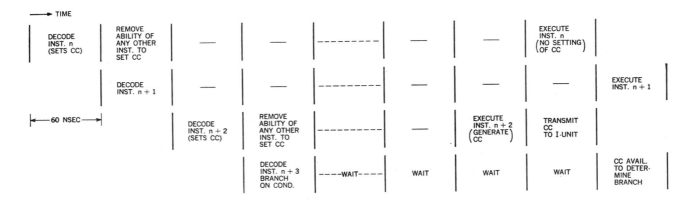

Figure 7 Condition code interlock.

completes instructions it decrements the appropriate counter(s), thus eventually freeing the register.

Branching leads to another sequential situation, since a disruption in the instruction supply is created. (Techniques employed to minimize or circumvent the storage access delay involved in obtaining the new instructions are discussed under *Instruction supplying* in the following section of this paper.) Conditional branching poses an additional delay in that the branch decision depends on the outcome of arithmetic operations in the execution units. The Model 91 has a relatively lower performance in cases for which a large percentage of conditional branch instructions lead to the branch being taken. The discontinuity is minimized, when the branch is not taken, through special handling of the condition code (CC) and the conditional branch instruction (BC). The condition code is a two-bit indicator, set according to the outcome of a variety of instructions, and can subsequently be interrogated for branching through the BC instruction. Since the code is to represent the outcome of the last decoded CC-affecting instruction, and since execution can be out of sequence, interlocks must be established to ensure this. This is accomplished, as illustrated in Fig. 7, by tagging each instruction at decode time if it is to set the CC. Simultaneously, a signal is communicated throughout the CPU to remove all tags from previously decoded but not executed instructions. Allowing only the execution of the tagged instruction to alter the code insures that the correct CC will be set. The decode hardware monitors the CPU for outstanding tags; only when none exists is the condition code considered valid for interrogation.

The organization assumes that, for a conditional branch, the CC will not be valid when the "branch-on-condition" (BC) is decoded (a most likely situation, considering that

most arithmetic and logical operations set the code). Rather than wait for a valid CC, fetches are initiated for two instruction double-words as a hedge against a successful branch. Following this, it is assumed that the branch will fail, and a "conditional mode" is established. In conditional mode, shown in Fig. 8, instructions are decoded and conditionally forwarded to the execution units, and concomitant operand fetches are initiated. The execution units are inhibited from completing conditional instructions. When a valid condition code appears, the appropriate branching action is detected and activates or cancels the conditional instructions. Should the no-branch guess prove correct, a substantial head start is provided by activating the conditionally issued and initiated operand fetches for a number of instructions. If the branch is successful, the previously fetched target words are activated and provide work while the instruction fetching is diverted to the new stream. (Additional optimizing techniques are covered under the discussion of branching in a subsequent section of this paper.)

Interrupts, as architecturally constrained, are a major bottleneck to performance in the assembly line organization. Strict adherence to a specification which states that an interrupt on instruction n should logically precede and inhibit any action from being taken on instruction $n + 1$ leaves two alternatives. The first would be to force sequentialism between instructions which may lead to an interrupt. In view of the variety of interrupt possibilities defined, this course would totally thwart high performance and is necessarily discarded. The second is to set aside sufficient information to permit recovery from any interrupt which might arise. In view of the pipeline and execution concurrency which allows the Model 91 to advance many instructions beyond n prior to its execution, and to

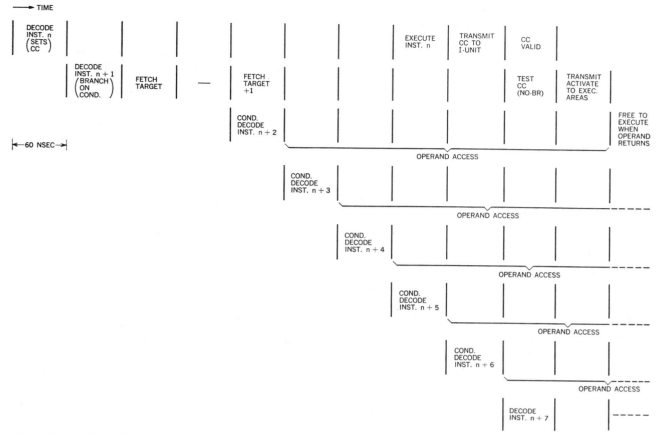

Figure 8 Conditional instruction issuing: the branch-on-condition philosophy.

execute independent instructions out of sequence ($n + m$ before n), the recovery problem becomes extremely complex and costly. Taking this approach would entail hardware additions to the extent that it would severely degrade the performance one is seeking to enhance. The impracticality of both alternatives by which the interrupt specifications could be met made it mandatory that the specifications themselves be altered. The architecture was compromised by removing the above-mentioned "precedence" and "inhibit" requirements. The specification change led to what is termed the "imprecise interrupt" philosophy of the Model 91 and reduced the interrupt bottleneck to an instruction supply discontinuity. The imprecise interrupt, and the manner in which the instruction discontinuity is minimized, are covered in the next section of the paper.

The bottlenecks discussed above gave rise to the major interlocks among the separate CPU areas. Within each of the areas, however, additional considerations hold. These are discussed as appropriate in the next section or in following papers.

Instruction unit

The central control functions for the Model 91 CPU are performed in the instruction unit. The objective here is to discuss these functions in terms of how they are performed and to include the reasons for selecting the present design. However, before proceeding with this discussion it will be useful to examine some over-all design considerations and decisions which directly affect the instruction unit functions. In approaching the design of the instruction unit, many program situations were examined, and it was found that while many short instruction sequences are nicely ordered, the trend is toward frequent branching. Such things as performing short work loops, taking new action based on data results, and calling subroutines are the bases upon which programs are built and, in many instances, these factors play a larger role in the use of available time than does execution. Consequently, emphasis on branch sequencing is required. A second finding was that, even with sophisticated execution algorithms, very few programs can cause answers actually to flow from the assembly line at an average rate in excess of one every two cycles. Inherent inter-instruction dependencies, storage and other hardware conflicts, and the frequency of operations requiring multi-cycle execution all combine to prevent it.

Consideration of branching and execution times indicates that, for overall balance, the instruction unit should be able to surge ahead of the execution units by issuing instructions at a faster-than-execution rate. Then, when a branch is encountered, a significant part of the instruction unit slowdown will be overlapped with execution catch-up. With this objective in mind it becomes necessary to consider what constitutes a fast issue rate and what "trade-offs" would be required to achieve it. It is easily shown that issuing at a rate in excess of one instruction per cycle leads to a rapid expansion of hardware and complexity. (Variable-length instructions, adjacent instruction interdependencies, and storage requirements are prime factors involved.) A one-cycle maximum rate is thereby established, but it too presents difficulties. The assembly line process requires that both instruction fetching and instruction issuing proceed concurrently in order to hide storage delays. It is found through program analysis that slightly more than two instructions will be obtained per 64-bit instruction fetch* and that approximately 80% of all instructions require an operand reference to storage. From this it is concluded that issuing the average instruction entails approximately 1.25 storage accesses: 0.45 (instruction fetches) + 0.80 (operand fetches). This figure, with the one-per-cycle issue rate goal, clearly indicates a need for either two address paths to storage and associated return capabilities, or for multiple words returned per fetch. In considering these options, the initial tendency is to separate instruction and operand storage access paths. However, multiple paths to storage give rise to substantial hardware additions and lead to severe control problems, particularly in establishing storage priorities and interlocks due to address dependencies. With a one-at-a-time approach these can be established on each new address as it appears, whereas simultaneous requests involve doing considerably more testing in a shorter time interval. Multiple address paths to storage were considered impractical because of the unfavorable compromise between hardware and performance.

The multiple-words-returned-per-fetch option was considered in conjunction with instruction fetching since the instruction stream is comprised of sequential words. To prevent excessive storage "busying" this approach requires multiple word readout at the storage unit along with a wider data return path. Also, the interleaving factor is altered from *sequential* to *multi-sequential*, i.e., rather than having sequential double words in different storage modules, groups of sequential words reside in the same module. The interlock problems created by this technique are modest, the change in interleaving technique has little performance effect,* and storage can be (is, in some cases) organized to read out multiple words, all of which make this approach feasible. However, packaging density (more hardware required for wide data paths), storage organization constraints, and scheduling were such that this approach was also discarded. As a consequence, the single-port storage bus, which allows sequential accessing of double words, was adopted. This fact, in conjunction with the 1.25 storage accesses required per instruction, leads to a lowering of the average maximum issue rate to 0.8 instructions per machine cycle. The instruction unit achieves the issue rate through an organization which allows concurrency by separating the instruction supplying from the instruction issuing function.

- *Instruction supplying*

Instruction supplying includes the provision of an instruction stream which will support the desired issue rate in a sequential (non-branch) environment, and the ability to switch readily to a new instruction stream when required because of branching or interrupts.

Sequential instruction fetching

Provision of a sequential string of instructions has two fundamental aspects, an initiation or start-up transient, and a steady-state function. The initial transient entails filling the assembly line ahead of the decode station with instructions. In hardware terms, this means initiating sufficient instruction fetches so that, following a wait of one access time, a continuous flow of instruction words will return from storage. Three double-word fetches are the minimum required to fill the assembly line, since approximately two instructions are contained within a double word, and the design point access time is six machine cycles. The actual design exceeds the minimum for several reasons, the first being that during start-up no operand requests are being generated (there are no instructions), and consequently the single address port to storage is totally available for instruction fetching. Second, the start-up delay provides otherwise idle time during which to

---

* Storage-to-storage (SS) instructions are not considered here. They can be viewed as macro-operations and are treated as such by the hardware. The macro-operations are equivalent to basic instructions, and the number of micro-instructions involved in performing an SS function indicates that many instruction fetches would be required to perform the same function using other System/360 instructions.

* This is more intuitive than analytical. Certainly for strictly random addressing, the interleave technique is irrelevant. However, in real applications, programs are generally localized with (1) the instructions sequential and (2) branches jumping tens or hundreds rather than thousands of words. Data is more random because, even though it is often ordered in arrays, quite frequently many arrays are utilized concurrently. Also, various data constants are used which tend to randomize the total use. A proper analysis must consider all these factors and so becomes complex. In any event, as long as the interleave factor remains fixed the interference appears little affected by small changes in the interleaving pattern.

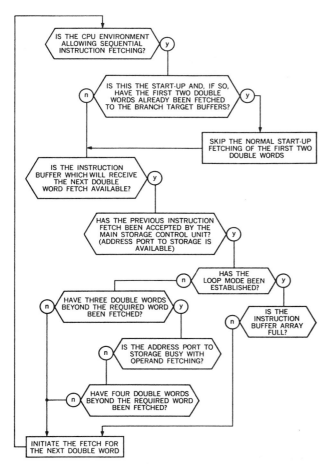

Figure 9 Flow chart of the sequential instruction-supply function.

initiate more fetches, and the eight double words of instruction buffering provide space into which the words can return. A third point is that, should storage requiring more than six cycles of access time be utilized, more fetching-ahead will be required. Finally, establishing an excess queue of instructions during the transient time will allow temporary maintenance of a full assembly line without any further instruction fetching. The significance of this action is that it allows the issuing of a short burst of instructions at a one-per-cycle rate. This follows from the fact that the single, normally shared storage address port becomes exclusively available to the issue function. A start-up fetching burst of five double instruction words was the design point which resulted when all of these factors had been considered.*

Steady-state instruction supplying serves the function

of maintaining a full assembly line by initiating instruction fetches at appropriate intervals. The address port to storage is multiplexed between instruction fetches and operand fetches, with instructions receiving priority in conflict situations. An additional optimization technique allows the instruction fetching to re-advance to the start-up level of five double words ahead if storage address time "slots" become available. A flow chart of the basic instruction fetch control algorithm is shown in Fig. 9,* while Fig. 10 is a schematic of the data paths provided for the total instruction supplying function. Some of the decision blocks contained in the flow chart result from the effects of branch instructions; their function will be clarified in the subsequent discussion of branching. There are two fundamental reasons for checking buffer availability in the algorithm. First, the instruction buffer array is a modulo-eight map of storage that is interleaved by sixteen. Second, fetches can return out of order because storage may be busy or of varying performance. For example, when a branch is encountered, point one above implies that the target may overlay a fetch which has not yet returned from storage. In view of the second point, it is necessary to ensure that the unreturned fetch is ignored, as it would be possible for a new fetch to return ahead of it. Proper sequencing is accomplished by "tagging" the buffers assigned to outstanding fetches, and preventing the initiation of a new fetch to a buffer so tagged.

Branch Handling

Branching adds to the complexity of the instruction supplying function because attempts are made to minimize discontinuities caused by the branching and the consequent adverse effects on the issue rate. The discontinuities result because for each branch the supply of instructions is disrupted for a time roughly equivalent to the greater of the storage access period (start-up transient previously mentioned), or the internal testing and "housekeeping" time required to make and carry out the branch decision. This time can severely limit the total CPU performance in short program loops. It has a somewhat less pronounced effect in longer loops because the branch time becomes a smaller percentage of the total problem loop time and, more important, the instruction unit has greater opportunity to run ahead of the execution units (see Fig. 11). This last makes more time available in which to overlap the branch time with execution catch-up.

The detrimental performance effect which stems from short loops led to a dual branch philosophy. The first aspect deals with branches which are either forward into the instruction stream,[†] beyond the prefetched instructions, or if backward from the branch instruction, greater

---

* The one disadvantage to over-fetching instructions is that the extra fetches may lead to storage conflicts, delaying the subsequently initiated operand fetches. This is a second-order effect, however, first because it is desirable for the instruction fetches to win conflicts unless these fetches are rendered unnecessary by an intervening branch instruction, and secondly because the sixteen-deep interleaving of storage significantly lowers the probability of the conflict situation.

* In this flow chart, unlabeled exits from decision blocks imply that a "wait" state will exist until the required condition has been satisfied.
† In the actual program the branch instruction would precede the target for this case.

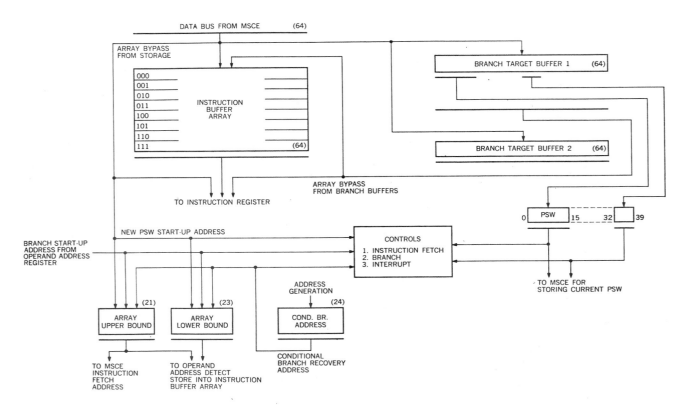

Figure 10 Data paths for the basic instruction supply.

than eight double-words back. In these situations the branch storage-delay is unavoidable. As a hedge against such a branch being taken, the branch sequencing (Fig. 12) initiates fetches for the first two double words down the target path. Two branch buffers are provided (Fig. 10—the instruction supply data flow) to receive these words, in order that the instruction buffer array will be unaffected if the result is a no branch decision. The branch house-keeping and decision making are carried on in parallel with the access time of the target fetches. If a branch decision is reached before the access has been completed, additional optimizing hardware routes the target fetch around the buffer and directly to the instruction register, from which it will be decoded. Minor disadvantages of the technique are that the "hedge" fetching results in a delay of the no-branch decision and may lead to storage conflicts. Consequently, a small amount of time is lost for a branch which "falls through."

The second aspect of the branch philosophy treats the case for which the target is backward within eight double words of the branch instruction. A separation of eight double words or less defines a "short" loop—this number being chosen as a hardware/performance compromise. Part of the housekeeping required in the branch sequencing is a "back eight" test. If this test is satisfied the instruction unit enters what is termed "loop mode." Two beneficial

results derive from loop mode. First, the complete loop is fetched into the instruction buffer array, after which instruction fetching ceases. Consequently, the address port to storage is totally available for operand fetching and a one instruction per cycle issue rate is possible. The second advantage gained by loop mode is a reduction by a factor of two to three in the time required to sequence the loop-establishing branch instruction. (For example, the "branch on index" instruction normally requires eight

Figure 11 Schematic representation of execution delays caused by (branch) discontinuities in the instruction issuing rate, for the case in which the issuing rate is faster than the execution rate.

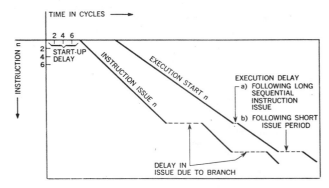

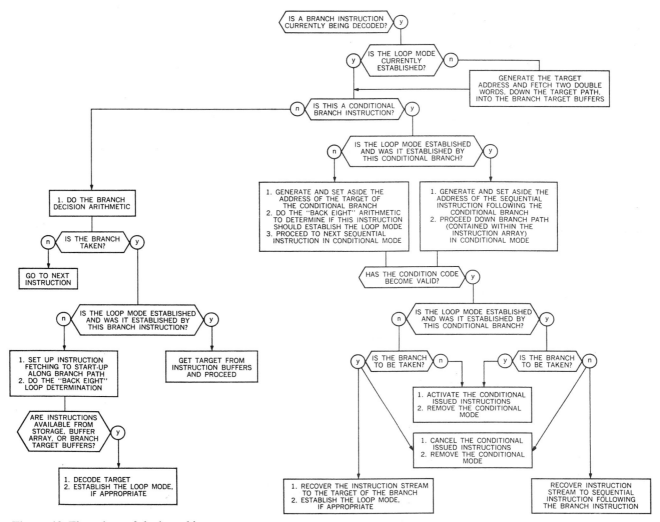

Figure 12 Flow chart of the branching sequence.

cycles for a successful branch, while in loop mode three cycles are sufficient.) In many significant programs it is estimated that the CPU will be in loop mode up to 30% of the time.

Loop mode may be established by all branch instructions except "branch and link." It was judged highly improbable that this instruction would be used to establish the type of short repetitious program loops to which loop mode is oriented. A conditional branch instruction, because it is data dependent and therefore less predictable in its outcome than other branch instructions, requires special consideration in setting up loop mode. Initial planning was to prevent looping with this instruction, but consultation with programmers has indicated that loops are frequently closed conditionally, since this allows a convenient means for loop breaking when exception conditions arise.

Furthermore, in these situations the most likely out-

come is often known and can be utilized to bias the branch decision whichever way is desirable. For such reasons, the "back eight" test is made during the sequencing of a conditional branch instruction, and the status is saved through conditional mode. Should it subsequently be determined that the branch is to be taken, and the "saved" status indicates "back eight," loop mode is established. Thereafter the role of conditional mode is reversed, i.e., when the conditional branch is next encountered, it will be assumed that the branch will be taken. The conditionally issued instructions are from the target path rather than from the no-branch path as is the case when not in loop mode. A cancel requires recovery from the branch guess. Figure 12 is a flow chart of this action. In retrospect, the conditional philosophy and its effects on loop mode, although significant to the performance of the CPU and conceptually simple, were found to require numerous interlocks throughout the CPU. The complications of conditional mode, coupled with the fact that it is primarily aimed at circumventing storage access delays, indicate that a careful re-examination of its usefulness will be called for as the access time decreases.

Interrupts

Interrupts, like branching, are another disruption to a smooth instruction supply. In the interrupt situation the instruction discontinuity is worsened because, following the recognition of the interrupt, two sequential storage access delays are encountered prior to receiving the next instruction.* Fortunately, and this is unlike branches, interrupts are relatively infrequent. In defining the interrupt function it was decided that the architectural "imprecise" compromise mentioned in the previous section would be invoked only where necessary to achieve the required performance. In terms of the assembly line concept, this means that interrupts associated with an instruction which can be uncovered during the instruction unit decode time interval will conform with the specifications. Consequently, only interrupts which result from address, storage, and execution functions are imprecise.

One advantage of this dual treatment is that System/360 compatibility is retained to a useful degree. For example, a programming strategy sometimes employed to call special subroutines involves using a selected invalid instruction code. The ensuing interrupt provides a convenient subroutine entry technique. Retaining the compatible interrupt philosophy through the decoding time interval in the Model 91 allows it to operate programs employing such techniques. The manifestation of this approach is illustrated in the flow chart of Fig. 13. In accordance with System/360 specifications, no further decoding is allowed once either a precise or an imprecise interrupt has been signalled. With the assembly line organization, it is highly probable that at the time of the interrupt there will be instructions still in the pipeline which should be executed prior to changing the CPU status to that of the interrupt routine. However, it is also desirable to minimize the effect of the interrupt on the instruction supply, so the new status word is fetched to the existing branch target buffer in parallel with the execution completion. After the return from storage of the new status word, if execution is still incomplete, further optimizing allows the fetching of instructions for the interrupt routine. Before proceeding, it becomes necessary to consider an implication resulting

---

* This arises from the architectural technique of indirectly entering the interrupt subroutines. In System/360 the interrupts are divided into classes. Each class is assigned a different, fixed low storage address which contains the status to which the CPU shall be set should an interrupt of the associated class occur. Part of this status is a new program address. Consequently, interrupting requires obtaining a new supply of instructions from storage indirectly, through the new status word.

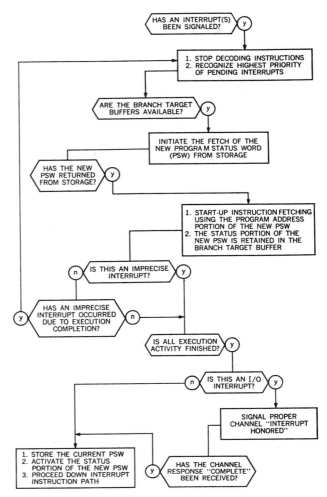

Figure 13 Flow chart of the interrupt sequence.

from the dual interrupt philosophy. Should a precise interrupt have initiated the action, it is possible that the execution "cleanup" will lead to an imprecise condition. In this event, and in view of the desire to maintain compatibility for precise cases, the logically preceding imprecise signal should cancel all previous precise action. The flow chart (Fig. 13) illustrates this cancel-recovery action. Should no cancel action occur (the more likely situation), the completion of all execution functions results, with one exception, in the release of the new status word and instruction supply. The I/O interrupts require special consideration because of certain peculiarities in the channel hardware (the System 360/Model 60–75 channel hardware is used). Because of them, the CPU-channel communication cannot be carried out in parallel with the execution completion. However, the relative infrequency of I/O interrupts renders negligible the degradation caused by this.

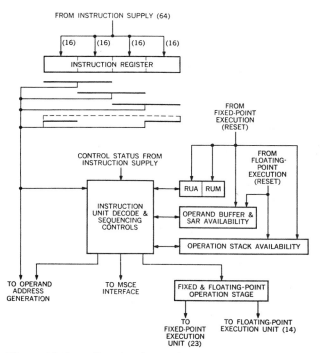

Figure 14 Data flow for instruction decoding and instruction issuing.

• *Instruction issuing*

The instruction-issuing hardware initiates and controls orderly concurrency in the assembly line process leading to instruction execution. It accomplishes this by scanning each instruction, in the order presented by the program, and clearing all necessary interlocks before releasing the instruction. In addition, should a storage reference be required by the operation, the issuing mechanism performs the necessary address calculations, initiates the storage action, and establishes the routing by which the operand and operation will ultimately be merged for execution. In addition, certain essential inter-instruction dependencies are maintained while the issue functions proceed concurrently.

In terms of the assembly line of Fig. 3, the moving of instructions to the decode area, the decode, and the operand address generation comprise the issue stations. The moving of instructions to the decode area entails the taking of 64-bit double-words, as provided by the instruction supply, and extracting from them the proper instruction half-words, one instruction at a time. The instruction register is the area through which this is accomplished (Fig. 14). The register efficiently handles variable-length instructions and provides a stable platform from which to decode. All available space in this 64-bit register is kept full of instructions yet to be decoded, provided only that the required new instruction information

tion has returned from storage. The decoder scans across the instruction register, starting at any half-word (16-bit) boundary, with new instructions refilling any space vacated by instruction issuing. The register is treated conceptually as a cylinder; i.e., the end of the register is concatenated with the beginning, since the decode scan must accommodate instructions which cross double-word boundaries.

The decoding station is the time interval during which instruction scanning and interlock clearing take place. Instruction-independent functions (interval timer update, wait state, certain interrupts and manual intervention) are subject to entry interlocks during this interval. Instruction-associated functions also have interlocks which check for such things as the validity of the scanned portion of the instruction register, whether or not the instruction starts on a half-word boundary, whether the instruction is a valid operation, whether an address is to be generated for the instruction (and if so, whether the address adder is available), and where the instruction is to be executed. In conjunction with this last point, should the fixed- or floating-point execution units be involved, availability of operation buffering is checked. Inter-instruction dependencies are the final class of interlocks which can occur during the decoding interval. These arise because of decision predictions which, if proven wrong, require that decoding cease immediately so that recovery can be initiated with a minimum of backup facilities.

Such occurrences as the discovery of a branch wrong guess or a store instruction which may alter the prefetched instruction stream generate these inter-instruction interlocks. Figure 15 illustrates the interlock function. The placement of a store instruction in the instruction stream, in particular, warrants further discussion because it presents a serious time problem in the instruction unit. The dilemma stems both from the concurrency philosophy and from the architectural specification that a store operation may alter the subsequent instruction. Recall that, through the pipeline concept, decoding can occur on successive cycles, with one instruction being decoded at the same time the address for the previous instruction is being generated. Therefore, for a decode which follows a store instruction, a test between the instruction counter and the storage address is required to detect whether or not the subsequent decode is affected by the store. Unless rather extensive recovery hardware is used, the decode, if affected, must be suppressed. However, the assembly line basic time interval is too short to both complete the detection and block the decode. The simplest solution would require a null decode time following each store issue. However, the frequency of store instructions is high enough that the performance degradation would be objectionable. The compromise solution which was adopted reduces the number of decoding delays by utilizing a truncated-address compare. The time requirements

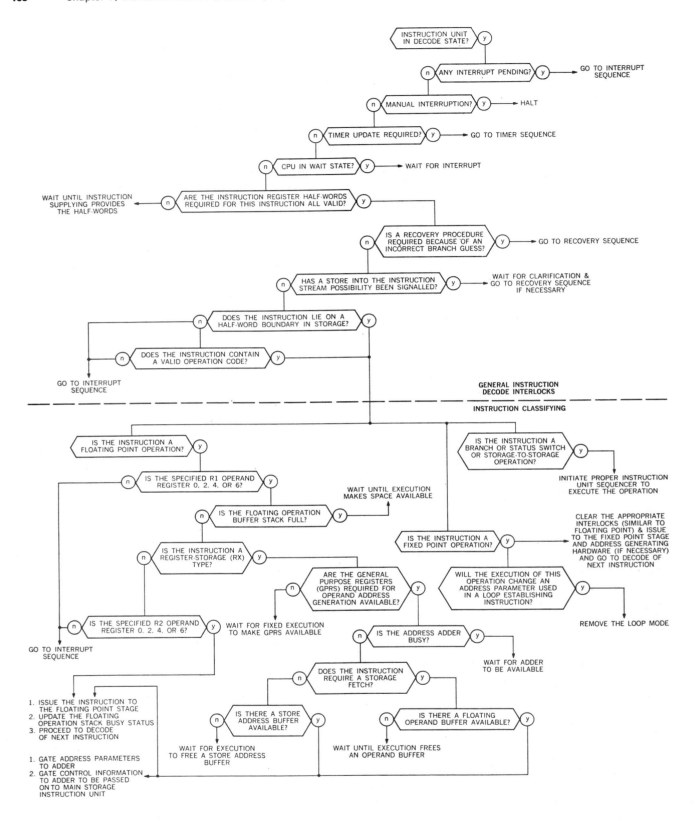

Figure 15 Decision sequence for instruction decoding and instruction issuing.

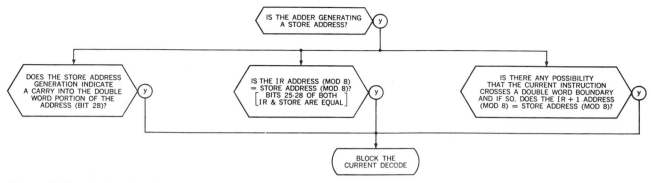

Figure 16 Decode interlock (established following the issue of a store instruction).

prohibit anything more than a compare of the low-order six bits of the storage address currently being generated, using the algorithm illustrated in Fig. 16.

The algorithm attaches relatively little significance to the low-order three adder bits (dealing with byte, half-word and full-word addresses) since the primary performance concern is with stores of double-words. It is seen, for example, that for the full-word case the probability of a carry into the double-word address is approximately 1/4, while for double-word handling it is negligible. The double-word address three-bit compare will occur with 1/8 probability while the word boundary crossover term has a probability of 1/16. (Probability that instruction can cross boundary, 1/2, $\times$ probability that the crossover is into the store-affected-word, 1/8). The two cases thus have the probabilities:

Full word $1/4 + 1/8 + 1/16 = 7/16$, and

Double-word $1/8 + 1/16 = 3/16$.

These figures indicate the likelihood of a decode time-interval delay following the issue of a store instruction. When such a decode delay is encountered, the following cycle is used to complete the test, that is, to check the total address to determine whether an instruction word has in fact been altered. To this effect, the generated storage address is compared with the upper and lower bounds of the instruction array (Fig. 16). A between-the-bounds indication results in a decode halt, a re-fetch of the affected instruction double-word, then resumption of normal processing. This second portion of the interlock is only slightly less critical in timing than the first. Figure 17 illustrates the re-fetch timing sequence. One difficulty with the store interlock is that in blocking the decode, it must inhibit action over a significant portion of the instruction unit. This implies both heavy loading and lengthy wire, each of which seriously hampers circuit performance. It was therefore

important that the unit be as small as possible and that the layout of the hardware constantly consider the interlock.

For each instruction, following the clearing of all interlocks, the decode decision determines whether to issue the instruction to an execution unit and initiate address generation, or to retain the instruction for sequencing within the instruction unit. The issuing to an execution unit and the operand fetching for storage-to-register (RX) instructions constitutes a controlled splitting operation; sufficient information is forwarded along both paths to effect a proper execution unit merge. For example, buffer assignment is carried in both paths so that the main storage control element will return the operand to the buffer which will be accessed by the execution unit when it prepares to execute the instruction. With this technique the execution units are isolated from storage and can be designed to treat all operations as involving only registers.

A final decoding function is mentioned here, to exemplify the sort of design considerations and hardware additions that are caused by performance-optimizing techniques. The branch sequencing is optimized so that no address generation is required when a branch which established the loop mode is re-encountered. This is done by saving the location, within the instruction array, of the target. It is possible, even if unlikely, that one of the instructions contained in a loop may alter the parameter originally used to generate the target address which is now being assumed. This possibility, although rare, does require hardware to detect the occurrence and terminate the loop mode. This hardware includes two 4-bit registers, required to preserve the addresses of the general purpose registers (X and B) utilized in the target address generation, and comparators which check these addresses against the sink address (R1) of the fixed-point instructions. Detection of a compare and termination of loop mode are necessary during the decoding interval to ensure that subsequent branch sequencing will be correct.

The address-generating time interval provides for the combining of proper address parameters and for the forwarding of the associated operation (fetch or store) control to the main storage control element through an interface register. A major concern, associated with the address parameters, was to decide where the physical location of the general purpose registers should be. This concern arises since the fixed-point execution unit, as well as the instruction unit, makes demands on the GPR's, while the packaging split will cause the registers to be relatively far from one of the units. It was decided to place them in the execution unit since, first, execution tends to change the registers while address generation merely examines their contents, and secondly, it was desired that a fixed-point execution unit be able to iteratively use any particular register on successive time intervals. In order to circumvent the resulting time delay (long wire separation) between the general purpose registers and the address adder, each register is fed via "hot" lines to the instruction unit. The gating of a particular GPR to the adder can thereby be implemented locally within the instruction unit, and no transmission delay is incurred unless the register contents have just been changed.

Placing the GPR's outside the instruction unit creates a delay of two basic time intervals before a change initiated by the instruction unit is reflected at the address parameter inputs from the GPRs. This delay is particularly evident when it is realized that the address generated immediately following such a GPR change generally requires the contents of the affected register as a parameter. For example, branch on index, branch on count, branch and link, and load address are instruction unit operations which change the contents of a GPR. Further, in loop situations the target of the branch frequently uses the changed register as an index quantity in its address. Performance demands led to the incorporating of controls which recognize the above situation and effect a by-pass

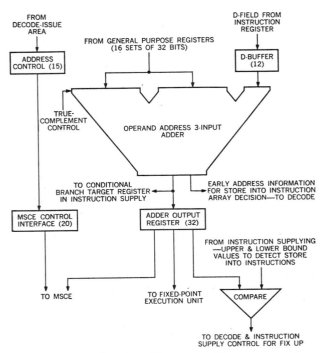

Figure 18 Data flow for address generation.

of the GPR. This entails substituting the content of the adder output register (which contains the new GPR data) for the content of the affected GPR. One performance cycle was saved by this technique.

In addition to address generation, the address adder serves to accomplish branch decision arithmetic, loop mode testing, and instruction counter value generation for various situations. In order to perform all of these functions, it was required that the adder have two 32-bit inputs and one input of 12 bits. One of the 32-bit inputs is complementable and a variety of fixed, single-bit inputs is provided for miscellaneous sequences. The data path is illustrated in Fig. 18.

Status switching and input/output

The philosophy associated with status switching instructions is primarily one of design expediency. Basic existing hardware paths are exercised wherever possible, and an attempt is made to adhere to the architectural interrupt specifications. When status switching instructions are encountered in conditional mode the instruction unit is halted and no action is taken until the condition is cleared.

The supervisor call (SVC) instruction is treated by the interrupt hardware as a precise interrupt. The same new status word pre-fetch philosophy is utilized in the load program status word (LPSW) operation.

Figure 17 Effect of the decode interlock on pre-fetched instructions.

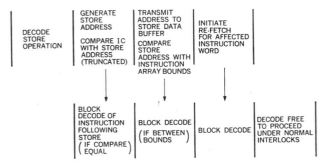

One difficulty encountered in conjunction with the start-up fetching of instructions following a status switch (or interrupt) is that a new storage protect key* is likely to obtain. Consequently, a period exists during which two protect keys are active, the first for previously delayed, still outstanding accesses associated with the current execution clean-up, and the second for the fetching of instructions. This situation is handled by sending both keys to the main storage control element and attaching proper control information to the instruction fetches.

The set program mask (SPM) implementation has a minor optimization: Whenever the new mask equals the current mask, the instruction completes immediately. Otherwise an execution clean-up is effected before setting the new mask to make certain that outstanding operations are executed in the proper mask environment.

I/O instructions, and I/O interrupts, require a wait for channel communications. The independent channel and CPU paths to storage demand that the CPU be finished setting up the I/O controls in storage before the channel can be notified to proceed. Once notified, the channel must interrogate the instruction-addressed device prior to setting the condition code in the CPU. This is

accomplished by lower-speed circuitry and involves units some distance away; consequently, I/O initiation times are of the order of 5–10 microseconds.

Acknowledgments

The authors wish to thank Mr. R. J. Litwiller for his interest, suggestions and design effort, and Messrs. J. G. Adler, R. N. Gustafson, P. N. Prentice and C. Zeitler, Jr. for their contributions to the design of the instruction unit.

References

1. G. M. Amdahl, G. A. Blaauw and F. P. Brooks, Jr., "Architecture of the IBM System/360," *IBM Journal* 8, 87 (1964).
2. W. Buchholz et al., *Planning a Computer System*, McGraw-Hill Publishing Co., Inc., New York, 1962.
3. R. J. Litwiller and J. G. Adler, private communication.
4. S. F. Anderson et al., "The IBM System/360 Model 91 Floating Point Execution Unit," *IBM Journal* 11, 34 (1967) (this issue).
5. R. M. Tomasulo, "An Efficient Algorithm for Exploiting Multiple Arithmetic Units," *IBM Journal* 11, 25 (1967) (this issue).
6. L. J. Boland, et al., "IBM System/360 Model 91 Storage System," *IBM Journal* 11, 54 (1967) (this issue).
7. M. J. Flynn and P. R. Low, "The IBM System/360 Model 91: Some Remarks on System Development" *IBM Journal* 11, 2 (1967) (this issue).

---

* The storage protect key is contained in the program status word (PSW). It is a tag which accompanies all storage requests, and from it the storage can determine when a protect violation occurs.

Received September 21, 1965.

Implementing Precise Interrupts in Pipelined Processors

JAMES E. SMITH, MEMBER, IEEE, AND ANDREW R. PLESZKUN, MEMBER, IEEE

Abstract—This paper describes and evaluates solutions to the precise interrupt problem in pipelined processors. An interrupt is *precise* if the saved process state corresponds with a sequential model of program execution where one instruction completes before the next begins. In a pipelined processor, precise interrupts are difficult to implement because an instruction may be initiated before its predecessors have completed.

The precise interrupt problem is described, and five solutions are discussed in detail. The first solution forces instructions to complete and modify the process state in architectural order. The other four solutions allow instructions to complete in any order, but additional hardware is used so that a precise state can be restored when an interrupt occurs. All the methods are discussed in the context of a parallel pipeline structure. Simulation results based on the CRAY-1S scalar architecture are used to show that the first solution results in a performance degradation of at least 16 percent. The remaining four solutions offer better performance, and three of them result in as little as a 3 percent performance loss. Several extensions, including vector architectures, virtual memory, and linear pipeline structures, are briefly discussed.

Index Terms—Performance simulation, pipelined computers, precise interrupts, process checkpointing, process recovery, virtual memory.

I. INTRODUCTION

MOST computer architectures are based on a sequential model of program execution in which an architectural program counter sequences through instructions one-by-one, finishing one before starting the next. In contrast, a high-performance implementation may be pipelined, permitting several instructions to be in some phase of execution at the same time. The use of a sequential architecture and a pipelined implementation clash at the time of an interrupt; pipelined instructions may modify the process state in an order different from that defined by the sequential architectural model. At the time an interrupt condition is detected, the hardware may not be in a state that is consistent with any specific program counter value.

When an interrupt occurs, the state of an interrupted process is typically saved by the hardware, the software, or by a combination of the two. The process state generally consists of the program counter, registers, and memory. If the saved process state is consistent with the sequential architectural model, then the interrupt is *precise*. To be more specific, the saved state should reflect the following conditions.

1) All instructions preceding the instruction indicated by the saved program counter have been executed and have modified the process state correctly.

2) All instructions following the instruction indicated by the saved program counter are unexecuted and have not modified the process state.

3) If the interrupt is caused by an exception condition raised by an instruction in the program, the saved program counter points to the interrupted instruction. The interrupted instruction may or may not have been executed, depending on the definition of the architecture and the cause of the interrupt. Whichever is the case, the interrupted instruction has either completed, or has not started execution.

If the saved process state is inconsistent with the sequential architectural model and does not satisfy the above conditions, then the interrupt is *imprecise*.

This paper describes and compares ways of implementing precise interrupts in pipelined processors. The methods used are designed to modify the state of an executing process in a carefully controlled way. The simple methods force all instructions to update the process state in the architectural order. Other, more complex methods save portions of the process state so that the proper state may be restored by the hardware at the time an interrupt occurs.

A. Classification of Interrupts

We consider interrupts belonging to two classes.

1) *Program interrupts,* sometimes referred to as "traps," result from *exception conditions* detected during fetching and execution of specific instructions. These exceptions may be due to software errors such as trying to execute an illegal opcode, numerical errors such as overflow, or they may be part of normal program execution as with page faults.

2) *External interrupts* are not caused by specific instructions and are often caused by sources outside the currently executing process, sometimes completely unrelated to it. I/O interrupts and timer interrupts are examples.

For a specific architecture, all interrupts may be defined to be precise or only a proper subset. Virtually every architecture, however, has some types of interrupts that must be precise. There are a number of conditions under which precise interrupts are either necessary or desirable.

1) For I/O and timer interrupts, a precise process state makes restarting possible.

2) In virtual memory systems, precise interrupts allow a process to be correctly restarted after a page fault has been serviced.

3) For software debugging, it is desirable for the saved state to be precise. This information can be helpful in isolating the exact instruction and circumstances that caused the exception condition.

4) For graceful recovery from arithmetic exceptions, software routines may be able to take steps, rescale floating point numbers for example, to allow a process to continue. Some end cases of modern floating point arithmetic systems might best be handled by software, gradual underflow in the proposed IEEE floating point standard [15], for example.

5) Unimplemented opcodes can be simulated by system software in a way transparent to the programmer if interrupts are precise. In this way, lower performance models of an architecture can maintain compatibility with higher performance models using extended instruction sets.

6) Virtual machines can be implemented if privileged instruction faults cause precise interrupts. Host software can simulate these instructions and return to the guest operating system in a user-transparent way.

B. Historical Survey

The precise interrupt problem is as old as the first pipelined computers [5]. The IBM 360/91 [3] was a well-known computer that produced imprecise interrupts under some circumstances, floating point exceptions, for example. Imprecise interrupts were a break with the IBM 360 architecture which made them even more noticeable. Subsequent IBM 360 and 370 implementations have used less aggressive pipeline designs where instructions modify the process state in strict program order, and interrupts are precise.[1] A more complete description of the method used in these "linear" pipeline implementations is in Section VIII-D.

Most pipelined implementations of general purpose architectures are similar to those used by IBM. These pipelines constrain all instructions to pass through the pipeline in order with a stage at the end where exception conditions are checked before the process state is modified. Examples include the Amdahl 470 and 580 [1], [2] and the Gould/SEL 32/87 [17].

The high-performance CDC 6600 [16], CDC 7600 [4], and Cray Research [8], [14] computers allow instructions to complete out of the architectural sequence. Consequently, they have some exception conditions that result in imprecise interrupts. In these machines, the advantages of precise interrupts have been sacrificed in favor of maximum parallelism and design simplicity. I/O interrupts in these machines are precise, and they do not implement virtual memory.

The CDC STAR-100 [11] and CYBER 200 [7] series machines also allow instructions to complete out of order, and they do support virtual memory. In these machines, the use of vector instructions further complicates the problem. The solution finally arrived at was the addition of an *invisible exchange package* [7]. The invisible exchange package resides in memory and captures machine-dependent state information resulting from partially completed instructions. A

related approach is used in pipelined array processors [9] which contain instructions that permit interrupt handlers to explicitly dump and restore the contents of certain pipeline segments. A similar method has been suggested for MIPS [10] where pipeline information is dumped at the time of an interrupt and restored to the pipeline when the process is resumed. This solution makes a process restartable although it is arguable whether it has all the features and advantages of an architecturally precise interrupt. For example, it might be necessary to have implementation-dependent software sift through the machine-dependent state in order to provide complete debug information.

The recently announced CDC CYBER 180/990 [6] is a pipelined implementation of a new architecture that supports virtual memory, and offers roughly the same performance as a CRAY-1S. To provide precise interrupts, the CYBER 180/990 uses a history buffer, to be described later in this paper, where state information is saved just prior to being modified. When an interrupt occurs, this "history" information is used to back the system up into a precise state.

C. Paper Overview

This paper concentrates on explaining and discussing basic methods for implementing precise interrupts in pipelined processors. We emphasize scalar architectures (as opposed to vector architectures) because of their applicability to a wider range of machines. Section II defines the model architecture to be used in describing precise interrupt implementations. The model architecture is very simple so that the fundamentals of the methods can be clearly described. Sections III–VI contain methods for implementing precise interrupts. Section III describes a simple method that is easy to implement, but which reduces performance. Section IV describes a higher performance variation where results may be bypassed to other instructions before the results are used to modify the process state. Sections V and VI describe methods where instructions are allowed to complete in any order, but where state information is saved so that a precise state may be restored when an interrupt occurs. Section VII presents simulation results. Experimental results based on these CRAY-1S simulations are presented and discussed. Section VIII contains a brief discussion of 1) saving additional state information, 2) supporting virtual memory, 3) precise interrupts when a data cache is used, 4) linear pipeline structures, and 5) vector instructions. Finally, Section IX discusses ways to solve the precise interrupt problem architecturally rather than in the implementation. These methods are based on an architectural model that is parallel instead of sequential.

II. PRELIMINARIES

A. Model Architecture

For describing the various techniques, a model architecture is chosen so that the basic methods are not obscured by details and unnecessary complications brought about by a specific architecture.

We choose a register–register architecture where all memory accesses are through registers and all functional operations involve registers. In this respect, it bears some similarity to the

---

[1] Except for the models 95 and 195 which were derived from the original model 91 design. Also, the models 85 and 165 had imprecise interrupts for the case of protection exceptions and addressing exceptions caused by store operations.

CDC and Cray architectures, but has only one set of registers. The load instructions are of the form $Ri = (Rj + disp)$. That is, the content of register Rj plus a displacement given in the instruction are added to form an effective address. The content of the addressed memory location is loaded into register Ri. Similarly, a store is of the form $(Rj + disp) = Ri$, where register Ri is stored at the address found by adding the content of register Rj and a displacement. The functional instructions are of the form $Ri = Rj$ op Rk, where op is the operation being performed. For unary operations, the degenerate form $Ri = $ op Rk is used. Conditional instructions are of the form $P = disp{:}Ri$ op Rj, where P is the program counter, the disp is the address of the branch target, and op is a relational operator, $=$, $>$, $<$, etc.

The only process state in the model architecture consists of the program counter, the general purpose registers, and main memory. The architecture is simple, has a minimal amount of process state, can be easily pipelined, and can be implemented in a straightforward way with parallel functional units like the CDC and Cray architectures.

Initially, we assume no operand cache. Similarly, condition codes are not used. They add other problems beyond precise interrupts when a pipelined implementation is used. Extensions for operand cache and condition codes are discussed in Section VIII.

A parallel pipeline implementation for the simple architecture is shown in Fig. 1. It uses an instruction fetch/decode pipeline which processes instructions in order. The final stage of the fetch/decode pipeline is an issue register where all register interlock conditions are checked. If there are no register conflicts, an instruction issues to one of the parallel functional units. Here, the memory access function is implemented as one of the functional units. The operand registers are read at the time an instruction issues. There is a single result bus that returns results to the register file. This bus may be reserved at the time an instruction issues or when an instruction is approaching completion. This assumes the functional unit times are deterministic. A new instruction can issue every clock period in the absence of register or result bus conflicts. Unless stated otherwise, the parallel pipeline structure of Fig. 1 is used throughout this paper.

Example 1: To demonstrate how an imprecise process state may occur in our model architecture, consider the following section of code which sums the elements of arrays A and B into array C.

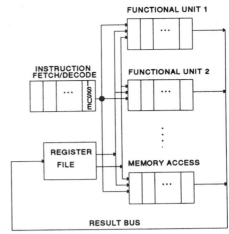

Fig. 1. Pipelined implementation of our model architecture. Not shown is the results shift register used to control the result bus.

Consider the instructions in statements 6 and 7. Although the integer add which increments the loop count will be issued after the floating point add, it will complete before the floating point add. The integer add will therefore change the process state before an overflow condition is detected in the floating point add. In the event of such an overflow, there is an imprecise interrupt.

B. Interrupts Prior to Instruction Issue

Before proceeding with the various precise interrupt methods, we first consider interrupts that occur prior to instruction issue because they are handled the same way by all the methods.

In the pipeline implementation of Fig. 1, instructions stay in sequence until the time they are issued. Furthermore, the process state is not modified by an instruction before it issues. This makes precise interrupts a simple matter when an exception condition can be detected prior to issue. Examples of such exceptions are privileged instruction faults and unimplemented instructions. This class also includes external interrupts which can be checked at the issue stage.

When such an interrupt condition is detected, instruction issuing is halted. Then, there is a wait while all previously issued instructions complete. After they have completed, the process is in a precise state, with the program counter value corresponding to the instruction being held in the issue

Statement			Comments	Execution Time
0		$R2 \leftarrow 0$	Init. loop index	
1		$R0 \leftarrow 0$	Init. loop count	
2		$R5 \leftarrow 1$	Loop inc. value	
3		$R7 \leftarrow 100$	Maximum loop count	
4	Loop:	$R1 \leftarrow (R2 + A)$	Load $A(I)$	11 clock periods
5		$R3 \leftarrow (R2 + B)$	Load $B(I)$	11 clock periods
6		$R4 \leftarrow R1 + fR3$	Floating add	6 clock periods
7		$R0 \leftarrow R0 + R5$	Inc. loop count	2 clock periods
8		$(R0 + C) \leftarrow R4$	Store $C(I)$	
9		$R2 \leftarrow R2 + R5$	Inc. loop index	2 clock periods
10		$P = Loop{:}R0\ !{=}\ R7$	cond. branch not equal	

register. The registers and main memory are in a state consistent with this program counter value.

Because exception conditions detected prior to instruction can be handled easily as described above, we will not consider them any further. Rather, we will concentrate on exception conditions detected after instruction issue.

III. IN-ORDER INSTRUCTION COMPLETION

With this method, instructions modify the process state only when all previously issued instructions are known to be free of exception conditions. This section describes a strategy that is most easily implemented when pipeline delays in the parallel functional units are fixed. That is, they do not depend on the operands, only on the function. Thus, the result bus can be reserved at the time of issue.

First, we consider a method commonly used to control the pipelined organization shown in Fig. 1. This method may be used regardless of whether precise interrupts are to be implemented. The precise interrupt methods described in this paper are integrated into this basic control strategy, however. To control the result bus, a ''result shift register'' is used; see Fig. 2. Here, the stages are labeled 1 through n, where n is the length of the longest functional unit pipeline. An instruction that takes i clock periods reserves stage i of the result shift register at the time it issues. If the stage already contains valid control information, then issue is held until the next clock period, and stage i is checked once again. An issuing instruction places control information in the result shift register. This control information identifies the functional unit that will be supplying the result and the destination register of the result. This control information is also marked ''valid'' with a validity bit. Each clock period, the control information is shifted down one stage toward stage one. When it reaches stage one, it is used during the next clock period to control the result bus so that the functional until result is placed in the correct result register.

Still disregarding precise interrupts, it is possible for a short instruction to be placed in the result pipeline in stage i when previously issued instructions are in stage j, $j > i$. This leads to instructions finishing out of the original program sequence. If the instruction at stage j eventually encounters an exception condition, the interrupt will be imprecise because the instruction placed in stage i will complete and modify the process state even though the sequential architecture model says i does not begin until j completes.

Example 2: If one considers the section of code presented in Example 1, and an initially empty result shift register (all the entries invalid), the floating point add would be placed in stage 6 while the integer add would be placed in stage 2. The result shift register entries shown in Fig. 2 reflect the state of the result shift register after the integer add issues. Notice that the floating point add entry is in stage 5 since one clock period has passed since it issued. As described above, this situation leads to instructions finishing out of the original program sequence.

A. Registers

To implement precise interrupts with respect to registers using the above pipeline control structure, an issuing instruc-

STAGE	FUNCTIONAL UNIT SOURCE	DESTN. REGISTER	VALID	PROGRAM COUNTER
1			0	
2	INTEGER ADD	0	1	7
3			0	
4			0	
5	FLT PT ADD	4	1	6
⋮	⋮	⋮	⋮	⋮
N			0	

Fig. 2. Result shift register.

tion using stage j should ''reserve'' stages $i < j$ as well as stage j. That is, the stages $i < j$ that were not previously reserved by other instructions are reserved, and they are loaded with null control information so that they do not affect the process state. This guarantees that instructions modifying registers finish in order.

There is logic on the result bus that checks for exception conditions in instructions as they complete. If an instruction contains a nonmasked exception condition, then control logic ''cancels'' all subsequent instructions coming on the result bus so that they do not modify the process state.

Example 3: For our sample section of code given in Example 1, assuming the the result shift register is initially empty, such a policy would have the floating point add instruction reserve stages 1–6 of the result shift register. When, on the next clock cycle, the integer add is in the issue register, it is prohibited from issuing because stage 2 is already reserved. Thus, the integer add must wait at the issue stage until stage 2 of the result shift register is no longer reserved. This would be five clock periods after the issue of the floating point add.

A generalization of this method is to determine, if possible, that an instruction is free of exception conditions prior to the time it is complete. Only result shift register stages that will finish before exceptions are detected need to be reserved (in addition to the stage that actually controls the result).

B. Main Memory

Store instructions modify the portion of process state that resides in main memory. To implement precise interrupts with respect to memory, one solution is to force store instructions to wait for the result shift register to be empty before allowing them to issue. Alternatively, stores can issue and be held in the load/store pipeline until all preceding instructions are known to be exception-free. Then the store can be released to memory.

To implement the second alternative, recall that memory can be treated as a special functional unit. Thus, as with any other instruction, the store can make an entry in the result shift register. This entry is defined as a *dummy* store. The dummy store does not cause a result to be placed in the register file, but is used for controlling the memory pipeline. The dummy store is placed in the result shift register so that it will not reach stage one until the store is known to be exception-free. When the dummy stores stage one, all previous instructions have completed without exceptions, and a signal is sent to the load/store unit to release the store to memory. If the store itself contains an exception condition, then the store is cancelled, all following load/store instructions are cancelled, and the store unit signals the pipeline control so that all instructions issued subsequent to the store are cancelled as they leave the result pipeline.

C. Program Counter

To implement precise interrupts with respect to the program counter, the result shift register is widened to include a field for the program counter of each instruction (see Fig. 2). This field is filled as the instruction issues. When an instruction with an exception condition appears at the result bus, its program counter is available and becomes part of the saved state.

IV. THE REORDER BUFFER

The primary disadvantage of the above method is that fast instructions may sometimes get held up at the issue register even though they have no dependencies and would otherwise issue. In addition, they block the issue register while slower instructions behind them could conceivably issue.

This leads us to a more complex, but more general solution. Instructions are allowed to finish out of order, but a special buffer called the *reorder buffer* is used to reorder them before they modify the process state.

A. Basic Method

The overall organization is shown in Fig. 3(a). The reorder buffer, Fig. 3(b), is a circular buffer with head and tail pointers. Entries between the head and tail are considered valid. When an instruction issues, the next available reorder buffer entry, pointed to by the tail pointer, is given to the issuing instruction. The tail pointer value is used as a tag to identify the entry in the buffer reserved for the instruction. The tag is placed in the result shift register along with the other control information. The tail pointer is then incremented, modulo the buffer size. The result shift register differs from the one used earlier because there is a field containing a reorder tag instead of a field specifying a destination register.

When an instruction completes, both results and exception conditions are sent to the reorder buffer. The tag from the result shift register is used to guide them to the correct reorder buffer entry. When the entry at the head of the reorder buffer contains valid results (its instruction has finished), then its exceptions are checked. If there are none, the results are written into the registers. If an exception is detected, issue is stopped in preparation for the interrupt, and all further writes into the register file are inhibited.

Example 4: The entries in the reorder buffer and result shift register shown in Fig. 3(b) reflect their state after the integer add from Example 2 has issued. Notice that the result shift register entries are very similar to those in the Fig. 2. The integer add will complete execution before the floating point add and its results will be placed in entry 5 of the reorder buffer. These results, however, will not be written into $R0$ until the floating point result, found in entry 4, has been placed in $R4$.

B. Main Memory

Preciseness with respect to memory is maintained in a manner similar to that in the in-order completion scheme

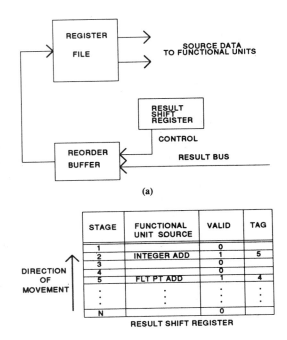

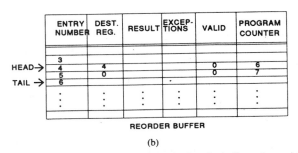

Fig. 3.   (a) Reorder buffer organization. (b) Reorder buffer and associated result shift register.

(Section III-B). The simplest method holds stores in the issue register until all previous instructions are known to be free of exceptions. In the more complex method, a store signal is sent to the memory pipeline as a "dummy" store is removed from the reorder buffer. Stores are allowed to issue, and block in the store pipeline prior to being committed to memory while they wait for their dummy counterpart.

C. Program Counter

To maintain preciseness with respect to the program counter, the program counter can be sent to a reserved space in the reorder buffer at issue time [shown in Fig. 3(b)]. While the program counter could be sent to the result shift register, it is expected that the result shift register will contain more stages than the reorder buffer and thus require more hardware. The length of the result shift register must be as long as the longest pipeline stage; as will be seen in Section VII, the number of entries in the reorder buffer can be quite small. When an instruction arrives at the head of the reorder buffer with an exception condition, the program counter found in the reorder buffer entry becomes part of the saved precise state.

D. Bypass Paths

While an improvement over the method described in Section III, the reorder buffer still suffers a performance penalty. A computed result that is generated out of order is held in the reorder buffer until previous instructions, finishing later, have updated the register file. An instruction dependent on a result being held in the reorder buffer cannot issue until the result has been written into the register file.

The reorder buffer method may, however, be modified to minimize some of the drawbacks of finishing strictly in order. In order for results to be used early, bypass paths may be provided from the entries in the reorder buffer to the register file output latches, see Fig. 4. These paths allow data being held in the reorder buffer to be used in place of register data. The implementation of this method requires comparators for each reorder buffer stage and operand designator. If an operand register designator of an instruction being checked for issue matches a register designator in the reorder buffer, then a multiplexer is set to gate the data from the reorder buffer to the register output latch. In the absence of other issue blockage conditions, the instruction is allowed to issue, and the data from the reorder data are used prior to being written into the register file.

There may be bypass paths from some or all of the reorder buffer entries. If multiple bypass paths exist, it is possible for more than one destination entry in the reorder buffer to correspond to a single register. Clearly only the *latest* reorder buffer entry that corresponds to an operand designator should generate a bypass path to the register output latch. To prevent multiple bypassing of the same register, when an instruction is placed in the reorder buffer, any entries with the same destination register designator must be inhibited from matching a bypass check.

When bypass paths are added, preciseness with respect to the memory and the program counter does not change from the previous method.

The greatest disadvantage with this method is the number of bypass comparators needed and the amount of circuitry required for the multiple bypass check. While this circuitry is conceptually simple, there is a great deal of it.

V. HISTORY BUFFER

The methods presented in this section and the next are intended to reduce or eliminate performance losses experienced with a simple reorder buffer, but without all the control logic needed for multiple bypass paths. Primarily, these methods place computed results in a working register file, but retain enough state information so a precise state can be restored if an exception occurs.

Fig. 5(a) illustrates the history buffer method. The history buffer is organized in a manner very similar to the reorder buffer. When an instruction issues, a buffer entry is loaded with control information, as with the reorder buffer, but the current value of the destination register (to be overwritten by the issuing instruction) is also read from the register file and written into the buffer entry. Results on the result bus are written directly into the register file when an instruction completes. Exception reports come back as an instruction

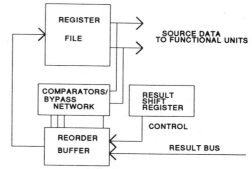

Fig. 4.   Reorder buffer method with bypasses.

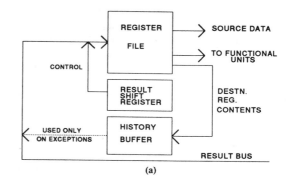

(a)

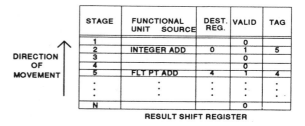

STAGE	FUNCTIONAL UNIT SOURCE	DEST. REG.	VALID	TAG
1			0	
2	INTEGER ADD	0	1	5
3			0	
4			0	
5	FLT PT ADD	4	1	4
⋮	⋮	⋮	⋮	⋮
N			0	

DIRECTION OF MOVEMENT

RESULT SHIFT REGISTER

ENTRY NUMBER	DEST. REG.	OLD VALUE	EXCEP-TIONS	VALID	PROGRAM COUNTER
3					
4	4	40800000		0	6
5	0	42		0	7
6					
⋮	⋮	⋮	⋮	⋮	⋮

HEAD → (entry 4)
TAIL → (entry 6)

HISTORY BUFFER

(b)

Fig. 5.   (a) History buffer organization. (b) History buffer and associated result shift register.

completes and are written into the history buffer. As with the reorder buffer, the exception reports are guided to the proper history buffer entry through the use of tags found in the result shift register. When the history buffer contains an element at the head that is known to have finished without exceptions, the history buffer entry is no longer needed and that buffer location can be reused (the head pointer is incremented). As with the reorder buffer, the history buffer can be shorter than the maximum number of pipeline stages. If all history buffer entries are used (the buffer is too small), issue must be blocked until an entry becomes available. Hence, the buffer should be long enough so that this seldom happens. The effect of the history buffer on performance is determined in Section VII.

Example 5: The entries in the history buffer and result shift register shown Fig. 5(b) correspond to our code in Example 1, after the integer add has issued. The only differences between this and the reorder buffer method shown in Fig. 3(b) are the addition of an "old value" field in the history buffer and a "destination register" field in the result shift register. The result shift register now looks like the one shown in Fig. 2.

When an exception condition arrives at the head of the buffer, the buffer is held, instruction issue is immediately halted, and there is a wait until pipeline activity completes. The active buffer entries are then emptied from tail to head, and the history values are loaded back into their original registers. The program counter value found in the head of the history buffer is the precise program counter.

To make main memory precise, when a store entry emerges from the buffer, it sends a signal that another store can be committed to memory. Stores can either wait in the issue register or can be blocked in the memory pipeline, as in the previous methods.

The extra hardware required by this method is in the form of a large buffer to contain the history information. Also the register file must have three read ports since the destination value as well as the source operands must be read at issue time. There is a slight problem if the basic implementation has a bypass of the result bus around the register file. In such a case, the bypass must also be connected into the history buffer.

VI. Future File

The future file method (Fig. 6) is similar to the history buffer method; however, it uses two separate register files. One register file reflects the state of the architectural (sequential) machine. This file will be referred to as the *architectural file*. A second register file is updated as soon as instructions finish and therefore runs ahead of the architectural file (i.e., it reflects the future with respect to the architectural file). This *future file* is the working file used for computation by the functional units.

Instructions are issued and results are returned to the future file in any order, just as in the original pipeline model. There is also a reorder buffer that receives results at the same time they are written into the future file. When the head pointer finds a completed instruction (a valid entry), the result associated with that entry is written in the architectural file.

Example 6: If we consider the code in Example 1 again, there is a period of time when the architecture file and the future file contain different entries. With this method, an instruction may finish out of order, so when the integer add finishes, the future file contains the new contents of $R0$. The architecture file, however, does not, and the new contents of $R0$ are buffered in the reorder buffer entry corresponding to the integer add. Between the time the integer add finishes and the time the floating point add finishes, the two files are different. Once the floating point finishes and its results are written into $R4$ of both files, $R0$ of the architecture file is written.

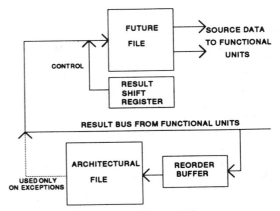

Fig. 6.   Future file organization.

Just as with the pure reorder buffer method, program counter values are written into the reorder buffer at issue time. When the instruction at the head of the reorder buffer has completed without error, its result is placed in the architectural file. If it completes with an error, the register designators associated with the buffer entries between the head and tail pointers are used to restore values in the future file from the architectural file.[2]

The primary advantage of the future file method is realized when the architecture implements interrupts via an "exchange" where all the registers are automatically saved in memory and new ones are restored (as is done in CDC and Cray architectures). In this case, the architectural file can be stored away immediately; no restoring is necessary as in the history buffer method. There is also no bypass problem as with the history buffer method.

VII. Performance Evaluation

To evaluate the effectiveness of our precise interrupt schemes, we use a CRAY-1S simulation system developed at the University of Wisconsin [13]. This trace-driven simulator is extremely accurate, due to the highly deterministic nature of the CRAY-1S, and gives the number of clock periods required to execute a program.

The scalar portion of the CRAY-1S is very similar to the model architecture described in Section II-A. Thus, casting the basic approaches into the CRAY-1S scalar architecture is straightforward.

For a simulation workload, the first 14 Lawrence Livermore Loops [12] were used. Because we are primarily interested in pipelined implementations of conventional scalar architectures, the loops were compiled by the Cray Fortran compiler with the vectorizer turned off.

In the preceding sections, five methods were described that could be used for guaranteeing precise interrupts. To evaluate the effect of these methods on system performance, the methods were partitioned into three groups. The first and second group, respectively, contain the in-order method and the simple reorder buffer method. The third group is com-

---

[2] The restoration is performed from the architectural file since the future file is the register file from which all execution takes place.

posed of the reorder buffer with bypasses, the history buffer, and the future file. This partitioning was performed because the methods in the third group result in identical system performance. This is because the future file has a reorder buffer embedded as part of its implementation, and the history buffer length constrains performance in the same way as a reorder buffer: when the buffer fills, issue must stop. All the simulation results are reported as for the reorder buffer with bypasses. They apply equally well for the history buffer and future file methods. The selection of a particular method depends not only on its effect on system performance but also the cost of implementation and the ease with which the precise CPU state can be restored.

For each precise interrupt method, both methods for handling stores were simulated. For those methods other than the in-order completion method, the size of the reorder buffer is a parameter. Sizing the buffer with too few entries degrades performance since instructions that might issue could block at the issue register. The blockage occurs because there is no room for a new entry in the buffer.

Table I shows the relative performance of the in-order, reorder buffer, and reorder buffer with bypass methods when the stores are held until the result shift register is empty. The results in the table indicate the relative performance of these methods with respect to the CRAY-1S across the first 14 Lawrence Livermore Loops; real CRAY-1S performance is 1.0. A relative performance greater than 1.0 indicates a degradation in performance. The number of entries in the reorder buffer varies from 3 to 10.

The simulation results for in-order completion are constant because this method does not depend on a buffer that reorders instructions. For all the methods, there is some performance degradation. Initially, when the reorder buffer is small, the in-order completion method produces the least performance degradation. A small reorder buffer (less than three entries) limits the number of instructions that can simultaneously be in some stage of execution. Once the reorder buffer size is increased beyond three entries, either of the other methods results in better performance. As expected, the reorder buffer with bypasses offers superior performance when compared to the simple reorder buffer. When the size of the buffer was increased beyond ten entries, simulation results indicated no further performance improvements. (Simulations were also run for buffer sizes of 15, 16, 20, 25, and 60.) One can expect at least 12 percent performance degradation when using a reorder buffer with bypasses and the first method for handling stores.

Table II indicates the relative performance when stores issue and wait at the same memory pipeline stage as for memory bank conflicts in the original CRAY-1S. After issuing, stores wait for their counterpart dummy store to signal that all previously issued register instructions have finished. Subsequent loads and stores are blocked from issuing.

As in Table I, the in-order completion results are constant across all entries. For the simple reorder buffer, the buffer must have at least five entries before it results in better performance than in-order completion. The reorder buffer with bypasses, however, requires only four entries before it is

TABLE I
RELATIVE PERFORMANCE FOR THE FIRST 14 LAWRENCE LIVERMORE LOOPS, WITH STORES BLOCKED UNTIL THE RESULTS PIPELINE IS EMPTY

Number of Entries	In-order Completion	Reorder Buffer	Reorder with Bypasses
3	1.2322	1.3315	1.3069
4	1.2322	1.2183	1.1743
5	1.2322	1.1954	1.1439
8	1.2322	1.1808	1.1208
10	1.2332	1.1808	1.1208

TABLE II
RELATIVE PERFORMANCE FOR THE FIRST 14 LAWRENCE LIVERMORE LOOPS, WITH STORES HELD IN THE MEMORY PIPELINE AFTER ISSUE

Number of Entries	In-order Completion	Reorder Buffer	Reorder with Bypasses
3	1.1560	1.3058	1.2797
4	1.1560	1.1724	1.1152
5	1.1560	1.1348	1.0539
8	1.1560	1.1167	1.0279
10	1.1560	1.1167	1.0279

performing more effectively than with in-order completion. Just as in Table I, having more than eight entries in the reorder buffer does not result in improved performance. Comparing Tables I and II, the second method for handling stores offers a clear improvement over the first method. If the second method is used with an eight-entry reorder buffer that has bypasses, a performance degradation of only 3 percent is experienced.

Clearly there is a tradeoff between performance degradation and the cost of implementing a method. For very little cost, the in-order completion method can be combined with the first method of handling stores. Selecting this "cheap" approach results in a 23 percent performance degradation. If this degradation is too great, either the second store method must be used with in-order completion or one of the more complex methods must be used. If the reorder buffer method is used, one should use a buffer with at least three or four entries.

It is important to note that in the performance study just described, some indirect causes for performance degradation were not considered. These include longer control paths that would tend to lengthen the clock period. Also, additional logic for supporting precise interrupts implies greater board area which implies more wiring delays which could also lengthen the clock period.

VIII. EXTENSIONS

In previous sections, we described methods that could be used to guarantee precise interrupts with respect to the registers, the main memory, and the program counter of our simple architectural model. In the following sections, we extend the previous methods to handle additional state information, virtual memory, cache memory, linear pipelines, and vectors.

A. Handling Other State Values

Most architectures have more state information than we have assumed in the model architecture. For example, a process may have state registers that point to page and segment tables, indicate interrupt mask conditions, etc. This additional state information can be precisely maintained with a method similar to that used for stores to memory. If using a reorder buffer, an instruction that changes a state register reserves a reorder buffer entry and proceeds to the part of the machine where the state change will be made. The instruction then waits there until receiving a signal to proceed from the reorder buffer. When its entry arrives at the head of the buffer and is removed, then the signal is sent to cause the state change.

In architectures that use condition codes, the condition codes are state information. Although the problem condition codes present to conditional branches is not totally unrelated to the topic here, solutions to the branch problem are not the primary topic of this paper. Hence, it is assumed that the conditional branch problem has been solved in some way, e.g., [3]. If a reorder buffer is being used, condition codes can be placed in the reorder buffer. That is, just as for data, the reorder buffer is made sufficiently wide to hold the condition codes. The condition code entry is then updated when the condition codes associated with the execution of an instruction are computed. Just as with data in the reorder buffer, a condition code entry is not used to change processor state until all previous instructions have completed without error (however, condition codes can be bypassed to the instruction fetch unit to speed up conditional branches).

Extension of the history buffer and future file methods to handle condition codes is very similar to that of the reorder buffer. For the history buffer, the condition code settings at the time of instruction issue must be saved in the history buffer. The saved condition codes can then be used to restore the processor state when an exception is detected.

B. Virtual Memory

Virtual memory is a very important reason for supporting precise interrupts; it must be possible to recover from page faults. First, the address translation section of the pipeline should be designed so that all the load/store instructions pass through it in order. In-order memory operations have been assumed throughout this paper. Depending on the method being used, the load/store instructions reserve time slots in the result pipeline and/or reorder buffer that are read no earlier than the time at which the instructions have been checked for exception conditions (especially page faults). For stores, these entries are not used for data; just for exception reporting and/ or holding a program counter value.

If there is an addressing fault, then the instruction is cancelled in the addressing pipeline, and all subsequent load/ store instructions are cancelled as they pass through the addressing pipeline. This guarantees that no additional loads or stores modify the process state. The mechanisms described in the earlier sections for assuring preciseness with respect to registers guarantee that nonload/store instructions following the faulting load/store will not modify the process state; hence, the interrupt is precise.

For example, if the reorder buffer method is being used, a page fault would be sent to the reorder buffer when it is detected. The tag assigned to the corresponding load/store

instruction guides it to the correct reorder buffer entry. The reorder buffer entry is removed from the buffer when it reaches the head. The exception condition in the entry causes all further entries of the reorder buffer to be discarded so that the process state is modified no further (no more registers are written). The program counter found in the reorder buffer entry is precise with respect to the fault.

C. Cache Memory

Thus far, we have assumed systems that do not use a cache memory. Inclusion of a cache in the memory hierarchy affects the implementation of precise interrupts. As we have seen, an important part of all the methods is that stores are held until all previous instructions are known to be exception-free. With a cache, stores may be made into the cache earlier, and for performance reasons should be. The actual updating of main memory, however, is still subject to the same constraints as before.

1) Store-Through Caches: With a store-through cache, the cache can be updated immediately, while the store-through to main memory is handled as in previous sections. That is, all previous instructions must first be known to be exception-free. Load instructions are free to use the cached copy, however, regardless of whether the store-through has taken place. This means that main memory is always in a precise state, but the cache contents may "run ahead" of the precise state. If an interrupt should occur while the cache is potentially in such a state, then the cache should be flushed. This guarantees that prematurely updated cache locations will not be used. However, this can lead to performance problems, especially for larger caches.

An alternative is to treat the cache in a way similar to the register files. One could, for example, keep a history buffer for the cache. Just as with registers, a cache location would have to be read just prior to writing it with a new value. This does not necessarily mean a performance penalty because the cache must be checked for a hit prior to the write cycle. In many high-performance cache organizations, the read cycle for the history data could be done in parallel with the hit check. Each store instruction makes a buffer entry indicating the cache location it has written. The buffer entries can be used to restore the state of the cache. As instructions complete without exceptions, the buffer entries are discarded. The future file can be extended in a similar way.

2) Write-Back Cache: A write-back cache is perhaps the cache type most compatible with implementing precise interrupts. This is because stores in a write-back cache are not made directly to memory; there is a built-in delay between updating the cache and updating main memory. Before an actual write-back operation can be performed, however, the reorder buffer should be emptied or should be checked for data belonging to the line being written back. If such data should be found, the write-back must wait until the data have been stored in the cache. If a history buffer is used, either a cache line must be saved in the history buffer, or the write-back must wait until the associated instruction has made its way to the end of the buffer. Notice that in any case, the write-back will sometimes have to wait until a precise state is reached.

D. Linear Pipeline Structures

An alternative to the parallel functional unit organizations we have been discussing is a linear pipeline organization. Refer to Fig. 7. Linear pipelines provide a more natural implementation of register–storage architectures like the IBM 370. Here, the same instruction can access a memory operand and perform some function on it. Hence, these linear pipelines have an instruction fetch/decode phase, an operand fetch phase, and an execution phase, any of which may be composed of one or several pipeline stages.

In general, reordering instructions after execution is not as significant an issue in such organizations because it is natural for instructions to stay in order as they pass through the pipe. Even if they finish early in the pipe, they proceed to the end where exceptions are checked before modifying the process state. Hence, the pipeline itself acts as a sort of reorder buffer.

The role of the result shift register is played by the control information that flows down the pipeline alongside the data path. Program counter values for preciseness may also flow down the pipeline so that they are available should an exception arise.

Linear pipelines often have several bypass paths connecting intermediate pipeline stages. A complete set of bypasses is typically not used, rather there is some critical subset selected to maximize performance while keeping control complexity manageable. Hence, using the terminology of this paper, linear pipelines typically achieve precise interrupts by using a reorder buffer method with bypasses.

E. Vectors

Implementing precise interrupts in a pipelined vector architecture is more difficult than for a scalar architecture. In this section, we consider extensions of our previous methods to vectors.

When considering precise interrupts with respect to vector instructions, preciseness must be carefully defined. Unlike the scalar instructions described thus far, vector instructions do not produce a single result and change the system state as they complete. Rather, they produce a series of results that change the system state over the course of many clock periods. The sequential architecture model, as applied to vectors, requires that one vector instruction completes its last result before the next begins producing results. Furthermore, requirement 3) for precise interrupts implies that a vector instruction must either complete in the presence of an exception condition, or it must be made to look as if it has not started. This implies that some buffering of vector results may be required in a pipelined implementation regardless of the method used for implementing precise interrupts.

There are two primary classes of vector architectures: those with vector registers, and those with memory-to-memory vector operations. For vector register architectures, we extend our earlier methods for maintaining scalar registers precisely. For memory-to-memory architectures, the second method for handling scalar stores to memory is extended.

1) Register Architectures: In-order completion (our first method) as extended to vectors implies that one instruction is finished producing results before the next begins. This implies

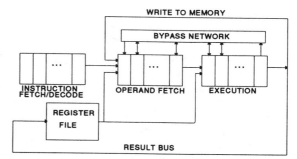

Fig. 7.   Example of a linear pipeline implementation.

no overlap of vectors with scalars, and no vector chaining. This can be implemented in instruction issue logic by blocking issue as long as a vector instruction is in progress.

There still remains the problem of interrupts that occur in the middle of the execution of a vector instruction. If the interrupt is an external interrupt, it is simply a matter of waiting until the instruction completes. For many types of program interrupts (e.g., page faults), however, it may not be possible to allow the instruction to complete, so it must be backed up. A simple solution is to buffer results and write them into a vector register after all results are complete, but this leads to performance problems. A vector instruction using the results must wait for the copy from the buffer to the register to complete. A better method is to have two copies of each vector register. A 1-bit pointer for each register indicates the "current" copy. When a vector operation is initiated, vector results are placed in the "new" (noncurrent) copy. When the vector instruction is complete, then the "current" pointer can be changed to the new copy. If there is a fault, then the pointer is not updated, and the register copy saved from before the vector instruction started remains the current copy.

A reorder buffer method can be used to permit limited overlap of scalar and vector operation. Due to the length of many vector operations, however, the buffer would have to be very long, or relatively little scalar operation would be possible. Also, unless bypasses are used, all the scalar instructions would have to be independent of each other. This would limit the usefulness of this method even more. For vectors, complete buffering of results would still be needed, but without bypasses, chaining would not be possible.

A practical method based on reorder buffers is to save scalars in the buffer as before, but save vector register pointers, rather than the vectors themselves, in the buffer. There would, again, be two copies of each vector register: a current copy and a new copy. A pointer to a specific vector register could appear in the buffer only once. This pointer would indicate not only a vector register, but which of the pair contains the new results. As the pointer is removed from the buffer, the "current" pointer for the vector would be updated. If a fault is detected, the pointer is not updated, so the old copy of the vector register is kept. This method overlaps dependent scalar operations with vectors, and chaining can be implemented by bypassing from the new copy pointed to by vector pointer in the buffer, rather than the current copy.

We now give an example of the method just described.

Consider the following two instructions: $V1 = V2 + V3$; $V3 = V1 \times V4$. Assume at the beginning of the sequence, the current pointer for $V1$ is 0. After the first vector instruction is issued, the vector designator $V1$ and 1 (the complement of its current pointer) are placed in the reorder buffer, and vector results are placed into copy 1 of $V1$ as they are generated. The previous values in copy 0 of $V1$ are retained. The second instruction can begin and chain to the first; here copy 1 of $V1$ is used for the chain. The chain is set up using the pointer found in the reorder buffer. After the first instruction is known to be complete without errors, the current pointer for $V1$ is updated to 1. Else if there is an error, it is kept at 0. Note that copy 0 of $V1$ can only be reused after the first instruction has completed.

With the history file method, the size of buffers is again a major problem; the file would be written as vector results are produced; vector chaining would imply multiple results being generated simultaneously so that the file would have to be able to support multiple simultaneous writes. Similarly, scalar results could be produced simultaneously with vector results so that they would probably need their own history file with some linkage between the two. A better method is to once again use pairs of vector registers. When a vector instruction is issued, it makes an entry in the history file indicating the vector register copy to be used as a backup. If a backup is required, the "current" pointer is adjusted to achieve the backup. As with the other methods, using pairs of vector registers requires that only one instruction that uses a specific vector register can be active in the system at any given time; one copy of the pair is used for new results, the other is used for saving old results.

By this time it should be clear that extending the future file method for vector registers can also easily be done with pairs of vector registers in a manner very similar to the history file method just described.

To summarize, the various methods for implementing precise interrupts can be extended for vector registers, but the cost is a doubling of the number of hardware registers plus some additional control hardware to keep track of the "current" pointers.

2) Memory-to-Memory Vectors: In the case of a memory-to-memory vector architecture, it may be necessary to buffer results in the CPU until all the operations associated with a vector instruction are completed without exception before allowing memory stores to begin. This is done in the most straightforward way by extending store method 2 described earlier, but it may require a much larger store buffer. This is the method used in the CDC CYBER 180/990 where vectors may contain up to 512 elements. In some architectures which used longer vector lengths, the size of this buffer may be prohibitive, however.

IX. ARCHITECTURAL SOLUTIONS

Thus far, we have assumed a sequential architectural model for execution, and have attempted to work around it for pipelined implementations. However, the root cause of the problem is the architectural model. Hence, it seems reasonable to solve the problem at the architectural level. That is, one might be able to define an architectural model where an interrupted state assumes an underlying parallel implementation. In this section, we briefly discuss a few such architectural solutions.

One architectural solution is to "freeze" the pipeline when an interrupt is detected, and simply "dump" the state of all the registers in the pipeline to memory as part of a saved context. Then, to restart the process, all the pipeline registers are restored, and the pipeline is started. Although this leads to processes that may be restarted, this approach has some disadvantages. One disadvantage is that freezing a pipe is difficult in practice due to fan-out problems. The fan-out problem comes from the need to control overwriting every pipeline stage. If writing all the stages is conditional on a single signal, for example a signal indicating no interrupt conditions, then the "no interrupt" condition must be fanned out to all the flip flops in all the registers in the pipeline. The large fan-out required for such a signal can lengthen the critical path of the pipeline control. Because of the tremendous fan-out for larger pipelined systems, this method may only be useful for the very smallest pipelined systems [10]. Such an approach also means that implementation details, for example the number of pipeline stages, become part of the architecture. This could lead to compatibility problems.

A variation of the above method, directed at vectors, is to define the vector architecture so that at the time of the interrupt, the intermediate state of vector instructions is saved. This information is primarily in the form of length counters. If done properly, a vector instruction is stopped in the middle, and restarting upon returning from the interrupt is accomplished by reissuing the stopped vector instruction.

Another architectural solution to the precise interrupt problem is to save a series of program counter values, ending with a final program counter value that is much like the one in the sequential model. Each program counter points to an instruction, prior to the final one, that has not been executed. To restart a process, the instructions pointed to by the series program counters must first be executed before the machine is in a precise state with respect to the final one.

Example 7: Again, we consider the code shown in Example 1 and the case where the floating point add overflows after the loop increment in statement 7 has completed. Using an architecture as defined above, in the event of floating point overflow in statement 6, the program counter pointing to statement 6 could be saved along with the program counter pointing to statement 8. A program counter for statement 7 is not needed because it has successfully completed. The overflow handler could "fix up" the overflow, possibly by rescaling, and then return to the process. Then using both saved program counters, the processor would execute statement 6 before resuming regular execution with statement 8.

Finally, one could save a sequence of instructions that must be executed before the saved program counter is precise. This has the advantage of fetching the instruction sequence as part of the context being restored. The program counter method requires first fetching the program counters as part of the restored context, then fetching the instructions themselves. In the example just given, the floating point add instruction itself would be saved, not its program counter. Then, as part of the return from the interrupt the processor would execute the floating point add before fetching instructions beginning with statement 8.

X. Summary and Conclusions

Five methods for implementing precise interrupts in the pipelined processors were described. These methods were then evaluated through simulations of a CRAY-1S implemented with these methods.

The first method forces in-order instruction completion, and our simulation study indicates a performance degradation of about 23 percent when store instructions are held in the instruction issue register and about 16 percent when stores are held in the memory pipeline. Performance is lost primarily because of added instruction issue blockages not related to data dependencies. The significant performance difference due to the way stores are handled is noteworthy.

To improve the performance provided by the first method, a reorder buffer is proposed to permit instructions to complete out of order, but to reorder the results going into the register file. For a reorder buffer of size eight, this method results in performance loss of 18 percent or 12 percent, depending on the way stores to memory are handled. Here performance is lost because results cannot be used because they are being held in the reorder buffer prior to result register update.

The third method studied adds bypass paths to the reorder buffer permitting data to be used prior to the result register update. With this method, performance loss is cut to 12 percent or 3 percent, again depending on the handling of stores. These final results indicate that performance losses can be significantly reduced, but only if stores are blocked in the memory pipeline to wait for previous instructions to complete.

The final two methods, the history buffer and future file methods, permit alternative implementations that give the same performance as with the reorder buffer using bypasses. The implementation differences among the final three methods are relatively minor, and any final choice should be based on technology related issues affecting implementation cost and complexity.

There are many other interesting issues related to implementing precise interrupts. These include the handling of virtual memory faults, caches, vectors, and alternative pipeline structures. Although they were briefly touched on in this paper, they deserve further research.

Finally, the basic concepts of process interruptability and restartability should be studied extensively. We feel that methods of saving and restoring state which do not rely on a serial model of execution are essential to the development of parallel general purpose systems.

Acknowledgment

The authors would like to thank R. G. Hintz and J. B. Pearson of the Control Data Corporation.

References

[1] Amdahl Corp., *Amdahl 470V/8 Computing System Machine Reference Manual,* pub. G1014.0-03A, Oct. 1981.
[2] ——, "580 Technical Introduction," 1980.
[3] D. W. Anderson, F. J. Sparacio, and F. M. Tomasulo, "The IBM system/360 Model 91: Machine philosophy and instruction-handling," *IBM J. Res. Develop.,* vol. 11, pp. 8–24, Jan. 1967.
[4] P. Bonseigneur, "Description of the 7600 computer system," *Computer Group News,* pp. 11–15, May 1969.
[5] W. Bucholz, Ed., *Planning a Computer System.* New York: McGraw-Hill, 1962.
[6] Control Data Corp., *CDC Cyber 180 Computer System Model 990 Hardware Reference Manual,* pub. 60462090, 1984.
[7] ——, *CDC CYBER 200 Model 205 Computer System Hardware Reference Manual,* Arden Hills, MN, 1981.
[8] Cray Research, Inc., *CRAY-1 Computer Systems, Hardware Reference Manual,* Chippewa Falls, WI, 1979.
[9] Floating Point Systems, *FPS-100 Programmers Reference Manual,* Beaverton, OR, 1980.
[10] J. Hennessy *et al.,* "Hardware/software tradeoffs for increased performance," in *Proc. Symp. Architectural Support Programming Languages Oper. Syst.,* Apr. 1982, pp. 2–11.
[11] R. G. Hintz and D. P. Tate, "Control data STAR-100 processor design," in *Proc. COMPCON 72, IEEE Comput. Soc. Conf. Proc.,* Sept. 1972, pp. 1–4.
[12] F. H. McMahon, "FORTRAN CPU performance analysis," Lawrence Livermore Labs., 1972.
[13] N. Pang and J. E. Smith, "CRAY-1 simulation tools," Tech. Rep. ECE-83-11, Univ. Wisconsin-Madison, Dec. 1983.
[14] R. M. Russell, "The CRAY-1 computer system," *Commun. ACM,* vol. 21, pp. 63–72, Jan. 1978.
[15] D. Stevenson, "A proposed standard for binary floating point arithmetic," *Computer,* vol. 14, pp. 51–62, Mar. 1981.
[16] J. E. Thornton, *Design of a Computer—The Control Data 6600.* Glenview, IL: Scott, Foresman, 1970.
[17] W. P. Ward, "Minicomputer blasts through 4 million instructions a second," *Electron.,* pp. 155–159, Jan. 13, 1982.

James E. Smith (S'74–M'76) received the B.S., M.S., and Ph.D. degrees from the University of Illinois in 1972, 1974, and 1976, respectively.

Since 1976, he has been on the faculty of the University of Wisconsin, Madison where he is an Associate Professor in the Department of Electrical and Computer Engineering. He spent the summer of 1978 with the IBM Thomas J. Watson Research Center, and from September 1979 until July 1981 he worked for the Control Data Corporation, Arden Hills, MN. While at CDC he participated in the design of the CYBER 180/990. He is currently on leave from the University of Wisconsin, working for the Astronautics Corporation of America on the design of a large scale scientific computer system.

Andrew R. Pleszkun (S'82–M'82) received the B.S. degree in electrical engineering from the Illinois Institute of Technology, Chicago, in 1977 and the M.S. and Ph.D. degrees in electrical engineering from the University of Illinois, Urbana, in 1979 and 1982, respectively.

He is an Assistant Professor in Computer Sciences Department at the University of Wisconsin, Madison. His research interests include computer architecture, with an emphasis on pipelined systems, and the impact of VLSI on computer architecture.

A STUDY OF BRANCH PREDICTION STRATEGIES

JAMES E. SMITH

Control Data Corporation
Arden Hills, Minnesota

ABSTRACT

In high-performance computer systems, performance losses due to conditional branch instructions can be minimized by predicting a branch outcome and fetching, decoding, and/or issuing subsequent instructions before the actual outcome is known. This paper discusses branch prediction strategies with the goal of maximizing prediction accuracy. First, currently used techniques are discussed and analyzed using instruction trace data. Then, new techniques are proposed and are shown to provide greater accuracy and more flexibility at low cost.

INTRODUCTION

It is well known[1-3,10] that in a highly parallel computer system, branch instructions can break the smooth flow of instruction fetching and execution. This results in delay, because a branch that is taken changes the location of instruction fetches and because the issuing of instructions must often wait until conditional branch decisions are made.

To reduce delay, one can attempt to predict the direction that a branch instruction will take and begin fetching, decoding, or even issuing instructions before the branch decision is made. Unfortunately, a wrong prediction may lead to more delay if, for example, instructions on the correct branch path need to be fetched or partially executed instructions on the wrong path need to be purged. The disparity between the delay for a correctly predicted branch and an incorrectly predicted branch points to the need for accurate branch prediction strategies.

This paper discusses branch prediction strategies with the goal of maximizing the likelihood of correctly predicting the outcome of a branch. First, previously suggested branch prediction techniques are discussed. Owing to the large number of variations and configurations, only a few representative strategies have been singled out for detailed study, although several are mentioned. Then, new techniques are proposed that provide more accuracy, less cost, and more flexibility than methods used currently.

Because of the wide variation in branching behavior between different applications, different programming languages, and even individual programs, there is no good analytic model for studying branch prediction. For this reason, we used instruction trace data to measure experimentally the accuracy of branch prediction strategies.

Originally, ten FORTRAN programs, primarily scientific, were chosen. It was found, however, that several were heavily dominated by inner loops, which made them very predictable by every strategy considered. Two programs, SCI2 and ADVAN, were chosen from this inner-loop-dominated class. Four other programs were not as heavily dominated by inner loops and were less predictable. All were chosen for the study.

The six FORTRAN programs used in this study were:

1. ADVAN: Calculates the solution of three simultaneous partial differential equations

2. SCI2:   Performs matrix inversion

3. SINCOS: Converts a series of points from polar to Cartesian coordinates

4. SORTST: Sorts a list of 10,000 integers using the shell sort algorithm[9]

5. GIBSON: An artificial program that compiles to instructions that roughly satisfy the so called GIBSON mix[5]

6. TBLLNK: Processes a linked list and contains a variety of conditional branches

The programs were compiled for a CDC CYBER 170 architecture.

Note that other than ADVAN and SCI2, the test programs were chosen for their unpredictability, and that a more typical scientific mix would contain more programs like ADVAN and SCI2.

Because of the method used for evaluating prediction strategies, any conclusions regarding their relative performance must be considered in light of the application area and the language used here. Nevertheless, the basic concepts and the strategies are of broader interest, because it is relatively straightforward to generate instruction traces and to measure prediction accuracy for other applications or languages.

Results published previously in this area appear in Shustek[6], who used instruction trace data to evaluate strategies for the IBM System 360/370 architecture. Ibbett[7] described the instruction pipeline of the MU5 computer and gave experimental results for a particular branch prediction strategy. A rather sophisticated branch predictor has been described for the S1 processor,[8] but as of this writing, no information appears to have been published regarding its accuracy. Branch prediction strategies have also been used in other high performance processors, but, again, experimental results have not been published.

Our study begins in the next section, with two branch prediction strategies that are often suggested. These strategies indicate the success that can reasonably be expected. They also introduce concepts and terminology used in this paper. Strategies are divided into two basic categories, depending on whether or not past history was used for making a prediction. In subsequent sections, strategies belonging to each of the categories are discussed, and further refinements intended to reduce cost and increase accuracy are presented. Levels of confidence are attached to branch predictions to minimize delay when there are varying degrees to which branch outcomes can be anticipated (for example, prefetching instructions is one degree, preissuing them is another). Conclusions are given in the final section.

TWO PRELIMINARY PREDICTION STRATEGIES

Branch instructions test a condition specified by the instruction. If the condition is true, the branch is *taken*: instruction execution begins at the target address specified by the instruction. If the condition is false, the branch is *not taken*, and instruction execution continues with the instruction sequentially following the branch instruction. An unconditional branch has a condition that is always true (the usual case) or is always false (effectively, a pass). Because unconditional branches typically are special cases of conditional branches and use the same operation codes, we did not distinguish

them when gathering statistics, and hence, unconditional branches were included.

A straightforward method for branch prediction is to predict that branches are either always taken or always not taken. Because most unconditional branches are always taken, and loops are terminated with branches that are taken to the top of the loop, predicting that all branches are taken results typically in a success rate of over 50%.

Strategy 1

- Predict that all branches will be taken.

Figure 1 summarizes the results of using strategy 1 on the six FORTRAN benchmarks.

From Figure 1, it is evident that the majority of branches are taken, although the success rates vary widely from program to program. This points to one factor that must be considered when evaluating prediction strategies: *program sensitivity*. The algorithm being programmed, as well as the programmer and the compiler, can influence the structure of the program and, consequently, the percentage of branches that are taken. High program sensitivity can lead to widely different prediction accuracies. This, in turn, can result in significant differences in program performance that may be difficult for the programmer of a high-level language to anticipate.

Strategy 1 always makes the same prediction every time a branch instruction is encountered. Because of this, strategy 1 is called *static*. It has been observed and documented,[6] however, that the likelihood of a conditional branch instruction at a particular location being taken is highly dependent on the way the same branch was decided previously. This leads to *dynamic* prediction strategies in which the prediction varies, based on branch history.

Strategy 2

- Predict that a branch will be decided the same way as it was on its last execution. If it has not been previously executed, predict that it will be taken.

The results (Figure 2) of using strategy 2, indicate that strategy 2 generally provides better accuracy than strategy 1. Unfortunately, strategy 2 is not physically realizable, because theoretically, there is no bound on the number on individual branch instructions that a program may contain. (In practice, however, it may be possible to record the history of a limited number of past branches; such strategies are discussed in a subsequent section.)

Strategies 1 and 2 provide standards for judging other branch prediction strategies. Strategy 1 is simple and inexpensive to implement, and any strategy that is seriously being considered for use should perform at least at the same level as strategy 1. Strategy 2 is widely recognized as being accurate, and if a feasible strategy comes close to (or exceeds) the accuracy of strategy 2, the strategy is about as good as can reasonably be expected.

Strategy 1 is apparently more program sensitive than strategy 2. Evidence of this is the wide variation in accuracy for strategy 1 and the much narrower variation for strategy 2 (Figures 1 and 2). Strategy 2 has a kind of second-order program sensitivity, however, in that a branch that has not previously been executed is predicted to be taken. Lower program sensitivity for dynamic prediction strategies is typical, as results throughout this paper show.

Finally, it is interesting that one aspect of branch behavior leads occasionally to better accuracy with strategy 1 than strategy 2. Often, a particular branch instruction is predominately decided one way (for example, a conditional branch that terminates a loop is most often taken). Sometimes, however, it is decided the other way (when "falling out of the loop"). These *anomalous decisions*, are treated differently by strategies 1 and 2. Strategy 1, if it is being used on a branch that is most often taken, leads to one incorrect prediction for each anomalous not taken decision. Strategy 2 leads to two incorrect predictions; one for the anomalous decision and one for the subsequent branch decision. The handling of anomalous decisions explains those instances in which strategy 1 outperforms strategy 2 and indicates that there may exist some strategies that consistently exceed the success rate of strategy 2.

STATIC PREDICTION STRATEGIES

Strategy 1 (always predict that a branch is taken) and its converse (always predict that a branch is not taken) are two examples of static prediction strategies. A further refinement of strategy 1 is to make a prediction based on the type of branch, determined, for example, by examining the operation code. This is the strategy used in some of the IBM System 360/370 models[9] and

attempts to exploit program sensitivities by observing, for example, that certain branch types are used to terminate loops, while others are used in IF-THEN-ELSE-type constructs.

Strategy 1a

- Predict that all branches with certain operation codes will be taken; predict that the others will not be taken.

The six CYBER 170 FORTRAN programs were examined, and it was found that "branch if negative", "branch if equal", and "branch if greater than or equal" are usually taken, so they are always predicted to be taken. Other operation codes are always predicted to be not taken. This strategy is somewhat tuned to the six benchmarks, because only the benchmarks were analyzed to determine which opcodes should be predicted to be taken. For this reason, the results for strategy 1a may be slightly optimistic.

Figure 3 shows the results for strategy 1a when it was applied to the CY170 programs. Generally, greater accuracy was achieved with strategy 1a than with strategy 1. The largest increase was in the GIBSON program in which the prediction accuracy was improved from 65.4% to 98.5%. The only program showing a decrease in accuracy was the SINCOS program in which there was a drop from 80.2% to 65.7%. The changes in both the GIBSON and SINCOS programs can be attributed to predicting that "branch if plus" was not taken. If it had been predicted as taken, the accuracy of the GIBSON program would have dropped nearly to its original value, and the accuracy of the SINCOS program would have risen nearly to its original value.

Other static strategies are possible. For example, predictions based on the direction of the potential branch or on the distance to the branch target can be made. Following is a detailed description of one of these strategies.

Strategy 3

- Predict that all backward branches (toward lower addresses) will be taken; predict that all forward branches will not be taken.

The thought behind strategy 3 is that loops are terminated with backward branches, and if all loop branches are correctly predicted, the overall accuracy will be high.

Figure 4 indicates that strategy 3 often worked well, sometimes exceeding strategy 2 (probably because of the anomalous decision case). There is, however, one program in which its performance was poor: in the SINCOS program, the accuracy for strategy 3 was about 35%. This indicates that program sensitivity is significant and that performance can suffer considerably for some programs.

A disadvantage of strategy 3, and of other strategies using the target address, is that the target address may need to be computed or compared with the program counter before a prediction can be make. This tends to make the prediction process slower than for other strategies.

DYNAMIC PREDICTION STRATEGIES

Some strategies base predictions on past branch history. Strategy 2 is an idealized strategy of this type, because it assumes knowledge of the history of all branch instructions. The strategies discussed in this section are actually realizable, because they use bounded tables to record a limited amount of past branch history.

Branch history can be used in several ways to make a branch prediction. One possibility is to use the outcome of the most recent execution of the branch instruction; this is done by strategy 2. Another possibility is to use more than one of the more recent executions to predict according to the way a majority of them were decided; this is done by strategy 7. A third possibility is to use only the first execution of the branch instruction as a guide; a strategy of this type, although accurate, has been found to be slightly less accurate than other dynamic strategies.

First, strategies are considered that base their predictions on the most recent branch execution (strategy 2). The most straightforward strategy is to use an associative memory that contains the addresses of the n most-recent branch instructions and a bit indicating whether the branch was taken or not taken. The memory is accessed with the address of the branch instruction to be predicted, and the taken or not taken bit is used to make the prediction.

If a branch instruction is not found in the table, two issues must be considered: (1) the prediction that is to be made, and (2) the table entry that should be replaced

to make room for the new branch instruction. First, if a branch instruction is not in the table, some static strategy must be reverted to for a default prediction. A good choice is to predict that the branch is taken as in strategy 2.

A more complex default strategy could be used (strategy 1a, for example), but using the simpler always predict taken strategy has a positive side effect. In particular, only branch instructions that are not taken need to be put into the table; then, the existence of a branch in the table implies it was previously not taken. Branches that were recently taken are given the proper prediction by default. One bit of memory is saved, but more importantly, histories of more branch instructions are effectively remembered. For example, if two out of the eight most-recent branch instructions executed are not taken, then all eight consume only two table entries, although all are predicted to have the same outcome as on their previous executions. A dual strategy is to use a default prediction of branch not taken and to maintain a table of branches most recently taken. Because most branch instructions are taken, however, this strategy is generally less accurate.

As far as replacement strategies, first-in first-out (FIFO) and least-recently used (LRU) seem to be two reasonable alternatives. For the application here, in which the sequence of branch instructions tends to be periodic because of the iterative structure of most programs, there is actually little difference between the FIFO and LRU strategies as far as prediction accuracy. The LRU strategy does appear to be more compatible with the scheme mentioned previously in which only branches that were not taken are recorded. Then, if a branch in the table is taken, it is purged from the table, and that table location is recorded as being least recently used. A branch that is taken subsequently fills the vacancy in the table rather than replacing a good table entry. Such a scheme for filling vacancies in the table fits naturally with the LRU replacement strategy.

Strategy 4

- Maintain a table of the most recently used branch instructions that are not taken. If a branch instruction is in the table, predict that it will not be taken; otherwise predict that it will be taken. Purge table entries if they are taken, and use LRU replacement to add new entries.

Figure 5 indicates the accuracy of strategy 4 for tables of 1, 2, 4, and 8 entries. In some cases, the accuracy was close to strategy 1 for small table sizes and became close to strategy 2 as the table size grew. This is because small table sizes are not big enough to contain all active branch instructions, and they keep replacing each other. As a result, few branch instructions are ever found in the table, and most branches are predicted as taken. As the table size becomes large enough to hold all active branches, they are all predicted as in strategy 2.

A variation[7] allows earlier predictions than with the strategies discussed thus far. In this variation, instruction words being fetched are compared with an associative memory to see whether the following word was in sequence or out of sequence the last time the word was accessed. If it is out of sequence, a memory alongside the associative memory gives the address of the out-of-sequence word, and instruction fetching can begin at the out-of-sequence location. In this way, the prediction is, in effect, made before decoding an instruction as a branch and even before decomposing the instruction word into separate instructions. The accuracy of this strategy (75%)[7] is lower than many of the strategies given here, partly because the default prediction is effectively that the branch will not be taken. The prediction, however, can be made earlier in the instruction-fetching sequence, and can therefore lead to a smoother stream of prefetched instructions.

Another possibility for implementing a dynamic strategy when the system contains cache memory is to store previous branch outcomes in the cache.[6, 8]

Strategy 5

- Maintain a bit for each instruction in the cache. If an instruction is a branch instruction, the bit is used to record if it was taken on its last execution. Branches are predicted to be decided as on their last execution; if a branch has not been executed, it is predicted to be taken (implemented by initializing the bit cache to taken when an instruction is first placed in cache).

Figure 6 shows the result of using strategy 5 when there is a 64-word instruction cache with 4 blocks of 16 words each; replacement in the cache is the LRU strategy. The results are close to strategy 2, as expected, because an instruction cache hit ratio is usually at least 90%.

There is also a strategy that is similar to strategy 5 except in its implementation.[8] A bit is maintained for each instruction in the cache, but the bit is not directly

used to make a branch prediction. First, a static prediction based on the operation code is made. Then, the prediction is exclusive ORed with the cache prediction bit. This changes the prediction if the bit is set. Whenever a wrong prediction is made, the cache prediction bit is complemented. In this way, branches are predicted as in strategy 5, but the prediction memory only needs to be updated when there is a wrong prediction. This is an advantage if there is a time penalty for updating the memory.

IMPROVED DYNAMIC STRATEGIES

Several dynamic strategies in the preceding section are quite accurate. In this section, they are refined to (1) use random access memory instead of associative memory and (2) deal with anomalous decisions more effectively.

In any of the strategies, there is always the possibility that a prediction may be incorrect, and there must be a mechanism for reversing a wrong prediction. This implies that there is room for error, and this fact can be used to replace associative memory with random access memory.

Instead of using the entire branch instruction's address for indexing into a table, it can be hashed down to a small number of bits. More than one branch instruction might hash to the same index, but at worst, an incorrect prediction would result, which could be compensated for.

The hashed address can be used to access a small random access memory that contains a bit indicating the outcome of the most recent branch instruction hashing to the same address. Hashing functions can be quite simple; for example, the low-order m bits of the address can be used, or the low-order m bits can be exclusive ORed with the next higher m bits. With these methods, branch instructions in the same vicinity will tend to hash to different indices.

Strategy 6

- Hash the branch instruction address to m bits and use this index to address a random access memory containing the outcome of the most recent branch instruction indexing the same location. Predict that the branch outcome will be the same.

Although it contributes negligibly to the results, the default prediction (when a location is accessed the first time) can be controlled by initializing the memory to all 0's or all 1's.

Figure 7 indicates the results of using strategy 6 for m equals 4 (a random access memory of 16 one-bit words). The exclusive OR hash was used. The results are similar to those of strategy 2.

A variation of strategy 6 can be used to deal with anomalous branch decisions more effectively. This variation uses random access memory words that contain a count rather than a single bit. Say the counts are initially 0 and the word length is n; the maximum count is $2^{n-1} - 1$, and the minimum count is -2^{n-1} (twos complement notation). When a branch instruction is taken, the memory word it indexes is incremented (up to the limit of $2^{n-1}) - 1$; when it is not taken, the memory word is decremented (down to the limit of -2^{n-1}).

When a branch instruction is to be predicted, its address is hashed, and the proper count is read out of random access memory. If the sign bit is 0 (a positive number or 0), the branch is predicted to be taken. If it is 1, the branch is predicted to be not taken. In this way, the histories of several of the more-recent branch executions determine a prediction rather than just that of the most recent branch execution. In the case of an anomalous branch decision, other preceding decisions tend to override the most recent anomalous decision, so only one incorrect prediction is made rather than two.

Strategy 7

Use strategy 6 with twos complement counts instead of a single bit. Predict that the branch will be taken if the sign bit of the accessed count is 0; predict that it will not be taken if the sign bit is 1. Increment the count when a branch is taken; decrement it when a branch is not taken.

Note that strategy 6 is actually a special case of strategy 7 with a count of one bit. Also, using a count tends to cause a "vote" when more than one branch instruction hashes to the same count.

Figure 8 summarizes the results of using strategy 7 with counts of 2 and 3 bits and with a hash index of 4 bits. The accuracy is quite good; in fact, it is usually as good as or better than any strategies looked at thus far. Also, a count of 2 bits often gives better accuracy than a count of one bit, but going to larger counters than 2 bits

does not necessarily give better results. This is partially attributed to the "inertia" that can be built up with a larger counter in which history in the too-distant past is used, or the history of an earlier branch instruction hashing to the same address influences predictions for a later branch instruction.

HIEARCHIAL PREDICTION

Generally, the farther an instruction is processed following a predicted branch, the greater the time penalty if the prediction is wrong. For example, if only instruction prefetches are based on a conditional branch prediction, the time penalty will probably be less than if instructions are not only prefetched but also preissued. That is, the time needed to redirect instruction prefetches is probably less than the "cleanup" time for instructions issued incorrectly.

Of course, the rewards are greater the farther an instruction is processed when the prediction turns out to be right. If a level of confidence can be attached to a branch prediction, then performance can be optimized by limiting the processing of an instruction based on the confidence that a branch prediction is correct.

Example

Assume that for CPU, if instruction prefetches are based on a branch prediction, an incorrect prediction leads to a 6 clock period (cp) delay to fetch the correct instructions. If the prediction is correct, but instructions are not issued before the outcome is known, there is a 3 cp delay to wait for the branch decision. If instructions are preissued anyway, and the prediction is correct, there is no delay at all, but if the prediction is incorrect, there is a total of a 12 cp delay.

Assume that overall, 70% of the branches can be predicted correctly. Half of the branches (Set A) can be predicted with 50% accuracy, and the other half (Set B) can be predicted with 90% accuracy. Further, assume that it is known at the time a prediction is made whether the branch instruction belongs to set A or set B.

The three possible strategies and their average delays are as follows:

1. Prefetch for all branches:
    (0.3 x 6 cp) + (0.7 x 3 cp) = 3.9 cp

2. Prefetch and preissue for all branches:

$(0.3 \times 12 \text{ cp}) + (0.7 \times 0 \text{ cp}) = 3.6 \text{ cp}$

3.   Prefetch for branches in set A; prefetch and
     preissue for branches in set B:
     $0.5 \times [(0.5 \times 3 \text{ cp}) + (0.5 \times 6 \text{ cp})] + 0.5 \times$
     $[(0.1 \times 12 \text{ cp}) + (0.9 \times 0 \text{ cp})] = 2.85 \text{ cp}$

The third strategy is best, because it risks the high 12
clock period penalty only when there is higher
confidence of being correct.

Strategy 7 provides a natural way of implementing such
a hierarchical prediction strategy. If a counter (of at least
2 bits) is at its maximum value when a prediction is to
be made, the last prediction must have been that the
branch would be taken, and it must have been correct.
A following similar prediction would then seem likely to
be correct. An analogous statement holds if a count is
at its minimum value.

Consequently, a prediction based on an extremal counter
value is a high-confidence prediction, and a prediction
based on any other counter value is a lower-confidence
prediction. Figure 9 summarizes the results of using
such an approach. A 16-word RAM is used with a
count of 3 bits.

In all cases studied, the predictions made at the counter
extremes were more accurate. The greatest variation in
accuracy was in the SORTST program in which 78.5%
of the predictions were made at the counter extremes
(-4, +3), and about 92% were correct. Of the 21.5% of
the predictions made away from the counter extremes,
only about 58% were accurate. The least variation was
in the ADVAN program in which the counters were
virtually always at their maximum values, and hierarchical
prediction would have been of no real value.

The counter method usually achieved what was
anticipated in making predictions with two confidence
levels. This method could be generalized if counter
ranges were broken into several intervals, a different
confidence level being attached to each.

CONCLUSIONS

This paper studied the accuracy of branch prediction
methods proposed elsewhere as well as new methods
proposed here. A summary of the strategies follows. In
the cases of strategies with several variations, only one
or two representatives are indicated. Figure 10 gives a
summary of the results.

Strategy 1:   Predict that all branches will be
                taken.

Strategy 1a: Predict that only certain branch
                operation codes will be taken.

Strategy 2:   Always predict that a branch will be
                decided as on its last execution.

Strategy 3:   Predict that only backward branches
                will be taken.

Strategy 4:   Maintain a table of the m most
                recent branches not taken. Predict
                that only branches found in table
                will be not taken.

Strategy 5:   Maintain a history bit in cache and
                predict according to the history bit in
                cache and predict according to the
                history bit (a 64-word instruction
                cache was used).

Strategy 6:   Hash the branch address to m bits
                and access a 2^m word RAM
                containing history bits, and predict
                according to the history bit.

Strategy 7:   Like Strategy 6, but use counters
                instead of a single history bit.

The dynamic methods tended to be more accurate. Of
the feasible strategies, strategy 7 was the most
accurate. It also had the advantage of using random
access memory rather than associative memory. For
attaching levels of confidence to predictions, strategy 7
was easily adapted and gave good results. At least for
the applications studied here, strategy 7 is probably the
best choice based on accuracy, cost, and flexibility.

REFERENCES

[1] D. W. Anderson et al. The IBM System/360 model 91:
Machine philosophy and instruction handling, *IBM Journal*
(Jan. 1967), 8-24.

[2] M. J. Flynn. Some computer organizations and their
effectiveness, *IEEE Transactions on Computers*, C-21 (Sept.
1972), 948-960.

[3] H. D. Shapiro. A comparison of various methods for detecting
and utilizing parallelism in a single instruction stream,
*Proceedings of the 1977 International Conference on Parallel
Processing* (Aug. 1977), 67-76.

[4]D. E. Knuth. *The Art of Computer Programming*, vol. 3—*Sorting and Searching* (Reading, Mass.: Addison–Wesley 1973), 84–95.

[5]J. C. Gibson. The Gibson mix (Report TR 00.2043), IBM Systems Development Division, 1970.

[6]L. J. Shustek. Analysis and performance of computer instruction sets (Report 205), Stanford Linear Accelerator Center, 1978.

[7]R. N. Ibbett. The MU5 instruction pipeline, *The Computer Journal*, 15 (Feb. 1972), 42–50.

[8]S1 Project Staff. Advanced digital computing technology base development for Navy applications: The S-1 project, Lawrence Livermore Laboratories (Technical report UCID 18038), 1978.

[9]I. Flores. Lookahead control in the IBM System 370 Model 165, *Computer*, 7 (Nov. 1974), 24–38.

[10]E. M. Riseman and C. C. Foster. The inhibition of potential parallelism by conditional jumps, *IEEE Transactions on Computers*, C-21 (Dec. 1972), 1405–1411.

Program	Prediction Accuracy
ADVAN	99.4
GIBSON	65.4
SCI2	96.2
SINCOS	80.2
SORTST	57.4
TBLLNK	61.5

Figure 1. Accuracy of Prediction (%) for Strategy 1

Program	Prediction Accuracy
ADVAN	98.9
GIBSON	97.9
SCI2	96.0
SINCOS	76.2
SORTST	81.7
TBLLNK	91.7

Figure 2. Accuracy of Prediction (%) for Strategy 2

PROGRAM	PREDICTED ACCURACY
ADVAN	99.4
GIBSON	98.5
SCI2	97.9
SINCOS	65.7
SORTST	82.5
TBLLNK	76.2

Figure 3. Accuracy of Prediction (%) for 1a on CY170 Kernels

PROGRAM	PREDICTION ACCURACY
GIBSON	81.9
SCI2	98.0
SINCOS	35.2
SORTST	82.5
TBLLNK	84.9

Figure 4. Accuracy of Prediction (%) for Strategy 3

PREDICTION ACCURACY

PROGRAM	Table Size			
	1	2	4	8
ADVAN	98.9	98.9	98.9	98.9
GIBSON	65.4	97.9	97.9	97.9
SCI2	96.1	96.1	96.0	96.0
SINCOS	76.2	76.2	76.2	76.2
SORTST	57.3	81.7	81.7	81.7
TBLLNK	61.5	61.5	91.7	91.7

Figure 5. Accuracy of Prediction (%) for Strategy 4

PROGRAM	PREDICTION ACCURACY CY170
ADVAN	98.9
GIBSON	97.0
SCI2	96.0
SINCOS	76.1
SORTST	81.7
TBLLNK	91.7

Figure 6. Accuracy of Prediction (%) for Strategy 5

PROGRAM	PREDICTION ACCURACY
ADVAN	98.9
GIBSON	97.9
SCI2	96.0
SINCOS	76.2
SORTST	81.7
TBLLNK	91.8

Figure 7. Accuracy of Prediction (%) for Strategy 6

	PREDICTION ACCURACY	
PROGRAM	2 BIT COUNTER	3 BIT COUNTER
ADVAN	99.4	99.4
GIBSON	97.9	97.3
SCI2	98.0	98.0
SINCOS	80.1	83.4
SORTST	84.7	81.7
TBLLNK	95.2	94.6

Figure 8. Accuracy of Prediction (%) for Strategy 7 for Counters of 2 and 3 Bits

PROGRAM	% Prediction Made At Extremes	% Correct at Extremes	% Correct Not At Extremes	% Correct Overall
ADVAN	99.3	99.4	87.8	99.4
GIBSON	91.3	98.3	86.8	97.3
SCI2	98.0	99.8	99.4	98.0
SINCOS	78.4	85.7	75.1	83.4
SORTST	78.5	92.1	57.7	84.7
TBLLNK	96.8	95.2	76.2	94.6

Figure 9. Accuracy of Hierarchical Prediction for Strategy 7 with 16-Word Memory and Counters of 3 Bits

STRATEGY

Kernel	1	1a	2	3	4		5	6	7
					1 entry	8 entries		16 wds	16 wds, 2 bits
ADVAN	99.4	99.4	98.9	99.2	98.9	98.9	98.9	98.9	99.4
GIBSON	65.4	98.5	97.9	81.9	65.4	97.9	97.0	97.9	97.9
SCI2	96.2	97.9	96.0	98.0	96.1	96.0	96.0	96.0	98.0
SINCOS	80.2	65.7	76.2	35.2	76.2	76.2	76.1	76.2	80.1
SORTST	57.4	82.5	81.7	82.5	57.3	81.7	81.7	81.7	84.7
TBLLNK	61.5	76.2	91.7	84.9	61.5	91.7	91.7	91.8	95.2

Figure 10. Summary of Results

Two-Level Adaptive Training Branch Prediction

Tse–Yu Yeh and Yale N. Patt
Department of Electrical Engineering and Computer Science
The University of Michigan
Ann Arbor, Michigan 48109-2122

Abstract

High-performance microarchitectures use, among other structures, deep pipelines to help speed up execution. The importance of a good branch predictor to the effectiveness of a deep pipeline in the presence of conditional branches is well-known. In fact, the literature contains proposals for a number of branch prediction schemes. Some are static in that they use opcode information and profiling statistics to make predictions. Others are dynamic in that they use run-time execution history to make predictions.

This paper proposes a new dynamic branch predictor, the Two-Level Adaptive Training scheme, which alters the branch prediction algorithm on the basis of information collected at run-time.

Several configurations of the Two-Level Adaptive Training Branch Predictor are introduced, simulated, and compared to simulations of other known static and dynamic branch prediction schemes. Two-Level Adaptive Training Branch Prediction achieves 97 percent accuracy on nine of the ten SPEC benchmarks, compared to less than 93 percent for other schemes. Since a prediction miss requires flushing of the speculative execution already in progress, the relevant metric is the miss rate. The miss rate is 3 percent for the Two-Level Adaptive Training scheme vs. 7 percent (best case) for the other schemes. This represents more than a 100 percent improvement in reducing the number of pipeline flushes required.

1   Introduction

Pipelining, at least as early as [18] and continuing to the present time [6], has been one of the most effective ways to improve performance on a single processor. On the other hand, branches impede machine performance due to pipeline stalls for unresolved branches. As pipelines get deeper or issuing bandwidth becomes greater, the negative effect of branches on performance increases.

Among different types of branches, conditional branches have to wait for the condition to be resolved and the target address to be calculated before the target instruction can be fetched. Unconditional branches have to wait for the target address to be calculated. In conventional computers, instruction issuing stalls until the target address is determined, resulting in pipeline bubbles. When the number of cycles taken to resolve a branch is large, the performance loss due to the pipeline stalls is considerable. There are two ways to reduce the loss: the first is to resolve the branch as early as possible to reduce the instruction fetch pipeline bubbles. The second is to provide fast fetching and decoding of the target instruction to reduce the execution pipeline bubbles. Branch prediction is a way to reduce the execution penalty due to branches by predicting, prefetching and initiating execution of the branch target before the branch is resolved.

Branch prediction schemes can be classified into static schemes and dynamic schemes depending on the information used to make predictions. Static branch prediction schemes can be as simple as predicting that all branches are not taken or predicting that all branches are taken. Predicting that all branches are taken can achieve approximately 68 percent prediction accuracy as reported by Lee and Smith [13]. In the dynamic instructions of the benchmarks used in this study, about 60 percent of conditional branches are taken. Static predictions can also be based on the opcode. Certain classes of branch instructions tend to branch more in one direction than the other. The branch direction can also be taken into consideration such as the Backward Taken and Forward Not Taken scheme [16] which is fairly effective in loop-bound programs, because it misses only once over all iterations of a loop. However, this scheme does not work well on programs with irregular branches. Profiling [12, 5] can also be used to predict the branch path by measuring the tendencies of the branches and presetting a static prediction bit in the opcode. However, program profiling has to be performed in advance with certain sample data sets which may have different branch tendencies than the data sets that occur at run-time.

Dynamic branch prediction takes advantage of the knowledge of branches' run-time behavior to make predictions. Lee and Smith proposed a structure they called a Branch Target Buffer [13] which uses 2-bit saturating up-down counters to collect history information which is then used to make predictions. The execution history dynamically changes the state of the branch's entry in the buffer. In their scheme, branch prediction is based on the state of the entry. The Branch Target Buffer design can also be simplified to record only the result of the last execution of the branch. Another dynamic scheme also proposed by Lee and Smith is the Static Training scheme [13] which uses the statistics collected from a pre-run of the program and a history pattern consisting of the last n run-time execution results of the branch to make a prediction. The major disadvantage of the Static Training scheme is that the program has to be run first to accumulate the statistics and the same statistics may not be applicable to different data sets.

There is serious performance degradation in deep-pipelined and/or superscalar machines caused by prediction misses due to the large amount of speculative work that has to be discarded [1, 8]. This is the motivation for proposing a new, higher-accuracy dynamic branch prediction scheme. The new scheme uses two levels of branch history information to make predictions. The first level is the history of the last n branches. The second is the branch behavior for the last s occurrences of that unique pattern of the last n branches. The history information is collected on the fly without executing the program beforehand, eliminating the major disadvantage of Static Training Prediction. The scheme proposed here is called Two-Level Adaptive Training Branch Prediction, because predictions are based not only on the record of the last n branches, but moreover on the record of the last s occurrences of the particular record of the last n branches.

Trace-driven simulations were used in this study. The Two-Level Adaptive Training branch prediction scheme as well as the other dynamic and static branch prediction schemes were simulated on the SPEC benchmark suite. By using Two-Level Adaptive Training Branch Prediction, the average prediction accuracy for the benchmarks reaches 97 percent, while most of the other schemes achieve under 93 percent. This represents more than 100 percent reduction in mispredictions by using the Two-Level Adaptive Training scheme. This reduction can lead directly to a large performance gain on a high-performance processor.

Section two gives an introduction to the proposed Two-Level Adaptive Training Branch Prediction scheme. Section three discusses the methodology used in this study and the simulated prediction models. Section four reports the simulation results of a wide selection of schemes including both the dynamic and the static branch predictors. Section five contains some concluding remarks.

2   Two-Level Adaptive Training Branch Prediction

The Two-Level Adaptive Training Branch Prediction scheme has the following characteristics:

- Branch prediction is based on the history of branches executed during the current execution of the program.

- Execution history pattern information is collected on the fly of the program execution by updating the pattern history information in the branch history pattern table of the predictor. Therefore, no pre-runs of the program are necessary.

2.1   Concept of Two-Level Adaptive Training Branch Prediction

The Two-Level Adaptive Training scheme has two major data structures, the branch history register (HR) and the branch history pattern table (PT), similar to those used in the Static Training scheme of Lee and Smith [13]. In Two-Level Adaptive Training, instead of accumulating statistics by profiling the programs, the execution history information on which branch predictions are based is collected by updating the contents of the history registers and the pattern history bits in the entries of the pattern table depending on the outcomes of the branches. The history register is a shift register which shifts in bits representing the branch results of the most recent history information. All the history registers are contained in a history register table (HRT). The pattern history bits represent the most recent branch results for the particular contents of the history register. Branch predictions are made by checking the pattern history bits in the pattern table entry indexed by the content of the history register for the particular branch that is being predicted.

Since the history register table is indexed by branch instruction addresses, the history register table is called

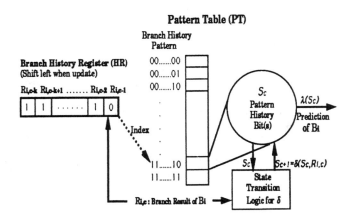

Figure 1: The structure of the Two-Level Adaptive Training scheme.

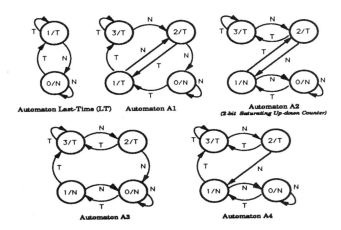

Figure 2: The state transition diagrams of the finite-state machines used for updating the pattern history in the pattern table entry.

a per-address history register table (PHRT). The pattern table is called a global pattern table, because all the history registers access the same pattern table.

The structure of Two-Level Adaptive Training Branch Prediction is shown in Figure 1. The prediction of a branch B_i is based on the history pattern of the last k outcomes of executing the branch; therefore, k bits are needed in the history register for each branch to keep track of the history. If the branch was taken, then a "1" is recorded; if not, a "0" is recorded. Since there are k bits in the history register, at most 2^k different patterns appear in the history register. In order to keep track of the history of the patterns, there are 2^k entries in the pattern table; each entry is indexed by one distinct history pattern.

When a conditional branch B_i is being predicted, the contents of its history register, HR_i, whose content is denoted as $R_{i,c-k}R_{i,c-k+1}......R_{i,c-1}$ for the last k outcomes of executing the branch, is used to address the pattern table. The pattern history bits S_c in the addressed entry $PT_{R_{i,c-k}R_{i,c-k+1}......R_{i,c-1}}$ in the pattern table are then used for predicting the branch. The prediction of the branch is

$$z_c = \lambda(S_c), \qquad (1)$$

where λ is the prediction decision function.

After the conditional branch is resolved, the outcome $R_{i,c}$ is shifted left into the history register HR_i in the least significant bit position and is also used to update the pattern history bits in the pattern table entry $PT_{R_{i,c-k}R_{i,c-k+1}......R_{i,c-1}}$. After being updated, the content of the history register becomes $R_{i,c-k+1}R_{i,c-k+2}......R_{i,c}$ and the state represented by the pattern history bits becomes S_{c+1}. The transition of the pattern history bits in the pattern table entry is done by the state transition function δ which takes

in the old pattern history bits and the outcome of the branch as inputs to generate the new pattern history bits. Therefore, the new pattern history bits S_{c+1} become

$$S_{c+1} = \delta(S_c, R_{i,c}) \qquad (2)$$

A straightforward combinational logic circuit is used to implement the function δ to update the pattern history bits in the entries of the pattern table. The transition function δ, pattern history bits S and the outcome R of the branch comprise a finite-state machine, which can be characterized by equations 1 and 2. Since the prediction is based on the pattern history bits, the finite-state machine is a Moore machine with the output z characterized by equation 1.

The state transition diagrams of the finite-state machines used in this study for updating the pattern history in the pattern table entry are shown in the Figure 2. The automaton *Last-Time* stores in the pattern history bit only the outcome of the last execution of the branch when the history pattern appeared. The next time the same history pattern appears the prediction will be what happened last time. Only one bit is needed to store the pattern history information. The automaton $A1$ records the results of the last two times the same history pattern appeared. Only when there is no taken branch recorded, the next execution of the branch when the history register has the same history pattern will be predicted as not taken; otherwise, the branch will be predicted as taken. The automaton $A2$ is a saturating up-down counter, which is also used, but differently, in Lee and Smith's Branch Target Buffer design [13]. The counter is incremented when the branch is taken and is decremented when the branch is not taken. The next execution of the branch will be predicted as taken when the counter value is greater than or equal to two; otherwise, the branch will be predicted as not taken. Automata $A3$ and $A4$ are both similar to $A2$.

Both Static Training and Two-Level Adaptive Training are dynamic branch predictors, because their predictions are based on run-time information, i.e. the dynamic branch history. The major difference between these two schemes is that the pattern history information in the pattern table changes dynamically in Two-Level Adaptive Training but is preset in Static Training from profiling. In Static Training, the input to the prediction decision function, λ, for a given branch history pattern is determined before execution. Therefore, the output of λ is determined before execution for a given branch history pattern. That is, the same branch predictions are made if the same history pattern appears at different times during execution. Two-Level Adaptive Training, on the other hand, updates the appropriate pattern history information with the actual result of each branch. As a result, given the same branch history pattern, different pattern history information can be found in the pattern table; therefore, there can be different inputs to the prediction decision function for Two-Level Adaptive Training. Predictions of Two-Level Adaptive Training change adaptively in accordance with the program execution behavior.

Since the pattern history bits change in Two-Level Adaptive Training, the predictor can adjust to the current branch execution behavior of the program to make proper predictions. With the updates, Two-Level Adaptive Training can still be highly accurate over many different programs and data sets. Static Training, on the contrary, may not predict well if changing data sets results in different execution behavior.

3 Implementation Methods

3.1 Implementations of the Per-address History Register Table

It is not feasible to have a big enough history register table for each static branch to have its own history register in real implementations. Therefore, two approaches are proposed for implementing the Per-address History Register Table.

The first approach is to implement the per-address register table as a set-associative cache. A fixed number of entries in the table are grouped together as a set. Within a set, the Least-Recently-Used (LRU) algorithm is used for replacement. The lower part of a branch address is used to index into the table and the higher part is used as a tag which is recorded in the entry allocated for the branch. The per-address history register table implemented in this way is called the Associative History Register Table (AHRT). When a

conditional branch is to be predicted, the branch's entry in the AHRT is located first. If the branch has an entry in the AHRT, the contents of the corresponding history register is used to address the pattern table. If the branch does not have an entry in the AHRT, a new entry is allocated for the branch. There is an extra cost for implementing the tag store in this approach.

The second approach is to implement the history register table as a hash table. The address of a conditional branch is used for hashing into the table. The per-address history table using this approach is called the Hash History Register Table (HHRT). Since collisions can occur when accessing a hash table, this implementation results in more interference in the execution history. As one would expect, the prediction accuracy for this approach is lower than what would be obtained with an AHRT, but the cost of the tag store is saved.

In this study, the above two practical approaches and the Ideal History Register Table (IHRT), in which there is a history register for each static conditional branch, were simulated for the Two-Level Adaptive Training Branch Predictor. The AHRT was simulated with two configurations: 512-entry 4-way set-associative and 256-entry 4-way set-associative. The HHRT was also simulated with 512 entries and 256 entries. The IHRT simulation data is provided to show how much accuracy is lost due to the history interference in the practical history register table designs.

3.2 Prediction Latency

The Two-Level Adaptive Training Branch Predictor needs two sequential table lookups to make a prediction. It is hard to squeeze the two lookups into one cycle, which is usually the requirement for a high-performance processor in determining the next instruction address. The solution to this problem is to perform the pattern table lookup with the updated history pattern of a branch at the time the history register is updated, produce a prediction from the pattern table, and store the prediction as a prediction bit in the history register table with the history register for the branch. Therefore, the next time the branch must be predicted, the prediction is available in the history register table, and the pattern table does not have to be accessed that cycle.

Another problem occurs when the prediction of a branch is required before the result of the previous execution of the branch has been confirmed. This case appears very often when a tight loop is being executed by a deep-pipelined superscalar machine, but not usually otherwise. Since this kind of branch has a high tendency to be taken, the branch is predicted taken and the machine does not have to stall until the previous branch result is confirmed.

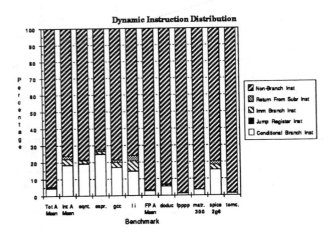

Figure 3: Distribution of dynamic instructions.

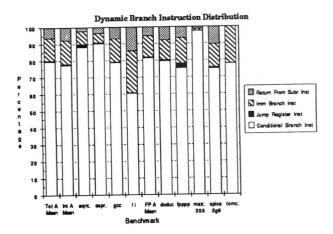

Figure 4: Distribution of dynamic branch instructions.

4   Methodology and Simulation Model

Trace-driven simulations were used in this study. A Motorola 88100 instruction level simulator (ISIM) is used for generating instruction traces. The instruction and address traces are fed into the branch prediction simulator which decodes instructions, predicts branches, and verifies the predictions with the branch results to collect statistics for branch prediction accuracy.

The branch instructions in the M88100 instruction set [4] are classified into four classes: conditional branches, subroutine return branches, immediate unconditional branches, and unconditional branches on registers. Instructions other than the branches are classified into the non-branch instruction class.

Conditional branches have to wait for condition codes in order to decide the branch targets. Subroutine return branches can be predicted by using a return address stack. A return address is pushed onto the stack when a subroutine is called and is popped as the prediction for the branch target address when a return instruction is detected. The return address prediction may miss when the return address stack overflows. For instruction sets without special instructions for returns from subroutines, the double stacks scheme proposed by Kaeli and Emma in [2] is able to perform the return address prediction. An immediate unconditional branch's target address is calculated by adding the offset in the instruction to the program counter; therefore, the target address can be generated immediately. Unconditional branches on registers have to wait for the register value which is the target address to become ready.

4.1   Description of Traces

Nine benchmarks from the SPEC benchmark suite are used in this branch prediction study. Five are float-

Benchmark Name	Number of Static Cnd. Br.	Benchmark Name	Number of Static Cnd. Br.
eqntott	277	espresso	556
gcc	6922	li	489
doduc	1149	fpppp	653
matrix300	213	spice2g6	606
tomcatv	370		

Table 1: The number of static conditional branches in each benchmark.

ing point benchmarks and four are integer benchmarks. The floating point benchmarks include *doduc*, *fpppp*, *matrix*300, *spice2g6* and *tomcatv* and the integer ones include *eqntott*, *espresso*, *gcc*, and *li*. *Nasa7* is not included because it takes too long to capture the branch behavior of all seven kernels. Among the five floating point benchmarks, *matrix*300 and *tomcatv* have repetitive loop execution; thus, a very high prediction accuracy is attainable. The integer benchmarks tend to have many conditional branches and irregular branch behavior. Therefore, it is on the integer benchmarks where the mettle of the branch predictor is tested.

Since this study focuses on the prediction for conditional branches, all benchmarks except fpppp and gcc were simulated for twenty million conditional branch instructions. The benchmarks *fpppp* and *gcc* finish execution before twenty millions conditional branches are executed. The number of dynamic instructions simulated for the benchmarks range from fifty million to 1.8 billion.

The dynamic instruction distribution is shown in Figure 3. About 24 percent of the dynamic instructions for the integer benchmarks and about 5 percent of the dynamic instructions for the floating point benchmarks are branch instructions.

The distribution of the dynamic branch instructions

| Model | HRT Implementation | | PT Implementation | |
Name	# of Entries	Entry Content	# of Entries	Entry Content
AT(AHRT(256,12SR), PT(2^{12},A2),)	256	12-bit SR	2^{12}	Atm A2
AT(AHRT(512,12SR), PT(2^{12},A2),)	512	12-bit SR	2^{12}	Atm A2
AT(AHRT(512,12SR), PT(2^{12},A3),)	512	12-bit SR	2^{12}	Atm A3
AT(AHRT(512,12SR), PT(2^{12},A4),)	512	12-bit SR	2^{12}	Atm A4
AT(AHRT(512,12SR), PT(2^{12},LT),)	512	12-bit SR	2^{12}	Atm LT
AT(AHRT(512,10SR), PT(2^{10},A2),)	512	10-bit SR	2^{10}	Atm A2
AT(AHRT(512,8SR), PT(2^8,A2),)	512	8-bit SR	2^8	Atm A2
AT(AHRT(512,6SR), PT(2^6,A2),)	512	6-bit SR	2^6	Atm A2
AT(HHRT(256,12SR), PT(2^{12},A2),)	256	12-bit SR	2^{12}	Atm A2
AT(HHRT(512,12SR), PT(2^{12},A2),)	512	12-bit SR	2^{12}	Atm A2
AT(IHRT(,12SR), PT(2^{12},A2),)	∞	12-bit SR	2^{12}	Atm A2
ST(AHRT(512,12SR), PT(2^{12},PB),Same)	512	12-bit SR	2^{12}	PB
ST(HHRT(512,12SR), PT(2^{12},PB),Same)	512	12-bit SR	2^{12}	PB
ST(IHRT(,12SR), PT(2^{12},PB),Same)	∞	12-bit SR	2^{12}	PB
ST(AHRT(512,12SR), PT(2^{12},PB),Diff)	512	12-bit SR	2^{12}	PB
ST(HHRT(512,12SR), PT(2^{12},PB),Diff)	512	12-bit SR	2^{12}	PB
ST(IHRT(,12SR), PT(2^{12},PB),Diff)	∞	12-bit SR	2^{12}	PB
LS(AHRT(512,A2),,)	512	Atm A2		
LS(AHRT(512,LT),,)	512	Atm LT		
LS(HHRT(512,A2),,)	512	Atm A2		
LS(HHRT(512,LT),,)	512	Atm LT		
LS(IHRT(,A2),,)	∞	Atm A2		
LS(IHRT(,LT),,)	∞	Atm LT		

AT – Two-Level Adaptive Training, ST – Static Training, LS – Lee and Smith's Branch Target Buffer Design, AHRT – Four-way Set-Associative History Register Table, HHRT – Hash History Register Table, IHRT – Ideal History Register Table, SR – Shift Register, Atm – Automaton, LT – Last-Time, PB – Preset Prediction Bit.

Table 2: Configurations of simulated branch predictors.

is shown in Figure 4. As can be seen from the distribution, about 80 percent of the dynamic branch instructions are conditional branches. The conditional branch is the branch class that should be studied to improve the prediction accuracy. The number of static conditional branches in the trace tapes of the benchmarks are listed in Table 1.

4.2   Simulation Model

Several configurations were simulated for the Two-Level Adaptive Training scheme. For the per-address history register table (PHRT), two practical implementations, the associative HRT (AHRT) and the hash HRT (HHRT), along with the ideal HRT (IHRT) were simulated. In order to distinguish the different schemes, the naming convention for the branch prediction schemes is *Scheme(History(Size, Entry_Content), Pattern(Size, Entry_Content), Data)*. *Scheme* specifies the scheme, for example, Two-Level Adaptive Training (AT), Static Training (ST), or Lee and Smith's

Branch Target Buffer design (LS). In *History(Size, Entry_Content)*, *History* is the implementation for keeping history information of branches, for example, IHRT, AHRT, or HHRT. *Size* specifies the number of entries in the implementation, and *Entry_Content* specifies the content in each entry. The content of an entry in the history register table can be any automaton shown in Figure 2 or a history register. In *Pattern(Size, Entry_Content)*, *Pattern* is the implementation for keeping history information for history patterns, *Size* specifies the number of entries in the implementation, and *Entry_Content* specifies the content in each entry. The content of an entry in the pattern history table can be any automaton shown in Figure 2. For Lee and Smith's Branch Target Buffer designs, the *Pattern* part is not included, because there is no pattern history information kept in their designs. *Data* specifies how the data sets are used. When *Data* is specified as *Same*, the same data set is used for both training and testing. When *Data* is specified as *Diff*, different data sets are used for training and testing. If *Data* is not specified, no training data set is needed for the shemes, as in Two-Level Adaptive Training schemes or Lee and Smith's Branch Target Buffer designs. The configuration and scheme of each simulation model in this study are listed in Table 2.

Since about 60 percent of branches are taken according to our simulation results, the contents of the history register usually should contain more 1's than 0's. Accordingly, all the bits in the history register of each entry in the HRT are initialized to 1's at the beginning of program execution. During execution, when an entry is re-allocated to a different static branch, the history register is not re-initialized.

The pattern history bits in the pattern table entries are also initialized at the beginning of execution. Since taken branches are more likely, for those pattern tables using automata, A1, A2, A3, and A4, all entries are initialized to state 3. For *Last-Time*, all entries are initialized to state 1 such that the branches at the beginning of execution will be more likely to be predicted taken.

In addition to the Two-Level Adaptive Training schemes, Lee and Smith's Static Training schemes and Branch Target Buffer designs, and some dynamic and static branch prediction schemes were simulated for comparison purposes. Lee and Smith's Static Training scheme is similar to the Two-Level Adaptive Training scheme with an IHRT but with the important difference that the prediction for a given pattern is pre-determined by profiling. The two practical approaches for the HRT were also simulated for Static Training with the same accessing method introduced above.

Lee and Smith's Branch Target Buffer designs were simulated with automata A2, A3, A4, and *Last-Time*. The static branch prediction schemes simulated include the Always Taken, Backward Taken and Forward Not taken, and a simple profiling scheme. The profiling scheme is done by counting the frequency of taken and not-taken for each static branch in the profiling execution. The predicted direction of a branch is the one the branch takes most frequently. Since the same data set was used for profiling and execution in this study, the prediction accuracy was calculated by taking the ratio of the sum of the larger number in the two numbers for two possible directions of every static branch over the total number of the dynamic conditional branch instructions.

5   Simulation Results

The simulation results presented in this section were run with the Two-Level Adaptive Training schemes, the Static Training Schemes, the Branch Target Buffer designs, and some static branch prediction schemes. Figures 5 through 10 show the prediction accuracy across the nine benchmarks. On the horizontal axis, the category labeled as "Tot G Mean" shows the geometric mean across all the benchmarks, "Int G Mean" shows the geometric mean across all integer benchmarks, and "FP G Mean" shows the geometric mean across all floating point benchmarks. The vertical axis shows the prediction accuracy scaled from 76 percent to 100 percent. This section concludes with a comparison between different branch prediction schemes.

5.1   Two-Level Adaptive Training

The Two-Level Adaptive Training schemes were simulated with different state transition automata, different HRT implementations, and different history register lengths to show their effects on prediction accuracy. The simulations of the Two-Level Adaptive Training scheme using an IHRT demonstrate the accuracy the scheme can achieve without history table miss effect and is used as a comparison to Lee and Smith's Static Training scheme which also uses the ideal history register table.

5.1.1   Effect of State Transition Automata

Figure 5 shows the efficiency of different state transition automata. Four state transition automata, $A2$, $A3$, $A4$, and *Last-Time* were simulated. $A1$ is not included, because early experiments indicated it was inferior to the other four-state automata, $A2$, $A3$, and $A4$. The scheme using *Last-Time* performs about 1 percent worse than the ones using the other automata which achieve similar accuracy around 97 percent. The four-state finite-state machines maintain more history information than the *Last-Time* which only records what happened last time; $A2$, $A3$, and $A4$ are therefore more tolerant to noise in the execution history.

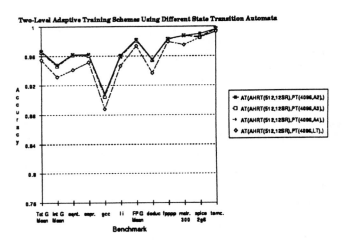

Figure 5: Two-Level Adaptive Training schemes using different state transition automata.

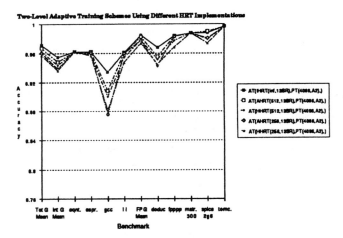

Figure 6: Two-Level Adaptive Training schemes using different history register table implementations.

In order to show the curves clearly in the following figures, each scheme is shown with the state transition automata $A2$ which usually performs the best among the state transition automata used in this study.

5.1.2   Effect of History Register Table Implementation

Figure 6 shows the effects of the HRT implementations on the prediction accuracy of the Two-Level Adaptive Training schemes. Every scheme in the graph was simulated with the same history register length. With the equivalent history register length, the IHRT scheme performs the best, the 512-entry AHRT scheme the second, the 512-entry HHRT scheme the third, the 256-entry AHRT scheme the fourth and the 256-entry HHRT scheme the worst, in the decreasing order of the HRT hit ratio. This is due to the increasing interference in the branch history as the hit ratio decreases.

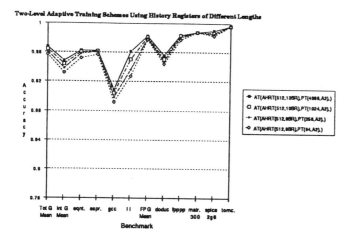

Figure 7: Two-Level Adaptive Training schemes using history registers of different lengths.

5.1.3 Effect of History Register Length

Figure 7 shows the effect of history register length on the prediction accuracy of Two-Level Adaptive Training schemes. The Two-Level Adaptive Training schemes using four different history register lengths were simulated. The accuracy increases for about 0.5 percent by lengthening the history registers for 2 bits. According to the simulation results, increasing the history register length often improves the prediction accuracy until the accuracy asymptote is reached.

5.2 Static Training

Static Training Branch Prediction examines the history pattern of the last n executions of a branch and the statistics gathered from profiling the program with a training data set to calculate the probabilities the branch will be taken or not-taken with the given history pattern to predict the branch path.

Although the accounting required to gather the the training statistics can be done in software, the Static Training scheme needs to keep track of the execution history of every static branch in the program, which requires hardware support. History registers must be used to keep track of the branch execution history of each static branch during run-time. When a branch is being predicted, its recorded history pattern is used to index the branch pattern table which contains preset branch prediction information. The preset prediction bit is then used for predicting the branch. Because the number of static branches varies from one program to another, the number of history registers required changes, which requires the hardware to offer a big enough table like IHRT to hold all the static branches in the programs. In order to consider the effects of practical implementations, in addition to the IHRT, the two practical HRT

Benchmark Name	Training Data Set	Testing Data Set
eqntott	NA	int_pri_3.eqn
espresso	cps	bca
gcc	cexp.i	dbxout.i
li	tower of hanoi	eight queens
doduc	tiny doducin	doducin
fpppp	NA	natoms
matrix300	NA	NA
spice2g6	short greycode.in	greycode.in
tomcatv	NA	NA

Table 3: Training and testing data sets of each benchmark.

implementations used in this study were simulated with the Static Training schemes. The cost to implement Static Training is not any less expensive than for Two-Level Adaptive Training, because the history register table and pattern table required by both schemes are similar. However, the state transition logic in the pattern table is simpler for the Static Training scheme.

In order to show the effects of the training data sets, the simulation results for the schemes (with *Same* in their names) which were trained and tested on the same data set and those for the schemes (with *Diff* in their names) which were trained and tested on different data sets are both presented. All the testing data sets are the same as those used by other schemes in order for a fair comparison. In the schemes which were trained and executed on the same data set, the results are the best the Static Training schemes can achieve with that data set, because the best predictions for branches are known beforehand.

Five of nine benchmarks were trained with other applicable data sets. The other four benchmarks, *eqntott*, *matrix*300, *fpppp*, and *tomcatv*, are excluded because there are no other applicable data sets or the applicable data sets are too similar to each other. The data sets used in training and testing are shown in Table 3.

The Static Training schemes with similar configurations to the Two-Level Adaptive Training schemes in Figure 6 are shown in Figure 8. The highest prediction accuracy of the schemes using the same data set for training and execution is about 97 percent. This is achieved by the Static Training scheme using 12 bit history registers and an IHRT. The accuracy is about the same as that achieved by the Two-Level Adaptive Training scheme using 12 bit history registers and an 512-entry 4-way AHRT. However, when different data sets are used for training and execution, the prediction accuracy for *gcc* and *espresso* is about 1 percent lower respectively. The drop in the accuracy for *li* is more significant. It is about 5 percent lower. For the floating point benchmarks, the degradations are not so apparent due to the regular branch behavior of the programs. The degradations are within 0.5 percent. Since the data

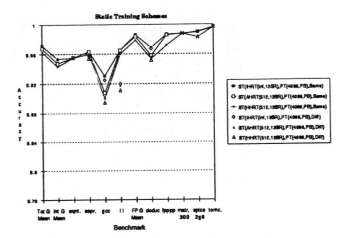

Figure 8: Prediction accuracy of Static Training schemes.

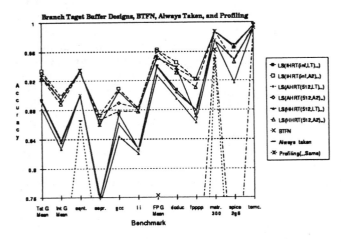

Figure 9: Prediction accuracy of Branch Target Buffer designs, BTFN, Always Taken, and the Profiling scheme.

for the Static Training Schemes using different data sets for training and testing is not complete, the average accuracy for the schemes is not graphed.

5.3   Other Schemes

Figure 9 shows the simulation results of Lee and Smith's Branch Target Buffer designs, Backward Taken and Forward Not taken (BTFN), Always Taken, and the profiling scheme. The Branch Target Buffer designs were simulated with automata, $A1$, $A2$, $A3$, $A4$, and $Last\text{-}Time$. Only the results of the designs using $A2$ and $Last\text{-}Time$ are shown in the figure, because the results of the designs using $A3$ and $A4$ are similar to those of the designs using $A2$. The designs using $A1$ predict about 2 to 3 percent lower than those using $A2$. Three buffer configurations, similar to IHRT, AHRT, and HHRT, were simulated. Using an IHRT in those schemes sets the upper

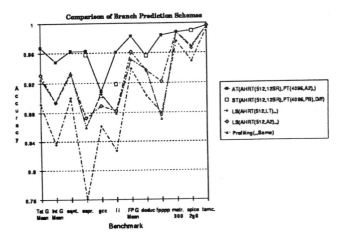

Figure 10: Comparison of branch prediction schemes

bound at 93 percent for the same schemes with practical HRT implementations. Using $Last\text{-}Time$ is about 4 percent lower than using $A2$.

BTFN and Always Taken predict poorly compared to the other schemes. Some of the data points fall below 76 percent.

The Backward Taken and Forward Not taken scheme (BTFN) is effective for the loop-bound benchmarks like matrix300 and tomcatv but not for other benchmarks. For the loop-bound benchmarks, the prediction accuracy is as high as 98 percent. However, for the other benchmarks, its accuracy is often lower than 70 percent. The average accuracy is approximate 69 percent.

The accuracy of the Always Taken scheme changes quite markedly from one benchmark to another. Its average is about 60 percent.

The simple profiling scheme simulated here is to run the program once to accumulate the statistics of how many times the branch is taken and how many times the branch is not taken for each branch. The prediction bit in the opcode of the branch is set or cleared depending on whether the taken branch count is larger than the not-taken branch count or not. The run-time prediction of the branch is made according to the prediction bit. The average of this scheme is about 92.5 percent. This scheme is fairly simple but at the cost of profiling and low prediction accuracy.

5.4   Comparison of Schemes

Figure 10 illustrates the comparison between the schemes mentioned above. The 512-entry 4-way AHRT was chosen for all the uses of HRT, because it is simple enough to be implemented. Two-Level Adaptive and Static training schemes are chosen on the basis of similar costs. At the top is the Two-Level Adaptive Training scheme whose average prediction accuracy is about 97 percent. As can be seen from the graph, the

Static Training scheme predicts about 1 to 5 percent lower than the top curve. The profiling scheme predicts almost as well as Lee and Smith's Branch Target Buffer design with accuracy around 92.5 percent. The scheme which predicts a branch with the last result of the execution of the branch achieves about 89 percent accuracy.

6 Concluding Remarks

This paper proposes a new branch predictor, Two-Level Adaptive Training. The scheme predicts a branch by examining the history of the last n branches and the branch behavior for the last s occurrences of that unique pattern of the last n branches.

The Two-Level Adaptive Training schemes were simulated with three HRT configurations: the IHRT which is an ideal history register table large enough to hold all static branches, the AHRT which is a set-associative cache, and the HHRT which is a hash table. The IHRT data was included to obtain upper bounds for each of the other schemes. A scheme using an AHRT usually has higher prediction accuracy than the same scheme using an HHRT of the same size, because the AHRT has lower miss rate than the HHRT.

Each Two-Level Adaptive Training scheme was simulated with various history register lengths. As seen from the simulation results, prediction accuracy is usually improved by lengthening the history register.

In addition to the Two-Level Adaptive Training scheme, several other dynamic or static branch prediction schemes such as Lee and Smith's Static Training schemes, Branch Target Buffer designs, Always Taken, Backward Taken and Forward Not taken, and a simple profiling scheme were simulated.

The Two-Level Adaptive Training scheme has been shown to have an average prediction accuracy of 97 percent on nine benchmarks from the SPEC benchmark suite. The prediction accuracy is about 4 percent better than most of the other static or dynamic branch prediction schemes, which means more than a 100 percent reduction in the number of pipeline flushes required. Since a prediction miss causes flushing of the speculative execution already in progress, the performance improvement on a high-performance processor can be considerable by using the Two-Level Adaptive Training scheme.

Deep-pipelining and superscalar execution are effective methods for exploiting instruction level parallelism to improve single processor performance. This effectiveness, however, depends critically on the accuracy of a good branch predictor. Two-Level Adaptive Training Branch Prediction is proposed as a way to support high performance processors by minimizing the penalty associated with mispredicted branches.

References

[1] M. Butler, T-Y Yeh, Y.N. Patt, M. Alsup, H. Scales, and M. Shebanow, "Instruction Level Parallelism is Greater Than Two", *Proceedings of the 18th International Symposium on Computer Architecture*, (May. 1991), pp. 276–286.

[2] D. R. Kaeli and P. G. Emma, "Branch History Table Prediction of Moving Target Branches Due to Subroutine Returns", *Proceedings of the 18th International Symposium on Computer Architecture*, (May 1991), pp. 34–42.

[3] Tse–Yu Yeh, "Two-Level Adaptive Training Branch Prediction", Technical Report, University of Michigan, (1991).

[4] Motorola Inc., "M88100 User's Manual", *Phoenix, Arizona*, (March 13, 1989).

[5] W.W. Hwu, T.M.Conte, and P.P.Chang, "Comparing Software and Hardware Schemes for Reducing the Cost of Branches", *Proceedings of the 16th International Symposium on Computer Architecture*, (May 1989).

[6] N.P. Jouppi and D. Wall, "Available Instruction-Level Parallelism for Superscalar and Superpipelined Machines.", *Proceedings of the Third International Conference on Architectural Support for Programming Languages and Operating Systems*, (April 1989), pp. 272-282.

[7] D. J. Lilja, "Reducing the Branch Penalty in Pipelined Processors ", *IEEE Computer*, (July 1988), pp.47-55.

[8] W.W. Hwu and Y.N. Patt, "Checkpoint Repair for Out-of-order Execution Machines", *IEEE Transactions on Computers*, (December 1987), pp.1496-1514.

[9] P. G. Emma and E. S. Davidson, "Characterization of Branch and Data Dependencies in Programs for Evaluating Pipeline Performance", *IEEE Transactions on Computers*, (July 1987), pp.859-876.

[10] J. A. DeRosa and H. M. Levy, "An Evaluation of Branch Architectures ", *Proceedings of the 14th International Symposium on Computer Architecture*, (June 1987), pp.10-16.

[11] D.R. Ditzel and H.R. McLellan, "Branch Folding in the CRISP Microprocessor: Reducing Branch Delay to Zero", *Proceedings of the 14th International Symposium on Computer Architecture*, (June 1987), pp.2-9.

HPS, A NEW MICROARCHITECTURE: RATIONALE AND INTRODUCTION

Yale N. Patt, Wen-mei Hwu, and Michael Shebanow

Computer Science Division
University of California, Berkeley
Berkeley, CA 94720

ABSTRACT

HPS (High Performance Substrate) is a new microarchitecture targeted for implementing very high performance computing engines. Our model of execution is a restriction on fine granularity data flow. This paper introduces the model, provides the rationale for its selection, and describes the data path and flow of instructions through the microengine.

1. Introduction

A computer system is a multilevel structure, algorithms at the top, gates and wires at the bottom. To achieve high performance, one must optimize at all levels of this structure. At most levels, the conventional wisdom suggests exploiting concurrency. Several proposals have been put forward as to how to do this. We also argue for exploiting concurrency, focusing in particular on the microarchitecture level.

1.1. Restricted Data Flow.

We are calling our engine HPS, which stands for High Performance Substrate, to reflect the notion that what we are proposing should be useful for implementing very dissimilar ISP architectures. Our model of the microengine (i.e., a restriction on classical fine granularity data flow) is not unlike that of Dennis [3], Arvind [2], and others, but with some very important differences. These differences will be discussed n detail in section 3.

For the moment, it is important to understand that unlike classical data flow machines, only a small subset of the entire program is in the HPS microengine at any one time. We define the "active window" as the set of ISP instructions whose corresponding data flow nodes are currently part of the data flow graph which is resident in the microengine. As the active window moves through the dynamic instruction stream, HPS executes the entire program.

1.2. Potential Limitations of Other Approaches.

We believe that an essential ingredient of high performance computing is the effective utilization of a lot of concurrency. Thus we see a potential limitation in microengines that are limited to one operation per cycle. Similarly, we see a potential limitation in a microengine that underutilizes its bandwidth to either instruction memory or data memory. Finally, although we appreciate the advantages of static scheduling, we see a potential limitation in a microengine that purports to execute a substantial number of operations each cycle, but must rely on a non-run-time scheduler for determining what to do next.

1.3. Outline of this paper.

This paper is organized in four sections. Section 2 delineates the fundamental reasons which led us to this new microarchitecture. Section 3 describes the basic operation of HPS. Section 4 offers some concluding remarks, and describes where our research in HPS is heading.

2. Rationale.

2.1. The Three Tier Model.

We believe that irregular parallelism in a program exists both locally and globally. Our mechanism exploits the local parallelism, but disregards global parallelism. Our belief is that the execution of an algorithm should be handled in three tiers. At the top, where global parallelism can best be identified, the execution model should utilize large granularity data flow, much like the proposal of the CEDAR project [4]. In the middle, where forty years of collected experience in computer processing can be exploited probably without harm, classical sequential control flow should be the model. At the bottom, where we want to exploit local parallelism, fine granularity data flow is recommended. Our three tier model reflects our conception that the top level should be algorithm oriented, the middle level sequential control flow ISP architecture oriented, and the bottom level microengine oriented.

2.2. Local Parallelism.

We feel obliged to re-emphasize the importance of local parallelism to our choice of execution model. Indeed, we chose this restricted form of data flow specifically because our studies have shown that the parallelism available from the middle control flow tier (i.e., the sequential control flow architecture) is highly localized. We argue that, by restricting the active instruction window, we can exploit almost all of the inherent parallelism in the program while incurring very little of the synchronization costs which would be needed to keep the entire program around as a total data flow graph.

2.3. Stalls, Bandwidth, and Concurrency.

We believe that a high performance computing engine should exhibit a number of characteristics. First, all its components must be kept busy. There must be few stalls, both in the flow of information (i.e., the path to memory, loading of registers, etc.) and in the processing of information (i.e., the functional units). Second, there must be a high degree of concurrency available, such as multiple paths to memory, multiple processing elements, and some form of pipelining, for example.

In our view, the restricted data flow model, with its out-of-order execution capability, best enables the above two requirements, as follows: The center of our model is the set of node tables, where operations await their operands. Instruction memory feeds the microengine at a constant rate with few stalls. Data memory and I/O supply and extract data at constant rates with few stalls. Functional units are kept busy by nodes that can fire. Somewhere in this system, there has to be "slack." The slack is in the nodes waiting in the node tables. Since nodes can execute out-of-order, there is no blocking due to unavailable data. Decoded instructions add nodes to the node tables and executed nodes remove them. The node tables tend to grow in the presence of data dependencies, and shrink as these dependencies become fewer. Meanwhile, our preliminary measurements support, the multiple components of the microengine are kept busy.

3. The HPS Model of Execution.

3.1. Overview.

An abstract view of HPS is shown in figure 1. Instructions are fetched and decoded from a dynamic instruction stream, shown at the top of the figure. The figure implies that the instruction stream is taken from a sequential control flow ISP architecture. We need to emphasize that this is not a necessary part of the HPS specification. Indeed, we are investigating having HPS directly process multinode words (i.e., the nodes of a directed graph) which would be produced as the target code of a (for example) C compiler. What is necessary is that, for each instruction, the output of the decoder which is presented to the Merger for handling by HPS is a data flow graph.

A very important part of the specification of HPS is the notion of the active instruction window. Unlike classical data flow machines, it is not the case that the

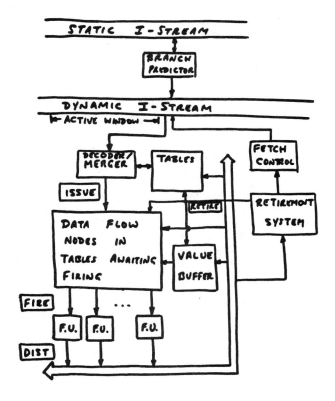

FIGURE 1.

data flow graph for the entire program is in the machine at one time. We define the active window as the set of ISP instructions whose corresponding data flow nodes are currently being worked on in the data flow microengine.

As the instruction window moves through the dynamic instruction stream, HPS executes the entire instruction stream. Parallelism which exists within the window is fully exploited by the microengine. This parallelism is limited in scope; ergo, the term "restricted data flow."

The Merger takes the data flow graph corresponding to each ISP instruction and, using a generalized Tomasulo algorithm to resolve any existing data dependencies, merges it into the entire data flow graph for the active window. Each node of the data flow graph is shipped to one of the node tables where it remains until it is ready to fire.

When all operands for a data flow node are ready, the data flow node fires by transmitting the node to the appropriate functional unit. The functional unit (an ALU, memory, or I/O device) executes the node and distributes the result, if any, to those locations where it is needed for subsequent processing: the node tables, the Merger (for resolving subsequent dependencies) and the Fetch Control Unit (for bringing new instructions into the active window). When all the data flow nodes for a particular instruction have been executed, the instruction is said to have executed. An instruction is retired from the active window when it has executed and all the instructions before it have retired. All side effects to memory are taken care of when an instruction retires from the active window. This is essential for the correct handling of precise interrupts [1].

The instruction fetching and decoding units maintain the degree of parallelism in the node tables by bringing new instructions into the active window, which results in new data flow nodes being merged into the data flow node tables.

3.2. Instruction Flow

Figure 2 shows the global data path of HPS. Instructions enter the data path as input to the Merger. This input is in the form of a data flow graph, one per instruction. The data flow graph can be the result of decoding an instruction in a classical sequential instruction stream, or it can be the output of a non-conventional compiler. In either case, the Merger sees a set of data flow nodes (and data dependencies), one for each operation that must be performed in the execution of that instruction. Operations are, for example, reads, writes, address computations and ALU functions. In the example of figure 3, the data flow graph corresponding to the VAX instruction ADDL3 #1000,A,B consists of three nodes: a memory read, memory write, and an ALU operation. Figure 3 also shows the structure of the three nodes and the five value buffer entries required for the instruction.

The Merger, using the Register Alias Table to resolve data dependencies not explicit in the individual instruction, forms the set of data flow nodes which are necessary to execute the instruction. Nodes are then transmitted to the appropriate node tables. Node tables, as we shall see, are content addressible memories, and thus should be kept small. The size of each node table is a function of the size of the active window and the decoding rate of the Von Neumann instruction stream. In our experiments with the VAX architecture, for example, an active window of 16 instructions, coupled with a decoding rate of eight nodes per cycle, required at most a 35 entry node table.

For each node, a slot is reserved in the global multi-port value buffer for storing the result of the operation of that node. The index of each slot is designated as a tag for the corresponding node, and is carried along with the node until it completes its execution. Value buffer slots are assigned in a circular queue, the size of the buffer being large enough to guarrantee retirement of an instruction before its value buffer slot is again needed. (In the case of our simulated implementation of the VAX architecture, an active window of 16 instructions, having approximately four nodes per instruction, means that a value buffer of 128 entries is more than adequate.)

A node remains in its node table until all of its operands are available, at which point it is ready to fire (i.e., it is executable). A node is fired by transmitting its operator, tag, and set of operands to one of the functional units associated with that node table. When execution completes, the result and its tag are distributed to each port of the value buffer. In the case of a result destined for a general purpose register, the corresponding tag is also transmitted to the Register Alias Table to update information stored there. The corresponding tag is also transmitted to the node tables for the purpose of setting the ready bits in those nodes awaiting this result.

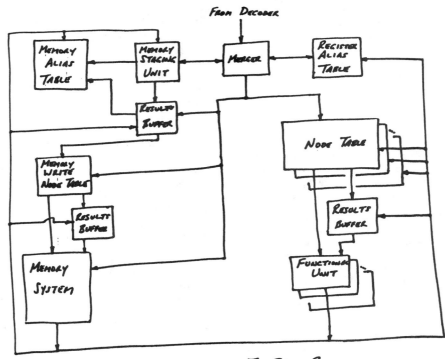

FIGURE 2. THE DATA PATH

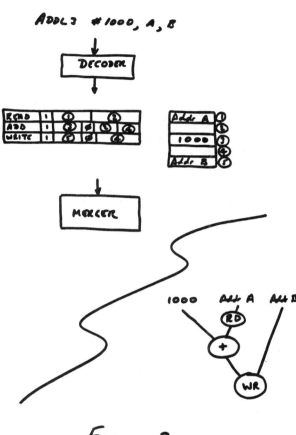

An Example From The VAX :

ADDL3 #1000, A, B

FIGURE 3.

Memory read and write nodes present additional complications. Although these will be discussed in greater detail in [7], a few observations here are in order. First is the fact that at the time memory access nodes are issued by the Merger (depending of course on the addressing structure of the target architecture), the address of the memory access may be unknown, and the addresses of other memory accesses which could block the node being issued may also be unknown. A Memory Alias Table and a Read Staging Unit are provided to handle these problems. Second is the fact that writes can occur out of order coupled with our requirement that exception handling must allow the machine state to be recovered "precisely." A Write Buffer and an algorithm for retiring instructions are provided for handling this problem.

One final observation about the processing of nodes must be made. The stages that a node goes through (i.e., merging, waiting for operands, firing, executing, and distributing its results) is independent of the other nodes in the node tables. That is, for example, the number of nodes firable in a given cycle is limited by the ability to detect that multiple nodes are firable and the number of functional units available for concurrent processing of

nodes. The number of results that can be distributed in a single cycle is a function of the bus structure and the organization of the node tables. The intent is that in each cycle, multiple nodes will be in each stage of the process.

3.3. Data Dependencies and their Resolution.

Fundamental to the correct, fast, out-of-order execution of operations in HPS is the handling of data dependencies and, as we will see, the absence of blocking in those cases where blocking is unnecessary. Since our locally concurrent implementation model has to conform to the target architecture, the local concurrency exploited must not cause incorrect execution results.

3.3.1. Data, Anti, and Output Dependencies.

A micro-operation B depends on another micro-operation A if B has to be executed after A in order to produce the correct result. There are three ways in which a micro-operation can depend on another micro-operation through register usage: data, anti, and output dependencies.

A data (read-after-write) dependency occurs when A is going to write to the register from which B is going to read. In this case, A supplies information essential to the execution of B. An anti (write-after-read) dependency occurs when A is going to read from the register to which B is going to write. An output (write-after-write) dependency occurs when A and B are going to write to the same register.

In the last two cases, the execution of A does not supply any information necessary for the execution of B. The only reason B depends on A is that a register has been allocated to two different temporary variables due to a shortage of registers. In fact, if we had an unlimited number of registers, different temporary variables would never have to be allocated to the same register and the second and the third dependencies would never occur. So, a proper renaming mechanism and extra buffer registers would remove anti and data dependencies. Then, the only type of dependency that could delay micro-operation execution would be a data dependency. In other words, a micro-operation could be executed as soon as its input operands are properly generated. This is exactly the description of a data flow execution model.

3.3.2. Our Modified Tomasulo Algorithm.

Our algorithm for enforcing data dependencies and removing anti and output dependencies is similar to the Tomasulo algorithm which was used in the Floating Point Unit of the IBM 360/91 [6]. During execution, the algorithm manages two major data structures: a register alias table and a set of node tables. Each entry in the register alias table keeps track of the dynamic information for a register necessary either to supply an input operand value or to establish dependency arcs. There are two fields in each register alias table entry. The first is a *ready* bit. This bit, if cleared, indicates that there is an active micro-operation which is going to supply the register value. The second field is the *tag* field which provides an index into a result buffer. This indicates where the register value can be found if the ready bit is set.

Each entry in a node table corresponds to a micro-operation and has an *operation* field, a *result tag* field, and two operand records. The *operation* field specifies the action that will be performed on the input operands. The *result tag* field provides the location in the result buffer that the result value will be shipped to after the execution of the micro-operation. Each operand record consists of two fields. The first is a *ready* bit. This bit is set when the input operand has been properly produced. The second field is the *tag* field which contains an index into the operand buffer. This indicates where the operand can be found if the ready bit is set.

A data path designed for our modified Tomasulo algorithm is presented in figure 2. There are two phases in each machine cycle: merging/scheduling and distribution. Initially all register alias table entries are ready and the initial register values are in result buffer entries whose index is in the *tag* fields of the corresponding register alias table entries.

Merging/Scheduling

A new micro-operation is assigned an entry in a node table and is given a unique *result tag* . First, the contents of both fields in the register alias table for each input operand are copied to the corresponding fields in the operand records of the new node table entry. Second, the *ready* bit of the register to be written by the micro-operation is reset and the *result tag* for the micro-operation is written into the *tag* field of the alias table entry. If both operands of a node are marked ready, this node can fire. The tags in the operand records are used to index into the result buffer and obtain the operand values. The *operation* and the operand values are sent to the function unit for execution. The *result tag,* which will be used to distribute the result, is also sent to the function unit.

Distribution

When a function unit finishes executing a micro-operation, the *result tag* of that micro-operation is used to select a result buffer entry and the result value is stored into the entry. The result tag is also distributed to the register alias table and the node table. Both the register alias table and the node table are content addressable memories. Entries in these tables are addressed by the value of the result tag. All of the register alias table entries and all of the operand records in the node table entries set their ready bit if the distributed *result tag* matches their *tag* field contents.

After execution, all the register alias table entries are ready and the corresponding register values are in the result buffer entries whose indices are in the *tag* fields.

The algorithm described above is a win on at least two counts. First, it removes anti and output dependencies without producing incorrect results. In fact, it can be shown that reservation schemes without renaming can not remove anti and output dependencies without producing incorrect results. Second, unlike Scoreboarding (for example), the issuing process never has to stall due to dependencies. It can also be shown that any reservation scheme without renaming will have to stall for some dependencies.

4. Concluding Remarks.

The purpose of this paper has been to introduce the HPS microarchitecture. Current research at Berkeley is taking HPS along four tracks. First, we are attempting to design, at high performance, three very dissimilar architectures: the microVAX, a C machine, and a Prolog processor. Equally important, we are investigating the limits of this microarchitecture, both from the standpoint of a minimal implementation and from the standpoint of a cadillac version.

As is to be expected, there are issues to be resolved before an effective HPS implementation can be achieved. For example, if HPS is to implement a sequential control based ISP architecture, then there are decoding issues, including the question of a node cache, which need to be decided. Second, HPS requires a data path that (1) has high bandwidth and (2) allows the processing of very irregular parallel data. Third, HPS needs a scheduler which can determine, in real-time, which nodes are firable and which are not. Fourth, the out-of-order execution of nodes requires additional attention to the design of the memory system, the instruction retirement and repair mechanisms, and the I/O system. These issues are the subject of a companion paper [7] in these Proceedings.

Acknowledgement.

The authors wish to acknowledge first the Digital Equipment Corporation for supporting very generously our research in a number of positive ways: Linda Wright, formerly Head of Digital's Eastern Research Lab in Hudson Massachusetts for providing an environment during the summer of 1984 where our ideas could flourish; Bill Kania, formerly with Digital's Laboratory Data Products Group, for providing major capital equipment grants that have greatly supported our ability to do research; Digital's External Research Grants Program, also for providing major capital equipment to enhance our ability to do research; and Fernando Colon Osorio, head of Advanced Development with Digital's High Performance Systems/Clusters Group, for providing funding of part of this work and first-rate technical interaction with his group on the tough problems. We also acknowledge the other members of the HPS group, Steve Melvin, Chien Chen, and Jia-juin Wei for their contributions to the HPS model as well as to this paper. Finally, we wish to acknowledge our colleagues in the Aquarius Research Group at Berkeley, Al Despain, presiding, for the stimulating interaction which characterizes our daily activity at Berkeley.

5. References.

1. Anderson, D. W., Sparacio, F. J., Tomasulo, R. M., "The IBM System/360 Model 91: Machine Philosophy and Instruction - Handling," IBM Journal of Research and Development, Vol. 11, No. 1, 1967, pp. 8-24.

2. Arvind and Gostelow, K. P., "A New Interpreter for Dataflow and Its Implications for Computer Architecture," Department of Information and Computer Science, University of California, Irvine, Tech. Report 72, October 1975.

3. Dennis, J. B., and Misunas, D. P., "A Preliminary Architecture for a Basic Data Flow Processor," Proceedings of the Second International Symposium on Computer Architecture, 1975, pp 126-132.

4. Gajski, D., Kuck, D., Lawrie, D., Sameh, A., "CEDAR -- A Large Scale Multiprocessor," Computer Architecture News, March 1983.

5. Keller, R. M., "Look Ahead Processors," Computing Surveys, vol. 7, no. 4, Dec. 1975.

6. Tomasulo, R. M., "An Efficient Algorithm for Exploiting Multiple Arithmetic Units," IBM Journal of Research and Development, vol. 11, 1967, pp 25 - 33. Principles and Examples, McGraw-Hill, 1982.

7. Patt, Y.N., Melvin, S.W., Hwu, W., and Shebanow, M.C., "Critical Issues Regarding HPS, a High Performance Microarchitecture, Proceedings of the 18th International Microprogramming Workshop, Asilomar, CA, December, 1985.

INSTRUCTION ISSUE LOGIC FOR HIGH-PERFORMANCE, INTERRUPTABLE PIPELINED PROCESSORS

Gurindar S. Sohi and Sriram Vajapeyam

Computer Sciences Department
University of Wisconsin-Madison
1210 West Dayton Street
Madison, Wisconsin 53706

Abstract

The performance of pipelined processors is severely limited by data dependencies. In order to achieve high performance, a mechanism to alleviate the effects of data dependencies must exist. If a pipelined CPU with multiple functional units is to be used in the presence of a virtual memory hierarchy, a mechanism must also exist for determining the state of the machine precisely. In this paper, we combine the issues of dependency-resolution and preciseness of state. We present a design for instruction issue logic that resolves dependencies dynamically and, at the same time, guarantees a precise state of the machine, without a significant hardware overhead. Detailed simulation studies for the proposed mechanism, using the Lawrence Livermore loops as a benchmark, are presented.

1. INTRODUCTION

As the demand for processing power increases, computer system designers are forced to use techniques that result in high-performance processing units. A widely used technique is *pipelining* [1], in which the overall logic of the system is split into several stages with each stage performing a sub-task of a complete task. Considerable overlap can be achieved because each stage can perform a sub-task for a different task. Pipelined CPUs have two major impediments to their performance: i) *data dependencies* and ii) *branch instructions*. An instruction cannot begin execution until its operands are available. If an operand is the result of a previous instruction, the instruction must wait till the previous instruction has completed execution, thereby degrading performance. The performance degradation due to branch instructions is even more severe. Not only must a conditional branch instruction wait for its condition to be known (resulting in "bubbles" in the pipeline), an additional penalty is incurred in fetching an instruction from the taken branch path to the instruction decode and issue stage.

A major problem that arises in pipelined computer design is that an interrupt can be *imprecise* [2,3]. This problem is especially severe in multiple functional unit computers in which instructions can complete execution out of program order [2,4]. For a high-performance, pipelined CPU, an adequate solution must be found for the imprecise interrupt problem and means must be provided for overcoming the performance-degrading factors.

1.1. Background and Previous Work

The detrimental effects of branch instructions can be alleviated by using *delayed* branch instructions. However, the utility of delayed branch instructions is limited for long pipelines. In such cases, other means must exist to alleviate the detrimental effects. A common approach is to use *branch prediction* [5,6]. Using prediction techniques, the probable execution path of a branch instruction is determined. Instructions from the predicted path can then be fetched into instruction buffers or even executed in a *conditional mode*[2,7,8]. While the conditional mode of execution will result in a higher pipeline throughput, especially if the outcome of the branches is predicted correctly, a hardware mechanism must exist which will allow the machine to recover from an incorrect sequence of conditional instructions.

Both hardware and software solutions exist to the data dependency problem. Software solutions use code scheduling techniques (combined with a large set of registers) to increase the dependency distance and to provide interlocks [9]. Hardware solutions employ *waiting stations* or *reservation stations* where an instruction can wait for its operands and allow subsequent instructions to proceed [10].

In a pipelined machine, imprecise interrupts can be caused by instruction-generated traps such as arithmetic exceptions and page faults. An imprecise interrupt can leave the machine in an irrecoverable state. While the occurrence of arithmetic exceptions is rare, the occurrence of page faults in a machine that supports virtual memory is not. Therefore, if virtual memory is to be used with a pipelined CPU, it is crucial that interrupts be precise. Several hardware solutions to the problem are described in [3]. We are unaware of any software solutions to the imprecise interrupt problem for multiple functional unit computers. A software solution will be extremely difficult, if not impossible. Not only must the software allow for the worst-case execution time for any instruction, it must also keep track of instructions that have completed out of program order and generate the appropriate code sequence to undo the effects of those instructions. In either case, some hardware support must be provided to maintain run time information.

1.2. Outline of the Paper

In this paper, we treat the problems of dependency resolution and imprecise interrupts simultaneously. Since a hardware mechanism must exist for implementing precise interrupts, why not extend this mechanism to resolve dependencies and allow out-of-order instruction execution?

In section 2, we discuss Tomasulo's dependency-resolution algorithm and extend it, giving several variations, so that the cost of implementing it is not prohibitive even for a large number of registers. In section 3, we discuss the problem of imprecise interrupts and present solutions. Section 4 describes a unit that resolves dependencies as well as implements precise interrupts. The precise interrupt and dependency-resolution mechanisms mutually aid and simplify each other. A simulation analysis of the proposed mechanism using several Livermore loops as benchmarks is carried out in section 5. Finally, we discuss how our mechanism might be used to alleviate the degradation due to branch instructions.

Throughout the paper, we discuss incremental modifications to the basic principles. Data supporting our claims for such modifications have been omitted for reasons of conciseness. However, we do present detailed simulation data for our final design.

1.3. Model Architecture

The model architecture that we use for our studies is presented in Figure 1. It has the same capabilities and executes the same instruction set as the scalar unit of the CRAY-1 [4, 11]. However, there is a major difference. In our architecture, all instructions, whether they are composed of 1 parcel (16 bits) or 2 parcels (32 bits) can issue in a single cycle if issue conditions are favorable. Therefore, the best-case execution time of a conditional branch instruction is 4 clock cycles after the condition is known as opposed to 5 clock cycles for the CRAY-1 [11]. The CRAY-1 was chosen because it represents a state-of-the-art scalar unit and its execution can be modeled precisely. The authors also had easy access to tools that could be used to generate instruction traces for the CRAY-1 scalar unit [12]. The model machine, therefore, consists of several functional units connected to a common result bus. Only one function can output data onto the result bus in any clock cycle. Instructions are fetched by the *Instruction Fetch Unit* and decoded and issued by the *Decode and Issue Unit*. Once dependencies have been resolved in the decode and issue unit, instructions are forwarded to the functional units for execution. The results of the functional units are written directly into the register file. The register file consists of 8 A, 8 S, 64 B and 64 T registers.

2.   DEPENDENCY RESOLUTION: OUT-OF-ORDER INSTRUCTION EXECUTION

When an instruction reaches the decode and issue stage in the pipeline, checks must be made to determine if the operands for the instruction are available, i.e., if all dependencies for this instruction have been resolved. If an operand is not available, the instruction must wait. Consequently, subsequent instructions cannot proceed even though they may be ready to exe-

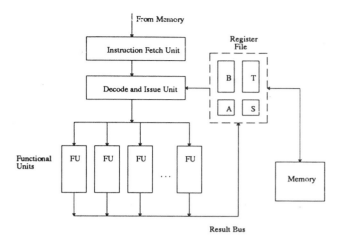

Figure 1. The Basic Architecture

cute. Subsequent instructions can proceed if the waiting instruction "steps aside," and allows other instructions to bypass it while it waits for its operands. Reservation stations permit an instruction to do this [10].

2.1. Tomasulo's Algorithm

Tomasulo's dependency-resolution algorithm was first presented for the floating-point unit of the IBM 360/91 [10]. An extension of this algorithm for the scalar unit of the CRAY-1 is presented in [13]. The algorithm operates as follows. An instruction whose operands are not available when it enters the decode and issue stage is forwarded to a *Reservation Station (RS)* associated with the functional unit that it will be using. It waits in the RS until its data dependencies have been resolved, i.e., its operands are available. Once at a reservation station, an instruction can resolve its dependencies by monitoring the Common Data Bus (the Result Bus in our model architecture). When all the operands for an instruction are available, it is dispatched to the appropriate functional unit for execution. The result bus can be reserved either when the instruction is dispatched to the functional unit[13] or soon before it is about the leave the functional unit [10].

Each source register is assigned a bit that determines if the register is busy. A register is busy if it is the destination of an instruction that is still in execution. A destination register is also called a *sink* register [10]. Each sink register is assigned a tag which identifies the result that must be written into the register. Since any register in the register file can be a sink, each register must be assigned a tag. Each reservation station has the following fields:

Source Operand 1			Source Operand 2			Destination
Ready	Tag	Contents	Ready	Tag	Contents	Register

If a source register is busy when the instruction reaches the issue stage, the tag for the source register is obtained and the instruction is forwarded to a reservation station. If the sink register is busy, the instruction fetches a new tag, updates the tag of the sink register and proceeds to a reservation station. The registers as well as the reservation stations monitor the result bus and update their contents when a matching tag is found. Memory is treated as a special functional unit. Details of the algorithm can be found in [10] and [13].

While this algorithm is straightforward and effective, it is expensive to implement because each register needs to be tagged and each tag needs associative comparison hardware to carry out the tag-matching process. This may not be practical if the number of *possible sink fields*, i.e., the number of registers is large. For our model architecture which has 8 A, 8 S, 64 B and 64 T registers, clearly the use of 144 tag-matching hardware units is impractical.

2.2. Extensions to Tomasulo's Algorithm

2.2.1. A Separate Tag Unit

On closer inspection we see that very few of all *possible* sink registers may actually be active, i.e., be waiting for a result at any given time. Therefore, if we associate a tag with *each possible* sink register, a lot of associative tag-matching hardware will be idle at any given time. Why not have a common tag pool and assign a tag only to a *currently active* sink register rather than associating a tag with each possible sink field? In Tomasulo's algorithm, a currently active register is one whose busy bit is on.

We consolidate the tags from all *currently active* registers into a *Tag Unit (TU)*. Each register now has only a single busy bit. At instruction issue time, if a source register is busy, the TU is queried for the current tag of the appropriate register and the tag is forwarded to the reservation stations. A new tag is obtained for the destination register of the instruction. If the destination register is not busy, acquiring such a tag from the TU is straightforward. If the destination register is busy, i.e., the TU already holds a tag for the register, a new tag is obtained and the instruction holding the old tag is informed that, while it may update the register, it may not *unlock* the register, i.e., clear the busy bit. Instruction issue blocks if no tag can be obtained, i.e., the TU is full.

As before, the instruction along with its associated tags/operands is forwarded to a reservation station where it waits for its operands to become ready. The result from a functional unit (along with its tag) is broadcast to all reservation stations and is also forwarded to the TU. Reservation stations monitor the result bus and gate in the result if the tag of the data on the result bus matches the tag stored in the reservation station. The TU forwards the result to the register specified in the appropriate slot of the TU. All registers are, therefore, updated only by the TU when their data is available and no direct connection is needed between the functional units and the register file. When the register has been updated by the TU, the corresponding tag is released and is marked free in the TU.

In order to ensure correct operation, i.e., only the latest tag for each register is used by all subsequent instructions and only the latest instruction updates the busy bit of the register,

we associate another bit with each TU entry. This bit indicates if the tag is the latest tag for the register and if the instruction has a *key* to *unlock* the register, i.e., clear the busy bit. The modified architecture that incorporates a Tag Unit and reservation stations associated with each functional unit is shown in Figure 2. The reservation stations are modified so that the result can be forwarded to the appropriate slot in the TU. The new reservation station has the following fields:

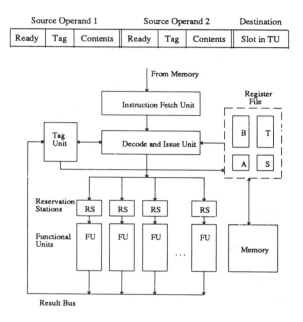

Figure 2. Issue Logic with a Tag Unit and Distributed Reservation Stations

2.2.1.1. Example

The operation of the Tag Unit is best illustrated by an example. Consider a TU that has 6 entries as shown in Figure 3. Each entry in the TU has a bit indicating if the tag is free, i.e., available for use by the issue logic, a bit indicating if the tag is the latest tag for the register and a field for the number of the destination register.

The TU is indexed by the tag number. Consider the execution of an instruction I_1 that adds the contents of registers S0 and S7 and put the result in S4. Assume that the state of the TU is as shown in Figure 3. When the issue logic decodes I_1, it attempts to get a *new* tag for the destination register S4 from the TU and obtains tag 3. Since the TU already has a tag for S4, the old tag (4) is updated to indicate that it no longer represents the latest copy of the register. Since S7's contents are valid, they can be read from the register file and forwarded to the reservation stations directly. However, since the contents of S0 are not valid, the latest tag for S0 (tag 2) must be obtained from the TU. The issue unit forwards a packet to the reservation station associated with the add functional unit. The packet contains the contents of S7, a tag (2) for S0 and a tag (3) for the destination register S4. When I_1 completes execution, i.e., leaves the add functional unit, the result is forwarded to all reservation stations that have a matching tag (3) and also to the TU. The TU forwards the result to the register

Tag Number	Register Number	Tag Free	Latest Copy
1	A0	N	Y
2	S0	N	Y
3	NIL	Y	Y
4	S4	N	Y
5	S0	N	N
6	S3	N	Y

Figure 3: A Tag Unit

file to be written into S4. Since tag 3 is the latest tag for S4, S4's busy bit can be reset when the data has been written into S4. Tag 3 is then marked free, i.e., is available for reuse by the issue logic.

2.2.2. Merging the Reservation Stations

If each functional unit has a separate set of reservation stations, it is likely that some functional unit will run out of reservation stations while the reservation stations associated with another functional unit are idle. As suggested in [13], we can combine all the reservation stations into a common *RS Pool* rather than having disjoint pools of reservation stations associated with each functional unit. All instructions that were previously issued to distributed reservation stations associated with the functional units now go to the common RS Pool. Instruction issue is blocked if no free reservation station is available, i.e., if the RS Pool is full. As instructions become ready in the RS Pool, they are issued to the functional units. All the other functions are as before.

An organization with merged reservation stations does have one disadvantage over distributed reservation stations - only one instruction can issue from the RS Pool to the functional units unless multiple paths are provided between the RS Pool and the functional units. On the other hand, a better use of the reservations stations results since the reservation stations can be shared amongst several functional units. We chose to provide only a single path from the RS Pool to the functional units because our simulations showed that multiple paths between the RS Pool and the functional units would not have a significant impact on performance. Rather than present detailed simulations to support our decision, we use an argument based on instruction flow to convince the reader. The RS Pool is essentially a reservoir of instructions that is filled by the decode and issue logic and drained by the functional units. Since the decode and issue logic can fill this reservoir at a maximum rate of 1 instruction per cycle, having a drain that is capable of draining more than 1 instruction per cycle will not be very useful in a steady state.

2.2.3. Merging the RS Pool with the Tag Unit

In the Tag Unit, there is one entry for every instruction that is present in either the RS Pool or in the functional units. Therefore, at any time, there is a one-to-one correspondence between the entries in the TU and the number of instructions in the reservation stations or the functional units. This suggests that we can combine the RS Pool and the Tag Unit into a single *RS Tag Unit (RSTU)*. In the RSTU, a reservation station is reserved at the same time that a tag is reserved. Of course, a

reservation station is wasted if it is associated with an instruction that is in a functional unit. However, as we shall see in section 4, this organization can easily be extended to allow for the implementation of precise interrupts. When an instruction issues, it obtains a tag from the RSTU and in doing so automatically reserves a reservation station. All the other functions are as before. Each entry in the RSTU is as follows:

Tag Number	Tag Free	Latest Copy	Source Operand 1		
Index	Yes/No	Yes/No	Ready	Tag	Contents

Source Operand 2			Destination
Ready	Tag	Contents	Register

3. IMPLEMENTATION OF PRECISE INTERRUPTS

Now we address the issue of precise interrupts. A complete description of several schemes that implement precise interrupts is given in [3]. The scheme of interest to us is the *reorder buffer*. The reorder buffer allows instructions to finish execution out of order but updates the state of the machine (registers, memory, etc.), i.e., *commits* the instructions in the order that the instructions were present in the program, thereby assuring that a precise state of the machine is recoverable at any time. By forcing an ordering of commitment amongst the instructions, the reorder buffer aggravates data dependencies - the value of a register cannot be read till it has been updated by the reorder buffer, even though the instruction that computed a value for the register may have completed already.

An alternative to a simple reorder buffer is to associate *bypass logic* with the reorder buffer. In such an organization, an instruction does not have to wait for the reorder buffer to update a source register; it can fetch the value from the reorder buffer (if it is available) and can issue. With a bypass mechanism, the issue rate of the machine is not degraded considerably if the size of the buffer is reasonably large [3]. However, a bypass mechanism is expensive to implement since it requires a search capability and additional data paths for each buffer entry.

4. MERGING DEPENDENCY RESOLUTION AND PRECISE INTERRUPTS

We note that the RSTU of section 2.2.3 can be modified to behave like a reorder buffer if it is forced to update the state of the machine in the order that the instructions are encountered. This is easily accomplished by managing the RSTU as a queue. Therefore, all that we have to do to implement precise interrupts in an architecture with a RSTU is to manage the RSTU like a queue. The modified logic is called the *Register Update Unit (RUU)*. The RUU is essentially the RSTU constrained to commit instructions in the order that the instructions were received by the decode and issue logic (and consequently by the RUU). The functional units remain unchanged. The modified architecture that uses a RUU to execute instructions out of program order and to ensure a precise state of the machine is given in Figure 4.

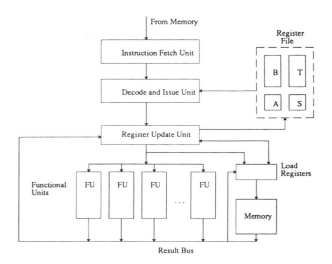

Figure 4. The Modified Architecture with a RUU

Note the absence of a direct path between the decode and issue logic and the functional units. In order to implement precise interrupts, every instruction must reserve an entry in the RUU. Since every instruction must pass through the RUU, no direct connection is needed between the decode and issue logic and the functional units. Also note that the CPU's interactions with the memory functional unit have been depicted in more detail. In the next few sections, we describe in some detail the operation of the modified architecture with a RUU.

4.1. Decode and Issue Unit

When an instruction is decoded, the issue logic requests an entry in the RUU. If no free entry is available, i.e., the RUU is full, instruction issue is blocked. If an entry is available, the issue logic obtains the position of the entry (an index into the RUU). It then forwards the contents of the source registers (if they are available) or a register identifier (the register number appended with some extra control bits to be used as a tag) to the selected reservation station in the RUU. Control bits for the destination register (a complete description of which follows in section 4.2.2) in the register file are updated and the identifier for the destination register forwarded to the RUU.

4.2. The Register Update Unit

The RUU is the unit that (i) determines which instruction should be issued to the functional units for execution, reserves the result bus and dispatches the instruction to the functional unit, (ii) determines which instruction can commit, i.e., update the state of the machine, (iii) monitors the result bus to resolve dependencies and (iv) provides tags to and accepts new instructions from the decode and issue logic. The RUU is managed like a queue using RUU_Head and RUU_Tail pointers. RUU slots that do not lie between RUU_Head and RUU_Tail are free. If RUU_Head = RUU_Tail, the RUU is full and cannot accept any more instructions from the decode and issue logic. In designing the RUU, we keep in mind that (i) it should not involve a large amount of comparison hardware and (ii) it should not affect the clock speed to an

intolerable extent. In the next few sections, we describe the components of the RUU in some more detail.

4.2.1. Source Operand Fields

The design of the source operand fields is straightforward. Each source operand field has a ready bit, a tag sub-field and a content sub-field as below:

Source Operand

Ready	Tag	Contents

If the operand is not ready, the tag sub-field monitors the result bus for a matching tag. If a match is detected, the data on the bus is gated into the content field.

4.2.2. Destination Field

Recall that in the RSTU of section 2.2.3, the issue logic needed to search the TU to obtain the correct tag for the source operand and to update the latest copy field for the destination register. Such a wide associative search may not acceptable because of the large amount of hardware required. If multiple instances of the same destination register are disallowed, no associative logic is necessary. An *instance* of a register is a new copy of the register. By providing a new instance for a busy destination register, the architecture can process several instructions that write into the same register simultaneously. Unfortunately, disallowing multiple instances of a destination register degrades performance [13]. However, all is not lost. As noted in [10], it is possible to eliminate the associative search and use a counter to provide multiple instances for each register *if we can guarantee that results return to the registers in order*. This is exactly the goal of the precise-interrupt mechanism. The implementation of precise interrupts, therefore, simplifies the design of the dependency resolution mechanism.

The scheme we use associates 2 n-bit counters (control bits) with each register in the register file. There is no busy bit. The counters, the *Number of Instances (NI)* and the *Latest Instance (LI)*, represent the number of instances of a register in the RUU and the number of the latest instance, respectively. When an instruction that writes into register Ri is issued to the RUU, both NI and LI are incremented. LI is incremented modulo n. Up to $2^n - 1$ instances of a register can be present in the RUU at any time; issue is blocked if NI for a destination register is $2^n - 1$. When an instruction leaves the RUU and updates the value of Ri, the associated NI is decremented. A register is free if NI = 0, i.e., there is no instruction in the RUU that is going to write into the register.

The register tag sent to the RUU now consists of the register number Ri appended with the LI counter. This guarantees that future instructions access the latest instance, i.e., obtain the latest copy of the register contents and that instructions already present in the RUU get the correct version of the data. In our experiments, each of these counters was 3 bits wide. A 3-bit counter ensured that, for our benchmark programs, an instruction never blocked in the decode and issue stage because an instance of a register was unavailable. Since we had a total of 144 registers, the tag field was 11 (8+3) bits wide. There is no need for a Latest Copy field in the RUU and no associative logic is needed to search within the RUU.

4.2.3. Bypass Logic in the RUU

One of the primary drawbacks of the simple reorder buffer presented in[3] is that performance may be degraded because instruction issue is blocked if a source register is busy even though its result may be present in the reorder buffer. This performance-degrading problem is easily rectified if bypass logic is provided so that a source operand could be read directly from the reorder buffer before it is written into the register file. Such bypass logic though simple, is cumbersome and expensive to implement. Does the RUU need such logic?

Consider an instruction I_i that uses the result of a previous instruction I_j. Recall that the reservation stations associated with the RUU already have the capability to monitor the result bus. Therefore, if I_j completes execution *after* I_i is issued to the RUU, I_i can gate in the result from I_j when it appears on the result bus. In this case, no bypass logic is needed. The only case that bypass logic might be helpful is when I_j has completed execution but has not committed, i.e., updated the register file, when I_i is issued to the RUU.

Rather that providing bypass logic for this case, we extend the monitoring capabilities of the reservation stations to monitor both the result bus and the RUU to register bus. This can be accomplished without a substantial increase in hardware. Therefore, I_i's dependency on I_j is resolved when I_j puts its result on the RUU to register bus if I_j has completed execution before I_i is issued to the RUU. If I_i is issued to the RUU before I_j completes, I_i's dependency on I_j can be resolved when I_j completes and puts its result on the result bus. Therefore, instruction I_i needs to wait in the decode and issue stage only if the RUU is full.

4.3. Interactions with Memory

Instructions that interact with the memory, i.e., load/store instructions, are handled in a special manner. Rather than using *Load* addresses, a *Store* data buffer and a *Conflict* buffer as in [13], we keep a set of *Load Registers* to resolve dependencies in the memory functional unit. The reservation stations for load/store instructions are provided by the RUU. The load registers contain the addresses of "currently active" memory locations. Each load register has the LI and NI counters to allow for multiple instances of a memory address.

If the address of a load/store operation is unavailable, subsequent load/store instructions in the RUU are not allowed to proceed. When a load instruction is allowed to proceed, it checks to see if the address for the load operation matches an address stored in the load registers. If a match occurs and the load register is not free (NI is nonzero) the load instruction simply forwards a tag to the RUU. The load operation *is not* submitted to the memory. The tag is the number of the load register appended with the LI counter. A match can occur if there is either a pending load or a pending store operation. In either case, the load need not be submitted to memory since the desired data can be obtained when the pending load or store operation completes. If a match occurs for a store instruction, the NI and LI counters are incremented and the new tag forwarded to the RUU.

If no match occurs for either operation, a free load register is obtained. A load register is free if there are no pending load or store instructions to the memory address held in the load register, i.e., NI = 0. The NI counter is set to 1 and the LI counter is set to 0. The load request is submitted to memory. The corresponding tag is also submitted to memory so that the data supplied by the memory may be read by the appropriate source operands in the RUU. Load/store instructions are not issued by the RUU if a free load register is not available. When the result for a load operation returns from the memory or the store operation is committed by the RUU, NI is decremented. The data and the address are forwarded to the memory in case of a store operation.

Note that decode and issue unit logic needs to search the load registers associatively for memory addresses. However, the hardware needed for this comparison is not very great for a small number of load registers. In our simulations, we used 6 load registers though 4 were sufficient for most cases.

4.4. Operation of the RUU

In each clock cycle, the RUU carries out 4 distinct tasks: (i) it accepts an instruction from the issue logic, (ii) it *commits* an instruction, i.e., updates the register file, (iii) it issues an instruction to the functional units and (iv) it monitors the busses for matching tags. This constitutes a lot of work; however, each of these tasks can be carried out *in parallel*.

Accepting a new task is straightforward. If an entry in the RUU is free, the issue logic updates the fields of the selected entry. If the instruction at the head of the RUU has finished execution, its results are forwarded to the register file. If the operands of an instruction in the RUU are ready, the instruction can issue to the functional units. Priority is first given to load/store instructions and then to an instruction which entered the RUU earlier. The RUU reserves the result bus when it issues an instruction to the functional units. The final task of monitoring the busses is left to the tag-matching logic in the source-operand fields. Each entry in the RUU is, therefore:

Source Operand 1			Source Operand 2		
Ready	Tag	Content	Ready	Tag	Content

Destination		Executed	Program Counter
Register,LI	Content	Yes/No	Content

The Program Counter field is needed for the implementation of precise interrupts [3]. For the sake of brevity, we have omitted the details of extra information that must be carried around with each instruction (such as tags and RUU entry numbers). The details of such information are obvious.

5. SIMULATION RESULTS

In order to evaluate the effectiveness of the RUU, we carried out trace-driven simulations. The benchmark programs used for all our simulations were the Lawrence Livermore loops [14]. The first 14 loops were chosen because they were readily available. Henceforth, we shall refer to them as LL1, LL2, ..., LL14. The simulations were carried out as follows.

The benchmark programs, as compiled by the CFT compiler for the scalar unit, were fed into the CRAY-1 simulator [12]. The CRAY-1 simulator generates an instruction trace for each program. Vector instructions are not used. Each instruction trace was then fed into our simulator to calculate the execution time and the relative speedup for different RUU sizes. Our simulator converts 2 parcel instructions to 1 parcel instructions when they are encountered.

In our simulations, the LI and NI counters were each 3 bits wide thereby allowing up to 7 instances of a register in the RUU. This was useful in loops 7, 8, 9 and 14 which updated the contents of registers frequently. We used 6 load registers so that the issue of a load/store instruction is never blocked because a load register is unavailable. Furthermore, an instruction left the RUU only when it was executed completely. Specifically, load instructions did not leave the RUU for at least 10 cycles after they were issued to the memory (the time taken for the result to come back from the memory).

Table 1 presents the speedups for a RUU with bypass logic over a simple CRAY-like instruction issue mechanism[13] for different sizes of the RUU. A speedup of greater than 1 implies that the instruction issue mechanism using a RUU is faster than the simple CRAY-like instruction issue mechanism. Note that the CRAY-like instruction issue mechanism does not implement precise interrupts. The average column is the average for all 14 loops. The results are quite encouraging. A RUU with a reasonable number of entries (8-12), not only speeds up execution, it also provides precise interrupts. We would like to point out that we have assumed that the clock period for our mechanism is the same as the clock period for the simple CRAY-like instruction issue mechanism. Unfortunately, we cannot verify this assumption till a hardware implementation is actually realized. If the clock periods are indeed different, the speedup factors would have to be normalized accordingly.

Since bypass logic is expensive, we decided to evaluate a RUU that did not have any bypass logic but its reservation stations monitored both the result bus and the RUU to register bus as discussed in section 4.2.3. The results are presented in Table 2. For many cases, the presence of bypass logic made a negligible difference, if any. On the average, a RUU with no bypass logic is still able to speed up the execution time and, at the same time, implement precise interrupts. The RUU is specially able to speedup loops that make heavy use of the B and T register files (loops 3, 4 and 8).

From tables 1 and 2, it may seem that a reasonably large sized RUU is needed to achieve a performance improvement. The main reason for the large RUU size is that, in our simulations, load instructions did not free a slot in the RUU till the instruction was completely executed (10 cycles). Consequently, instruction issue is blocked because of unavailable RUU slots. If, as in [3], we had allowed load instructions to free RUU slots as soon as it was determined that they would not cause exceptions, much smaller RUU sizes would be needed. Even for the presented results we note that an architecture with a RUU of size 10 has comparable hardware requirements to an architecture that associates only a *single* reservation station with each of the functional units and does not associate any tags with the registers.

6. BRANCH PREDICTION AND CONDITIONAL INSTRUCTIONS

As mentioned earlier, the performance degradation due to branches can be reduced by conditionally executing instructions from a predicted branch path. Several architectures employ this approach [2, 8, 15]. To allow conditional execution of instructions, a hardware mechanism is needed that would allow the machine to recover from an incorrect branch prediction.

The RUU provides a very powerful mechanism for *nullifying* instructions, be the instructions valid instructions or instructions that executed in a *conditional mode*. Valid instructions may be nullified because of an interrupt caused by a previous instruction; conditionally executed instructions may be nullified if they are from an incorrect execution path. Therefore, the conditional execution of instructions with a RUU is very easy. If the decode and issue unit predicts the outcome of branches and actually executes instructions from a predicted path in a conditional mode, recovery from incorrect branch predictions can be achieved very easily without duplicating the register file. We can identify such instructions through the use of an additional field in the RUU and prevent them from being committed until they are proven to be from a correct path. Furthermore, there is no hard limit to the number of branches that can be predicted in a branch path; the RUU can provide multiple instances of a register for the different paths. This is in contrast to the approach taken in [15]. Extending the RUU to accommodate branch prediction and conditional execution is a topic for future research.

7. CONCLUSION

In this paper, we have combined the issues of hardware dependency-resolution and implementation of precise interrupts. We devised a scheme that can resolve dependencies and thereby allow out-of-order instruction execution without associating tag-matching hardware with each register. Such a scheme can, therefore, be used even in the presence of a large number of registers without a substantial hardware cost. Then we extended the scheme to incorporate precise interrupts. The precise interrupt and the dependency-resolution mechanisms mutually aid and simplify each other. We evaluated the performance of the resulting hardware that allows out-of-order instruction execution and also implements precise interrupts using several Livermore loops as the benchmark. The results are quite encouraging. The combined mechanism, called the RUU, is able to implement precise interrupts and is able to

achieve a significant performance improvement over a simple instruction issue mechanism without a substantial cost in hardware. We noted that this mechanism can easily be extended to support conditional execution of instructions from a predicted branch path.

Acknowledgments

This work was supported in part by the University of Wisconsin Graduate Research Committee. The authors would like to thank Jim Goodman, Andy Pleszkun, Jim Smith and the anonymous reviewers for their useful comments.

Table 1: Relative Speedups with Bypass Logic

Benchmark	RUU Size										
	4	6	8	10	12	14	16	18	20	30	50
LL1	0.95	1.04	1.26	1.48	1.59	1.78	1.78	1.78	1.78	1.78	1.94
LL2	0.76	0.92	1.04	1.20	1.22	1.22	1.22	1.22	1.22	1.22	1.70
LL3	1.00	1.05	1.27	1.42	1.76	1.76	1.84	1.94	2.05	2.05	2.05
LL4	1.02	1.13	1.20	1.28	1.37	1.78	1.78	1.78	1.78	1.78	1.78
LL5	0.87	0.98	1.19	1.26	1.34	1.40	1.44	1.44	1.44	1.44	2.02
LL6	0.81	1.01	1.17	1.26	1.34	1.40	1.46	1.49	1.50	1.50	2.04
LL7	0.81	1.10	1.43	1.60	1.73	1.84	1.94	1.97	1.91	1.96	2.01
LL8	0.54	0.78	0.93	1.04	1.09	1.15	1.16	1.16	1.15	1.24	1.60
LL9	0.70	0.90	1.06	1.16	1.22	1.27	1.32	1.42	1.42	1.41	1.80
LL10	0.83	1.01	1.06	1.17	1.20	1.20	1.20	1.20	1.20	1.20	1.75
LL11	0.71	0.75	0.93	1.03	1.03	1.03	1.03	1.03	1.03	1.03	1.39
LL12	0.93	1.00	1.33	1.47	1.55	1.55	1.55	1.55	1.55	1.55	1.69
LL13	0.82	1.09	1.18	1.35	1.41	1.50	1.52	1.53	1.57	1.68	1.79
LL14	0.90	1.13	1.31	1.38	1.43	1.55	1.83	1.89	1.95	2.06	2.09
Average	0.85	0.99	1.17	1.29	1.37	1.44	1.48	1.50	1.51	1.53	1.81

Table 2: Relative Speedups with No Bypass Logic

Benchmark	RUU Size										
	4	6	8	10	12	14	16	18	20	30	50
LL1	0.91	1.02	1.22	1.30	1.30	1.34	1.34	1.34	1.34	1.34	1.87
LL2	0.74	0.88	1.01	1.17	1.19	1.19	1.19	1.19	1.19	1.19	1.68
LL3	1.00	1.05	1.27	1.42	1.76	1.76	1.84	1.94	2.05	2.05	2.05
LL4	0.97	1.02	1.08	1.14	1.36	1.46	1.46	1.52	1.54	1.47	1.77
LL5	0.82	0.95	1.06	1.10	1.10	1.10	1.10	1.10	1.10	1.10	1.90
LL6	0.77	0.93	1.01	1.06	1.10	1.10	1.10	1.10	1.08	1.19	2.05
LL7	0.81	1.05	1.21	1.26	1.31	1.24	1.24	1.27	1.28	1.62	2.00
LL8	0.54	0.76	0.91	0.98	0.99	1.05	1.06	1.06	1.09	1.11	1.56
LL9	0.69	0.88	1.04	1.11	1.14	1.19	1.18	1.17	1.19	1.20	1.80
LL10	0.83	1.00	1.03	1.14	1.13	1.14	1.14	1.14	1.14	1.16	1.75
LL11	0.69	0.75	0.93	1.03	1.03	1.03	1.03	1.03	1.03	1.03	1.39
LL12	0.93	1.00	1.33	1.47	1.55	1.55	1.55	1.55	1.55	1.55	1.69
LL13	0.82	1.02	1.16	1.27	1.39	1.35	1.44	1.45	1.45	1.39	1.70
LL14	0.83	0.95	1.05	1.04	1.07	1.08	1.20	1.18	1.23	1.53	1.98
Average	0.82	0.94	1.10	1.18	1.25	1.26	1.29	1.30	1.31	1.35	1.79

References

[1] P. M. Kogge, *The Architecture of Pipelined Computers*. New York: McGraw-Hill, 1981.

[2] D. W. Anderson, F. J. Sparacio, and R. M. Tomasulo, "The IBM System/360 Model 91: Machine Philosophy and Instruction-Handling," *IBM Journal of Research and Development*, pp. 8-24, January 1967.

[3] J. E. Smith and A. R. Pleszkun, "Implementation of Precise Interrupts in Pipelined Processors," *Proc. 12th Annual Symposium on Computer Architecture*, pp. 36-44, June 1985.

[4] R. M Russel, "The CRAY-1 Computer System," *CACM*, vol. 21, pp. 63-72, January 1978.

[5] J. E. Smith, "A Study of Branch Prediction Strategies," *Proc. 8th International Symposium on Computer Architecture*, pp. 135-148, May 1981.

[6] J. K. F. Lee and A. J. Smith, "Branch Prediction Strategies and Branch Target Buffer Design," *IEEE Computer*, vol. 17, pp. 6-22, January 1984.

[7] P. Y. T. Hsu and E. S. Davidson, "Highly Concurrent Scalar Processing," *Proc. 13th Annual Symposium on Computer Architecture*, pp. 386-395, June 1986.

[8] A. Pleszkun, J. Goodman, W. C. Hsu, R. Joersz, G. Bier, P. Woest, and P. Schecter, "WISQ: A Restartable Architecture Using Queues," in *Proc. 14th Annual Symposium on Computer Architecture*, Pittsburgh, PA, June, 1987.

[9] J. Hennessy, N. Jouppi, F. Baskett, T. Gross, and J. Gill, "Hardware/Software Tradeoffs for Increased Performance," *Proc. Int. Symp. on Arch. Support for Prog. Lang. and Operating Sys.*, pp. 2-11, March 1982.

[10] R. M. Tomasulo, "An Efficient Algorithm for Exploiting Multiple Arithmetic Units," *IBM Journal of Research and Development*, pp. 25-33, January 1967.

[11] *CRAY-1 Computer Systems, Hardware Reference Manual*. Chippewa Falls, WI: Cray Research, Inc., 1982.

[12] N. Pang and J. E. Smith, "CRAY-1 Simulation Tools," Tech. Report ECE-83-11, University of Wisconsin-Madison, Dec. 1983.

[13] S. Weiss and J. E. Smith, "Instruction Issue Logic for Pipelined Supercomputers," *Proc. 11th Annual Symposium on Computer Architecture*, pp. 110-118, June 1984.

[14] F. H. McMahon, *FORTRAN CPU Performance Analysis*. Lawrence Livermore Laboratories, 1972.

[15] W. Hwu and Y. N Patt, "HPSm, a High Performance Restricted Data Flow Architecture Having Minimal Functionality," *Proc. 13th Annual Symposium on Computer Architecture*, pp. 297-307, June 1986.

IBM

Journal of
Research and Development

Volume 34, Number 1, January 1990

by G. F. Grohoski

Machine organization of the IBM RISC System/6000 processor

Machine organization of the IBM RISC System/6000 processor

by G. F. Grohoski

The IBM RISC System/6000* processor is a second-generation RISC processor which reduces the execution pipeline penalties caused by branch instructions and also provides high floating-point performance. It employs multiple functional units which operate concurrently to maximize the instruction execution rate. By employing these advanced machine-organization techniques, it can execute up to four instructions simultaneously. Approximately 11 MFLOPS are achieved on the LINPACK benchmarks.

Introduction

This paper describes the machine organization of the IBM RISC System/6000* (RS/6000) processor. Companion papers in this issue describe the instruction-

* RISC System/6000 is a trademark of International Business Machines Corporation.

set architecture [1] and the organization of the floating-point dataflow [2]. The next section describes the motivation for the original design work. The third section describes the problems inherent in a highly overlapped multiple-execution-unit design, and the solutions which were developed for them. The fourth section describes modifications to the original design point introduced during the implementation.

Motivation for the design

• *Evolution of 801-based machine organizations*
In the early 1980s various projects at the IBM Thomas J. Watson Research Center examined aspects of high-performance Reduced Instruction-Set Computer (RISC) designs. From earlier work [3] based on the experimental 801 computer, it was clear that RISC processors offered many advantages over conventional CISC (Complex Instruction-Set Computer) designs such as the IBM System/370. First, the amount of logic required to implement the architecture naturally led to a compact, efficient design which could potentially be brought to market in a short period of time. A fast cycle time could be supported, since control could be hard-wired, and a simple dataflow effectively supported the instruction set. Ignoring finite cache effects, the 801 inherently executed nearly one instruction per clock cycle.

John Cocke believed that a suitably augmented scalar RISC processor could effectively compete with larger and more expensive vector processors by using multiple execution units and by dispatching several instructions per cycle.

The notion of using multiple functional units which operate concurrently to improve performance was examined in early computer designs, notably the IBM System/360 Model 91 [4] and the CDC 6600 [5]. One basic question was how far a RISC machine organization could be pushed: Could a sustained rate of less than one cycle per instruction be achieved? How much hardware would be required? Would the cycle time be lengthened enough to offset any gain in cycles per instruction? What architecture changes would be required to effectively support a multiple-execution-unit 801 design?

This so-called superscalar approach was studied in the Cheetah project at the Watson Research Center in 1982–1983.† The Cheetah machine organization used separate branch, fixed-point, and floating-point execution units to speed instruction processing. Significant changes were made to the 801 architecture to facilitate the implementation of a multiple-execution-unit design and to expose this design to the compiler. The RS/6000 machine organization owes much to that of the Cheetah machine; important differences between the two will be discussed where appropriate.

The target technology of the superscalar studies was bipolar ECL. By 1984 it became clear that CMOS was achieving a level of integration, chip size, and circuit performance which allowed high-performance RISC processors to be packaged on a few chips. The resulting cost and cost/performance advantages of this design point were dramatic.

The AMERICA project was undertaken to study further the implementation of a multiple-execution-unit 801 design in CMOS. The author, working with John Cocke and Gregory Chaitin, wrote a cycle-by-cycle simulator of the machine organization (called a "timer" in IBM parlance) to demonstrate clearly the processing power of the machine organization, to validate the organizational concepts, and possibly to be used as the initial logic specification for a prototype. Some areas of the machine organization, such as the interrupt synchronization mechanism, were developed during the following year.

The end result of this work was a combination of machine organization, instruction-set architecture, and compiler techniques which allowed a VLSI CMOS processing unit to perform at a level comparable to those of ECL vector processors such as the Cray-1.

• *AMERICA machine organization*
Figure 1 depicts the organization of the AMERICA processor; the organization of the RS/6000 processor is

identical. It consists of several functional units, each partitioned onto one chip (except for the data cache). The instruction cache unit (ICU) fetches instructions and executes branch and LCR (Condition Register Logic) instructions. It dispatches two instructions per cycle to the fixed-point unit and floating-point unit, and receives condition-code information from each unit over dedicated buses. A two-word instruction-reload bus refills an instruction cache line when a miss occurs. The fixed-point unit (FXU) executes fixed-point instructions, performs address calculations for floating-point loads and stores, and contains the address translation, directories, and controls for the data cache. It controls the PBUS, an internal processor bus used to communicate cache-miss and store-back information to the memory interface, and to transfer architected registers between the FXU and ICU. The floating-point unit (FPU) is a high-speed chip which is capable of executing floating-point loads in parallel with arithmetic instructions. One fixed-point, one floating-point, one branch, and one LCR instruction can be executed simultaneously. The system control unit (SCU) contains the memory and I/O interface and controls. The data-cache unit (DCU) contains 64-Kbyte data-cache arrays and data-cache buffers. More details on the actual implementation can be found in [6]. This paper is concerned primarily with the ICU, the FXU, and the control interface to the FPU.

To understand the operation of the AMERICA processor, consider the following 2D graphics transform. The RS/6000 pipeline is nearly identical, except that floating-point loads and stores work differently. It rotates a list of points (x_i, y_i) through an angle θ and displaces them by an amount $(x_{\text{dis}}, y_{\text{dis}})$ to produce a new set of points (x_i', y_i'), stored in the same locations as the original set. An RS/6000 pseudoassembly code excerpt for this routine is given below:

```
      FL FR0, sin theta        ;load rotation matrix
      FL FR1, −sin theta       ;constants
      FL FR2, cos theta
      FL FR3, xdis             ;load x and y
      FL FR4, ydis             ;displacements
      MTCTR i                  ;load Count register
                               ;with loop count
LOOP  UFL FR8, x(i)            ;load x(i)
      FMA FR10, FR8, FR2, FR3  ;form x(i)*cos + xdis
      UFL FR9, y(i)            ;load y(i)
      FMA FR11, FR9, FR2, FR4  ;form y(i)*cos + ydis
      FMA FR12, FR9, FR1, FR10 ;form −y(i)*sin + FR10
      FST FR12, x(i)'          ;store x(i)'
      FMA FR13, FR8, FR0, FR11 ;form x(i)*sin + FR11
      FST FR13, y(i)'          ;store y(i)'
      BCT LOOP                 ;continue for all points
```

---

† T. K. M. Agerwala and D. Prener, "Cheetah Principles of Operation," IBM internal document, IBM Thomas J. Watson Research Center, Yorktown Heights, NY, May 1982.

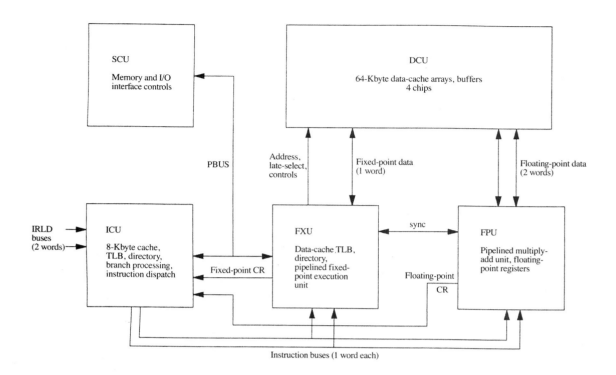

General organization of the AMERICA and RISC System/6000 processors.

UFL is an update-form floating-point load that auto-increments the address to use for the next point. FMA is a multiply-add instruction that accepts four register operands. The second and third operands are multiplied together, added to the fourth operand, and stored in the first. FST stores a floating-point result in memory. BCT is a special loop-closing branch instruction which examines a value in the Count register; if it is greater than zero, the branch is taken. The Count register is auto-decremented.

Following is a description of the cycle-by-cycle execution of the inner loop in the AMERICA machine organization; a diagram is shown in **Figure 2**. (The actual RS/6000 pipeline is described later in more detail.)

IF   The instruction-fetch cycle of the processor. The instruction cache is accessed and four instructions are fetched from the cache arrays and placed into instruction buffers.

Disp/BRE During this cycle, up to four instructions are examined for dispatching. Branch and LCR instructions are executed, if they can be removed from the buffer. The target addresses for branch instructions are generated. Fixed- and floating-point instructions are transmitted to the fixed- and floating-point units.

FXD During this cycle the fixed-point unit decodes fixed-point instructions and accesses the register file for operands.

FXE The fixed-point unit executes instructions during this cycle. For load and store instructions, the address is generated, and the data-cache translation look-aside buffers (TLBs) and directories are searched. The array address is transmitted to the data-cache arrays and latched.

C   During this cycle the data-cache arrays are accessed. Based upon a late-select signal from the fixed-point unit, which chooses data from one of the four sets of the data cache, data is returned to either the fixed- or floating-point units.

	1	2	3	4	5	6	7	8	9
IF	UFL8 UFL9 FMA FMA	FMA FMA FST FST	BCT		UFL8 UFL9 FMA FMA	FMA FMA FST FST	BCT		
Disp/BRE		UFL8 FMA	UFL9 FMA	FMA (BCT) FST	FMA BCT FST	UFL8 FMA	UFL9 FMA		
FXD			UFL8 FMA	UFL9 FMA	FMA FST	FMA FST	UFL8 FMA	UFL9 FMA	FMA FST
FXE				UFL8	UFL9	FST	FST	UFL8	UFL9
C					UFL8	UFL9			UFL8
WB									
PD			UFL8 FMA	UFL9 FMA	FMA FST	FMA FST	UFL8 FMA	UFL9 FMA	FMA FST
Remap				UFL8 FMA	UFL9 FMA	FMA FST	FMA FST	UFL8 FMA	UFL9 FMA
FPD					FMA	FMA	FMA	FMA	FMA
FPE1						FMA	FMA	FMA	FMA
FPE2							FMA	FMA	FMA
FPWB								FMA	FMA

Figure 2

AMERICA processor pipeline showing cycle-by-cycle execution of the inner loop (see pp. 39-40 for definitions and discussion of the terms at the left).

WB	During this cycle the fixed-point unit writes the results of instructions to the register file. For RR instructions, this cycle is in parallel with the cache access cycle. Data for loads is written into the register file during this cycle.
PD	This is the floating-point pre-decode cycle. It is at the same pipeline level as FXD. During this cycle instructions are pre-decoded in preparation for renaming.
Remap	During this cycle the registers of floating-point instructions are mapped to physical registers.
FPD	This is the floating-point decode cycle. The registers are read out for floating-point arithmetic instructions.
FPE1	The first cycle of the multiply-add pipeline.
FPE2	The second and final cycle of the multiply-add pipeline.
FPWB	During this cycle the results of floating-point arithmetic instructions are written to the floating-point register file.

During cycle 1 the first four instructions starting at LOOP are fetched. During cycle 2 the first load and multiply are dispatched to the floating-point unit. The next four instructions are also fetched.

During cycle 3 the second instruction pair is dispatched to the fixed- and floating-point units. The first pair is in fixed-point decode and floating-point pre-decode. The fixed-point unit will execute the floating-point load and discard the multiply-add. The floating-point unit will send both instructions to the rename stage. The loop-closing BCT instruction, along with three subsequent instructions (not shown), is being fetched from the instruction cache.

During cycle 4 the fixed-point unit generates the address for the first floating-point load. The floating-point unit renames the floating-point load and the multiply-add. The second instruction pair is in fixed-point decode and floating-point pre-decode. The instruction cache dispatches the third instruction pair, and branch-scanning logic looks five instructions deep in the instruction buffer to generate the target address of the BCT.

During cycle 5, the instruction cache fetches the top of the loop. The fourth instruction pair is dispatched to the fixed- and floating-point units, and the BCT is executed. The first FMA is in floating-point decode; the first floating-point load is accessing the data cache. At the end of this cycle, the data will return and the FMA will enter the floating-point execution pipeline, since all of its registers are free. The fixed-point unit is generating the address for the second floating-point load.

During cycle 6 the second floating-point load is accessing the data cache. The second floating-point multiply-add will decode, since all required registers are available. The address of the first floating-point store is being generated; it will be placed in a store data address buffer at the end of the cycle. When the data is produced in cycle 10 (not shown), the store will be written to the data cache at the first free cache cycle.

Several points are notable. The BCT causes no pipeline delays, and as far as the fixed- and floating-point units are concerned, no branch ever occurs. The floating-point pipeline is kept 100% busy, and produces two floating-point results each cycle (one multiply and one add). Ignoring finite cache effects, this computation proceeds at 50 MFLOPS in the inner loop on AMERICA at a 40-ns clock cycle. Due to problems encountered during the implementation of the floating-point unit, the RS/6000 processor executes this code at a 28-MFLOP rate. The remainder of this paper describes how this processing rate was achieved.

Problems of a multiple-execution-unit design approach

A RISC design which uses multiple functional units simultaneously executes several instructions per cycle; therefore, several instructions must be fetched each cycle. The effect of branch instructions on the pipeline must be reduced, because it is relatively greater than in a machine which executes only a single instruction per cycle. The execution units must be synchronized when interrupts occur, to maintain sequential program consistency and to ensure that arithmetic operations are performed using the correct data in the correct order.

If the effect of branch instructions can be mitigated and the floating-point and fixed-point units can be

supplied with instructions and data at a high rate, a large increase in processor performance is possible. The central requirements which needed to be addressed were the following:

1. Design a low-latency, high-bandwidth instruction-fetching mechanism.
2. Overlap the execution of branch instructions with fixed-point and floating-point instructions.
3. Overlap the fixed-point and floating-point units in order to keep the floating-point unit supplied with data.
4. Maintain the effects of sequential program execution while executing several instructions in parallel.
5. Design a high-performance floating-point execution unit.

The solutions to the first four requirements, developed during the AMERICA project, are discussed here. The design of the floating-point dataflow is discussed in [2].

• *Instruction fetching*
The instruction-fetching mechanism must have a low latency so that the execution units remain busy when the target of a taken branch is being fetched. This argues for a cache which can be accessed in one machine cycle.

While the processor can execute four instructions per machine cycle, it more commonly executes three instructions (a branch, a fixed-point, and a floating-point instruction) per machine cycle in heavy floating-point code. The cache must at least match this rate. In order to help overlap the execution of branch instructions with fixed- and floating-point instructions, the branch-scanning logic, as it looks through the instruction buffers, must detect a branch somewhat in advance of its execution. This means that the instruction-cache bandwidth must be greater than the raw bandwidth required by the execution pipelines.

In view of the high bandwidth required, an on-chip dedicated instruction cache was designed which could be accessed in one cycle. In order to fetch multiple instructions per cycle, a new cache organization was developed.

All instructions are four bytes (one word) in length. The first design choice was to build an instruction cache which, given an arbitrary byte address, truncated the four low-order bits and returned the resulting quadword (QW)-aligned set of four instructions. However, this did not supply the processor with the required number of instructions if, for example, an instruction branched to the last word in a QW. In this case only one instruction would be supplied to the execution units, and this would seriously degrade loop performance. Possibly the

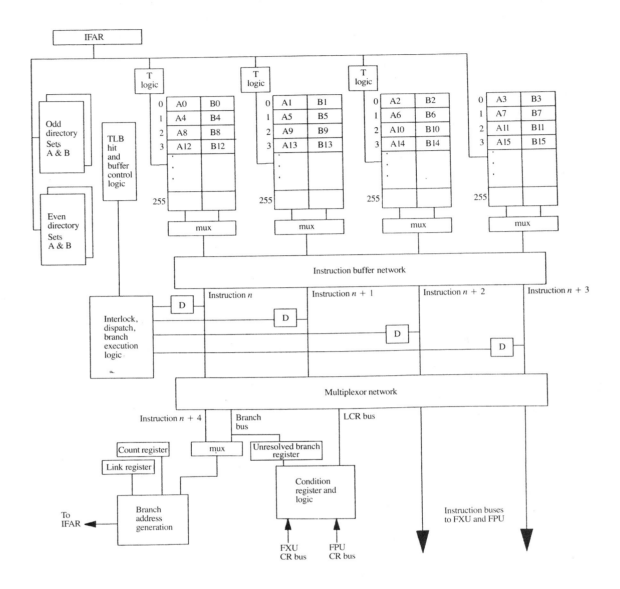

Figure 3

General organization of the instruction cache and branch-processing unit.

compiler and loader could be directed to QW-align all branch targets for loops, but this would increase code size and could lead to additional complications.

Consider the instruction-cache arrays to be composed of four smaller, independent arrays, each fetching one instruction per cycle. By controlling the address presented to each array and interleaving the instructions among the cache arrays, four instructions can always be fetched, as long as they reside in the same cache line. **Figure 3** diagrams the organization of the cache arrays for a two-

way set-associative cache with a line size of 16 instructions (64 bytes).

Each subsequent instruction is placed into a different cache array, computed modulo 4. If the actual word linewidth of each array is two instructions, instruction 0 of associativity sets A and B occupies row I of cache array 0. Row I of cache array 1 contains instruction 1 of a given cache line, and so on. In this case one cache line is split into four rows of a cache array. Consider how four sequential instructions in a cache line, regardless of the address of the first instruction of the group, can be fetched.

In order to fetch instructions 0, 1, 2, and 3 of a given cache line, the same row address can be presented to all cache arrays. This is precisely the QW-aligned case mentioned above. In order to fetch instructions 1, 2, 3, and 4 of a cache line, the row address for cache array 0 must be incremented, since instruction 4 resides in the next row. This is determined by address bit 28 (bit 0 is the high-order bit of a 32-bit address).

By considering all 16 possibilities of the starting address of a word in a cache line, it is seen that cache arrays 0, 1, and 2 need to have their row addresses incremented, while array 3 does not. The T logic of Figure 3 provides the row incrementation and selection functions.

By interleaving the cache arrays and providing the necessary row incrementation, row-selection multiplexors, and row-selection logic, four instructions can be fetched each cycle as long as they are contained in the same cache line. If the group of four is within the last three instructions of a cache line, it spans two cache lines. In this case, only 3, 2, or 1 instructions can be fetched. On the average, this organization allows $(13/16) \times 4 + (1/16) \times 3 + (1/16) \times 2 + (1/16) \times 1 = 3.625$ instructions to be fetched each machine cycle.

- *Branch delays*

Reducing the delays caused by branches in a pipelined machine has been one of the classical challenges of computer design. Consequently, many approaches have been developed. The objective, of course, is to have branches take zero execution cycles. Branches reduce the effective throughput of the pipeline by causing several types of delays; following is a description of these delays and the state of the art in reducing them in 1984:

- It takes time to fetch the target of a successful (taken) branch. During this time the execution pipeline may be starved of instructions.

  There are several approaches which reduce the target-fetch delay. First, the branch-target address can be calculated while the branch is in the early stages of the execution pipeline. This generally requires a separate branch-target address adder. Then, the address can be provided to the instruction-fetching mechanism to fetch the branch target before the outcome is known. If the branch is not taken, the branch-target instructions can be discarded. If the target is fetched, a pipeline delay can be introduced if too few sequential instructions are available to the execution pipeline to cover the delay of re-fetching the sequential path. Generally, then, the target address is fetched based upon some prediction of the branch being taken.

Another technique, typically useful for IBM System/370 processors [7], is to store the calculated branch-target address in a table which is indexed using the address of the branch instruction. When the branch instruction is fetched, its address is used to access the table, which provides the branch-target address. Logic is provided which ensures that the table contains the proper branch-target address by invalidating the table entry for the branch if the register which the branch uses for its target address is changed.

To further reduce the target-fetch delay, a branch-target buffer [8] can be provided which stores the target address of a branch and the first several instructions from a branch target. Once the branch-target address has been computed, it can be presented to the branch-target buffer, where the target address is compared with the addresses of branch targets contained in the buffer. If a match is found, no request need be made to the instruction-fetching mechanism until the outcome of the branch is known. If taken, the instruction-fetching mechanism is given the address of the instruction just beyond the last instruction stored in the matching entry in the branch-target buffer. If no match is found, the branch target can be fetched. It is added to the buffer by replacing a buffer entry which has not been referenced recently. The effectiveness of a branch-target buffer depends on the fraction of taken branches whose targets are found in the buffer.

Yet another technique common to RISC machines is to use some variant of the so-called branch-with-execute instruction [3, 8]. An instruction which originally preceded a branch is moved behind the branch by the compiler. This subject instruction is executed whether or not the branch is taken. If the branch is not taken, no penalty is incurred. If the branch is taken, at least one instruction is available to the execution pipeline while the branch target is being fetched. Variations on this technique utilize more subject instructions, or can choose instructions from the target of the branch to be used as subject instructions. With this form, termed branch-or-skip, if the branch is not taken the execute instructions must be skipped, possibly introducing some delay. This form is used when the branch is unconditional or has a high likelihood of being taken. The Cheetah machine used up to four subject instructions in both branch-with-execute and branch-or-skip forms.

These execute-form branches have several drawbacks. Architectural and implementation complications result if the subject instruction causes an interrupt. If the interrupt handler returns to the subject instruction once its interrupt has been serviced, the branch may be taken or not taken. If it is to be taken, the machine must "remember" the branch target address. Or the interrupt handler may examine a bit which denotes the interrupting instruction as the subject of a branch-with-execute, reexecute the subject instruction, and then return either to the target of the branch or to the next sequential instruction following the subject, depending upon the interrupt handler's determination of the branch outcome. Alternatively, the interrupt handler may return directly to the branch instruction and reexecute the subject instruction. In this case the branch instruction must not alter any registers (or the interrupt handler must undo the effects of the changes). Whichever course is chosen, the situation becomes even more complicated if multiple subject instructions are used.

Nor can subject instructions always be found. Because of dependencies in basic blocks, subject instructions can be used to fill the execution slot only about 60% of the time [3].

- Conditional branches require an execution unit to set a condition code. There is typically some pipeline latency before the condition code is available and the outcome of the branch can be determined, which stalls the execution of the branch instruction.

In order to reduce the delays caused by waiting for the condition code to become available, several techniques can be employed. Branch-prediction techniques can be combined with branch-target buffers or decode history tables [8, 9] to reduce branch delays. Smith [10] examined several branch-prediction strategies. A branch can be guessed taken, or not taken, as a function of history (the branch history table [9] or its variants) or of branch type, or based on a bit placed in the instruction and set by the compiler. Prediction simply allows the machine to proceed down either the sequential or the target path. Since the outcome of the branch is uncertain, the pipeline must treat the instructions in a conditional fashion and be able to undo any changes to the architected machine state if a wrong prediction has been made. Alternatively, machines have been proposed which proceed down both paths [7], although this requires the duplication of hardware and in general has been too costly to implement.

- Branches also typically proceed through the execution pipeline, thereby consuming at least one pipeline slot and delaying subsequent fixed-point instructions. This is the case with most current RISC machines [11–14].

In Cheetah, a separate branch-execution unit was provided to eliminate this pipeline delay. In order for this to be most effective, architecture changes were made to decouple the branch and fixed-point execution units (these are described in [1]).

In a machine which can execute several instructions per cycle, the effects of these branch delays are magnified.

The approach chosen for AMERICA was the following. First, a separate branch-execution unit was provided. This allowed for the possibility of zero-cycle branches. Second, logic was provided to scan through the instruction buffers for branches, to generate the branch-target address, and to determine the branch outcome if possible. If the branch outcome was undefined, instructions would be dispatched from the sequential path to the fixed- and floating-point execution units in a conditional fashion. When the branch outcome was determined, these instructions would either be executed, and the branch-target instructions discarded, or canceled, and the branch-target instructions transmitted to the execution units. (The notion of combining branch-address generation logic and instruction-cache accessing had also occurred to other researchers [15], but they did not consider fully integrating a separate branch-processing unit and an instruction cache.)

The justification for this simplistic strategy was the following. Gross branch statistics available from 801 instruction studies indicated that branches comprised approximately 20% of all instructions (in fixed-point code). Approximately one third of the branches were unconditional; another third were used to terminate do-loops of the form do $i = 1$, n; and the final third were conditional. If a separate branch-execution unit is used, with proper scanning ahead to overlap branch execution with the execution of fixed-point instructions, unconditional branches should cause no pipeline delay provided the branch target is in the cache. Using the loop-closing branch instruction, which is basically an unconditional branch for the first $n - 1$ iterations, should also cause no delay. Of the remaining conditional branches, about half are taken, and half are not taken. The branches not taken should cause no delay, since they would be predicted not taken. The branches taken would cause some delay, estimated to be two pipeline cycles. Thus, branches, instead of requiring one cycle each to execute, would require approximately $(5/6) \times 0 + (1/6) \times 2$, or about 0.33 cycles on the average.

Some form of branch prediction for conditional branches could further reduce the delay. One strategy would be to have a branch history table for conditional branches whose outcome is unknown when they are first encountered. However, the published effectiveness of most branch-prediction strategies is skewed because unconditional branches are included in the prediction mechanism. This raises their apparent effectiveness substantially. Our feeling was that the remaining conditional branches were essentially random in nature and that typical branch-prediction techniques would not be very effective. A branch-prediction mechanism would require some significant space to implement. Furthermore, in order to decode down the target path, and dispatch target instructions to the fixed- and floating-point units, additional logic would have to be added to the instruction-cache unit. This logic would at most eliminate the 0.33-cycle delay entirely, if both streams were decoded; otherwise, it might perform worse if a branch were predicted to be taken but was not taken. For these reasons, sophisticated branch prediction, such as a branch history table, was not implemented.

Branch-with-execute and branch-or-skip were not utilized. Assuming that the branch-processing unit and branch-scanning logic run far enough ahead of the fixed- and floating-point execution units, the branch target can be fetched in time to avoid pipeline execution delays for most taken branches. Not-taken branches do not benefit from branch-with-execute. Certain implementation difficulties could be avoided (801 implementations were notorious for having problems with bugs in branch-with-execute), and the architecture could be simplified, if these branches were not architected. Branch-with-execute can provide one advantage: The branch is effectively moved forward in the instruction stream, allowing the branch-scanning logic to detect it earlier. (Referring to Figure 2, if the BCT were an execute-form branch, it would be detected one cycle earlier, and the target could be fetched one cycle earlier. The branch-scanning logic would only have to look four instructions deep to detect the branch.) This potential advantage was offset by simply looking further ahead in the instruction buffers for a branch.

To illustrate the design, several branch-execution examples are depicted in **Figure 4**, which illustrates the RS/6000 pipeline delays. Figure 4(a) shows an unconditional branch, and 4(b) its associated pipeline behavior. The pipeline cycle names are the same as in Figure 2. At the end of the fixed-point execution cycle (FXE), condition-code results are transmitted to the branch unit so that conditional branches can be resolved in the following cycle.

Figures 4(c) and 4(d) depict a conditional branch which is not taken. Figures 4(e) and 4(f) depict a taken conditional branch whose condition is set two fixed-point instructions before the branch, causing a one-cycle pipeline delay. Figures 4(g) and 4(h) depict a taken conditional branch which causes no pipeline delay.

Note that the only branches which typically cause any pipeline delay are taken conditional branches that depend upon a fixed-point compare which cannot be scheduled with three or more instructions between it and the branch. Thus, the AMERICA branch-processing approach is robust and simple. Although sophisticated branch-prediction techniques are not used, branch instructions cause a fraction of the pipeline delay of most other RISC machines.

• *Overlap of fixed-point and floating-point units*
Several problems needed to be solved. One was how to synchronize the fixed- and floating-point units to maintain precise interrupts and still allow a high rate of instruction processing. The second was how to allow floating-point loads to proceed when the state of the floating-point register file was unknown to the fixed-point unit. The third was how, with the fixed-point unit performing address calculations for floating-point loads and stores, to ensure that the correct data was loaded into or stored from the floating-point register file.

Synchronization
One design goal was to keep the fixed- and floating-point units overlapped sufficiently that the execution rate of floating-point code would depend only upon either 1) the rate at which data could be fetched from the data cache or 2) the rate at which arithmetic operations could be performed, considering the effects of dependencies, by the floating-point arithmetic dataflow. That is, the MFLOP rate of the processor should not be limited by the instruction-processing characteristics and synchronization requirements of the pipeline. The synchronization scheme must allow the simultaneous processing of fixed- and floating-point instructions. It must also maintain precise interrupts for loads, stores, and trap instructions. When an interrupt for one of these instructions occurs during the execution phase of the fixed-point pipeline, all prior instructions must complete, and no subsequent instructions may alter the machine state. A final objective of the synchronization scheme was that it be simple to debug, preferably by inspection.

The synchronization scheme which was used in the AMERICA timer is diagrammed in **Figure 5**. The major pipeline stages are depicted. In the fixed-point unit, a set of instruction-prefetch buffers (IPB0–IPB3) feeds two decode registers, D0 and D1. The IPBs allow the branch unit to get ahead of the fixed- and floating-point units. A mux (multiplexer, not shown) between D0 and D1 feeds the selected fixed-point instruction to the register file and pipeline controls. This instruction is then logically fed to the execute cycle, where ALU, shift, address translation, and cache-directory operations are completed.

On the floating-point side, a mirror image of the instruction buffers and decode registers is provided. Decode registers PD0 and PD1 feed the rename registers (register renaming is discussed shortly) R0 and R1. These registers feed floating-point instruction-decode buffers (IDB) which in turn feed the floating-point decode register. The IDBs are provided so that the fixed-point unit is not held up waiting for floating-point arithmetic instructions to complete.

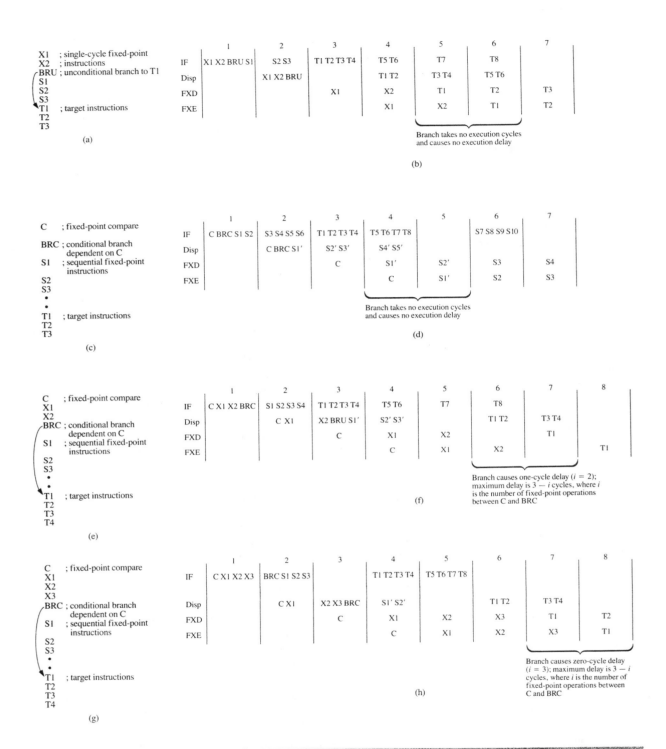

Figure 4

Examples of branch execution: (a) An unconditional branch. (b) Pipeline behavior for the branch shown in (a). (c), (d) A conditional branch that is not taken. (e), (f) A conditional branch that is taken and causes a one-cycle pipeline delay. (g), (h) A conditional branch that is taken and causes no pipeline delay.

The fixed-point unit and the early stages of the floating-point unit are kept in lock step by synchronization signals which are passed between the two units. During fixed-point decode, pipeline-hold conditions produce a signal which prevents the floating-point unit from pre-decoding. Thus, registers D0 and PD0 and D1 and PD1 always contain the same instruction. Similarly, during the fixed-point execute phase, signals are generated and passed to the floating-point unit which tell whether the instruction in execution completed, or caused an interrupt. The instruction in fixed-point execution is always in either register R0 or R1. Only floating-point loads, stores, and arithmetic instructions pass from registers R0 and R1 to the IDB and decode stages. Fixed-point instructions that enter R0 and R1 are discarded as soon as they are executed by the fixed-point unit (or are interrupted). If an instruction in fixed-point execution causes an interrupt, the contents of registers R1, D0, D1, PD0, PD1, and both sets of instruction buffers are purged. Additionally, the contents of R0 may or may not be purged, depending upon whether the content of R0 is a floating-point load, store, or other fixed-point instruction. If so, it is purged, since it is precisely the instruction causing the interrupt. If not, it must be a prior floating-point arithmetic instruction, and is allowed to proceed.

Similarly, a hold signal can be produced by logic in the floating-point rename stage. If the IDB becomes full, or the renaming mechanism runs out of rename registers, the floating-point unit tells the fixed-point unit to hold execution.

Figures 5(a–f) illustrate the operation of this synchronization scheme on one iteration of the loop of Example 1. In Figure 5(a), the first two instructions have been dispatched to the fixed- and floating-point units. The fixed-point unit decodes the floating-point load and discards the FMA. The floating-point unit pre-decodes both instructions and transfers them to the rename stage.

In Figure 5(b), the next two instructions enter D0, PD0, D1, and PD1. The fixed-point unit is performing the address generation and translation for UFL FR8. Similarly, the floating-point unit is remapping UFL FR8 and FMA FR10. If the UFL should cause an interrupt, the fixed-point unit informs the floating-point unit via the cancel line to cancel all instructions in rename and above. Any instructions in the IDBs or floating-point decode are not affected. Similarly, if the floating-point unit runs out of IDB space or rename registers, it informs the fixed-point unit to hold in the execution stage.

In Figure 5(c), the second UFL is in fixed-point execution, and the first FMA has entered floating-point decode. At the end of this cycle, the floating-point data returns from the data cache, and execution of the FMA starts as data is bypassed to the execution pipeline.

Figure 5(d) continues the sequence. In Figures 5(e) and 5(f), the instructions from the next iteration of the loop have entered decode and pre-decode and the process repeats.

This synchronization scheme allows the floating-point and fixed-point units to operate in an overlapped manner without inhibiting the processing rate of the pipeline, and it maintains precise interrupts. It is easy to debug, since the contents of registers must correspond to one another. Although it adds two stages to the floating-point pipeline, this does not affect the processing of floating-point arithmetic instructions that need data from the data cache, since the data does not return until the floating-point decode cycle. It does, however, mean that the branch unit must wait an additional two cycles before resolving a conditional branch that depends on a floating-point compare. In the code sequences which were studied, this did not cause any great delay, since the compare typically depended upon a floating-point load (directly or indirectly) and thus could not have been executed any sooner.

Register renaming
When the fixed-point unit performs address generation and initiates the data-cache request for a floating-point load, the floating-point register denoted as the target of the load is overwritten with new data. The floating-point load can be considered to define a new value of the floating-point register (FPR). The FPR cannot be overwritten until all prior floating-point instructions which reference the old value of the register have accessed that value.

In the simplest implementations, the fixed-point unit is prevented from initiating a floating-point load until the floating-point unit signals that all previous floating-point operations are complete. In a coprocessor arrangement, this is acceptable; however, it severely limits fixed–floating-point overlap, which is required for high floating-point performance. With respect to Figure 5, the question is, when a floating-point load is in fixed-point execution, how is the fixed-point unit to know that the request can be sent to the cache? If the data returns too early, it will overwrite a value in the register file which may still be needed.

There are several solutions to this problem. One of the most elegant was invented by Tomasulo for the IBM System/360 Model 91 [16]. Floating-point data buffers are provided in the floating-point unit. When the instruction unit executes a floating-point load, it reserves one of these buffers. The instruction unit can proceed as long as the data buffers are not full. The load instruction is sent to the floating-point unit, so that the data can be placed in the floating-point register file at the appropriate point in the program sequence. When the load is decoded

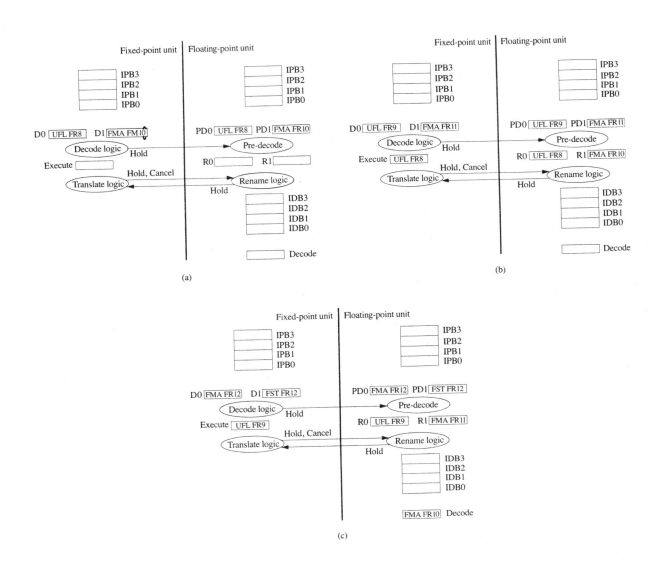

Figure 5

Fixed-point–floating-point synchronization scheme used in the AMERICA timer: (a) First two instructions dispatched to fixed- and floating-point units. (b) Next two instructions enter D0, PD0, D1, and PD1. (c), (d) Second UFL in fixed-point execution, and first FMA enters floating-point decode; sequence continues. (e), (f) First instructions from next iteration of the loop enter decode and pre-decode; process repeats.

by the floating-point unit, the data is transferred to the register file from the buffer, once it is available.

A second approach was examined in the Cheetah machine. Two copies of the floating-point registers were architected. The primary floating-point registers, 32 in number, were used by the arithmetic unit. The backup registers, also 32 in number, were used by the fixed-point unit to load data from the data cache. Receive (RCV) instructions moved data from the backup register to the

primary register. The RCV operation could be coded as a bit in a floating-point arithmetic instruction.

This procedure worked in the following manner. A floating-point load would load the backup register with data. The first floating-point arithmetic instruction to use the data would have its RCV bit set for that register field. The data would be transferred from the backup register to the primary register. A valid bit would denote whether or not the backup register was in use. If it was, a

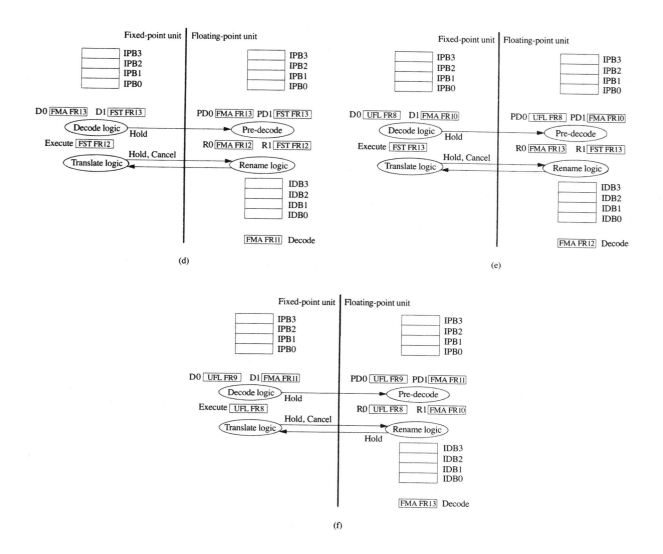

(d)   (e)

(f)

Figure 5 Continued

subsequent floating-point load to that register could not proceed and would be held up by the fixed-point unit. Otherwise, the fixed-point unit could effectively pre-load the next value of the FPR. This was particularly useful in floating-point loops, where the fixed-point unit would typically reach the top of the loop before the floating-point unit. Instead of waiting for the floating-point unit to catch up, it could proceed with loads and overlap them with the execution of prior floating-point code.

However, the backup registers doubled the size of the register file, and might not be utilized uniformly by the compiler. Receive and transmit operations were another chore for the compiler to get right. In a straightforward

implementation, 32 valid wires must be exposed to the fixed-point unit.

Simple interlocking, as in a typical coprocessor implementation, was too slow. The Cheetah approach was cumbersome. Instead, a variant of the Tomasulo approach, called register renaming, was developed.

A load of a floating-point register creates a new semantic value for that register. If there were a pool of physical registers, greater than the number of architected registers, the extra registers could serve as a dynamic buffer to hold data for floating-point loads executed by the fixed-point unit but not yet encountered by the floating-point unit. As long as there were some free

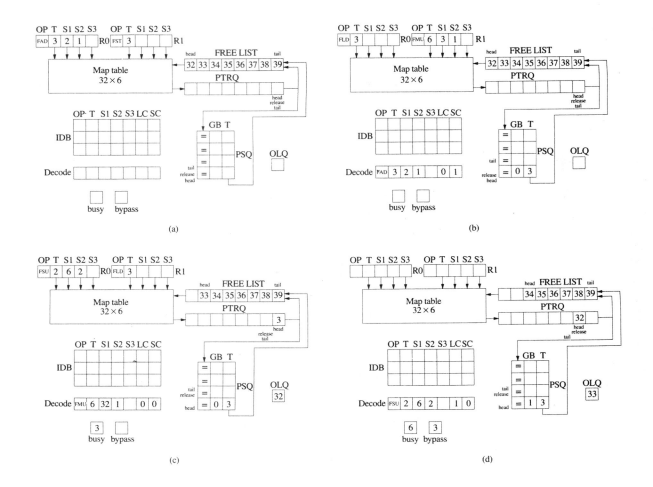

Figure 6

Register-renaming structure: (a) Map table initialized to identity. (b) Floating-point add passes from rename into decode. (c) Floating-point add in execution. (d) Store removed and tag returned to free list. (e) Subtract can decode, releasing register tag 32, which is returned during next cycle. (f), (g) Subtract completes execution.

physical registers, floating-point loads could be processed by the fixed-point unit without regard to the actual state of particular floating-point registers. Internal floating-point control logic would determine when to use the value in the buffer pool based on the decoding of floating-point loads and the registers being used by instructions in execution.

The organization that was adopted is illustrated in **Figure 6**. R0 and R1 are the rename registers. They contain an opcode field, a target-register field, and three source-register fields.

The map table is a 32-entry, 6-bit-wide table which maintains the correspondence of an architected register

to a physical register. For instance, if the entry for register 12 is 38, then physical register 38 currently contains the contents of architected register 12.

The free list (FL) contains a list of currently unassigned physical registers. In the initial state, the map table is initialized to identity and the remaining registers are placed on the free list. Since there are 40 physical registers, the FL can contain a maximum of eight entries. The FL is maintained as a circular queue and uses a head pointer and a tail pointer.

The pending-target return queue (PTRQ) contains those physical registers which are being used by instructions in the IDB or decode phases, and will

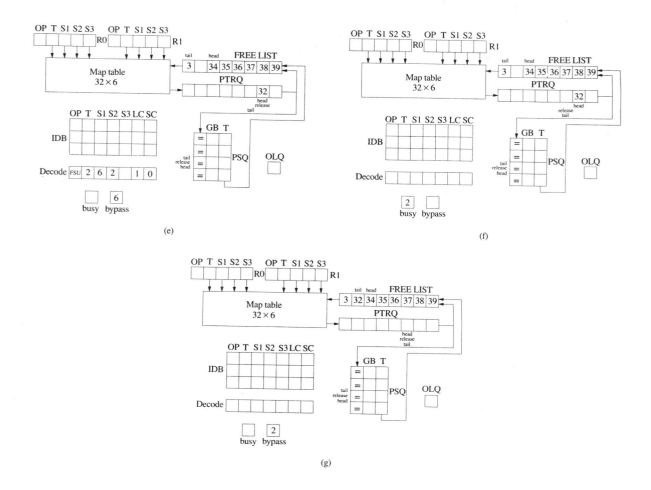

(e)

(f)

(g)

Figure 6 Continued

become free as soon as these instructions pass decode. It also has a maximum size of 8. Like the FL, it is maintained as a circular queue with head and tail pointers. It also has an additional pointer. The release pointer keeps register tags on the PTRQ until all prior arithmetic instructions which could have required the data in the corresponding physical register have decoded.

The decode stage contains floating-point arithmetic instructions. The instruction-decode buffers (IDB) buffer instructions which have been renamed but which cannot enter decode. They allow the fixed-point unit to run ahead of the floating-point arithmetic pipeline. The decode and IDB registers each contain load-count (LC) and store-count (SC) fields. When an instruction decodes, the LC field is used to increment the release pointer for the PTRQ, in order to release physical registers to the

free list. In a similar way, the SC field increments the release pointer of the store queue to allow floating-point stores to be performed.

The BUSY and BYPASS registers contain the physical register number of the floating-point instruction currently in the first and second execution stages. If any register field of an instruction in decode compares with the BUSY register, it is prevented from decoding. If a source field compares with the BYPASS register, the data is read from the execution pipeline and not from the register file.

The outstanding load queue (OLQ) contains the physical register number of the next floating-point load whose data will return from the cache. It stops instructions from decoding if they require data which has not returned from the data cache.

When floating-point stores are renamed, they are placed on the pending-store queue (PSQ). This eliminates the need for them to go through the floating-point decode phase. They remain on the queue until they are released by an arithmetic instruction decoding. Once released, they may be performed if their data is available.

When an instruction enters the rename phase (registers R0 and R1), what happens next depends upon the instruction type.

Floating-point arithmetic instructions When an arithmetic instruction is renamed, the contents of the map table are not altered. Each 5-bit architected register number is replaced by a 6-bit physical register tag. The instruction proceeds to the decoder, or, if the decoder is full, to an IDB position. If the arithmetic instruction is in R1, its LC and SC fields are set to 0. If it is in R0, these fields are set to 1 if there is a floating-point load or store in R1.

Once renamed, the arithmetic instruction enters the decode stage, if the decode stage is empty or is becoming empty; otherwise it is placed into an IDB. If the IDB is full, the pipeline backs up, and the fixed-point unit is told to stop executing instructions.

Once in decode, the arithmetic instruction reads out the contents of its physical registers. If the contents of any of its physical registers are not valid, because they are being loaded from memory or are being computed in the pipeline, the instruction remains in decode. These conditions are checked by comparing each physical register field with the OLQ and BUSY registers. When the instruction can successfully decode, it enters the arithmetic pipeline. The store-count field increments the release pointer of the PSQ to allow subsequent floating-point stores to be performed. The load-count field increments the release pointer of the PTRQ to release unneeded physical registers. These registers are then placed on the free list, as long as there are no stores on the store queue using this register which have not been done.

Floating-point stores When a floating-point store enters the rename stage, the target register is renamed to a physical register. The store could have been placed in the IDB or Decode stages, like arithmetic instructions. However, since the fixed-point unit executes fixed-point instructions and throws away floating-point arithmetic instructions, the floating-point unit must process loads or stores and arithmetic instructions in parallel. Otherwise, it will slow down the fixed-point unit. Thus, if the store were placed into the decoder, the decoder would have to inspect two instructions per cycle.

Instead, it is placed on the pending-store queue (PSQ). It remains there until the value of the physical register it is trying to store is available. Before leaving rename, the store causes the store-count field of the most recent prior arithmetic instruction to be incremented. This is because the last instruction which could have produced the result is that arithmetic instruction (or a load). The store count keeps the store from being performed until all prior arithmetic instructions have decoded.

Before the store is actually performed (before the fixed-point unit is notified that data is available), several conditions must be met. First, the store must be at the head of the PSQ, since stores are done in order. The physical register tag of the store at the head of the queue must not be coming from the pipeline, or be busy from memory. These conditions are checked by comparing the physical register tag with the contents of the BUSY tag and the OLQ. Once the data is valid, the store is performed. If the give-back bit is set (see below), the tag is returned to the free list.

A few more words about floating-point stores are in order. While the fixed-point unit generates the address for a floating-point store, it must know when the data will be available. Again, in many coprocessor schemes, it would simply wait for the floating-point unit to produce the data and stop executing subsequent instructions. The RISC System/6000 uses a store-data buffer similar to that of the System/360 Model 91 [16] to allow the fixed-point unit to proceed to execute subsequent instructions. It works in the following way.

After generating the address for a floating-point store, the fixed-point unit places the address in a pending-store queue. When the floating-point unit removes the store from the store queue, it places the data in a data buffer on the floating-point chip, and informs the fixed-point unit that the data is available. Now that the data and address are available, the fixed-point unit can perform the store on any subsequent cycle.

Floating-point loads A floating-point load, since it defines a new semantic value for the architected register, causes the map table to be updated. When a load enters the rename stage, the map table is accessed for the target register. The tag stored there is placed on the PTRQ. It cannot be returned immediately to the free list since there may be pending floating-point arithmetic and store instructions which still need the value in that physical register. The tag at the head of the free list is written into the map-table entry. If there are no free tags, the fixed-point unit is informed to stop executing instructions.

The new physical register tag is then placed on the OLQ, and the LC field of the most recent prior arithmetic instruction is incremented.

Tags are returned to the free list from the PTRQ in the following way. The contents of a physical register become unused (free) when the last arithmetic instruction or store referencing that physical register has been performed. For arithmetic instructions, this occurs when they complete decode. For stores, this occurs when they are removed from the store queue. When a load causes a new logical-to-physical mapping, the last instruction which could have used that physical register was the most recent arithmetic instruction, or floating-point store. (It may actually never have been used for many, many instructions.) Thus, when the most recent prior arithmetic instruction has decoded or store has been performed, that physical register can be returned to the free list.

Several mechanisms could have been used to determine this. The most straightforward would have been to compare the old physical register tag to all outstanding register fields of instructions in an IDB or the decoder, and to stores on the store queue. The last instruction to have matched would then be told to return the tag to the free list when it decoded or was removed from the store queue. This would have required up to 20 comparators, and 20 latch bits to ensure that the instruction returned the register.

An alternate method was developed. First, it is sufficient to let only arithmetic instructions return tags to the free list, if, before doing so, they check (via comparators) the contents of the store queue to ensure that there are no pending stores of this physical register. Then, each time a load renames a register, the old register tag is placed on the PTRQ. A counter, the load count (LCT) associated with each arithmetic instruction, is incremented. When the load decodes, the LCT field is used by the PTRQ controls to release that number of tags to the free list. This method eliminates the need for comparators with the IDB and decode stages. However, comparators and a bit are required for each store-queue entry. **Table 1** illustrates the procedure.

The operation of this example is shown in Figure 6. In Figure 6(a), the map table is initialized to identity, and all physical registers are free. The decoder, IDB, arithmetic pipeline, OLQ, and PSQ are empty. A floating-point add and a store are in registers R0 and R1. They are renamed, and pass to the decoder and the PSQ. The store-count field of the add is set to 1.

In Figure 6(b) the floating-point add has passed from rename into decode, since all required physical registers are free. Its store count increments the release pointer of the PSQ to release the store. A floating-point load and a multiply are in rename. The load causes a new mapping for architected register 3. It places the old mapping for register 3 on the PTRQ, and replaces it with register 32 from the free list. The release pointer for the PTRQ will automatically be incremented, since the add in decode (the most recent arithmetic instruction) will read out the

Table 1 Register renaming for floating-point load instructions.

Original stream	Rename table	Free head	Renamed stream	PTRQ
FADD R3, R2, R1	(1, 1); (2, 2); (3, 3)	32	R3, R2, R1	
FST R3	(3, 3)	32	R3	
FLD R3	(3, 3)	32	PR32	3
FMUL R6, R3, R1	(1, 1); (3, 32); (6, 6)	33	R6, R32, R1	
FSUB R2, R6, R2	(2, 2); (6, 6); (2, 2)	33	R2, R6, R2	
FLD R3	(3, 32)	33	PR33	32

old value. The load will be placed on the OLQ. The multiply will be renamed, after which it passes into decode, with its LC and SC fields set to 0.

During the next cycle [Figure 6(c)], the floating-point add is in execution. Its target register is in the BUSY register. The store of register 3, while released, cannot be performed since the data is being produced by the add and is not yet available. The load is on the OLQ, and the data will return from the data cache during this cycle. The PTRQ controls will try to place physical register 3 on the free list. However, the store still needs the old value. The give-back bit for the store will be set. The multiply is in decode and will decode during this cycle, since there are no register interlocks. The last two instructions, the subtract and the final load, are in rename and will proceed into the decoder and the OLQ during the next cycle. The load count field of the subtract is set to 1.

During the next cycle [Figure 6(d)], the store can be removed, since the data is available from the add. Since its give-back bit is set, it will also return the tag to the free list. The last load is on the OLQ. The subtract must wait for the multiply to execute and will remain in decode.

During the next cycle [Figure 6(e)], the subtract can decode, releasing register tag 32 on the PTRQ. It is returned during the next cycle. One cycle later [Figures 6(f) and 6(g)], the subtract completes execution.

While register renaming appears to be a fairly complex control mechanism, it elegantly allows fixed- and floating-point instructions to be overlapped to take maximum advantage of each execution unit. In conjunction with the fixed–floating-point synchronization scheme, precise interrupts are maintained between fixed- and floating-point operations.

• *Maintaining the consistency of the instruction stream*
In a highly overlapped machine, interrupts may be precise or imprecise. An interrupt is precise if, when it is processed, no subsequent instructions have begun execution and all prior instructions have completed. Precise interrupts force the machine to preserve the view of a machine which executes one instruction at a time,

finishing it before processing the next one. Imprecise interrupts, on the other hand, allow the processor to leave the instruction stream in the neighborhood of the interrupt in a fragmented, but recoverable, state. For instance, all prior instructions may have executed, and some subsequent instructions may have begun execution and updated architected registers. In this case, it may not be possible to re-execute them. Imprecise interrupts therefore require the architecture to provide a means for reconstructing the instruction stream around the point of the interrupt, so that post-interrupt processing software can recreate the sequential state of the machine.

Due to the pipeline complexity of the AMERICA machine organization, it would have been difficult to architect a facility for handling interrupts in an imprecise fashion, which would have accounted for the many possibilities for instruction execution past the point of an interrupt. Therefore, precise interrupts were specified for all program-generated interrupts.

In order to guarantee precise interrupts, each interrupt type was analyzed, and a means of handling each in a precise fashion was developed. External, asynchronous interrupts were handled by stopping instruction dispatch and waiting for the pipeline to drain. If an instruction in the pipeline caused an interrupt, that interrupt was taken. Other interrupt conditions, such as invalid instructions, were detected in the ICU during the dispatch cycle, causing a wait for the pipeline to drain in a similar fashion.

The following mechanism was developed to ensure that interrupts resulting from the execution of load, store, or trap instructions by the fixed-point unit were precise. These three types of instructions are termed interrupt-causing (IC) instructions, although they are not the only instructions which can cause interrupts.

The fixed–floating-point synchronization scheme ensures that precise interrupts are maintained between the fixed- and floating-point units. Since no floating-point instructions could cause interrupts in AMERICA, the remaining need was to synchronize the branch-processing unit with the fixed-point unit.

From the pipeline structure it is apparent that branches and LCR operations executed by the branch unit change the count, link, and condition registers before the branch unit is informed that a prior IC instruction has caused an interrupt. Therefore, any changes to these registers must be undone to reflect their state at the time of the interrupt. In addition, the address of the IC instruction must be saved in SRR0 so that interrupt-handling software can process it.

The program counter stack (PCS) mechanism was developed to handle this. Each cycle, as instructions are dispatched to the execution units, logic-records the relationship of branches and LCR instructions which

modify the count, link, and condition registers to IC instructions. The addresses of IC instructions are also recorded on a stack. If a branch or LCR instruction is executed before a prior IC instruction has been executed, the old value of the count, link, or condition register is saved on a backup stack for that register.

As IC instructions are executed by the fixed-point unit, entries are removed from the PCS; old entries for the count, link, or condition registers are removed from their backup stacks, since no interrupt has occurred. When an IC instruction causes an interrupt, the head entry on the backup stacks is written to that register, and the address of the IC instruction saved on the PCS is saved in SRR0. Consider the following example:

```
1000   L        ;Load which will cause an interrupt
1004   CRAND    ;LCR instruction which modifies CR
1008   BL       ;Branch and Link changing LR
```

Assume that these three instructions are dispatched during one cycle. The address of the load, 1000, is recorded on the PCS, and the load is sent to the fixed-point unit. The old value of the condition-register field modified by the CRAND instruction is recorded on the CR backup stack. The branch-and-link updates the value of the link register to 100C hex, and causes the old value of the link register to be placed on the link-register backup queue. Status bits are set which reflect the fact that changes to the CR and LR were made after an interrupt-causing instruction. When the load interrupts several cycles later, the PCS is accessed. The address stored there is placed in SRR0. The status bits cause the values for the link register and condition register to be restored, erasing any changes to the machine state.

Design of the IBM RISC System/6000 processor
During the implementation of the RS/6000 processor, several notable changes were made to the processor specification. Additionally, several areas of the machine were developed in greater detail.

• *Instruction cache*
As originally specified, the instruction-fetching mechanism could fetch four instructions per cycle as long as they were within the first 13 instructions of a cache line (out of a total of 16). While implementing the array access logic, it was noted that the same interleaving principle could be applied to the cache directories. By splitting the cache directories into even and odd components and supplying a "row-incrementation feature" to the even directory, four instructions could be fetched even if two cache lines were crossed. If the first instruction of the group was in an even cache line, the odd directory could be accessed with the same row address to search for the remaining instructions in the

successor cache line. Similarly, if the first instruction was in an odd cache line, the next cache line would be contained in the next congruence class in the even directory, requiring that the row address be incremented. This feature complicated the hit logic and replicated some comparators, but was introduced at no cycle-time penalty. As a result, assuming that both lines are present in a cache, four instructions can always be fetched as long as the lines are in the same 4-Kbyte virtual page. This case could also have been handled by interleaving the instruction TLB into even and odd pages, but this was not worth the implementation cost.

The instruction cache is organized as an 8-Kbyte, two-way set-associative cache, which has a 64-byte (16-instruction) line size. The size of the instruction cache was limited by that which could fit on the 12.7-mm-square chip used for implementing the RS/6000 processors. With an 8-Kbyte instruction cache, a miss ratio of less than 2% is expected. A 64-byte line size was chosen for three reasons. Simulation of IBM System/370 processors with this line size indicated that larger lines tended to increase miss ratios at this cache size. The package available dictated that the reload bus from memory be two instructions wide. With a 64-byte line size, eight cycles over this bus are required to reload a cache line when a miss occurs. A 128-byte line would require 16 cycles, and would tie up the instruction cache for too long. A cache with 32-byte lines requires twice the directory space of a cache with 64-byte lines. A two-way set-associative cache was used, since the behavior of a direct-mapped cache is worse, and the performance gain of a four-way set-associative cache is marginally superior to that of a two-way set-associative cache. Also, properly designed, the two-way set-associative cache would not lengthen the machine cycle, since there are many other paths in other pipeline cycles which could equally well determine the cycle time.

- *Branch processing*

One path that was known to be critical in AMERICA was the condition-code-setting path from the fixed-point unit to the branch unit. In one cycle the fixed-point unit was to execute a compare-type instruction and transmit the resulting condition code to the ICU chip, where the branch-resolution logic would determine the outcome in time to switch the instruction stream. The time taken to resolve the branch and perform the stream switch took longer than originally anticipated, so it was delayed until the next cycle. As a result, the compare-branch penalty was increased to three cycles from two cycles, as illustrated in Figure 4. Nevertheless, in the Dhrystone 1.1 benchmark [17], of 64 branches in the inner loop, only 20 cause any delay. The total delay is 46 cycles, so that branches are executed at the rate of 46/64 = 0.72 cycles per instruction. This is a considerable improvement over

the 1+ cycles per branch instruction typical of most current RISC processors.

- *Condition register*

One of the prime examples of how the 801 architecture was changed to support concurrent execution of many instructions is embodied in the condition register (CR) [1]. It contains eight fields, each of which can be designated to hold the results of a compare-type operation. It is located in the instruction cache and branch-processing unit. By having one interlock bit per field, eight outstanding operations can be maintained. When an instruction is dispatched to the fixed- or floating-point units, which sets CR field 0, the corresponding interlock bit is set. Subsequent instructions which try to read or to set that field remain in the instruction buffers. Eventually the fixed-point or floating-point unit executes the instruction, and the ICU is informed via the condition-register bus from that unit. Then, the interlock bit is reset. Since instructions which set the condition register can be dispatched conditionally, and canceled, any corresponding condition-register interlock bits which were set must be reset. A similar reset occurs for compares which are dispatched after IC instructions that interrupt. This is performed and maintained by the PCS.

During the implementation, the amount of space dedicated to resolving condition-register interlocks in the dispatch and PCS logic became too large. Four interlock bits were introduced, so that four outstanding operations to the condition register could be maintained.

- *Synchronization of fixed-point and floating-point units*

The design of the fixed-point unit was such that instructions were held off in the execution phase rather than in the decode phase. As a result, the decode hold line shown in Figure 5 was not necessary. Also, the hold/cancel signal generated by the fixed-point unit was too late to make a chip crossing to the floating-point unit in one cycle. Therefore, instructions were permitted to enter floating-point decode, where they would be held off and canceled. This meant that, potentially, one rename cycle would have to be undone. Furthermore, many bugs were found in the synchronization scheme, so a counter was added to the fixed-point unit. Each time the floating-point unit shifted instructions out of rename, the shift amount was transmitted to the fixed-point unit. The fixed-point unit subtracted the number of instructions it shifted; the value of the difference specified the buffer position in the fixed-point unit of the instruction which was in R0 in the floating-point unit.

- *Register renaming and floating-point control*

Originally both floating-point arithmetic instructions and floating-point loads caused new logical-to-physical

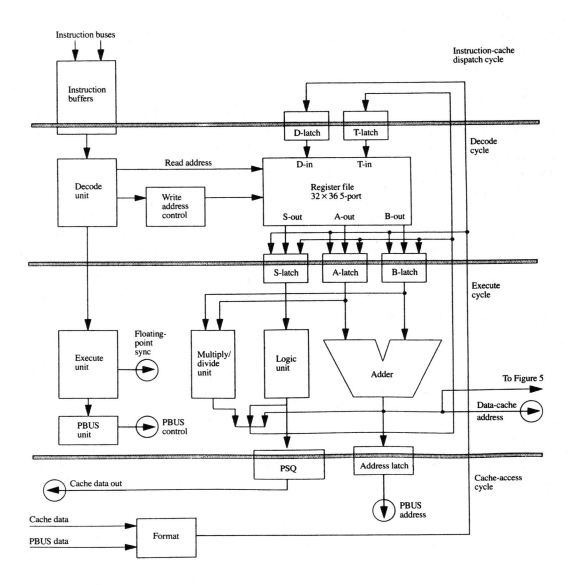

Figure 7

General organization and pipelining of the fixed-point unit.

register mappings for their targets. Remapping arithmetic instructions complicates the renaming logic, since more ports are required on the PTRQ and the free list. It is only useful if arithmetic instructions can be executed out of order. In a sequence such as

```
FDIV FR0,      ;FR0 gets divide
FST FR0,       ;store FR0
FADD FR0,      ;FR0 used for add result
```

the floating-point add could proceed. Sequences like this would not occur frequently, since the RS/6000 processor has 32 floating-point registers. Since the floating-point unit executed floating-point arithmetic instructions in sequence, there was no need to remap floating-point arithmetic instructions. This simplified the remap logic by requiring fewer ports on the AVRQ and PTRQ, as well as reducing the control logic complexity.

Another significant change was that the RISC System/6000 uses the IEEE floating-point arithmetic format, while AMERICA used the IBM System/370 format. This necessitated several changes to the controls.

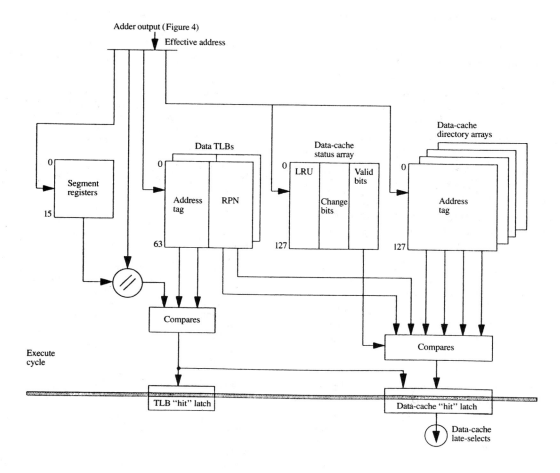

Figure 8

General organization and pipelining of the data TLB and data-cache directory/status arrays.

The most significant was that floating-point stores were required to proceed through the floating-point decoder, so that any normalizations were performed properly. This is described in more detail in [2]. This degraded floating-point performance substantially in peak floating-point loops. For example, using the 2D graphics example described above, the RS/6000 machine takes seven cycles per loop iteration as opposed to four in AMERICA. On balance, however, this degradation is less severe; while the potential AMERICA LINPACK performance was approximately 15 MFLOPS, the RISC System/6000 achieves nearly 11 MFLOPS.

• *Fixed-point execution, data-cache access, and address translation*
The RS/6000 FXU is diagrammed in **Figure 7**. The basic 801 fixed-point execution-unit organization was sufficient

to provide an instruction execution rate close to one cycle per instruction. Thus, it was not a primary area of focus for improvement. However, some attention was given to making loads and stores operate quickly by placing the data-cache TLBs (translation look-aside buffers) and the data-cache directories on the fixed-point chip. Initial studies indicated that the following pipeline structure could be utilized. Starting at the beginning of the execution cycle, the address is generated by the ALU. This requires approximately one-half cycle. In the second half cycle, the segment registers are accessed, the virtual address generated, and the TLB and directories are searched in parallel. At the end of the cycle, it is known whether or not the access resulted in a hit or miss, and whether or not the access was permitted or caused a data storage interrupt. Also, during the last half cycle, the address is transmitted across a chip boundary to the data-cache arrays and latched. This is diagrammed in **Figure 8**.

At the beginning of the next cycle, the late-selects are generated to select one of the four sets in the four-way set-associative data cache, and are sent to the data-cache chips. In parallel, the data-cache arrays are accessed to provide one word from each of four sets. The late-selects then select one word, which is transmitted to the fixed-point unit. It is formatted (sign-extended, rotated) as necessary, bypassed to the ALU and shifter, and latched for writing into the register file during the next cycle.

This cache organization therefore provides data in two execution cycles. An instruction using a register being loaded must wait one cycle before being executed. About two thirds of the time, the load can be scheduled back by the compiler, and this delay can be covered.

Summary

The IBM RISC System/6000 machine organization uses multiple execution units to achieve high performance. A separate instruction cache which fetches four instructions per cycle effectively eliminates pipeline starvation. A robust branch-processing unit removes the execution pipeline penalties of most branch instructions without using a branch history table or elaborate branch-prediction mechanisms. By overlapping the execution of floating-point loads and stores with floating-point arithmetic operations, high floating-point performance is achieved. Precise interrupts are maintained to simplify system-interrupt handlers. The result is a powerful, robust processing platform which gives high system performance across a wide spectrum of application programs.

Acknowledgments

The author would like to thank the many people of IBM Austin without whom the processor could not have been designed. Although too many contributed to be listed here, the contributions of several people are notable. Chuck Moore, Ed Boufarah, and C. C. Lee helped implement the instruction cache and branch-processing unit. Jim Kahle, Larry Thatcher, Dennis Gregoire, Paul Harvey, and Brian Bakoglu worked on the fixed-point unit. Myhong Nguyenphu, Daniel Cocanougher, Richard Fry, Pat Mills, Oscar Mitchell, and Troy Hicks worked on the floating-point unit. Brett Olsson analyzed the branch performance of the RISC System/6000 on the Dhrystone 1.1 benchmark.

References

1. R. R. Oehler and R. D. Groves, "IBM RISC System/6000 Processor Architecture," *IBM J. Res. Develop.* **34**, 23–36 (1990, this issue).
2. R. K. Montoye, E. Hokenek, and S. L. Runyon, "Design of the IBM RISC System/6000 Floating-Point Execution Unit," *IBM J. Res. Develop.* **34**, 59–70 (1990, this issue).
3. G. Radin, "The 801 Minicomputer," *Proceedings of the Symposium on Architectural Support for Programming Languages and Operating Systems,* in *ACM SIGARCH Computer Architecture News* **10**, No. 2, 39–47 (1982).
4. D. W. Anderson, F. J. Sparacio, and R. M. Tomasulo, "The IBM System/360 Model 91: Machine Philosophy and Instruction-Handling," *IBM J. Res. Develop.* **11**, 8–24 (1967).
5. J. E. Thornton, *Design of a Computer—The Control Data 6600,* Scott, Foresman, & Co., Glenview, IL, 1970.
6. *IBM RISC System/6000 Technology,* Order Number SA23-2619, 1990; available through IBM branch offices.
7. J. F. Hughes et al., "Decode Branch History Table," *IBM Tech. Disclosure Bull.* **25**, 2396–2398 (1982).
8. J. K. Lee and A. J. Smith, "Branch Prediction Strategies and Branch Target Buffer Designs," *IEEE Computer Magazine* **17**, 6–22 (1984).
9. J. J. Losq, "Generalized History Table for Branch Prediction," *IBM Tech. Disclosure Bull.* **25**, 99–101 (1982).
10. J. E. Smith, "A Study of Branch Prediction Strategies," *Proceedings of the 8th Symposium on Computer Architecture,* Institute of Electrical and Electronics Engineers, May 1981, pp. 135–148.
11. R. B. Garner et al., "The Scalable Processor Architecture (SPARC)," *Proceedings of COMPCON '88,* Institute of Electrical and Electronics Engineers, 1988, pp. 278–293.
12. C. Rowen et al., "RISC VLSI Design for System Level Performance," *VLSI Systems Design,* pp. 81–88 (March 1988).
13. M. Johnson, "System Considerations in the Design of the AMD 29000," *IEEE Micro,* pp. 28–41 (August 1987).
14. Tom Manuel, "Taking a Close Look at the Motorola 88000," *Electronics,* pp. 75–78 (April 28, 1988).
15. D. A. Patterson et al., "Architecture of a VLSI Instruction Cache for a RISC," *Proceedings of the 10th Annual Symposium on Computer Architecture,* Institute of Electrical and Electronics Engineers, 1983, pp. 108–116.
16. R. M. Tomasulo, "An Efficient Algorithm for Exploiting Multiple Arithmetic Units," *IBM J. Res. Develop.* **11**, 25–33 (1967).
17. R. P. Weicker, "Dhrystone: A Synthetic Systems Programming Benchmark," *Commun. ACM* **27**, 1013–1030 (October 1984).

Received February 28, 1989; accepted for publication January 17, 1990

Gregory F. Grohoski *IBM Advanced Workstations Division, 11400 Burnet Road, Austin, Texas 78758.* Mr. Grohoski received a B.S. with distinction in electrical engineering from Cornell University in 1980 and an M.S. in electrical engineering from the University of Illinois at Urbana-Champaign in 1981. That same year he joined the IBM Research Division at the Thomas J. Watson Research Center in Yorktown Heights, New York, where he worked on high-performance RISC machine designs. In 1986 he transferred to IBM Austin to work on the RISC System/6000 project. Mr. Grohoski holds two IBM Invention Achievement Awards and an IBM Outstanding Technical Achievement Award; he has applied for five patents. He is currently an Advisory Engineer in the hardware architecture group.

THE MIPS R10000 SUPERSCALAR MICROPROCESSOR

Kenneth C. Yeager

Silicon Graphics, Inc.

Out-of-order superscalar microprocessors execute instructions beyond those stalled by cache misses. This minimizes the time lost due to latency by completing other instructions and initiating subsequent cache refills early.

The Mips R10000 is a dynamic, superscalar microprocessor that implements the 64-bit Mips 4 instruction set architecture. It fetches and decodes four instructions per cycle and dynamically issues them to five fully-pipelined, low-latency execution units. Instructions can be fetched and executed speculatively beyond branches. Instructions graduate in order upon completion. Although execution is out of order, the processor still provides sequential memory consistency and precise exception handling.

The R10000 is designed for high performance, even in large, real-world applications with poor memory locality. With speculative execution, it calculates memory addresses and initiates cache refills early. Its hierarchical, nonblocking memory system helps hide memory latency with two levels of set-associative, write-back caches. Figure 1 shows the R10000 system configuration, and the R10000 box lists its principal features.

Out-of-order superscalar processors are inherently complex. To cope with this complexity, the R10000 uses a modular design that locates much of the control logic within regular structures, including the active list, register map tables, and instruction queues.

Design rationale

Memory bandwidth and latency limit the performance of many programs. Because packaging and system costs constrain these resources, the processor must use them efficiently.

The R10000 implements register mapping and nonblocking caches, which complement each other to overlap cache refill operations. Thus, if an instruction misses in the cache, it must wait for its operand to be refilled, but other instructions can continue out of order. This increases memory use and reduces effective latency, because refills begin early and up to four refills proceed in parallel while the processor executes other instructions. This type of cache design is called "nonblocking," because cache refills do not block subsequent accesses to other cache lines.

Processors rely on compiler support to optimize instruction sequencing. This technique is especially effective for data arrays, such as those used in many floating-point applications. For these arrays, a sophisticated compiler can optimize performance for a specific cache organization. However, compiler optimization is less effective for the scalar values of many integer applications, because the compiler has difficulty predicting which instructions will generate cache misses.

The R10000 design includes complex hardware that dynamically reorders instruction execution based on operand availability. This hardware immediately adapts whenever cache misses delay instructions. The processor looks ahead up to 32 instructions to find possible parallelism. This instruction window is large enough to hide most of the latency for refills from the secondary cache. However, it can hide only a fraction of main memory latency, which is typically much longer.

It is relatively easy to add nonblocking caches to an out-of-order processor, because it already contains mechanisms that coordinate dependencies between instructions.

Implementation

We implemented the initial R10000 microprocessor using 0.35-μm CMOS technology on a 16.64×17.934-mm chip. This 298-mm² chip contains 6.8 million transistors, including 4.4 million in its primary cache arrays. We implemented data paths and time-critical control logic in full custom design, making wide use of dynamic and latch-based logic. We synthesized the less critical circuits using static register-based logic.

Mips R10000

This processor features a four-way superscalar RISC processor that

- fetches and decodes four instructions per cycle,
- speculatively executes beyond branches, with a four-entry branch stack,
- uses dynamic out-of-order execution,
- implements register renaming using map tables, and
- achieves in-order graduation for precise exceptions.

Five independent pipelined execution units include

- a nonblocking load/store unit,
- dual 64-bit integer ALUs,
- 64-bit, IEEE Std 754-1985 floating-point units,
- a pipelined adder with two-cycle latency, and
- a pipelined multiplier with two-cycle latency.

The hierarchical, nonblocking memory subsystem includes

- on-chip, two-way-associative primary caches—32-Kbyte instruction cache and 32-Kbyte, two-way interleaved data cache,
- an external, two-way-associative secondary cache—128-bit-wide, synchronous static RAM, and
- a 64-bit multiprocessor system interface with split transaction protocol.

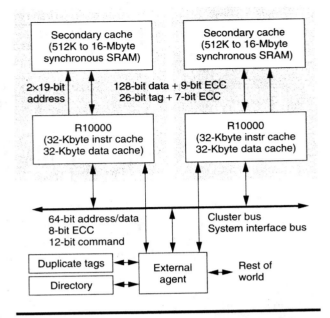

Figure 1. System configuration. The cluster bus directly connects as many as four chips.

System flexibility

Alternate configurations allow the R10000 to operate in a wide range of systems—as a uniprocessor or in a multiprocessor cluster. The system maintains cache coherency using either snoopy or directory-based protocols. The R10000's secondary cache ranges from 512 Kbytes to 16 Mbytes.

Operation overview

Figure 2 (next page) shows a block diagram and a pipeline timing diagram for the R10000. There are six nearly independent pipelines.

The instruction fetch pipeline occupies stages 1 through 3. In stage 1, the R10000 fetches and aligns the next four instructions. In stage 2, it decodes and renames these instructions and also calculates target addresses for jump and branch instructions. In stage 3, it writes the renamed instructions into the queues and reads the busy-bit table to determine if the operands are initially busy. Instructions wait in the queues until all their operands are ready.

The five execution pipelines begin when a queue issues an instruction in stage 3. The processor reads operands from the register files during the second half of stage 3, and execution begins in stage 4. The integer pipelines occupy one stage, the load pipeline occupies two, and the floating-point pipelines occupy three. The processor writes results into the register file during the first half of the next stage.

The integer and floating-point sections have separate instruction queues, register files, and data paths. This separation reduces maximum wire lengths and allows fully parallel operation. Together, the two register files need more free registers than would a combined unit, but they are physically smaller, because each register has fewer read and write ports.

Instruction fetch

For good performance, the processor must fetch and decode instructions at a higher bandwidth than it can execute them. It is important to keep the queues full, so they can look ahead to find instructions to issue out of order. Ultimately, the processor fetches more instructions than it graduates, because it discards instructions occurring after mispredicted branches.

The processor fetches instructions during stage 1, as shown in Figure 3. The instruction cache contains address tag and data sections. To implement two-way set associativity, each section has two parallel arrays. The processor compares the two tag addresses to translated physical addresses to select data from the correct way. The small, eight-entry instruction translation look-aside buffer (TLB) contains a subset of the translations in the main TLB.

The processor fetches four instructions in parallel at any word alignment within a 16-word instruction cache line. We implemented this feature with a simple modification to the cache's sense amplifiers, as shown in Figure 4. Each sense amplifier is as wide as four bit columns in the memory array, and a 4-to-1 multiplexer selects one column (which represents one instruction) for fetching. The R10000 fetches unaligned instructions using a separate select signal for each instruction. These instructions rotate, if necessary, so that they are decoded in order. This ordering reduces the amount of dependency logic.

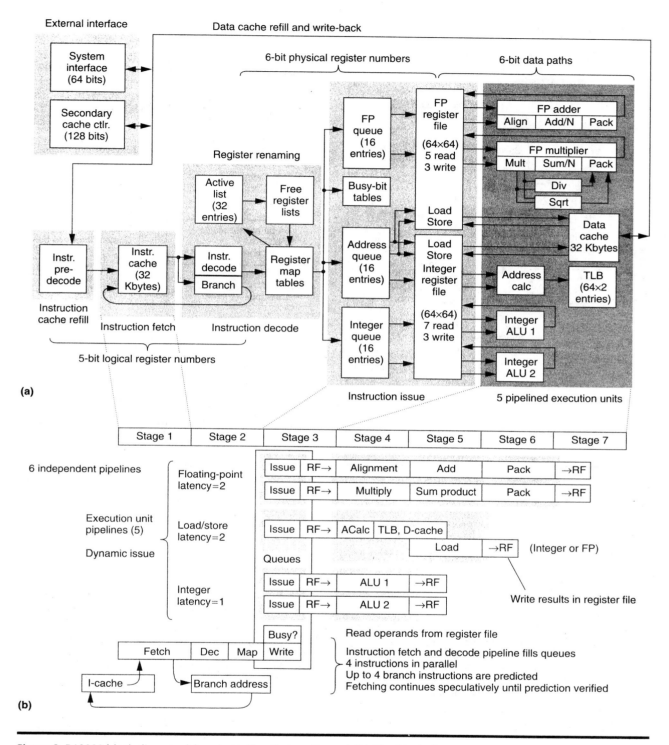

Figure 2. R10000 block diagram (a) and pipeline timing diagram (b). The block diagram shows pipeline stages left to right to correspond to pipeline timing.

Usually, the processor decodes all four instructions during the next cycle, unless the queues or active list is full. Instructions that are not immediately decoded remain in an eight-word instruction buffer, simplifying timing for sequential fetching.

Branch unit

Branch instructions occur frequently and must execute quickly. However, the processor cannot usually determine the branch direction until several or even many cycles after

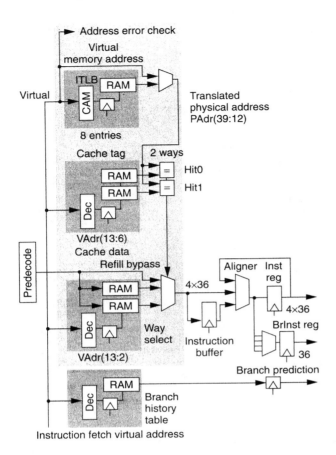

Figure 3. Instruction fetch, pipeline stage 1.

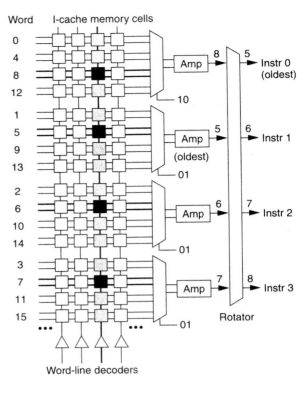

Figure 4. Unaligned fetching from instruction cache.

decoding the branch. Thus, the processor predicts the direction a conditional branch will take and fetches instructions speculatively along the predicted path. The prediction uses a 2-bit algorithm based on a 512-entry branch history table. This table is indexed by bits 11:3 of the address of the branch instruction. Simulations show an 87 percent prediction accuracy for Spec92 integer programs.

In the Mips architecture, the processor executes the instruction immediately following a jump or branch before executing instructions at the target address. In a pipelined scalar processor, this delay slot instruction can be executed for free, while the target instruction is read from the cache. This technique improved branch efficiency in early RISC microprocessors. For a superscalar design, however, it has no performance advantage, but we retained the feature in the R10000 for compatibility.

When the program execution takes a jump or branch, the processor discards any instructions already fetched beyond the delay slot. It loads the jump's target address into the program counter and fetches new instructions from the cache after a one-cycle delay. This introduces one "branch bubble" cycle, during which the R10000 decodes no instructions.

Branch stack. When it decodes a branch, the processor saves its state in a four-entry branch stack. This contains the

alternate branch address, complete copies of the integer and floating-point map tables, and miscellaneous control bits. Although the stack operates as a single logical entity, it is physically distributed near the information it copies.

When the branch stack is full, the processor continues decoding only until it encounters the next branch instruction. Decoding then stalls until resolution of one of the pending branches.

Branch verification. The processor verifies each branch prediction as soon as its condition is determined, even if earlier branches are still pending. If the prediction was incorrect, the processor immediately aborts all instructions fetched along the mispredicted path and restores its state from the branch stack.

Fetching along mispredicted paths may initiate unneeded cache refills. In this case, the instruction cache is nonblocking, and the processor fetches the correct path while these refills complete. It is easier and often desirable to complete such refills, since the program execution may soon take the other direction of the branch, such as at the end of a loop.

A 4-bit branch mask, corresponding to entries within the branch stack, accompanies each instruction through the queues and execution pipelines. This mask indicates which pending branches the instruction depends on. If any of these branches was mispredicted, the processor will abort the instruction when that branch decision is reversed. Whenever the R10000 verifies a branch, it resets the corresponding mask bits throughout the pipeline.

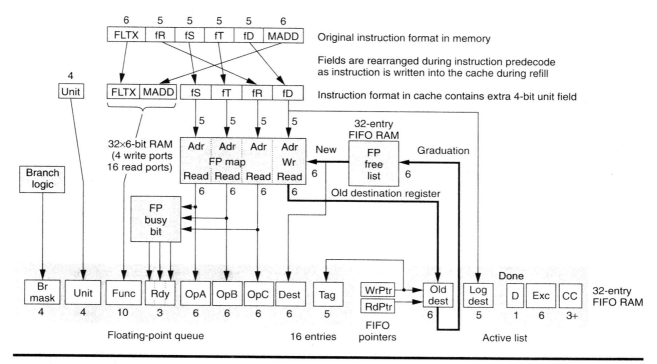

Figure 5. Register renaming, pipeline stage 2. The R10000 rearranges fields during instruction predecode as it writes the instruction into the cache during refill. The instruction format in the cache contains an extra 4-bit unit field.

Decode logic

The R10000 decodes and maps four instructions in parallel during stage 2 and writes them into the appropriate instruction queue at the beginning of stage 3.

Decoding stops if the active list or a queue becomes full, but there are very few decode restrictions that depend on the type of instructions being decoded. The principal exception involves integer multiply and divide instructions. Their results go into two special registers—Hi and Lo. No other instructions have more than one result register. We did not add much logic for these infrequently used instructions; instead, they occupy two slots in the active list. Once the processor decodes such an instruction, it does not decode any subsequent instructions during the same cycle. (In addition, it cannot decode an integer multiply or divide as the fourth instruction in a cycle.)

Instructions that read or modify certain control registers execute serially. The processor can only execute these instructions, which are mostly restricted to rare cases in the kernel operating system mode, when the pipeline is empty. This restriction has little effect on overall performance.

Register mapping

Figure 5 illustrates the R10000's register-mapping hardware. To execute instructions out of their original program order, the processor must keep track of dependencies on register operands, memory addresses, and condition bits. (The condition bits are eight bits in the status register set by floating-point compare instructions.) To determine register dependencies, the R10000 uses register renaming. It determines memory address dependencies in the address queue. It sets each condition bit operand during decode if its value is known. If not, it renames the bit with the tag of the floating-point compare instruction that will eventually set its value.

From a programmer's perspective, instructions execute sequentially in the order the program specifies. When an instruction loads a new value into its destination register, that new value is immediately available for subsequent instructions to use. However, a superscalar processor performs several instructions simultaneously, and their results are not immediately available for subsequent instructions. Frequently, the next sequential instruction must wait for its operands to become valid, but the operands of later instructions may already be available.

The R10000 achieves higher performance by executing these later instructions out of order, but this reordering is invisible to the programmer. Any result it generates out of order is temporary until all previous instructions have completed. Then this instruction graduates, and its result is committed as the processor's state. Until it graduates, an instruction can be aborted if it follows an exception or a mispredicted branch. The previous contents of its logical destination register can be retrieved by restoring its previous mapping.

In most processors, there is no distinction between logical register numbers, which are referenced within instruction fields, and physical registers, which are locations in the hardware register file. Each instruction field directly addresses the corresponding register. Our renaming strategy, however, dynamically maps the logical-register numbers into physical-register numbers. The processor writes each new result into a new physical register. After mapping, the processor determines dependencies simply by comparing physical-register numbers; it no longer must consider instruction order. Again, the existence of these physical registers and the mapping of logical registers to physical registers are invisible to the programmer.

The R10000 executes instructions dynamically after resolving all dependencies on previous instructions. That is, each instruction must wait until all its operands have been computed. Then the R10000 can execute that instruction, regardless of the original instruction sequence. To execute instructions correctly, the processor must determine when each operand register is ready. This can be complicated, because logical-register numbers may be ambiguous in terms of operand values. For example, if several instructions specifying the same logical register are simultaneously in the pipeline, that register may load repeatedly with different values.

There must be more physical than logical registers, because physical registers contain both committed values and temporary results for instructions that have completed but not yet graduated. A logical register may have a sequence of values as instructions flow through the pipeline. Whenever an instruction modifies a register, the processor assigns a new physical register to the logical destination register and stores these assignments in register map tables. As the R10000 decodes each instruction, it replaces each of the logical-register fields with the corresponding physical-register number.

Each physical register is written exactly once after each assignment from the free list. Until it is written, it is busy. If a subsequent instruction needs its value, that instruction must wait until it is written. After the register is written, it is ready, and its value does not change. When a subsequent instruction changes the corresponding logical register, that result is written into a new physical register. When this subsequent instruction graduates, the program no longer needs the old value, and the old physical register becomes free for reuse. Thus, physical registers always have unambiguous values.

There are 33 logical (numbers 1 through 31, Hi, and Lo) and 64 physical integer registers. (There is no integer register 0. A zero operand field indicates a zero value; a zero destination field indicates an unstored result.) There are 32 logical (numbers 0 through 31) and 64 physical floating-point registers.

Register map tables. Separate register files store integer and floating-point registers, which the processor renames independently. The integer and floating-point map tables contain the current assignments of logical to physical registers. The processor selects logical registers using 5-bit instruction fields. Six-bit addresses in the corresponding register files identify the physical registers.

The floating-point table maps registers f0 through f31 in a 32×6-bit multiport RAM. The integer table maps registers r1 through r31, Hi, and Lo in a 33×6-bit multiport RAM. (There is special access logic for the Hi and Lo registers, the implicit destinations of integer multiply and divide instructions.)

These map tables have 16 read ports and four write ports which map four instructions in parallel. Each instruction reads the mappings for three operand registers and one destination register. The processor writes the current operand mappings and new destination mapping into the instruction queues,

while the active list saves previous destination mappings.

The R10000 uses 24 five-bit comparators to detect dependencies among the four instructions decoded in parallel. These comparators control bypass multiplexers, which replace dependent operands with new assignments from the free lists.

Free lists. The integer and floating-point free lists contain lists of currently unassigned physical registers. Because the processor decodes and graduates up to four instructions in parallel, these lists consist of four parallel, eight-deep, circular FIFOs.

Active list. The active list records all instructions currently active within the processor, appending each instruction as the processor decodes it. The list removes instructions when they graduate, or if a mispredicted branch or an exception causes them to abort. Since up to 32 instructions can be active, the active list consists of four parallel, eight-deep, circular FIFOs.

Each instruction is identified by 5-bit tag, which equals an address in the active list. When an execution unit completes an instruction, it sends its tag to the active list, which sets its done bit.

The active list contains the logical-destination register number and its old physical-register number for each instruction. An instruction's graduation commits its new mapping, so the old physical register can return to the free list for reuse.

When an exception occurs, however, subsequent instructions never graduate. Instead, the processor restores old mappings from the active list. The R10000 unmaps four instructions per cycle—in reverse order, in case it renamed the same logical register twice. Although this is slower than restoring a branch, exceptions are much rarer than mispredicted branches. The processor returns new physical registers to the free lists by restoring their read pointers.

Busy-bit tables. For each physical register, integer and floating-point busy-bit tables contain a bit indicating whether the register currently contains a valid value. Each table is a 64×1-bit multiport RAM. The tables sets a bit busy when the corresponding register leaves the free list. It resets the bit when an execution unit writes a value into this register. Twelve read ports determine the status of three operand registers for each of four newly decoded instructions. The queues use three other ports for special-case instructions, such as moves between the integer and floating-point register files.

Instruction queues

The R10000 puts each decoded instruction, except jumps and no operation NOPs, into one of three instruction queues, according to type. Provided there is room, the queues can accept any combination of new instructions.

The chip's cycle time constrained our design of the queues. For instance, we dedicated two register file read ports to each issued instruction to avoid delays arbitrating and multiplexing operand buses.

Integer queue. The integer queue contains 16 entries in no specific order and allocates an entry to each integer instruction as it is decoded. The queue releases the entry as soon as it issues the instruction to an ALU.

Instructions that only one of the ALUs can execute have priority for that ALU. Thus, branch and shift instructions have priority for ALU 1; integer multiply and divide have priority

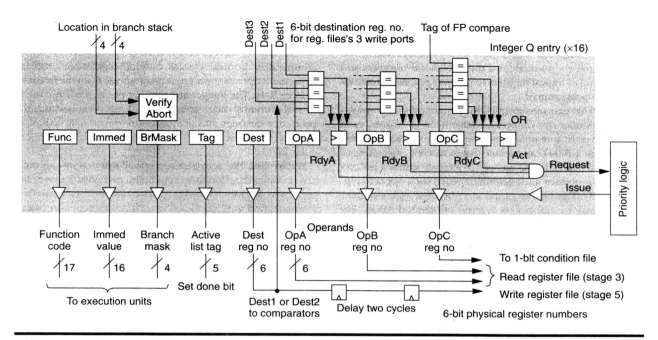

Figure 6. Integer instruction queue, showing only one issue port. The queue issues two instructions in parallel.

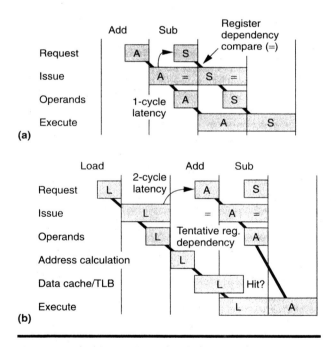

Figure 7. Releasing register dependency in the integer queue (a) and tentative issue of an instruction dependent on an earlier load instruction (b).

for ALU 2. For simplicity, location in the queue rather than instruction age determines priority for issue. However, a round-robin request circuit raises the priority of old instructions requesting ALU 2.

Figure 6 shows the contents of an integer queue entry. It contains three operand select fields, which contain physical-register numbers. Each field contains a ready bit, initialized from the busy-bit table. The queue compares each select with the three destination selects corresponding to write ports in the integer register file. Any comparator match sets the corresponding ready bit. When all operands are ready, the queue can issue the instruction to an execution unit.

Operand C contains either a condition bit value or the tag of the floating-point compare instruction that will set its value. In total, each of the 16 entries contains ten 6-bit comparators.

The queue issues the function code and immediate values to the execution units. The branch mask determines if the instruction aborted because of a mispredicted branch. The tag sets the done bit in the active list after the processor completes the instruction.

The single-cycle latency of integer instructions complicated integer queue timing and logic. In one cycle, the queue must issue two instructions, detect which operands become ready, and request dependent instructions. Figure 7a illustrates this process.

To achieve two-cycle load latency, an instruction that depends on the result of an integer load must be issued tentatively, assuming that the load will be completed successfully. The dependent instruction is issued one cycle before it is executed, while the load reads the data cache. If the load fails, because of a cache miss or a dependency, the issue of the dependent instruction must be aborted. Figure 7b illustrates this process.

Address queue. The address queue contains 16 entries. Unlike the other two queues, it is a circular FIFO that preserves the original program order of its instructions. It allocates an entry when the processor decodes each load or store instruction and removes the entry after that instruction graduates. The queue uses instruction order to determine memory dependencies and to give priority to the oldest instruction.

When the processor restores a mispredicted branch, the address queue removes all instructions decoded after that branch from the end of the queue by restoring the write pointer. The queue issues instructions to the address calculation unit using logic similar to that used in the integer queue, except that this logic contains only two register operands.

The address queue is more complex than the other queues. A load or store instruction may need to be retried if it has a memory address dependency or misses in the data cache.

Two 16-bit×16-bit matrixes track dependencies between memory accesses. The rows and columns correspond to the queue's entries. The first matrix avoids unnecessary cache thrashing by tracking which entries access the same cache set (virtual addresses 13:5). Either way in a set can be used by instructions that are executed out of order. But if two or more queue entries address different lines in the same cache set, the other way is reserved for the oldest entry that accesses that set. The second matrix tracks instructions that load the same bytes as a pending store instruction. It determines this match by comparing double-word addresses and 8-bit byte masks.

Whenever the external interface accesses the data cache, the processor compares its index to all pending entries in the queue. If a load entry matches a refill address, it passes the refill data directly into its destination register. If an entry matches an invalidated command, that entry's state clears.

Although the address queue executes load and store instructions out of their original order, it maintains sequential-memory consistency. The external interface could violate this consistency, however, by invalidating a cache line after it was used to load a register, but before that load instruction graduates. In this case, the queue creates a soft exception on the load instruction. This exception flushes the pipeline and aborts that load and all later instructions, so the processor does not use the stale data. Then, instead of continuing with the exception, the processor simply resumes normal execution, beginning with the aborted load instruction. (This strategy guarantees forward progress because the oldest instruction graduates immediately after completion.)

Store instructions require special coordination between the address queue and active list. The queue must write into the data cache precisely when the store instruction graduates.

The Mips architecture simulates atomic memory operations with load-link (LL) and store-conditional (SC) instruction pairs. These instructions do not complicate system design, because they do not need to lock access to memory. In a typical sequence, the processor loads a value with an LL instruction, tests and modifies it, and then conditionally stores it with an SC instruction. The SC instruction writes into memory only if there was no conflict for this value and the link word remains in the cache. The processor loads its result register with a one or zero to indicate if memory was written.

Floating-point queue. The floating-point queue contains 16 entries. It is very similar to the integer queue, but it does not contain immediate values. Because of extra wiring delays, floating-point loads have three-cycle latency.

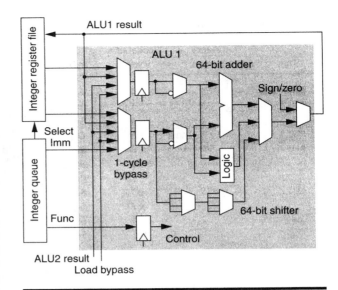

Figure 8. ALU 1 block diagram.

Register files

Integer and floating-point register files each contain 64 physical registers. Execution units read operands directly from the register files and write results directly back. Results may bypass the register file into operand registers, but there are no separate structures, such as reservation stations or reorder buffers in the wide data paths.

The integer register file has seven read ports and three write ports. These include two dedicated read ports and one dedicated write port for each ALU and two dedicated read ports for the address calculate unit. The integer register's seventh read port handles store, jump-register, and move-to-floating-point instructions. Its third write port handles load, branch-and-link, and move-from-floating-point instructions.

A separate 64-word×1-bit condition file indicates if the value in the corresponding physical register is non-zero. Its three write ports operate in parallel with the integer register file. Its two read ports allow integer and floating-point conditional-move instructions to test a single condition bit instead of an entire register. This file used much less area than two additional read ports in the register file.

The floating-point register file has five read and three write ports. The adder and multiplier each have two dedicated read ports and one dedicated write port. The fifth read port handles store and move instructions; the third write port handles load and move instructions.

Integer execution units

During each cycle, the integer queue can issue two instructions to the integer execution units.

Integer ALUs. Each of the two integer ALUs contains a 64-bit adder and a logic unit. In addition, ALU 1 contains a 64-bit shifter and branch condition logic, and ALU 2 contains a partial integer multiplier array and integer-divide logic. Figure 8 shows the ALU 1 block diagram. Each ALU has two 64-bit operand registers that load from the register file. To

Table 1. Latency and repeat rates for integer instructions.

Unit	Latency (cycles)	Repeat rate (cycles)	Instruction
Either ALU	1	1	Add, subtract, logical, move Hi/Lo, trap
ALU 1	1	1	Integer branches
ALU 1	1	1	Shift
ALU 1	1	1	Conditional move
ALU 2	5/6	6	32-bit multiply
	9/10	10	64-bit multiply (to Hi/Lo registers)
ALU 2	34/35	35	32-bit divide
	66/67	67	64-bit divide
Load/store	2	1	Load integer
	—	1	Store integer

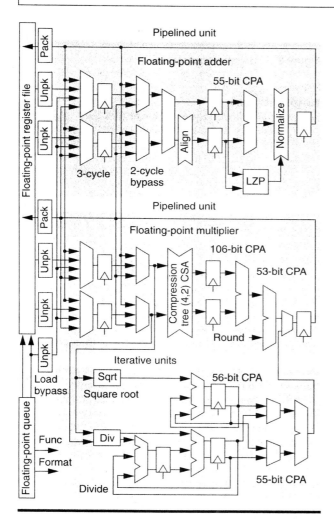

Figure 9. Floating-point execution units block diagram.

achieve one-cycle latency, the three write ports of the register file bypass into the operand register.

The integer queue controls both ALUs. It provides function

codes, immediate values, bypass controls, and so forth.

Integer multiplication and division. ALU 2 iteratively computes integer multiplication and division. As mentioned earlier, these instructions have two destination registers, Hi and Lo. For multiply instructions, Hi and Lo contain the high and low halves of a double-precision product. For divide instructions, they contain the remainder and quotient.

ALU 2 computes integer multiplication using Booth's algorithm, which generates a partial product for each two bits of the multiplier. The algorithm generates and accumulates four partial products per cycle. ALU 2 is busy for the first cycle after the instruction is issued, and for the last two cycles to store the result.

To compute an integer division, ALU 2 uses a nonrestoring algorithm that generates one bit per cycle. ALU 2 is busy for the entire operation.

Table 1 lists latency and repeat rates for common integer instructions.

Floating-point execution units

Figure 9 shows the mantissa data path for these units. (Exponent logic is not shown.) The adder and multiplier have three-stage pipelines. Both units are fully pipelined with a single-cycle repeat rate. Results can bypass the register file for either two-cycle or three-cycle latency. All floating-point operations are issued from the floating-point queue.

Floating-point values are packed in IEEE Std 754 single- or double-precision formats in the floating-point register file. The execution units and all internal bypassing use an unpacked format that explicitly stores the hidden bit and separates the 11-bit exponent and 53-bit mantissa. Operands are unpacked as they are read, and results are packed before they are written back. Packing and unpacking are implemented with two-input multiplexers that select bits according to single- or double precision formats. This logic is between the execution units and register file.

Floating-point adder. The adder does floating-point addition, subtraction, compare, and conversion operations. Its first stage subtracts the operand exponents, selects the larger operand, and aligns the smaller mantissa in a 55-bit right shifter. The second stage adds or subtracts the mantissas, depending on the operation and the signs of the operands.

A magnitude addition can produce a carry that requires a one-bit shift right for post normalization. Conceptually, the processor must round the result after generating it. To avoid extra delay, a dual, carry-chain adder generates both +1 and +2 versions of the sum. The processor selects the +2 chain if the operation requires a right shift for post normalization.

On the other hand, a magnitude subtraction can cause massive cancellation, producing high-order zeros in the result. A leading-zero prediction circuit determines how many high-order zeros the subtraction will produce. Its output controls a 55-bit left shifter that normalizes the result.

Floating-point multiplier. The multiplier does floating-point multiplication in a full double-precision array. Because it is slightly less busy than the adder, it also contains the multiplexers that perform move and conditional-move operations.

During the first cycle, the unit Booth-encodes the 53-bit mantissa of the multiplier and uses it to select 27 partial products. (With Booth encoding, only one partial product is needed for each two bits of the multiplier.) A compression tree uses an array of (4, 2) carry-save adders, which sum four bits into two sum and carry outputs. During the second cycle, the resulting 106-bit sum and carry values are combined using a 106-bit carry-propagate adder. A final 53-bit adder rounds the result.

Floating-point divide and square root. Two independent iterative units compute floating-point division and square-root operations. Each unit uses an SRT algorithm that generates two bits per iteration stage. The divide unit cascades two stages within each cycle to generate four bits per cycle.

These units share register file ports with the multiplier. Each operation preempts two cycles. The first cycle issues the instruction and reads its operands from the register file. At the end of the operation, the unit uses the second cycle to write the result into the register file.

Table 2 lists latency and repeat rates for common floating-point instructions.

Memory hierarchy

Memory latency has a major impact on processor performance. To run large programs effectively, the R10000 implements a nonblocking memory hierarchy with two levels of set-associative caches. The on-chip primary instruction and data caches operate concurrently, providing low latency and high bandwidth. The chip also controls a large external secondary cache. All caches use a least-recently-used (LRU) replacement algorithm.

Both primary caches use a virtual address index and a physical-address tag. To minimize latency, the processor can access each primary cache concurrently with address translation in its TLB. Because each cache way contains 16 Kbytes (four times the minimum virtual page size), two of the virtual index bits (13:12) might not equal bits in the physical address tag. This technique simplifies the cache design. It works well, as long as the program uses consistent virtual indexes to reference the same page. The processor stores these two virtual address bits as part of the secondary-cache tag. The secondary-cache controller detects any violations and ensures that the primary caches retain only a single copy of each cache line.

Load/store unit. Figure 10 contains a block diagram of the load/store unit and the data cache. The address queue issues load and store instructions to the address calculation unit and the data cache. When the cache is not busy, a load

Unit	Latency (cycles)	Repeat rate (cycles)	Instruction
Add	2	1	Add, subtract, compare
Multiply	2	1	Integer branches
Divide	12	14	32-bit divide
	19	21	64-bit divide
Square root	18	20	32-bit square root
	33	35	64-bit square root
Load/store	3	1	Load floating-point value
	—	1	Store floating-point value

Table 2. Latency and repeat rates for floating-point instructions.

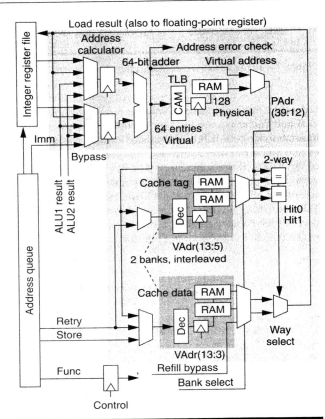

Figure 10. Address calculation unit and data cache block diagram.

instruction simultaneously accesses the TLB, cache tag array, and cache data array. This parallel access results in two-cycle load latency.

Address calculation. The R10000 calculates virtual memory addresses as the sum of two 64-bit registers or the sum of a register and a 16-bit immediate field. Results from the ALUs or the data cache can bypass the register files into the operand registers. The TLB translates these virtual addresses to physical addresses.

Memory address translation (TLB). The Mips-4 architecture defines 64-bit addressing. Practical implementations

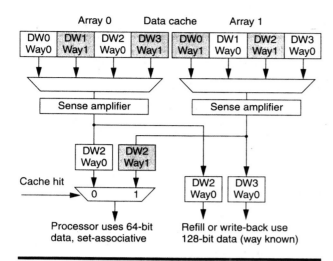

Figure 11. Arrangement of ways in the data cache.

Primary instruction cache. The 32-Kbyte instruction cache contains 8,192 instruction words, each predecoded into a 36-bit format. The processor can decode this expanded format more rapidly than the original instruction format. In particular, the four extra bits indicate which functional unit should execute the instruction. The predecoding also rearranges operand- and destination-select fields to be in the same position for every instruction. Finally, it modifies several opcodes to simplify decoding of integer or floating-point destination registers.

The processor simultaneously fetches four instructions in parallel from both cache ways, and the cache hit logic selects the desired instructions. These instructions need not be aligned on a quad-word address, but they cannot cross a 16-word cache line (see Figure 3).

Primary data cache. The data cache interleaves two 16-Kbyte banks for increased bandwidth. The processor allocates the tag and data arrays of each bank independently to the four following requesting pipelines:

- external interface (refill data, interventions, and so on),
- tag check for a newly calculated address,
- retrying a load instruction, and
- graduating a store instruction.

To simplify interfacing and reduce the amount of buffering required, the external interface has priority for the arrays it needs. Its requests occur two cycles before cache reads or writes, so the processor can allocate the remaining resources among its pipelines.

The data cache has an eight-word line size, which is a con-

reduce the maximum address width to reduce the cost of the TLB and cache tag arrays. The R10000's fully-associative translation look-aside buffer translates 44-bit virtual addresses into 40-bit physical addresses. This TLB is similar to that of the R4000, but we increased it to 64 entries. Each entry maps a pair of virtual pages and independently selects a page size of any power of 4 between 4 Kbytes and 16 Mbytes. The TLB consists of a content-addressable memory (CAM section), which compares virtual addresses, and a RAM section, which contains corresponding physical addresses.

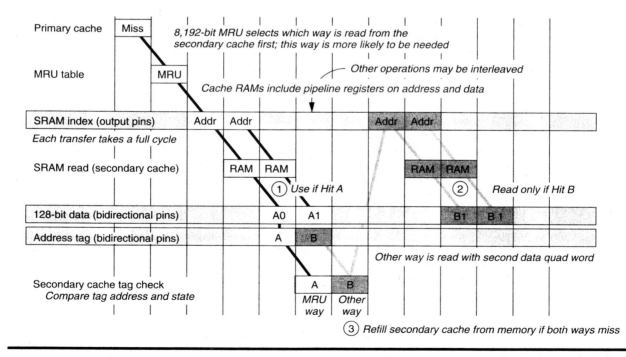

Figure 12. Refill from the set-associative secondary cache. In this example, the secondary clock equals the processor's internal pipeline clock. It may be slower.

venient compromise. Larger sizes reduce the tag RAM array area and modestly reduce the miss rate, but increase the bandwidth consumed during refill. With an eight-word line size, the secondary-cache bandwidth supports three or four overlapped refills.

Each of the data cache's two banks comprises two logical arrays to support two-way set associativity. Unlike the usual arrangement, however, the cache ways alternate between these arrays to efficiently support different-width accesses, as Figure 11 shows.

The processor simultaneously reads the same double word from both cache ways, because it checks the cache tags in parallel and later selects data from the correct way. It discards the double word from the incorrect way. The external interface refills or writes quad words by accessing two double words in parallel. This is possible because it knows the correct cache way in advance.

This arrangement makes efficient use of the cache's sense amplifiers. Each amplifier includes a four-to-one multiplexer anyway, because there are four columns of memory cells for each amplifier. We implemented this feature by changing the select logic.

Secondary cache. We used external synchronous static RAM chips to implement the 512-Kbyte to 16-Mbyte, two-way set-associative secondary cache. Depending on system requirements, the user can configure the secondary-cache line size at either 16 or 32 words.

Set associativity reduces conflict misses and increases predictability. For an external cache, however, this usually requires special RAMs or many more interface pins. Instead, the R10000 implements a two-way pseudo-set-associative secondary cache using standard synchronous SRAMs and only one extra address pin.

Figure 12 shows how cache refills are pipelined. The single group of RAMs contains both cache ways. An on-chip bit array keeps track of which way was most recently used for each cache set. After a primary miss, two quad words are read from this way in the secondary cache. Its tag is read along with the first quad word. The tag of the alternate way is read with the second quad word by toggling of the extra address pin.

Three cases occur: If the first way hits, data becomes available immediately. If the alternate way hits, the processor reads the secondary cache again. If neither way hits, the processor must refill the secondary cache from memory.

Large external caches require error correction codes for data integrity. The R10000 stores both a 9-bit ECC code and a parity bit with each data quad word. The extra parity bit reduces latency because it can be checked quickly and stop the use of bad data. If the processor detects a correctable error, it retries the read through a two-cycle correction pipeline.

We can configure the interface to use this correction pipeline for all reads. Although this increases latency, it allows redundant lock-step processors to remain synchronized in the presence of correctable errors.

System interface

The R10000 communicates with the outside world using a 64-bit split-transaction system bus with multiplexed address and data. This bus can directly connect as many as four R10000 chips in a cluster and overlaps up to eight read requests.

The system interface dedicates substantial resources to support concurrency and out-of-order operation. Cache refills are nonblocking, with up to four outstanding read requests from either the secondary cache or main memory. These are controlled by the miss handling table.

The cached buffer contains addresses for four outstanding read requests. The memory data returned from these requests is stored in the four-entry incoming buffer, so that it can be accepted at any rate and in any order. The outgoing buffer holds up to five "victim" blocks to be written back to memory. The buffer requires the fifth entry when the bus invalidates a secondary-cache line.

An eight-entry cluster buffer tracks all outstanding operations on the system bus. It ensures cache coherency by interrogating and, if necessary, by invalidating cache lines.

Uncached loads and stores execute serially when they are the oldest instructions in the pipeline. The processor often uses uncached stores for writing to graphics or other peripheral devices. Such sequences typically consist of numerous sequentially or identically addressed accesses. The uncached buffer automatically gathers these into 32-word blocks to conserve bus bandwidth.

Clocks. An on-chip phase-locked loop (PLL) generates all timing synchronously with an external system interface clock. For system design and upgrade flexibility, independent clock divisors give users the choice of five secondary-cache and seven system interface clock frequencies. To allow more choices, we base these clocks on a PLL clock oscillating at twice the pipeline clock. When the pipeline operates at 200 MHz, the PLL operates at 400 MHz, and the user can configure the system interface to run at 200, 133, 100, 80, 66.7, 57, or 50 MHz. In addition, the user can separately configure the secondary-cache to frequencies between 200 and 66.7 MHz.

Output drivers. Four groups of buffers drive the chip's output pins. The user can configure each group separately to conform to either low-voltage CMOS or HSTL standards. The buffer design for each group has special characteristics.

Figure 13 (next page) illustrates how these buffers connect. The system interface buffer contains additional open-drain pull-down transistors, which provide the extra current needed to drive HSTL Class-2 multidrop buses.

We designed the secondary-cache data buffer to reduce overlap current spikes when switching, because nearly 200 of these signals can switch simultaneously.

The cache address buffer uses large totem pole transistors to rapidly drive multiple distributed loads. The cache clock buffer drives low-impedance differential signals with minimum output delay. A low-jitter delay element precisely aligns these clocks. This delay is statically configured to adjust for propagation delays in the printed circuit board clock net, so the clock's rising edge arrives at the cache simultaneously with the processor's internal clock.

Test features. For economical manufacture, a microprocessor chip must be easy to test with high fault coverage. The R10000 observes internal signals with ten 128-bit linear-feedback shift registers. These internal test points partition

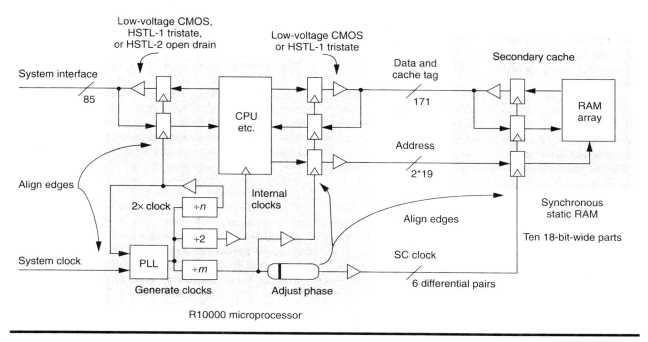

Figure 13. Clocks and output drivers.

the chip into three fully observed sections.

The registers are separate structures that do not affect the processor's logic or add a noticeable load to the observed signals. They use the processor's clock to ensure synchronous behavior and avoid any special clock requirements. They are useful for debugging or production testing.

Performance

We are currently shipping 200-MHz R10000 microprocessors in Silicon Graphics' Challenge servers, and several vendors will soon ship the R10000 in systems specifically designed to use its features. We project that such a system—with a 200-MHz R10000 microprocessor, 4-Mbyte secondary cache (200 MHz), 100-MHz system interface bus, and 180-ns memory latency—will have the following performance:

- SPEC95int (peak)   9
- SPEC95fp (peak)   19

We scaled these benchmark results from the performance of an R10000 running in an actual system in which the processor, cache, and memory speeds were proportionately slower. We compiled the benchmarks using early versions of the Mips Mongoose compiler.

Acknowledgments

The R10000 was designed by the Mips "T5" project team, whose dedication made this chip a reality. The figures in this article are derived from the author's design notes, and are used with permission from Mips Technologies, Inc.

Kenneth C. Yeager is a microprocessor designer at Mips Technologies Inc. (a subsidiary of Silicon Graphics Inc.), where he participated in the conception and design of the R10000 superscalar microprocessor. His research interests include the architecture, logic, and circuit implementation of high-performance processors. Yeager received BS degrees in physics and electrical engineering from the Massachusetts Institute of Technology.

Direct questions concerning this article to the author at Silicon Graphics Inc., M/S 10L-175, 2011 N. Shoreline Blvd., Mountain View, CA 94043; yeager@mti.sgi.com.

AN AGGRESSIVE, SUPERSCALAR MICROPROCESSOR, the R10000 features fast clocks and a nonblocking, set-associative memory subsystem. Its design emphasizes concurrency and latency-hiding techniques to efficiently run large real-world applications. **L**

The Journal of Supercomputing, 7, 9–50 (1993)

Instruction-Level Parallel Processing: History, Overview, and Perspective

B. RAMAKRISHNA RAU AND JOSEPH A. FISHER
Hewlett-Packard Laboratories, 1501 Page Mill Road, Bldg. 3U, Palo Alto, CA 94304

(October 20, 1992)

Abstract. Instruction-level parallelism (ILP) is a family of processor and compiler design techniques that speed up execution by causing individual machine operations to execute in parallel. Although ILP has appeared in the highest performance uniprocessors for the past 30 years, the 1980s saw it become a much more significant force in computer design. Several systems were built and sold commercially, which pushed ILP far beyond where it had been before, both in terms of the amount of ILP offered and in the central role ILP played in the design of the system. By the end of the decade, advanced microprocessor design at all major CPU manufacturers had incorporated ILP, and new techniques for ILP had become a popular topic at academic conferences. This article provides an overview and historical perspective of the field of ILP and its development over the past three decades.

Keywords. Instruction-level parallelism, VLIW processors, superscalar processors, pipelining, multiple operation issue, speculative execution, scheduling, register allocation.

1. Introduction

Instruction-level parallelism (ILP) is a family of processor and compiler design techniques that speed up execution by causing individual machine operations, such as memory loads and stores, integer additions, and floating point multiplications, to execute in parallel. The operations involved are normal RISC-style operations, and the system is handed a single program written with a sequential processor in mind. Thus an important feature of these techniques is that like circuit speed improvements, but unlike traditional multiprocessor parallelism and massive parallel processing, they are largely transparent to users. VLIWs and superscalars are examples of processors that derive their benefit from instruction-level parallelism, and software pipelining and trace scheduling are example software techniques that expose the parallelism that these processors can use.

Although small amounts of ILP have been present in the highest performance uniprocessors of the past 30 years, the 1980s saw it become a much more significant force in computer design. Several systems were built and sold commercially, which pushed ILP far beyond where it had been before, both in terms of the amount of ILP offered and in the central role ILP played in the design of the system. By the early 1990s, advanced microprocessor design at all major CPU manufacturers incorporated ILP, and new techniques for ILP became a popular topic at academic conferences. With all of this activity we felt that, in contrast to a report on suggested future techniques, there would be great value in gathering, in an archival reference, reports on experience with real ILP systems and reports on the measured potential of ILP. Thus this special issue of *The Journal of Supercomputing*.

1.1. ILP Execution

A typical ILP processor has the same type of execution hardware as a normal RISC machine. The differences between a machine with ILP and one without is that there may be more of that hardware, for example, several integer adders instead of just one, and that the control will allow, and possibly arrange, simultaneous access to whatever execution hardware is present.

Consider the execution hardware of a simplified ILP processor consisting of four functional units and a branch unit connected to a common register file (Table 1). Typically ILP execution hardware allows multiple-cycle operations to be pipelined, so we may assume that a total of four operations can be initiated each cycle. If in each cycle the longest latency operation is issued, this hardware could have ten operations "in flight" at once, which would give it a maximum possible speedup of a factor of ten over a sequential processor with similar execution hardware. As the papers in this issue show, this execution hardware resembles that of several VLIW processors that have been built and used commercially, though it is more limited in its amount of ILP. Several superscalar processors now being built also offer a similar amount of ILP.

There is a large amount of parallelism available even in this simple processor. The challenge is to make good use of it—we will see that with the technology available today, an ILP processor is unlikely to achieve nearly as much as a factor of ten on many classes of programs, though scientific programs and others can yield far more than that on a processor that has more functional units. The first question that comes to mind is whether enough ILP exists in programs to make this possible. Then, if this is so, what must the compiler and hardware do to successfully exploit it? In reality, as we shall see in Section 4, the two questions have to be reversed; in the absence of techniques to find and exploit ILP, it remains hidden, and we are left with a pessimistic answer.

Figure 1a shows a very large expression taken from the inner loop of a compute-intensive program. It is presented cycle by cycle as it might execute on a processor with functional units similar to those shown in Table 1, but capable of having only one operation in flight

Table 1. Execution hardware for a simplified ILP processor.

Functional Unit	Operations Performed	Latency
Integer unit 1	Integer ALU operations	1
	Integer multiplication	2
	Loads	2
	Stores	1
Integer unit 2/branch unit	Integer ALU operations	1
	Integer multiplication	2
	Loads	2
	Stores	1
	Test-and-branch	1
Floating point unit 1	Floating point operations	3
Floating point unit 2		

In our ILP record of execution (Figure 1b), both effects are evident: In cycle 1, four operations are issued; in cycle 2, two more operations are issued even though neither multiply in cycle 1 has yet completed execution.

This special issue of *The Journal of Supercomputing* concerns itself with the technology of systems that try to attain the kind of record of execution in Figure 1b, given a program written with the record of execution in Figure 1a in mind.

1.2. Early History of Instruction-Level Parallelism

In small ways, instruction-level parallelism factored into the thinking of machine designers in the 1940s and 1950s. Parallelism that would today be called horizontal microcode appeared in Turing's 1946 design of the Pilot ACE [Carpenter and Doran 1986] and was carefully described by Wilkes [1951]. Indeed, in 1953 Wilkes and Stringer wrote, "In some cases it may be possible for two or more micro-operations to take place at the same time" [Wilkes and Stringer 1953].

The 1960s saw the appearance of transistorized computers. One effect of this revolution was that it became practical to build reliable machines with far more gates than was necessary to build a general-purpose CPU. This led to commercially successful machines that used this available hardware to provide instruction-level parallelism at the machine-language level. In 1963 Control Data Corporation started delivering its CDC 6600 [Thornton 1964, 1970], which had ten functional units—integer add, shift, increment (2), multiply (2), logical branch, floating point add and divide. Any one of these could start executing in a given cycle whether or not others were still processing data-independent earlier operations. In this machine the hardware decided, as the program executed, which operation to issue in a given cycle; its model of execution was well along the way toward what we would today call superscalar. Indeed, in many ways it strongly resembled its direct descendant, the scalar portion of the CRAY-1. The CDC 6600 was the scientific supercomputer of its day.

Also during the 1960s, IBM introduced, and in 1967–68 delivered, the 360/91 [IBM 1967]. This machine, based partly on IBM's instruction-level parallel experimental Stretch processor, offered less instruction-level parallelism than the CDC 6600, having only a single integer adder, a floating point adder, and a floating point multiply/divide. But it was far more ambitious than the CDC 6600 in its attempt to rearrange the instruction stream to keep these functional units busy—a key technology in today's superscalar designs. For various nontechnical reasons the 360/91 was not as commercially successful as it might have been, with only about 20 machines delivered [Bell and Newell 1971]. But its CPU architecture was the start of a long line of successful high-performance processors. As with the CDC 6600, this ILP pioneer started a chain of superscalar architectures that has lasted into the 1990s.

In the 1960s, research into "parallel processing" often was concerned with the ILP found in these processors. By the mid-1970s the term was used more often for multiple processor parallelism and for regular array and vector parallelism. In part, this was due to some very pessimistic results about the availability of ILP in ordinary programs, which we discuss below.

```
CYCLE  1 xseed1 = xseed * 1309
CYCLE  2 nop
CYCLE  3 nop
CYCLE  4 yseed1 = yseed * 1308
CYCLE  5 nop
CYCLE  6 nop
CYCLE  7 xseed2 = xseed1 + 13849
CYCLE  8 yseed2 = yseed1 + 13849
CYCLE  9 xseed = xseed2 && 65535
CYCLE 10 yseed = yseed2 && 65535
CYCLE 11 tseed1 = tseed * 1307
CYCLE 12 nop
CYCLE 13 nop
CYCLE 14 vseed1 = vseed * 1306
CYCLE 15 nop
CYCLE 16 nop
CYCLE 17 tseed2 = tseed1 + 13849
CYCLE 18 vseed2 = vseed1 + 13849
CYCLE 19 tseed = tseed2 && 65535
CYCLE 20 vseed = vseed2 && 65535
CYCLE 21 xsq = xseed * xseed
CYCLE 22 nop
CYCLE 23 nop
CYCLE 24 ysq = yseed * yseed
CYCLE 25 nop
CYCLE 26 nop
CYCLE 27 xysumsq = xsq + ysq
CYCLE 28 tsq = tseed * tseed
CYCLE 29 nop
CYCLE 30 nop
CYCLE 31 vsq = vseed * vseed
CYCLE 32 nop
CYCLE 33 nop
CYCLE 34 tvsumsq = tsq + vsq
CYCLE 35 plc = plc + 1
CYCLE 36 tp = tp + 2
CYCLE 37 if xysumsq > radius goto @xy-no-hit
```
(a)

	INT ALU	INT ALU	FLOAT ALU	FLOAT ALU
CYCLE 1	tp=tp+2	plc=plc+1	vseed1=vseed*1306	tseed1=tseed*1307
CYCLE 2			yseed1=yseed*1308	xseed1=xseed*1309
CYCLE 3	nop			
CYCLE 4	vseed2=vseed1+13849	tseed2=tseed1+13849		
CYCLE 5	yseed2=yseed1+13849	xseed2=xseed1+13849		
CYCLE 6	yseed=yseed2&&65535	xseed=xseed2&&65535		
CYCLE 7	vseed=vseed2&&65535	tseed=tseed2&&65535	ysq=yseed*yseed	xsq=xseed*xseed
CYCLE 8			vsq=vseed*vseed	tsq=tseed*tseed
CYCLE 9	nop			
CYCLE 10	xysumsq=xsq+ysq			
CYCLE 11	tvsumsq=tsq+vsq	if xysumsq>radius goto @xy-no-hit		

(b)

Figure 1. (a) An example of the sequential record of execution for a loop. (b) The instruction-level parallel record of execution for the same loop.

at a time. Figure 1b shows the same program fragment as it might be executed on the hardware indicated in Table 1.

Note that several of the cycles in Figure 1a contain no-ops. This is because the sequential processor must await the completion of the three-cycle latency multiply issued in cycle 1 before issuing the next operation. (These no-ops would not appear in the text of a program, but are shown here as the actual record of what is executed each cycle.) Most instruction-level parallel processors can issue operations during these no-op cycles, when previous operations are still in flight, and many can issue more than one operation in a given cycle.

1.3. Modern Instruction-Level Parallelism

In the late 1970s the beginnings of a new style of ILP, called very long instruction word (VLIW), emerged on several different fronts. In many ways VLIWs were a natural outgrowth of horizontal microcode, the first ILP technology, and they were triggered, in the 1980s, by the same changes in semiconductor technology that had such a profound impact upon the entire computer industry.

For sequential processors, as the speed gap between writeable and read-only memory narrowed, the advantages of a small, dedicated, read-only control store began to disappear. One natural effect of this was to diminish the advantage of microcode; it no longer made as much sense to define a complex language as a compiler target and then interpret this in very fast read-only microcode. Instead, the vertical microcode interface was presented as a clean, simple compiler target. This concept was called RISC [Hennessy, Jouppi, Baskett et al. 1982; Patterson and Sequin 1981; Radin 1982]. In the 1980s the general movement of microprocessor products was towards the RISC concept, and instruction-level parallel techniques fell out of favor. In the minisupercomputer price-bracket though, one innovative superscalar product, the ZS-1, which could issue up to two instructions each cycle, was built and marketed by Astronautics [Smith et al. 1987].

The same changes in memory technology were having a somewhat different effect upon horizontally microcoded processors. During the 1970s a large market had grown in special-ized signal processing computers. Not aimed at general-purpose use, these CPUs hard-wired FFTs and other important algorithms directly into the horizontal control store, gaining tremendous advantages from the instruction-level parallelism available there. When fast, writeable memory became available, some of these manufacturers, most notably Floating Point Systems [Charlesworth 1981], replaced the read-only control store with writeable mem-ory, giving users access to instruction-level parallelism in far greater amounts than the early superscalar processors had. These machines were extremely fast, the fastest processors by far in their price ranges, for important classes of scientific applications. However, despite attempts on the part of several manufacturers to market their products for more general, everyday use, they were almost always restricted to a narrow class of applications. This was caused by the lack of good system software, which in turn was caused by the idiosyn-cratic architecture of processors built for a single application, and by the lack at that time of good code generation algorithms for ILP machines with that much parallelism.

As with RISC, the crucial step was to present a simple, clean interface to the compiler. However, in this case the clean interface was horizontal, not vertical, so as to afford greater ILP [Fisher 1983; Rau, Glaeser, and Greenawalt 1982]. This style of architecture was dubbed VLIW [Fisher 1983]. Code generation techniques, some of which had been developed for generating horizontal microcode, were extended to these general-purpose VLIW machines so that the compiler could specify the parallelism directly [Fisher 1981; Rau and Glaeser 1981].

In the 1980s VLIW CPUs were offered commercially in the form of capable, general-purpose machines. Three computer start-ups—Culler, Multiflow, and Cydrome—built VLIWs with varying degrees of parallelism [Colwell et al. 1988; Rau et al. 1989]. As a group these companies were able to demonstrate that it was possible to build practical ma-chines that achieved large amounts of ILP on scientific and engineering codes. Although, for various reasons, none was a lasting business success, several major computer manufac-turers acquired access to the technologies developed at these start-ups and there are several active VLIW design efforts underway. Furthermore, many of the compiler techniques devel-oped with VLIWs in mind, and reported upon in this issue, have been used to compile for superscalar machines as well.

1.3.1. ILP in the 1990s. Just as had happened 30 years ago when the transistor became available, CPU designers in the 1990s now have offered to them more silicon space on a single chip than a RISC processor requires. Virtually all designers have begun to add some degree of superscalar capability, and some are investigating VLIWs as well. It is a safe bet that by 1995 virtually all new CPUs will embody some degree of ILP.

Partly as a result of this commercial resurgence of interest in ILP, research into that area has become a dominant feature of architecture and systems conferences of the 1990s. Unfor-tunately, those researchers who found themselves designing state-of-the-art products at com-puter start-ups did not have the time to document the progress that was made and the large amount that was learned. Virtually everything that was done by these groups was relevant to what designers wrestle with today.

2. ILP Architectures

The end result of instruction-level parallel execution is that multiple operations are simul-taneously in execution, either as a result of having been issued simultaneously or because the time to execute an operation is greater than the interval between the issuance of succes-sive operations. How exactly are the necessary decisions made as to when an operation should be executed and whether an operation should be speculatively executed? The alter-natives can be broken down depending on the extent to which these decisions are made by the compiler rather than by the hardware and on the manner in which information regard-ing parallelism is communicated by the compiler to the hardware via the program.

A computer architecture is a contract between the class of programs that are written for the architecture and the set of processor implementations of that architecture. Usually this contract is concerned with the instruction format and the interpretation of the bits that con-stitute an instruction, but in the case of ILP architectures it extends to information embedded in the program pertaining to the available parallelism between the instructions or operations in the program. With this in mind, ILP architectures can be classified as follows.

- *Sequential architectures*: architectures for which the program is not expected to convey any explicit information regarding parallelism. Superscalar processors are representative of ILP processor implementations for sequential architectures [Anderson et al. 1967; Apollo Computer 1988; Bahr et al. 1991; Blanck and Krueger 1992; DeLano et al. 1992; Diefendorff and Allen 1992; IBM 1990; Intel 1989b; Keller et al. 1975; Popescu et al. 1991; Smith et al. 1987; Thompson 1964].

- *Dependence architectures*: architectures for which the program explicitly indicates the dependences that exist between operations. Dataflow processors [Arvind and Gostelow 1982; Arvind and Kathail 1981; Gurd et al. 1985] are representative of this class.

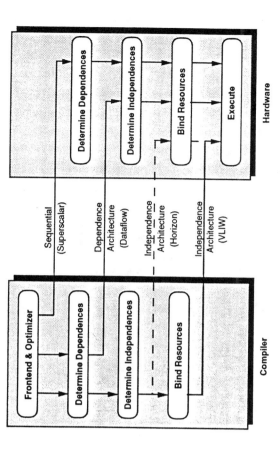

Figure 2. Division of responsibilities between the compiler and the hardware for the three classes of architecture.

When the operation is independent of all other operations it may begin execution. At this point the hardware must make the scheduling decision of when and where this operation is to execute.

A superscalar processor[1] strives to issue an instruction every cycle so as to execute many instructions in parallel, even though the hardware is handed a sequential program. The problem is that a sequential program is constructed with the assumption only that it will execute correctly when each instruction waits for the previous one to finish, and that is the only order that the architecture guarantees to be correct. The first task, then, for a superscalar processor is to understand, for each instruction, which other instructions it actually is dependent upon. With every instruction that a superscalar processor issues, it must check whether the instruction's operands (registers or memory locations that the instruction uses or modifies) interfere with the operands of any other instruction in flight, that is, one that is either

- already in execution or
- has been issued but is waiting for the completion of interfering instructions that would have been executed earlier in a sequential execution of the program.

If either of these conditions is true, the instruction in question must be delayed until the instructions on which it is dependent have completed execution. For each waiting operation, these dependences must be monitored to determine the point at which neither condition is true. When this happens, the instruction is independent of all other uncompleted instructions and can be allowed to begin executing at any time thereafter. In the meantime the processor may begin execution of subsequent instructions that prove to be independent

---

- *Independence architectures*: architectures for which the program provides information as to which operations are independent of one another. Very long instruction word (VLIW) processors [Charlesworth 1981; Colwell et al. 1988; Rau et al. 1989] are examples of the class of independence architectures.

In the context of this taxonomy, vector processors [Hintz and Tate 1972; Russell 1978; Watson 1972] are best thought of as processors for a sequential, CISC (complex instruction set computer) architecture. The complex instructions are the vector instructions that do possess a stylized form of instruction-level parallelism internal to each vector instruction. Attempting to execute multiple instructions in parallel, whether scalar or vector, incurs all of the same problems that are faced by a superscalar processor. Because of their stylized approach to parallelism, vector processors are less general in their ability to exploit all forms of instruction-level parallelism. Nevertheless, vector processors have enjoyed great commercial success over the past decade. Not being true ILP processors, vector processors are outside the scope of this special issue. (Vector processors have received a great deal of attention elsewhere over the past decade and have been treated extensively in many books and articles, for instance, the survey by Dongarra [1986] and the book by Schneck [1987].) Also, certain hybrid architectures [Danelutto and Vanneschi 1990; Franklin and Sohi 1992; Wolfe and Shen 1991], which also combine some degree of multithreading with ILP, fall outside of this taxonomy for uniprocessors.

If ILP is to be achieved, between the compiler and the run-time hardware, the following functions must be performed:

1. The dependences between operations must be determined.
2. The operations that are independent of any operation that has not as yet completed must be determined.
3. These independent operations must be scheduled to execute at some particular time, on some specific functional unit, and must be assigned a register into which the result may be deposited.

Figure 2 shows the breakdown of these three tasks, between the compiler and run-time hardware, for the three classes of architecture.

2.1. Sequential Architectures and Superscalar Processors

The program for a sequential architecture contains no explicit information regarding the dependences that exist between instructions. Consequently, the compiler need neither identify parallelism nor make scheduling decisions since there is no explicit way to communicate this information to the hardware. (It is true, nevertheless, that there is value in the compiler performing these functions and ordering the instructions so as to facilitate the hardware's task of extracting parallelism.) In any event, if instruction-level parallelism is to be employed, the dependences that exist between instructions must be determined by the hardware. It is only necessary to determine dependences with sequentially preceding operations that are in flight, that is, those that have been issued but have not yet completed.

of all sequentially preceding instructions in flight. Once an instruction is independent of all other ones in flight, the hardware must also decide exactly when and on which available functional unit to execute the instruction. The Control Data CDC 6600 used a mechanism, called the *scoreboard*, to perform these functions [Thornton 1964]. The IBM System/360 Model 91, built in the early 1960s, used an even more sophisticated method known as Tomasulo's algorithm to carry out these functions [Tomasulo 1967].

The further goal of a superscalar processor is to issue *multiple* instructions every cycle. The most problematic aspect of doing so is determining the dependences between the operations that one wishes to issue simultaneously. Since the semantics of the program, and in particular the essential dependences, are specified by the sequential ordering of the operations, the operations must be processed in this order to determine the essential dependences. This constitutes an unacceptable performance bottleneck in a machine that is attempting parallel execution. On the other hand, eliminating this bottleneck can be very expensive, as is always the case when attempting to execute an inherently sequential task in parallel. An excellent reference on superscalar processor design and its complexity is the book by Johnson [1991].

A number of superscalar processors have been built during the past decade including the Astronautics' ZS-1 decoupled access minisupercomputer [Smith 1989; Smith et al. 1987], Apollo's DN10000 personal supercomputer [Apollo 1988; Bahr et al. 1991], and, most recently, a number of microprocessors [Blanck and Krueger 1992; DeLano et al. 1992; Diefendorff and Allen 1992; IBM 1990; Intel 1989b; Popescu et al. 1991].

Note that an ILP processor need not issue multiple operations per cycle in order to achieve a certain level of performance. For instance, instead of a processor capable of issuing five instructions per cycle, the same performance could be achieved by pipelining the functional units and instruction issue hardware five times as deeply, speeding up the clock rate by a factor of five but issuing only one instruction per cycle. This strategy, which has been termed *superpipelining* [Jouppi 1989], goes full circle back to the single-issue, superscalar processing of the 1960s. Superpipelining may result in some parts of the processor (such as the instruction unit and communications buses) being less expensive and better utilized and other parts (such as the execution hardware) being more costly and less well used.

2.2. Dependence Architectures and Dataflow Processors

In the case of dependence architectures the compiler or the programmer identifies the parallelism in the program and communicates it to the hardware by specifying, in the executable program, the dependences between operations. The hardware must still determine, at run time, when each operation is independent of all other operations and then perform the scheduling. However, the inherently sequential task, of scanning the sequential program in its original order to determine the dependences, has been eliminated.

The objective of a dataflow processor is to execute an instruction at the earliest possible time subject only to the availability of the input operands and a functional unit upon which to execute the instruction [Arvind and Gostelow 1982; Arvind and Kathail 1981]. To do so, it counts on the program to provide information about the dependences between instructions. Typically, this is accomplished by including in each instruction a list of successor

instructions. (An instruction is a successor of another instruction if it uses as one of its input operands the result of that other instruction.) Each time an instruction completes, it creates a copy of its result for each of its successor instructions. As soon as all of the input operands of an instruction are available, the hardware fetches the instruction, which specifies the operation to be performed and the list of successor instructions. The instruction is then executed as soon as a functional unit of the requisite type is available. This property, whereby the availability of the data triggers the fetching and execution of an instruction, is what gives rise to the name of this type of processor. Because of this property, it is redundant for the instruction to specify its input operands. Rather, the input operands specify the instruction! If there is always at least one instruction ready to execute on every functional unit, the dataflow processor achieves peak performance.

Computation within a basic block typically does not provide adequate levels of parallelism. Superscalar and VLIW processors use control parallelism and speculative execution to keep the hardware fully utilized. (This is discussed in greater detail in Sections 3 and 4.) Dataflow processors have traditionally counted on using control parallelism alone to fully utilize the functional units. A dataflow processor is more successful than the others at looking far down the execution path to find abundant control parallelism. When successful, this is a better strategy than speculative execution since every instruction executed is a useful one and the processor does not have to deal with error conditions raised by speculative operations.

As far as the authors are aware, there have been no commercial products built based on the dataflow architecture, except in a limited sense [Schmidt and Caesar 1991]. There have, however, been a number of research prototypes built, for instance, the ones built at the University of Manchester [Gurd et al. 1985] and at MIT [Papadopoulos and Culler 1990].

2.3. Independence Architectures and VLIW Processors

In order to execute operations in parallel, the system must determine that the operations are independent of one another. Superscalar processors and dataflow processors represent two ways of deriving this information at run time. In the case of the dataflow processor the explicitly provided dependence information is used to determine when an instruction may be executed so that it is independent of all other concurrently executing instructions. The superscalar processor must do the same, but since programs for it lack any explicit information, it must also first determine the dependences between instructions. In contrast, for an independence architecture the compiler identifies the parallelism in the program and communicates it to the hardware by specifying which operations are independent of one another. This information is of direct value to the hardware, since it knows with no further checking which operations it can execute in the same cycle. Unfortunately, for any given operation, the number of operations of which it is independent is far greater than the number of operations on which it is dependent, so it is impractical to specify all independences. Instead, for each operation, independences with only a subset of all independent operations (those operations that the compiler thinks are the best candidates to execute concurrently) are specified.

By listing operations that could be executed simultaneously, code for an independence architecture may be very close to the record of execution produced by an implementation of that architecture additionally requires that programs specify where (on which functional unit) and when (in which cycle) the operations are executed, then the hardware makes no run time decisions at all and the code is virtually identical to the desired record of execution. The VLIW processors that have been built to date are of this type and represent the predominant examples of machines with independence architectures. The program for a VLIW processor specifies exactly which functional unit each operation should be executed on and exactly when each operation should be issued so as to be independent of all operations that are being issued at the same time as well as of those that are in execution. A particular processor implementation of a VLIW architecture could choose to disregard the scheduling decisions embedded in the program, making them at run time instead. In doing so, the processor would still benefit from the independence information but would have to perform all of the scheduling tasks of a superscalar processor. Furthermore, when attempting to execute concurrently two operations that the program did not specify as being independent of each other, it must determine independence, just as a superscalar processor must.

With a VLIW processor it is important to distinguish between an instruction and an operation. An operation is a unit of computation, such as an addition, memory load, or branch, which would be referred to as an instruction in the context of a sequential architecture. A VLIW instruction is the set of operations that are intended to be issued simultaneously. It is the task of the compiler to decide which operations should go into each instruction. This process is termed *scheduling*. Conceptually, the compiler schedules a program by emulating at compile time what a dataflow processor, with the same execution hardware, would do at run time. All operations that are supposed to begin at the same time are packaged into a single VLIW instruction. The order of the operations within the instruction specifies the functional unit on which each operation is to execute. A VLIW program is a transliteration of a desired record of execution that is feasible in the context of the given execution hardware.

The compiler for a VLIW machine specifies that an operation be executed speculatively merely by performing speculative code motion, that is, scheduling an operation before the branch that determines that it should, in fact, be executed. At run time, the VLIW processor blindly executes this operation exactly as specified by the program, just as it would for a nonspeculative operation. Speculative execution is virtually transparent to the VLIW processor and requires little additional hardware. When the compiler decides to schedule an operation for speculative execution, it can arrange to leave behind enough of the state of the computation to assure correct results when the flow of the program requires that the operation be ignored. The hardware required for the support of speculative code motion consists of having some extra registers, of fetching some extra instructions, and of suppressing the generation of spurious error conditions. The VLIW compiler must perform many of the same functions that a superscalar processor performs at run time to support speculative execution, but it does so at compile time.

The earliest VLIW processors built were the so-called attached array processors [Charlesworth 1981; Floating Point Systems 1979; IBM 1976; Intel 1989a; Ruggiero and Coryell 1969] of which the best known were the Floating Point Systems products, the AP-120B, the FPS-164, and the FPS-264. The next generation of products were the minisupercomputers: Multiflow's Trace series of machines [Colwell et al. 1988; Colwell et al. 1990] and Cydrome's Cydra 5 [Beck et al. 1993; Rau 1988; Rau et al. 1989] and the Culler machine for which, as far as we are aware, there is no published description in the literature. Over the last few years the VLIW architecture has begun to show up in microprocessors [Kohn and Margulis 1989; Labrousse and Slavenburg 1988, 1990a, 1990b; Peterson et al. 1981].

Other types of processors with independence architectures have been built or proposed. A superpipelined machine may issue only one operation per cycle, but if there is no superscalar hardware devoted to preserving the correct execution order of operations, the compiler will have to schedule them with full knowledge of dependences and latencies. From the compiler's point of view these machines are virtually the same as VLIWs, though the hardware design of such a processor offers some tradeoffs with respect to VLIWs. Another proposed independence architecture, dubbed *Horizon* [Thistle and Smith 1988], encodes an integer H into each operation. The architecture guarantees that all of the next H operations in the instruction stream are data-independent of the current operation. All the hardware has to do to release an operation, then, is to assure itself that no more than H subsequent operations are allowed to issue before this operation has completed. The hardware does all of its own scheduling, unlike the VLIWs and deeply pipelined machines that rely on the compiler, but the hardware is relieved of the task of determining data dependence. The key distinguishing features of these three ILP architectures are summarized in Table 2.

Table 2. A comparison of the instruction-level parallel architecture discussed in this paper.

	Sequential Architecture	Dependence Architecture	Independence Architecture
Additional information required in the program	None	Complete specification of dependences between operations	Minimally, a partial list of independences. Typically, a complete specification of when and where each operation is to be executed
Typical kind of ILP processor	Superscalar	Dataflow	VLIW
Analysis of dependences between operations	Performed by hardware	Performed by the compiler	Performed by the compiler
Analysis of independent operations	Performed by hardware	Performed by hardware	Performed by the compiler
Final operation scheduling	Performed by hardware	Performed by hardware	Typically, performed by the compiler
Role of compiler	Rearranges the code to make the analysis and scheduling hardware more successful	Replaces some analysis hardware	Replaces virtually all the analysis and scheduling hardware

3. Hardware and Software Techniques for ILP Execution

Regardless of which ILP architecture is considered, certain functions must be performed if a sequential program is to be executed in an ILP fashion. The program must be analyzed to determine the dependences; the point in time at which an operation is independent, of all operations that are as yet not complete, must be determined; scheduling and register allocation must be performed; often, operations must be executed speculatively, which in turn requires that branch prediction be performed. All these functions must be performed. The choice is, first, whether they are to be performed by the compiler or by run-time hardware and, second, which specific technique is to be used. These alternatives are reviewed in the rest of this section.

3.1. Hardware Features to Support ILP Execution

Instruction-level parallelism involves the existence of multiple operations in flight at any one time, that is, operations that have begun, but not completed, executing. This implies the presence of execution hardware that can simultaneously process multiple operations. This has, historically, been achieved by two mechanisms: first, providing multiple, parallel functional units and, second, pipelining the functional units. Although both are fairly similar from a compiler's viewpoint—the compiler must find enough independent operations to keep the functional units busy—they have their relative strengths and weaknesses from a hardware viewpoint.

In principle, pipelining is the more cost-effective way of building ILP execution hardware. For the relatively low cost of adding pipeline latches within each functional unit, the amount of ILP can be doubled, tripled, or more. The limiting factors in increasing the performance by this means are the data and clock skews and the latch setup and hold times. These issues were studied during the 1960s and 1970s, and the upper limits on the extent of pipelining were determined [Chen 1971; Cotten 1965, 1969; Fawcett 1975; Hallin and Flynn 1972]. However, the upper limit on pipelining is not necessarily the best from the viewpoint of achieved performance. Pipelining adds delays to the execution time of individual operations (even though multiples of them can be in flight on the same functional unit). Beyond a certain point, especially on computations that have small amounts of parallelism, the increase in the latency counterbalances the benefits of the increase in ILP, yielding lower performance [Kunkel and Smith 1986]. Parallelism achieved by adding more functional units does not suffer from this drawback, but has its own set of disadvantages. First, the amount of functional unit hardware goes up in linear proportion to the parallelism. Worse, the cost of the interconnection network and the register files goes up proportional to the square of the number of functional units since, ideally, each functional unit's output bus must communicate with every functional unit's input buses through the register file. Also, as the number of loads on each bus increases, so must the cycle time or the extent of pipelining, both of which degrade performance on computation with little parallelism.

The related techniques of pipelining and overlapped execution were employed as early as in the late 1950s in computers such as IBM's STRETCH computer [Bloch 1959; Buchholz 1962] and UNIVAC's LARC [Eckert et al. 1959]. Traditionally, overlapped execution refers to the parallelism that results from multiple active instructions, each in a different one of the phases of instruction fetch, decode, operand fetch, and execute, whereas pipelining is used in the context of functional units such as multipliers and floating point adders [Chen 1975; Kogge 1981]. (A potential source of confusion is that, in the context of RISC processors, overlapped execution and pipelining, especially when the integer ALU is pipelined, of have been referred to as *pipelining* and *superpipelining*, respectively [Jouppi 1989].)

The organization of the register files becomes a major issue when there are multiple functional units operating concurrently. For ease of scheduling, it is desirable that every operation (except loads and stores) be register-register and that the register file be the hub for communication between all the functional units. However, with each functional unit performing two reads and one write per cycle from or to the register file, the implementation of the register file becomes problematic. The chip real estate of a multiported register file is proportional to the product of the number of read ports and the number of write ports. The loading of multiple read ports on each register cell slows down the access time. For these reasons, highly parallel ILP hardware is structured as multiple clusters of functional units, with all the functional units within a single cluster sharing the same multiported register files [Colwell et al. 1988; Colwell et al. 1990; Fisher 1983; Fisher et al. 1984]. Communication between clusters is slower and occurs with lower bandwidth. This places a burden upon the compiler to partition the computation intelligently across the clusters; an inept partitioning can result in worse performance than if just a single cluster were used.

The presence of multiple, pipelined function units places increased demands upon the instruction issue unit. In a fully sequential processor, each instruction is issued after the previous one has completed. Of course, this totally defeats the benefits of parallel execution hardware. However, if the instruction unit attempts to issue an instruction every cycle, care must be taken not to do so if an instruction, upon which this one is dependent, is still not complete. The scoreboard in the CDC 6600 [Thornton 1964] was capable of issuing an instruction every cycle until an output dependence was discovered. In the process, instructions following one that was waiting on a flow dependence could begin execution. This was the first implementation of an out-of-order execution scheme. Stalling instruction issue is unnecessary on encountering an output dependence if register renaming is performed. The Tomasulo algorithm [Tomasulo 1967], which was implemented in the IBM System/360 Model 91 [Anderson et al. 1967], is the classical scheme for register renaming and has served as the model for subsequent variations [Hwu and Patt 1986, 1987; Oehler and Blasgen 1991; Popescu et al. 1991; Weiss and Smith 1984]. A different, programmatically controlled register renaming scheme is obtained by providing rotating register files, that is, base-displacement indexing into the register file using an instruction-provided displacement off a dedicated base register [Advanced Micro Devices 1989; Charlesworth 1981; Rau 1988; Rau et al. 1989]. Although applicable only for renaming registers across multiple iterations of a loop, rotating registers have the advantage of being considerably less expensive in their implementation than are other renaming schemes.

The first consideration given to the possibility of issuing multiple instructions per cycle from a sequential program was by Tjaden and Flynn [1970]. This line of investigation into the logic needed to perform multiple-issue was continued by various researchers [Acosta et al. 1986; Dwyer and Torng 1992; Hwu and Patt 1986, 1987; Tjaden and Flynn 1973;

Uht 1986; Wedig 1982]. This idea, of multiple instruction issue of sequential programs, was probably first referred to as superscalar execution by Agerwala and Cocke [1987]. A careful assessment of the complexity of the control logic involved in superscalar processors is provided by Johnson [1991]. An interesting variation on multiple-issue, which made use of architecturally visible queues to simplify the out-of-order execution logic, was the decoupled access/execute architecture proposed by Smith [1982] and subsequently developed as a commercial product [Smith 1989; Smith et al. 1987].

A completely different approach to achieving multiple instruction issue, which grew out of horizontal microprogramming, was represented by attached-processor products such as the Floating Point Systems AP-120B [Floating Point Systems 1979], the Polycyclic project at ESL [Rau and Glaeser 1981; Rau, Glaeser, and Greenwalt 1982; Rau, Glaeser, and Picard 1982], the Stanford University MIPS project [Hennessy, Jouppi, Przyblski et al. 1982] and the ELI project at Yale [Fisher 1983; Fisher et al. 1984]. The concept is to have the compiler decide which operations should be issued in parallel and to group them in a single, long instruction. This style of architecture, which was dubbed a *very long instruction word* (VLIW) architecture [Fisher 1983], has the advantage that the instruction issue logic is trivial in comparison to that for a superscalar machine, but suffers the disadvantage that the set of operations that are to be issued simultaneously is fixed once and for all at compile time. One of the implications of issuing multiple operations per instruction is that one needs the ability to issue (and process) multiple branches per second. Various types of multiway branches, each corresponding to a different detailed model of execution or compilation, have been suggested [Colwell et al. 1988; Ebcioglu 1988; Fisher 1980; Nicolau 1985a].

The first obstacle that one encounters when attempting ILP computation is the generally small size of basic blocks. In light of the pipeline latencies and the interoperation dependences, little instruction-level parallelism is to be found. It is important that operations from multiple basic blocks be executed concurrently if a parallel machine is to be fully utilized. Since the branch condition, which determines which block is to be executed next, is often resolved only at the end of a basic block, it is necessary to resort to speculative execution, that is, continuing execution along one or more paths before it is known which way the branch will go. Dynamic schemes for speculative execution [Hwu and Patt 1986, 1987; Smith and Pleszkun 1988; Sohi and Vajapayem 1987] must provide ways to

• terminate unnecessary speculative computation once the branch has been resolved,
• undo the effects of the speculatively executed operations that should not been executed,
• ensure that no exceptions are reported until it is known that the excepting operation should, in fact, have been executed, and
• preserve enough execution state at each speculative branch point to enable execution to resume down the correct path if the speculative execution happened to proceed down the wrong one.

All this can be expensive in hardware. The alternative is to perform speculative code motion at compile time, that is, move operations from subsequent blocks up past branch operations into preceding blocks. These operations will end up being executed before the branch that they were supposed to follow; hence, they are executed speculatively. Such code motion is fundamental to global scheduling schemes such as trace scheduling [Ellis

1985; Fisher 1979, 1981]. The hardware support needed is much less demanding: first, a mechanism to ensure that exceptions caused by speculatively scheduled operations are reported if and only if the flow of control is such that they would have been executed in the nonspeculative version of the code [Mahlke, Chen et al. 1992] and, second, additional architecturally visible registers to hold the speculative execution state. A limited form of speculative code motion is provided by the "boosting" scheme [Smith et al. 1992; Smith et al. 1990].

Since all speculative computation is wasted if the wrong path is followed, it is important that accurate branch prediction be used to guide speculative execution. Various dynamic schemes of varying levels of sophistication and practicality have been suggested that gather execution statistics of one form or another while the program is running [Lee and Smith 1984; McFarling and Hennessy 1986; Smith 1981; Yeh and Patt 1992]. The alternative is to use profiling runs to gather the appropriate statistics and to embed the prediction, at compile time, into the program. Trace scheduling and superblock scheduling [Hwu et al. 1989; Hwu et al. 1993] use this approach to reorder the control flow graph to reflect the expected branch behavior. Hwu and others claim better performance than with dynamic branch prediction [Hwu et al. 1989]. Fisher and Freudenberger [1992] have examined the extent to which branch statistics gathered using one set of data are applicable to subsequent runs with different data. Although static prediction can be useful for guiding both static and dynamic speculation, it is not apparent how dynamic prediction can assist static speculative code motion.

Predicted execution is an architectural feature that permits the execution of individual operations to be determined by an additional, Boolean input. It has been used to selectively squash operations that have been moved up from successor blocks into the delay slots of a branch operation [Ebcioglu 1988; Hsu and Davidson 1986]. In its more general form [Beck et al. 1993; Rau 1988; Rau et al. 1989] it is used to eliminate branches in their entirety over an acyclic region of a control flow graph [Dehnert and Towle 1993; Dehnert et al. 1989; Mahlke, Lin et al. 1992] that has been IF-converted [Allen et al. 1983].

3.2. ILP Compilation

3.2.1. Scheduling. Scheduling algorithms can be classified based on two broad criteria. The first one is the nature of the control flow graph that can be scheduled by the algorithm. The control flow graph can be described by the following two properties:

• whether it consists of a single basic block or multiple basic blocks, and
• whether it is an acyclic or cyclic control flow graph.

Algorithms that can only schedule single acyclic basic blocks are known as *local scheduling* algorithms. Algorithms that jointly schedule multiple basic blocks (even if these are multiple iterations of a single static basic block) are termed *global scheduling* algorithms. Acyclic global scheduling algorithms deal either with control flow graphs that contain no cycles or, more typically, cyclic graphs for which a self-imposed scheduling barrier exists

at least the late 1960s [Agerwala 1976; Davidson et al. 1981; DeWitt 1975; Fisher 1979; 1981; Kleir and Ramamoorthy 1971; Landskov et al. 1989; Ramamoorthy and Gonzalez 1969; Tokoro et al. 1977; Tsuchiya and Gonzalez 1974, 1976; Wood 1978]. Since scheduling is known to be NP-complete [Coffman 1976], the initial focus was on defining adequate heuristics [Dasgupta and Tartar 1976; Fisher 1979; Gonzalez 1977; Mallett 1978; Ramamoorthy and Gonzalez 1969; Ramamoorthy and Tsuchiya 1974]. The consensus was that list scheduling using the highest-level-first priority scheme [Adam et al. 1974; Fisher 1979] is relatively inexpensive computationally (a one-pass algorithm) and near-optimal most of the time. Furthermore, this algorithm has no difficulty in dealing with nonunit execution latencies.

The other dimension in which local scheduling matured was in the degree of realism of the machine model. From an initial model in which each operation used a single resource for a single cycle (the simple resource usage model) and had unit latency, algorithms for local scheduling were gradually generalized to cope with complex resource usage and arbitrary latencies [Dasgupta and Tartar 1976; DeWitt 1975; Kleir 1974; Mallett 1978; Ramamoorthy and Tsuchiya 1974; Tsuchiya and Gonzalez 1974; Yau et al. 1974] culminating in the fully general resource usage "microtemplate" model proposed in [Tokoro et al. 1981], and which was known in the hardware pipeline design field as a reservation table [Davidson 1971]. In one form or another, this is now the commonly used machine model in serious instruction schedulers. This machine model is quite compatible with the highest-level-first list scheduling algorithm and does not compromise the near-optimality of this algorithm [Fisher 1981].

3.2.1.2. Global Acyclic Scheduling. A number of studies have established that basic blocks are quite short—typically about 5–20 instructions on the average—so whereas local scheduling can generate a near-optimal schedule, data dependences and execution latencies conspire to make the optimal schedule itself rather disappointing in terms of its speedup over the original sequential code. Further improvements require overlapping the execution of successive basic blocks, which is achieved by global scheduling.

Early strategies for global scheduling attempted to automate and emulate the ad hoc techniques that hand coders practiced of first performing local scheduling of each basic block and then attempting to move operations from one block to an empty slot in a neighboring block [Tokoro et al. 1981; Tokoro et al. 1978]. The shortcoming of such an approach is that, during local compaction, too many arbitrary decisions have already been made that failed to take into account the needs of and opportunities in the neighboring blocks. Many of these decisions might need to be undone before the global schedule can be improved.

In one very important way the mindset inherited from microprogramming was an obstacle to progress in global scheduling. Traditionally, code compaction was focused on the objective of reducing the size of the microprogram so as to allow it to fit in the microprogram memory. In the case of individual basic blocks the objectives of local compaction and local scheduling are aligned. This alignment of objectives is absent in the global case. Whereas global code compaction wishes to minimize the sum of the code sizes for the individual basic blocks, global scheduling must attempt to minimize the total execution time of all the basic blocks. In other words, global scheduling must minimize the sum of the code sizes of the individual basic blocks *weighted by the number of times each basic block is executed*. Thus, effective global scheduling might actually increase the size of the program

at each back edge in the control flow graph. As a consequence of these scheduling barriers, back edges present no opportunity to the scheduler and are therefore irrelevant to it. Acyclic schedulers can yield better performance on cyclic graphs by unrolling the loop, a transformation which though easier to visualize for cyclic graphs with a single back edge, can be generalized to arbitrary cyclic graphs. The benefit of this transformation is that the acyclic scheduler now has multiple iterations' worth of computation to work with and overlap. The penalty of the scheduling barrier is amortized over more computation. Cyclic global scheduling algorithms attempt to directly optimize the schedule across back edges as well. Each class of scheduling algorithms is more general than the previous one and, as we shall see, attempts to build on the intuition and heuristics of the simpler, less general algorithm. As might be expected, the more general algorithms experience greater difficulty in achieving near-optimality or of even articulating intuitively appealing heuristics.

The second classifying criterion is the type of machine for which scheduling is being performed, which in turn is described by the following assumed properties of the machine:

- finite versus unbounded resources
- unit latency versus multiple cycle latency execution, and
- simple resource usage patterns for every operation (i.e., each operation uses just one resource for a single cycle, typically during the first cycle of the operation's execution) versus more complex resource usage patterns for some or all of the operations.

Needless to say, real machines have finite resources, generally have at least a few operations that have latencies greater than one cycle, and often have at least a few operations with complex usage patterns. We believe that the value of a scheduling algorithm is proportional to the degree of realism of the assumed machine model.

Finally, the scheduling algorithm can also be categorized by the nature of the process involved in generating the schedule. At one extreme are one-pass algorithms that schedule each operation once and for all. At the other extreme are algorithms that perform an exhaustive, branch-and-bound style of search for the best schedule. In between is a spectrum of possibilities such as iterative but nonexhaustive search algorithms or incremental algorithms that make a succession of elementary perturbations to an existing legal schedule to nudge it toward the final solution. This aspect of the scheduling algorithm is immensely important in practice. The further one diverges from a one-pass algorithm, the slower the scheduler gets until, eventually, it is unacceptable in a real-world setting.

3.2.1.1. Local Scheduling. Scheduling, as a part of the code generation process, was first studied extensively in the context of microprogramming. Local scheduling is concerned with generating as short a schedule as possible for the operations within a single basic block; in effect a scheduling barrier is assumed to exist between adjacent basic blocks in the control flow graph. Although it was typically referred to as *local code compaction*,[2] the similarity to the job of scheduling tasks on processors was soon understood [Adam et al. 1974; Baker 1974; Coffman 1976; Coffman and Graham 1972; Fernandez and Bussel 1973; Gonzalez 1977; Hu 1961; Kasahara and Narita 1984; Kohler 1975; Ramamoorthy et al. 1972], and a number of notions and algorithms from scheduling theory were borrowed by the microprogramming community. Attempts at automating this task have been made since

by greatly lengthening an infrequently visited basic block in order to slightly reduce the length of a high-frequency basic block. This difference between global compaction and global scheduling, which was captured neither by the early ad hoc techniques nor by the syntactically-driven hierarchical reduction approach proposed by Wood [1979], was noted by Fisher [1979, 1981].

Furthermore, the focus of Fisher's work was on reducing the length of those *sequences* of basic blocks that are frequently executed by the program. These concepts were captured by Fisher in the global scheduling algorithm known as *trace scheduling* [Fisher 1979, 1981]. Central to this procedure is the concept of a trace, which is an acyclic sequence of basic blocks embedded in the control flow graph, that is, a path through the program that could conceivably be taken for some set of input data. Traces are selected and scheduled in order of their frequency of execution. The next trace to be scheduled is defined by selecting the highest frequency basic block that has not yet been scheduled as the seed of the trace. The trace is extended forward along the highest frequency edge out of the last block of the trace as long as that edge is also the most frequent edge into the successor block and as long as the successor block is not already part of the trace. Likewise, the trace is extended backwards, as well, from the seed block. The selected trace is then scheduled as if it were a single block; that is, there is no special consideration given to branches, except that they are constrained to remain in their original order. Implicit in the resulting schedule is interblock code motion along the trace in either the upward or downward direction. Matching off-trace code motions must be performed as prescribed by the rules of interblock code motion specified by Fisher. This activity is termed *bookkeeping*. Therafter, the next trace is selected and scheduled. This procedure is repeated until the entire program has been scheduled. The key property of trace scheduling is that, unlike previous approaches to global scheduling, the decisions as to whether to move an operation from one block to another, where to schedule it, and which register to allocate to hold its result (see Section 3.2.2 below) are all made jointly rather than in distinct compiler phases.

Fisher and his coworkers at Yale went on to implement trace scheduling in the Bulldog compiler as part of the ELI project [Fisher 1983; Fisher et al. 1986]. This trace scheduling implementation and other aspects of the Bulldog compiler have been extensively documented by Ellis [1986]. The motion of code downwards across branches and upwards across merges results in code replication. Although this is generally acceptable as the price to be paid for better global schedules, Fisher recognized the possibility that the greediness of highest-level-first list scheduling could sometimes cause more code motion and, hence, replication then is needed to achieve a particular schedule length [Fisher 1981]. Su and his colleagues have recommended certain heuristics for the list scheduling of traces to address this problem [Grishman and Su 1983; Su and Ding 1985; Su et al. 1984]. Experiments over a limited set of test cases indicate that these heuristics appear to have the desired effect.

The research performed in the ELI project formed the basis of the production-quality compiler that was built at Multiflow. One of the enhancements to trace scheduling implemented in the Multiflow compiler was the elimination of redundant copies of operations caused by bookkeeping. When an off-trace path, emanating from a branch on the trace, rejoins the trace lower down, an operation that is moved above the rejoin and all the way to a point above the branch can make the off-trace copy redundant under the appropriate circumstances. The original version of trace scheduling, oblivious to such situations, retains

two copies of the operation. Gross and Ward [1990] describe an algorithm to avoid such redundancies. Freudenberger and Ruttenberg [1992] discuss the integrated scheduling and register allocation in the Multiflow compiler. Lowney and others provide a comprehensive description of the Multiflow compiler [1993].

Hwu and his colleagues on the IMPACT project have developed a variant of trace scheduling that they term *superblock scheduling* [Chang, Mahlke et al. 1991; Hwu and Chang 1988]. In an attempt to facilitate the task of incorporating profile-driven global scheduling into more conventional compilers, they separate the trace selection and code replication from the actual scheduling and bookkeeping. To do this, they limit themselves to only moving operations up above branches, never down, and never up past merges. To make this possible, they outlaw control flow into the interior of a trace by means of tail duplication, that is, creating a copy of the trace below the entry point and redirecting the incoming control flow path to that copy. Once this is done for each incoming path, the resulting trace consists of a sequence of basic blocks with branches out of the trace but no incoming branches except to the top of the trace. This constitutes a superblock, also known as an *extended basic block* in the compiler literature. Chang and Hwu [1988] have studied different trace selection strategies and have measured their relative effectiveness. A comprehensive discussion of the results and insights from the IMPACT project are provided in this special issue [Hwu et al. 1993].

Although the global scheduling of linear sequences of basic blocks represents a major step forward, it has been criticized for its total focus on the current trace and neglect of the rest of the program. For instance, if there are two equally frequent paths through the program that have basic blocks in common, it is unclear as part of which trace these blocks should be scheduled. One solution is to replicate the code as is done for superblock scheduling. The other is to generalize trace scheduling to deal with more general control flow graphs. Linn [1988] and Hsu and Davidson [1986] proposed profile-driven algorithms for scheduling trees of basic blocks in which all but the root basic block have a single incoming path. Nicolau [1985a, 1985b] attempted to extend global scheduling to arbitrary, acyclic control flow graphs using percolation scheduling. However, since percolation scheduling assumes unbounded resources, it cannot realistically be viewed as a scheduling algorithm. Percolation scheduling was then extended to nonunit execution latencies (but still with unbounded resources) [Nicolau and Potasman 1990].

The development of practical algorithms for the global scheduling of arbitrary, acyclic control flow graphs is an area of active research. Preliminary algorithms, assuming finite resources have been defined by Ebcioglu [Ebcioglu and Nicolau 1989; Moon and Ebcioglu 1992] and by Fisher [1992]. These are both generalizations of trace scheduling. However, there are numerous difficulties in the engineering of a robust and efficient scheduler of this sort. The challenges in this area of research revolve around finding pragmatic engineering solutions to these problems.

A rather different approach to global acyclic scheduling has been pursued in the IMPACT project [Mahlke, Lin et al. 1992]. An arbitrary, acyclic control flow graph, having a single entry can be handled by this technique. The control flow graph is IF-converted [Allen et al. 1983; Park and Schlansker 1991] so as to eliminate all branches internal to the flow graph. The resulting code, which is similar to a superblock in that it can only be entered at the top but has multiple exits, is termed a *hyperblock*. This is scheduled in much the same manner as a superblock except that two operations with disjoint predicates (i.e., operations that cannot both be encountered on any single path through the original flow graph) may be scheduled to use the same resources at the same time. After scheduling, reverse IF-conversion is performed to regenerate the control flow graph. Portions of the schedule in which *m* predicates are active yield 2^m versions of the code.

3.2.1.3. Cyclic Scheduling. As with acyclic flow graphs, instruction-level parallelism in loops is obtained by overlapping the execution of multiple basic blocks. With loops, however, the multiple basic blocks are the multiple iterations of the same piece of code. The most natural extension of the previous global scheduling ideas to loops is to unroll the body of the loop some number of times and to then perform trace scheduling, or some other form of global scheduling, over the unrolled loop body. This approach was suggested by Fisher [Fisher et al. 1981]. A drawback of this approach is that no overlap is sustained across the back edge of the unrolled loop. Fisher and others went on to propose a solution to this problem, which is to continue unrolling and scheduling successive iterations until a repeating pattern is detected in the schedule. The repeating pattern can be rerolled to yield a loop whose body is the repeating schedule. As we shall see, this approach was subsequently pursued by various researchers. In the meantime, loop scheduling moved off in a different direction, which, as is true of most VLIW scheduling work, had its roots in hardware design.

Researchers concerned with the design of pipelined functional units, most notably Davidson and coworkers, had developed the theory of and algorithms for the design of hardware controllers for pipelines to maximize the rate at which functions could be evaluated [Davidson 1971, 1974; Davidson et al. 1975; Patel 1976; Patel and Davidson 1976; Thomas and Davidson 1974]. The issues considered here were quite similar to those faced by individuals programming the innermost loops of signal processing algorithms [Cohen 1978; Kogge 1973, 1974, 1977a, 1977b; Kogge and Stone 1973] on the early peripheral array processors [Floating Point Systems 1979; IBM 1976; Ruggiero and Coryell 1969]. In both cases the objective was to sustain the initiation of successive function evaluations (loop iterations) before prior ones had completed. Since this style of computation is termed pipelining in the hardware context, it was dubbed *software pipelining* in the programming domain [Charlesworth 1981].

Early work in software pipelining consisted of ad hoc hand-coding techniques [Charlesworth 1981; Cohen 1978]. Both the quality of the schedules and the attempts at automating the generation of software pipelined schedules were hampered by the architecture of the early array processors. Nevertheless, Floating Point Systems developed, for the FPS-164 array processor, a compiler that could software pipeline a loop consisting of a single basic block [Touzeau 1984]. Weiss and Smith [1987] note that a limited form of software pipelining was present both in certain hand-coded libraries for the CDC 6600 and also as a capability in the Fortran compiler for the CDC 6600.

The general formulation of the software pipelining process for single basic block loops was stated by Rau and others [Rau and Glaeser 1981; Rau, Glaeser, and Picard 1982] drawing upon and generalizing the theory developed by Davidson and his coworkers on the design of hardware pipelines. This work identified the attributes of a VLIW architecture that make it amenable to software pipelining, most importantly, the availability of conflict-free access to register storage between the output of a functional unit producing a result

and the functional unit that uses that result. This provides freedom in scheduling each operation and is in contrast to the situation in array processors where, due to limited register file bandwidth, achieving peak performance required that a majority of the operations be scheduled to start at the same instant that their predecessor operations completed so that they could pluck their operands right off the result buses.

Rau and others also presented a condition that has to be met by any legal software pipelined schedule—the *modulo constraint*—and derived lower bounds on the rate at which successive iterations of the loop can be started, that is, the *initiation interval* (II). (II is also the length of the software pipelined loop, measured in VLIW instructions, when no loop unrolling is employed.) This lower bound on II, the *minimum initiation interval* (MII), is the maximum of the lower bound due to the resource usage constraints (ResMII) and the lower bound due to the cyclic data dependence constraints caused by recurrences (RecMII). This lower bound is applicable both to vectorizable loops as well as those with arbitrary recurrences and for operation latencies of arbitrary length. A simple, deterministic software pipelining algorithm based on list scheduling, the modulo scheduling algorithm, was shown to achieve the MII, thereby yielding an asymptotically optimal schedule. This algorithm was restricted to DO loops whose body is a single basic block being scheduled on a machine in which each operation has a simple pattern of resource usage, viz., the resource usage of each operation can be abstracted to the use of a single resource for a single cycle (even though the latency of the operation is not restricted to a single cycle). The task of generating an optimal, resource-constrained schedule for loops with arbitrary recurrences is known to be NP-complete [Hsu 1986; Lam 1987] and any practical algorithm must utilize heuristics to guide a generally near-optimal process. These heuristics were only broadly outlined in this work.

Three independent sets of activity took this work and extended it in various directions. The first one was the direct continuation at Cydrome, over the period 1984–88, of the work done by Rau and others [Dehnert et al. 1989; Dehnert and Towle 1993]. In addition to enhancing the modulo scheduling algorithm to handle loops with recurrences and arbitrary acyclic control flow in the loop body, attention was paid to coping with the very complex resource usage patterns that were the result of compromises forced by pragmatic implementation considerations. Complex recurrences and resource usage patterns make it unlikely that a one-pass scheduling algorithm, such as list scheduling, will be able to succeed in finding a near-optimal modulo schedule, even when one exists, and performing an exhaustive search was deemed impractical. Instead, an iterative scheduling algorithm was used that could unschedule and reschedule operations. This iterative algorithm is guided by heuristics based on dynamic slack-based priorities. The initial attempt is to schedule the loop with the II equal to the MII. If unsuccessful, the II is incremented until a modulo schedule is achieved.

Loops with arbitrary acyclic control flow in the loop body are dealt with by performing IF-conversion [Allen et al. 1983] to replace all branching by predicated (guarded) operations. This transformation, which assumes the hardware capability of predicated execution [Rau 1988; Rau et al. 1989], yields a loop with a single basic block that is then amenable to the modulo scheduling algorithm [Dehnert et al. 1989]. A disadvantage of predicated modulo scheduling is that the ResMII must be computed as if all the operations in the body of the loop are executed each iteration, whereas, in reality, only those along one of the control flow paths are actually executed. As a result, during execution, some fraction of the operations in an instruction are wasted. Likewise, the RecMII is determined by the worst-case dependence chain across all paths through the loop body. Both contribute to a degree of suboptimality that depends on the structure of the loop.

Assuming the existence of hardware to support both predicated execution and speculative execution [Mahlke, Chen et al. 1992], Cydrome's modulo scheduling algorithm has been further extended to handle WHILE loops and loops with conditional exits [Tirumalai et al. 1990]. The problem that such loops pose is that it is not known until late in one iteration whether the next one should be started. This eliminates much of the overlap between successive iterations. The solution is to start iterations speculatively, in effect, by moving operations from one iteration into a prior one. The hardware support makes it possible to avoid observing exceptions from operations that should not have been executed, without overlooking exceptions from nonspeculative operations.

Independently of the Cydrome work, Hsu [1986] proposed a modulo scheduling algorithm for single basic block loops with general recurrences that recognizes each strongly connected class (SCC) of nodes in the cyclic dependence graph as a distinct entity. Once the nodes in all the SCCs have been jointly scheduled at the smallest possible II using a combinatorial search, the nodes in a given SCC may only be rescheduled as a unit and at a time that is displayed by a multiple of II. This rescheduling is performed to enable the remaining nodes that are not part of any SCC to be inserted into the schedule. Hsu also described an II extension technique that can be used to take a legal modulo schedule for one iteration and trivially convert it into a legal modulo schedule for a larger II without performing any scheduling. This works with simple resource usage patterns. With complex patterns a certain amount of rescheduling would be required, but less than starting from scratch.

Lam's algorithm, too, utilizes the SCC structure but list schedules each SCC separately, ignoring the inter-iteration dependences [Lam 1987, 1988]. Thereafter, an SCC is treated as a single pseudo-operation with a complex resource usage pattern, employing the technique of hierarchical reduction proposed by Wood [1979]. After this hierarchical reduction has been performed, the dependence graph of the computation is acyclic and can be scheduled using modulo scheduling. With an initial value equal to the MII, the II is iteratively increased until a legal modulo schedule is obtained. By determining and fixing the schedule of each SCC in isolation, Lam's algorithm can result in SCCs that cannot be scheduled together at the minimum achievable II.

On the other hand, the application of hierarchical reduction enables Lam's algorithm to cope with loop bodies containing structured control flow graphs without any special hardware support such as predicated execution. Just as with the SCCs, structured constructs such as IF-THEN-ELSE are list scheduled and treated as atomic objects. Each leg of the IF-THEN-ELSE is list scheduled separately and the union of the resource usages represents that of the reduced IF-THEN-ELSE construct. This permits loops with structured flow of control to be modulo scheduled. After modulo scheduling, the hierarchically reduced IF-THEN-ELSE pseudo-operations must be expanded. Each portion of the schedule in which m IF-THEN-ELSE pseudo-operations are active must be expanded into 2^m control flow paths with the appropriate branching and merging between the paths.

Since Lam takes the union of the resource usages in a conditional construct while predicated modulo scheduling takes the sum of the usages, the former approach should yield the smaller MII. However, since Lam separately list schedules each leg of the conditional creating pseudo-operations with complex resource usage patterns, the II that she actually achieves should deviate from the MII to a greater extent. Warter and others have implemented both techniques and have observed that, on the average, Lam's approach results in smaller MIIs but larger IIs [Warter et al. 1992]. This effect increases for processors with higher issue rates. Warter and others go on to combine the best of both approaches in their enhanced modulo scheduling algorithm. They derive the modulo schedule as if predicated execution were available, except that two operations from the same iteration are allowed to be scheduled on the same resource at the same time if their predicates are mutually exclusive, that is, they cannot both be true. This is equivalent to taking the union of the resource usages. Furthermore, it is applicable to arbitrary, possibly unstructured, acyclic control flow graphs in the loop body. After modulo scheduling, the control flow graph is regenerated much as in Lam's approach. Enhanced modulo scheduling results in MIIs that are as small as for hierarchical reduction, but as with predicated modulo scheduling, the achieved II is rarely more than the MII.

Yet another independent stream of activity has been the work of Su and his colleagues [Su et al. 1984; Su et al. 1986]. When limited to loops with a single basic block, Su's URPR algorithm is an ad hoc approximation to modulo scheduling and is susceptible to significant suboptimality when confronted by nonunit latencies and complex resource usage patterns. The essence of the URPR algorithm is to unroll and schedule successive iterations until the first iteration has completed. Next the smallest contiguous set of instructions, which contain at least one instance of each operation in the original loop, is identified. After deleting multiple instances of all operations, this constitutes the software pipelined schedule. This deletion process introduced "holes" in the schedule and the attendant suboptimality. Also, for nonunit latencies, there is no guarantee that the schedule, as constructed, can loop back on itself without padding the schedule out with no-op cycles. This introduces further degradation.

Subsequently, Su extended URPR to the GURPR* algorithm for software pipelining loops containing control flow [Su et al. 1987; Su and Wang 1991a, 1991b]. GURPR* consists of first performing global scheduling on the body of the loop and then using a URPR-like procedure, as if each iteration was IF-converted, to derive the repeating pattern. Finally, as with enhanced modulo scheduling, a control flow graph is regenerated. The shortcomings of URPR are inherited by GURPR*. Warter and others, who have implemented GURPR* within the IMPACT compiler, have found that GURPR* performs significantly worse than hierarchical reduction, predicated modulo scheduling, or enhanced module scheduling [Warter et al. 1992].

The idea proposed by Fisher and others of incrementally unrolling and scheduling a loop until the pattern repeats [Fisher et al. 1981] was pursued by Nicolau and his coworkers, assuming unbounded resources, initially for single basic block loops [Aiken and Nicolau 1988b] and then, under the title of perfect pipelining, for multiple basic block loops [Aiken and Nicolau 1988a; Nicolau and Potasman 1990]. The latter was subsequently extended to yield a more realistic algorithm assuming finite resources [Aiken and Nicolau 1991].
For single basic block loops the incremental unrolling yields a growing linear trace, the

expansion of which is terminated once a repeating pattern is observed. In practice there are complications since the various SCCs might proceed at different rates, never yielding a repeating pattern. For multiple basic block loops, the unrolling yields a growing tree of schedules, each leaf of which spawns two further leaves when a conditional branch is scheduled. A new leaf is not spawned if the (infinite) tree, of which it would be the root, is identical to another (infinite) tree (of which it might be the leaf) whose root has already been generated.

This approach addresses a shortcoming of all the previously mentioned approaches to software pipelining multiple basic block loops. In general, both RecMII and ResMII are dependent upon the specific control flow path followed in each iteration. Whereas the previous approaches had to use a single, constant, conservative value for each one of these lower bounds, the unrolling approach is able to take advantage of the branch history of previous iterations in deriving the schedule for the current one. However, there are some drawbacks as well. One handicap that such unrolling schemes have is a lack of control over the greediness of the process of initiating iterations. Starting successive iterations as soon as possible, rather than at a measured rate that is in balance with the completion rate, cannot reduce the average initiation interval but can increase the time to enter the repeating pattern and the length of the repeating pattern. Both contribute to longer compilation times and larger code size. A second problem with unrolling schemes lies in their implementation; recognizing that one has arrived at a previously visited state, to which one can wrap back instead of further expanding the search tree, is quite complicated, especially in the context of finite resources, nonunit latencies, and complex resource usage patterns.

The cyclic scheduling algorithm developed by the IBM VLIW research project [Ebcioglu and Nakatani 1989; Gasperoni 1989; Moon and Ebcioglu 1992; Nakatani and Ebcioglu 1990] might represent a good compromise between the ideal and the practical. Stripped to the essentials, this algorithm applies a cut set, termed a *fence*, to the cyclic graph, which yields an acyclic graph. This reduces the problem to that of scheduling a general, acyclic graph—a simpler problem. Once this is done the fence is moved and the acyclic scheduling is repeated. As this process is repeated, all the cycles in the control flow graph acquire increasingly tight schedules. The acyclic scheduling algorithm used by Ebcioglu and others is a resource-constrained version of percolation scheduling [Ebcioglu and Nicolau 1989; Moon and Ebcioglu 1992].

Software pipelining was also implemented in the compiler for the product line marketed by another minisupercomputer company, Culler Scientific. Unfortunately, we do not believe that any publication describing their implementation of software pipelining exists. Quite recently, software pipelining has been implemented in the compilers for HP's PA-RISC line of computers [Ramakrishnan 1992].

3.2.1.4. *Scheduling for RISC and Superscalar Processors.* Seemingly conventional scalar processors can sometimes benefit from scheduling techniques. This is due to small amounts of ILP in the form of, for instance, branch delay slots and shallow pipelines. Scheduling for such processors, whether RISC or CISC, has generally been less ambitious and more ad hoc than that for VLIW processors [Auslander and Hopkins 1982; Gross and Hennessy 1982; Hennessy and Gross 1983; Hsu 1987; McFarling and Hennessy 1986]. This was a

direct consequence of the lack of parallelism in those machines and the corresponding lack of opportunity for the scheduler to make a big difference. Furthermore, the limited number of registers in those architectures made the use of aggressive scheduling rather unattractive. As a result, scheduling was viewed as rather peripheral to the compilation process, in contrast to the central position it occupied for VLIW processors and, to a lesser extent, for more highly pipelined processors [Rymarczyk 1982; Sites 1978; Weiss and Smith 1987]. Now, with superscalar processors growing in popularity, the importance of scheduling, as a core part of the compiler, is better appreciated and a good deal of activity has begun in this area [Bernstein and Rodeh 1991; Bernstein et al. 1991; Golumbic and Rainish 1990; Jain 1991; Smotherman et al. 1991], unfortunately, sometimes unaware of the large body of literature that already exists.

3.2.2. *Register Allocation.* In conventional, sequential processors, instruction scheduling is not an issue. The program's execution time is barely affected by the order of the instruction, only by the number of instructions. Accordingly, the emphasis of the code generator is on generating the minimum number of instructions and using as few registers as possible [Aho et al. 1977a, 1977b; Aho and Sethi 1976; Bruno and Sethi 1976; Sethi 1975; Sethi and Ullman 1970]. However, in the context of pipelined or multiple-issue processors, where instruction scheduling is important, the issue of the phase-ordering between it and register allocation has been a topic of much debate. There are advocates both for performing register allocation before scheduling [Gibbons and Muchnick 1986; Hennessy and Gross 1983; Jain 1991] as well as for performing it after scheduling [Auslander and Hopkins 1982; Chang, Lavery, and Hwu 1991; Goodman and Hsu 1988; Warren 1990]. Each phase-ordering has its advantages and neither one is completely satisfactory.

The most important argument in favor of performing register allocation first is that whereas a better schedule may be desirable, code that requires more registers than are available is just unacceptable. Clearly, achieving a successful register allocation must supersede the objective of constructing a better schedule. The drawback of performing scheduling first, oblivious of the register allocation, is that shorter schedules tend to yield greater register pressure. If a viable allocation cannot be found, spill code must be inserted. At this point, in the case of a statically scheduled processor, the schedule just constructed may no longer be correct. Even if it is, it may be far from the best one possible, for either a VLIW or superscalar machine, since the schedule was built without the spill code in mind. In machines whose load latency is far greater than that of the other operations, the time penalty of the spill code may far exceed the benefits of the better schedule obtained by performing scheduling first.

Historically, the merit of performing register allocation first was that processors had little instruction-level parallelism and few registers, so whereas there was much to be lost by a poor register allocation, there was little to be gained by good scheduling. It was customary, therefore, to perform register allocation first, for instance using graph coloring [Chaitin 1982; Chow and Hennessy 1984, 1990] followed by a postpass scheduling step that considered individual basic blocks [Gibbons and Muchnick 1986; Hennessy and Gross 1983].

From the viewpoint of instruction-level parallel machines, the major problem with performing register allocation first is that it introduces antidependences and output dependences that can constrain parallelism and the ability to construct a good schedule. To some extent this is inevitable; the theoretically optimal combination of schedule and allocation might contain additional arcs due to the allocation. The real concern is that, when allocation is done first, an excessive number of ill-advised and unnecessary arcs might be introduced due to the insensitivity of the register allocator to the scheduling task. On pipelined machines, whose cache access time is as short as or shorter than the functional unit latencies, the benefits of a schedule unconstrained by register allocation may outweigh the penalties of the resulting spill code.

Scheduling prior to register allocation, known as prepass scheduling, was used in the PL.8 compiler [Auslander and Hopkins 1982]. In evolving this compiler to become the compiler for the superscalar IBM RISC System/6000, the suboptimality of inserting spill code after the creation of the schedule became clear and a second, postpass scheduling step was added after the register allocation [Warren 1990]. During the postpass the scheduler honors all the dependences caused by the register allocation, which in turn was aware of the preferred instruction schedule provided by the prepass scheduler. The IMPACT project at the University of Illinois has demonstrated the effectiveness of this strategy for multiple-issue processors [Chang, Lavery, and Hwu 1991]. Instead of employing the graph coloring paradigm, Hendren and others make use of the richer information present in interval graphs, which are a direct temporal representation of the span of the lifetimes [Hendren et al. 1992]. This assumes that the schedule or, at least, the instruction order has already been determined and that a postpass scheduling step will follow.

Irrespective of which one goes first, a shortcoming of all strategies discussed so far is that the first phase makes its decisions with no consideration of their impact on the subsequent phase. Goodman and Hsu [1988] have addressed this problem by developing two algorithms—one, a scheduler that attempts to keep the register pressure below a limit provided to it, and the second, a register allocation algorithm that is sensitive to its effect on the critical path length of the DAG and thus to the effect on the eventual schedule.

For any piece of code on a given processor, there is some optimal schedule for which register allocation is possible. Scheduling twice, once before and then after register allocation, is an approximation of achieving this ideal. Simultaneous scheduling and register allocation is another strategy for attempting to find a near-optimal schedule and register allocation. Simultaneous scheduling and register allocation is currently understood only in the context of acyclic code, specifically, a single basic block or a linear trace of basic blocks. The essence of the idea is that at each time an operation is scheduled, an available register is allocated to hold the result. Also, if this operation constitutes the last use of the contents of one of the source registers, that register is made available once again for subsequent allocation. When no register is available to receive the result of the operation being scheduled, a register must be spilled. The register holding the datum whose use is furthest away in the future is spilled. This approach was used in the FPS-164 compiler at the level of individual basic blocks [Touzeau 1984] as well as across entire traces [Ellis 1985; Freudenberger and Ruttenberg 1992; Lowney et al. 1993]. An important concept developed by the ELI project at Yale and by Multiflow was that of performing hierarchical, profile-driven, integrated global scheduling and register allocation. Traces are picked in decreasing order of frequency and integrated scheduling and allocation are performed on each. The scheduling and allocation decisions made for traces that have been processed form constraints on the corresponding decisions for the remaining code. This is a far more systematic approach than other ad hoc, priority-based schemes with the same objective. A syntax-based hierarchical approach to global register allocation has been suggested by Callahan and Koblenz [1991].

If a loop is unrolled some number of times and then treated as a linear trace of basic blocks [Fisher et al. 1981], simultaneous trace scheduling and register allocation can be accomplished, but with some loss of performance due to the emptying of pipelines across the back edge. In the case of modulo scheduling, which avoids this performance penalty, no approach has yet been advanced for simultaneous register allocation. Since doing register allocation in advance is unacceptably constraining on the schedule, it must be performed following modulo scheduling. A unique situation encountered with modulo scheduled loops is that the lifetimes are often much longer than the initiation interval. Normally, this would result in a value being overwritten before its last use has occurred. One solution is to unroll the kernel of a modulo scheduled loop a sufficient number of times to ensure that no lifetime is longer than the length of the replicated kernel [Lam 1987, 1988]. This is known as *modulo variable expansion*. In addition to techniques such as graph coloring, the heuristics proposed by Hendren and others [1992] and by Rau and others [1992] may be applied after modulo variable expansion. The other solution for register allocation is to assume the dynamic register renaming provided by the rotating register capability of the Cydra 5. The entity that the register allocator works with are vector lifetimes, that is, the entire sequence of (scalar) lifetimes defined by a particular operation over the execution of the loop [Dehnert and Towle 1993; Dehnert et al. 1989; Rau et al. 1992]. Lower bounds on the number of registers needed for a modulo scheduled loop have been developed by Mangione-Smith and others [1992]. The strategy for recovering from a situation, in which no allocation can be found for the software pipelined loop, is not well understood. Some options have been outlined [Rau et al. 1992], but their detailed implementation, effectiveness, and relative merits have as yet to be investigated.

3.2.3. Other ILP Compiler Topics. Although scheduling and register allocation are at the heart of ILP compilation, a number of other analyses, optimizations, and transformations are crucial to the generation of high-quality code. Currently, schedulers treat a procedure call as a barrier to code motion. Thus, in-lining of intrinsics and user procedures is very important in the high frequency portions of the program [Dehnert and Towle 1993; Linn 1988; Lowney et al. 1993].

Certain loop-oriented analyses and optimizations are specific to modulo scheduling. IF-conversion and the appropriate placement of predicate-setting operations are needed to modulo schedule loops with control flow [Allen et al. 1983; Dehnert and Towle 1993; Dehnert et al. 1989; Park and Schlansker 1991]. The elimination of subscripted loads and stores that are redundant across multiple iterations of a loop can have a significant effect upon both the ResMII and the RecMII [Callahan et al. 1990; Dehnert and Towle 1993; Rau 1992]. This is important for trace scheduling unrolled loops as well [Lowney et al. 1993]. Recurrence back-substitution, and other transformations that reduce the RecMII have a major effect on the performance of all software pipelined loops [Dehnert and Towle 1993]. Most of these transformations and analyses are facilitated by the dynamic single-assignment representation for inner loops [Dehnert and Towle 1993; Rau 1992].

On machines with multiple, identical clusters, such as the Multiflow Trace machines, it is necessary to decide which part of the computation will go on each cluster. This is a nontrivial task; whereas increased parallelism argues in favor of spreading the computation over the clusters, this also introduces intercluster move operations into the computation, whose latency can degrade performance if the partitioning of the computation across clusters is not done carefully. An algorithm for performing this partitioning was developed by Ellis [1986] and was incorporated into the Multiflow compiler [Lowney et al. 1993].

An issue of central importance to all ILP compilation is the disambiguation of memory references, that is, deciding whether two memory references definitely are to the same memory location or definitely are not. Known as dependence analysis, this has become a very well developed topic in the area of vector computing over the past twenty years [Zima and Chapman 1990]. For vector computers the compiler is attempting to prove that two references in different iterations are *not* to the same location. No benefit is derived if it is determined that they *are* to the same location since such loops cannot be vectorized. Consequently, the nature of the analysis, especially in the context of loops containing conditional branching, has been approximate. This is a shortcoming from the point of view of ILP processors that can benefit both if the two references are or are not to the same location. A more precise analysis than dependence analysis, involving data flow analysis, is required. Also, with ILP processors, memory disambiguation is important outside of loops as well as within them. Memory disambiguation within traces was studied in the ELI project [Ellis 1985; Nicolau 1984] and was implemented in the Multiflow compiler [Lowney et al. 1993]. Memory disambiguation, in the context of innermost loops, was implemented in the Cydra 5 compiler [Dehnert and Towle 1993; Rau 1992] and was studied by Callahan and Koblenz [1991].

4. Available ILP

4.1. Limit Studies and Their Shortcomings

Many experimenters have attempted to measure the maximum parallelism available in programs. The goal of such limit studies is to

throw away all considerations of hardware and compiler practicality and measure the greatest possible amount of ILP inherent in a program.

Limit studies are simple enough to describe: Take an execution trace of the program, and build a data precedence graph on the operations, eliminating false antidependences caused by the write-after-read usage of a register or other piece of hardware storage. The length in cycles of the serial execution of the trace gives the serial execution time on hardware with the given latencies. The length in cycles of the critical path though the data dependence graph gives the shortest possible execution time. The quotient of these two is the available speedup. (In practice, an execution trace is not always gathered. Instead, the executed stream is processed as the code runs, greatly reducing the computation or storage required, or both.)

These are indeed maximum parallelism measures in some sense, but they have a critical shortcoming that causes them to miss accomplishing their stated goal; they do not consider transformations that a compiler might make to enhance ILP. Although we mostly mean transformations of a yet-unknown nature that researchers may develop in the future, even current state-of-the-art transformations are rarely reflected in limit studies. Thus we have had, in recent years, the anomalies of researchers stating an "upper limit" on available parallelism in programs that is lower than what has already been accomplished with those same programs, or of new results that show the maximum available parallelism to be significantly higher than it was a few years ago, before a new set of code transformations was considered.

There is a somewhat fatuous argument that demonstrates just how imprecise limit studies must be; recalling that infinite hardware is available, we can replace computations in the code with table lookups. In each case we will replace a longer—perhaps very long—computation with one that takes a single step. While this is obviously impractical for most computations with operands that span the (finite, but large) range of integers or floating point numbers representable on a system, it is only impractical in the very sense in which practicality is to be discarded in limit studies. And even on practicality grounds, one cannot dismiss this argument completely; in a sense it really does capture what is wrong with these experiments. There are many instances of transformations, some done by hand, others automatically, that reduce to this concept. Arithmetic and transcendental functions are often sped up significantly by the carefully selected use of table lookups at critical parts of the computation. Modern compilers can often replace a nested set of IF-THEN tests with a single lookup in which hardware does an indirect jump through a lookup table. Limit studies have no way of capturing these transformations, the effect of which could be a large improvement in available ILP.

Even in current practice the effect of ignoring sophisticated compiling is extreme. Transformations such as tree height reduction, loop conditioning, loop exchange, and so forth can have a huge effect on the parallelism available in code. A greater unknown is the research future of data structure selection to improve ILP. A simple example can show this effect. The following code finds the maximum element of a linked list of data:

```
this-ptr = head-ptr;
max-so-far = most-neg-number;
while this-ptr {
    if this-ptr.data > max-so-far
        then max-so-far = this-ptr.data;
    this-ptr = this-ptr.next }
```

From simple observation the list of elements chained from head-ptr cannot be circular. If the compiler had judged it worthwhile, it could have stored these elements in an array and done the comparisons pairwise, in parallel, without having to chase the pointers linearly. This example is not as farfetched as it might seem. Vectorization took 20 years to go from the ability to recognize the simplest loop to the sophisticated vectorizers we have today. There has been virtually no work done on compiler transformations to enhance ILP.

Limit studies, then, are in some sense finding the maximum parallelism available, but in other ways are finding the minimum. In these senses they find the maximum parallelism:

- Disambiguation can be done perfectly, well beyond what is practical.
- There are infinitely many functional units available.
- There are infinitely many registers available.
- Rejoins can be completely unwound.

In other senses, they represent a minimum, or an existence proof that at least a certain amount of parallelism exists, since potentially important processes have been left out:

- Compiler transformations to enhance ILP have not been done.
- Intermediate code generation techniques that boost ILP have not been done.

Perhaps it is more accurate to say that a limit study shows that the maximum parallelism available, in the absence of practicality considerations, is *at least* the amount measured.

4.1.1. Early Experiments. The very first ILP limit studies demonstrated the effect we wrote of above: The experimenters' view of the techniques by which one could find parallelism was limited to the current state of the art, and the experimenters missed a technique that is now known to provide most of the available ILP, the motion of operations between basic blocks of code. Experiments done by Tjaden and Flynn [1970] and by Foster and Riseman [1972] (and, anecdotally, elsewhere) found that there was only a small amount (about a factor of two to three) of improvement due to ILP available in real programs. This was dubbed the *Flynn bottleneck*. By all accounts, these pessimistic and, in a sense, erroneous experiments had a tremendous dampening effect on the progress of ILP research. The experiments were only erroneous in the sense of missing improvements; certainly they did correctly what they said they did.

Interestingly, one of the research teams doing these experiments saw that under the hypothesis of free and infinite hardware, one would not necessarily have to stop finding ILP at basic block boundaries. In a companion paper to the one mentioned above, Riseman and Foster [1972] put forward a hardware-intensive solution to the problem of doing operations speculatively: They measured what would happen if one used duplicate hardware at conditional jumps, and disregarded the one that went in the wrong direction. They found a far larger amount of parallelism: Indeed, they found more than an order of magnitude more than they could when branches were a barrier. Some of the programs they measured could achieve arbitrarily large amounts of parallelism, depending only on data set size. But in an otherwise insightful and visionary piece of work, the researchers lost sight of the fact that they were doing a limit study, and in their tone and abstract emphasized how impractical it would be to implement the hardware scheme they had suggested. (They found that to get a factor-of-ten ILP speedup, one had to be prepared to cope with 16 unresolved branches at the worst point of a typical program. Their scheme would require, then, 2^{16} sets of hardware to do so. Today, as described in most of the papers in this issue, we try to get much of the benefit of the same parallelism without the hardware cost by doing code motions that move operations between blocks and having the code generator make sure that the correct computation is ultimately done once the branches settle.)

4.1.2. Contemporary Experiments. We know of no other ILP limit studies published between then and the 1980s. In 1981 Nicolau and Fisher [1981, 1984] used some of the apparatuses being developed for the Yale Bulldog compiler to repeat the experiment done by Riseman and Foster, and found virtually the same results.

In the late 1980s architects began to look at superscalar microprocessors and again started a series of limit studies. Interestingly, the most notorious of these [Jouppi and Wall 1989] again neglected the possibility of code motions between blocks. Unsurprisingly, the Flynn bottleneck appeared again, and only the factor of 2–3 parallelism found earlier was found. Two years later Wall [1991] did the most thorough limit study to date and accounted for speculative execution, memory disambiguation, and other factors. He built an elaborate model and published available ILP speedup under a great many scenarios, yielding a wealth of valuable data but no simple answers. The various scenarios allow one to try to bracket what really might be practical in the near future, but are subject to quite a bit of interpretation. In examining the various scenarios presented, we find that settings that a sophisticated compiler might approach during the coming decade could yield speedups ranging from 7 to 60 on the sample programs, which are taken from the SPEC suite and other standard benchmarks. (It is worth noting that Wall himself is much more pessimistic. In the same results he sees an average ceiling of about 5, and the near impossibility of attaining even that much.) Lam and Wilson [1992] did an experiment to measure the effects of different methods of eliminating control flow barriers to parallelism. When their model agreed with Wall's, their results were similar. Butler and Patt [Butler et al. 1991] considered models with a large variety of numbers of functional units and found that with good branch prediction schemes and speculative execution, a wide range of speedup was available.

4.2. Experiments That Measure Attained Parallelism

In contrast to the limit studies, some people have built real or simulated ILP systems and have measured their speedup against real or simulated nonparallel systems. When simulated systems have been involved, they have been relatively realistic systems, or systems that the researchers have argued would abstract the essence of realistic systems in such a way that the system realities should not lower the attained parallelism. Thus the experiments represent something closer to true lower bounds on available parallelism.

Ellis [1986] used the Bulldog compiler to generate code for a hypothetical machine. His model was unrealistic in several aspects, most notably the memory system, but realistic implementations should have little difficulty exploiting the parallelism he found. Ellis measured the speedups obtained on 12 small scientific programs for both a "realistic" machine (corresponding to one under design at Yale) and an "ideal" machine, with limitless hardware and single-cycle functional units. He found speedups ranging from no speedup to 7.6 times speedup for the real model, and a range of 2.7 to 48.3 for the ideal model.

In this issue there are three papers that add to our understanding of the performance of ILP systems. The paper by Hwu and others [1993] considers the effect of a realistic compiler that uses superblock scheduling. Lowney and others [1993] and Schuette and Shen [1993] compare the performance of the Multiflow TRACE 14/300 with current microprocessors from MIPs and IBM, respectively.

Fewer studies have been done to measure the attained performance of software pipelining. Warter and others [1992] consider a set of 30 *doall* loops with branches found in the Perfect and SPEC benchmark sets. Relative to a single-issue machine without modulo scheduling, they find a 6-time speedup on a hypothetical 4-issue machine and a 10-time speedup on a hypothetical 8-issue machine. Lee and others [1993] combined superblock scheduling and software pipelining for a machine capable of issuing up to seven operations per cycle. On a mix of loop-intensive (e.g., LINPACK) and "scalar" (e.g., Spice) codes, they found an average of one to four operations issued per cycle, with two to seven operations in flight.

5. An Introduction to This Special Issue

In this special issue of *The Journal of Supercomputing* we have attempted to capture the most significant work that took place during the 1980s in the area of instruction-level parallel processing. The intent is to document both the theory and the practice of ILP computing. Consequently, our emphasis is on projects that resulted in implementations of serious scope, since it is this reduction to practice that exposes the true merit and the real problems of ideas that sound good on paper.

During the 1980s the bulk of the advances in ILP occurred in the form of VLIW processing, and this special issue reflects it with papers on Multiflow's Trace family and on Cydrome's Cydra 5. The paper by Lowney and others [1993] provides an overview of the Trace hardware and an in-depth discussion of the compiler. The paper by Schuette and Shen [1993] reports on an evaluation performed by the authors of the TRACE 14/300 and a comparison of it to the superscalar IBM RS/6000. The Cydra 5 effort is documented by two papers: one by Beck, Yen, and Anderson [1993] on the Cydra 5 architecture and hardware implementation, and the other by Dehnert and Towle [1993] on the Cydra 5 compiler. (While reading the descriptions of these large and bulky minisupercomputers, it is worthwhile to bear in mind that they could easily fit on a single chip in the near future!) The only important superscalar product of the 1980s was Astronautics' ZS-1 minisupercomputer. Although we wanted to include a paper on it in this special issue, that did not come to pass. The paper by Hwu and others [1993] reports on IMPACT, the most thorough implementation of an ILP compiler that has occurred in academia.

Notes

1. The first machines of this type that were built in the 1960s were referred to as *look-ahead* processors. Subsequently, machines that performed out-of-order execution, while issuing multiple operations per cycle, came to be termed *superscalar* processors. Since look-ahead processors are only quantitatively different from superscalar processors, we shall drop the distinction and refer to them, too, as superscalar processors.

2. We shall consistently refer to this code generation activity as *scheduling*.

References

Acosta, R.D., Kjelstrup, J., and Torng, H.C. 1986. An instruction issuing approach to enhancing performance in multiple function unit processors. *IEEE Trans. Comps.*, C-35, 9 (Sept.): 815–828.

Adam, T.L., Chandy, K.M., and Dickson, J.R. 1974. A comparison of list schedules for parallel processing systems. *CACM*, 17, 12 (Dec.): 685–690.

Advanced Micro Devices. 1989. *Am29000 Users Manual.* Pub. no. 10620B, Advanced Micro Devices, Sunnyvale, Calif.

Agerwala, T. 1976. Microprogram optimization: A survey. *IEEE Trans. Comps.*, C-25, 10 (Oct.): 962–973.

Agerwala, T., and Cocke, J. 1987. High performance reduced instruction set processors. Tech. rept. RC12434 (#55845), IBM Thomas J. Watson Research Center, Yorktown Heights, N.Y.

Aho, A.V., and Johnson, S.C. 1976. Optimal code generation for expression trees. *JACM*, 23, 3 (July): 488–501.

Aho, A.V., Johnson, S.C., and Ullman, J.D. 1977a. Code generation for expressions with common subexpressions. *JACM*, 24, 1 (Jan.): 146–160.

Aho, A.V., Johnson, S.C., and Ullman, J.D. 1977b. Code generation for machines with multiregister operations. In *Proc., Fourth ACM Symp. on Principles of Programming Languages*, pp. 21–28.

Aiken, A., and Nicolau, A. 1988a. Optimal loop parallelization. In *Proc., SIGPLAN '88 Conf. on Programming Language Design and Implementation* (Atlanta, June), pp. 308–317.

Aiken, A., and Nicolau, A. 1988b. Perfect pipelining: A new loop parallelization technique. In *Proc., 1988 European Symp. on Programming*, Springer Verlag, New York, pp. 221–235.

Aiken, A., and Nicolau, A. 1991. A realistic resource-constrained software pipelining algorithm. In *Advances in Languages and Compilers for Parallel Processing* (A. Nicolau, D. Gelernter, T. Gross, and D. Padua, eds.), Pitman/MIT Press, London, pp. 274–290.

Allen, J.R., Kennedy, K., Porterfield, C., and Warren, J. 1983. Conversion of control dependence to data dependence. In *Proc., Tenth Annual ACM Symp. on Principles of Programming Languages* (Jan.): pp. 177–189.

Anderson DW., Sparacio, F.J., and Tomasulo, R.M. 1967. The System/360 Model 91: Machine philosophy and instruction handling. *IBM J. Res. and Dev.*, 11, 1 (Jan.): 8–24.

Apollo Computer. 1988. *The Series 10000 Personal Supercomputer: Inside a New Architecture.* Publication no. 002402-007 2-88, Apollo Computer, Inc., Chelmsford, Mass.

Arvind and Gostelow, K. 1982. The U-interpreter. *Computer*, 15, 2 (Feb.): 12–49.

Arvind and Kathail, V. 1981. A multiple processor dataflow machine that supports generalised procedures. In *Proc., Eighth Annual Symp. on Computer Architecture* (May): pp. 291–302.

Auslander, M., and Hopkins, M. 1982. An overview of the PL.8 compiler. In *Proc., ACM SIGPLAN Symp. on Compiler Construction* (Boston, June), pp. 22–31.

Bahr, R., Ciavaglia, S., Flahive, B., Kline, M., Mageau, P., and Nickel, D. 1991. The DN10000TX: A new high-performance PRISM processor. In *Proc., COMPCON '91*, pp. 90–95.

Baker, K.R. 1974. *Introduction to Sequencing and Scheduling.* John Wiley, New York.

Beck, G.R., Yen, D.W.L., and Anderson T.L. 1993. The Cydra 5 minisupercomputer: Architecture and implementation. *The J. Supercomputing*, 7, 1/2: 143–180.

Bell, C.G., and Newell, A. 1971. *Computer Structures: Readings and Examples.* McGraw-Hill, New York.

Bernstein, D., and Rodeh, M. 1991. Global instruction scheduling for superscalar machines. In *Proc., SIGPLAN '91 Conf. on Programming Language Design and Implementation* (June), pp. 241–255.

Bernstein, D., Cohen, D., and Krawczyk, H. 1991. Code duplication: An assist for global instruction scheduling. In *Proc., 24th Annual Internat. Symp. on Microarchitecture* (Albuquerque, N.Mex.), pp. 103–113.

Blanck, G., and Krueger, S. 1992. The SuperSPARC™ microprocessor. In *Proc., COMPCON '92*, pp. 136–141.

Bloch, E. 1959. The engineering design of the STRETCH computer. In *Proc., Eastern Joint Computer Conf.*, pp. 48–59.

Bruno, J.L., and Sethi, R. 1976. Code generation for a one-register machine. *JACM*, 23, 3 (July): 502–510.

Buchholz, W., ed. 1962. *Planning a Computer System: Project Stretch.* McGraw-Hill, New York.

Butler, M., Yeh, T., Patt, Y., Alsup, M., Scales, H., and Shebanow, M. 1991. Single instruction stream parallelism is greater than two. In *Proc., Eighteenth Annual Internat. Symp. on Computer Architecture* (Toronto), pp. 276–286.

Callahan, D., and Koblenz, B. 1991. Register allocation via hierarchical graph coloring. In *Proc., SIGPLAN '91 Conf. on Programming Language Design and Implementation* (Toronto, June), pp. 192–203.

Callahan, D., Carr, S., and Kennedy, K. 1990. Improving register allocation for subscripted variables. In *Proc., ACM SIGPLAN '90 Conf. on Programming Language Design and Implementation*, (White Plains, N.Y., June), pp. 53–65.

Carpenter, B.E., and Doran, R.W., eds. 1986. *A.M. Turing's ACE Report of 1946 and Other Papers.* MIT Press, Cambridge, Mass.

Chaitin, G.J. 1982. Register allocation and spilling via graph coloring. In *Proc., ACM SIGPLAN Symp. on Compiler Construction* (Boston, June), pp. 98–105.

Chang, P.P., and Hwu, W.W. 1988. Trace selection for compiling large C application programs to microcode. In *Proc., 21st Annual Workshop on Microprogramming and Microarchitectures* (San Diego, Nov.), pp. 21–29.

Chang, P.P., and Hwu, W.W. 1992. Profile-guided automatic inline expansion for C programs. Software—Practice and Experience, 22, 5 (May): 349–376.

Chang, P.P., Lavery, D.M., and Hwu, W.W. 1991. The importance of prepass code scheduling for superscalar and superpipelined processors. Tech. Rept. no. CRHC-91-18, Center for Reliable and High-Performance Computing, Univ. of Ill, Urbana-Champaign, Ill.

Chang, P.P., Mahlke, S.A., Chen, W.Y., Warter, N.J., and Hwu, W.W. 1991. IMPACT: An architectural framework for multiple-instruction-issue processors. In Proc., 18th Annual Internat. Symp. on Computer Architecture (Toronto, May), pp. 266–275.

Charlesworth, A.E. 1981. An approach to scientific array processing: The architectural design of the AP-120B/FPS-164 family. Computer, 14, 9: 18–27.

Chen, T.C. 1971. Parallelism, pipelining, and computer efficiency. Computer Design, 10, 1 (Jan.): 69–74.

Chen, T.C. 1975. Overlap and pipeline processing. In Introduction to Computer Architecture (H.S. Stone, ed.), Science Research Associates, Chicago, pp. 375–431.

Chow, F., and Hennessy, J. 1984. Register allocation by priority-based coloring. In Proc., ACM SIGPLAN Symp. on Compiler Construction (Montreal, June), pp. 222–232.

Chow, F.C., and Hennessy, J.L. 1990. The priority-based coloring approach to register allocation. ACM Trans. Programming Languages and Systems, 12 (Oct.): 501–536.

Coffman, J.R., ed. 1976. Computer and Job-Shop Scheduling Theory. John Wiley, New York.

Coffman, E.G., and Graham, R.L. 1972. Optimal scheduling for two processor systems. Acta Informatica, 1, 3: 200–213.

Cohen, D. 1978. A methodology for programming a pipeline array processor. In Proc., 11th Annual Microprogramming Workshop (Asilomar, Calif., Nov.), pp. 82–89.

Colwell, R.P., Nix, R.P., O'Donnell, J.J., Papworth, D.B., and Rodman, P.K. 1988. A VLIW architecture for a trace scheduling compiler. IEEE Trans. Comps., C-37, 8 (Aug.): 967–979.

Colwell, R.P., Hall, W.E., Joshi, C.S., Papworth, D.B., Rodman, P.K., and Tornes, J.E. 1990. Architecture and implementation of a VLIW supercomputer. In Proc., Supercomputing '90 (Nov.), pp. 910–919.

Cotten, L.W. 1965. Circuit implementation of high-speed pipeline systems. In Proc., AFIPS Fall Joint Computing Conf., pp. 489–504.

Cotten, L.W. 1969. Maximum-rate pipeline systems. In Proc., AFIPS Spring Joint Computing Conf., 581–586.

Danelutto, M., and Vanneschi, M. 1990. VLIW in-the-large: A model for fine grain parallelism exploitation of distributed memory multiprocessors. In Proc., 23rd Annual Workshop on Microprogramming and Microarchitecture (Nov.), pp. 7–16.

Dasgupta, S., and Tartar, J. 1976. The identification of maximal parallelism in straight-line microprograms. IEEE Trans. Comps., C-25, 10 (Oct.): 986–991.

Davidson, E.S. 1971. The design and control of pipelined function generators. In Proc., 1971 Internat. IEEE Conf. on Systems, Networks, and Computers (Oaxtepec, Mexico, Jan.), pp. 19–21.

Davidson, E.S. 1974. Scheduling for pipelined processors. In Proc., 7th Hawaii Conf. on Systems Sciences, pp. 58–60.

Davidson, S., Landskov, D., Shriver, B.D., and Mallett, P.W. 1981. Some experiments in local microcode compaction for horizontal machines. IEEE Trans. Comps., C-30, 7: 460–477.

Davidson, E.S., Shar, L.E., Thomas, A.T., and Patel, J.H. 1975. Effective control for pipelined computers. In Proc., COMPCON '90 (San Francisco, Feb.), pp. 181–184.

Dehnert, J.C., and Towle, R.A. 1993. Compiling for the Cydra 5. The J. Supercomputing, 7, 1/2: 181–227.

Dehnert, J.C., Hsu, P.Y-T., and Bratt, J.P. 1989. Overlapped loop support in the Cydra 5. In Proc., Third Internat. Conf. on Architectural Support for Programming Languages and Operating Systems (Boston, Apr.), pp. 26–38.

DeLano, E., Walker, W., Yetter, J., and Forsyth, M. 1992. A high speed superscalar PA-RISC processor. In Proc., COMPCON '92 (Feb.), pp. 116–121.

DeWitt, D.J. 1975. A control word model for detecting conflicts between microprograms. In Proc., 8th Annual Workshop on Microprogramming (Chicago, Sept.), pp. 6–12.

Diefendorff, K., and Allen, M. 1992. Organization of the Motorola 88110 superscalar RISC microprocessor. IEEE Micro, 12, 2 (Apr.): 40–63.

Dongarra, J.J. 1986. A survey of high performance computers. In Proc., COMPCON '86 (Mar.), pp. 8–11.

Dwyer, H., and Torng, H.C. 1992. An out-of-order superscalar processor with speculative execution and fast, precise interrupts. In Proc., 25th Annual Internat. Symp. on Microarchitecture (Portland, Ore., Dec.), pp. 272–281.

Ebcioglu, K. 1988. Some design ideas for a VLIW architecture for sequential-natured software. In Parallel Processing (Proc., IFIP WG 10.3 Working Conf. on Parallel Processing, Pisa, Italy) (M. Cosnard, M.H. Barton, and M. Vanneschi, eds.), North-Holland, pp. 3–21.

Ebcioglu, K., and Nakatani, T. 1989. A new compilation technique for parallelizing loops with unpredictable branches on a VLIW architecture. In Languages and Compilers for Parallel Computing (D. Gelernter, A. Nicolau, and D. Padua, eds.), Pitman/MIT Press, London, pp. 213–229.

Ebcioglu, K., and Nicolau, A. 1989. A global resource-constrained parallelization technique. In Proc., 3rd Internat. Conf. on Supercomputing (Crete, Greece, June), pp. 154–163.

Eckert, J.P., Chu, J.C., Tonik, A.B., and Schmitt, W.F. 1959. Design of UNIVAC-LARC System: I. In Proc., Eastern Joint Computer Conf., pp. 59–65.

Ellis, J.R. 1986. Bulldog: A Compiler for VLIW Architectures. MIT Press, Cambridge, Mass.

Fawcett, B.K. 1975. Maximal clocking rates for pipelined digital systems. M.S. thesis, Univ. of Ill., Urbana-Champaign, Ill.

Fernandez, E.B., and Bussel, B. 1973. Bounds on the number of processors and time for multiprocessor optimal schedule. IEEE Trans. Comps., C-22, 8 (Aug.): 745–751.

Fisher, J.A. 1979. The optimization of horizontal microcode within and beyond basic blocks: An application of processor scheduling with resources, Ph.D. thesis, New York Univ., New York.

Fisher, J.A. 1980. 2^N-way jump microinstruction hardware and an effective instruction binding method. In Proc., 13th Annual Workshop on Microprogramming (Colorado Springs, Colo., Nov.), pp. 64–75.

Fisher, J.A. 1981. Trace scheduling: A technique for global microcode compaction. IEEE Trans. Comps., C-30, 7 (July): 478–490.

Fisher, J.A. 1983. Very long instruction word architectures and the ELI-512. In Proc., Tenth Annual Internat. Symp. on Computer Architecture (Stockholm, June), pp. 140–150.

Fisher, J.A. 1992. Trace Scheduling-2, an extension of trace scheduling. Tech. rept., Hewlett-Packard Laboratories.

Fisher, J.A., and Freudenberger, S.M. 1992. Predicting conditional jump directions from previous runs of a program. In Proc., Fifth Internat. Conf. on Architectural Support for Programming Languages and Operating Systems (Boston, Oct.), pp. 85–95.

Fisher, J.A., Landskov, D., and Shriver, B.D. 1981. Microcode compaction: Looking backward and looking forward. In Proc., 1981 Nat. Computer Conf., pp. 95–102.

Fisher, J.A., Ellis, J.R., Ruttenberg, J.C., and Nicolau, A. 1984. Parallel processing: A smart compiler and a dumb machine. In Proc., ACM SIGPLAN '84 Symp. on Compiler Construction (Montreal, June), pp. 37–47.

Floating Point Systems. 1979. FPS AP-120B Processor Handbook. Floating Point Systems, Inc., Beaverton, Ore.

Foster, C.C., and Riseman, E.M. 1972. Percolation of code to enhance parallel dispatching and execution. IEEE Trans. Comps., C-21, 12 (Dec.): 1411–1415.

Franklin, M., and Sohi, G.S. 1992. The expandable split window paradigm for exploiting fine-grain parallelism. In Proc. 19th Annual International Symp. on Computer Architecture (Gold Coast, Australia, May), pp. 58–67.

Freudenberger, S.M., and Ruttenberg, J.C. 1992. Phase ordering of register allocation and instruction scheduling. In Code Generation—Concepts, Tools, Techniques: Proc., Internat. Workshop on Code Generation, May 1991 (R. Giegerich, and S.L. Graham, eds.), Springer-Verlag, London, pp. 146–172.

Gasperoni, F. 1989. Compilation techniques for VLIW architectures. Tech. rept. RC 14915, IBM Research Div., T.J. Watson Research Center, Yorktown Heights, N.Y.

Gibbons, P.B., and Muchnick, S.S. 1986. Efficient instruction scheduling for a pipelined architecture. In Proc., ACM SIGPLAN '86 Symp. on Compiler Construction (Palo Alto, Calif., July), pp. 11–16.

Golumbic, M.C., and Rainish, V. 1990. Instruction scheduling beyond basic blocks. IBM J. Res. and Dev., 34, 1 (Jan.): 93–97.

Gonzalez, M.J. 1977. Deterministic processor scheduling. ACM Computer Surveys, 9, 3 (Sept.): 173–204.

Goodman, J.R., and Hsu, W.-C. 1988. Code scheduling and register allocation in large basic blocks. In Proc., 1988 Internat. Conf. on Supercomputing (St. Malo, France, July), pp. 442–452.

Grishman, R., and Su, B. 1983. A preliminary evaluation of trace scheduling for global microcode compaction. IEEE Trans. Comps., C-32, 12 (Dec.): 1191–1194.

Gross, T.R., and Hennessy, J.L. 1982. Optimizing delayed branches. In Proc., 15th Annual Workshop on Microprogramming (Oct.), pp. 114–120.

Gross, T., and Ward, M. 1990. The suppression of compensation code. In *Advances in Languages and Compilers for Parallel Computing* (A. Nicolau, D. Gelernter, T. Gross, and D. Padua, eds.), Pitman/MIT Press, London, pp. 260-273.

Gurd, J., Kirkham, C.C., and Watson, I. 1985. The Manchester prototype dataflow computer. *CACM*, 28, 1(Jan.): 34-52.

Hallin, T.G., and Flynn, M.J. 1972. Pipelining of arithmetic functions. *IEEE Trans. Comps.*, C-21, 8 (Aug.): 880-886.

Hendren, L.J., Gao, G.R., Altman, E.R., and Mukerji, C. 1992. Register allocation using cyclic interval graphs: A new approach to an old problem. ACAPS Tech. Memo 33, Advanced Computer Architecture and Program Structures Group, McGill Univ., Montreal.

Hennessy, J.L., and Gross, T. 1983. Post-pass code optimization of pipelined constraints. *ACM Trans. Programming Languages and Systems*, 5, 3 (July): 422-448.

Hennessy, J., Jouppi, N., Baskett, F., Gross, T., and Gill, J. 1982. Hardware/software tradeoffs for increased performance. In *Proc., Symp. on Architectural Support for Programming Languages and Operating Systems* (Palo Alto, Calif., Mar.) pp. 2-11.

Hennessy, J. Jouppi, N., Przybylski, S., Rowen, C., Gross, T., Baskett, F., and Gill, J. 1982. MIPS: A microprocessor architecture. In *Proc., 15th Annual Workshop on Microprogramming* (Palo Alto, Calif., Oct.), pp. 17-22.

Hintz, R.G., and Tate, D.P. 1972. Control Data STAR-100 processor design. In *Proc., COMPCON '72* (Sept.), pp. 1-4.

Hsu, P.Y.T. 1986. Highly concurrent scalar processing. Ph.D. thesis, Univ. of Ill., Urbana-Champaign, Ill.

Hsu, P.Y.T., and Davidson, E.S. 1986. Highly concurrent scalar processing. In *Proc., Thirteenth Annual Internat. Symp. on Computer Architecture*, pp. 386-395.

Hsu, W-C. 1987. Register allocation and code scheduling for load/store architectures. Comp. Sci. Tech. Rept. no. 722, Univ. of Wisc., Madison.

Hu, T.C. 1961. Parallel sequencing and assembly line problems. *Operations Research*, 9, 6: 841-848.

Hwu, W.W., and Chang, P.P. 1988. Exploiting parallel microprocessor microarchitectures with a compiler code generator. In *Proc., 15th Annual Internat. Symp. on Computer Architecture* (Honolulu, May), pp. 45-53.

Hwu, W.W., and Patt, Y.N. 1986. HPSm, a high performance restricted data flow architecture having minimal functionality. In *Proc., 13th Annual Internat. Symp. on Computer Architecture* (Tokyo, June), pp. 297-306.

Hwu, W.W., and Patt, Y.N. 1987. Checkpoint repair for out-of-order execution machines. *IEEE Trans. Comps.*, C-36, 12 (Dec.): 1496-1514.

Hwu, W.W., Conte, T.M., and Chang, P.P. 1989. Comparing software and hardware schemes for reducing the cost of branches. In *Proc., 16th Annual Internat. Symp. on Computer Architecture* (May), pp. 224-233.

Hwu, W.W., Mahlke, S.A., Chen, W.Y., Chang, P.P., Warter, N.J., Bringmann, R.A., Ouellette, R.G., Hank, R.E., Kiyohara, T., Haab, G.E., Holm, J.G., and Lavery, D.M. 1993. The superblock: An effective technique for VLIW and superscalar compilation. *The J. Supercomputing*, 7, 1/2: 229-248.

IBM 1967. *IBM J. Res. and Dev.*, 11, 1 (Jan.). Special issue on the System/360 Model 91.

IBM 1976. *IBM 3838 Array Processor Functional Characteristics.* Pub. no. 6A24-3639-0, file no. S370-08, IBM Corp., Endicott, N.Y.

IBM 1990. *IBM J. Res. and Dev*, 34, 1 (Jan.). Special issue on the IBM RISC System/6000 processor.

Intel 1989a. *i860 64-Bit Microprocessor Programmer's Reference Manual.* Pub. no. 240329-001, Intel Corp., Santa Clara, Calif.

Intel 1989b. *80960CA User's Manual.* Pub. no. 270710-001, Intel Corp., Santa Clara, Calif.

Jain, S. 1991. Circular scheduling: A new technique to perform software pipelining. In *Proc., ACM SIGPLAN '91 Conf. on Programming Language Design and Implementation* (June), pp. 219-228.

Johnson, M. 1991. *Superscalar Microprocessor Design.* Prentice-Hall, Englewood Cliffs, N.J.

Jouppi, N.P. 1989. The nonuniform distribution of instruction-level and machine parallelism and its effect on performance. *IEEE Trans. Comps.*, C-38, 12 (Dec.): 1645-1658.

Jouppi, N.P., and Wall, D. 1989. Available instruction level parallelism for superscalar and superpipelined machines. In *Proc., Third Internat. Conf. on Architectural Support for Programming Languages and Operating Systems* (Boston, Apr.), pp. 272-282.

Kasahara, H., and Narita, S. 1984. Practical multiprocessor scheduling algorithms for efficient parallel processing. *IEEE Trans. Comps.*, C-33, 11 (Nov.): 1023-1029.

Keller, R.M. 1975. Look-ahead processors. *Computing Surveys* 7, 4 (Dec.): 177-196.

Kleir, R.L. 1974. A representation for the analysis of microprogram operation. In *Proc., 7th Annual Workshop on Microprogramming* (Sept.), pp. 107-118.

Kleir, R.L., and Ramamoorthy, C.V. 1971. Optimization strategies for microprograms. *IEEE Trans. Comps.*, C-20, 7 (July): 783-794.

Kogge, P.M. 1973. Maximal rate pipelined solutions to recurrence programs. In *Proc., First Annual Symp. on Computer Architecture* (Univ. of Fla., Gainesville, Dec.), pp. 71-76.

Kogge, P.M. 1974. Parallel solution of recurrence problems. *IBM J. Res. and Dev.*, 18, 2 (Mar.): 138-148.

Kogge, P.M. 1977a. Algorithm development for pipelined processors. In *Proc., 1977 Internat. Conf. on Parallel Processing* (Aug.), p. 217.

Kogge, P.M. 1977b. The microprogramming of pipelined processors. In *Proc., 4th Annual Symp. on Computer Architecture* (Mar.), pp. 63-69.

Kogge, P.M. 1981. *The Architecture of Pipelined Computers.* McGraw-Hill, New York.

Kogge, P.M., and Stone, H.S. 1973. A parallel algorithm for the efficient solution of a general class of recurrence equations. *IEEE Trans. Comps.*, C-22, 8 (Aug.): 786-793.

Kohler, W.H. 1975. A preliminary evaluation of the critical path method for scheduling tasks on multiprocessor systems. *IEEE Trans. Comps.*, C-24, 12 (Dec.): 1235-1238.

Kohn, L., and Margulis, N. 1989. Introducing the Intel i860 64-bit microprocessor. *IEEE Micro*, 9, 4 (Aug.): 15-30.

Kunkel, S.R., and Smith, J.E. 1986. Optimal pipelining in supercomputers. In *Proc., 13th Annual Internat. Symp. on Computer Architecture* (Tokyo, June), pp. 404-411.

Labrousse, J., and Slavenburg, G.A. 1988. CREATE-LIFE: A design system for high performance VLSI circuits. In *Proc., Internat. Conf. on Circuits and Devices*, pp. 365-360.

Labrousse, J., and Slavenburg, G.A. 1990a. A 50 MHz microprocessor with a VLIW architecture. In *Proc., ISSCC '90* (San Francisco), pp. 44-45.

Labrousse, J., and Slavenburg, G.A. 1990b. CREATE-LIFE: A modular design approach for high performance ASICs. In *Proc., COMPCON '90* (San Francisco), pp. 427-433.

Lam, M.S-L. 1987. A systolic array optimizing compiler. Ph.D. thesis, Carnegie Mellon Univ., Pittsburgh.

Lam. M. 1988. Software pipelining: An effective scheduling technique for VLIW machines. In *Proc., ACM SIGPLAN '88 Conf. on Programming Language Design and Implementation* (Atlanta, June). pp. 318-327.

Lam, M.S., and Wilson, R.P. 1992. Limits of control flow on parallelism. In *Proc., Nineteenth Internat. Symp. on Computer Architecture* (Gold Coast, Australia, May), pp. 46-57.

Landskov, D., Davidson, S., Shriver, B., and Mallett, P.W. 1980. Local microcode compaction techniques. *ACM Computer Surveys*, 12, 3 (Sept.): 261-294.

Lee, J.K.F., and Smith, A.J. 1984. Branch prediction strategies and branch target buffer design. *Computer*, 17, 1 (Jan.): 6-22.

Lee, M., Tirumalai, P.P., and Ngai, T-F. 1993. Software pipelining and superblock scheduling: Compilation techniques for VLIW machines. In *Proc., 26th Annual Hawaii Internat. Conf. on System Sciences* (Hawaii, Jan.), vol. 1, pp. 202-213.

Linn, J.L. 1988. Horizontal microcode compaction. In *Microprogramming and Firmware Engineering Methods* (S. Habib, ed.), Van Nostrand Reinhold, New York, pp. 381-431.

Lowney, P.G., Freudenberger, S.M., Karzes, T.J., Lichtenstein, W.D., Nix, R.P., O'Donnell, J.S., and Ruttenburg, J.C. 1993. The Multiflow trace scheduling compiler. *The J. Supercomputing*, 7, 1/2: 51-142.

Mahlke, S.A., Chen, W.Y., Hwu, W.W., Rau, B.R., and Schlansker, M.S. 1992. Sentinel scheduling for VLIW and superscalar processors. In *Proc., Fifth Internat. Conf. on Architectural Support for Programming Languages and Operating Systems* (Boston, Oct.), pp. 238-247.

Mahlke, S.A., Lin, D.C., Chen, W.Y., Hank, R.E., and Bringmann, R.A. 1992. Effective compiler support for predicated execution using the hyperblock. In *Proc., 25th Annual Internat. Symp. on Microarchitecture* (Dec.), pp. 45-54.

Mallett, P.W. 1978. Methods of compacting microprograms. Ph.D. thesis, Univ. of Southwestern La., Lafayette, La.

Mangione-Smith, W., Abraham, S.G., and Davidson, E.S. 1992. Register requirements of pipelined processors. In *Proc., Internat. Conf. on Supercomputing* (Washington, DC, July).

McFarling, S., and Hennessy, J. 1986. Reducing the cost of branches. In *Proc., Thirteenth Internat. Symp. on Computer Architecture* (Tokyo, June), pp. 396-403.

Moon, S-M., Ebcioglu, K. 1992. An efficient resource-constrained global scheduling technique for superscalar and VLIW processors. In *Proc., 25th Annual Internat. Symp. on Microarchitecture* (Portland, Ore., Dec.), pp. 55-71.

Rau, B.R., Lee, M., Tirumalai, P., and Schlansker, M.S. 1992. Register allocation for software pipelined loops. In Proc., SIGPLAN '92 Conf. on Programming Language Design and Implementation (San Francisco, June 17–19), pp. 283–299.

Rau, B.R., Yen, D.W.L., Yen, W., and Towle, R.A. 1989. The Cydra 5 departmental supercomputer: Design philosophies, decisions and trade-offs. Computer, 22, 1 (Jan.): 12–34.

Riseman, E.M., and Foster, C.C. 1972. The inhibition of potential parallelism by conditional jumps. IEEE Trans. Comps., C-21, 12 (Dec.): 1405–1411.

Ruggiero, J.F., and Coryell, D.A. 1969. An auxiliary processing system for array calculations. IBM Systems J., 8, 2: 118–135.

Russell, R.M. 1978. The CRAY-1 computer system. CACM, 21: 63–72.

Rymarczyk, J. 1982. Coding guidelines for pipelined processors. In Proc., Symp. on Architectural Support for Programming Languages and Operating Systems (Palo Alto, Calif., Mar.), pp. 12–19.

Schmidt, U., and Caesar, K. 1991. Datawave: A single-chip multiprocessor for video applications. IEEE Micro, 11, 3 (June): 22.

Schneck, P.B. 1987. Supercomputer Architecture. Kluwer Academic, Norwell, Mass.

Schuette, M.A., and Shen, J.P. 1993. Instruction-level experimental evaluation of the Multiflow TRACE 14/300 VLIW computer. The J. Supercomputing, 7, 1/2: 249–271.

Sethi, R. 1975. Complete register allocation problems. SIAM J. Computing, 4, 3: 226–248.

Sethi, R., and Ullman, J.D. 1970. The generation of optimal code for arithmetic expressions, JACM, 17, 4 (Oct.): 715–728.

Sites, R.L. 1978. Instruction ordering for the CRAY-1 computer. Tech. rept. 78-CS-023, Univ. of Calif., San Diego.

Smith, J.E. 1981. A study of branch prediction strategies. In Proc., Eighth Annual Internat. Symp. on Computer Architecture (May), pp. 135–148.

Smith, J.E. 1982. Decoupled access/execute architectures. In Proc., Ninth Annual Internat. Symp. on Computer Architecture (Apr.), pp. 112–119.

Smith, J.E. 1989. Dynamic instruction scheduling and the Astronautics ZS-1. Computer, 22, 1 (Jan.): 21–35.

Smith, J.E., and Pleszkun, A.R. 1988. Implementing precise interrupts in pipelined processors. IEEE Trans. Comps., C-37, 5 (May): 562–573.

Smith, J.E., Dermer, G.E., Vanderwarn, B.D., Klinger, S.D., Roszewski, C.M., Fowler, D.L., Scidmore, K.R., and Laudon, J.P. 1987. The ZS-1 central processor. In Proc., Second Internat. Conf. on Architectural Support for Programming Languages and Operating Systems (Palo Alto, Calif., Oct.), pp. 199–204.

Smith, M.D., Horowitz, M., and Lam, M. 1992. Efficient superscalar performance through boosting. In Proc., Fifth Internat. Conf. on Architectural Support for Programming Languages and Operating Systems (Boston, Oct.), pp. 248–259.

Smith, M.D., Lam, M.S., and Horowitz, M.A. 1990. Boosting beyond static scheduling in a superscalar processor. In Proc., Seventeenth Internat. Symp. on Computer Architecture (June), pp. 344–354.

Smotherman, M., Krishnamurthy, S., Aravind, P.S., and Hunnicutt, D. 1991. Efficient DAG construction and heuristic calculation for instruction scheduling. In Proc., 24th Annual Internat. Workshop on Microarchitecture (Albuquerque, N.M., Nov.), pp. 93–102.

Sohi, G.S., and Vajapayem, S. 1987. Instruction issue logic for high-performance, interruptable pipelined processors. In Proc. 14th Annual Symp. on Computer Architecture (Pittsburgh, June), pp. 27–36.

Su, B., and Ding, S. 1985. Some experiments in global microcode compaction. In Proc., 18th Annual Workshop on Microprogramming (Asilomar, Calif., Nov.), pp. 175–180.

Su, B., and Wang, J. 1991a. GURPR*: A new global software pipelining algorithm. In Proc., 24th Annual Workshop on Microprogramming (Albuquerque, N.M., Nov.), pp. 212–216.

Su, B., and Wang, J. 1991b. Loop-carried dependence and the general URPR software pipelining approach. In Proc., 24th Annual Hawaii Internat. Conf. on System Sciences (Hawaii, Jan.).

Su, B., Ding, S., and Jin, L. 1984. An improvement of trace scheduling for global microcode compaction. In Proc., 17th Annual Workshop on Microprogramming (New Orleans, Oct.), pp. 78–85.

Su, B., Ding, S., and Xia, J. 1986. URPR—An extension of URCR for software pipelining. In Proc. 19th Annual Workshop on Microprogramming (New York, Oct.), pp. 104–108.

Su, B., Ding, S., Wang, J., and Xia, J. 1987. GURPR—A method for global software pipelining. In Proc., 20th Annual Workshop on Microprogramming (Colorado Springs, Colo., Dec.), pp. 88–96.

Nakatani, T., and Ebcioglu, K. 1990. Using a lookahead window in a compaction-based parallelizing compiler. In Proc., 23rd Annual Workshop on Microprogramming and Microarchitecture (Orlando, Fla., Nov.), pp. 57–68.

Nicolau, A. 1984. Parallelism, memory anti-aliasing and correctness for trace scheduling compilers. Ph.D. thesis, Yale Univ., New Haven, Conn.

Nicolau, A. 1985a. Percolation scheduling: A parallel compilation technique. Tech. Rept. TR 85-678, Dept. of Comp. Sci., Cornell, Ithaca, N.Y.

Nicolau, A. 1985b. Uniform parallelism exploitation in ordinary programs. In Proc., Internat. Conf. on Parallel Processing (Aug.), pp. 614–618.

Nicolau, A., and Fisher, J.A. 1981. Using an oracle to measure parallelism in single instruction stream programs. In Proc., Fourteenth Annual Microprogramming Workshop (Oct.), pp. 171–182.

Nicolau, A., and Fisher, J.A. 1984. Measuring the parallelism available for very long instruction word architectures. IEEE Trans. Comps., C-33, 11 (Nov.): 968–976.

Nicolau, A., and Potasman, R. 1990. Realistic scheduling: Compaction for pipelined architectures. In Proc., 23rd Annual Workshop on Microprogramming and Microarchitecture (Orlando, Fla., Nov.), pp. 69–79.

Oehler, R.R., and Blasgen, M.W. 1991. IBM RISC System/6000: Architecture and performance. IEEE Micro, 11, 3 (June): 14.

Papadopoulos, G.M., and Culler, D.E. 1990. Monsoon: An explicit token store architecture. In Proc., Seventeenth Internat. Symp. on Computer Architecture (Seattle, May), pp. 82–91.

Park, J.C.H., and Schlansker, M.S. 1991. On predicated execution. Tech. Rept. HPL-91-58, Hewlett Packard Laboratories.

Patel, J.H. 1976. Improving the throughput of pipelines with delays and buffers. Ph.D. thesis, Univ. of Ill., Urbana-Champaign, Ill.

Patel, J.H., and Davidson, E.S. 1976. Improving the throughput of a pipeline by insertion of delays. In Proc., 3rd Annual Symp. on Computer Architecture (Jan.), pp. 159–164.

Patterson, D.A., and Sequin, C.H. 1981. RISC I: A reduced instruction set VLSI computer. In Proc., 8th Annual Symp. on Computer Architecture (Minneapolis, May), pp. 443–450.

Peterson, C., Sutton, J., and Wiley, P., 1991. iWarp: A 100-MOPS, LIW microprocessor for multicomputers. IEEE Micro, 11, 3 (June): 26.

Popescu, V., Schultz, M., Spracklen, J., Gibson, G., Lightner, B., and Isaman, D. 1991. The Metaflow architecture. IEEE Micro, 11, 3 (June): 10.

Radin, G. 1982. The 801 minicomputer. In Proc., Symp. on Architectural Support for Programming Languages and Operating Systems (Palo Alto, Calif., Mar.), pp. 39–47.

Ramakrishnan, S. 1992. Software pipelining in PA-RISC compilers. Hewlett-Packard J. (July): 39–45.

Ramamoorthy, C.V., and Gonzalez, M.J. 1969. A survey of techniques for recognizing parallel processable streams in computer programs. In Proc., AFIPS Fall Joint Computing Conf., pp. 1–15.

Ramamoorthy, C.V., and Tsuchiya, M. 1974. A high level language for horizontal microprogramming. IEEE Trans. Comps., C-23: 791–802.

Ramamoorthy, C.V, Chandy, K.M., and Gonzalez, M.J. 1972. Optimal scheduling strategies in a multiprocessor system. IEEE Trans. Comps., C-21, 2 (Feb.): 137–146.

Rau, B.R. 1988. Cydra 5 Directed Dataflow architecture. In Proc., COMPCON '88 (San Francisco, Mar.), pp. 106–113.

Rau, B. R. 1992. Data flow and dependence analysis for instruction level parallelism. In Fourth Internat. Workshop on Languages and Compilers for Parallel Computing (U. Banerjee, D. Gelernter, A. Nicolau, and D. Padua, eds.), Springer-Verlag, pp. 236–250.

Rau, B.R., and Glaeser, C.D. 1981. Some scheduling techniques and an easily schedulable horizontal architecture for high performance scientific computing. In Proc., Fourteenth Annual Workshop on Microprogramming (Oct.), pp. 183–198.

Rau, B.R., Glaeser, C.D., and Greenawalt, E.M. 1982. Architectural support for the efficient generation of code for horizontal architectures. In Proc., Symp. on Architectural Support for Programming Languages and Operating Systems (Palo Alto, Calif., Mar.), pp. 96–99.

Rau, B.R., Glaeser, C.D., and Picard, R.L. 1982. Efficient code generation for horizontal architectures: Compiler techniques and architectural support. In Proc., Ninth Annual Internat. Symp. on Computer Architecture (Apr.), pp. 131–139.

Thistle, M.R., and Smith, B.J. 1988. A processor architecture for Horizon. In *Proc., Supercomputing '88,* (Orlando, Fla., Nov.), pp. 35–41.

Thomas, A.T., and Davidson, E.S. 1974. Scheduling of multiconfigurable pipelines. In *Proc., 12th Annual Allerton Conf. on Circuits and Systems Theory* (Allerton, Ill.), pp. 658–669.

Thornton, J.E. 1964. Parallel operation in the Control Data 6600. In *Proc., AFIPS Fall Joint Computer Conf.,* pp. 33–40.

Thornton, J.E. 1970. *Design of a Computer—The Control Data 6600.* Scott, Foresman, Glenview, Ill.

Tirumalai, P., Lee, M., and Schlansker, M.S. 1990. Parallelization of loops with exits on pipelined architectures. In *Proc., Supercomputing '90* (Nov.), pp. 200–212.

Tjaden, G.S., and Flynn, M.J. 1970. Detection and parallel execution of parallel instructions. *IEEE Trans. Comps.,* C-19, 10 (Oct.): 889–895.

Tjaden, G.S., and Flynn, M.J. 1973. Representation of concurrency with ordering matrices. *IEEE Trans. Comps.,* C-22, 8 (Aug.): 752–761.

Tokoro, M., Tamura, E., and Takizuka, T. 1981. Optimization of microprograms. *IEEE Trans. Comps.,* C-30, 7 (July): 491–504.

Tokoro, M., Takizuka, T., Tamura, E., and Yamaura, I. 1978. A technique of global optimization of microprograms. In *Proc., 11th Annual Workshop on Microprogramming* (Asilomar, Calif., Nov.), pp. 41–50.

Tokoro, M., Tamura, E., Takase, K., and Tamaru, K. 1977. An approach to microprogram optimization considering resource occupancy and instruction formats. In *Proc., 10th Annual Workshop on Microprogramming* (Niagara Falls, N.Y., Nov.), pp. 92–108.

Tomasulo, R.M. 1967. An efficient algorithm for exploiting multiple arithmetic units. *IBM J. Res. and Dev.,* 11, 1 (Jan.): 25–33.

Touzeau, R.F. 1984. A FORTRAN compiler for the FPS-164 scientific computer. In *Proc., ACM SIGPLAN '84 Symp. on Compiler Construction* (Montreal), pp. 48–57.

Tsuchiya, M., and Gonzalez, M.J. 1974. An approach to optimization of horizontal microprograms. In *Proc., Seventh Annual Workshop on Microprogramming* (Palo Alto, Calif., Apr.), pp. 85–90.

Tsuchiya, M., and Gonzalez, M.J. 1976. Toward optimization of horizontal microprograms, *IEEE Trans. Comps.,* C-25, 10 (Oct.): 992–999.

Uht, A.K. 1986. An efficient hardware algorithm to extract concurrency from general-purpose code. In *Proc., Nineteenth Annual Hawaii Conf. on System Sciences* (Jun.), pp. 41–50.

Wall, DW. 1991. Limits of instruction-level parallelism. In *Proc., Fourth Internat. Conf. on Architectural Support for Programming Languages and Operating Systems* (Santa Clara, Calif., Apr.), pp. 176–188.

Warren, H.S. 1990. Instruction scheduling for the IBM RISC System/6000 processor. *IBM J. Res. and Dev.,* 34, 1 (Jan.): 85–92.

Warter, N.J., Bockhaus, J.W., Haab, G.E., and Subramanian, K. 1992. Enhanced modulo scheduling for loops with conditional branches. In *Proc., 25th Annual Internat. Symp. on Microarchitecture* (Portland, Ore., Dec.), pp. 170–179.

Watson, W.J. 1972. The TI ASC—A highly modular and flexible super computer architecture. In *Proc., AFIPS Fall Joint Computer Conf.,* pp. 221–228.

Wedig, R.G. 1982. Detection of concurrency in directly executed language instruction streams. Ph.D. thesis, Stanford Univ., Stanford, Calif.

Weiss, S., and Smith, J.E. 1984. Instruction issue logic for pipelined supercomputers. In *Proc., 11th Annual Internat. Symp. on Computer Architecture,* pp. 110–118.

Weiss, S., and Smith, J.E. 1987. A study of scalar compilation techniques for pipelined supercomputers. In *Proc., Second Internat. Conf. on Architectural Support for Programming Languages and Operating Systems* (Palo Alto, Calif., Oct.), pp. 105–109.

Wilkes, M.V. 1951. The best way to design an automatic calculating machine. In *Proc., Manchester Univ. Comp. Inaugural Conf.* (Manchester, England, July), pp. 16–18.

Wilkes, M.V., and Stringer,J.B. 1953. Microprogramming and the design of the control circuits in an electronic digital computer. In *Proc., The Cambridge Philosophical Society, Part 2* (Apr.), pp. 230–238.

Wolfe, A., and Shen, J.P. 1991. A variable instruction stream extension to the VLIW architecture. In *Proc., Fourth Internat. Conf. on Architectural Support for Programming Languages and Operating Systems* (Santa Clara, Calif., Apr.), pp. 2–14.

Wood, G. 1978. On the packing of micro-operations into micro-instruction words. In *Proc., 11th Annual Workshop on Microprogramming* (Asilomar, Calif., Nov.), pp. 51–55.

Wood, G. 1979. Global optimization of microprograms through modular control constructs. In *Proc., 12th Annual Workshop on Microprogramming* (Hershey, Penn.), pp. 1–6.

Yau, S.S., Schowe, A.C. and Tsuchiya, M. 1974. On storage optimization of horizontal microprograms. In *Proc., Seventh Annual Workshop on Microprogramming* (Palo Alto, Calif.), pp. 98–106.

Yeh, T.Y., and Patt, Y.N. 1992. Alternative implementations of two-level adaptive branch prediction. In *Proc., Nineteenth Internat. Symp. on Comp. Architecture* (Gold Coast, Australia, May), pp. 124–134.

Zima, H., and Chapman, B. 1990. *Supercompilers for Parallel and Vector Computers.* Addison-Wesley, Reading, Mass.

Dataflow and Multithreading

5.1 Dataflow Computers

Most computers today are based on a *sequential execution model*, where instructions of a program are executed in an implied (sequential) order. This model closely resembles the way processors were implemented in their early days, where program instructions were processed one at a time. The sequential execution model also led to instruction sets and programming languages with sequential execution semantics. Today, almost all programs are written in programming languages and compiled to instruction sets that have an implied execution order.

To maximize parallelism, ordering constraints must be minimized. Ideally, the execution of an instruction should be constrained only by dependence relationships and not by any other ordering constraints. Therefore, to achieve high performance in the sequential execution model, means are needed to discover and extract parallelism from the serial specification, and to execute these operations on parallel hardware. Dataflow is a computing model that has been proposed to overcome the performance limitations of the traditional sequential computing model. Many of the limitations of the traditional (sequential) model have to do with exposing and extracting parallelism hidden as a result of serial program semantics, exploiting it on parallel hardware, and maintaining the implied program ordering.

The idea of dataflow is to have a computing engine that has no ordering constraints on operation execution other than data (and control) dependences that exist in the computation. Computation is represented as a dataflow graph, which captures the data dependence relationships between the operations. Control dependences are treated just like data dependences (by using a SWITCH operator to gate data values using a Boolean condition). By not imposing a "total order" on program execution, opportunities for parallelism are not artificially constrained. In the absence of a total order, other rules are needed to determine the order in which operations should be executed. The dataflow model uses a data-driven (or dependence-driven) rule governing the execution of operations.

A dataflow program consists of blocks of instructions, or *code blocks*, whose execution is governed by the dataflow "firing" rule. The dynamic state of a code block, analogous to a stack frame, resides in a *token store*. When an operation executes, it "wakes up" other operations in the token store that depend on it, and when the operands of an operation are ready, it can be "fired." Different types of dataflow computers use different means to wake up operations. The classic *tagged-token dataflow architecture* (TTDA), which is described in the paper by Arvind and Nikhil, uses an associative token store [3]. When an operation executes, it creates one or two result tokens, each with a tag indicating the instance of an instruction that needs the token. The token store is searched (associatively) to see if another token with the same tag is present. If such a match is found, then the new instruction becomes ready to execute. Otherwise, the token is left in the token store. Because token stores can be large, associative searching is implemented via hashing [9,14]. A more recent proposal, the *explicit token store* (ETS) dataflow machine eliminates the need to do an associative search in the token store [13] by mapping dynamic instances of code blocks to a linear (addressable) memory; a token can be forwarded directly to the consuming instructions at known memory addresses.

Even though the dataflow execution model eliminates artificial ordering constraints, conventional programming languages have ordering constraints that might be carried through by the translation process, just as a (conventional) program is compiled into a dataflow executable. To overcome this problem, dataflow researchers have proposed dataflow languages such as Id [2], which are devoid of artificial ordering constraints.

A dataflow computing system (language, compiler, instruction set, and execution hardware) allows parallelism to be exposed and exploited to its fullest. However, the abundance of parallelism is not necessarily a good thing: Means must exist to deal with this parallelism [4]. These means include large token stores to handle all the operations that are waiting to execute, means to manage the token store, and means to schedule the (hundreds or thousands) of operations that are ready to execute so that they can execute on the limited amount of available hardware. In many cases, constraining the amount of parallelism actually allows for more efficient solutions!

5. 2 Multithreaded Computers

Multithreaded computers are computers that can execute instructions from more than one execution thread. The term *multithreaded*, however, is a heavily overloaded term in computer science in general, and in computer architecture in particular. A thread is a piece of code together with a state (registers and memory); instructions from a thread modify this state as they execute. In its most common usage, multiple threads imply multiple different programs (or processes). However, computer architects, especially processor architects, are rarely concerned with computer designs that improve the overall throughput when processing a workload consisting of several programs. Rather, they are concerned about improving the time that it takes to execute a single program. In this context, multiple threads refer to different (generally independent) portions of a single program; for example, the different iterations of a loop. In either case, a multithreaded processor can also be viewed as an alternate way of implementing a parallel processor (albeit a small-scale one).

To support multiple threads, multithreaded processors have to provide hardware resources to implement the thread context, that is, the state for each thread. Recall that state for a thread generally resides in two name spaces: registers and memory. Multithreaded processors typically provide a separate register file for each thread. However, the (physical) memory is shared amongst the different threads just as it would be in a nonmultithreaded processor running a multiprogrammed workload.

The most common use of multithreading is to improve the utilization of a resource. For example, when a processor is idling while waiting for the result of a long-latency memory operation, processor utilization (and overall processing throughput) can be improved if the processor switches execution to a different thread, and instructions from that thread are executed during cycles that would otherwise have been idle. By performing work during otherwise dead cycles, the processor is able to tolerate long latencies. Accordingly, many also view multithreading as a means for tolerating long latencies. However, the beneficial effect of tolerating the latency on the execution time of a single program only shows up if the operations that are overlapped with the long-latency operation are from the same program; that is, the multiple threads are threads of the same program.

Multithreading has a cost overhead, in that additional hardware must be provided to handle state from multiple threads. In addition, it has performance overheads related to thread switching that can impact single-thread performance. First, switching to a different thread can incur an overhead, depending on how the register contexts of the different threads are implemented. The impact of this overhead can be reduced by having more hardware that allows switches between threads to take place without any time penalty. Second, once a thread is switched out, it might not be restarted immediately after its long-latency operation is finished, resulting in increased execution time for the thread (versus a scenario where the thread was not switched out, and was able to resume execution immediately on completion of its long-latency operation). The tradeoff between thread switching and single-thread performance has been central to the design of multithreaded processors over the decades, and several different switching policies have been proposed.

One commonly used thread-switching policy is to switch to a different thread on every cycle. This policy is relatively straightforward to implement. Moreover, if there are as many threads as there are stages in the processing pipeline, there is only one instruction from any thread in the processing pipeline. This obviates the need for hardware dedicated to overcoming the problems of overlapping the processing of instructions from a single thread (for example, dependence checking logic, branch prediction hardware, etc.). The drawback of this approach, however, is that the performance of a single thread is sacrificed.

Another policy is to keep processing a single thread until a long-latency operation (such as a cache miss) is encountered and switch to a new thread at that point [1]. This degrades single-thread performance less than the previous proposal (the issue of restarting a thread on completion of its long-latency operation still exists) but is more involved. There have been several other proposals for thread-switching policies.

Most of the multithreading policies studied until the 1990s were aimed at processors that can execute only a single operation in a clock cycle. For these processors, it made sense only to switch threads after a clock cycle (or after multiple cycles), because at least one operation should be executed from a thread once it has been selected, and this took at least one clock cycle. The advent of multiple-issue long instruction word (LIW) and superscalar processors in the late 1980s and 1990s caused researchers to rethink the notion of thread switching. Multiple-issue processors allow multiple operations to be launched in every clock cycle, and not all of these issue slots might be usable by a given thread in a given clock cycle. In this case, the possibility of thread switching at a granularity of less than a clock cycle (i.e., within a clock cycle) arises: Issue slots within a clock cycle that are unused by the primary thread could be used for operations from another thread. This could potentially be a win-win situation: A single thread continues its execution unperturbed, and other threads get to use execution slots that would otherwise have not been used. Of course, this assumes that the hardware and software complexity is not increased, and that the different threads do not cause interfere in other resources of the machine (e.g., caches, memory systems, and interconnects). Executing operations from multiple threads in a single clock cycle is called *simultaneous multithreading*.

With a simultaneous-multithreading policy allowing multithreading without sacrificing single-thread per-formance, and with semiconductor technology allowing sufficient hardware resources to build (register) contexts for multiple threads on a single chip, computer architects are considering multithreading support even in general-purpose processors.

The reader may ask: Dataflow and multithreading appear to be very different concepts, so why are we lumping them together in a single chapter? It is true that dataflow and multithreading are different concepts. However, a lot of multithreading research has been carried out within the dataflow context for reasons we discuss next.

The objective of dataflow is to expose and exploit parallelism, and this requires parallel hardware. Parallel hardware introduces latencies that may not exist in non-parallel hardware, such as latencies resulting from traversing interconnection structures, and due to distributing resources such as memory. In the data-driven execution model, where an operation wakes up when its predecessor operation communicates a value to it, latencies introduced by parallel hardware aggravate the interoperation communication latency, and we have to tolerate this latency by overlapping this communication with other (independent) computations. Moreover, a code block of a dataflow program can be viewed as a "thread."[1] Because the dynamic execution of a dataflow program results in several such "threads" being active at the same time, it is natural to design machines that can handle multiple such threads.

5.3 Discussion of Included Papers

Next, we present a brief discussion of the papers reprinted in this chapter.

5.3.1 Dennis and Misunas's "A Preliminary Architecture for a Basic Data-Flow Processor" [6]

The paper by Dennis and Misunas was the first paper to describe the architecture of an entire processor based on data-driven execution principles. Here, the program is a dataflow program, and the proposal is for a processor that executes a dataflow program. This was not the earliest description of *dataflow execution* principles, however: Tomasulo's algorithm [18], implemented in the IBM 360/91, applied dataflow principles (which were not called dataflow at the time) to come up with hardware that allowed data-driven execution of a small number of instructions. Note, however, that this

---

[1]If we characterize machines on a multithreading spectrum based on the length of the threads that they support, pure classical dataflow (e.g., MIT TTDA) has threads with a length of one operation. It is possible to think of threads of a dataflow machine consisting of several operations that are executed together (e.g., MIT Monsoon).

group of instructions was not represented as a dataflow program. Rather, they were created dynamically by sequencing through a more traditional control flow program.

5.3.2 Arvind and Nikhil's "Executing a Program on the MIT TTDA" [3]

The early work by Dennis and his colleagues provided the spark for a significant amount of research on dataflow processors at several institutions worldwide in addition to the continuing research at MIT. The paper by Arvind and Nikhil presents a snapshot of the work in dataflow at MIT (as well as at other places) circa 1987. In addition to describing the architecture of the MIT tagged-token dataflow architecture (TTDA) computer, it discusses several other aspects of dataflow computing. The paper starts out by describing the dataflow language Id. As mentioned earlier, dataflow proponents believe that more conventional languages introduce ordering constraints on operations (perhaps unintentionally) that can only serve to obscure parallelism. The paper then describes how Id programs can be compiled into dataflow graphs and an architecture for interpreting (i.e., executing) programs represented as dataflow graphs.

5.3.3 Smith's "Architecture and Applications of the HEP Multiprocessor" [15]

The paper by Smith describes aspects of the heterogeneous element processor (HEP) built by Denelcor. The HEP was an early example of a (publicly documented) machine that used multithreaded execution for processing the "main" instruction stream(s). Earlier machines used multithreading for some aspects of processing (e.g., the input/output units of the MIT TX-2 and the peripheral processors of the CDC 6600). Other multithreaded machines were proposed (and some were even built) prior to HEP, but documentation about such machines is not readily available.

The paper also describes of a novel synchronization mechanism (full-empty bits) and of Fortran extensions that would allow an application to be compiled in order to make use of the multithreaded architecture and the synchronization features of the HEP.

5.3.4 Tullsen et al.'s "Exploiting Choice: Instruction Fetch and Issue on an Implementable Simultaneous Multithreading Processor" [20]

Multithreaded architectures that switched threads every cycle (or every few cycles) were not seriously considered by architects of mainstream general-purpose processors, because they were viewed as sacrificing single-thread latency in favor of multiple-thread throughput. And limited chip resources called into question the utility of expending hardware to support multiple thread contexts, especially if single-thread performance was going to be compromised.

The advent of wide-issue machines resulted in a new form of multithreading, one in which operations from multiple threads were issued *in the same cycle*. This form of multithreading could improve multiple-thread throughput without compromising single-thread latency (assuming that interthread interference did not degrade single-thread latency; e.g., resulting from increased cache misses). There were several proposals for this type of multithreading in the 1990s, both within the context of statically scheduled wide-issue machines [12, 21] as well as within the context of dynamically scheduled wide-issue machines [5, 11, 19, 20, 22].

The paper by Tullsen et al. discusses several issues that need to be considered when implementing simultaneous multithreading on top of a dynamically scheduled superscalar processor. They show how the basic mechanisms of a superscalar processor could be extended to allow multiple simultaneous processing of instructions from multiple threads. Though the threads in this proposal are different programs, it is easy to see how they could be different parts of the same program.

5.4 Looking Ahead

Despite its promise, the dataflow computing model has not been adopted in mainstream processor design. There are several reasons for this. First, it is not practical to give up traditional serial programming languages and instruction sets entirely. Second, the main source of the "power" of the dataflow model (no artificial ordering constraints, and consequently no well-defined, reproducible state) results in several practical problems. Perhaps the most important of these is the difficulty of debugging.[2] A discussion of some of these limitations can be found in a paper by Gajski, et al. [8]. The computer architect is then faced with the question: Can we apply some of the principles of dataflow computing to more practical computing situations? The answer to this question so far has been a resounding *yes*. The dataflow paradigm continues to serve as the inspiration for many innovations in ILP processors, whose goal is to achieve dataflow-like execution, but

---

[2]Parallel machines without artificial ordering constraints (i.e., synchronization) have very similar problems.

starting out with an imperative language and a practical microarchitecture. Modern dynamically scheduled superscalar processors are one example of this influence, called *micro dataflow* machines by some. In the future, the dataflow model (coupled with suitable speculation techniques) is likely to continue to be the inspiration for many upcoming innovations in exploiting parallelism. Future innovators are likely to benefit from a thorough understanding of dataflow concepts and their evolution. And the dataflow computing model is likely to evolve to include different forms of speculation, including speculation that even removes the one ordering constraint in the dataflow model: data dependences.

Future processors are also likely to be influenced by multithreading techniques. Recall that one way of viewing a multithreaded processor is an implementation of a parallel processor (with several resources that are shared). As technology allows "parallel processing" capability to be put on a single chip, different ways of incorporating "parallel processing" functionality need to be considered. Multithreading techniques that are likely to succeed are techniques that do not hinder single-thread latency. Ideally, multithreading might even be used to *improve* single-program performance rather than simply be a means for improving multiple-thread throughput. This can be done using *thread-level speculation*, as has been proposed in several recent research projects [7, 10, 16, 17].

5.5 References

[1] A. Agarwal, B.-H. Lim, D. Kranz, and J. Kubiatowicz, "APRIL: A processor architecture for multiprocessing," *Proceedings of the 17th Annual International Symposium on Computer Architecture*, pp. 104–114, May 1990.

[2] Arvind, K. Gostelow, and W. Plouffe, "An asynchronous programming language and computing machine," Tech. Rep. TR-114a, Department of Information and Computer Science, University of California, Irvine, Dec. 1978.

[3] Arvind and R. S. Nikhil, "Executing a program on the MIT tagged-token dataflow architecture," *IEEE Transactions on Computers*, 39(3):300–318, Mar. 1990.

[4] D. E. Culler and Arvind, "Resource requirements of dataflow programs," *Proceedings of the 15th Annual International Symposium on Computer Architecture*, pp. 141–150, May 1998.

[5] G. E. Daddis, Jr. and H. C. Torng, "The concurrent execution of multiple instruction streams on superscalar processors," *International Conference on Parallel Processing*, pp. I:76–83, Aug. 1991.

[6] J. B. Dennis and D. P. Misunas, "A preliminary architecture for a basic dataflow processor," *Proceedings of the 2nd Annual Symposium on Computer Architecture*, pp. 126–132, Dec. 1974.

[7] P. K. Dubey, K. O'Brien, K. O'Brien, and C. Barton, "Single-program speculative multithreading (SPSM) architecture: Compiler-assisted fine-grained multithreading," *Proceedings of the Conference on Parallel Architectures and Compilation Techniques*, pp. 109–121, June 1995.

[8] D. Gajski, D. Padua, D. Kuck, and R. Kuhn, "A second opinion on data flow machines and languages," *IEEE Computer*, pp. 58–69, Feb. 1982.

[9] J. R. Gurd, C. C. Kirkham, and I. Watson, "The Manchester prototype dataflow computer," *Communications of the ACM*, vol. 28, 1985.

[10] L. Hammond, M. Willey, and K. Olukotun, "Data speculation support for a chip multiprocessor," *Proceedings of the 8th International Conference on Architectural Support for Programming Languages and Operating Systems*, pp. 58–69, Oct. 1998.

[11] H. Hirata, K. Kimura, S. Nagamine, Y. Mochizuki, A. Nishimura, Y. Nakase, and T. Nishizawa, "An elementary processor architecture with simultaneous instruction issuing from multiple threads," *Proceedings of the 19th Annual International Symposium on Computer Architecture*, pp. 136–145, May 1992.

[12] S. W. Keckler and W. J. Dally, "Processor coupling: Integrating compile time and runtime scheduling for parallelism," *Proceedings of the 19th Annual International Symposium on Computer Architecture*, Queensland, Australia, pp. 202–213, 1992.

[13] G. M. Papadopoulos and D. E. Culler, "Monsoon: An explicit token-store architecture," *Proceedings of the 17th Annual International Symposium on Computer Architecture*, pp. 82–91, May 1990.

[14] T. Shimada, K. Hiraki, K. Nishida, and S. Sekiguchi, "Evaluation of a prototype data flow processor of the SIGMA-1 for scientific computations," *Proceedings of the 13th Annual International Symposium on Computer Architecture*, pp. 226–234, June 1986.

[15] B. Smith, "Architecture and applications of the HEP multiprocessor computer system," *Proceedings of the International Society for Optical Engineering*, pp. 241–248, 1982.

[16] G. S. Sohi, S. E. Breach, and T. N. Vijaykumar, "Multiscalar processors," *Proceedings of the 22nd Annual International Symposium on Computer Architecture*, pp. 414–425, June 1995.

[17] J. G. Steffan and T. C. Mowry, "The potential for using thread-level data speculation to facilitate automatic parallelization," *Proceedings of the 4th International Symposium on High-Performance Computer Architecture*, Feb. 1998.

[18] R. M. Tomasulo "An efficient algorithm for exploiting multiple arithmetic units," *IBM Journal of Research and Development*, pp. 25–33, Jan. 1967.

[19] D. M. Tullsen, S. J. Eggers, and H. M. Levy, "Simultaneous multithreading: Maximizing on-chip parallelism," *Proceedings of the 22nd Annual International Symposium on Computer Architecture*, pp. 392–403, June 1995.

[20] D. M. Tullsen, S. J. Eggers, J. S. Emer, H. M. Levy, J. L. Lo, and R. L. Stamm, "Exploiting choice: Instruction fetch and issue on an implementable simultaneous multithreading processor," *Proceedings of the 23rd Annual International Symposium on Computer Architecture*, pp. 191–202, May 1996.

[21] A. Wolfe and J. P. Shen, "A variable instruction stream extension to the VLIW architecture," *Proceedings of the 4th International Conference on Architectural Support for Programming Languages and Operating Systems*, pp. 2–14, Apr. 1991.

[22] W. Yamamoto and M. Nemirovsky, "Increasing superscalar performances through multistreaming," *Proceedings of the Conference on Parallel Architectures and Compilation Techniques*, pp. 49–58, June 1995.

A Preliminary Architecture for a Basic Data-Flow Processor[*]

Jack B. Dennis and David P. Misunas
Project MAC
Massachusetts Institute of Technology

Abstract: A processor is described which can achieve highly parallel execution of programs represented in data-flow form. The language implemented incorporates conditional and iteration mechanisms, and the processor is a step toward a practical data-flow processor for a Fortran-level data-flow language. The processor has a unique architecture which avoids the problems of processor switching and memory/processor interconnecion that usually limit the degree of realizable concurrent processing. The architecture offers an unusual solution to the problem of structuring and managing a two-level memory system.

Introduction

Studies of concurrent operation within a computer system and of the representation of parallelism in a programming language have yielded a new form of program representation, known as data flow. Execution of a data-flow program is data-driven; that is, each instruction is enabled for execution just when each required operand has been supplied by the execution of a predecessor instruction. Data-flow representations for programs have been described by Karp and Miller [8], Rodriguez [11], Adams [1], Dennis and Fosseen [5], Bährs [2], Kosinski [9, 10], and Dennis [4].

We have developed an attractive architecture for a processor that executes elementary data-flow programs [6, 7]. The class of programs implemented by this processor corresponds to the model of Karp and Miller [8]. These data-flow programs are well suited to representing signal processing computations such as waveform generation, modulation and filtering, in which a group of operations is to be performed once for each sample (in time) of the signals being processed. This elementary data-flow processor avoids the problems of processor switching and processor/memory interconnection present in attempts to adapt conventional Von Neuman type machines for parallel computation. Sections of the machine communicate by the transmission of fixed size information packets, and the machine is organized so that the sections can tolerate delays in packet transmission without compromising effective utilization of the hardware.

We wish to expand the capabilities of the data-flow architecture, with the ultimate goal of developing a general purpose processor using a generalized data-flow language such as described by Dennis [4], Kosinski [9, 10] and Bährs [2]. As an intermediate step, we have developed a preliminary design for a basic data-flow processor that executes programs expressed in a more powerful language than the elementary machine, but still not achieving a generalized capability. The language of the basic machine is that described by Dennis and Fosseen [5], and includes constructs for expressing conditional and iterative execution of program parts.

In this paper we present solutions to the major problems faced in the development of the basic machine. A straightforward solution to the incorporation of decision capabilities in the machine is described. In addition, the growth in program size and complexity with the addition of the decision capability requires utilization of a two-level memory system. A design is presented in which only active instructions are in the operational memory of the processor, and each instruction is brought to that memory only when necessary for program execution, and remains there only as long as it is being utilized.

[*]The work reported here was supported by the National Science Foundation under research grant GJ-34671.

The Elementary Processor

The Elementary Processor is designed to utilize the elementary data-flow language as its base language. A program in the elementary data-flow language is a directed graph in which the nodes are operators or links. These nodes are connected by arcs along which values (conveyed by tokens) may travel. An operator of the schema is _enabled_ when tokens are present on all input arcs. The enabled operator may _fire_ at any time, removing the tokens on its input arcs, computing a value from the operands associated with the input tokens, and associating that value with a result token placed on its output arc. A result may be sent to more than one destination by means of a link which removes a token on its input arc and places tokens on its output arcs bearing copies of the input value. An operator or a link cannot fire unless there is no token present on any output arc of that operator or link.

An example of a program in the elementary data-flow language is shown in Figure 1 and represents the following simple computation:

```
input a, b
    y := (a+b)/x
    x := (a*(a+b))+b
output y, x
```

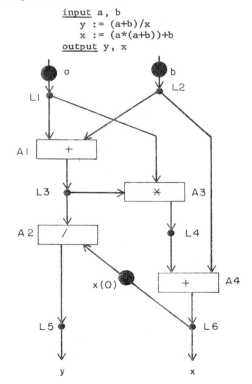

Figure 1. An elementary data-flow program.

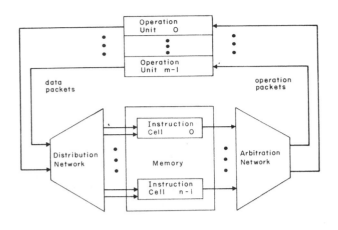

Figure 2. Organization of the elementary data-flow processor.

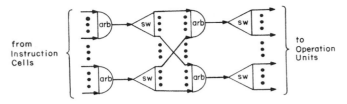

Figure 5. Structure of the Arbitration Network.

tration Network which directs it to an appropriate Operation Unit by decoding the instruction portion of the packet.

The result of an operation leaves an Operation Unit as one or more <u>data packets</u>, consisting of the computed value and the address of a register in the Memory to which the value is to be delivered. The <u>Distribution Network</u> accepts data packets from the Operation Units and utilizes the address of each to direct the data item through the network to the correct register in the Memory. The Instruction Cell containing that register may then be enabled if an instruction and all operands are present in the Cell.

Many Instruction Cells may be enabled simultaneously, and it is the task of the Arbitration Network to efficiently deliver operation packets to Operation Units and to queue operation packets waiting for each Operation Unit. A structure for the Arbitration Network providing a path for operation packets from each Instruction Cell to each Operation Unit is presented in Figure 5. Each <u>Arbitration Unit</u> passes packets arriving at its input ports one-at-a-time to its output port, using a round-robin discipline to resolve any ambiguity about which packets should be sent next. A <u>Switch Unit</u> assigns a packet at its input to one of its output ports, according to some property of the packet, in this case the operation code.

The Distribution Network is similarly organized using Switch Units to route data packets from the Operation Units to the Memory Registers specified by the destination addresses. A few Arbitration Units are required so data packets from different Operation Units can enter the network simultaneously.

Since the Arbitration Network has many input ports and only a few output ports, the rate of packet flow will be much greater at the output ports. Thus, a serial representation of packets is appropriate at the input ports to minimize the number of connections to the Memory, but a more parallel representation is required at the output ports so a high throughput may be achieved. Hence, serial-to-parallel conversion is performed in stages within the Arbitration Network. Similarly, parallel-to-serial conversion of the value portion of each result packet occurs within the Distribution Network.

The Operation Units of the processor are pipelined in

The rectangular boxes in Figure 1 are operators, and each arithmetic operator in the above computation is reflected in a corresponding operator in the program. The small dots are links. The large dots represent tokens holding values for the initial configuration of the program.

In the program of Figure 1, links L1 and L2 are initially enabled. The firing of L1 makes copies of the value a available to operators A1 and A3; firing L2 presents the value b to operators A1 and A4. Once L1 and L2 have fired (in any order), operator A1 is enabled since it will have a token on each of its input arcs. After A1 has fired (completing the computation of a + b), link L3 will become enabled. The firing of L3 will enable the concurrent firing of operators A2 and A3, and so on.

The computations represented by an elementary program are performed in a data-driven manner; the enabling of an operator is determined only by the arrival of values on all input links, and no separate control signals are utilized. Such a scheme prompted the design of a processor organized as in Figure 2.

A data-flow schema to be executed is stored in the <u>Memory</u> of the processor. The Memory is organized into <u>Instruction Cells</u>, each Cell corresponding to an operator of the data-flow program. Each Instruction Cell (Figure 3) is composed of three <u>registers</u>. The first register holds an instruction (Figure 4) which specifies the operation to be performed and the address(es) of the register(s) to which the result of the operation is to be directed. The second and third registers hold the operands for use in execution of the instruction.

When a Cell contains an instruction and the necessary operands, it is <u>enabled</u> and signals the <u>Arbitration Network</u> that it is ready to transmit its contents as an <u>operation packet</u> to an <u>Operation Unit</u> which can perform the desired function. The operation packet flows through the Arbi-

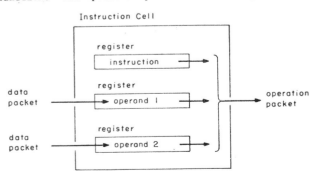

Figure 3. Operation of an Instruction Cell.

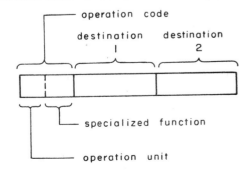

Figure 4. Instruction format.

Figure 6. Links of the basic data-flow language.

order to allow maximum throughput. The destination address(es) of an instruction are entered into identity pipelines of the Operation Units and are utilized to form data packets with the result when it appears.

A more detailed explanation of the elementary processor and its operation is given in [6]. We have completed designs for all units of the elementary processor in the form of speed-independent interconnections of a small set of basic asynchronous module types. These designs are presented in [7].

The Basic Data-Flow Language

Our success in the architecture of the elementary data-flow processor led us to consider applying the concepts to the architecture of machines for more complete data-flow languages. For the first step in generalization, we have chosen a class of data-flow programs that correspond to a formal data-flow model studied by Dennis and Fosseen [5].

The representation of conditionals and iteration in data-flow form requires additional types of links and actors. The types of links and actors for the basic data-flow language are shown in Figures 6 and 7.

Data values pass through data links in the manner presented previously. The tokens transmitted by control links are known as <u>control</u> <u>tokens</u>, and each conveys a value of either <u>true</u> or <u>false</u>. A control token is generated at a decider which, upon receiving values from its input arcs, applies its associated predicate, and produces either a <u>true</u> or <u>false</u> control token at its output arc.

The control token produced at a decider can be combined with other control tokens by means of a Boolean operator (Figure 7f), allowing a decision to be built up from simpler decisions.

Control tokens direct the flow of data tokens by means of T-gates, F-gates, or merge actors (Figure 7c, d, e). A T-gate passes the data token on its input arc to its output arc when it receives a control token conveying

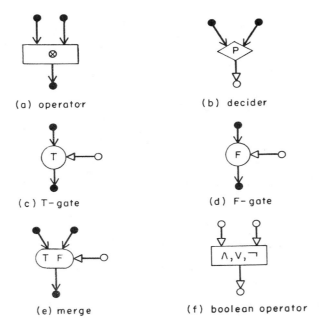

Figure 7. Actors of the basic data-flow language.

the value <u>true</u> at its control input. It will absorb the data token on its input arc and place nothing on its output arc if a <u>false</u>-valued control token is received. Similarly, the F-gate will pass its input data token to its output arc only on receipt of a <u>false</u>-valued token on the control input. Upon receipt of a <u>true</u>-valued token, it will absorb the data token.

A merge actor has a true input, a false input, and a control input. It passes to its output arc a data token from the input arc corresponding to the value of the control token received. Any tokens on the other input are not affected.

As with the elementary schemas, a link or actor is not enabled to fire unless there is no token on any of its output arcs.

Using the actors and links of the basic data-flow language, conditionals and iteration can be easily represented. In illustration, Figure 8 gives a basic data-flow program for the following computation:

<u>input</u> y, x
n := 0
<u>while</u> y < x <u>do</u>
   y := y + x
   n := n + 1
   <u>end</u>
<u>output</u> y, n

The control input arcs of the three merge actors carry <u>false</u>-valued tokens in the initial configuration so the input values of x and y and the constant 0 are admitted as initial values for the iteration. Once these values have been received, the predicate y < x is tested. If it is true, the value of x and the new value for y are cycled back into the body of the iteration through the T-gates and two merge nodes. Concurrently, the remaining T-gate and merge node return an incremented value of the iteration count n. When the output of the decider is <u>false</u>, the current values of y and n are delivered through the two F-gates, and the initial configuration is restored.

The Basic Data-Flow Processor

Two problems must be faced in adapting the design of the

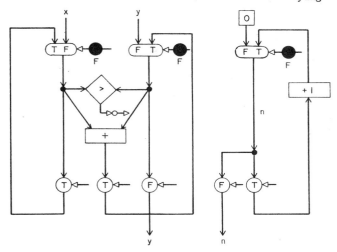

Figure 8. Data-flow representation of the basic program.

elementary data-flow processor for basic data-flow programs. The first task is to expand the architecture of the elementary machine to incorporate decision capability by implementing deciders, gates and merges. A fairly straightforward solution to this problem will be presented.

However, in contrast to elementary data-flow programs, the nodes of a basic data-flow program do not fire equally often during execution. As computation proceeds, different parts of the program become active or quiescent as iterations are initiated and completed, and as decisions lead to selection of alternate parts of a program for activation. Thus it would be wasteful to assign a Cell to each instruction for the duration of program execution. The basic data-flow processor must have a multi-level memory system such that only the active instructions of a program occupy the Instruction Cells of the processor. In the following sections we first show how decision capability may be realized by augmenting the elementary processor; then we show how an auxiliary memory system may be added so the Instruction Cells act as a cache for the most active instructions.

Decision Capability

The organization of a basic data-flow processor without the two-level memory is shown in Fig. 9. As in the elementary processor, each Instruction Cell consists of three Registers and holds one instruction together with spaces for receiving its operands. Each instruction corresponds to an operator, a decider, or a Boolean operator of a basic data-flow program. The gate and merge actors of the data-flow program are not represented by separate instructions; rather, the function of the gates is incorporated into the instructions associated with operators and deciders in a manner that will be described shortly, and the function of the merge actors is implemented for free by the nature of the Distribution Network.

Instructions that represent operators are interpreted by the Operation Units to yield data packets as in the elementary processor. Instructions that represent deciders or Boolean operators are interpreted by the Decision Units to yield <u>control packets</u> having one of the two forms

$$\left\{ \underline{gate}, \begin{bmatrix} \underline{true} \\ \underline{false} \end{bmatrix}, \langle address \rangle \right\}$$

$$\left\{ \underline{value}, \begin{bmatrix} \underline{true} \\ \underline{false} \end{bmatrix}, \langle address \rangle \right\}$$

A gate-type control packet performs a gating function at the addressed operand register. A value-type control packet provides a Boolean operand value to an Instruction Cell that represents a Boolean operator.

The six formats for the contents of Instruction Cells in the basic processor are given in Figure 10. The use of each Register is specified in its leftmost field:

    I   instruction register
    D   operand register for data values
    B   operand register for Boolean values

Only Registers specified to be operand registers of consistent type may be addressed by instructions of a valid program.

The remaining fields in the Instruction Cell formats are: an instruction code, op, pr or bo, that identifies the class and variation of the instruction in the Cell; from one to three destination addresses d1, d2, d3 that specify target operand registers for the packets generated by instruction execution; in the case of deciders and Boolean operators, a <u>result tag</u> t1, t2, t3 for each destination that specifies whether the control packet is of gate-type (tag = <u>gate</u>) or of value type (tag = <u>value</u>); and, for each operand register, a <u>gating code</u> g1, g2 and either a <u>data receiver</u> v1, v2 or a <u>control receiver</u> c1, c2.

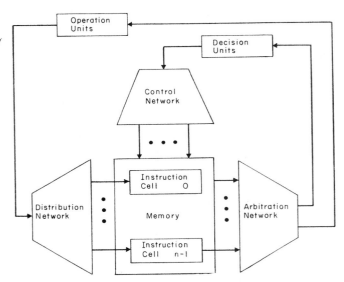

Figure 9. Organization of a basic data-flow processor without two-level memory.

The gating codes permit representation of gate actors that control the reception of operand values by the operator or decider represented by the Instruction Cell. The meanings of the code values are as follows:

code value	meaning
<u>no</u>	the associated operand is not gated.
<u>true</u>	an operand value is accepted by arrival of a <u>true</u> gate packet; discarded by arrival of a <u>false</u> gate packet.
<u>false</u>	an operand value is accepted by arrival of a <u>false</u> gate packet; discarded by arrival of a <u>true</u> gate packet.
<u>cons</u>	the operand is a constant value.

The structure of a data or control receiver (Fig. 11) provides space to receive a data or Boolean value, and two flag fields in which the arrival of data and control packets is recorded. The <u>gate flag</u> is changed from <u>off</u> to <u>true</u> or <u>false</u> by a true or false gate-type control packet; the value flag is changed from <u>off</u> to <u>on</u> by a data packet or value type control packet according to the type of receiver.

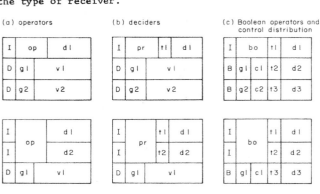

(a) operators   (b) deciders   (c) Boolean operators and control distribution

op – operation code
pr – predicate code   } instruction codes
bo – Boolean operation code

d1, d2, d3   destination addresses
t1, t2, t3   result tags
g1, g2   gating codes
v1, v2   data receivers
c1, c2   control receivers

Figure 10. Instruction Cell formats for the basic processor.

Receiver:

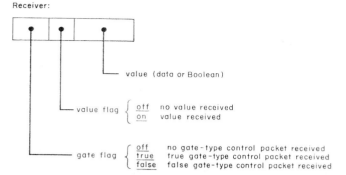

value (data or Boolean)

value flag ⎰ off   no value received
          ⎱ on   value received

gate flag ⎰ off   no gate-type control packet received
          ⎨ true   true gate-type control packet received
          ⎩ false false gate-type control packet received

Figure II. Structure and states of receivers.

Instruction Cell Operation

The function of each Instruction Cell is to receive data and control packets, and, when the Cell becomes enabled, to transmit an operation or decision packet through the Arbitration Network and reset the Instruction Cell to its initial status. An Instruction Cell becomes enabled just when all three of its registers are enabled. A register specified to act as an instruction register is always enabled. Registers specified to act as operand registers change state with the arrival of packets directed to them. The state transitions and enabling rules for data operand registers are defined in Fig. 12.

In Fig. 12 the contents of an operand register are represented as follows:

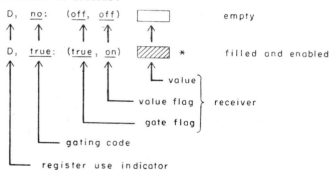

The asterisk indicates that the Register is enabled. Events denoting arrival of data and control packets are labelled thus:

    d   data packet
    t   true gate-type control packet
    f   false gate-type control packet

With this explanation of notation, the state changes and enabling rules given in Fig. 12 should be clear. Similar rules apply to the state changes and enabling of Boolean operand registers. Note that arrival of a gate-type control packet that does not match the gating code of the Register causes the associated data packet to be discar-

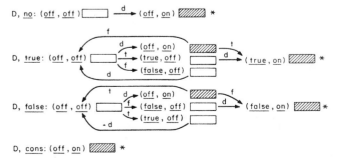

Figure 12. State transition and enabling rules for data operand registers.

ded, and resets the Register to its starting condition.

The operation packets sent to Operation Units and **decision packets** sent to Decision Units consist of the entire contents of the Instruction Cell except for the gating codes and receiver status fields. Thus the packets sent through the Arbitration Network have the following formats:

To the Operation Units:

    op, v1, v2, d1
    op, v1, d1, d2

To the Decision Units:

    pr, v1, v2, t1, d1
    pr, v1, t1, d1, t2, d2
    bo, c1, c2, t1, d1, t2, d2, t3, d3
    bo, c1, t1, d1, t2, d2, t3, d3

An initial configuration of Instruction Cells corresponding to the basic data-flow program of Fig. 8 is given in Fig. 13. For simplicity, Cells containing control distribution and data forwarding instructions are not shown. Instead, we have taken the liberty of writing any number of addresses in the destination fields of instructions.

The initial values of x and y are placed in Registers 2 and 5. Cells 1 and 2, containing these values, are then enabled and present to the Arbitration Network the operation packets

$$\left\{ \begin{array}{c} \underline{ident};\ 8,\ 11,\ 14 \\ x \end{array} \right\}$$

and

$$\left\{ \begin{array}{c} \underline{ident};\ 7,\ 13,\ 20 \\ y \end{array} \right\}$$

These packets are directed to an identity Operation Unit which merely creates the desired data packets with the values of x and y and delivers the packets to the Distribution Network.

Upon receipt by the Memory of the data packets directed to Registers 7 and 8, cell 3 will be enabled and will transmit its decision packet to a Decision Unit to perform the **less** than function. The result of the decision will be returned through the Control Network as five control packets. If the result is **true**, Cells 4, 5 and 6 will be enabled and will send their contents through the

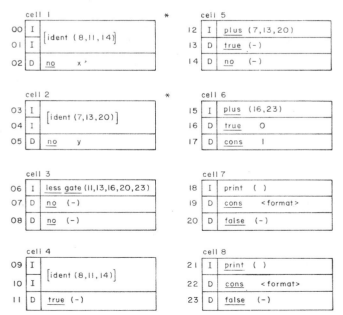

Figure 13. Instruction Cell initialization for the basic data-flow program in Figure 8.

Arbitration Network to Operation Units capable of performing the identity and addition operations. If the result of the decision is <u>false</u>, output cells 7 and 8 will be enabled, and cells 4, 5, and 6 will have their gated operands deleted.

<u>Two-Level Memory Hierarchy</u>

The high level of parallel activity achievable in data-flow processors makes a unique form of memory hierarchy feasible: the Instruction Cells are arranged to act as a cache for the most active instructions of the data-flow program. Individual instructions are retrieved from auxiliary memory (the Instruction Memory) as they become required by the progress of computation, and instructions are returned to the Instruction Memory when the Instruction Cells holding them are required for more active parts of the program.

The organization of a basic data-flow processor with Instruction Memory is given in Fig. 14.

<u>Instruction Memory</u>

The Instruction Memory has a storage location for each possible register address of the basic processor. These storage locations are organized into groups of three locations identified by the address of the first location of the group. Each group can hold the contents of one Instruction Cell in the formats already given in Fig. 10.

A <u>memory command packet</u> {a, <u>retr</u>} presented to the <u>command</u> port of the Instruction Memory, requests retrieval of an <u>instruction packet</u> {a, x} in which x is the Cell contents stored in the group of locations specified by address a. The instruction packet is delivered at the <u>retrieve</u> port of the Instruction Memory.

An instruction packet {a, x} presented at the <u>store</u> port of the Instruction Memory requests storage of Cell contents x in the three-location group specified by address a. However, the storage is not effective until a memory command packet {a, <u>store</u>} is received by the Instruction

Memory at its <u>command</u> port, and any prior retrieval request has been honored. Similarly, retrieval requests are not honored until prior storage requests for the group have taken effect.

We envision that the Instruction Memory would be designed to handle large numbers of storage and retrieval requests concurrently, much as the input/output facilities of contemporary computer systems operate under software control.

<u>Cell Block Operation</u>

For application of the cache principle to the basic data-flow processor, an Instruction Memory address is divided into a <u>major address</u> and a <u>minor address</u>, each containing a number of bits of the address. One Cell Block of the processor is associated with each possible major address. All instructions having the same major address are processed by the Instruction Cells of the corresponding Cell Block. Thus the Distribution and Control Networks use the major address to direct data packets, control packets, and instruction packets to the appropriate Cell Block. The packets delivered to the Cell Block include the minor address, which is sufficient to determine how the packet should be treated by the Cell Block.

Operation and decision packets leaving a Cell Block have exactly the same format as before. Instruction packets leaving a Cell Block have the form {m, x} where m is a minor address and x is the contents of an Instruction Cell. The major address of the Cell Block is appended to each instruction packet as it travels through the Arbitration Network. In the same way, memory command packets leave the Cell Block with just a minor address, which is augmented by the major address of the Cell Block during its trip through the Memory Command Network.

Fig. 15 shows the structure of a Cell Block. Each Instruction Cell is able to hold any instruction whose major address is that of the Cell Block. Since many more instructions share a major address than there are Cells in a Cell Block, the Cell Block includes an Association Table which has an entry {m, i} for each Instruction Cell: m is the minor address of the instruction to which the Cell is assigned, and i is a Cell status indicator whose values have significance as follows:

<u>status value</u>	<u>meaning</u>
<u>free</u>	the Cell is not assigned to any instruction
<u>engaged</u>	the Cell has been engaged for the instruction having minor address m, by arrival of a data or control packet
<u>occupied</u>	the Cell is occupied by an instruction with minor address m

The Stack element of a Cell Block holds an ordering of the Instruction Cells as candidates for displacement of their contents by newly activated instructions. Only Cells in <u>occupied</u> status are candiates for displacement.

Operation of a Cell Block can be specified by giving two procedures -- one initiated by arrival of a data or control packet at the Cell Block, and the other activated by arrival of an instruction packet from the Instruction Memory.

<u>Procedure</u> 1: Arrival of a data or control packet {n, y} where n is a minor address and y is the packet content.

<u>step</u> 1. Does the Association Table have an entry with minor address n? If so, let p be the Cell corresponding to the entry, and go to step 5. Otherwise continue with step 2.

<u>step</u> 2. If the Association Table shows that no Instruction Cell has status <u>free</u>, go to step 3. Otherwise let p be a Cell with status <u>free</u>. Let the Associa-

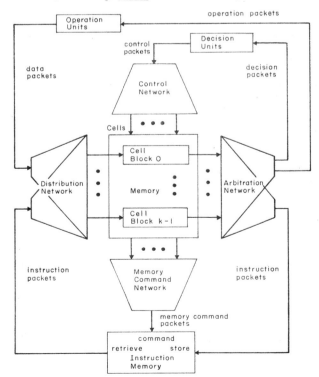

Figure 14. Organization of the basic data-flow processor with auxiliary memory.

Operation Units

operation packets

Decision Units

control packets

data packets

decision packets

Control Network

Cells

Cell Block 0

Distribution Network

Memory

Arbitration Network

Cell Block k-1

instruction packets

Memory Command Network

instruction packets

memory command packets

command
retrieve   store
Instruction Memory

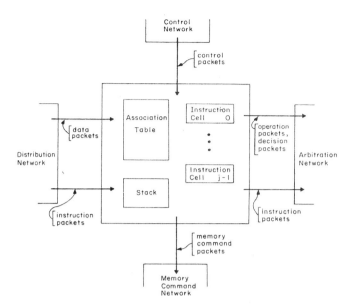

Figure 15. Structure of a Cell Block.

tion Table entry for p be {m, free}; go to step 4.

step 3. Use the Stack to choose a Cell p in occupied status for preemption; let the Association Table entry for p be {m, occupied}; transmit the contents z of Cell p as an instruction packet {m, z} to the Instruction Memory via the Arbitration Network; transmit the memory command packet {m, store} to the Instruction Memory through the Memory Command Network.

step 4. Make an entry {n, engaged} for Cell p in the Association Table; transmit the memory command packet {n, retr} to the Instruction Memory via the Memory Command Network.

step 5. Update the operand register of Cell p having minor address n according to the content y of the data or control packet (the rules for updating are those given in Fig. 12). If Cell p is occupied the state change of the register must be consistent with the instruction code or the program is invalid. If Cell p is engaged, the changes must be consistent with the register status left by preceding packet arrivals.

step 6. If Cell p is occupied and all three registers are enabled (according to the rules of Fig. 12), the Cell p is enabled: transmit an operation or decision packet to the Operation Units or Decision Units through the Arbitration Network; leave Cell p in occupied status holding the same instruction with its operand registers reset (receivers empty with the gate and value flags set to off). Change the order of Cells in the Stack to make Cell p the last candidate for displacement.

Procedure 2: Arrival of an instruction packet {n, x} with minor address n and content x.

step 1. Let p be the Instruction Cell with entry {n, engaged} in the Association Table.

step 2. The status of the operand registers of Cell p must be consistent with the content x of the instruction packet, or the program is invalid. Update the contents of Cell p to incorporate the instruction and operand status information in the instruction packet.

step 3. Change the Association Table entry for Cell p from {n, engaged} to {n, occupied}.

step 4. If all registers of Cell p are enabled, then

Cell p is enabled: transmit an operation or decision packet to the Operation Units or Decision Units through the Arbitration Network; leave Cell p in occupied status holding the same instruction with its operand registers reset. Change the order of Cells in the Stack to make Cell p the last candidate for displacement.

Conclusion

The organization of a computer which allows the execution of programs represented in data-flow form offers a very promising solution to the problem of achieving highly parallel computation. Thus far, the design of two processors, the elementary and the basic data-flow processors, has been investigated. The elementary processor is attractive for stream-oriented signal processing applications. The basic processor described here is a first step toward a highly parallel processor for numerical algorithms expressed in a Fortran-like data-flow language. However, this goal requires further elaboration of the data-flow architecture to encompass arrays, concurrent activation of procedures, and some means of exploiting the sort of parallelism present in vector operations. We are optimistic that extensions of the architecture to provide these features can be devised, and we are hopeful that these concepts can be further extended to the design of computers for general-purpose computation based on more complete data-flow models such as presented by Dennis [4].

References

1. Adams, D. A. A Computation Model With Data Flow Sequencing. Technical Report CS 117, Computer Science Department, School of Humanities and Sciences, Stanford University, Stanford, Calif., December 1968.

2. Bährs, A. Operation patterns (An extensible model of an extensible language). Symposium on Theoretical Programming, Novosibirsk, USSR, August 1972 (preprint).

3. Dennis, J. B. Programming generality, parallelism and computer architecture. Information Processing 68, North-Holland Publishing Co., Amsterdam 1969, 484-492.

4. Dennis, J. B. First version of a data flow procedure language. Symposium on Programming, Institut de Programmation, University of Paris, Paris, France, April 1974, 241-271.

5. Dennis, J. B., and J. B. Fosseen. Introduction to Data Flow Schemas. November 1973 (submitted for publication).

6. Dennis, J. B., and D. P. Misunas. A computer architecture for highly parallel signal processing. Proceedings of the ACM 1974 National Conference, ACM, New York, November 1974.

7. Dennis, J. B., and D. P. Misunas. The Design of a Highly Parallel Computer for Signal Processing Applications. Computation Structures Group Memo 101, Project MAC, M.I.T., Cambridge, Mass., July 1974.

8. Karp, R. M., and R. E. Miller. Properties of a model for parallel computations: determinacy, termination, queueing. SIAM J. Appl. Math. 14 (November 1966), 1390-1411.

9. Kosinski, P. R. A Data Flow Programming Language. Report RC 4264, IBM T. J. Watson Research Center, Yorktown Heights, N. Y., March 1973.

10. Kosinski, P. R. A data flow language for operating systems programming. Proceedings of ACM SIGPLAN-SIGOPS Interface Meeting, SIGPLAN Notices 8, 9 (September 1973), 89-94.

11. Rodriguez, J. E. A Graph Model for Parallel Computation. Report TR-64, Project MAC, M.I.T., Cambridge, Mass., September 1969.

Executing a Program on the MIT Tagged-Token Dataflow Architecture

ARVIND, SENIOR MEMBER, IEEE, AND RISHIYUR S. NIKHIL, MEMBER, IEEE

Abstract—The MIT Tagged-Token Dataflow project has an unconventional, but integrated approach to general-purpose high-performance parallel computing. Rather than extending conventional sequential languages, we use Id, a high-level language with fine-grained parallelism and determinacy implicit in its operational semantics. Id programs are compiled to dynamic dataflow graphs, a parallel machine language. Dataflow graphs are directly executed on the MIT Tagged-Token Dataflow Architecture (TTDA), a novel multiprocessor architecture. Dataflow research has advanced significantly in the last few years; in this paper, we provide an overview of our current thinking, by describing example Id programs, their compilation to dataflow graphs, and their execution on the TTDA. Finally, we describe related work and the status of our project.

Index Terms—Dataflow architectures, dataflow graphs, functional languages, implicit parallelism, *I*-structures, MIMD machines.

I. INTRODUCTION

THERE are several commercial and research efforts currently underway to build parallel computers with performance far beyond what is possible today. Among those approaches that can be classified as general-purpose, "multiple instruction multiple data" (MIMD) machines, most are evolutionary in nature. For architectures, they employ interconnections of conventional von Neumann machines. For programming, they rely upon conventional sequential languages (such as Fortran, C, or Lisp) extended with some parallel primitives, often implemented using operating system calls. These extensions are necessary because the automatic detection of adequate parallelism remains a difficult problem, in spite of recent advances in compiler technology [28], [2], [35].

Unfortunately, a traditional von Neumann processor has fundamental characteristics that reduce its effectiveness in a parallel machine. First, its performance suffers in the presence of long memory and communication latencies, and these are unavoidable in a parallel machine. Second, they do not provide good synchronization mechanisms for frequent task switching between parallel activities, again inevitable in a parallel machine. Our detailed technical examination of these issues may be found in [11]. In [25], Iannucci explores architectural changes to remedy these problems, inspired by dataflow architectures.

Furthermore, traditional programming languages are not easily extended to incorporate parallelism. First, loss of determinacy adds significant complexity to establishing correctness (this includes debugging). Second, it is a significant added complication for the programmer to manage parallelism explicitly—to identify and schedule parallel tasks small enough to utilize the machine effectively but large enough to keep the resource-management overheads reasonable.

In contrast, our dataflow approach is quite unconventional. We begin with *Id*, a high-level language with fine-grained parallelism *implicit* in its operational semantics. Despite this potential for enormous parallelism, the semantics are also *determinate*. Programs in Id are compiled into *dataflow graphs*, which constitute a parallel machine language. Finally, dataflow graphs are executed directly on the *Tagged-Token Dataflow Architecture* (TTDA), a machine with purely data-driven instruction scheduling, unlike the sequential program counter-based scheduling of von Neumann machines.

Dataflow research has made great strides since the seminal paper on dataflow graphs by Dennis [18]. Major milestones have been: the *U*-Interpreter for dynamic dataflow graphs [9], the first version of Id [10], the Manchester Dataflow machine [22] and, most recently, the ETL Sigma-1 in Japan [48], [23]. But much has happened since then at all levels—language, compiling, and architecture—and dataflow, not being a mainstream approach, requires some demystification. In this paper, we provide an accurate snapshot as of early 1987, by providing a fairly detailed explanation of the compilation and execution of an Id program. Because of the expanse of topics, our coverage of neither the language and compiler nor the architecture can be comprehensive; we provide pointers to relevant literature for the interested reader.

In Section II, we present example programs expressed in Id, our high-level parallel language. We take the opportunity to explain the parallelism in Id, and to state our philosophy about parallel languages in general. In Section III, we explain dataflow graphs as a parallel machine language and show how to compile the example programs. In Section IV, we describe the MIT Tagged-Token Dataflow Architecture and show how to encode and execute dataflow graphs. Finally, in Section V we discuss some characteristics of the machine, compare it to other approaches, and outline future research directions.

Before we plunge in, a word about our program examples. First, we are not concerned here with algorithmic cleverness. Improving an algorithm is always a possibility, but is outside the scope of this paper—we concentrate here only on efficient execution of a given algorithm. Second, even though in our research we are concerned primarily with large programs, the examples here are necessarily small because of limitations of space. However, even these small examples will reveal an abundance of issues relating to parallelism.

II. PROGRAMMING IN ID

We believe that it is necessary for a parallel programming language to have the following characteristics.

• It must insulate the programmer from details of the machine such as the number and speed of processors, topology and speed of the communication network, etc.

• The parallelism should be implicit in the operational semantics, thus freeing the programmer from having to identify parallelism explicitly.

• It must be *determinate*, i.e., if an algorithm, by itself, is determinate, then so should its coding in the parallel language. The programmer should not have to establish this determinacy by explicit management of scheduling and synchronization.

The last point is worth elaboration. Varying machine configurations and machine loads can cause the particular schedule for parallel activities in a program to be nondeterministic. However, the result computed should depend only on the program inputs and should not vary with the particular schedule chosen. It is a notoriously difficult task for the programmer to guarantee determinacy by explicitly inserting adequate synchronization. On the other hand, functional programming languages guarantee determinacy automatically, because of the Church–Rosser property.

Id is a high-level language—a functional programming language augmented with a determinate, parallel data-structuring mechanism called *I-structures*. I-structures are array-like data structures related to *terms* in logic programming languages, and were developed to overcome deficiencies in the purely functional approach (see [12] for a detailed discussion of this topic).

The exposition here relies on the intuition of the reader. The precise syntax and operational semantics of Id (expressed as rewrite rules) may be found in [34] and [13], respectively.

A. An Example Problem: Moving a Graphic Object

A graphics package requires a function to move objects around on the screen. For example, as shown in Fig. 1, we may want to "drag" a shape to a new position. A k-sided shape can be represented by a vector of k points, and a point in an n-dimensional space can itself be represented by a vector of n numbers. The distance and direction that we want the shape to move can also be represented as an n-dimensional vector. Given such a representation for a shape S and movement d, the new shape S' can be computed by simply adding vector d to each point of S. In order to explain Id, we develop the program move_shape which, given an S and a d, will produce the new

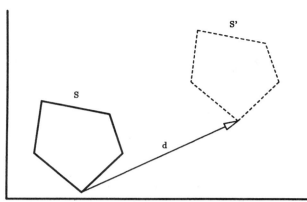

Fig. 1.   Moving a shape in a two-dimensional space.

shape. Along the way, we will define some functions that are useful in other contexts as well.

To simplify the exposition here, we assume that n is a constant, even though in Id we could discover n by querying the index bounds of, say, d. Also, we use the words "array" and "vector" synonymously.

B. Vector Sum

We begin by writing a function that moves a single point, i.e., a function that can add two vectors:

```
Def vsum A B =
    { C = array (1,n) ;
      {For j From 1 To n Do
          C[j] = A[j] + B[j]}
    In
      C } ;
```

This defines a function vsum that takes two vector arguments A and B and returns a vector result C. The body of the function is a block (the outer braces). The first statement in the block allocates the vector C with index bounds 1 to n. The second statement, the For-loop, fills it with the appropriate contents. Finally, the block's *return expression* (after the keyword In) indicates that the new vector is returned as the value of the block (which is the value of the function).

It is, of course, obvious to the reader, and perhaps can be deduced by a compiler, that the iterations of the loop are independent of each other, and hence can be done in parallel. But Id's semantics reveal much more parallelism than this. In any block, the return expression and the statements are all executed in parallel, subject only to data dependencies. Thus, the allocation of vector C can proceed in parallel with the unfolding of the loop and evaluation of all the subexpressions $A[j] + B[j]$. The array allocator returns a *descriptor* for the new vector (a pointer to memory). When C is finally available, all the pending stores $C[j] = \cdots$ can proceed.

Furthermore, the vector descriptor can be returned as the value of the function vsum even before the For-loop has terminated. This is because arrays in Id have I-structure semantics, eliminating read–write races. Array locations are initially empty, and they may be written at most once, at which point they become full. A reader of an array location is automatically deferred until it is full. In functional languages, a data structure whose elements can be read before all the elements of the data structure have been defined is called *nonstrict*. In this sense, all data structures in Id, including *I*-structures, are nonstrict. Generally, nonstrictness increases the opportunity for parallelism, in addition to increasing the expressive power of functional languages.

Functions can be called merely by juxtaposing them with their arguments. The expression

   vsum *e*1 *e*2

represents the *application* of vsum to two arguments, the values of the expressions *e*1 and *e*2.

Functions are nonstrict in the same sense as data structures. When evaluating the function-call expression (vsum *e*1 *e*2), the output vector C can be allocated and returned, and the loop unfolded, even before *e*1 and *e*2 have produced vsum's *input* vectors A and B. The expressions $A[j]$ and $B[j]$ simply suspend until descriptors for A and B arrive. Because of this nonstrict behavior, Id can dynamically adjust to, and exploit, variations in producer–consumer (or "pipelined") parallelism, even if it depends on the inputs of the program.

We reassure the reader that the above informal explanations of the parallelism in Id will be made more precise in Sections III and IV.

C. Higher Order Functions: map_array

A very interesting and useful feature of functional languages like Id is currying, which allows us to give meaning to expressions like (vsum A). Such expressions are called *partial applications*. Suppose we write

   move_point = vsum A ;

Then, the application (move_point p) is equivalent to the expression (vsum A p), and will compute a new point which is a distance A away from p. In other words, move_point is itself a legitimate unary function that adds vector A to its argument. Functions viewed in this higher order sense are said to be *curried*; they can be partially applied to their arguments, one at a time, to produce successively more specialized functions.[1]

In order to move each point of a shape, we will first write a function for the following general paradigm:

"Do something (f) to each element of an array (X) and return an array (Y) containing the results."

This can be expressed in Id as follows:

   Def map_array f X = { l,u = bounds X ;
               Y = array (l,u) ;
               {For j From l To u Do
                  $Y[j]$ = f $X[j]$]]
            In
               Y] ;

Note that one of the arguments (f) is itself a function. The first statement queries the index bounds of X and binds them to

the names l and u. The second statement allocates a new array Y with the same bounds. The loop fills each $Y[j]$ with the result of applying the function f to $X[j]$. The value of the block, Y, is also the value of the function.

So, to move a shape, we simply say

   Def move_shape S d = map_array (vsum d) S ;

i.e., to each point in the shape S, we apply vsum d, thus computing a corresponding point displaced by d, and we collect the resulting points into an array (the result shape).

Of course, we could have written move_shape as a loop iterating over S and doing a vsum with d in each iteration. However, the recommended style for programming in Id is to use abstractions like make_array [8]. The abstractions are inexpensive—our compiler is sophisticated enough to produce code for the above program that is as efficient as one written directly using nested loops. In fact, with a handful of generally useful abstractions like map_array, one rarely needs to write loops explicitly at all. However, in this paper we use loops to minimize the gap between the source program and dataflow graphs, so that the translation is easier to understand.

D. Another Example: Inner Product

The inner product of two vectors may be written in Id as follows:

   Def ip A B = { s = 0
            In
               {For j From 1 To n Do
                  Next s = s + $A[j]$ * $B[j]$
                  Finally s }} ;

In the first statement of the block, the value of a running sum s is bound to zero for the first iteration of the loop. During the jth iteration of the loop, the s for the next (i.e., $j+1$st) iteration is bound to the sum of s for the current iteration and the product of the jth elements of the vectors. The value of s after the nth iteration is returned as the value of the loop, block, and function.

Id loops differ radically from loops in conventional languages like Pascal. All iterations execute in parallel (after some initial unfolding), except where constrained by data dependencies. In ip, all $2n$ array selections and n multiplications may proceed in parallel, but the n additions are sequentialized.[2] The variables j and s do not refer to single *locations* which are updated on each iteration (as in Pascal); rather, every iteration has its own copy of j and s.

III. DATAFLOW GRAPHS AS A TARGET FOR COMPILATION

In this section, we describe *dataflow graphs*, which we consider to be an excellent parallel machine language and a suitable target for programs written in high-level languages like Id. This idea was first expressed by Dennis in a seminal paper in 1974 [18]. The version we present here reflects 1) an augmentation from "static" to "dynamic" dataflow graphs that significantly increases the available parallelism [10], [9],

---

[1] It is to support currying notationally that parentheses are optional in function applications. For example, the curried application f x y z would be written $(((f\ x)\ y)\ z)$ in Lisp.

[2] Of course, a different definition for ip could use a divide-and-conquer method to parallelize the additions.

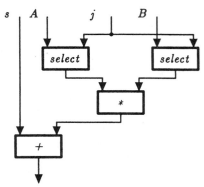

Fig. 2.   Dataflow graph for $s + A[j] * B[j]$.

and 2) the introduction of numerous significant details and optimizations developed subsequently.

A. Basics

A dataflow graph consists of *operators* (or instructions) connected by directed *arcs* that represent data dependencies between the operators. Each operator may have one or more input and output arcs. Arcs may be named—the names correspond to program variables. Fig. 2 shows the graph for a simple subexpression of the inner product program *ip*.

The fork for *j* at the top of the figure can be regarded as a separate one-input, two-output operator, but since *any* operator can have more than one output, it would usually be incorporated as part of the preceding operator (not shown).

Data values between operators are carried on *tokens* which are said to *flow* along the arcs. In a dataflow machine, this is represented by including a *destination* in the token, that is, the address of the instruction (operator) at the end of the arc. (So, except in special signal processing architectures, one should *never* think of the dataflow graph as representing physical wiring between function modules.)

An operator is ready to *fire*, i.e., execute, when there are tokens on all its input arcs. Firing an operator involves consuming all its input tokens, performing the designated operation on the values carried on the tokens, and producing a result token on each output arc. Fig. 3 shows a possible firing sequence for our simple expression.

Tokens on the *A* and *B* arcs carry only *descriptors* (or pointers) to the *I*-structures themselves which reside in a memory called *I-structure storage*. (We discuss this in detail in Section III-C.) Note that the firing sequence is unspecified: operators may fire as soon as tokens arrive at their inputs; many operators may fire at the same time, and the execution times of the operators may vary.

The compilation of constants requires some care. In most cases, such as the constant 1 in the expression $j + 1$, it is incorporated as an immediate operand into the + instruction itself, making it effectively a unary " + 1" operator. However, if necessary, a constant can be compiled as an operator with one *trigger* input and one output (see Fig. 4). Such a situation may arise, for example, if both inputs to an instruction are constants. The data value on a trigger token is irrelevant. Whenever the trigger token arrives, the operator

emits an output token carrying the constant. We discuss trigger arcs in Section III-E.

B. Functions

The body of a function definition is an expression; its dataflow graph will have

- an input arc for each formal parameter, and
- an output arc for each result.

There are two major issues to be addressed: 1) when one function *invokes* (i.e., calls) another, how should the graph of the caller be linked to the graph for the body of the callee, and 2) how to handle multiple invocations of a function that may overlap in time (due to recursion, calls from parallel loops, etc). We address the latter issue first.

1) Contexts and Firing Rules: Because of parallel invocations and recursion, a function can have many simultaneous activations. Therefore, we need a way to distinguish tokens within a function's graph that logically belong to different activations. One way to handle this would be to copy the entire graph of the function body for each activation. However, in the TTDA we avoid this overhead by keeping a single copy of the function body, and by *tagging* each token with a *context* identifier that specifies the activation to which it belongs.[3]

The reader should think of a context exactly as a "frame pointer," i.e., one should regard the set of tokens corresponding to a function activation as the contents of a frame (or "activation record") for that function. The dataflow graph for the function corresponds to its fixed code. A token carries the address of an instruction in this fixed code, and a dynamic context that specifies the frame for a particular invocation of the function. The format of a token can now be seen:

$$\langle c.s, \ v \rangle_p.$$

Here, *c* is the context, *s* is the address of the destination instruction, *v* is the datum, and *p* is the *port* identifying which input of the instruction this token is meant for. The value *c.s* is called the *tag* of the token.[4] To simplify hardware implementation, we limit the number of inputs per instruction to two (with no loss of expressive power). Thus, *p* designates the "left" or "right" port. We have written *p* as a subscript for convenience; we will drop it whenever it is obvious from the graph.

Tokens corresponding to many activations may flow simultaneously through a graph. The normal firing rule for operators must therefore be changed so that tokens from different activations are not confused:

- An operator is ready to fire when a *matched* set of input tokens arrives, i.e., a set of tokens for all its input ports that have the same tag *c.s*.
- When the operator fires, the output value is tagged with *c.t*., i.e., the instruction in the same context that is to receive this token.

---

[3] Of course, this does not preclude also making copies of the function body across processors, to avoid congestion.

[4] The "tag" terminology is historical. It may be more appropriate to call it a "continuation," because it specifies what must be done subsequently with the value on the token.

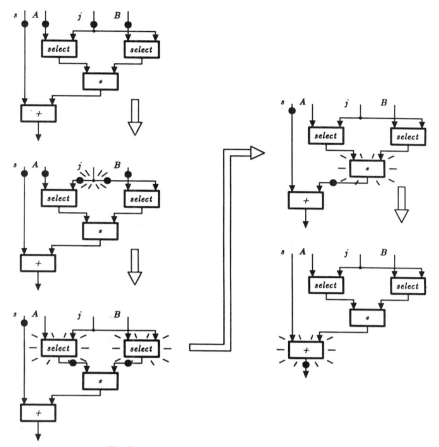

Fig. 3.   A firing sequence for "$s + A[i] * B[i]$."

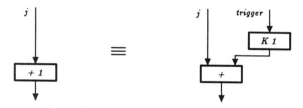

Fig. 4.   Dataflow graphs for constants.

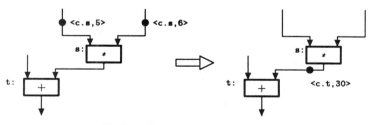

Fig. 5.   Firing rule for "$*$" operator.

This is summarized using the following notation:

$$\text{op} : \langle c.s, v1 \rangle_l \times \langle c.s, v2 \rangle_r \Rightarrow \langle c.t, (v1 \text{ op } v2) \rangle.$$

For clarity, we will consistently follow the convention that the operator is located at address s, and its destination is located at address t. Fig. 5 shows the tag manipulation for the firing of the $*$ operator.

2) Function Linkage: In order to handle function calls, it is necessary

- to allocate a new context (i.e., a new frame) for the callee,
- for the caller to send argument tokens, including a "return continuation," to the new context, and

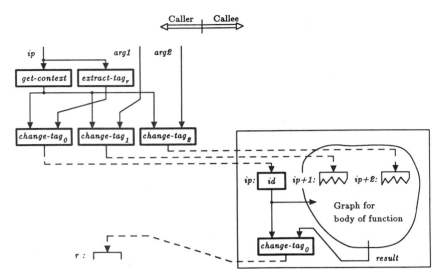

Fig. 6.   Dataflow graph for function call and return linkage.

- for the callee to send result tokens back to the caller's context using the return continuation.

While reading the following description, the reader may want to refer to Fig. 6, where the graph for the function call, (ip arg1 arg2) is shown. It is assumed that r is the address of the instruction expecting the result of the function call. Thus, the return continuation is $c.r$, where c is the context of the caller. By convention, the return continuation implicitly becomes the zeroth argument. Function linkage requires instructions to manipulate contexts on tokens. The two key instructions for this purpose are extract_tag$_r$ and change_tag$_j$.

Extract_tag$_r$ is a family of monadic instructions parameterized by an address and is used by a caller to construct a return continuation for the instruction at r in the current context:

$$\text{extract\_tag}_r : \langle c.s, \_\rangle \Rightarrow \langle c.t, c.r\rangle.$$

It takes a trigger input (whose value is irrelevant) and uses the current context c to produce a tag $c.r$ as its output datum.

Change_tag$_j$ is a family of dyadic instructions parameterized by a small constant j, and is used by the caller to send arguments to the callee:

$$\text{change\_tag}_j : \langle c.s, c'.t'\rangle_l \times \langle c.s, v\rangle_r \Rightarrow \langle c'.(t'+j), v\rangle_l.$$

Here, v is an argument value, c' is the context of the callee, and $t'+j$ is the address of the instruction in the callee that is to receive this argument. Change_tag$_j$ is also used by the callee to send results back to the caller. In this case, v is a result value, c' is the context of the caller, and $t'+j$ is the address of the instruction in the caller that is to receive the result. Although not shown here, note that it is possible to return multiple results. By convention, the receiving instructions for multiple arguments (or results) are placed at contiguous addresses t', $t'+1$, $t'+2$, etc. Thus, for example, to send the second argument, the compiler uses a change_tag$_2$ instruction.

It is not possible to depict the output arc of change_tag graphically, because the destination of its output token is not determined statically—it depends on the left input data value.

We call such arcs *dynamic arcs* and show them in figures using dashed lines.

All that remains is to allocate a new context for the callee. For this, we use the following "operator:"

$$\text{get\_context} : \langle c.s, f\rangle \Rightarrow \langle c.t, \text{new\_}c.f\rangle.$$

The input is a destination address f (the callee function's entry point), and the output is new_$c.f$, where new_c is a new, unique context identifier. The astute reader will immediately realize that there is something special about the get_context "operator." Whereas all operators described so far were purely functional (outputs depended only on the inputs), this "operator" needs some internal state so that it can produce a new unique context each time it is called. The way this is achieved is discussed in Section III-I—get_context is actually an abbreviation for a call to a special dataflow graph called a *manager*.

Now we have described the machinery used in Fig. 6 for linking function calls and returns. This linkage mechanism is only one of a number of possibilities that we have investigated.

It is important to note that the call/return scheme supports *nonstrict* functions. As suggested in Fig. 6, the zeroth argument (the return continuation) may be received by an identity instruction (*id*) that forks it and uses it as a "trigger" (to be described in Section III-E) to initiate computation in the body of the function before any of the "normal" arguments arrive. Furthermore, it is even possible for the function to return a result before the normal arguments arrive. An example of such a function is the vsum program of Section II-B, where the allocation of the result vector c does not depend on the argument vectors A and B. Thus, the part of vsum that allocates C and returns its pointer to the caller can be triggered as soon as the return continuation arrives. When the normal arguments A and B arrive, other parts of vsum will execute concurrently, filling in C's components. Our experiments show that this kind of overlap due to nonstrictness is a significant source of additional parallelism [7].

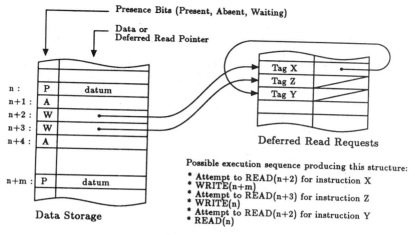

Fig. 7. *I*-structure memory.

C. I-structures

In the simple model of dataflow graphs, all data are carried on tokens. *I*-structures are a way of introducing a limited notion of state into dataflow graphs, without compromising parallelism or determinacy. *I*-structures reside in a global memory which has atypical read–write semantics. A token representing an *I*-structure carries only a *descriptor* of, i.e., a pointer to, an *I*-structure. When an *I*-structure token moves through a fork, only the token and not the whole *I*-structure, is duplicated, so that there can be many pointers to a structure.

A "producer" dataflow graph writes into an *I*-structure location while several other "consumer" dataflow graphs read that location. However, *I*-structure semantics require that consumers should wait until the value becomes available. Furthermore, determinacy is preserved by disallowing multiple writes or testing for the emptiness of an *I*-structure location. Even though our general discussion of TTDA architectures is in Section IV, we would like to shore up the reader's intuition about *I*-structures by presenting the *I*-structure storage model here.

1) I-Structure Storage: An *I*-structure store is a memory module with a controller that handles *I*-structure read and write requests, as well as requests to initialize the storage. The structure of the memory is shown in Fig. 7. In the data storage area, each location has some extra *presence bits* that specify its state: "present," "absent," or "waiting." When an *I*-structure is allocated in this area, all its locations are initialized to the absent state.

When a "read token" arrives, it contains the address of the location to be read and the tag for the instruction that is waiting for the value. If the designated location's state is present, the datum is read and sent to that instruction. If the state is absent or waiting, the read is *deferred*, i.e., the tag is *queued* at that location. The queue is simply a linked list of tags in the *deferred read requests* area.

When a "write token" arrives, it contains the address of the location to be written and the datum to be written there. If the location's state is absent, the value is written there and the state changed to present. If the location's state is waiting, the

value is written there, its state is changed to present, and the value is also sent to all the destinations queued at the location. If the location's state is already present, it is an error.

As an aside, we would like to point out that dataflow processors with *I*-structure storage are able to tolerate high memory latencies and synchronization costs. We have given extensive reasons in [11] why it is difficult to do so in a parallel machine based on the von Neumann model.

We now return to the discussion of *I*-structures at the Id and dataflow graph level.

2) I-Structure Select Operation: The architecture takes no position on the representation of *I*-structure descriptors. One possible representation is simply a pointer to the base of the array, with its index bounds stored just below the base. In order to evaluate the expression $A[j]$, the address a to be read must be computed from the descriptor A and the index j. The address computation may also perform bounds checking (see Fig. 8). The *I-fetch* operator then sends a "read token" to the *I*-structure storage controller with address a, along with the continuation $c.t$.

At the *I*-structure memory, if the location a has the present state, i.e., it is not empty and contains a value v, the value is sent in a token $\langle c.t, v \rangle$ to the instruction at $c.t$. If the location is in the absent state, i.e., it is empty, it is changed to the waiting state, and the continuation $c.t$ is simply *queued* at that location.

Thus, all memory reads are so-called *split-phase* reads, i.e., the request and the reply are not synchronous. The processor is free to execute any number of other enabled dataflow instructions during the memory fetch. In fact, the destination $c.t$ may be on an entirely different processor.

3) I-Structure Assignment: An *I*-structure assignment

$$A[j] = v$$

is translated into the dataflow graph shown in Fig. 9.

As in the select operation, the address a of the *I*-structure location is computed, based on the descriptor A and the index j. The *I-store* operator then sends a "write token" to the appropriate *I*-structure memory.

When the write token arrives there, the location may be in

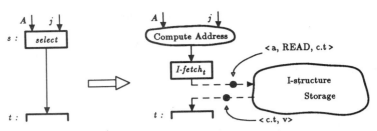

Fig. 8.   Dataflow graph for *I*-structure selection.

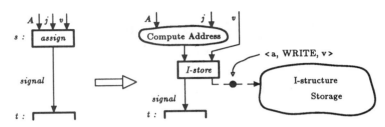

Fig. 9.   Dataflow graph for *I*-structure assignment.

the absent state or in the waiting state, i.e., there are some destinations queued there from prior memory reads. The value v is written to location a, and the state is changed to present. If it was in the waiting state, a copy of v is also sent to all destinations that were queued at a.

If the location is already in the present state, i.e., it already contains a value from a previous write token, it is treated as a run-time error, since an *I*-structure location may written to at most once.

The *I-store* operator, in addition to generating the write-token $\langle a, \text{WRITE}, v \rangle$, also generates a *signal* token for the destination $c.t$. The signal is used, ultimately, to detect the termination of the function activation containing this *I-store* instruction. This is to ensure that the function's context is not reclaimed before all its activity has ceased. (Note that this signal does *not* imply that the actual memory write has taken place—the write token may still be on its way to *I*-structure memory.)

In some resource-management situations, it may be necessary to *know* that the write has completed at the memory unit. This can be achieved simply by doing a fetch to the same location and waiting for the response—*I*-structure semantics ensures that it cannot come back until the write has occurred.

4) I-Structure Allocation: *I*-structure allocation is required by the Id expression

$$\text{array } (l,u).$$

Just like the get_context "operator," we can think of a get_storage operator

$$\text{get\_storage} : \langle c.s, \text{size} \rangle \Rightarrow \langle c.t, A \rangle$$

where size is computed from l and u, and A is the descriptor for the allocated array. Like get_context, this is also implemented by a call to a *manager* (see Section III-I). The storage allocator manager

- allocates a free area of *I*-structure memory,

- initializes all locations to the absent (i.e., empty) state, and

- sends the descriptor to the instruction at $c.t$.

Manager calls are split phase operations, like the select operation. Hence, the processor can execute other instructions while storage is being allocated.

5) Discussion: The write-once semantics that we have described supports the high-level determinacy requirements of Id. However, architecturally, and at the dataflow graph level, it is trivial to implement other memory operations as well. An "exchange" operation for managers is described in Section III-I. One could have ordinary, imperative writes as well (the storage allocator needs this). In fact, it is not difficult to include a small ALU in the *I*-structure controller to perform *fetch-and-add* style instructions [21], [41], [29].

D. Well-Behaved Graphs and Signals

When a function is invoked, some machine resources (e.g., a frame, registers) must be dynamically allocated for that invocation. We refer to these resources collectively as a *context*. Because machine resources are finite, the resources in a context must be recycled when that activation terminates. However, parallelism complicates the detection of termination. The termination of a function is no longer synonymous with the production of the result token. Because functions are nonstrict, and because there are instructions that do not return results (e.g., *I-store*), a result can be returned before all operators within the function body have executed. If resources are released before termination, there may be tokens still in transit that arrive at a nonexistent context, or worse, at a recycled context (a manifestation of the "dangling pointer" problem).

How, then, can we determine when it is safe to reclaim the resources used by a function activation? We do so by imposing an inductively-defined structure on dataflow graphs; such graphs are called *well-behaved*. We insist that all graphs have at least one input and at least one output. Then, a graph is well-behaved if

    1) initially, there are no tokens in the graph;

    2) given exactly one token on every input, ultimately exactly one token is produced on every output;

    3) when all output tokens have been produced, there are no tokens left in the graph, i.e., the graph is *self-cleaning*.

To ensure that all our graphs are well-behaved, we construct them inductively. We start with primitive well-behaved graphs and build larger composite graphs using composition rules, or *graph schemas*, that preserve well-behavedness.

Most graph primitives are already well-behaved (+ , *, · · ·). For some operators, such as *I-store*, it is necessary to introduce an artificial output called a *signal* to make it well-behaved. Signal tokens do not carry any meaningful values; they are used only to detect that a graph has executed.

For composite graphs, there may be many nested graphs that only produce signals. In the conditional schema (Section III-G), some data arcs may be used in one arm but not in the other. All such signals and dangling arcs are combined by feeding them into a "synchronization tree," which is a tree of dyadic synchronization operators, each of which emits a signal token on its output when it has received tokens on both its inputs. Thus, a composite graph can itself be made well-behaved by augmenting it with a suitable synchronization tree. Some examples are shown in later sections, but we gloss over many subtleties, notably signal generation for conditionals and loops; these are explained in detail in [43].

E. Code Blocks and Triggers

Apart from the common misconception that dataflow graphs represent an interconnection of hardware modules, another major misconception about dataflow is that decisions about the distribution of work on the machine are taken dynamically at the level of individual instructions. This naturally leads to fears of intolerable overheads.

The dataflow graph for a program is divided into units called *code blocks*. Each user-defined function is compiled as a separate code block. Inner loops (i.e., loops that are contained within other loops) are also compiled as separate code blocks. Of course, because of compiler transformations (such as lambda lifting [27]) and optimizations (such as in-line function expansion), there may no longer be a one-to-one correspondence between code blocks and source program functions and loops.

The "function call" mechanism described in Section III-B is, in fact, the general mechanism by which any code block invokes another. Thus, it is the code block that is the unit of dynamic distribution of work in the TTDA, at which resource allocation decisions are taken. In contrast, *within* a code block, the *work* is distributed automatically with some hardware support, as described in Section IV-C.

Every code block has one or more input arcs and one or more output arcs. One of the input arcs is designated as the trigger input and one of the output arcs the termination-signal output. When a code block B_1 invokes a code block B_2,

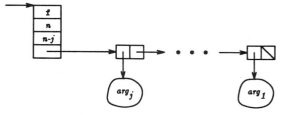

Fig. 10.   Representation of a closure.

- B_1 (the caller) acquires a context for B_2 (the callee) from a manager (see Section III-I). This may involve loading code for B_2 in one or more processors.
- B_1 sends a trigger token to B_2. Usually, the return continuation token (i.e., the implicit zeroth argument) can be used as the trigger.
- B_1 sends other input tokens to B_2 (and, perhaps, continues its own execution).
- B_2 returns result(s) to B_1 (and, perhaps, continues its own execution).
- One of the "results" from B_2 is a termination signal. Often, one of the data results can be used as a termination signal.
- B_1 deallocates the context for B_2. If there is more than one output arc from B_2 back to B_1, then B_1 will need a synchronization tree to ensure that all these tokens have arrived before it deallocates B_1's context.

The top level computation of a program begins by injecting a trigger token into the outermost code block. Inner code blocks, in turn, get their triggers from their callers. The reader is referred to [43] for the details of generation and propagation of signals and triggers.

F. Higher Order Functions

Every function has a syntactically derived property called its *arity* (≥ 1) which is the number of arguments in its definition. For example, vsum has arity 2. In Section III-B, we saw how to compile expressions representing the application of a known, arity n function to n arguments [e.g., (ip arg1 arg2)]. But what about expressions where the function is applied to fewer than n arguments? (An example is the expression (vsum d) described in Section II-C.)

The "partial application" of a function of arity n to one argument produces a function that requires $n - 1$ arguments. When this, in turn, is applied to another argument, it produces a function that requires $n - 2$ arguments, and so on. Finally, when a function is applied to its last argument, the "full application," or invocation, of Section III-B can be performed.

Function values are represented by a data structure called a *closure*. Fig. 10 depicts the situation after a function f of arity n has been applied to j arguments. A closure contains:

- the entry address of the function f;
- its arity n;
- $n - j$, the number of arguments remaining;
- a list of the j argument values collected so far.

The degenerate case of a closure is the function value itself (for example, the token ip at the top left of Fig. 6); it is a

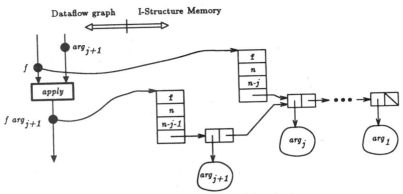

Fig. 11. Dataflow graph for partial applications.

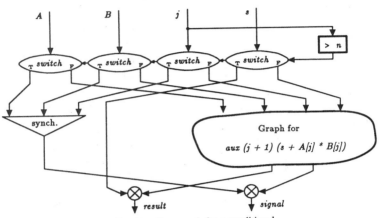

Fig. 12. Dataflow graph for a conditional.

closure with n arguments remaining and an empty list of arguments collected so far.

For general applications, we use a dyadic *apply* schema. The *apply* schema is not a primitive operator, but we will describe its behavior here without expanding it into a more detailed dataflow graph.

The left input to the *apply* schema is a closure for a function f of arity n, $n - j$ remaining arguments, and list of j collected arguments. The right input to *apply* is the next argument.

Suppose $n - j > 1$; then, this is a partial application to the $j + 1$st argument. The output of *apply* is a new closure containing the same function and arity, but with decremented arguments-remaining ($n - j - 1$) and an augmented argument list incorporating this argument. This is depicted in Fig. 11. Note that the input and output closures *share* the first j arguments.

When $n - j = 1$, the current argument is the final argument for f, and f can now be invoked. In this case, *apply* performs a full function call, as shown in Fig. 6.

Since closures and argument-lists are implemented using I-structures, the *apply* schema can return the new closure even before the argument token on its right input has arrived—the allocation of the new cell in the argument list can be done immediately. When the argument finally arrives, it will be stored in the argument list. Thus, the *apply* schema is consistent with the nonstrict semantics of full function calls. The reader is referred to [43] for further details.

The general *apply* schema is of course not inexpensive. However, most applications are detectable as full-arity applications at compile time, in which case the call-return linkage is generated directly. For those familiar with the literature on compiling graph reduction, the general *apply* schema is needed only in those places where a graph *must* be constructed instead of a direct function call.

G. Conditionals

Consider the following expression (part of a tail-recursive formulation of the ip inner product function, not shown):

> If ($j > n$) Then s
> Else aux ($j + 1$) ($s + A[j] * B[j]$).

The graph for the conditional is shown in Fig. 12.

The output of the $> n$ operator is actually forked four ways to the side inputs of the four *switch* operators; the abbreviation in the picture is for clarity only.

A true token at the side input of a *switch* copies the token from the top input to the T output. A false token at the side input of a *switch* copies the token from the top input to the F output. The $\otimes$ node simply passes tokens from either input to its output. The $\otimes$ node is only a notational device and does not actually exist in the encoding of a dataflow graph—the outputs of the two arms of the conditional are sent directly to the appropriate destination. The T outputs of the A, B, and j

switches are routed to a *synchronization tree* to produce the termination signal for the true arm of the conditional.

Note that the *switch* operator is not well-behaved by itself—given a token on each of its two inputs, it produces a token on only one of its outputs. However, when used in the context of a structured conditional schema, the overall graph is well-behaved. The reader should convince himself that after a token has appeared on each of the output arcs no token could remain in the graph.

H. Loops

Loops are an efficient implementation of tail-recursive functions. In Id, the programmer may express a computation directly as a loop, or the compiler may recognize tail-recursive forms and transform them to loops.

(The impatient reader may safely skip to Section III-I, but we invite you to scan the intermediate subsection headings, hoping that you will be tempted to come back!)

We will discuss only while-loops here, using this version of the function ip which is equivalent to the for-loop version:

Def ip A B = { s = 0 ;
$\quad\quad\quad\quad j = 1$
$\quad\quad$ In
$\quad\quad\quad$ {While ($j <= n$) Do
$\quad\quad\quad\quad$ Next $j = j + 1$;
$\quad\quad\quad\quad$ Next $s = s + A[j] * B[j]$
$\quad\quad\quad$ Finally s }} ;

1) Circulating Variables and Loop Constants: The body of the loop contains expressions with free variables j, s, A, and B. Two of them, j and s, are bound on each iteration using Next—we call these *circulating* variables. The dataflow graph for the loop body has an input arc and an output arc for every circulating variable. The remaining two, A and B, are invariant over all iterations of the loop, and are thus called *loop constants*. It is possible to think of loop constants as if they too, were circulating, using the trivial statements

next A = A ;
next B = B.

However, implementing them in this way would incur unnecessary overheads, and so we give them special treatment.

With every loop, we associate a region of memory in its context (frame) called its *constant area*. Before the loop body executes, there is a graph called the *loop prelude* that stores the loop constants in the constant area. Within the loop body, every reference to a loop constant is translated into a simple memory fetch from the constant area.

The dataflow graph for our loop is shown in Fig. 13. For the moment, ignore the operators labeled D and D-reset. The loop prelude stores A and B in the constant area. j and s circulate around the loop as long as the $j <= n$ output is true.

2) Loop Iteration Context: Because of the asynchronous nature of execution, it is possible that the j tokens circulate much faster than the s tokens. This means that since the loop condition depends only on j, many j tokens corresponding to different iterations may pile up on the right-hand inputs of the select operators. Thus, we need a mechanism to distinguish the

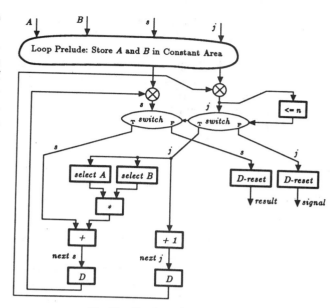

Fig. 13.   Dataflow graph for a loop.

tokens corresponding to different iterations. This is performed by the D and D_reset operators. The D operator merely changes the context of its input token to a new context; the D-reset operator resets the context of its input token to the original context of the entire loop.

We could use the general get_context mechanism for this, but this would be equivalent to implementing the loop using general recursion. Instead, we assume that the get_context call that is used when invoking a code block containing a loop actually preallocates several contexts C_0, C_1, $\cdots$, for the different iterations of the loop, and returns C_0, the identifier of the first one. The structure of context identifiers is such that given the identifier C_i, we can compute the identifiers C_{i+1} and C_0. The former computation is performed by the D operator, which is an identity operator that simply increments the context of its input token from C_i to C_{i+1}, and the latter computation is performed by the D-reset operator, which is an identity operator that resets the context of its input token to C_0. The i part of the context field is called the *iteration number*. In effect, a block of resources is preallocated for the loop which is then able to perform its own resource management locally.

The astute reader will recognize that the loop-iteration-context mechanism is not sufficient to handle nested loops—tokens can still get confused. For this reason, every nested loop is packaged as a separate code block, like a procedure call, and given its own, unique context when it is invoked.

3) Loop Throttling: There remains the problem of how large should be the contiguous block of contexts for a loop. One of the problems in parallel machines is the difficulty of controlling enormous amounts of parallelism. For example, unfolding 100 000 iterations of a loop on a 256-processor machine could swamp the machine. A related point is this: in a real machine, there will be only a fixed number of bits to represent the iteration number of contexts. Hence, there is a possibility of overflow, if the loop unfolds too fast.

There is an elegant solution to these problems based on the simple observation that *all* inputs to the loop body are controlled by the bank of switch operators at the top of the loop, and these, in turn, are all controlled by a single Boolean value from the loop predicate. Any particular iteration of the loop can proceed only if the corresponding Boolean token arrives at the switches. Thus, by controlling the delivery of these Boolean tokens to the switches, we can regulate the rate at which the loop unfolds.

Suppose we wanted to limit the unfolding of a loop to some k, i.e., no more than k iterations are to exist simultaneously. The general form of a k-throttled loop is shown in Fig. 14.

The Boolean input to the switches is now *gated* using $\boxtimes$, a two-input operator that fires when both inputs arrive, copying one of them to its output. By gating this token, we can hold back an iteration of the loop. The loop prelude primes the gate with the first $k - 1$ loop iteration contexts $C_0, \cdots, C_{k-2}$, which allows the first $k - 1$ Booleans to go through, which, in turn, allows the first $k - 1$ iterations to proceed. At the bottom of the loop, each circulating variable goes through a D_k operator which increments the loop iteration context from i to $i + 1$, modulo k. Thus, the loop iteration context is the same for the ith and the $i + k$th iteration.

The reader should convince himself that tokens with contexts C_0 and C_{k-1}, inclusive, may now be sitting at the inputs to the switches. In order to prevent mismatching unrelated tokens, we must allow the C_{k-1} iteration to proceed only after the C_0 iteration is over.

The outputs of all the D_k operators are combined using a synchronization tree. When a signal token appears at the output of the tree with context C_1, we know that the C_0 iteration has terminated completely, and that there are no more C_0 tokens extant. (Recall that the loop body is itself well-behaved, by induction, so that we know that all instructions in it, including *I-stores*, have completed.) When triggered by the signal token, the D_k^{-2} operator enables the gate with a token carrying context C_{k-1} (hence the "-2" in the name, since $(k - 1) = (1 - 2) \bmod k$).

The value k may be specified as a compile-time or load-time pragma, or may be dynamically generated based on the current load on the machine. In our current graph interpreter, the user can specify it on a per loop basis at load time. There is also some code generated by the compiler, which we have glossed over, to consume the k extra tokens left at the gate when the loop terminates; for full details see [6] and [16].

Loop throttling amounts to inserting extra data dependencies in the dataflow graph. Because of this, it is possible for a throttled loop to deadlock where the unthrottled loop would not. Consider this example:

```
{ a = array (1,10) ;
  a[10] = 1 ;
  {For j From 1 To 9 Do
     a[j] = 2 * a[j+1] }}.
```

The loop unfolds forward, but the data dependencies go backward, so that $a[9]$ becomes defined first, which enables $a[8]$ to become defined, which enables $a[7]$ to become defined, and so on. If the unfolding is throttled too much (e.g.,

$k = 5$), the loop will deadlock, since the iteration that defines $a[9]$ cannot execute.

This example is pathological; it would have been more natural to write it with a For-downto loop instead of a For-to loop, in which case the deadlock problem does not arise. In our experience, programs rarely have dependencies that run counter to the loop direction.

To avoid deadlock, the compiler may do some analysis to choose adequately large loop bounds or to change the loop direction, but this is of course undecidable in general. The programmer also has recourse to using general recursion to avoid deadlocks due to throttled loops.

I. Managers

In any machine supporting a general-purpose programming, various resources need to be allocated and deallocated dynamically, e.g., frame and heap allocation and deallocation. We call the entities that perform these services *resource managers*. In a sequential language, such managers may not be clearly distinguishable as they are often distributed and embedded within the program itself. However, in any parallel language, these services must be shared by multiple processes (we will call them *clients*) and thus need special treatment.

Even though the bulk of a resource manager may be written as an ordinary procedure (mapping resource requests to resources), the entry and exit are handled quite differently from ordinary procedure calls. First, each resource manager must have private data structures that are shared across all calls to that manager. Second, multiple calls to a manager must be serialized so that the manipulation of these data structures is done consistently. Typically, this serialization is performed in the nondeterministic order in which requests arrive.

On a conventional machine, concurrent accesses to a manager are usually operating system calls (e.g., file allocation) and are implemented using interrupts and interrupt handlers. Serialized entry is ensured by disabling interrupts, setting semaphore locks, etc. This kind of programming is notorious for its difficulty and high probability of error. The dataflow approach offers a very clean and elegant solution to these problems, allowing significant internal parallelism within the manager itself. We present one possible implementation.

Resource managers are ordinary Id programs that run continuously and concurrently with the main application program. While no special hardware is necessary, managers do use privileged instructions that allow them to manipulate the state of the machine. For example, the *I*-structure memory manager uses special instructions to reset presence bits, update its memory map (such as free lists), etc.

Access to a manager is mediated by a shared *serializing queue* of requests, shown in Fig. 15. All data structures shown in the figure are located in *I*-structure memory. The queue is a chain of two-slot *entries*, where the first slot holds a request and the second slot points to the next entry in the queue. The second slot of the last entry (a) is empty (in the *I*-structure sense). The clients' interface to the manager is m, an indirection cell that always points to the last entry in the queue.

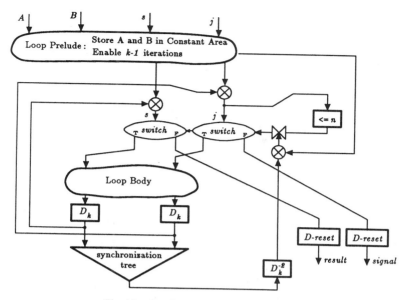

Fig. 14.   Dataflow graph for throttled loops.

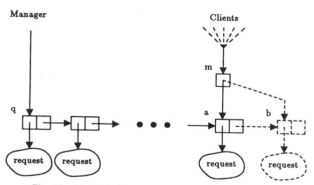

Fig. 15.   Serializing input queue for a resource manager.

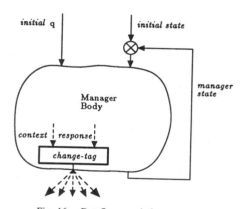

Fig. 16.   Dataflow graph for a manager.

Clients use m to attach their requests to the end of the queue, in some nondeterministic order. The manager holds a reference to q, the current head of the queue. After consuming the request in the first slot of q, it uses the second slot to refer to the next entry in the queue, and so on. If the manager runs ahead of the requests, it suspends automatically when it tries to read the empty slot at the end of the queue.

Suppose a client wishes to send a request, such as ''get a context for function ip,'' to the context manager. First, it *creates a new entry b*, a two-slot I-structure, and puts the request in $b[1]$. The client then executes (exchange $m\ b$), an I-structure operation that simultaneously fetches a, the current tail of the queue and stores b, the new tail, into m. The exchange is performed *atomically* at the I-structure memory, to ensure that two clients executing this code simultaneously do not corrupt the shared data structure. Finally, the client enqueues b by storing b in $a[2]$.

The request to a manager generally contains several pieces of information, according to software convention. For example, we may have a manager exclusively for allocating and deallocating contexts (see Section III-B2). The request constructed by get_context may contain

• a request type (''allocate''/''deallocate''),
• the name of the callee function (so that the manager knows what resources to allocate), and
• a return continuation $c.t$ for the managers' response (the instruction that receives the output of get_context).

Some requests, such as release_context, may not require a return continuation. The mechanism also allows other pragmatic information to be packaged with the request, such as loop bounds, priorities, etc.

Similarly, get_storage and release_storage expand into calls to a manager for heap storage, with request containing the size of the memory request.

A manager is shown in outline in Fig. 16. Each manager is initialized with an *initial state* containing data structures representing available resources and a reference to q, the head of its serializing queue. A request is taken off the queue, and together with the current *state*, enters the manager body (which is an ordinary dataflow graph) to actually allocate/ deallocate the resource. It uses the change_tag operator and the return continuation that was packaged with the request to send the response back to the client. Finally, the manager body produces a *next state* which is fed back, ready to be combined with the next request. The behavior of a manager is abstractly modeled as follows:

{WHILE true DO
    request = $q[1]$;
    next state = manager_body request state ;
    next q = $q[2]$ }.

As pointed out earlier, the manager will automatically suspend when it tries to read the empty *I*-structure slot at the end of the queue. Using loop bounding, we can limit it to one iteration at a time. The manager body itself can have significant internal parallelism.

The manager need not respond to requests in the order in which they were received. For example, in order to favor small requests over large, a heap allocator needs the ability to defer a large request. In such cases, the manager simply stores the pending request in its state variable and examines the next request. Thus, dataflow managers permit *all* the flexibility one normally expects in resource managers, such as priority queues, preemptive resource allocation, etc.

As in any resource management system, there are some bootstrapping issues. For example, storage for the queue entry for a storage allocation request must not itself need a call to the storage manager. These issues are no different from those in conventional systems, and are handled similarly.

If all requests for a particular kind of resource (e.g., heap storage) went to a single manager, it is, of course, likely to become a bottleneck. This can be addressed in standard ways. For example, we may partition the resource into separate domains, each managed by a local manager. These managers may negotiate with each other occasionally to balance resource usage across the machine. The communication between managers is no different from the communication between parts of any other Id program.

Functional programmers will recognize that the manager queue performs a ''nondeterministic'' merge. However, managers are significantly easier to use than the nondeterministic merge operator, which cannot adequately cope with systems in which the users of a resource manager are dynamically determined. The reader is invited to see [4] for more details, including a programming methodology for managers.

Dataflow graphs provide all the *mechanisms* necessary to implement managers; what remains is to decide the *policies* encoded therein. This is a major area for research (see [17]), both in our project and elsewhere. Currently, a major obstacle is the general lack of experience in the research community with large, parallel applications.

IV. DATAFLOW GRAPHS AS A MACHINE LANGUAGE FOR THE TTDA

We have seen that dataflow graphs are a good target for a compiler for a high-level programming language such as Id. Our experiments have confirmed that the tagged-token semantics for executing dataflow graphs exposes large amounts of parallelism, even in conventional algorithms [7]. In this section, we describe the MIT Tagged-Token Dataflow Archi-

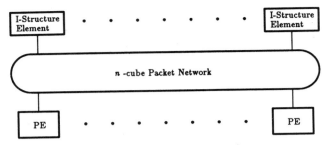

Fig. 17.   Top-level view of TTDA.

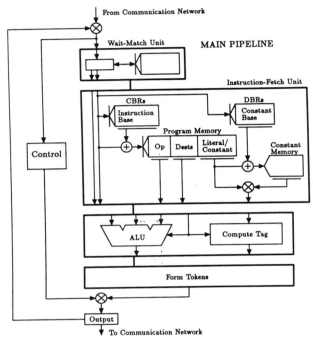

Fig. 18.   A processing element.

tecture (TTDA), a machine architecture for directly executing dataflow graphs.

A. Architecture

At a sufficiently abstract level, the TTDA looks no different from a number of other parallel MIMD machines (Fig. 17)—it has a number of identical processing elements (PE's) and storage units interconnected by an *n*-cube packet network. As usual, there are many packaging alternatives—for example, a PE and storage unit may be physically one unit—but we do not explore such choices here. However, it is important that the storage units are addressed uniformly in a *global address space*; thus, they can be regarded as a multiported, interleaved memory.

Each PE is a dataflow processor. Each storage unit is an *I*-structure storage unit, which was described in Section III-C. A single PE and a single *I*-structure unit constitute a complete dataflow computer. To simplify the exposition, we will first describe the operation of the machine as if it had only one PE and *I*-structure unit; in Section IV-C, we discuss multiprocessor operation.

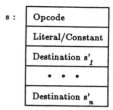

Fig. 19. Representation of an instruction.

B. Single Processor Operation

The architecture of a single processing element is shown in Fig. 18. The main pipeline is the central feature of the PE.

1) Representation of Dataflow Graphs and Contexts: Recall (from Section III-E) that a program is translated into a set of basic dataflow graphs called code blocks. The graph for a code block is encoded as a linear sequence of instructions in program memory. The assignment of instructions to addresses in the linear sequence is arbitrary, except for the call-return linkage convention mentioned in Section III-B. As an engineering decision, every instruction has no more than two inputs. Thus, every instruction in the graph is encoded as shown in Fig. 19.

The literal/constant field in an instruction may be a literal value or an offset into the constant area in constant memory. The destinations are merely the addresses of the successor instructions in the graph. To facilitate relocation, addressing within a code block is relative, i.e., destination addresses are encoded as offsets from the current instruction.

A specific invocation of a code block is determined by a *context*, which identifies two registers: a code block register (CBR) which points to the base address in program memory for the code block's instructions, and a database register (DBR) which points to the base address for the constant area in constant memory.

The get_context manager-call discussed in Sections III-B and III-I must therefore

- allocate a CBR/DBR pair and space in constant memory for the designated function,
- initialize the CBR/DBR to point to the instruction and constant base addresses, and
- return the CBR/DBR number as the context.

2) Operation of the Main Pipeline: Tokens entering the main pipeline go through the following units in sequence.

Wait–Match Unit: The *wait–match unit* (WM) is a memory containing a pool of waiting tokens. If the entering token is destined for a monadic operator, it goes straight through WM to the instruction-fetch unit. Otherwise, the token is destined for a dyadic operator and the tokens in WM are examined to see if the other operand has already arrived, i.e., if WM contains another token with the same tag. If so, a *match* occurs: that token is extracted from WM, and the two tokens are passed on to the instruction-fetch unit. If WM does not contain the partner, then this token is deposited into WM to wait for it.

The wait–match unit is thus the *rendezvous* point for pairs of arguments for dyadic operators. It has the semantics of an associative memory, but can be implemented using hashing.

Instruction-Fetch Unit: The tag on the operand tokens entering the instruction-fetch unit identifies an instruction to be fetched from program memory (via a CBR). The fetched instruction may include a literal or offset into the constant area, and a list of destination instruction offsets. The tag also specifies a DBR; using the constant base address found there and the constant offset in the instruction, any required constants from the constant area are now fetched from constant memory.

All this information—the data values from the tokens; a constant from the constant area or a literal from the instruction, the opcode from the instruction, the destination offsets from the instruction, and the context itself—is passed on to the next stage, the ALU, and compute-tag unit.

ALU and Compute-Tag Unit: The ALU and compute-tag units are actually two ALU's operating in parallel. The ALU unit is a conventional one that takes the operand/literal/constant data values and the opcode, performs the operation, and produces a result.

The compute-tag unit takes the CBR and DBR numbers from the context and the instruction offsets for the destinations, and computes the tags for the output of the operator. Recall that the tag for two instructions in the same code block invocation will differ only in the instruction offset.

The ALU result and the destination tags are passed to the form-tokens unit.

Form-Tokens Unit: The form-tokens unit takes the data value(s) from the ALU and the tags from the compute tag and combines them into result tokens.

Output tokens emerging at the bottom of the pipe are routed according to their destination addresses: back to the top of the PE, or into the network to the *I*-structure unit, or, in a multiprocessor, to other PE's and *I*-structure units. The global address space makes this routing straightforward.

The main pipeline can be viewed as two simpler pipelines—the wait–match unit and everything below it. Once tokens enter the lower pipeline, there is nothing further to block them. Pipeline stages do not share any state, so there are no complications such as reservation bits, etc.

3) The Control Unit: The control unit receives special tokens that can manipulate any part of the PE's state—for example, tokens that initialize code-block registers, store values into constant memory and program memory, etc. These tokens are typically produced by various managers such as the context manager.

The control section also contains any connection to the outside world, such as input–output channels.

C. Multiprocessor Operation

In a multiprocessor machine, all memories (program, constant, *I*-structure) are globally addressed. Thus, one can implement any desired form of interleaving. The simplest distribution of code on the TTDA is to allocate an entire code block to a PE. However, the TTDA has a sophisticated *mapping* mechanism that also allows a code block to be allocated *across* a group of PE's, thereby exploiting the internal parallelism within them. For example, it is possible to load a copy of a loop procedure on several PE's, and distribute different iterations of the loop on different PE's according to some prespecified hash function on the tags. The hash function to be used is stored in a MAP register which like the CBR and DBR is loaded at the time of procedure activation. In fact it is also possible to execute a code block on several PE's by loading only parts of it on different PE's. When a token is produced at the output of either a PE or an *I*-structure unit, its tag specifies exactly which PE or *I*-structure unit it must go to. The token is sent there directly, i.e., there is no broadcasting.

It is important to note that the program does not have to be recompiled for different mapping schemes. The machine code (dataflow graph) is independent of the mapping schemes and the machine configuration. Furthermore, the number of instructions executed does not vary with the machine configuration.

D. Discussion

It is important to realize that the PE architecture shown here is *the* hardware interpreter for dataflow graphs—it is not an abstraction to be implemented at a lower level by a conventional processor.

Any parallel machine must support mechanisms for fast synchronization and process switching. The TTDA supports these at the *lowest* level of the architecture, without any busy–waiting. Every wait–match operation and every *I*-structure read and write operation is a synchronization event directly supported in hardware. Sequential threads may be interleaved at the level of individual instructions. Unlike von Neumann machines, switching between threads does not involve any overheads of saving and restoring registers, loading and flushing caches, etc. All memory reads are *split phase*, i.e., between the request-to-read and the datum-reply there may be an arbitrary number of other instructions executed. Thus, the latency (roundtrip time) of memory reads, which is bound to be high in a parallel machine, is masked by doing useful work in the interval; the overall throughput of the interconnection network is more critical than its latency.

V. Comparison to Other Work

An invariant in our approach to the problem of high-speed, general-purpose parallel computing has been the belief that it cannot be solved at any single level. The goal will be achieved only with synergy between the language, the compiler, and the architecture.[5] This cannot be achieved by simple extensions to conventional sequential languages and architectures—the problems of determinacy, cost of synchronization and context switches, and intolerance of memory latency are insurmountable in the pure von Neumann framework.

A. Languages and Compiling

Our research on languages is constrained mainly by the two requirements of *implicitly* parallel semantics and *determinacy*.

Originally (i.e., in [10], 1978), Id was simply intended as a convenient textual encoding of dataflow graphs which are

---

[5] The RISC experience has demonstrated this tight coupling even on sequential machines.

tedious to draw explicitly. Over the years, Id has evolved in the direction of higher level features and greater abstraction. Today, the functional subset of Id is as powerful and abstract as other modern functional languages such as SML [31], LML [15], and Miranda [46]. Like these other functional languages, Id can be explained and understood purely in terms of the concept of *reduction*, without any recourse to dataflow graphs (such an explanation may be found in [13]).

I-structures and managers extend Id beyond functional languages. *I*-structures were originally introduced only as a characterization of certain "monotonic" constructions of functional arrays ([14], 1980). It was only in 1986 that the connection with logic variables became clear, and *I*-structures were clearly incorporated into the language [12]. A recent development is the "array comprehension" notation by which the programmer can stay within the functional subset and largely avoid the explicit use of *I*-structures [34]. We believe that the treatment of arrays is one of Id's unique features. Managers in Id are used for expressing explicit nondeterminism and are more expressive than the "merge" operator often used to express nondeterminism in functional languages.

It is also interesting to compile Id for sequential and parallel architectures using von Neumann processors. The major complication here arises from Id's nonstrict semantics which makes it quite difficult to achieve efficient partitioning of code into sequential von Neumann threads. This has recently been a very active area for research. Outside our group, this has been the primary focus of the *graph-reduction* [45] community, where an additional motivation has been "lazy evaluation," which is one way to achieve nonstrict semantics. Work on compiling for sequential von Neumann machines may be found in [26] and [19], and for parallel von Neumann machines in [37] and [20]. Within our group, we have recently embarked upon a project to tackle this problem systematically and at a more fundamental level [44], cleanly separating out the issue of nonstrictness from the issue of laziness. This work has, in fact, strengthened our conviction that dataflow architectures are good architectures in which to implement parallel graph reduction.

Another language associated prominently with dataflow is SISAL [30] (which, in turn, was influenced by both Id and VAL, another early dataflow language [1]). Id and SISAL differ in many ways; most notably:

- SISAL deliberately omits higher order functions in favor of simplicity.
- Current implementations of SISAL have strict semantics, although we have been informed that the SISAL specification takes no position on strictness.
- SISAL arrays are purely functional, and are extensible, i.e., the index bounds can grow. It is possible to define some arrays monolithically using the "forall" construct. In addition, there is an incremental update operation that conceptually produces a new array from an old one, differing at one index. If implemented naively, this implies some sequentialization and a heavy use of array storage, but it is the aim of SISAL researchers to use program analysis to alleviate this problem. In contrast, Id arrays are not extensible, and instead of incremental updates, the Id programmer uses bulk or mono-

lithic operators like map_array (the programmer can code new bulk operators himself, using higher order functions). The nonstrictness of Id is crucial in allowing bulk operators to be used when an array is defined using recurrences.

• Both Id and SISAL are statically and strongly typed. However, SISAL's type-system is monomorphic, and requires type declarations by the programmer, whereas Id has a polymorphic type system, and types are automatically inferred by the compiler.

Most current SISAL research focuses on compiling to existing multiprocessors, except at Manchester University, where the target is the Manchester dataflow machine. A major contribution of the SISAL effort has been to define IF1, an intermediate language to which SISAL programs are first translated. IF1 is a dataflow graph language, although not at a sufficiently detailed level to be a directly executable machine language. Proper documentation of IF1 and tools for manipulating it have allowed diverse research groups to target SISAL to their machines. However, none of the current implementations of SISAL can match the performance of conventional languages on parallel or sequential machines.

Lucid is another language known as a dataflow language [47] because, though textually a functional language, the operational interpretation often given to Lucid programs is one of networks of *filter* functions connected by arcs carrying infinite sequences of values. High-level iteration constructs are used to specify the filters and their interconnections. Unlike our dataflow graphs that constitute a machine language, Lucid's networks are at a much more abstract level and do not address such issues as tagging, data structure representations, etc. Current implementations of Lucid interpret such networks in von Neumann code. Insofar as Lucid can be viewed denotationally as a purely functional language, it should also be amenable to our compilation techniques. As a programming language, Lucid does not have higher order functions, arrays, user-defined data types, type checking, etc., although we understand that such features are under consideration.

B. Dataflow Architectures

The first tagged-token dynamic dataflow interpreter was the *U*-Interpreter developed in 1977 [9]. In the *U*-Interpreter, contexts and iteration numbers on tags were completely abstract entities, with no physical interpretation. Indeed, for procedure calls, each context carried within it the entire chain of its parent contexts. The TTDA is an evolution of the *U*-Interpreter in the direction of a realizable architecture. Contexts now have a physical interpretation—they are directly related to machine resources, referring to code block registers, database registers, constant areas, and so on. Detailed, explicit mechanisms have been developed to invoke new contexts and restore old ones. Loop-bounding techniques have been developed in recognition that resources are bounded (including the iteration field on a token). Finally, *I*-structure memory has been developed to deal with data structures.

Of course, the TTDA is not the end of the evolutionary path from the *U*-Interpreter. Our current view is embodied in the Monsoon dataflow processor architecture [36], which we describe briefly in the next section.

The tagged-token dataflow idea was also developed independently at Manchester University, where the first dataflow machine was built [22]. It consisted of one processing element and introduced the idea of "waiting–matching" functions. This made it possible to implement an "*I*-structure store" in the waiting–matching section itself. Although the Manchester machine was too small to run any actual applications, it was able to demonstrate that pipelines in a dataflow processor can be kept busy almost effortlessly.

The most complete and impressive dataflow machine to date is the Sigma-1, built by researchers at Japan's Electro-Technical Laboratory [23], [48]. It embodies nearly all the ideas discussed in this paper. The current implementation consists of 128 processors and 128 *I*-structure stores and has just gone into operation (early 1988). It has already demonstrated a performance of 170 MFLOPS on a small integration problem. It is programmed in dataflow C, a derivative subset of the C programming language. There is a paucity of software for Sigma-1, although we think it would be straightforward to develop an Id compiler for it.

In Japan, there is also related work at the NTT under the direction of Dr. Amamiya [3], [40]. NEC has also built some dataflow machines, including a commercial signal-processing chip [32], [42].

A more detailed survey of dataflow architectures may be found in [5].

C. Project Status and Plans: Id and the Monsoon Machine

Our current research (December 1988) continues to cover a spectrum from languages to compilers to architectures.

On the Id language, we are working on further improvements in data-structuring facilities, development of an automatic incremental, polymorphic type-checker with overloading, and language constructs for resource managers.

The central vehicle of our compiler research is the Id compiler implemented by Traub [43]. Issues we are currently investigating revolve around optimization techniques: use of type information to improve object code, code motion and transformation, fast function calls and loops, fast resource management, and reducing the overhead of dynamic resource management by moving some of those activities into in-line code.

To support this research, we have constructed *Id World*, an integrated programming environment for Id and the TTDA [33] running on workstations such as Lisp machines. In addition to sophisticated edit–compile–debug–run support, Id World measures and plots parallelism profiles, instruction counts, and other emulated TTDA machine statistics. The first version of Id World was released under license from MIT on April 15, 1987.

In our laboratory, programs can also be run on two other facilities without recompilation. The Multiprocessor Emulation Facility (MEF) is a collection of 32 TI Explorer Lisp Machines interconnected by a high-speed network that we built and has been operational since January 1986. An event-driven simulator provides the detailed timing information essential for designing a real dataflow processor.

The Monsoon Machine: We are sufficiently encouraged by the experiments conducted to date that we are proceeding with the construction of a 256-node, 1 BIPS (billion instructions per second) machine. The architecture of this machine is called "Monsoon" and was proposed by Papadopoulos and Culler [36]. It is another evolutionary step from the TTDA (and ultimately from the *U*-Interpreter) in which the resources for a code block have a direct correspondence to "frames" or "activation records" of conventional systems. The idea is basically to allocate a "frame" of wait–match storage on each code-block invocation. This frame interpretation allows the wait–match store to be a fast, *directly addressable* memory, whereas in the TTDA it had the semantics of a potentially slow associative memory.

A context, then, is merely the pointer to a frame. Tokens now have the format $\langle S, R, v \rangle_p$ where S is a pointer to an instruction in program memory, R is a pointer to the frame, v is the datum, and p, as before, the port. The instruction now contains the offset of a location in its frame where its input tokens wait to rendezvous. When a token arrives, S is used first to fetch the instruction. The offset r encoded in the instruction, together with R, is used to interrogate exactly one location, $R + r$, in wait–match memory. If empty, this token is deposited there to wait. If full, the partner token is extracted, and the instruction is dispatched.

Interestingly, it is also possible to view R as an *I*-structure address and specify fancy *I*-structure operations using S. With minor modification to the empty/full states associated with the token-store elements, *I*-structures can be implemented on the same PE hardware.

This new architecture eliminates the CBR/DBR registers of the TTDA and thus simplifies one of its resource management problems. By combining PE's and *I*-structures it reduces the engineering effort. Most importantly, our current software will run on this machine with minimal changes in the Id compiler.

A prototype single-processor Monsoon board has been operational in our laboratory since October 1988. Single-processor boards to be plugged into workstations are expected to be available in early 1990. A 16-node multiprocessor containing Monsoon processors, *I*-structure memory, and a switching network is expected to be ready by the end of 1990.

D. Macrodataflow or Pure Dataflow?

We are often asked why we take such a "fine-grained" approach to dataflow instead of using a hybrid computation model which may be termed *macrodataflow*. Rather than adopting dataflow scheduling at the individual instruction level, one considers larger chunks or "grains" of conventional von Neumann instructions that are scheduled using a program counter, with the grains themselves being scheduled in dataflow fashion.

First, we have reason to believe that the compilation problem for macrodataflow is significantly harder. Choosing an appropriate grain size and partitioning a program into such grains is a very difficult problem [38], [24], [25], [44].

Second, the macrodataflow approach requires an ability to switch a von Neumann processor very rapidly between the threads representing different grains, and no one has yet shown convincing solutions to this problem. The Denelcor HEP [39] was one attempt at such a multithreaded architecture; however, it still had inadequate support for synchronization, with some degree of busy–waiting and a limited namespace for synchronization events.

However, the appeal of a hybrid dataflow machine cannot be denied, as it represents an evolutionary step away from a von Neumann machine. Such a "von Neumann-Dataflow" machine has been studied recently in our group by Iannucci [25]. We believe that further synthesis of the dataflow and von Neumann computation models is very likely.

E. The Future

Our main research focus is determined by our belief that declarative languages on dataflow architectures constitute the right combination for general-purpose, parallel computing. However, our experiments have given us increasing confidence that Id can be a competitive language for other multiprocessors, and that dataflow architectures can competitively support other parallel languages such as parallel Fortran or C. These are exciting alternatives which we hope will attract more research attention in the future, both within our group and without.

ACKNOWLEDGMENT

The ideas presented in this paper are due to the efforts of the very talented students and research staff of the Computation Structures Group of the Laboratory for Computer Science at MIT. While every member of the group is typically interested in, and contributes to several aspects of the project, we mention here some rough areas of specialization: Languages and Reduction: K. Pingali and V. Kathail; Demand-driven evaluation: Pingali and S. Heller; Compilers: Kathail originally, then K. Traub, and now J. Hicks; Architecture: D. Culler, B. Iannucci, and G. Papadopoulos; Resource Management: Culler and P. Barth; Id World: D. Morais and R. Soley; Simulator: S. Brobst, A. Chien and G. Maa; Emulator: Culler, Morais, and Traub; MEF: Papadopoulos, Soley and A. Boughton.

Our thanks to the referees for detailed comments which spurred a major reworking of this paper, and to P. Barth, S. Brobst, D. Culler, G. Papadopoulos, L. Snyder, R. Soley, and N. Tarbet for a careful reading and comments on the revision.

REFERENCES

[1] W. B. Ackerman and J. B. Dennis, "VAL—A value-oriented algorithmic language: Preliminary reference manual," Tech. Rep. TR-218, Computat. Structures Group, MIT Lab. for Comput. Sci., 545 Technology Square, Cambridge, MA 02139, June 1979.

[2] J. Allen and K. Kennedy, "PFC: A program to convert FORTRAN to parallel form," Tech. Rep. MASC-TR82-6, Rice Univ., Houston, TX, Mar. 1982.

[3] M. Amamiya, R. Hasegawa, O. Nakamura, and H. Mikami, "A list-oriented data flow machine," in *Proc. Nat. Comput. Conf.*, AFIPS, 1982, pp. 143–151.

[4] Arvind and J. D. Brock, "Resource managers in functional programming," *J. Parallel Distrib. Comput.*, vol. 1, no. 1, Jan. 1984.

[5] Arvind and D. E. Culler, "Dataflow architectures," in *Annual Reviews in Computer Science, Vol. 1*. Palo Alto, CA: Annual Reviews Inc., 1986, pp. 225–253.

[6] ——, "Managing resources in a parallel machine," in *Fifth Generation Computer Architectures, 1986*. New York: Elsevier Science Publishers, B.V., 1986, pp. 103–121.

[7] Arvind, D. E. Culler, and G. L. Maa, "Assessing the benefits of fine-grained parallelism in dataflow programs," *Int. J. Supercomput. Appl.*, vol. 2, no. 3, Fall 1988.

[8] Arvind and K. Ekanadham, "Future scientific programming on parallel machines," *J. Parallel Distrib. Comput.*, vol. 5, no. 5, Oct. 1988.

[9] Arvind and K. Gostelow, "The U-Interpreter," *IEEE Comput. Mag.*, vol. 15, Feb. 1982.

[10] Arvind, K. Gostelow, and W. Plouffe, "An asynchronous programming language and computing machine," Tech. Rep. TR-114a, Dep. Inform. Comput. Sci., Univ. of California, Irvine, CA, Dec. 1978.

[11] Arvind and R. A. Iannucci, "Two fundamental issues in multiprocessing," in *Proc. DFVLR—Conf. 1987 Parallel Processing Sci. Eng.*, BonnBad Godesberg, W. Germany, June 25–29, 1987.

[12] Arvind, R. S. Nikhil, and K. K. Pingali, "I-Structures: Data structures for parallel computing," in *Proc. Workshop Graph Reduction*, Santa Fe, New Mexico. Berlin, Germany: Springer-Verlag, Sept./Oct. 1986. Lecture Notes in Computer Science 279.

[13] ——, "Id Nouveau reference manual, Part II: Semantics," Tech. Rep., Computat. Structures Group, MIT Lab. Comput. Sci., 545 Technology Square, Cambridge, MA 02139, Apr. 1987.

[14] Arvind and R. E. Thomas, "I-structures: An efficient data type for parallel machines," Tech. Rep. TM 178, Computat. Structures Group, MIT Lab. for Comput. Sci., 545 Technology Square, Cambridge, MA 02139, Sept. 1980.

[15] L. Augustsson and T. Johnsson, "Lazy ML user's manual," Tech. Rep. (Preliminary Draft), Programming Methodology Group Rep., Dep. Comput. Sci., Chalmers Univ. of Technol. and Univ. of Goteborg, S-421 96 Goteborg, Sweden, Jan. 1988.

[16] D. E. Culler, "Resource management for the tagged token dataflow architecture," Tech. Rep. TR-332, Computat. Structures Group, MIT Lab. for Comput. Sci., 545 Technology Square, Cambridge, MA 02139, 1985.

[17] ——, "Effective dataflow execution of scientific applications," Ph.D. dissertation, Lab. Comput. Sci., Massachusetts Instit. Technol., Cambridge, MA, 02139, 1989.

[18] J. B. Dennis, "First version of a data flow procedure language," in *Proc. Programming Symp.*, G. Goos and J. Hartmanis, Eds. Paris, France, 1974. Berlin, Germany: Springer-Verlag, 1974. Lecture Notes in Computer Science 19.

[19] J. Fairbairn and S. C. Wray, "TIM: A simple abstract machine for executing supercombinators," in *Proc. 1987 Functional Programming Comput. Architecture Conf.*, Portland, OR, Sept. 1987.

[20] B. Goldberg and P. Hudak, "Alfalfa: Distributed graph reduction on a hypercube multiprocessor," Tech. Rep., Dep. Comput. Sci., Yale Univ., New Haven, CT, Nov. 1986.

[21] A. Gottlieb, R. Grishman, C. Kruskal, K. McAuliffe, L. Rudolph, and M. Snir, "The NYU Ultracomputer—Designing an MIMD shared memory parallel computer," *IEEE Trans. Comput.*, vol. C-32, no. 2, pp. 175–189, Feb. 1983.

[22] J. R. Gurd, C. Kirkham, and I. Watson, "The Manchester prototype dataflow computer," *Commun. ACM*, vol. 28, no. 1, pp. 34–52, Jan. 1985.

[23] K. Hiraki, S. Sekiguchi, and T. Shimada, "System architecture of a dataflow supercomputer," Tech. Rep., Comput. Syst. Division, Electrochemical Lab., 1-1-4 Umezono, Sakura-mura, Niihari-gun, Ibaraki, 305, Japan, 1987.

[24] P. Hudak and B. Goldberg, "Serial combinators: "Optimal" grains of parallelism," in *Proc. Functional Programming Languages Architures.* Nancy, France, pp. 382–399. Berlin, Germany: Springer-Verlag, Sept. 1985, Lecture Notes in Computer Science 201.

[25] R. A. Iannucci, "A dataflow/von Neumann hybrid architecture," Ph.D. dissertation, Lab. for Comput. Sci., Massachusetts Institute of Technology, Cambridge, MA 02139, May 1988.

[26] T. Johnsson, "Efficient compilation of lazy evaluation," *ACM SIGPLAN Notices*, vol. 19, no. 6, pp. 58–69, June 1984. *Proc. ACM SIGPLAN '84 Symp. Compiler Construction*.

[27] ——, "Lambda lifting: Transforming programs to recursive equations," in *Proc. Functional Programming Languages and Comput. Architecture*, Nancy, France. Berlin, Germany: Springer-Verlag, Sept. 1985. Lecture Notes in Computer Science 201.

[28] D. J. Kuck, R. Kuhn, D. Padua, B. Leasure, and M. Wolfe, "Dependence graphs and compiler optimizations," in *Proc. 8th ACM Symp. Principles Programming Languages*, Jan. 1981, pp. 207–218.

[29] D. J. Kuck, D. Lawrie, R. Cytron, A. Sameh, and D. Gajski, "The architecture and programming of the Cedar System," Tech. Rep. Cedar No. 21, Lab. for Advanced Supercomput., Dep. Comput. Sci., Univ. of Illinois at Urbana-Champaign, Aug. 12, 1983.

[30] J. McGraw, S. Skedzielewski, S. Allan, D. Grit, R. Oldehoeft, J. Glauert, P. Hohensee, and I. Dobes, "Sisal reference manual," Tech. Rep., Lawrence Livermore Nat. Lab., 1984.

[31] R. Milner, "A proposal for standard ML," in *Proc. 1984 ACM Symp. Lisp Functional Programming*, Aug. 1984, pp. 184–197.

[32] NEC, *Advanced Product Information User's Manual: μPD7281*, NEC Electronics Inc., Mountain View, CA, 1985.

[33] R. S. Nikhil, "Id World reference manual," Tech. Rep., Computat. Structures Group, MIT Lab. for Comput. Sci., 545 Technology Square, Cambridge, MA 02139, Apr. 1987.

[34] ——, "Id (Version 88.1) reference manual," Tech. Rep. CSG Memo 284, MIT Lab. for Comput. Sci., 545 Technology Square, Cambridge, MA 02139, Aug. 1988.

[35] D. A. Padua and M. J. Wolfe, "Advanced compiler optimizations for supercomputers," *Commun. ACM*, vol. 29, no. 12, Dec. 1986.

[36] G. M. Papadopoulos, "Implementation of a general-purpose dataflow multiprocessor," Ph.D. dissertation, Lab. for Comput. Sci., Massachusetts Instit. Technol., Cambridge, MA 02139, Aug. 1988.

[37] S. L. Peyton-Jones, C. Clack, J. Salkild, and M. Hardie, "GRIP—A high performance architecture for parallel graph reduction," in *Proc. 3rd Int. Conf. Functional Programming Comput. Architecture*, Portland, OR, Sept. 1987.

[38] V. Sarkar and J. Hennessy, "Partitioning parallel programs for macro-dataflow," in *Proc. 1986 ACM Conf. Lisp Functional Programming*, Cambridge, MA, Aug. 4–6, 1986, pp. 202–211.

[39] B. J. Smith, "A pipelined, shared resource MIMD computer," in *Proc. 1978 Int. Conf. Parallel Processing*, 1978, pp. 6–8.

[40] N. Takahashi and M. Amamiya, "A dataflow processor array system: Design and analysis," in *Proc. 10th Int. Symp. Comput. Architecture*, Stockholm, Sweden, June 1983, pp. 243–250.

[41] P. Tang, C.-Q. Zhu, and P.-C. Yew, "An implementation of Cedar synchronization primitives," Tech. Rep. Cedar No. 32, Lab. for Advanced Supercomput., Dep. Comput. Sci., Univ. of Illinois at Urbana-Champaign, Apr. 3, 1984.

[42] T. Temma, S. Hasegawa, and S. Hanaki, "Dataflow processor for image processing," in *Proc. 11th Int. Symp. Mini and Microcomputers*, Monterey, CA, pp. 52–56, 1980.

[43] K. R. Traub, "A compiler for the MIT tagged token dataflow architecture," Master's thesis, Tech. Rep. TR-370, MIT Lab. for Comput. Sci., Cambridge, MA 02139, Aug. 1986.

[44] ——, "Sequential implementation of non-strict languages," PhD dissertation, MIT Lab. for Comput. Sci., 545 Technology Square, Cambridge, MA 02139, May 1988.

[45] D. A. Turner, "A new implementation technique for applicative languages," *Software: Practice and Experience*, vol. 9, no. 1, pp. 31–49, 1979.

[46] ——, "Miranda, A non-strict functional language with polymorphic types," in *Proc. Functional Programming Languages Comput. Architecture*, Nancy, France. Berlin, Germany: Springer-Verlag, Sept. 1985. Lecture Notes in Computer Science 201, pp. 1–16.

[47] W. W. Wadge and E. A. Ashcroft, *Lucid, The Dataflow Programming Language*. London, England: Academic, 1985.

[48] T. Yuba, T. Shimada, K. Hiraki, and H. Kashiwagi, "Sigma-1: A dataflow computer for scientific computation," Tech. Rep., Electrotechnical Lab., 1-1-4 Umesono, Sakuramura, Niiharigun, Ibaraki 305, Japan, 1984.

Architecture and applications of the HEP multiprocessor computer system

Burton J. Smith
Denelcor, Inc., 14221 E. 4th Avenue, Aurora, Colorado 80011

Abstract

The HEP computer system is a large scale scientific parallel computer employing shared-resource MIMD architecture. The hardware and software facilities provided by the system are described, and techniques found to be useful in programming the system are also discussed.

Introduction

The HEP computer system[1] is a large scale scientific parallel computer employing shared-resource MIMD architecture[2]. In this particular implementation, the processors are pipelined to support many concurrent processes, with each pipeline segment responsible for a different phase of instruction interpretation. Each processor has its own program memory, general purpose registers, and functional units; a number of these processors are connected to shared data memory modules by means of a very high speed pipelined packet switching network. The extensive use of pipelining in conjunction with the shared resource idea is synergistic in several useful and important ways, and results in a very flexible and effective architecture. For example, the switch used to interconnect processors and memories is modular, and is designed to allow a given system to be field-expanded. The increased memory access times that result from greater physical distances can be compensated for by using more processes in each processor because the switch is pipelined.

An overall block diagram of a typical HEP configuration is shown in Figure 1. The switch network shown has 28 nodes; it interconnects four processors, four data memory modules, an I/O cache module, an I/O control processor, and four other I/O devices. Systems of this kind can be built to include as many as 16 processors, 128 data memory modules, and 4 I/O cache modules. Each processor performs 10 million instructions per second (MIPS), and the switch bandwidth is 10 million 64 bit words per second in every network link. Data memory module bandwidth is 10 million 64 bit words per second, and each I/O cache supports sequential or random access I/O at sustained rates of 32 million bytes per second.

The remainder of this paper discusses the hardware and software architecture of the system. An overview will be given of each of the major components of the system, followed by a programmer's view of the facilities provided by these components.

Processor and data memory

A simplified diagram of the HEP processor internal organization is shown in Figure 2. The process status word (PSW) contains the program counter and other state information for a HEP process; these PSW's circulate in a control loop which includes a queue, an incrementer, and a pipelined delay. The delay is such that a particular PSW cannot circulate around the control loop any faster than data can circulate around the data loop consisting of register memory and the function units. As the program counter in a circulating PSW increments to point to successive instructions in program memory, the function units are able to complete each instruction in time to allow the next instruction for that PSW to be influenced by its effects. The control and data loops are pipelined in eight 100 nanosecond segments, so that as long as at least eight PSW's are in the control loop the processor executes 10 million instructions per second. A particular process cannot execute faster that 1.25 million instructions per second, and will execute at a lesser rate if more than eight PSW's are in the control loop.

The PSW contains a 20 bit program counter to allow for program memory configurations ranging from 32K to 1024K words. Each instruction in program memory is 64 bits long, and typically consists of an opcode and three register memory addresses. These addresses can be modified by the addition of an index value from the PSW to allow reentrant programming. The register memory consists of 2048 general purpose 64 bit registers, augmented by a 4096 location constant memory. Constant memory may only be modified by supervisor processes.

One of the function units, the scheduler function unit (SFU), is responsible for implementing load and store instructions to transmit data between register memory and data memory. When such an instruction is executed, the SFU sends a switch message packet containing a 32 bit data memory address, a return address identifying both processor and process, and 64 bits of data if a store instruction was executed. The SFU also removes the process that executed the instruction from the control loop, and does not reinsert it until a response packet is received from the switch. When that response packet arrives, the SFU writes the data portion of the response in the appropriate register if a load instruction was executed. In order to perform these functions, the SFU is equipped with a queue similar to the queue in the control loop of the processor proper, and a process migrates freely between these two queues as it initiates and completes data memory reference instructions.

The various function units of the HEP processor support the data types shown in Figure 3. The floating point formats are sign-magnitude and use a seven bit, excess 64 hexadecimal exponent. Integer formats are twos complement. The various precisions for each data type are implemented by loading and storing partial words in data memory using either the leftmost or rightmost part of the register. In addition, load instructions can specify sign extension instead of zero extension for right justified partial word load instructions.

The floating point operations implemented by the processor are floating point add, subtract, multiply, divide, and floating point compare instructions that optionally produce integer 1, floating point 1.0, or a 64 bit vector of all 1's as "true" values and zero as "false" values. Unnormalized floating point add and subtract are also implemented, as are conversion instructions between floating point and integer (the Fortran functions FLOAT, INT, and AINT). Integer functions are add, subtract, multiply, arithmetic shift, and compare instructions analogous to those for floating point. Both halves of the 128 bit twos complement product of two integers are available. Bit vector instructions include all sixteen Boolean functions, logical and circular shifts, instructions which return the numeric bit position of the leftmost "1" or "0" in a register, and instructions which set or reset a bit at a given numeric position in a register.

The control instructions available provide not only for the loading, storing and modification of the executing PSW to implement conditional branches and subroutine calls, but also for the conditional creation and termination of processes. These latter functions are performed by ordinary (unprivileged) instructions, and allow the user to control the amount of concurrency with very low overhead. A supervisor call instruction allows user processes to create supervisor processes, which in turn may execute privileged instructions to manage the user processes and perform I/O.

Cooperating parallel processes must have some way of synchronizing with each other to allow data sharing. In HEP, this facility is provided by associating an access state with each register memory and data memory location. In data memory, the access states are "full" and "empty"; a load instruction can be made to wait until the addressed location is "full" and indivisibly (i.e., without allowing an intervening reference to the location) set the location "empty". Similarly, a store instruction can wait for "empty" and then set "full" at any location in data memory. In register memory, an instruction can require that both sources be "full" and the destination "empty", and then set both sources "empty" and the destination "full". To ensure the indivisibility of this kind of operation, a third access state, "reserved", is set in the destination register location when the source data are sent to the function units, and only when the function unit stores the result is the destination set "full". No instruction can successfully execute if any of the registers it uses is "reserved".

A process failing to execute an instruction because of improper register access state is merely reinserted in the queue with an unincremented program counter so that it will reattempt the instruction on its next turn for execution. A process executing a load or store instruction that fails because of improper data memory access state is reinserted in the SFU queue and generates a new switch message on its next attempt.

One simple way to exploit the parallelism available in HEP is to run several independent programs simultaneously. To protect independent programs from each other, base and limit registers in program memory, register memory, and data memory are associated with processes. A set of processes having the same protection domain (the same base and limit register values) is called a task. HEP support up to seven user tasks and seven corresponding supervisor tasks in each processor. When a user process executes a create instruction, the new process runs in the same task as the originating process; privileged instructions exist to allow supervisors to create processes in any task or to kill all of the processes in a task.

A HEP job consists of one or more tasks, normally intended to execute on a like number of processors. The tasks making up a job have disjoint allocations in program and register memory, but an identical allocation in data memory to allow them to share data and synchronize. Supervisor calls are used by a process in one task to create a process in a different task of the same job. When a job is submitted to the system, the user specifies the maximum number of processes that will ever be active in each task; the operating system only loads the job when it can guarantee that there are enough processes available in each processor. The maximum number of user processes supported by a processor is 50, and these may be distributed in any way whatsoever among the seven (or fewer) user tasks.

Switch

The HEP switch is a synchronous, modular packet switching network consisting of an arbitrary number of nodes. Each node is connected to its neighbors (which may be processors, data memory modules, or other nodes) by three full-duplex ports. Each node receives three message packets on each of its three ports every 100 nanoseconds, and attempts to route the messages in such a way that the distance from each message to its addressed destination is reduced. To accomplish this, each node has three routing tables, one per port, which are initialized when the system is initialized. The tables are indexed by the destination address and contain the identification of the preferred port out of which the packet should be sent.

When a conflict for a port occurs, the node does not enqueue messages; instead, it routes all messages immediately to output ports. It is the responsibility of the neighbors of the node to make sure that incorrectly routed messages eventually reach their correct destinations. To help accomplish this, each message contains a priority which is initially 1 and is incremented whenever a message is routed incorrectly. In a conflict between messages of differing priority, the message with the highest priority is routed correctly. As a consequence, devices connected to the switch must immediately reinsert arriving messages not addressed to them in preference to inserting new messages.

Empty messages are just those of priority zero; zero priority messages do not increase in priority and always lose conflicts. Also, since the ports of the switch nodes and the devices connected to it are full duplex, an Eulerian circuit of the switch is guaranteed to exist. Such an Eulerian circuit traverses every port exactly once in each direction. Packets with the maximum priority of 15 are sent on such an Eulerian circuit, independent of destination address, to ensure that no conflicts between two of these messages occur. When a priority 15 message eventually reaches its addressed destination, it is recognized and removed from the switch in the normal manner. Like the routing table data, the Eulerian circuit information is loaded into each switch node when the system is initialized.

Each switch node checks the parity of the incoming messages, and also checks that the routing it performs is a permutation of the ports. If a check fails, the switch node signals the diagnostic and maintenance subsystem of the HEP that an error has occurred. The failing port or node, or a failed processor or memory for that matter, can be removed from the system just by reprogramming the routing tables to reflect the reduced configuration. To avoid splitting the system in half, the graph of the switch must be at least biconnected; that is, there must exist two disjoint paths from any node to any other. If the port connecting a processor or a memory to the switch fails in either direction, the effect is the same as if the processor or memory itself fails.

The propagation delay for a message in the switch is 50 nanoseconds for each port traversed. The pipeline rate is one message per 100 nanoseconds per port. To ensure that message routing conflicts are synchronized, the switch must be two-colorable, so that messages conflict at nodes of one color on even multiples of 50 nanoseconds and at the other color on odd multiples. Excepting this constraint, the graph of the switch is totally arbitrary. Adjacent nodes may be separated by up to four meters of connecting wire to allow a great deal of flexibility in system configuration. A HEP system may be field-expanded by adding processors, memories, and switch nodes up to the maximum allowed.

I/O facilities

The HEP High Speed I/O Subsystem (HSIOS) includes from one to four I/O cache modules, each of which serves as a buffer between the switch and 32 I/O channels. Each I/O channel can support transfer rates up to 2.5 million bytes per second. The I/O cache supports this transfer rate by all channels simultaneously, and can concurrently transfer 80 million bytes per second via its switch port for a total bandwidth of 160 million bytes per second. An I/O cache can range in size from 8 million to 128 million bytes in 8 million byte increments, so that the maximum amount of I/O cache memory implementable in a single HEP system is 512 million bytes. The reason for this large amount of memory is to allow a large page size to be used in conjunction with a large number of disks or tapes. The large page size (40 kilobytes nominal) means that mechanical delays can be made insignificant compared to data transfer times to increase channel utilization, and the large number of channels allows data to be distributed across many disks to provide high I/O bandwidth through the use of parallelism. The distribution of data is provided for by interleaving logical records among many files, one file per disk, and is accomplished not by the file system itself but by the library I/O routines that the user calls. In this way, the management of distributed data is entirely under the user's control, allowing him to exchange reliability for speed as required by his application.

The I/O channels are controlled by an I/O control processor (IOCP). The IOCP is interrupted both by the channels, when I/O operations are completed, and by arrivals of switch messages from supervisor processes running in the processors. The function of the IOCP is to schedule the I/O requests from the supervisors on the channels. To a supervisor, the IOCP-switch interface appears as a sequence of special memory locations in the data memory address space, and an I/O request is made by storing the request at one of these special locations. When the switch message arrives at the IOCP-switch interface, the IOCP services the interrupt by acquiring the message from the interface and enqueueing it internally on a queue served by the I/O channel that was requested. When the request reaches the head of the queue, it is serviced; on completion, a response message is loaded into the switch interface and sent back to the processor from which the request came. The effect seen by the supervisor process itself is extremely simple; a page I/O request was made and completed by executing a store instruction. The fact that the store instruction may have taken several milliseconds to execute has no effect on the performance of the processor if enough processes remain in the control loop.

When a file is opened, the number of cache frames allocated to the file may be specified as a parameter (the default quantity is 2). Another parameter specifies the sequential direction (forward or backward). All data transfer instructions perform sequential I/O in the specified direction, and the supervisor handling the requests attempts to "read ahead" and "write behind" the pages surrounding the current file position. To accomplish random I/O, a separate command is implemented to allow the current file position to be changed. This feature allows caching of data to proceed concurrently with user processing.

A HEP file consists of a header page and zero or more data pages. The header is kept in the I/O cache as long as the file is open, and contains either the data itself or pairs of pointers to the disk locations of the data pages and the cache frames holding those pages, if any. Since all pages are the same size, both disk and cache space allocation are performed using bit tables and are extremely fast; this is an important consideration when a large number of supervisor processes are all attempting to allocate space in parallel. To the user, a file appears to be a randomly addressable sequence of records or words, and there are no "access methods" provided by the file system itself.

When a user process executes a supervisor call to perform I/O, the supervisor process first computes the page or pages containing the data from the current file position and from the amount of data to be transferred. It then verifies that those pages are in the cache, requesting them, from the IOCP as necessary. Next, it transfers the data between the cache and the user's buffer, and changes the current file position based on the sequential direction (forward or backward). Finally, the supervisor schedules page "write behind" and "read ahead" with the IOCP as required, and returns to the user without waiting for the IOCP. If a page was never modified, it is not written on the disk by "write behind". Moreover, a reference count is maintained for each cached page and for the file as a whole to allow a file to be multiply opened by a large number of processes. A page is actually uncached only when its reference count is zero, and the file header itself is uncached when the file reference count is zero.

Fortran extensions

Two kinds of extensions were added to HEP Fortran to allow the programmer to write explicit parallel algorithms. The first class of extensions allows parallel process creation. In HEP Fortran, a CREATE statement, syntactically similar to a CALL, causes a subroutine to run in parallel with its creator. The RESUME statement, syntactically like RETURN, causes the caller of a subroutine to resume execution in parallel with the subroutine. If a subroutine was CREATEd, a RESUME has no effect, and a RETURN causes the termination of the process executing the subroutine if the subroutine was CREATEd or if it previously executed a RESUME.

The second extension allows the programmer to use the access states provided by the HEP hardware. Any variable whose name begins with the character "$" is called an asynchronous variable, and has the property that an evaluation of the variable waits until the associated location is "full" and sets it "empty" while fetching its value. An assignment to the variable waits until the variable is "empty" and then sets it "full" while storing the new value. A PURGE statement is used to unconditionally set the access state to "empty".

HEP Fortran generates fully reentrant code, and dynamically allocates registers and local variables in data memory as required by the program. For example, it is often useful to place a CREATE statement in a loop so that several parallel processes will execute identical programs on different local data. An example is shown in Figure 4; in this instance, the program creates NPROCS-1 processes all executing subroutine S, and then itself executes the subroutine S by calling it, with the result that NPROCS processes are ultimately executing S. The parameter $IP is used here to identify each process uniquely. Since parameter addresses rather that values are passed, $IP is asynchronous and is filled by the creating program and emptied within S. This prevents the creating program from changing the value of $IP until S has made a copy of it. The asynchronous variable $NP is used to record the number of processes executing S. When S is finished, $NP is decremented, and when the creating program discovers that $NP has reached zero, all NPROCS processes have completed execution of S (excepting possibly the RETURN statement).

HEP programming

The facilities provided by the HEP hardware and software are clearly well suited to pipelining as a means of parallel algorithm implementation. The access states "full" and "empty" can be viewed as a mechanism for passing messages between processes using single-word queues. It is also clear that a location can be used to implement a critical section merely by requiring processes to empty the location upon entry and fill it upon exit. Other common synchronization mechanisms can be implemented using similar techiques. Processes can be dynamically initiated and terminated to avoid busy waiting.

One frequently occurring situation in parallel programming involves the computation of recurrences of the form

$$X = X \text{ op } Y$$

where op is commutative and associative and Y does not depend on X. One example occurs in the use of $NP in Figure 4; another obvious example is vector inner product. The difficulties with merely writing

$$\$X = \$X \text{ op } Y$$

are twofold. First, all processes are competing for access to $X and interfere with each other; second, the final value of $X often must be made available to the various processes in some independent way, perhaps involving another recurrence similar to the recurrence for $NP in Figure 4.

One attractive method which avoids these difficulties requires log P locations for each of the P processes. The method simultaneously computes the final value of X and broadcasts it to the P processes in time O(log P). The idea is to implement an appropriate interconnection network (in software) that has the required computational property at each element. In this case, the property required is that the two identical element outputs be the result of applying op to the two inputs. One HEP Fortan program to accomplish this task is shown in Figure 5 with op = + and with a Staran flip network[3] interconnection.

Notice that since the function used to compute K from I is always a bijection, there is no conflict for the elements of $A by the processes. That is, only one process is attempting to fill a given location in $A and only one process is attempting to empty it. Overtaking by processes is not possible because of this fact. In addition, the same array $A can be reused immediately to perform a different function (e.g., global minimum) as long as the same network topology is used. Analogous techniques, sometimes requiring other network topologies, can be used to permute the elements of X, to sort X, to perform fast Fourier transforms, and so forth.

Another important HEP programming technique allows processes to schedule themselves. In the simplest case, a number of totally independent computational steps is to be performed that significantly exceeds the number of processes available; moreover, the execution time of the steps may be widely varying. The self-scheduling idea is to allow each process to acquire the next computational step dynamically when it finishes the previous one. In a more complex situation involving dependencies and priorities, the processes might perform a significant amount of computation in scheduling themselves, but in most cases the method is quite efficient. Figure 6 shows an example of an ordinary DO loop in which all iterations are presumed independent; Figure 7 is a parallel version of Figure 6 which uses self-scheduling. One of the most attractive benefits of self-scheduling a loop is that there is no need to worry about poor process utilization resulting from an unsatisfactory a priori schedule.

Conclusions

The HEP computer system represents a unique and very flexible architecture. First, its modularity is exceptional even for an MIMD computer. Second, the availability of a very natural synchronization primitive at every memory location allows the programmer a large amount of freedom in developing parallel algorithms. Finally, a mechanism is provided to allow the user to control the number of processes dynamically in order to take advantage of varying amounts of parallelism in a problem.

References

1. Smith, B.J., "A Pipelined, Shared Resource MIMD Computer," Proceedings of the 1978 International Conference on Parallel Processing, pp. 6-8.

2. Flynn, M.J., "Some Computer Organizations and their Effectiveness, IEEE Transactions on Computers, Vol. 21, pp. 948-960 (Sept. 1972).

3. Batcher, K.E., "The Flip Network in Staran," Proceedings of the 1976 International Conference on Parallel Processing, pp. 65-71.

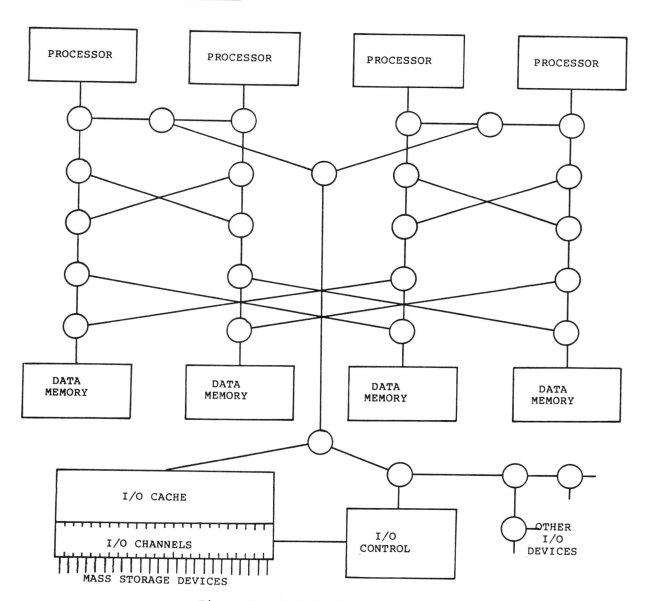

Figure 1. A typical HEP system

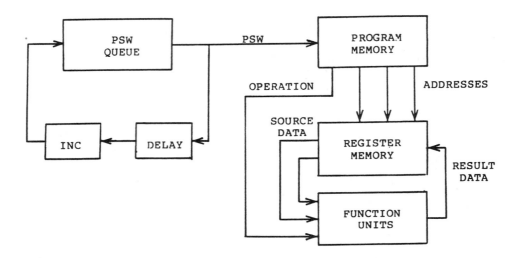

Figure 2. Simplified HEP processor

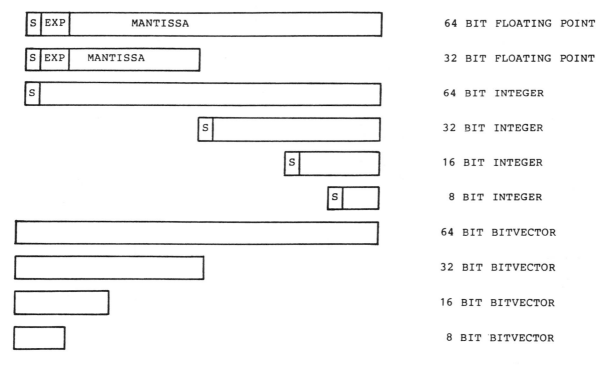

Figure 3. Data types

```
            :
            :
      PURGE $IP, $NP
      $NP = NPROCS
      DO 10 I = 2, NPROCS
      $IP = I-1
      CREATE S($IP,$NP)
   10 CONTINUE
      $IP = NPROCS
      CALL S($IP,$NP)
C     WAIT FOR ALL PROCESSES TO FINISH
   20 N = $NP
      $NP = N
      IF (N .NE. 0) GO TO 20
            :
            :
      SUBROUTINE S($IP,$NP)
      MYNUM = $IP
            :
            :
      $NP = $NP-1
      RETURN
      END
            :
            :
```

Figure 4.   HEP Fortran example

```
C     REPLACE EACH ELEMENT OF THE VECTOR X
C     BY THE SUM OF THE ELEMENTS OF X
C     USING THE INITIALLY EMPTY ARRAY $A.
C     P = 2**L PROCESSES EXECUTE THIS PROGRAM.
C     THE PROCESS IDENTIFER IS I.
      DIMENSION X(P), A(P,L)
      JPOW = 2
C     JPOW IS 2 TO THE J POWER
      DO 10 J = 1,L
C     COMPUTE THE PROCESS K = (I-1) EXOR(JPOW/2)+1
C     WITH WHICH THIS PROCESS WILL EXCHANGE DATA
      K = ((I-1)/JPOW)*JPOW + MOD (I-1 + JPOW/2,JPOW)+1
      JPOW = JPOW*2
C     NOW EXCHANGE DATA AND ACCUMULATE
      $A(K,J) = X(I)
      X(I) = X(I) + $A(I,J)
   10 CONTINUE
```

Figure 5.   Summation by network simulation

```
      DO 10 I = J, K, L
            :
            :
   10 CONTINUE
```

Figure 6.   A DO loop

```
      PURGE $IV
      $IV = J
C     CREATE ANY NUMBER OF PROCESSES EXECUTING
    1 I = $IV
C     THIS PROCESS HAS SEIZED AN ITERATION INDEX
C     LET ANOTHER PROCESS OBTAIN THE NEXT INDEX
      $IV = I + L
C     TERMINATE IF THROUGH
      IF (I .GT. K) RETURN
            :
            :
      GO TO 1
```

Figure 7. A self-scheduled loop

Exploiting Choice: Instruction Fetch and Issue on an Implementable Simultaneous Multithreading Processor

Dean M. Tullsen*, Susan J. Eggers*, Joel S. Emer[†], Henry M. Levy*,
Jack L. Lo*, and Rebecca L. Stamm[†]

*Dept of Computer Science and Engineering
University of Washington
Box 352350
Seattle, WA 98195-2350

[†]Digital Equipment Corporation
HLO2-3/J3
77 Reed Road
Hudson, MA 01749

Abstract

Simultaneous multithreading is a technique that permits multiple independent threads to issue multiple instructions each cycle. In previous work we demonstrated the performance potential of simultaneous multithreading, based on a somewhat idealized model. In this paper we show that the throughput gains from simultaneous multithreading can be achieved *without* extensive changes to a conventional wide-issue superscalar, either in hardware structures or sizes. We present an architecture for simultaneous multithreading that achieves three goals: (1) it minimizes the architectural impact on the conventional superscalar design, (2) it has minimal performance impact on a single thread executing alone, and (3) it achieves significant throughput gains when running multiple threads. Our simultaneous multithreading architecture achieves a throughput of 5.4 instructions per cycle, a 2.5-fold improvement over an unmodified superscalar with similar hardware resources. This speedup is enhanced by an advantage of multithreading previously unexploited in other architectures: the ability to favor for fetch and issue those threads most efficiently using the processor each cycle, thereby providing the "best" instructions to the processor.

1   Introduction

Simultaneous multithreading (SMT) is a technique that permits multiple independent threads to issue multiple instructions each cycle to a superscalar processor's functional units. SMT combines the multiple-instruction-issue features of modern superscalars with the latency-hiding ability of multithreaded architectures. Unlike conventional multithreaded architectures [1, 2, 15, 23], which depend on fast context switching to share processor execution resources, all hardware contexts in an SMT processor are active simultaneously, competing each cycle for all available resources. This dynamic sharing of the functional units allows simultaneous multithreading to substantially increase throughput, attacking the two major impediments to processor utilization — long latencies and limited per-thread parallelism. Tullsen, *et al.*, [27] showed the potential of

an SMT processor to achieve significantly higher throughput than either a wide superscalar or a multithreaded processor. That paper also demonstrated the advantages of simultaneous multithreading over multiple processors on a single chip, due to SMT's ability to dynamically assign execution resources where needed each cycle.

Those results showed SMT's potential based on a somewhat idealized model. This paper extends that work in four significant ways. First, we demonstrate that the throughput gains of simultaneous multithreading are possible *without* extensive changes to a conventional, wide-issue superscalar processor. We propose an architecture that is more comprehensive, realistic, and heavily leveraged off existing superscalar technology. Our simulations show that a minimal implementation of simultaneous multithreading achieves throughput 1.8 times that of the unmodified superscalar; small tuning of this architecture increases that gain to 2.5 (reaching throughput as high as 5.4 instructions per cycle). Second, we show that SMT need not compromise single-thread performance. Third, we use our more detailed architectural model to analyze and relieve bottlenecks that did not exist in the more idealized model. Fourth, we show how simultaneous multithreading creates an advantage previously unexploitable in other architectures: namely, the ability to choose the "best" instructions, from all threads, for both fetch and issue each cycle. By favoring the threads most efficiently using the processor, we can boost the throughput of our limited resources. We present several simple heuristics for this selection process, and demonstrate how such heuristics, when applied to the fetch mechanism, can increase throughput by as much as 37%.

This paper is organized as follows. Section 2 presents our baseline simultaneous multithreading architecture, comparing it with existing superscalar technology. Section 3 describes our simulator and our workload, and Section 4 shows the performance of the baseline architecture. In Section 5, we examine the instruction fetch process, present several heuristics for improving it based on intelligent instruction selection, and give performance results to differentiate those heuristics. Section 6 examines the instruction issue process in a similar way. We then use the best designs chosen from our fetch and issue studies in Section 7 as a basis to discover bottlenecks for further performance improvement. We discuss related work in Section 8 and summarize our results in Section 9.

This research was supported by ONR grants N00014-92-J-1395 and N00014-94-1-1136, NSF grants CCR-9200832 and CDA-9123308, NSF PYI Award MIP-9058439, the Washington Technology Center, Digital Equipment Corporation, and fellowships from Intel and the Computer Measurement Group.

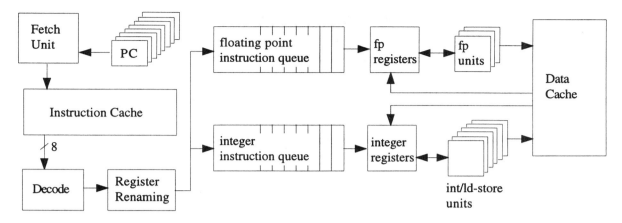

Figure 1: **Our base simultaneous multithreading hardware architecture.**

2   A Simultaneous Multithreading Processor Architecture

In this section we present the architecture of our simultaneous multithreading processor. We show that the throughput gains provided by simultaneous multithreading are possible without adding undue complexity to a conventional superscalar processor design.

Our SMT architecture is derived from a high-performance, out-of-order, superscalar architecture (Figure 1, without the extra program counters) which represents a projection of current superscalar design trends 3-5 years into the future. This superscalar processor fetches up to eight instructions per cycle; fetching is controlled by a conventional system of branch target buffer, branch prediction, and subroutine return stacks. Fetched instructions are then decoded and passed to the register renaming logic, which maps logical registers onto a pool of physical registers, removing false dependences. Instructions are then placed in one of two instruction queues. Those instruction queues are similar to the ones used by the MIPS R10000 [20] and the HP PA-8000 [21], in this case holding instructions until they are issued. Instructions are issued to the functional units out-of-order when their operands are available. After completing execution, instructions are retired in-order, freeing physical registers that are no longer needed.

Our SMT architecture is a straightforward extension to this conventional superscalar design. We made changes only when necessary to enable simultaneous multithreading, and in general, structures were not replicated or resized to support SMT or a multithreaded workload. Thus, nearly all hardware resources remain completely available even when there is only a single thread in the system. The changes necessary to support simultaneous multithreading on that architecture are:

- multiple program counters and some mechanism by which the fetch unit selects one each cycle,

- a separate return stack for each thread for predicting subroutine return destinations,

- per-thread instruction retirement, instruction queue flush, and trap mechanisms,

- a thread id with each branch target buffer entry to avoid predicting phantom branches, and

- a larger register file, to support logical registers for all threads plus additional registers for register renaming. The size of the register file affects the pipeline (we add two extra stages) and the scheduling of load-dependent instructions, which we discuss later in this section.

Noticeably absent from this list is a mechanism to enable simultaneous multithreaded scheduling of instructions onto the functional units. Because any apparent dependences between instructions from different threads are removed by the register renaming phase, a conventional instruction queue (IQ) designed for dynamic scheduling contains all of the functionality necessary for simultaneous multithreading. The instruction queue is shared by all threads and an instruction from any thread in the queue can issue when its operands are available.

We fetch from one program counter (PC) each cycle. The PC is chosen, in round-robin order, from among those threads not already experiencing an I cache miss. This scheme provides simultaneous multithreading at the point of issue, but only fine-grain multithreading of the fetch unit. We will look in Section 5 at ways to extend simultaneous multithreading to the fetch unit. We also investigate alternative thread priority mechanisms for fetching.

A primary impact of multithreading on our architecture is on the size of the register file. We have a single register file, as thread-specific logical registers are mapped onto a completely shared physical register file by the register renaming. To support eight threads, we need a minimum of $8*32 = 256$ physical integer registers (for a 32-register instruction set architecture), plus more to enable register renaming. Access to such a large register file will be slow, almost certainly affecting the cycle time of the machine.

To account for the size of the register file, we take two cycles to read registers instead of one. In the first cycle values are read into a buffer closer to the functional units. The instruction is sent to a similar buffer at the same time. The next cycle the data is sent to a functional unit for execution. Writes to the register file are treated similarly, requiring an extra *register write* stage. Figure 2 shows the pipeline modified for two-phase register access, compared to the pipeline of the original superscalar.

The two-stage register access has several ramifications on our architecture. First, it increases the pipeline distance between *fetch* and *exec*, increasing the branch misprediction penalty by 1 cycle. Second, it takes an extra cycle to write back results, requiring an extra level of bypass logic. Third, increasing the distance between

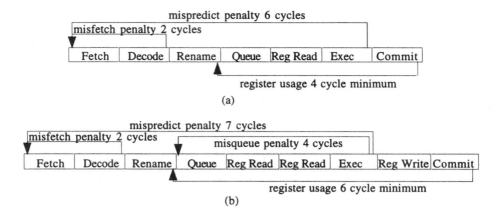

Figure 2: **The pipeline of (a) a conventional superscalar processor and (b) that pipeline modified for an SMT processor, along with some implications of those pipelines.**

queue and *exec* increases the period during which wrong-path instructions remain in the pipeline after a misprediction is discovered (the misqueue penalty in Figure 2). Wrong-path instructions are those instructions brought into the processor as a result of a branch misprediction. Those instructions consume instruction queue slots, renaming registers and possibly issue slots, all of which, on an SMT processor, could be used by other threads.

This pipeline does not increase the inter-instruction latency between most instructions. Dependent (single-cycle latency) instructions can still be issued on consecutive cycles, for example, as long as inter-instruction latencies are predetermined. That is the case for all instructions but loads. Since we are scheduling instructions a cycle earlier (relative to the *exec* cycle), load-hit latency increases by one cycle (to two cycles). Rather than suffer this penalty, we schedule load-dependent instructions assuming a 1-cycle data latency, but squash those instructions in the case of an L1 cache miss or a bank conflict. There are two performance costs to this solution, which we call *optimistic issue*. Optimistically issued instructions that get squashed waste issue slots, and optimistic instructions must still be held in the IQ an extra cycle after they are issued, until it is known that they won't be squashed.

The last implication of the two-phase register access is that there are two more stages between *rename* and *commit*, thus increasing the minimum time that a physical register is held by an in-flight instruction. This increases the pressure on the renaming register pool.

We assume, for each machine size, enough physical registers to support all active threads, plus 100 more registers to enable renaming, both for the integer file and the floating point file; i.e., for the single-thread results, we model 132 physical integer registers, and for an 8-thread machine, 356. We expect that in the 3-5 year time-frame, the scheme we have described will remove register file access from the critical path for a 4-thread machine, but 8 threads will still be a significant challenge. Nonetheless, extending our results to an 8-thread machine allows us to see trends beyond the 4-thread numbers and anticipates other solutions to this problem. The number of registers available for renaming determines the number of instructions that can be in the processor between the *rename* stage and the *commit* stage.

This architecture allows us to address several concerns about simultaneous multithreaded processor design. In particular, this paper shows that:

- Instruction scheduling is no more complex than on a dynamically scheduled superscalar.

- Register file data paths are no more complex than in the superscalar, and the performance implications of the register file and its extended pipeline are small.

- The required instruction fetch throughput is attainable, even without any increase in fetch bandwidth.

- Unmodified (for an SMT workload) cache and branch prediction structures do not thrash on that workload.

- Even aggressive superscalar technologies, such as dynamic scheduling and speculative execution, are not sufficient to take full advantage of a wide-issue processor without simultaneous multithreading.

We have only presented an outline of the hardware architecture to this point; the next section provides more detail.

2.1 Hardware Details

The processor contains 3 floating point functional units and 6 integer units; four of the six integer units also execute loads and stores. The peak issue bandwidth out of the two instruction queues is therefore nine; however, the throughput of the machine is bounded by the peak fetch and decode bandwidths, which are eight instructions per cycle. We assume that all functional units are completely pipelined. Table 1 shows the instruction latencies, which are derived from the Alpha 21164 [8].

We assume a 32-entry integer instruction queue (which handles integer instructions and all load/store operations) and a 32-entry floating point queue, not significantly larger than the HP PA-8000 [21], which has two 28-entry queues.

The caches (Table 2) are multi-ported by interleaving them into banks, similar to the design of Sohi and Franklin [26]. We model lockup-free caches and TLBs. TLB misses require two full memory accesses and no execution resources. We model the memory subsystem in great detail, simulating bandwidth limitations and access conflicts at multiple levels of the hierarchy, to address the concern

Instruction Class	Latency
integer multiply	8,16
conditional move	2
compare	0
all other integer	1
FP divide	17,30
all other FP	4
load (cache hit)	1

Table 1: **Simulated instruction latencies**

	ICache	DCache	L2	L3
Size	32 KB	32 KB	256 KB	2 MB
Associativity	DM	DM	4-way	DM
Line Size	64	64	64	64
Banks	8	8	8	1
Transfer time	1 cycle	1	1	4
Accesses/cycle	var (1-4)	4	1	1/4
Cache fill time	2 cycles	2	2	8
Latency to next level	6	6	12	62

Table 2: **Details of the cache hierarchy**

that memory throughput could be a limiting condition for simultaneous multithreading.

Each cycle, one thread is given control of the fetch unit, chosen from among those not stalled for an instruction cache (I cache) miss. If we fetch from multiple threads, we never attempt to fetch from threads that conflict (on an I cache bank) with each other, although they may conflict with other I cache activity (cache fills).

Branch prediction is provided by a decoupled branch target buffer (BTB) and pattern history table (PHT) scheme [4]. We use a 256-entry BTB, organized as four-way set associative. The 2K x 2-bit PHT is accessed by the XOR of the lower bits of the address and the global history register [18, 30]. Return destinations are predicted with a 12-entry return stack (per context).

We assume an efficient, but not perfect, implementation of dynamic memory disambiguation. This is emulated by using only part of the address (10 bits) to disambiguate memory references, so that it is occasionally over-conservative.

3   Methodology

The methodology in this paper closely follows the simulation and measurement methodology of [27]. Our simulator uses emulation-based, instruction-level simulation, and borrows significantly from MIPSI [22], a MIPS-based simulator. The simulator executes unmodified Alpha object code and models the execution pipelines, memory hierarchy, TLBs, and the branch prediction logic of the processor described in Section 2.

In an SMT processor a branch misprediction introduces wrong-path instructions that interact with instructions from other threads. To model this behavior, we fetch down wrong paths, introduce those instructions into the instruction queues, track their dependences, and issue them. We eventually squash all wrong-path instructions a cycle after a branch misprediction is discovered in the *exec* stage. Our throughput results only count useful instructions.

Our workload comes primarily from the SPEC92 benchmark suite [7]. We use five floating point programs (alvinn, doduc, fpppp, ora, and tomcatv) and two integer programs (espresso and xlisp) from that suite, and the document typesetting program TeX. We assign a distinct program to each thread in the processor: the multi-programmed workload stresses our architecture more than a parallel program by presenting threads with widely varying program characteristics and with no overlap of cache, TLB or branch prediction usage. To eliminate the effects of benchmark differences, a single data point is composed of 8 runs, each T * 300 million instructions in length, where T is the number of threads. Each of the 8 runs uses a different combination of the benchmarks.

We compile each program with the Multiflow trace scheduling compiler [17], modified to produce Alpha code. In contrast to [27], we turn off trace scheduling in the compiler for this study, for two reasons. In our measurements, we want to differentiate between useful and useless speculative instructions, which is easy with hardware speculation, but not possible for software speculation with our system. Also, software speculation is not as beneficial on an architecture which features hardware speculation, and in some cases is harmful. However, the Multiflow compiler is still a good choice for our compilation engine, because of the high quality of the loop unrolling, instruction scheduling and alignment, and other optimizations, as well as the ease with which the machine model can be changed. The benchmarks are compiled to optimize single-thread performance on the base hardware.

4   Performance of the Base Hardware Design

In this section we examine the performance of the base architecture and identify opportunities for improvement. Figure 3 shows that with only a single thread running on our SMT architecture, the throughput is less than 2% below a superscalar without SMT support. The drop in throughput is due to the longer pipeline (described in Section 2) used by the SMT processor. Its peak throughput is 84% higher than the superscalar. This gain is achieved with virtually no tuning of the base architecture for simultaneous multithreading. This design combines low single-thread impact with high speedup for even a few threads, enabling simultaneous multithreading to reap benefits even in an environment where multiple processes are running only a small fraction of the time. We also note, however, that the throughput peaks before 8 threads, and the processor utilization, at less than 50% of the 8-issue processor, is well short of the potential shown in [27].

We make several conclusions about the potential bottlenecks of this system as we approach 8 threads, aided by Figure 3 and Table 3. Issue bandwidth is clearly not a bottleneck, as the throughput represents a fraction of available issue bandwidth, and our data shows that no functional unit type is being overloaded. We appear to have enough physical registers. The caches and branch prediction logic are being stressed more heavily at 8 threads, but we expect the latency-hiding potential of the additional threads to make up for those drops. The culprit appears to be one or more of the following three problems: (1) IQ size — IQ-full conditions are common, 12 to 21% of cycles total for the two queues; (2) fetch throughput — even in those cycles where we don't experience an IQ-full condition, our data shows that we are sustaining only 4.2 useful instructions fetched per cycle (4.5 including wrong-path); and (3) lack of parallelism — although the queues are reasonably full, we find fewer

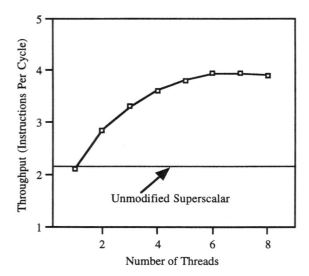

Figure 3: Instruction throughput for the base hardware architecture.

Metric	Number of Threads		
	1	4	8
out-of-registers (% of cycles)	3%	7%	3%
I cache miss rate	2.5%	7.8%	14.1%
-misses per thousand instructions	6	17	29
D cache miss rate	3.1%	6.5%	11.3%
-misses per thousand instructions	12	25	43
L2 cache miss rate	17.6%	15.0%	12.5%
-misses per thousand instructions	3	5	9
L3 cache miss rate	55.1%	33.6%	45.4%
-misses per thousand instructions	1	3	4
branch misprediction rate	5.0%	7.4%	9.1%
jump misprediction rate	2.2%	6.4%	12.9%
integer IQ-full (% of cycles)	7%	10%	9%
fp IQ-full (% of cycles)	14%	9%	3%
avg (combined) queue population	25	25	27
wrong-path instructions fetched	24%	7%	7%
wrong-path instructions issued	9%	4%	3%

Table 3: The result of increased multithreading on some low-level metrics for the base architecture.

than four out of, on average, 27 instructions per cycle to issue. We expect eight threads to provide more parallelism, so perhaps we have the wrong instructions in the instruction queues.

The rest of this paper focuses on improving this base architecture. The next section addresses each of the problems identified here with different fetch policies and IQ configurations. Section 6 examines ways to prevent issue waste, and Section 7 re-examines the improved architecture for new bottlenecks, identifying directions for further improvement.

5   The Fetch Unit — In Search of Useful Instructions

In this section we examine ways to improve fetch throughput without increasing the fetch bandwidth. Our SMT architecture shares a single fetch unit among eight threads. We can exploit the high level of competition for the fetch unit in two ways not possible with single-threaded processors: (1) the fetch unit can fetch from multiple threads at once, increasing our utilization of the fetch bandwidth, and (2) it can be selective about which thread or threads to fetch from. Because not all paths provide equally useful instructions in a particular cycle, an SMT processor can benefit by fetching from the thread(s) that will provide the best instructions.

We examine a variety of fetch architectures and fetch policies that exploit those advantages. Specifically, they attempt to improve fetch throughput by addressing three factors: fetch efficiency, by partitioning the fetch unit among threads (Section 5.1); fetch effectiveness, by improving the quality of the instructions fetched (Section 5.2); and fetch availability, by eliminating conditions that block the fetch unit (Section 5.3).

5.1   Partitioning the Fetch Unit

Recall that our baseline architecture fetches up to eight instructions from one thread each cycle. The frequency of branches in typical instruction streams and the misalignment of branch destinations make it difficult to fill the entire fetch bandwidth from one thread,

even for smaller block sizes [5, 24]. In this processor, we can spread the burden of filling the fetch bandwidth among multiple threads. For example, the probability of finding four instructions from each of two threads should be greater than that of finding eight from one thread.

In this section, we attempt to reduce *fetch block fragmentation* (our term for the various factors that prevent us from fetching the maximum number of instructions) by fetching from multiple threads each cycle, while keeping the maximum fetch bandwidth (but not necessarily the I cache bandwidth) constant. We evaluate several fetching schemes, which are labeled *alg.num1.num2*, where *alg* is the fetch selection method (in this section threads are always selected using a round-robin priority scheme), *num1* is the number of threads that can fetch in 1 cycle, and *num2* is the maximum number of instructions fetched per thread in 1 cycle. The maximum number of total instructions fetched is always limited to eight. For each of the fetch partitioning policies, the cache is always 32 kilobytes organized into 8 data banks; a given bank can do just one access per cycle.

RR.1.8 — This is the baseline scheme from Section 4. Each cycle one thread fetches as many as eight instructions. The thread is determined by a round-robin priority scheme from among those not currently suffering an I cache miss. In this scheme the I cache is indistinguishable from that on a single-threaded superscalar. Each cache bank has its own address decoder and output drivers; each cycle, only one of the banks drives the cache output bus, which is 8 instructions (32 bytes) wide.

RR.2.4, RR.4.2 — These schemes fetch fewer instructions per thread from more threads (four each from two threads, or two each from four threads). If we try to partition the fetch bandwidth too finely, however, we may suffer *thread shortage*, where fewer threads are available than are required to fill the fetch bandwidth.

For these schemes, multiple cache addresses are driven to each cache data bank, each of which now has a multiplexer before its address decoder, to select one cache index per cycle. Since the cache banks are single-ported, bank-conflict logic is needed to ensure that each address targets a separate bank. RR.2.4 has two cache output

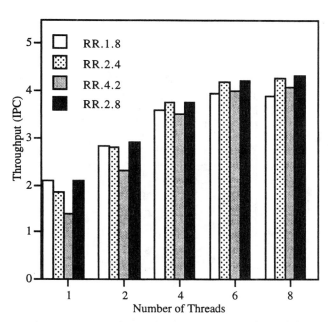

Figure 4: Instruction throughput for the different instruction cache interfaces with round-robin instruction scheduling.

buses, each four instructions wide, while RR.4.2 has four output buses, each two instructions wide. For both schemes, the total width of the output buses is 8 instructions (identical to that in RR.1.8), but additional circuitry is needed so each bank is capable of driving any of the multiple (now smaller) output buses, and is able to select one or none to drive in a given cycle. Also, the cache tag store logic must be replicated or multiple-ported in order to calculate hit/miss for each address looked up per cycle.

Thus, the hardware additions are: the address mux; multiple address buses; selection logic on the output drivers; the bank conflict logic; and multiple hit/miss calculations. The changes required for RR.2.4 would have a negligible impact on area and cache access time. The changes for RR.4.2 are more extensive, and would be more difficult to do without affecting area or access time. These schemes actually reduce the latency in the decode and rename stages, as the maximum length of dependency chains among fetched instructions is reduced by a factor of 2 and 4, respectively.

RR.2.8 — This scheme attacks fetch block fragmentation without suffering from thread shortage by fetching eight instructions more flexibly from two threads. This can be implemented by reading an eight-instruction block for each thread (16 instructions total), then combining them. We take as many instructions as possible from the first thread, then fill in with instructions from the second, up to eight total. Like RR.2.4, two addresses must be routed to each cache bank, then multiplexed before the decoder; bank-conflict logic and two hit/miss calculations per cycle are necessary; and each bank drives one of the two output buses. Now, however, each output bus is eight instructions wide, which doubles the bandwidth out of the cache compared to any of the previous schemes. This could be done without greatly affecting area or cycle time, as the additional bussing could probably be done without expanding the cache layout. In addition, logic to select and combine the instructions is necessary, which might or might not require an additional pipe stage. Our simulations assume it does not.

Figure 4 shows that we can get higher maximum throughput by splitting the fetch over multiple threads. For example, the RR.2.4 scheme outperforms RR.1.8 at 8 threads by 9%. However, better maximum throughput comes at the cost of a 12% single-thread penalty; in fact, RR.2.4 does not surpass RR.1.8 until 4 threads. The RR.4.2 scheme needs 6 threads to surpass RR.1.8 and never catches the 2-thread schemes, suffering from thread shortage.

The RR.2.8 scheme provides the best of both worlds: few-threads performance like RR.1.8 and many-threads performance like RR.2.4. However, the higher throughput of this scheme puts more pressure on the instruction queues, causing IQ-full conditions at a rate of 18% (integer) and 8% (fp) with 8 threads.

With the RR.2.8 scheme we have improved the maximum throughput by 10% without compromising single-thread performance. This was achieved by a combination of (1) partitioning the fetch bandwidth over multiple threads, and (2) making that partition flexible. This is the same approach (although in a more limited fashion here) that simultaneous multithreading uses to improve the throughput of the functional units [27].

5.2 Exploiting Thread Choice in the Fetch Unit

The efficiency of the entire processor is affected by the quality of instructions fetched. A multithreaded processor has a unique ability to control that factor. In this section, we examine fetching policies aimed at identifying the "best" thread or threads available to fetch each cycle. Two factors make one thread less desirable than another. The first is the probability that a thread is following a wrong path as a result of an earlier branch misprediction. Wrong-path instructions consume not only fetch bandwidth, but also registers, IQ space, and possibly issue bandwidth. The second factor is the length of time the fetched instructions will be in the queue before becoming issuable. We maximize the throughput of a queue of bounded size by feeding it instructions that will spend the least time in the queue. If we fetch too many instructions that block for a long time, we eventually fill the IQ with unissuable instructions, a condition we call *IQ clog*. This restricts both fetch and issue throughput, causing the fetch unit to go idle and preventing issuable instructions from getting into the IQ. Both of these factors (wrong-path probability and expected queue time) improve over time, so a thread becomes more desirable as we delay fetching it.

We define several fetch policies, each of which attempts to improve on the round-robin priority policy using feedback from other parts of the processor. The first attacks wrong-path fetching, the others attack IQ clog. They are:

BRCOUNT — Here we attempt to give highest priority to those threads that are least likely to be on a wrong path. We do this by counting branch instructions that are in the decode stage, the rename stage, and the instruction queues, favoring those with the fewest unresolved branches.

MISSCOUNT — This policy detects an important cause of IQ clog. A long memory latency can cause dependent instructions to back up in the IQ waiting for the load to complete, eventually filling the queue with blocked instructions from one thread. This policy prevents that by giving priority to those threads that have the fewest outstanding D cache misses.

ICOUNT — This is a more general solution to IQ clog. Here priority is given to threads with the fewest instructions in decode, rename, and the instruction queues. This achieves three purposes: (1) it prevents any one thread from filling the IQ, (2) it gives highest

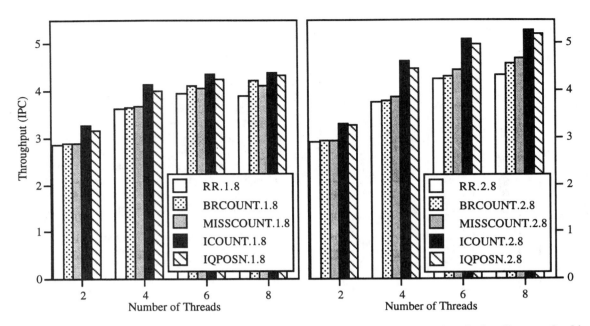

Figure 5: Instruction throughput for fetching based on several priority heuristics, all compared to the baseline round-robin scheme. The results for 1 thread are the same for all schemes, and thus not shown.

priority to threads that are moving instructions through the IQ most efficiently, and (3) it provides a more even mix of instructions from the available threads, maximizing the parallelism in the queues. If cache misses are the dominant cause of IQ clog, MISSCOUNT may perform better, since it gets cache miss feedback to the fetch unit more quickly. If the causes are more varied, ICOUNT should perform better.

IQPOSN — Like ICOUNT, IQPOSN strives to minimize IQ clog and bias toward efficient threads. It gives lowest priority to those threads with instructions closest to the head of either the integer or floating point instruction queues (the oldest instruction is at the head of the queue). Threads with the oldest instructions will be most prone to IQ clog, and those making the best progress will have instructions farthest from the head of the queue. This policy does not require a counter for each thread, as do the previous three policies.

Like any control system, the efficiency of these mechanisms is limited by the feedback latency resulting, in this case, from feeding data from later pipeline stages back to the fetch stage. For example, by the time instructions enter the *queue* stage or the *exec* stage, the information used to fetch them is three or (at least) six cycles old, respectively.

Both the branch-counting and the miss-counting policies tend to produce frequent ties. In those cases, the tie-breaker is round-robin priority.

Figure 5 shows that all of the fetch heuristics provide speedup over round-robin. Branch counting and cache-miss counting provide moderate speedups, but only when the processor is saturated with many threads. Instruction counting, in contrast, produces more significant improvements regardless of the number of threads. IQPOSN provides similar results to ICOUNT, being within 4% at all times, but never exceeding it.

The branch-counting heuristic does everything we ask of it. It reduces wrong-path instructions, from 8.2% of fetched instructions to 3.6%, and from 3.6% of issued instructions to 0.8% (RR.1.8 vs.

BRCOUNT.1.8 with eight threads). And it improves throughput by as much as 8%. Its weakness is that the wrong-path problem it solves is not large on this processor, which has already attacked the problem with simultaneous multithreading. Even with the RR scheme, simultaneous multithreading reduces fetched wrong-path instructions from 16% with one thread to 8% with 8 threads.

Cache miss counting also achieves throughput gains as high as 8% over RR, but in general the gains are much lower. It is not particularly effective at reducing IQ clog, as we get IQ-full conditions 12% of the time on the integer queue and 14% on the floating point queue (for MISSCOUNT.2.8 with 8 threads). These results indicate that IQ clog is more than simply the result of long memory latencies.

Metric	1 Thread	8 Threads RR	8 Threads ICOUNT
integer IQ-full (% of cycles)	7%	18%	6%
fp IQ-full (% of cycles)	14%	8%	1%
avg queue population	25	38	30
out-of-registers (% of cycles)	3%	8%	5%

Table 4: **Some low-level metrics for the round-robin and instruction-counting priority policies (and the 2.8 fetch partitioning scheme).**

The instruction-counting heuristic provides instruction throughput as high as 5.3 instructions per cycle, a throughput gain over the unmodified superscalar of 2.5. It outperforms the best round-robin result by 23%. Instruction counting is as effective at 2 and 4 threads (in benefit over round-robin) as it is at 8 threads. It nearly eliminates IQ clog (see IQ-full results in Table 4) and greatly improves the mix of instructions in the queues (we are finding more issuable instructions despite having fewer instructions in the two queues). Intelligent fetching with this heuristic is of greater benefit than partitioning the fetch unit, as the ICOUNT.1.8 scheme consistently

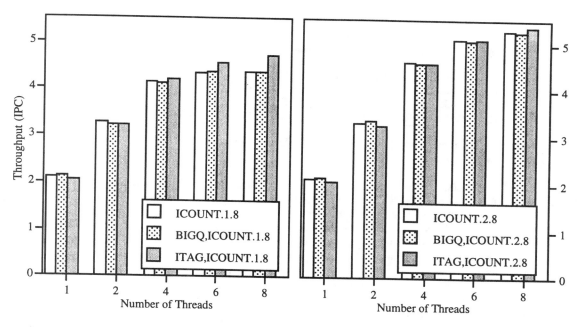

Figure 6: **Instruction throughput for the 64-entry queue and early I cache tag lookup, when coupled with the ICOUNT fetch policy.**

outperforms RR.2.8.

Table 4 points to a surprising result. As a result of simultaneous multithreaded instruction issue and the ICOUNT fetch heuristics, we actually put *less* pressure on the same instruction queue with eight threads than with one, having sharply reduced IQ-full conditions. It also reduces pressure on the register file (vs. RR) by keeping fewer instructions in the queue.

BRCOUNT and ICOUNT each solve different problems, and perhaps the best performance could be achieved from a weighted combination of them; however, the complexity of the feedback mechanism increases as a result. By itself, instruction counting clearly provides the best gains.

Given our measurement methodology, it is possible that the throughput increases could be overstated if a fetch policy simply favors those threads with the most inherent instruction-level parallelism or the best cache behavior, thus achieving improvements that would not be seen in practice. However, with the ICOUNT.2.8 policy, the opposite happens. Our results show that this scheme favors threads with lower single-thread ILP, thus its results include a higher sample of instructions from the slow threads than either the superscalar results or the RR results. If anything, then, the ICOUNT.2.8 improvements are understated.

In summary, we have identified a simple heuristic that is very successful at identifying the best threads to fetch. Instruction counting dynamically biases toward threads that will use processor resources most efficiently, thereby improving processor throughput as well as relieving pressure on scarce processor resources: the instruction queues and the registers.

5.3 Unblocking the Fetch Unit

By fetching from multiple threads and using intelligent fetch heuristics, we have significantly increased fetch throughput and efficiency. The more efficiently we are using the fetch unit, the more we stand to lose when it becomes blocked. In this section we examine schemes that prevent two conditions that cause the fetch unit to miss fetch

opportunities, specifically IQ-full conditions and I cache misses. The two schemes are:

BIGQ — The primary restriction on IQ size is not the chip area, but the time to search it; therefore we can increase its size as long as we don't increase the search space. In this scheme, we double the sizes of the instruction queues, but only search the first 32 entries for issue. This scheme allows the queues to buffer instructions from the fetch unit when the IQ overflows.

ITAG — When a thread is selected for fetching but experiences a cache miss, we lose the opportunity to fetch that cycle. If we do the I cache tag lookups a cycle early, we can fetch around cache misses: cache miss accesses are still started immediately, but only non-missing threads are chosen for fetch. Because we need to have the fetch address a cycle early, we essentially add a stage to the front of the pipeline, increasing the misfetch and mispredict penalties. This scheme requires one or more additional ports on the I cache tags, so that potential replacement threads can be looked up at the same time.

Although the BIGQ scheme improves the performance of the round-robin scheme (not shown), 1.5-2% across the board, Figure 6 shows that the bigger queues add no significant improvement to the ICOUNT policy. In fact, it is actually detrimental for several thread configurations. This is because the buffering effect of the big queue scheme brings instructions into the issuable part of the instruction queue that may have been fetched many cycles earlier, using priority information that is now out-of-date. The results indicate that using up-to-date priority information is more important than buffering.

These results show that intelligent fetch heuristics have made the extra instruction queue hardware unnecessary. The bigger queue by itself is actually *less* effective at reducing IQ clog than the ICOUNT scheme. With 8 threads, the bigger queues alone (BIGQ,RR.2.8) reduce IQ-full conditions to 11% (integer) and 0% (fp), while instruction counting alone (ICOUNT.2.8) reduces them to 6% and 1%. Combining BIGQ and ICOUNT drops them to 3% and 0%.

Early I cache tag lookup boosts throughput as much as 8%

| Issue | Number of Threads | | | | | Useless Instructions | |
Method	1	2	4	6	8	wrong-path	optimistic
OLDEST	2.10	3.30	4.62	5.09	5.29	4%	3%
OPT_LAST	2.07	3.30	4.59	5.09	5.29	4%	2%
SPEC_LAST	2.10	3.31	4.59	5.09	5.29	4%	3%
BRANCH_FIRST	2.07	3.29	4.58	5.08	5.28	4%	6%

Table 5: **Instruction throughput (instructions per cycle) for the issue priority schemes, and the percentage of useless instructions issued when running with 8 threads.**

over ICOUNT. It is most effective when fetching one thread (ICOUNT.1.8, where the cost of a lost fetch slot is greater). However, it improves the ICOUNT.2.8 results no more than 2%, as the flexibility of the 2.8 scheme already hides some of the lost fetch bandwidth. In addition, ITAG lowers throughput with few threads, where competition for the fetch slots is low and the cost of the longer misprediction penalty is highest.

Using a combination of partitioning the fetch unit, intelligent fetching, and early I cache tag lookups, we have raised the peak performance of the base SMT architecture by 37% (5.4 instructions per cycle vs. 3.9). Our maximum speedup relative to a conventional superscalar has gone up proportionately, from 1.8 to 2.5 times the throughput. That gain comes from exploiting characteristics of a simultaneous multithreading processor not available to a single-threaded machine.

High fetch throughput makes issue bandwidth a more critical resource. We focus on this factor in the next section.

6 Choosing Instructions For Issue

Much as the fetch unit in a simultaneous multithreading processor can take advantage of the ability to choose which threads to fetch, the issue logic has the ability to choose instructions for issue. A dynamically scheduled single-threaded processor may have enough ready instructions to be able to choose between them, but with an SMT processor the options are more diverse. Also, because we have higher throughput than a single-threaded superscalar processor, the issue bandwidth is potentially a more critical resource, so avoiding issue slot waste may be more beneficial.

In this section, we examine issue priority policies aimed at preventing issue waste. Issue slot waste comes from two sources, wrong-path instructions (resulting from mispredicted branches) and optimistically issued instructions. Recall (from Section 2) that we optimistically issue load-dependent instructions a cycle before we have D cache hit information. In the case of a cache miss or bank conflict, we have to squash the optimistically issued instruction, wasting that issue slot.

In a single-threaded processor, choosing instructions least likely to be on a wrong path is always achieved by selecting the oldest instructions (those deepest into the instruction queue). In a simultaneous multithreading processor, the position of an instruction in the queue is no longer the best indicator of the level of speculation of that instruction, as right-path instructions are intermingled in the queues with wrong-path.

The policies we examine are OLDEST_FIRST, our default issue algorithm up to this point, OPT_LAST and SPEC_LAST, which only issue optimistic and speculative instructions (more specifically, any instruction behind a branch from the same thread in the

instruction queue), respectively, after all others have been issued, and BRANCH_FIRST, which issues branches as early as possible in order to identify mispredicted branches quickly. The default fetch algorithm for each of these schemes is ICOUNT.2.8.

The strong message of Table 5 is that issue bandwidth is not yet a bottleneck. Even when it does become a critical resource, the amount of improvement we get from not wasting it is likely to be bounded by the percentage of our issue bandwidth given to useless instructions, which currently stands at 7% (4% wrong-path instructions, 3% squashed optimistic instructions). Because we don't often have more issuable instructions than functional units, we aren't able to and don't need to reduce that significantly. The SPEC_LAST scheme is unable to reduce the number of useless instructions at all, while OPT_LAST brings it down to 6%. BRANCH_FIRST actually increases it to 10%, as branch instructions are often load-dependent; therefore, issuing them as early as possible often means issuing them optimistically. A combined scheme (OPT_LAST and BRANCH_FIRST) might reduce that side effect, but is unlikely to have much effect on throughput.

Since each of the alternate schemes potentially introduces multiple passes to the IQ search, it is convenient that the simplest mechanism still works well.

7 Where Are the Bottlenecks Now?

We have shown that proposed changes to the instruction queues and the issue logic are unnecessary to achieve the best performance with this architecture, but that significant gains can be produced by moderate changes to the instruction fetch mechanisms. Here we examine that architecture more closely (using ICOUNT.2.8 as our new baseline), identifying likely directions for further improvements.

In this section we present results of experiments intended to identify bottlenecks in the new design. For components that are potential bottlenecks, we quantify the size of the bottleneck by measuring the impact of relieving it. For some of the components that are not bottlenecks, we examine whether it is possible to simplify those components without creating a bottleneck. Because we are identifying bottlenecks rather than proposing architectures, we are no longer bound by implementation practicalities in these experiments.

The Issue Bandwidth — The experiments in Section 6 indicate that issue bandwidth is not a bottleneck. In fact, we found that even an infinite number of functional units increases throughput by only 0.5% at 8 threads.

Instruction Queue Size — Results in Section 5 would, similarly, seem to imply that the size of the instruction queues was not a bottleneck, particularly with instruction counting; however, the schemes we examined are not the same as larger, searchable queues, which would also increase available parallelism. Nonetheless, the experiment with larger (64-entry) queues increased throughput by less than 1%, despite reducing IQ-full conditions to 0%.

Fetch Bandwidth — Although we have significantly improved fetch throughput, it is still a prime candidate for bottleneck status. Branch frequency and PC alignment problems still prevent us from fully utilizing the fetch bandwidth. A scheme that allows us to fetch as many as 16 instructions (up to eight each from two threads), increases throughput 8% to 5.7 instructions per cycle. At that point, however, the IQ size and the number of physical registers each become more of a restriction. Increasing the instruction queues to 64 entries and the excess registers to 140 increases performance another 7% to 6.1 IPC. These results indicate that we have not yet completely removed fetch throughput as a performance bottleneck.

Branch Prediction — Simultaneous multithreading has a dual effect on branch prediction, much as it has on caches. While it puts more pressure on the branch prediction hardware (see Table 3), it is more tolerant of branch mispredictions. This tolerance arises because SMT is less dependent on techniques that expose single-thread parallelism (e.g., speculative fetching and speculative execution based on branch prediction) due to its ability to exploit inter-thread parallelism. With one thread running, on average 16% of the instructions we fetch and 10% of the instructions we execute are down a wrong path. With eight threads running and the ICOUNT fetch scheme, only 9% of the instructions we fetch and 4% of the instructions we execute are wrong-path.

Perfect branch prediction boosts throughput by 25% at 1 thread, 15% at 4 threads, and 9% at 8 threads. So despite the significantly decreased efficiency of the branch prediction hardware, simultaneous multithreading is much less sensitive to the quality of the branch prediction than a single-threaded processor. Still, better branch prediction is beneficial for both architectures. Significant improvements come at a cost, however; a better scheme than our baseline (doubling the size of both the BTB and PHT) yields only a 2% gain at 8 threads.

Speculative Execution — The ability to do speculative execution on this machine is not a bottleneck, but we would like to know whether eliminating it would create one. The cost of speculative execution (in performance) is not particularly high (again, 4% of issued instructions are wrong-path), but the benefits may not be either.

Speculative execution can mean two different things in an SMT processor, (1) the ability to issue wrong-path instructions that can interfere with others, and (2) the ability to allow instructions to issue before preceding branches from the same thread. In order to guarantee that no wrong-path instructions are issued, we need to delay instructions 4 cycles after the preceding branch is issued. Doing this reduces throughput by 7% at 8 threads, and 38% at 1 thread. Simply preventing instructions from passing branches only lowers throughput 1.5% (vs. 12% for 1 thread). Simultaneous multithreading (with many threads) benefits much less from speculative execution than a single-threaded processor; it benefits more from the ability to issue wrong-path instructions than from allowing instructions to pass branches.

Memory Throughput — While simultaneous multithreading hides memory latencies effectively, it is less effective if the problem is memory throughput, since it does not address that problem. For that reason, our simulator models memory throughput limitations at multiple levels of the cache hierarchy, and the buses between them. With our workload, we never saturate any single cache or bus, but in some cases there are significant queueing delays for certain levels of the cache. If we had infinite bandwidth caches (i.e., the same cache latencies, but no cache bank or bus conflicts), the throughput would only increase by 3%.

Register File Size — The number of registers required by this machine is a very significant issue. While we have modeled the effects of register renaming, we have not set the number of physical registers low enough that it is a significant bottleneck. In fact, setting the number of excess registers to infinite instead of 100 only improves 8-thread performance by 2%. Lowering it to 90 reduces performance by 1%, and to 80 by 3%, and 70 by 6%, so there is no sharp drop-off point. The ICOUNT fetch scheme is probably a factor in this, as we've shown that it creates more parallelism with fewer instructions in the machine. With four threads and fewer excess registers, the reductions were nearly identical.

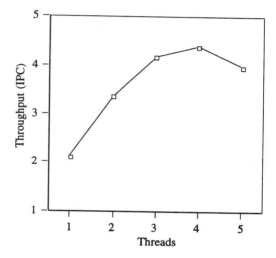

Figure 7: **Instruction throughput for machines with 200 physical registers and from 1 to 5 hardware contexts.**

However, this does not completely address the total size of the register file, particularly when comparing different numbers of threads. An alternate approach is to examine the maximize performance achieved with a given set of physical registers. For example, if we identify the largest register file that could support the scheme outlined in Section 2, then we can investigate how many threads to support for the best performance. The tradeoff arises because supporting more hardware contexts leaves fewer (excess) registers available for renaming. The number of renaming registers, however, determines the total number of instructions the processor can have in-flight. It is difficult to predict the right register file size that far into the future, but in Figure 7 we illustrate this type of analysis by finding the performance achieved with 200 physical registers. That equates to a 1-thread machine with 168 excess registers or a 4-thread machine with 72 excess registers, for example. In this case there is a clear maximum point at 4 threads.

In summary, fetch throughput is still a bottleneck in our proposed architecture. It may no longer be appropriate to keep fetch and issue bandwidth in balance, given the much greater difficulty of filling the fetch bandwidth. Also, register file access time will likely be a limiting factor in the number of threads an architecture can support.

8   Related Work

A number of other architectures have been proposed that exhibit simultaneous multithreading in some form. Tullsen, *et al.*, [27] demonstrated the potential for simultaneous multithreading, but did not simulate a complete architecture, nor did that paper present a specific solution to register file access or instruction scheduling. This paper presents an architecture that realizes much of the potential demonstrated by that work, simulating it in detail.

Hirata, *et al.*, [13] present an architecture for a multithreaded superscalar processor and simulate its performance on a parallel ray-tracing application. They do not simulate caches or TLBs and their architecture has no branch prediction mechanism. Yamamoto, *et al.*, [29] present an analytical model of multithreaded superscalar performance, backed up by simulation. Their study models perfect branching, perfect caches and a homogeneous workload (all threads running the same trace). Yamamoto and Nemirovsky [28] simulate an SMT architecture with separate instruction queues and up to four threads. Gulati and Bagherzadeh [11] model a 4-issue machine with four hardware contexts and a single compiler-partitioned register file.

Keckler and Dally [14] and Prasadh and Wu [19] describe architectures that dynamically interleave operations from VLIW instructions onto individual functional units.

Daddis and Torng [6] plot increases in instruction throughput as a function of the fetch bandwidth and the size of the dispatch stack, a structure similar to our instruction queue. Their system has two threads, unlimited functional units, and unlimited issue bandwidth.

In addition to these, Beckmann and Polychronopoulus [3], Gunther [12], Li and Chu [16], and Govindarajan, *et al.*, [10] all discuss architectures that feature simultaneous multithreading, none of which can issue more than one instruction per cycle per thread.

Our work is distinguished from most of these studies in our dual goals of maintaining high single-thread performance and minimizing the architectural impact on a conventional processor. For example, two implications of those goals in our architecture are limited fetch bandwidth and a centralized instruction scheduling mechanism based on a conventional instruction queue.

Most of these studies either model infinite fetch bandwidth (with perfect caches) or high-bandwidth instruction fetch, each context fetching from a private cache. However, Hirata, *et al.*, and Daddis and Torng both model limited fetch bandwidth (with zero-latency memory), using round-robin priority, our baseline mechanism; neither model the instruction cache, however. Gulati and Bagherzadeh fetch from a single thread each cycle, and even look at thread selection policies, but find no policy with improvement better than intelligent round robin.

Also, only a few of these studies use any kind of centralized scheduling mechanism: Yamamoto, *et al.*, model a global instruction queue that only holds ready instructions; Govindarajan, *et al.*, and Beckmann and Polychronopoulus have central queues, but threads are very restricted in the number of instructions they can have active at once; Daddis and Torng model an instruction queue similar to ours, but they do not couple that with a realistic model of functional units, instruction latencies, or memory latencies. Gulati and Bagherzadeh model an instruction window composed of four-instruction blocks, each block holding instructions from a single thread.

The M-Machine [9] and the Multiscalar project [25] combine multiple-issue with multithreading, but assign work onto processors at a coarser level than individual instructions. Tera [2] combines LIW with fine-grain multithreading.

9   Summary

This paper presents a simultaneous multithreading architecture that:

- borrows heavily from conventional superscalar design, requiring little additional hardware support,

- minimizes the impact on single-thread performance, running only 2% slower in that scenario, and

- achieves significant throughput improvements over the superscalar when many threads are running: a 2.5 throughput gain at 8 threads, achieving 5.4 IPC.

The fetch improvements result from two advantages of simultaneous multithreading unavailable to conventional processors: the ability to partition the fetch bandwidth over multiple threads, and the ability to dynamically select for fetch those threads that are using processor resources most efficiently.

Simultaneous multithreading achieves multiprocessor-type speedups without multiprocessor-type hardware explosion. This architecture achieves significant throughput gains over a superscalar using the same cache sizes, fetch bandwidth, branch prediction hardware, functional units, instruction queues, and TLBs. The SMT processor is actually less sensitive to instruction queue and branch prediction table sizes than the single-thread superscalar, even with a multiprogrammed workload.

Acknowledgments

We would like to thank Tryggve Fossum for his support of this work and for numerous suggestions. And we would like to thank Bert Halstead and Rishiyur Nikhil for several valuable discussions, and the referees for their helpful comments. We would also like to thank John O'Donnell from Equator Technologies, Inc. for access to the source for the Multiflow compiler.

References

[1]   A. Agarwal, B.H. Lim, D. Kranz, and J. Kubiatowicz. APRIL: a processor architecture for multiprocessing. In *17th Annual International Symposium on Computer Architecture*, pages 104–114, May 1990.

[2]   R. Alverson, D. Callahan, D. Cummings, B. Koblenz, A. Porterfield, and B. Smith. The Tera computer system. In *International Conference on Supercomputing*, pages 1–6, June 1990.

[3]   C.J. Beckmann and C.D. Polychronopoulos. Microarchitecture support for dynamic scheduling of acyclic task graphs. In *25th Annual International Symposium on Microarchitecture*, pages 140–148, December 1992.

[4]   B. Calder and D. Grunwald. Fast and accurate instruction fetch and branch prediction. In *21st Annual International Symposium on Computer Architecture*, pages 2–11, April 1994.

[5] T.M. Conte, K.N. Menezes, P.M. Mills, and B.A. Patel. Optimization of instruction fetch mechanisms for high issue rates. In *22nd Annual International Symposium on Computer Architecture*, pages 333–344, June 1995.

[6] G.E. Daddis, Jr. and H.C. Torng. The concurrent execution of multiple instruction streams on superscalar processors. In *International Conference on Parallel Processing*, pages I:76–83, August 1991.

[7] K.M. Dixit. New CPU benchmark suites from SPEC. In *COMPCON, Spring 1992*, pages 305–310, 1992.

[8] J. Edmondson and P. Rubinfield. An overview of the 21164 AXP microprocessor. In *Hot Chips VI*, pages 1–8, August 1994.

[9] M. Fillo, S.W. Keckler, W.J. Dally, N.P. Carter, A. Chang, Y. Gurevich, and W.S. Lee. The M-Machine multicomputer. In *28th Annual International Symposium on Microarchitecture*, November 1995.

[10] R. Govindarajan, S.S. Nemawarkar, and P. LeNir. Design and peformance evaluation of a multithreaded architecture. In *First IEEE Symposium on High-Performance Computer Architecture*, pages 298–307, January 1995.

[11] M. Gulati and N. Bagherzadeh. Performance study of a multithreaded superscalar microprocessor. In *Second International Symposium on High-Performance Computer Architecture*, pages 291–301, February 1996.

[12] B.K. Gunther. *Superscalar performance in a multithreaded microprocessor*. PhD thesis, University of Tasmania, December 1993.

[13] H. Hirata, K. Kimura, S. Nagamine, Y. Mochizuki, A. Nishimura, Y. Nakase, and T. Nishizawa. An elementary processor architecture with simultaneous instruction issuing from multiple threads. In *19th Annual International Symposium on Computer Architecture*, pages 136–145, May 1992.

[14] S.W. Keckler and W.J. Dally. Processor coupling: Integrating compile time and runtime scheduling for parallelism. In *19th Annual International Symposium on Computer Architecture*, pages 202–213, May 1992.

[15] J. Laudon, A. Gupta, and M. Horowitz. Interleaving: A multithreading technique targeting multiprocessors and workstations. In *Sixth International Conference on Architectural Support for Programming Languages and Operating Systems*, pages 308–318, October 1994.

[16] Y. Li and W. Chu. The effects of STEF in finely parallel multithreaded processors. In *First IEEE Symposium on High-Performance Computer Architecture*, pages 318–325, January 1995.

[17] P.G. Lowney, S.M. Freudenberger, T.J. Karzes, W.D. Lichtenstein, R.P. Nix, J.S. ODonnell, and J.C. Ruttenberg. The multiflow trace scheduling compiler. *Journal of Supercomputing*, 7(1-2):51–142, May 1993.

[18] S. McFarling. Combining branch predictors. Technical Report TN-36, DEC-WRL, June 1993.

[19] R.G. Prasadh and C.-L. Wu. A benchmark evaluation of a multi-threaded RISC processor architecture. In *International Conference on Parallel Processing*, pages I:84–91, August 1991.

[20] Microprocessor Report, October 24 1994.

[21] Microprocessor Report, November 14 1994.

[22] E.G. Sirer. Measuring limits of fine-grained parallelism. Senior Independent Work, Princeton University, June 1993.

[23] B.J. Smith. Architecture and applications of the HEP multiprocessor computer system. In *SPIE Real Time Signal Processing IV*, pages 241–248, 1981.

[24] M.D. Smith, M. Johnson, and M.A. Horowitz. Limits on multiple instruction issue. In *Third International Conference on Architectural Support for Programming Languages and Operating Systems*, pages 290–302, 1989.

[25] G.S. Sohi, S.E. Breach, and T.N. Vijaykumar. Multiscalar processors. In *22nd Annual International Symposium on Computer Architecture*, pages 414–425, June 1995.

[26] G.S. Sohi and M. Franklin. High-bandwidth data memory systems for superscalar processors. In *Fourth International Conference on Architectural Support for Programming Languages and Operating Systems*, pages 53–62, April 1991.

[27] D.M. Tullsen, S.J. Eggers, and H.M. Levy. Simultaneous multithreading: Maximizing on-chip parallelism. In *22nd Annual International Symposium on Computer Architecture*, pages 392–403, June 1995.

[28] W. Yamamoto and M. Nemirovsky. Increasing superscalar performance through multistreaming. In *Conference on Parallel Architectures and Compilation Techniques*, pages 49–58, June 1995.

[29] W. Yamamoto, M.J. Serrano, A.R. Talcott, R.C. Wood, and M. Nemirosky. Performance estimation of multistreamed, superscalar processors. In *Twenty-Seventh Hawaii International Conference on System Sciences*, pages I:195–204, January 1994.

[30] T.-Y. Yeh and Y. Patt. Alternative implementations of two-level adaptive branch prediction. In *19th Annual International Symposium on Computer Architecture*, pages 124–134, May 1992.

Memory Systems

6.1 Introduction

The function of a computer's memory system is simple—writing, storing, and reading data stored at addressable locations in electronic, magnetic, or other media. Nevertheless, in modern practice, the implementation complexity of memory systems rivals that of processing. Furthermore, the resources devoted to memory systems dwarfs those spent on processing. Even most of the transistors used in modern microprocessors are memory system components: registers, translation lookaside buffers (TLBs), one or two level-one caches and, increasingly, level-two cache tags and/or data. Burks, Goldstein, and von Neumann foresaw this trend in 1946 [2]:

Ideally one would desire an indefinitely large memory such that any particular . . . word would be immediately available—i.e., in a time which is somewhat or considerably shorter than the operation time of a fast electronic multiplier. This may be assumed to be practical at the level of about 100 μsec. Hence the availability time for a word in memory should be 5 to 50 μsec. It is equally desirable that words may be replaced with new words at about the same rate. It does not seem possible physically to achieve such capacity. We are therefore forced to recognize the possibility of constructing a hierarchy of memories, each of which has greater capacity than the preceding but which is less quickly accessible.

These words remain prophetic half a century later as gigahertz superscalar processors read and write words at a rate seven orders of magnitude faster than Burks et al. considered. What has changed is our understanding of how to engineer memory hierarchies.

In theory, memory hierarchies can be characterized by Hennessy and Patterson's [7] four questions that assume the "upper" level is caching the "lower" level and data are moved between them in "blocks":

- Where can a block be placed in the upper level? (Block placement)
- How is a block found if it is in the upper level? (Block identification)
- Which blocks should be replaced on a miss? (Block replacement)
- What happens on a write? (Write strategy)

In practice, memory hierarchy design bifurcates into design issues for hardware caches and virtual memory. Other examples of what could be considered memory hierarchy design, such as register allocation, file I/O, tape archiving, and proxy server URL caching are, in practice, not considered part of the memory system.

For these reasons, this chapter will concentrate on the development of hardware caches, virtual memory, and then some interactions between them. We assume that readers are familiar with caches and virtual memory through the reading of textbooks such as Hennessy and Patterson [7, ch. 5]. Therefore, we will not devote space to introducing the basic concepts. Some readers many also notice that our selection of readings does not include some of the great survey articles that taught many people about caches and virtual memory. Notable among these are Smith's 1982 cache survey [17] and Denning's 1970 virtual memory survey [5]. We instead concentrate on the primary sources that have developed the field. Nevertheless, Smith and Denning's surveys are good reading for those interested in seeing historical snapshots of the state of the art.

Even though this chapter focus on architectural issues, it is important to remember the fundamental role of the technologies of memory. Modern computers are not possible without economical large memories. The first technology to meet the challenge was the ferrite core memory developed in the late 1940s by MIT's Project Whirlwind. Core used a two-dimensional array of magnetic donuts with row and column control signals that constructively interacted only at the addressed bit. Core was eventually supplanted by a second memory technology still in unchallenged dominance today: semiconductor memory. Furthermore, the characteristics of semiconductor memories deployed continues to change rapidly as packages and protocols evolve (e.g., SDRAMs, Rambus, and integrated circuits that combine logic and dynamic RAM [16]). These economical memory technologies—together with non-volatile magnetic storage (e.g., disks)—are arguably more critical to economical computers than the comparatively few transistors used for processing.

6.2 Cache Origins

A hardware cache is an application of memory hierarchy principles yielding a hardware upper level that caches information from main memory (or a lower level cache) in a manner functionally transparent to software. Block placement, block identification, block replacement, and write strategy are handled by hardware. Block placement is usually limited to much less than the whole cache (direct-mapped or set-associative) to ease the implementation of associative block identification. Blocks are identified by explicitly storing either a main memory address (physical address) or a program address (virtual address). Block replacement uses simple hardware algorithms, such as least-recently used (LRU), pseudo-LRU, or random. Writes either update memory on replacements (write-back) or on all writes (write-through). Write misses may or may not allocate new cache blocks.

6.2.1 Wilkes's "Slave Memories and Dynamic Storage Allocation" [23]

Maurice Wilkes invented the cache with the seminal observation that Gordon Scarrott's instruction buffering ideas could be applied to data as well as instructions.[1] Wilkes presents his ideas for data caches ("slave memory") in a 1.5-page 1965 paper. The paper includes three direct-mapped cache designs that are not important in and of themselves. What is important is that the paper brought out the potential of caching to the world, in general, and the IBM System/360 Model 85 designers, in particular.

6.2.2 Liptay's "Structural Aspects of the System/360 Model 85, Part II: The Cache" [12]

The first commercial realization of the cache concept came just 3 years later in the IBM System/360 Model 85 [12]. The Model 85's cache was so effective that it derailed interest in the much more complex out-of-order microarchitectural techniques of the cache-less Model 91 (e.g., Tomasulo's Algorithm) [1].

Liptay's paper is important, because it describes the first commercial cache and the first cache performance studies. In modern terms, the Model 85's 16 Kbyte cache is divided into 16 fully associative 1 Kbyte blocks (called "sectors" in the paper). Large blocks reduce the amount of expensive tag logic. Each block is further

---

[1]Personal communication with Maurice V. Wilkes on 10 August 1998. Gordon Scarrott was with International Computers and Tabulators, the major British computer company of the period.

subdivided into sixteen 64-byte subblocks (called "blocks" in the paper) with per-subblock valid bits. A block hit and subblock miss loads a 64-byte subblock and sets its valid bit. A block miss replaces the LRU block and performs a subblock miss. The cache uses write-through with no write allocation, so block replacement is trivial.

Performance evaluations used trace-driven simulation to find an average hit ratio of 96.8% and mean performance relative to an ideal system of 81%. Also studied were alternative caches of larger size, larger block size, more limited associativity, and a pseudo-LRU replacement algorithm. This work was very impressive for appearing only 3 years after the first cache paper.

6.3 Cache Advances

Of the hundreds of memory system papers that have been written, it is hard to select just a few. These next three represent key qualitative advances in different dimensions. Kroft introduces lockup-free or non-blocking caches. Goodman outlines a snooping cache coherence protocol. Jouppi gives some techniques made practical as custom VLSI replaces discrete RAM chips at the fast end of the memory hierarchy.

6.3.1 Kroft's "Lockup-Free Instruction Fetch/Prefetch Cache Organization" [11]

Until the 1990s, a cache miss stalled the processor until the miss was handled. This approach was so common it was usually an unstated assumption. For two reasons, handling one miss at time—called a *blocking* or *lockup* cache—becomes problematic when cache miss occurences become very large relative to the number of cache hits. First, the processor and cache cannot hide the latency of a cache miss by overlapping it with other work. Second, the memory bandwidth available is limited to the cache block size divided by the cache miss latency [18]. On the other hand, building an *n*-way *non-blocking* or *lockup-free cache* that allows up to *n* outstanding misses provides both latency tolerance and memory bandwidth up to *n* times that of a blocking cache. Of course, a nonblocking cache is useless unless its processor is capable of doing useful work, usually including memory references, while one or more misses are outstanding.

Kroft presented the first design for a nonblocking cache in 1981, a full decade before common commercial use. The paper focuses on specific details of one design, but this design has served as a basis for many commercial

designs that followed. Key are *n miss information/status holding* (MSHR) registers. Each MSHR register holds information pertinent to one outstanding miss. On a cache reference, MSHRs are searched concurrently with the main cache to suppress a main memory reference on a cache miss, but MSHR hit. Specific MSHR state is needed to keep track of the block's address, where the block will go into the cache, how much of the block has been returned from memory so far, which words have outstanding reads (including transaction identifiers), and which words have been (partially or totally) overwritten by stores. Kroft reports, without analysis, that four MSHR registers can be supported with a 10% increase to overall cache cost. Today, most caches are nonblocking, and we expect the trend toward nonblocking to continue.

6.3.2 Goodman's "Using Cache Memory to Reduce Processor-Memory Traffic" [6]

Entering the 1980s, caches were prized for reducing effective memory latency in uniprocessors. Caches were also used in small-way multiprocessors (e.g., two-way systems from IBM) where coherence was maintained by generating "cross invalidations" on every write. There were also complex (in late 1970s technology) schemes for using a centralized directory to reduce the negative effects of frequent invalidations [21].

Goodman's paper entered with two contributions. First, he observed that caches can be used to reduce bandwidth (as well as latency). This observation is typical of influential ideas. It changed the way people think sufficiently that it now seems too obvious to be a contribution. Goodman noted that bandwidth is reduced more by using write-back instead of write-through. A write-back cache with B-word blocks, a miss ratio m, a fraction d block dirty at replacement time multiplies the bandwidth required from/to memory by a factor of $m \times B \times (1 + d)$. The factor is much less than 1.0 for reasonable miss ratios. In addition, Goodman advocated using subblocking so that small subblocks could be transferred on misses (transfer blocks), whereas address tags are associated with larger blocks (address blocks).

Goodman's caches could reduce bandwidth requirements enough that a multiprocessor could use a bus as an interconnect, provided the cache coherence problem could be simply solved for write-back caches. Goodman's second contribution was to solve this problem with the *write-once* protocol, the first snooping coherence protocol. On the first write to a block, the write-once protocol performs a write-through that also invalidates other cached copies. On subsequent writes, write-back is used. Write-once spawned a series of alternative snooping protocols that were then unified with Sweazey and Smith's MOESI framework [19]. Today, snooping on a bus is considered a solved research problem and is a solution used in all but the largest commercial multiprocessors.

6.3.3 Jouppi's "Improving Direct-Mapped Cache Performance by the Addition of a Small Fully-Associative Cache and Prefetch Buffers" [9]

Memory system performance is frequently improved by devoting more resources to larger or more levels of traditional caches. Alternatively, one could spend some of those resources on special buffers and additional logic to accelerate traditional caches. This alternative does not work so well at the board level, because the chips for small special buffers could use as much board area as that of a traditional cache. The special buffer alternative is much more viable in future systems, where many caches are implemented in custom logic on microprocessor chips. Here the die area of special buffers is roughly proportion to special buffer capacity. Thus, adding 1-Kbyte buffer (plus logic for using it) next to a 64-Kbyte cache might increase die area only 1–3%. So what special buffers are useful? Jouppi gives some initial answers, but, we believe, researchers of the future will find many more.

Specifically, Jouppi proposes two types of special buffers: *victim caches* and *stream buffers* (and *miss caches* that are obsoleted by victim caches). A victim cache is a small, fully associative buffer behind a cache that holds recently replaced blocks and can provide them much faster than memory can (or the next level of cache). A victim cache reduces the negative effect of conflict misses by providing conflicting blocks faster than misses to memory can. A stream buffer prefetches blocks from memory into the stream buffer at addresses sequentially after a miss. Blocks are moved from the stream buffer into the cache only if they are actually referenced. Multiple stream buffers can prefetch after multiple misses. Stream buffers can be extended to nonunit stride prefetching [13]. Thus, stream buffers reduce both capacity and compulsory misses.

6.3.4 Cache Directions

Three other major cache trends are also apparent. First, one level of cache is increasingly being replaced by two levels. This change is occurring because memory

is getting much slower relative to processors, causing caches to spend more time missing. One option was to make caches larger so they would miss less often. Very large caches, however, could slow down the common case of a cache hit. Thus, designers searched for another way to reduce the miss time. A solution was to add a level-two cache to exploit locality in level-one cache misses [14]. Multiple levels of caches. however, make maintaining coherence more difficult, as we will see for Wang, Baer, and Levy's paper [22].

Second, instruction cache design is getting much more complex, because modern superscalar processors can require many instructions per cycle. Furthermore, increased issues widths and branch speculation make it possible that instructions fetched in a given cycle must come from two or more basic blocks. This forced researchers toward multiported caches [24] and trace caches that contiguously cache dynamically contiguous instructions that may not be contiguous in memory [15].

Third, multiprocessor cache issues are moving well beyond simple snooping, as discussed in the shared-memory multiprocessor papers of Chapter 9.

6.4 Virtual Memory

Virtual memory is an application of memory hierarchy principles that allows main memory to cache information from magnetic disks or other secondary storage media. Virtual memory systems use a combination of operating system and hardware support to move and cache data in blocks called *pages*. Page placement is done by the operating system, usually by considering all free page frames as equivalent. Page identification begins by placing all code and data in a virtual address space that is unconcerned with the level (memory or disk) or location (physical address or disk address) at which the information actually resides. Virtual memory systems could follow caches and do page identification by explicitly storing virtual addresses with each page frame. Instead, most modern virtual memory systems use a level of indirection through a page table to translate a virtual address into main memory's physical addresses. Page tables are large and must be stored in memory. To avoid doing one (or more) extra memory references per memory reference, recent translations are cached in a special hardware cache called a *translation lookaside buffer* (TLB). Thus, the common case of page identification is performed completely in hardware by the TLB. Page replacement is handled by the operating system, usually using some approximation to LRU. Write strategy is always write-back with write-allocation.

We have selected two papers pertinent to virtual memory. Kilburn et al. describe the first implementation of virtual memory in the Manchester Atlas. Clark and Emer describe the virtual memory state of the art circa 1980.

6.4.1 Kilburn et al.'s "One-Level Storage System" [10]

Virtual memory was both first proposed and first implemented in the Manchester Altas. Kilburn et al. describe the Atlas in general and its virtual memory system in particular. Even though the general description provides a history lesson, we will concentrate on the virtual memory aspects described mostly in sections 3 and 5. What is most important is that the Altas introduced many seminal concepts: address translation, demand paging, page-fault interrupts, reference bits, and multiprogramming made more transparent by virtual memory.

Specifically, programs running on the Atlas use virtual addresses to transparently access 50-bit (four character) words actually stored in a 16-K-word main memory (ferrite core "central store") or on a 96-K-word magnetic drum. Main memory held 32 512-word pages. The virtual address for each page was stored in a "page address register" (PAR). The 32 PARs can be thought of as "cache tags" for memory's 32 pages or as 32-entry fully associative TLB that maps all memory. On a program memory reference, the 32 PARs are associatively searched. On a match ("equivalence"), memory data is returned. If there is not a match, an interrupt is generated that context-switches the processor to a page fault handler. If main memory has a free page, the handler loads the page from drum and resumes the program. Otherwise, it must first replace a page. The Altas includes reference bits (use digits) to aid page replacement but uses a replacement policy much more complex that a modern approximations to LRU (the learning program). It probably took experimental data from actual operation to inform designers that a simpler policy would suffice.

6.4.2 Clark and Emer's "Performance of the VAX-11/780 Translation Buffer: Simulation and Measurement" [9]

Clark and Emer describe and evaluate a state-of-the-art virtual memory system from the late-1970s: the memory system of DEC VAX-11/780. The VAX-11 architecture was the first widely successful 32-bit architecture designed specifically with virtual memory in mind and represents the state of the art some twenty years after the Atlas. Clark and Emer introduce how the VAX-11 page tables translate 32-bit virtual addresses

without occupying too much physical memory, describe how the VAX-11/780's TLB operates, and present influential performance results from system monitoring.

VAX-11 divided a 32-bit virtual address space into three 1-Gbyte regions: system space (S0), a process space for program text and heap (P0), and process space for stack (P1). Paging was done with 512-byte pages (probably too small even for 1978). Translation information for pages was stored in a page table entry (PTE) in a linear page table. The index within a page table for a page's PTE could be obtained by selecting high-order virtual address bits. The S0 page table resided at a well-known physical address. P0 and P1 are process specific and reside at a well-known address in S0 virtual space. A context switch can change the P0/P1 page tables but not the S0 page table. P0/P1 page table overhead is reduced two ways. First, P0 and P1 grow toward each other and have limit registers to avoid allocating PTEs for unallocated pages. Second, P0/P1 PTEs reside in S0 virtual space and can be paged. This means, however, that a user reference can suffer two page faults—one for the user page and one for the corresponding PTE—but that the physical memory devoted to page tables is dramatically reduced from the naive 32 Mbytes (4 bytes/PTE $\times$ 4 Gbytes / 512 bytes/PTE).

All VAX-11 implementations accelerated address translation with a TLB. The VAX-11/780's TLB contained 128 translations. It was two-way set-associative with random replacement. Half the sets were devoted to S0 translations and half to P0/P1 translations. The P0/P1 were flushed on context switches. Data references access the TLB before accessing the VAX-11/780's cache. Instruction references saved the translation of the current instruction page and bypassed the TLB on sequential instructions that did not cross a page boundary.

The paper used a combination of system monitoring and trace-driven simulation to evaluate the VAX-11/780's TLB. Results were so influential that they are now mostly well known: Operating system reference miss ratios are much higher than user miss ratios, data misses per instruction are consistently greater than instruction misses per instruction, "double" TLB misses were rare, and the VAX-11/780's TLB was adequate (adding only 0.7 cycles to the VAX-11/780's 10 cycles per instruction).

6.4.3 Virtual Memory Directions

We see three major trends in virtual memory systems. First, some TLBs must translate enormous regions of memory; for example, to avoid TLB misses on accesses to multiple-gigabyte database buffer pools. Moreover, TLBs are now on microprocessor chips that must be deployed in both personal computers and large servers. A "one-size-fits-all" TLB is often overkill for a personal computer and is still inadequate for a large server. One answer is to augment the virtual memory system to also support large, aligned superpages (e.g., 4 Mbytes). Superpages, however, complicate the operating system and the TLB and are not (yet) easy to use in general [20].

Second, commercial microprocessors are making the transition from 32-bit to 64-bit virtual addresses. Larger addresses make it more difficult to do translation quickly. To make matters worse, many modern language systems wish to do dynamic memory allocation sparsely distributed about the virtual address space. These trends make more desirable page table designs that perform address translation via hashing physical addresses [3, 8]. This is because these *inverted* or *hashed* page tables occupy memory in proportion to physical memory size, not virtual address space size.

Third, the interactions between caches and TLBs is becoming more difficult as we discuss next.

6.5 Cache and Virtual Memory Interactions

Conventionally, address translation is performed before cache access, making the cache a *physical* cache. Even so, address translation can be implemented in parallel with the first part of a cache access if the cache can be indexed with bits within the page offset (that do not change in translation). This requires that the cache size not exceed the page size times the cache's associativity. Today, however, we often want level-one caches that are larger than a typical page size (4 Kbytes or 8 Kbytes) times the associativity (1–4). These physical caches require address translation to complete before the cache access begins.

Alternatively, researchers have long argued for virtual caches that are indexed and tagged with virtual addresses [17]. Virtual caches do not require address translation on cache hits. Virtual caches, however, have not been widely deployed because of issues of synonyms and context switch requirements. *Synonyms* are two different virtual pages that map to the same physical page. Context switches force a virtual cache to deal with the same virtual page (from different contexts) mapping to different physical pages.

In our view, virtual caches may become more important in future systems. Solutions exist to the synonym and context switching problems (e.g., as discussed next by Wang et al. [22]). Today's superscalar processors can perform many instructions per cycle. Tomorrow's will do many memory references per cycle. Performing multiple address translations per cycle may prove complex enough to make virtual cache more attractive.

6.5.1 Put It All Together: Wang, Baer, and Levy's "Organization and Performance of a Two-Level Virtual-Real Cache Hierarchy" [22]

Wang, Baer, and Levy present a case study that nicely incorporates (1) multiple levels of cache, (2) virtual caches, and (3) cache coherence. Level-one (L1) caches are virtual to ease address translation concerns. Level-two (L2) caches are physical and always contain a superset of the blocks in the L1 caches, called *multilevel inclusion*. Cache coherence is done on physical addresses by the L2 caches. L2 cache blocks maintain pointers to L1 cache blocks to solve the synonym problem and forward pertinent coherence traffic.

The specifics of Wang et al.'s solution are as follows. Each L2 cache block includes some extra state and a pointer, the *vpointer*, indicating where the block is in the level one (if it is). (Multiple pointers are needed when the L1 block size is smaller than the L2 block size.) The pointer size is usually small, because it is $\log_2$ of the number of L1 cache block less the number of index bits that do not change in address translation. Coherence requests only go to the L1 cache for valid vpointers. Furthermore, an L1 miss that finds a vpointer to another L1 block knows it has encountered an active synonym, which it remaps or moves. L1 blocks contain a second valid bit, *sv*, which is reset on a context switch. Blocks with valid set and sv reset have valid data whose mapping needs to be reverified with the L2 cache. Thus, Wang et al.'s solution maintains three invariants: (1) An L1 block always has a corresponding L2 block that points back to it; (2) a block is present in the L1 cache at (at most) one virtual address even if synonyms exist; and (3) an L1 virtual tag is valid for this context if sv is set.

The inclusion of Wang et al.'s design cache study should not be construed as a prediction that most future memory hierarchies will follow their design. In particular, many current systems use physical level-one caches and do not maintain inclusion, especially for instruction caches.

6.6 References

[1] D. W. Anderson, F. J. Sparacio, and R. M. Tomasulo, "The IBM System/360 Model 91: Machine philosophy and instruction-handling" *IBM Journal*, 11(1):8–24, Jan. 1967.

[2] A. W. Burks, H. H. Goldstine, and J. von Neumann "Preliminary discussion of the logical design of an electronic computing instrument," Tech. rep., U.S. Army Ordinance Department, 1946.

[3] A. Chang and M. F. Mergen, "801 storage: Architecture and programming," *ACM Transactions on Computer Systems*, 6(1):28–50, Feb. 1988.

[4] D. W. Clark and J. S. Emer, "Performance of the VAX-11/780 translation buffer: Simulation and measurement," *ACM Transactions on Computer Systems*, 3(1):31–62, Feb. 1985.

[5] P. J. Denning, "Virtual memory," *ACM Computing Surveys*, 2(3):153–189, Sept. 1970.

[6] J. R. Goodman, "Using cache memory to reduce processor-memory traffic," *Proceedings of the 10th Annual International Symposium on Computer Architecture*, pp. 124–131, 1983.

[7] J. L. Hennessy and D. A. Patterson, *Computer Architecture: A Quantitative Approach*, 2nd ed. San Francisco, CA: Morgan Kaufmann, 1996.

[8] J. Huck and J. Hays, "Architectural support for translation tables management in large address space machines," *Proceedings of the 20th Annual International Symposium on Computer Architecture*, pp. 39–50, May 1993.

[9] N. P. Jouppi, "Improving direct-mapped cache performance by the addition of a small fully-associative cache and prefetch buffers," *The 17th Annual International Symposium on Computer Architecture*, pp. 364–373, May 1990.

[10] T. Kilburn, D. B. G. Edwards, M. J. Lanigan, and F. H. Sumner, "One-level storage system," *IRE Transactions*, EC-11(2):223–235, 1962.

[11] D. Kroft, "Lockup-free instruction fetch/prefetch cache organization," *Proceedings of the 8th Annual Symposium on Computer Architecture*, pp. 81–87, May 1981.

[12] J. S. Liptay, "Structural aspects of the system/360 Model 85, part II: The cache," *IBM Systems Journal*, 7(1):15–21, 1968.

[13] S. Palacharla and R. E. Kessler, "Evaluating stream buffers as a secondary cache replacement," *Proceedings of the 21st Annual International Symposium on Computer Architecture*, pp. 24–33, Apr. 1994.

[14] S. Przybylski, M. Horowitz, and J. Hennessy, "Characteristics of performance-optimal multi-level cache hierarchies," *Proceedings of the 16th Annual International Symposium on Computer Architecture*, pp. 114–121, June 1989.

[15] E. Rotenberg, S. Bennett, and J. E. Smith, "Trace cache: A low latency approach to high bandwidth instruction fetching," *Proceedings of the International Symposium on Microarchitecture*, pp. 24–34, Dec. 1996.

[16] K. Sakamura, "Special issue on advanced DRAM technology," *IEEE Micro*, 17(6), 1997.

[17] A. J. Smith, "Cache memories," *ACM Computing Surveys*, 14(3):473–530, 1982.

[18] G. Sohi and M. Franklin, "High-bandwidth data memory systems for superscalar processors," *Proceedings of the Fourth International Conference on Architectural Support for Programming Languages and Operating Systems*, pp. 53–62, Santa Clara, CA, 1991.

[19] P. Sweazey and A. J. Smith, "A class of compatible cache consistency protocols and their support by the IEEE futurebus," *Proceedings of the 13th Annual International Symposium on Computer Architecture*, pp. 414–423, June 1986.

[20] M. Talluri and M. D. Hill, "Surpassing the TLB performance of superpages with less operating system support," *Proceedings of the Sixth International Conference on Architectural Support for Programming Languages and Operating Systems*, pp. 171–182, San Jose, CA, 1994.

[21] C. K. Tang, "Cache system design in the tightly compled multiprocessor system," *Proceedings of the AFIPS National Computing Conference*, pp. 749–753, June 1976.

[22] W.-H. Wang, J.-L. Baer, and H. M. Levy, "Organization and performance of a two-level virtual-real cache hierarchy," *Proceedings of the 16th Annual International Symposium on Computer Architecture*, pp. 140–148, June 1989.

[23] M. V. Wilkes, "Slave memories and dynamic storage allocation," *IEEE Transactions on Electronic Computers*, EC-14(2):270–271, 1965.

[24] T.-Y. Yeh, D. Marr, and Y. N. Patt, "Increasing the instruction fetch rate via multiple branch prediction and branch address cache," *Proceedings of the 1993 ACM International Conference on Supercomputing*, pp. 51–61, July 1993.

Slave Memories and Dynamic Storage Allocation

M. V. WILKES

SUMMARY

The use is discussed of a fast core memory of, say, 32 000 words as a slave to a slower core memory of, say, one million words in such a way that in practical cases the effective access time is nearer that of the fast memory than that of the slow memory.

INTRODUCTION

In the hierarchic storage systems used at present, core memories are backed up by magnetic drums or disks which are, in their turn, backed up by magnetic tape. In these systems it is natural and efficient for information to be moved in and out of the core memory in blocks. The situation is very different, however, when a fast core memory is backed up by a large slow core memory, since both memories are truly random access and there is no latency time problem. The time spent in transferring to the fast memory words of a program which are not used in a subsequent running is simply wasted.

I wish in this note to draw attention to the use of a fast memory as a slave memory. By a slave memory I mean one which automatically accumulates to itself words that come from a slower main memory, and keeps them available for subsequent use without it being necessary for the penalty of main memory access to be incurred again. Since the slave memory can only be a fraction of the size of the main memory, words cannot be preserved in it indefinitely, and there must be wired into the system an algorithm by which they are progressively overwritten. In favorable circumstances, however, a good proportion of the words will survive long enough to be used on subsequent occasions and a distinct gain of speed results. The actual gain depends on the statistics of the particular situation.

Slave memories have recently come into prominence as a way of reducing instruction access time in an otherwise conventional computer.[1,2] A small, very-high-speed memory of, say, 32 words, accumulates instructions as they are taken out of the main memory. Since instructions often occur in small loops a quite appreciable speeding up can be obtained.

One method of designing a slave memory for instructions is as follows. Suppose that the main memory has $64K$ words (where $K = 1024$) and, therefore, 16 address bits, and that the slave memory has 32 words and, therefore, 5 address bits. The slave memory is constructed with a word length equal to that of the main memory plus 11 extra bits, which will be referred to as *tag* bits. An instruction extracted from register r of the main memory is copied into register r (mod 32) of the slave memory and, at the same time, the 11 most significant bits of r are copied into the 11 tag bits. For example, suppose $r = 10\ 259$, that is, $320.2^5 + 19$. The instruction from this register is copied into register 19 of the slave and the number 320 is copied into the tag bits of that register.

Whenever an instruction is required, the slave is first examined to see whether it already contains that instruction. This is done by accessing the register that might contain the instruction [namely, register r (mod 32)], and examining the tag bits to see whether they are equal to the 11 most significant digits of r. If they are, the instruction is taken from the slave; otherwise, it is obtained from the main memory and a copy left in the slave. If the system is to preserve full freedom for the programmer to modify instructions in the accumulator, it is necessary that every time a writing operation is to take place, the slave shall be examined to see whether it contains the word about to be updated. If it does, then the word must be updated in the slave as well as in the main memory.

LARGE SLAVE MEMORY

So far the slave principle has been applied to very small super-speed memories associated with the control of a computer. There would, however, appear to be possibilities in the use of a normal sized core memory as a slave to a large core memory, and I will now discuss various ways in which this might be done. I shall be concerned primarily with a computer system designed for on-line time-sharing in which a large number of user programs are held in auxiliary storage and activated, in turn, according to a sequence determined by a scheduling algorithm. When activated, each program runs until it is either completed or held up by an input/output wait, or until the period of time allocated to it by the scheduling algorithm is exhausted. Another program is then activated. See Corbató.[3]

Consider a computer in which a working memory of, say, $32K$ and 1-μs access time is backed up by a large core memory of, say, one million words and 8-μs access time. In the simplest scheme to be described, programs are split into $32K$ word blocks, each user making use of one or more blocks for his program. The large core memory is provided with a base register, which contains the starting address of the $32K$ block currently active. What we wish to avoid is transferring the whole block to the fast core memory every time it becomes active; this would be wasteful since chances are only a small fraction of the $32K$ words will actually be accessed before the block ceases to be active. If the fast core memory is operated on the slave principle, no word is copied into it until that word has actually been called for by the program. When this happens, the word is automatically copied by the hardware into the fast memory, and the fact that copying has taken place is indicated by the first of two tag bits being changed from a 0 to a 1. When any reference to storage takes place the fast memory is accessed first,[4] and, if the first tag bit is a 1, no reference is made to the large memory; this is true whether reading or writing is called for. If a word in the fast memory is changed, a second tag bit is changed from 0 to 1. Two tag bits are all that are required in this system.

As time goes on, the fast memory will accumulate all the words of the program in active use. When the number in the base register is changed so that a new program becomes active in the place of the one currently active (a change that is brought about by the supervisor), a scan of the fast memory is initiated. Each register is examined in turn and, if the first tag bit is a 0, no action is taken for that register. No action is similarly taken if the first tag bit is a 1 and the second tag bit is a 0. If, however, both tag bits are 1's, the word in the register under examination is copied into its appropriate place in the large memory.

Many variants of the simple scheme are possible. The tag bits may, for example, be stored in a separate superspeed memory. A

[1] Takahashi, S., H. Nishino, K. Yoshihiro, and K. Fuchi, System design of the ETL Mk-6 computers. *Information Processing 1962 (Proc. IFIP Congress 62),* Amsterdam, The Netherlands: North Holland Publishing Co., 1963, p 690.
[2] *Ferranti Computing Systems; Atlas 2,* London: Ferranti Ltd., 1963.

[3] Corbató, F. J. *Proc. 1962 Internat'l Federation of Information Processing Congress,* Amsterdam, The Netherlands: North-Holland Publishing Co., 1963, p 711.
[4] If the design of the large core memory permits, access to it can be initiated simultaneously with access to the fast memory, and cancelled if it turns out not to be required.

1024-word memory, each having 64 bits, would be suitable; such a memory could be made with an access time of about 100 ns, and would enable the scanning process to be completed more rapidly. Similarly, a number of base registers could be provided and the fast core memory divided into sections, each serving as a slave to a separate program block in the main memory. Such a provision would, in principle, enable short programs belonging to a number of users to remain in the fast memory while some other user was active, being displaced only when the space they occupied was required for some other purpose. This would present the designer of the supervisor with problems similar to those presented by an Atlas-type system of dynamic storage allocation.[5]

An alternative, and perhaps more attractive, scheme would be to retain $32K$ (or whatever the size of the fast memory may be) as the block length, but to arrange that the fast memory acts as a slave to more than one block in the main memory, it being recognized that this will lead to some overwriting of information in the slave, but will, nevertheless, on the average, be advantageous. Suppose, for example, that there are seven base registers, each containing an address of a register in the main memory at which a program block starts. Four tag bits are necessary, the first three containing either zeros or the number of one of the base registers. The fourth tag bit indicates whether a word has been altered while in the slave.

At any given time, one of the seven program blocks is active. Whenever access is required to a word in the memory, the hardware looks to see whether that word is to be found in the slave. This is done by reading the word in the appropriate place in the slave and comparing the first 3 tag bits with the number of the base register corresponding to the program block then active. If there is agreement, and if a reading operation is to be performed, the word from

[5] Kilburn, T., D. B. G. Edwards, M. J. Lanigan, and F. H. Sumner, One level storage system, *IRE Trans. on Electronic Computers*, vol 11, Apr 1962, pp 223–235.

the slave is used and operation proceeds. If the three tag bits are all zero, the word is obtained from the main memory and a copy put into the slave memory for future use. If the three tag bits are not zero but correspond to another base register, the fourth digit is examined. If this is a zero, action proceeds as before, the word in the slave being overwritten by the word from the new program block. If, however, the fourth bit is a 1, indicating that the word has been altered while in the slave, that word is copied back into its proper place in the main memory before being overwritten by the word from the new program block. In the case of a writing operation the sequence of events is similar, except that the fourth tag bit is made into a 1 when a word in the slave is modified. Thus, if the seven programs become active in turn, they may be said to share the slave between them and, if each runs in short bursts, there is a fair chance that only a few words belonging to a particular program block get overwritten in the slave before that program block is activated again.

There will, normally, be more than seven program blocks ready to take their turn for running and the supervisor will, from time to time, change the address in one of the base registers. When this happens, a scan of the slave is initiated, and all words which belong to the program block being displaced and which have a 1 in the fourth bit of the tag, are copied into the main memory.

On the face of it, the scheme just outlined appears to offer the basis for a satisfactory two-level core storage system without involving too high a degree of complexity in the hardware.

Acknowledgment

The author wishes to express his gratitude to Prof. R. M. Fano, Director of Project MAC, for inviting him to participate in the project. He is also grateful to his colleagues in Cambridge, England, for discussions, particularly to Dr. D. J. Wheeler and N. E. Wiseman, who designed the slave memory of Atlas 2. G. Scarrot first suggested the idea of a slave memory to them.

The cache, a high-speed buffer establishing a storage hierarchy in the Model 85, is discussed in depth in this part, since it represents the basic organizational departure from other SYSTEM/360 *computers.*

Discussed are organization and operation of the cache, including the mechanisms used to locate and retrieve data needed by the processor.

The internal performance studies that led to use of the cache are described, and simulated performance of the chosen configuration is compared with that of a theoretical system having an entire 80-nanosecond main storage. Finally, the effects of varying cache parameters are discussed and tabulated.

Structural aspects of the System/360 Model 85

II The cache

by J. S. Liptay

Among the objectives of the Model 85 is that of providing a SYSTEM/360 compatible processor with both high performance and high throughput. One of the important ingredients of high throughput is a large main storage capacity (see the accompanying article in Part I). However, it is not feasible to provide a large main storage with an access time commensurate with the 80-nanosecond processor cycle of the Model 85. A longer access time can be partially compensated for by an increase in overlap, greater buffering, deeper storage interleaving, more sophistication in the handling of branches, and other improvements in the processor. All of these factors only partially compensate for the slower storage, and, therefore, we decided to use a storage hierarchy instead.

The storage hierarchy consists of a 1.04-microsecond main storage and a small, fast store called a cache,[1] which is integrated into the CPU. The cache is not addressable by a program, but rather is used to hold the contents of those portions of main storage that are currently being used. Most processor fetches can then be handled by referring to the cache, so that most of the time the processor has a short access time. When the program starts operating on data in a different portion of main storage, the data in that portion must be loaded into the cache and the data from some other portion removed. This activity must take place without program assistance, since the Model 85 must be compatible with the rest of the SYSTEM/360 line.

This paper discusses organization of the cache and the studies that led to its use in the Model 85 and to selecting of values for its parameters.

Figure 1 Assignment of cache sectors to main storage sectors

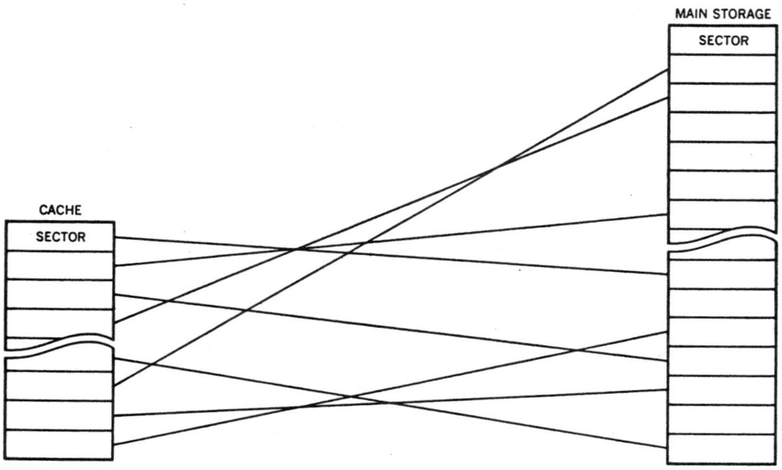

Cache organization

The main storage units that can be used on the Model 85 are the IBM 2365-5 and the 2385. They have a 1.04-microsecond cycle time and make available capacities from 512K bytes to 4096K bytes (K = 1024). The cache is a 16K-byte integrated storage, which is capable of operating every processor cycle. Optionally, it can be expanded to 24K bytes or 32K bytes.

Both the cache and main storage are logically divided into sectors, each consisting of 1K contiguous bytes starting on 1K-byte boundaries. During operation, a correspondence is set up between cache sectors and main storage sectors in which each cache sector is assigned to a single different main storage sector. However, because of the limited number of cache sectors, most main storage sectors do not have any cache sectors assigned to them (see Figure 1). Each of the cache sectors has a 14-bit sector address register, which holds the address of the main storage sector to which it is assigned.

assigning
cache
sectors

The assignment of cache sectors is dynamically adjusted during operation, so that they are assigned to the main storage sectors that are currently being used by the program. If the program causes a fetch from a main storage sector that does not have a cache sector assigned to it, one of the cache sectors is then reassigned to that main storage sector. To make a good selection of a cache sector to reassign, enough information is maintained to order the cache sectors into an activity list. The sector at the top of the list is the one that was most recently referred to, the second one is the next most recently referred to, and so forth. When a cache sector is referred to, it is moved to the top of the list, and the intervening ones are moved down one position. This is not meant to imply an actual movement of sectors within the cache, but rather refers to a logical ordering of the sectors. When it is necessary to reassign a sector, the one selected is the one at the bottom of the activity list. This cache sector is the one that has gone the longest without being referred to.

When a cache sector is assigned to a different main storage sector, the contents of all of the 1K bytes located in that main storage sector are not loaded into the cache at once. Rather, each sector is divided into 16 blocks of 64 bytes, and the blocks are loaded on a demand basis. When a cache sector is reassigned, the only block that is loaded is the one that was referred to. If they are required, the remaining blocks are loaded later, one at a time. Each block in the cache has a bit associated with it to record whether it has been loaded. This "validity bit" is turned on when the block is loaded and off when the sector is reassigned.

Store operations always cause main storage to be updated. If the main storage sector being changed has a cache sector assigned to it, the cache is also updated; otherwise, no activity related to the cache takes place. Therefore, store operations cannot cause a cache sector to be reassigned, a block to be loaded, or the activity list to be revised. Since all of the data in the cache is also in main storage, it is not necessary on a cache sector reassignment to move any data from the cache to main storage. All that is required is to change the sector address register, reset the validity bits, and initiate loading of a block. The processor is capable of buffering one instruction requesting the storing of information in main storage, so that it can proceed with subsequent instructions even if execution of the store instruction cannot be initiated immediately.

store operations

Two processor cycles are required to fetch data that is in the cache. The first cycle is used to examine the sector address registers and the validity bits to determine if the data is in the cache. The second cycle is then used to read the data out of the cache. However, requests can normally be overlapped, so that one request can be processed every cycle. If the data is not present in the cache, additional cycles are required while the block is loaded into the cache from main storage.

The storage word size on which the Model 85 operates internally is 16 bytes. This is the width of the data paths to and from the storage units, and is the amount the processor can store or fetch with a single request. Because a single 2365-5 storage unit operates on an 8-byte-wide interface, two units are paired together and operated simultaneously. Except for the 512K configuration, main storage is interleaved four ways. Since a block is 64 bytes, four fetches to main storage are required to load one block into the cache. With four-way interleaving, this means one request to each basic storage module. To improve performance, the first basic storage module referred to during each block load is the one containing the 16 bytes wanted by the processor. In addition to being loaded into the cache, the data is sent directly to the processor, so that execution can proceed as soon as possible (see Figure 2).

On the Model 85, channels store and fetch data by way of the

Figure 2   Timing for a block load

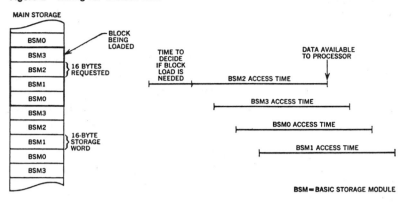

processor. Channel fetches are processed by getting the required data from main storage without referring to the cache. Channel stores are handled the same way as processor stores. In this way, if a channel changes data that is in the cache, the cache is updated but the channels do not have any part of the cache devoted to them.

Performance studies

Among the questions that had to be answered to determine whether the cache approach should be taken were: (1) how effective is it, and (2) does its effectiveness vary substantially from one program to another? The principal tools used to answer these questions are the tracing and timing techniques referred to in Part I. The tracing technique produces an instruction-by-instruction trace of a program operating under the SYSTEM/360 Operating System. The output is a sequence of "trace tapes," which contain every instruction executed, whether in the problem program or the operating system, and the necessary information to determine how long it takes to be executed. These trace tapes contain about 250,000 instructions each and are used as input to a timing program, which determines, cycle-by-cycle, how the Model 85 would execute that sequence of instructions. These techniques are intended to determine internal performance and do not provide any information concerning throughput. An intensive investigation preceded selection of the programs used in this study.

cache
effectiveness

In order to measure the effectiveness of the cache, we postulated a system identical to the Model 85 except that the storage hierarchy is replaced by a single-level storage operating at cache speed. The performance of such a system is that which would be achieved by the Model 85 if it always found the data it wanted in the cache and if it never encountered interference in main storage due to stores. Therefore, it represents an upper limit on the performance of the Model 85; how close the Model 85 approaches this ideal can serve as a measure of how effective the cache is. Nineteen trace tapes

Figure 3   Model 85 performance relative to single-level storage operating at cache speed

Figure 4   Probability of finding fetched data in cache

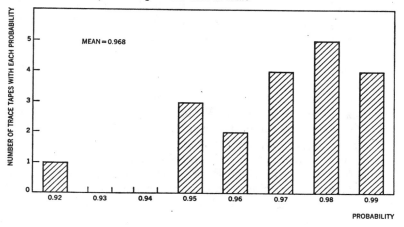

were timed for both the Model 85 and the postulated system, and the performance of the Model 85 was expressed as a percentage of the performance of the ideal system. Figure 3 shows the distribution of performance data obtained. The average was 81 percent of the performance of the ideal system, with a range between 66 and 94 percent.

An important statistic related to cache operation is the probability of finding the data wanted for a fetch in the cache. Figure 4 shows the distribution of this probability for the same 19 trace tapes used for Figure 3. The average probability was 0.968. It is worth noting that, if the addresses generated by a program were random, the probability of finding the data wanted in the cache would be much less than 0.01. Therefore, it can be said that what makes the cache work is the fact that *real programs are not random in their addressing patterns.*

Table 1 Average performance relative to an ideal system with cache size and number of sectors varied — Block size = 64 bytes

Number of cache bytes	Number of sectors		
	8	16	32
8K	0.693	0.744	0.793
16K	0.765	0.825	0.861
32K	0.857	0.891	0.902

Selection of cache parameters

Before the final cache design was established, a great deal of effort was expended on the choice of cache parameters.[2] The tools used to make the choice were the trace and timing programs. From among the trace tapes available, we picked five representative ones and ran them for many cache configurations, varying cache size, sector size, and block size. Tables 1 and 2 show the results obtained. In Table 1, block size is always 64 bytes; in Table 2, the number of sectors is always sixteen. In both cases, performance is compared with that of a single-level storage operating at cache speed. The selection of a 16K byte cache with 16 sectors and 64 bytes per block was made as the best balance between cost and performance.

replacement algorithms

The choice of an algorithm for the selection of a sector to reassign was also the object of careful study. From among the algorithms proposed, two were selected as likely candidates and incorporated into the timing program for study.

For one algorithm, the cache sectors are partitioned with an equal number of sectors in each partition. An activity list is maintained for each partition reflecting the use of the sectors within it. Each partition has a binary address, and when a main storage sector needs to be assigned a position in the cache, the low-order bits of its sector address are used to select one of the partitions. The sector at the bottom of that partition's activity list is the one chosen for reassignment.

This algorithm was studied for 1, 2, 4, 8, and 16 partitions. When there is only one partition, the algorithm becomes the Model 85 replacement algorithm. At the opposite extreme, when there are sixteen partitions, there is only one sector in each, and the idea of an activity list for each partition is meaningless. In this case, the choice of a cache sector to reassign depends only on the low-order address bits of the main storage sector for which a place is being found in the cache, and consequently each main storage sector has only one possible place where it can be put in the cache.

The second algorithm involves a single usage bit for each cache sector. When a sector is referred to, its usage bit is turned on if it is not already on. When the last sector bit is turned on, all of the other bits are turned off and the process continues. If a sector has to be reassigned, it is selected randomly from among those with their usage bits off.

Table 2 Average performance relative to an ideal system with cache size and number of bytes per block varied – Number of sectors = 16

Number of cache bytes	Number of bytes per block		
	64	128	256
8K	0.744		
16K	0.825	0.810	0.781
32K	0.891	0.885	0.870

Table 3 Comparative performance using different cache sector replacement algorithms

algorithm	performance
1 partition*	1.000
2 partitions	0.990
4 partitions	0.987
8 partitions	0.979
16 partitions	0.933
usage bits	0.931

* Replacement algorithm chosen for the Model 85

Table 3 summarizes the results obtained. The choice of the activity list was made because it provided the best balance between cost and performance.

Summary comment

The inclusion of a storage hierarchy represents one of the major advances in system organization present in the Model 85. Although the concept of a storage hierarchy is not new, the successful implementation of a nanosecond/microsecond level of hierarchy was inhibited until now by the lack of a suitable technology. As implemented in the Model 85, the fast monolithic storage physically integrated with the CPU logic yields the desired machine speed, while the large core storage yields the desired storage capacity, the combination being transparent to the user. It is likely that with future progress in technology this nanosecond/microsecond hierarchy is not merely an innovation that worked out well for the Model 85, but rather it is a fundamental step forward that will be incorporated into most large systems of the future.

CITED REFREENCE AND FOOTNOTE

1. The term cache is synonymous with high-speed buffer, as used in other Model 85 documentation.
2. D. H. Gibson, "Considerations in block-oriented systems design," *AFIPS Conference Proceedings, Spring Joint Computer Conference* **30**, Academic Press, New York, New York, 75–80 (1967).

LOCKUP-FREE INSTRUCTION FETCH/PREFETCH CACHE ORGANIZATION

DAVID KROFT

Control Data Canada, Ltd.
Canadian Development Division
Mississauga, Ontario, Canada

ABSTRACT

In the past decade, there has been much literature describing various cache organizations that exploit general programming idiosyncrasies to obtain maximum hit rate (the probability that a requested datum is now resident in the cache). Little, if any, has been presented to exploit: (1) the inherent dual input nature of the cache and (2) the many-datum reference type central processor instructions.

No matter how high the cache hit rate is, a cache miss may impose a penalty on subsequent cache references. This penalty is the necessity of waiting until the missed requested datum is received from central memory and, possibly, for cache update. For the two cases above, the cache references following a miss do not require the information of the datum not resident in the cache, and are therefore penalized in this fashion.

In this paper, a cache organization is presented that essentially eliminates this penalty. This cache organizational feature has been incorporated in a cache/memory interface subsystem design, and the design has been implemented and prototyped. An existing simple instruction set machine has verified the advantage of this feature; future, more extensive and sophisticated instruction set machines may obviously take more advantage. Prior to prototyping, simulations verified the advantage.

INTRODUCTION

A cache buffer[1,2] is a small, fast memory holding most recently accessed data and its surrounding neighbors. Because the access time of this buffer is usually an order of magnitude greater than main or central memory, and the standard software practice is to localize data, the effective memory access time is considerably reduced when a cache buffer is included. The cost increment for this when compared with the cost of central memory along with the above access time advantage infers cost effectiveness.

Now, accepting the usefulness of a cache buffer, one looks into ways of increasing its effectiveness; that is, further decreasing the effective memory access time. Considerable research has been done to fine tune a cache design for various requirements.[3,6] This fine tuning consisted of selecting optimal total cache buffer size, block size (the number of bytes to be requested on a cache miss), space allocation, and replacement algorithms to maximize hit rate. Another method presented to increase the hit rate was selective prefetching.[7] All these methods assume the cache can handle *only* one request at a time; on a miss, the cache stays busy servicing the request until the data is received from memory and, possibly, for cache buffer update.

In this paper, a cache organization is presented that increases the effectiveness of a normal cache inclusion by using the inherent dual input nature of an overall cache and the many data reference instructions. In other words, it would be extremely useful to pipeline the requests into the cache at the cache hit throughput rate regardless of any misses. If this could be accomplished then all fetch and/or prefetch of instructions could be totally transparent to the execution unit. Also, for instructions that require a number of data references, the requests could be almost entirely overlapped. Obviously, requests could not be streamed into the cache at the hit throughput rate indefinitely. There is a limit. This organization's limit is imposed by the number of misses that have not been completely processed that the cache will keep track of simultaneously without lockup.

ORGANIZATION

In addition to the standard blocks, this cache organization requires the following:

1. One unresolved miss information/status holding register (MSHR) for each miss that will be handled concurrently.

2. One n way comparator, in which n is the number of MSHR registers, for registering hits on data in transit from memory.

3. An input stack to hold the total number of received data words possibly outstanding . The size of this stack, consequently, is equal to the

block size in words times the number of MSHR registers.

4. MSHR status update and collecting networks.

5. The appropriate control unit enhancement to accommodate 1 through 4.

Figure 1 is a simplified block diagram of the cache organization. (A set-associative operation is assumed.) Included are the required blocks for a set-associative cache (tag arrays and control, cache buffer), the central memory interface blocks (memory requestor, memory receiver), and the cache enhancement blocks (miss info holding registers, miss comparator and status collection, input stack). The miss info holding registers hold all necessary information to (1) handle the central memory received data properly and (2) inform the main cache control, through the miss comparator and status collector, of all hit and other status of data in transit from memory. The input stack is necessary to leave the main cache buffer available for overlapped reads and writes. Note that this organization allows for data just received from memory or in the input stack to be sent immediately to the requesting CPU units.

Of course, the number of MSHR registers is important. As with set size (blocks per set), the incremental value decreases rapidly with the number of registers. This is good, because the cost increases significantly with the number of registers. Figure 2 presents a qualitative curve. The average delay time is caused by lockout on outstanding misses. This delay time, of course, is also dependent on cache input request and hit rates. In the degenerate case, 1 MSHR register of reduced size is required; 2 MSHR registers allow for overlap while one miss is outstanding, but still would lock up the cache input on multiple misses outstanding. Owing to cost considerations and incremental effectiveness gained on increasing the number of MSHR registers, 4 registers appear to be optimal.[8]

The necessary information contained within one of these MSHR registers includes the following: First, the cache buffer address, along with the input request address, is required. The cache buffer address is kept to know where to place the returning memory data; the input request address is saved to determine if, on subsequent requests, the data requested is on its way from central memory. Second, input request identification tags, along with the send-to-CPU status, are stored. This information permits the cache to return to CPU requesting units only the data requested and return it with its identification tag. Third, in-input-stack

indicators are used to allow for reading data directly from the input stack. Fourth, a code (for example, one bit per byte for partial write) is held for each word to indicate what bytes of the word have been written to the cache buffer. This code controls the cache buffer write update and allows dispensing of data for buffer areas that have been totally written after requested. The cache, thus, has the capability of processing partial write input requests "on the fly" without purging. (Of course, this partial write code may not be incorporated if the cache block is purged on a partial write request to a word in a block in transit from memory.) Last, some control information (the register contains valid information only for returning requested data, but not for cache buffer update and the number of words of the block that have been received and written, if required, into the cache buffer) is needed. Therefore, each MSHR register contains:

1. Cache buffer address

2. Input request address

3. Input identification tags (one per word)

4. Send-to-CPU indicators (one per word)

5. In-input-stack indicators (one per word)

6. Partial write codes (one per word)

7. Number of words of blocks processed

8. Valid information indicator

9. Obsolete indicator (information *not* valid for cache update or MSHR hit on data in transit)

OPERATION

The operation can be split into two basic parts: memory receiver/input stack operations and tag array control operations. For memory receiver/input stack operations, the fields of MSHR interrogated are the following:

1. Send-to-CPU indicator

2. Input identification tags

3. Cache buffer address

4. Partial write codes

5.   Obsolete indicator

6.   Valid indicator

When a word is received from memory, it is sent to the CPU requesting unit if the send-to-CPU indicator is set; the appropriate identification tag accompanies the data. This word is also written into the input stack if the word's space has not been previously totally written in the cache buffer or if MSHR is not obsolete (invalid for cache update). The words of data are removed from this input stack on a first-in, first-out basis and are written into the cache buffer using fields 3 and 4. Of course, MSHR must hold valid information when interrogated, or an error signal will be generated.

A slight diversion is necessary at this point to explain cache data tagging. On a miss, the cache requests a block of words. Along with each word, a cache tag is sent. This tag points to the particular assigned MSHR and indicates the word of the block. Note that the cache saves in MSHR the requesting unit's identification tag. This tagging closes the remaining open link for the handling of data returned from memory and removes all restrictions on memory on the order of responses.

If a particular processor/memory interface allows for a data width of a block of words for cache to central memory requests, the cache data tagging may be simplified by merely pointing to the particular assigned MSHR. If, however, all other data paths are still one word wide, the main operations would be essentially unchanged. Consequently, this extended interface would *not* significantly reduce the control complexity or the average lockout time delay per request.

The fields of the MSHR updated during memory receiver/input stack operations are the following:

1.   In-input-stack indicators

2.   Partial write codes

3.   Number of words of block processed

4.   Valid information indicator (being used indicator)

The in-input-stack indicators are set when the data word is written into the input stack and cleared when data is removed from the input stack and written into the cache buffer. The partial write code is set to indicate totally written when the data word from central memory indicates the cache buffer. In addition, whenever a data word is disposed of because of being

totally written or having an obsolete MSHR, or is written into the cache buffer, the number-of-words-processed counter is incremented. On number-of-words-processed counter overflow (all words for a block have been received), the valid or used MSHR indicator is cleared.

For tag array control operations, the following fields of MSHRs are interrogated:

1.   Input request addresses

2.   Send-to-CPU indicators

3.   In-input-stack indicators

4.   Partial write codes

5.   Valid indicator

6.   Obsolete indicator

Fields 1, 5, and 6 are used along with current input request address and the n way MSHR comparator to determine if there is a hit on previously missed data still being handled (previous miss hit). Fields 2, 3, and 4 produce one of the following states for the previous miss hit:

- Partially written (Partial write code has at least one bit set.)

- Totally written (Partial write code is all 1's.)

- In-input-stack

- Already-asked-for (Send-to-CPU indicator is already set.)

Figure 3 indicates the actions followed by the tag array control under all the above combinations for a previous miss hit. On a miss, a MSHR is assigned, and the following is performed:

1.   Valid indicator set

2.   Obsolete indicator cleared

3.   Cache buffer address saved in assigned MSHR

4.   Input request address saved in assigned MSHR

5.   Appropriate send-to-CPU indicator set and others cleared

6.   Input identification tag saved in appropriate
     position

7.   All partial write codes associated with assigned
     MSHR cleared

8.   All MSHRs pointing to same cache buffer address
     purged (Set partial write code to all 1's)

Note that actions 5 and 6 will vary if the cache function
was a prefetch (all send-to-CPU indicators are cleared,
and no tag is saved). Action 8 prevents data from a
previous allocation of a cache buffer block from
overwriting the present allocation's data. On a miss and
previous miss hit (the cache buffer block was reallocated
for the same input address before all data was
received), MSHR is set obsolete to prevent possible
subsequent multiple hits in the MSHR comparator.

SIMULTANEITY

A previous miss hit on a data word just being received
is definitely possible. Depending on the control
operation, this word may have its corresponding
send-to-CPU indicator's output forced to the send
condition or may be read out of the input stack on the
next minor cycle.

DIAGNOSABILITY

To diagnose this cache enhancement more readily,
cache input functions should be added to clear and set
the valid indicators of the MSHR registers. This would
allow the following error conditions to be forced:

* Cache tag points to nonvalid MSHR register

* Multiple hit with MSHR comparator

* Previous miss hit status—totally written and not
  partially written

All other fields of the MSHR registers may be verified
by using these special cache input functions in
combination with the standard input functions with all
combinations of addresses, identification tags and data.

CONCLUSIONS

This cache organization has been designed, prototyped,
and verified. The design allows for the disabling of the
MSHR registers. Using this capability, the direct effect
of the number of MSHR registers on the execution
times of a number of applications was noted. The
reduced execution times of these applications directly
demonstrated the effectiveness of this enhancement. (It
is beyond the scope of this paper to analyze
quantitatively the average lockout delay/request with
respect to the number of enabled MSHR registers for
different cache input rates and hit rates [cache buffer
sizes]. This analysis will be reported in future work.)
The cost of the 4 MSHR additions to the design was
about 10% of the total cache cost.

ACKNOWLEDGMENT

The author thanks Control Data Canada for the opportunity to
develop the new cache organization presented in this paper.

REFERENCES

[1]C. J. Conti. Concepts of buffer storage, *IEEE Computer Group News*, 2 (March 1969).

[2]R. M. Meade. How a cache memory enhances a computer's performance, *Electronics* (Jan. 1972).

[3]K. R. Kaplan and R. O. Winder. Cache-based computer systems, *IEEE Computer* (March 1973).

[4]J. Bell, D. Casasent, and C. G. Bell. An investigation of alternative cache organizations. *IEEE Transactions on Computers*, C-23 (April 1974).

[5]J. H. Kroeger and R. M. Meade (of Cogar Corporation, Woppingers Fall, NY). Cache buffer memory specification.

[6]A. V. Pohm, O. P. Agrawal, and R. N. Monroe. The cost and performance tradeoffs of buffered memories. *Proceedings of the IEEE*, 63 (Aug. 1973).

[7]A. J. Smith. Sequential program prefetching in memory hierachies, *IEEE Computer* (Dec 1978).

[8]G. H. Toole. Instruction lookahead and execution traffic considerations for the _____ cache design (Development division internal paper), Control Data-Canada, 1975.

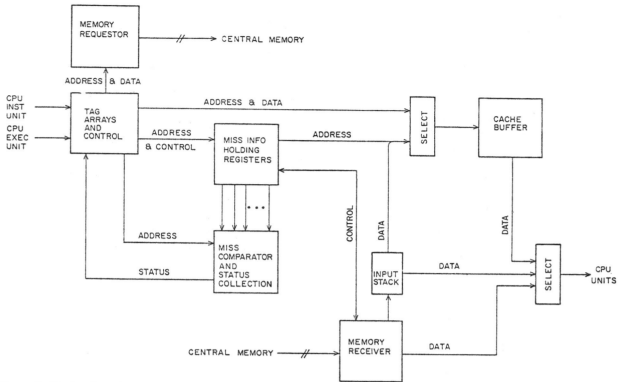

Figure 1. Cache Organization

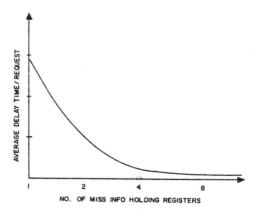

Figure 2. Qualitative Curve for Lockout Delay

INPUT FUNCTION	PARTIALLY WRITTEN	TOTALLY WRITTEN	IN INPUT STACK	ALREADY ASKED FOR	ACTION
READ	NO	NO	NO	NO	SET SEND – TO – CPU BIT SAVE IDENT
READ	NO	NO	NO	YES	READ FROM CENTRAL MEMORY (BY – PASS)
READ	NO	NO	YES	X	READ FROM STACK
READ	YES	NO	X	X	READ FROM CENTRAL MEMORY (BY – PASS)
RFAD	YES	YES	X	X	READ FROM CACHE BUFFER
PREFETCH	X	X	X	X	NO ACTION
WRITE	X	X	X	X	WRITE BYTES TO CACHE BUFFER. SET APPROPRIATE PARTIAL WRITE BITS.

WHERE X IS DON'T CARE

Figure 3. Previous Miss Hit Operations

USING CACHE MEMORY TO REDUCE PROCESSOR-MEMORY TRAFFIC

James R. Goodman

Department of Computer Sciences
University of Wisconsin-Madison
Madison, WI 53706

ABSTRACT—The importance of reducing processor-memory bandwidth is recognized in two distinct situations: single board computer systems and microprocessors of the future. Cache memory is investigated as a way to reduce the memory-processor traffic. We show that traditional caches which depend heavily on spatial locality (look-ahead) for their performance are inappropriate in these environments because they generate large bursts of bus traffic. A cache exploiting primarily temporal locality (look-behind) is then proposed and demonstrated to be effective in an environment where process switches are infrequent. We argue that such an environment is possible if the traffic to backing store is small enough that many processors can share a common memory and if the cache data consistency problem is solved. We demonstrate that such a cache can indeed reduce traffic to memory greatly, and introduce an elegant solution to the cache coherency problem.

1. Introduction

Because there are straightforward ways to construct powerful, cost-effective systems using random access memories and single-chip microprocessors, semiconductor technology has, until now, had the greatest impact through these components. High-performance processors, however, are still beyond the capability of a single-chip implementation and are not easily partitioned in a way which can effectively exploit the technology and economics of VLSI. An interesting phenomenon has occurred in the previous decade as a result of this disparity. Memory costs have dropped radically and consistently for computer systems of all sizes. While the component cost of a CPU (single-chip implementations excluded) has declined significantly over the same period, the reduction has been less dramatic. A result is that the amount of memory thought to be appropriate for a given speed processor has grown dramatically in recent years. Today small minicomputers have memory as large as that of the most expensive machines of a decade ago.

The impact of VLSI has been very different in microprocessor applications. Here memory is still regarded as an expensive component in the system, and those familiar primarily with a minicomputer or mainframe environment are often scornful of the trouble to which microprocessor users go to conserve memory. The reason, of course, is that even the small memory in a microprocessor is a much larger portion of the total system cost than the much larger memory on a typical main frame system. This results from the fact that memory and processors are implemented in the same technology.

1.1. A Super CPU

With the advances to VLSI occurring now and continuing over the next few years, it will become possible to fabricate circuits that are one to two orders of magnitude more complex than currently available microprocessors. It will soon be possible to fabricate an extremely high-performance CPU on a single chip. If the entire chip is devoted to the CPU, however, it is not a good idea. Extrapolating historical trends to predict future component densities, we might expect that within a few years we should be able to purchase a single-chip processor containing at least ten times as many transistors as occur in, say, the MC68000. For the empirical rule known as Grosch's law [Grosch53], $P = k\ C^g$, where P is some measure of performance, C is the cost, and k and g are constants, Knight[Knight66] concluded that g is at least 2, and Solomon[Solomon66] has suggested that $g \approx 1.47$. For the IBM System/370 family, Siewiorek determined that $g \approx 1.6$ [Siewiorek82]. While Grosch's law breaks down in the comparison of processors using different technology or architectures, it is realistic for predicting improvements within a single technology. Siewiorek in fact suggests that it holds "by definition."

Assuming $g = 1.5$ and using processor-memory bandwidth as our measure of performance, Grosch's law predicts that a processor containing 10 times as many transistors as a current microprocessor would require 30 times the memory bandwidth.[1] The Motorola MC68000, running at 10 MHz, accesses data from memory at a maximum rate of 5 million bytes per second, using more than half its pins to achieve this rate. Although packaging technology is rapidly increasing the pins available to a chip, it is unlikely that the increase will be 30-fold (the 68000 has 64 pins). We would suggest a factor of two is realistic. Although some techniques are clearly possible to increase the transfer rate into and out of the 68000, supplying such a processor with data as fast as needed is a severe constraint. One of the designers of the 68000, has stated that all modern microprocessors — the 68000

---

[1]This is a conservative estimate, in fact, because it ignores predictable decreases in gate delays.

included — are already bus-limited [Tredennick82].

1.2. On-chip Memory

One alternative for increased performance without proportionally increasing processor-memory bandwidth is to introduce memory on the same chip with the CPU. With the ability to fabricate chips containing one to two million transistors, it should be possible — using only a portion of the chip — to build a processor significantly more powerful than any currently available single-chip CPU. While devoting the entire chip to the CPU could result in a still more powerful processor, introducing on-chip memory offers a reduction in memory access time due to the inherently smaller delays as compared to inter-chip data transfers. If most accesses were on-chip, it might actually perform as fast as the more powerful processor.

Ideally, the chip should contain as much memory as the processor "needs" for main storage. Conventional wisdom today says that a processor of the speed of current microprocessors needs at least 1/4 megabytes of memory [Lindsay81]. This is certainly more than is feasible on-chip, though a high performance processor could probably use substantially more than that. Clearly all the primary memory for the processor cannot be placed on the same chip with a powerful CPU. What is needed is the top element of a memory hierarchy.

1.3. Cache Memory

The use of cache memory, however, has often aggravated the bandwidth problem rather than reduce it. Smith [Smith82] says that optimizing the design has four general aspects:

(1) maximizing the hit ratio,

(2) minimizing the access time to data in the cache,

(3) minimizing the delay due to a miss, and

(4) minimizing the overheads of updating main memory, maintaining multicache consistency, etc.

The result is often a larger burst bandwidth requirement from main storage to the cache than would be necessary without a cache. For example, the cache on the IBM System/370 model 168, is capable of receiving data from main memory at a rate of 100 megabytes per second [IBM76]. It supplies data to the CPU at less than 1/3 that rate. The reason is that to exploit the spatial locality in memory references, the data transferred from backing store into the cache is fetched in large blocks, resulting in requirements of very high bandwidth bursts of data. We have measured the average bandwidth on an IBM System/370 model 155, and concluded that the *average* backing-store-to-cache traffic is less than the cache-to-CPU traffic.

The design of cache memory for mini-computers demanded greater concern for bus bandwidth. The designers of the PDP-11 models 60 and 70 clearly recognized that small block sizes were necessary to keep main memory traffic to a minimum [Bell78].

Lowering the bandwidth from backing store to the cache can be accomplished in one of two ways:

(1) small blocks of data are brought from backing store to the cache, or

(2) long delays occur while a block is being brought in, independent of (and in addition to) the access time of the backing store.

While it is possible to bring in the word requested initially (read through), thus reducing the wait on a given reference, the low bandwidth memory interface will remain busy long after the initial transfer is completed, resulting in long delays if a second backing storage

operation is required.

We therefore have explored the effectiveness of a cache which exploits primarily or exclusively temporal locality, i.e., the blocks fetched from backing store are only the size needed by the CPU (or possibly slightly larger). In considering ways to evaluate this strategy, we identified a commercial environment that contained many of the same constraints and seemed amenable to the same kinds of solutions. This environment is the marketplace of the single-board computer running on a standard bus such as Multibus[2] or Versabus.[3] We have chosen to study this environment in an attempt to gain insight into the original, general scheme.

2. The Single Board Computer Application

A single board computer typically contains a microprocessor and a substantial amount of memory, though small enough that it must be used carefully. If needed, access to additional random access memory is through the bus, which is designed for generality and simplicity, not for high performance. Multibus, in particular, was defined in the early 70's to offer an inexpensive means of communication among a variety of sub-systems. Although originally introduced by Intel Corporation, it has found wide acceptance, having been proposed — in a slightly modified form — as the IEEE P796 bus standard [IEEE80]. Currently, several hundred vendors offer Multibus-compatible cards.

While the market has rapidly developed for products using this bus, its applications are limited by the severe constraint imposed by the bandwidth of Multibus. Clearly the bus bandwidth could be increased by increasing the number of pins, and by modifying the protocol. Its broad popularity and the availability of components to implement its protocol mean, however, that it is likely to survive many years in its present form. Thus a large market exists for a computer-on-a-card which, much as if it were all on a single chip, has severe limitations on its communications with the rest of the system.

We decided to determine if a cache memory system could be implemented effectively in the Multibus environment. To that end we have designed a cache to be used with a current-generation microprocessor. In addition, we have done extensive simulation of cache performance, driven by memory trace data. We have identified a new component which is particularly suited for VLSI implementation and have demonstrated its feasibility by designing it [Ravishankar83]. This component, which implements the tag memory for a dynamic RAM cache intended for a microprocessor, is similar in many respects to the recently announced TMS 2150 [TI82].

Multibus systems have generally dealt with the problem of limited bus bandwidth by removing most of the processor-memory accesses from the bus. Each processor card has its own local memory, which may be addressable to others through the Multibus. While this approach has much in common with ours, we believe that the allocation of memory — local or remote — should be handled by the system, freeing the programmer of this task. In typical Multibus applications, considerable effort is expended guaranteeing that the program running is primarily resident on-board. This approach is viable for a static partitioning of tasks. Results to date have been much less satisfactory, however, for the more general situation where a number of processors are dynamically allocated. (For efficiency reasons it also precludes the use of shared code segments).

---

[2]Multibus is a trademark of Intel Corporation.

[3]Versabus is a trademark of Motorola.

In many environments, a simple dynamic hardware allocation scheme can efficiently determine what memory locations are being accessed frequently and should therefore be kept in local memory — better than the programmer who often has little insight into the dynamic characteristics of his program. There are environments where the programmer is intimately familiar with the behavior of his program and can generate code to take advantage of it. In this environment the time spent running a program is often much more substantial than the time developing the program. This explains, for example, why an invisible cache is not appropriate on the CRAY-1. We believe that freeing the programmer from concern about memory allocation is essential where programmer productivity is critical.

2.1. A Single-Board Computer with Cache

To evaluate our approach, we proposed a single-board computer containing, (possibly along with other things) a CPU and no local memory except a cache, with backing store provided through Multibus. Thus we picked an important problem in its own right: Can we build a cache that works with a Multibus system supporting multiple processors? In particular, how many processors can we support running in parallel on Multibus? We believe that a system which could reasonably support five to 10 processors would be a significant advance. This can't be compared directly against current systems because a single processor overloads the Multibus. Thus local memories must be heavily exploited if performance is important.

Earlier analyses [Kaplan73, Bell74, Rao78, Patel82] have used the cache hit ratio or something closely related to measure performance. The important criterion here is to maximize use of the bus, not the hit ratio, or even necessarily to optimize processor performance. We optimize system performance by optimizing bus utilization, achieving higher performance by minimizing individual processors' bus requirements, and thereby supporting more processors reasonably well. We allow individual processors to sit idle periodically rather than tie up the bus fetching data which they might not use. This implies that the cache stale data problem must be solved effectively. We present a new solution in section 3.

2.2. Switching Contexts

Where bus bandwidth is limited, a task switch is a major disturbance, since the cache must effectively be reloaded at this time. The processor is momentarily reduced to accesses at the rate at which the bus can supply them. While this problem seems unavoidable, it need not be serious if task switching is minimized. We are providing an environment which allows many processors to work out of a single monolithic memory in parallel. If more parallel tasks are required, more processors can be used. We point out that the current Multibus alternative is to move the program into local memory, an operation which also swamps the bus. The task switch merely makes this operation implicit, and avoids bringing across the bus data which are never actually used. Writing the old data out is also no worse than the alternative, since we only write that which has been changed and which has not been already purged.

There may be certain cases — an interrupt handling program, for example — where a particular program does not flush the cache, but uses only a small portion of it. Provisions could be made to allow such a program to be locked in the cache. Alternatively, a separate cache might be provided for such a program Our studies indicate that a relatively small cache can be effective for a single program, so it may be possible to keep separate caches around for individual processes if the number is

small. We would suggest taking this one step further and providing an additional processor for each cache. An interesting question then arises as to the cost of dynamically assigning processes to processors. Our proposal allows this assignment, though clearly at some performance penalty.

3. Cache Coherency

It is well-known that multiple caches present serious problems because of the redundancy of storage of a single logical memory location [Tang76, Censier78, Rao78]. The most common method among commercial products for dealing with this, the stale data problem, is to create a special, high-speed bus on which addresses are sent whenever a write operation is performed by any processor. This solution has weaknesses [Censier78] which have generally limited commercial implementations to two processors. In the single-chip processor or single-board computer environments, it has the added weakness that it requires a number of extra I/O pins.

An alternative approach, implemented in C.mmp [Hoogendoorn77] and proposed by Norton [Norton82], is to require the operating system to recognize when inconsistencies might occur and take steps to prevent them under those circumstances. This solution is unappealing because the cache is normally regarded as an architecture-independent feature, invisible to the software.

A third approach, variations of which have been proposed by Censier and Feautrier [Censier78], Tang [Tang76], Widdoes [Widdoes79], and Yen and Fu [Yen82], is to use some form of tagged main memory, keeping track of individual blocks in this way to prevent inconsistency. Individual blocks are temporarily designated as *private* for a particular processor so that it may modify it repeatedly without reference to main memory. The tag must be set whenever such a critical section is entered and reset whenever the critical section is left, i.e., the modified word is written back to main storage. This approach requires substantial hardware, and appears infeasible for a large number of caches, since an operation in a central place is required at the entry or exit of any critical section.

Our approach has much in common with the third approach, but allows the critical section information to be distributed among the caches, where it already resides. In addition, we use the normal read and write operations, with no tag bits in main memory, to accomplish the synchronization. A related scheme [Amdahl82] which uses a special bus to convey the notice of entry or exit from a critical section, has been implemented in a commercial product, but has not been published to our knowledge. We call our scheme *write-once*.

3.1. Write-Through or Write-Back?

While the choice between write-through (also known as store-through) and write-back (also known as store-back or copy-back) has no bearing on the read hit ratio, it has a major impact on bus traffic, particularly as the hit ratio approaches 100%. In the limit, when the hit ratio is 100%, write-back results in no bus traffic at all, while write-through requires at least one bus cycle for each write operation. Norton [Norton82] concluded that using write-back instead of write-through for a hypothetical processor typically would reduce the bus traffic by more than 50% and if the processes ran to completion bus traffic would be decreased by a factor of 8. For typical read-to-write and hit ratios and when task switching is infrequent, our simulations have given strong evidence that write-back generates substantially less bus traffic than write-through.

But write-back has more severe coherency problems than write-through, since even main memory does not always contain the current version of a particular memory location.

3.2. A New Write Strategy: Write-Once

We propose a new write strategy which solves the stale data problem and produces minimal bus traffic. The replacement technique requires the following structure. Associated with each block in the cache are two bits defining one of four states for the associated data:

Invalid　There is no data in the block.

Valid　There is data in the block which has been read from backing store and has not been modified.

Reserved　The data in the block has been locally modified exactly once since it was brought into the cache and the change has been transmitted to backing store.

Dirty　The data in the block has been locally modified more than once since it was brought into the cache and the latest change has not been transmitted to backing store.

Write-once requires rapid access to the address tags and state bit pairs concurrently with accesses to the address tags by the CPU. This can most easily be achieved by creating two (identical) copies of the tag memory. Censier [Censier78] claims that duplication is "the usual way out" for resolving collisions between cache invalidation requests and normal cache references. This is not a large cost, since a single chip design of this part of the cache — using present technology — is quite feasible. Further, we have discovered a way to reduce substantially the number of tags required. In addition, the same chip type could be used for both instances. This is a natural way to partition the cache in VLSI because it results in a maximal logic-to-pin ratio. We have designed and submitted for fabrication such a chip [Ravishankar83].

The two copies always contain exactly the same address data, because they are always written simultaneously. While one unit is used in the conventional way to support accesses by the CPU, a second monitors all accesses to memory via the Multibus. For each such operation, it checks for the address in the local cache. If a match is found on a write operation, it notifies the cache controller, and the appropriate block in the cache is marked *invalid*. If a match is found on a read operation, nothing is done unless the block has been modified, i.e., its state is *reserved* or *dirty*. If it is just *reserved*, the state is changed to *valid*. If it is *dirty*, the local systems inhibits the backing store from supplying the data. It then supplies the data itself.[4] On the same bus access or immediately following it, the data must be written to backing store. In addition, for either *reserved* or *dirty* data, the state is changed to *valid*.

This scheme achieves coherency in the following way. Initially write-through is employed. However, an additional goal is achieved upon writing. All other caches are purged of the block being written, so the cache writing through the bus now is guaranteed the only copy except for backing store. It is so identified by being marked *reserved*. If it is purged at this point, no write is necessary to backing store, so this is essentially write-through. If another write occurs, the block is marked *dirty*. Now write-back is employed and, on purging, the data must be rewritten to backing store.

Write-once has the desirable feature that units accessing backing store need not have a cache, and need not know whether others do or not. A cache is responsible for maintaining consistency exactly for those cases where it might create a violation, i.e., whenever it writes to a location. Thus it is possible to mix in an arbitrary way systems which employ a cache and those which do not; the latter would probably be I/O devices. Considerable care must be exercised, however, when a write operation over the bus modifies less than an entire block.

4. Simulation

We designed a cache memory system to work on Multibus. To validate our design before building it we did extensive simulation using memory trace data. To date we have performed extensive simulations for six traces, all running under UNIX:[5]

EDC　The UNIX editor *ed* running a script.

ROFFAS　The old UNIX text processor program *roff*.

TRACE　The program, written in assembly language, which generated the above traces for the PDP-11.

NROFF　The program *nroff* interpreting the Berkeley macro package *-me*.

CACHE　The trace-driven cache simulator program.

COMPACT　A program using an on-line algorithm which compresses files using an adaptive Huffman code.

The first three traces are for a PDP-11, while the latter three are for a VAX. While the PDP-11 does not run on Multibus, its instruction set is similar to many microprocessors which do, and the programs used for tracing were of the kind we envision for such a system. The PDP-11 is similar in many ways to the MC68000, and has in common with the 8086 a limited addressing capability.

While the VAX also does not run on Multibus, it is an example of a modern instruction set and, therefore is a reasonable example of the kind of processor likely to appear in a single-chip CPU in the future. It also has a larger address space which, as shown in section 4.3, is significant. We are actually using virtual addresses, but all of the programs we ran are small enough to fit into main memory. Since we are tracing only a single process, we conclude that there is no significant difference between virtual and real addresses.

In addition to cache parameters, miss ratios vary greatly depending on the program running. For the each of the above traces, a wide and unpredictable variation occurred as we varied a single parameter. Thus plotting parameters for the individual traces was often not enlightening. Averaging over the three traces in each category gave much more revealing results, providing data that suggested a continuous function for many of the variables studied. Thus all our results are actually the average of three programs, each running alone.

4.1. Effect of Write Strategy on Bus Traffic

Although write-through normally generates less bus traffic than write-back, the latter can be worse if the hit ratio is low and the block size is large. Under write-back, when a dirty block is purged, the entire block must be written out. With write-through, only that portion which was modified must be written. We found that write-back is decisively superior to write-through except (1) when cache blocks are very large, or (2) when the cache size is very small.

---

[4]There is a mechanism in Multibus which allows this capability. Unfortunately, it is rarely used, not well-defined, and requires that local caches respond very rapidly. Versabus has a much cleaner mechanism by which this end can be accomplished.

[5]UNIX and NROFF are trademarks of Bell Laboratories.

Write-once results in bus traffic roughly equal to the better of the two. We have found cache parameters for which it actually performs better on the average than either write-through or write-back for a number of programs. This was a surprising result, since write-once was developed to assure coherency, not to minimize bus traffic. The replacement scheme outperforms both write-through and write-back whenever the total number of sets is about 16. For example, for a 4-way set associative, 2048-byte cache with a block size of 32 bytes, the average bus traffic for three PDP-11 programs for which we have traces was 30.768% for write-through, 17.55% for write-back, and 17.38% for write-once.

4.2. Cold Start vs. Warm Start

An important consideration in determining cache hit ratio and bus traffic is the cold start period known as the *lifetime function* [Easton78], during which time many misses occur because the cache is empty. This is defined as the period until as many cache misses have occurred as the total number of blocks in the cache. This initial burst of misses is amortized over all accesses, so the longer the trace analyzed, the lower the miss ratio obtained. In addition to the initiation of a program and occasional switches of environments, a cold start generally occurs whenever there is a task switch. Thus an important assumption in traditional cache evaluation is the frequency of task switching. We have argued that task switching must be very infrequent in our system. Thus we can more nearly approach in practice the warm start hit ratios, and thus it is appropriate to use very long traces of a single program, and assume a warm start. We did that initially, using the full length of the PDP-11 traces available to us (1,256,570 memory accesses). We noted, however, that for even much shorter traces than we were running, there was little difference between warm start and cold start statistics. Since cold start statistics are easier to generate, we normally used them. Unless stated otherwise, our results are from cold start, but at least 10 times the lifetime function in total length.

4.3. Cache Size

In general, we were surprised at the effectiveness of a small cache. For the PDP-11 traces with a cache of 2K bytes or larger, we discovered that essentially no misses occurred after the cold start period. These are not trivial programs, but were run on a machine which has only 64K bytes for both instructions and data. The programs are very frugal in their use of memory, and the entire working set apparently can fit in the cache.

The VAX traces do not exhibit the same locality observed with the PDP-11, and a 64K-byte cache was not large enough to contain the entire working set of the program. This may be a result of the larger address space available, the more complex instruction set, or more complex programs. In all cases the programs were spread out over a much larger memory space than for the PDP-11 traces. For this comparison we used a small block size of 4 bytes. This may have had a greater impact on the VAX than on PDP-11 traces.

We found that reducing the size of the cache (below 4K bytes for the PDP-11) increased the miss ratio and the bus traffic — in general the two correlate well with respect to this parameter. Fig. 1 shows the average miss ratio and bus traffic as a function of total cache size for the PDP-11 traces. For this and all results given, the miss ratio includes writes. The bus traffic is given as a percent of the number of accesses that would be required if no cache were present. Fig. 2 shows the same data for the VAX traces.

4.4. Block Size

Our cache design incorporates extremely small blocks, depending heavily on temporal locality. Easton and Fagin [Easton78] claim that page size and miss ratios are independent for warm start, but highly dependent for cold start. If true, this can be explained by the observation that hits in the cache on cold start depend heavily on spatial locality, while temporal locality provides many hits when it is warm. Spatial locality, however, is strongly correlated to block size, being directly proportional in the extreme case of strictly sequential memory accesses. Our simulations partially confirm Easton's observation. In particular, we found that, as block size is increased, miss ratios generally decline up to a point, then increase for either warm or cold starts. However, for small block sizes, the warm start miss ratio is marginally lower than for the cold start case, while for large block sizes, the two numbers are nearly identical. See figs. 3-7. This is encouraging since we have argued for restricted task switches: our environment is more that of a warm start than is the traditional environment. In many simulations we were able to get very high hit ratios once the cold start period ended. For small blocks transferred, however, this period (the lifetime function) is longer. Our simulations show very clearly that reducing the block size down to a single transfer across the bus dramatically decreases the hit ratio, particularly for cold starts, but also decreases bus traffic significantly. In general, we observed that increasing the transfer block size from one bus cycle to two typically decreases the miss ratio by 30 to 50%, while increasing the bus traffic by 10 to 20%. This relation holds for the first two doublings. These results, e.g., fig. 3, are relatively more pessimistic for small block sizes than those reported by Strecker in [Bell78].

We have made the assumption that access time is related linearly to block size. In many cases this is not true. It is essentially true for the Multibus, since only two bytes can be fetched at a time, and arbitration is overlapped with bus operations. For a single-chip implementation, it would almost certainly be worthwhile to provide the capability for efficient multiple transfers over a set of wires into the processor. This has not been incorporated in our analysis, but will undoubtedly suggest a somewhat larger transfer block size.

4.4.1. Lowering the Overhead of Small Blocks

Small blocks are costly in that they greatly increase the overhead of the cache: an address tag and the two state bits are normally stored in the cache for each block transferred. We reduced this overhead by splitting the notion of block into two parts:

(1) The *transfer block* is the amount of data transferred from backing store into the cache on a read miss.

(2) The *address block* is the quantum of storage for which a tag is maintained in the cache. It is always a power of two larger than a transfer block. An effective cache can be implemented by keeping the transfer block small but making the address block larger.

For most commercial products containing a cache, the address block size is the same as the transfer block size, though we know of one example [IBM74] where the address block contained two transfer blocks. The IBM System/360 Model 85 [Liptay68] in fact is a special case of this, *viz.*, a direct-mapped cache, where the Model 85 "sector," consisting of 1K bytes, corresponds to our address block. Each sector contains 16 transfer blocks, which were called simply "blocks."

4.4.2. The Effect of Large Address Blocks

The use of address blocks larger than transfer blocks means that only data from one address block in backing store can occupy any of the blocks making up an address block in the cache. There are cases where the appropriate transfer block is empty, but other transfer blocks in the same address block must be purged so that the new address block can be allocated. We examined this for various sizes of address blocks and found that the miss ratio increased very slowly up to a point. For the situation shown in fig. 7, the miss ratio had only risen by about 30% when the address block contained 64 bytes for the PDP-11 traces. That point was reached for the VAX traces when it contained 32-byte address blocks.

We predicted that the bus traffic would correlate well with miss ratio with respect to this parameter. To our surprise, the bus traffic actually *declined* initially as we increased the address block size. The decline was small, but consistent for the PDP-11 trace tapes, eventually climbing over the base line when the address block was 16 or 32 transfer blocks. The phenomenon was smaller, but discernible for the VAX traces as well, though in all cases the bus traffic started increasing sooner. This situation is shown in fig. 8.

We initially suspected that our simulation might be faulty. That was not the case, and eventually we were able to explain it and verify it. The write-once algorithm requires a bus operation whenever a block is modified initially (set to *reserved.*) However, reservations could be made on the basis of either transfer blocks or address blocks. We had put the choice into the simulator, but had not experimented with it, reserving at the address block level. This in fact reduces the number of bus writes necessary for reservation because of spatial locality of writes: an address block already *reserved* need only be marked *dirty* when any transfer block within it is modified. This would seem to increase greatly the traffic whenever the block is purged from the cache, but in fact the effect is small: only those transfer blocks which have actually been modified need be written back.

We demonstrated that this was indeed responsible for the behavior noted by changing the reservations to the transfer block level. The simulation results then exhibited the originally predicted behavior, correlating closely with the miss ratio.

We conclude that minimum bus traffic is generated with minimum transfer block sizes. The miss ratio may be substantially improved by using slightly larger transfer blocks, in which case bus traffic does not increase greatly. Using larger address blocks reduces the cost of the tag memory considerably. It initially has only a minor effect on miss ratio, which is more than offset by the savings in writes due to the more efficient reservation of modified blocks

4.5. Other Design Aspects Studied

4.5.1. Write Allocation

Write allocation, also known as *fetch on write*, means that a block is allocated in the cache on a write miss as well as on a read miss. While it seems natural for write-back, it typically is not used with write-through. It is essential for write-once to assure coherency. Our early simulations showed that it was highly desirable for write-back and write-once, and superior even for write-through with small blocks. This was true using both the measures of miss ratio and bus traffic. In all results presented, write allocation was employed.

4.5.2. Associativity

We ran a number of simulations varying the associativity all the way from direct mapped to fully associative. While this is clearly an important parameter, we have little new to report, i.e., fully associative cache is the best,

but 2-way set associative is not much worse, and 4-way set associative is somewhere in between. (But see [Smith83]). We had hoped to find that a high degree of associativity would improve performance, because such an organization is much more feasible in the VLSI domain, but results were negative. For results reported here we have assumed a 4-way, set associative cache.

4.5.3. Replacement Algorithm

Replacement strategy has been the subject of another study using the same simulator and traces [Smith83]. In order to limit its significance, which seems to be orthogonal to the issues raised here, we have assumed true LRU replacement among the elements of each set in all cases.

4.5.4. Bus Width

The width of the data paths between units is an important parameter in that it is closely related to bandwidth. We have the capability to specify the bus width both from backing store to cache and from cache to CPU. For the purposes of this study, we have assumed in all cases that the VAX memory supplies 4 bytes to the cache in one bus cycle, while the PDP-11 memory supplies 2 bytes. An 8-byte transfer therefore is counted as two cycles for the VAX and 4 for the PDP-11.

We assumed that the cache supplied one word — 16 bits for the PDP-11 and 32 bits for the VAX — to the CPU on each request. However, the intelligence of the processor determines how often the same word must be fetched. The trace tapes contain all memory references. We filtered these with the assumption that on instruction fetches the same word would not be fetched without an intervening instruction fetch. No filtering was done on data fetches.

5. Summary

Our simulations indicate that a single board computer with a 4K-byte cache can perform reasonably well with less than 10% of the accesses required to its primary memory without a cache. The PDP-11 traces suggest a number as low as 3%. While the VAX numbers are higher, additional declines will be experienced by increasing the size of the cache beyond 4K bytes.

An important result is the use of the write-once algorithm to guarantee consistent data among multiple processors. We have shown that this algorithm can be implemented in a way that degrades performance only trivially (ignoring actual collisions, which are rare), and performs better than either pure write-back or write-through in many instances.

The use of small transfer block sizes can be coupled with large address blocks to build an inexpensive cache which performs effectively in the absence of frequent process switches. The low bus utilization and the solution to the stale data problem make possible an environment for which this condition is met. Even though the miss ratio increases, bus traffic initially declines as the address block is enlarged, holding the transfer block constant. Therefore larger address blocks should be used for reserving memory for modification even if small blocks are used for transfer of data.

The approach advocated here is appropriate only for a system containing a single logical memory. This is significant because it depends on the serialization of memory accesses to assure consistency. It has applications beyond those studied here, however. For example, the access path to memory could be via a ring network, or any other technique in which every request passes every processor. This extension seems particularly applicable at the for maintaining consistency for a file system or a common virtual memory being supplied to multiple processors through a common bus such as Ethernet.

Clearly there are many environments for which this model is inappropriate — response to individual tasks may be unpredictable, for example. However, we believe that such a configuration has many potential applications and can be exploited economically if the appropriate VLSI components are designed. We have investigated the design of such components and believe that they are both feasible and well-suited for VLSI [Ravishankar83].

Our analysis indicates that the cache approach is reasonable for a system where bandwidth between the CPU and most of its memory is severely limited. We have demonstrated through simulation of real programs that a cache memory can be used to significantly reduce the amount of communication a processor requires. While we were interested in this for a single-chip microcomputer of the future, we have also demonstrated that such an approach is feasible for one or more currently popular commercial markets.

6. Acknowledgements

This material is based upon work supported by the National Science Foundation under Grant MCS-8202952.

We thank Dr. A. J. Smith for providing the PDP-11 trace tapes upon which much of our early work depended. We also wish to thank T.-H. Yang for developing the VAX trace facility. P. Vitale and T. Doyle contributed much through discussions and by commenting on an early draft of the manuscript.

7. References

[Amdahl 82] C. Amdahl, *private communication*, March 82.

[Bell 74] J. Bell, D. Casasent, and C. G. Bell, "An investigation of alternative cache organizations," *IEEE Trans. on Computers*, Vol. C-23, No. 4, April 1974, pp. 346-351.

[Bell 78] C. Bell, J. Judge, J. McNamara, *Computer engineering: a DEC view of hardware system design*, Digital Press, Bedford, Mass., 1978.

[Censier 78] L. M. Censier and P. Feautrier, "A new solution to coherence problems in multicache systems," *IEEE Trans. on Computers*, Vol. C-27, No. 12, December 1978, pp. 1112-1118.

[Easton 78] M. C. Easton and R. Fagin, "Cold-start vs. warm-start miss ratios," *CACM*, Vol. 21, No. 10, October 1978, pp. 866-872.

[Grosch 53] H. A. Grosch, "High Speed Arithmetic: the Digital Computer as a Research Tool," *Journal of the Optical Society of America*, Vol. 43, No. 4, (April 1953).

[Hoogendoorn 77] C. H. Hoogendoorn, "Reduction of memory interference in multiprocessor systems," *Proc. 4th Annual Symp. Comput. Arch.*, 1977, pp. 179-183.

[IBM 74] "System/370 model 155 theory of operation/diagrams manual (volume 5): buffer control unit," IBM System Products Division, Poughkeepsie, N.Y., 1974.

[IBM 76] "System/370 model 168 theory of operation/diagrams manual (volume 1)," Document No. SY22-6931-3, IBM System Products Division, Poughkeepsie, N.Y., 1976.

[IEEE 80] "Proposed microcomputer system bus standard (P796 bus)," *IEEE Computer Society Subcommittee Microcomputer System Bus Group*, October 1980.

[Kaplan 73] K. R. Kaplan and R. O. Winder, "Cache-based computer systems," *Computer*, March 1973, pp. 30-36.

[Knight 66] J. R. Knight, "Changes in computer performance," *Datamation*, Vol. 12, No. 9, September 1966, pp. 40-54.

[Lindsay 81] "Cache Memory for Microprocessors," *Computer Architecture News, ACM - SIGARCH*, Vol. 9, No. 5, (August 1981), pp. 6-13.

[Liptay 68] "J. S. Liptay, "Structural aspects of the System/360 Model 85, Part II: the cache," *IBM Syst. J.*, Vol. 7, No. 1, 1968, pp. 15-21.

[Norton 82] R. L. Norton and J. L. Abraham, "Using write back cache to improve performance of multiuser multiprocessors," *1982 Int. Conf. on Par. Proc.*, IEEE cat. no. 82CH1794-7, 1982, pp. 326-331.

[Patel 82] "Analysis of multiprocessor with private cache memories," J. H. Patel, *IEEE Trans. on Computers*, Vol. C-31, No. 4, April 1982, pp. 296-304.

[Rao 78] G. S. Rao, "Performance Analysis of Cache Memories," *Journal of the ACM*, Vol. 25, July 1978, pp. 378-395.

[Ravishankar 83] C. V. Ravishankar and J. Goodman, "Cache implementation for multiple microprocessors," *Digest of Papers, Spring COMPCON 83*, IEEE Computer Society Press, March 1983.

[Siewiorek 82] D. P. Siewiorek, C. G. Bell, and A. Newell, *Computer Structures: Principles and Examples*, McGraw-Hill, New York, N.Y., 1982.

[Smith 82] A. J. Smith, "Cache memories," *Computing Surveys*, Vol. 14, No. 3, September 1982, pp. 473-530.

[Smith 83] J. E. Smith and J. R. Goodman, "A study of instruction cache organizations and replacement policies," *Tenth Annual Symposium on Computer Architecture*, June 1983.

[Solomon 66] M. B. Solomon, Jr., "Economies of Scale and the IBM System/360," *CACM*, Vol. 9, No. 6, June 1966, pp. 435-440.

[Tang 76] C. K. Tang, "Cache system design in the tightly coupled multiprocessor system," *AFIPS Proc., NCC*, Vol. 45, pp. 749-753, 1976.

[TI 82] *Texas Instruments MOS Memory Data Book*, Texas Instruments, Inc., Memory Division, Houston, Texas, pp. 106-111, 1982.

[Tredennick 82] N. Tredennick, "The IBM micro/370 project," public lecture for *Distinguished Lecturer Series*, Computer Sciences Department, University of Wisconsin-Madison, March 31, 1982.

[Widdoes 79] L. C. Widdoes, "S-1 Multiprocessor architecture (MULT-2)," *1979 Annual Report — the S-1 Project, Volume 1: Architecture*, Lawrence Livermore Laboratories, Tech. Report UCID 18619, 1979.

[Yen 82] W. C. Yen and K. S. Fu, "Coherence problem in a multicache system," *1982 Int. Conf. on Par. Proc.*, IEEE cat. no. 82CH1794-7, 1982, pp. 332-339.

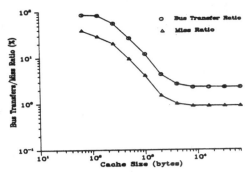

Fig. 1. Bus Transfer and Miss Ratios vs. Cache Size; blocks are 4 bytes; PDP-11 traces. The bus transfer ratio is the number of transfers between cache and main store relative to those necessary if there were no cache.

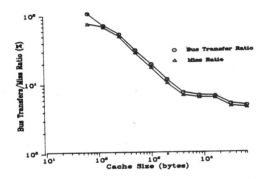

Fig. 2. Bus Transfer and Miss Ratios vs. Cache Size; 4-byte blocks; VAX-11 traces.

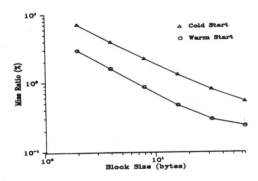

Fig. 3. Miss Ratio vs. Block Size for warm and cold starts; PDP-11 traces.

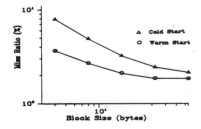

Fig. 4. Miss Ratio vs. Block Size for warm and cold starts; VAX-11 traces.

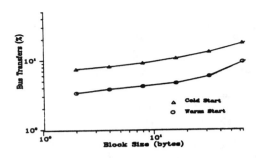

Fig. 5. Bus Transfer Ratio vs. Block Size for warm and cold starts; PDP-11 traces.

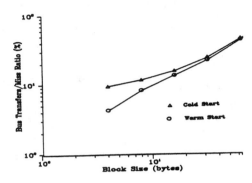

Fig. 6. Bus Transfer Ratio vs. Block Size for warm and cold starts; VAX-11 traces.

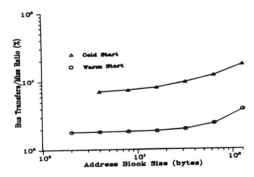

Fig. 7. Miss ratio vs. Address Block Size for warm and cold starts.

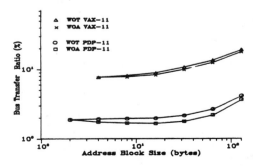

Fig. 8. Bus Transfer Ratio vs. Address Block Size for warm and cold starts; WOA: address blocks are reserved. WOT: transfer blocks are reserved.

Improving Direct-Mapped Cache Performance by the Addition of a Small Fully-Associative Cache and Prefetch Buffers

Norman P. Jouppi

Digital Equipment Corporation Western Research Lab

100 Hamilton Ave., Palo Alto, CA 94301

Abstract

Projections of computer technology forecast processors with peak performance of 1,000 MIPS in the relatively near future. These processors could easily lose half or more of their performance in the memory hierarchy if the hierarchy design is based on conventional caching techniques. This paper presents hardware techniques to improve the performance of caches.

Miss caching places a small fully-associative cache between a cache and its refill path. Misses in the cache that hit in the miss cache have only a one cycle miss penalty, as opposed to a many cycle miss penalty without the miss cache. Small miss caches of 2 to 5 entries are shown to be very effective in removing mapping conflict misses in first-level direct-mapped caches.

Victim caching is an improvement to miss caching that loads the small fully-associative cache with the victim of a miss and not the requested line. Small victim caches of 1 to 5 entries are even more effective at removing conflict misses than miss caching.

Stream buffers prefetch cache lines starting at a cache miss address. The prefetched data is placed in the buffer and not in the cache. Stream buffers are useful in removing capacity and compulsory cache misses, as well as some instruction cache conflict misses. Stream buffers are more effective than previously investigated prefetch techniques at using the next slower level in the memory hierarchy when it is pipelined. An extension to the basic stream buffer, called *multi-way stream buffers*, is introduced. Multi-way stream buffers are useful for prefetching along multiple intertwined data reference streams.

Together, victim caches and stream buffers reduce the miss rate of the first level in the cache hierarchy by a factor of two to three on a set of six large benchmarks.

1. Introduction

Cache performance is becoming increasingly important since it has a dramatic effect on the performance of advanced processors. Table 1-1 lists some cache miss times and the effect of a miss on machine performance. Over the last decade, cycle time has been decreasing much faster than main memory access time. The average number of machine cycles per instruction has also been decreasing dramatically, especially when the transition from CISC machines to RISC machines is included. These two effects are multiplicative and result in tremendous increases in miss cost. For example, a cache miss on a VAX 11/780 only costs 60% of the average instruction execution time. Thus even if every instruction had a cache miss, the machine performance would slow down by only 60%! However, if a RISC machine like the WRL Titan [10] has a miss, the cost is almost ten instruction times. Moreover, these trends seem to be continuing, especially the increasing ratio of memory access time to machine cycle time. In the future a cache miss all the way to main memory on a superscalar machine executing two instructions per cycle could cost well over 100 instruction times! Even with careful application of well-known cache design techniques, machines with main memory latencies of over 100 instruction times can easily lose over half of their potential performance to the memory hierarchy. This makes both hardware and software research on advanced memory hierarchies increasingly important.

Machine	cycles per instr	cycle time (ns)	mem time (ns)	miss cost (cycles)	miss cost (instr)
VAX11/780	10.0	200	1200	6	.6
WRL Titan	1.4	45	540	12	8.6
?	0.5	4	280	70	140.0

Table 1-1: The increasing cost of cache misses

This paper investigates new hardware techniques for increasing the performance of the memory hierarchy. Section 2 describes a baseline design using conventional caching techniques. The large performance loss due to the memory hierarchy is a detailed motivation for the techniques discussed in the remainder of the paper. Techniques for reducing misses due to mapping conflicts (i.e., lack of associativity) are presented in Section 3. An extension to prefetch techniques called stream buffering is evaluated in Section 4. Section 5 summarizes this work and evaluates promising directions for future work.

2. Baseline Design

Figure 2-1 shows the range of configurations of interest in this study. The CPU, floating-point unit, memory management unit (e.g., TLB), and first level instruction and data caches are on the same chip or on a single high-speed module built with an advanced packaging technology. (We will refer to the central processor as a single chip in the remainder of the paper, but chip or module is implied.) The cycle time off this chip is 3 to 8 times longer than the instruction issue rate (i.e., 3 to 8 instructions can issue in one off-chip clock cycle). This is obtained either by having a very fast on-chip clock (e.g., superpipelining [8]), by issuing many instructions per cycle (e.g., superscalar or VLIW), and/or by using higher speed technologies for the processor chip than for the rest of the system (e.g., GaAs vs. BiCMOS).

The expected size of the on-chip caches varies with the implementation technology for the processor, but higher-speed technologies generally result in smaller on-chip caches. For example, quite large on-chip caches should be feasible in CMOS but only small caches are feasible in the near term for GaAs or bipolar processors. Thus, although GaAs and bipolar are faster, the higher miss rate from their smaller caches tends to decrease the actual system performance ratio between GaAs or bipolar machines and dense CMOS machines to less than the ratio between their gate speeds. In all cases the first-level caches are assumed to be direct-mapped, since this results in the fastest effective access time [7]. Line sizes in the on-chip caches are most likely in the range of 16B to 32B. The data cache may be either write-through or write-back, but this paper does not examine those tradeoffs.

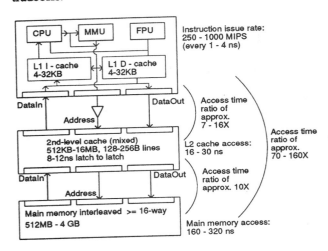

Figure 2-1: Baseline design

The second-level cache is assumed to range from 512KB to 16MB, and to be built from very high speed static RAMs. It is assumed to be direct-mapped for the same reasons as the first-level caches. For caches of this size access times of 16 to 30ns are likely. This yields an access time for the cache of 4 to 30 instruction times. The relative speed of the processor as compared to the access time of the cache implies that the second-level cache must be pipelined in order for it to provide sufficient bandwidth. For example, consider the case where the first-level cache is a write-through cache. Since stores typically occur at an average rate of 1 in every 6 or 7 instructions, an unpipelined external cache would not have even enough bandwidth to handle the store traffic for access times greater than seven instruction times. Caches have been pipelined in mainframes for a number of years [12], but this is a recent development for workstations. Recently cache chips with ECL I/O's and registers or latches on their inputs and outputs have appeared; these are ideal for pipelined caches. The number

of pipeline stages in a second-level cache access could be 2 or 3 depending on whether the pipestage going from the processor chip to the cache chips and the pipestage returning from the cache chips to the processor are full or half pipestages.

In order to provide sufficient memory for a processor of this speed (e.g., several megabytes per MIP), main memory should be in the range of 512MB to 4GB. This means that even if 16Mb DRAMs are used that it will contain roughly a thousand DRAMs. The main memory system probably will take about ten times longer for an access than the second-level cache. This access time is easily dominated by the time required to fan out address and data signals among a thousand DRAMs spread over many cards. Thus even with the advent of faster DRAMs, the access time for main memory may stay roughly the same. The relatively large access time for main memory in turn requires that second-level cache line sizes of 128 or 256B are needed. As a counter example, consider the case where only 16B are returned after 320ns. This is a bus bandwidth of 50MB/sec. Since a 10 MIP processor with this bus bandwidth would be bus-bandwidth limited in copying from one memory location to another [11], little extra performance would be obtained by the use of a 100 to 1,000 MIP processor. This is an important consideration in the system performance of a processor.

Several observations are in order on the baseline system. First, the memory hierarchy of the system is actually quite similar to that of a machine like the VAX 11/780 [3, 4], only each level in the hierarchy has moved one step closer to the CPU. For example, the 8KB board-level cache in the 780 has moved on-chip. The 512KB to 16MB main memory on early VAX models has become the board-level cache. Just as in the 780's main memory, the incoming transfer size is large (128-256B here vs. 512B pages in the VAX). The main memory in this system is of similar size to the disk subsystems of the early 780's and performs similar functions such as paging and file system caching.

The actual parameters assumed for our baseline system are 1,000 MIPS peak instruction issue rate, separate 4KB first-level instruction and data caches with 16B lines, and a 1MB second-level cache with 128B lines. The miss penalties are assumed to be 24 instruction times for the first level and 320 instruction times for the second level. The characteristics of the test programs used in this study are given in Table 2-1. These benchmarks are reasonably long in comparison with most traces in use today, however the effects of multiprocessing have not been modeled in this work. The first-level cache miss rates of these programs running on the baseline system configuration are given in Table 2-2.

program name	dynamic instr.	data refs.	total refs.	program type
ccom	31.5M	14.0M	45.5M	C compiler
grr	134.2M	59.2M	193.4M	PC board CAD
yacc	51.0M	16.7M	67.7M	Unix utility
met	99.4M	50.3M	149.7M	PC board CAD
linpack	144.8M	40.7M	185.5M	100x100 numeric
liver	23.6M	7.4M	31.0M	LFK (numeric)
total	484.5M	188.3M	672.8M	

Table 2-1: Test program characteristics

The effects of these miss rates are given graphically in Figure 2-2. The region below the solid line gives the net performance of the system, while the region above the solid line gives the performance lost in the memory hierarchy. For example, the difference between the top dotted line and the bottom dotted line gives the performance lost due to first-level data cache misses. As can be seen in Figure 2-2, most benchmarks lose over half of their potential performance in first level cache misses. Only relatively small amounts of performance are lost to second-level cache misses. This is primarily due to the large second-level cache size in comparison to the size of the programs executed. Longer traces [2] of larger programs exhibit significant numbers of second-level cache misses. Since the test suite used in this paper is too small for significant second-level cache activity, second-level cache misses will not be investigated in detail, but will be left to future work.

program name	baseline miss rate instr.	data
ccom	0.096	0.120
grr	0.061	0.062
yacc	0.028	0.040
met	0.017	0.039
linpack	0.000	0.144
liver	0.000	0.273

Table 2-2: Baseline system first-level cache miss rates

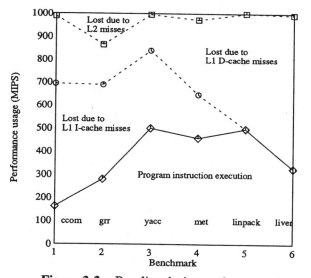

Figure 2-2: Baseline design performance

Since the exact parameters assumed are at the extreme end of the ranges described (maximum performance processor with minimum size caches), other configurations would lose proportionally less performance in their memory hierarchy. Nevertheless, any configuration in the range of interest will lose a substantial proportion of its potential performance in the memory hierarchy. This means that the greatest leverage on system performance will be obtained by improving the memory hierarchy performance, and not by attempting to further increase the performance of the CPU (e.g., by more aggressive parallel issuing of instructions). Techniques for improving the performance of the baseline memory

hierarchy at low cost are the subject of the remainder of this paper. Finally, in order to avoid compromising the performance of the CPU core (comprising of the CPU, FPU, MMU, and first level caches), any additional hardware required by the techniques to be investigated should reside outside the CPU core (i.e., below the first level caches). By doing this the additional hardware will only be involved during cache misses, and therefore will not be in the critical path for normal instruction execution.

3. Reducing Conflict Misses: Miss Caching and Victim Caching

Misses in caches can be classified into four categories: conflict, compulsory, capacity [7], and coherence. Conflict misses are misses that would not occur if the cache was fully-associative and had LRU replacement. Compulsory misses are misses required in any cache organization because they are the first references to an instruction or piece of data. Capacity misses occur when the cache size is not sufficient to hold data between references. Coherence misses are misses that occur as a result of invalidation to preserve multiprocessor cache consistency.

Even though direct-mapped caches have more conflict misses due to their lack of associativity, their performance is still better than set-associative caches when the access time costs for hits are considered. In fact, the direct-mapped cache is the only cache configuration where the critical path is merely the time required to access a RAM [9]. Conflict misses typically account for between 20% and 40% of all direct-mapped cache misses [7]. Figure 3-1 details the percentage of misses due to conflicts for our test suite. On average 39% of the first-level data cache misses are due to conflicts, and 29% of the first-level instruction cache misses are due to conflicts. Since these are significant percentages, it would be nice to "have our cake and eat it too" by somehow providing additional associativity without adding to the critical access path for a direct-mapped cache.

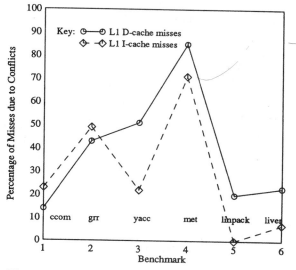

Figure 3-1: Conflict misses, 4KB I and D, 16B lines

3.1. Miss Caching

We can add associativity to a direct-mapped cache by placing a small *miss cache* on-chip between a first-level cache and the access port to the second-level cache (Figure 3-2). A miss cache is a small fully-associative cache containing on the order of two to five cache lines of data. When a miss occurs, data is returned not only to the direct-mapped cache, but also to the miss cache under it, where it replaces the least recently used item. Each time the upper cache is probed, the miss cache is probed as well. If a miss occurs in the upper cache but the address hits in the miss cache, then the direct-mapped cache can be reloaded in the next cycle from the miss cache. This replaces a long off-chip miss penalty with a short one-cycle on-chip miss. This arrangement satisfies the requirement that the critical path is not worsened, since the miss cache itself is not in the normal critical path of processor execution.

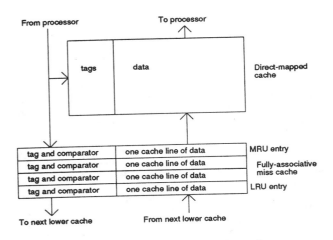

Figure 3-2: Miss cache organization

The success of different miss cache organizations at removing conflict misses is shown in Figure 3-3. The first observation to be made is that many more data conflict misses are removed by the miss cache than instruction conflict misses. This can be explained as follows. Instruction conflicts tend to be widely spaced because the instructions within one procedure will not conflict with each other as long as the procedure size is less than the cache size, which is almost always the case. Instruction conflict misses are most likely when another procedure is called. The target procedure may map anywhere with respect to the calling procedure, possibly resulting in a large overlap. Assuming at least 60 different instructions are executed in each procedure, the conflict misses would span more than the 15 lines in the maximum size miss cache tested. In other words, a small miss cache could not contain the entire overlap and so would be reloaded repeatedly before it could be used. This type of reference pattern exhibits the worst miss cache performance.

Data conflicts, on the other hand, can be quite closely spaced. Consider the case where two character strings are being compared. If the points of comparison of the two strings happen to map to the same line, alternating references to different strings will always miss in the cache. In this case a miss cache of only two entries

would remove all of the conflict misses. Obviously this is another extreme of performance and the results in Figure 3-3 show a range of performance based on the program involved. Nevertheless, for 4KB data caches a miss cache of only 2 entries can remove 25% percent of the data cache conflict misses on average,[1] or 13% of the data cache misses overall. If the miss cache is increased to 4 entries, 36% percent of the conflict misses can be removed, or 18% of the data cache misses overall. After four entries the improvement from additional miss cache entries is minor, only increasing to a 25% overall reduction in data cache misses if 15 entries are provided.

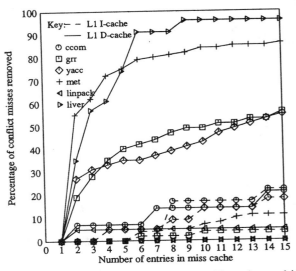

Figure 3-3: Conflict misses removed by miss caching

Since doubling the data cache size results in a 32% reduction in misses (over this set of benchmarks when increasing data cache size from 4K to 8K), each additional line in the first level cache reduces the number of misses by approximately 0.13%. Although the miss cache requires more area per bit of storage than lines in the data cache, each line in a two line miss cache effects a 50 times larger marginal improvement in the miss rate, so this should more than cover any differences in layout size.

Comparing Figure 3-3 and Figure 3-1, we see that the higher the percentage of misses due to conflicts, the more effective the miss cache is at eliminating them. For example, in Figure 3-1 *met* has by far the highest ratio of conflict misses to total data cache misses. Similarly, *grr* and *yacc* also have greater than average percentages of conflict misses, and the miss cache helps these programs significantly as well. *linpack* and *ccom* have the lowest

---

[1]Throughout this paper the average reduction in miss rates is used as a metric. This is computed by calculating the percent reduction in miss rate for each benchmark, and then taking the average of these percentages. This has the advantage that it is independent of the number of memory references made by each program. Furthermore, if two programs have widely different miss rates, the average percent reduction in miss rate gives equal weighting to each benchmark. This is in contrast with the percent reduction in average miss rate, which weights the program with the highest miss rate most heavily.

percentage of conflict misses, and the miss cache removes the lowest percentage of conflict misses from these programs. This results from the fact that if a program has a large percentage of data conflict misses then they must be clustered to some extent because of their overall density. This does not prevent programs with a small number of conflict misses such as *liver* from benefiting from a miss cache, but it seems that as the percentage of conflict misses increases, the percentage of these misses removable by a miss cache increases.

3.2. Victim Caching

Consider a system with a direct-mapped cache and a miss cache. When a miss occurs, data is loaded into both the miss cache and the direct-mapped cache. In a sense, this duplication of data wastes storage space in the miss cache. The number of duplicate items in the miss cache can range from one (in the case where all items in the miss cache map to the same line in the direct-mapped cache) to all of the entries (in the case where a series of misses occur which do not hit in the miss cache).

To make better use of the miss cache we can use a different replacement algorithm for the small fully-associative cache [5]. Instead of loading the requested data into the miss cache on a miss, we can load the fully-associative cache with the victim line from the direct-mapped cache instead. We call this *victim caching* (see Figure 3-4). With victim caching, no data line appears both in the direct-mapped cache and the victim cache. This follows from the fact that the victim cache is loaded only with items thrown out from the direct-mapped cache. In the case of a miss in the direct-mapped cache that hits in the victim cache, the contents of the direct-mapped cache line and the matching victim cache line are swapped.

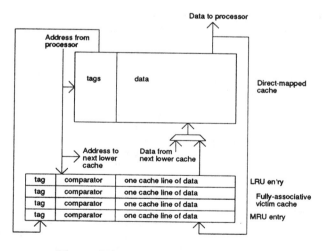

Figure 3-4: Victim cache organization

Depending on the reference stream, victim caching can either be a small or significant improvement over miss caching. The magnitude of this benefit depends on the amount of duplication in the miss cache. Victim caching is always an improvement over miss caching.

As an example, consider an instruction reference stream that calls a small procedure in its inner loop that conflicts with the loop body. If the total number of con-

flicting lines between the procedure and loop body were larger than the miss cache, the miss cache would be of no value since misses at the beginning of the loop would be flushed out by later misses before execution returned to the beginning of the loop. If a victim cache is used instead, however, the number of conflicts in the loop that can be captured is doubled compared to that stored by a miss cache. This is because one set of conflicting instructions lives in the direct-mapped cache, while the other lives in the victim cache. As execution proceeds around the loop and through the procedure call these items trade places.

The percentage of conflict misses removed by victim caching is given in Figure 3-5. Note that victim caches consisting of just one line are useful, in contrast to miss caches which must have two lines to be useful. All of the benchmarks have improved performance in comparison to miss caches, but instruction cache performance and the data cache performance of benchmarks that have conflicting long sequential reference streams (e.g., *ccom* and *linpack*) improve the most.

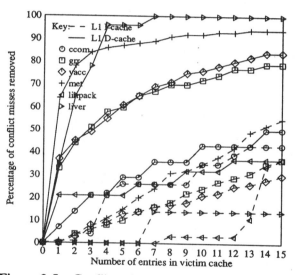

Figure 3-5: Conflict misses removed by victim caching

3.3. The Effect of Direct-Mapped Cache Size on Victim Cache Performance

Figure 3-6 shows the performance of 1, 2, 4, and 15 entry victim caches when backing up direct-mapped data caches of varying sizes. In general smaller direct-mapped caches benefit the most from the addition of a victim cache. Also shown for reference is the total percentage of conflict misses for each cache size. There are two factors to victim cache performance versus direct-mapped cache size. First, as the direct-mapped cache increases in size, the relative size of the victim cache becomes smaller. Since the direct-mapped cache gets larger but keeps the same line size (16B), the likelihood of a tight mapping conflict which would be easily removed by victim caching is reduced. Second, the percentage of conflict misses decreases slightly from 1KB to 32KB. As we have seen previously, as the percentage of conflict misses decreases, the percentage of these misses removed by the victim cache decreases. The first effect dominates, however, since as the percentage of conflict misses increases with very large caches (as in [7]), the victim cache performance only improves slightly.

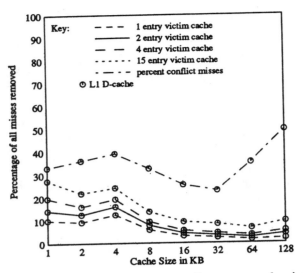

Figure 3-6: Victim cache: vary direct-map cache size

3.4. The Effect of Line Size on Victim Cache Performance

Figure 3-7 shows the performance of victim caches for 4KB direct-mapped data caches of varying line sizes. As one would expect, as the line size at this level increases, the number of conflict misses also increases.

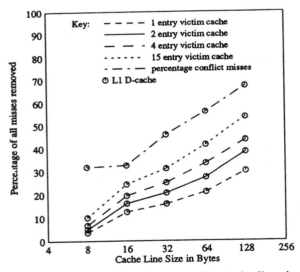

Figure 3-7: Victim cache: vary data cache line size

The increasing percentage of conflict misses results in an increasing percentage of these misses being removed by the victim cache. Systems with victim caches can benefit from longer line sizes more than systems without victim caches, since the victim caches help remove misses caused by conflicts that result from longer cache lines. Note that even if the area used for data storage in the victim cache is held constant (i.e., the

number of entries is cut in half when the line size doubles) the performance of the victim cache still improves or at least breaks even when line sizes increase.

3.5. Victim Caches and Second-Level Caches

As the size of a cache increases, a larger percentage of its misses are due to conflict and compulsory misses and fewer are due to capacity misses. (Unless of course the cache is larger than the entire program, in which case only compulsory misses remain.) Thus victim caches might be expected to be useful for second-level caches as well. Since the number of conflict misses increases with increasing line sizes, the large line sizes of second-level caches would also tend to increase the potential usefulness of victim caches.

One interesting aspect of victim caches is that they violate inclusion properties [1] in cache hierarchies. However, the line size of the second level cache in the baseline design is 8 to 16 times larger than the first-level cache line sizes, so this violates inclusion as well.

Note that a first-level victim cache can contain many lines that conflict not only at the first level but also at the second level. Thus, using a first-level victim cache can also reduce the number of conflict misses at the second level. In investigating victim caches for second-level caches, both configurations with and without first-level victim caches will need to be considered.

A thorough investigation of victim caches for megabyte second-level caches requires traces of billions of instructions. At this time we only have victim cache performance for our smaller test suite, and work on obtaining victim cache performance for multi-megabyte second-level caches is underway.

4. Reducing Capacity and Compulsory Misses

Compulsory misses are misses required in any cache organization because they are the first references to a piece of data. Capacity misses occur when the cache size is not sufficient to hold data between references. One way of reducing the number of capacity and compulsory misses is to use prefetch techniques such as longer cache line sizes or prefetching methods [13, 6]. However, line sizes can not be made arbitrarily large without increasing the miss rate and greatly increasing the amount of data to be transferred. In this section we investigate techniques to reduce capacity and compulsory misses while mitigating traditional problems with long lines and excessive prefetching.

A detailed analysis of three prefetch algorithms has appeared in [13]. *Prefetch always* prefetches after every reference. Needless to say this is impractical in our base system since many level-one cache accesses can take place in the time required to initiate a single level-two cache reference. This is especially true in machines that fetch multiple instructions per cycle from an instruction cache and can concurrently perform a load or store per cycle to a data cache. *Prefetch on miss* and *tagged prefetch* are more promising techniques. On a miss *prefetch on miss* always fetches the next line as well. It can cut the number of misses for a purely sequential reference stream in half. *Tagged prefetch* can do even better. In this technique each block has a tag bit associated with it. When a block is prefetched, its tag bit is set to zero. Each time a block is used its tag bit is set to one. When a block undergoes a zero to one transition its successor block is prefetched. This can reduce the number of misses in a purely sequential reference stream to zero, if fetching is fast enough. Unfortunately the large latencies in the base system can make this impossible. Consider Figure 4-1, which gives the amount of time (in instruction issues) until a prefetched line is required during the execution of *ccom*. Not surprisingly, since the line size is four instructions, prefetched lines must be received within four instruction-times to keep up with the machine on uncached straight-line code. Because the base system second-level cache takes many cycles to access, and the machine may actually issue many instructions per cycle, tagged prefetch may only have a one-cycle-out-of-many head start on providing the required instructions.

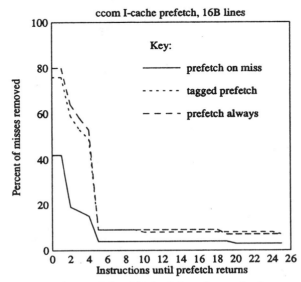

Figure 4-1: Limited time for prefetch

4.1. Stream Buffers

What we really need to do is to start the prefetch before a tag transition can take place. We can do this with a mechanism called a *stream buffer* (Figure 4-2). A stream buffer consists of a series of entries, each consisting of a tag, an available bit, and a data line.

When a miss occurs, the stream buffer begins prefetching successive lines starting at the miss target. As each prefetch request is sent out, the tag for the address is entered into the stream buffer, and the available bit is set to false. When the prefetch data returns it is placed in the entry with its tag and the available bit is set to true. Note that lines after the line requested on the miss are placed in the buffer and not in the cache. This avoids polluting the cache with data that may never be needed.

Subsequent accesses to the cache also compare their address against the first item stored in the buffer. If a reference misses in the cache but hits in the buffer the cache can be reloaded in a single cycle from the stream buffer. This is much faster than the off-chip miss penalty. The stream buffers considered in this section are simple FIFO queues, where only the head of the queue has a tag comparator and elements removed from the buffer must be removed strictly in sequence without

skipping any lines. In this simple model non-sequential line misses will cause a stream buffer to be flushed and restarted at the miss address even if the requested line is already present further down in the queue.

When a line is moved from a stream buffer to the cache, the entries in the stream buffer can shift up by one and a new successive address is fetched. The pipelined interface to the second level allows the buffer to be filled at the maximum bandwidth of the second level cache, and many cache lines can be in the process of being fetched simultaneously. For example, assume the latency to refill a 16B line on a instruction cache miss is 12 cycles. Consider a memory interface that is pipelined and can accept a new line request every 4 cycles. A four-entry stream buffer can provide 4B instructions at a rate of one per cycle by having three requests outstanding at all times. Thus during sequential instruction execution long latency cache misses will not occur. This is in contrast to the performance of tagged prefetch on purely sequential reference streams where only one line is being prefetched at a time. In that case sequential instructions will only be supplied at a bandwidth equal to one instruction every three cycles (i.e., 12 cycle latency / 4 instructions per line).

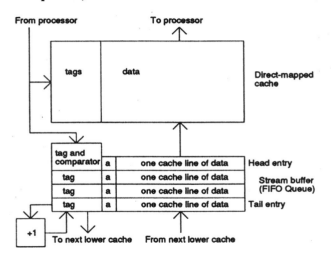

Figure 4-2: Sequential stream buffer design

Figure 4-3 shows the performance of a four-entry instruction stream buffer backing a 4KB instruction cache and a data stream buffer backing a 4KB data cache, each with 16B lines. The graph gives the cumulative number of misses removed based on the number of lines that the buffer is allowed to prefetch after the original miss. (In practice the stream buffer would probably be allowed to fetch until the end of a virtual memory page or a second-level cache line. The major reason for plotting stream buffer performance as a function of prefetch length is to get a better idea of how far streams continue on average.) Most instruction references break the purely sequential access pattern by the time the 6th successive line is fetched, while many data reference patterns end even sooner. The exceptions to this appear to be instruction references for *liver* and data references for *linpack*. *liver* is probably an anomaly since the 14 loops of the program are executed sequentially, and the first 14 loops do not generally call other procedures or do excessive branching, which would cause the sequential miss pattern to break. The data reference pattern of *linpack* can be understood as follows. Remember that the stream buffer is only responsible for providing lines that the cache misses on. The inner loop of *linpack* (i.e., saxpy) performs an inner product between one row and the other rows of a matrix. The first use of the one row loads it into the cache. After that subsequent misses in the cache (except for mapping conflicts with the first row) consist of subsequent lines of the matrix. Since the matrix is too large to fit in the on-chip cache, the whole matrix is passed through the cache on each iteration. The stream buffer can do this at the maximum bandwidth provided by the second-level cache. Of course one prerequisite for this is that the reference stream is unit-stride or at most skips to every other or every third word. If an array is accessed in the non-unit-stride direction (and the other dimensions have non-trivial extents) then a stream buffer as presented here will be of little benefit.

experience the greatest improvement (it changes from 7% to 60% reduction), all of the programs benefit to some extent.

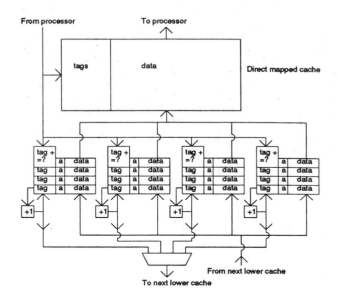

Figure 4-4: Four-way stream buffer design

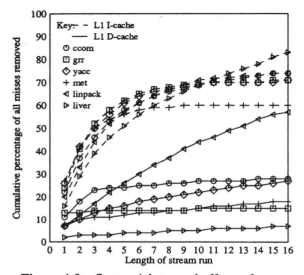

Figure 4-3: Sequential stream buffer performance

4.2. Multi-Way Stream Buffers

Overall, the stream buffer presented in the previous section could remove 72% of the instruction cache misses, but it could only remove 25% of the data cache misses. One reason for this is that data references tend to consist of interleaved streams of data from different sources. In order to improve the performance of stream buffers for data references, a multi-way stream buffer was simulated (Figure 4-4). It consists of four stream buffers in parallel. When a miss occurs in the data cache that does not hit in any stream buffer, the stream buffer hit least recently is cleared (i.e., LRU replacement) and it is started fetching at the miss address.

Figure 4-5 shows the performance of the multi-way stream buffer on our benchmark set. As expected, the performance on the instruction stream remains virtually unchanged. This means that the simpler single stream buffer will suffice for instruction streams. The multi-way stream buffer does significantly improve the performance on the data side, however. Overall, the multi-way stream buffer can remove 43% of the misses for the six programs, almost twice the performance of the single stream buffer. Although the matrix operations of *liver*

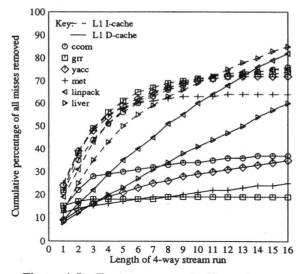

Figure 4-5: Four-way stream buffer performance

4.3. Stream Buffer Performance vs. Cache Size

Figure 4-6 gives the performance of single and 4-way stream buffers with 16B lines as a function of cache size. The instruction stream buffers have remarkably constant performance over a wide range of cache sizes. The data stream buffer performance generally improves as the cache size increases. This is especially true for the single stream buffer, whose performance increases from a 15% reduction in misses for a data cache size of 1KB to a 35% reduction in misses for a data cache size of 128KB. This is probably because as the cache size increases, it can contain data for reference patterns that access several sets of data, or at least all but one of the sets. What misses that remain are more likely to consist of very long single sequential streams. For example, as the cache size increases the percentage of compulsory misses increase, and these are more likely to be sequential in nature than data conflict or capacity misses.

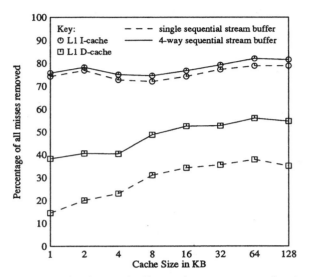

Figure 4-6: Stream buffer performance vs. cache size

4.4. Stream Buffer Performance vs. Line Size

Figure 4-7 gives the performance of single and 4-way stream buffers as a function of the line size in the stream buffer and 4KB cache. The reduction in misses provided by a single data stream buffer falls by a factor of 6.8 going from a line size of 8B to a line size of 128B, while a 4-way stream buffer's contribution falls by a factor of 4.5. This is not too surprising since data references are often fairly widely distributed. In other words if a piece of data is accessed, the odds that another piece of data 128B away will be needed soon are fairly low. The single data stream buffer performance is especially hard hit compared to the multi-way stream buffer because of the increase in conflict misses at large line sizes.

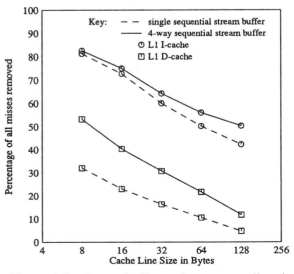

Figure 4-7: Stream buffer performance vs. line size

The instruction stream buffers perform well even out to 128B line sizes. Both the 4-way and the single stream buffer still remove at least 40% of the misses at 128B line sizes, coming down from an 80% reduction with 8B lines. This is probably due to the large granularity of conflicting instruction reference streams, and the fact that many procedures are more than 128B long.

5. Conclusions

Small miss caches (e.g., 2 to 5 entries) have been shown to be effective in reducing data cache conflict misses for direct-mapped caches in range of 1K to 8K bytes. They effectively remove tight conflicts where misses alternate between several addresses that map to the same line in the cache. Miss caches are increasingly beneficial as line sizes increase and the percentage of conflict misses increases. In general it appears that as the percentage of conflict misses increases, the percent of these misses removable by a miss cache also increases, resulting in an even steeper slope for the performance improvement possible by using miss caches.

Victim caches are an improvement to miss caching that saves the victim of the cache miss instead of the target in a small associative cache. Victim caches are even more effective at removing conflict misses than miss caches.

Stream buffers prefetch cache lines after a missed cache line. They store the line until it is requested by a cache miss (if ever) to avoid unnecessary pollution of the cache. They are particularly useful at reducing the number of capacity and compulsory misses. They can take full advantage of the memory bandwidth available in pipelined memory systems for sequential references, unlike previously discussed prefetch techniques such as tagged prefetch or prefetch on miss. Stream buffers can also tolerate longer memory system latencies since they prefetch data much in advance of other prefetch techniques (even prefetch always). Stream buffers can also compensate for instruction conflict misses, since these tend to be relatively sequential in nature as well.

Multi-way stream buffers are a set of stream buffers that can prefetch down several streams concurrently. Multi-way stream buffers are useful for data references that contain interleaved accesses to several different large data structures, such as in array operations. However, since the prefetching is of sequential lines, only unit stride or near unit stride (2 or 3) access patterns benefit.

The performance improvements due to victim caches and due to stream buffers are relatively orthogonal for data references. Victim caches work well where references alternate between two locations that map to the same line in the cache. They do not prefetch data but only do a better job of keeping data fetched available for use. Stream buffers, however, achieve performance improvements by prefetching data. They do not remove conflict misses unless the conflicts are widely spaced in time, and the cache miss reference stream consists of many sequential accesses. These are precisely the conflict misses not handled well by a victim cache due to its relatively small capacity. Over the set of six benchmarks, on average only 2.5% of 4KB direct-mapped data cache misses that hit in a four-entry victim cache also hit in a four-way stream buffer for *ccom*, *met*, *yacc*, *grr*, and *liver*. In contrast, *linpack*, due to its sequential data access patterns, has 50% of the hits in the victim cache also hit in a four-way stream buffer. However only 4% of *linpack*'s cache misses hit in the victim cache (it benefits least from victim caching among the six benchmarks), so this is still not a significant amount of overlap between stream buffers and victim caching.

Figure 5-1 shows the performance of the base system with the addition of a four entry data victim cache, a instruction stream buffer, and a four-way data stream buffer. (The base system has on-chip 4KB instruction and 4KB data caches with 24 cycle miss penalties and 16B lines to a three-stage pipelined second-level 1MB cache with 128B lines and 320 cycle miss penalty.) The lower solid line in Figure 5-1 gives the performance of the original base system without the victim caches or buffers while the upper solid line gives the performance with buffers and victim caches. The combination of these techniques reduces the first-level miss rate to less than half of that of the baseline system, resulting in an average of 143% improvement in system performance for the six benchmarks. These results show that the addition of a small amount of hardware can dramatically reduce cache miss rates and improve system performance.

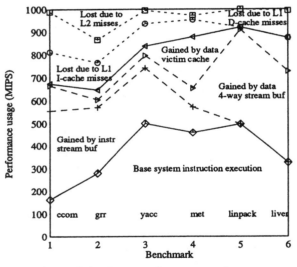

Figure 5-1: Improved system performance

This study has concentrated on applying victim caches and stream buffers to first-level caches. An interesting area for future work is the application of these techniques to second-level caches. Also, the numeric programs used in this study used unit stride access patterns. Numeric programs with non-unit stride and mixed stride access patterns also need to be simulated. Finally, the performance of victim caching and stream buffers needs to be investigated for operating system execution and for multiprogramming workloads.

Acknowledgements

Mary Jo Doherty, John Ousterhout, Jeremy Dion, Anita Borg, Richard Swan, and the anonymous referees provided many helpful comments on an early draft of this paper. Alan Eustace suggested victim caching as an improvement to miss caching.

References

1. Baer, Jean-Loup, and Wang, Wenn-Hann. On the Inclusion Properties for Multi-Level Cache Hierarchies. The 15th Annual Symposium on Computer Architecture, IEEE Computer Society Press, June, 1988, pp. 73-80.

2. Borg, Anita, Kessler, Rick E., Lazana, Georgia, and Wall, David W. Long Address Traces from RISC Machines: Generation and Analysis. Tech. Rept. 89/14, Digital Equipment Corporation Western Research Laboratory, September, 1989.

3. Digital Equipment Corporation, Inc. *VAX Hardware Handbook, volume 1 - 1984*. Maynard, Massachusetts, 1984.

4. Emer, Joel S., and Clark, Douglas W. A Characterization of Processor Performance in the VAX-11/780. The 11th Annual Symposium on Computer Architecture, IEEE Computer Society Press, June, 1984, pp. 301-310.

5. Eustace, Alan. Private communication.

6. Farrens, Matthew K., and Pleszkun, Andrew R. Improving Performance of Small On-Chip Instruction Caches . The 16th Annual Symposium on Computer Architecture, IEEE Computer Society Press, May, 1989, pp. 234-241.

7. Hill, Mark D. *Aspects of Cache Memory and Instruction Buffer Performance*. Ph.D. Th., University of California, Berkeley, 1987.

8. Jouppi, Norman P., and Wall, David W. Available Instruction-Level Parallelism For Superpipelined and Superscalar Machines. Third International Conference on Architectural Support for Programming Languages and Operating Systems, IEEE Computer Society Press, April, 1989, pp. 272-282.

9. Jouppi, Norman P. Architectural and Organizational Tradeoffs in the Design of the MultiTitan CPU. The 16th Annual Symposium on Computer Architecture, IEEE Computer Society Press, May, 1989, pp. 281-289.

10. Nielsen, Michael J. K. Titan System Manual. Tech. Rept. 86/1, Digital Equipment Corporation Western Research Laboratory, September, 1986.

11. Ousterhout, John. Why Aren't Operating Systems Getting Faster As Fast As Hardware? Tech. Rept. Technote 11, Digital Equipment Corporation Western Research Laboratory, October, 1989.

12. Smith, Alan J. "Sequential program prefetching in memory hierarchies." *IEEE Computer 11*, 12 (December 1978), 7-21.

13. Smith, Alan J. "Cache Memories." *Computing Surveys* (September 1982), 473-530.

One-Level Storage System*

T. KILBURN†, D. B. G. EDWARDS†, M. J. LANIGAN†, AND F. H. SUMNER†

Summary—After a brief survey of the basic Atlas machine, the paper describes an automatic system which in principle can be applied to any combination of two storage systems so that the combination can be regarded by the machine user as a single level. The actual system described relates to a fast core store-drum combination. The effect of the system on instruction times is illustrated, and the tape transfer system is also introduced since it fits basically in through the same hardware. The scheme incorporates a "learning" program, a technique which can be of greater importance in future computers.

I. INTRODUCTION

IN A UNIVERSAL high-speed digital computer it is necessary to have a large-capacity fast-access main store. While more efficient operation of the computer can be achieved by making this store all of one type, this step is scarcely practical for the storage capacities now being considered. For example, on Atlas it is possible to address 10^6 words in the main store. In practice on the first installation at Manchester University a total of 10^5 words are provided, but though it is just technically feasible to make this in one level it is much more economical to provide a core store (16,000 words) and drum (96,000 words) combination.

Atlas is a machine which operates its peripheral equipment on a time division basis, the equipment "interrupting" the normal main program when it requires attention. Organization of the peripheral equipment is also done by program so that many programs can be contained in the store of the machine at the same time. This technique can also be extended to include several main programs as well as the smaller subroutines used for controlling peripherals. For these reasons as well as the fact that some orders take a variable time depending on the exact numbers involved, it is not really feasible to "optimum" program transfers of information between the two levels of store, *i.e.*, core store and drum, in order to eliminate the long drum access time of 6 msec. Hence a system has been devised to make the

* Received September 11, 1961.
† Department of Computer Engineering, University of Manchester, Manchester, England.

core drum store combination appear to the programmer as a single level of storage, the requisite transfers of information taking place automatically. There are a number of additional benefits derived from the scheme adopted, which include relative addressing so that routines can operate anywhere in the store, and a "lock out" facility to prevent interference between different programs simultaneously held in the store.

II. THE BASIC MACHINE

The arrangement of the basic machine is shown in Fig. 1. The available storage space is split into three sections; the private store which is used solely for internal machine organization, the central store which includes both core and drum store, in which all words are addressed and is the store available to the normal user, and finally the tape store, which is the conventional backing-up large capacity store of the machine. Both the private store and the main core store are linked with the main accumulator, the *B*-store, and the *B*-arithmetic unit. However the drum and tape stores only have access to these latter sections of the machine via the main core store.

The machine order code is of the single address type, and a comprehensive range of basic functions are provided by normal engineering methods. Also available to the programmer are a number of extra functions termed "extracodes" which give automatic access to and subsequent return from a large number of built-in subroutines. These routines provide

1) A number of orders which would be expensive to provide in the machine both in terms of equipment and also time because of the extra loading on certain circuits. An example of this is the order:
   Shift accumulator contents $\pm n$ places where n is an integer.
2) The more complex mathematical operations, *e.g.*, sin x, log x, etc.,
3) Control orders for peripheral equipments, card readers, parallel printers, etc.,
4) Input-output conversion routines,
5) Special programs concerned with storage allocation to different programs being run simultaneously, monitoring routines for fault finding and costing purposes, and the detailed organization of drum and tape transfers.

All this information is permanently required and hence is kept in part of the private store termed the "fixed store"[1] which operates on a "read only" basis. This store consists of a woven wire mesh into which a pattern of small "linear" ferrite slugs are inserted to represent digital information. The information content can only be changed manually and will tend to differ only in detail between the different versions of the Atlas computer. In Muse this store is arranged in two units each of 4096 words, a unit consisting of

[1] T. Kilburn and R. L. Grimsdale, "A digital computer store with a very short read time," *Proc. IEE*, vol. 107, pt. B, pp. 567–572; November, 1960.

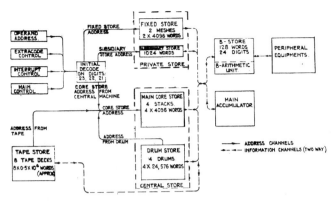

Fig. 1—Layout of basic machine.

16 columns of 256 words, each word being 50 bits. The access time to a word in any one column is about 0.4 μsec. If a change of column address is required, this figure increases by about 1 μsec due to switching transients in the read amplifiers. Subsequent accesses in the new column revert to 0.4 μsec. The store operates in conjunction with a subsidiary core store of 1024 words which provides working space for the fixed store programs, and has a cycle time of about 1.8 μsec. There are certain safeguards against a normal machine user gaining access to addresses in either part of the private store, though in effect he makes use of this store through the extracode facility.

The central store of the machine consists of a drum and core store combination, which has a maximum addressable capacity of about 10^6 words. In Muse the central store capacity is about 96,000 words contained on 4 drums. Any part of this store can be transferred in blocks of 512 words to/from the main core store, which consists of four separate stacks, each stack having a capacity of 4096 words.

The tape system provides a very large capacity backing store for the machine. The user can effect transfers of variable amounts of information between this store and the central store. In actual fact such transfers are organized by a fixed store program which initiates automatic transfers of blocks of 512 words between the tape store and the main core store. The system can handle eight tape decks running simultaneously, each producing or demanding a word on average every 88 μsec.

The main core store address can thus be provided from either the central machine, the drum, or the tape system. Since there is no synchronization between these addresses, there has to be a priority system to allocate addresses to the core store. The drum has top priority since it delivers a word every 4 μsec, the tape next priority since words can arise every 11 μsec from 8 decks and the machine uses the core store for the rest of the available time. A priority system necessarily takes time to establish its priority, and so it has been arranged that it comes into effect only at each drum or tape request. Thus the machine is not slowed down in any way when no drum or tape transfers take place. The effect of drum and tape transfers on machine speed is given in Appendix I.

To simplify the control commands given to the drum, tape, and peripheral equipment in the machine, the orders all take the form $b \to S$ or $s \to B$ and the identification of the required command register is provided by the address S. This type of storage is clearly widely scattered in the machine but is termed collectively the V-store.

In the central machine the main accumulator contains a fast adder[2] and has built-in multiplication and division facilities. It can deal with fixed or floating point numbers and its operation is completely independent of the B-store and B-arithmetic unit. The B-store is a fast core store (cycle time 0.7 μsec) of 120 twenty-four bit words operating in a word selected partial flux switching mode.[3] Eight "fast" B lines are also provided in the form of flip-flop registers. Of these, three are used as control lines, termed main, extracode, and interrupt controls respectively. The arrangement has the advantage that the control numbers can be manipulated by the normal B-type orders, and the existence of three controls permits the machine to switch rapidly from one to another without having to transfer control numbers to the core store. Main control is used when the central machine is obeying the current program, while the extracode control is concerned with the fixed store subroutines. The interrupt control provides the means for handling numerous peripheral equipments which "interrupt" the machine when they either require or are providing information. The remaining "fast" B lines are mainly used for organizational procedures, though $B124$ is the floating point accumulator exponent.

The operating speed of the machine is of the order of 0.5×10^6 instructions per second. This is achieved by the use of fast transistor logic circuitry, rapid access to storage locations, and an extensive overlapping technique. The latter procedure is made possible by the provision of a number of intermediate buffer storage registers, separate access mechanisms to the individual units of core store and parallel operation of the main accumulator and B-arithmetic units. The word length throughout the machine is 48 bits which may be considered as two half-words of 24 bits each. All store transfers between the central machine, the drum and tape stores are parity checked, there being a parity digit associated with each half-word. In the case of transfers within the central store (i.e., between main core store and drum) the parity digits associated with a given word are retained throughout the system. Tape transfers are parity checked when information is transferred to and from the main core store, and on the tape itself a check sum technique involving the use of two closely spaced heads is used.

The form of the instruction, which allows for two B-modifications, and the allocation of the address digits is shown in Fig. 2(a). Half of the addressable store locations

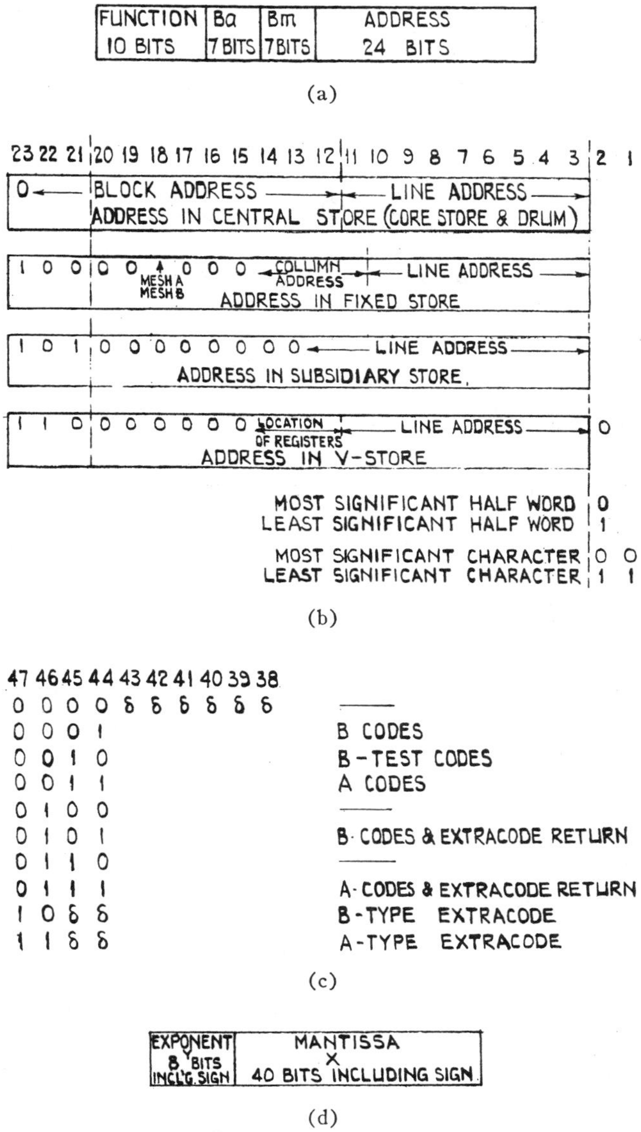

[2] T. Kilburn, D. B. H. Edwards and D. Aspinall, "A parallel arithmetic unit using a saturated transistor fast-carry circuit," *Proc. IEE*, vol. 107, pt. B, pp. 573–584; November, 1960.
[3] D. B. G. Edwards, M. J. Lanigan and T. Kilburn, "Ferrite-core memory systems with rapid cycle times," *Proc. IEE*, vol. 107, pt. B, pp. 585–598; November, 1960.

Fig. 2—Interpretation of a word. (a) Form of instruction. (b) Allocation of address digits. (c) Function of decoding. (d) Floating point number $X8^Y$.

are allocated to the central store which is identified by a zero in the most significant digit of the address. [See Fig. 2(b).] This address can be further subdivided into block address, and line address in a block of 512 words. The least significant digits, 0 and 1, make it possible to address 6 bit characters in a half word and digit 2 specifies the half word.

The function number is split into several sections, each section relating to a particular set of operations, and these are listed in Fig. 2(c). The machine orders fall into two broad classes, and these are

1) *B codes:* These involve operations between a B line specified by the B_A digits in the instruction and a core store line whose address can be modified by the contents of a B line determined by the B_m digits. There are a total of 128 B lines, one of which, B_0, al-

ways contains zero. Of the other lines 90 are available to the machine user, 7 are special registers previously mentioned, and a further 30 are used by extra-code orders.

2) *A codes:* These involve operations between the Accumulator and a core store line whose address can now be doubly modified first by contents of B_m and then by the contents of B_A. Both fixed and floating point orders are provided, and in the latter case numbers take the form of $X8^Y$, the digit allocation of X and Y being shown in Fig. 2(d). When fixed point working occurs, use is made only of the X digits.

III. ONE LEVEL STORE CONCEPT

The choice of system for the fast access store in a large scale computer is governed by a number of conflicting factors which include speed and size requirements, economic and technical difficulties. Previously the problem has been resolved in two extreme cases either by the provision of a very large core store, *e.g.*, the 2.5 megabit[4] store at M.I.T., or by the use of a small core store (40,000 bits) expanded to 640,000 bits by a drum store as in the Ferranti Mercury[5] computer. Each of these methods has its disadvantages, in the first case, that of expense, and in the second case, that of inconvenience to the user, who is obliged to program transfers of information between the two types of store and this can be time consuming. In some instances it is possible for an expert machine user to arrange his program so that the amount of time lost by the transfers in the two-level storage arrangement is not significant, but this sort of "optimum" programming is not very desirable. Suitable interpretative coding[6] can permit the two-level system to appear as one level. The effect is, however, accompanied by an effective loss of machine speed which, in some programs and depending on details of machine design can be quite severe, varying typically, for example, between one and three.

The two-level storage scheme has obvious economic advantages, and inconvenience to the machine user can be eliminated by making the transfer arrangements completely automatic. In Atlas a completely automatic system has been provided with techniques for minimizing the transfer times. In this way the core and drum are merged into an apparent single level of storage with good performance and at moderate cost. Some details of this arrangement on the Muse are now provided.

The central store is subdivided into blocks of 512 words as shown by the address arrangements in Fig. 2(b). The main core store is also partitioned into blocks of this size

which for identification purposes are called pages. Associated with each of these core store page positions is a "page address register" (P.A.R.) which contains the address of the block of information at present occupying that page position. When access to any word in the central store is required the digits of the demanded block address are compared with the contents of all the page address registers. If an "equivalence" indication is obtained then access to that particular page position is permitted. Since a block can occupy any one of the 32 page positions in the core store it is necessary to modify some digits of the demanded block address to conform with the page positions in which an equivalence was obtained.

These processes are necessarily time consuming but by providing a by-pass of this procedure for instruction accesses (since, in general, instruction loops are all contained in the same block) then most of this time can be overlapped with a useful portion of the machine or core store rhythm. In this way information in the core store is available to the machine at the full speed of the core store and only rarely is the over-all machine speed effected by delays in the equivalence circuitry.

If a "not equivalence" indication is obtained when the demanded block address is compared with the contents of the P.A.R.'s then that address, which may have been B-modified, is first stored in a register which can be accessed as a line of the V-store. This permits the central machine easy access to this address. An "interrupt" also occurs which switches operation of the machine over to the interrupt control, which first determines the cause of the interrupt and then, in this instance, enters a fixed store routine to organize the necessary transfers of information between drum and core store.

A. Drum Transfers

On each drum, one track is used to identify absolute block positions around the drum periphery. The records on these tracks are read into the θ registers which can be accessed as lines of the V-store and this permits the present angular drum position to be determined, though only in units of one block. In this way the time needed to transfer any block while reading from the drums can be assessed. This time varies between 2 and 14 msec since the drum revolution time is 12 msec and the actual transfer time 2 msec.

The time of a writing transfer to the drums has been reduced by writing the block of information to the first available empty block position on any drum. Thus the access time of the drum can be eliminated provided there are a reasonable number of empty blocks on the drum. This means, however, that transfers to/from the drum have to be carried out by reference to a directory and this is stored in the subsidiary store and up-dated whenever a transfer occurs.

When the drum transfer routine is entered the first action is to determine the absolute position on a drum of the required block. The order is then given to carry out the transfer to an empty page position in the core store. The

[4] W. N. Papian, "High-speed computer stores 2.5 megabits," *Electronics,* vol. 30; October, 1957.
[5] K. Lonsdale and E. T. Warburton, "Mercury: a high speed digital computer," *Proc. IEE,* vol. 103, pt. B (suppl. 2), pp. 174–183; 1956.
  T. Kilburn, D. B. G. Edwards, and C. E. Thomas, "The Manchester University Mark II Digital Computing Machine," *Proc. IEE,* vol. 103, pt. B (suppl. 2), pp. 247–268; 1956.
[6] R. A. Brooker, "Some techniques for dealing with two-level storage," *The Computer Journal,* vol. 2; 1960.

transfer occurs automatically as soon as the drum reaches the correct angular position. The page address register in the vacant position in the core store is set to a specific block number for drum transfers. This technique simplifies the engineering with regard to the provision of this number from the drum and also provides a safeguard against transferring to the wrong block.

As soon as the order asking for a read transfer from the drum has been given the machine continues with the drum transfer program. It is now concerned with determining a block to be transferred back from the core store to the drum. This is necessary to ensure an empty core store page

access to that page position can then be made from the central machine. It is clear that the L.O. digit can also be used to prevent interference between programs when several different ones are being held in the machine at the same time.

In Section III it was stated that addresses demanding access to the core store could arise from three distinct sources, the central machine, the drum, and the tape. These accesses are complicated because of 1) the equivalence technique, and 2) the lock out digit. The various cases and the action that takes place are summarized in Table I.

TABLE I

Comparison of Demanded Block Address with Contents of the P.A.R.'s Resultant State of Equivalence and Lock Out Circuits

Source of Address	Equivalence Lock out = 0 [E.Q.]	Not Equivalence [N.E.Q.]	Equivalence Lock out = 1 [E.Q. & L.O.]
1. Central Machine	Access to required page position	Enter drum transfer routine	Not available to this program
2. Drum System	Access to required page position	Fault condition indicated	Fault condition indicated
3. Tape System	Access to required page position	Fault condition indicated	Fault condition indicated

position when the next read transfer is required. The block in the core store to be transferred has to be carefully chosen to minimize the number of transfers in the program and this optimization process is carried out by a learning program, details of which are given in Section V. The operation of this program is assisted by the provision of the "use" digits which are associated with each page position of the core store.

To interchange information between the core store and drums, two transfers, a read from and a write to the drum are necessary. These have to be done sequentially but could occur in either order. The technique of having a vacant page position in the core store permits a read transfer to occur first and thus allows the time for the learning program to be overlapped either into the waiting period for the read transfer or into the transfer time itself. In the time remaining after completion of the learning program an entry is made into the over-all supervisor program for the machine, and a decision is taken concerning what the machine is to do until the drum transfer is completed. This might involve a change to a different main program.

A program could ask for access to information in a page position while a drum or tape transfer is taking place to that page. This is prevented in Atlas by the use of a "lock out" (L.O.) digit which is provided with each Page Address Register. When a lock out digit is set at 1, access to that page is only permitted when the address has been provided either by the drum system, the tape system, or the interrupt control. The latter case permits all transfers from paper tape, punched card, and other peripheral equipments, to be handled without interference from the main program. When the transfer of a block has been completed the organizing program resets the L.O. digit to zero and

The provision of the Page Address Registers, the equivalence circuitry, and the learning program have permitted the core store and drum to be regarded by the ordinary machine user as a one level store, and the system has the additional feature of "floating address" operation, i.e., any block of information can be stored in any absolute position in either core or drum store. The minimum access time to information in this store is obviously limited by the core store and its arrangement and this is now discussed.

B. Core Store Arrangement

The core store is split into four stacks, each with individual address decoding and read and write mechanisms. The stacks are then combined in such a way that common channels into the machine for the address, read and write digits are time shared between the various stacks. Sequential address positions occur in two stacks alternately and a page position which contains a block of 512 sequential addresses is thus arranged across two stacks. In this way it is possible to read a pair of instructions from consecutive addresses in parallel by increasing the size of the read channel. This permits two instructions to be completely obeyed in three store "accesses." The choice of this particular storage arrangement is discussed in Appendix II.

The coordination of these four stacks is done by the "core stack coordinator" and some features of this are now discussed, starting with the operation of a single stack.

C. Operation of a Single Stack of Core Store

The storage system employed is a coincident current M.I.T. system arranged to give parallel read out of 50 digits. The reading operation is destructive and each read phase of the stack cycle is followed by a write phase during which the information read out may be rewritten. This is achieved by a set of digit staticizors which are loaded during the read phase and are used to control the inhibit current drivers during the write phase. When new information is to be written into the store a similar sequence is followed, except that the digit staticizors are loaded with the new information during the read phase. A diagram indicating the different types of stack cycle is shown in Fig. 3.

There is a small delay W_D ($\simeq$100 mμsec) between the "stack request" signal, SR, and the start of the read phase to allow for setting of the address state and the address decoding. The output information from the store appears in the read strobe period, which is towards the end of the read phase. In general, the write phase starts as soon as the read phase ends. However, the start of the write phase may be held up until the new information is available from the central machine. This delay is shown as W_w in Fig. 3(c). The interval T_A between the stack request and the read strobe is termed the stack access time, and in practice this is approximately one third of the cycle time T_C. Both T_A and T_C are functions of the storage system and assuming that W_w is zero have typical values of 0.7 μsec and 1.9 μsec respectively. A holdup gate in the request channel prevents the next stack request occurring before the end of the preceding write phase.

D. *Operation of the Main Core Store with the Central Machine*

A schematic diagram of the essentials of the main core store control system is shown in Fig. 4. The control signals SA_1 and SA_2 indicate whether the address presented is that of a single word or a pair of sequentially addressed instructions. Assuming that the flip-flop F is in the reset condition, either of these signals results in the loading of the buffer address register (B.A.R.). This loading is done by the signal B.A.B.A. which also indicates that the buffer register in the central machine has become free.

In dealing with the first request the block address digits in the B.A.R. are compared with the contents of all the page address registers. Then one of the indications summarized in Table I and indicated in Fig. 4 is obtained. Assuming access to the required store stack is permitted then a set C.S.F. signal is given which resets the flip-flop F. If this occurs before the next access request arises, then the speed of the system is not store-limited. In most cases SET CSF is generated when the equivalence operation on

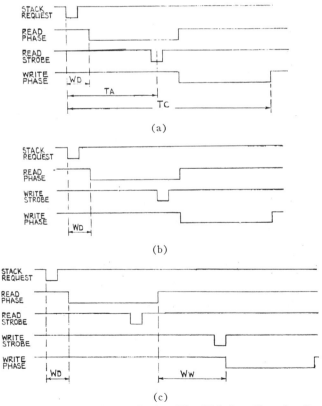

T_A = Access time, T_C = Cyclic time, W_D = Wait for address decoding and loading of address register, W_w = Wait for release of write hold up.

Fig. 3—Basic types of stack cycle. (a) Read order ($s{\to}A$). (b) Write order ($a{\to}s$). (c) Read-write order ($b+s{\to}S$).

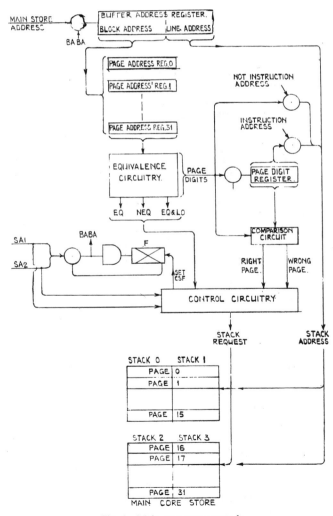

Fig. 4—Main core store control.

the demanded block address is complete, and the read phase of the appropriate stack (or stacks) has started. Until this time the information held in the B.A.R. must not be allowed to change. In Fig. 5 a flow diagram is shown for the various cases which can arise in practice.

When a single address request is accepted it is necessary to obtain an "equivalence" indication and form the page location digits before the stack request can be generated. The SET CSF signal then occurs as soon as the read phase starts. If a "not equivalent" or "equivalent and locked out" indication is obtained a stack request is not generated, and the contents of the B.A.R. are copied in to a line of the *V*-store before SET CSF is generated.

When access to a pair of addresses is requested (*i.e.,* an instruction pair) the stack requests are generated on the assumption that these instructions are located in the same page position as the last pair requested, *i.e.,* the page position digits are taken from the page digit register. (See Fig. 4.) In this way the time required to obtain the equivalent indication and form the page location digits is not included in the over-all access time of the system. The assumption will normally be true, except when crossing block boundaries. The latter cases are detected and corrected by comparing the true position page digits obtained

as a result of the equivalence operation with the contents of the page digit register and a "right page" or "wrong page" indication is obtained. (See Fig. 4.) If a wrong page is accessed this is indicated to the central machine and the read out is inhibited. The true page location digits are copied into the page digit register, so that the required instruction pair will be obtained when next requested. The read out to the central machine is also inhibited for "not equivalent" or "equivalent and locked out" indications.

In Fig. 5 the waiting time indicated immediately before the stack request is generated can arise for a number of reasons.

1) The preceding write phase of that stack has not yet finished.
2) The central machine is not yet ready either to accept information from the store, or to supply information to it.
3) It is necessary to ensure a certain minimum time between successive read strobes from the core store stacks to allow satisfactory operation of the parity circuits, which take about 0.4 μsec to check the information. This time could be reduced, but as it is only possible to get such a condition for a small part of the normal instruction timing cycle it was not thought to be an economical proposition.

The basic machine timing is now discussed.

IV. INSTRUCTION TIMES

In high-speed computers, one of the main factors limiting speed of operation is the store cycle time. Here a number of techniques, *e.g.,* splitting the core store into four separate stacks and extracting two instructions in a single cycle, have been adopted despite a fast basic cycle time of 2 μsec in order to alleviate this situation. The time taken to complete an instruction is dependent upon

1) The type of instruction (which is defined by the function digits),
2) The exact location of the instruction and operand in the core or fixed store since this can affect the access time,
3) Whether or not the operand address is to be modified,
4) In the case of floating point accumulator orders, the actual numbers themselves,
5) Whether drum and/or tape transfers are taking place.

The approximate times for various instructions are given in Table II. These figures relate to the times between completing instructions when a long sequence of the same type of instruction is obeyed. While this method is not ideal, it is necessary because in practice obeying one instruction is overlapped in time with some part of three other instructions. This makes the detailed timing complicated, and so the timing sequence is developed slowly by first considering instructions obeyed one after another. It is convenient to make these instructions a sequence of floating point additions with both instruction and operand in the core store and with the operand address single *B*-modified.

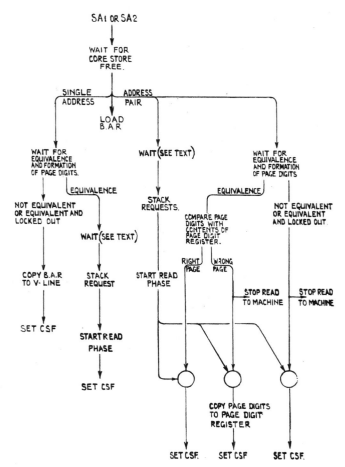

Fig. 5—Flow diagram of main core store control.

TABLE II
APPROXIMATE INSTRUCTION TIMES

Type of Instruction	Number of Modifications of Address	Instruction in Core Store. Operands in Core Store. Time in μsec	Instructions in Fixed Store. Operands in Core Store. Time in μsec	Instructions in Fixed Store. Operands in Fixed Store. Time in μsec
Floating Point Addition	0	1.4	1.65	1.2
	1	1.6	1.65	1.2
	2	2.03	1.9	1.9
Floating Point Multiplication	0, 1 or 2	4.7	4.7	4.7
Floating Point Division	0, 1 or 2	13.6	13.6	13.6
Add Store Line to an Index Register	0	1.53	1.65	1.15
	1	1.85	1.85	1.85
Add Index Register to Store Line and Rewrite to Store Line	0	1.63	1.65	—
	1	1.8	1.7	—

To obey this instruction the central machine makes two requests to the core store, one for the instruction and the second for the operand. After the instruction is received in the machine the function part has to be decoded and the operand address modified by the contents of one of the B registers before the operand request can be made. Finally, after the operand has been obtained the actual accumulator addition takes place to complete the instruction. The time from beginning to end of one instruction is 6.05 μsec and an approximate timing schedule is as follows in Table III.

If no other action is permitted in the time required to complete the instruction (steps 1 to 8 in Table III), then the different sections of the machine are being used very inefficiently, e.g., the accumulator adder is only used for less than 1.1 μsec. However, the organization of the computer is such that the different sections such as store stacks, accumulator and B-arithmetic unit, can operate at the same time. In this way several instructions can be started before the first has finished, and then the effective instruction time is considerably reduced. There have, of course, to be certain safeguards when for example an instruction is dependent in any way on the completion of a preceding instruction.

In the time sequence previously tabulated, by far the longest time was that between a request in the central machine for the core store and the receipt in the central machine of the information from that store. This effective access time of 1.75 μsec is made up as shown in Table IV. It has been reduced in practice by the provision of two buffer registers, one in the central machine and the other in the core stack coordinator. These allow the equivalence and transfer times to be overlapped with the organization of requests in the central machine.

In this way, provided the machine can arrange to make requests fast enough, then the effective access time is reduced to 0.8 μsec. Further, since three accessses are needed to complete two instructions (one for an instruction pair and one for each of the two operands) the theoretical minimum time of an instruction is 1.2 μsec $3 \times 0.8/2$ and it then becomes store limited. Reference to Table III

TABLE III*
TIMING SEQUENCE FOR FLOATING POINT ADDITION
(Instructions and Operands in the Core Store)

Sequence	Time Interval Between Steps μsec	Total Time μsec
1. Add 1 to Main Control (Addition time)	0.3	0
2. Make Instruction Request (Transfer times, equivalence time and stack access time)	1.75	0.3
3. Receive Instruction in Central Machine (Load register and decode)	0.2	2.05
4. Function decoding complete (Single address modification)	0.85	2.25
5. Request Operand (Transfer times, equivalence time and stack access time)	1.75	3.10
6. Receive Operand in Central Machine (Load register)	0.1	4.85
7. Start Addition in Accumulator (Average floating point addition, including shift round and standardise)	1.1	4.95
8. Instruction complete		6.05

* In step 4, time is for single address modification. Times for no modification and two modifications are 0.25 μsec and 1.55 μsec respectively.

TABLE IV
EFFECTIVE STORE ACCESS TIME

Sequence	Total Time μsec
1. Request in Central Machine	0
2. Request in Core Stack Coordinator	0.25
3. Equivalence complete and request made to selected stack	0.95
4. Information in Core Stack Coordinator	1.65
5. Information in Central Machine	1.75

shows that the arithmetic operation takes 1.2 μsec to complete so that, on the average, the capabilities of the store and the accumulator are well matched.

Another technique for reducing store access time for instructions has also been adopted. This permits the read cycles of the two stacks to start assuming that the same page will be referred to as in the previous instruction pair.

This, of course, will normally be true and there is sufficient time to take corrective procedures should the page have been changed. The limit of 1.2 μsec per instruction is not reduced by this technique, but the possibility of reaching this limit under other conditions is enhanced.

A schematic diagram of the practical timing of a sequence of floating point addition orders is shown in Fig. 6. The overlapping is not perfect and in the time between successive instruction pairs the computer is obeying four instructions for 25 per cent of the time, three for 56 per cent and two for 19 per cent. It is therefore to be expected that the practical time for the complete order is greater than the theoretical minimum time; it is in fact approximately 1.6 μsec.

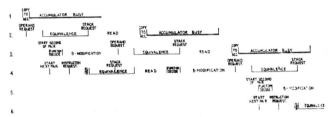

Fig. 6—Timing diagram for a sequence of floating point addition orders. (Single address modification.)

For certain types of functions the reading of the next pair of instructions before completing both instructions of the first pair would be incorrect, e.g., functions causing transfer of control. Such situations are recognized during the function decoding, and the request for the next instruction pair is held up until a suitable time.

In a sequence of floating point addition orders with the operand addresses unmodified the limit is again 1.2 μsec while the time obtained is 1.4 μsec. For accumulator orders in which the actual accumulator operation imposes a limit in excess of 2 μsec then the actual time is equal to this limit.

Perhaps a more realistic way of defining the speed of the computer is to give the time for a typical inner loop of instructions. A frequently occurring operation in matrix work in the formation of the scalar product of two vectors, this requires a loop of five instructions:

1) Element of first vector into accumulator. (Operand B-modified.)
2) Multiply accumulator by element of second vector. (Operand B-modified.)
3) Add partial product to accumulator.
4) Copy accumulator to store line containing partial product.
5) Alter count to select next elements and repeat.

The time for this loop with instructions and operands on the core store is 12.2 μsec. The value of the overlapping technique is shown by the fact that the time from starting the first instruction to finishing the second is approximately 10 μsec.

When the drum or tape systems are transferring information to or from the core store then the rate of obeying instructions which also use the core store will be affected. The affect is discussed in more detail in Appendix I. The degree of slowing down is dependent upon the time at which a drum or tape request occurs relative to machine requests. It also depends on the stacks used by the drum or tape and those being used by the central machine. The approximate slowing down is by a factor of 25 per cent during a drum transfer and by 2 per cent for each active tape channel. (See Appendix I.)

V. The Drum Transfer Learning Program

The organization of drum transfers has been described in Section IIA. After the transfer of the required block from the drum to the core store has been initiated, the organizing program examines the state of the core store, and if empty pages still exist, no further action is taken. However, if the core store is full it is necessary to arrange for an empty page to be made available for use at the next nonequivalence. The selection of the page to be transferred could be made at random; this could easily result in many additional transfers occurring, as the page selected could be one of those in current use or one required in the near future. The ideal selection, which would minimize the total number of transfers, could only be made by the programmer. To make this ideal selection the programmer would have to know, 1) precisely how his program operated, which is not always the case, and 2) the precise amount of core store available to his program at any instant. This latter information is not generally available as the core store could be shared by other central machine programs, and almost certainly by some fixed store program organizing the input and output of information from slow peripheral equipments. The amount of core store required by this fixed store program is continuously varying.[7] The only way the ideal pattern of transfers can be approached is for the transfer program to monitor the behavior of the main program and in so doing attempt to select the correct pages to be transferred to the drum. The techniques used for monitoring are subject to the condition that they must not slow down the operation of the program to such an extent that they offset any reduction in the number of transfers required. The method described occupies less than 1 per cent of the operating time, and the reduction in the number of transfers is more than sufficient to cover this.

That part of the transfer program which organizes the selection of the page to be transferred has been called the "learning" program. In order for this program to have some data on which to operate, the machine has been designed to supply information about the use made of the different pages of the core store by the program being monitored.

[7] T. Kilburn, D. J. Howarth, R. B. Payne and F. H. Sumner, "The Manchester University Atlas Operating System. Part I: Internal Organisation," The Computer Journal, vol. 4; October, 1961.

With each page of the core store there is associated a "use" digit which is set to "1" whenever any line in that page is accessed. The 32 "use" digits exist in two lines of the V-store and can be read by the learning program, the reading automatically resetting them to zero. The frequency with which these digits are read is governed by a clock which measures not real time but the number of instructions obeyed in the operation of the main program. This clock causes the learning program to copy the "use" digits to a list in the subsidiary store every 1024 instructions. The use of an instruction counter rather than a normal clock to measure "time" for the learning program is due to the fact that the operations of the main program may be interrupted at random for random lengths of time by the operation of peripheral equipments. With an instruction counter the temporal pattern of the blocks used will be the same on successive runs through the same part of the program. This is essential if the learning program is to make use of this pattern to minimize the number of transfers.

When a nonequivalence occurs and after the transfer of the required block has been arranged, the learning program again adds the current values of the "use" digits to the list and then uses this list to bring up to date two sets of times also kept in the subsidiary store. These sets consist of 32 values of t and T, one of each for each page of the core store. The value of t is the length of time since the block in that page has been used. The value of T is the length of the last period of inactivity of this block. The accuracy of the values of t and T is governed by the frequency with which the "use" digits are inspected.

The page to be written to the drum is selected by the application in turn of three simple tests to the values of t and T.

1) Any page for which $t > T+1$,

or 2) That page with $t \neq 0$ and $(T-t)$ max,

or 3) That page with T_{max} (all $t=0$).

The first rule selects any page which has been currently out of use for longer than its last period of inactivity. Such a page has probably ceased to be used by the program and is therefore an ideal one to be transferred to the drum. The second rule ignores all pages with $t=0$ as they are in current use, and then selects the one which, if the pattern of use is maintained, will not be required by the program for the longest time. If the first two rules fail to select a page the third ensures that if the page finally selected is wrong, in that it is immediately required again, then, as in this case, T will become zero and the same mistake will not be repeated.

For all the blocks on the drum a list of values of τ is kept. The values of τ are set when the block is transferred to the drum:

τ = Time of transfer—value of t for transferred page.

When a block is transferred to the core store the value of τ is used to set the value of T.

T = Time of transfer—value of τ for this block
= Length of last period of inactivity.

For the block transferred from the drum t is set to 0.

In order to make its decision the learning program has only to update two short lists and apply at the most three simple rules; this can easily be done during the 2 msec transfer time of the block required as a result of the nonequivalence. As the learning program uses only fixed and subsidiary store addresses it is not slowed down during the period of the drum transfer.

The over-all efficiency of the learning program cannot be known until the complete Atlas system is working. However, the value of the method used has been investigated by simulating the behavior of the one-level store and learning program on the Mercury computer at Manchester University. This has been done for several problems using varying amounts of store in excess of the core store available. One of these was the problem of forming the product A of two 80th order matrices B and C. The three matrices were stored row by row each one extending over 14 blocks, only 14 pages of core store were assumed to be avilable. The method of multiplication was

$b_{11} \times$ 1st row of C = partial answer to 1st row of A,
$b_{12} \times$ 2nd row of C + partial answer = second partial answer, etc.,

thus matrix B was scanned once, matrix C 80 times and each row of matrix A 80 times.

Several machine users were asked to spend a short time writing a program to organize the transfers for a general matrix multiplication problem. In no case when the method was applied to the above problem were fewer than 357 transfers required. A program written specifically for this problem which paid great attention to the distribution of the rows of the matrices relative to block divisions required 234 transfers. The learning program required 274 transfers, the gain over the human programmer was chiefly due to the fact that the learning program could take full advantage of the occasions when the rows of A existed entirely within one block.

Many other problems involving cyclic running of single or multiple sets of data were simulated, and in no case did the learning program require more transfers than an experienced human programmer.

A. Prediction of Drum Transfers

Although the learning program tends to reduce the number of transfers required to a minimum, the transfers which do occur still interrupt the operation of the program for from 2 to 14 msec as they are initiated by nonequivalence interrupts. Some or all of this time loss could be avoided by organizing the transfers in advance. A very experienced programmer having sole use of the core store could arrange his own transfers in such a way that no unnecessary ones ever occurred and no time was ever wasted waiting for transfers to be completed. This would require a great deal of effort and would only be worthwhile for a program that was going to occupy the machine for a long time. By using the data accumulated by the learning program it is possible to recognize simple patterns in the use made by a program of the various blocks of the one level store. In this way a prediction program could forecast the blocks required in the near future and organize the transfers. By recording the success or failure of these forecasts the program could be made self-improving. For the matrix multiplication problem discussed above the pattern of use of the blocks containing matrix C is repeated 80 times, and a considerable degree of success could be obtained with a simple prediction program.

VI. Conclusions

A specific system for making a core-drum store combination appear as a single level store has been described. While this is the actual system being built for the Atlas machine the principles involved are applicable to combinations of other types of store. For example, a tunnel diode-fast core store combination for an even faster machine. An alternative which was considered for Atlas, but which was not as attractive economically, was a fast core-slow core store combination. The system too can be extended to three levels of storage, and indeed if 10^6 words of total storage had to be provided then it would be most economical to provide it on a third level of store such as a file drum.

The automatic system does require additional equipment and introduces some complexity, since it is necessary to overlap the time taken for address comparison into the store and machine operating time if it is not to introduce any extra time delays. Simulated tests have shown that the organization of drum transfers are reasonably efficient and other advantages which accrue, such as efficient allocation of core storage between different programs and store lock out facilities are also invaluable. No matter how intelligent a programmer may be he can never know how many programs or peripheral equipments are in operation when his program is running. The advantage of the automatic system is that it takes into account the state of the machine as it exists at any particular time. Furthermore if as in normal use there is some sort of regular machine rhythm even through several programs, there is the possibility of making some sort of prediction with regard to the transfers necessary. This involves no more hardware and will be done by program. However, this stage will probably be left until results on the actual system are obtained.

It can be seen that the system is both useful and flexible in that it can be modified or extended in the manner previously indicated. Thus despite the increase in equipment, the advantages which are derived completely justify the building of this automatic system.

VII. Appendix I

Organization of the Access Requests to the Core Store

There are three sources of access requests to the core store, namely the central machine, the drum, and the tape systems. In deciding how the sequence of requests from all three sources are to be serialized and placed in some sort of order, a number of facts have to be considered. These are

1) All three sources are asynchronous in nature.
2) The drum and tape systems can make requests at a fairly high rate compared with the store cycle time of approximately 2 μsec. For example, the drum provides a request every 4 μsec and the tape system every 11 μsec when all 8 channels are operative.
3) The drum and tape systems can only be stopped in multiples of a block length, i.e., 512 words. This means that any system devised for accessing the core store must deal with both the average rates of drum drum and tape requests specified in 2). Only the central machine can tolerate requests being stopped at any time and for any length of time. From these facts a request priority can be stated which is
   a) Drum request.
   b) Tape request.
   c) Central machine request.
4) A machine request can be accepted by the core store, but because there is no place available to accept the core store information, its cycle is inhibited and further requests held up. In the case of successive division orders this time can be as long as 20 μsec, in which case 5 drum requests could be made. To avoid having an excessive amount of buffer storage for the drum two techniques are possible:
   a) When drums or tapes are operative do not permit machine requests to be accepted until there is a place available to put the information.
   b) Store the machine request and then permit a drum or tape request.
   The latter scheme has been adopted because it can be accommodated more conveniently and it saves a small amount of time.
5) If the central machine is using the private store then it is desirable for drum and tape transfers to the core store not to interfere with or slow down the central machine in any way.
6) When the central machine, drum and tape are sharing the core store then the loss of central machine speed should be roughly proportional to the activity of the drum or tape systems. This means that drum or tape requests must "break" into the normal machine request channel as and when required.

The system which accommodates all these points is now discussed. Whenever a drum or tape request occurs inhibit signals are applied to request channel into the core stack coordinator and also to the stack request channels from this coordinator. This results in a "freezing" of the state of flip-flop F (Fig. 5) and this state is then inspected (Fig. 7, point X). If the state is "busy" this means that a machine order has been stopped somewhere between the loading of the buffer address register (B.A.R.) and the stack request. Normally this time interval can vary from about 0.5 μsec if there are no stack request holdups, to 20 μsec in the case of certain accumulator holdups. In either case sufficient time is allowed after the inspection to ensure that the equivalence operation has been completed. If an equiva-

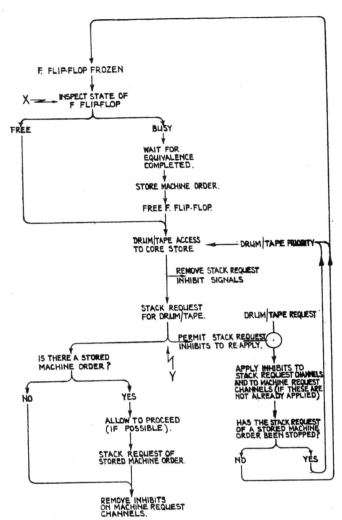

Fig. 7—Drum and tape break in systems.

lence indication is obtained all the information relevant to this machine order (*i.e.,* the line address, page digits, stack(s) required and type of stack order) are stored for future reference. Use is made here of the page digit register provided to allow the by-pass on the equivalence circuitry for instruction accesses. The core store is then made free for access by the drum or the tape. If the core store had been found to be free on inspection, the above procedure is omitted.

A drum or tape access (as decided by the priority circuit) to the core store then occurs, which removes the inhibits on the stack request channels. When the stack request for the drum or tape cycle is initiated these inhibits are allowed to reapply. At this stage (Fig. 7, point *Y*), if there is a stored machine order it is allowed to proceed if possible. The inhibits on the machine request channels are removed when the stack request for the stored machine order occurs. If there is no stored machine order this is done immediately, and the central machine is again allowed access to the core store. However, another drum or tape request can arise before the stack request of the

stored machine order occurs, in particular because this latter order may still be held up by the central machine. If this is the case the drum or tape is allowed immediate access and a further attempt is made to complete the stored machine order when this drum or tape stack request occurs.

If the stored machine order was for an operand, the content of the page digit register will correspond to the location of this operand. The next machine request for an instruction pair will then almost certainly result in a "wrong page" indication. This is prevented by arranging that the next instruction pair access does not by-pass the equivalence circuitry.

The effect on the machine speed when the drum or tapes are transferring information to or from the core store is dependent upon two factors. First, upon the proportion of time during which the buffer register in the core coordinator is busy dealing with machine requests, and secondly, upon the particular stacks being used by the central machine and the drum or tape. If the computer is obeying a program with instructions and operands on the fixed or subsidiary store then the rate of obeying instructions is unaffected by drum or tape transfers. A drum or tape interrupt occuring when the B.A.R. is free prevents any machine address being accepted onto this buffer for 1.0 μsec. However, if the B.A.R. is busy then the next machine request to the core store is delayed until 1.8 μsec after the interrupt if different stacks are being used, or until 3.4 μsec after the interrupt if the stacks are the same.

When the machine is obeying a program with instructions and operands on the core store the slowing down during drum transfers can be by a factor of two if instructions, operands, and drum requests use the same stacks. It is also possible for the machine to be unaffected. The effect on a particular sequence of orders can be seen by considering the one discussed in Section IV and illustrated in Fig. 6. In this sequence the instructions are on stacks 0 and 1 while the operands are on stacks 2 and 3. If the drum or tape is transferring alternately to stacks 0 and 1 then the effect of any interrupt within the 3.2 μsec of an instruction pair is to increase this time by between 0.5 and 3.4 μsec depending upon where the interrupt occurred. The average increase is 1.8 μsec and for a tape transfer with interrupts every 88 μsec the computer can obey instructions at 98 per cent of the normal rate. During drum transfers the interrupts occur every 4 μsec which would suggest a slowing down to 60 per cent of normal. However, for any regular sequence of orders the requests to the core store by the machine and by the drum rapidly become synchronized with the result in this particular case that the machine can still operate at 80 per cent of its normal speed.

Appendix II

Methods of Division of the Main Core Store

The maximum frequency with which requests can be dealt with by a single stack core store is governed by the cycle time of the store. If the store is divided into several stacks which can be cycled independently then the limit imposed on the speed of the machine by the core store is reduced. The degree of division which is chosen is dependent upon the ratio of core store cycle time to other machine operations and also upon the cost of the multiple selection mechanisms required.

Considering a sequence of orders in which both the instruction and operand are in the core store, then for a single stack store the limit imposed on the operating speed by the store is two cycle times per order, *i.e.*, 4 μsec in Atlas. This is significantly larger than the limits imposed by other sections of the computer (Section IV). If the store is divided into two stacks and instructions and operands are separated, then the limit is reduced to 2 μsec which is still rather high. The provision of two stacks permits the addressing of the store to be arranged so that successive addresses are in alternate stacks. It is therefore possible by making requests to both stacks at the same time to read two instructions together, so reducing the number of access times to three per instruction pair. Unfortunately such an arrangement of the store means that operands are always on the same stacks as instruction pairs, and the limit imposed by the cycle time is still 2 μsec per order even if the two operand requests in the instruction pair are to different stacks and occur at the same time.

Division into any number of stacks with the addressing system working through each stack in turn cannot reduce the limit below 2 μsec since successive instructions normally occur in successive addresses and are therefore in the same stack. However, four stacks arranged in two pairs reduces the limit to 1 μsec as the operands can always be arranged to be on different stacks from the instruction pairs. In order to reduce the limit to 0.5 μsec it is necessary to have eight stacks arranged in two sets of four and to read four instructions at once, which would increase the complexity of the central machine.

The limit of 1 μsec is quite sufficient and further division with the stacks arranged in pairs only enables the limit to be more easily obtained by suitable location of the instructions and operands.

The location of instructions and operands within the core store is under the control of the drum transfer program; thus when there are several stacks instructions and operands are separated wherever possible. Under these

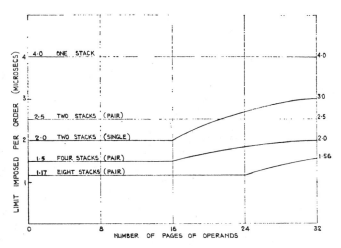

Fig. 8—Limit imposed by cycle time on operating speed for difficult divisions of the core store.

conditions it is possible to calculate the limit imposed on the operating speed by the cycle time for different divisions of the core store. The results are shown in Fig. 8, for stacks arranged in pairs instructions are read in pairs and in all cases both instructions and operands are assumed to be on the core store. Operands are assumed to be selected at random from the operand space, for instance in the case of two stacks arranged as a pair, successive operand requests have equal probability of being to the same stack or to alternate stacks.

The limit imposed by a four stack store is never severe compared with other limitations, for example the sequence of floating point addition orders discussed in Section IV required 1.6 μsec per order with ideal distribution of instructions and operands. Division into eight stacks, although it reduces the limit, will not have an equivalent effect on the over-all operating speed, and such a division was not considered to be justified.

ACKNOWLEDGMENT

The authors gratefully acknowledge the contributions made to this work by all members of the Atlas computer team at both Manchester University and Ferranti Ltd.

Performance of the VAX-11/780 Translation Buffer: Simulation and Measurement

DOUGLAS W. CLARK AND JOEL S. EMER
Digital Equipment Corporation

A virtual-address translation buffer (TB) is a hardware cache of recently used virtual-to-physical address mappings. The authors present the results of a set of measurements and simulations of translation buffer performance in the VAX-11/780. Two different hardware monitors were attached to VAX-11/780 computers, and translation buffer behavior was measured. Measurements were made under normal time-sharing use and while running reproducible synthetic time-sharing work loads. Reported measurements include the miss ratios of data and instruction references, the rate of TB invalidations due to context switches, and the amount of time taken to service TB misses. Additional hardware measurements were also made with half the TB disabled. Trace-driven simulations of several programs were also run; the traces captured system activity as well as user-mode execution. Several variants of the 11/780 TB structure were simulated.

Categories and Subject Descriptors: B.3.2 [Memory Structures]: Design Styles—associative memories; cache memories; virtual memory; B.3.3 [Memory Structures]: Performance Analysis and Design Aids—simulation; C.1.1 [Processor Architectures]: Single Data Stream Architectures—VAX

General Terms: Design, Experimentation, Measurement, Performance

Additional Key Words and Phrases: Translation buffer, translation look-aside buffer, miss ratio, hardware monitor, trace-driven simulation

1. INTRODUCTION

Virtual-memory systems profit from the use of a fast hardware cache of virtual-to-physical address translations. This cache, here called a *translation buffer* (TB), is sometimes known as a Directory Look-Aside Table (DLAT) or a Translation Look-aside Buffer (TLB). Translation buffers are widely used, but their performance is rarely reported (see [17, 18]). In this paper we report the performance of the translation buffer used in the Digital Equipment Corporation VAX-11/780 computer [5, 20]. We use two methods: trace-driven simulation and direct measurement of the hardware.

Virtual memory requires a translation of each virtual address generated by a program into a physical address, which is used to reference real memory. Most

virtual-memory systems use two levels of mapping, in which an address is interpreted first as belonging to a *segment* and then translation is performed for the specified *page* within the segment. Determination of a segment address from a virtual address may be simple, as in the VAX or the IBM System/370 [2], or complex, as in the Intel iAPX 432 [10].

If the virtual memory is large, the tables required to hold the page translations are typically so big that they must be stored in main memory. Therefore, in general, each virtual-memory reference logically requires one or more extra memory references just to do the translation.

A translation buffer is a high-speed associative cache of recently used virtual-to-physical address translations. Its purpose is to eliminate the need for the extra memory references most of the time by taking advantage of the principle of *locality* [4]. When an address translation is present in the TB, main memory need not be read to perform the translation; instead the mapping is performed in hardware with the aid of the buffer. This event is called a translation buffer *hit*. When a desired translation is not in the buffer—a TB *miss*—the necessary table or tables must be referenced and the translation constructed and inserted into the TB, perhaps displacing a previous entry. The time lost servicing TB misses is one of the costs of supporting virtual memory.

Optimizing TB performance involves a cost/performance evaluation of three items: the TB miss rate, the time to perform a virtual-to-physical translation for a TB hit, and the time required to fill a TB entry following a miss. The miss rate is directly related to the TB configuration, where bigger and more associative is better. But cost constraints, timing limitations on the associative hardware, and practical consideration of the depth of available RAM memory chips lead to designs with limited size and associativity. The translation time for a TB hit is generally highly constrained by the machine cycle time and cache access requirements, which can also place restrictions on the feasibility of some configurations. Finally, the fill time is related to memory reference times and the implementation of the translation algorithm.

In the rest of this paper we study the consequences of these design trade-offs on performance of the VAX-11/780. After giving some necessary definitions in Section 2, we discuss in Section 3 the techniques we used to characterize the 11/780 TB. Section 4 presents the raw miss data as measured and simulated, and categorizes the sources of the misses. Section 5 reports measurements of the TB miss service time and illustrates its impact on overall CPU performance. Section 6 examines the frequency of some architectural events that affect TB performance, such as context switches and branches. Section 7 discusses performance of alternative TB configurations, and Section 8 concludes the paper.

2. DEFINITIONS

2.1 VAX Virtual Memory

VAX virtual memory consists of a 32-bit address space that is divided into three usable regions or segments. These regions are selected by the top two bits of the virtual address. They are referred to as the *system-space* region (S0), and two *process-space* regions (P0 and P1). Each region is in turn partitioned into pages

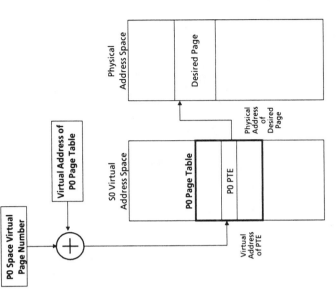

Fig. 2.   Process space virtual page translation.

P1 address translation is nearly identical. In this case the well-known address points to a page table that is expected to grow backward (from high-numbered pages to low-numbered pages). This convention was adopted because the high end of the P1 region is expected to contain a large stack which grows downward.

One final characteristic of the VAX virtual memory architecture is that the S0 address space is common to all processes, while each process has distinct P0 and P1 address spaces. This has important ramifications for the implementation of the TB, because the processor must guarantee that the P0 and P1 translations of one process are not mistakenly used to translate addresses for another process. This is typically handled by removing all process-space translations from the TB on each process context switch; we will call this operation a *flush*.

The flush operation can have a significant impact on TB performance. Upon resuming execution of a process there will be "extra" misses that result solely from filling entries that had been flushed. Two other operations of the VAX result in the flushing of TB entries: TB Invalidate Single (TBIS) and TB Invalidate All (TBIA). These operations, which are invoked by special VAX instructions, result in either a single mapping or the entire TB being flushed. It is important to quantify the frequency of these various TB flushes to understand their impact on TB performance.

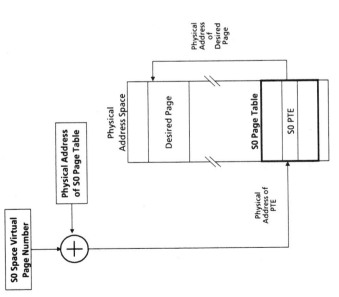

Fig. 1.   System space virtual page translation.

of fixed size. Each page contains 512 bytes, and the low-order 9 bits of each address determine the byte within the page containing the desired reference.

Since virtual-to-physical address translation in the S0 region is simplest, we will consider it first. Given a virtual address, the translation for a given page can be found by looking at the proper *page table entry* (PTE) in a list of translations, called the *S0 page table*. The page table is a vector of translations containing one entry for each page, starting at page 0 of the region. This page table resides at a well-known address in *physical* memory, so the hardware can directly access the desired address to perform a translation. Figure 1 illustrates this process.

Process-space (P0) translations are only one step harder, since the P0 page table has the same structure as the S0 table, except that in order to save physical memory, it resides at a well-known address in the S0 region of the *virtual* memory space. Thus, to translate a P0 address, it is necessary to have the translation for the S0 page that contains the P0 page-table entry. This requirement implies that when a P0 TB miss is handled, the P0 PTE reference may cause another TB miss. This need for two page-table look-ups is referred to as a *double miss*. Note that further nested misses cannot occur, because the S0 page table resides at a *physical* memory address, which requires no translation. Figure 2 illustrates a P0 translation.

For a complete description of the VAX/VMS virtual memory structure, see [7, 13].

2.2 VAX-11/780 TB

The 11/780 TB is structured in the same manner as the tag-matching mechanism associated with main memory data caches [19]. Figure 3 illustrates this. The TB consists of a number of *rows*, where each row consists of a set of virtual-to-physical translations. To perform a translation, the virtual address is divided into two fields. The first field consists of the low-order bits of the address and is used to select the byte within the page. This number, called the *offset*, does not participate in the translation process but is retained to access the proper byte within the physical page selected. The other field consists of the virtual page number of the desired reference. It is used to determine if the translation is present in the TB. The page number is divided into two fields. The first, called the *row index*, is used to select a row within the TB. If the desired translation is to be found in the TB, it must be contained in this row. The other field is called the *tag* and contains sufficient information to identify uniquely a virtual address among all those that may reside in the selected row. This tag is compared against all the tags of the translations currently stored in the selected row of the TB. A translation hit occurs if there is a tag match. In this event the physical address of the page is extracted from the TB and combined with the saved offset to create the address for the desired reference to physical memory.

The structure of a TB is defined by the number of *rows* it contains and the number of tag entries that are compared in parallel when a row is selected, usually referred to as the *set size* or *associativity* of the TB. The total number of translations in the TB is referred to as the *size* of the TB.

Different implementations of the VAX architecture can have different types of translation buffers. The VAX model 11/780 TB considered in this paper has the following characteristics: its size is 128 translations; its structure is 2-way set-associative; and it uses random replacement on a miss. The 128 translations are evenly divided between system space and process space. Thus the 11/780 TB appears to be two separate translation buffers, each 64 entries in size, and each devoted to one address space. Other VAX implementations (all divided equally between system and process space) are as follows:

Model	Size (translations)	Associativity
11/780	128	2-way
11/750	512	2-way
11/730	128	1-way
11/785	512	2-way
8600	512	1-way

As we noted above, each entry of a VAX TB maps one 512-byte page. For any fixed size TB, bigger pages are always better: more memory is mapped at no added cost, resulting in fewer misses. Bigger is not always better, however, for overall paging behavior. The choice of page size is a trade-off involving the TB as well as other hardware and software components of the virtual memory system.

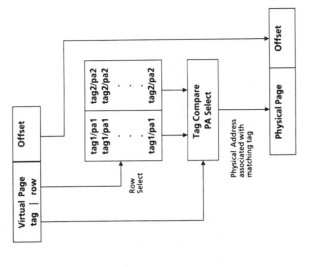

Fig. 3. 11/780 TB configuration.

Figure 4 is a simplified picture of the 11/780 address paths relevant to the TB. Translation requests are made both by the CPU for operand data (referred to as *D-stream* references) and by the 8-byte prefetching Instruction Buffer or IB (referred to as *I-stream* references). Every D-stream reference needs to use the TB, but since I-stream prefetching is strictly sequential, one I-stream reference to the TB can cover a set of consecutive references to memory. The Virtual Instruction Buffer Address register (VIBA) holds the prefetch pointer, and the Physical Instruction Buffer Address register (PIBA) holds its corresponding physical address. The IB's references to memory use the PIBA directly, bypassing the TB (see Figure 4). This works until one of two events interrupts sequential prefetching: a branch instruction or a sequential prefetch across a page boundary. A branch requires a reload of VIBA, and both branches and page crossings result in a TB reference to reload the PIBA.

The presence of the VIBA–PIBA registers complicates the task of measuring TB performance. The usual measure, namely, the *miss ratio*, is the number of misses divided by the number of references. In the 11/780's case, what exactly should be denoted by an I-stream "reference"? We discuss this question in the next section.

The technology of the 11/780 is 1975–76 vintage Schottky-TTL SSI and MSI. The processor is implemented on twenty 12-inch-by-15-inch boards (five more boards implement the Floating Point Accelerator). About one and one-third boards are devoted to the TB and its attendant hardware, with one-third of a board for the tag and data RAMs alone. Thus, about 6 or 7 percent of the hardware cost of the processor (neglecting memory and I/O) is spent for the TB.

from the instructions of other architectures, it does allow easy comparison with other VAX implementations by abstracting some of the organization-specific characteristics that are not related to TB performance. For example, comparison of widely varying instruction buffer structures will show nearly identical numbers of misses per instruction, even if one structure repeatedly reads the same location while the other does not. Similarly, the misses per instruction metric will not be as sensitive to data-path access widths as misses per hardware reference. Finally, we have found that this metric, along with the average number of cycles per instruction and the number of cycles to service a TB miss, allows simple computation of the relative importance of the TB miss service time to processor performance. (See [1, 12] for other uses of this metric.)

In order to make both of our metrics easier to deal with, we will multiply them by 100, reporting misses per 100 instructions and miss ratios as percentages between 0 and 100.

3. METHODS

Apart from analytic modeling, there are two approaches to understanding the performance of a computer system component such as a TB: simulation and measurement. Both approaches have advantages and disadvantages.

Simulation requires no special hardware and is quite flexible, since variations in hardware structure can easily be evaluated. Simulation experiments are reproducible. On the other hand, simulation can be inaccurate if the structure of the simulated model does not closely match the structure of the actual hardware. Certain aspects of performance may require an impractical amount of detail in the simulation. It may also be difficult to create an accurate representation of the real work load, especially if that workload must include the interactions of many distinct instruction streams. Simulation is also expensive in computational resources: simulated hardware typically runs orders of magnitude slower than real hardware and requires large amounts of storage.

Direct measurement of the hardware has complementary advantages and disadvantages. There is no question concerning accuracy, of course, nor is there any problem with the speed of the experiments. But variations in the hardware structure—an enlargement of the TB, for example—are generally not possible to measure, and measurements of a real work load are not reproducible. Perhaps the biggest difficulty with measurement is the inescapable requirement for some sort of instrument and the need to connect it correctly but harmlessly to the system under test.

Three independent TB studies done at Digital attempted to characterize the 11/780 TB in support of new VAX processor development. Both measurements and simulation techniques were used. The first study used a commercial hardware monitor, the second used a monitor specially designed and built for VAX measurements, and the third used trace-driven simulation. In the remainder of this section we will discuss these three experimental approaches in detail. The three techniques do not yield fully comparable sets of results, so our presentation of data may sometimes use results from one or two of them; where possible, however, we report results from all three experimental settings.

Common to all our experiments was the use of the VMS operating system (version 2) [6, 13] on 11/780s with Floating Point Accelerators. The VMS null

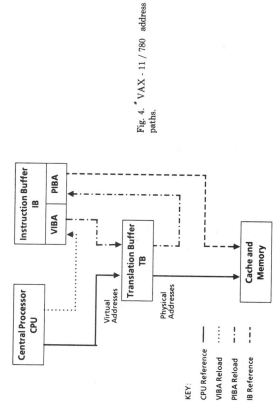

Fig. 4. 'VAX-11/780 address paths.

KEY:
CPU Reference ———
VIBA Reload ·······
PIBA Reload –·–·–
IB Reference – – –

Filling of TB entries on the 11/780 is performed by CPU microcode routines. Handling of D-stream reference TB misses is simplest, since these routines are entered via a microcode trap when the miss occurs. I-stream misses are more complex. The IB hardware first sets a state bit indicating that it received notification of an I-stream TB miss. Eventually the CPU finds an insufficient number of bytes in the IB, notices that the bit is set, and calls the microcode routine to do the fill.

2.3 Performance Metrics

We will use two different performance metrics in this paper. The first is the simple miss ratio. For the D-stream, this is just the number of misses divided by the number of data references made by the program. In the 11/780, data references are all for a 4-byte *longword* of data, and therefore data items that are longer than a longword will result in multiple references, as will references to any data item that crosses a longword boundary.

For the I-stream miss ratio, we will follow the hardware. The TB miss ratio will be the number of misses caused by the IB divided by the number of TB requests (reloadings of PIBA) made by the IB. This makes these I-stream numbers 11/780-specific; other implementations of the VAX architecture might have quite different I-stream TB miss ratios, even with a similar TB. The difficulty in determining the exact number of references makes comparison of miss ratios especially difficult, and the difficulty can be compounded when trying to contrast performance between machines with different architectures.

A second metric will help eliminate some of this dependence on the specific processor organization. This metric is the number of TB misses *per instruction*. Although this metric is clearly VAX-specific, since VAX instructions are different

process, which runs when the system is idle, was excluded from all measurements. The null process was excluded because its trivial code structure (branch to self, waiting for an interrupt) results in no TB misses and would therefore bias the results in proportion to the amount of time the CPU was idle.

3.1 Plugboard Hardware Monitor

A Dynaprobe™ Model 7916 hardware monitor (manufactured by NCR COM-TEN, Inc.) was used in the first set of experiments. Seventeen measurement probes were attached to 11/780 backpanel pins and in three instances to new signals created with added logic on one processor board. The Dynaprobe has a logic plugboard that was used to refine these signals into the quantities actually counted.

The Dynaprobe was used in two different experimental settings. In the first, the Dynaprobe was simply run all day long, measuring whatever happened to be running on the VAX that day. The particular VAX we measured was an 11/780 used at a Digital engineering site. This machine was used for general-purpose time-sharing, including editing, program development, simulation, electronic mail, and so on. Measurements were taken on three days; the three sets of results will be called Dyn-DAY1, Dyn-DAY2, and Dyn-DAY3 (DAY for DAY-long measurement). During the period of these experiments, roughly 30 users were logged on in the middle of the day.

The only major parameter that varied across the experiments was the main memory size. For the Dynaprobe time-sharing measurements, an 11/780 with 5 Mbytes of interleaved memory was used.

Although realistic, these experiments are not repeatable, since the computational load varies greatly over time. A second experimental setting addressed this problem. In it, a Remote Terminal Emulator (RTE) [9, 21] provided a real-time simulation of 40 time-sharing users connected to the VAX. The RTE is a PDP-11 with 40 asynchronous terminal interfaces; output characters generated by the VAX are seen as terminal input characters by the VAX from canned user scripts and vice versa. The work load was designed to simulate a general time-sharing load in an educational program-development environment. Some of the simulated users were editing, compiling, linking, and executing programs in various languages; some were updating indexed files; and some were doing numerical computation. For these experiments the 11/780's memory was reduced to 3 Mbytes. In later experiments with another hardware monitor we used the RTE to emulate an engineering and commercial environment; these are described later. Five-minute segments of this work load were measured. The two repetitions of this experiment will be called Dyn-EDU1 and Dyn-EDU2.

In the Dynaprobe measurements PDP-11 compatibility mode was excluded along with the VMS null process. Compatibility mode was excluded because some of the hardware signals measured do not accurately reflect compatibility mode execution.

3.2 Micro-PC Histogram Measurement

A second set of measurements were collected via a special-purpose hardware monitor that enabled us to create histograms of microcode execution in the VAX-11/780 processor. This micro-Program Counter, or μPC, monitor consists of a general purpose histogram count board that has 16,000 addressable count loca-

tions (or histogram buckets) and is capable of incrementing the count in a selected location at a rate commensurate with the microcode execution rate of the VAX-11/780. In conjunction with the histogram count board, a processor-specific interface board was required to provide the address of a histogram count bucket and control lines to signal when a count should be made. For these experiments the interface board addressed a distinct histogram bucket for each microcode location in the processor's control store, and a count was taken for each microinstruction executed. The capacity of the counters was sufficient to collect data for 1 to 2 hours of heavy processing on the CPU.

The histogram collection board was designed as a UNIBUS device, and UNIBUS commands were used to start and stop data collection, as well as to clear and read the histogram count buckets. Coincidentally, since the 11/780 has a UNIBUS, the histogram collection monitor could be installed directly on the system being measured, obviating the cost and nuisance of using a second machine for the hardware monitor. This was a further convenience, as the data collected was immediately available on a machine of sufficient capacity to do the data reduction. Note, however, that while actually monitoring microcode execution, the data collection hardware is totally passive, causing no UNIBUS activity and having no effect on the execution of programs on the system.

Since much of the activity in the 11/780 processor is under direct microcode control, the frequency of many events can be determined through examination of the relative execution counts of various microinstructions. Of particular interest for this study were the characteristics and service times of various activities associated with translation buffer fills and flushes.

The μPC histogram data is especially useful, since it forms a general resource from which the answers to many questions concerning the operation of the 11/780 running the same work load can be obtained simply by doing additional interpretation of the raw histogram data [8].

The major disadvantage of this method of hardware monitoring is that certain hardware events are not visible to the microcode. For example, the counts of instruction-stream memory references are not available because they are made by a distinct portion of the processor not under direct control of the microcode. Another characteristic of this measurement technique is that the analysis produces only average behavior characterizations of the processor over the measurement interval, since no measures of the variation of the statistics during the measurement are collected.

The μPC histogram measurements were taken in two different experimental settings: live time-sharing and synthetic RTE-generated loads. The live time-sharing measurements were taken from two different machines within Digital engineering. The first machine belonged to the research group and was used for general time-sharing and some performance data analysis. The general-purpose time-sharing was similar to that measured with the Dynaprobe, consisting of text-editing, program development, and electronic mail. This machine was relatively lightly loaded and had approximately 15 users logged in during the measurement interval. Measurements taken on this machine will be referred to as μPC-TS1 (TS for time-sharing).

The second time-sharing measurements were taken from a machine being used by a group in the initial stages of development of a VAX CPU. The load on this machine consisted of the same type of general purpose time-sharing as in μPC-TS1, with the addition of some circuit simulation and microcode development. This machine had a heavier load, with approximately 30 users logged in during the measurement interval. Measurements taken on this machine will be referred to as μPC-TS2.

The remaining measurements were taken under RTE-generated loads. These loads provided a more repeatable measurement environment and were used to test the system in environments different from those available inside Digital engineering. The three measurements of this type were taken in an educational environment, an engineering/scientific environment, and a commercial transaction-processing environment, respectively. The educational environment, which we will refer to as μPC-EDU, is the same load as used for the Dynaprobe measurements. The engineering load consisted of 40 users doing program development and scientific computations. This load will be called μPC-SCI. And finally, the commercial load consisted of 32 users doing transactional database inquiries and updates. This load will be denoted μPC-COM.

As with the Dynaprobe measurements, the VMS null process was excluded. The PDP-11 compatibility mode, however, was not. The percentage of time each measurement spent in PDP-11 mode was as follows:

TS1:	9.5 percent
TS2:	3.3 percent
EDU:	0.3 percent
SCI:	4.0 percent
COM:	0.3 percent

All of these experiments ran on machines with 8 Megabytes of memory, and each experiment lasted about one hour. Note that the Dyn-EDU1 and EDU2 experiments differ from μPC-EDU in memory size and measurement duration.

3.3 Trace-Driven Simulation

Trace-driven simulation works as follows. A program of interest is executed interpretively, and a record is made of each of its memory references. The *address trace* that results is then used to drive a simulation of the translation buffer under study. Instruction tracing features are provided in the VAX architecture, so it was relatively easy to generate address traces [22].

The major disadvantages of simulation fall into three major categories:

(1) limitations in the scope of the address trace itself;
(2) the inability to properly model multiprocess effects; and
(3) the cost of modeling the performance of a sufficient number of program traces to achieve a "representative" measure of the performance of the translation buffer, especially in those cases where detailed modeling of the hardware is required to assess the interactions and impact of TB references from various hardware units.

Our simulation effort strove to overcome some of these difficulties. We will consider each in turn.

Most trace-driven simulations have been based on traces obtained from the user-mode execution of the subject program. Since it is easiest to do simulations directly from a user program image or to do trace traps during the user-mode execution of a program, these techniques have been most popular for the generation of address traces. Unfortunately, except in cases of batch-style computation-intensive applications, much of the processor's time is spent within the operating system. This time is spent doing I/O processing, system services, and interrupts. Therefore, we developed a trace technique that allows tracing to occur during all modes of processor operation and that therefore enabled us to capture much more of the processor's activity. This trace facility allowed us to capture all the system service execution with the exception of certain time-dependent interrupt service operations, and instruction faults. Of course, slowing down the subject program while tracing it was unavoidable, and consequently the relative timing between the program and its I/O was changed. This in turn could change the context-switching behavior of the program.

The second difficulty with trace generation is the inability to incorporate accurately the effect that other processes have on the execution of the process being simulated. The primary manifestation of this effect is the fact that the process being simulated may be removed from execution temporarily, and the state that it has built up in the TB will be lost. Interrupts also result in short pauses in program execution.

Pauses in program execution can be defined as falling into two categories: voluntary and involuntary waits. Voluntary waits are those pauses in execution that are a direct consequence of program execution. Examples of voluntary waits are waiting for disk or terminal I/O or page-fault service. The typical technique of adding TB flushes at random intervals will not properly model these program-dependent pauses. However, since our multimode instruction traces include all the code leading up to most I/O waits, including the VAX save process context instruction (SVPCTX), our TB simulator can detect and model these pauses properly. Page-fault activity is more difficult to obtain, since it can be load dependent, and we felt that small traces would have an inordinate number of page faults for their size. Therefore in our simulations we did not explicitly calculate where page faults would occur, but treated them as a component of the involuntary waits.

Involuntary waits result primarily when a higher priority process preempts the CPU. This event is basically load-dependent, and therefore its frequency was set as a parameter in the simulation with a value determined from other measurements. In addition, a process that has exceeded the limit of its time slice on the CPU is removed from execution. The frequency of this event is a system parameter that is easily incorporated into a simulation. In practice on VMS systems, the process time-out is relatively infrequent and was not considered.

In general, each time a program is removed from execution there is the opportunity for the state of the TB to be lost to some degree. The loss may be almost total if there is a process context switch, which causes the process-space section of the TB to be flushed, and sufficient references are made to S0 space that its contents are completely changed. On the other hand, the loss may be minimal if the cause was a short burst of interrupt processing. In the simulations

Table I. Miss Ratios in the Dynaprobe Experiments (Percent)

		I-stream	D-stream	Total
Process	Dyn-DAY1	1.0	0.8	0.9
	Dyn-DAY2	1.5	0.9	1.1
	Dyn-DAY3	0.7	0.6	0.7
	Dyn-EDU1	1.1	1.0	1.0
	Dyn-EDU2	1.1	0.9	1.0
System	Dyn-DAY1	19.4	4.8	6.9
	Dyn-DAY2	17.5	4.0	5.8
	Dyn-DAY3	15.4	5.4	7.2
	Dyn-EDU1	31.7	6.2	9.5
	Dyn-EDU2	32.5	6.7	10.0
Total	Dyn-DAY1	3.9	1.7	2.2
	Dyn-DAY2	2.9	1.4	1.8
	Dyn-DAY3	3.5	1.6	1.9
	Dyn-EDU1	6.5	2.4	3.2
	Dyn-EDU2	5.9	2.4	3.1

we ran, it was assumed that any context switch resulted in a complete flush of the process half of the TB but had no effect on the system half.

The traces we used in these studies were derived from a number of Digital utilities available under VMS. A study conducted by Jain [11], which characterized the work loads at a number of VAX sites at educational institutions, has shown that on average more than half of all computation time was spent in system programs. Therefore, considering the limited number of benchmarks that could be run, we selected some of the more heavily used system utilities in an effort to obtain a set of traces that would be representative of a large fraction of the work on such VAX/VMS systems.

The utility traces that we used were:

DIR   A directory listing of the files in a user's file directory (47,212 instructions)

FORT   A FORTRAN compilation (2,293,007 instructions)

LINK   The LINKing of a program (481,301 instructions)

MAIL   The interactive sending and receiving of electronic mail messages (284,986 instructions)

EDT   The interactive use of the VAX/VMS standard screen editor (1,050,746 instructions)

RNO   The execution of a text processing utility (2,704,570 instructions)

SORT   The SORTing of an ASCII file (2,158,468 instructions)

The simulation experiments will be referred to as Sim-DIR, Sim-FORT, etc.

4. TB MISSES

This section will present most of the basic TB miss data. We look first at miss ratios, the most common metric of TB performance, and then proceed to consider more detailed data and other performance metrics.

4.1 Miss Ratios

Table I presents miss ratios for the Dynaprobe experiments, calculated separately for I-stream versus D-stream and for process space versus system space. (As we mentioned above, I-stream miss ratios are only available in the Dynaprobe data.) Row, column, and overall totals represent miss data pooled over the corresponding categories; for example, the total I-stream miss ratio is calculated without distinguishing process from system activity. Recall that the 11/780 TB is split into process and system halves, each of which holds a mixture of I-stream and D-stream translations.

These miss ratios are strikingly and consistently different across the four categories. The I-stream miss ratios are all greater than the corresponding D-stream miss ratios, particularly in system space. Part of the explanation for this lies in our definition of the I-stream miss ratio: only branches and page-crossings are counted as TB references.

System space miss ratios are much higher than process space miss ratios, particularly in the I-stream. We offer three informal hypotheses:

(1) System code and data structures are simply bigger than process code and data structures. In an average locality interval, system code involves more pages than process code and will have higher TB miss ratios in both I-stream and D-stream.

(2) In addition to being larger, system data structures are more complex than process data structures. They are more likely to be pointer-rich structures such as queues and linked lists, and therefore are more likely to involve multiple pages. A higher D-stream miss ratio results.

(3) System loops have fewer iterations than process loops. I-stream processing only needs the TB for branches and page-crossings, so once a loop's pages are in the TB, further iterations are highly unlikely to cause TB misses. The greater the number of iterations, the lower the I-stream miss ratio for that part of the program.

Although some of these miss ratios look quite large, the overall percentages (bottom right corner of the table) are reasonably small: two to three percent. This, of course, is due to the distribution of TB references across the four categories. Figure 5 shows the distribution of references and misses across the four categories for Dyn-DAY3; the other experiments are similar. Process references account for more than three-quarters of all references, but because of their lower miss ratios, they account for less than one-third of the misses.

4.2 Misses per Instruction

In this section we examine the TB miss behavior using the misses-per-instruction metric. Tables II–IV tabulate misses per instruction for the Dynaprobe, μPC monitor, and simulation experiments, respectively. Just as above, misses are categorized as arising from I-stream or D-stream references, and from process-space or system-space references. The μPC measurements are an exception, since the process-space/system-space distinction was not available.

Note that these miss rates are not relative to the number of references of each type, or to the type of instruction issuing the reference, but are simply the number of misses over all instructions.

Table III. TB Misses per 100 Instructions (µPC)

	I-stream	D-stream	Total
Total µPC-TS1	0.92	2.10	3.02
µPC-TS2	0.83	2.12	2.95
µPC-EDU	0.99	2.12	3.11
µPC-SCI	0.70	1.80	2.50
µPC-COM	1.24	2.18	3.41

Table IV. TB Misses per 100 Instructions (Simulator)

		I-stream	D-stream	Total
Process	Sim-DIR	0.17	0.57	0.73
	Sim-FORT	0.40	1.42	1.82
	Sim-LINK	0.46	1.41	1.87
	Sim-MAIL	0.15	0.54	0.69
	Sim-EDT	0.27	1.05	1.32
	Sim-RNO	0.50	1.37	1.87
	Sim-SORT	0.12	0.51	0.63
System	Sim-DIR	1.04	0.92	1.96
	Sim-FORT	0.02	0.02	0.04
	Sim-LINK	0.54	0.94	1.48
	Sim-MAIL	1.39	1.37	2.75
	Sim-EDT	0.70	1.02	1.72
	Sim-RNO	0.03	0.05	0.07
	Sim-SORT	0.15	0.38	0.53
Total	Sim-DIR	1.21	1.48	2.69
	Sim-FORT	0.41	1.45	1.86
	Sim-LINK	1.00	2.35	3.35
	Sim-MAIL	1.54	1.91	3.44
	Sim-EDT	0.97	2.07	3.04
	Sim-RNO	0.53	1.41	1.94
	Sim-SORT	0.27	0.89	1.17

The misses-per-instruction metric gives a good indication of the relative impact of TB misses on the processor performance, since the number of misses determines the amount of time expended in filling TB entries. In fact, the hardware monitor measurements show remarkable consistency in the relative impact of each reference type. The D-stream miss rate was consistently greater than the I-stream miss rate for both process space and system space. In 100 instructions in a time-sharing load, there are roughly two D-stream misses and one I-stream miss. This implies that there is greater locality in the I-stream than in the D-stream. Therefore, if one were to consider distinct TBs for I-stream and D-stream references, a smaller one could be used for the I-stream.

The system-space miss rate was consistently greater than the process-space miss rate regardless of whether the reference was from the I-stream or D-stream. This is particularly interesting, since the system portion of the TB is not flushed

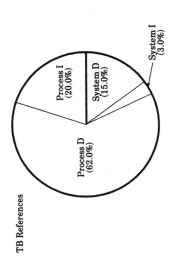

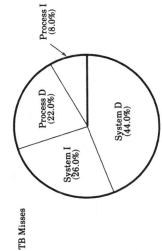

Fig. 5. Distribution of references and misses in Dyn-Day3.

Table II. TB Misses per 100 Instructions (Dynaprobe)

		I-stream	D-stream	Total
Process	Dyn-DAY1	0.23	0.73	0.96
	Dyn-DAY2	0.42	0.73	1.15
	Dyn-DAY3	0.18	0.50	0.69
	Dyn-EDU1	0.23	0.77	1.00
	Dyn-EDU2	0.24	0.77	1.00
System	Dyn-DAY1	0.87	1.26	2.13
	Dyn-DAY2	0.48	0.69	1.17
	Dyn-DAY3	0.62	1.03	1.64
	Dyn-EDU1	1.44	1.91	3.34
	Dyn-EDU2	1.32	1.88	3.21
Total	Dyn-DAY1	1.10	1.99	3.10
	Dyn-DAY2	0.90	1.41	2.32
	Dyn-DAY3	0.80	1.53	2.33
	Dyn-EDU1	1.67	2.67	4.34
	Dyn-EDU2	1.56	2.65	4.21

Table V. Types of TB Misses (Percent)*

	P0	P1	Double	S0
μPC-TS1	46.7	8.2	3.1	42.0
μPC-TS2	31.0	6.2	3.4	59.4
μPC-EDU	19.4	9.0	3.4	68.1
μPC-SCI	28.5	5.0	3.0	63.4
μPC-COM	16.4	9.2	4.8	69.6

*This table actually shows the types of PTE references, which are very nearly the same as the types of TB misses. See the text for details.

Table VI. Type of I-stream Misses in μPC Experiments (Percent)

	Branch target	Page-crossing		
	Opcode	Opcode	First specifier	Other specifier
μPC-TS1	93			7
μPC-TS2	94			6
μPC-EDU	95			5
μPC-SCI	94			6
μPC-COM	95			5

Table VII. Type of I-Stream Misses in Simulation Experiments (Percent)

	Branch target	Page-crossing		
	Opcode	Opcode	First specifier	Other specifier
Sim-DIR	91	9		
Sim-FORT	76	24		
Sim-LINK	64	36		
Sim-MAIL	86	14		
Sim-EDT	82	18		
Sim-RNO	68	32		
Sim-SORT	74	26		

on context switches. As we hypothesized above, this may be a consequence of the types of data structures and program structures typical of system code. But it also implies that it may be most cost-effective to increase the size of the system portion of the TB so that it is larger than the process portion.

4.3 Double Misses

As described in Section 2.1, the virtual memory of the VAX is divided into three regions, the system space, S0, and two regions of process space, P0 and P1. Furthermore, the page tables for the process-space regions are held in the S0 region of the virtual address space to avoid allocating physical memory for the page tables of every process. However, this results in the possibility of *double* TB misses. To assess the impact of these misses, we used the μPC histograms to measure the relative frequency of the page table look-ups from each of the following reference sources: P0 space, P1 space, S0 space due to double misses, and normal S0 space references. (Practically all of these look-ups were for TB misses; the rest were for protection-checking probe operations used in some VAX instructions.) Table V summarizes these results.

The table shows again the large proportion of TB misses attributable to system-space references. It also shows that P0 misses in turn greatly outnumber P1 misses. This we presume is due to the fact that P1 holds the stacks, which have inherently good locality of reference. Finally, the table shows that only a small number of page table references were for double misses. This implies that the D-allocation of process page tables in virtual memory had only a small cost in terms of multiple page-table translations.

4.4 I-stream Details

I-stream TB misses have two sources: explicit branches in the program and prefetches that cross a page boundary. There are two slightly incompatible observations of this distinction to report. A miss due to page-crossing can happen on any byte of an instruction. A VAX instruction consists of an opcode byte followed by a variable number of operand specifiers of various sizes [7, 20]. There are three types of page-crosses: on the opcode byte itself, on any byte of the first operand specifier, and on any byte of any later specifier. The μPC method could not distinguish branch-type misses from those due to the first two types of page cross; results are shown in Table VI. The simulation runs, on the other hand, could clearly distinguish between branch misses and all page-cross misses; these results are shown in Table VII.

Not surprisingly, most I-stream misses are due to branches, which therefore become a more important candidate for efficient service of TB misses than I-stream page crossings.

4.5 D-stream Details

The μPC and simulation experiments allowed us to separate D-stream TB references and misses into reads and writes. Table VIII shows the miss ratios of read and write references from the D-stream. Modify references here count as one read followed by one write, where the write will never miss. Dynaprobe D-stream miss ratios were presented in Table I, and they are similar to the ones given here.

Reads appear to be two to four times as likely to miss as writes. A simple hypothesis to explain this is that within a locality interval, data is more likely to be written after it is read than before. Thus the reference that brings an entry into the TB is more likely to be a read than a write.

4.6 Modify Bit Characterization

In order to support the paging strategy of the operating system, the VAX architecture provides help in indicating which pages have been modified. A PTE bit called the *M-bit* (modify bit) is set whenever a page that has not yet been marked as modified is written into. There is an M-bit associated with each virtual page, and it resides in the page-table entry for the page. A copy of the M-bit resides in the TB entry for any page whose translation is present in the TB.

Table VIII. D-Stream Miss Ratios (Percent)

	Read	Write	Total
μPC-TS1	2.13	1.11	1.76
μPC-TS2	2.58	0.64	1.93
μPC-EDU	2.17	0.79	1.67
μPC-SCI	1.75	0.78	1.43
μPC-COM	2.34	0.76	1.80
Sim-DIR	2.28	0.71	1.65
Sim-FORT	1.73	0.54	1.25
Sim-LINK	2.55	1.17	1.99
Sim-MAIL	2.67	0.73	1.89
Sim-EDT	2.32	0.70	1.67
Sim-RNO	1.46	0.61	1.13
Sim-SORT	0.93	0.60	0.83

Table IX. M-Bit Setting Rate (Settings per 100 Instructions)

	Write with TB miss	Write with TB hit	Total
μPC-TS1	0.0095	0.0022	0.0117
μPC-TS2	0.0011	0.0007	0.0018
μPC-EDU	0.0031	0.0016	0.0047
μPC-SCI	0.0042	0.0026	0.0067
μPC-COM	0.0026	0.0017	0.0044

Table X. Time in TB Miss Service (Average Cycles per Miss)

	Nonstalled	Stalled	Total
Dyn-DAY1	—	—	21.5
Dyn-DAY2	—	—	21.7
Dyn-DAY3	—	—	21.8
Dyn-EDU1	—	—	22.1
Dyn-EDU2	—	—	22.1
μPC-TS1	18.6	2.4	21.0
μPC-TS2	18.1	3.5	21.6
μPC-EDU	18.0	3.8	21.8
μPC-SCI	18.2	3.8	21.9
μPC-COM	17.6	4.0	21.7

Setting the M-bit can occur in two circumstances, depending upon whether the current reference has resulted in a TB miss or a TB hit. The latter case arises if at some time in the past the page was read and a translation put into the TB, but the current reference is the first to modify the page. Setting the M-bit in cases of TB misses is easy, since a check can be incorporated in the TB fill service. Setting the M-bit on TB hits is handled as a special microcode exception case on memory references.

M-bit setting operations are overheads incurred for virtual memory support, and their performance impact is proportional to their frequency of occurrence. We used the μPC histogram measurements to find the frequency of setting the M-bit. Table IX shows the average rate of M-bit settings, for cases of both TB hits and misses.

It is clear from the table that the frequency of M-bit settings is two orders of magnitude less than the frequency of TB misses, and consequently the few microoperations required to set the M-bit will have an insignificant effect on 11/780 performance.

5. TIME IN TB MISS SERVICE

In the VAX-11/780, TB misses are handled by microcode routines that read the required PTE from memory and insert it in the TB. The time spent doing this is a major performance cost of the TB: cycles so spent are lost to the running program. (If the PTE indicates that the page is not currently in main memory, i.e., a *page fault*, then the TB miss microcode must yield control to memory-management software, which will bring it in. Time spent this way is a major performance cost of paged virtual memory and is a function of the size of main memory, speed of the disk, memory-management algorithm, and so on. See [14] for a discussion of VAX/VMS memory management.)

We measured TB miss time in the Dynaprobe and μPC experiments. The μPC histogram gives the result directly, reporting execution counts for the microinstructions in the TB service routines. In the Dynaprobe experiments we marked the entries and exits of these routines by using hardware intended to mark the locations of microcode patches. The Dynaprobe counted cycles between entry and exit. Cycles in the 11/780 are 200 nanoseconds long.

The TB miss routine must locate the appropriate page table, read the proper PTE from memory, and write the mapping into the TB. The routine in its simplest form is roughly 17 microinstructions long; there is some minor additional overhead (one or two cycles) on entry and exit. The PTE, of course, may not be in the *cache*. Hence reading it may provoke a cache miss and a processor wait, or *stall*, of about 6 cycles, depending on other simultaneous memory activity [3]. The μPC measurements separated the TB routine's cycles into stalled and nonstalled cycles; the Dynaprobe measurements did not.

Table X shows the results. These results include the routine entry and exit overhead, and double misses count here (as throughout this paper) as two TB misses. According to the table, TB misses take about 22 cycles each, including the cache stall and the overhead. The average length of the cache stall is 3.5 cycles. Since a cache miss usually takes 6 cycles, we conclude that the PTE is, on average, in the cache about 40 percent of the time.

What is the performance cost of the TB service time? Combining the time-per-miss results and miss-rate measurements of Section 4.2 with a knowledge of the total time required for instruction execution provides an understanding of the amount of time attributable to TB service and its relation to the total execution time of an instruction. Since TB service time is added explicitly to time for base instruction execution, the effect of TB service on the 11/780 can be represented by the simple formula,

$$cpi_{total} = cpi_{base} + cpi_{tb},$$

Table XII. Context Switches (LDPCTX) from Dynaprobe and μPC

	Average headway		Average number of process space misses per interval
	Time (ms)	Instructions	
Dyn-DAY1	11	5,140	82
Dyn-DAY2	17	8,600	152
Dyn-DAY3	14	7,350	64
Dyn-EDU1	7.8	3,250	35
Dyn-EDU2	8.0	3,400	37
μPC-TS1	13.7	7,100	83
μPC-TS2	11.2	5,660	83
μPC-EDU	12.7	5,660	49
μPC-SCI	21.3	10,600	89
μPC-COM	9.5	4,350	35

Table XI. Time in TB Miss Service

	VAX MIPS	cpi_{base}	+	cpi_{tb}	=	cpi_{total}	Service time as percent of all cycles
Dyn-DAY1	0.46	10.08		0.67		10.75	6.2
Dyn-DAY2	0.50	9.42		0.50		9.92	5.1
Dyn-DAY3	0.51	9.31		0.51		9.82	5.2
Dyn-EDU1	0.42	11.00		0.96		11.96	8.0
Dyn-EDU2	0.43	10.81		0.93		11.74	7.9
μPC-TS1	0.52	8.97		0.63		9.60	6.6
μPC-TS2	0.50	9.28		0.64		9.92	6.4
μPC-EDU	0.45	10.53		0.68		11.21	6.0
μPC-SCI	0.50	9.51		0.55		10.06	5.5
μPC-COM	0.46	10.15		0.74		10.89	6.8

where

$$cpi_{total} = total \ cycles \ per \ instruction,$$

$$cpi_{base} = cycles \ per \ instruction$$

exclusive of TB miss service,

$$cpi_{tb} = cycles \ per \ instruction \ for \ TB \ service,$$

m_{tb} = TB misses per instruction (see Table II),

$t_{service}$ = TB miss service time in cycles (see Table X).

and

$$cpi_{tb} = m_{tb} \times t_{service}$$

Table XI shows the execution rate of the 11/780 and its decomposition into the time spent in base execution and in TB service as determined in the Dynaprobe and μPC measurements. The first section of the table shows the execution rate measured in millions of VAX instructions per second (VAX MIPS). Note that this measure is specific to the VAX architecture and cannot be used to compare different architectures. The next section of the table shows the application of the above formula to determine the number of instruction cycles dedicated to TB service relative to total instruction execution. (A more detailed timing model of the 11/780 is given in [8].)

Enhancing the 11/780 TB structure does not, it appears, offer much leverage for increasing the performance of the processor. Even if there were no TB misses at all, performance could be improved by only 5–8 percent. And even a TB of infinite size could not realize this improvement because of the misses due to context-switching. In the next section we discuss these misses, and in Section 7 we look at some finite variations of the 11/780 TB structure.

6. CONTROL FLOW CHANGES

6.1 Context Switches

In the VAX architecture, a process context switch is accomplished by a save-process-context instruction (SVPCTX) followed by a load-process-context instruction (LDPCTX). In VMS, other methods with less overhead are used to

transfer control to and from the system and to service interrupts; full context switches happen only when one user process is replaced by another. A context switch changes process state, including the process virtual address space. This is typically accomplished by invalidating all of the process-space entries in the TB. Since context-switching is thus responsible for some portion of the TB misses, it is important to know how often it occurs. (The TB flush itself takes 40 cycles on the 11/780.)

Table XII describes context-switching in the Dynaprobe and μPC experiments. The average *headway* is the average length of the interval between switches, here measured in milliseconds and in VAX instructions (but, as usual, not counting the null process). The length of a context-switch interval is a complex function of system load and hardware configuration. These lengths vary widely. According to the table, there were from 3200 to 10,600 instructions in the average interval. The longest and shortest intervals were observed in the RTE experiments. In the real time-sharing runs the average interval ranged between 5100 and 8600 instructions.

Roughly speaking, the shorter the average context interval, the greater the number of misses per average instruction. This can be seen by comparing Table XII with Tables II and III. In particular, the worst TB performance is found in the Dyn-EDU workloads, which have the shortest average intervals. This we attribute to the fact that these experiments used the smallest amount of main memory.

Table XII also shows the number of process-space misses in the average interval. This turned out to be, to us, surprisingly low. Indeed, only one of the numbers shown in the table is much greater than the maximum number of process-space entries in the TB, namely 64. This led us to investigate, through simulation, how many misses could be attributed purely to filling up empty slots in the TB. (Unfortunately, neither hardware monitor allowed this to be measured directly.)

When the new process being execution after a context switch, it will at first experience TB misses solely on account of the process TB being empty; these misses fill an empty slot and will be called *fills*. Once some fills have occurred,

Table XIII. Context Switches in the Simulations

	Average headway (instructions)	Flushes due to SVPCTX (percent)	Process-space misses per context interval		
			Fills	Bumps	Total
Sim-DIR	4,721	50.0	22.6	12.0	34.6
Sim-FORT	9,926	0.4	49.7	131.0	180.7
Sim-LINK	7,763	21.0	39.5	105.5	145.0
Sim-MAIL	6,064	38.3	29.1	12.9	42.0
Sim-EDT	1,812	81.7	16.4	7.5	23.9
Sim-RNO	9,729	2.5	47.8	133.9	181.7
Sim-SORT	9,679	3.1	25.2	36.1	61.3

Table XIV. Average TB Invalidate Headway (Instructions)

	TBIS	TBIA
μPC-TS1	4,110	8,730,000
μPC-TS2	10,190	2,410,000
μPC-EDU	3,410	934,000
μPC-SCI	2,960	*
μPC-COM	5,330	*

* Never occurred.

the process can miss on an address that maps to an occupied TB slot; these misses replace one valid entry with another and will be called *bumps*. Every process-space miss is either a fill or a bump. We distinguish between these because only bumps can be reduced by enlarging or restructuring the TB. The number of fills in a particular context interval cannot be reduced, and may likely be increased, with a bigger or more associative TB.

As mentioned in Section 3.3, not all context switches could be recorded in our simulation traces. In particular, those due to VAX traps and faults (such as page faults) were not seen. To compensate for this, the simulated TB was arbitrarily flushed every 10,000 instructions, in addition to the flushes due to SVPCTX instructions in the traces.

Table XIII gives the results on context-switching in the simulations. There is fairly wide variation in all of the reported statistics. In particular, the total number of process misses per context interval has a wider range than the values seen in the measurements (Table XII). The three runs with the smallest percentage of flushes from SVPCTX are the three with the smallest amount of system activity.

The shorter the interval, the greater the ratio of fills to bumps is likely to be. Table XIII shows that the three programs with the shortest average intervals (DIR, MAIL, and EDT) are also the three in which fills actually outnumber bumps. In these three and in SORT, less than half of the available 64 entries were filled in the average interval.

These results show that for the 11/780 style of TB design, the process-space miss rate contains a significant irreducible component. Whereas we can expect steady enlargement of the system part of the TB to yield steady reduction of the system miss rate, we cannot expect any reduction in the rate of process-space fills. Indeed, the limiting value for the number of fills per interval as the TB grows is the average number of virtual pages touched in one context interval.

The number of fills could be reduced if process-space TB entries were tagged with a unique process ID number. A TB hit would then require matching both the virtual address and the requesting process' ID. Context switches would not need to flush anything from the TB. No such ID number exists in the VAX architecture, however, and we have not explored this design alternative.

6.2 TB Invalidations

The μPC histogram measurements allowed us to measure two other events that flush TB entries. These were two special VAX instructions: TB Invalidate Single (TBIS) and TB Invalidate All (TBIA). TBIS is used by VMS when a single page-table entry is changed and it is necessary to make sure that the TB does not maintain a stale translation. TBIA is used by VMS to clear the entire TB when massive changes have been made to the page tables and it is easier to clear the entire TB than to figure out which pages to invalidate.

Table XIV shows the average instruction headway between executions of TBIS and TBIA. The average headway between executions of TBIS is in about the same range as the context-switch headway. If we assume that every TBIS caused one additional miss (the worst-case assumption), then we would expect one or two of these per context interval. TBIA is so infrequent that its effects are negligible. TBIS and TBIA, then, do not affect TB performance very much.

6.3 PC Changes

As was reported above, most I-stream TB references are due to branch instructions. Branches are very common, a property the VAX architecture shares with many others (see [15, 16]). Table XV shows that roughly one quarter of all VAX instructions executed in all our experiments changed the PC. This number includes explicit branches, both conditional and unconditional, as well as subroutine and procedure calls. (The actual measurements in the Dynaprobe and μPC experiments counted instruction buffer flushes; these occur very slightly more often than once every branch instruction, since they occur on traps, faults, interrupts, and resumptions of interruptible instructions.)

The Dynaprobe and simulation experiments allowed the branches to be classified according to whether the destination instruction was in process or system space. The results are shown in Table XV. All of the Dynaprobe runs and most of the simulation runs showed a much higher branch frequency in process space than in system space. In fact, according to the Dynaprobe results, an instruction in process space is about twice as likely to branch as one in system space.

Why should this be so? Here are three possible explanations:

(1) Most system code was written in VAX assembly language, and most process

Table XVI. Effects of Hardware Reduction of the TB

	DAY		EDU	
	Full TB*	Half TB	Full TB*	Half TB
Process space misses per 100 instructions	0.93	4.52	1.00	3.33
System space misses per 100 instructions	1.65	3.76	3.28	5.72
Total misses per 100 instructions	2.58	8.28	4.28	9.05
Time spent in miss service (percent of cycles)	5.5	14.5	8.0	14.5
VAX MIPS	0.494	0.431	0.420	0.382
Relative performance	1.00	0.87	1.00	0.91

* Full TB numbers are unweighted averages.

Table XV. Instructions That Change the PC (Percent)

	Process space	System space	Total
Dyn-DAY1	31	16	28
Dyn-DAY2	33	14	30
Dyn-DAY3	28	19	27
Dyn-EDU1	30	14	25
Dyn-EDU2	30	13	26
μPC-TS1	—	—	27
μPC-TS2	—	—	29
μPC-EDU	—	—	26
μPC-SCI	—	—	24
μPC-COM	—	—	27
Sim-DIR	34	22	23
Sim-FORT	31	21	30
Sim-LINK	23	25	24
Sim-MAIL	27	21	22
Sim-EDT	29	20	26
Sim-RNO	26	23	25
Sim-SORT	23	24	23

flushes are a likely culprit: in Section 6 we showed that for three of the simulations, 32 entries would not be enough to accommodate all of the fills in the average context interval. Certainly 32 entries are too few for the system as well, but explicit full flushes of the system half of the TB do not occur, so the degradation in TB performance was not as pronounced as for process space.

7.2 Simulation Of TB Configuration Alternatives

The 11/780 hardware provides only a limited capability to vary the configuration of the TB. Simulation was necessary to evaluate TB configurations beyond those alternatives. Using simulation, we investigated the effect of size and associativity on miss rate, and the effect of separating the TB into process and system halves. In general, we have explored the design space around the 11/780.

The first parameters to be investigated were the size and associativity of the TB. Figure 6 shows TB miss rate versus TB size while holding the associativity constant at 2-way. It shows results for each of the simulated programs, and the solid dot represents the 11/780 measurement reported in Section 7.1. The figure shows that doubling the size of the 11/780 TB will result in an average savings of approximately 1.1 misses per 100 instructions. Using the results from Section 5, this would correspond to a 2.3 percent decrease in execution time for these benchmarks. Doubling the size again results in a further savings of 0.4 misses per 100 instructions, for a total reduction in execution time of 3.3 percent.

Figure 7 shows TB performance for the same set of TB sizes with a 1-way associative or direct-mapped configuration. Note that in both these charts, size is measured in number of TB slots, which is one of the principal determinants of the cost of the TB. Again the solid dot is used to represent the 11/780 measurement reported in Section 7.1. Comparison of Figures 6 and 7 shows that the reduction in miss rate gained by taking a direct-mapped TB and making it 2-way associative is almost equivalent to doubling its size.

Some details of the miss rates in the EDT benchmark are illustrated in Figure 8. The EDT benchmark was selected for illustration because its miss rate closely

code in some high-level language. With this greater degree of control over the code, VMS programmers avoided branches where possible.

(2) VMS programmers coded conditional branches so that they were more likely to fail (fall through) than succeed. High-level language programs cannot generally do this.

(3) It was hypothesized in Section 4.1 that system data structures were more complicated than process structures, and that system loops were iterated less than process loops. These characteristics could yield code with fewer branches.

Since conditional branches that fail to branch are not counted as PC-changing instructions, the dynamic frequency of instructions that *might* change the PC is even higher than shown in Table XV.

7. VARIATIONS OF THE TB STRUCTURE

7.1 Hardware Measurement Of TB Configuration Alternatives

By setting some special control bits at system boot time, one can reconfigure the 11/780's TB from 128-entry, 2-way associative to 64-entry, direct-mapped. This preserves the process/system split, with 32 entries for each. We did this in the Dynaprobe setting and collected one set of data for an additional DAY and one set for an additional segment of the EDU workload. Table XVI shows the results.

The miss rate increased by a factor of about 2 to 3 with the smaller TB, as did the percentage of total cycles spent in miss service. But process and system misses changed very differently. The size reduction had a much greater effect on process-space misses, which were increased by a factor of 3 to 5, than it did on system misses, which were increased by around a factor of 2. The context-switch

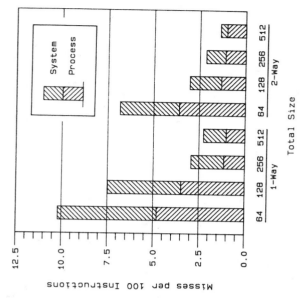

Fig. 8.   TB miss rate (EDT benchmark).

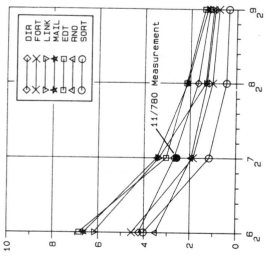

Fig. 6.   TB miss rate versus size (2-way associative).

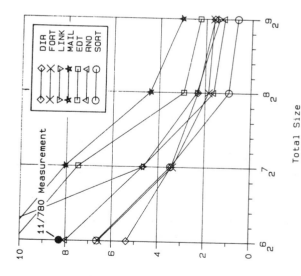

Fig. 7.   TB miss rate versus size (1-way associative).

resembles the aggregate miss rates measured with the Dynaprobe and μPC monitors. The bar chart illustrates the effect on miss rate as the size of the TB is increased from 64 to 512 tag entries and for both 1-way and 2-way associativity. Furthermore, the total miss rate is shown as being composed of two components: a process-space miss component, which is the bottom part of each bar, and a system-space miss component, which is the top part of each bar.

The figure shows the steady decline in the system-space component of the miss rate as the size of the TB increases. This behavior is to be expected, since the system half of a larger TB will allow more of the program's system-space translations to be resident in the TB, resulting in less contention for individual tag locations. In contrast to this behavior is the asymptotic approach of the process-space component of the miss rate to a much larger value of approximately one miss per 100 instructions. This is due to the frequent flushes of the process-space half of the TB. Even with large TB sizes there remains a significant number of *fills* following each flush (see Section 6.1).

Is there an overall advantage to having a separate system TB? Let a *split* TB be one with separate system and process halves, and let a *joint* TB be one in which process and system entries are combined. As was noted earlier, the advantage of a split TB is that system-space translations need not be flushed on process context switches. We assume that a joint TB, on the other hand, must be completely flushed on a process context switch. (An alternative, feasible in VLSI, would be to flush from a joint TB only the process-space entries.)

432   Chapter 6 / Memory Systems

Table XVII. Least Size at Which Split TB Is Superior

	1-way	2-way
Sim-DIR	<64	<64
Sim-FORT	256	512
Sim-LINK	256	256
Sim-MAIL	<64	<64
Sim-EDT	256	128
Sim-RNO	256	128
Sim-SORT	512	256

8. CONCLUSION

We used three different techniques to study and evaluate translation buffer performance in the VAX-11/780. The Dynaprobe technique allowed direct access to hardware signals and was thus the best of the three for evaluating exactly what the hardware was doing. Its major drawbacks were that necessary hardware signals were not always conveniently available on the backpanel, and that *all* signals of interest had to be specified by the experimenter beforehand. The microPC histogram technique was more restricted in scope, since it could measure only phenomena expressed in the microprogram PC. However, it did allow the experimenter to measure new quantities after the fact. Simulation was the most flexible technique, allowing us to look at variations of the TB configuration as described in Section 7, but only gross performance characteristics could be seen. Timing information, in particular, was not available.

The simulation data show that selected single programs do have TB behavior similar to the aggregate behavior of real time-sharing systems. The data also emphasize the importance of choosing a program with significant system activity. The programs with the best simulated TB performance (FORT, RNO, and SORT) were also the ones with the fewest system-space misses and were not good representatives of the time-sharing systems. (We note in passing that FORTRAN compilers are frequent subjects of simulation experiments.) The editor EDT turned out to be a fair representative of the larger experiments when its system references were counted, but if only process misses and process instructions were counted, its miss rate per 100 instructions would decrease from 3.0 to 2.1.

Our measurements provided a good characterization of the impact of the TB on instruction performance. The product of the miss rate per instruction and the average service time per miss gives the time cost of the TB per average VAX instruction. We observed a typical miss rate of about 3 per 100 instructions and a service time of about 22 cycles per miss. This yields a cost of around 0.7 cycles out of the 10 spent in the average instruction.

The 11/780 was the first VAX, and thus its TB design choices were made without the benefit of extensive VAX simulation and measurement results such as ours. In view of this, our results, generally speaking, validate VAX architectural choices and 11/780 implementation choices concerning the TB. Its size and associativity seem about right (Section 7.2); the allocation of process page tables

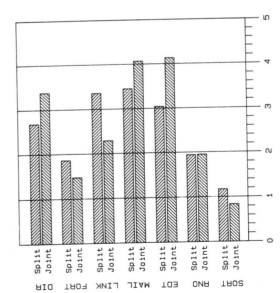

Fig. 9. TB miss rate for split and joint TBs.

Figure 9 illustrates the split versus joint comparison for TBs otherwise configured like the 11/780's. The figure indicates that for this set of benchmarks a split TB is not universally superior. Examination of those programs for which the joint TB was better (FORT, LINK, and SORT) revealed them to be those with miss rates larger for process space than for system space.

In general, a joint TB helps reduce a high process- or system-space miss rate by giving each address space additional TB entries. The three programs noted above benefited from the additional process-space entries. However, a joint TB will not be as effective at reducing a high system-space miss rate, because it must also offset the cost of flushing system entries on context switches. Furthermore, for either address space, the additional TB entries are bought at the expense of sharing the entries with the other space. This sharing exposes one space's entries to being bumped by misses in the other space.

Since the benefit of a joint TB is essentially manifest as an apparent increase in size, and simply increasing TB size ceases to be effective as the TB gets too large, one expects that for very small TBs a joint TB will be superior. Conversely, as the TB size increases, a split TB becomes superior. Table XVII illustrates this effect by listing the crossover sizes for the benchmarks simulated for both 1-way and 2-way associative TBs. The table also indicates that increasing associativity tends to reduce the size at which it is better to split the TB. This follows since increasing associativity makes the TB appear larger, thereby reducing the benefit of having a joint TB.

in virtual memory does not produce many double misses (Section 4.3); and the microcode implementation of the TB service routines has acceptable performance cost (Section 5).

The results do not settle the question of split versus joint TB. Some of the simulated programs (at least the portions captured in our traces) would perform slightly better if the 11/780 TB did not differentiate system from process entries. As we discussed in Section 7, the joint organization is better for small TBs, and the split organization is better for large TBs; the 11/780's TB size seems to be near the boundary between small and large in this sense.

There is some room for performance enhancement of the 11/780 TB. It could be made bigger: a fourfold increase in size might cut the miss rate by a little more than half (Figure 6). A very much bigger TB could hold *all* of the system-space page mappings, but flushes due to process context switches prevent a like elimination of process misses. An architectural change that could help in this regard would be to tag each process TB entry with a unique process ID. This would eliminate flushing, but of course, unless the TB were quite big, context switching might accomplish *de facto* flushes by gradually replacing one process' tagged entries with another's. One final place where performance could be improved would be through the addition of hardware assists in the TB service routine. Cutting the 22 cycles we measured in half, for example, would speed up the 11/780 by around 3 percent. The benefit of any of these changes must, of course, be balanced against the corresponding cost, both in added logic and in potential increases in cycle time.

ACKNOWLEDGMENTS

The Dynaprobe experiments were done jointly with J. J. Grady. Bob Stewart, the designer of the 11/780 TB, helped us determine where to put our measurement probes and helped interpret the results. Garth Wiebe and Jean Hsiao developed the μPC histogram system. Dennis Ting developed the multimode trace facility, and Dave Orbits helped develop the simulator. Helpful comments on earlier drafts of this paper were offered by Dileep Bhandarkar, Wayne Cardoza, Dick Flower, Israel Gat, Kevin Koch, Jud Leonard, Matt Reilly, Alan Smith, Bob Stewart, Bob Supnik, Mark Truhlar, and Deborra Zukowski.

REFERENCES

1. ALPERT, D., CARBERRY, D., YAMAMURA, M., CHOW, Y., AND MAK, P. 32-bit processor chip integrates major system functions. *Electronics 56,* 14 (July 14, 1983), 113–119.
2. CASE, R. P., AND PADEGS, A. Architecture of the IBM System/370. *Commun. ACM 21,* 1 (Jan. 1978), 73–96.
3. CLARK, D. W. Cache performance in the VAX-11/780. *ACM Trans. Comput. Syst. 1,* 1 (Feb. 1983), 24–37.
4. DENNING, P. J. On modeling program behavior. In *Proceedings of the Spring Joint Computer Conference, Volume 40.* AFIPS Press, Arlington, Va., 1972, pp. 937–944.
5. DIGITAL EQUIPMENT CORP. TB/Cache/SBI Control technical description—VAX-11/780 implementation. Doc. No. EK-MM780-TD-001, Digital Equipment Corp., Maynard, Mass., Apr. 1978.
6. DIGITAL EQUIPMENT CORP. VAX/VMS internals and data structures. Doc. No. AA-K785A-TE, Digital Equipment Corp., Maynard, Mass., 1981.
7. DIGITAL EQUIPMENT CORP. VAX-11 architecture reference manual. Doc. No. EK-VAXAR-RM-001, Digital Equipment Corp., Maynard, Mass., May 1982.
8. EMER, J. S., and CLARK, D. W. A characterization of processor performance in the VAX-11/780. In *Proceedings of the 11th Annual Symposium on Computer Architecture* (Ann Arbor, Mich., June 5–7). IEEE, New York, 1984, pp. 301–310.
9. GREENBAUM, H. J. A simulator of multiple interactive users to drive a time-shared computer system. Master's thesis, Project MAC Rep. MAR-TR-54, MIT, Cambridge, Mass., Oct. 1968.
10. INTEL CORP. Intel iAPX 432 general data processor architecture reference manual, preliminary ed. Intel Corp., Aloha, Oreg., 1981.
11. JAIN, R. K. Workload characterization using image accounting. In *Proceedings of the Computer Performance Evaluation Users Group 18th Meeting* (Washington, D.C., Oct.). National Bureau of Standards, Washington, D.C., 1982, pp. 111–120.
12. KAPLAN, K. R., and WINDER, R. O. Cache-based computer systems. *IEEE Computer 6,* 3 (Mar. 1973), 30–36.
13. LEVY, H. M., and ECKHOUSE, R. H. *Computer Programming and Architecture: The VAX-11.* Digital Press, Bedford, Mass., 1980.
14. LEVY, H. M., and LIPMAN, P. H. Virtual memory management in the VAX/VMS operating system. *IEEE Computer 15,* 3 (Mar. 1982), 35–41.
15. MCDANIEL, G. An analysis of a mesa instruction set using dynamic instruction frequencies. In *Symposium on Architectural Support for Programming Languages and Operating Systems* (Palo Alto, Calif., Mar. 1–3). ACM, New York, 1982, pp. 167–176.
16. PEUTO, B. L., AND SHUSTEK, L. J. An instruction timing model of CPU performance. In *Proceedings of the 4th Annual Symposium on Computer Architecture,* (Silver Spring, Md., Mar. 23–25). IEEE, New York, 1977, pp. 165–178.
17. SATYANARAYANAN, M., and BHANDARKAR, D. Design trade-offs in VAX-11 translation buffer organization. *IEEE Computer 14,* 12 (Dec. 1981), 103–111.
18. SCHROEDER, M. D. Performance of the GE-645 associative memory while Multics is in operation. In *Proceedings of the ACM SIGOPS Workshop on System Performance Evaluation* (Cambridge, Mass., Apr.). ACM, New York, 1971, pp. 227–245.
19. SMITH, A. J. Cache memories. *ACM Comput. Surv. 14,* 3 (Sept. 1982), 473–530.
20. STRECKER, W. D. VAX-11/780—A virtual address extension for the PDP-11 family computers. In *Proceedings of the National Computer Conference, vol. 47,* AFIPS Press, Reston, Va., 1978.
21. WATKINS, S. W. and ABRAMS, M. D. Survey of remote terminal emulators. NBS Special Pub. 500-4, Apr. 1977.
22. WIECEK, C. A. A case study of VAX-11 instruction set usage for compiler execution. In *Symposium on Architectural Support for Programming Languages and Operating Systems* (Palo Alto, Calif., Mar. 1–3). ACM, New York, 1982, pp. 177–184.

Received January 1984; revised 7 November 1984; accepted 16 November 1984

Organization and Performance of a Two-Level Virtual-Real Cache Hierarchy

Wen-Hann Wang, Jean-Loup Baer and Henry M. Levy

Department of Computer Science, FR-35
University of Washington
Seattle, WA 98195

Abstract

We propose and analyze a two-level cache organization that provides high memory bandwidth. The first-level cache is accessed directly by virtual addresses. It is small, fast, and, without the burden of address translation, can easily be optimized to match the processor speed. The virtually-addressed cache is backed up by a large physically-addressed cache; this second-level cache provides a high hit ratio and greatly reduces memory traffic. We show how the second-level cache can be easily extended to solve the synonym problem resulting from the use of a virtually-addressed cache at the first level. Moreover, the second-level cache can be used to shield the virtually-addressed first-level cache from irrelevant cache coherence interference. Finally, simulation results show that this organization has a performance advantage over a hierarchy of physically-addressed caches in a multiprocessor environment.

Keywords: Caches, Virtual Memory, Multiprocessors, Memory Hierarchy, Cache Coherence.

1   Introduction

Virtually-addressed caches are becoming commonplace in high-performance multiprocessors due to the need for rapid cache access [11, 3, 17]. A virtually-addressed cache can be accessed more quickly than a physically-addressed cache because it does not require a preceding virtual-to-physical address translation. However, virtually-addressed caches have several problems as well. For example:

1. They must be capable of handling synonyms, that is, multiple virtual addresses that map to the same physical address.

2. While address translation is not required before a virtual cache lookup, address translation is still needed following a miss.

3. In a multiprocessor system, the use of a virtually-addressed cache may complicate cache coherence because bus addresses are physical, therefore a reverse translation may be required.

4. I/O devices use physical addresses as well, also requiring reverse translation.

5. A virtual cache may need to be invalidated on a context switch because virtual addresses are unique to a single process.

None of these problems is insolvable by itself, and several schemes have been proposed for managing virtual caches. For example, dual tag sets, one virtual and one physical, can be used for each cache entry [7, 6]. As another example, the SPUR system restricts the use of address space, prohibits caching of I/O buffers, and requires bus transmission of both virtual and physical addresses [11]. However, these schemes tend to have performance shortcomings or unpleasant implications for system software. Virtually-addressed caches are fundamentally complicated, and this time or space complexity reduces the ability of the cache to match the ever-increasing needs of modern processors.

To attack this problem, we propose a two-level cache organization involving a virtually-addressed first-level cache and a physically-addressed second-level cache (recent studies of two-level uniprocessor and multiprocessor caches can be found in [4, 5, 12, 13]). The small first-level cache can be fast to meet the requirements of high-speed processors; it is virtually addressed to avoid the need for address translation. The large second-level cache will reduce miss ratios and memory traffic; it is physically addressed to simplify the I/O and multiprocessor coherence problems. Furthermore, we show how the second-level cache can be utilized to solve the synonym problem and to shield the first-level cache from irrelevant cache coherence traffic. Overall, we believe that this two-level virtual-real organization simplifies the design of the first-level, where performance is crucial, while solving some of the difficult problems at the second level, where time and space are more easily available.

Our organization involves the use of pointers in the two caches to keep track of the mappings between virtual cache and physical cache entries [7]. We also provide a translation buffer at the second level which operates in parallel with first-level cache lookups in case a miss requires reverse translation. Trace-driven simulations are used to demonstrate the advantages of a two-level V-R (virtual-real) cache over a hierarchy of real-addressed caches in a multiprocessor environment.

The rest of this paper is organized as follows. Section 2 describes the approaches taken in solving various problems related to virtual address caches and presents some design choices for high performance multiprocessor caches. Section 3 gives the specific organization of a V-R two-level cache hierarchy and its detailed operational description. Section 4 presents performance results from simulations, and conclusions are drawn in section 5.

2 Design issues of two-level V-R caches for high performance multiprocessors

This section addresses some important issues in the design of two level V-R caches and motivates our design choices. A more detailed operational description of our approach is given in the following section. The proposed architecture for this evaluation is a shared-bus multiprocessor where each processor has a private, two-level, V-cache–R-cache hierarchy as shown in Figure 1.

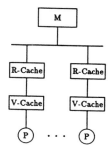

Figure 1: Shared-bus organization

Write policies

For a two-level cache, the write policy can be selected independently at each level. In the literature, write-through has been proposed as the most reasonable write policy for the first-level cache in a two-level hierarchy, while write-back is advocated for the second level [10, 8, 13]. A major motivation for the choice of write-through at the first level is that cache coherence control is simplified. In this case, the first- and second-level caches will always contain identical values.

There are several problems, however, with using a first-level write-through cache. First, assuming no write-allocate, write-through caches will have smaller hit ratios than write-back caches. Second, a write takes longer under write-through because the second-level cache must be updated as well; primary memory may also need to be updated depending on the write policy for the second level.

The reduced write latency with write-through can be greatly hidden by the use of write buffers between the first and second levels, but several write buffers may be needed. Table 1, for example, shows that in the execution of the VAX program *pops* (cf. section 4), 30% of writes are due to procedure calls, each of which typically generates six or more successive writes. Table 2 shows the inter-write interval distribution for a snapshot (411,237 references) of the same trace using a 16K direct-mapped cache with a 16-byte block size. As can be seen, the high percentage of short inter-write intervals confirms the need for several buffers.

Unfortunately, while write buffers can reduce the write latency of the first-level cache, they re-introduce a complexity that write-through was intended to avoid, namely cache coherence. Write buffers can hold modified data for which other processors might encounter a miss. Thus, cache coherency control must be provided for the write buffers on every cache coherence transaction.

These difficulties lead us to favor the write-back policy for our virtually-addressed cache at the first level.

no. of wr. per call	count	total writes
1	3	3
2	2	4
3	0	0
4	2	8
5	2	10
6	4123	24738
7	1266	8862
8	1246	9968
9	2634	23706
10	797	7970
11	539	5929
12	441	5292
13	0	0
14	0	0
15	0	0
16	43	688
no. of wr. due to proc. call		87178
total no. of writes		283057

Table 1: Number of writes due to procedure calls

interval	count
1	4589
2	1015
3	1270
4	786
5	1482
6	687
7	63
8	481
9	735
10 and larger	3245

Table 2: Inter-write intervals (snapshot of 411,237 references)

The synonym problem

As previously noted, a two-level V-R organization can be used to solve the synonym problem. The solution requires the use of a *reverse translation table* [15] for detecting synonyms, and a natural place to put that table is at the second level.

Our two-level organization permits and detects synonyms, but guarantees that at most one copy of a data element exists in the V-cache at any time. Each second-level cache block will have a pointer to its first-level child block, if one exists. If we guarantee an inclusion property, where the R-cache contains a superset of the tags in the V-cache, the reverse translation information can be stored in log(V-cache size/page size) superset bits in each R-cache block. For each entry in the R-cache with a child in the V-cache, these extra bits, together with the page offset, provide the V-cache location of its child.

When a miss occurs in the V-cache, the virtual address is translated (using a second-level translation buffer) and the R-cache is accessed. If an R-cache hit occurs, the R-cache checks whether the data is also in the V-cache under another virtual address (a synonym). If so, it simply invalidates that V-cache copy and moves the data to the new virtual address in the V-cache. Thus, while a data element can have synonyms, it is always stored in the V-cache using the last virtual address with which it was accessed.[1]

---

[1]Note that our approach in dealing with the synonym problem has some similarities to Goodman's approach [7]. One can view our approach as moving Goodman's real directory from being just for snooping to being associated with the level two cache. This move provides two benefits. First, it hides the cost of Goodman's extra, real directory by making it the level two cache directory. Second, it reduces the misses caused by real-address collisions via making the real directory much bigger.

Context switching

In a multiprogramming environment, addresses are unique to each process and therefore the V-cache must be flushed whenever a context switch occurs. This might be costly for a large virtually-addressed cache. For small caches we believe the penalty on hit ratios will be negligible and this is confirmed by our simulation results (cf. Section 4). However, if a write-back policy is used for the V-cache, a substantial number of write-backs may occur at each context switch, which greatly increases context-switch latency.

Another solution to avoid the address mapping conflict is to attach a process identifier to each tag entry of the V-cache. This approach does not improve the hit ratio for a small V-cache [1], but can avoid the large number of write-backs at context switch time. Unfortunately, this approach increases the complexity of a two-level hierarchy because the V-cache needs to be purged or selectively flushed when a TLB entry of an inactive process is replaced by an entry of the active process, or a process-id is reassigned.

We wish to have the benefits of reduced context-switch latency without needing to flush the V-cache when a TLB entry changes. Our approach meets these goals by invalidating all V-cache blocks on a context switch but *not* writing them back at that time. Instead, each block is written back only when it is replaced, that is, when a new block is read into that cache slot. The writes are thus distributed in time where the latency can be hidden using write-back buffers.

To implement this scheme, we add two new fields to each V-cache block. First, we add a *swapped-valid bit*, which is set for each V-cache block on a context switch. Upon a replacement, if the V-cache finds a block with swapped-valid set, it checks whether that block is also marked both dirty and valid; if so, that block must be written back. Second, we add an *r-pointer*, which is the low-order bits of the page number, to each V-cache block. The r-pointer, together with the page offset, is sufficient to link a V-cache entry to its corresponding location in the R-cache. This linkage makes a write-back or a state check efficient, since there is no need for an address translation. This approach uses space comparable to that of the process identifier scheme, but without its disadvantages.

Table 3 shows the effect of the swapped-valid bit; here we see the inter-write interval from the same benchmark as Table 2 when the swapped-valid bit is used. Because swapped write-backs are typically far apart from other (swapped) write-backs, a single write-back buffer is sufficient to overlap swapped write-backs with processor execution. Our simulations show that with a single buffer the amount of stalling on a swapped write-back is indeed negligible. On the other hand, if the incremental write-back is not used we need to write back over a hundred blocks at context switching time for this specific benchmark. Notice that the number of write-backs needed due to context switching is a function of cache size, cache organization, the duration of the running state of a process, and the workload.

Cache coherence

While two-level caches are attractive, cache coherence control is complicated by a two-level scheme. Without special attention to the coherence problem, the first-level cache will be disturbed by every coherency request on the bus. A solution to this problem is to use the second-level cache as a filter to shield the first-level cache from irrelevant interference. In order to achieve this, we need to impose an inclusion property where the tags of the

interval	count
1	2
2	3
3	0
4	2
5	5
6	0
7	1
8	2
9	1
10 and larger	119

Table 3: Write interval with write-back and swapped write-back (snapshot of 411,237 references)

second-level cache are a superset of the tags of its child cache. We say that a multilevel cache hierarchy has the inclusion property if this superset relation holds. Imposing inclusion is also essential for solving the synonym problem as stated above.

In a multiprocessor environment, the inclusion property cannot be held even with a global LRU replacement [4]. In [5] the following replacement algorithm was proposed as one of the conditions to impose the inclusion.

- First level: Any replacement algorithm will do (e.g., LRU). Notify the second level cache of the block being replaced.

- Second level: Replace a block which does not exist in the first level (this is done by checking an inclusion bit; there is one inclusion bit per block to indicate whether the block is present in the first level).

The general problem with inclusion is its implications for a large set size in the second level (i.e., high associativity). By following the same approach as in [5], and letting S_i be the number of sets, B_i be the block size, and $size(i)$ be the cache size of a level i cache, we can show that in order to impose inclusion under the above replacement algorithm, the set-associativity of the second-level cache A_2 must be:

$$A_2 \geq \frac{size(1)}{pagesize} \times \frac{B_2}{B_1}$$

under the usual practical situations where $S_2 > S_1$, $B_2 \geq B_1$, $size(2) > size(1)$ and $B_1 S_1 \geq pagesize^2$.

In practical cases, this constraint can be too strict to be feasible. For example, if the V-cache is 16K bytes, the page size is 4K bytes, and B_2 is 4 times as large as B_1, even with a direct-mapped V-cache we need a 16-way R-cache to achieve the inclusion.

To relax the strict constraint on the set-associativity of the R-cache, we change the replacement rule of the R-cache to operate as follows: replace a block with the inclusion bit clear if there is one; otherwise replace a block according to some predefined replacement algorithm and invalidate the corresponding V-cache block. Note that the latter won't happen very often since the R-cache is much larger than the V-cache. For example, the analysis of the multiprocessor trace, pops (over 3 million memory references), shows that only 21 inclusion invalidations are needed if the V cache is 16K bytes, 2-way set-associative with a 16 byte block size and the R cache is 256K bytes with same set size and block size.

---

[2] if $B_1 S_1 < pagesize$ the results of [5] apply.

3 Organization of a V-R two-level cache

A simplified organizational block diagram of a V-R two-level cache is given in Figure 2. The V-cache is accessed via virtual addresses, which are also forwarded to the TLB at the second level so that address translation can proceed concurrently with the access to the V-cache. This translation and the access to the R-cache are aborted if there is a valid hit in the V-cache. A number of tag and control bits that we call tag entry are associated with data blocks in both caches as shown in Figure 3. Each tag entry in the V-cache contains a tag, an r-pointer, a dirty bit, a valid bit and a swapped-valid bit. The r-pointer contains the lower log(R-cache-size/page-size) bits of the real address page number. Together with the page offset, it can be used to address the related entry in the R-cache. The swapped-valid bit is used to indicate whether the entry belongs to a swapped process. This is needed in order to avoid a large context switch overhead, as previously described.

Each tag entry in the R-cache tag store contains a tag and a number of subentries, one subentry per V-cache block since we allow larger block sizes in the R-cache. A subentry contains an inclusion bit that indicates whether a copy of the data is in the V-cache or not, a buffer bit that indicates if a copy of the data is in a write buffer of the V-cache, a few state bits for sharing status and cache coherence control (with other R-caches), two

dirty bits, one for V-cache dirty and for R-cache dirty, and a v-pointer which contains the lower log(V-cache-size/page-size) bits of the virtual page number. Together with the page offset, the v-pointer can be used to address the entry in the V-cache.

In order to properly provide the data and manage cache coherence and synonyms, we list in Table 4 the communication buses between the V-cache and the R-cache. The following is a detailed operational description of a two-level V-R cache.

For simplicity, let us assume that an invalidation protocol is used at the R-cache level although our scheme will also work for other protocols as well. An invalidation protocol invalidates all other cache copies before updating shared data in the local cache. Write-backs to memory are performed when a dirty block moves from one cache hierarchy to another. A number of existing protocols belong to this category [16].

V-R hierarchy algorithm

1. Read hit in V-cache. Give the data to the processor. The hit signal is sent to the R-cache to abort the R-cache and TLB accesses.

2. Read miss in V-cache. Raise the replacement signal if a V-cache block needs to be replaced to give room to the incoming new data. Give the R-cache both the v-pointer, which is the V-cache location for the new data, and the r-pointer, which is the R-cache location of the block being replaced. If the replaced block in V-cache is clean, the

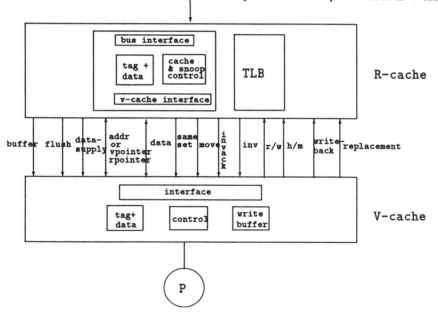

Figure 2: V-R cache organization

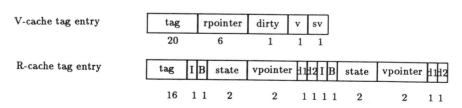

Figure 3: Contents of tag stores (assume page size is 4K, C_1 is 16K and C_2 is 256K, $B_2 = 2 \times B_1$.)

From V to R:	
read/write	tells the R-cache whether the current request is a read or a write.
replacement	tells the R-cache that a V-cache block needs to be replaced.
hit/miss(v-pointer, r-pointer)	tells the R-cache whether the current access results in a hit or a miss in the V-cache. If it is a miss, the target v-pointer gives the V-cache slot for the new data and the r-pointer gives the R-cache entry where the inclusion bit is to be erased if the block to be replaced is clean, or where the buffer bit is to be set if the block is dirty. If it is a hit the R-cache access is aborted.
write back(r-pointer)	tells the R-cache that the data in the write buffer will be written back to the place pointed to by the r-pointer.
From R to V:	
sameset(v-pointer)	tells the V-cache that there is a synonym copy in the same set; no need to write back; and the data is available under v-pointer.
move(v-pointer)	tells the V-cache that there is a synonym copy in a different set; the data is available under v-pointer.
data supply(r-pointer)	tells the V-cache that the data is ready to be loaded and gives its location in the R-cache to be stored as part of the tag entry.
invalidation(v-pointer)	tells the V-cache to invalidate the data under v-pointer.
flush(v-pointer)	tells the V-cache to flush the data under v-pointer.
invalidation(buffer)	tells the V-cache to invalidate the data in the buffer.
flush(buffer)	tells the V-cache to flush the data in the buffer.
invack	tells the V-cache that the coherency has been cleared and that it can update the data.

Table 4: V-R interface

R-cache resets the inclusion bit. If the block is dirty, the V-cache copies the block into the write buffer and the R-cache sets the buffer bit to indicate that the block is still in the write buffer of the V-cache. This bit gets reset when the write-back occurs or when the write-back is canceled (see below).

(a) Hit in R-cache.

    i. The data is in the V-cache under another virtual address. The R-cache tests whether the two locations are in the same set. If so, a *sameset* signal is sent to the V-cache so that the write-back can be canceled if the replaced block is dirty; the R-cache will reset the buffer bit if the replaced block is dirty, or it will set the inclusion bit if the replaced block is clean[3]. If the blocks are in different sets, the R-cache sends a move(v-pointer) to the V-cache so that the data can be stored at the new location. Valid bits are set to valid. The v-pointer tag entry of the R-cache is modified accordingly. Notice that in both cases the v-tag is updated to reflect the new virtual address.

    ii. No other copy in V-cache. R-cache raises the data supply signal and sends the block to the V-cache. The R-cache also supplies the r-pointer to the V-cache to set up the link information. R-cache sets the inclusion bit and the v-pointer and the V-cache stores the r-pointer, sets the valid bits, and resets the dirty bit.

(b) Miss in R-cache. Proceeds as described in the cache coherence subsection. Gets a clean copy and then back to (a)ii.

3. Write hit on clean block in V-cache. Wait till the R-cache raises the *invack* signal (cf. the cache coherence subsection); then update the data and set the dirty bit in the V-cache.

4. Write miss in V-cache. The replacement proceeds as in the case of a read miss.

---
[3]the inclusion bit was reset earlier to reflect the replacement.

(a) Hit in R-cache. Resolve the cache coherency (cf. below); resolve the synonyms as in the case of a read miss; load the block into V-cache; update the data and sets the dirty bit in the V-cache.

(b) Miss in R-cache. Proceed as described in the cache coherence subsection; get a clean copy, load the block into the V-cache and the R-cache and set appropriate pointers and inclusion as in the case for a read; update the data, and set the dirty bit in the V-cache.

It is worth noticing that the cost of handling a synonym is approximately the same as a first-level miss and second-level hit. This observation will be used in our performance evaluations.

Cache coherence

Processor induced:

1. Read miss in the V-cache and in the R-cache. Initiate a read-miss bus transaction and get the block. Set the state of the block as shared if another cache acknowledges having this block; otherwise set the state as private.

2. Write hit on a clean block in the V-cache. Check the state in the R-cache. If private, raises the *invack* to let the V-cache proceed; sets the vdirty bit in the R-cache. Otherwise, the R-cache initiates an invalidation bus transaction and when it is completed, raise the *invack* signal and set the vdirty bit in the R-cache.

3. Write miss in the V-cache.

    (a) Hit in the R-cache. Check the state in the R-cache. If shared, initiate an invalidation bus transaction. Supply the block to the V-cache when the transaction is completed and set the vdirty bit in the R-cache.

    (b) Miss in the R-cache. Initiate a read-modified-write bus transaction; get the block; reset the rdirty bit in the R-cache and set the vdirty bit in the R-cache.

Bus induced:

1. Read-miss. Acknowledge the sharing status if in possession of the requested block and:

(a) If the block is modified in the V-cache, the R-cache sends a flush(v-pointer) to V-cache and gets the block, updates itself, changes its state to shared, resets the vdirty bit, resets the rdirty bit, supplies the block to the requesting cache and updates the memory.

(b) If the block is modified in the write buffer of V-cache, R-cache sends a flush(buffer) to V-cache and gets the block, updates itself, changes its state to shared, resets vdirty bit, resets the rdirty bit, resets the inclusion bit, supplies the block to the requesting cache and updates the memory.

(c) If the block is dirty in the R-cache, the R-cache supplies the block to the requesting cache, updates the memory, changes its state to shared, and resets its dirty bit.

(d) Otherwise, memory supplies the block.

2. Invalidation. The R-cache invalidates its own entry if present and checks the inclusion bit. If it is set, the corresponding entry in the V-cache is invalidated. This is done by issuing invalidate(v-pointer) to the V-cache.

3. Read-modified-write. Treated as a read-miss followed by an invalidation.

Replacement

(a) V-cache: Any replacement algorithm will do (e.g., LRU).

(b) R-cache: Replace a block with all inclusion bits (i.e., for each subentry) reset. If there is none (this might happen if we follow the strategy of the end of section 2), randomly choose one block and invalidate the copy (or copies if $B_2 > B_1$) in the V-cache.

4   Performance

In this section, we compare the relative performance of virtual-real (V-R) and real-real (R-R) two-level caches. We also examine the merits of splitting the first-level virtually-addressed cache into I and D caches. Finally, we measure the effect of the R-cache in shielding the V-cache from irrelevant cache coherence interference.

To gather the performance figures, we use trace-driven simulations and three parallel program traces: pops, thor and abaqus [2, 14]. In pops and thor, context switches occur rarely while they are frequent in abaqus. Table 5 gives a summary of some characteristics of these traces.

Relative performance of V-R and R-R two-level caches

To compare the performance of V-R and R-R two-level caches, we gather the hit ratios at different levels; the hit ratios are then used in generic memory access time equations to predict relative performances. We assume that the inclusion property defined previously also holds for the R-R two-level cache. For simplicity, we consider only direct-mapped caches at both levels.

The generic access time equation of a two-level cache hierarchy is as follows:

T_{acc} = Prob(hit at level 1) × access time at level 1
+ Prob(hit at level 2 & miss at level 1) × access time at level 2
+ Prob(miss at level 1 and 2) × memory access time

that is:

$$T_{acc} = h_1 t_1 + (1 - h_1)h_2 t_2 + (1 - h_1 - (1 - h_1)h_2)t_m$$

where h_1, h_2 are hit ratios at levels 1 and 2, t_1 and t_2 are access times at the two levels, and t_m is the memory access time including the bus overhead.

Because the second-level caches are the same for both V-R and R-R organizations, and because inclusion holds, the number of misses and the traffic from the second-level cache are the same in both organizations. Therefore the third term in the above equation is the same for both V-R and R-R organizations. Assuming that handling a synonym has a cost equivalent of handling a miss in the first-level cache that hits in the second-level cache, the relative performance where there is a hit in the hierarchy can be estimated solely on the first two terms of the above equation.

Table 6 shows the hit ratios at both levels of V-R and R-R organizations for the three traces under three different pairs of first and second-level cache sizes. Figures 4, 5 and 6 depict the relative performance of the two organizations under different degrees of assumed R-cache degradation due to address translation overhead. These figures plot the relative performance of the two hierarchies with $t_2 = 4t_1$ vs. the percentage of slow down due to address translation for various first-level/second-level cache sizes. The points on the y-axis correspond to no slow down at all. From these figures we can draw the following conclusions.

Let us assume that there is no time penalty involved in performing a virtual-real address translation in conjunction with the access to the first level cache. When context switches occur rarely, as is the case for the first two traces (Figures 4 and 5), the performances of the V-R and R-R hierarchies are almost indistinguishable (the points on the y-axis are the same). When context switches are frequent, as in the third trace (Figure 6), the V-R hierarchy is slower by 2 to 6% depending on the size of the V-cache (a larger V-cache seems to imply a larger relative degradation).

Now, let us assume a time penalty for the translation. There are two possible reasons for this penalty. The first is that TLB access and cache access cannot be completely overlapped as soon as the cache size is larger than the page size multiplied by the set associativity. Second, even if there were total overlap, there would still be an extra comparison necessary to check the validity of a cache hit. From the observations of the previous paragraph, it is clear that the V-R hierarchy will perform better in the case of rare context-switches. The relative improvement is approximately equal to the overhead of address translation. What is interesting is to see the cross-over point for the case of frequent context-switches. From Figure 6, we see that the V-R hierarchy will have a better performance when the address translation slows down the first level R-cache access by 6% or more.

Since 6% is a conservative figure for the penalty due to the insertion of a TLB at the first level, it appears that the V-R hierarchy is a better solution. Its performance is as good as that of an R-R hierarchy and its cost is less since the TLB does not have to be

trace	num. of cpus	total refs	instr count	data read	data write	context switch count
thor	4	3283k	1517k	1390k	376k	21
pops	4	3286k	1718k	1285k	283k	7
abaqus	2	1196k	514k	600k	82k	292

Table 5: Characteristics of traces

trace	thor			pops			abaqus		
sizes	4K/64K	8K/128K	16K/256K	4K/64K	8K/128K	16K/256K	4K/64K	8K/128K	16K/256K
h1VR	.925	.957	.968	.928	.943	.954	.852	.873	.888
h1RR	.925	.958	.969	.928	.943	.954	.857	.889	.908
h2VR	.692	.531	.463	.609	.608	.567	.551	.559	.585
h2RR	.691	.526	.449	.608	.608	.563	.536	.493	.498

Table 6: hit ratios

trace	thor			pops			abaqus		
sizes	.5K/64K	1K/128K	2K/256K	.5K/64K	1K/128K	2K/256K	.5K/64K	1K/128K	2K/256K
h1VR	.755	.828	.872	.727	.882	.909	.766	.793	.822
h1RR	.755	.828	.872	.727	.882	.909	.767	.797	.827
h2VR	.905	.883	.867	.897	.810	.781	.716	.728	.739
h2RR	.905	.883	.867	.897	.810	.781	.715	.723	.732

Table 7: Hit ratios for small first-level caches

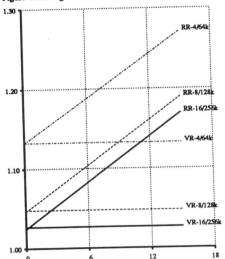

Figure 4: Average access time vs. slow-down of R-cache (thor)

First-level R-cache slow-down percentage

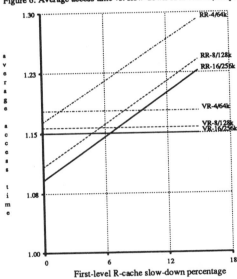

Figure 6: Average access time vs. slow-down of R-cache (abaqus)

First-level R-cache slow-down percentage

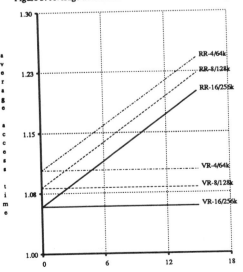

Figure 5: Average access time vs. slow-down of R-cache (pops)

First-level R-cache slow-down percentage

implemented in fast logic. Another advantage is that problems such as TLB coherence can also be handled at the second level.

The results presented above assumed 4K to 16K first-level caches, which may be impractical for some advanced technologies, such as GaAs. However, we believe that the V-R organization is even more attractive for hierarchies with smaller first-level caches. Our results in Table 7 show that for smaller first-level caches (e.g., .5K to 2K), the first-level hit ratios of V-R and R-R organizations are nearly identical. Therefore, performance of a V-R hierarchy will be superior given any penalty for a TLB lookup. In addition, for technologies in which space is at a premium, we can trade the first-level TLB of an R-R hierarchy for a larger first-level cache in a V-R hierarchy. This in turn provides larger hit ratios and hence smaller average access time.

Splitting the first-level virtually-addressed cache

There are a number of reasons why it is advantageous to split the first-level cache into separate I and D caches. First, the bandwidth can almost be doubled for pipelined processors where an instruction fetch can occur at the same time as a data fetch of a previous instruction (e.g., the IBM801 and Motorola 88000). Second, each I and D cache is smaller and has the potential to be optimized for its speed. Third, and this pertains mostly to V-caches, the I cache is simpler than the D cache since it does not need to handle the synonym and the cache coherence problems provided that self-modifying programs are not permitted. A disadvantage, however, is that we need more wirings or pins for the processor and cache module. It is important to assess, however, if splitting the cache into I & D components will improve performance.

Our results in Table 8, 9 and 10 show that the hit ratios of split I&D caches are very close to that of a unified I&D cache and are not necessarily worse. In these tables, the I and D separate caches are of equal sizes (i.e., in the 4K example the I-cache and the D-cache are each 2K). Similar results have been found in [9, 13]. Thus, we would advocate such a split for a V-R hierarchy.

thor	4K/64K	8K/128K	16K/256K
data read split	0.924	0.937	0.945
unified	0.913	0.938	0.950
data write split	0.952	0.962	0.969
unified	0.946	0.966	0.972
instruction split	0.957	0.963	0.989
unified	0.930	0.973	0.984
overall split	0.942	0.952	0.968
unified	0.925	0.957	0.968

Table 8: Hit ratios of level 1 caches for the thor trace

pops	4K/64K	8K/128K	16K/256K
dataread split	0.902	0.912	0.923
unified	0.900	0.915	0.926
data write split	0.936	0.946	0.955
unified	0.937	0.948	0.958
instruction split	0.947	0.966	0.978
unified	0.948	0.963	0.974
overall split	0.928	0.944	0.955
unified	0.928	0.943	0.954

Table 9: Hit ratios of level 1 caches for the pops trace

abaqus	4K/64K	8K/128K	16K/256K
data read split	0.795	0.818	0.837
unified	0.806	0.829	0.845
data write split	0.841	0.861	0.875
unified	0.847	0.857	0.895
instruction split	0.920	0.947	0.949
unified	0.907	0.926	0.938
overall split	0.852	0.876	0.888
unified	0.852	0.873	0.888

Table 10: Hit ratios of level 1 caches for the abaqus trace

Shielding cache coherence interference

An important advantage of the two-level approach is that the R-cache can shield the V-cache from irrelevant cache coherence interference. For example, on a read miss bus request, the R-cache needs to send a flush request to its V-cache only when the V-cache contains a modified copy of the data; otherwise the V-cache will not be disrupted. Note that this shielding effect is achieved because the inclusion property holds in our V-R two-level cache. Imposing inclusion might not seem to be essential for an R-R two-level hierarchy because the synonym problem is not present. However, the results in Tables 11, 12 and 13, which give the number of coherence messages being percolated to each first-level cache, show that a V-R two-level cache has much less coherence interference at the first level than that of an R-R two-level cache without inclusion. The results also show that inclusion is important in an R-R two-level cache since it results in approximately the same savings in coherence messages to the first-level cache.[4]

We believe that the shielding effect on cache coherence will be more prominent as the number of processors increases. This is due to the fact that more bus coherence requests will be generated from a larger number of processors, and without the shielding, a first-level cache will be disrupted more often. Our results in Tables 11, 12 (4 cpus) and 13 (2 cpus) reflect this effect. For example, on the average, the first-level cache of a V-R hierarchy encounters about half the coherence messages than that of the R-R hierarchy without inclusion for the two processor trace (cf. Table 13), whereas for four processor traces the first-level cache of the V-R hierarchy encounters from three to six times fewer coherence messages. We plan to further confirm this observation when we are in possession of larger-scale traces.

5   Conclusions

One of the most challenging issues in computer design is the support of high memory bandwidth. In this paper, we have proposed

---

[4] We notice that RR with inclusion has over 10% fewer coherence messages than that of VR for the abaqus trace. This discrepancy is due to a large amount of inclusion invalidations incurred in this specific trace due to a large number of context switchings.

pops	4K/64K			8K/128K			16K/256K		
cpu	VR	RR(incl)	RR(no incl)	VR	RR(incl)	RR(no incl)	VR	RR(incl)	RR(no incl)
0	6717	7113	23804	7237	7707	20783	8309	8854	19468
1	10015	10351	30523	10606	11027	26128	11771	12357	24258
2	9518	9861	30063	10143	11027	26407	11344	11906	24817
3	9368	9963	31311	10001	10650	27528	11144	12061	25932

Table 11: Number of coherence messages to the first-level cache

thor	4K/64K			8K/128K			16K/256K		
cpu	VR	RR(incl)	RR(no incl)	VR	RR(incl)	RR(no incl)	VR	RR(incl)	RR(no incl)
0	3755	3743	23005	4342	4317	21773	5785	4473	18123
1	4144	4139	27056	4727	4722	23538	5473	5170	18304
2	4229	4229	27005	4810	4820	23915	5561	5229	18776
3	4135	4129	25210	4699	4692	21593	6797	5103	16231

Table 12: Number of coherence messages to the first-level cache

abaqus	4K/64K			8K/128K			16K/256K		
cpu	VR	RR(incl)	RR(no incl)	VR	RR(incl)	RR(no incl)	VR	RR(incl)	RR(no incl)
0	10961	8436	18855	11677	9379	21295	11067	9853	22603
1	10527	8029	20726	10547	9528	24202	10599	10028	26845

Table 13: Number of coherence messages to the first-level cache

a two-level cache hierarchy to address this issue. We have argued that the first level cache is best accessed directly by virtual addresses. We back up the small virtually-addressed cache by a large second-level cache. A virtually-addressed first-level cache does not require address translation and can be optimized to match the processor speed. Through the use of a swapped-valid bit, we avoid the clustering of write-backs at context switching time. The distribution of these write-backs is more evenly spread over time. The large second-level cache provides a high hit ratio and reduces a large amount of memory traffic. We have shown how the second-level cache can be easily extended to solve the synonym problem resulting from the use of a virtually-addressed cache at the first level. Furthermore, the second-level cache can be used effectively to shield the virtually-addressed first-level cache from irrelevant cache coherence interference.

Our simulation results show that when context switches are rare, the virtually-addressed cache option has comparable performance to its physically-addressed counterpart, even assuming no address translation overhead. When context switches occur frequently, the virtually-addressed cache option has a performance edge when a small address translation penalty is taken into account, and the smaller the virtually-addressed cache the larger the relative performance edge. We also advocate splitting the virtually-addressed cache into separated instruction and data caches. This approach has the potential of doubling the memory bandwidth since our results show that the hit ratios of split instruction and data caches are very close to that of a single I&D cache.

As a final remark, we note that cache performance is workload dependent. In this study we have confined ourselves to a limited VAX multiprocessor workload. We plan to enlarge our workload sample as soon as we are in possession of other multiprocessor traces.

Acknowledgment
This work was supported in part by National Science Foundation (Grants No. CCR-8702915 and CCR-8619663), Boeing Computer Services, Digital Equipment Corporation (the System Research Center and the External Research Program) and a GTE fellowship. The experimental part of this study could not have been possible without Dick Sites who made the traces available to us and Anant Agarwal who allowed us to share his postprocessing programs and who patiently answered our many questions. We also thank the members of the "Computer Architecture lunch", especially Tom Anderson, Jon Bertoni, Sanglyul Min and John Zahorjan for their excellent comments and suggestions.

References

[1] Agarwal, A., R. L. Sites and M. Horowitz. ATUM: A new technique for capturing address traces using microcode. In *Proc. 13th Symposium on Computer Architecture*, pages 119–127, 1986.

[2] Agarwal, A., R. Simoni, J. Hennessy and M. Horowitz. An evaluation of directory schemes for cache coherence. In *Proc. 15th Symposium on Computer Architecture*, pages 280–289, 1988.

[3] Atkinson, R. R. and E. M. McCreight. The dragon processor. In *Proc. Architectural Support for Programming Languages and Operating Systems(ASPLOS-II)*, pages 65–69, 1987.

[4] Baer, J.-L. and W.-H. Wang. Architectural choices for multi-level cache hierarchies. In *Proc. 16th International Conference on Parallel Processing*, pages 258–261, 1987.

[5] Baer, J.-L. and W.-H. Wang. On the inclusion property for multi-level cache hierarchies. In *Proc. 15th Symposium on Computer Architecture*, pages 73–80, 1988.

[6] Cheriton, D.R., G. Slavenburg and P. Boyle. Software-controlled caches in the VMP multiprocessor. In *Proc. 13th Symposium on Computer Architecture*, pages 367–374, 1986.

[7] Goodman, J. Coherency for multiprocessor virtual address caches. In *Proc. Architectural Support for Programming Languages and Operating Systems(ASPLOS-II)*, pages 72–81, 1987.

[8] Goodman, J. and P.J. Woest. The Wisconsin multicube: A new large-scale cache-coherent multiprocessor. In *Proc. 15th Symposium on Computer Architecture*, pages 422–431, 1988.

[9] Haikala, I.J. and P.H. Kutvonen. Split cache organizations. In *Proc. Performance '84*, pages 459–472, 1984.

[10] Hattori,A., Koshino,M. and S.Kamimoto. Three-level hierarchical storage system for FACOM M-380/382. In *Proc. Information Processing IFIP*, pages 693–697, 1983.

[11] Hill,M. et al. Design decisions in SPUR. *Computer*, 19(11):8–22, November 1986.

[12] Przybylski, Steven A. *Performance-Directed Memory Hierarchy Design*. Ph.D Dissertation, Stanford University, 1988.

[13] Short R.T. and H.M. Levy. A simulation study of two-level caches. In *Proc. 15th Symposium on Computer Architecture*, pages 81–88, 1988.

[14] Sites, R.L. and A. Agarwal. Multiprocessor cache analysis using ATUM. In *Proc. 15th Symposium on Computer Architecture*, pages 186–195, 1988.

[15] Smith,A.J. Cache memories. *Computing Surveys*, 14(3):473–530, September 1982.

[16] Sweazey, P. and A.J. Smith. A class of compatible cache consistency protocols and their support by the IEEE futurebus. In *Proc. 13th Symposium on Computer Architecture*, pages 414–423, 1986.

[17] Cheng, Ray. Virtual address cache in UNIX. In *Proc. USENIX Conference*, pages 217–224, June 1987.

I/O: Storage Systems, Networks, and Graphics

In this chapter, we start with an economic basis for the status of I/O in a system context. We then present the I/O system of a modern PC as a case study for the application of I/O concepts. We conclude with some of the key papers in the evolution and analysis of I/O. The basic concepts underlying I/O have already been well covered in the I/O chapter in Hennessy and Patterson's *Computer Architecture: A Quantitative Approach* [2], and we will not duplicate them here.

7.1 I/O Economics

The I/O system of a computer often accounts for the majority of its cost. For example, even in a $700 PC (including the monitor), the processor and memory together likely cost less than $150. The most expensive component is the monitor, which in such a system would likely cost $150 by itself. The disk is also rather expensive, costing close to $100. The CD-ROM drive, floppy, graphics accelerator, modem, motherboard, case, and power supply can account for the remaining $200.

The common wisdom is that the performance of I/O systems has been lagging for decades, and will cause computer system performance to imminently hit a wall, yet it still receives very little academic attention. It is certainly true that I/O issues receive relatively little academic attention, and the performance of I/O devices is often a drag on total system performance. But given the economic analysis above on the components of a low-cost PC, you can begin to understand why this is so. Faster I/O capabilities generally cost more money. With I/O already being the dominant system cost, the marginal returns for doubling I/O speed (and perhaps doubling I/O cost and close to doubling system cost) are not good. Instead, it makes more sense to provide a faster CPU (being the relatively cheaper component) so that the slower (and more expensive) I/O system is saturated. As a more concrete example, with disks costing $100 and providing more storage capacity than the average PC user needs, it currently does not make economic sense to have RAID on a desktop.

Thus, some of the more important trends in I/O involve reducing its cost for a given level of performance or increasing its performance (in terms of capacity or speed) for a given level of cost. Since Moore's law does not apply to wires on a connector, the substitution of semiconductor components for electromechanical components is also an important trend in I/O systems. For example, one aspect behind the recent appearance of the universal serial bus (USB) is the replacement of large numbers of wires by a smaller number of wires driven and sensed by high-speed semiconductors in I/O devices (some of which used to be so simple as to almost be passive, such as the keyboard and mouse). Also of key importance in the ever-increasing storage density of magnetic disks are higher and higher speed interface electronics of ever increasing complexity. Recent advancements in disk technology such as partial response maximum likelihood (PRML) [11] require a digital signal processor (DSP) in the disk read channel to separate bits that are effectively overlapping each other. As another example, the number of pixels on a cathode-ray tube (CRT) monitor is limited by electromechanical considerations and the cost of very large monitors is prohibitively expensive (e.g., 2,000 × 2,000 pixel displays currently cost $35,000). Full-screen antialiasing of computer-generated images by graphics accelerators can increase the visual quality of a monitor to be equivalent to a monitor with two to three times its actual resolution. However, it requires much larger frame buffer memories to implement. As time goes by and semiconductor components scale while electromechanical components do not, it will make more economic sense to use additional semiconductor resources to produce full-screen antialiased images rather than to purchase a higher resolution monitor. Real-time antialiasing technology was pioneered in the Silicon Graphics RealityEngine, a graphics supercomputer, and within a few years will likely migrate down to PCs via the benefits of Moore's Law. As a final example, the WebTV system eliminates a per-user disk, CD-ROM, floppy, and monitor, replacing a private local disk with a shared remote disk, and replacing a dedicated monitor with the CRT monitor of the user's television. This saves a large percentage of a PC's cost as well as relieving the user of system management responsibilities.

7.2 PC I/O Case Study

The PC on your desk top or side provides an excellent case study of I/O systems. This is especially true now that large computer systems are adopting multiple instances of standard PC I/O busses to reduce their total system costs. PC components are always cheaper than specialized proprietary components for a given level of functionality for two reasons. First, PC components are manufactured in huge volumes and benefit from economies of scale. Second, because they are designed to support industry standards, there are many different competing manufacturers producing the components, many of which are operating financially with low margins or are losing money.

In the following case study, we focus primarily on I/O busses. Discussion of I/O components is well covered in the papers later in this section and in the I/O chapter of Hennessy and Patterson's *Computer Architecture: A Quantitative Approach* [2]. I/O busses are important because they can be a bottleneck between high-performance I/O devices and high-performance CPUs. This is exacerbated by several factors. First, to have economies of scale in development of third-party I/O devices (i.e., graphics accelerators, video capture cards, data acquisition cards, etc.), the same add-in card must be usable for many years, even though PC systems are changing each year. Because the volume of these add-in cards is lower than that of the base system, development costs need to be spread over several years to reduce the option cost. This is more of a factor for more specialized cards; for example, laboratory data acquisition cards will evolve less rapidly than will PC graphics accelerators bought by hordes of avid gamers. As a result, general-purpose I/O busses tend to evolve rather slowly—and also in a backward compatible manner. Backward compatibility means that a new I/O bus will support older previous generation I/O devices designed for the same bus family.

When a new bus is introduced, increased cost considerations tend to limit the amount of performance headroom designed into the bus. However, as years go by and the bus evolves, the presence of older I/O devices on a bus can reduce its performance to that of earlier generation busses and act as a system performance bottleneck.

The most important busses and interfaces on a PC today are the serial port, parallel port, ISA, PCI, AGP, PCMCIA, USB, IDE, and SCSI. We give a brief overview of some of the interesting issues with each of these interfaces. For more details, the reader is encouraged to see any of a number of PC reference books or online guides. The references to useful online guides can be found on this reader's Web companion. A good book on the subject is *The Indispensable PC Hardware Book* by Hans-Peter Messmer [5].

7.2.1 Serial Port

The serial port implements the RS-232C (Recommended Standard 232C from the EIA [Electronic Industries Alliance]) which was developed in 1969. It supports communication rates as low as 110 baud in order to support old teletype equipment. Baud is a measure of how often a bit-serial line changes state. The unit baud is named after Jean Maurice Emile Baudot, who was an officer in the French Telegraph Service. In the late nineteenth century, he invented the first uniform-length 5-bit code for characters of the alphabet. The original RS-232C standard only supported communication rates up to 20 Kbaud; however, newer devices can often run up to 115 Kbaud over short distances with good cables.

7.2.2 Parallel Port

The parallel port on a PC is derived from a Centronics printer port. This port consists of 8 bits of parallel data output and was originally defined by Centronics in the 1970s and refined by Epson. The maximum data transfer rate achievable with this interface is approximately 150 Kbytes/s but is extremely software intensive. By the late 1980s there was a demand for high-speed bidirectional communication for external I/O devices such as scanners. Two standards were defined to provide this (Extended Parallel Port [EPP] and Extended Capabilities Port [ECP]) and were later combined into the IEEE 1284 standard in 1994. This new standard allows bidirectional communication of up to 1 Mbyte/s as well as daisy chaining multiple devices on the port.

7.2.3 ISA Bus

The ISA bus is derived from the main 8-bit internal data bus of the original 1981 IBM PC. In this PC, it was used to connect the CPU with the memory and I/O devices. This bus had a 20-bit address field (capable of addressing up to 1 Mbyte). The second-generation IBM PC/XT used an Intel 8086 with a 16-bit data bus but still kept the same I/O slots for compatibility. With the introduction of the Intel 80286-based IBM PC/AT in 1984 (AT for Advanced Technology), these I/O slots were extended in an upward-compatible manner. A second set of 36 contacts was added next to the original 62 contacts of the original 8-bit PC card slot to extend the data bus to 16 bits. After many years of confusion resulting from different clock speeds and timings, the interface was standardized to the industry standard architecture (ISA) bus. The bus is specified to run at a maximum clock frequency of 8.33 MHz. This gives a maximum speed of 16 Mbytes/s, but speeds of 3 Mbytes/s are more common because of wait cycles needed by memory or slow I/O devices. The ISA bus provides for DMA transfers in order to reduce the demand on the CPU. Unfortunately, because it is derived from the main bus of the original PC, it requires each adapter card to select one of a limited number of interrupt request (IRQ) vectors. Installation of ISA cards originally required the setting of jumpers on the cards to select addresses and IRQs. This made adding new adapter cards tricky as they could conflict with existing cards. For Windows 95, Microsoft and Intel introduced Plug-and-Play extensions to the ISA bus, which allowed users to install cards without setting jumpers or switches. Many expansion cards for lower performance devices in the late 1990s still only connect to the original 62 contacts of the 8-bit bus in order to reduce cost.

7.2.4 PCI Bus

The Peripheral Component Interconnect (PCI) bus was developed by Intel and introduced in 1993 for Pentium systems. The PCI bus has a 32-bit-wide data bus and can operate at speeds of 33 MHz. This gives it a peak speed of 133 Mbytes/s. Address and data are multiplexed on the same signals, so for single-word transfers, this immediately cuts the peak speed in half. Read cycles also require a cycle to turn around the bus, slowing the speed down to one third the peak rate for independent single-word system reads. However, the PCI bus provides a burst transfer capability, which allows performance closer to the peak speed of the bus for longer transfers (because in that case more than one data cycle follows an address cycle). The PCI bus also allows I/O devices to become the bus master and control the transfer of bursts of data.

A major advance of the PCI bus is that it is decoupled from the processor and memory of the PC by a chipset that contains transfer buffers, and it has its own interrupt system, which is decoupled from the IRQs of the processor. The transfer buffers allow the PCI bus to run without memory wait states and asynchronously in parallel with the processor. This is key in obtaining transfer rates approaching the peak rates. It also allows independent scalability of the memory and I/O systems, including their clock speeds. The separate interrupt structure enables the PCI chipset circuitry to handle the identification of cards and work with the operating system and BIOS to automatically set resource allocations for compatible peripheral cards. This makes installing new cards easy. Extensions to the PCI bus, expanding it to 64 bits and 66 MHz have been developed; however, they are still rare in practice.

7.2.5 AGP

When displaying video or 3-D graphics, a PCI bus shared between a graphics accelerator and other I/O devices can become a bottleneck. In order to speed up graphics and free up the PCI bus for other I/O, Intel introduced the Advanced Graphics Port (AGP) in 1997. The AGP is similar to a specialized version of the PCI bus, dedicated to graphics accelerators. The AGP is a port and not a bus, because it connects only the (primary) system graphics accelerator to the system chipset. Because it always consists of only two interconnected devices instead of from two to seven or more, the electrical signaling on the AGP can operate faster. The original AGP operates at 66 MHz, twice the speed of the PCI bus. AGP2X transfers data on both edges of the port clock and provides bandwidths up to 533 Mbytes/s. Further speed doubling to AGP4X has already been defined.

7.2.6 PCMCIA

The Personal Computer Memory Card International Association (PCMCIA) has designed a series of standards for credit-card sized devices. Originally it was conceived as a means to provide additional memory for portable devices (the 3.3-mm-thick type-I form factor standardized in 1990). This form factor was later expanded to the 5.0-mm type II, which can support plug-in modem cards and network interfaces. A final 10.5-mm type-III format can support miniature disk drives. Of the three formats, the type-II slot is by far the most common. Larger slots are designed to accept any card of a smaller type. The original specifications covered cards with 8- and 16-bit data widths operating at ISA clock frequencies (8.33 MHz), whereas the CardBus specification of 1996 supports widths of 32 bits and speeds of 33 MHz, the same as the standard PCI bus. The cards and interface are also designed to be hot swappable, so that a limited number of slots can be used in different ways within one user session. The big advantage of the PCMCIA interface is that it allows common modems and other standard devices to be used in a wide variety of platforms, decreasing their cost and increasing the product diversity. Before PCMCIA standards, different products had different interfaces; hence, any plug-in products were specialized, low volume, high cost, and of limited diversity.

7.2.7 USB

The Universal Serial Bus (USB) provides a bandwidth of up to a maximum of 12 Mbits/s. This is adequate to service the needs of low-performance PC peripherals, such as pointing devices, keyboards, modems, and low-resolution, low-frame-rate cameras. USB devices are attached to a computer through a tree topology using multiport hubs for expansion. The USB connection consists of a differential data pair and two power connections. Low-power devices (such as keyboards or mice) can obtain their power from the bus. USB devices include plug-and-play mechanisms that support hot connection and disconnection of devices. USB communication consists of sending data packets. It provides both asynchronous communication and isochronous communication, in which specific devices are granted guaranteed use of a portion of the available bus bandwidth. This style of communication is important in multimedia applications, which typically face stringent latency limits. Two important advantages of the USB are that it does not require users to open up the PC case to add peripherals, and that it is inexpensive because it only has four wires.

7.2.8 FireWire/IEEE 1394

FireWire was a high-speed external serial interface originally developed by Apple Computer, which later became IEEE standard 1394. IEEE 1394 uses a six-conductor cable consisting of power, ground, and differential data and strobe signals. It currently supports speeds up to 800 Mbits/s, which makes it useful for high-quality video devices. Like USB, IEEE 1394 enables plug-and-play peripheral connectivity, provides power to peripherals, and supports isochronous data transfers. Because of its higher speed, IEEE 1394 costs more than USB, so lower speed devices will still use USB rather than IEEE 1394. In order to obtain such high speeds over serial lines, IEEE 1394 requires a fast and rather complicated interface chip on both ends of the wire. This is an example of the trend of complex silicon substituting for more-expensive electromechanical components.

7.2.9 IDE

In late 1984, Compaq, working with Western Digital, Imprimis, and Seagate, initiated the development of the Intelligent Drive Electronics (IDE) interface. Before this, disk drives in PCs had very low-level interfaces to their disk drives, because the cost of adding an intelligent controller to each disk drive was prohibitive. However, initial IDE designs had many incompatibilities, so in 1989 the standard was redefined as the AT Attachment (ATA) standard. Today IDE and ATA are synonymous. An IDE/ATA bus is 16 bits wide, dating from the 16-bit data bus in the PC/AT. The initial IDE/ATA spec allowed a total of two drives per channel and supported DMA rates of up to 8.3 Mbytes/s. This was expanded to 16.6 Mbyte/s in EIDE (Enhanced IDE) and ATA-2. (Unfortunately, different manufacturers call their compatible standard drives incompatible names.) The ATA-2 interface was also expanded to cover CD-ROMs and tape drives by adding additional protocol capabilities called the ATA Packet Interface (ATAPI). Finally, the maximum performance has been extended to 33.3 Mbytes/s in the Ultra ATA/DMA-33 generation and 66.6 Mbytes/s in the Ultra ATA/DMA-66 generation. However, even in this generation, it does not implement a split-transaction (pended) protocol [2], so the typical performance can be significantly below the peak performance. The maximum IDE bus length is limited to 18 in. because it uses a flat (untwisted pair) unshielded ribbon cable. This cable is inexpensive, but it was originally designed for transfer speeds of only 8.3 Mbytes/s. This means IDE is only useful within a PC enclosure.

7.2.10 SCSI

The original Small Computer Systems Interface (SCSI) standard was derived from the Shugart Associates System Interface (SASI). SCSI-I was approved by ANSI in 1986 as standard X3.131-1986. It only defined an 8-bit-wide bus operating with a 5-MHz maximum transfer speed over a 50-conductor cable. The advanced SCSI-2 specification was approved by ANSI in 1990. It defined extensions to 16 bits ("wide") and 10 MHz ("fast") and increased the maximum number of devices supported on a bus from 8 to 16. This required a new high-quality 68-conductor twisted-pair cable, improved connectors, and active termination, which provided much better signal integrity. Command queuing, which allows multiple outstanding transactions, was also added in SCSI-2. This provides significant advantages over IDE in high-performance systems with multiple devices. Finally, SCSI-2 added command enhancements to operate with a wide variety of devices such as removable media storage devices and scanners. More recently, 20-MHz ("ultra") SCSI devices have appeared. These have maximum transfer rates of 20 Mbytes/s if "narrow" or

40 Mbytes/s if "wide." The maximum SCSI cable length is proportional to its speed; 5-MHz systems can support 6-m cable lengths, whereas 20-MHz systems are limited to 1.5-m cables. To overcome the reduced cabling length of the higher speed interfaces, differential SCSI (which has a maximum cable length of 25 m) was introduced in all of the above variants. This cable is required for the latest 80-Mbyte/s Ultra2 SCSI, which uses low-voltage differential signaling over distances up to 12 m.

Because of their focus on higher performance systems such as servers, it is common to find support for hardware-implemented RAID built into SCSI host adapters. For high-end systems, a variant called single connector attachment (SCA) was developed which uses 80-pin connectors and cables that add power to the 68-pin interface and allows hot swapping and reconfiguration of drives. Because of its more complex cabling and interface and its lower volume, a SCSI disk is usually 1.5–2 times more expensive than an IDE disk of the same capacity.

7.3 Summary

I/O devices will continue to dominate computer system cost, because they are based on electromechanical devices that do not scale at the same rate as Moore's Law. Thus, it will continue to make economic sense for their performance to often be a limit to overall system performance, as the marginal cost of higher CPU performance is less. Note that although disk *capacity* has been keeping up with Moore's Law, it is largely driven by lithographical reduction in thin film read/write head sizes and by improvements in the electronics, which are driven by lithography. However, the minimum cost of a disk drive has been scaling much more slowly than its capacity. For example, current disks of the same physical size as disks from three years ago may hold four times as much data, but their prices are still roughly equal.

As long as Moore's Law continues to hold, it will also continue to make economic sense to replace more and more electromechanical components with semiconductor components. Examples of these include high-speed serial interconnects, full-screen antialiasing, and I/O devices shared between multiple PCs.

Finally, the development of low-volume specialized I/O devices must be amortized over many years. Furthermore, because I/O devices are a large part of system cost, many users benefit from upgrading their computer systems while keeping some of their existing

I/O devices. These two factors, as well as others, make I/O standards very important. It also exerts pressure from the marketplace to improve I/O standards in a backward-compatible manner.

7.4 Discussion of Included Papers

The papers we have included begin with a historical taxonomy of I/O techniques and then present key papers in storage, networks, and graphics.

7.4.1 Smotherman's "A Sequencing-Based Taxonomy of I/O Systems and Review of Historical Machines" [11]

A wide variety of I/O techniques have been used throughout the history of computers. Smotherman proposes an I/O taxonomy and provides a wealth of historical references and a brief overview of each type of machine. These techniques are basic in nature and reappear in today's machines, both in I/O structures as well as processors. For example, the MIT TX-2 in 1957 had thirty-three program counters and was a forerunner of multithreaded machines today. Similarly, PCs have been moving up the I/O evolutionary ladder and the recent intelligent I/O (I2O) proposals introduce I/O processors in PCs, which have been present since the 1950s and 1960s in large processors.

7.4.2 Ruemmler and Wilkes's "An Introduction to Disk Drive Modeling" [10]

Disk drives have been part of computer systems since the 1950s. At various times, some have proposed that semiconductors or exotic technologies would replace or supplant disk drives. However, disk drives have continued to scale in cost, capacity, reliability, and performance for decades and have remained key components of computer systems.

Ruemmler and Wilkes is an excellent reference for understanding and modeling recent disk drives. First, it describes the operation of the various components of a disk drive from the I/O device driver, SCSI bus, and disk controller through the cache within the disk drive, data layout on the disk, and finally head positioning effects. It then develops a series of models for disk drive operation of increasing complexity and validates these models against actual measured data. A good understanding of disk drive operation as provided by this paper is essential for those interested in higher level I/O architectures such as RAID.

7.4.3 Patterson, Gibson, and Katz's "A Case for Redundant Arrays of Inexpensive Disks (RAID)" [9]

Supercomputers like the Cray-1 in the 1970s could afford to stripe files across multiple disks for higher performance. However, it wasn't until more recently that disks became cheap enough for the distribution of files across multiple disks to be more widely applicable. This first RAID paper expanded beyond striping to offer a range of improvements in performance and reliability by using RAIDs.

7.4.4 Metcalfe and Boggs's "Ethernet: Distributed Packet Switching for Local Computer Networks" [6]

Computer networks come in two principal types: those between computer systems, such as local area networks, and networks within large computer systems, such multicomputer meshes. Metcalfe and Boggs's classic paper introduced the Ethernet, which was the first successful local area network and was a key part of the development of distributed systems. Although originally developed at 3 Mbits/s, Ethernet quickly scaled to 10 Mbits/s. More recently, it has scaled to 100 Mbits/s and even 1 Gbits/s, as well as switched (i.e., point-to-point) configurations.

7.4.5 Ni and McKinley's "A Survey of Wormhole Routing Techniques in Direct Networks" [8]

Ni and McKinley is an excellent reference for the interconnection networks common in large-scale multiprocessors today. It begins with an overview of direct network topologies, routing, flow control, and switching. It then describes wormhole routing, where segments of a packet travel through a network in a pipelined fashion. Issues related to deadlock in deterministic, adaptive, and reconfigurable network routing are covered as well.

7.4.6 Akeley's "RealityEngine Graphics" [1]

Akeley's paper presents one of most important graphics architectures of the early 1990s. This architecture was implemented then as a graphics supercomputer. However, graphics supercomputer architectures have been migrating down to workstation, and most recently, PC graphics architectures as technology and integration advance.

A number of significant advances in computer graphics hardware were introduced in the Reality Engine. The RealityEngine provided a combination of more than one million triangles per second performance combined with trilinear mip-mapped texture mapping and full-scene antialiasing. (Antialiasing removes or reduces the stairsteps, jaggies, and crawlies in simple pixel-based graphics.) The first two features are becoming common in workstations and PCs today, whereas antialiasing will likely start to appear in the next generation of workstation graphics. The GL graphics language developed for the RealityEngine and its siblings has developed into the OpenGL standard, ensuring that many of today's graphics accelerators implement the same features in similar ways.

7.5 References

A good historical overview of disk and tape technology can be found in *Magnetic Recording: The First 100 Years* by Mee, Daniel, and Clark [4]. Recent articles of interest on disk technology include Wood and Hodges [13] and Tsang, Chen, and Yogi [12].

Other approaches to high-end graphics architecture can be found in Molnar, Eyles, and Poulton [7]. McCormack et al. present the Neon single-chip graphics accelerator in [3]. Other sources for papers on graphics architectures include recent proceedings of the SIGGRAPH/Eurographics Workshop on Graphics Hardware. I/O Web references are given on this reader's companion Web site.

[1]   K. Akeley, "RealityEngine graphics," *SIGGRAPH '93 Proceedings*, pp. 109–116, 1993.

[2]   J. L. Hennessy and D. A. Patterson, *Computer Architecture: A Quantitative Approach*, San Francisco, CA: Morgan Kaufmann, 2nd ed. 1996.

[3]   J. McCormack et al., "Implementing Neon: A 256-Bit graphics accelerator," *IEEE Micro*, 19(2):58–69, 1999.

[4]   C. D. Mee, E. D. Daniel, and M. H. Clark. *Magnetic Recording: The First 100 Years*. Piscataway, N. J.: IEEE Press, 1999.

[5]   H. P. Messmer, *The Indispensable PC Hardware Book*, Reading, MA: Addison-Wesley-Longman, 3rd ed. 1997.

[6]   R. M. Metcalf and D. R. Boggs, "Ethernet: Distributed packet switching for local computer networks," *Communications of the ACM*, 19(7):395–404, 1976.

[7]   S. Molnar, J. Eyles, and J. Poulton, "Pixelflow: High-speed rendering using image composition," *SIGGRAPH '92 Proceedings*, pp. 231–240, 1992.

[8]   L. M. Ni and P. K. McKinley, "A survey of wormhole routing techniques in direct networks," *IEEE Computer*, 26(2):62–76, 1993.

[9]   D. Patterson, G. Gibson, and R. Katz, "A Case for redundant arrrays of inexpensive disks (RAID)," *Proceedings of the ACM SIGMOD Conference*, pp. 109–116, June 1988.

[10]   C. Ruemmler and J. Wilkes, "An introduction to disk drive modeling," *IEEE Computer*, 27(3):17–28, 1994.

[11]   M. Smotherman, "A sequencing-based taxonomy of I/O systems and review of historical machines," *ACM Computer Architecture News*, 17(5):5–15, 1989.

[12]   C. Tsang, M. M. Chen, and T. Yogi. "Gigabit density magnetic recording," *Proceedings of the IEEE*, 83(9):134–1359, 1993.

[13]   C. Wood and P. Hodges, "DASD trends: Cost, performance, and form factor," *Proceedings of the IEEE*, 81(4):573–585, 1993.

A Sequencing-Based Taxonomy of I/O Systems and Review of Historical Machines

Mark Smotherman

Dept. of Computer Science
Clemson University, Clemson, SC 29634-1906
INTERNET: mark@hubcap.clemson.edu

Abstract

A new taxonomy for I/O systems is proposed that is based on the program sequencing necessary for the control of I/O devices. A review of historical machines demonstrates the need for a more comprehensive categorization than previously published and reveals the historical firsts of I/O interrupts in the NBS DYSEAC, DMA in the IBM SAGE (AN/FSQ-7), the interrupt vector concept in the Lincoln Labs TX-2, and fully symmetric I/O in the Burroughs D-825 multiprocessor.

Introduction

Textbook presentations of I/O systems typically identify only four categories (i.e. the methods of data transfer):

1) program-controlled I/O (i.e. polling),
2) interrupt-driven I/O,
3) DMA, and
4) channel I/O.

Blaauw and Brooks present a broader categorization in their manuscript, *Computer Architecture* [10]. They identify essentially seven distinct types of I/O systems:

I. Dependent I/O
  A. direct
  B. single instruction overlap
    1. private buffer per device
    2. shared buffer
      a. dedicated to I/O usage
      b. general buffer in main memory
II. Autonomous I/O
  A. channel (specialized controller/processor)
  B. peripheral processor (generalized processor)
    1. homogeneous multiprocessor structure
    2. heterogeneous multiprocessor structure

However, after reviewing the historical development of I/O systems, I am led to believe that there is a much richer design space and more differences between machines than suggested by either of the categorizations above. For uniprocessors, I believe that the major issue is the method of transfer initiation; thus, major categories are synchronous I/O versus the several different ways in which overlapped I/O operations can be initiated. For each of the overlapped operations, I believe they should be subdivided according to their method of completion reporting. Furthermore, the major multiprocessor issue of symmetry in I/O should be handled separately.

The method of transfer is an indication of the level of functionality of the I/O subsystem, that is, how often and how much the CPU is involved in the actual transfer. This ranges from the CPU doing all to sophisticated peripheral processing units, and it applies to all initiation/completion reporting categories. Within this range, I draw a distinction between a controller that can transfer only one block before requiring CPU intervention and a controller that can transfer multiple blocks in a scatter/gather type of operation (in which the blocks are identified to the controller by a chain of descriptors). Some designers and authors call a controller with the latter capability an I/O channel. Indeed, Bell and Newell categorize controllers with scatter/gather capability as Pios, since they consider the chain of block descriptors to be a series of jump instructions [8]. However, in this taxonomy I reserve the term I/O channel for a specialized I/O processor that fetches instructions with identifiable opcode fields. Moreover, I also use the distinction made by Blaauw and Brooks between I/O channels and I/O processors, which is the general ability to count. That is, an I/O processor should have the ability to maintain a loop or event count that is unrelated to the transfer of a given number of words or characters per block.

For multiprocessors, the method of initiation is not as important as the symmetry of the initiation; therefore, this symmetry or lack of it becomes the basis of the major categories. The method of completion reporting is the basis of subcategories, and symmetry in interruption is explicitly identified.

A classification of historical machines serves to demonstrate the usefulness of the proposed taxonomy and also serves as a guided tour of the history of I/O systems. For older machines with multiple I/O options, I have chosen to classify them according to their established use (e.g. the IBM S/360 has synchronous I/O capability, but it is rarely used). Some multiprocessors appear in the first section; this is because they represent the first use of a given transfer initiation method.

Not all categories are populated with machines. This may be the result of omissions on my part, or the category may indeed be unfruitful. I would like to characterize the reasons for the latter occurrence.

A Sequencing-Based Taxonomy

I. CPU - I/O INTERACTION
  A. Synchronous transfer
  B. Asynchronous transfer
  1. interlocked instruction to start transfer
    a. synchronization by interlock
    b. synchronization by polling
      i. separate instructions to poll and transfer data
      ii. controller transfers words of block (i.e. DMA)
      iii. controller with scatter/gather capability (often called an I/O channel)
      iv. I/O channel (with specialized I/O instruction set)
      v. I/O processor
    c. synchronization by interrupt
      i. separate instruction to transfer data
      ii. controller transfers words of block (i.e. DMA)
      iii. controller with scatter/gather capability (often called an I/O channel)
      iv. I/O channel (with specialized I/O instruction set)
      v. I/O processor
  2. conditional instruction to start transfer
    a. synchronization by polling
    b. synchronization by interrupt
  3. mailbox deposit to start transfer (i.e. single entry)
    a. synchronization by polling
    b. synchronization by interrupt
  4. queue insert to start transfer (i.e. multiple entries)
    a. synchronization by polling
    b. synchronization by queueing
    c. synchronization by interrupt

     5. asynchronous instruction to start transfer
       a. synchronization by polling
       b. synchronization by interrupt

II. MULTIPROCESSOR I/O
  A. Asymmetric initiation
     1. synchronization by polling
     2. synchronization by asymmetric interrupt
     3. synchronization by symmetric interrupt
  B. Symmetric initiation
     1. synchronization by polling
     2. synchronization by queueing
     3. synchronization by asymmetric interrupt
     4. synchronization by symmetric interrupt

A Review of Historical Machines

I. CPU - I/O INTERACTION

A. Synchronous transfer

ERA 1103 (1953) - word-at-a-time interlocked I/O [8]. Bell and Newell and Blaauw and Brooks credit a UNIVAC 1103A as the first computer to use the interrupt concept [8,10], in which a batch machine was preempted to start data collection from a NASA wind tunnel [44]; however, see also the UNIVAC I and NBS DYSEAC.

IBM 702 (1953) - block interlocked I/O [5,6]. The CPU stalls while a block of characters is transferred from an I/O device buffer. The 702 introduced the control unit concept.

IBM 1401 (1959) [5,6]. This machine was originally designed as a printer controller but found widespread use as a small business computer. It uses one opcode per I/O device, and these include reading a card into memory locations 0 to 79, punching a card from other locations, and printing from a third set of locations. The CPU stalls while the characters are transferred. An example of its ease of use is that a card duplicating program can be written in about 20 characters and punched onto one card.

B. Asynchronous transfer

1. interlocked instruction to start transfer

a. synchronization by interlock

UNIVAC I (1951) - buffered I/O [8,23,56]. There is one 60-word tape buffer for input and one for output. An initial input instruction starts the transfer to the buffer and then releases the CPU for overlapped instruction execution; a subsequent input instruction dumps the buffer to memory, starts the next transfer, and then releases the CPU. If a subsequent input instruction is issued too early then an interlock stalls the CPU. I/O errors halt the CPU, and the operator must diagnose the problem. Codd credits the UNIVAC I as "one of the earliest machines to be equipped with program interruption" since he states that an arithmetic overflow would cause the program to stop [17]; Eckert also mentions several checks that can stop the machine [23]. However, interrupts were apparently never used for I/O completion.

IBM 701 (1952) - "copy logic" [5,6,10,14,50]. After an initial prepare to read (or write) instruction, the program must issue a copy instruction for each word in the transfer. A loop is coded to update the memory addresses and issue the copies, and the loop may also perform superficial processing such as character code conversion. The copy instruction is interlocked so that an early issue is stalled until the I/O device can provide/accept the next word. At end of file the copy instruction causes a one-instruction skip, and at the end of block it causes a two-instruction skip.

b. *synchronization by polling*

i. separate instructions to poll and transfer data

PDP-1 (1959) [7]. This machine provided conditional skips on I/O buffer register contents, which are apparently used to poll for transfer completion.

PDP-8 (1965) [7,8]. Conditional skips on control unit status registers are used for polling.

ii. controller transfers words of block (i.e. DMA)

(Whirlwind I, 1951 - Everett states, "In general the computer continues to run during terminal equipment wait times," but explains no further [29].)

IBM SAGE (or AN/FSQ-7, started 1952, operational 1955) - DMA operation [3]. I/O operations start block transfers of data to/from drum buffers that proceed in parallel with further CPU operations. A controller generates the sequential memory addresses for the block and decrements a counter, while the CPU has a conditional branch to test completion of the transfer. Transfers are interlocked so that the CPU is stalled if a second transfer is attempted before the previous one ends. Jacobs states "the input/output (I/O) break, or memory cycle stealing," was introduced in SAGE [37], and Serrell, et al., identify "computation in parallel with I/O" as a significant new feature of SAGE [48].

(see also UNIVAC 1107)

iii. controller with scatter/gather capability (often called an I/O channel)

Honeywell 800 (1963) - hardware-assisted multiprogramming [34,35,42,43]. This machine implements eight virtual processors, each having 2 program counters and an individual interrupt vector base register. On each memory cycle the hardware scans on a priority basis for activity on eight input controllers, then eight output controllers, and then the CPU. Within the CPU the hardware scans the virtual processors in a cyclic manner (with various exceptions for multiple memory cycle operations). (Papers are unclear about program I/O synchronization.)

iv. I/O channel (with specialized I/O instruction set)

(see IBM 709)

v. I/O processor

(example unknown)

c. *synchronization by interrupt*

i. separate instruction to transfer data

NBS DYSEAC (1954) - introduced I/O interrupt [38,39]. This machine has two program counters; an I/O signal causes the CPU to switch PCs. A bit in each instruction can force a switch back between PCs. Codd states, "in the NBS DYSEAC the very significant step was made of extending interruption to input-output operations" [17].

Lincoln TX-2 (1957 paper) - "multiple sequence" [30]. This machine contains 33 program counters; each I/O device has a dedicated PC and operates at a fixed priority (i.e. forerunner of interrupt vector). Each instruction has break and dismiss bits: break is used to indicate points at which a higher-priority sequence can take over, while dismiss is used to allow lower-priority sequences to resume. Blaauw and Brooks classify this machine as having PPUs [10], but I see the explicit instruction bits as a recognition of the sharing of a single CPU. Thus, I consider this machine closer to interrupt vectoring than to virtual PPUs.

PDP-1 (1959) [7]. Bell, et al., credit the "16-channel sequence break system" to TX-2 influence (actual operation not described) [7].

ii. controller transfers words of block (i.e. DMA)

UNIVAC 1107 (1962) [11,12]. Controller uses a single I/O control word, which contains a memory address, address increment/decrement flag, and a word count. Interrupt occurs on zero count when specified by Load Channel commands.

iii. controller with scatter/gather capability (often called an I/O channel)

IBM 7070 (1958) - "priority processing" (I/O interrupt) [51]. An I/O completion causes the CPU to switch to an uninterruptible "priority routine," and the return address is stored in a register. The machine provides scatter/gather capability using a chain of record definition words.

IBM STRETCH (started 1954, delivered 1961) [10,15,22]. The I/O exchange acts as a byte multiplexor. I/O completion is part of a comprehensive interrupt vector facility, in which each vector contains a single instruction to be executed outside the normal instruction cycle. These instructions can be single-instruction fixups or subroutine calls. In general, interrupt nesting is allowed; however, I/O is treated as a single cause.

iv. I/O channel (with specialized I/O instruction set)

IBM 709 (1957) - introduction of channel I/O [5,6,32]. The CPU must execute two instructions in sequence to start I/O. A read select or write select instruction is first used to select a given device, and then a channel-specific instruction is used to reset and start any of the maximum of six channels (766s). The address field of the reset and start instruction is used to carry the channel program address. Some device select instructions are interlocked so that the CPU is stalled if a second select is issued before a previous one ends. The reset and select instructions, however, immediately act upon the channels, which were much more sophisticated than the later IBM S/360 channels. Polling can be used for I/O completion, while interruption ("data-channel trap") is available as an extra cost feature. Apparently, all installations chose to use the interrupt feature [M. Rubinstein, personal communication].

IBM 7090 (1958) [8,10]. The optional "data-channel trap" feature of the 709 architecture is included as standard equipment. An interrupt vector with a pair of saved-PC and new-PC locations for each channel is used to resolve I/O completion traps. The later version channels (7909) can themselves be interrupted by external events and are capable of dealing with I/O retries without CPU intervention.

v. I/O processor

UNIVAC LARC (started 1954, delivered 1960) [20,24,25]. High-level request packets (e.g. record number or key) are sent to an I/O processor, which also performs services such as device queueing. The requesting processor is interrupted when its request is complete.

2. *conditional instruction to start transfer*

   a. *synchronization by polling*

   (example unknown)

   b. *synchronization by interrupt*

   IBM S/360 (1964) [1,8-10]. The Start I/O instruction sets the condition code according to success of initiation (path may be busy and CPU must perform queueing, or error may exist). Channel I/O is the method of transfer, but a less complex channel instruction set is provided than that for 7090 channels.

3. *mailbox deposit to start transfer*

   a. *synchronization by polling*

   CDC 6600 (1965) - virtual PPUs [8,28,47,54,55,57]. In the typical OS structure, PPUs are assigned to devices and poll reserved main memory locations (input mailboxes) to determine I/O requests for that device. After starting a device, a PPU will poll the device until completion and will then place a completion notice in its output mailbox. Programs running on the CPU can poll the output mailbox; otherwise, they can be suspended until the PPU running the OS sees the completion notice and resumes the program by an exchange jump. Before an output transfer the PPU must move the data from the shared main memory to its local memory, likewise after an input transfer the PPU must move the data from its local memory to the shared main memory. The execution of ten virtual PPUs is accomplished by time-sharing a single execution unit.

   b. *synchronization by interrupt*

   (example unknown)

4. *queue insert to start transfer*

   a. *synchronization by polling*

   Burroughs B7700 (1972) [20,28,47]. Reserved locations exist in main memory that define head and tail pointers to I/O device request queues and I/O completion block queues. Queue manipulations by the CPU and I/O modules are atomic actions. Any IOM can handle any device, but a start I/O instruction issued by the CPU begins IOM processing on a specified device queue. IOM processing continues until an error, interrupt, or empty queue. The CPU polls the completion block queue, or, optionally, interrupts can be generated on completion of each request.

   (see also IBM S/370 XA where path busy queueing is handled by the channel subsystem)

   b. *synchronization by queueing*

   Honeywell Series 60 Level 64 (1974) [4]. Microcoded semaphore operations are used in I/O processing. On I/O completion, the controller inserts a completion message into a queue and signals the corresponding general semaphore.

ELXSI System 6400 (1987) [45]. This machine uses message passing as a synchronization mechanism between both OS processes and I/O controllers. An I/O processor notifies the controller that a message is pending, but it is the responsibility of the controller to handle queues, including out-of-order processing and error handling.

    c. synchronization by interrupt

(see also IBM S/370 XA where path busy queueing is handled by the channel subsystem)

  5. asynchronous instruction to start transfer

    a. synchronization by polling

(example unknown)

    b. synchronization by interrupt

IBM S/370 (1970) [16,47]. SIOF (start I/O fast release) is used to release the CPU after a channel has fetched its CAW but before the channel has determined if the I/O operation can be successfully initiated. An interrupt occurs if the device or path is busy. The designers assumed these conditions would be infrequent, but on later systems the interrupt overhead canceled out any performance gain from the fast release of CPU.

II. MULTIPROCESSOR I/O

A. Asymmetric initiation

  1. synchronization by polling

(example unknown)

  2. synchronization by asymmetric interrupt

Burroughs B5500 (1964) [8,10,28]. This machine provides up to two CPUs, but only the master CPU can initiate I/O. An ITI instruction to test for pending interrupt at end of interrupt handling prevents unnecessary context switching. The I/O channels and CPUs are crossbarred with memory modules; also the I/O channels are crossbarred with all the peripherals.

IBM S/370 MP (1974) [16,28,47]. Channels and devices are dedicated to a particular CPU.

  3. synchronization by symmetric interrupt

UNIVAC 1100 Model 80 (1976) [11,12,47]. This machine provides up to four CPUs, but I/O must be initiated by either of the two CPUs that connect to the storage interface unit that controls memory access for the I/O device. I/O is directed to the cache in the SIU rather than directly to main memory. I/O interrupts are made available to the two CPUs in alternation and for a limited amount of time each; if one CPU doesn't respond to the interrupt within the available period, the interrupt is passed on to the next CPU in sequence.

B. Symmetric initiation

1. synchronization by polling

Plessey System 250 (1972) - memory-mapped I/O with capability protection [19,26,27,33,40]. A design philosophy of reliability and security led the designers to reject I/O channels in favor of additional CPUs and to reject interprocessor and device-processor interrupts. The advantages of this approach lie in the simplified problem of component sparing, the prevention of disruptions from unplanned external events, and the ease of hardware isolation in the case of component failure. Device drivers obtain I/O requests from memory queues and poll device registers until transfers are complete. An interrupt-like system is also available in which each processor periodically (100 microsec.) examines a common status word for interrupt-like requests; however, various papers differ on its use in I/O.

(see also B-7700)

(see also IBM S/370 XA option of masking off subclasses and using Test Subchannel)

2. synchronization by queueing

Intel 432 (1981) - a layered, intelligent peripheral subsystem and object-oriented design [36]. GDPs (i.e. CPUs) can request an I/O operation by sending a message object to a device request port object. An I/O process on an interface processor (IP) owns this port and responds by sending a message to an attached processor (AP) (i.e. placing the necessary information in the local memory of the AP and interrupting the AP). The IP has responsibility to protect the 432 core system logically using capabilities and physically using separate busses, while the AP is a more conventional microprocessor (e.g. 8086) and may use polling, byte-at-a-time interrupts, or DMA controllers for the actual I/O transfer. The device driver on the AP formats a reply message from the I/O buffers in its local memory and sends it to the I/O process on the IP, which then sends a message object to the corresponding device reply port object.

(see also ELXSI System 6400)

3. synchronization by asymmetric interrupt

Ramo-Wooldridge RW-400 (1960) [8,20,28,46]. Multiple computers (CPUs with local memories) can connect over a crossbar exchange to specialized processors called buffer memories and from there to any one of multiple I/O controllers. Interrupts are available, but the papers are unclear as to whether the connection between a buffer memory and I/O controller must be maintained for an interrupt to be sent. Curtin states that connection requests can only be made by the computers or buffer memories but that a computer can request that a buffer memory start I/O operations and then later transfer data from the buffer memory into its local memory [20]. Enslow indicates that a complete system was never built [28].

Univac 1108-MP (1967) [28,47,49]. Any CPU can initiate I/O operations, but interrupts are directed to a single prespecified processor.

GE-655 (1969, later renamed Honeywell 6000) [28,47]. Any CPU can initiate I/O operations, but interrupts are directed to a single control processor (which is determined by manually set switches).

4. synchronization by symmetric interrupt

Burroughs D-825 (1960) [2,8,28,53]. All interrupts are transmitted to each processor; an OS-controlled mask register in each processor determines if it will respond to a given interrupt.

IBM S/360 Model 67 (1966) [31]. I/O handling on this dual processor system is similar to D-825.

IBM S/370 XA (1983) - subchannel per device [18,21]. Any CPU can start I/O on any device, and any CPU can accept an interrupt. Optionally, interrupt requests from subchannels can be assigned to one of eight maskable interruption subclasses, and priority schemes can be programmed so that certain high priority programs can be interrupted by only a small number of subclasses. If all CPUs mask off a certain subclass, the interruption status is held pending in the channel system and can be accepted later by use of the test subchannel instruction. A test pending interruption instruction is also available and is used to avoid an immediate context switch after a LPSW is executed by the interrupt handler. Path busy queueing is handled by the channel subsystem.

Data General MV/20000 (1985). Any processor can start I/O on any channel. Channels either send interrupts to a processor identified by an OS-set register in the channel or according to device directed interrupt mode, which uses an OS-controlled table in main memory to map device numbers to processor numbers.

Sequent Balance (1986) - intelligent interrupt bus [52]. The SLIC bus interrupts the processor currently running the program with least priority.

Concluding Remarks

I would like to gather responses and corrections to this new taxonomy and to the historical information in the review section. An additional categorization under synchronization by interrupt might be the determination of the interrupt handler location. For example, the PDP-8 has one interrupt location, while the PDP-11 provides a single, large interrupt vector table yielding the possibility of hardware identification of a separate interrupt handler for each of several I/O devices. (Interrupt vector tables, as we use them today, apparently originated with IBM Stretch, which along with the Honeywell 800 provided a base address register for the current table. Thus, different processes could use different tables.) Finally, the RCA 601 required that the user specify the address of the appropriate interrupt handler as part of the Start I/O instruction [41].

Three other issues might also deserve explicit categorization: in all systems, the recognition of unsolicited input (e.g. PDP-8) versus locking each input unit until a read is issued (e.g. IBM S/360); in systems with cache memory, I/O to cache (UNIVAC 1100/80) versus I/O to memory (S/370); and, in systems with virtual memory, I/O controllers with virtual address mapping (Honeywell DPS-8) versus I/O controllers requiring premapped physical addresses (S/370).

Acknowledgements: I wish to thank Randolph Bentson at Colorado State, Hank Dietz at Purdue, Dan Kern at Univ. of Washington, Philip Koch at Dartmouth, Jim Haynes at UC Santa Cruz, John Levine at ISC, Barry Margolin at Thinking Machines Corp., Robert Olson at ELXSI, Dan Pierson at Encore, Marv Rubinstein at ISC, Dan Siewiorek at Carnegie Mellon, Jan Stubbs at NCR, Chris Thomson at Myrias Research, and Steve Wilson for their comments and suggestions on earlier drafts of this paper.

References

[1] G.M. Amdahl, G.A. Blaauw, and F.P. Brooks, Jr., "Architecture of the IBM System/360," *IBM J. Research and Development 8*, 2 (April 1964) 87-101.

[2] J.P. Anderson, S.A. Hoffman, J. Shifman, and R.J. Williams, "D-825 - A Multiple Computer System for Command and Control," in *Proc. AFIPS FJCC*, 1962, pp. 89-96.

[3] M.M. Astrahan, B. Housman, J.F. Jacobs, R.P. Mayer, and W.H. Thomas, "Logical Design of the Digital Computer for the SAGE System," *IBM J. Research Development 1*, 1, (January 1957) 76-83.

[4] T. Atkinson, "Architecture of Series 60/Level 64," *Honeywell Comp. J. 8*, 2 (1974) 94-106.

[5] C.J. Bashe, W. Buchholz, G.V. Hawkins, J.J. Ingram, and N. Rochester, "The Architecture of IBM's Early Computers," *IBM J. Research Development 25*, 5 (September 1981) 363-375.

[6] C.J. Bashe, L.R. Johnson, J.H. Palmer, and E.W. Pugh, *IBM's Early Computers.* Cambridge, MA: The MIT

Press, 1986.

[7] C.G. Bell, J.C. Mudge, and J.E. McNamara, *Computer Engineering: A DEC View of Hardware Systems Design.* Bedford, MA: Digital Press, 1978.

[8] C.G. Bell and A. Newell, *Computer Structures: Readings and Examples.* New York: McGraw-Hill, 1971.

[9] G.A. Blaauw and F.P. Brooks, Jr., "The Structure of System/360, Part I - Outline of the Logical Structure," *IBM Systems J. 3*, 2 (1964) 119-135.

[10] G.A. Blaauw and F.P. Brooks, Jr., *Computer Architecture*, 1983 manuscript.

[11] B.R. Borgerson, M.L. Hanson, and P.A. Hartley, "The Evolution of the Sperry Univac 1100 Series: A History, Analysis, and Projection," *Comm. ACM 21*, 1 (January 1978) 25-43.

[12] B.R. Borgerson, M.D. Godfrey, P.E. Hagerty, and T.R. Rykken, "The Architecture of the Sperry Univac 1100 Series Systems," in *Proc. Intl. Symp. Comp. Architecture*, April 1979, pp. 137-146.

[13] J. Bouvard, "Operating System for the 800/1800," *Datamation 10*, 5 (May 1964) 29-34.

[14] W. Buchholz, "The System Design of the IBM Type 701 Computer," *Proc. TRE 41*, 10 (October 1953) 1262-1275.

[15] W. Buchholz (ed.), *Planning a Computer System.* New York: McGraw-Hill, 1962.

[16] R.P. Case and A. Padegs, "Architecture of the IBM System/370," *Comm. ACM 21*, 1 (January 1978) 73-96.

[17] E.F. Codd, "Multiprogramming," pp. 77-153, in F.L. Alt and M. Rubinoff (eds.), *Advances in Computers, Vol. 3.* New York: Academic Press, 1962.

[18] R.L. Cormier, R.J. Dugan, and R.R. Guyette, "System/370 Extended Architecture: The Channel Subsystem," *IBM J. Res. Dev. 27*, 3 (May 1983) 206-218.

[19] D.C. Cosserat, "A Capability Oriented Multi-Processor System for Real-Time Applications," in *Proc. Intl. Conf. Computer Communications*, Washington, DC, 1972, pp. 282-289.

[20] W.A. Curtin, "Multiple Computer Systems," pp. 245-303, in F.L. Alt (ed.), *Advances in Computers, Vol. 4.* New York: Academic Press, 1964.

[20] R.W. Doran, *Computer Architecture: A Structured Approach.* New York: Academic Press, 1979.

[21] R.J. Dugan, "System/370 Extended Architecture: A Program View of the Channel Subsystem," in *Proc. Intl. Symp. Comp. Architecture*, 1983, pp. 270-276.

[22] S.W. Dunwell, "Design Objectives for the IBM STRETCH Computer," in *Proc. EJCC*, 1956, pp. 20-22.

[23] J.P. Eckert, J.R. Weiner, H.F. Welsh, and H.F. Mitchell, "The UNIVAC system," in *Proc. Joint AIEE-IRE Conf.*, Philadelphia, February 1952, pp. 6-14.

[24] J.P. Eckert, "UNIVAC Larc, The Next Step in Computer Design," in *Proc. EJCC*, 1956, pp. 16-20.

[25] J.P. Eckert, J.C. Chu, A.B. Tonik, and W.F. Schmitt, "Design of Univac-LARC System: I," in *Proc. EJCC*, 1959, pp. 59-65.

[26] D.M. England, "Architectural Features of System 250," in *Operating Systems: Intl. Computer State of the Art Report, Vol. 14.* Maindenhead, England: Infotech, 1972, pp. 395-427.

[27] D.M. England, "Operating System of System 250," in *Proc. Intl. Switching Symp.*, Cambridge, MA, June 1972, pp. 525-529.

[28] P.H. Enslow, Jr. (ed.), *Multiprocessors and Parallel Processing.* New York: John Wiley and Sons, 1974.

[29] R.R. Everett, "The Whirlwind I Computer," in *Proc. Joint AIEE-IRE Computer Conf.*, Philadelphia, December 1951, pp. 70-74.

[30] J.W. Forgie, "The Lincoln TX-2 Input-Output System," in *Proc. WJCC*, 1957, pp. 156-160.

[31] C.T. Gibson, "Time-Sharing in the IBM System 360: Model 67," in *Proc. AFIPS SJCC*, 1966, pp. 61-78.

[32] J.L. Greenstadt, "The IBM 709 Computer," in *New Computers, Report from the Manufacturers ACM Conf.*, 1957, pp. 92-98.

[33] D. Halton, "Hardware of the System 250 for Communication Control," in *Proc. Intl. Switching Symp.*, Cambridge, MA, June 1972, pp. 530-536.

[34] S.D. Harper, "Automatic Parallel Processing," in *Proc. Conf. Computing and Data Processing Society of Canada*, 1960, pp. 321-331.

[35] T.F. Hatch and J.B. Geyer, "Hardware/Software Interaction on the Honeywell Model 8200," in *Proc. AFIPS FJCC*, 1968, pp. 891-901.

[36] Intel, *iAPX 432 Interface Processor Architecture Reference Manual*. Santa Clara, CA: Intel, 1981.

[37] J.F. Jacobs, *The SAGE Air Defense System - A Personal History*. Bedford, MA: MITRE Corp., 1986.

[38] A.L. Leiner, "System Specifications for the DYSEAC," *JACM 1*, 2 (April 1954) 57-81.

[39] A.L. Leiner and S.N. Alexander, "System Organization of DYSEAC," *IRE Trans. on Elect. Computers EC-3*, 1 (March 1954) 1-10.

[40] H.M. Levy, "The Plessey System 250," chapter 4 of *Capability-Based Computer Systems*. Bedford, MA: Digital Press, 1984.

[41] A.T. Ling and K. Kozarsky, "The RCA 601 System Design," in *Proc. EJCC*, New York, December 1960, pp. 173-177.

[42] N. Lourie, H. Schrimpf, R. Reach, and W. Kahn, "Arithmetic and Control Techniques in a Multiprogram Computer," in *Proc. EJCC*, 1959, pp. 75-81.

[43] B.A. Maynard (ed.), "Honeywell 800 System," in *Manual of Computer Systems*. London: Gee and Company, 1964.

[44] J. Mercel, "Program Interrupt on the Univac Scientific Computer," in *Proc. WJCC*, San Francisco, February 1956, pp. 52-53.

[45] R.A. Olson, "Parallel Processing in a Message-Based Operating System," *IEEE Software 2*, 4 (July 1985) pp. 39-49.

[46] R.E. Porter, "The RW-400 - A New Polymorphic Data System," *Datamation 6*, 1, (Jan./Feb. 1960) 8-14.

[47] M. Satyanarayanan, *Multiprocessors: A Comparative Study*. Englewood Cliffs, NJ: Prentice-Hall, 1980.

[48] R. Serrell, M.M. Astrahan, G.W. Patterson, and I.B. Pyne, "The Evolution of Computing Machines and Systems," *Proc. IRE 50*, 5 (May 1962) 1039-1058.

[49] D.C. Stanga, "Univac 1108 Multiprocessor System," in *Proc. AFIPS SJCC*, vol. 30, Atlantic City, NJ, April 1967, pp. 67-74.

[50] L.D. Stevens, "Engineering Organization of Input and Output for the IBM 701 Electronic Data-Processing Machine," in *Proc. Joint AIEE-IRE-ACM Computer Conf.*, New York, December 1952, pp. 81-85.

[51] J. Svigals, "IBM 7070 Data Processing System," in *Proc. WJCC*, San Francisco, 1959, pp. 222-231.

[52] S. Thakkar, P. Gifford, and G. Fielland, "The Balance Multiprocessor System," *IEEE MICRO*, (February 1988) 57-69.

[53] R.N. Thompson and J.A. Wilkinson, "The D825 Automatic Operating and Scheduling Program," in *Proc. AFIPS SJCC*, 1963, pp. 41-49.

[54] J.E. Thornton, "Parallel Operation in the Control Data 6600," in *Proc. AFIPS SJCC*, 1964, pp. 33-44.

[55] J.E. Thornton, *Design of a Computer: The Control Data 6600*. Glenview, IL: Scott, Foresman and Co., 1970.

[56] H.F. Welsh and H. Lukoff, "The Uniservo - Tape Reader and Recorder," in *Proc. Joint AIEE-IRE-ACM Computer Conf.*, New York, December 1952, pp. 47-53.

[57] R. Wilson, "CDC SCOPE 3.2," in R.M. McKeag, R. Wilson, and D. Huxtable, *Studies in Operating Systems*. New York: Academic Press, 1976.

An Introduction to Disk Drive Modeling

Chris Ruemmler and John Wilkes

Hewlett-Packard Laboratories

odern microprocessor technology is advancing at an incredible rate, and speedups of 40 to 60 percent compounded annually have become the norm. Although disk storage densities are also improving impressively (60 to 80 percent compounded annually), performance improvements have been occurring at only about 7 to 10 percent compounded annually over the last decade. As a result, disk system performance is fast becoming a dominant factor in overall system behavior.

Naturally, researchers want to improve overall I/O performance, of which a large component is the performance of the disk drive itself. This research often involves using analytical or simulation models to compare alternative approaches, and the quality of these models determines the quality of the conclusions; indeed, the wrong modeling assumptions can lead to erroneous conclusions. Nevertheless, little work has been done to develop or describe accurate disk drive models. This may explain the commonplace use of simple, relatively inaccurate models.

We believe there is much room for improvement. This article demonstrates and describes a calibrated, high-quality disk drive model in which the overall error factor is 14 times smaller than that of a simple first-order model. We describe the various disk drive performance components separately, then show how their inclusion improves the simulation model. This enables an informed trade-off between effort and accuracy. In addition, we provide detailed characteristics for two disk drives, as well as a brief description of a simulation environment that uses the disk drive model.

Much research in I/O systems is based on disk drive simulation models, but how good are they? An accurate simulation model should emphasize the performance-critical areas.

Characteristics of modern disk drives

To model disk drives, we must understand how they behave. Thus, we begin with an overview of the current state of the art in nonremovable magnetic disk drives with embedded SCSI (Small Computer Systems Interconnect) controllers, since these are widely available.

Disk drives contain a *mechanism* and a *controller*. The mechanism is made up of the recording components (the rotating disks and the heads that access them) and the positioning components (an arm assembly that moves the heads into the correct position together with a track-following system that keeps it in place). The disk controller contains a microprocessor, some buffer memory, and an interface to the SCSI bus. The controller manages the storage and retrieval of data to and from the mechanism and performs mappings between incoming logical addresses and the physical disk sectors that store the information.

Below, we look more closely at each of these elements, emphasizing features that need to be considered when creating a disk drive model. It will become clear that not all these features are equally important to a model's accuracy.

The recording components. Modern disks range in size from 1.3 to 8 inches in diameter; 2.5, 3.5, and 5.25 inches are the most common sizes today. Smaller disks have less surface area and thus store less data than their larger counterparts; however, they consume less power, can spin faster, and have smaller seek distances. Historically, as storage densities have increased to where 2-3 gigabytes can fit on a single disk, the next-smaller diameter in the series has become the most cost-effective and hence the preferred storage device.

Increased storage density results from two improvements. The first is better linear recording density, which is determined by the maximum rate of flux changes that can be recorded and read back; current values are around 50,000 bits per inch and will approximately double by the end of the decade. The second comes from packing the separate tracks of data more closely together, which is how most of the improvements are occurring. Current values are about 2,500 tracks

per inch, rising to perhaps 20,000 TPI by the end of the decade. The product of these two factors will probably sustain a growth rate above 60 percent per year to the end of the decade.

A single disk contains one, two, or as many as a dozen platters, as shown in Figure 1. The stack of platters rotates in lockstep on a central spindle. Although 3,600 rpm was a de facto standard for many years, spindle rotation speed has increased recently to as much as 7,200 rpm. The median rotation speed is increasing at a compound rate of about 12 percent per year. A higher spin speed increases transfer rates and shortens rotation latencies (the time for data to rotate under the head), but power consumption increases and better bearings are required for the spindle. The spin speed is typically quoted as accurate within 0.5 to 1 percent; in practice, the disk speeds vary slowly around the nominal rate. Although this is perfectly reasonable for the disk's operation, it makes it nearly impossible to model the disk's rotational position some 100-200 revolutions after the last known operation. Fortunately, many I/O operations occur in bursts, so the uncertainty applies only to the first request in the burst.

Each platter surface has an associated disk head responsible for recording (writing) and later sensing (reading) the magnetic flux variations on the platter's surface. The disk drive has a single read-write data channel that can be switched between the heads. This channel is responsible for encoding and decoding the data stream into or from a series of magnetic phase changes stored on the disk. Significant fractions of the

encoded data stream are dedicated to error correction. The application of digital signal processing may soon increase channel speeds above their current 100 megabits per second. (Multichannel disks can support more than one read/write operation at a time, making higher data transfer rates possible. However, these disks are relatively costly because of technical difficulties such as controlling the cross talk between the concurrently active channels and keeping multiple heads aligned on their platters simultaneously. The latter is becoming more difficult as track densities increase.)

The positioning components. Each data surface is set up to store data in a series of concentric circles, or tracks. A single stack of tracks at a common distance from the spindle is called a cylinder. Today's typical 3.5-inch disk has about 2,000 cylinders. As track densities increase, the notion of vertical alignment that is associated with cylinders becomes less and less relevant because track alignment tolerances are simply too fine. Essentially, then, we must consider the tracks on each platter independently.

To access the data stored in a track, the disk head must be moved over it. This is done by attaching each head to a disk arm — a lever that is pivoted near one end on a rotation bearing. All the disk arms are attached to the same rotation pivot, so that moving one head causes the others to move as well. The rotation pivot is more immune to linear shocks than the older scheme of mounting the head on a linear slider.

The positioning system's task is to

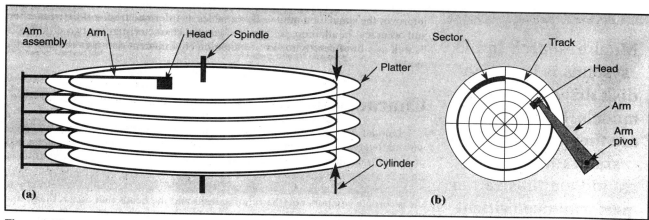

Figure 1. The mechanical components of a disk drive; (a) side view, (b) top view.

ensure that the appropriate head gets to the desired track as quickly as possible and remains there even in the face of external vibration, shocks, and disk flaws (for example, nonconcentric and noncircular tracks).

Seeking. The speed of head movement, or seeking, is limited by the power available for the pivot motor (halving the seek time requires quadrupling the power) and by the arm's stiffness. Accelerations of 30-40g are required to achieve good seek times, and too flexible an arm can twist and bring the head into contact with the platter surface. Smaller diameter disks have correspondingly reduced distances for the head to move. These disks have smaller, lighter arms that are easier to stiffen against flexing — all contributing to shorter seek times.

A seek is composed of

- a *speedup*, where the arm is accelerated until it reaches half of the seek distance or a fixed maximum velocity,
- a *coast* for long seeks, where the arm moves at its maximum velocity,
- a *slowdown*, where the arm is brought to rest close to the desired track, and
- a *settle*, where the disk controller adjusts the head to access the desired location.

Very short seeks (less than, say, two to four cylinders) are dominated by the settle time (1-3 milliseconds). In fact, a seek may not even occur; the head may just resettle into position on a new track. Short seeks (less than 200-400 cylinders) spend almost all of their time in the constant-acceleration phase, and their time is proportional to the square root of the seek distance plus the settle time. Long seeks spend most of their time moving at a constant speed, taking time that is proportional to distance plus a constant overhead. As disks become smaller and track densities increase, the fraction of the total seek time attributed to the settle phase increases.

"Average" seek times are commonly used as a figure of merit for disk drives, but they can be misleading. Such averages are calculated in various ways, a situation further complicated by the fact that independent seeks are rare in practice. Shorter seeks are much more common,[1,2] although their overall frequency is very much a function of the workload and the operating system driving the disk.

If disk requests are completely independent of one another, the average seek distance will be one third of the full stroke. Thus, some sources quote the one-third-stroke seek time as the "average." Others simply quote the full-stroke time divided by three. Another way is to sum the times needed to perform one seek of each size and divide this sum by the number of different seek sizes. Perhaps the best of the commonly used techniques is to weight the seek time by the number of possible seeks of each size: Thus, there are $N - 1$ different single-track seeks

---

Average seek times, commonly used as a disk drive figure of merit, can be misleading.

---

that can be done on a disk with N cylinders, but only one full-stroke seek. This emphasizes the shorter seeks, providing a somewhat better approximation to measured seek-distance profiles. What matters to people building models, however, is the seek-time-versus-distance profile. We encourage manufacturers to include these in their disk specifications, since the only alternative is to determine them experimentally.

The information required to determine how much power to apply to the pivot motor and for how long on a particular seek is encoded in tabular form in the disk controller. Rather than every possible value, a subset of the total is stored, and interpolation is used for intermediate seek distances. The resulting fine-grained seek-time profile can look rather like a sawtooth.[1]

Thermal expansion, arm pivot-bearing stickiness, and other factors occasionally make it necessary to recalibrate these tables. This can take 500-800 milliseconds. Recalibrations are triggered by temperature changes and by timers, so they occur most frequently just after the disk drive is powered up. In steady-state conditions, recalibration occurs only once every 15-30 minutes. Obviously, this can cause difficulties with real-time or guaranteed-bandwidth systems (such as multimedia file servers), so disk drives are now appearing with modified controller firmware that either avoids these visible recalibrations completely or allows the host to schedule their execution.

Track following. Fine-tuning the head position at the end of a seek and keeping the head on the desired track is the function of the track-following system. This system uses positioning information recorded on the disk at manufacturing time to determine whether the disk head is correctly aligned. This information can be embedded in the target surface or recorded on a separate dedicated surface. The former maximizes capacity, so it is most frequently used in disks with a small number of platters. As track density increases, some form of embedded positioning data becomes essential for fine-grained control — perhaps combined with a dedicated surface for coarse positioning data. However, the embedded-data method alone is not good at coping with shock and vibration because feedback information is only available intermittently between data sectors.

The track-following system is also used to perform a head switch. When the controller switches its data channel from one surface to the next in the same cylinder, the new head may need repositioning to accommodate small differences in the alignment of the tracks on the different surfaces. The time taken for such a switch (0.5-1.5 ms) is typically one third to one half of the time taken to do a settle at the end of a seek. Similarly, a track switch (or cylinder switch) occurs when the arm has to be moved from the last track of a cylinder to the first track of the next. This takes about the same time as the end-of-seek settling process. Since settling time increases as track density increases, and the tracks on different platters are becoming less well aligned, head-switching times are approaching those for track switching.

Nowadays, many disk drives use an aggressive, optimistic approach to head settling before a read operation. This means they will attempt a read as soon as the head is near the right track; after all, if the data are unreadable because the settle has not quite completed, nothing has been lost. (There is enough error correction and identification data in a misread sector to ensure that the data are not wrongly interpreted.) On the other hand, if the data are available, it might just save an entire revolution's delay. For obvious reasons, this approach is not taken for a settle that immediately precedes a write. The difference in the settle times for reads and writes can be as much as 0.75 ms.

Data layout. A SCSI disk appears to its client computer as a linear vector of addressable blocks, each typically 256–1,024 bytes in size. These blocks must be mapped to physical sectors on the disk, which are the fixed-size data-layout units on the platters. Separating the logical and physical views of the disk in this way means that the disk can hide bad sectors and do some low-level performance optimizations, but it complicates the task of higher level software that is trying to second-guess the controller (for example, the 4.2 BSD Unix fast file system).

• *Zoning.* Tracks are longer at the outside of a platter than at the inside. To maximize storage capacity, linear density should remain near the maximum that the drive can support; thus, the amount of data stored on each track should scale with its length. This is accomplished on many disks by a technique called zoning, where adjacent disk cylinders are grouped into zones. Zones near the outer edge have more sectors per track than zones on the inside. There are typically 3 to 20 zones, and the number is likely to double by the end of the decade. Since the data transfer rate is proportional to the rate at which the media passes under the head, the outer zones have higher data transfer rates. For example, on a Hewlett-Packard C2240 3.5-inch disk drive, the burst transfer rate (with no intertrack head switches) varies from 3.1 megabytes per second at the inner zone to 5.3 MBps at the outermost zone.[3]

• *Track skewing.* Faster sequential access across track and cylinder boundaries is obtained by skewing logical sector zero on each track by just the amount of time required to cope with

the most likely worst-case head- or track-switch times. This means that data can be read or written at nearly full media speed. Each zone has its own track and cylinder skew factors.

• *Sparing.* It is prohibitively expensive to manufacture perfect surfaces, so disks invariably have some flawed sectors that cannot be used. Flaws are found through extensive testing during manufacturing, and a list is built and recorded on the disk for the controller's use.

So that flawed sectors are not used, references to them are remapped to other portions of the disk. This process, known as *sparing*, is done at the granularity of single sectors or whole tracks. The simplest technique is to remap a

---

By far the most important feature to model is the data-caching characteristics of the disk.

---

bad sector or track to an alternate location. Alternatively, *slip sparing* can be used, in which the logical block that would map to the bad sector and the ones after it are "slipped" by one sector or by a whole track. Many combinations of techniques are possible, so disk drive designers must make a complex trade-off involving performance, expected bad-sector rate, and space utilization. A concrete example is the HP C2240 disk drive, which uses both forms of track-level sparing: slip-track sparing at disk format time and single-track remapping for defects discovered during operation.

The disk controller. The disk controller mediates access to the mechanism, runs the track-following system, transfers data between the disk drive and its client, and, in many cases, manages an embedded cache. Controllers are built around specially designed microprocessors, which often have digital signal processing capability and special interfaces that let them control

hardware directly. The trend is toward more powerful controllers for handling increasingly sophisticated interfaces and for reducing costs by replacing previously dedicated electronic components with firmware.

Interpreting the SCSI requests and performing the appropriate computations takes time. Controller microprocessor speed is increasing just about fast enough to stay ahead of the additional functions the controller is being asked to perform, so controller overhead is slowly declining. It is typically in the range 0.3-1.0 ms.

Bus interface. The most important aspects of a disk drive's host channel are its topology, its transfer rate, and its overhead. SCSI is currently defined as a bus, although alternative versions are being discussed, as are encapsulations of the higher levels of the SCSI protocol across other transmission media, such as Fibre Channel.

Most disk drives use the SCSI bus operation's synchronous mode, which can run at the maximum bus speed. This was 5 MBps with early SCSI buses; differential drivers and the "fast SCSI" specification increased this to 10 MBps a couple of years ago. Disks are now appearing that can drive the bus at 20 MBps ("fast, wide"), and the standard is defined up to 40 MBps. The maximum bus transfer rate is negotiated between the host computer SCSI interface and the disk drive. It appears likely that some serial channel such as Fibre Channel will become a more popular transmission medium at the higher speeds, partly because it would have fewer wires and require a smaller connector.

Because SCSI is a bus, more than one device can be attached to it. SCSI initially supported up to eight addresses, a figure recently doubled with the use of wide SCSI. As the number of devices on the bus increases, contention for the bus can occur, leading to delays in executing data transfers. This matters more if the disk drives are doing large transfers or if their controller overheads are high.

In addition to the time attributed to the transfer rate, the SCSI bus interfaces at the host and disk also require time to establish connections and decipher commands. On SCSI, the cost of the low-level protocol for acquiring control of the bus is on the order of a few microseconds if the bus is idle. The SCSI protocol also allows a disk drive to disconnect from the bus and reconnect later once it has data to transfer. This cycle may take 200 µs but allows other devices to access the bus while the disconnected device processes data, resulting in a higher overall throughput.

In older channel architectures, there was no buffering in the disk drive itself. As a result, if the disk was ready to transfer data to a host whose interface was not ready, then the disk had to wait an entire revolution for the same data to come under the head again before it could retry the transfer. In SCSI, the disk drive is expected to have a speed-matching buffer to avoid this delay, masking the asynchrony between the bus and the mechanism.

Since most SCSI drives take data off the media more slowly than they can send it over the bus, the drive partially fills its buffer before attempting to commence the bus data transfer. The amount of data read into the buffer before the transfer is initiated is called the *fence*; its size is a property of the disk controller, although it can be specified on modern SCSI disk drives by a control command. Write requests can cause the data transfer to the disk's buffer to overlap the head reposition-

ing, up to the limit permitted by the buffer's size. These interactions are illustrated in Figure 2.

Caching of requests. The functions of the speed-matching buffer in the disk drive can be readily extended to include some form of caching for both reads and writes. Caches in disk drives tend to be relatively small (currently 64 kilobytes to 1 megabyte) because of space limitations and the relatively high cost of the dual-ported static RAM needed to keep up with both the disk mechanism and the bus interface.

• *Read-ahead.* A read that hits in the cache can be satisfied "immediately," that is, in just the time needed for the controller to detect the hit and send the data back across the bus. This is usually much quicker than seeking to the data and reading it off the disk, so most modern SCSI disks provide some form of read caching. The most common form is read-ahead — actively retrieving and caching data that the disk expects the host to request momentarily.

As we will show, read caching turns out to be very important when it comes to modeling a disk drive, but it is one of the least well specified areas of disk system behavior. For example, a read

that partially hits in the cache may be partially serviced by the cache (with only the noncached portion being read from disk), or it may simply bypass the cache altogether. Very large read requests may always bypass the cache. Once a block has been read from the cache, some controllers discard it; others keep it in case a subsequent read is directed to the same block.

Some early disk drives with caches did on-arrival read-ahead to minimize rotation latency for whole-track transfers; as soon as the head arrived at the relevant track, the drive started reading into its cache. At the end of one revolution, the full track's worth of data had been read, and this could then be sent to the host without waiting for the data after the logical start point to be reread. (This is sometimes — rather unfortunately — called a "zero-latency read" and is also why disk cache memory is often called a track buffer.) As tracks get longer but request sizes do not, on-arrival caching brings less benefit; for example, with 8-Kbyte accesses to a disk with 32-Kbyte tracks, the maximum benefit is only 25 percent of a rotation time.

On-arrival caching has been largely supplanted by simple read-ahead in which the disk continues to read where

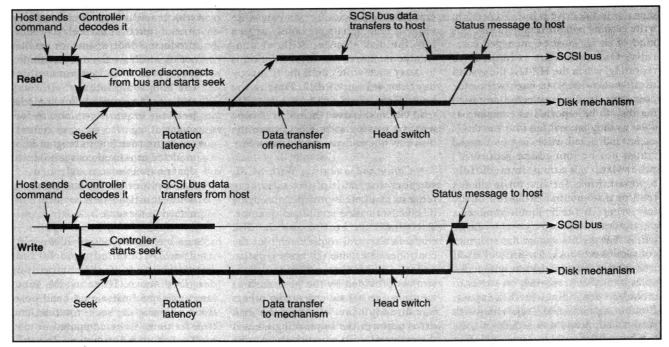

Figure 2. Overlap of bus phases and mechanism activity. The low-level details of bus arbitration and selection have been omitted for simplicity.

the last host request left off. This proves to be optimal for sequential reads and allows them to proceed at the full disk bandwidth. (Without read-ahead, two back-to-back reads would be delayed by almost a full revolution because the disk and host processing time for initiating the second read request would be larger than the inter-sector gap.) Even here there is a policy choice: Should the read-ahead be aggressive, crossing track and cylinder boundaries, or should it stop when the end of the track is reached? Aggressive read-ahead is optimal for sequential access, but it degrades random accesses because head and track switches typically cannot be aborted once initiated, so an unrelated request that arrives while the switch is in progress can be delayed.

A single read-ahead cache can provide effective support for only a single sequential read stream. If two or more sequential read streams are interleaved, the result is no benefit at all. This can be remedied by segmenting the cache so that several unrelated data items can be cached. For example, a 256-Kbyte cache might be split into eight separate 32-Kbyte cache segments by appropriate configuration commands to the disk controller.

• *Write caching.* In most disk drives, the cache is volatile, losing its contents if power to the drive is lost. To perform write caching and prevent data loss, this kind of cache must be managed carefully. One technique is immediate reporting, which the HP-UX file system uses to allow back-to-back writes for user data. It allows selected writes to the disk to be reported as complete as soon as they are written into the disk's cache. Individual writes can be flagged "must not be immediate-reported"; otherwise, a write is immediately reported if it is the first write since a read or a sequential extension of the last write. This technique optimizes a particularly common case — large writes that the file system has split into consecutive blocks. To protect itself from power failures, the file system disables immediate reporting on writes to metadata describing the disk layout. Combining immediate reporting with read-ahead means that sequential data can be written and read from adjacent disk blocks at the disk's full throughput.

Volatile write-cache problems go away if the disk's cache memory can be made nonvolatile. One technique is battery-backed RAM, since a lithium cell can provide 10-year retention. Thus equipped, the disk drive is free to accept all the write requests that will fit in its buffer and acknowledge them all immediately. In addition to the reduced latency for write requests, two throughput benefits also result: (1) Data in a write buffer are often overwritten in place, reducing the amount of data that must be written to the mechanism, and (2) the large number of stored writes makes it possible for the controller to schedule them in near-optimal fashion, so that each takes less time to perform. These issues are discussed in more detail elsewhere.[2]

Simulation is used because disk drives cannot be accurately modeled analytically.

As with read caching, there are several possible policies for handling write requests that hit data previously written into the disk's cache. Without nonvolatile memory, the safest solution is to delay such writes until the first copy has been written to disk. Data in the write cache must also be scanned for read hits; in this case, the buffered copy must be treated as primary, since the disk may not yet have been written to.

• *Command queuing.* With SCSI, support for multiple outstanding requests at a time is provided through a mechanism called command queuing. This allows the host to give the disk controller several requests and let the controller determine the best execution order — subject to additional constraints provided by the host, such as "do this one before any of the others you already have." Letting the disk drive perform the sequencing gives it the potential to do a better job by using its detailed knowledge of the disk's rotation position.[4,5]

Modeling disk drives

With this understanding of the various disk drive performance factors, we are ready to model the behavior of the drives we have just described. We describe our models in sufficient detail to quantify the relative importance of the different components. That way a conscious choice can be made as to how much detail a disk drive performance model needs for a particular application. By selectively enabling various features, we arrive at a model that accurately imitates the behavior of a real drive.

Related work. Disk drive models have been used ever since disk drives became available as storage devices. Because of their nonlinear, state-dependent behavior, disk drives cannot be modeled analytically with any accuracy, so most work in this area uses simulation. Nonetheless, the simplest models merely assume a fixed time for an I/O, or they select times from a uniform distribution. The more elaborate models acknowledge that a disk I/O has separate seek, rotation, and transfer times, but most fail to model these components carefully. Consider, for example, that

• seek times are often modeled as a linear function of seek distance, producing poor results for smaller seeks, which are the most common;
• uniform distributions are used for the rotational latency, although they are inappropriate for nonindependent requests, which are frequent;
• media transfer times are ignored or modeled as a fixed constant dependent on transfer size; and
• bus contention is often ignored when multiple devices are connected to the same bus.

Some previously described work[2,6-8] used more detailed models that avoided many of the limitations described above. These models simulated axial and rotational head positions, allowing the seek, rotation, and transfer times to be computed instead of drawn from a distribution. This article is an extension of simulation work described earlier.[2]

Table 1. Characteristics of the two disk drives analyzed in this article.

Disk Type	Formatted Capacity	Cylinders	Size	Rotational Speed	Average 8KB access	Host Interconnect Type	Max Speed
HP C2200A	335 MB	1,449	5.25"	4,002 rpm	33.6 ms	HP-IB	1.2 MBps
HP 97560	1.3 GB	1,935	5.25"	4,002 rpm	22.8 ms	SCSI-2	10 MBps

The simulator. We built our event-based simulator in C++ using a version of the AT&T tasking library[9] modified locally to support time as a *double* type rather than a *long* type. The tasking library provides a simple but effective simulation environment. In it, tasks represent independent units of activity; when they call *delay(time)*, the simulated time advances. A task can also wait for certain low-level events; it is easy to construct a variety of synchronization mechanisms on top of these primitives. The basic ideas are readily applicable to other simulation environments.

We model a disk drive as two tasks and some additional control structures (Figure 3). One task models the mechanism, including the head and platter (rotation) positions. This task accepts requests of the form "read this much from here" and "seek to there" and executes them one at a time. It also handles the data layout mapping between logical blocks and physical sectors. A second task, the direct memory access engine (DMA engine), models the SCSI bus interface and its transfer engine. This task accepts requests of the form "transfer this request between the host and the disk" and handles them one at a time. A cache object buffers requests between the two tasks and is used in a classic producer-consumer style to manage the asynchronous interactions between the bus interface and the disk mechanism tasks.

The disk drive model fits into a larger system that has items for representing the SCSI bus itself (a semaphore, so that only one device can use the bus at a time), the host interface, synthetic and trace-driven workload generator tasks, and a range of statistics-gathering and -reporting tools.

The disk-related portions of our simulation system consist of about 5,800 lines of commented C++ code. There are also around 7,000 lines of other infrastructure. The simulator can pro-

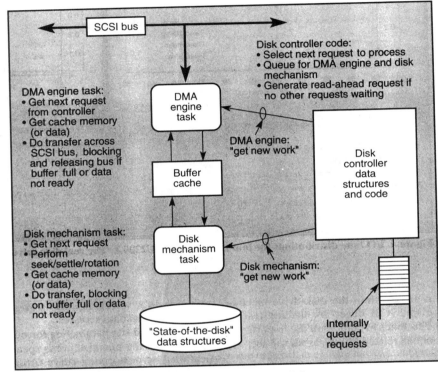

Figure 3. Simulation model structure for a single disk drive.

cess about 2,000 I/Os per second on an HP9000 Series 800 Model H50 system, which has a 96-MHz PA-RISC 7100 processor. This allows about 1 million requests to be serviced in approximately 10 minutes.

Traces. For this study, we selected representative week-long samples from a longer trace series of HP-UX (Unix) computer systems. The systems and the traces have been described in much greater detail elsewhere.[2]

For each request, the traces included data such as start and finish times with a granularity of 1 microsecond, disk address and transfer length, flags such as read/write, and whether the request was marked synchronous or not by the file system. The start time corresponds to the moment when

the disk driver gives the request to the disk, and the finish time corresponds to when the "request completed" interrupt fires. The results we present here do not include time spent queued in the disk driver.

Table 1 describes the disks we singled out for analysis. Since our purpose is to show how the different components of a disk drive model contribute to its accuracy, we selected a noncaching disk drive (the HP C2200A[10]) as our first example so that the cache would not interfere with our analysis of the disk mechanism itself. Later we use the HP 97560 disk drive[11] to show the effects of adding caching. The HP C2200A has an HP-IB (IEEE-488) bus instead of a SCSI interface. From a modeling perspective, the only major difference is that the HP-IB bus

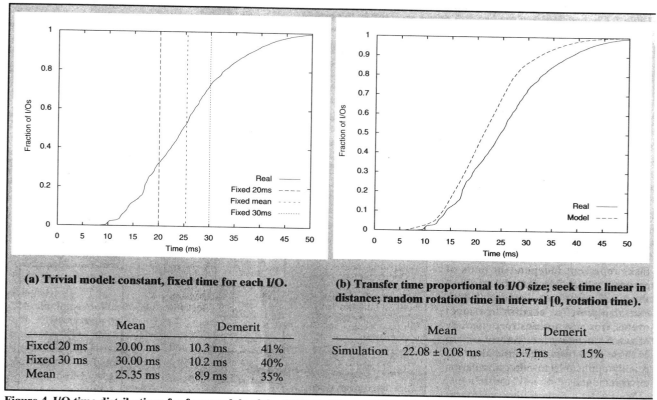

(a) Trivial model: constant, fixed time for each I/O.

(b) Transfer time proportional to I/O size; seek time linear in distance; random rotation time in interval [0, rotation time).

	Mean	Demerit	
Fixed 20 ms	20.00 ms	10.3 ms	41%
Fixed 30 ms	30.00 ms	10.2 ms	40%
Mean	25.35 ms	8.9 ms	35%

	Mean	Demerit	
Simulation	22.08 ± 0.08 ms	3.7 ms	15%

Figure 4. I/O time distributions for four models of the C2200A. The real disk drive has a mean I/O time of 25.36 ± 0.09 ms.

is slower than the disk drive mechanism; SCSI buses are usually faster. This tends to emphasize the importance of bus-related effects, as we will see.

Evaluation. For comparison, we need a metric to evaluate the models. A simple mean execution time for a request is of some value in calibrating a model to the real world, though it provides little differentiation between models. Instead, we plot the time distribution curves for the real drive and the model output and use the root mean square of the horizontal distance between these two curves as our metric. We call this the demerit figure of the model and present it in both absolute terms (as a difference in milliseconds) and relative terms (as a percentage of the mean I/O time). The real trace has a demerit figure of zero — that is, it matches itself exactly.

We encourage other researchers using disk drive models to publish their demerit figures (and preferably the calibration curves). It is important to use a test workload similar to the kind of data one wishes to analyze. For example, a synthetic random I/O load is of little use in calibrating a model that is

being used for workloads with a great many sequential data accesses.

We obtained the parameters for our models from the manufacturer's specifications, by performing curve fitting against the traces, and by direct measurement on the disk drives themselves.

No modeling. The simplest possible "model" uses a constant, fixed time for each I/O. Figure 4a plots two typical values from the literature (20 ms and 30 ms), together with the actual mean I/O time for the week's traced data. This model is not good. Even using the mean I/O time rather than a fixed estimate results in a demerit factor that is 35 percent of the average I/O time.

A simple model. To do better requires remembering state information between requests and modeling the effect of an I/O's length. A straightforward model that does this has the following combination of features:

- a seek time that is linear with the distance, using the single-cylinder and full-stroke seek times pub-

lished in the disk drive specification (see Figure 5),
- no head-settle effects or head-switching costs,
- a rotational delay drawn from a uniform distribution over the interval [0, rotation time),
- a fixed controller overhead, and
- a transfer time linear with the length of the request. (There is an asymmetry in transfer rates across the HP-IB bus: Reads run at 1 MBps, writes at 1.2 MBps. On the C2200A, the media transfer rate of 1.9 MBps is faster than the HP-IB bus, so bus speed dominates.)

Figure 4b shows how this new model fares. We are now at a demerit of only 15 percent of a mean I/O time. This is better, but the demerit itself is still two to three times larger than many of the effects that I/O system designers wish to investigate.

Modeling head-positioning effects. The previous model used a seek time that was a linear function of distance. However, this is not a particularly good match, as Figure 5 shows. The mean difference

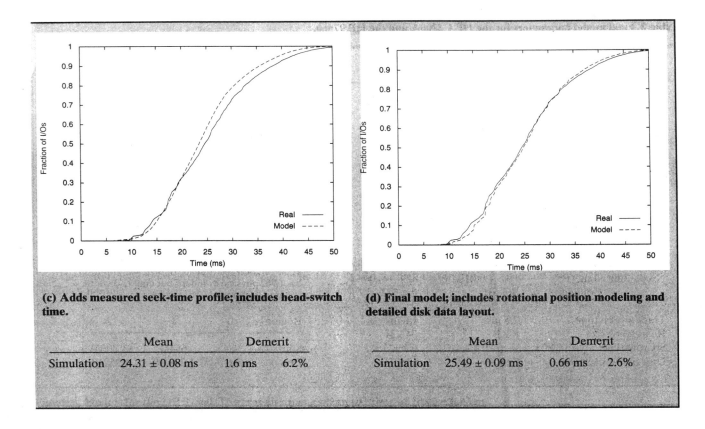

(c) Adds measured seek-time profile; includes head-switch time.

	Mean	Demerit	
Simulation	24.31 ± 0.08 ms	1.6 ms	6.2%

(d) Final model; includes rotational position modeling and detailed disk data layout.

	Mean	Demerit	
Simulation	25.49 ± 0.09 ms	0.66 ms	2.6%

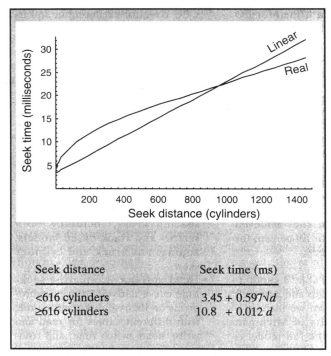

Seek distance	Seek time (ms)
<616 cylinders	$3.45 + 0.597\sqrt{d}$
≥616 cylinders	$10.8 + 0.012\,d$

Figure 5. The graph displays the measured-seek-time-versus-distance curve for the C2200A and a linear interpolation between the manufacturer's published single-cylinder and full-stroke seek times. The accompanying table shows the formula we used to model the real curve.

between the linear seek model and the real one is 2.66 ms, which is a 9 percent error by itself. The table in Figure 5 describes the model we used to approximate the measured seek-time profile for this disk drive. Computing the better model is trivial — a six-line rather than a single-line calculation.

Since we were improving our positioning calculations, we also took the opportunity to model the costs of head and track switching. This was achieved by determining which track and cylinder the request started on and where it ended, and then adding a fixed cost of 2.5 ms for each head and track switch needed to get from the start of the request to its end. Figure 4c shows that the demerit figure has more than halved to 6.2 percent of a mean I/O time.

Modeling rotation position. Only two important performance components are left to model on the C2200A: detailed rotational latency and spare-sector placement. By keeping track of the rotational position of the disk, we can explicitly calculate the rotational latency rather than just drawing it from a uniform distribution. This is done by calculating how many times the disk would have revolved since the start of the simulation, assuming it was spinning at exactly its nominally rated speed. The C2200A uses track and cylinder skewing and sector-based sparing with one spare sector per track. This needs to be accounted for in mapping logical blocks to the physical sectors.

Adding all these factors results in the data shown in Figure 4d. This is a good match, with the model fitting the real disk drive to within 2.6 percent. Table 2 lists all the parameters used in this final model.

Table 2. Final model parameters for the HP C2200A and the HP 97560.

Parameter	HP C2200A	HP 97560
Sector size	256 bytes	512 bytes
Cylinders	1,449	1,962
Tracks per cylinder	8	19
Data sectors per track	113	72
Number of zones	1	1
Track skew	34 sectors	8 sectors
Cylinder skew	43 sectors	18 sectors
Revolution speed	4,002 RPM	4,002 RPM
Controller interface	HP-IB	SCSI-II
Controller reads	1.1 ms	2.2 ms
Overhead writes	5.1 ms	2.2 ms
Seek time short (ms)	$3.45 + 0.597\sqrt{d}$	$3.24 + 0.400\sqrt{d}$
Seek time long (ms)	$10.8 + 0.012d$	$8.00 + 0.008d$
Seek time boundary	$d = 616$	$d = 383$
Track switch time	2.5 ms	1.6 ms
Read fence size	8 KB	64 KB
Sparing type	sector*	track**
Disk buffer cache size	32 KB	128 KB

*The HP C2200A also does track sparing, but the spare regions are at the beginning and end of the data region, so they have no effect on simulation performance. The HP C2200A has one spare sector at the end of each track (giving it 114 sectors per track).

**The HP 97560 does track sparing and has dedicated sparing regions embedded in the data area. The table below shows where the three data regions are located physically on the HP 97560 disk, using the format "cylinder/track" to indicate boundaries in the physical sector space of the disk. This disk has 1,962 physical cylinders, but only 1,935 of these are used to store data; the rest are spares.

Region	0	1	2
Start	1/4	654/0	1,308/0
End	646/3	1,298/18	1,952/18

Modeling data caching. In the discussion so far we have used the C2200A disk drive because it has no buffer cache. When a cache is added to a disk drive, however, complications can arise. This is shown in Figure 6a, where a model incorporating all the features described so far is used to simulate an HP 97560 SCSI disk drive that uses both read-ahead and immediate reporting. The large disparity at small completion times is due to the caching, since about 50 percent of the requests are completed in 3 ms or less. Clearly, caching needs to be modeled if we are to get results closely matching the real disk drive. A demerit of 112 percent is not acceptable!

We added aggressive read-ahead and immediate reporting to the model, as described in the section "Caching of requests." This gave the results shown in Figure 6b. We consider this quite a good match, since the demerit is now only 5.7 percent of the mean I/O time; and since this mean is only half that of the C2200A, the absolute value of the error is comparable.

Two major remaining components can be modeled more accurately: (1) the actual bus speeds achieved in a particular system (these may be less than the drive's rated speed if the host I/O controller imposes a lower rate), and (2) the detailed disk drive controller overheads, which are frequently a combination of interactions between the previous request and the current one; these overheads also depend on the size of the request. Modeling at this level of detail requires heroic efforts, such as applying logic analyzers to SCSI buses. Bruce Worthington and Greg Ganger at the University of Michigan took this approach and managed to fine-tune the controller-overhead and bus-transfer components of a model similar to ours. They achieved demerit figures of 0.4 to 1.9 percent for an HP C2247 disk drive.[12]

Model summary. Table 3 summarizes the different models and how well they did; at the bottom we include a line for the University of Michigan model also. Clearly, the full model is necessary if a good match is required. Since it is not particularly onerous to implement, we encourage others to adopt it. Our full model includes the following details (parameters are provided in Table 2):

- The host I/O device driver: the CPU costs for executing it, and its queuing strategy.
- The SCSI bus, including bus contention effects.
- Disk controller effects: fixed controller overhead, SCSI bus disconnects during mechanism delays, and overlapped bus transfers and mechanism activity.
- Disk buffer cache, including read-ahead, write-behind (immediate reporting), and producer-consumer interlocks between the mechanism and bus transfers.
- Data layout model: reserved sparing areas, including both sector- and track-based models, zoning, and track and cylinder skew.
- Head movement effects: a seek-time curve derived from measurements on the real disks; settle time, with different values for read and write; head-switch time; and rotation latency.

As with any model, we chose to ignore some things. For example, we do not believe it worthwhile to try to model soft-error retries and the effects

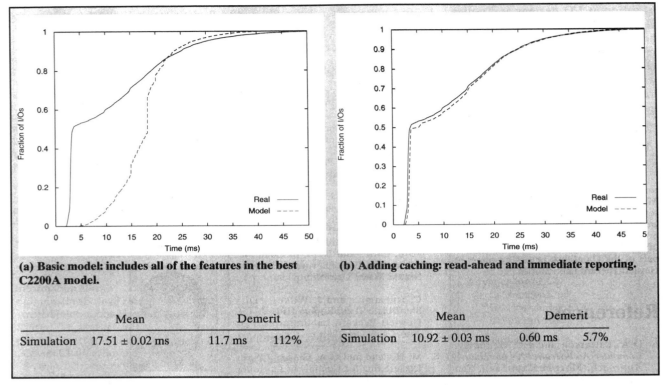

(a) Basic model: includes all of the features in the best C2200A model.

(b) Adding caching: read-ahead and immediate reporting.

	Mean	Demerit			Mean	Demerit
Simulation	17.51 ± 0.02 ms	11.7 ms	112%	Simulation	10.92 ± 0.03 ms	0.60 ms	5.7%

Figure 6. Models for the HP 97560. The real disk had a mean I/O time of 10.47 ± 0.03 ms.

of individual spared sectors or tracks. Likewise, other features (such as a disk drive's sparing policy) are not in themselves very important, although an accurate understanding of the layout effects of sparing is necessary to model rotational positioning effects well.

An accurate model of a disk drive is essential for obtaining good simulation results from I/O studies. Failure to model disk drive behavior can result in quantitative — and in extreme cases, qualitative — errors in an analysis. Careful modeling is neither too difficult nor too costly. We have provided data that enables designers to quantitatively determine the benefits to be gained from investing effort in a disk drive model.

By far the most important feature to model is the data-caching characteristics of the disk (112 percent relative demerit if this is ignored). The next most important features to get right are the data transfer model, including overlaps between mechanism activity and the bus transfers (20 percent demerit), and the seek-time and head-switching costs (9 percent demerit). Although in our evaluation of the C2200A the transfer model

Table 3. Performance figures for the models of three disk drives show greater accuracy as features are added to the model.

Feature	Demerit		Disk Type
Constant mean time	8.9 ms	35%	
Basic model	3.7 ms	15%	HP C2200A
Add head positioning	1.3 ms	6%	
Add rotation position	0.5 ms	3%	
No caching	11.7 ms	112%	HP 97560
Add caching	0.6 ms	6%	
Controller costs	~0.2 ms	1%	HP C2247

had a greater effect than the positioning model, the relative importance will probably be reversed for SCSI drives because there the bus is generally faster than the disk mechanism.

Finally, modeling the rotational position and detailed data layout improved model accuracy by a further factor of nearly two. Modeling rotational position accurately is important for systems that emphasize sequential transfers, which modern file systems are becoming increasingly adept at doing.

Even a good model needs careful calibration and tuning. For example, some of the values we used to get a good fit in our models differ from the manufacturer's published specifications. In addition, we did not have space here to present the quantitative effects of modeling zoning (although our model handles it). These features and others may become particularly important when a workload has large data transfers.

We plan to use our refined disk drive simulation model to explore a variety of different I/O designs and policy choies at host and disk drive levels. We hope to make the source code of our model available to interested researchers later this year, together with calibrated model parameters for a longer list of disk drive types than we have space to describe here. ■

Acknowledgments

Pei Cao contributed greatly to the simulator of which our disk model is a part, and Marvin Keshner provided information on several of the underlying storage technology trends. Tim Sullivan and Patricia Jacobson provided helpful feedback on earlier drafts of this article. This work was performed as part of the DataMesh research project at Hewlett-Packard Laboratories.

References

1. D.A. Patterson and J.L. Hennessy, *Computer Architecture: A Quantitative Approach*, Morgan Kaufmann, San Mateo, Calif., 1990.

2. C. Ruemmler and J. Wilkes, "Unix Disk Access Patterns," *Proc. Winter 1993 Usenix Conf.*, Usenix, Sunset Beach, Calif., Jan. 1993, pp. 405-420.

3. Hewlett-Packard Co., Boise, Idaho, *HP C2240 Series 3.5-Inch SCSI-2 Disk Drive: Technical Reference Manual*, part number 5960-8346, 2nd ed., Apr. 1992.

4. M. Seltzer, P. Chen, and J. Ousterhout, "Disk Scheduling Revisited," *Proc. Winter 1990 Usenix Conf.*, Usenix, Sunset Beach, Calif., Jan. 1990, pp. 313-323.

5. D.M. Jacobson and J. Wilkes, "Disk-Scheduling Algorithms Based on Rotational Position," Tech. Report HPL-CSP-91-7, Hewlett-Packard Laboratories, Palo Alto, Calif., Feb. 1991.

6. C.A. Thekkath, J. Wilkes, and E.D. Lazowska, "Techniques for File System Simulation," published simultaneously as Tech. Reports HPL-92-131 and 92-09-08, Hewlett-Packard Laboratories, Palo Alto, Calif., and Dept. of Computer Science and Eng., Univ. of Washington, Seattle, Wash., Oct. 1992.

7. C. Ruemmler and J. Wilkes, "Disk Shuffling," Tech. Report HPL-91-156, Hewlett-Packard Laboratories, Palo Alto, Calif., Oct. 1991.

8. M. Holland and G.A. Gibson, "Parity Declustering for Continuous Operation in Redundant Disk Arrays," *Proc. Fifth Int'l Conf. Architectural Support for Programming Languages and Operating Systems*, published as a special issue of *Computer Architecutre News*, Vol. 20, 1992, pp. 23-35.

9. *Unix System V AT&T C++ Language System Release 2.0, Selected Readings*, AT&T select code 307-144, 1989.

10. Hewlett-Packard Co., Boise, Idaho, *HP Series 6000 Disk Storage Systems Owner's Manual for Models 335H, 670H, and 670XP*, part number C2200-90901, Feb. 1990.

11. Hewlett-Packard Co., Boise, Idaho, *HP 97556, 97558, and 97560 5.25-Inch SCSI Disk Drives: Technical Reference Manual*, part number 5960-0115, June 1991.

12. B. Worthington, G. Ganger, and Y. Patt, "Scheduling Algorithms for Modern Disk Drives," to be published in *Proc. ACM SIGMetrics Conf.*, May 1994.

Chris Ruemmler is a software engineer at Hewlett-Packard, where he works in the area of performance analysis. His technical interests include architectural design, system performance, and operating systems. He graduated with BA and MS degrees in computer science (1991 and 1993, respectively) from the University of California at Berkeley.

John Wilkes has worked since 1982 as a researcher and project manager at Hewlett-Packard Laboratories. His current research interest is high-performance, high-availability storage systems. He is also interested in performance modeling, and interconnects and resource management for scalable systems. He enjoys interacting with the academic research community. Wilkes graduated from the University of Cambridge with BA and MA degrees in physics (1978 and 1980, respectively) and a Diploma and PhD in computer science (1979 and 1984, respectively).

A Case for Redundant Arrays of Inexpensive Disks (RAID)

David A. Patterson, Garth Gibson, and Randy H. Katz

Computer Science Division
Department of Electrical Engineering and Computer Sciences
571 Evans Hall
University of California
Berkeley, CA 94720
(pattrsn@ginger.berkeley.edu)

Abstract. Increasing performance of CPUs and memories will be squandered if not matched by a similar performance increase in I/O. While the capacity of Single Large Expensive Disks (SLED) has grown rapidly, the performance improvement of SLED has been modest. Redundant Arrays of Inexpensive Disks (RAID), based on the magnetic disk technology developed for personal computers, offers an attractive alternative to SLED, promising improvements of an order of magnitude in performance, reliability, power consumption, and scalability. This paper introduces five levels of RAIDs, giving their relative cost/performance, and compares RAID to an IBM 3380 and a Fujitsu Super Eagle.

1. Background: Rising CPU and Memory Performance

The users of computers are currently enjoying unprecedented growth in the speed of computers. Gordon Bell said that between 1974 and 1984, single chip computers improved in performance by 40% per year, about twice the rate of minicomputers [Bell 84]. In the following year Bill Joy predicted an even faster growth [Joy 85]:

$$MIPS = 2^{Year-1984}$$

Mainframe and supercomputer manufacturers, having difficulty keeping pace with the rapid growth predicted by "Joy's Law," cope by offering multiprocessors as their top-of-the-line product.

But a fast CPU does not a fast system make. Gene Amdahl related CPU speed to main memory size using this rule [Siewiorek 82]:

Each CPU instruction per second requires one byte of main memory;

If computer system costs are not to be dominated by the cost of memory, then Amdahl's constant suggests that memory chip capacity should grow at the same rate. Gordon Moore predicted that growth rate over 20 years ago:

$$transistors/chip = 2^{Year-1964}$$

As predicted by Moore's Law, RAMs have quadrupled in capacity every two [Moore 75] to three years [Myers 86].

Recently the ratio of megabytes of main memory to MIPS has been defined as *alpha* [Garcia 84], with Amdahl's constant meaning alpha = 1. In part because of the rapid drop of memory prices, main memory sizes have grown faster than CPU speeds and many machines are shipped today with alphas of 3 or higher.

To maintain the balance of costs in computer systems, secondary storage must match the advances in other parts of the system. A key meas-
ure of magnetic disk technology is the growth in the maximum number of bits that can be stored per square inch, or the bits per inch in a track times the number of tracks per inch. Called M.A.D., for maximal areal density, the "First Law in Disk Density" predicts [Frank87] :

$$MAD = 10^{(Year-1971)/10}$$

Magnetic disk technology has doubled capacity and halved price every three years, in line with the growth rate of semiconductor memory, and in practice between 1967 and 1979 the disk capacity of the average IBM data processing system more than kept up with its main memory [Stevens81].

Capacity is not the only memory characteristic that must grow rapidly to maintain system balance, since the speed with which instructions and data are delivered to a CPU also determines its ultimate performance. The speed of main memory has kept pace for two reasons:
(1) the invention of caches, showing that a small buffer can be managed automatically to contain a substantial fraction of memory references;
(2) and the SRAM technology, used to build caches, whose speed has improved at the rate of 40% to 100% per year.

In contrast to primary memory technologies, the performance of single large expensive magnetic disks (SLED) has improved at a modest rate. These *mechanical* devices are dominated by the seek and the rotation delays: from 1971 to 1981, the raw seek time for a high-end IBM disk improved by only a factor of two while the rotation time did not change[Harker81]. Greater density means a higher transfer rate when the information is found, and extra heads can reduce the average seek time, but the raw seek time only improved at a rate of 7% per year. There is no reason to expect a faster rate in the near future.

To maintain balance, computer systems have been using even larger main memories or solid state disks to buffer some of the I/O activity. This may be a fine solution for applications whose I/O activity has locality of reference and for which volatility is not an issue, but applications dominated by a high rate of random requests for small pieces of data (such as transaction-processing) or by a low number of requests for massive amounts of data (such as large simulations running on supercomputers) are facing a serious performance limitation.

2. The Pending I/O Crisis

What is the impact of improving the performance of some pieces of a problem while leaving others the same? Amdahl's answer is now known as Amdahl's Law [Amdahl67]:

$$S = \frac{1}{(1-f) + f/k}$$

where:
  S = the effective speedup;
  f = fraction of work in faster mode; and
  k = speedup while in faster mode.

Suppose that some current applications spend 10% of their time in I/O. Then when computers are 10X faster--according to Bill Joy in just over three years--then Amdahl's Law predicts effective speedup will be only 5X. When we have computers 100X faster--via evolution of uniprocessors or by multiprocessors--this application will be less than 10X faster, wasting 90% of the potential speedup.

While we can imagine improvements in software file systems via buffering for near term I/O demands, we need innovation to avoid an I/O crisis [Boral 83].

3. A Solution: Arrays of Inexpensive Disks

Rapid improvements in capacity of large disks have not been the only target of disk designers, since personal computers have created a market for inexpensive magnetic disks. These lower cost disks have lower performance as well as less capacity. Table I below compares the top-of-the-line IBM 3380 model AK4 mainframe disk, Fujitsu M2361A "Super Eagle" minicomputer disk, and the Conner Peripherals CP 3100 personal computer disk.

Characteristics	IBM 3380	Fujitsu M2361A	Conners CP3100	3380 v. 3100	2361 v 3100
				(>1 means 3100 is better)	
Disk diameter (inches)	14	10.5	3.5	4	3
Formatted Data Capacity (MB)	7500	600	100	.01	.2
Price/MB(controller incl.)	$18-$10	$20-$17	$10-$7	1-2.5	1.7-3
MTTF Rated (hours)	30,000	20,000	30,000	1	1.5
MTTF in practice (hours)	100,000	?	?	?	?
No. Actuators	4	1	1	.2	1
Maximum I/O's/second/Actuator	50	40	30	.6	.8
Typical I/O's/second/Actuator	30	24	20	.7	.8
Maximum I/O's/second/box	200	40	30	.2	.8
Typical I/O's/second/box	120	24	20	.2	.8
Transfer Rate (MB/sec)	3	2.5	1	.3	.4
Power/box (W)	6,600	640	10	660	64
Volume (cu. ft.)	24	3.4	.03	800	110

Table I. *Comparison of IBM 3380 disk model AK4 for mainframe computers, the Fujitsu M2361A "Super Eagle" disk for minicomputers, and the Conners Peripherals CP 3100 disk for personal computers. By "Maximum I/O's/second" we mean the maximum number of average seeks and average rotates for a single sector access. Cost and reliability information on the 3380 comes from widespread experience [IBM 87] [Gawlick87] and the information on the Fujitsu from the manual [Fujitsu 87], while some numbers on the new CP3100 are based on speculation. The price per megabyte is given as a range to allow for different prices for volume discount and different mark-up practices of the vendors. (The 8 watt maximum power of the CP3100 was increased to 10 watts to allow for the inefficiency of an external power supply, since the other drives contain their own power supplies).*

One surprising fact is that the number of I/Os per second per actuator in an inexpensive disk is within a factor of two of the large disks. In several of the remaining metrics, including price per megabyte, the inexpensive disk is superior or equal to the large disks. •

The small size and low power are even more impressive since disks such as the CP3100 contain full track buffers *and* most functions of the traditional mainframe controller. Small disk manufacturers can provide such functions in high volume disks because of the efforts of standards committees in defining higher level peripheral interfaces, such as the ANSI X3.131-1986 Small Computer System Interface (SCSI). Such standards have encouraged companies like Adeptec to offer SCSI interfaces as single chips, in turn allowing disk companies to *embed* mainframe controller functions at low cost. Figure 1 compares the traditional mainframe disk approach and the small computer disk approach. The same SCSI interface chip embedded as a controller in every disk can also be used as the direct memory access (DMA) device at the other end of the SCSI bus.

Such characteristics lead to our proposal for building I/O systems as arrays of inexpensive disks, either interleaved for the large transfers of supercomputers [Kim 86][Livny 87][Salem86] or independent for the many small transfers of transaction processing. Using the information in Table I, 75 inexpensive disks potentially have 12 times the I/O bandwidth of the IBM 3380 and the same capacity, with lower power consumption and cost.

4. Caveats

We cannot explore all issues associated with such arrays in the space available in this paper, so we concentrate on fundamental estimates of

price-performance and reliability. Our reasoning is that if there are no advantages in price-performance or terrible disadvantages in reliability, then there is no need to explore further. We characterize a transaction-processing workload to evaluate performance of a collection of inexpensive disks, but remember that such a collection is just one hardware component of a complete tranaction-processing system. While designing a complete TPS based on these ideas is enticing, we will resist that temptation in this paper. Cabling and packaging, certainly an issue in the cost and reliability of an array of many inexpensive disks, is also beyond this paper's scope.

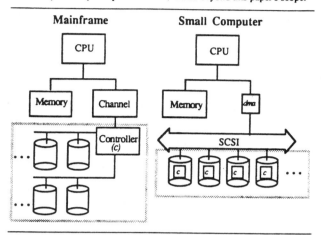

Figure 1. *Comparison of organizations for typical mainframe and small computer disk interfaces. Single chip SCSI interfaces such as the Adaptec AIC-6250 allow the small computer to use a single chip to be the DMA interface as well as provide an embedded controller for each disk [Adeptec 87]. (The price per megabyte in Table I includes everything in the shaded boxes above.)*

5. And Now The Bad News: Reliability

The unreliability of disks forces computer systems managers to make backup versions of information quite frequently in case of failure. What would be the impact on reliability of having a hundredfold increase in disks? Assuming a constant failure rate--that is, an exponentially distributed time to failure--and that failures are independent--both assumptions made by disk manufacturers when calculating the Mean Time To Failure (MTTF)--the reliability of an array of disks is:

$$MTTF \ of \ a \ Disk \ Array \ = \ \frac{MTTF \ of \ a \ Single \ Disk}{Number \ of \ Disks \ in \ the \ Array}$$

Using the information in Table I, the MTTF of 100 CP 3100 disks is 30,000/100 = 300 hours, or less than 2 weeks. Compared to the 30,000 hour (> 3 years) MTTF of the IBM 3380, this is dismal. If we consider scaling the array to 1000 disks, then the MTTF is 30 hours or about one day, requiring an adjective worse than dismal.

Without fault tolerance, large arrays of inexpensive disks are too unreliable to be useful.

6. A Better Solution: RAID

To overcome the reliability challenge, we must make use of extra disks containing redundant information to recover the original information when a disk fails. Our acronym for these Redundant Arrays of Inexpensive Disks is *RAID*. To simplify the explanation of our final proposal and to avoid confusion with previous work, we give a taxonomy of five different organizations of disk arrays, beginning with mirrored disks and progressing through a variety of alternatives with differing performance and reliability. We refer to each organization as a RAID *level*.

The reader should be forewarned that we describe all levels as if implemented in hardware solely to simplify the presentation, for RAID ideas are applicable to software implementations as well as hardware.

Reliability. Our basic approach will be to break the arrays into reliability groups, with each group having extra "check" disks containing redundant information. When a disk fails we assume that within a short time the failed disk will be replaced and the information will be reconstructed on to the new disk using the redundant information. This time is called the mean time to repair (MTTR). The MTTR can be reduced if the system includes extra disks to act as "hot" standby spares; when a disk fails, a replacement disk is switched in electronically. Periodically a human operator replaces all failed disks. Here are other terms that we use:

D = total number of disks with data (not including extra check disks);
G = number of data disks in a *group* (not including extra check disks);
C = number of check disks in a group;
$n_G = D/G$ = number of groups;

As mentioned above we make the same assumptions that disk manufacturers make--that failures are exponential and independent. (An earthquake or power surge is a situation where an array of disks might not fail independently.) Since these reliability predictions will be very high, we want to emphasize that the reliability is only of the the disk-head assemblies with this failure model, and not the whole software and electronic system. In addition, in our view the pace of technology means extremely high MTTF are "overkill"--for, independent of expected lifetime, users will replace obsolete disks. After all, how many people are still using 20 year old disks?

The general MTTF calculation for single-error repairing RAID is given in two steps. First, the group MTTF is:

$$MTTF_{Group} = \frac{MTTF_{Disk}}{G+C} * \frac{1}{\text{Probability of another failure in a group before repairing the dead disk}}$$

As more formally derived in the appendix, the probability of a second failure before the first has been repaired is:

$$\text{Probability of Another Failure} = \frac{MTTR}{MTTF_{Disk}/(\text{No. Disks}-1)} = \frac{MTTR}{MTTF_{Disk}/(G+C-1)}$$

The intuition behind the formal calculation in the appendix comes from trying to calculate the average number of second disk failures during the repair time for X single disk failures. Since we assume that disk failures occur at a uniform rate, this average number of second failures during the repair time for X first failures is

$$\frac{X*MTTR}{MTTF \text{ of remaining disks in the group}}$$

The average number of second failures for a single disk is then

$$\frac{MTTR}{MTTF_{Disk}/\text{ No. of remaining disks in the group}}$$

The MTTF of the remaining disks is just the MTTF of a single disk divided by the number of good disks in the group, giving the result above.

The second step is the reliability of the whole system, which is approximately (since $MTTF_{Group}$ is not quite distributed exponentially):

$$MTTF_{RAID} = \frac{MTTF_{Group}}{n_G}$$

Plugging it all together, we get:

$$MTTF_{RAID} = \frac{MTTF_{Disk}}{G+C} * \frac{MTTF_{Disk}}{(G+C-1)*MTTR} * \frac{1}{n_G}$$

$$= \frac{(MTTF_{Disk})^2}{(G+C)*n_G * (G+C-1)*MTTR}$$

$$MTTF_{RAID} = \frac{(MTTF_{Disk})^2}{(D+C*n_G)*(G+C-1)*MTTR}$$

Since the formula is the same for each level, we make the abstract numbers concrete using these parameters as appropriate: D=100 total data disks, G=10 data disks per group, $MTTF_{Disk}$ = 30,000 hours, $MTTR$ = 1 hour, with the check disks per group C determined by the RAID level.

Reliability Overhead Cost. This is simply the extra check disks, expressed as a percentage of the number of data disks D. As we shall see below, the cost varies with RAID level from 100% down to 4%.

Useable Storage Capacity Percentage. Another way to express this reliability overhead is in terms of the percentage of the total capacity of data disks *and* check disks that can be used to store data. Depending on the organization, this varies from a low of 50% to a high of 96%.

Performance. Since supercomputer applications and transaction-processing systems have different access patterns and rates, we need different metrics to evaluate both. For supercomputers we count the number of reads and writes per second for large blocks of data, with large defined as getting at least one sector from each data disk in a group. During large transfers all the disks in a group act as a single unit, each reading or writing a portion of the large data block in parallel.

A better measure for transaction-processing systems is the number of **individual** reads or writes per second. Since transaction-processing systems (e.g., debits/credits) use a read-modify-write sequence of disk accesses, we include that metric as well. Ideally during small transfers each disk in a group can act independently, either reading or writing independent information. In summary supercomputer applications need a *high data rate* while transaction-processing need a *high I/O rate.*

For both the large and small transfer calculations we assume the minimum user request is a sector, that a sector is small relative to a track, and that there is enough work to keep every device busy. Thus sector size affects both disk storage efficiency and transfer size. Figure 2 shows the ideal operation of large and small disk accesses in a RAID.

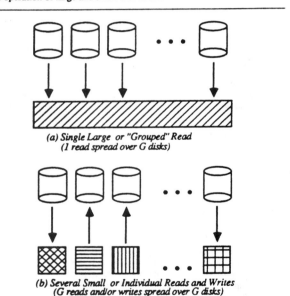

(a) Single Large or "Grouped" Read
(1 read spread over G disks)

(b) Several Small or Individual Reads and Writes
(G reads and/or writes spread over G disks)

Figure 2. *Large transfer vs. small transfers in a group of G disks.*

The six performance metrics are then the number of reads, writes, and read-modify-writes per second for both large (grouped) or small (individual) transfers. Rather than give absolute numbers for each metric, we calculate efficiency: the number of events per second for a RAID relative to the corresponding events per second for a single disk. (This is Boral's I/O bandwidth per gigabyte [Boral 83] scaled to gigabytes per disk.) In this paper we are after fundamental differences so we use simple, deterministic throughput measures for our performance metric rather than latency.

Effective Performance Per Disk. The cost of disks can be a large portion of the cost of a database system, so the I/O performance per disk--factoring in the overhead of the check disks--suggests the cost/performance of a system. This is the bottom line for a RAID.

7. First Level RAID: Mirrored Disks

Mirrored disks are a traditional approach for improving reliability of magnetic disks. This is the most expensive option we consider since all disks are duplicated ($G=1$ and $C=1$), and every write to a data disk is also a write to a check disk. Tandem doubles the number of controllers for fault tolerance, allowing an optimized version of mirrored disks that lets reads occur in parallel. Table II shows the metrics for a Level 1 RAID assuming this optimization.

MTTF	Exceeds Useful Product Lifetime	
	(4,500,000 hrs or > 500 years)	
Total Number of Disks	2D	
Overhead Cost	100%	
Useable Storage Capacity	50%	
Events/Sec vs. Single Disk	Full RAID	Efficiency Per Disk
Large (or Grouped) Reads	2D/S	1.00/S
Large (or Grouped) Writes	D/S	.50/S
Large (or Grouped) R-M-W	4D/3S	.67/S
Small (or Individual) Reads	2D	1.00
Small (or Individual) Writes	D	.50
Small (or Individual) R-M-W	4D/3	.67

Table II. *Characteristics of Level 1 RAID. Here we assume that writes are not slowed by waiting for the second write to complete because the slowdown for writing 2 disks is minor compared to the slowdown S for writing a whole group of 10 to 25 disks. Unlike a "pure" mirrored scheme with extra disks that are invisible to the software, we assume an optimized scheme with twice as many controllers allowing parallel reads to all disks, giving full disk bandwidth for large reads and allowing the reads of read-modify-writes to occur in parallel.*

When individual accesses are distributed across multiple disks, average queueing, seek, and rotate delays may differ from the single disk case. Although bandwidth may be unchanged, it is distributed more evenly, reducing variance in queueing delay and, if the disk load is not too high, also reducing the expected queueing delay through parallelism [Livny 87]. When many arms seek to the same track then rotate to the described sector, the average seek and rotate time will be larger than the average for a single disk, tending toward the worst case times. This affect should not generally more than double the average access time to a single sector while still getting many sectors in parallel. In the special case of mirrored disks with sufficient controllers, the choice between arms that can read any data sector will reduce the time for the average read seek by up to 45% [Bitton 88].

To allow for these factors but to retain our fundamental emphasis we apply a slowdown factor, S, when there are more than two disks in a group. In general, $1 \leq S \leq 2$ whenever groups of disk work in parallel. With synchronous disks the spindles of all disks in the group are synchronous so that the corresponding sectors of a group of disks pass under the heads simultaneously,[Kurzweil 88] so for synchronous disks there is no slowdown and $S = 1$. Since a Level 1 RAID has only one data disk in its group, we assume that the large transfer requires the same number of disks acting in concert as found in groups of the higher level RAIDs: 10 to 25 disks.

Duplicating all disks can mean doubling the cost of the database system or using only 50% of the disk storage capacity. Such largess inspires the next levels of RAID.

8. Second Level RAID: Hamming Code for ECC

The history of main memory organizations suggests a way to reduce the cost of reliability. With the introduction of 4K and 16K DRAMs, computer designers discovered that these new devices were subject to losing information due to alpha particles. Since there were many single bit DRAMs in a system and since they were usually accessed in groups of 16 to 64 chips at a time, system designers added redundant chips to correct single errors and to detect double errors in each group. This increased the number of memory chips by 12% to 38%--depending on the size of the group--but it significantly improved reliability.

As long as all the data bits in a group are read or written together, there is no impact on performance. However, reads of less than the group size require reading the whole group to be sure the information is correct, and writes to a portion of the group mean three steps:

1) a read step to get all the rest of the data;
2) a modify step to merge the new and old information;
3) a write step to write the full group, including check information.

Since we have scores of disks in a RAID and since some accesses are to groups of disks, we can mimic the DRAM solution by bit-interleaving the data across the disks of a group and then add enough check disks to detect and correct a single error. A single parity disk can detect a single error, but to correct an error we need enough check disks to identify the disk with the error. For a group size of 10 data disks (G) we need 4 check disks (C) in total, and if $G = 25$ then $C = 5$ [Hamming50]. To keep down the cost of redundancy, we assume the group size will vary from 10 to 25.

Since our individual data transfer unit is just a sector, bit-interleaved disks mean that a large transfer for this RAID must be at least G sectors. Like DRAMs, reads to a smaller amount implies reading a full sector from each of the bit-interleaved disks in a group, and writes of a single unit involve the read-modify-write cycle to all the disks. Table III shows the metrics of this Level 2 RAID.

MTTF		Exceeds Useful Lifetime			
		G=10		G=25	
		(494,500 hrs		(103,500 hrs	
		or >50 years)		or 12 years)	
Total Number of Disks		1.40D		1.20D	
Overhead Cost		40%		20%	
Useable Storage Capacity		71%		83%	
Events/Sec	Full RAID	Efficiency Per Disk		Efficiency Per Disk	
(vs. Single Disk)		L2	L2/L1	L2	L2/L1
Large Reads	D/S	.71/S	71%	.86/S	86%
Large Writes	D/S	.71/S	143%	.86/S	172%
Large R-M-W	D/S	.71/S	107%	.86/S	129%
Small Reads	D/SG	.07/S	6%	.03/S	3%
Small Writes	D/2SG	.04/S	6%	.02/S	3%
Small R-M-W	D/SG	.07/S	9%	.03/S	4%

Table III. *Characteristics of a Level 2 RAID. The L2/L1 column gives the % performance of level 2 in terms of level 1 (>100% means L2 is faster). As long as the transfer unit is large enough to spread over all the data disks of a group, the large I/Os get the full bandwidth of each disk, divided by S to allow all disks in a group to complete. Level 1 large reads are faster because data is duplicated and so the redundancy disks can also do independent accesses. Small I/Os still require accessing all the disks in a group, so only D/G small I/Os can happen at a time, again divided by S to allow a group of disks to finish. Small Level 2 writes are like small R-M-W because full sectors must be read before new data can be written onto part of each sector.*

For large writes, the level 2 system has the same performance as level 1 even though it uses fewer check disks, and so on a per disk basis it outperforms level 1. For small data transfers the performance is dismal either for the whole system or per disk; all the disks of a group must be accessed for a small transfer, limiting the maximum number of simultaneous accesses to D/G. We also include the slowdown factor S since the access must wait for all the disks to complete.

Thus level 2 RAID is desirable for supercomputers but inappropriate for transaction processing systems, with increasing group size increasing the disparity in performance per disk for the two applications. In recognition of this fact, Thinking Machines Incorporated announced a Level 2 RAID this year for its Connection Machine supercomputer called the "Data Vault," with G = 32 and C = 8, including one hot standby spare [Hillis 87].

Before improving small data transfers, we concentrate once more on lowering the cost.

9. Third Level RAID: Single Check Disk Per Group

Most check disks in the level 2 RAID are used to determine which disk failed, for only one redundant parity disk is needed to detect an error. These extra disks are truly "redundant" since most disk controllers can already detect if a disk failed: either through special signals provided in the disk interface or the extra checking information at the end of a sector used to detect and correct soft errors. So information on the failed disk can be reconstructed by calculating the parity of the remaining good disks and then comparing bit-by-bit to the parity calculated for the original full group. When these two parities agree, the failed bit was a 0; otherwise it was a 1. If the check disk is the failure, just read all the data disks and store the group parity in the replacement disk.

Reducing the check disks to one per group (C=1) reduces the overhead cost to between 4% and 10% for the group sizes considered here. The performance for the third level RAID system is the same as the Level 2 RAID, but the effective performance per disk increases since it needs fewer check disks. This reduction in total disks also increases reliability, but since it is still larger than the useful lifetime of disks, this is a minor point. One advantage of a level 2 system over level 3 is that the extra check information associated with each sector to correct soft errors is not needed, increasing the capacity per disk by perhaps 10%. Level 2 also allows all soft errors to be corrected "on the fly" without having to reread a sector. Table IV summarizes the third level RAID characteristics and Figure 3 compares the sector layout and check disks for levels 2 and 3.

MTTF		Exceeds Useful Lifetime	
		G=10	G=25
		(820,000 hrs or >90 years)	(346,000 hrs or 40 years)
Total Number of Disks		1.10D	1.04D
Overhead Cost		10%	4%
Useable Storage Capacity		91%	96%

Events/Sec (vs. Single Disk)	Full RAID	Efficiency Per Disk			Efficiency Per Disk		
		L3	L3/L2	L3/L1	L3	L3/L2	L3/L1
Large Reads	D/S	.91/S	127%	91%	.96/S	112%	96%
Large Writes	D/S	.91/S	127%	182%	.96/S	112%	192%
Large R-M-W	D/S	.91/S	127%	136%	.96/S	112%	142%
Small Reads	D/SG	.09/S	127%	8%	.04/S	112%	3%
Small Writes	D/2SG	.05/S	127%	8%	.02/S	112%	3%
Small R-M-W	D/SG	.09/S	127%	11%	.04/S	112%	5%

Table IV. Characteristics of a Level 3 RAID. The L3/L2 column gives the % performance of L3 in terms of L2 and the L3/L1 column gives it in terms of L1 (>100% means L3 is faster). The performance for the full systems is the same in RAID levels 2 and 3, but since there are fewer check disks the performance per disk improves.

Park and Balasubramanian proposed a third level RAID system without suggesting a particular application [Park86]. Our calculations suggest it is a much better match to supercomputer applications than to transaction processing systems. This year two disk manufacturers have announced level 3 RAIDs for such applications using synchronized 5.25 inch disks with G=4 and C=1: one from Maxtor and one from Micropolis [Maginnis 87].

This third level has brought the reliability overhead cost to its lowest level, so in the last two levels we improve performance of small accesses without changing cost or reliability.

10. Fourth Level RAID: Independent Reads/Writes

Spreading a transfer across all disks within the group has the following advantage:

- Large or grouped transfer time is reduced because transfer bandwidth of the entire array can be exploited.

But it has the following disadvantages as well:

- Reading/writing to a disk in a group requires reading/writing to all the disks in a group; levels 2 and 3 RAIDs can perform only one I/O at a time per group.
- If the disks are not synchronized, you do not see average seek and rotational delays; the observed delays should move towards the worst case, hence the S factor in the equations above.

This fourth level RAID improves performance of small transfers through parallelism--the ability to do more than one I/O per group at a time. We no longer spread the individual transfer information across several disks, but keep each individual unit in a single disk.

The virtue of bit-interleaving is the easy calculation of the Hamming code needed to detect or correct errors in level 2. But recall that in the third level RAID we rely on the disk controller to detect errors within a single disk sector. Hence, if we store an individual transfer unit in a single sector, we can detect errors on an individual read without accessing any other disk. Figure 3 shows the different ways the information is stored in a sector for

RAID levels 2, 3, and 4. By storing a whole transfer unit in a sector, reads can be independent and operate at the maximum rate of a disk yet still detect errors. Thus the primary change between level 3 and 4 is that we interleave data between disks at the sector level rather than at the bit level.

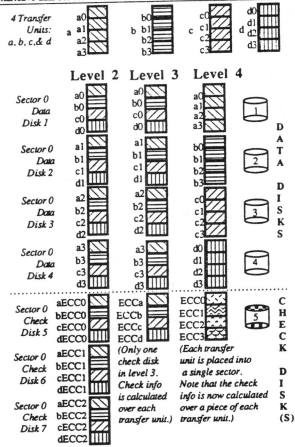

Figure 3. Comparison of location of data and check information in sectors for RAID levels 2, 3, and 4 for G=4. Not shown is the small amount of check information per sector added by the disk controller to detect and correct soft errors within a sector. Remember that we use physical sector numbers and hardware control to explain these ideas, but RAID can be implemented by software using logical sectors and disks.

At first thought you might expect that an individual write to a single sector still involves all the disks in a group since (1) the check disk must be rewritten with the new parity data, and (2) the rest of the data disks must be read to be able to calculate the new parity data. Recall that each parity bit is just a single exclusive OR of all the corresponding data bits in a group. In level 4 RAID, unlike level 3, the parity calculation is much simpler since, if we know the old data value and the old parity value as well as the new data value, we can calculate the new parity information as follows:

new parity = (old data xor new data) xor old parity

In level 4 a small write then uses 2 disks to perform 4 accesses--2 reads and 2 writes--while a small read involves only one read on one disk. Table V summarizes the fourth level RAID characteristics. Note that all small accesses improve--dramatically for the reads--but the small read-modify write is still so slow relative to a level 1 RAID that its applicability to transaction processing is doubtful. Recently Salem and Garcia-Molina proposed a Level 4 system [Salem 86].

Before proceeding to the next level we need to explain the performance of small writes in Table V (and hence small read-modify-writes since they entail the same operations in this RAID). The formula for the small writes divides D by 2 instead of 4 because 2 accesses can proceed in parallel: the old data and old parity can be read at the same time and the new data and new parity can be written at the same time. The performance of small writes is also divided by G because the single check disk in a group must be read and written with every small write in that group, thereby limiting the number of writes that can be performed at a time to the number of groups.

The check disk is the bottleneck, and the final level RAID removes this bottleneck.

MTTF		Exceeds Useful Lifetime	
		$G=10$ (820,000 hrs or >90 years)	$G=25$ (346,000 hrs or 40 years)
Total Number of Disks		1.10D	1.04D
Overhead Cost		10%	4%
Useable Storage Capacity		91%	96%

Events/Sec (vs. Single Disk)	Full RAID	Efficiency Per Disk L4 L4/L3 L4/L1			Efficiency Per Disk L4 L4/L3 L4/L1		
Large Reads	D/S	.91/S	100%	91%	.96/S	100%	96%
Large Writes	D/S	.91/S	100%	182%	.96/S	100%	192%
Large R-M-W	D/S	.91/S	100%	136%	.96/S	100%	146%
Small Reads	D	.91	1200%	91%	.96	3000%	96%
Small Writes	D/2G	.05	120%	9%	.02	120%	4%
Small R-M-W	D/G	.09	120%	14%	.04	120%	6%

Table V. *Characteristics of a Level 4 RAID. The L4/L3 column gives the % performance of L4 in terms of L3 and the L4/L1 column gives it in terms of L1 (>100% means L4 is faster). Small reads improve because they no longer tie up a whole group at a time. Small writes and R-M-Ws improve some because we make the same assumptions as we made in Table II: the slowdown for two related I/Os can be ignored because only two disks are involved.*

11. Fifth Level RAID: No Single Check Disk

While level 4 RAID achieved parallelism for reads, writes are still limited to one per group since every write must read and write the check disk. The final level RAID distributes the data and check information across all the disks--including the check disks. Figure 4 compares the location of check information in the sectors of disks for levels 4 and 5 RAIDs.

The performance impact of this small change is large since RAID level 5 can support multiple individual writes per group. For example, suppose in Figure 4 above we want to write sector 0 of disk 2 and sector 1 of disk 3. As shown on the left Figure 4, in RAID level 4 these writes must be sequential since both sector 0 and sector 1 of disk 5 must be written. However, as shown on the right, in RAID level 5 the writes can proceed in parallel since a write to sector 0 of disk 2 still involves a write to disk 5 but a write to sector 1 of disk 3 involves a write to disk 4.

These changes bring RAID level 5 near the best of both worlds: small read-modify-writes now perform close to the speed per disk of a level 1 RAID while keeping the large transfer performance per disk and high useful storage capacity percentage of the RAID levels 3 and 4. Spreading the data across all disks even improves the performance of small reads, since there is one more disk per group that contains data. Table VI summarizes the characteristics of this RAID.

Keeping in mind the caveats given earlier, a Level 5 RAID appears very attractive if you want to do just supercomputer applications, or just transaction processing when storage capacity is limited, or if you want to do both supercomputer applications *and* transaction processing.

12. Discussion

Before concluding the paper, we wish to note a few more interesting points about RAIDs. The first is that while the schemes for disk striping and parity support were presented as if they were done by hardware, there is no necessity to do so. We just give the method, and the decision between hardware and software solutions is strictly one of cost and benefit. For example, in cases where disk buffering is effective, there is no extra disks reads for level 5 small writes since the old data and old parity would be in main memory, so software would give the best performance as well as the least cost.

In this paper we have assumed the transfer unit is a multiple of the sector. As the size of the smallest transfer unit grows larger than one

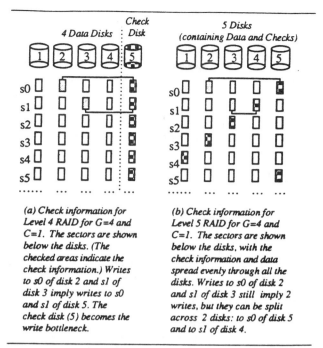

(a) Check information for Level 4 RAID for G=4 and C=1. The sectors are shown below the disks. (The checked areas indicate the check information.) Writes to s0 of disk 2 and s1 of disk 3 imply writes to s0 and s1 of disk 5. The check disk (5) becomes the write bottleneck.

(b) Check information for Level 5 RAID for G=4 and C=1. The sectors are shown below the disks, with the check information and data spread evenly through all the disks. Writes to s0 of disk 2 and s1 of disk 3 still imply 2 writes, but they can be split across 2 disks: to s0 of disk 5 and to s1 of disk 4.

Figure 4. *Location of check information per sector for Level 4 RAID vs. Level 5 RAID.*

MTTF		Exceeds Useful Lifetime	
		$G=10$ (820,000 hrs or >90 years)	$G=25$ (346,000 hrs or 40 years)
Total Number of Disks		1.10D	1.04D
Overhead Cost		10%	4%
Useable Storage Capacity		91%	96%

Events/Sec (vs. Single Disk)	Full RAID	Efficiency Per Disk L5 L5/L4 L5/L1			Efficiency Per Disk L5 L5/L4 L5/L1		
Large Reads	D/S	.91/S	100%	91%	.96/S	100%	96%
Large Writes	D/S	.91/S	100%	182%	.96/S	100%	192%
Large R-M-W	D/S	.91/S	100%	136%	.96/S	100%	144%
Small Reads	(1+C/G)D	1.00	110%	100%	1.00	104%	100%
Small Writes	(1+C/G)D/4	.25	550%	50%	.25	1300%	50%
Small R-M-W	(1+C/G)D/2	.50	550%	75%	.50	1300%	75%

Table VI. *Characteristics of a Level 5 RAID. The L5/L4 column gives the % performance of L5 in terms of L4 and the L5/L1 column gives it in terms of L1 (>100% means L5 is faster). Because reads can be spread over all disks, including what were check disks in level 4, all small I/Os improve by a factor of 1+C/G. Small writes and R-M-Ws improve because they are no longer constrained by group size, getting the full disk bandwidth for the 4 I/O's associated with these accesses. We again make the same assumptions as we made in Tables II and V: the slowdown for two related I/Os can be ignored because only two disks are involved.*

sector per drive--such as a full track with an I/O protocol that supports data returned out-of-order--then the performance of RAIDs improves significantly because of the full track buffer in every disk. For example, if every disk begins transferring to its buffer as soon as it reaches the next sector, then S may reduce to less than 1 since there would be virtually no rotational delay. With transfer units the size of a track, it is not even clear if synchronizing the disks in a group improves RAID performance.

This paper makes two separable points: the advantages of building I/O systems from personal computer disks and the advantages of five different disk array organizations, independent of disks used in those array. The later point starts with the traditional mirrored disks to achieve acceptable reliability, with each succeeding level improving:

- *the data rate*, characterized by a small number of requests per second for massive amounts of sequential information (supercomputer applications);

- *the I/O rate*, characterized by a large number of read-modify-writes to a small amount of random information (transaction-processing);
- or *the useable storage capacity*;

or possibly all three.

Figure 5 shows the performance improvements per disk for each level RAID. The highest performance per disk comes from either Level 1 or Level 5. In transaction-processing situations using no more than 50% of storage capacity, then the choice is mirrored disks (Level 1). However, if the situation calls for using more than 50% of storage capacity, or for supercomputer applications, or for combined supercomputer applications and transaction processing, then Level 5 looks best. Both the strength and weakness of Level 1 is that it duplicates data rather than calculating check information, for the duplicated data improves read performance but lowers capacity and write performance, while check data is useful only on a failure.

Inspired by the space-time product of paging studies [Denning 78], we propose a single figure of merit called the *space-speed product*: the useable storage fraction times the efficiency per event. Using this metric, Level 5 has an advantage over Level 1 of 1.7 for reads and 3.3 for writes for $G=10$.

Let us return to the first point, the advantages of building I/O system from personal computer disks. Compared to traditional Single Large Expensive Disks (SLED), Redundant Arrays of Inexpensive Disks (RAID) offer significant advantages for the same cost. Table VII compares a level 5 RAID using 100 inexpensive data disks with a group size of 10 to the IBM 3380. As you can see, a level 5 RAID offers a factor of roughly 10 improvement in performance, reliability, and power consumption (and hence air conditioning costs) and a factor of 3 reduction in size over this SLED. Table VII also compares a level 5 RAID using 10 inexpensive data disks with a group size of 10 to a Fujitsu M2361A "Super Eagle". In this comparison RAID offers roughly a factor of 5 improvement in performance, power consumption, and size with more than two orders of magnitude improvement in (calculated) reliability.

RAID offers the further advantage of modular growth over SLED. Rather than being limited to 7,500 MB per increase for $100,000 as in the case of this model of IBM disk, RAIDs can grow at either the group size (1000 MB for $11,000) or, if partial groups are allowed, at the disk size (100 MB for $1,100). The flip side of the coin is that RAID also makes sense in systems considerably smaller than a SLED. Small incremental costs also makes hot standby spares practical to further reduce MTTR and thereby increase the MTTF of a large system. For example, a 1000 disk level 5 RAID with a group size of 10 and a few standby spares could have a calculated MTTF of over 45 years.

A final comment concerns the prospect of designing a complete transaction processing system from either a Level 1 or Level 5 RAID. The drastically lower power per megabyte of inexpensive disks allows systems designers to consider battery backup for the whole disk array--the power needed for 110 PC disks is less than two Fujitsu Super Eagles. Another approach would be to use a few such disks to save the contents of battery backed-up main memory in the event of an extended power failure. The smaller capacity of these disks also ties up less of the database during reconstruction, leading to higher availability. (Note that Level 5 ties up all the disks in a group in event of failure while Level 1 only needs the single mirrored disk during reconstruction, giving Level 1 the edge in availability).

13. Conclusion

RAIDs offer a cost effective option to meet the challenge of exponential growth in the processor and memory speeds. We believe the size reduction of personal computer disks is a key to the success of disk arrays, just as Gordon Bell argues that the size reduction of microprocessors is a key to the success in multiprocessors [Bell 85]. In both cases the smaller size simplifies the interconnection of the many components as well as packaging and cabling. While large arrays of mainframe processors (or SLEDs) are possible, it is certainly easier to construct an array from the same number of microprocessors (or PC drives). Just as Bell coined the term "multi" to distinguish a multiprocessor made from microprocessors, we use the term "RAID" to identify a disk array made from personal computer disks.

With advantages in cost-performance, reliability, power consumption, and modular growth, we expect RAIDs to replace SLEDs in future I/O systems. There are, however, several open issues that may bare on the practicality of RAIDs:

- What is the impact of a RAID on latency?
- What is the impact on MTTF calculations of non-exponential failure assumptions for individual disks?
- What will be the real lifetime of a RAID vs. calculated MTTF using the independent failure model?
- How would synchronized disks affect level 4 and 5 RAID performance?
- How does "slowdown" S actually behave? [Livny 87]
- How do defective sectors affect RAID?
- How do you schedule I/O to level 5 RAIDs to maximize write parallelism?
- Is there locality of reference of disk accesses in transaction processing?
- Can information be automatically redistributed over 100 to 1000 disks to reduce contention?
- Will disk controller design limit RAID performance?
- How should 100 to 1000 disks be constructed and physically connected to the processor?
- What is the impact of cabling on cost, performance, and reliability?
- Where should a RAID be connected to a CPU so as not to limit performance? Memory bus? I/O bus? Cache?
- Can a file system allow differ striping policies for different files?
- What is the role of solid state disks and WORMs in a RAID?
- What is the impact on RAID of "parallel access" disks (access to every surface under the read/write head in parallel)?

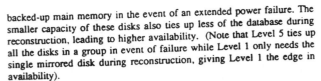

Characteristics	RAID 5L (100,10) (CP3100)	SLED (IBM 3380)	RAID v. SLED (>1 better for RAID)	RAID 5L (10,10) (CP3100)	SLED (Fujitsu M2361)	RAID v. SLED (>1 better for RAID)
Formatted Data Capacity (MB)	10,000	7,500	1.33	1,000	600	1.67
Price/MB (controller incl.)	$11-$8	$18-$10	2.2-.9	$11-$8	$20-$17	2.5-1.5
Rated MTTF (hours)	820,000	30,000	27.3	8,200,000	20,000	410
MTTF in practice (hours)	?	100,000	?	?	?	?
No. Actuators	110	4	22.5	11	1	11
Max I/O's/Actuator	30	50	.6	30	40	.8
Max Grouped RMW/box	1250	100	12.5	125	20	6.2
Max Individual RMW/box	825	100	8.2	83	20	4.2
Typ I/O's/Actuator	20	30	.7	20	24	.8
Typ Grouped RMW/box	833	60	13.9	83	12	6.9
Typ Individual RMW/box	550	60	9.2	55	12	4.6
Volume/Box (cubic feet)	10	24	2.4	1	3.4	3.4
Power/box (W)	1100	6,600	6.0	100-1000	640	5.8
Min. Expansion Size (MB)	100-1000	7,500	7.5-75	100-1000	600	0.6-6

Figure 5. *Plot of Large (Grouped) and Small (Individual) Read-Modify-Writes per second per disk and useable storage capacity for all five levels of RAID (D=100, G=10). We assume a single S factor uniformly for all levels, with S=1.3 where it is needed.*

Table VII. *Comparison of IBM 3380 disk model AK4 to Level 5 RAID using 100 Conners & Associates CP 3100s disks and a group size of 10 and a comparison of the Fujitsu M2361A "Super Eagle" to a level 5 RAID using 10 inexpensive data disks with a group size of 10. Numbers greater than 1 in the comparison columns favor the RAID.*

Acknowledgements

We wish to acknowledge the following people who participated in the discussions from which these ideas emerged: Michael Stonebraker, John Ousterhout, Doug Johnson, Ken Lutz, Anapum Bhide, Gaetano Boriello, Mark Hill, David Wood, and students in SPATS seminar offered at U. C. Berkeley in Fall 1987. We also wish to thank the following people who gave comments useful in the preparation of this paper: Anapum Bhide, Pete Chen, Ron David, Dave Ditzel, Fred Douglis, Dieter Gawlick, Jim Gray, Mark Hill, Doug Johnson, Joan Pendleton, Martin Schulze, and Hervé Touati. This work was supported by the National Science Foundation under grant # MIP-8715235.

Appendix: Reliability Calculation

Using probability theory we can calculate the $MTTF_{Group}$. We first assume independent and exponential failure rates. Our model uses a biased coin with the probability of heads being the probability that a second failure will occur within the MTTR of a first failure. Since disk failures are exponential:

Probability(at least one of the remaining disks failing in MTTR)
$$= [1 - (e^{-MTTR/MTTF_{Disk}})^{(G+C-1)}]$$

In all practical cases

$$MTTR << \frac{MTTF_{Disk}}{G+C}$$

and since $(1 - e^{-X})$ is approximately X for $0 < X << 1$:

Probability(at least one of the remaining disks failing in MTTR)
$$= MTTR*(G+C-1)/MTTF_{Disk}$$

Then that on a disk failure we flip this coin:

heads => a system crash, because a second failure occurs before the first was repaired;

tails => recover from error and continue.

Then
$$MTTF_{Group} = Expected[Time\ between\ Failures]$$
$$* Expected[no.\ of\ flips\ until\ first\ heads]$$

$$= \frac{Expected[Time\ between\ Failures]}{Probability(heads)}$$

$$= \frac{MTTF_{Disk}}{(G+C)*(MTTR*(G+C-1)/MTTF_{Disk})}$$

$$MTTF_{Group} = \frac{(MTTF_{Disk})^2}{(G+C)*(G+C-1)*MTTR}$$

Group failure is not precisely exponential in our model, but we have validated this simplifying assumption for practical cases of MTTR << MTTF/(G+C). This makes the MTTF of the whole system just $MTTF_{Group}$ divided by the number of groups, n_G.

References

[Bell 84]   C.G. Bell, "The Mini and Micro Industries," *IEEE Computer*, Vol. 17, No. 10 (October 1984), pp. 14-30.

[Joy 85]   B. Joy, presentation at ISSCC '85 panel session, Feb. 1985.

[Siewiorek 82]   D.P. Siewiorek, C.G. Bell, and A. Newell, *Computer Structures: Principles and Examples*, p. 46.

[Moore 75]   G.E. Moore, "Progress in Digital Integrated Electronics," *Proc. IEEE Digital Integrated Electronic Device Meeting*, (1975), p. 11.

[Myers 86]   G.J. Myers, A.Y.C. Yu, and D.L. House, "Microprocessor Technology Trends," *Proc. IEEE*, Vol. 74, no. 12, (December 1986), pp. 1605-1622.

[Garcia 84]   H. Garcia-Molina, R. Cullingford, P. Honeyman, R. Lipton, "The Case for Massive Memory," Technical Report 326, Dept. of EE and CS, Princeton Univ., May 1984.

[Myers 86]   W. Myers, "The Competitiveness of the United States Disk Industry," *IEEE Computer*, Vol. 19, No. 11 (January 1986), pp. 85-90.

[Frank 87]   P.D. Frank, "Advances in Head Technology," presentation at *Challenges in Disk Technology Short Course*, Institute for Information Storage Technology, Santa Clara University, Santa Clara, California, December 15-17, 1987.

[Stevens 81]   L.D. Stevens, "The Evolution of Magnetic Storage," *IBM Journal of Research and Development*, Vol. 25, No. 5, Sept. 1981, pp. 663-675.

[Harker 81]   J.M. Harker *et al.*, "A Quarter Century of Disk File Innovation," *ibid.*, pp. 677-689.

[Amdahl 67]   G.M. Amdahl, "Validity of the single processor approach to achieving large scale computing capabilities," *Proceedings AFIPS 1967 Spring Joint Computer Conference* Vol. 30 (Atlantic City, New Jersey April 1967), pp. 483-485.

[Boral 83]   H. Boral and D.J. DeWitt, "Database Machines: An Ideas Whose Time Has Passed? A Critique of the Future of Database Machines," *Proc. International Conf. on Database Machines*, Edited by H.-O. Leilich and M. Misskoff, Springer-Verlag, Berlin, 1983.

[IBM 87]   "IBM 3380 Direct Access Storage Introduction," IBM GC 26-4491-0, September 1987.

[Gawlick 87]   D. Gawlick, private communication, Nov., 1987.

[Fujitsu 87]   "M2361A Mini-Disk Drive Engineering Specifications," (revised) Feb., 1987, B03P-4825-0001A.

[Adaptec 87]   AIC-6250, *IC Product Guide*, Adaptec, stock # DB0003-00 rev. B, 1987, p. 46.

[Livny 87]   Livny, M., S. Khoshafian, H. Boral, "Multi-disk management algorithms," *Proc. of ACM SIGMETRICS*, May 1987.

[Kim 86]   M.Y. Kim, "Synchronized disk interleaving," *IEEE Trans. on Computers*, vol. C-35, no. 11, Nov. 1986.

[Salem 86]   K. Salem and Garcia-Molina, H., "Disk Striping," *IEEE 1986 Int. Conf. on Data Engineering*, 1986.

[Bitton 88]   D. Bitton and J. Gray, "Disk Shadowing," *in press*, 1988.

[Kurzweil 88]   F. Kurzweil, "Small Disk Arrays - The Emerging Approach to High Performance," presentation at Spring COMPCON 88, March 1, 1988, San Francisco, CA.

[Hamming 50]   R. W. Hamming, "Error Detecting and Correcting Codes," *The Bell System Technical Journal*, Vol XXVI, No. 2 (April 1950), pp. 147-160.

[Hillis 87]   D. Hillis, private communication, October, 1987.

[Park 86]   A. Park and K. Balasubramanian, "Providing Fault Tolerance in Parallel Secondary Storage Systems," Department of Computer Science, Princeton University, CS-TR-057-86, Nov. 7, 1986.

[Maginnis 87]   N.B. Maginnis, "Store More, Spend Less: Mid-range Options Abound,"*Computerworld*, Nov. 16, 1987, p. 71.

[Denning 78]   P.J. Denning and D.F. Slutz, "Generalized Working Sets for Segment Reference Strings," *CACM*, vol. 21, no. 9, (Sept. 1978) pp. 750-759.

[Bell 85]   Bell, C.G., "Multis: a new class of multiprocessor computers,"*Science*, vol. 228 (April 26, 1985) 462-467.

Computer   G. Bell, S. Fuller and
Systems   D. Siewiorek, Editors

Ethernet: Distributed Packet Switching for Local Computer Networks

Robert M. Metcalfe and David R. Boggs
Xerox Palo Alto Research Center

Ethernet is a branching broadcast communication system for carrying digital data packets among locally distributed computing stations. The packet transport mechanism provided by Ethernet has been used to build systems which can be viewed as either local computer networks or loosely coupled multiprocessors. An Ethernet's shared communication facility, its Ether, is a passive broadcast medium with no central control. Coordination of access to the Ether for packet broadcasts is distributed among the contending transmitting stations using controlled statistical arbitration. Switching of packets to their destinations on the Ether is distributed among the receiving stations using packet address recognition. Design principles and implementation are described, based on experience with an operating Ethernet of 100 nodes along a kilometer of coaxial cable. A model for estimating performance under heavy loads and a packet protocol for error controlled communication are included for completeness.

Key Words and Phrases: computer networks, packet switching, multiprocessing, distributed control, distributed computing, broadcast communication, statistical arbitration
CR Categories: 3.81, 4.32, 6.35

1. Background

One can characterize distributed computing as a spectrum of activities varying in their degree of decentralization, with one extreme being remote computer networking and the other extreme being multiprocessing. Remote computer networking is the loose interconnection of previously isolated, widely separated, and rather large computing systems. Multiprocessing is the construction of previously monolithic and serial computing systems from increasingly numerous and smaller pieces computing in parallel. Near the middle of this spectrum is local networking, the interconnection of computers to gain the resource sharing of computer networking and the parallelism of multiprocessing.

The separation between computers and the associated bit rate of their communication can be used to divide the distributed computing spectrum into broad activities. The product of separation and bit rate, now about 1 gigabit-meter per second (1 Gbmps), is an indication of the limit of current communication technology and can be expected to increase with time:

Activity	Separation	Bit rate
Remote networks	> 10 km	< .1 Mbps
Local networks	10–.1 km	.1–10 Mbps
Multiprocessors	< .1 km	> 10 Mbps

1.1 Remote Computer Networking

Computer networking evolved from telecommunications *terminal-computer* communication, where the object was to connect remote terminals to a central computing facility. As the need for *computer-computer* interconnection grew, computers themselves were used to provide communication [2, 4, 29]. Communication *using* computers as packet switches [15–21, 26] and communications *among* computers for resource sharing [10, 32] were both advanced by the development of the Arpa Computer Network.

The Aloha Network at the University of Hawaii was originally developed to apply packet radio techniques for communication between a central computer and its terminals scattered among the Hawaiian Islands [1, 2]. Many of the terminals are now minicomputers communicating among themselves using the Aloha Network's Menehune as a packet switch. The Menehune and an Arpanet Imp are now connected, providing terminals on the Aloha Network access to computing resources on the U.S. mainland.

Just as computer networks have grown across continents and oceans to interconnect major computing facilities around the world, they are now growing down corridors and between buildings to interconnect minicomputers in offices and laboratories [3, 12, 13, 14, 35].

1.2 Multiprocessing

Multiprocessing first took the form of connecting an I/O controller to a large central computer; IBM's Asp is a classic example [29]. Next, multiple central processors were connected to a common memory to provide more power for compute-bound applications [33]. For certain of these applications, more exotic multiprocessor architectures such as Illiac IV were introduced [5].

More recently minicomputers have been connected in multiprocessor configurations for economy, reliability, and increased system modularity [24, 36]. The trend has been toward decentralization for reliability; loosely coupled multiprocessor systems depend less on shared central memory and more on *thin wires* for interprocess communication with increased component isolation [18, 26]. With the continued thinning of interprocessor communication for reliability and the development of distributable applications, multiprocessing is gradually approaching a local form of distributed computing.

1.3 Local Computer Networking

Ethernet shares many objectives with other local networks such as Mitre's Mitrix, Bell Telephone Laboratory's Spider, and U.C. Irvine's Distributed Computing System (DCS) [12, 13, 14, 35]. Prototypes of all four local networking schemes operate at bit rates between one and three megabits per second. Mitrix and Spider have a central minicomputer for switching and bandwidth allocation, while DCS and Ethernet use distributed control. Spider and DCS use a ring communication path, Mitrix uses off-the-shelf CATV technology to implement two one-way busses, and our experimental Ethernet uses a branching two-way passive bus. Differences among these systems are due to differences among their intended applications, differences among the cost constraints under which trade-offs were made, and differences of opinion among researchers.

Before going into a detailed description of Ethernet, we offer the following overview (see Figure 1).

2. System Summary

Ethernet is a system for local communication among computing stations. Our experimental Ethernet uses tapped coaxial cables to carry variable length digital data packets among, for example, personal minicomputers, printing facilities, large file storage devices, magnetic tape backup stations, larger central computers, and longer-haul communication equipment.

The shared communication facility, a branching Ether, is passive. A station's Ethernet interface connects bit-serially through an interface cable to a transceiver which in turn taps into the passing Ether. A packet is broadcast onto the Ether, is heard by all stations, and is copied from the Ether by destinations which select it according to the packet's leading address bits. This is broadcast packet switching and should be distinguished from store-and-forward packet switching, in which routing is performed by intermediate process-

ing elements. To handle the demands of growth, an Ethernet can be extended using packet repeaters for signal regeneration, packet filters for traffic localization, and packet gateways for internetwork address extension.

Control is completely distributed among stations, with packet transmissions coordinated through statistical arbitration. Transmissions initiated by a station defer to any which may already be in progress. Once started, if interference with other packets is detected, a transmission is aborted and rescheduled by its source station. After a certain period of interference-free transmission, a packet is heard by all stations and will run to completion without interference. Ethernet controllers in colliding stations each generate random retransmission intervals to avoid repeated collisions. The mean of a packet's retransmission intervals is adjusted as a function of collision history to keep Ether utilization near the optimum with changing network load.

Even when transmitted without source-detected interference, a packet may still not reach its destination without error; thus, packets are delivered *only with high probability*. Stations requiring a residual error rate lower than that provided by the bare Ethernet packet transport mechanism must follow mutually agreed upon packet protocols.

3. Design Principles

Our object is to design a communication system which can grow smoothly to accommodate several buildings full of personal computers and the facilities needed for their support.

Like the computing stations to be connected, the communication system must be inexpensive. We choose to distribute control of the communications facility among the communicating computers to eliminate the reliability problems of an active central controller, to avoid creating a bottleneck in a system rich in parallelism, and to reduce the fixed costs which make small systems uneconomical.

Ethernet design started with the basic idea of packet collision and retransmission developed in the Aloha Network [1]. We expected that, like the Aloha Network, Ethernets would carry bursty traffic so that conventional synchronous time-division multiplexing (STDM) would be inefficient [1, 2, 21, 26]. We saw promise in the Aloha approach to distributed control of radio channel multiplexing and hoped that it could be applied effectively with media suited to local computer communication. With several innovations of our own, the promise is realized.

Ethernet is named for the historical *luminiferous ether* through which electromagnetic radiations were once alleged to propagate. Like an Aloha radio transmitter, an Ethernet transmitter broadcasts completely-addressed transmitter-synchronous bit sequences called packets onto the Ether and hopes that they are heard by

Fig. 1. A two-segment Ethernet.

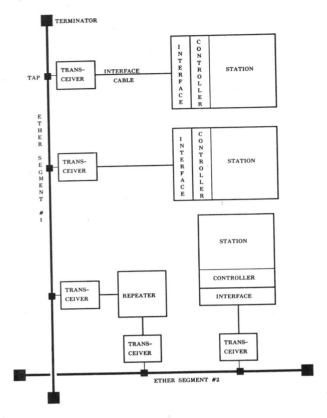

the intended receivers. The Ether is a logically passive medium for the propagation of digital signals and can be constructed using any number of media including coaxial cables, twisted pairs, and optical fibers.

3.1 Topology

We cannot afford the redundant connections and dynamic routing of store-and-forward packet switching to assure reliable communication, so we choose to achieve reliability through simplicity. We choose to make the shared communication facility passive so that the failure of an active element will tend to affect the communications of only a single station. The layout and changing needs of office and laboratory buildings leads us to pick a network topology with the potential for convenient incremental extention and reconfiguration with minimal service disruption.

The topology of the Ethernet is that of an unrooted tree. It is a *tree* so that the Ether can branch at the entrance to a building's corridor, yet avoid multipath interference. There must be only one path through the Ether between any source and destination; if more than one path were to exist, a transmission would interfere with itself, repeatedly arriving at its intended destination having travelled by paths of different length. The Ether is *unrooted* because it can be extended from any of its points in any direction. Any station wishing to join

an Ethernet taps into the Ether at the nearest convenient point.

Looking at the relationship of interconnection and control, we see that Ethernet is the dual of a star network. Rather than *distributed* interconnection through many separate links and *central* control in a switching node, as in a star network, the Ethernet has *central* interconnection through the Ether and *distributed* control among its stations.

Unlike an Aloha Network, which is a star network with an outgoing broadcast channel and an incoming multi-access channel, an Ethernet supports many-to-many communication with a single broadcast multi-access channel.

3.2 Control

Sharing of the Ether is controlled in such a way that it is not only possible but probable that two or more stations will attempt to transmit a packet at roughly the same time. Packets which overlap in time on the Ether are said to *collide*; they interfere so as to be unrecognizable by a receiver. A station recovers from a detected collision by abandoning the attempt and retransmitting the packet after some dynamically chosen random time period. Arbitration of conflicting transmission demands is both distributed and statistical.

When the Ether is largely unused, a station transmits its packets at will, the packets are received without error, and all is well. As more stations begin to transmit, the rate of packet interference increases. Ethernet controllers in each station are built to adjust the mean retransmission interval in proportion to the frequency of collisons; sharing of the Ether among competing station-station transmissions is thereby kept near the optimum [20, 21].

A degree of cooperation among the stations is required to share the Ether equitably. In demanding applications certain stations might usefully take transmission priority through some systematic violation of equity rules. A station could usurp the Ether by not adjusting its retransmission interval with increasing traffic or by sending very large packets. Both practices are now prohibited by low-level software in each station.

3.3 Addressing

Each packet has a source and destination, both of which are identified in the packet's header. A packet placed on the Ether eventually propagates to all stations. Any station can copy a packet from the Ether into its local memory, but normally only an active destination station matching its address in the packet's header will do so as the packet passes. By convention, a zero destination address is a wildcard and matches all addresses; a packet with a destination of zero is called a *broadcast packet*.

3.4 Reliability

An Ethernet is probabilistic. Packets may be lost due to interference with other packets, impulse noise on the

Ether, an inactive receiver at a packet's intended destination, or purposeful discard. Protocols used to communicate through an Ethernet must assume that packets will be received correctly at intended destinations *only with high probability.*

An Ethernet gives its *best efforts* to transmit packets successfully, but it is the responsibility of processes in the source and destination stations to take the precautions necessary to assure reliable communication of the quality they themselves desire [18, 21]. Recognizing the costliness and dangers of promising "error-free" communication, we refrain from guaranteeing reliable delivery of any single packet to get both economy of transmission and high reliability averaged over many packets [21]. Removing the responsibility for reliable communication from the packet transport mechanism allows us to tailor reliability to the application and to place error recovery where it will do the most good. This policy becomes more important as Ethernets are interconnected in a hierarchy of networks through which packets must travel farther and suffer greater risks.

3.5 Mechanisms

A station connects to the Ether with a *tap* and a *transceiver.* A tap is a device for physically connecting to the Ether while disturbing its transmission characteristics as little as possible. The design of the transceiver must be an exercise in paranoia. Precautions must be taken to insure that likely failures in the transceiver or station do not result in pollution of the Ether. In particular, removing power from the transceiver should cause it to disconnect from the Ether.

Five mechanisms are provided in our experimental Ethernet for reducing the probability and cost of losing a packet. These are (1) carrier detection, (2) interference detection, (3) packet error detection, (4) truncated packet filtering, and (5) collision consensus enforcement.

3.5.1 Carrier detection. As a packet's bits are placed on the Ether by a station, they are phase encoded (like bits on a magnetic tape), which guarantees that there is at least one transition on the Ether during each bit time. The passing of a packet on the Ether can therefore be detected by listening for its transitions. To use a radio analogy, we speak of the presence of *carrier* as a packet passes a transceiver. Because a station can sense the carrier of a passing packet, it can delay sending one of its own until the detected packet passes safely. The Aloha Network does not have carrier detection and consequently suffers a substantially higher collision rate. Without carrier detection, efficient use of the Ether would decrease with increasing packet length. In Section 6 below, we show that with carrier detection, Ether efficiency increases with increasing packet length.

With carrier detection we are able to implement *deference*: no station will start transmitting while hearing carrier. With deference comes *acquisition*: once a packet transmission has been in progress for an Ether end-to-

end propagation time, all stations are hearing carrier and are deferring; the Ether has been acquired and the transmission will complete without an interfering collision.

With carrier detection, collisions should occur only when two or more stations find the Ether silent and begin transmitting simultaneously: within an Ether end-to-end propagation time. This will almost always happen immediately after a packet transmission during which two or more stations were deferring. Because stations do not now randomize after deferring, when the transmission terminates, the waiting stations pile on together, collide, randomize, and retransmit.

3.5.2 Interference detection. Each transceiver has an interference detector. Interference is indicated when the transceiver notices a difference between the value of the bit it is receiving from the Ether and the value of the bit it is attempting to transmit.

Interference detection has three advantages. First, a station detecting a collision knows that its packet has been damaged. The packet can be scheduled for retransmission immediately, avoiding a long acknowledgment timeout. Second, interference periods on the Ether are limited to a maximum of one round trip time. Colliding packets in the Aloha Network run to completion, but the truncated packets resulting from Ethernet collisions waste only a small fraction of a packet time on the Ether. Third, the frequency of detected interference is used to estimate Ether traffic for adjusting retransmission intervals and optimizing channel efficiency.

3.5.3 Packet error detection. As a packet is placed on the Ether, a checksum is computed and appended. As the packet is read from the Ether, the checksum is recomputed. Packets which do not carry a consistent checksum are discarded. In this way transmission errors, impulse noise errors, and errors due to undetected interference are caught at a packet's destination.

3.5.4 Truncated packet filtering. Interference detection and deference cause most collisions to result in *truncated packets* of only a few bits; colliding stations detect interference and abort transmission within an Ether round trip time. To reduce the processing load that the rejection of such obviously damaged packets would place on listening station software, truncated packets are filtered out in hardware.

3.5.5 Collision consensus enforcement. When a station determines that its transmission is experiencing interference, it momentarily jams the Ether to insure that all other participants in the collision will detect interference and, because of deference, will be forced to abort. Without this *collision consensus enforcement* mechanism, it is possible that the transmitting station which would otherwise be the last to detect a collision might not do so as the other interfering transmissions successively abort and stop interfering. Although the packet may look good to that last transmitter, different path lengths between the colliding transmitters and the intended receiver will cause the packet to arrive damaged.

4. Implementation

Our choices of 1 kilometer, 3 megabits per second, and 256 stations for the parameters of an experimental Ethernet were based on characteristics of the locally distributed computer communication environment and our assessments of what would be marginally achievable; they were certainly not hard restrictions essential to the Ethernet concept.

We expect that a reasonable maximum network size would be on the order of 1 kilometer of cable. We used this working number to choose among Ethers of varying signal attenuation and to design transceivers with appropriate power and sensitivity.

The dominant station on our experimental Ethernet is a minicomputer for which 3 megabits per second is a convenient data transfer rate. By keeping the peak rate well below that of the computer's path to main memory, we reduce the need for expensive special-purpose packet buffering in our Ethernet interfaces. By keeping the peak rate as high as is convenient, we provide for larger numbers of stations and more ambitious multiprocessing communications applications.

To expedite low-level packet handling among 256 stations, we allocate the first 8-bit byte of the packet to be the destination address field and the second byte to be the source address field (see Figure 2). 256 is a number small enough to allow each station to get an adequate share of the available bandwidth and approaches the limit of what we can achieve with current techniques for tapping cables. 256 is only a convenient number for the lowest level of protocol; higher levels can accomodate extended address spaces with additional fields inside the packet and software to interpret them.

Our experimental Ethernet implementation has four major parts: the Ether, transceivers, interfaces, and controllers (see Figure 1).

4.1 Ether

We chose to implement our experimental Ether using low-loss coaxial cable with off-the-shelf CATV taps and connectors. It is possible to mix Ethers on a single Ethernet; we use a smaller-diameter coax for convenient connection within station clusters and a larger-diameter coax for low-loss runs between clusters. The cost of coaxial cable Ether is insignificant relative to the cost of the distributed computing systems supported by Ethernet.

4.2 Transceivers

Our experimental transceivers can drive a kilometer of coaxial cable Ether tapped by 256 stations transmitting at 3 megabits per second. The transceivers can *endure* (i.e. work after) sustained direct shorting, improper termination of the Ether, and simultaneous drive by all 256 stations; they can *tolerate* (i.e. work during) ground differentials and everyday electrical noise, from typewriters or electric drills, encountered when stations are separated by as much as a kilometer.

An Ethernet transceiver attaches directly to the Ether which passes by in the ceiling or under the floor. It is powered and controlled through five twisted pairs in an interface cable carrying transmit data, receive data, interference detect, and power supply voltages. When unpowered, the transceiver disconnects itself electrically from the Ether. Here is where our fight for reliability is won or lost; a broken transceiver can, but should not, bring down an entire Ethernet. A watchdog timer circuit in each transceiver attempts to prevent pollution of the Ether by shutting down the output stage if it acts suspiciously. For transceiver simplicity we use the Ether's base frequency band, but an Ethernet could be built to use any suitably sized band of a frequency division multiplexed Ether.

Even though our experimental transceivers are very simple and can tolerate only limited signal attenuation, they have proven quite adequate and reliable. A more sophisticated transceiver design might permit passive branching of the Ether and wider station separation.

4.3 Interface

An Ethernet interface serializes and deserializes the parallel data used by its station. There are a number of different stations on our Ethernet; an interface must be built for each kind.

Each interface is equipped with the hardware necessary to compute a 16-bit cyclic redundancy checksum (CRC) on serial data as it is transmitted and received. This checksum protects only against errors in the Ether and specifically not against errors in the parallel portions of the interface hardware or station. Higher-level software checksums are recommended for applications in which a higher degree of reliability is required.

A transmitting interface uses a packet buffer address and word count to serialize and phase encode a variable number of 16-bit words which are taken from the station's memory and passed to the transceiver, preceded by a start bit (called SYNC in Figure 2) and followed by the CRC. A receiving interface uses the appearance of carrier to detect the start of a packet and uses the SYNC bit to acquire bit phase. As long as carrier stays on, the interface decodes and deserializes the incoming bit stream depositing 16-bit words in a packet buffer in the station's main memory. When carrier goes away, the interface checks that an integral number of 16-bit words has been received and that the CRC is correct. The last word received is assumed to be the CRC and is not copied into the packet buffer.

These interfaces ordinarily include hardware for accepting only those packets with appropriate addresses in their headers. Hardware address filtering helps a station avoid burdensome software packet processing when

Fig. 2. Ethernet packet layout.

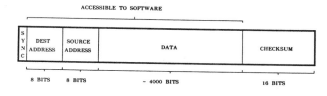

the Ether is very busy carrying traffic intended for other stations.

4.4 Controller

An Ethernet controller is the station-specific low-level firmware or software for getting packets onto and out of the Ether. When a source-detected collision occurs, it is the source controller's responsibility to generate a new random retransmission interval based on the updated collision count. We have studied a number of algorithms for controlling retransmission rates in stations to maintain Ether efficiency [20, 22]. The most practical of these algorithms estimate traffic load using recent collision history.

Retransmission intervals are multiples of a *slot*, the maximum time between starting a transmission and detecting a collision, one end-to-end round trip delay. An Ethernet controller begins transmission of each new packet with a mean retransmission interval of one slot. Each time a transmission attempt ends in collision, the controller delays for an interval of random length with a mean twice that of the previous interval, defers to any passing packet, and then attempts retransmission. This heuristic approximates an algorithm we have called Binary Exponential Backoff (see Figure 3) [22].

When the network is unloaded and collisions are rare, the mean seldom departs from one and retransmissions are prompt. As the traffic load increases, more collisions are experienced, a backlog of packets builds up in the stations, retransmission intervals increase, and retransmission traffic backs off to sustain channel efficiency.

5. Growth

5.1 Signal Cover

One can expand an Ethernet just so far by adding transceivers and Ether. At some point, the transceivers and Ether will be unable to carry the required signals. The *signal cover* can be extended with a simple unbuffered *packet repeater*. In our experimental Ethernet, where because of transceiver simplicity the Ether cannot be branched passively, a simple repeater may join any number of Ether *segments* to enrich the topology while extending the signal cover.

We operate an experimental two-segment packet repeater, but hope to avoid relying on them. In branching

the Ether and extending its signal cover, there is a trade-off between using sophisticated transceivers and using repeaters. With increased power and sensitivity, transceivers become more expensive and less reliable. The introduction of repeaters into an Ethernet makes the centrally interconnecting Ether active. The failure of a transceiver will sever the communications of its owner; the failure of a repeater partitions the Ether severing many communications.

5.2 Traffic Cover

One can expand an Ethernet just so far by adding Ether and packet repeaters. At some point the Ether will be so busy that additional stations will just divide more finely the already inadequate bandwidth. The *traffic cover* can be extended with an unbuffered traffic-filtering repeater or *packet filter*, which passes packets from one Ether segment to another only if the destination station is located on the new segment. A packet filter also extends the signal cover.

5.3 Address Cover

One can expand an Ethernet just so far by adding Ether, repeaters, and traffic filters. At some point there will be too many stations to be addressed with the Ethernet's 8-bit addresses. The *address cover* can be extended with *packet gateways* and the software addressing conventions they implement [7]. Addresses can be expanded in two directions: *down* into the station by adding fields to identify destination ports or processes within a station, and *up* into the internetwork by adding fields to identify destination stations on remote networks. A gateway also extends the traffic and signal covers.

There can be only one repeater or packet filter connecting two Ether segments; a packet repeated onto a segment by multiple repeaters would interfere with itself. However, there is no limit to the number of gateways connecting two segments; a gateway only repeats packets addressed to itself as an intermediary. Failure of the single repeater connecting two segments partitions the network; failure of a gateway need not partition the net if there are paths through other gateways between the segments.

6. Performance

We present here a simple set of formulas with which to characterize the performance expected of an Ethernet when it is heavily loaded. More elaborate analyses and several detailed simulations have been done, but the following simple model has proven very useful in understanding the Ethernet's distributed contention scheme, even when it is loaded beyond expectations [1, 20, 21, 22, 23, 27].

We develop a simple model of the performance of a loaded Ethernet by examining alternating Ether time periods. The first, called a *transmission interval*, is that during which the Ether has been acquired for a successful packet transmission. The second, called a *contention interval*, is that composed of the retransmission slots of Section 4.4, during which stations attempt to acquire control of the Ether. Because the model's Ethernets are loaded and because stations defer to passing packets before starting transmission, the slots are synchronized by the tail of the preceding acquisition interval. A slot will be empty when no station chooses to attempt transmission in it and it will contain a collision if more than one station attempts to transmit. When a slot contains only one attempted transmission, then the Ether has been acquired for the duration of a packet, the contention interval ends, and a transmission interval begins.

Let P be the number of bits in an Ethernet *packet*. Let C be the peak *capacity* in bits per second, carried on the Ether. Let T be the *time* in seconds of a slot, the number of seconds it takes to detect a collision after starting a transmission. Let us assume that there are Q stations continuously *queued* to transmit a packet; either the acquiring station has a new packet immediately after a successful acquisition or another station comes ready. Note that Q also happens to give the total *offered load* on the network which for this analysis is always 1 or greater. We assume that a queued station attempts to transmit in the current slot with probability $1/Q$, or delays with probability $1-(1/Q)$; this is known

to be the optimum statistical decision rule, approximated in Ethernet stations by means of our load-estimating retransmission control algorithms [20, 21].

6.1 Acquisition Probability

We now compute A, the probability that exactly one station attempts a transmission in a slot and therefore *acquires* the Ether. A is $Q*(1/Q)*((1 - (1/Q))**(Q - 1))$; there are Q ways in which one station can choose to transmit (with probability $(1/Q)$) while $Q - 1$ stations choose to wait (with probability $1 - (1/Q)$). Simplifying,

$$A = (1 - (1/Q))^{(Q-1)}.$$

6.2 Waiting Time

We now compute W, the mean number of slots of *waiting* in a contention interval before a successful acquisition of the Ether by a station's transmission. The probability of waiting no time at all is just A, the probability that one and only one station chooses to transmit in the first slot following a transmission. The probability of waiting 1 slot is $A*(1 - A)$; the probability of waiting i slots is $A*((1 - A)**i)$. The mean of this geometric distribution is

$$W = (1 - A)/A.$$

6.3 Efficiency

We now compute E, that fraction of time the Ether is carrying good packets, the *efficiency*. The Ether's time is divided between transmission intervals and contention intervals. A packet transmission takes P/C seconds. The mean time to acquisition is $W*T$. Therefore, by our simple model,

$$E = (P/C)/((P/C) + (W*T)).$$

Table I presents representative performance figures (i.e. E) for our experimental Ethernet with the indicated packet sizes and number of *continuously queued* stations. The efficiency figures given do not account for inevitable reductions due to headers and control packets nor for losses due to imprecise control of the retransmission parameter $1/Q$; the former is straightforwardly protocol-dependent and the latter requires analysis beyond the scope of this paper. Again, we feel that all of the Ethernets in the table are overloaded; normally loaded Ethernets will usually have a Q much less than 1 and exhibit behavior not covered by this model.

For our calculations we use a C of 3 megabits per second and a T of 16 microseconds. The slot duration T must be long enough to allow a collision to be detected or at least twice the Ether's round trip time. We limit in software the maximum length of our packets to be near 4000 bits to keep the latency of network access down and to permit efficient use of station packet buffer storage.

For packets whose size is above 4000 bits, the efficiency of our experimental Ethernet stays well above 95

Fig. 3. Collision control algorithm.

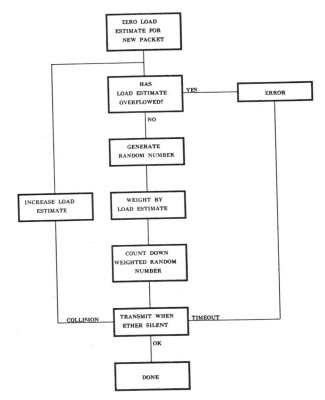

percent. For packets with a size approximating that of a slot, Ethernet efficiency approaches $1/e$, the asymptotic efficiency of a slotted Aloha network [27].

7. Protocol

There is more to the construction of a viable packet communication system than simply providing the mechanisms for packet transport. Methods for error correction, flow control, process naming, security, and accounting must also be provided through higher-level protocols implemented on top of the Ether control protocol described in Sections 3 and 4 above. [7, 10, 12, 21, 28, 34]. Ether control includes packet framing, error detection, addressing and multi-access control; like other line control procedures, Ethernet is used to support numerous network and multiprocessor architectures [30, 31].

Here is a brief description of one simple error-controlling packet protocol. The EFTP (Ethernet File Transfer Protocol) is of interest both because it is relatively easy to understand and implement correctly and because it has dutifully carried many valuable files during the development of more general and efficient protocols.

7.1. General Terminology

In discussing packet protocols, we use the following generally useful terminology. A packet is said to have a *source* and a *destination*. A flow of data is said to have a *sender* and a *receiver*, recognizing that to support a flow of data some packets (typically acknowledgments) will be sourced at the receiver and destined for the sender. A connection is said to have a *listener* and an *initiator* and a service is said to have a *server* and a *user*. It is very useful to treat these as orthogonal descriptors of the participants in a communication. Of course, a server is usually a listener and the source of data-bearing packets is usually the sender.

7.2 EFTP

The first 16 bits of all Ethernet packets contain its interface-interpretable destination and source station addresses, a byte each, in that order (see Figure 2). By software convention, the second 16 bits of all Ethernet packets contain the packet type. Different protocols use disjoint sets of packet types. The EFTP uses 5 packet types: data, ack, abort, end, and endreply. Following the 16-bit type word of an EFTP packet are 16 bits of sequence number, 16 bits of length, optionally some 16-bit data words, and finally a 16-bit software checksum word (see Figure 4). The Ethernet's hardware checksum is present only on the Ether and is not counted at this level of protocol.

It should be obvious that little care has been taken to cram certain fields into just the right number of bits. The emphasis here is on simplicity and ease of pro-

gramming. Despite this disclaimer, we do feel that it is more advisable to err on the side of spacious fields; try as you may, one field or another will always turn out to be too small.

The software checksum word is used to lower the probability of an undetected error. It serves not only as a backup for the experimental Ethernet's serial hardware 16-bit cyclic redundancy checksum (in Figure 2), but also for protection against failures in parallel data paths within stations which are not checked by the CRC. The checksum used by the EFTP is a 1's complement add and cycle over the entire packet, including header and content data. The checksum can be ignored at the user's peril at either end; the sender may put all 1's (an impossible value) into the checksum word to indicate to the receiver that no checksum was computed.

7.2.1 Data transfer. The 16-bit words of a file are carried from sending station to receiving station in data packets consecutively numbered from 0. Each data packet is retransmitted periodically by the sender until an ack packet with a matching sequence number is returned from the receiver. The receiver ignores all damaged packets, packets from a station other than the sender, and packets whose sequence number does not match either the expected one or the one preceding. When a packet has the expected sequence number, the packet is acked, its data is accepted as part of the file, and the sequence number is incremented. When a packet arrives with a sequence number one less than that expected, it is acknowledged and discarded; the presumption is that its ack was lost and needs retransmission [21].

7.2.2 End. When all the data has been transmitted, an end packet is sent with the next consecutive sequence number and than the sender waits for a matching endreply. Having accepted an end packet in sequence, the data receiver responds with a matching endreply and then *dallys* for some reasonably long period of time (10 seconds). Upon getting the endreply, the sending station transmits an echoing endreply and is free to go off with the assurance that the file has been transferred successfully. The dallying receiver then gets the echoed endreply and it too goes off assured.

Table I. Ethernet Efficiency.

Q	$P = 4096$	$P = 1024$	$P = 512$	$P = 48$
1	1.0000	1.0000	1.0000	1.0000
2	0.9884	0.9552	0.9143	0.5000
3	0.9857	0.9447	0.8951	0.4444
4	0.9842	0.9396	0.8862	0.4219
5	0.9834	0.9367	0.8810	0.4096
10	0.9818	0.9310	0.8709	0.3874
32	0.9807	0.9272	0.8642	0.3737
64	0.9805	0.9263	0.8627	0.3708
128	0.9804	0.9259	0.8620	0.3693
256	0.9803	0.9257	0.8616	0.3686

Fig. 4. EFTP packet layout.

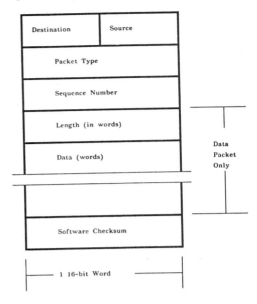

The comparatively complex end-dally sequence is intended to make it practically certain that the sender and receiver of a file will agree on whether the file has been transmitted correctly. If the end packet is lost, the data sender simply retransmits it as it would any packet with an overdue acknowledgement. If the endreply from the data receiver is lost, the data sender will time out in the same way and retransmit the end packet which will in turn be acknowledged by the dallying receiver. If the echoed endreply is lost, the dallying receiver will be inconvenienced having to wait for it, but when it has timed out, the receiver can nevertheless be assured of successful transfer of the file because the end packet has been received.

At any time during all of this, either side is free to decide communication has failed and just give up; it is considered polite to send an abort packet to end the communication promptly in the event of, say, a user-initiated abort or a file system error.

7.2.3 EFTP shortcomings. The EFTP has been very useful, but its shortcomings are many. First, the protocol provides only for file transfer from station to station in a single network and specifically not from process to process within stations either on the same network or through a gateway. Second, process rendezvous is degenerate in that there are no mechanisms for finding processes by name or for convenient handling of multiple users by a single server. Third, there is no real flow control. If data arrives at a receiver unable to accept it into its buffers, the data can simply be thrown away with complete assurance that it will be retransmitted eventually. There is no way for a receiver to quench the flow of such wasted transmissions or to expedite retransmission. Fourth, data is transmitted in integral numbers of 16-bit

words belonging to unnamed files and thus the EFTP is either terribly restrictive or demands some nested file transfer formats internal to its data words. And fifth, functional generality is lost because the receiver is also the listener and server.

8. Conclusion

Our experience with an operating Ethernet leads us to conclude that our emphasis on distributed control was well placed. By keeping the shared components of the communication system to a minimum and passive, we have achieved a very high level of reliability. Installation and maintenance of our experimental Ethernet has been more than satisfactory. The flexibility of station interconnection provided by broadcast packet switching has encouraged the development of numerous computer networking and multiprocessing applications.

Acknowledgments. Our colleagues at the Xerox Palo Alto Research Center, especially Tat C. Lam, Butler W. Lampson, John F. Shoch, and Charles P. Thacker, have contributed in many ways to the evolution of Ethernet ideas and to the construction of the experimental system without which such ideas would be just so much speculation.

Received May 1975; revised December 1975

References
1. Abramson, N. The Aloha system. AFIPS Conf. Proc., Vol. 37, 1970 FJCC, AFIPS Press, Montvale, N.J., 1970, pp. 281–285.
2. Abramson, N. and Kuo, F.F. *Computer-Communication Networks.* Prentice-Hall, Englewood Cliffs, N.J., 1975.
3. Ashenhurst, R.L., and Vonderohe, R.H. A hierarchical network. *Datamation 21*, 2 (Feb. 1975), 40–44.
4. Baran, P. On distributed communications. Rand Corp. Memo RM-3420-PR, Aug. 1964.
5. Barnes, G.H., Brown, R.M., Kato, M., Kuck, D.J., Slotnick, D.L., and Stokes, R.A. The Illiac IV Computer. *IEEE Trans. Computers C-17*, 8 (Aug. 1968), 758–770.
6. Binder, R., Abramson, N., Kuo, F., Okinaka, A., and Wax, D. Aloha packet broadcasting—a retrospect. AFIPS Conf. Proc., Vol. 44, 1975 NCC, AFIPS Press, Montvale, N.J., 1975.
7. Cerf, V.G., and Kahn, R.E. A protocol for packet network intercommunication. *IEEE Trans. Comm. COMM-22*, 5 (May 1974), 637–648.
8. The shrinking world: computer networks and communications. *Computer 7*, 2 (Feb. 1974).
9. Distributed-function computer architectures. *Computer 7*, 3 (March 1974).
10. Crocker, S.D., Heafner, J.F., Metcalfe, R.M., and Postel, J.B. Function-oriented protocols for the Arpa computer network. AFIPS Conf. Proc., Vol. 40, 1972 SJCC, AFIPS Press, Montvale, N.J., 1972, pp. 271–279.
11. Crowther, W.R., Heart, F.E., McKenzie, A.A., McQuillan, J.M., and Walden, D.C. Issues in packet-switching network design. AFIPS Conf. Proc., Vol. 44, 1975 NCC, AFIPS Press, Montvale, N.J., 1975, pp. 161–175.
12. Farber, D.J., et al. The distributed computing system. Proc. 7th Ann. IEEE Computer Soc. International Conf., Feb. 1973, pp. 31–34.
13. Farber, D.J., A ring network. *Datamation 21*, 2 (Feb. 1975), 44–46.
14. Fraser, A.G. A virtual channel network. *Datamation 21*, 2 (Feb. 1975), 51–53.

15. Heart, F.E., Kahn, R.E., Ornstein, S.M., Crowther, W.R., and Walden, D.C. The interface message processor for the Arpa computer network, AFIPS Conf. Proc., Vol. 36, 1970 SJCC, AFIPS Press, Montvale, N.J., 1970, pp. 551–567.

16. Heart, F.E., Ornstein, S.M., Crowther, W.R., and Barker, W.B. A new minicomputer-multiprocessor for the Arpa network. AFIPS Conf. Proc., Vol. 42, 1972 SJCC, AFIPS Press, Montvale, N.J., 1972, pp. 529–537.

17. Kahn, R.R. The organization of computer resources into a packet ratio network. AFIPS Conf. Proc., Vol. 44, 1975 NCC, AFIPS Press, Montvale, N.J., 1975, pp. 177–186.

18. Metcalfe, R.M. Strategies for interprocess communication in a distributed computing system. Proc. Symp. on Computer Commun. Networks and Teletraffic. Polytechnic Press, New York, 1972.

19. Metcalfe, R.M. Strategies for Operating Systems in Computer Networks, Proc. ACM National Conf., August 1972, pp. 278–281.

20. Metcalfe, R.M. Steady-state analysis of a slotted and controlled aloha system with blocking. Proc. 6th Hawaii Conf. on System Sci. Jan. 1973, pp. 375–380.

21. Metcalfe, R.M. Packet communication. Harvard Ph.D. Th., Project Mac TR-114, Dec. 1973.

22. Metcalfe, R.M. Distributed algorithms for a broadcast queue. Talk given at Stanford University in November 1974 and at the University of California at Berkeley in February 1975, paper in preparation.

23. Murthy, P. Analysis of a carrier-sense random-access system with random packet length. Aloha System Tech. Rep. B75-17, U. of Hawaii, May 1975.

24. Ornstein, S.M., Crowther, W.R., Kraley, M.F., Bressler, R.D., Michel, A., and Heart, F.E. Pluribus—a reliable multiprocessor. AFIPS Conf. Proc., Vol. 44, 1975 NCC, AFIPS Press, Montvale, N.J., 1970, pp. 551–559.

25. Retz, D.L. Operating system design considerations for the packet switching environment. AFIPS Conf. Proc., Vol. 44, 1975 NCC, AFIPS Press, Montvale, N.J., 1970, pp. 155–160.

26. Roberts, L., and Wessler, B. Computer network development to achieve resource sharing. AFIPS Conf. Proc., Vol. 36, 1970 SJCC, AFIPS Press, Montvale, N.J., 1970, pp. 543–549.

27. Roberts, L. Capture effects on Aloha channels. Proc. 6th Hawaii Conf. on System Sci., Jan. 1973.

28. Rowe, L.A. The distributed computing operating system. Tech. Rep. 66, Dep. of Information and Computer Sci., U. of California, Irvine, June 1975.

29. Rustin, R. (Ed.) Computer Networks (Proc. Courant Computer Sci. Symp. 3, December 1970), Prentice-Hall, Englewood Cliffs, N.J., 1970.

30. *IBM synchronous data link control—general information.* IBM Systems Development Div., Pub. Center, Research Triangle Park, N.C., 1974.

31. *IBM system network architecture—general information.* IBM Systems Development Div., Pub. Center, Research Triangle Park, N.C., 1975.

32. Thomas, R.H. A resource sharing executive for the Arpanet. AFIPS Conf. Proc., Vol. 42, 1973 NCC, AFIPS Press, Montvale, N.J., 1973, pp. 155–163.

33. Thornton, J.E. *Design of a Computer: the Control Data 6600.* Scott Foresman and Co., Glenview, Ill. 1970.

34. Walden, D.C. A system for interprocess communication in a resource sharing computer network. *Comm. ACM, 15,* 4 (April 1972), 221–230.

35. Willard, D.G. Mitrix: A sophisticated digital cable communications system Proc. National Telecommunications Conf., Nov. 1973.

36. Wulf, W., and Levin, R. C.mmp—a multi-mini-processor, AFIPS Conf. Proc., Vol. 41, 1972 FJCC, AFIPS Press, Montvale, N.J., 1972.

A Survey of Wormhole Routing Techniques in Direct Networks

Lionel M. Ni and Philip K. McKinley

Michigan State University

Efficient routing of messages is critical to the performance of direct network systems. The popular wormhole routing technique faces several challenges — particularly flow control and deadlock avoidance.

Massively parallel computers with thousands of processors are considered the most promising technology to achieve teraflops computational power. Such large-scale multiprocessors are usually organized as ensembles of nodes, where each node has its own processor, local memory, and other supporting devices. These nodes may have different functional capabilities. For example, the set of nodes may include vector processors, graphics processors, I/O processors, and symbolic processors.

The way the nodes are connected to one another varies among machines. In a direct network architecture, each node has a point-to-point, or direct, connection to some number of other nodes, called neighboring nodes. Direct networks have become a popular architecture for constructing massively parallel computers because they scale well; that is, as the number of nodes in the system increases, the total communication bandwidth, memory bandwidth, and processing capability of the system also increase. Figure 1 shows a generic multiprocessor with a set of nodes interconnected through a direct network.

Because they do not physically share memory, nodes must communicate by passing messages through the network. Message size may vary, depending on the application. For efficient and fair use of network resources, a message is often divided into packets prior to transmission. A packet is the smallest unit of communication that contains routing and sequencing information; this information is carried in the packet header. Neighboring nodes may send packets to one another directly, while nodes that are not directly connected must rely on other nodes in the network to relay packets from source to destination. In many systems, each node contains a separate router to handle such communication-related tasks. Although a router's function could be performed by the corresponding local processor, dedicated routers are used to allow overlapped computation and communication within each node.

Figure 2 shows the architecture of a generic node. Each router supports some number of input and output channels. Normally, every input channel is paired with a corresponding output channel. Internal channels connect the local processor/memory to the router. Although it is common to provide only one pair of internal channels, some systems use more internal channels to avoid a communication bottleneck between the local processor/memory and the router. External channels are used for communication between routers and, therefore, between nodes. In this article, unless otherwise specified, the term *channel* will refer to an external channel. By connecting the input channels of one node to the output channels of other nodes, the topology of the direct network is defined. A packet sent between two nodes that are not neighboring must be forwarded by routers along multiple external channels. Usually, a crossbar is used to allow all possible connections between the input and output channels within the router. The sequential list of channels traversed by such a packet is called a path, and the number of channels in the path is called the path length.

The programmer of a multiprocessor based on a direct network can invoke various system primitives to send messages between processes executing on different nodes. Writing such a message-passing program has been traditionally difficult and error prone. Systems used in this manner have been referred to as message-passing multicomputers.[1] Recently, an alternative approach has been pursued, whereby a sophisticated compiler generates data-movement operations from shared-memory parallel programs. For a user, the shared-memory programming paradigm is usually simpler and more intuitive than dealing with the low-level details of message passing. Systems used in this manner have been referred to as scalable shared-memory multiprocessors.[2]

Whether a direct network system is used to support a message-passing or a shared-memory programming paradigm, the time required to move data between nodes is critical to system performance, as it effectively determines what granularity levels of parallelism are possible in executing an application program. A metric commonly used to evaluate a direct network system is *communication latency*, which is the sum of three values: start-up latency, network latency, and blocking time.

Start-up latency is the time required for the system to handle the packet at both the source and destination nodes. Its value depends mainly on the design of system software and the interface between local processors and routers. Start-up latency can be further decomposed into sending latency and receiving latency — the start-up latencies incurred at the sending node and the receiving node, respectively. The network latency equals the elapsed time

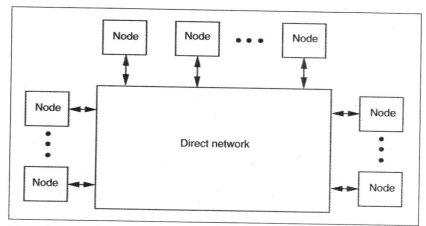

Figure 1. A generic multiprocessor based on a direct network.

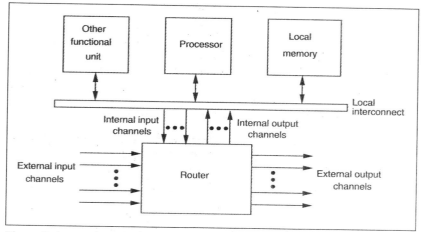

Figure 2. A generic node architecture.

after the head of a packet has entered the network at the source until the tail of the packet emerges from the network at the destination. Start-up latency and network latency are static for a given system; that is, the sum of their values reflects the latency of packets sent in the absence of other network traffic and transient system activities.

The blocking time includes all possible delays encountered during the lifetime of a packet. These delays are due mainly to conflicts over the use of shared resources, for example, delays due to channel contention, in which two packets simultaneously require the same channel. Blocking time reflects the dynamic behavior of the network resulting from the passing of multiple packets; it may be high if the network traffic is heavy or unevenly distributed.

The communication latency of a direct network depends on several architectural characteristics; one of the most

important is the type of switching technology used by routers to transfer data from input channels to output channels. A variety of switching techniques have been used in direct networks. One method, called *wormhole routing*,[3] has become quite popular in recent years. This article surveys the research contributions and commercial ventures related to wormhole routing. We review the properties of direct networks, then describe in detail the operation and characteristics of wormhole routing. By its nature, wormhole routing is particularly susceptible to deadlock situations, in which two or more packets may block one another indefinitely. Deadlock avoidance is usually guaranteed by the routing algorithm, which selects the path a packet takes. We describe several approaches to deadlock-free routing, along with a technique that allows multiple *virtual* channels to share the same physical channel. In addition, we discuss sev-

Direct network topologies

There are many ways to interconnect nodes in a direct network. Most of the popular direct network topologies fall in the general category of either n-dimensional meshes or k-ary n-cubes because their regular topologies simplify routing.

Formally, an n-dimensional mesh has $k_0 \times k_1 \times \ldots \times k_{n-2} \times k_{n-1}$ nodes, k_i nodes along each dimension i, where $k_i \geq 2$. Each node x is identified by n coordinates, $\sigma_{n-1}(x)$, $\sigma_{n-2}(x), \ldots, \sigma_1(x), \sigma_0(x)$, where $0 \leq \sigma_i(x) \leq k_i - 1$ for $0 \leq i \leq n - 1$. Two nodes x and y are neighbors if and only if $\sigma_i(x) = \sigma_i(y)$ for all i, $0 \leq i \leq n - 1$, except one, j, where $\sigma_j(y) = \sigma_j(x) \pm 1$. Thus, nodes have from n to $2n$ neighbors, depending on their location in the mesh.

In a k-ary n-cube, all nodes have the same number of neighbors. The definition of a k-ary n-cube differs from that of an n-dimensional mesh in that all of the k_i's are equal to k and two nodes x and y are neighbors if and only if $\sigma_i(x) = \sigma_i(y)$ for all i, $0 \leq i \leq n - 1$, except one, j, where $\sigma_j(y) = (\sigma_j(x) \pm 1) \mod k$. The use of modular arithmetic in the definition results in *wraparound* channels in the k-ary n-cube, which are not present in the n-dimensional mesh. A k-ary n-cube contains k^n nodes. If $k = 2$, then every node has n neighbors, one in each dimension. If $k > 2$, then every node has $2n$ neighbors, two in each dimension.

Several special cases of the n-dimensional meshes and k-ary n-cubes have been proposed or implemented as direct network topologies. When $n = 1$, the k-ary n-cube collapses to a ring with k nodes. The hypercube is a symmetric network and a special case of both the n-dimensional mesh and the k-ary n-cube. A hypercube is an n-dimensional mesh in which $k_i = 2$ for all i, $0 \leq i \leq n - 1$, that is, a 2-ary n-cube. Figure A1 depicts a binary 4-cube, or 16-node hypercube. When $n = 2$, the topology is a 2D torus with k^2 nodes. Figure A2 illustrates a 3-ary 2D torus. Figure A3 shows a $3 \times 3 \times 3$ 3D mesh, which results from removing the wraparound channels from a 3-ary 3-cube.

Hypercubes, low-dimensional meshes, and tori can be compared in terms of their bisection width η, that is, the minimum number of channels that must be removed to partition the network into two equal subnetworks. To make a fair comparison, we consider networks in which the number of nodes is $N = 2^{2n}$. Three possible network topologies containing this number of nodes are a $2n$-cube, a $2^n \times 2^n$ 2D mesh, and a $2^n \times 2^n$ 2D torus. The bisection widths of these three topologies are $\eta_{hypercube} = 2^{2n-1}$, $\eta_{2D mesh} = 2^n$, and $\eta_{2D torus} = 2^{n+1}$, respectively. The bisection density is the product of η and the channel width W and can be used as a measure of the network cost. If all of the

networks have the same bisection density, then
$$W_{2D mesh}/W_{hypercube} = 2^{n-1} = \sqrt{N}/2$$
and
$$W_{2D torus}/W_{hypercube} = 2^{n-2} = \sqrt{N}/4.$$
In other words, for the same cost, the 2D mesh and the 2D torus can support wider channels and thereby offer higher channel bandwidth. However, the low-dimensional networks have larger diameters, which is the maximum distance between two nodes. The diameters of the topologies are $2n$, $2^{n+1} - 2$, and $2^n - 1$, respectively.

Both the hypercube and the torus are symmetric networks in that there exists a homomorphism that maps any node of the graph representing the network graph onto any other node.[1] Mesh networks, on the other hand, are asymmetric because the wraparound channels are absent. Assuming uniform traffic between nodes, channels near the center of the mesh are likely to experience higher traffic density than channels on the periphery. In addition, the network diameter is doubled. On the other hand, it is easier to provide deadlock-free routing in mesh networks than in torus networks. Furthermore, in a 2D layout, long wraparound wires connecting boundary nodes are eliminated to further reduce the wire complexity and increase the potential clock rate. In fact, the network bisection width is reduced by half.

Most direct network topologies used in wormhole-routed systems are low-dimensional meshes and hypercubes. The Intel Touchstone Delta, the Intel Paragon, and the Symult 2010 use a 2D mesh; the MIT J-machine and Caltech's Mosaic use a 3D mesh; and the Ncube-2/3 uses a hypercube.

Further information on direct network topologies is available from several sources. Reed and Fujimoto offer an analysis of many direct network topologies and discuss the treatment of many other issues related to multicomputer design.[1] Dally provides a performance analysis of k-ary n-cube topologies[2] and also deals with wire limit issues and constraints with regard to direct network topologies.[3]

References

1. D.A. Reed and R.M. Fujimoto, *Multicomputer Networks: Message-Based Parallel Processing*, MIT Press, Cambridge, Mass., 1987.

2. W.J. Dally, "Performance Analysis of k-ary n-cube Interconnection Networks," *IEEE Trans. Computers*, June 1990, Vol. 39, No. 6, pp. 775-785.

3. W.J. Dally, "Wire-Efficient VLSI Multiprocessor Communication Networks," *Proc. Stanford Conf. Advanced Research in VLSI*, P. Losleben, ed., MIT Press, Cambridge, Mass., Mar. 1987, pp. 391-415.

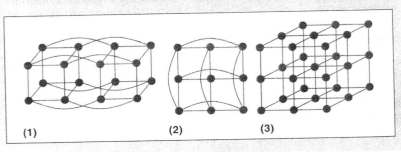

(1)　　　　(2)　　　　(3)

Figure A. Direct network topologies: (1) 2-ary 4-cube (hypercube); (2) 3-ary 2-cube (torus); (3) $3 \times 3 \times 3$ 3D mesh.

eral open issues related to wormhole routing.

Characteristics of direct networks

The average communication latency in a direct network depends on several network properties. A direct network is characterized by four factors: topology, routing, flow control, and switching.

Topology. The topology of a network, usually modeled as a graph, defines how the nodes are interconnected by channels. If every node is connected directly to every other node, the network topology is fully connected, or complete. Although complete topologies obviate forwarding of packets by intermediate nodes, they are practical only for very small networks because the number of physical connections per node is limited by rigid constraints, such as the number of available pins and pads on the router and the amount of VLSI area available for communication-related hardware. These engineering and scaling difficulties preclude networks with large complete topologies.

Therefore, many direct networks use a fixed, *multiple-hop* topology, such as a hypercube or two-dimensional mesh, each of which is a special case of k-ary n-cubes or n-dimensional meshes. (See the "Direct network topologies" sidebar for detailed definitions.) In multiple-hop topologies, packets may traverse one or more intermediate nodes before reaching the destination. Some computers provide basic cells that can be configured as different topologies, depending on the application. For example, if each router has one input channel and one output channel, the only feasible interconnection topology is a unidirectional ring. If each router has two input channels and two output channels, possible interconnection topologies include a bidirectional linear array and a bidirectional ring. With enough input and output channels, direct networks of arbitrary size and topology can be constructed.

Two conflicting requirements of a direct network are that it must accommodate a large number of nodes and exhibit a low network latency. As the number of nodes increases, the number of wires needed to interconnect them

also increases. The complexity of the connection is said to be *wire limited:* the more edges in a topology, the more difficult that topology is to fabricate in a limited area.

Several parameters are used to study this problem. The *bisection width* of a topology is the minimum number of channels that must be removed, or cut, to partition the network into two subnetworks, each containing half the nodes in the network. The channel width is the number of bits that can be transmitted simultaneously on a physical channel between two adjacent nodes, and the channel rate is the peak rate at which bits can be transferred over each individual line of a physical channel. The channel bandwidth, which is the product of the channel width and the channel rate, determines the communication performance of a direct network. Bisection density, the product of bisection width and the channel width, can be used as a measure of network cost. For a given bisection density, a large bisection width dictates a small channel width.

For a given number of network nodes, low-dimensional mesh networks have much lower bisection widths than, say, hypercubes; consequently, they can offer wider channels and a higher channel bandwidth for a given bisection density (see "Direct network topologies" sidebar for details). A disadvantage of low-dimensional networks is that the average distance between nodes is relatively large. For systems in which the network latency depends on the path length, the hypercube is a popular choice of topology because of its relatively small internode distance. However, in other systems, such as those that support wormhole routing, the network latency is almost independent of the path length when there is no contention and the packet length is relatively large. Low-dimensional meshes are popular topologies for such systems because the negative effects of their large internode distance are minimized.

Routing. A direct network topology must allow every node to send packets to every other node. In the absence of a complete topology, routing determines the path selected by a packet to reach its destination. Efficient routing is critical to the performance of direct networks.

Routing can be classified in several ways. In *source routing*, the source node

selects the entire path before sending the packet. Each packet must carry this routing information, increasing the packet size. Furthermore, the path cannot be changed after the packet has left the source. Most direct network systems use *distributed routing.* In this approach, each router, upon receiving the packet, decides whether it should be delivered to the local processor or forwarded to a neighboring router. In the latter case, the routing algorithm is invoked to determine which neighbor should be sent the packet. In a practical router design, the routing decision process must be as fast as possible to reduce the network latency. A good routing algorithm should also be easily implemented in hardware. Furthermore, the decision process usually does not require global state information of the network. Providing such information to each router creates additional traffic and requires additional storage space in each router.

Routing can also be classified as deterministic or adaptive. In deterministic routing, the path is completely determined by the source and destination addresses. This method is also referred to as oblivious routing. A routing technique is adaptive if, for a given source and destination, the path taken by a particular packet depends on dynamic network conditions, such as the presence of faulty or congested channels.

A routing algorithm is said to be minimal if the path selected is one of the shortest paths between the source and destination pair. Using a minimal routing algorithm, every channel visited will bring the packet closer to the destination. A nonminimal routing algorithm allows packets to follow a longer path, usually in response to current network conditions. If nonminimal routing is used, care must be taken to avoid a situation in which the packet will continue to be routed through the network but never reach the destination.

Flow control. A network consists of many channels and buffers. Flow control deals with the allocation of channels and buffers to a packet as it travels along a path through the network. A resource collision occurs when a packet cannot proceed because some resource that it requires is held by another packet. Whether the packet is dropped, blocked in place, buffered, or rerouted through another channel depends on the flow control policy. A good flow control policy should avoid channel congestion while reducing the network latency.

The allocation of channels and their associated buffers to packets can be viewed from two perspectives. The routing algorithm determines which output channel is selected for a packet arriving on a given input channel. Therefore, routing can be referred to as the *output selection policy*. Since an outgoing channel can be requested by packets arriving on many different input channels, an *input selection policy* is needed to determine which packet may use the output channel. Possible input selection policies include round robin, fixed channel priority, and first come, first served. The input selection policy affects the fairness of routing algorithms.

Switching techniques

Early direct networks used store-and-forward switching borrowed from the computer network community. In this approach, when a packet reaches an intermediate node, the entire packet is stored in a packet buffer. The packet is then forwarded to a selected neighboring node when the next output channel is available and the neighboring node has an available buffer. This switching strategy was adopted in the research prototype Cosmic Cube and several first-generation commercial multicomputers, including the iPSC-1, Ncube 1, Ametek 14, and FPS T-series. Store-and-forward switching is simple, but it has two major drawbacks. First, each node must buffer every incoming packet, consuming memory space. Second, the network latency is proportional to the distance between the source and destination nodes. The network latency is $(L/B)D$, where L is the packet length, B is the channel bandwidth, and D is the length of the path between the source and destination nodes.

To decrease the amount of time spent transmitting data, Kermani and Kleinrock introduced the virtual cut-through method for computer communication networks. In virtual cut-through, a packet is stored at an intermediate node only if the next required channel is busy. The network latency is $(L_h/B)D + L/B$, where L_h is the length of the header field. When $L \gg L_h$, the second term, L/B, will dominate, and the distance D will produce a negligible effect on the network latency. The research prototype Harts, developed at the University of Michigan, is a hexagonal mesh multicomputer that adopts virtual cut-through switching. Felperin et al. provide a good survey of routing algorithms based on store-and-forward or virtual cut-through switching mechanisms.[1]

In circuit switching, a physical circuit is constructed between the source and destination nodes during the circuit establishment phase. In the packet transmission phase, the packet is transmitted along the circuit to the destination. During this phase, the channels constituting the circuit are reserved exclusively for the circuit; hence, there is no need for buffers at the intermediate nodes. In the circuit termination phase, the circuit is torn down as the tail of the packet is transmitted.

The network latency for circuit switching is $(L_c/B)D + L/B$, where L_c is the length of the control packet transmitted to establish the circuit. If $L_c \ll L$, the distance D has a negligible effect on the network latency. If a circuit cannot be established because a desired channel is being used by other packets, the circuit is said to be blocked. Depending on the way blocked circuits are handled, the partial circuit may be torn down, with establishment to be attempted later. This policy is called *loss mode*. Some second-generation multicomputers, such as Intel's iPSC-2 and iPSC/860, use circuit switching. Grunwald and Reed present a detailed performance study of different circuit switching techniques.[2]

Wormhole routing also uses a cut-through approach to switching. A packet is divided into a number of *flits* (flow control digits) for transmission. The header flit (or flits) governs the route. As the header advances along the specified route, the remaining flits follow in a pipeline fashion. If the header flit encounters a channel already in use, it is blocked until the channel becomes available. Rather than buffering the remaining flits by removing them from the network channels, as in virtual cut-through, the flow control within the network blocks the trailing flits and they remain in flit buffers along the established route. The network latency for wormhole routing is $(L_f/B)D + L/B$, where L_f is the length of each flit, B is the channel bandwidth, D is the path length, and L is the length of the message. If $L_f \ll L$, the path length D will not significantly affect the network latency unless it is very large.

Both computer networks and direct networks can implement and share the above switching techniques. Since cut-through switching does not have to buffer the entire packet before forwarding it to the next node, the data-link-level protocol is eliminated. This is good for direct networks, as the network complexity and overhead are further reduced. However, because of the high transmission error rate in computer networks, eliminating the data-link-level protocol will delay the detection of a transmission error. The error will be detected by an end-to-end acknowledgment provided at the transport layer. This is the main reason that cut-through switching is not normally used in computer networks.

Figure B compares the communication latency of wormhole routing with that of store-and-forward switching and circuit switching in a contention-free network. In this case, the behavior of virtual cut-through is the same as that of wormhole routing, so virtual cut-through is not shown explicitly. The channel propagation delay is typically small relative to L/B and is ignored here. For example, in the Intel Touchstone Delta, the time to transmit one flit on a channel is 75 nanoseconds for packets traveling in the same direction and 150 nanoseconds for packets that change direction. Even for a channel a foot long, the propagation delay is only 1.5 nanoseconds. The delay in transmitting a "ready" signal from the destination to the source in circuit switching is also ignored.

The figure shows the activities of each node over time when a packet is transmitted from a source node S to the destination node D through three intermediate nodes, $I1$, $I2$, and $I3$. The time required to transfer the packet between the source processor and its router, and between the last router and the destination processor, is ignored. Unlike store-and-forward switching, both circuit switching and

Switching. While the input and output selection policies determine how a packet uses channels as it traverses an intermediate router, switching is the actual mechanism that removes data from an input channel and places it on an output channel. Network latency is

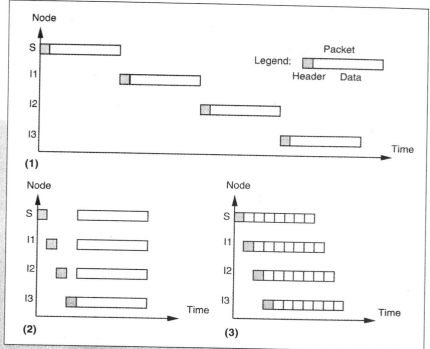

Figure B. Comparison of different switching techniques: (1) store-and-forward switching; (2) circuit switching; (3) wormhole routing.

wormhole routing have communication latencies that are nearly independent of the distance between the source and destination nodes.

This characteristic is confirmed by measurements on actual machines. Figure C plots the communication latency versus path length for a 1-Kbyte packet transmitted using three switching techniques: store-and-forward switching (on a 64-node Ncube-1 at Michigan State University), circuit switching (on a 32-node iPSC/2 at the University of Missouri–Rolla), and wormhole routing (on a 64-node Ncube-2 at Purdue University). The latencies of both circuit switching and wormhole routing demonstrate virtually no sensitivity to distance. In these measurements, the traffic is generated such that there is no channel contention. Thus, the communication latency does not include the blocking time.

The first commercial multiprocessor to adopt wormhole routing was the Ametek 2010, which used a 2D mesh topology. This machine was renamed Symult 2010 and ceased production in 1990. The Ncube-2, announced in 1989, also uses wormhole routing in a hypercube. Intel/DARPA's Touchstone Delta, delivered in 1991, uses wormhole routing based on a 2D mesh, as does the Intel Paragon, announced in 1991. The research prototype J-machine, built at the Massachusetts Institute of Technology in 1991, uses wormhole routing in a 3D mesh. Both Intel/CMU's iWarp and the Transputer IMS T9000 family use wormhole routing in their basic building-block nodes. Additional material and complete references for these machines are available in the literature.[3]

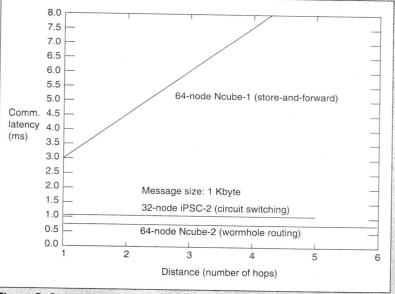

Figure C. Communication latency in milliseconds versus distance for transmitting a 1-Kbyte message.

References

1. S.A. Felperin et al., "Routing Techniques for Massively Parallel Communication," *Proc. IEEE*, Vol. 79, No. 4, Apr. 1991, pp. 488-503.

2. D.C. Grunwald and D.A. Reed, "Networks for Parallel Processors: Measurements and Prognostications," *Proc. Third Conf. Hypercube Concurrent Computers and Applications*, Vol. 1, ACM, New York, Jan. 1988, pp. 610-619.

3. L.M. Ni and P.K. McKinley, "A Survey of Routing Techniques in Wormhole Networks," Tech. Report MSU-CPS-ACS-46, Dept. of Computer Science, Michigan State University, East Lansing, Mich., Oct. 1991.

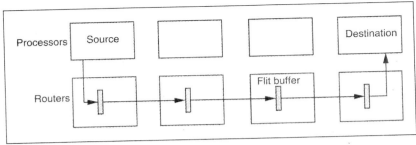

Figure 3. Wormhole routing.

highly dependent on the switching technique used. Four switching techniques have been adopted in direct networks: store-and-forward, circuit switching, virtual cut-through, and wormhole routing (see "Switching techniques" sidebar on pages 66-67). In store-and-forward switching, also called packet switching, when a packet reaches an intermediate node, the entire packet is stored in a packet buffer. The packet is then forwarded to a selected neighboring node when the next channel is available and the neighboring node has an available packet buffer. In circuit switching, a physical circuit is constructed between the source and destination nodes. After the packet has been transmitted along the circuit to the destination, the circuit is torn down. In virtual cut-through, the packet header is examined upon arrival at an intermediate node. The packet is stored at the intermediate node only if the next required channel is busy; oth-

erwise, it is forwarded immediately without buffering.

Circuit switching and virtual cut-through are both based on the concept of cut-through, which can significantly reduce the network latency. Specifically, the delay introduced by each intermediate router is small. If the start-up latency (about 385 microseconds in Ncube-1 and 150 microseconds in Ncube-2) is very large relative to the delay at each router, the network latency contributes little to the communication latency unless the path is very long. However, as network traffic increases, the blocking time, which is a function of the path length, may become significant.

Wormhole routing

Although both virtual cut-through and circuit switching offer low network la-

tencies that are relatively independent of path length, virtual cut-through requires that blocked packets be buffered, and circuit switching makes it difficult to support sharing of channels among packets. Wormhole routing, proposed by Dally and Seitz,[3] was designed to overcome these difficulties while offering similar network latency.

Wormhole routing also uses a cut-through approach to switching. A packet is divided into a number of *flits* (flow control digits) for transmission. The size of a flit depends on system parameters, in particular the channel width. Normally, the bits constituting a flit are transmitted in parallel between two routers. The header flit (or flits) of a packet governs the route. As the header advances along the specified route, the remaining flits follow in a pipeline fashion, as shown in Figure 3. If the header flit encounters a channel already in use, it is blocked until the channel becomes available. Rather than buffering the remaining flits by removing them from the network channels, as in virtual cut-through, the flow control within the network blocks the trailing flits and they remain in flit buffers along the established route. Once a channel has been acquired by a packet, it is reserved for the packet. The channel is released when the last, or tail, flit has been transmitted on the channel.

The pipelined nature of wormhole routing produces two positive effects. First, the absence of network conten-

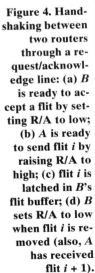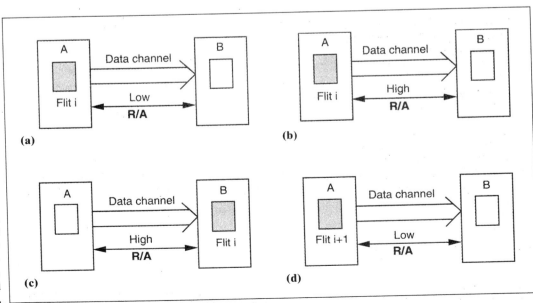

Figure 4. Handshaking between two routers through a request/acknowledge line: (a) *B* is ready to accept a flit by setting R/A to low; (b) *A* is ready to send flit *i* by raising R/A to high; (c) flit *i* is latched in *B*'s flit buffer; (d) *B* sets R/A to low when flit *i* is removed (also, *A* has received flit *i* + 1).

tion makes the network latency relatively insensitive to path length. Second, large packet buffers at each intermediate node are obviated; only a small FIFO (first in, first out) flit buffer is required. In some wormhole-routed systems, such as the Ncube-2 and Symult 2010, the flit buffer can hold only one flit. Other systems, such as the J-machine, a fine-grained system built at the Massachusetts Institute of Technology, have demonstrated improved network performance by using larger flit buffers. In the extreme, when the flit buffers are as large as the packets themselves, the behavior of wormhole routing resembles that of virtual cut-through.

If a large-scale wormhole-routed network is to be constructed, the effects of propagation delay make it difficult to distribute a high-speed synchronous clock to all nodes over a physically large area. Therefore, a popular approach has been self-timed circuit design,[4] in which flits passing between two adjacent nodes must use a handshaking protocol. In the example in Figure 4, a unidirectional channel from router A connects to router B. A single-wire request/acknowledge (R/A) line is associated with the channel. The R/A line can be raised only by router A, the requesting side, and lowered only by router B, the acknowledging side. When A is ready to send a flit to B, A must wait until the R/A line is low. A then places the data on the data channel and raises the R/A line to high. Router B will lower the R/A line when it has removed the flit from the flit buffer (or, in the case of large flit buffers, if there is an empty flit slot in the buffer).

The way wormhole-routed packets acquire and use channels leads to other advantages over circuit switching. In circuit switching, once a channel is assigned to a packet, it cannot be used by other packets until the channel is released. In contrast, wormhole routing allows a channel to be shared by many packets. We discuss this *virtual channel* concept later. Furthermore, wormhole routing allows packet replication, in which copies of a flit can be sent on multiple output channels. Packet replication is useful in supporting broadcast and multicast communication.[5] By its nature, circuit switching does not permit packet replication.

Wormhole routing has been a popular switching technique in new-genera-

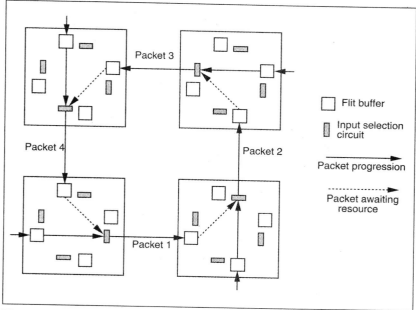

Figure 5. An example of channel deadlock involving four packets.

tion direct networks. The first commercial multicomputer to adopt wormhole routing was the Ametek 2010, which used a 2D mesh topology. (This machine was later renamed the Symult 2010.) The Ncube-2, which uses a hypercube topology, has also adopted wormhole routing. The Intel Touchstone Delta and Intel Paragon use wormhole routing in a 2D mesh. Finally, MIT's research prototype J-machine uses wormhole routing in a 3D mesh.

Deadlock

Switching strategy and the routing algorithm used are among several factors that affect communication latency. One situation that can postpone packet delivery indefinitely is deadlock, in which a set of packets may become blocked forever in the network. Deadlock can occur if packets are allowed to hold some resources while requesting others. In store-and-forward and virtual cut-through switching, the resources are buffers. In circuit switching and wormhole routing, the resources are channels. Because blocked packets holding channels (and their corresponding flit buffers) remain in the network, wormhole routing is particularly susceptible to deadlock. Figure 5 shows an example of channel deadlock involving four rout-

ers and four packets. Each packet is holding a flit buffer while requesting the flit buffer being held by another packet.

One way to solve the deadlock problem is to allow the preemption of packets involved in a potential deadlock situation. Preempted packets can be either rerouted or discarded. The former policy gives rise to adaptive nonminimal routing techniques. The latter policy requires that the packets be recovered at the source and retransmitted. Because of requirements for low latency and reliability, packet preemption is not used in most direct network architectures.

More commonly, deadlock is avoided by the routing algorithm. By ordering network resources and requiring that packets request and use these resources in strictly monotonic order, circular wait — a necessary condition for deadlock — is avoided. Hence, deadlock involving these resources cannot arise.

In wormhole-routed networks, channels are the critical resources. A *channel dependence graph*[6] can be used to develop a deadlock-free routing algorithm. The channel dependence graph for a direct network and a routing algorithm is a directed graph $D = G(C, E)$, where the vertex set $C(D)$ consists of all the unidirectional channels in the

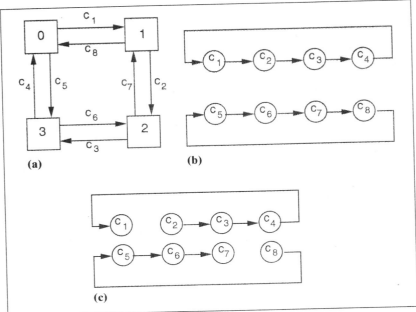

Figure 6. A four-node network and the corresponding channel dependence graphs: (a) a direct network with four nodes; (b) channel dependence graph; (c) channel dependence graph based on restricted minimal routing.

network, and the edge set $E(D)$ includes all the pairs of connected channels, as defined by the routing algorithm. In other words, if $(c_i, c_j) \in E(D)$, then c_i and c_j are, respectively, an input channel and an output channel of a node, and the routing algorithm may route packets from c_i to c_j. A routing algorithm for a direct network is deadlock-free if and only if there is no cycle in the channel dependence graph.[6]

Figure 6 demonstrates the channel dependence graph method. The four nodes shown in Figure 6a can be considered as a ring, a 2×2 mesh, a 2-cube, a 4-ary 1-cube, or a 2×2 torus. Assuming a packet can be delivered through any minimal routing path, the corresponding channel dependence graph is shown in Figure 6b. Since there are two cycles in the channel dependence graph, deadlock is possible. One way to avoid deadlock is to disallow packets to be forwarded from channel c_1 to c_2 and from c_7 to c_8. The resulting channel dependence graph is shown in Figure 6c. It can be easily verified that the routing is still minimal. However, to send a packet from node 0 to node 2, the packet must be forwarded through node 3, as the

path through node 1 is no longer permitted.

Deterministic routing

One approach to designing a deadlock-free routing algorithm for a wormhole-routed network is to ensure that cycles are avoided in the channel dependence graph. This can be achieved by assigning each channel a unique number and allocating channels to packets in strictly ascending (or descending) order. If the behavior of the algorithm is independent of current network conditions, it is deterministic.

Dimension-ordered routing. A channel numbering scheme often used in n-dimensional meshes is based on the dimension of channels. In dimension-ordered routing, each packet is routed in one dimension at a time, arriving at the proper coordinate in each dimension before proceeding to the next dimension. By enforcing a strictly monotonic order on the dimensions traversed, deadlock-free routing is guaranteed. Hypercube and 2D mesh topologies each use a deadlock-free minimal deterministic routing algorithm. Both algorithms are based on the concept of dimension ordering.

In an n-cube, each node is represented using an n-bit binary number. Each node has n outgoing channels, and the ith channel corresponds to the ith dimension. In the E-cube routing algorithm, the packet header carries the destination node address d. When a node v in the n-cube receives a packet, the E-cube routing algorithm computes $c = d$

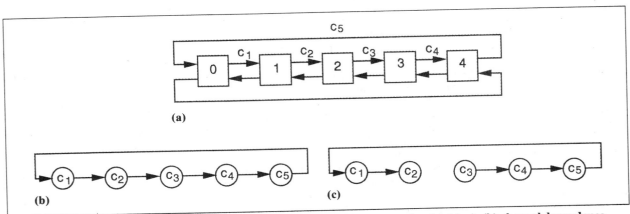

Figure 7. A five-node ring topology and channel dependence graphs: (a) 5-ary 1-cube (ring); (b) channel dependence graph; (c) channel dependence graph for deadlock-free nonminimal deterministic routing.

$\oplus\ v$, where $\oplus$ is the exclusive-OR operation. If $c = 0$, the packet is forwarded to the local processor. Otherwise, the packet is forwarded on the outgoing channel in the kth dimension, where k is the position of the rightmost (alternatively, leftmost) 1 in c.

In a 2D mesh, each node is represented by its position (x, y) in the mesh. In the XY routing algorithm, packets are sent first along the X dimension and then along the Y dimension. In other words, at most one turn is allowed, and that turn must be from the X dimension to the Y dimension. Let (s_x, s_y) and (d_x, d_y) denote the addresses of a source and destination node, respectively. Furthermore, let $(g_x, g_y) = (d_x - s_x, d_y - s_y)$. XY routing can be implemented by placing g_x and g_y in the first two flits, respectively, of the packet. When the first flit of a packet arrives at a router, it is decremented or incremented, depending on whether it is greater than 0 or less than 0. If the result is not equal to 0, the packet is forwarded in the same dimension and direction it arrived in. If the result equals 0 and the packet arrived on the Y dimension, the packet is delivered to the local processor. If the result equals 0 and the packet arrived on the X dimension, the flit is discarded and the next flit is examined upon arrival. If that flit is 0, the packet is delivered to the local processor; otherwise, the packet is forwarded in the Y dimension. Using this method, the largest possible 2D mesh with an 8-bit flit is 128×128. To construct a larger mesh, either the flit size must be increased or the flit buffer must be able to store multiple flits.

Routing in general k-ary n-cubes. For k-ary n-cube topologies with $k > 4$, it is impossible to construct a deadlock-free minimal deterministic routing algorithm. This result is true even when $n = 1$, as illustrated by the one-dimensional ring topology shown in Figure 7a, where $k = 5$. (The case of $k = 4$ was demonstrated in Figure 6, where deterministic minimal routing *is* possible.) Since only minimal routing is allowed, there are two disjoint channel dependence graphs. Figure 7b shows one of these; recall that the vertices represent channels, as labeled. To break the cycle, one of the edges must be deleted. However, in that case, minimal routing cannot be guaranteed. For example, if the edge between c_2 and c_3 is deleted, as shown in Figure 7c, then packets arriving at node 2 on channel c_2 cannot depart on channel c_3. Hence, packets sent from node 1 to node 3 must take a nonminimal path. Thus, a deadlock-free nonminimal deterministic routing algorithm is obtained. By using this technique, deadlock-free nonminimal deterministic routing algorithms can be developed for general k-ary n-cube topologies.[6]

Adaptive routing

The main disadvantage of deterministic routing is that it cannot respond to dynamic network conditions, such as congestion. An adaptive routing algorithm for a wormhole-routed network, however, must address the deadlock issue. To do so often requires the use of additional channels; in particular, some adjacent nodes must be connected by multiple pairs of opposite unidirectional channels. These pairs of channels may share one or more physical channels. The concept of virtual channels will be discussed later. To simplify the discussion, we will not distinguish between physical and virtual channels in this section.

Minimal adaptive routing. One general adaptive routing technique works by partitioning the channels into disjoint subsets. Each subset constitutes a corresponding subnetwork. Packets are routed through different subnetworks, depending on the location of destination nodes.

Figure 8 illustrates the application of this method to a 2D mesh. As Figure 8a shows, the mesh contains an additional pair of channels added to the Y dimension. The network can be partitioned into two subnetworks called the $+X$ subnetwork and the $-X$ subnetwork, each having a pair of channels in the Y dimension and a unidirectional channel in the X dimension. The $+X$ subnetwork is shown in Figure 8b. If the destination node is to the right of the source, that is, if $d_x > s_x$, the packet will be routed through the $+X$ subnetwork. If $d_x < s_x$, the $-X$ subnetwork is used. If $d_x = s_x$, the packet can be routed using either subnetwork.

This double Y-channel routing algorithm is minimal and fully adaptive; that is, a packet can be delivered through any of the shortest paths. The algorithm can be proved to be deadlock-free by ordering the channels appropriately.[7] Such an ordering of the channels in the $+X$ subnetwork is shown in Figure 8b. For any pair of source and destination nodes, the channels will be traversed in descending order, no matter which shortest paths are taken. Hence, deadlock cannot occur. In Figure 8b, for example, any of the minimal paths from node $(1,0)$ to node $(2,2)$ — specifically, (25, 24, 18), (25, 17, 14), and (16, 15, 14) — are valid.

Providing deadlock-free minimal fully adaptive routing algorithms for the hypercube, 2D torus, or more general k-ary n-cube topologies may require additional channels. Linder and Harden[7] have shown that a k-ary n-cube can be partitioned into 2^{n-1} subnetworks, $n + 1$ levels per subnetwork, and k^n channels per level. The number of additional channels increases rapidly with n. While this approach does provide minimal fully adaptive routing, the cost associated with

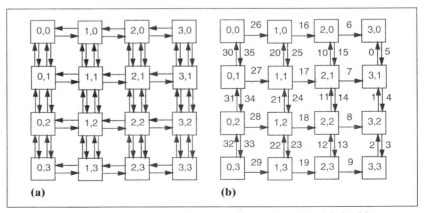

Figure 8. Adaptive double Y-channel routing for a 2D mesh: (a) double Y-channel 2D mesh; (b) $+X$ subnetwork and labeling.

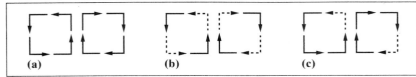

Figure 9. An illustration of the turn model in a 2D mesh: (a) abstract cycles in a 2D mesh; (b) four turns (solid arrows) allowed in XY routing; (c) six turns (solid arrows) allowed in west-first routing.

the additional channels makes it impractical when n is large.

Nonminimal adaptive routing. If minimal routing is not required, deadlock-free adaptive routing can be provided using fewer additional channels. If r pairs of channels connect every pair of adjacent nodes, then the following nonminimal adaptive routing algorithms, proposed by Dally and Aoki,[8] can be applied to k-ary n-cube and mesh topologies. Both of these algorithms allow the packets to take a longer path if there is no shortest path with all its channels available.

In the *static dimension reversal routing algorithm*, there are r pairs of channels between any two adjacent nodes. The network is partitioned into r subnetworks. The class-i ($0 \leq i \leq r - 1$) subnetwork consists of all the ith pair channels. The packet header carries an additional class field c initially set to 0. Packets with $c < r - 1$ can be routed in any direction in the class-c subnetwork; thus, the route may be nonminimal. However, each time a packet is routed from a high-dimensional channel to a low-dimensional channel, that is, reverse

to the dimension ordering, the c field is increased by 1. Once the value of c has reached $r - 1$, the packet must use the deterministic dimension-ordered routing described earlier for the remainder of the path. The additional channels allow a packet to be routed in reverse dimension order. The parameter r limits the number of times this can happen, and hence dictates the degree of adaptivity of the routing algorithm.

In the *dynamic dimension reversal routing algorithm*, the channels are divided into two nonempty classes: adaptive and deterministic. Packets originate in the adaptive channels, where they can be routed in any direction with no limit on the number of times the packet can be routed in reverse dimension order. However, a packet with $c = p$ is not allowed to wait on a channel currently occupied by a packet with $c = q$ if $p \geq q$. A packet that reaches a node where all permissible output channels are occupied by packets whose values of c are less than or equal to its own must switch to the deterministic class of channels. When a packet enters the deterministic channels, it must follow the dimension-ordered routing described

earlier and cannot reenter the adaptive channels. Since it is impossible for a circular wait to occur among packets in the adaptive channels, because of the way c is used, it can be easily shown that the algorithm is deadlock-free. An important design issue concerns how many channels are classified as adaptive and how many are deterministic between each pair of adjacent nodes.

The turn model. Given a network topology and the associated set of channels, adaptive routing algorithms are usually developed in an ad hoc way. The turn model proposed by Glass and Ni[9] provides a systematic approach to the development of maximally adaptive routing algorithms, both minimal and nonminimal, for a given network without adding channels. As Figure 5 shows, deadlock occurs because the packet routes contain turns that form a cycle. The following six steps can be used to develop maximally adaptive routing algorithms for n-dimensional meshes and k-ary n-cubes:

(1) Classify channels according to the direction in which they route packets.
(2) Identify the turns that occur between one direction and another, omitting 0-degree and 180-degree turns.
(3) Identify the simple cycles these turns can form.
(4) Prohibit one turn in each cycle.
(5) In the case of k-ary n-cubes, incorporate as many turns as possible that involve wraparound channels.
(6) Add 180-degree and 0-degree turns, which are needed for nonminimal routing algorithms or if there are multiple channels in the same direction.

The case of a 2D mesh illustrates the use of the turn model. There are eight possible turns and two possible abstract cycles, as shown in Figure 9a. Cycles among packets may result if the turns are not restricted, as illustrated in Figure 5. The deterministic XY routing algorithm prevents deadlock by prohibiting four of the turns, as shown in Figure 9b. The remaining four turns cannot form a cycle, but neither do they allow any adaptiveness.

The fundamental concept behind the turn model is to prohibit the smallest number of turns such that cycles are prevented. In fact, for a 2D mesh, only two turns need to be prohibited. Figure 9c shows six turns allowed, suggesting

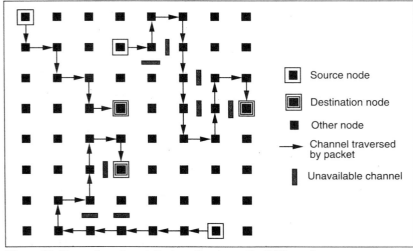

Source node
Destination node
Other node
Channel traversed by packet
Unavailable channel

Figure 10. Examples of west-first routing in an 8×8 2D mesh.

the corresponding *west-first routing algorithm:* First route a packet west, if necessary, and then adaptively south, east, and north. The two turns prohibited in Figure 9c are the two turns to the west. Therefore, to travel west, a packet must begin in that direction.

Figure 10 shows three example paths for the west-first algorithm. The channels marked as unavailable are either faulty or being used by other packets. One of the paths shown is minimal, while the other two paths are nonminimal, resulting from routing around unavailable channels. Because cycles are avoided, west-first routing is deadlock-free. For minimal routing, the algorithm is fully adaptive if the destination is on the right-hand side (east) of the source; otherwise, it is deterministic. If nonminimal routing is allowed, the algorithm is adaptive in either case. There are other ways to select six turns so as to prohibit cycles, although the selection of the two prohibited turns is not arbitrary.[9]

By applying the turn model to the hypercube, an adaptive routing algorithm, namely P-cube routing, can be developed. Let $s = \sigma_{n-1}(s), \sigma_{n-2}(s), \ldots, \sigma_0(s)$ and $d = \sigma_{n-1}(d), \sigma_{n-2}(d), \ldots, \sigma_0(d)$ be the source and destination nodes, respectively, in an n-cube. The set E consists of all the dimension numbers in which s and d differ. The size of E is the Hamming distance between s and d. Thus, $i \in E$ if $\sigma_i(s) \neq \sigma_i(d)$. E is divided into two disjoint subsets, E_0 and E_1, where $i \in E_0$ if $\sigma_i(s) = 0$ and $\sigma_i(d) = 1$, and $j \in E_1$ if $\sigma_i(s) = 1$ and $\sigma_i(d) = 0$.

The fundamental concept of P-cube routing is to divide the routing selection into two phases. In the first phase, a packet is routed through the dimensions in E_0, in any order. In the second phase, the packet is routed through the dimensions in E_1. A similar algorithm was proposed by Konstantinidou[10]; however, the P-cube routing algorithm can be systematically generalized to handle nonminimal routing as well.[9]

Routing in reconfigurable networks

In the examples cited thus far, one or more routing algorithms have been developed for each type of direct network topology. It is possible for the network topology itself to be reconfigurable. For example, by using basic building-block nodes such as Intel/CMU's iWarp cells or elements of the Transputer IMS T9000 family, different network topologies can be constructed from a given set of components. In this case, the router must be flexible or programmable to allow for the implementation of different deadlock-free routing algorithms. Two techniques are general enough to accommodate any topology, given a specific routing algorithm for each topology, while permitting the router design to be relatively simple.

Source routing. The first approach is source routing, mentioned earlier. Depending on the underlying network topology, the source node specifies the routing path on the basis of a deadlock-free deterministic routing algorithm. The packet must carry complete routing information in the packet header. Since the header itself must be transmitted through the network, thereby consuming network bandwidth, it is important to minimize header length.

One source-routing method that achieves this goal is called street-sign routing. The header is analogous to a set of directions given to a driver in a city. Only the names of the streets that the driver must turn on, along with the direction of the turn, are needed. Street-sign routing is used in iWarp, where each router has four pairs of channels corresponding to four cardinal directions ($+X, -X, +Y, -Y$). By default, packets arriving from the input channel in $+X$ (or $+Y$) will be forwarded to the output channel in $-X$ (or $-Y$), and vice versa. The source overrides this default by including in the header the addresses of all nodes at which a different action is to be taken.

There are two possible actions. The packet has either reached the destination or it must make a turn. For each turn, the header must contain the node address and the direction of the turn. Furthermore, this information must occur in the header according to the order in which nodes are reached. Upon receiving each header flit, the router compares the node address in the flit to the local node address. If they match, the packet either turns or is sent to the destination, as specified in the header flit; otherwise, the packet will be forwarded through the default output channel. By incorporating the concept of a default direction, the packet header can be kept short, requiring less time to generate and transmit. An appropriate header-generation algorithm can be designed for each of the possible topologies that may be configured.

Table-lookup routing. Another approach that is amenable to reconfigurable topologies is to perform routing by using table lookup. An obvious implementation is to place a lookup table at each node, with the number of entries in the table equal to the number of nodes in the network. Given a destination node address carried in the header, the corresponding entry in the table indicates which outgoing channel should be used to forward the packet. Such an implementation is not practical, however, because the size of the lookup table places an artificial upper bound on the network size, and the large table is inefficient in the use of chip area.

One way to reduce the table size is to define a range of addresses to be associated with each outgoing channel.[5] For example, each node of the 4×3 2D mesh shown in Figure 11a is assigned a label $\ell(x, y)$. Consider the node $(1,1)$, which is labeled 4. Let d be the label of

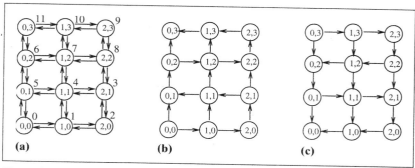

Figure 11. The labeling of a 4×3 mesh: (a) physical network; (b) high-channel network; (c) low-channel network.

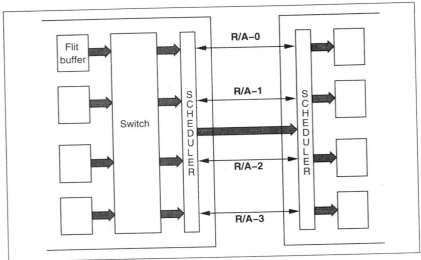

Figure 12. Four virtual channels share a unidirectional physical channel.

the destination address in a packet. Each routing table requires only four entries, one for each outgoing channel. For example, the routing table at node (1,1) will contain the following information. For $d \geq 7$, the packet will be routed using the $+Y$ channel. For $5 \leq d < 7$, $1 < d \leq 3$, and $d \leq 1$, the packet will be routed through channels $-X$, $+X$, and $-Y$, respectively.

In table-lookup routing, the most important issue is how to assign appropriate labels to nodes so that minimal, deadlock-free routing results. One such strategy for a 2D mesh topology with N nodes assigns a label to each node on the basis of its position in a particular Hamiltonian path of the network graph[5]; the first node in the path is labeled 0, and the last node in the path is labeled $N-1$. A label assignment function ℓ for an $m \times n$ mesh that results in minimal routing is

$$\ell(x,y) = \begin{cases} y*n+x & \text{if } y \text{ is even} \\ y*n+n-x-1 & \text{if } y \text{ is odd} \end{cases}$$

This labeling effectively divides the network into two subnetworks, shown in Figures 11b and 11c. The *high-channel subnetwork* contains all of the channels whose direction is from lower labeled nodes to higher labeled nodes, and the *low-channel subnetwork* contains all of the channels whose direction is from higher labeled nodes to lower labeled nodes. Since both subnetworks are acyclic, it is easily shown that this table-lookup routing algorithm is deadlock-free.

A deadlock-free table-lookup rout-

ing algorithm for the hypercube is also given by Lin and Ni.[5] For the hypercube, the label assignment function ℓ for a node with address $d_{n-1}d_{n-2}\ldots d_0$ is

$$\ell\left(d_{n-1}d_{n-2}\ldots d_0\right) = \sum_{i=0}^{n-1}\left(c_i \overline{d_i} 2^i + \overline{c_i} d_i 2^i\right)$$

where $c_{n-1} = 0$, $c_{n-j} = d_{n-1} \oplus d_{n-2} \oplus \ldots \oplus d_{n-j+1}$ for $1 < j \leq n$. A similar technique is used in the Inmos IMS T9000 transputer, where it is referred to as interval labeling.

Virtual channels

Some adaptive routing algorithms require multiple pairs of channels between adjacent nodes. Implementing each channel in a wormhole-routed network with a separate set of physical wires is very expensive. Furthermore, in most applications the channel utilization is not high. One way to address this problem is to multiplex several virtual channels on a single physical communication channel. Each virtual channel has its own flit buffer, control, and data path.[11] In some designs, such as those of the Intel Touchstone and Intel/CMU iWarp, several unidirectional channels in the same direction share a single physical unidirectional channel; in other designs,[4] unidirectional virtual channels in opposite directions share a physical bidirectional channel.

Through virtual channels, a physical network can be divided into multiple disjoint logical networks, thereby facil-

itating adaptive routing algorithms. Virtual channels are useful in three other ways. First, by increasing the degree of connectivity in the network, they facilitate the mapping onto a particular physical topology of applications in which processes communicate according to another logical topology. For example, an application in which processes communicate according to a hexagonal array can be mapped onto a 2D mesh. Second, even when the application and the architecture have the same topology, extra connections may still be needed to route around congested or faulty nodes. Third, virtual channels provide the ability to deliver guaranteed communication bandwidth to certain classes of packets. For example, it is important that some bandwidth be reserved to support system-related functions, such as debugging, monitoring, and system diagnosis. By time-multiplexing virtual channels onto physical channels using a fair schedule, availability of some minimum bandwidth can be guaranteed to each virtual channel as long as the number of virtual channels sharing the same physical channel is bounded.

The most important issue concerning virtual channels is the multiplexing and arbitration of a physical channel among many virtual channels. The multiplexing technique should be designed to maximize channel utilization. Specifically, if m virtual channels share a physical channel with bandwidth W, and k virtual channels are active, where $1 \leq k \leq m$, then each active virtual channel should have an effective bandwidth of W/k. Since the number of active virtual channels is a function of time, the router should be able to dynamically allocate channel bandwidth to the active virtual channels.

Figure 12 illustrates the sharing of four virtual channels over a unidirectional physical channel. A dedicated single-bit Request/Acknowledge wire exists between an input virtual channel and an output virtual channel of two adjacent nodes, as shown in Figure 4. The scheduler multiplexes data from the virtual channels over the physical channel. A fair scheduling discipline, such as round-robin, can be used. To preserve bandwidth, only those virtual channels that have a nonempty flit buffer at the sending side and a nonfull flit buffer at the receiving side may participate in the scheduling decision. In other words, among all of the low R/A lines, the scheduler on the sending side will decide which output channel with a nonempty flit buffer can raise its R/A line to high and use the physical channel.

Using a pair of opposite unidirectional channels between two adjacent nodes simplifies control. However, if these two unidirectional channels are not fully utilized, one may be busy while the other is idle. Combining two unidirectional channels into a single bidirectional channel will increase channel utilization. Assuming the bandwidth of each unidirectional channel is B, the bandwidth of the corresponding bidirectional channel will be $2B$. If only one of the nodes has packets to transmit, it can use the full bandwidth. The design of a bidirectional channel must provide a fair and efficient arbitration scheme between two sides. One such arbitration method is based on the concept of token passing,[4] in which a single-bit arbitration line is used to transfer control of the channel between two adjacent nodes.

The virtual channel concept is not without drawbacks. As the number of virtual channels increases, the scheduling becomes more complicated, requiring additional hardware complexity and potentially increasing network latency. The sharing of bandwidth may also increase latency. Consider the following scenario in which a communication path traverses multiple physical channels, each of which supports many virtual channels. If the bandwidth of each physical channel is W and there is no sharing with other virtual channels, the effective bandwidth of the communication path is W. On the other hand, if one of the physical channels along the path is shared with three other packets, that channel becomes a bottleneck and the effective bandwidth of the entire path is reduced to $W/4$, even though the available bandwidth of all other channels in the path is W. The trade-off between increased network throughput and longer communication latency should be considered when deciding whether to use virtual channels.

Open issues

As we have described, wormhole routing algorithms have already been subjected to extensive research. However, we should briefly mention several related topics that have only recently received attention from the research community.

The primary research tools used thus far to study the performance of wormhole routing algorithms have been analysis and simulation, in which either uniform or generic parameterized workloads have been used to evaluate routing algorithms. To account for the characteristics of specific application software, traces of communication in actual parallel programs must be incorporated into such models. More research is needed in this direction before a realistic and practical performance comparison study on the algorithms presented in this article can be conducted. In addition, researchers need simulation programs that efficiently model variations of wormhole routing, including virtual channels, large flit buffers, and sophisticated input and output selection policies.

A major goal in the design of direct networks is to minimize the constituent elements of communication latency so that such systems can support a finer grain of parallelism. Start-up latency, which may include time for memory and buffer coping, can significantly degrade performance. Methods to reduce start-up latency deserve further investigation, although significant progress in this area has been reported recently. The MIT J-machine uses special hardware to achieve a start-up latency of 2 microseconds, and the Ncube-3 is claimed to exhibit a start-up latency of 5 microseconds.

A related issue concerns the number of internal channels connecting the local processor/memory to the router. Most commercial multiprocessors support a single pair of internal channels, which may become a bottleneck for packets entering and leaving the direct network. One system that supports multiple pairs of internal channels is the Intel/CMU iWarp. The appropriate number of internal channels and their cost/performance trade-offs require further study.

Since the normal behavior of wormhole-routed networks is still a subject of intense research, this article has not addressed the issues of fault tolerance or reliable routing, which are desirable in highly reliable systems. The traditional "replace-and-reboot" approach is used in most existing direct network systems. Investigation of routing and flow control methods for injured wormhole-routed direct networks will likely receive much attention when research in this area becomes more mature and demand increases for highly reliable parallel computing environments.

Finally, this article has surveyed routing algorithms for single-destination, or unicast, communication. Another area of intensive research concerns one-to-many, or multicast, communication. Broadcast is a special case of multicast in which a message is delivered to all nodes in the network. Efficient multicast communication has been shown to be useful in applications such as parallel simulation and parallel search, as well as in operations such as replication and barrier synchronization, found in data parallel languages. Ongoing research concerning multicast communication in wormhole-routed systems includes the study of deadlock-free, hardware-supported multicast routing algorithms[5] and software-based multicast communication.[12] In spite of these efforts, much of the wormhole multicast problem, especially performance evaluation of multicast protocols under actual workloads, remains open to study.

Direct network architectures are strong candidates for use in massively parallel computers, as evidenced by many successful commercial and experimental multicomputers and scalable shared-memory multiprocessors. The characteristics of direct networks, as reflected by the communication latency metric, are critical to the performance of such systems. Wormhole routing, the most promising switching technique, has been adopted in several new massively parallel computers. However, wormhole routing also raises unique technical challenges in routing and flow control — in particular, the development of routing algorithms that avoid deadlock. The problem is complicated by the need for adaptive routing and reconfigurable topologies. We have tried to elucidate such issues while surveying various strategies that have been used or proposed to address them. ∎

Acknowledgments

We would like to thank Xiaola Lin and Christopher Glass for their invaluable contributions to this work. Thanks are also due to the anonymous reviewers for their many insightful comments and suggestions for improvement.

This research was supported in part by National Science Foundation Grants ECS-8814027, CDA-9121641, and MIP-9204066, and by an Ameritech Faculty Fellowship.

References

1. W.C. Athas and C.L. Seitz, "Multicomputers: Message-Passing Concurrent Computers," *Computer*, Vol. 21, No. 8, Aug. 1988, pp. 9-25.

2. S. Thakkar et al., "Scalable Shared-Memory Multiprocessor Architectures," *Computer*, Vol. 23, No. 6, June 1990, pp. 71-83.

3. W.J. Dally and C.L. Seitz, "The Torus Routing Chip," *J. Distributed Computing*, Vol. 1, No. 3, 1986, pp. 187-196.

4. W.J. Dally and P. Song, "Design of a Self-Timed VLSI Multicomputer Communication Controller," *Proc. Int'l Conf. Computer Design*, IEEE CS Press, Los Alamitos, Calif., Order No. 2473, 1987, pp. 230-234.

5. X. Lin and L.M. Ni, "Deadlock-Free Multicast Wormhole Routing in Multicomputer Networks," *Proc. 18th Int'l Symp. Computer Architecture*, IEEE CS Press, Los Alamitos, Calif., Order No. 2146, 1991, pp. 116-125.

6. W.J. Dally and C.L. Seitz, "Deadlock-Free Message Routing in Multiprocessor Interconnection Networks," *IEEE Trans. Computers*, Vol. C-36, No. 5, May 1987, pp. 547-553.

7. D.H. Linder and J.C. Harden, "An Adaptive and Fault-Tolerant Wormhole Routing Strategy for *k*-ary *n*-cubes," *IEEE Trans. Computers*, Vol. 40, No. 1, Jan. 1991, pp. 2-12.

8. W.J. Dally and H. Aoki, "Adaptive Routing Using Virtual Channels," tech. report, MIT Laboratory for Computer Science, Sept. 1990. To appear in *IEEE Trans. Parallel and Distributed Systems*.

9. C.J. Glass and L.M. Ni, "The Turn Model for Adaptive Routing," *Proc. 19th Int'l Symp. Computer Architecture*, IEEE CS Press, Los Alamitos, Calif., Order No. 2940, 1992, pp. 278-287.

10. S. Konstantinidou, "Adaptive, Minimal Routing in Hypercubes," *Proc. Sixth MIT Conf. Advanced Research in VLSI*, MIT Press, Cambridge, Mass., 1990, pp. 139-153.

11. W.J. Dally, "Virtual-Channel Flow Control," *IEEE Trans. Parallel and Distributed Systems*, Vol. 3, No. 2, Mar. 1992, pp. 194-205.

12. P.K. McKinley et al., "Unicast-Based Multicast Communication in Wormhole-Routed Networks," *Proc. 1992 Int'l Conf. Parallel Processing*, Vol. II, IEEE CS Press, Los Alamitos, Calif., Order No. 3155, 1992, pp. 10-19.

Lionel M. Ni is a professor in the Department of Computer Science and director of the Advanced Computer Systems Laboratory at Michigan State University. His research interests include computer architecture, parallel processing, and distributed computing.

Ni received a BS in electrical engineering from National Taiwan University in 1973, an MS in electrical and computer engineering from Wayne State University in 1977, and a PhD in electrical engineering from Purdue University in 1980. He is a member of the ACM, the Society for Industrial and Applied Mathematics, and the IEEE Computer Society, and he serves on the editorial board of the *Journal of Parallel and Distributed Computing* and *IEEE Transactions on Computers*.

Philip K. McKinley is an assistant professor in the Department of Computer Science at Michigan State University and was previously a member of technical staff at Bell Laboratories. His research interests include scalable architectures and software, optical communications, and multicast communication for parallel processing and computer networks.

McKinley received a BS in mathematics and computer science from Iowa State University in 1982, an MS in computer science from Purdue University in 1983, and a PhD in computer science from the University of Illinois at Urbana-Champaign in 1989. He is a member of ACM and the IEEE Computer Society.

RealityEngine Graphics

Kurt Akeley
Silicon Graphics Computer Systems*

Abstract

The RealityEngine™ graphics system is the first of a new generation of systems designed primarily to render texture mapped, antialiased polygons. This paper describes the architecture of the RealityEngine graphics system, then justifies some of the decisions made during its design. The implementation is near-massively parallel, employing 353 independent processors in its fullest configuration, resulting in a measured fill rate of over 240 million antialiased, texture mapped pixels per second. Rendering performance exceeds 1 million antialiased, texture mapped triangles per second. In addition to supporting the functions required of a general purpose, high-end graphics workstation, the system enables realtime, "out-the-window" image generation and interactive image processing.

CR Categories and Subject Descriptors: I.3.1 **[Computer Graphics]:** Hardware Architecture; I.3.7 **[Computer Graphics]:** Three-Dimensional Graphics and Realism - *color, shading, shadowing, and texture*

1   Introduction

This paper describes and to a large extent justifies the architecture chosen for the RealityEngine graphics system. The designers think of this system as our first implementation of a third-generation graphics system. To us a generation is characterized not by the scope of capabilities of an architecture, but rather by the capabilities for which the architecture was primarily designed – the target capabilities with maximized performance. Because we designed our first machine in the early eighties, our notion of first generation corresponds to this period. Floating point hardware was just becoming available at reasonable prices, framebuffer memory was still quite expensive, and application-specific integrated circuits (ASICs) were not readily available. The resulting machines had workable transformation capabilities, but very limited framebuffer processing capabilities. In particular, smooth shading and depth buffering, which require substantial framebuffer hardware and memory, were not available. Thus the target capabilities of first-generation machines were the transformation and rendering of flat-shaded points, lines, and polygons. These primitives were not lighted, and hidden surface elimination, if required, was accomplished by algorithms implemented by the application. Examples of such systems are the Silicon Graphics Iris 3000 (1985) and the Apollo DN570 (1985). Toward the end of the first-generation period advances in technology allowed lighting, smooth shading, and depth buffering to be implemented, but only with an order of magnitude less performance than was available to render flat-shaded lines and polygons. Thus the target capability of these machines remained first-generation. The Silicon Graphics 4DG (1986) is an example of such an architecture.

Because first-generation machines could not efficiently eliminate hidden surfaces, and could not efficiently shade surfaces even if the application was able to eliminate them, they were more effective at rendering wireframe images than at rendering solids. Beginning in 1988 a second-generation of graphics systems, primarily workstations rather than terminals, became available. These machines took advantage of reduced memory costs and the increased availability of ASICs to implement deep framebuffers with multiple rendering processors. These framebuffers had the numeric ability to interpolate colors and depths with little or no performance loss, and the memory capacity and bandwidth to support depth buffering with minimal performance loss. They were therefore able to render solids and full-frame scenes efficiently, as well as wireframe images. The Silicon Graphics GT (1988)[11] and the Apollo DN590 (1988) are early examples of second-generation machines. Later second-generation machines, such as the Silicon Graphics VGX[12] the Hewlett Packard VRX, and the Apollo DN10000[4] include texture mapping and antialiasing of points and lines, but not of polygons. Their performances are substantially reduced, however, when texture mapping is enabled, and the texture size (of the VGX) and filtering capabilities (of the VRX and the DN10000) are limited.

The RealityEngine system is our first third-generation design. Its target capability is the rendering of lighted, smooth shaded, depth buffered, texture mapped, antialiased triangles. The initial target performance was 1/2 million such triangles per second, assuming the triangles are in short strips, and 10 percent intersect the viewing frustum boundaries. Textures were to be well filtered (8-sample linear interpolation within and between two mipmap[13] levels) and large enough (1024×1024) to be usable as true images, rather than simply as repeated *textures*. Antialiasing was to result in high-quality images of solids, and was to work in conjunction with depth buffering, meaning that no application sorting was to be required. Pixels were to be filled at a rate sufficient to support 30Hz rendering of full-screen images. Finally, the performance on second-generation primitives (lighted, smooth shaded, depth buffered) was to be no lower than that of the VGX, which renders roughly 800,000 such mesh triangles per second. All of these goals were achieved.

The remainder of this paper is in four parts: a description of the architecture, some specifics of features supported by the architecture, alternatives considered during the design of the architecture, and finally some appendixes that describe performance and implementation details.

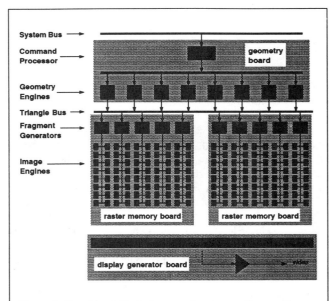

Figure 1. Board-level block diagram of an intermediate configuration with 8 Geometry Engines on the geometry board, 2 raster memory boards, and a display generator board.

2   Architecture

The RealityEngine system is a 3, 4, or 6 board graphics accelerator that is installed in a MIPS RISC workstation. The graphics system and one or more MIPS processors are connected by a single system bus. Figure 1 is a board-level block diagram of the RealityEngine graphics accelerator. The geometry board comprises an input FIFO, the Command Processor, and 6, 8, or 12 Geometry Engines. Each raster memory board comprises 5 Fragment Generators (each with its own complete copy of the texture memory), 80 Image Engines, and enough framebuffer memory to allocate 256 bits per pixel to a 1280×1024 framebuffer. The display generator board supports all video functions, including video timing, genlock, color mapping, and digital-to-analog conversion. Systems can be configured with 1, 2, or 4 raster memory boards, resulting in 5, 10, or 20 Fragment Generators and 80, 160, or 320 Image Engines.

To get an initial notion of how the system works, let's follow a single triangle as it is rendered. The position, color, normal, and texture coordinate commands that describe the vertexes of the triangle in object coordinates are queued by the input FIFO, then interpreted by the Command Processor. The Command Processor directs all of this data to one of the Geometry Engines, where the coordinates and normals are transformed to eye coordinates, lighted, transformed to clip coordinates, clipped, and projected to window coordinates. The associated texture coordinates are transformed by a third matrix and associated with the window coordinates and colors. Then window coordinate slope information regarding the red, green, blue, alpha, depth, and texture coordinates is computed.

The projected triangle, ready for rasterization, is then output from the Geometry Engine and broadcast on the Triangle Bus to the 5, 10, or 20 Fragment Generators. (We distinguish between pixels generated by rasterization and pixels in the framebuffer, referring to the former as fragments.) Each Fragment Generator is responsible for the rasterization of 1/5, 1/10, or 1/20 of the pixels in the frame-

buffer, with the pixel assignments finely interleaved to insure that even small triangles are partially rasterized by each of the Fragment Generators. Each Fragment Generator computes the intersection of the set of pixels that are fully or partially covered by the triangle and the set of pixels in the framebuffer that it is responsible for, generating a fragment for each of these pixels. Color, depth, and texture coordinates are assigned to each fragment based on the initial and slope values computed by the Geometry Engine. A subsample mask is assigned to the fragment based on the portion of each pixel that is covered by the triangle. The local copy of the texture memory is indexed by the texture coordinates, and the 8 resulting samples are reduced by linear interpolation to a single color value, which then modulates the fragment's color.

The resulting fragments, each comprising a pixel coordinate, a color, a depth, and a coverage mask, are then distributed to the Image Engines. Like the Fragment Generators, the Image Engines are each assigned a fixed subset of the pixels in the framebuffer. These subsets are themselves subsets of the Fragment Generator allocations, so that each Fragment Generator communicates only with the 16 Image Engines assigned to it. Each Image Engine manages its own dynamic RAM that implements its subset of the framebuffer. When a fragment is received by an Image Engine, its depth and color sample data are merged with the data already stored at that pixel, and a new aggregate pixel color is immediately computed. Thus the image is complete as soon as the last primitive has been rendered; there is no need for a final framebuffer operation to resolve the multiple color samples at each pixel location to a single displayable color.

Before describing each of the rendering operations in more detail, we make the following observations. First, after it is separated by the Command Processor, the stream of rendering commands merges only at the Triangle Bus. Second, triangles of sufficient size (a function of the number of raster memory boards) are processed by almost all the processors in the system, avoiding only 5, 7, or 11 Geometry Engines. Finally, small to moderate FIFO memories are included at the input and output of each Geometry Engine, at the input of each Fragment Generator, and at the input of each Image Engine. These memories smooth the flow of rendering commands, helping to insure that the processors are utilized efficiently.

2.1   Command Processor

That the Command Processor is required at all is primarily a function of the OpenGL™ [8][7] graphics language. OpenGL is modal, meaning that much of the state that controls rendering is included in the command stream only when it changes, rather than with each graphics primitive. The Command Processor distinguishes between two classes of this modal state. OpenGL commands that are expected infrequently, such as matrix manipulations and lighting model changes, are broadcast to all the Geometry Engines. OpenGL commands that are expected frequently, such as vertex colors, normals, and texture coordinates, are shadowed by the Command Processor, and the current values are bundled with each rendering command that is passed to an individual Geometry Engine. The Command Processor also breaks long connected sequences of line segments or triangles into smaller groups, each group passing to a single Geometry Engine. The size of these groups is a tradeoff between the increased vertex processing efficiency of larger groups (due to shared vertexes within a group) and the improved load balancing that results from smaller groups. Finally, because the Command Processor must interpret each graphics command, it is also able to detect invalid command sequences and protect the

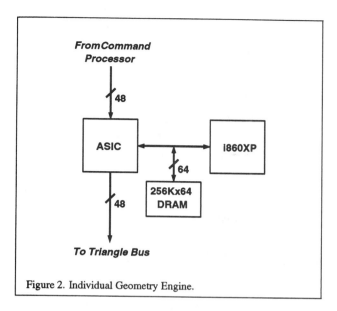

Figure 2. Individual Geometry Engine.

subsequent processors from their effects.

Non-broadcast rendering commands are distributed to the Geometry Engines in pure round-robin sequence, taking no account of Geometry Engine loading. This approach was chosen for its simplicity, and is efficient because the processing requirements of primitives are usually very similar, and because the input and output FIFOs of each Geometry Engine smooth the imbalances due to data-dependent processing such as clipping.

2.2   Geometry Engines

The core of each Geometry Engine is an Intel i860XP processor. Operating at 50MHz, the combined floating point multiplier and ALU can achieve a peak performance of 100 MFLOPS. Each Intel processor is provided 2 Mbytes of combined code/data dynamic memory, and is supported by a single ASIC that implements the input and output FIFOs, a small register space from which the i860XP accesses incoming commands, and specialized data conversion facilities that pack computed slope data into a format accepted by the Fragment Generators. (Figure 2.)

All Geometry Engine code is first developed in C, which is cross compiled for the i860XP on MIPS RISC development systems. Code that is executed frequently is then re-coded in i860XP assembly code, showing the greatest improvement in performance where scheduling of the vector floating point unit is hand optimized. The assembly code is written to conform to the compiler's link conventions, so that hand-coded and compiled modules are interchangeable for development and documentation purposes.

Most floating point arithmetic is done in single precision, but much of the texture arithmetic, and all depth arithmetic after projection transformation, must be done in double precision to maintain the required accuracy. After transformation, lighting, and clipping, the rasterization setup code treats each parameter as a plane equation, computing its signed slope in the positive X and Y screen directions. Because the parameters of polygons with more than 3 vertexes may be non-planar, the Geometry Engine decomposes all polygons to triangles.

2.3   Triangle Bus

The Triangle Bus acts as a crossbar, connecting the output of each Geometry Engine to the inputs of all the Fragment Generators. Because all Geometry Engine output converges at this bus, it is a potential bottleneck. To avoid performance loss, the Triangle Bus was designed with bandwidth to handle over one million shaded, depth buffered, texture mapped, antialiased triangles per second, more than twice the number of primitives per second that were anticipated from an 8 Geometry Engine system. This performance cushion allows the later-conceived 12 Geometry Engine system to render at full performance, in spite of the greater than expected performance of the individual engines.

In addition to broadcasting the rasterization data for triangles to the Fragment Generators, the Triangle Bus broadcasts point and line segment descriptions, texture images, and rasterization mode changes such as blending functions.

2.4   Fragment Generators

Although each Fragment Generator may be thought of as a single processor, the data path of each unit is actually a deep pipeline. This pipeline sequentially performs the initial generation of fragments, generation of the coverage mask, texture address generation, texture lookup, texture sample filtering, texture modulation of the fragment color, and fog computation and blending. These tasks are distributed among the four ASICs and eight dynamic RAMs that comprise each Fragment Generator. (Figure 3.)

Fragments are generated using Pineda arithmetic[9], with the algorithm modified to traverse only pixels that are in the domain of the Fragment Generator. A coverage mask is generated for 4, 8, or 16 sample locations, chosen on a regular 8×8 subsample grid within the square boundaries of the pixel. The hardware imposes no constraints on which subset of the 64 subsample locations is chosen, except that the same subset is chosen for each pixel. The subset may be changed by the application between frames.

Depth and texture coordinate sample values are always computed at the center-most sample location, regardless of the fragment coverage mask. The single depth sample is later used by the Image Engines to derive accurate depth samples at each subpixel location, using the X and Y depth slopes. Taking the texture sample at a consistent location insures that discontinuities are avoided at pixels that span multiple triangles. Color sample values are computed at the center-most sample location only if it is within the perimeter of the triangle. Otherwise the color sample is taken at a sample location within the triangle perimeter that is near the centroid of the covered region. Thus color samples are always taken within the triangle perimeter, and therefore never wrap to inappropriate values.

Based on a level-of-detail (LOD) calculation and the texture coordinate values at the fragment center, the addresses of the eight texels nearest the sample location in the mipmap of texture images are produced. Eight separate banks of texture memory are then accessed in parallel at these locations. The 8 16-bit values that result are merged with a trilinear blend, based on the subtexel coordinates and the LOD fraction, resulting in a single texture color that varies smoothly from frame to frame in an animation. The entire bandwidth of the 8-bank texture memory is consumed by a single Fragment Engine, so each Fragment Engine includes its own complete copy of all texture images in its texture memory, allowing all Fragment Generators to operate in parallel. Separate FIFO memories on the address and data ports of each texture memory bank

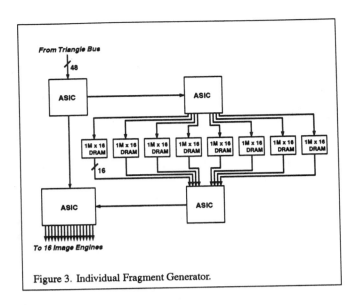

Figure 3. Individual Fragment Generator.

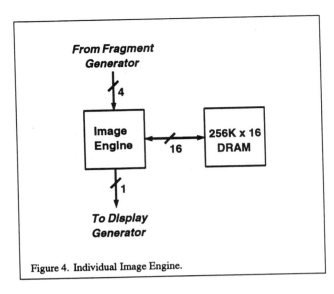

Figure 4. Individual Image Engine.

insure that random page boundary crossings do not significantly degrade the bandwidth available from the dynamic RAMs.

The last ASIC in the Fragment Generator applies the texture color to the fragment's smooth shaded color, typically by modulation. It then indexes its internal fog table with the fragment's depth value and uses the resulting fog blend factor (computed by linear interpolation between the two nearest table entries) to blend the fragment color with the application-defined fog color.

2.5 Image Engines

Fragments output by a single Fragment Generator are distributed equally among the 16 Image Engines connected to that generator. When the triangle was first accepted by the Fragment Generator for processing, its depth slopes in the X and Y screen directions were broadcast to each Image Engine, which stored them for later use. When an Image Engine accepts a fragment, it first uses these two slope values and the fragment's depth sample value to reconstruct the depth values at each subpixel sample location. The arithmetic required for this operation is simplified because the subpixel sample locations are fixed to a regular 8 × 8 grid. The calculations are linear because depth values have been projected to window coordinates just like the X and Y pixel coordinates. At each sample location corresponding to a '1' in the fragment's coverage mask, the computed depth value is compared to the depth value stored in the framebuffer. If the comparison succeeds, the framebuffer color at that subsample location is replaced by the fragment color, and the framebuffer depth is replaced by the derived fragment depth. If any change is made to the pixel's contents, the aggregate pixel color is recomputed by averaging the subpixel sample colors, and is immediately written to the displayable color buffer that will contain the final image.

Each Image Engine controls a single 256K × 16 dynamic RAM that comprises its portion of the framebuffer. (Figure 4.) When the framebuffer is initialized, this memory is partitioned equally among 4K, 8K, or 16K pixels, resulting in pixels with 1024, 512, or 256 bits. All subsample depth and color samples, as well as the one, two, or four displayable color buffers and other auxiliary buffers, are stored in this memory. By default, colors are stored

with 12 bits per red, green, blue, and alpha component in both the displayable buffers and the subpixel samples. Depth values are 32 bits each, and are normally required only for each subpixel sample, not for the displayable color buffer or buffers. Color and depth sample resolutions can be reduced to 8,8,8 and 24 bits to allow more samples to be stored per pixel. The 4K partition stores 8 high-resolution samples per pixel, or 16 low-resolution samples per pixel, in addition to two displayable color buffers of the same resolution. The 8K partition stores 4 high-resolution samples per pixel, or 8 low-resolution samples per pixel, again with two displayable color buffers of the same resolution. The 16K partition cannot be used to support multisample antialiasing.

Because the number of raster memory boards (1, 2, or 4) and the number of pixels per Image Engine (4K, 8K, or 16K) are independent, the RealityEngine system supports a wide variety of framebuffer dimensions, color and depth resolutions, and subpixel samples. For example, a single raster board system supports 16-sample antialiasing at 640 × 512 resolution or aliased rendering at 1280 × 1024 resolution, and a 4-board system supports 8-sample antialiasing at true HDTV (1920 × 1035) resolution or 16-sample antialiasing at 1280 × 1024 resolution.

2.6 Display Hardware

Each of the 80 Image Engines on the raster memory board drives a single-bit, 50 MHz path to the display board, delivering video data at 500 MBytes per second. All 160 single-bit paths of a two raster memory board configuration are active, doubling the peak video data rate. The paths are time multiplexed by pairs of raster memory boards in the four board configuration. Ten crossbar ASICs on the display board assemble the 80 or 160 single-bit streams into individual color components or color indexes. Color components are then dithered from 12 bits to 10 bits and gamma corrected using 1024 × 8 lookup tables. The resulting 8-bit color components drive digital-to-analog converters and are output to the monitor. Color indexes are dereferenced in a 32K-location lookup table, supporting separate color lookup tables for each of up to 40 windows on the screen. Per-pixel display modes, such as the color index offset, are supported by a combination of Image Engine and display board hardware, driven by window ID bits stored in the framebuffer [1].

3   Features

This section provides additional information regarding the architecture's antialiasing, texture mapping, stereo, and clipping capabilities.

3.1   Antialiasing

The architecture supports two fundamentally different antialiasing techniques: alpha and multisample. Alpha antialiasing of points and lines is common to second generation architectures. Alpha antialiasing is implemented using subpixel and line-slope indexed tables to generate appropriate coverage values for points and lines, compensating for the subpixel position of line endpoints. Polygon coverage values are computed by counting the '1's in the full precision 8×8 coverage mask. The fragment alpha value is scaled by the fractional coverage value, which varies from 0.0, indicating no coverage, to 1.0, indicating complete coverage. If pixel blending is enabled, fragments are blended directly into the color buffer – no subpixel sample locations are accessed or required. Alpha antialiasing results in higher quality points and lines than does multisample antialiasing, because the resolution of the filter tables is greater than the 4 bit equivalent of the 16-sample mask. While alpha antialiased primitives should be rendered back-to-front or front-to-back (depending on the blend function being used) to generate a correct image, it is often possible to get an acceptable point or line image without such sorting. Alpha antialiased polygons, however, must be sorted near to far to get an acceptable image. Thus this technique is efficiently applied to polygons only in 2D scenes, such as instrument panels, where primitive ordering is fixed and a slight increase in quality is desired.

Multisample antialiasing has already been described. Its principal advantage over alpha antialiasing is its order invariance - points, lines, and polygons can be drawn into a multisample buffer in any order to produce the same final image. Two different mask generation techniques are supported in multisample mode, each with its own advantages and disadvantages. The default mask generation mode is called point sampled; the alternate mode is area sampled. A point sampled mask is geometrically accurate, meaning that each mask bit is set if and only if its subpixel location is within the perimeter of the point, line, or polygon outline. (Samples on the primitive's edge are included in exactly one of the two adjacent primitives.) Such masks insure the correctness of the final image, at the expense of its filtered quality. The final image is correct because all the samples that comprise it are geometrically valid - none having been taken outside their corresponding primitives. It is poorly sampled because the number of bits set in the mask may not closely correspond to the actual area of the pixel that is covered by the primitive, and the final filtering quality depends on this correspondence. Area sampling attempts to insure that the number of '1's in the sample mask is correct plus or minus 1/2 a sample, based on the actual coverage of pixel area by the primitive. (Figure 5.) In order to accomplish this, area sampled masks necessarily include samples that are outside the primitive outline, resulting in image artifacts such as polygon protrusions at silhouettes and T-junctions. Area sampled masks are implemented with a technique that is related to the one described by Andreas Schilling[10]. Point and area sampling can be selected by the application program on a per-primitive basis.

The desirable multisample property of order invariance is lost if alpha transparency and pixel blending are used. Alpha does sometimes carry significant information, usually as a result of the alpha channel in the texture application. For example, trees are

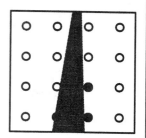

The single sample selected by the point sample method is darkened.   The three samples selected by the area sample method are darkened.

Figure 5. A narrow triangle intersected with a single, 16-sample pixel. The three samples selected by the area sample method accurately represent the fact that almost 20 percent of the pixel is covered by the triangle.

often drawn as single polygons, using an alpha matte to express their shape. In order to handle alpha transparency without requiring pixel blending, the Image Engines have the ability to convert fragment alpha values to pseudo-random masks, which are then logically ANDed with the fragment's coverage mask. This method, while not geometrically accurate, provides usable antialiasing of texture mattes, and is order invariant.

3.2   Texture Mapping

In addition to the 2-dimension texture maps described in the architecture section, 1- and 3-dimension maps are also supported. The eight million texel memory associated with each Fragment Generator stores 2D mipmapped images up to 1024×1024, and 3D non-mipmapped images up to $256 \times 256 \times 64$. Thus 3D textures can be used to render volumetric images of substantial resolution, at rates up to 30 frames per second. The S, T, and R texture coordinates of each fragment are computed by interpolating S/W, T/W, R/W, and 1/W, then doing the correct divisions at each pixel, resulting in perspective-corrected mapping. Level-of-detail is also computed for each pixel, based on the worst-case of the four pixel-to-texel X and Y ratios.

Linear filtering of the nearest texels and mipmap levels is supported for 1D, 2D, and 3D textures, blending a total of 16 texel colors in the 3D mode. In the 2D case such linear filtering is commonly known as trilinear. Bicubic interpolation is supported for 2D, nonmipmapped textures, again blending 16 texels. There is no support for cubic filtering of 1D or 3D textures, or of any mipmapped textures. The default 16-bit texel size supports RGBA texels at 4-bits per component, RGB texels at 5-bits per component (6 bits for green), intensity-alpha texels at 8-bits per component, and intensity texels at 12-bits per component. 32-bit and 48-bit texels can be specified by the application with proportional loss of performance. The maximum RBGA texel resolution is 12-bits per component, equal to the maximum framebuffer color resolution.

Texture magnification can be done by extrapolation of mipmap levels, resulting in a sharpening of the highest resolution mipmap image, or the highest resolution image can be blended with a replicated 256×256 detail image, greatly increasing the apparent resolution of the texture without requiring excessive texture storage. Filter functions for RGB and for alpha can be specified separately to improve the quality of texture mattes. Finally, texture memory can be loaded from the application processor's memory at the rate of 80 million 16-bit texels per second, allowing the application to treat texture memory as a managed cache of images.

3.3   Stereo in a Window

Image Engine memory can be configured with separate left and right color buffers for both the visible and nonvisible displayable color buffers, resulting in a total of four 48-bit color buffers per pixel. The display hardware alternately displays the left and right buffer contents of the visible buffers of all windows so configured, and drives a sync signal that can be used to control screen or head-mounted shutters. This stereo-in-a-window capability is both formally and practically compatible with the X protocol: formally because neither framebuffer dimensions nor pixel aspect ratio are changed when it is enabled or disabled, and practically because it allows monoscopic windows such as menus to be rendered and displayed correctly. To reduce eye fatigue, it is advisable to select a reduced-dimension framebuffer when the window system is initialized, allowing the frame display rate to be increased to 90+ Hz within the 140 MHz pixel limit of the display board.

3.4   Fast Clipping

RealityEngine polygon clipping is faster than that of our earlier designs for two fundamental reasons: it is implemented more efficiently, and it is required less often. Higher efficiency results from the MIMD Geometry Engine architecture. Because each of the engines executes an independent code sequence, and because each has significant input and output FIFOs, random clipping delays affect only a single engine and are averaged statistically across all the engines. Also, because each Geometry Engine comprises only a single processor, all of that engine's processing power can be devoted to the clipping process. SIMD architectures are less efficient because all processors are slowed when a single processor must clip a polygon. Pipelines of processors, and even MIMD arrangements of short pipelines, are less efficient because only a fraction of available processing power is available to the clipping process.

The requirement for clipping is reduced through a technique we call scissoring. Near and far plane clipping are done as usual, but the left, right, bottom, and top frustum edges are moved well away from the specified frustum, and all triangles that fall within the expanded frustum are projected to extended window coordinates. If culling is done by the application, almost no triangles will actually intersect the sides of the expanded frustum. Projected triangles that are not fully within the viewport are then scissored to match the edges of the viewport, eliminating the portions that are not within the viewport. The Pineda rasterization algorithm that is employed easily and efficiently handles the additional rectilinear edges that result, and no fragment generation performance is lost on scissored regions.

4   Design Alternatives

We think that the most interesting part of design is the alternatives considered, and the reasons for choices, rather than the details of the result. This section highlights some of these alternatives, in roughly decreasing order of significance.

4.1   Single-pass Antialiasing

Multi-pass accumulation buffer antialiasing using an accumulation buffer [3] is order invariant, and produces high-quality images in 10 to 20 passes. Further, a system that was fast enough to render 10 to 20 full scene images per frame would be a fantastic generator of aliased images. So why design a complex, multisample framebuffer to accomplish the same thing in one pass? The answer is that significantly more hardware would be required to implement a multi-pass machine with equivalent performance. This is true not only because the multi-pass machine must traverse and transform the object coordinates each pass, but in particular because texture mapping would also be performed for each pass. The component costs for traversal, transformation, parameter interpolation, and texture mapping constitute well over half of the multisample machine cost, and they are not replicated in the multisample architecture. A competing multi-pass architecture would have to replicate this hardware in some manner to achieve the required performance. Even the PixelFlow architecture[6], which avoids repeated traversal and transformation by buffering intermediate results, must still rasterize and texture map repeatedly.

4.2   Multisample Antialiasing

Multisample antialiasing is a rather brute-force technique for achieving order invariant single-pass antialiasing. We investigated alternative sorting buffer techniques derived from the A-buffer algorithm[2], hoping for higher filter quality and correct, single-pass transparency. These techniques were rejected for several reasons. First, sort buffers are inherently more complex than the multisample buffer and, with finite storage allocations per pixel, they may fail in undesirable ways. Second, any solution that is less exact than multisampling with point sampled mask generation will admit rendering errors such as polygon protrusions at silhouettes and T-junctions. Finally, the multisample algorithm matches the single-sample algorithm closely, allowing OpenGL pixel techniques such as stencil, alpha test, and depth test to work identically in single or multisample mode.

4.3   Immediate Resolution of Multisample Color

Our initial expectation was that rendering would update only the multisample color and depth values, requiring a subsequent resolution pass to reduce these values to the single color values for display. The computational expense of visiting all the pixels in the framebuffer is high, however, and the resolution pass damaged the software model, because OpenGL has no explicit scene demarcations. Immediate resolution became much more desirable when we realized that the single most common resolution case, where the fragment completely replaces the pixel's contents (i.e. the fragment mask is all ones and all depth comparisons pass) could be implemented by simply writing the fragment color to the color buffer, making no change to the 4, 8, or 16 subsample colors, and specially tagging the pixel. Only if the pixel is subsequently partially covered by a fragment is the color in the color buffer copied to the appropriate subsample color locations. This technique increases the performance in the typical rendering case and eliminates the need for a resolution pass.

4.4 Triangle Bus

All graphics architectures that implement parallel primitive processing and parallel fragment/pixel processing must also implement a crossbar somewhere between the geometry processors and the framebuffer[5]. While many of the issues concerning the placement of this crossbar are beyond the scope of this paper, we will mention some of the considerations that resulted in our Triangle Bus architecture. The RealityEngine Triangle Bus is a crossbar between the Geometry Engines and the Fragment Generators. Described in RealityEngine terms, architectures such as the Evans & Sutherland Freedom Series™ implement Geometry Engines and Fragment Generators in pairs, then switch the resulting fragments to the appropriate Image Engines using a fragment crossbar network. Such architectures have an advantage in fragment generation efficiency, due both to the improved locality of the fragments and to only one Fragment Generator being initialized per primitive. They suffer in comparison, however, for several reasons. First, transformation and fragment generation rates are linked, eliminating the possibility of tuning a machine for unbalanced rendering requirements by adding transformation or rasterization processors. Second, ultimate fill rate is limited by the fragment bandwidth, rather than the primitive bandwidth. For all but the smallest triangles the quantity of data generated by rasterization is much greater than that required for geometric specification, so this is a significant bottleneck. (See Appendix 2.) Finally, if primitives must be rendered in the order that they are specified, load balancing is almost impossible, because the number of fragments generated by a primitive varies by many orders of magnitude, and cannot be predicted prior to processor assignment. Both OpenGL and the core X renderer require such ordered rendering.

The PixelFlow[6] architecture also pairs Geometry Engines and Fragment Generators, but the equivalent of Image Engines and memory for a 128×128 pixel tile are also bundled with each Geometry/Fragment pair. The crossbar in this architecture is the compositing tree that funnels the contents of rasterized tiles to a final display buffer. Because the framebuffer associated with each processor is smaller than the final display buffer, the final image is assembled as a sequence of 128×128 logical tiles. Efficient operation is achieved only when each logical tile is rasterized once in its entirety, rather than being revisited when additional primitives are transformed. To insure that all primitives that correspond to a logical tile are known, all primitives must be transformed and sorted before rasterization can begin. This substantially increases the system's latency, and requires that the rendering software support the notion of frame demarcation. Neither the core X renderer nor OpenGL support this notion.

4.5 12-bit Color

Color component resolution was increased from the usual 8 bits to 12 bits for two reasons. First, the RealityEngine framebuffer stores color components in linear, rather than gamma-corrected, format. When 8-bit linear intensities are gamma corrected, single bit changes at low intensities are discernible, resulting in visible banding. The combination of 12-to-10 bit dithering and 10-bit gamma lookup tables used at display time eliminates visible banding. Second, it is intended that images be computed, rather than just stored, in the RealityEngine framebuffer. Volume rendering using 3D textures, for example, requires back-to-front composition of multiple slices through the data set. If the framebuffer resolution is just sufficient to display an acceptable image, repeated compositions will degrade the

Figure 6. A scene from a driving simulation running full-screen at 30 Hz.

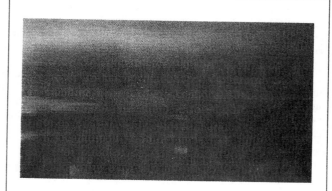

Figure 7. A 12x magnified subregion of the scene in figure 6. The sky texture is properly sampled and the silhouettes of the ground and buildings against the sky are antialiased.

resolution visibly. The 12-bit components allow substantial framebuffer composition to take place before artifacts become visible.

Conclusion

The RealityEngine system was designed as a high-end workstation graphics accelerator with special abilities in image generation and image processing. This paper has described its architecture and capabilities in the realm of image generation: 20 to 60 Hz animations of full-screen, fully-textured, antialiased scenes. (Figures 6 and 7.) The image processing capabilities of the architecture have not been described at all; they include convolution, color space conversion, table lookup, histogramming, and a variety of warping and mapping operations using the texture mapping hardware. Future developments will investigate additional advanced rendering features, while continually reducing the cost of high-performance, high-quality graphics.

Acknowledgments

It was a privilege to be a part of the team that created RealityEngine. While many team members made important contributions to the design, I especially acknowledge Mark Leather for developing the multisample antialiasing technique that was eventually adopted, and for designing a remarkable integrated circuit (the Image Engine) that implemented his design. Also, special thanks to Doug Voorhies, who read and carefully marked up several drafts of this paper. Finally, thanks to John Montrym, Dan Baum, Rolf van Widenfelt, and the anonymous reviewers for their clarifications and insights.

Appendix 1: Measured Performance

The two most significant performance categories are transform rate: the number of primitives per second that can be processed by the Geometry Engines, and fill rate: the number of fragments per second that can be generated and merged into the framebuffer. Running in third-generation mode (lighting, smooth shading, depth buffering, texturing and multisample antialiasing) a 12 Geometry Engine system can process 1.5 million points, 0.7 million connected lines, and 1.0 million connected triangles per second. In second-generation mode (lighting, smooth shading, and depth buffering) the same system can process 2.0 million points, 1.3 million connected lines, and 1.2 million connected triangles per second. Measured third-generation fill rates for 2 and 4 raster board systems are 120 and 240 million fragments per second. Measured second-generation fill rates for 1, 2, and 4 raster board systems are 85, 180, and 360 million fragments per second. The third-generation fill rate numbers are somewhat dependent on rendering order, and are therefore chosen as averages over a range of actual performances.

Appendix 2: Bandwidth and other Statistics

Triangle Bus, fragment transfer path, and Image Engine to framebuffer memory bandwidths are in roughly the ratios of 1:10:20. Specific numbers for the typical two raster board configuration are 240 Mbyte/sec on the Triangle Bus, 3,200 Mbyte/sec aggregate on the 160 Fragment Generator to Image Engine busses, and 6,400 Mbyte/sec aggregate on the 160 Image Engine to framebuffer connections.

Because the 6,400 Mbyte/sec framebuffer bandwidth is so much larger than the bandwidth required to refresh a monitor (roughly 800 Mbyte/sec at $1280 \times 1024 \times 76$Hz) we implement the framebuffer memory with dynamic RAM rather than video RAM, accepting the 12 percent fill rate degradation in favor of the lower cost of commodity memory. Geometry Engine memory and texture memory are also implemented with commodity, 16-bit data path dynamic RAM. Total dynamic memory in the maximally configured system is just over 1/2 Gigabyte.

References

[1] AKELEY, KURT AND TOM JERMOLUK. High-Performance Polygon Rendering. In *Proceedings of SIGGRAPH '88* (August 1988), pp. 239–246.

[2] CARPENTER, LOREN. The A-buffer, An Antialiased Hidden Surface Method. In *Proceedings of SIGGRAPH '84* (July 1984), pp. 103–108.

[3] HAEBERLI, PAUL AND KURT AKELEY. The Accumulation Buffer: Hardware Support for High-Quality Rendering. In *Proceedings of SIGGRAPH '90* (August 1990), pp. 309–318.

[4] KIRK, DAVID AND DOUGLAS VOORHIES. The Rendering Architecture of the DN10000VS. In *Proceedings of SIGGRAPH '90* (August 1990), pp. 299–308.

[5] MOLNAR, STEVEN. *Image-Composition Architectures for Real-Time Image Generation*. University of North Carolina at Chapel Hill, Chapel Hill, NC, 1991.

[6] MOLNAR, STEVEN, JOHN EYLES AND JOHN POULTON. PixelFlow: High-Speed Rendering Using Image Composition. In *Proceedings of SIGGRAPH '92* (July 1992), pp. 231–240.

[7] NEIDER, JACQUELINE, MASON WOO AND TOM DAVIS. *OpenGL Programming Guide*. Addison Wesley, 1993.

[8] OPENGL ARCHITECTURE REVIEW BOARD. *OpenGL Reference Manual*. Addison Wesley, 1992.

[9] PINEDA, JUAN. A Parallel Algorithm for Polygon Rasterization. In *Proceedings of SIGGRAPH '88* (August 1988), pp. 17–20.

[10] SCHILLING, ANDREAS. A New Simple and Efficient Antialiasing with Subpixel Masks. In *Proceedings of SIGGRAPH '91* (July 1991), pp. 133–141.

[11] SILICON GRAPHICS, INC. *Iris 4DGT Technical Report*. Silicon Graphics, Inc., Mountain View, CA, 1988.

[12] SILICON GRAPHICS, INC. *Technical Report - Power Series*. Silicon Graphics, Inc., Mountain View, CA, 1990.

[13] WILLIAMS, LANCE. Pyramidal Parametrics. In *Proceedings of SIGGRAPH '83* (July 1983), pp. 1–11.

CHAPTER 8

Single Instruction Multiple Data (SIMD) Parallelism

8.1 Introduction

Computer architects have always looked for alternate models for building computers, especially for different computing scenarios. An important computing scenario involves carrying out the same (or almost the same) sequence of operations on different elements of a large data set. Such a situation arises, for example, when carrying out common mathematical operations and transformations on matrices or when processing the pixels of an image. In such situations, the traditional computing model in which the processing unit is responsible for fetching an instruction from memory, decoding it, and processing it, and where a single instruction operates on a single data element, is not very efficient. With hundreds (or even thousands) of processing units being applied to a computation, having each of them fetch instructions from memory is wasteful if they are all going to be fetching the same (or almost the same) set of instructions! This waste takes on two forms: (1) storage to store multiple copies of the same set of instructions (program), and (2) logic associated with each processing unit to fetch instructions. The single instruction multiple data (SIMD) model is a computing model that is designed to overcome this waste.

In the canonical model of a SIMD computer, elements of a data structure(s) are distributed across multiple storage elements that are closely tied to the processing units (or elements). For example, an image consisting of 1024×1024 pixels might be divided into 256 subimages consisting of 64×64 pixels each, and distributed to 256 processor-memory elements.

These multiple processor-memory elements are connected to a controller. The program is stored in a memory associated with the controller. The controller sequences through the program (similar to a traditional processor) determining what computation needs to be performed and then sends this computation to the multiple processing elements. The processing elements each perform the computation in lock step (in some cases, a processing element might choose not to perform a computation, based on the value of a flag; i.e., treat the command as a NOP). When all processing elements have performed their command, the controller proceeds to the next command. A computer closely resembling the canonical SIMD computer described above was the ILLIAC IV, built in the 1960s [2]. SIMD principles, however, have been applied and implemented in a variety of different ways.

One important class of SIMD computers are massively parallel processors such as the Goodyear MPP [3] and the Thinking Machines CM-2 [10]. These machines consist of hundreds or thousands of processing elements (connected via an interconnection network to storage elements, to other processing elements, and to other entities, such as I/O elements). Because it has been impractical to build computers with thousands of fast processing elements (the power requirements would be enormous even if the hardware costs are tractable), such massively parallel computers typically sacrifice processing element speed in order to have more processing elements. The processing elements are typically bit-serial, taking multiple clock cycles to carry out a single 32-bit or a 64-bit computation, but taking a minimal amount of hardware to do so (for example, a simple single-bit versus a 64-bit ALU with carry lookahead logic). Because the objective is to carry out a computation consisting of many millions of independent operations, the massive parallelism makes up for the slow speed of a single n-bit operation.

Vector machines, such as the Cray-1, borrow some of the principles of SIMD computing, though they are generally not considered to be "pure" SIMD machines by many computer architects. A single vector instruction specifies a single operation on multiple data elements, so a vector instruction can be considered to be a SIMD instruction. However, vector machines typically do not have arrays of processing elements that are controlled by a master controller. Instead, vector instructions are fetched by the processor (typically by the instruction fetch logic in the scalar unit of a vector machine) and given to the vector unit. The manner in which a vector instruction is executed depends on the available hardware. For example, the elements of a vector can be operated on one at a time, using a single (typically pipelined) execution unit, or many at a time, if multiple execution units are available. In a sense, the scalar unit of a vector processor acts as the controller for the vector unit, which is based on the SIMD model.

The SIMD style of processing derives its power from many sources. First, SIMD instructions, which express multiple computations in a single instruction, are a very compact and regular means of specifying a desired set of operations. The single instruction single data (SISD) model requires loop control instructions (i.e., branches), in addition to the computation instructions themselves, as well as hardware to fetch and process these instructions. Second, because an SIMD instruction specifies a full set of operations that have to be performed, this set of operations can be scheduled for execution on parallel hardware with a degree of certainty in the (execution) timing of the operations—these operations can be launched to make full use of the available execution (or memory) bandwidth. Furthermore, regularity in hardware, and not having to deal with uncertainty, simplifies hardware designs. Third, because the processing units do not have to fetch instructions, not only do they not need instruction fetch hardware, they do not have to deal with uncertainties in the instruction fetching process (e.g., cache misses). Fourth, because the operations in a SIMD instruction

are executed with known timing characteristics (a common mode is lock-step operation of all the processing elements), no explicit synchronization is needed to coordinate the multiple operations.[1]

The main drawback of the SIMD style of processing is its lack of applicability to a wide variety of problems—not every computing problem involves applying the same set of operations on lots of regular data elements. And for applications where massive and regular data parallelism does not exist, the potential degradation in sequential processing speed limits the performance that can be achieved with SIMD computation. (The tradeoff between the available parallelism and the speed of a sequential computation was the subject of Gene Amdahl's famous Amdahl's Law paper [1]—a paper written to educate readers about this tradeoff, when many were arguing for using parallel processing principles, possibly at the expense of serial processing performance, for designing general-purpose computers.)

The canonical SIMD model and its variants do away with the problem of instruction fetching by the processing elements and its consequences. However, there is still a need to transfer data between the data memory and the individual processing elements. This results in: (1) enormous demands on processor-memory interconnect bandwidth and (2) performance degradation as the latency of memory (relative to the processor speed) increases. Rather than bring data to the processing elements, an alternative approach is to integrate the processing elements with the memory storage, that is, "move the processing to the memory."

The SIMD model, and its variants, are more applicable to the goal of "moving computation to the memory," as the processing elements in the SIMD model do little else other than carry out arithmetic operations. (They do not require hardware to store program instructions, fetch instructions, etc.) Integrating such simple computation elements (especially single-bit elements) with storage elements is easier than integrating more-complex processing elements. In the latter case, either storage is sacrificed (hardware that could be used to build storage is used for the more-complex processing element) or the resulting structure is simply a miniversion of a "vanilla" processing structure (i.e., separate processing and storage units) without a tight integration between processor and memory.

---

[1]Some argue that an alternate way of viewing this lack of synchronization is that, essentially, a barrier synchronization is performed as a part of every instruction execution, as sufficient time must be provided to allow all constituent operations of the instruction to complete.

8.2 Discussion of Included Papers

Next, we present a brief discussion on the papers reprinted in this chapter.

8.2.1 Flynn's "Very High-Speed Computing Systems" [4]

This classic paper, written by Mike Flynn in the mid-1960s, develops a taxonomy to characterize the different paradigms for building computers. By taking the cross product of the number of instruction streams that are being processed (single or multiple) and the number of data elements that are being processed (single or multiple), Flynn proposed four paradigms for computer design: (1) SISD, (2) SIMD, (3) multiple instruction, multiple data (MIMD), and (4) multiple instruction, single data (MISD). Flynn's taxonomy is widely used even today, more than thirty years after it was first proposed.

8.2.2 Kuck and Stokes's "The Burroughs Scientific Processor (BSP)" [8]

The paper by Kuck and Stokes describes the design of the BSP, a SIMD array processor with a unique instruction set and memory system. Unlike its predecessor, the ILLIAC-IV, the BSP parallel processor uses a "dance-hall" architecture with processors and memory modules on opposite ends of an interconnection network. A "system-level pipeline," the FAPAS pipeline governs the operation of the system—in any clock cycle, for common vector operations, 16 data items are being fetched from memory, 16 items are in the alignment network from memory to the processors, 16 operations are being executed in the processors, 16 results are on their way from the processors to memory, and 16 values are being stored in memory. To keep this pipeline full, the BSP uses a unique instruction set. Instructions, also called vector forms, can specify a chain of computations to be performed on elements of vectors. For example, a PENTAD instruction can be used to specify a computation expression of four operations on five input vectors. If the same computation is expressed with more traditional vector instructions, it would translate into a sequence of four dyadic vector instructions, which are *dependent* on each other. In other words, an instruction in the BSP can specify multiple *dependent* operations, whereas other instruction sets that specify multiple operations specify *independent* operations. The dependent vector forms of the BSP allow an entire high-level computation to be expressed in a single instruction, making the entire computation "visible" to the hardware controller, which can then decide how best

to schedule the execution of the constituent operations (including overlapping operations from different vector forms).

Another unique aspect of the BSP is its memory system—it consists of 17 (a prime number) memory banks. To prevent a degradation in pipeline throughput, the memory must be designed to have no bank conflicts for common array-access patterns (column, row, diagonal, back diagonal, subarray), and this requires a prime number of memory banks [9].

The BSP also provided special hardware to "parallelize" recurrence vector forms. Later, SIMD machines (e.g., the Thinking Machines CM-2) provided more elaborate forms of this hardware (also called parallel-prefix hardware). An excellent paper by Hillis and Steele shows how parallel prefix operations can be used to "parallelize" sequential computations [6].

8.2.3 Gokhale, Holmes, and Iobst's "Processing in Memory: The Terasys Massively Parallel PIM Array" [5]

The paper by Gokhale, Holmes, and Iobst describes a novel system ("Processor in Memory (PIM)"), which incorporates processing functions along with memory hardware. M single-bit processors are built into a memory chip consisting of $M \times M$ bits of storage, allowing arithmetic operations to be carried out on all the bits in a row of storage. By providing processing ability in the memory, the need to move data from memory to the processing elements and back to the memory is avoided, eliminating performance problems created by the latency of such data transfers and obviating the need for high-bandwidth processor-memory interconnects.

8.3 Looking Ahead

Although many of the SIMD computing principles were developed with the context of stand-alone SIMD parallel computers, such as the ILLIAC-IV, the Burroughs BSP, the Goodyear MPP and the Thinking Machines CM-2, it is unlikely that we will be seeing large-scale, pure-SIMD machines in the forseeable future. The reason for this is that the way multiprocessors are built today, and are likely to be built in the near future, is to start out with general-purpose microprocessors. We are unlikely to see many SIMD multiprocessors with custom-designed processors. However, as workloads change, and are more amenable to the SIMD style of processing, we are likely to see SIMD principles being adopted in the design of mainstream processor architectures. For example, to support multimedia workloads, many general-purpose architectures have added "multimedia extension" instructions that are based on SIMD principles: a single operation being performed on multiple data elements. Much of the SIMD-like support found to date is of a very basic variety (e.g., execute eight 8-bit operations in parallel on a 64-bit ALU)—a far cry from the plethora of powerful operations found in traditional SIMD computers. As semiconductor technology allows more arithmetic units to be built on a processing chip, more multimedia applications emerge, and program sequencing (and other aspects of instruction processing) become more cumbersome, one can expect to see more SIMD principles being applied in general-purpose processors. And some of these SIMD instructions might even look like the vector forms of the BSP: multiple dependent operations specified in a single instruction.

SIMD principles are also likely to be used in integrated processor-memory chips. Because hardware resources are not sufficient to allow both a sizable amount of memory as well as a powerful processor (based on currently known models for high-performance instruction processing) to be built on a single chip, such chips have to rely on multiple, simple processing elements to achieve the desired processing rate, and the SIMD model is an ideal model for organizing the processing elements. A recent proposal for an integrated processor-memory element, IRAM, proposes a vector processor integrated with DRAM [7].

8.4 References

[1]   G. Amdahl, "Validity of the single processor approach to achieving large scale computing capabilities," *AFIPS Spring Joint Computer Conference*, pp. 483–485, 1967.

[2]   G. H. Barnes, R. M. Brown, M. Kato, D. J. Kuck, D. L. Slotnick and R. A. Stokes, "The ILLIAC IV computer," *IEEE Transactions on Computers*, C-17(8):746–757, 1968.

[3]   K. E. Batcher, "Architecture of a massively parallel processor," *Proceedings of the 7th Annual Symposium on Computer Architecture*, pp. 168–173, May 1980.

[4]   M. J. Flynn, "Very high-speed computing systems," *Proceedings of the IEEE*, 54(12):1901–1909, 1966

[5]   M. Gokhale, B. Holmes, and K. Iobst, "Processing in memory: The Terasys massively parallel PIM array," *IEEE Computer*, 28(4):23–31, 1995.

[6]   W. D. Hillis and G. L. Steele, "Data parallel algorithms," *Communications of the ACM*, pp. 1170–1183, Dec. 1986.

[7]   C. E. Kozyrakis, S. Perissakis, D. A. Patterson, T. Anderson, K. Asanovic, N. Cardwell, R. Fromm, J. Golbus, B. Gribstad, K. Keeton, R. Thomas, N. Treuhaft, and K. Yelick, "Scalable processors in the billion-transistor era: IRAM," *IEEE Computer*, 30(9):75–78, 1997.

[8]   D. J. Kuck and R. A. Stokes, "The Burroughs scientific processor (BSP)," *IEEE Transactions on Computers*, C-31(5):363–376, 1982.

[9]   D. H. Lawrie and C. R. Vora, "The prime memory system for array access," *IEEE Transactions on Computers*, C-31(5):435–442, 1982.

[10] L. W. Tucker and G. G. Robertson, "Architecture and applications of the connection machine," *IEEE Computer*, 21(8):26–39, 1988.

Very High-Speed Computing Systems

MICHAEL J. FLYNN, MEMBER, IEEE

Abstract—Very high-speed computers may be classified as follows:

1) Single Instruction Stream–Single Data Stream (SISD)
2) Single Instruction Stream–Multiple Data Stream (SIMD)
3) Multiple Instruction Stream–Single Data Stream (MISD)
4) Multiple Instruction Stream–Multiple Data Stream (MIMD).

"Stream," as used here, refers to the sequence of data or instructions as seen by the machine during the execution of a program.

The constituents of a system: storage, execution, and instruction handling (branching) are discussed with regard to recent developments and/or systems limitations. The constituents are discussed in terms of concurrent SISD systems (CDC 6600 series and, in particular, IBM Model 90 series), since multiple stream organizations usually do not require any more elaborate components.

Representative organizations are selected from each class and the arrangement of the constituents is shown.

INTRODUCTION

MANY SIGNIFICANT scientific problems require the use of prodigious amounts of computing time. In order to handle these problems adequately, the large-scale scientific computer has been developed. This computer addresses itself to a class of problems characterized by having a high ratio of computing requirement to input/output requirements (a partially de facto situation caused by the unavailability of matching input/output equipment). The complexity of these processors, coupled with the advancement of the state of the computing art they represent, has focused attention on scientific computers. Insight thus gained is frequently a predictor of computer developments on a more universal basis. This paper is an attempt to explore large scientific computing equipment, reviewing possible organizations starting with the "concurrent" organizations which are presently in operation and then examining the other theoretical organizational possibilities.

ORGANIZATION

The computing process, in its essential form, is the performance of a sequence of instructions on a set of data.

Each instruction performs a combinatorial manipulation (although, for economy, subsequencing is also involved) on one or two elements of the data set. If the element were a single bit and only one such bit could be manipulated at any unit of time, we would have a variation of the Turing machine—the strictly serial sequential machine.

The natural extension of this is to introduce a data set whose elements more closely correspond to a "natural" data quantum (character, integer, floating point number, etc.). Since the size of datum has increased, so too has the number of combinatorial manipulations that can be performed (manipulations on two n bit arguments have 2^{2n} possible outcomes). Of course, attention is restricted to those operations which have arithmetic or logical significance.

A program consists of an ordered set of instructions. The program has considerably fewer written (or stored) instructions than the number of machine instructions to be performed. The difference is in the recursions or "loops" which are inherent in the program. It is highly advantageous if the algorithm being implemented is highly recursive. The basic mechanism for setting up the loops is the conditional branch instructions.

For convenience we adopt two working definitions: *Instruction Stream* is the sequence of instructions as performed by the machine; *Data Stream* is the sequence of data called for by the instruction stream (including input and partial or temporary results). These two concepts are quite useful in categorizing computer organizations in an attempt to avoid the ubiquitous and ambiguous term "parallelism." Organizations will be characterized by the multiplicity of the hardware provided to service the Instruction and Data Streams. The mutiplicity is taken as the maximum possible number of *simultaneous* operations (instructions) or operands (data) being in the same phase of execution *at the most constrained* component of the organization.

Several questions are immediately evident: what is an instruction; what is an operand; how is the "constraining component" found? These problems can be answered better by establishment of a reference. If the IBM 704 were compared to the Turing machine, the 704 would appear highly parallel. On the other hand, if a definition were made in terms of the "natural" data unit called for by a problem,

the situation would be equally untenable, since in many problems one would consider a large matrix of data a unit. Thus we arbitrarily select a reference organization: the IBM 704-709-7090. This organization is then regarded as the prototype of the class of machines which we label:

1) Single Instruction Stream–Single Data Stream (SISD).

Three additional organizational classes are evident.

2) Single Instruction Stream–Multiple Data Stream (SIMD)
3) Multiple Instruction Stream-Single Data Stream (MISD)
4) Multiple Instruction Stream–Multiple Data Stream (MIMD).

Before continuing, we define two additional useful notions.

Bandwidth is an expression of time-rate of occurrence. In particular, computational or execution bandwidth is the number of instructions processed per second and storage bandwidth is the retrieval rate of operand and operation memory words (words/second).

Latency or latent period is the total time associated with the processing (from excitation to response) of a particular data unit at a phase in the computing process.

Thus far, categorization has depended on the multiplicity of simultaneous events at the system's component which imposes the most constraints. The ratio of the number of simultaneous instructions being processed to this constrained multiplicity is called the *confluence* (or concurrence) of the system.

Confluence is illustrated in Fig. 1 for an SISD organization. Its effect is to increase the computational bandwidth (instructions processed/second) by maximizing the utility

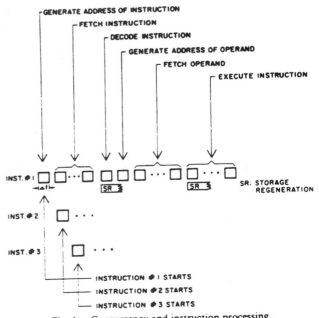

Fig. 1. Concurrency and instruction processing.

of the constraining component (or "bottleneck"). The processing of the first instruction proceeds in the phases shown. In order to increase the computational speed, we begin processing instruction 2 as soon as instruction 1 completes its first phase. Clearly, it is desirable to minimize the time in each phase, but there is no advantage in minimizing below the time required by a particular phase or mechanism. Suppose, for a given organization, that the instruction decoder is an absolute serial mechanism with resolution time. Δt. If the average instruction preparation and execution time is t_c, then the computational bandwidth may be improved by $t_c/\Delta t$. Thus if only one instruction can be handled at a time at the bottleneck, then the maximum achievable performance is $1/\Delta t$. (1 being the multiplicity of the constraint.)

In order to process a given number of instructions in a particular unit of time, a certain bandwidth of memory must be achieved to insure an ample supply of operands and operations in the form of instructions. Similarly, the data must be operated on (executed) at a rate consistent with the desired computational rate.

CONSTITUENTS OF THE SYSTEM

We will treat storage, execution, and instruction handling (branching) as the major constituents of a system. Since multiple stream organizations usually represent multiple attachments of one or more of the above constituents, we lose no generality in discussing the constituents of a system as they have evolved in SISD organizations. Indeed, confluent SISD organizations—by their nature—must allow arbitrary interaction between elements of the data stream or instruction stream. Multiple stream organization may limit this interaction, thus simplifying some of the considerations in an area. Therefore, for now, we shall be mainly concerned with techniques to extend computational performance in a context of a confluent SISD system. We will further assume that the serial mechanism which constrains the organization is the decoding of instructions. Thus, on the average, the processing of one instruction per decode cycle will be an upper limit on performance.

The relationship between the constituents is shown in Fig. 2 for the SISD organization.

A. Storage

The instruction and data streams are assumed sequential. Thus, accessing to storage will also be sequential. If there were available storage whose access mechanism could be operated in one decode cycle and this accessing could be repeated every cycle, the system would be relatively simple. The only interference would develop when operands had to be fetched in a pattern conflicting with the instructions. Unfortunately, accessing in most storage media is considerably slower than decoding. This makes the use of interleaving techniques necessary to achieve the required memory bandwidth (see Fig. 3). In the interleaving scheme, n memories are used. Words are distributed in each of the memories sequentially (modulo n). In memory i is stored word i, $n + i$, and $2n + i$, etc. However, the accessing mechanism does not alter the latency situation for the system, and this must be included in the design. Memory bandwidth must be sufficient to handle the accessing of instructions and operands, the storage of results and input–output traffic [9]. The amount of input–output bandwidth is problem-dependent. Large memory requirements will necessitate transfer of blocks of data to and from memory. The resulting traffic will be inversely proportional to the overall size of the memory. However, an increase in the size of the memory to minimize this interference also acts to increase the bulk of the memory, and usually the interconnection distance. The result, then, may be an increase in the latency caused by these communications problems.

Figure 3 was generated after the work of Flores [9] and assumes completely random address requests. The "waiting time" is the average additional amount of time (over the access time) required to retrieve an item due to conflicting

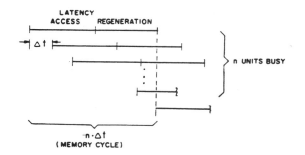

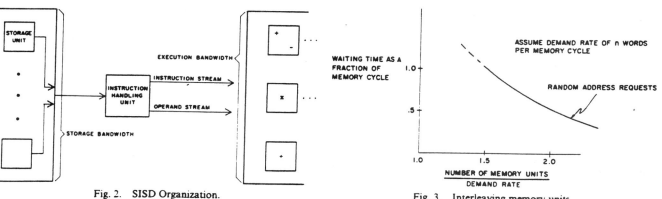

Fig. 2.   SISD Organization.

Fig. 3.   Interleaving memory units.

requests. Since memory requests are usually sequential for instructions and at least regular for data, the result is overly pessimistic for all but heavily branch-dependent problems. Typical programs will experience about half the waiting time shown.

This latency in the system greatly increases the complexity of the control mechanism for the storage system. The storage unit must now include queuing mechanisms to organize, fetch, and store requests which are in process or could not be honored due to conflicts. These queuing registers, containing outstanding service requests, must be continually compared against new requests for service. Extensive control interlocks must be made available to serve at least the following functions [2], [3]:

1) direct the fetched word to the appropriate requestor;
2) prevent out-of-sequence fetch-store or store-fetch in the same memory location;
3) eliminate duplicate requests of the same memory location (especially where the memory location contains more than one instruction or data unit);
4) analyze "keys" or "boundaries" where fetch or store memory protection are used.

In addition, confluent computing systems frequently employ buffers to minimize traffic requirements on the memory [2]. An instruction buffer might contain the next n instructions in the sequence as well as a history of m instructions together with several levels of alternate paths of branch.

The presence of a historical picture of instructions (in the instruction buffer) allows for the opportunity to store small loops, thus avoiding the penalty of reaccessing instructions. An operand buffer is used by the execution unit as its intrinsic storage medium. The instruction unit would restructure instructions that called for operands from memory into instructions which call for the contents of these registers. The instruction unit would, after decoding the instruction, initiate the requests for the appropriate operands and direct their placement into the operand buffer. Thus the execution unit would act as an independent computer, whose storage would be limited to the contents of this buffer, and whose instructions would be in a shortened format.

B. Execution

We center our discussion on the floating-point instructions since they are the most widely used in large scientific computing, and require the most sophisticated execution. In order to achieve the appropriate bandwidth levels, we can repeat the deployment scheme that was used for memory, only here the independent units will be dedicated to servicing one class of instructions. In addition to directly increasing the bandwidth by providing a number of units, the specialization of the unit aids in execution efficiency in several other ways. In particular, each unit might act as a small insular unit of logic, hence minimizing intra-unit wire communication problems. Secondly, the dedicated unit has fewer logical decisions to make than a universal unit.

Thirdly, the unit may be implemented in a more efficient fashion.

One may also consider "pipelining" techniques [6] to improve the bandwidth within a particular insular unit, in addition to optimizing an algorithm to minimize latent time. "Pipelining" is a process wherein natural points in the decision-making hardware are sought to latch up intermediate results and resuscitate the use of the unit. The latching may include extra decision elements for storage, but these may also be used in aiding the control of time skew (differences) in the various parallel paths.

1) Floating Add–Subtract Operations: Floating add–subtract operations consist of three basic parts. First, the justification of the fractional parts of the two operands by the amount of the difference of the exponents. Second, the adding of the fractional parts (or appropriate complement). Third, the postnormalization of the fraction if the result has a leading zero in a significant position or an overflow occurs. Because of the decision-making (shifting) problems associated with the exponent handling, a normal latch point for pipelining the two add operations in one unit (duplexing the unit) is at the interface from the preshift into the adder or after the first level of the adder structure. The floating add class of instruction has been reported [5] to operate in the 120 nanosecond range for a duplexed unit with 56-bit fraction (Systems 360 format).

2) Floating Multiply [5], [10], [12], [13]: The essential decision process of the multiplication algorithm is the addition of the multiplicand to itself by as many times as are indicated by the multiplier. If there are n bits in a multiplier and multiplicand, then the multiplicand must be added to itself n times with a one-place shift before each addition. Standard techniques exist for reducing the number of additions (e.g., multiplier bits: 1111. may be treated as $+10000. -1.$) required by encoding the multiplier into a lesser number of signed bits, say $n/2$. Once this is done, Wallace [12] suggests the direct addition of the $n/2$, n-bit, shifted multiplicands.

The basic decision element in adding of each bit of the $n/2$ operands is the so-called binary full adder, which takes three inputs of equal significance and produces two outputs, one of the same significance, the sum, and one of higher significance, the carry. By the associative law, the carry is injected into any available lower level add structure of the appropriate significance. (The net effect is sometimes referred to as a flush adder.) The final result, of course, is the reduction of the $n/2$ multiples into two result segments —the sums and the carries—which are then assimilated by a conventional carry-propagate adder with an anticipation mechanism. The basic problem is the implementation of this algorithm. For large n, the plane segments that partition the algorithm are inconsistent with conventional packaging sizes and interconnection limitations (see below).

Consider a simpler variation [Fig. 4(b)] [5]: here only n/m multiples of the multiplicand are retired per iteration (m iterations are required). The n/m multiples are decoded into $n/2m$ additions of the multiplier. These multiples are then inserted into the first level of the adder tree [Fig. 4(b)]. Now the add assimilation of both carries and sums proceeds as before with the introduction of intermediate staging points where the results are temporarily latched. The storage points act as skew (relative timing) control and improve the overall execution bandwidth efficiency of the algorithm. After the first set of multiples has been inserted into the first level of the tree and assimilated, it is latched at the first latch point. The storage point serves to decouple the first level from subsequent levels of the hardware; therefore the first set of multiples may now proceed to be absorbed in the second level and, simultaneously, a second set of multiples may be inserted into the first level of the tree. The process continues and, at the bottom of the tree, the carries and sums are assimilated in an adder with carry propagation. Notice that the latency in this variation may be twice that of the original algorithm. Also notice that

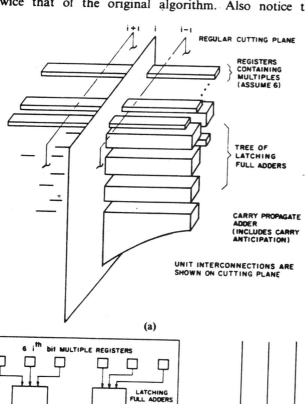

(a)

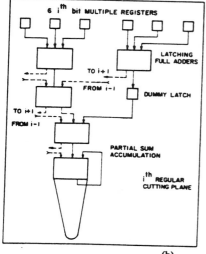

(b)

Fig. 4. Outline of a multiplier tree.

potential bandwidth in this algorithm has not suffered since a second multiplication may proceed independently as soon as the last set of multiples is inserted and has passed the first level of the tree. Implementations of this second scheme have yielded a performance of 180 nanoseconds for a floating-point multiply including post shifting and exponent updating (56-bit fraction, Systems 360 format).

Figure 4, parts (a) and (b) are three-dimensional representations of the second variation of the multiply algorithm. Figure 4(a) is an isometric projection and Fig. 4(b) is a cross-section (or "regular cutting plane") and profile view. This representation was chosen to illustrate some of the difficulties of implementing high-speed systems in general. It is well known [1] that propagation delay and nonuniform transmission line loading are major factors in the switching speed of a logic stage. One would, therefore, desire a physical package consistent with the "natural" communication pattern of the algorithm so that the implementation could be optimized. The difficulties of a planar package are obvious. Communications between "regular cutting planes" [profile view, Fig. 4(b)] must be made axially in the physical implementation. Indeed, there is no assurance that the capacity of the physical package-plane will match the requirements of the regular cutting plane—several package-planes may be required.

Notice that the first variation of the algorithm had much more extensive requirements per plane, thus its implementation would very likely be less efficient than the second variation.

3) Floating Point Divide [5], [10], [11]: Historically, divide has been limited by the fact that the iterative process was dependent on previous partial results. Recently, attention has been given to techniques which do not have this limitation. These techniques include use of Newton-Raphson iterations for series approximations to quotients.

Assume

$$\text{Quotient} = \frac{a}{b}$$

Let

$$\frac{1}{b} = \frac{1}{1-(-x)} = 1 - x + x^2 - x^3 + \cdots \pm x^n \mp \cdots$$

which can be rewritten as

$$\frac{1}{b} = (1-x)(1+x^2)(1+x^4)\cdots(1+x^{2m})$$

Thus:

$$\text{Quotient} = a \cdot (1-x) \cdot (1+x^2) \cdot (1+x^4) \cdots (1+x^{2m}).$$

Recall that in binary the factor $(1+x^m)$ is related to $(1-x^m)$ by a complementation operation. Thus, the denominator is rewritten as $(1+x)$, complemented to form $(1-x)$, the product is $(1-x^2)$ which is complemented to form $(1+x^2)$, which continues the development.

Notice that the speed is substantially enhanced by the presence of a high-speed multiplier. In fact, as many as two multiplications might proceed simultaneously. one for the quotient development and one for the next denominator term, if the hardware permits. In forcing quick convergence of the series, usually a table lookup arrangement is used to provide the first approximation for the quotient. Thereafter, subsequent iterations develop double the precision of the first approximation. Floating-point divides under 700 nanoseconds have been reported using this scheme [5].

4) Algorithms for Achieving Maximum Efficiency in the Concurrent Execution of Independent Units: One of the purposes in having independent units dedicated to individual instruction types is to improve the execution of each of the instruction classes. The other advantage is that these independent units may operate concurrently and serve to increase the overall bandwidth of the execution unit. Tomasulo [4] describes an elegant algorithm to allow the achievement of maximum efficiency in the concurrent execution of units (Fig. 5, illustration from Amdahl [1]). The operation of this algorithm takes advantage of the latent time following the issuing of the request to access the operands from storage into the memory in the execution area (either virtual or addressable buffers). When an instruction is forwarded to the execution area, a word in the execution unit memory is reserved for its operand, but the operand has not yet arrived. For example, if the instruction to be performed consisted of a multiply, then it could be immediately forwarded to the multiplication unit. The

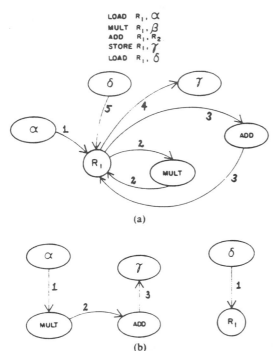

(a)

(b)

Fig. 5. Effect of Tomasulo concurrency algorithm. (a) Sequence with conventional dependency. (b) Sequence as performed after tag was forwarded.

multiplier would require a tag representing the operand. The execution area is provided with a common data bus and the tag representing the operand is broadcast on the bus one cycle early, then the execution functional units examine their queues of required operands and gate in immediately an appropriate one without waiting for it to go to the buffer storage. The tag forwarding frees the buffer storage of having any responsibility for this particular operand. Of course, at the same time, a load could then be executed into that same word. Thus, the second load instruction and the multiply instruction could proceed concurrently in a fashion impossible before. Results, as they become available, might also be forwarded to units (the adder in Fig. 5) requesting action by a similar mechanism, rather than proceeding directly to storage, whether virtual or addressed. This avoids intermediate stops and hence improves overall efficiency of execution by improving the overlap in the concurrency system.

C. Branching

Assume for the moment that memory bandwidth and execution bandwidth have now been arranged so that they more than satisfy the requirement of one instruction processed per decode cycle. What then would limit the performance of a SISD system? If it is assumed that there are a fixed number of data-dependent branch points in a given program, then, by operating in a confluent or other high-speed mode, we essentially bring the branch points closer together. However, the resolution time of the data-dependent branch point is basically fixed for a system with a given execution and/or accessing latency.

The basic retrogressive factor is the presence of branch dependencies in the instruction stream. Among the many types of branch instructions, we have [2], [7]:

1) *Execute:* The operand which is fetched is to be treated as an instruction (or an instruction counter). This presents some problems since the access latency is inserted into the instruction stream. It is essentially the same problem as indirect addressing or a double operand fetch. One could anticipate some of this difficulty by keeping ahead in the instruction stream. However, this particular instruction does not pose a series degradation problem because its use is normally restricted to linkages.

2) *Branch Unconditional:* The effective address so generated becomes the contents of the instruction counter. This subclass of instruction presents the same problem as execute.

3) *Branch on Index:* The contents of an index register is decremented by one on each iteration until the register is zero, upon which the alternate path is taken. Only the access latency is a factor since zero can be anticipated.

4) *Data-Dependent Branch:* The paths of the branch are determined by the condition (sign, bit, status, etc.) of some data cell. Invariably, this condition is dependent on the execution of a previously issued instruction.

Here the degradation is serious and unavoidable. First the execution of the condition-generating data must be completed. Then, the test is made and the path is selected. Now, the operands can be fetched and confluency can be restored. It is presumed that both instruction paths were previously fetched—but note that this is done only at the expense of greater memory bandwidth requirements. Another slight improvement can be made if the operands are fetched for one alternative path so long as the unresolved branch path is not executed (to avoid serious recovery and reconstruction problems if the guess proves wrong).

Of the two "loop closing" or conditional branch instructions, Branch on Index has less degradation due to resolution of latency than Data-Dependent Branch. When an option exists (as in the performance of a known number of iterations) the programmer should select the former.

Assuming that the Data-Dependent Branch-resolving latency is a constant for any particular machine, we may show its relationship (Fig. 6) to performance by assuming various percentages (of occurrence in executed code) of this type instruction. The latency represents the sum of average execution time plus operand access time from memory.

Figure 6 assumes that the organization under consideration has enough confluency to perform one instruction/cycle on the average without branch-resolution interruptions. To resolve the branch, it is generally necessary to fully execute and test the result of the preceding instruction. During this time, fetching of instructions and data may proceed for one branch path and possibly a few instructions may be fetched for the alternate. Fetching of both paths doubles the bandwidth required and increases the waiting time (Fig. 3). Thus the latency includes an average execution time, test time, and a percentage (wrong path guesses) of the operand-access time.

Notice that while we have studied degradation due to

latency for the SISD organization, multiple stream organizations may exhibit branch-induced degradation due to either this same phenomenon or an analog spatial inefficiency in which only one path activates or determines the outcome of a dependency.

CLASSES OF ORGANIZATION

In this section we shall consider each of the organizational classes listed in the first section of the paper. We will remark on or illustrate representative systems that fall into each class. The various configurations are by no means exhaustive.

A. Confluent SISD

The confluent SISD processor (IBM STRETCH [7], CDC 6600 series [8], IBM 360/90 series [2]–[5]) achieves its power by overlapping the various sequential decision processes which make up the execution of the instruction (Figs. 1 and 2). In spite of the various schemes for achieving arbitrarily high memory bandwidth and execution bandwidth, there remains an essential constraint in this type of organization. As we implied before, this bottleneck is the decoding of one instruction in a unit time, thus, no more than one instruction can be retired in the same time quantum, on the average. If one were to try to extend this organization by taking two, three, or n different instructions in the same decode cycle, and no limitations were placed on instruction interdependence, the number of instruction types to be classified would be increased by the combinatorial amount (M different instructions taken n at a time represents M^n different outcomes) and the decoding mechanism would be correspondingly increased in complexity. On the other hand, one could place restrictions on the occurrence of either specified types of instructions or instruction dependencies. This, in turn, narrows the class of problems for which the machine is suitable and/or demands restrictive programming practices. Indeed, this is a characteristic of multiple stream organizations since the multiplicity (or "parallelism") implies independent simultaneous action.

B. SIMD [14]–[18]

SIMD-type structures have been proposed by Unger [14], Slotnik [15] (SOLOMON, ILLIAC IV), Crane and Githens [16], and, more recently, by Hellerman [17].

SOLOMON is the classic SIMD. There are n universal execution units each with its own access to operand storage. The single instruction stream acts simultaneously on the n operands without using confluence techniques. Increased performance is gained strictly by using more units. Communication between units is restricted to a predetermined neighborhood pattern and must also proceed in a universal, uniform fashion [Fig. 7(a)]. (Note: SOLOMON has been superseded by ILLIAC IV as a system being actively developed, which is no longer completely SIMD.)

The difficulties with SIMD are:

1) Latency in the instruction stream for SIMD branches is now replaced by latency in the data stream caused by

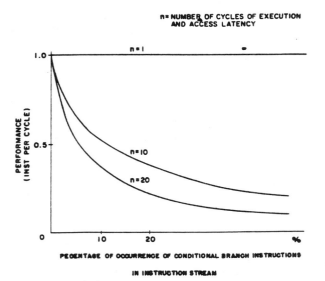

Fig. 6.   Degradation due to data-dependent branch instructions.

operand communication (forwarding) problems.

2) Presently, the number of classes of problems whose operand streams have the required communication regularity is not well established. SIMD organizations are inconsistent with standard algorithmic techniques (including, and especially, compiler techniques).

3) The universality of the execution units deprive them of maximum efficiency.

C. MISD

These structures have received much less attention [18], [19]. An example of such a structure is shown in Fig. 7(b). It basically employs the high bandwidth dedicated execution unit as described in the confluent SISD section. This unit is then shared by *n* virtual machines operating on program sequences independent of one another. Each virtual machine has access to the execution hardware once per cycle. Each virtual machine, of course, has its own

private instruction memory and interaction between instruction streams occurs only via the common data memory. Presumably, if there are N instruction units then the bandwidth of the common data storage must be N times greater than the individual instruction storage. This requirement could be substantially reduced by use of a modified version of Tomasulo's tag-forwarding algorithm and a separate common forwarding bus.

Another version of this [Fig. 7(c)] would force forwarding of operands. Thus the data stream presented to Execution Unit 2 is the resultant of Execution Unit 1 operating its instruction on the source data stream. The instruction that any unit performs may be fixed (specialized such that the interconnection (or setup) of units must be flexible), semifixed (such that the function of any unit is fixed for one pass of a data file) or variable (so that the stream of instructions operates at any point on the single data stream). Under such an arrangement, only the first execution unit sees the source data stream and while it is processing the *i*th operand the *i*th execution unit is processing the *i*th derivation of the first operand of the source stream.

D. MIMD

If we reconstruct the organization of Fig. 7(b) so that the data and instruction streams are maintained together in private memories, we have an example of MIMD. There is no interaction or minimum interaction allowed between these virtual machines. So long as the latent time for execution of any operation is less than the memory cycle, no problems arise due to branching. Thus, such an arrangement allows maximum advantage of the allowable bandwidths of execution unit and memory unit. Of course, such an approach might well be criticized on the basis that the requirement of independence of the instruction sequences does not address itself to the requirements of large scientific problems. It would be better suited to the needs of the timesharing and/or utility environment.

This restricted MIMD points up the shortcoming of our organizational definitions. The specifications fail to include a classification of how the streams may interact, thus a restricted MIMD may be organizationally much simpler than a confluent SISD.

General MIMD structures have been more widely described [20]–[23] with large-scale multiplicity being envisioned by Holland [21] and more restricted implementations being undertaken by Burroughs and Univac [23].

In his original proposal, Holland considers an array of processors each with a one-word storage. The modules are independent and are capable of concurrent execution. The processors have arithmetic ability but communication is limited by their need to "build a path" to the appropriate operand. In path building, the displacement and direction of the operand is specified and the intervening module processors form a vinculum.

Such an arrangement might solve some of the essential blockage problems of SISD and SIMD, since independent program segments proceed simultaneously. Also, memory bandwidth is always adequate.

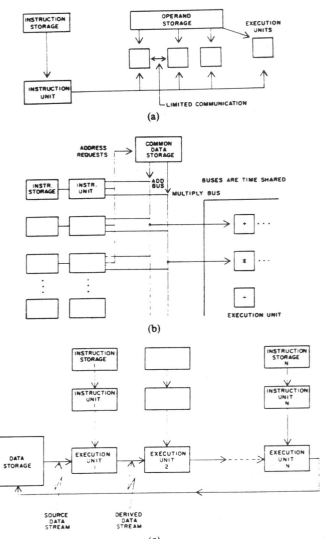

Fig. 7.   (a) SIMD. (b) MISD. Converts to MIMD if instructions and data are privately maintained (together). (c) MISD.

The difficulties with such an arrangement of MIMD generally include [20]:

1) interconnections between units, which pose serious interference problems
2) the universal nature of the individual module, which limits its efficiency
3) the class of problems which could utilize MIMD organization, which is presently small.

SYSTEMS REQUIREMENTS

The effectiveness of the overall computing processes must be measured on a basis much larger than performance (nanoseconds per instruction) alone. Even on this primitive basis, it is obvious that different instruction repertoire may imply substantially different effectiveness with the same average nanosecond per instruction ratio.

Despite our original assumption that the very large problem does not employ significant input/output, it is soon realized that this requirement is unduly restrictive. Presently, high-speed systems remain so limited. It may be some time before broader effective utilization may be realized through new developments in input/output equipment.

Of course, the overall measure of efficiency of the processor is the number of correctly completed computations and programs done over an extended period of time. Included in this measure is the reliability and the maintainability of the system. Complex systems with very large numbers of components are naturally very difficult to maintain, unless features which provide fault location are included. A major component of such features would be checking (or fault detection) of all operations and data transfers. On detection of error, hardware-aided diagnostics should be provided so that servicing and maintenance might be readily and easily accomplished. If checking is not included in the hardware, then it is, of course, incumbent on the user to program a thorough check of his results. This, of course, represents an overhead which penalizes the effective performance and utilization of the equipment.

Notice that some of the suggested organizations cater to restrictive problem sets—particularly the SIMD, where multiple operands are executed by the same instruction stream. Such organizations are clearly limited for general-purpose processing where there may be many interactions between operand elements. Similarly, with the MISD organizations, in the organization shown on Fig. 7(b), a number of independent instruction streams are involved and their very independence precludes MISD use on one large problem composed of essential dependencies; this, of course, is typical of large scale scientific programming.

CONCLUSIONS

Conventional Single Instruction Stream-Single Data Stream (SISD) processors may be enhanced by concurrency (confluence) of instruction handling, operand acquisition, and execution. There is, however, a limitation of the order of the execution of one instruction per instruction decoding

time, and this may be further degraded by the occurrence of "conditional branch" instructions.

By multiplexing the instruction stream or the data stream or both, new classes of processors which do not necessarily share this limit are developed. Their effectiveness depends on the nature of the problem and it is an open question as to whether new algorithms which will serve to extend their usefulness can be developed.

ACKNOWLEDGMENT

The author is indebted to D. Jacobsohn and R. Aschenbrenner of the Argonne National Laboratory for several valuable discussions on some of the material.

REFERENCES

[1] G. M. Amdahl and M. J. Flynn, "Engineering aspects of large high speed computer design," *Proc. Symp. on Microelectronics and Large Systems.* Washington, D. C.: Spartan. 1965, pp. 77–95.
[2] D. W. Anderson. F. J. Sparacio. and R. M. Tomasulo. "The Model 91: machine philosophy and instruction handling," *IBM J. Res. and Dev..* November 1966.
[3] L. J. Boland. G. D. Granito. A. U. Marcotte. B. M. Messina, and J. W. Smith, "The Model 91 storage system." *ibid.*
[4] R. M. Tomasulo. "An efficient algorithm for automatic exploitation of multiple execution units," *ibid.*
[5] S. F. Anderson. J. Earle. R. E. Goldschmidt, and D. M. Powers, "The Model 91 execution unit," *ibid.*
[6] L. W. Cotton. "Circuit implementation of high-speed pipeline systems," *1965 Proc. AFIPS FJCC.* p. 489.
[7] W. Buchholz. Ed., *Planning a Computer System.* New York: McGraw-Hill, 1962.
[8] J. E. Thornton. "Parallel operation in the Control Data 6600," *Proc. AFIPS 1964 FJCC,* pt. II, pp. 33–40.
[9] I. Flores. "Derivation of a waiting-time factor for a multiple bank memory," *J. ACM,* vol. 11, pp. 265–282, July 1964.
[10] M. Lehman, D. Senzig, and J. Lee, "Serial arithmetic techniques," *Proc. AFIPS 1965 FJCC,* pp. 715–725.
[11] R. E. Goldschmidt, "An algorithm for high-speed division," M.S. thesis, Mass. Inst. Tech., Cambridge, June 1965.
[12] C. S. Wallace. "A suggestion for a fast multiplier," *IEEE Trans. on Electronic Computers,* vol. EC-13, pp. 14–17, February 1964.
[13] D. Jacobsohn. "A suggestion for a fast multiplier," *IEEE Trans. on Electronic Computers (Correspondence),* vol. EC-13, p. 754, December 1964.
[14] S. H. Unger, "A computer oriented toward spatial problems," *Proc. IRE,* pp. 17–44, October 1958.
[15] D. L. Slotnick, W. C. Borch, and R. C. McReynolds, "The Solomon Computer—a preliminary report," *Proc. 1962 Workshop on Computer Organization.* Washington, D. C.: Spartan, 1963, pp. 66–92.
[16] B. A. Crane and J. A. Githens, "Bulk processing in distributed logic Memory," *IEEE Trans. on Electronic Computers,* vol. EC-14, pp. 186–196, April 1965.
[17] H. Hellerman. "Parallel processing of algebraic expressions," *IEEE Trans. on Electronic Computers,* vol. EC-15, pp. 82–91, February 1966.
[18] D. N. Senzig and R. V. Smith, "Computer organization for array processing," *Proc. AFIPS 1965 FJCC,* pp. 117–129.
[19] R. Aschenbrenner and G. Robinson, "Intrinsic multi-processing," Argonne National Laboratory, Argonne, Ill., ANL Tech. Memo. 121, June 1964.
[20] W. Comfort. "Highly parallel machines," *Proc. 1962 Workshop on Computer Organization.* Washington, D. C.: Spartan, 1963, pp. 126–155.
[21] J. H. Holland. "A universal computer capable of executing an arbitrary number of sub-programs simultaneously," *1959 Proc. EJCC,* pp. 108–113.
[22] R. Reiter. "A study of a model for parallel computation." University of Michigan, Ann Arbor, Tech. Rept., ISL-65-4, July 1965.
[23] D. R. Lewis and G. E. Mellen. "Stretching LARC's capability by 100—a new multiprocessor system," presented at the 1964 Symp. on Microelectronics and Large Systems. Washington, D. C.

The Burroughs Scientific Processor (BSP)

DAVID J. KUCK, MEMBER, IEEE, AND RICHARD A. STOKES

Abstract—The Burroughs Scientific Processor (BSP), a high-performance computer system, performed the Department of Energy LLL loops at roughly the speed of the CRAY-1. The BSP combined parallelism and pipelining, performing memory-to-memory operations. Seventeen memory units and two crossbar switch data alignment networks provided conflict-free access to most indexed arrays. Fast linear recurrence algorithms provided good performance on constructs that some machines execute serially. A system manager computer ran the operating system and a vectorizing Fortran compiler. An MOS file memory system served as a high bandwidth secondary memory.

Index Terms—Conflict-free array access, high-speed computer, parallel computer, pipeline computer, scientific computing, vectorizing compiler.

I. INTRODUCTION

FROM the beginning of the Burroughs Scientific Processor (BSP) design activity, we attempted to develop a system with high performance and reliability that is practical to manufacture, easy to use, and produces high quality numerical results. It is not possible to substantiate the success or failure in achieving these goals because the product was cancelled before user installations were realized. However, a full prototype system was operational for several months on customer benchmarks and demonstrated the practicality of the architecture. A number of points of technical merit have surfaced and are presented herein.

Because of the market place for which the BSP was intended, we chose Fortran as the main programming language for the machine. This choice leads to a need for array-oriented memory and processor schemes. It also leads to various control mechanisms that are required for Fortran program execution. To design a cost-effective and user-oriented system, more than programming languages must be considered; characteristics of the types of programs to be run on the machine must be carefully considered. We have throughout the design effort paid attention to the syntax of Fortran and also the details of "typical" scientific Fortran programs.

In the past 10 years several high performance systems have been built, including the pipelined CDC STAR (CYBER-205) [12], CRAY-1 [22], MU5 [24], and TI ASC [29], as well as Burroughs Illiac IV (BBKK68) and PEPE [9], the Goodyear Aerospace STARAN [21], and the ICL DAP [10], all parallel

Manuscript received June 5, 1978; revised December 3, 1981. This work was supported in part by the National Science Foundation under Grant US NSF MCS77-27910 and the Burroughs Corporation, Paoli, PA.
D. J. Kuck is with the Department of Computer Science, University of Illinois, Urbana, IL 61801.
R. A. Stokes is with the Burroughs Corporation, Paoli, PA 19301.

machines. While parallelism and pipelining are effective ways of improving system speed for a given technology (circuit and memory family, etc.), they both have shortcomings. Some pipelines perform better, the longer the vectors are that they have to process. The performance of other pipeline systems depends on vector lengths matching high-speed register set sizes. Parallel systems perform best on vectors whose length is a multiple of the number of processors available. Either type of system performs adequately if vector sizes are very large relative to the machine, but as these systems are used in wider application areas, short vector performance becomes more important. Other limitations of most pipeline processors have been that the arithmetic operations to be pipelined can reasonably be broken into only a limited number of segments and that overlapping of several instructions in one pipeline leads to unreasonable control problems.

Another important characteristic of high performance machines is the level of the language they execute. The CDC STAR and TI ASC, for example, have in their machine languages scalar and very high-level vector instructions, while ILLIAC IV, on the other hand, has a traditionally very low level machine language. A high-level machine language that is well matched to source programs can make compilation and control unit design easier and also helps ensure high system performance. A difficulty of array instructions can be that the setup time for instructions effectively stretches the pipeline length out intolerably.

System Overview

In the BSP we have combined parallelism and pipelining, and have provided array instructions that seem well matched to user programs. The machine has a five segment, memory-to-memory data pipeline, plus earlier instruction-setup pipeline segments. The data pipeline executes instructions that represent whole array assignment statements, recurrence system evaluations, etc., in contrast to most machines in which one or two arithmetic operations may be pipelined together. The BSP has 17 parallel memories, 16 parallel processors, and two data alignment networks. Since most instructions can be set up in the control pipeline preceding the data pipeline, instruction setup overhead should be insignificant in most cases. Thus, we have attempted to balance those architectural features that can provide good speedups with various overheads that can degrade or ruin system performance.

Another important factor in most supercomputers is I/O speed. If a very high speed processor is connected to standard disks, system performance may collapse because of I/O bound computations. The BSP has a high performance semiconductor file memory. This is used as a backup memory and to provide a smooth flow of jobs to and from the BSP.

Certain technological decisions were dictated by a Burroughs parallel development of a standard circuit and packaging design called Burroughs Current Mode Logic (BCML). A relatively long clock period was established in order to reduce the number of pipeline segments (for both data flow and instruction setup), avoid the complexities of high frequency clock distribution, and to facilitate manufacturing and testing the machine. The memory cycle time, the time to align 16 words between memories and processors (in either direction), and the time for many processor operations are all one 160 ns clock period; two clocks are required for floating-point addition and multiplication. In terms of these major events per clock, we attempted to lay out an array instruction set whose performance in the final system could be easily estimated during the design period.

A very important point in predicting system performance, and hence rationally choosing between design alternatives, is the determinacy of the system's behavior. We attempted to remove as much uncertainty as possible by several design choices. First, a parallel memory system was designed that provides conflict-free access to multidimensional arrays for most of the standard access patterns observed in programs. For cost reasons a parallel memory is required to achieve adequate bandwidth, and our design guarantees that for most instructions the effective bandwidth will be exactly at its maximum capacity. Since array elements are accessed in a different order from that in which they are processed, data alignment networks are needed along the path from memory to the processors and from the processors back to memory. These alignment networks also operate in a conflict-free way for most common operations. Finally, to guarantee that the memory-to-memory data pipeline is seldom broken, an array instruction set was designed. For example, a single BSP instruction can handle a whole assignment statement (with up to five right-hand side arguments) nested in one or two loops. The instruction can represent a number of 16 element slices of the operands, as long vector operations are automatically sliced and the slices overlapped in the memory-to-memory pipeline. Furthermore, as one vector assignment statement instruction ends, the next one can be overlapped with it in the pipeline. So for short vector operations there is usually no problem in keeping the pipeline full, since several different Fortran level instructions may be in operation at once.

Thus, for a wide class of instructions it was possible to predict the system performance (up to the clock speed) very early in the design process (1973). Furthermore, it has been possible during the later stages of design to make tradeoffs in these terms. Array instructions have also been very beneficial in allowing logic designers and compiler writers to communicate with each other about their own design efforts and to make tradeoffs in concrete performance terms.

A Fortran compiler has been implemented that vectorizes ANS Fortran programs, thus allowing old programs to be run without expensive reprogramming efforts. Vector extensions to Fortran are also provided to allow users to "improve" certain parts of old programs, if desired, or to write new programs in efficient ways. The vectorizer not only handles array operations, it also substantially speeds up linear recurrences—as found, for example, in processes that reduce vectors to scalars (e.g., inner product, polynomial evaluation, etc.)—and effectively handles many conditional branches within loops.

For some applications, numerical stability is a serious problem. The BSP does high quality rounding (approximate R*) rounding of its 36-bit mantissas and also provides double precision hardware operations. Furthermore, interrupts are generated for standard floating-point faults. Error detection and correction are provided throughout the system and automatic instruction retry is provided to ease the burden on the user in some cases.

The BSP and its file memory form a high-speed computing system that may be viewed as standing inside a computational envelope. This envelope is serviced by a *system manager* that can be a Burroughs B6700, B6800, B7700, or B7800. This front-end general-purpose system provides the following:

- compilation of BSP programs,
- archival storage for the BSP,
- data communication and time-sharing services to a user community,
- other languages and computation facilities.

Thus, a typical user will interactively generate compiled program and data files on the system manager, pass them to the BSP for execution, and have results returned via the system manager with permanent files maintained on the system manager's disks. Most job scheduling and operating system activities for the BSP are carried out on the system manager, so the BSP is dedicated to high-speed execution of user application programs.

II. System Overview

Fig. 1 shows a block diagram of the BSP and the system manager. The BSP itself consists of three major parts: the control processor, the parallel processor, and the file memory. In this section some characteristics of these parts of the BSP will be presented. In subsequent sections we will give more details about how they operate.

A. Control Processor (CP)

The control processor is a high-speed element of the BSP that provides the supervisory interface to the system manager in addition to controlling the parallel processor and the file memory. The CP consists of a scalar processor unit, a parallel processor control unit, a control memory, and a control and maintenance unit.

The CP executes some serial or scalar portions of user programs utilizing an arithmetic element (similar to one of the 16 arithmetic elements in the parallel processor) that contains additional capabilities to perform integer arithmetic and indexing operations. The CP also performs task scheduling, file memory allocation, and I/O management under control of the BSP operating system.

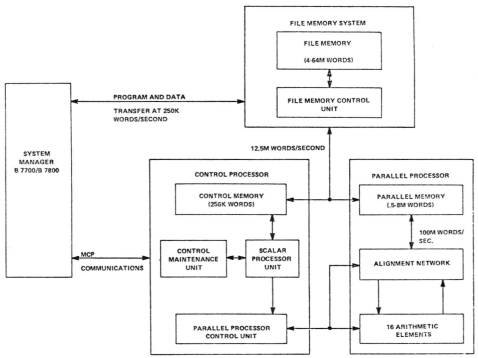

Fig. 1. BSP system diagram.

Scalar Processor Unit (SPU): The scalar processor unit processes all operating system and user program instructions that are stored in control memory. It has a clock frequency of 12.5 MHz and is able to perform up to 1.5 million floating-point operations/s. All array instructions and certain scalar operations are passed to the parallel processor control unit, which queues them for execution on the parallel processor.

Parallel Processor Control Unit (PPCU): The PPCU receives array instructions from the scalar processor unit. The instructions are validated and transformed into microsequences that control the operation of all 16 arithmetic elements in the parallel processor. Vectors of any length are handled automatically by the PPCU hardware, relieving the programmer and compiler of this burden.

Control Memory (CM): The control memory is used to store portions of the operating system and all user programs as they are being executed. It is also used to store data values that are operands for those instructions executed by the scalar processor unit. The control memory is a 4K bit/chip NMOS memory with a 160 ns cycle time. Capacity of the memory is 256K words; each word consists of 48 data bits and 8 bits for error detection and correction. Four words are accessed simultaneously, giving a minimum effective 40 ns access time per 48 bit word.

Control and Maintenance Unit (CMU): The control and maintenance unit serves as the direct interface between the system manager and the rest of the control processor for initialization, communication of supervisory commands, and maintenance. It communicates with the input/output processor of the system manager. The CMU has access to critical data paths and registers of the BSP, so that it can perform state

analysis and circuit diagnostics under control of maintenance software running on the system manager.

B. Parallel Processor (PP)

The parallel processor performs array-oriented computations at high speeds by executing 16 identical operations simultaneously in its 16 arithmetic elements. Data for the array operations are stored in a parallel memory (PM) consisting of 17 memory modules. Parallel memory is accessed by the arithmetic elements through input and output alignment networks. A memory-to-memory data pipeline is formed by the five steps (fetch, align, process, align, store) and overlap in the pipeline provides significant performance benefits.

Parallel Memory (PM): The parallel memory is used only to hold data arrays for the parallel processor and consists of 17 memory units, each of which may contain from 32K to 512K words, making a total of from 0.5 to 8 million words. It is a 4K bit/chip NMOS memory with a 160 ns cycle time as in the control processor memory. Each word contains 48 data bits and 8 bits for error detection and correction. The maximum rate of data transfer between the PM and the arithmetic elements is 10^8 words/s. The organization of the PM permits simultaneous access to most commonly referenced components of an indexed array, such as rows, columns, or diagonals. For some operands the compiler must choose between allocating storage in PM or CM, and performance can suffer if this is not done properly.

The Alignment Networks (AN): The BSP has two alignment networks: the input alignment network for data fetching and the output alignment network for data stores. Both units contain full crossbar switching networks as well as hardware for broadcasting data to several destinations and for resolving conflicts if several sources seek the same destination. This permits general-purpose interconnectivity between the arithmetic array and the memory storage modules. It is the combined function of the memory storage scheme and the alignment networks that supports the conflict-free capabilities of the parallel memory. The output alignment network is also used for interarithmetic element switching to support special functions such as the data compress and expand operations and the fast Fourier transform algorithm.

Arithmetic Elements (AE): At any time all of the arithmetic elements are executing the same instruction on different data values. The arithmetic elements operate at a clock frequency of 6.25 MHz and are able to complete the most common arithmetic operations in two clock periods. Each arithmetic element can perform a floating-point add, subtract, or multiply in 320 ns, so the BSP is capable of executing up to 50 million floating-point operations/s. Each arithmetic element can perform a floating-point divide in 1280 ns and extract a square root in 2080 ns.

C. File Memory (FM)

The file memory is a high-speed secondary storage device that is loaded by the system manager with BSP tasks and task files. These tasks are then queued for execution by the control processor. The FM is also used to store scratch files and output files produced during execution of a BSP program. It is the only peripheral device under the direct control of the BSP; all other peripheral devices are controlled by the system manager.

The FM utilizes high-speed semiconductor memory as its storage medium; it combines a 1 ms access time with a 12.5M word/s transfer rate. Since it is entirely semiconductor, the reliability of the file memory is much greater than that of conventional rotating storage devices.

III. Languages and Their Translation

The BSP can be regarded as a high performance Fortran machine, although many of the ideas in the design are useful for various languages. In this section we present some details of the vector form language seen by the PPCU and discuss how vector forms can be obtained from Fortran programs by a vectorizing compiler. The essential elements of many numerical algorithms are represented by these vector forms and numerical programs in most languages could be reduced to the same set of vector forms. However, the large collection of Fortran programs existing in the numerical computation community has dictated that the primary language of the BSP be Fortran. Nevertheless, vector extensions to Fortran are provided so that users may write new programs in a more convenient language than Fortran, and also to allow faster translation and possibly faster executable BSP code. We conclude this section with a sketch of the BSP vector Fortran extensions.

A. Vector Forms

The parallel processor control unit sequences the five stages of the data pipeline: fetch, align, process, align, store (FAPAS). In this pipeline several instructions corresponding to Fortran statements may be in execution at one time. To clarify this process, several definitions are required; these will lead to an understanding of the parallel processor control unit and compiler.

The BSP has a total of 64 *vector forms* that may be grouped in the following four types:
1) array expression statements,
2) recurrence and reduction statements,
3) expand, compress, random store, and fetch, and
4) parallel memory transmissions to and from control memory and file memory.

Array expression statements include indexing and evaluating right-hand side array expressions ranging from monad to pentad (five right-hand side operands), plus the assignment of the resulting values to parallel memory. A separate vector form exists for each possible parse of each right-hand side expression. The array operations are performed in an element by element fashion and allow scalars and array variables of one or two dimensions to be mixed on the right-hand side. For example,

DO 5 $I = 1, 30$
   DO 5 $J = 7, 25$
5     $X(I, J) = (A(I, J + 1) * 0.5 + B(I + 1, J))$
         $* X(I, J + 1) + C(J)$

would be compiled as a single vector form. This vector form can be regarded as a six-address instruction that contains the four array arithmetic operation specifications and the assignment operation.

Recurrence vector forms correspond to assignment statements with data dependence loops. For example,

DO 3 $I = 1, 25$
3    $Y(I) = F(I) * Y(I - 1) + G(I)$

has a right-hand side that uses a result computed on the previous iteration. This recurrence produces an array of results, while others lead to a scalar result and are called *reductions*. For example, a polynomial evaluation by Horner's rule leads to the reduction

    $P = C(O)$
DO 5 $I = 1, 25$
5    $P = C(I) + Y * P.$

Both of these are recurrences that can be represented by a linear system of the form $x = Ax + b$, where A is a lower triangular matrix with a single band, one diagonal below the main diagonal, and x is an unknown vector. We will refer to a linear recurrence of dimension n and order m as an $R\langle n, m \rangle$ recurrence, where n is the dimension of the matrix A and $m + 1$ is the bandwidth of matrix A. Thus, the above program leads to an $R\langle 25, 1 \rangle$ system. Fast efficient algorithms exist for solving such systems and the $R\langle n, 1 \rangle$ solver of [7] and [23] for small n and the $R\langle n, 1 \rangle$ solver of [6] for large n have been built into the BSP. For wider bandwidth recurrences the column sweep algorithm [15] is more efficient and it is used in the BSP. However, the user is not concerned with any of these considerations, since the vector forms described have array control unit hardware for their direct execution, as we shall see shortly.

Note that all recurrences would have to be executed serially without these algorithms. With them, $R\langle n, m\rangle$ systems (1 < $m \leq 16$ will obtain speedups proportional to m. For $m = 1$ and n of moderate size (say, 50 to 100), a speedup of 5 to 6 can be obtained, with greater speedups for large n. By speedup we mean time reduction compared to a hypothetical BSP with just one AE.

The third type of vector forms involves various sparse array operations. For example, in the case of a Fortran variable with subscripted subscripts, e.g., $A(B(I))$, no guarantee can be made concerning conflict-free access to the array A. In this case the indexing hardware generates a sequence of addresses that allows access to one operand per clock and these are then processed in parallel in the arithmetic elements. These are called *random store* and *random fetch* vector forms. Sparse arrays may be stored in memory in a compressed form and then expanded to their natural array positions using the input alignment network. After processing, the results may be compressed for storage by the output alignment network. These are called *compressed vector operand* and *compressed vector result* vector forms and they use control bit vectors that are packed, such that one 48 bit word is used for accesses to three 16 element vector slices.

A list illustrating the above three classes of vector forms is found in Table I. The mnemonics and comments should give an idea of what these vector forms do.

The fourth class of vector forms is used for I/O. Scalar and array assignments are made to control memory and parallel memory depending on whether they are to be processed in the scalar processor unit or the parallel processor, respectively; however, it is occasionally necessary to transmit data back and fourth between these memories. Transmissions to file memory are standard I/O types of operations.

These four types of vector forms comprise the entire set of array functions performed by the BSP. At the vector form level, the array processor may be regarded as arbitrarily large; thus, vector code generation is simplified in the compiler because it can transform Fortran programs into objects that map easily into vector forms, as we shall see shortly. However, in most Fortran programs some parameters are not defined at compile time (e.g., loop limits), so some run-time source language processing remains. This is carried out by the scalar processing unit of the control processor, and when it is finished the parallel processor is controlled by a template sequencing mechanism (see Section IV-D).

Vector forms are very high-level instructions with many parameters. For example, an array expression statement vector form corresponds to an assignment statement parse tree and leads to the execution of up to four operations on operands that may be combinations of scalars and one- or two-dimensional arrays. The following is a sketch of how the scalar processing

unit (SPU) initiates the execution of a vector form in the parallel processor control unit (PPCU).

Consider a triad vector form

$RBV, Z = (A\ op_1\ B)op_2\ C, OBV$

where Z, A, B, and C are vector descriptors, op_1 and op_2 are operators, and RBV and OBV are optional result and bit-vector descriptors, respectively. Bit vectors may be used to specify the elements of an array to be operated on or stored; they are optional (but not shown) for a number of the entries in Table I. In executing the triad, the SPU issues the following sequence of instructions that describe the vector form to the PPCU:

VFORM TRIAD, op_1, op_2
OBV
RBV
VOPERAND A
VOPERAND B
VOPERAND C
VRESULT Z.

The VFORM instruction contains bits that name the first template (see Section IV-D) to be executed, specify actual operator names, indicate the presence of bit-vectors, and specify the program countercontents; it also contains other synchronization and condition bits. The OBV and RBV descriptors give the bit-vector starting addresses and lengths. The VOPERAND and VRESULT instructions give the start of the vector relative to an array location, the location of the array, the volume of the array, the skip distance between vector elements to be accessed, and optionally the skip distance between the start of subsequent vectors in a nested pair of loops. The VFORM instruction is preceded by a VLEN instruction that specifies the level of loop nesting and array dimensions. At this point, all source language parameters have been bound and run-time source language processing ends. The remaining processing done by the PPCU, e.g., array bounds checking, is the same for all operations. We shall return to a discussion of template sequencing in Section IV.

B. Fortran Vectorizer

In ordinary Fortran programs it is possible to detect many array operations that easily can be mapped into BSP vector forms. This is accomplished in the BSP compiler by a program called the Fortran vectorizer. We will not attempt a complete description of the vectorizer here, but we will sketch its organization, emphasizing a few key steps. For more discussion of these ideas, see [15], [17], and [4].

First, consider the generation of a program graph based on data dependences. Each assignment statement is represented by a graph node, and directed arcs are drawn between nodes to indicate that one node is to be executed before another. Algorithms for data dependence graph construction are well known [1], [4] and will not be discussed here. It should be observed that some compilers have used naive algorithms, for example, checking only variable names. The BSP algorithm does a detailed subscript analysis and thus builds a high quality graph with few redundant arcs, thereby leading to more array operations and fewer recurrences.

TABLE I

Vector Forms

MONAD	It accepts one vector set operand, does one monadic operation on it and produces one vector set result.	$Z \leftarrow op\ A$
DYAD	It accepts two vector set operands, does one operation on them and produces one vector set result.	$Z \leftarrow A\ op\ B$
VSDYAD	It is similar to the DYAD except that operand B is a scalar.	$Z \leftarrow A\ op\ B$
EXTENDED DYAD	It accepts two vector set operands, does one operation and produces two vector set results.	$(Z1, Z2) \leftarrow A\ op\ B$
DOUBLE PRECISION DYAD	It accepts four vector set operands (i.e., two double precision operands), performs one operation and produces two vector set results.	$(Z1, Z2) \leftarrow (A1, A2)\ op\ (B1, B2)$
DUAL-DYAD	It accepts four vector set operands, does two operations and produces two vector set results.	$Z \leftarrow A\ op_1\ B$ $Y \leftarrow C\ op_2\ D$
TRIAD	It accepts three vector set operands, does two operations and produces one vector set result.	$Z \leftarrow (A\ op_1\ B)\ op_2\ C$
TETRAD1	It accepts four set operands, does three operations and produces one vector set result.	$Z \leftarrow ((A\ op_1\ B) op_2\ C)\ op_3\ D$
TETRAD2	It is similar to the TETRAD1 except for the order of operations.	$Z \leftarrow (A\ op_1\ B) op_2\ (C\ op_3\ D)$
PENTAD1	It accepts five vector set operands, does four operations and produces one vector set result.	$Z \leftarrow (((A\ op_1\ B) op_2\ C)\ op_3\ D) op_4\ E$
PENTAD2	It is similar to the PENTAD1 except for the order of operations.	$Z \leftarrow ((A\ op_1\ B) op_2\ (C\ op_3\ D)) op_4\ F$
PENTAD3	It is similar to the PENTAD1 except for the order of operations.	$Z \leftarrow ((A\ op_1\ B) op_2\ C)\ op_3\ (D\ op_4\ E)$
AMTM	It is similar to the MONAD and is used to transmit from parallel memory to control memory.	$Z \leftarrow op\ A$
TMAM	It accepts 6 vector set operands from control memory to transmit to parallel memory.	$Z \leftarrow A1(0,0),\ A2(0,0)$ $A3(0,0),\ A4(0,0),$ $A5(0,0),\ A6(0,0)$
COMPRESS	It accepts a vector set operand, compresses it under a bit vector operand control and produces a vector set result.	$X \leftarrow A,\ BVO$
EXPAND	It accepts a vector operand, expands it under a bit vector control and produces a vector set result.	$X \leftarrow V,\ BVO$
MERGE	It is the same as the EXPAND except that the vector set result elements corresponding to a zero bit in BV are not changed in the parallel memory.	$X \leftarrow V,\ BVO$
RANDOM FETCH	It performs the following operation $Z(j,k) \leftarrow U(I(j,k))$, where U is a vector and I is an index vector set.	
RANDOM STORE	It performs the following operation $X(I(j,k)) \leftarrow A(j,k)$, where X is a vector and I is an index vector set.	
REDUCTION	It accepts one vector set operand and produces one vector result given by $X(i) \leftarrow A(i,0)\ op\ A(i,1)\ op\ A(i,2)\ op\ A(i,3)\ \ldots\ A(i,L)$, where op must be a commutative and associative operator.	

TABLE I (CONTINUED)

DOUBLE-PRECISION REDUCTION	It accepts two vector set operands (one double-precision vector set) and produces two vector results (one d.p. vector) given by $(X_1(i), X_2(i)) \leftarrow (A_1(i,0), A_2(i,0))$ op $(A_1(i,1), A_2(i,1))$ op ... $(A_1(i,L), A_2(i,L))$, where op must be a commutative and associative operator.
GENERALIZED DOT PRODUCT	It accepts two vector set operands and produces one vector result given by $X(i) \leftarrow \{A(i,0)$ op_2 $B(i,0)\}$ op_1 $\{A(i,1)$ op_2 $B(i,1)\}$ op_1 ... $\{A(i,L)$ op_2 $B(i,L)\}$, where op_1 must be a commutative and associative operator.
RECURRENCE-1L	It accepts two vector set operands and produces one vector result given by $X(i) \leftarrow (\{...\{(B(i,0)$ op_1 $A(i,1))$ op_2 $B(i,1)\}$ op_1 ...$\}$ op_1 $A(1,L))$ op_2 $B(i,L)$ where op_2 can be ADD or IOR and op_1 can be MULT or AND.
PARTIAL REDUCTION	It accepts one vector set operand and produces one vector set result given by $Z(i,j) \leftarrow Z(i,j-1)$ op $A(i,j)$, where op must be a commutative and associative operator.
RECURRENCE-1A	It accepts two vector set operands and produces one vector set result given by $Z(i,j) \leftarrow \{Z(i,j-1)$ op_1 $A(i,j)\}$ op_2 $B(i,j)$, where op_1 can be MULT or AND and op_2 can be ADD or IOR.

As an example, consider the following program:

    DO 5 I = 1, 25
1       $A(I) = 3 * B(I)$
         DO 3 J = 1, 35
3            $X(I, J) = A(I) * X(I, J - 1) + C(J)$
5       $B(I) = 2 * B(I + 1)$.

A dependence graph for this program is shown in Fig. 2, where nodes are numbered according to the statement label numbers of the program. Node 1 has an arc to node 3 because of the $A(I)$ dependence and node 3 has a self-loop because $X(I, J - 1)$ is used one J iteration after it is generated. The crossed arc from node 1 to node 5 is an antidependence arc [16] indicating that statement 1 must be executed before statement 5 to ensure that $B(I)$ on the right-hand side of statement 1 is an initial value and not one computed by statement 5. Arcs from above denote initial values being supplied to each of the three statements: array B to statements 1 and 5, and array C to statement 3. The square brackets denote the scope of loop control for each of the DO statements.

Given a data dependence graph, loop control can be distributed down to individual assignment statements or collections of statements with internal loops of data dependences. In our example there is one loop (containing just one statement) and two individual assignment statements. After the distribution of loop control, the graph of Fig. 2 may be redrawn as shown in Fig. 3.

The graph of Fig. 3 can easily be mapped into BSP vector forms. Statements 1 and 5 go into array expression statement vector forms directly since they are both dyads. Had they had more than five right-hand side variables, their parse trees would have been broken into two or more array expression statement vector forms and joined by a temporary array assignment. Statement 3 can be split into 25 independent re-

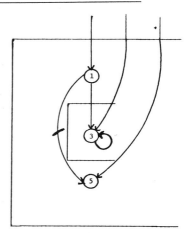

Fig. 2.   Data dependence graph.

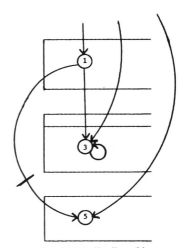

Fig. 3.   Graph with distributed loop control.

currence systems, each with a bandwidth of 1 caused by the $J - 1$ to J dependence, resulting in 25 independent $R\langle 35, 1\rangle$ systems, each of which maps into a recurrence vector form. Alternatively, it can be computed as a series of 35 array expression statement vector forms (triads). The maximum speed choice is made based on the loop limits.

The above cases are rather simple constructs, but they are typical of those found in existing Fortran programs. Several kinds of more complex cases are possible. If arrays with subscripted subscripts occur, they are compiled using the random fetch or store vector forms mentioned earlier. If recurrences with nonlinear right-hand sides occur, e.g., $X(I) = A(I) * X(I - 1) * X(I - 2) + B(I)$, then serial code is compiled. To this point we have ignored conditional statements inside loops, another problem that in the past has caused serial code to be compiled.

A number of IF statements can in fact be handled in parallel in the BSP. For a theoretical discussion of various types of IF's, see [14], where examples and measurements of the frequency of various types of IF's are presented. It turns out that many of the commonly found IF's can be handled in the BSP by using standard vector forms which include bit vectors. In this way, certain IF statements can be combined with assignment statements in a single vector form. For example, consider the following program:

```
        DO 1 I = 1, 92, 2
            DO J = 1, 46
1               IF(A(I, J).LT.0) B(I, J) = A(I, J) * 3.5.
```

This loop can be mapped into a single array expression statement vector form with bit-vector control that performs the parallel tests and makes the appropriate assignments to $B(I, J)$. By using loop distribution, many of the IF's found in ordinary Fortran programs can be transformed into such vector operations that allow substantial speedups on the BSP. Of course, there is also a residual set of IF's that must be compiled as serial code.

A traditional objection to array computers was that too many of the statements found in ordinary programs could not be vectorized and would have to be executed in a traditional sequential manner. In the BSP a combination of software and hardware innovations has led to a system that avoids most of these traditional objections. Of primary software importance are the distribution of loop control, fast algorithms to solve linear recurrences, and the vectorization of IF statements. Also of key importance is a good test for data dependence between subscripted variables, the appropriate introduction of additional subscripts to variables of lower dimension than their depth of loop nesting, and the transformation of scalar expressions inside loops as well as their substitution into subscripts. After a source program has been mapped into vector forms it is ready for execution.

C. Fortran Language Extensions

To provide users with language conveniences for writing new programs and to allow rewriting old programs that are difficult to vectorize automatically, several language extensions are being provided in the BSP software. Some of these extensions are also part of the proposed new ANS Fortran. The extensions may be categorized in four cases as array description, array operation, control, and I/O statements; we shall deal with them in that order, providing only a quick sketch of the ideas.

Arrays may be declared with the colon notation, using positive and negative subscripts, e.g., REAL $A(0:3, 0:3, -3:3)$ declares a $4 \times 4 \times 7$ array. Portions of declared arrays may be renamed for easy reference using an ARRAY statement as the following example shows:

```
        REAL A(100, 100)
        ARRAY ROW 2(J = 1:100) = A(2, J),
            DIAG(I = 1:100) = A(I, I)
```

identifies ROW 2 as a vector consisting of the second row of A and DIAG as the main diagonal of A. No storage is allocated or data are moved by an ARRAY statement, only additional array descriptors are created.

Array operations can be specified in various ways. If A and B are declared arrays, then $A = 0$ sets all elements of A to zero and $B = B + 1$ adds 1 to all elements of B. If A is two-dimensional, then $A(*, 0) = 2$ sets column zero of A to 2. Arithmetic, relational, and logical operators may be applied to pairs of arrays that are congruent, in which case element by element operations are performed. Furthermore, bit-vectors may be used to control array operations by use of the WHERE statement as follows. Assume that A and B are 500 element vectors, then

$$\text{WHERE}(A.GE.0)\ B = B + A$$

is equivalent to

```
        DO 10 I = 1, 500
10          IF (A(I).GE.0) B(I) = B(I) + A(I).
```

This is generalized to a block-structured WHERE DO that contains a sequence of OTHERWISE statements and ends with an END WHERE. PACK and UNPACK statements are provided to allow sparse arrays to be compressed and expanded, respectively; multidimensional arrays may be packed into vectors based on logical tests. There is also an IF-THEN-ELSE construct and an END DO that does not require a label in its DO statement. For scalars or congruent arrays, the exchange statement

$$A = = B$$

exchanges A and B in memory.

A collection of intrinsic functions is also provided, one set generalizes the standard scalar intrinsics to arrays (e.g., transcendental functions of the elements of an array) and the other set provides some standard array operations (e.g., dot product, matrix product, max of an array, etc.).

User programs can control I/O without supervisor intervention and without buffering by using the DIRECT statement which names an array that appears in a following READ statement. Execution of statements after the READ continues simultaneously with the input until the DIRECT named variable is encountered on the right-hand side of an assignment statement, at which point execution is suspended until the READ is completed.

IV. System Operation

In this section we give more details of the overall system operation. First, the parallel memory and its conflict-free structure are discussed (Section IV-A), and this is followed (Section IV-B) by the alignment networks that stand between the parallel memory and the arithmetic elements, which are discussed in Section IV-C. Section IV-D ties these components of the parallel processor together by detailing the template sequencing as carried out by the parallel processor control unit.

This also relates back to Section III-A, where it was pointed out that source programs are first mapped by software into vector forms which in turn are mapped by hardware into a sequence of templates. The template sequencing mechanism is one of the key points in achieving high system utilization through pipelining and overlap of vector forms in the BSP. This section concludes with a discussion of the high performance file memory used for secondary storage in the BSP.

A. Parallel Memory

The BSP parallel memory consists of 17 memory modules, each with a 160 ns cycle time; and since we access 16 words per cycle, this provides a maximum effective 10 ns memory cycle time. This is well balanced with the arithmetic elements which perform floating point addition and multiplication at the rate of (320 ns/16 operations) = 20(ns/operation), since each operation requires 2 arguments and temporary registers are provided in the arithmetic elements. Note that only array accessing (including I/O) uses parallel memory, since programs and scalars are held in control memory. Thus, perfect balance between parallel memory and floating-point arithmetic may be achieved for triad vector forms since three arguments and one result (four memory accesses) are required for two arithmetic operations. For longer vector forms, since temporaries reside in registers, only one operand is required per operation, so there is substantial parallel memory bandwidth remaining for I/O.

The total memory size ranges from 0.5 to 8 million 48 bit words. Eight parity bits provide single error correction and double error detection.

The main innovation in the parallel memory of the BSP is its 17 modules. In past supercomputers it has been common to use a number of parallel memory modules, but such memory systems are vulnerable to serious bandwidth degradation due to conflicts. For example, if 16 memories were used and a 16 × 16 array were stored with rows across the units and one column in each memory unit, then column access would be sequential.

Various storage schemes have been invented to avoid such memory conflicts. For example, arrays may be skewed [16] so that rows and columns can be accessed without conflict, and other related skewing schemes may be found with other useful properties. However, it is easy to show [5] that in general it is impossible to access rows, columns, and diagonals of square arrays without conflict if any power of two number of memory modules is used. Of course, various ad hoc procedures may be contrived, e.g., different skewing schemes for different arrays, but in the long run these are a compiler writer's (or user's) nightmare. A uniform, conflict-free procedure carried out by the hardware would be far superior for users of the system.

Early in the design of the BSP we decided to build the best possible parallel memory in this respect, and thereby avoid as many software implementation and performance problems as possible. For this reason we settled on a 17 memory module system that would provide conflict-free array access to most common array partitions, and yet have little redundant memory bandwidth since only one memory unit is unused per cycle.

With 17 memory modules it is clear that conflict-free access to one-dimensional arrays is possible for any arithmetic se-

quence index pattern except every 17th element. For two-dimensional arrays with a skewing distance of 4, conflict-free access is possible for rows, columns, diagonals, back-diagonals, and other common partitions, including arithmetic sequence indexing of these partitions [5]. The method extends to higher numbers of dimensions in a straightforward way.

One mundane characteristic of some Fortran programs can cause a problem here, namely, the use of COMMON in subroutine parameter passing. If used in the most general ways, this forces the storage of arrays in a contiguous way across parallel memory. In this case conflict-free access can still be guaranteed to any arithmetic sequence of physical memory addresses, as long as the difference between addresses is not a multiple of 17. This may force some array dimensions to be adjusted slightly for conflict-free access to all of the desired patterns.

To access parallel memory a set of 16 memory addresses must be generated. Assume that addresses are to a linear address space, i.e., multidimensional arrays have been mapped into a one-dimensional array, and that the array is stored across the memory modules beginning with module 0, through module 16, continuing in module 0, and so on. Then to access address α we must generate a *module number* μ and an *index* i in that module. These are defined by[1]

$$\mu = \alpha \pmod{17}$$

$$i = \left\lfloor \frac{\alpha}{16} \right\rfloor$$

since there are 17 memory modules and we access 16 numbers (one for each AE) per memory cycle. Notice that this wastes $\frac{1}{17}$ of the address space, a minor penalty for the conflict-free access it provides. Address generation hardware for the memory system is somewhat complex, but can be done in parallel for a sequence of addresses in one clock using the scheme described in [18]. This hardware also generates indices to set the alignment networks appropriately for each memory access.

B. Alignment Networks

The separation of data alignment functions from processing and memory activities is another departure of the BSP from most previous computers. As discussed earlier, the BSP has an input alignment network (IAN) connecting parallel memory to the arithmetic elements, and an output alignment network (OAN) connecting the arithmetic elements either to themselves or to parallel memory. Alignment of the elements of two arrays is sometimes required by the parallel memory and sometimes required by program or algorithm constraints, as the following examples illustrate.

Suppose we want to add together two rows of a matrix, element by element. The origins of the rows will in general be stored in different memory modules, so one row must be shifted relative to the other to align them for addition. Now if we want to add the odd elements of one row to the elements of another row (half as long), the first row will have to be "squeezed" as well as shifted to align proper pairs of operands. Similar alignment problems arise in row-column, column-diagonal, etc., pairings. Since we must store arrays consistently in parallel memory, the output alignment network is used to satisfy

[1] We use $\lfloor x \rfloor$ to denote the integer part of x.

the storage requirements and indexing patterns of the variable on the left-hand side of each assignment statement.

The above uses of the alignment networks hold for recurrence and reduction vector forms. In these cases, data may be aligned after fetching via the IAN, but now the OAN is useful between processing steps. As a simple example, consider the summation of 32 numbers. This may be done in five steps, each step consisting of an addition followed by an output alignment network mapping of the AE's into the AE's in the form of a tree, which reduces the 32 numbers to one in $\log_2 32$ steps. Similarly, other reduction operations may be carried out using the OAN; these include such operations as finding the maximum or minimum of a set of numbers. Notice that for any such operations the reduction to a set of 16 numbers is carried out using all 16 processors, and after that the number of processors used is halved on each step.

In solving more general linear recurrences, a vector of results is produced, e.g., an $R\langle n, 1\rangle$ system leads to n results. Again, the OAN is used for an AE to AE mapping of intermediate results. Other important algorithms also require data alignment between operations; the FFT [20] and the Batcher merge and sort algorithms [2] are examples. These and other algorithms can be implemented directly in the BSP using microprogrammed AN sequencing patterns. Each alignment operation takes one clock in a FAPAS pipeline sequence. In array expression statement vector forms most are overlapped, while in recurrence vector forms the later alignments must be alternated with arithmetic.

In the course of some of the above algorithms, certain vector positions are vacated during the course of the computation, e.g., reduction operations reduce a vector to a scalar. An effective way of handling this is to have the IAN introduce *null elements* into the computation at appropriate points. In AE operations null elements are handled as follows:

$$\text{operand} \leftarrow \text{null } \theta \text{ operand}$$
$$\text{operand} \leftarrow \text{operand } \theta \text{ null}$$
$$\text{null} \leftarrow \text{null } \theta \text{ null}$$

for any operator θ. Memory modules block the storing of a null. Nulls are also used when a vector length is not equal to a multiple of 16, so the last slice of the vector is padded out with nulls by the IAN.

The alignment networks are constructed from multiplexers and are generalizations of crossbar switches. In addition to the permutation functions of crossbars, the alignment networks can also broadcast an input element to any selected set of destinations. Furthermore, the random store and fetch vector forms, as well as the compress and expand operations, use the alignment networks to carry out their mappings. Control of the AN's is closely related to PM control. As was pointed out in Section IV-A, memory addressing information and AN control indices are generated by the same hardware control unit.

The two alignment networks have similar control in that they are both source initiated; conceptually, for the IAN the memories specify which AE to transmit to and for the OAN, the AE's specify which memory they want to store to. In certain cases, e.g., random store and fetch, the AE's actually

generate memory addresses as suggested here, whereas in the standard array expression statement or recurrence vector forms all of the addressing is carried out by a special control unit hardware. Conflict resolution hardware is provided to sequence certain alignments in several steps. For more AN details, see [18].

C. Arithmetic Element

The 16 arithmetic elements are microprogrammed, being sequenced by the parallel processor control unit using a wide (128 bit) microcode word. Besides the arithmetic operations expected in a scientific processor, the BSP has a rich set of nonnumeric operations that include field manipulation, editing, and Fortran format conversion operators. Floating-point addition, subtraction, and multiplication require two 160 ns clocks each, floating-point division requires 1280 ns, and the square root operation requires 2080 ns; the latter two use Newton–Raphson iterations that start with ROM values selected in each AE [11].

Single precision floating-point arithmetic is carried out using normalized signed magnitude numbers with 36 bits of mantissa and 10 bits of exponent, providing about 11 decimal digits of precision with a range between approximately 5.56×10^{-309} and 8.99×10^{307}. Four guard digits are retained within the AE and R* rounding is carried out using these four bits. Given that most alignment shifts are small [25], this should provide a good approximation of full R* rounding. Double-precision operations are carried out in the hardware (a double length product is always generated) about four times slower than single precision. The range of double precision numbers is the same as for single precision, and the precision is twice as great. Characters are stored as 8 bit EBCDIC bytes, packed six to a word.

Although they are not seen by users, each AE has a file of 10 registers, in addition to the standard registers used in the course of various operations. These are very convenient for holding intermediate results in the course of evaluating vector forms. The register assignment is done within the vector forms and the number of registers necessary to ensure high system performance was thus decided when the machine was designed. This is in contrast to building a machine first and then studying register allocation as a later compiler design question.

To add to the system reliability each AE contains residue checking hardware to check the arithmetic operations. Two-bit, modulo 3, residue calculations are carried out for each exponent and mantissa. To enhance the diagnosability of the entire system, the AE's (actually the AE-alignment network interfaces) contain Hamming code generators, detectors, and correctors for the data path loop from the AE's through the alignment networks and memory, and back to the AE's. This allows control information to be included in the Hamming code in order to check for failures in the control hardware of the parallel memory and alignment networks as well as the data paths mentioned above. The eight parity bits allow single error correction and double error detection. Most double-bit parity failures and all residue check failures lead to an instruction retry (see Section IV-D).

D. *Template Sequencing*

The execution of a vector form must be broken into a sequence of elemental array sequences called templates. This is done by the parallel processor control unit which issues a sequence of (one or more) *templates* to execute each vector form. The template provides the control framework in which vector forms are executed. Because it is desirable to overlap the execution of these template in the FAPAS pipeline, appropriate matching must be found in one template to accommodate the next template. For example, the fetching of operands for the next template may occur before the storing of the results from the previous template. In terms of such matching, *template families* have been defined with respect to the interface characteristics of their front and back templates. Each is said to have a front and back family number.

During execution the PPCU chooses templates on the basis of the vector form and the family numbers. For example, in executing a dyad followed by a triad, the PPCU will match the front family of the first triad template with the back family of the last dyad template. Then (assuming that there are more than 16 triad operations to perform) a second triad template will be chosen by matching its front family with the back family of the first triad template. Within three templates this reaches a cycle of one or two templates that repeats until the end of this particular vector form execution.

It is important to realize that the FAPAS overlap between templates as well as the arithmetic element register allocation for each one is done at machine design time. This leads to an *a priori* understanding of the machine's performance over a wide range of computations and also allows more vector operation overlap than might be possible otherwise, since all possible template combinations have been considered at machine design time.

This is in contrast to most previous high performance machines, wherein such overlap attempts are made at compile time or execution time. For example, in the CDC 6600 [27] and its successors, the control unit SCOREBOARD attempts run-time overlap and this is aided by compile-time transformations [26]. In the IBM 360/91 an overlap mechanism was built into the processor [28] in an effort to sequence several functional units at once. Most previous high performance machines seem to have overlap mechanisms that combine compile-time and run-time (control unit and processor) overlap decisions in ways similar to these. In some cases, however, certain common functions can be chained together (e.g., multiply and add for inner product in the CRAY-1), although in the CRAY-1, for example, intricate run-time considerations dictate whether or not chaining is possible [8].

The five-stage FAPAS pipeline may have four templates in process at once, and five more templates may be in various stages of setup in the PPCU pipeline that precedes execution. The amount of such overlap that exists at any moment depends, of course, on the width of individual templates. However, it is clear from an analysis of the templates that for most of the common Fortran constructs a very high percentage of processor and memory utilization can be expected in the BSP. Notice that there is overlap between templates of one vector form as well as overlap between different vector forms.

Due to the fact that the BSP executes a very high-level array language, complex hazard checking can be performed. As was mentioned in the discussion of template families, one template's fetches may begin before a previous template's store has been executed. In some cases, two previous stores may be pending while a third template's fetch is executed. This leads to *data dependence hazards* that must be checked before executing such memory accesses, i.e., if a fetch is for data that are to be stored by a previous template, the fetch must be delayed until after the store. Such hazard checking is carried out for up to two stores before a fetch by a combination of software and hardware in the BSP.

To clarify the above ideas, consider the following example program:

```
    DO 1 I = 1, 40
  1   Y(I) = A(I) + B(I)
    DO 2 I = 1, 90
  2   Z(I) = (C(I) + D(I)) * E(I).
```

This would be compiled as a dyad vector form followed by a triad; the dyad would be executed using $3 \left(= \left\lceil \frac{40}{16} \right\rceil \right)$ templates and the triad using $6 \left(= \left\lceil \frac{90}{16} \right\rceil \right)$ templates. Fig. 4 shows a FAPAS pipeline timing diagram for the execution of these templates.

In Fig. 4 notice that three distinct dyad templates are used:[2] dyad (2, 3), dyad (3, 6), and dyad (6, 7). The last memory cycle on clock 3 is provided for a previous template—some waste can be expected when beginning or ending a computation—but otherwise all memory cycles are occupied until clock 8. Notice also that after processing begins, the first three templates use $\frac{2}{3}$ of the processor clocks until clock 12.

The triad processing begins with three distinct templates: triad (2, 4), triad (4, 8), and triad (8, 8). It then continues in a steady state with triad (8, 8) templates. Except for one last clock at the dyad interface, the triad templates operate with total utilization of both the parallel memory and the parallel processor. Generally speaking, longer templates achieve very high utilization of the system hardware.

The total number of clocks required to execute this sequence of templates is 39, and since the original program contains 220 floating-point operations, the effective speed of this computation is greater than 35 million floating-point operations/s (Mflops). Assuming processing overlap at the beginning and end of this sequence, only 36 clocks are required for processing and on this basis a rate of more than 38 Mflops is achieved.

The use of vector forms and templates allows the easy implementation of a number of desirable features. The basic idea is that templates can be regarded as global microinstructions (the PPCU is microprogrammed) or "macroinstructions" that sequence the entire parallel processor. Consequently, even with

---

[2] The parenthesized numbers are the front family and back family identification numbers. The back family number of one must match the front family number of the next.

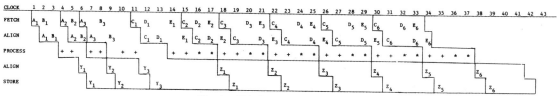

Fig. 4.   Triad template sequencing.

a set of overlapped templates in progress, it is easy to delay the entire parallel processor. This is easiest to think of in terms of Fig. 4. For example, if an error occurs, a vertical slice is made through Fig. 4 at the end of some clock period and all further steps may be deferred until the interrupt is handled. Also, longer operations than addition and multiplication (i.e., division or square root) can simply be handled by extending the process step for sufficiently many clocks and deferring all other tracks in the FAPAS diagram, resuming them when the longer operation is complete; double precision is implemented in a similar manner. Furthermore, instruction retry is facilitated by this ability to break the FAPAS sequence at any step and back up to the beginning of a vector form, since memory stores are prevented in case of an error.

The distinction between data pipelining and overlap here and in other machines should be clear at this point. The BSP pipelines each template through the five FAPAS segments, in contrast to traditional pipelining of arithmetic operations; the individual operations being decomposed are array assignment statements, recurrences, etc., in the BSP. A sequence of templates can be likened to a sequence of additions in an arithmetic pipeline. On the other hand, most modern machines are overlapped in the sense that memory and arithmetic can be performed simultaneously, based on run-time lookahead. In the BSP the analogous process is overlap between vector forms, as was illustrated in Fig. 4.

Run-time lookahead schemes are limited by data hazards, jumps, and various other resource conflicts. By complex analysis of source programs, much more simultaneity is possible. For the BSP, many IF and GOTO statements are replaced by bit-vector modifications of vector forms, so even these difficulties of standard run-time lookahead schemes are often avoided.

Globally, the PPCU may be viewed as accepting a single stream of array instructions, namely, vector forms, and producing five streams of array instructions to sequence the FAPAS segments. Thus, in the terminology of [16], the BSP array processor is a SIAMEA (single instruction array/multiple execution array) machine. Of course, the scalar processor unit also may execute instructions from a given Fortran program simultaneously with the parallel processor.

E. File Memory

The BSP file memory consists of two sections, the file storage units and the file memory controller. This is the secondary memory of the BSP, with longer term storage being provided on conventional disks and other I/O devices attached to the system manager (see Fig. 1).

During the BSP design phase several semiconductor technologies showed promise as high-speed secondary memory devices, in competition with conventional head-per-track disks. Charge-coupled device (CCD) and random access memory (RAM) chips were considered because they provide very attractive characteristics, they were well along in development, and their price outlook seemed likely to be competitive with head-per-track disks. As a result, an MOS RAM was chosen to provide the BSP file memory with a very low latency and a high transfer rate, which is expected to perform with good reliability and maintainability at a reasonable cost.

The file storage unit is built with semiconductor high density memory devices that provide a transfer rate of two words every 160 ns with a maximum latency of less than 1 ms. Nonaddressed modules are operated at $\frac{1}{4}$ that clock rate to conserve power, yet provide the refresh needed for the volatile devices. Each file storage unit is organized in 4 M ($M = 2^{20}$) word sections and may contain 4 sections for a total of 16 M words of 48 data bits plus 8 parity bits. Two words are accessed in

$$\text{parallel for a transfer rate of } 112 \text{ bits}/160 \text{ ns} = \frac{2 \text{ words}}{160 \text{ ns}} = 12.5$$

$\times 10^6$ word/s. A file memory system may contain up to 4 file memory units for maximum file memory capacity of 64 M (64 $\times 10^6$) words. Thus, the file memory provides a backup storage of one to two orders of magnitude the size of parallel memory.

Consider the file memory in relation to a typical BSP computation. For example, a block of 32K words may be read at an overall effective rate of about 10^7 words/s. Since the BSP operates at a maximum of 50 Mflops, this means that only 5 floating-point operations need be performed per I/O word to balance the I/O and processing rates. To sustain this, output must be considered as well so the ratio becomes 10 floating-point operations per I/O word, for balance. These ratios seem well within the range of most large scientific calculations (whose ratios often range up to 100 or more).

The file memory stands between the BSP and the system manager. The file memory controller can transmit data to and from the BSP parallel memory or control memory as well as the system manager I/O processor (see Fig. 1), the latter at the 0.25×10^6 words/s maximum channel speed of the system manager. I/O instructions are passed between the BSP control processor and the file memory controller.

The file memory controller (FMC) contains buffer areas to match the file memory speed with that of the system manager. I/O requests from the BSP and system manager are queued in the FMC in a 32 entry queue. Normally, the slower system manager receives highest priority and the BSP requests are handled in a first-in, first-out manner.

The file memory can be addressed to the word level and a block to be transmitted can be any number of words. The FMC converts logical addresses into physical addresses. A logical address contains a file name, a starting address in the file, a block length, and a destination (or source) memory address. File protection is provided by FMC hardware that allows any combination of four access modes: system manager READ or WRITE and BSP user program READ or WRITE. When operating in problem state, BSP I/O instructions can be executed with no supervisor program intervention at all for error-free transmissions. Synchronization bit registers are provided that allow BSP user programs to test for I/O completion without supervisor program intervention. The FMC also contains hardware for I/O instruction retry for all errors not automatically corrected. Thus, a number of situations that might traditionally have required slow, operation system intervention are handled by FMC hardware in the BSP.

Task switching within the BSP takes less than one-half second, but the speed of flow of jobs from the system manager, through file memory, and into the parallel memory and control memory, depends on many details of individual jobs.

V. Conclusion

We have outlined the organization of the BSP, a high performance scientific computer. Its key features include high quality, fast arithmetic, conflict-free access to arrays in parallel memory, separate data alignment networks, a pipelined control unit that sequences a high-level data pipeline and can overlap the execution of its vector form language, and a semiconductor file memory for secondary storage. Many error-checking and correcting features are included throughout the system to enhance its reliability and maintainability. Software was provided on a system manager computer that handles most operating system functions and has a Fortran vectorizing compiler that can also handle vector extensions.

The BSP system design effort began in early 1973, and led to an operational prototype machine in 1978. The maximum system speed is 50 million floating-point operations/s. The system performed as a "class 6" computer by running the Department of Energy LLL loops at speeds in excess of 20 Mflops. In fact, its average speed is almost identical to the average speed of the CRAY-1 on these benchmarks. A major design goal was a system that could achieve a high sustained performance over a wide variety of scientific and engineering calculations using standard Fortran programs. It is estimated that 20–40 Mflops could be achieved for a broad range of Fortran computations.

Acknowledgment

The authors are grateful to the entire BSP design team for years of work in the development of this system.

References

[1] U. Banerjee, "Data dependence in ordinary programs," M.S. thesis, Dep. Comput. Sci., Univ. of Illinois, Urbana-Champaign, Rep. 76-837, Nov. 1976.
[2] K. E. Batcher, "Sorting networks and their applications," in *Proc. AFIPS Spring Joint Comput. Conf.*, vol. 32, 1968, pp. 307–315.
[3] G. H. Barnes, R. M. Brown, M. Kato, D. J. Kuck, D. L. Slotnick, and R. A. Stokes, "The ILLIAC IV computer," *IEEE Trans. Comput.*, vol. C-17, pp. 746–757, Aug. 1968.
[4] U. Banerjee, S. C. Chen, D. J. Kuck, and R. A. Towle, "Time and parallel processor bounds for Fortran-like loops," *IEEE Trans. Comput.*, vol. C-28, pp. 660–670, Sept. 1979.
[5] P. Budnik and D. J. Kuck, "The organization and use of parallel memories," *IEEE Trans. Comput.*, vol. C-20, pp. 1566–1569, Dec. 1971.
[6] S. C. Chen, D. J. Kuck, and A. H. Sameh, "Practical parallel band triangular system solvers," *ACM Trans. Math. Software*, vol. 4, pp. 270–277, Sept. 1978.
[7] S. C. Chen and D. J. Kuck, "Time and parallel processor bounds for linear recurrence systems," *IEEE Trans. Comput.*, vol. C-24, pp. 701–717, July 1975.
[8] "The CRAY-1 computer," *Preliminary Reference Manual*, Cray Res. Inc., Chippewa Falls, WI, 1975.
[9] P. H. Enslow, Ed., *Multiprocessors and Parallel Processing.* New York: Wiley-Interscience, 1974.
[10] P. M. Flanders, D. J. Hunt, S. F. Reddaway, and D. Parkinson, "Efficient high speed computing with the distributed array processor," in *High Speed Computer and Algorithm Organization.* New York: Academic, 1977, pp. 113–128.
[11] D. D. Gajski and L. P. Rubinfield, "Design of arithmetic elements for Burroughs scientific processor," in *Proc. 4th Symp. Comput. Arithmetic*, Santa Monica, CA, 1978, pp. 245–256; also in *Proc. 1978 LASL Workshop Vector and Parallel Processors*, Los Alamos, NM, 1978.
[12] R. G. Hintz and D. P. Tate, "Control data STAR-100 processor design," in *Proc. IEEE COMPCON 1972*, Sept. 1972, pp. 1–4.
[13] D. J. Kuck, "ILLIAC IV software and application programming," *IEEE Trans. Comput.*, vol. C-17, pp. 758–770, Aug. 1968.
[14] ——, "Parallel processing of ordinary programs," in *Advances in Computers*, vol. 15, M. Rubinoff and M. C. Yovits, Eds. New York: Academic, 1976, pp. 119–179.
[15] ——, "A survey of parallel machine organization and programming," *ACM Comput. Surveys*, vol. 9, pp. 29–59, Mar. 1977.
[16] ——, *The Structure of Computers and Computations*, Vol. I. New York: Wiley, 1978.
[17] D. J. Kuck, Y. Muraoka, and S. C. Chen, "On the number of operations simultaneously executable in Fortran-like programs and their resulting speed-up," *IEEE Trans. Comput.*, vol. C-21, pp. 1293–1310, Dec. 1972.
[18] D. H. Lawrie and C. R. Vora, "Multidimensional parallel access computer memory system," U.S. Patent No. 4,051,551, Sept. 27, 1977.
[19] ——, "The prime memory system for array access," *IEEE Trans. Comput.*, vol. C-31, this issue, pp. 435–442.
[20] M. C. Pease, "An adaptation of the fast Fourier transform for parallel processing," *J. Ass. Comput. Mach.*, vol. 15, pp. 252–264, Apr. 1968.
[21] J. A. Rudolph, "A production implementation of an associative array processor—STARAN," in *Proc. 1972 AFIPS Fall Joint Comput. Conf.*, vol. 41, 1972, pp. 229–241.
[22] R. M. Russell, "The CRAY-1 computer system," *Commun. Ass. Comput. Mach.*, vol. 21, pp. 63–72, Jan. 1978.
[23] A. H. Sameh and R. P. Brent, "Solving triangular systems on a parallel computer," *SIAM J. Numer. Anal.*, vol. 14, pp. 1101–1113, Dec. 1977.
[24] F. H. Sumner, "MU5—An assessment of the design," in *Proc. IFIP Congress, Information Processing 1974.* Amsterdam, The Netherlands: North-Holland, 1974, pp. 133–136.
[25] D. W. Sweeney, "An analysis of floating-point addition," *IBM Syst. J.*, vol. 4, no. 1, pp. 31–42, 1965.
[26] J. F. Thorlin, "Code generation for PIE (Parallel Instruction Execution) computers," in *Proc. AFIPS Spring Joint Comput. Conf.*, 1967, pp. 641–643.

[27] J. E. Thornton, *Design of a Computer, the Control Data 6600.* Glenview, IL: Scott, Foresman, and Co., 1970.

[28] R. M. Tomasulo, "An efficient algorithm for exploiting multiple arithmetic units," *IBM J. Res. Develop.*, vol. 11, pp. 25–33, Jan. 1967.

[29] W. J. Watson, "The TI ASC-A highly modular and flexible super computer architecture," in *Proc. 1972 AFIPS Fall Joint Comput. Conf.*, 1972, pp. 221–228.

pirical analysis of real programs, and the design of high-performance processing, switching, and memory systems for classes of computation ranging from numerical to nonnumerical. The latter work includes the study of interactive text processing and database systems, from the point of view of both the computer and the user.

Dr. Kuck has served as an Editor for a number of professional journals, including the IEEE TRANSACTIONS ON COMPUTERS, and is presently an area editor of the *Journal of the Association for Computing Machinery*. Among his publications are *The Structure of Computers and Computations*, vol. I. He has consulted with many computer manufacturers and users and is the founder and president of Kuck and Associates, Inc., an architecture and optimizing compiler company.

David J. Kuck (S'59–M'69) was born in Muskegon, MI, on October 3, 1937. He received the B.S.E.E. degree from the University of Michigan, Ann Arbor, in 1959, and the M.S. and Ph.D. degrees from Northwestern University, Evanston, IL, in 1960 and 1963, respectively.

From 1963 to 1965 he was a Ford Postdoctoral Fellow and Assistant Professor of Electrical Engineering at the Massachusetts Institute of Technology, Cambridge. In 1965 he joined the Department of Computer Science, University of Illinois, Urbana, where he is now a Professor. Currently, his research interests are in the coherent design of hardware and software systems. This includes the development of the PARAFRASE system, a program transformation facility for array and multiprocessor machines. His recent computer systems research has included theoretical studies of upper bounds on computation time, em-

Richard A. Stokes was born in the Bronx, NY, on June 30, 1931. He received the A.B. degree in mathematics from St. Michael's College, Winooski, VT, and the B.S.E. degree in computer science from George Washington University, Washington, DC.

Following military service he joined the National Security Agency where he was involved in the early application of magnetic cores and transistor to computer design. In 1960 he joined the Martin Company as project leader in the development of CRT graphic displays. In 1964 he joined the Burroughs Corporation, Paoli, PA, as a Staff Engineer working on the design of the B 8501 computer. Later he became Lead Engineer in the development of the Illiac IV computer. In 1976 he was made General Manager of the plant responsible for the design and manufacture of the BSP. He holds several patents in computer design including the B 8501, the Illiac IV, and BSP.

Processing in Memory: The Terasys Massively Parallel PIM Array

Maya Gokhale
David Sarnoff Research Center*

Bill Holmes and Ken Iobst
Supercomputing Research Center

*The work reported here was done while the author was at the Supercomputing Research Center, Bowie, Maryland.

The PIM prototype in a workstation environment delivers supercomputer performance at a fraction of the cost. The next step is to incorporate PIM chips into Cray-3 memory.

SIMD processor arrays provide superior performance on fine-grained massively parallel problems in which all parallel threads do the same operations most of the time. However, this fine-grained synchrony limits the application space of SIMD (single instruction, multiple-data) machines. If there are many alternative data-dependent actions among the parallel threads, the total execution time is the *sum* of the alternatives rather than the maximum single-thread execution time. Additionally, if the application is not inherently load-balanced, performance can degrade seriously: Most of the processors finish their work quickly and become idle, while a few processors end up with the lion's share of the work. Thus, the economics of purchasing a high-performance computer often dictate giving up peak performance on a small application set (massively parallel SIMD) in favor of more modest improvement over a larger range of applications (general-purpose MIMD).

Ideally, one platform would provide the advantages of a SIMD array for applications well suited to SIMD processing without penalizing less well-structured applications. That is, a SIMD array would be integrated into the architecture of a high-performance computer, so some applications could benefit from the SIMD array while others could still run on the more flexible high-performance "carrier" (host). Researchers at the Supercomputing Research Center (SRC) have carried this notion one step further. We have integrated the SIMD array so closely into the architecture of the high-performance host that the hardware comprising the SIMD array can be used either as a SIMD processor array or as additional conventional memory.[1]

SRC researchers have designed and fabricated a processor-in-memory (PIM) chip, a standard 4-bit memory augmented with a single-bit ALU controlling each column of memory. In principle, PIM chips can replace the memory of any processor, including a supercomputer. To validate the notion of integrating SIMD computing into conventional processors on a more modest scale, we have built a half dozen Terasys workstations, which are Sun Microsystems' Sparcstation-2 workstations in which 8 megabytes of address space consist of PIM memory holding 32K single-bit ALUs. We have designed and implemented a high-level parallel language, called data-parallel bit C (dbC), for Terasys and demonstrated that dbC applications using the PIM memory as a SIMD array run at the speed of multiple Cray-YMP processors. Thus, we can deliver supercomputer performance for a small fraction of supercomputer cost.

Since the successful creation of the Terasys research prototype, we have begun work on processing in memory in a supercomputer setting. In a collaborative research project, we are working with Cray Computer to incorporate a new Cray-designed implementation of the PIM chips into two octants of Cray-3 memory.

TERASYS WORKSTATION

A Terasys workstation (see Figure 1) consists of

- a Sun Sparc-2 processor,
- an SBus interface card residing in the Sparc cabinet,
- a Terasys interface board, and
- one or more PIM array units.

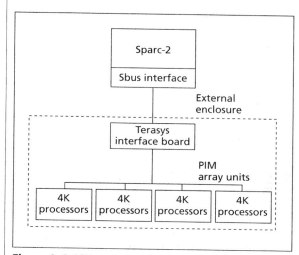

Figure 1. A 16K processor Terasys workstation.

Related work

The notion of computing in memory has been with us for several decades. For example, Stone[1] proposed a logic-in-memory computer consisting of an enhanced cache memory array that serves as a high-speed buffer between CPU and conventional memory.

More recently, a group at the University of Toronto has designed a computational RAM—conventional RAM with SIMD processors added to the send amplifiers in a 4-Mbit DRAM process.[2]

In the commercial realm, Hitachi markets a video DRAM chip with limited processing in the memory. This chip, the HM53642 series, is a $65K \times 4$-bit multiport CMOS video DRAM with simple logic operators on each of the 4 bit-planes.

Our data-parallel C is similar to MasPar's MPL[3] and Thinking Machines' C*.[4] Wavetracer's MultiC[5] had user-defined bit lengths, but did not have the bit extraction/insertion or generic bit-length features. Our generic SIMD interface is patterned after the CM-2 Paris instruction set.[5]

References

1. H.S. Stone, "A Logic-in-Memory Computer," *IEEE Trans. Computers*, Jan. 1970, pp. 73-78.
2. D.G. Elliott, W.M. Snelgrove, and M. Stunn, "A Memory SIMD Hybrid and its Application," *Proc. Custom IC Conf.*, IEEE, Piscateway, N.J., 1992.
3. *MasPar Application Language (MPL) Reference Manual*, MasPar, Pub-9302-0000 01/90, 1990.
4. *The MultiC Programming Language*, Wavetracer, Pub-00001-001-1.00, 1994.
5. *Paris Reference Manual*, Thinking Machines, Cambridge, Mass., Tech. Rep. Version 5.0, 1989.

The Terasys interface board and PIM array units fit into an external enclosure. The system can accommodate up to eight PIM array units, with 4K processors per array unit, giving a maximum configuration of 32,768 PIM processors.

A data parallel program resides on the Sparc. Conventional sequential instructions are executed by the Sparc. Operations on data parallel operands are conveyed as memory writes through the Terasys interface board to PIM memory and cause the single bit ALUs to perform the specified operations at the specified row address across all the columns of the memory.

An instruction written to the PIM array is actually a 12-bit address in a 4K entry table of horizontal microcode, which is generated on a per-program basis. The selected table entry is the real instruction, which is sent from the Terasys interface board to the PIM array units.

For global communications among the processors there are three networks: global OR, partitioned OR, and parallel prefix network. Level 0 of the PPN serves as a bidirectional linear nearest-neighbor network.

In the following sections, we describe the PIM chip and single-bit processor, the three interprocessor communication networks, the PIM array unit, and the Terasys interface board.

Processor-in-memory chip

The PIM integrated circuit, with slightly over one million transistors on 1-micron technology, contains $2K \times 64$ bits of SRAM, 64 custom-designed single-bit processors, plus control and error detection circuitry.[2] Figure 2 shows the PIM chip. Solid lines outline conventional memory components, while dotted lines delimit the added PIM circuitry.

In conventional memory mode, the chip is configured as a $32K \times 4$-bit SRAM with an 11-bit row address and a 4-bit column address. In response to the row address signals, it loads the selected row into a 64-bit register. The column address selects a 4-bit nibble (one of 16 nibbles composing the 64-bit register).

To operate in PIM mode, the chip is activated by one of 25 command bits from the Terasys interface board. Command mode initiates an internal row operation with 64 processors operating on one of 2K rows of memory. The processors can perform a local operation and optionally read/write the global OR, partitioned OR, and parallel prefix lines.

PIM processor

The PIM processor is a bit-serial processor that accesses and processes bits to/from a 2-Kbit column of attached memory. Functionally, the processor is divided into upper and lower halves. The upper half performs the actual computations on the data, while the lower half performs routing and masking operations. Data is brought in from the processors' attached memory through the load line, circulates through the logic as specified by the program, and is written back to memory via the store line. Figure 3 is a simplified diagram of the processor.

Three primary registers, denoted A, B, and C, supply data to the ALU. The registers have three primary input lines for receiving data, each of which also can be inverted to receive the logical NOT of that input.

At each clock cycle, the pipelined ALU can either load data from memory or store data to memory, but not both at the same time. Also, on each clock cycle, the ALU produces three outputs that can be either selected for storage (under mask control) or selected for recirculation. Additionally, data can be sent to other processors via the routing network.

The processor can input data through a multiplexer (MUX) from either the parallel prefix network, the global OR network, the partitioned OR network, or the internal mask/register control (see the "Network and mask" line at lower right in Figure 3).

Indirect addressing

Indirect addressing signifies an operation $A[i]$, where each processor has its own instances of A and i. To perform this operation, the processors must access different memory locations simultaneously.

We decided against hardware support for indirect addressing in the current PIM implementation for two major reasons. First, introducing indirect addressing registers on a per-processor basis would reduce the number of processors per chip. Second, the error detection and correction circuitry, which operates on a row basis, would not operate correctly in the presence of per-processor indirect addressing registers. Thus, we opted for indirect addressing through microcode. To make this operation efficient, we have the compiler emit array-bound information as part of an indexing operation. This allows the microcoded indexing subroutine to limit the number of locations to query to the number of array elements rather than the entire 2K bits.

In indirect addressing, each processor holds its private instance of an array. The application can also use a single array A in Sparc conventional memory, which is shared by all PIM processors. Each processor can index this shared table with its unique index i that is in PIM memory. An optimized microcode routine, which is a factor of 8 faster than the more general per-processor table lookup, is provided for this operation in a Fortran-based library called Passwork (Parallel SIMD Workbench).[3]

Interprocessor communication

A simple linear interconnect, augmented by global OR, partitioned OR, and parallel prefix networks, has been incorporated into the PIM design. This allows the PIM processor to

- compute a global OR or partitioned OR signal in one tick,
- send one bit of data to a left or right neighbor in one tick, and
- perform parallel prefix operations in log (number-of-processors) ticks per bit.

GLOBAL OR. The logical OR network combines signals from all processors and returns a single bit result to the host. GOR is performed across all 32K processors in hardware. This signal is used to conditionally control instruction execution: One of two instructions can be selected based on the value of the GOR signal. The microcode programmer has access to the GOR signal at the host processor through a GOR register containing the last 32 GORs generated by the system.

PARTITIONED OR NETWORK. In contrast to the GOR, which performs only many-to-one communication, the POR network can be used for many-to-one or one-to-many communication among groups of processors. The 32K processors in the Terasys workstation can be partitioned, starting with 2 processors per partition and increasing in

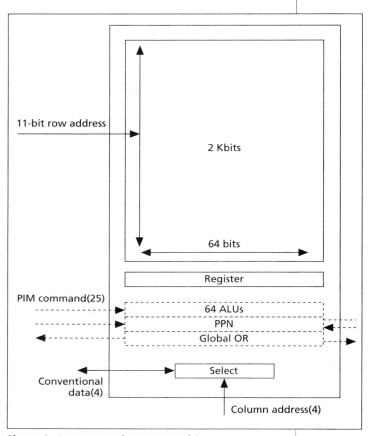

Figure 2. A processor-in-memory chip.

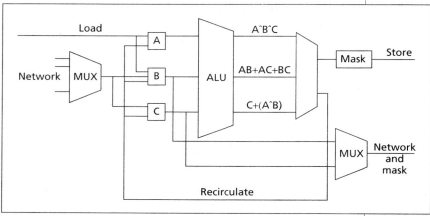

Figure 3. A processor-in-memory processor.

powers of 2 up to 32K processors per partition. Within a partition, an OR tree is formed from all the processors in the partition, and the result is fed back to them. POR hardware support is provided for groups of 64, 128, 256, and 512 processors. Other groupings are implemented in software.

The POR network is useful in matrix-pivoting operations. Disjoint matrices in different POR partitions can have different pivot points. The pivot information can be broadcast from one processor in each partition to all processors in that same partition. This is accomplished by using the internal mask to select a particular processor in each partition and then performing the POR operation, where only the signal from the selected processor is moved up the OR tree and fed back to the other processors in the partition.

PARALLEL PREFIX NETWORK (PPN). The PPN consists of 15 levels, settable by the programmer. It can be used for nearest-neighbor communication and for linear scan operations, which are useful for accumulating partial results such as sums or other associative operations.

At level 0, the PPN is a one-dimensional communications path used to transfer data among the processors, so that all processors can send to either the left or right neighbor in one tick. At higher levels, the PPN is a few-to-many communication path.

At level 0, each selected processor i sends data to its immediate neighbor to the left $(i-1)$ or to the right $(i+1)$. Levels 1-15 send data to the left only. At level 1, the PPN enables even-numbered processors i to send data to two left neighbors $i-1$ and $i-2$. At PPN level 2, processors 0, 4, 8, ... can send to the four left neighbors. Succeeding PPN levels expand at a power of 2, until at level 15, one data source broadcasts to all 32K processors.

The PPN network can be set to either the toroidally wrapped mode, where processor 0 gets its data from processor 32,767, or to "fill" mode, where processor 0 input data is fixed at 0 or 1. Three other levels of toroidally wrapped data are also supported at the 8-bank, bank, and chip levels.

Levels 0-9 of the PPN, which correspond to the PPN up to the memory bank (see "PIM array unit" below), are implemented in hardware. Levels above the memory bank are implemented in software.

GENERAL DATA MOVEMENT. Unstructured interprocessor data communication is through the host processor. For general any-to-any communication, PIM data values are sent to the host, transposed from bit-serial to bit-parallel representation, permuted in conventional memory, transposed again, and sent back to the PIM memory. This operation is time-consuming on the Terasys workstation. In the new vector supercomputer PIM array, where this operation will use the gather-scatter hardware, performance will be comparable to general communication networks in massively parallel processors such as SP-2 or MasPar.[4]

PIM array unit

A PIM array unit contains eight banks of PIM memory spread over two boards. Each bank contains eight PIM

> **E**ach of eight banks of PIM memory contains eight PIM chips—a total of 64 chips or 4,096 PIM processors per array unit.

chips—a total of 64 chips or 4,096 PIM processors per array unit. In addition to housing the 64 PIM chips, the array unit performs extended global OR and parallel prefix functions and provides a three-level partitioned OR tree.

Terasys interface board

Read and write operations to PIM memory are sent to the Terasys interface board. High-order bits of the address field tell the interface logic whether the operation is a normal memory operation or a PIM command pair. If they indicate PIM command mode, the interface board splits the combined commands into two individual commands. This command pairing allows a doubling of the command transfer rate. The Sparc-2 can transfer one command pair every 200 nanoseconds. The command issue rate to the PIM chips is 100 ns per command.

Each command is an index into a 4K lookup table. The lookup table contains 25-bit microcode instructions. Thus, out of a possible 2^{25} instructions, each program can use up to 4,096. The Twist (Terasys Workstation Interface Software Tools) microcode assembler generates the lookup table automatically. The table is loaded into the interface board when a Terasys program is initiated.

This board also provides PIM timers, selects one of two PIM commands based on the global OR signal's current value, and registers 31 bits of global OR history.

DATA-PARALLEL BIT C

The Terasys programming language dbC is an ANSI C superset based on a tightly synchronous (variously called data parallel, "single thread of control," or SIMD) parallel programming model. In dbC, arbitrary-length bit streams are treated as first-class objects in the parallel domain.[5,6] Our goals in designing dbC were to support

- a simple, easy-to-use programming model so that programmers can rapidly become productive on Terasys and other PIM-based systems;
- efficient data-parallel computation on SIMD machines; and
- computation on arbitrary bit-length integers in the parallel domain.

Data-parallel extensions

dbC data parallel extensions follow language conventions set by C* and MPL.

PARALLEL DATA. dbC adds a new memory attribute to C data declarations, the keyword "poly." A poly variable is instantiated on each processor, so that a reference to a poly variable in an expression is an aggregate reference that affects each active processor. dbC supports all the standard C data types in the parallel domain. It also supports parallel pointers. Pointers can point between serial and parallel domains and within the parallel domain, providing language support for indirect addressing. Pointers may not point from the memory of one processor to the memory of another; interprocessor communication intrinsics must be called to access data from another processor.

PARALLEL EXPRESSIONS. Polys can be used in C expressions just as normal C (mono) variables. An expression *a* op *b* is parallel if either *a* or *b* is parallel. If the other operand is serial, it is promoted to parallel, and the operation is performed in the parallel domain.

dbC has infix reduction operators such as |= (reduce with OR operator) that, when applied to a parallel expression, yield a serial value. Reductions are computed using the global OR and parallel prefix networks.

PARALLEL CONTROL CONSTRUCTS. dbC extends the standard C guarded control constructs (if, while, do, and for) to the parallel domain. The <guard> controlling the statement determines whether the statement is serial or parallel. If the <guard> is parallel, the statement is parallel. The escape statements *break*, *continue*, and *return* have parallel versions. A break or continue in a parallel loop is parallel. A return from a function returning a parallel result (even *poly void*) has parallel semantics. Gotos are not allowed in parallel constructs.

In addition to the C control constructs, dbC provides a masked *where* construct and an *all* block. Parallel code in an all block is executed by all processors regardless of previous processor activity. An all block may contain any serial or parallel code, including parallel if/where and parallel loops.

Bit extensions

The generality of dbC's bit constructs facilitates computation over arbitrarily sized data.

BIT-LENGTH SPECIFIERS. dbC extends C's bit-field feature to allow any parallel integer variable (or integer component of a structured variable) to specify a length. Although the syntax of the bit-length specifier is identical to the C bit field, the semantics are quite different. The C bit field represents a compromise between the desire to access bits and the difficulty of supporting efficient bit access in the word-oriented domain. A bit field declared to be 6 bits long in C might really occupy a full memory word (32 or 64 bits). A variable or structure component declared as "poly int:6" in dbC is guaranteed to use exactly 6 bits of parallel memory.

When two parallel operands are used in a binary operation, their bit lengths determine the number of bit operations required to compute the result. Thus, the user controls both

- storage allocation at the bit level (particularly useful on Terasys, where each processor has only 2,048 bits of memory) and
- the bit-serial complexity of operations, since the bit lengths of the operands determine the number of sub-operations required to perform an operation.

Figure 4 illustrates poly declarations with bit lengths.

BIT EXTRACTION AND INSERTION. dbC also has two bit-oriented operators, bit insertion and bit extraction,

```
poly unsigned x:4;  /* 4-bit logical variable x */
typedef unsigned poly int33:33;  /* 33-bit logical, user-defined type */
poly int y: 1000;  /* arbitrarily large variables are supported */
typedef poly struct
  {  int33 A[50];
     int33 B;
     char c;
  }  S;  /* poly structure */
```

Figure 4. Parallel variables in dbC (data-parallel bit C), the Terasys high-level programming language.

```
poly x:10, y:11
x[4:8] = y[0:4];     /* start/end index */
x[4+:5] = y[0+:5];   /* bit length notation */
```

Figure 5. Bit insertion and extraction in dbC.

```
void func(poly x:?)
{ ... }

    ...
    poly y_5:5, z_7:7;
    func(y_5);        /* pass 5 bits to func */
    func(z_7);        /* pass 7 bits to func */
    ...
```

Figure 6. Generic bit-length parameters.

illustrated in Figure 5. A parallel variable *x* may be indexed *x*[*a*:*b*], where *a* indicates the starting bit position and *b* the ending bit position, inclusive. On the right-hand side of an assignment, this notation means that *b* − *a* + 1 bits are extracted from *x* starting at bit offset *a*. When this "slice" notation is used to index a variable on the left-hand side, bit insertion is performed. As a shorthand, *x*[*a*:] is equivalent to *x*[*a*:*a*], meaning one bit at offset *a* is accessed. An alternative notation is also illustrated in the figure. The +: infix operator in an index expression *a*+:*b* means that the starting index is *a* and the bit length is *b*.

GENERIC BIT LENGTHS. To make it easier to write subroutines that can operate on parameters of any bit length, dbC provides a generic bit-length construct. The bit length of a parameter to a function may be "?," indicating that the length is to be determined at runtime at each invocation of the function. Figure 6 illustrates the use of generic bit length in the parameter *x* to function func. The function is called twice, first with a parameter of bit length 5, and the second time with a parameter of bit length 7.

COMMUNICATION. The interprocessor communication intrinsic DBC_net_send transfers data between nearest neighbors in a linear topology at level 0 in the parallel prefix network. In addition, the DBC_send intrinsic can be used for any-to-any communication; this general data movement between processors is done through the Sparc conventional memory.

Intrinsics are also provided to transfer data between serial and parallel domains, both one processor at a time and with block transfer. The intrinsics are overloaded, so the same name is used (for example, DBC_read_from_proc(x, pe_number)) regardless of the data type of x.

Example

Figure 7 illustrates both the data-parallel and the bit-oriented extensions to dbC. This function computes the greatest common divisor of two 68-bit parallel variables. The algorithm uses a parallel while loop to iteratively divide int2 by int1. As int1 and int2 become smaller at each iteration, the number of bits required for time-consuming bit-serial division is also reduced.

The outer while loop is a parallel loop. This loop iterates until int1 is 0 on every processor; processors fall out of the loop, becoming inactive, as their int1 values become 0. The inner for loop is serial because the test expression bits_per_divide > 0 is serial. The inner loop determines the minimum number of bits required for the next divide. As the algorithm proceeds, fewer and fewer bits are used for each divide operation.

Thus, as soon as a processor finds a nonzero bit in either int1 or int2 (the OR-reduce expressions), the for loop terminates. The intrinsic DBC_Divmod computes the quotient and remainder of int2 divided by int1. In this call, only the minimum number of bits is used for the division (real_isize + 1 bit).

The assignments into int1 and int2 illustrate both bit extraction and bit insertion. Real_isize number of bits are extracted from int1 and rem and inserted into int2 and int1.

Twist microcode library

dbC translates all code involving parallel operands into a generic three-address memory-to-memory SIMD assembly code. The generic SIMD is then mapped to the various platforms on which dbC programs run, including the CM-2, Splash-2,[7,8] and workstation clusters, in addition to Terasys. The Terasys Workstation Inter-face Software Tools (Twist) microcode library maps the generic SIMD instruction set to Terasys.

This subroutine library[9] performs basic operations such as

- parallel memory allocation and release,
- basic arithmetic and logical operations on poly operands of arbitrary bit length,
- random parallel-number generation,
- indexed address calculation and indirect addressing,
- global combining and broadcasts,
- parallel prefix operations such as scans and segmented scans,
- nearest-neighbor communication and generalized communication, and
- data transfer between host memory and PIM memory.

So that knowledge available to the compiler about operands can be passed to the runtime system, there are often several forms of an instruction. For example, there are eight variations to the add instruction for each of the basic data types (unsigned integer, signed integer, and floating point). This allows the microcode library to optimize for such properties as

- number of operands, because if the destination is the same as one source, only two operands are required in a binary operation;
- the number of bit lengths being passed, either 1, 2, or 3;
- whether or not an operand is a constant being broadcast as part of the instruction; and
- whether the instruction is to be masked or performed unconditionally, since unmasked instructions are faster. (If a store instruction is conditional, the microcode must load and save the original value at the store address, so that when a value is ready to be stored, inactive processors will store the original value back. This is a slower sequence than an unconditional store, in which the original value does not have to be read.)

The Twist microcode assembler extracts those microinstructions required by the program and builds the instruction lookup

```
#define ISIZE 68

typedef poly unsigned wide_int:ISIZE;

wide_int GCD(wide_int int1, wide_int int2)
    {
        wide_int result, rem;
        int bits_per_divide, real_isize;

        while (int1 !=0)
          {
            for (bits_per_divide = ISIZE-1; bits_per_divide>=0; bits_per_divide—)
              {
                /* position past leading zeros of int1 and int2 to
                    reduce the complexity of divide. */

                real_isize = bits_per_divide;
                if (l=(int1[bits_per_divide:]) != 0) break;      /* OR-reduce across ... */
                if (l=(int2[bits_per_divide:]) != 0) break;      /* ... active processors */
              }
            DBC_Divmod(&result, &rem, int2[0:real_isize-1], int1[0:real_isize-1]);

/* clear top bits of int2 and int1 */
            if (real_isize < ISIZE)
              {
                int2[real_isize:ISIZE-1] = 0;
                int1[real_isize:ISIZE-1] = 0;
              }

            int2[0:real_isize-1] = int1[0:real_isize-1];
            int1[0:real_isize-1] = rem[0:real_isize-1];
          }

        return result;
    }
```

Figure 7. A greatest-common-divisor function in dbC.

table. The lookup table is downloaded to the Terasys interface board upon program initiation. In addition to the microcode library, we provide a

- dbC simulator
- microcode emulator, and
- Fortran-based development system with the same functionality as Twist, the Parallel SIMD Simulation Workbench (Password).[3,10]

APPLICATIONS AND PERFORMANCE

The Terasys workstation—fully populated with 32K processors and assuming an instruction issue rate of 100 ns—delivers 3.2×10^{11} peak bit operations per second. Microcoded applications have achieved and, in one case, surpassed this theoretical peak. (The program surpassing the peak uses superscalar techniques that do two bit operations in one tick by using both the upper and lower parts of the processor.)

Applications profile

Applications such as DNA sequence match, low-level image processing, and tridiagonal solvers and other matrix algorithms are well suited to the Terasys workstation. In general, problems having

- largely independent computation,
- primarily linear nearest-neighbor communication,
- global data-parallel operations, and
- data of nonstandard integer sizes

are especially well suited to the Terasys architecture.

At SRC, we've written approximately 20 applications for Terasys, and we've observed a performance range of five to 50 Cray-YMP single processor equivalents on these applications. A representative tree-search application written in the high-level dbC language ran at eight YMP equivalents with no performance tuning. A pseudorandom number generator written in Password produced 2×10^{10} pseudorandom bits per second or about 20 Cray-YMP equivalents.[11] For these applications, performance of the YMP version is either an actual measured figure or a best-case estimate of bit operations, assuming no memory access delays.

In addition to running SRC applications, Terasys has been used for image-processing applications by researchers at the University of Massachusetts at Lowell. We report on one of their applications below.

Real-time color imaging and visualization

Researchers at the Institute for Visualization and Perception Research and the Computer Science Department at the University of Massachusetts at Lowell have used Terasys to investigate applications of real-time color imaging and visualization.[12]
A particularly interesting application is an

interactive environment that provides near real-time manipulation of medical imaging data.

Typically, radiologists view pairs of magnetic resonance images (MRIs) taken at different frequencies side by side to find diagnostic information. One image usually has better contrast, while the other has better shape and fine detail information. Both images contribute to the diagnostic process. The goal of the medical imaging application written for Terasys is to integrate the images into a single picture, in which all diagnostic information is clearly and immediately visible. Further, the system lets the user modify viewing parameters dynamically and watch the display change in response.

COLOR ICON. In geometric coding, each datum is represented by a small graphical element or icon, whose visual features are controlled by the data. For this project, the group developed a general color icon to integrate data from multiple images. Information in multiple images can be combined into a single display by having the pixel values in the separate images control the three color coordinates of the corresponding pixel in the integrated display.

The color icon is represented by a square box of pixels. In the RGB color model, each corner of the box may have up to three associated parameters, one for each of the red, green, and blue components. The three parameters determine the color of that corner. Intermediate pixels have values interpolated from the corner points. This allows merging up to 12 data-set parameters. The single image is represented, then, by a square display of icons, where each icon is typically a 5×5 pixel matrix.

For the MRI application, the input data consists of a pair of gray-scale images with values at each pixel position ranging from 0 (black) to 255 (white). The values are normalized to the range (0, 1). The images are combined by associating each image with one of the three parameters of the Generalized Lightness, Hue, and Saturation (GLHS) color model. Since there are only two images in this appli-

Cost estimates

The Terasys prototype, including hardware and system software, was assembled by a team of about 10 people over two years. The Terasys interface board was designed and built in-house, as were the array unit boards. The chips were fabricated at a silicon foundry.

Since Terasys is a research prototype, it's difficult to estimate costs. The cost of the PIM chip is particularly hard to estimate, since SRAM prices are so sensitive to production volume. A 16-Kbit SRAM, configured as 4K × 4 bits with 25-ns access time, can be purchased in quantities of 1,000 for $3.67. A 256-Kbit device, configured as 32K × 8 bits at 25 ns, costs $7.00. The PIM SRAM, with 128 Kbits (64 × 2,048) and a 30-ns access time, falls between these two parts in density. However, the PIM chip package is more expensive than the DIP packaging of standard SRAMs. Factoring in all these variables, and especially the fact that we cannot expect chip volume to be anything close to that of standard SRAMs, a conservative per-chip cost estimate would be around $100 or $32,000 for 32K processors. We price the host workstation and PIM cabinet at approximately $10,000.

cation, the third parameter is set to an arbitrary value chosen by the user. The GLHS parameters are transformed into (red, green, blue) triples required by the display hardware.

> **A** PIM array within a vector supercomputer would create a vector/parallel/SIMD hybrid, where the SIMD array could also function as additional memory.

INTERACTIVE DISPLAY. A unique feature is that the user can modify display parameters (controls) interactively. The simplest control is the "region of interest." Since the entire image cannot be displayed at once, only a portion is displayed. The user may drag the region selector over a small representation of the image to view other areas of interest.

The size of the icon box—that is, the number of pixels in the icon's height and width—can also be changed interactively. The color model used to calculate display colors can also be modified. The user can switch between the RGB and GLHS color models. While using the GLHS color model, the user can set values for each of the three variables (which determine how much of that component will appear in the displayed color) by dragging a point around a triangle, with one variable being maximized at each corner. The display is updated as the point moves within the triangle. Sliding bars can be used to dynamically change the input data's minimum and maximum thresholds. Once again, the display changes as the sliders change, letting the user adjust the parameters to extract the maximum information from the display.

MAPPING TO TERASYS PROCESSORS. A straightforward mapping of icon rendering to processors would associate an $M \times N$ icon with each processor, letting the processors compute independently without interprocessor communication. However, this approach was not used because with this mapping, the data is not arranged correctly for display and must be reshuffled in the Sparc memory before it can go to the frame buffer. Since the display time rather than the calculation time is the dominant factor, the method used is to load the data in the order required by the display hardware, and to use the linear nearest-neighbor network to exchange values needed to render an icon.

Using the latter method, a 4K Terasys can render 64×64 icons (a 320×320 pixel window) at a frame rate of 20 frames/second. The current implementation—which copies data from PIM memory into Sparc memory, from Sparc memory into a frame buffer; and then uses X-based display software to display the image—can display data at five frames per second. Alternatives to more closely match the display rate to the generation rate include bypassing the X display code to write directly into the frame buffer, and perhaps incorporating the frame buffer directly onto the Terasys hardware, thus eliminating the need to transfer displays over the Sbus.

THE PIM CHIP EMBODIES THE CONCEPT OF SIMD PROCESSING within the memory subsystem of conventional computers. We have built a system at one data point within that space, the Terasys workstation, which incorporates PIM processors in a Sparc-2. Programmed in the high-level dbC language, the Terasys workstation can deliver supercomputer performance at a very reasonable cost.

We are now exploring with Cray Computer the design of a PIM array within a vector supercomputer, the Cray-3/ SuperScalable System. This configuration would create a vector/parallel/SIMD hybrid, where the SIMD array could also function as additional memory. With the faster CPU cycle time of the vector supercomputer, issuing instructions to the PIM chips would not be a dominant factor, as it has been with the Sparc-2 and SBus on Terasys. This hybrid machine uses the supercomputer's gather-scatter hardware for efficient communication among the PIM processors. In the current design, the PIM memory will replace two octants of a Cray-3 memory system, serving as 512K processors, or 16 megawords of memory. Future generations of such a machine with 1K processors per PIM chip will be capable of 10^{15} bit operations per second, that is, a peta bitop supercomputer. ∎

Acknowledgments

The PIM chip is the invention of Ken Iobst, Dave Resnick, and Ken Wallgren. The following people have contributed to the Terasys project: Don Becker, Charlie Bostick, Harold Conn, Maya Gokhale, Bill Gromen, Howard Gordon, David Hickey, Bill Holmes, Jason Kassoff, Bob Kimble, Dan Kopetzky, Jennifer Marsh, Fred More, Alan Murray, Mark Norder, Phil Pfeiffer, Lou Podrazik, Judith Schlesinger, Paul Schneck, Al Schwartz, Doug Sweely, Tom Turnbull, and Lucak Womack.

We gratefully acknowledge the assistance of Rob Erbacher, Stu Smith, and Pat Mullins in preparing the section on applications and performance. We are indebted to the anonymous referees for their reviews of an earlier draft of this article.

References

1. P. Schneck, "Wire Problems and Parallel Computation," *Comm. ACM*, Vol. 36, No. 1, Jan. 1993, p. 20.
2. J. Marsh and M. Norder, "PIM Chip Specifications," Tech. Report TR-93-088, Supercomputing Research Center, Bowie, Md., 1993.
3. K. Iobst and T. Turnbull, "Passwork User's Guide," Tech. Report TR-90-014 (third edition), Supercomputing Research Center, Bowie, Md., 1993.
4. D. Smitley and K. Iobst, "Bit-Serial SIMD on the CM-s and the Cray-s," *J. Parallel and Distributed Computing*, Vol. 11, No. 2, Feb. 1991, pp. 135-145.
5. J. Schlesinger and M. Gokhale, "dbC Reference Manual," Tech. Report TR-93-109, Supercomputing Research Center, Bowie, Md., 1993.
6. M. Gokhale and J. Schlesinger, "A Data-Parallel C and its Platforms," *Proc. Fifth Symp. Frontiers of Massively Parallel Computation,* IEEE CS Press, Los Alamitos, Calif., 1995, pp 194-202.
7. M. Gokhale and R. Minnich, "FPGA Programming in a Data-Parallel C," *Proc. IEEE Workshop FPGAs for Custom Computing Machines*, 1993, pp. 94-101.

8. M. Gokhale and B. Schott, "Data-Parallel C on a Reconfigurable Logic Array," Tech. Report TR-94-121, Supercomputing Research Center, Bowie, Md., 1994.

9. J. Schlesinger and D. Kopetsky, "Terasys, Microcode, and TWIST," Tech. Report TR-94-119, Supercomputing Research Center, Bowie, Md., 1994.

10. K. Iobst and T. Turnbull, "Terasys Reference Manual," Tech. Report TR-90-103 (third edition), Supercomputing Research Center, Bowie, Md., 1993.

11. S. Arno and K. Iobst, "Petasys Supercomputer and a Class of Pseudorandom Number Generators," Tech. Report TR-92-069, Supercomputing Research Center, Bowie, Md., 1991.

12. R. Erbacher, G. Grinstein, and S. Smith, "Implementing an Interactive Visualization System on a SIMD Architecture," Tech. Report, University of Massachusetts, Lowell, 1994.

Maya Gokhale is the group head of Systems Software for High Performance Computing at the David Sarnoff Research Center, Princeton, New Jersey. Previously, she was a research staff member at the Supercomputing Research Center, Bowie, Maryland, working in languages and compilers for high-performance computers. Prior to joining SRC in 1988, she was an assistant professor at the University of Delaware. She also has seven years of industry experience with Burroughs and Hewlett-Packard as a design engineer. Gokhale received a BS in mathematics from Wake Forest University in 1972 and the MSE and PhD degrees in computer science from the University of Pennsylvania in 1977 and 1983, respectively.

Bill Holmes has been with the Supercomputing Research Center since 1987 as manager of the Horizon, Splash, and Terasys projects. Before that, he worked for NASA/Goddard, providing computer support to spacecraft missions. Holmes received a BS degree in mathematics from LaSalle University in 1966 and an MS in mathematics from Georgetown University in 1971.

Ken Iobst is the chief architect of processing-in-memory machines at the Supercomputing Research Center, Bowie, Maryland. He is the inventor of the Bit-Serial Orthogonal Transformation Instruction used in Cray Research vector machines and of the processing-in-memory chip used in the Cray-3/Super Scalable System. He received his BS degree in electrical engineering from Drexel University in 1971 and his MS and PhD degrees in electrical engineering/computer science from the University of Maryland in 1974 and 1981.

Multiprocessors and Multicomputers

9.1 Introduction

Most computers today use a single microprocessor as a central processor. Such systems—called *uniprocessors*—satisfy most users, because their processing power has been growing at a compound annual rate of about 50%. Nevertheless, some users and applications desire more power. Online transaction processing (OLTP) systems wish to handle more users, weather forecasters seek more fidelity in tomorrow's forecast, and virtual reality systems wish to do more accurate visual effects. If one wants to go five times faster, what are the alternatives to waiting four years ($1.5^4 \approx 5$ times)?

One approach to going faster is to try to build a faster processor using more gates in parallel and/or with a more exotic technology. This is the approach used by supercomputers of the 1970s and 1980s. The Cray-1 [30], for example, used an 80-MHz clock in 1976. Microprocessors did not reach this clock rate until the early 1990s.

Today, however, the exotic processor approach is not economically viable. Microprocessors provide the fastest computing engines by integrating tens (soon hundreds) of millions of transistors together with short wires to form complex pipelines and integrated memory systems. Designs are then carefully tuned and implemented with an expensive fabrication technology. A microprocessor's sales must reach millions of units to adequately amortize up-front costs. A customized microprocessor would not ship in enough volume to amortize the design and testing costs for complex pipelines and integrated memory systems. A processor that is not a microprocessor could use an exotic technology but would have longer wires—and hence longer wire delays—and the same design and testing cost problems.

Therefore, the only viable alternative for going faster than a uniprocessor is to employ multiple microprocessors and connect them in some fashion so that they can cooperate on the same problem. Because uniprocessors have long separated memory systems and I/O systems, it should not be surprising that the two alternatives for connecting processors are via the memory system and via the I/O system. In either case, processors in these systems execute instructions independently and, therefore, are *multiple instruction multiple data* (MIMD) systems, not single instruction multiple data (SIMD) systems, as were described in Chapter 8.

Shared-memory multiprocessors join multiple processors with a logically shared memory. Hardware ensures that a store by a processor to a physical address will be visible to all other processors. Thus, normal loads and stores can be used for communication. Shared-memory multiprocessors also tend to have a logically shared I/O system. Implementing shared-memory multiprocessors is challenging, because good performance dictates that the logically shared memory (and I/O) be physically distributed.

Multiple processors can alternatively be joined via the I/O system. With this approach, each processor can reside in a conventional computer *node* augmented with a network interface (NI). The NI, which usually resides on an I/O bus, could be a standard NI (e.g., for Ethernet) that supports standard network protocols (e.g., TCP/IP) to connect nodes with a local area network or even the Internet. We do not examine this case further, but instead refer readers to networking texts, such as Peterson and Davie [28].

We will instead examine systems that connect computers via custom NIs and/or custom networks. The NIs and networks of these systems—sometimes called *multicomputers*—vary from specialized (e.g., for the Intel line of multicomputers) to something that is close to a local area network (e.g., Myricom Myrinet [6]). Unlike shared-memory multiprocessors, multicomputers do not use stores and loads for communication. Instead, hardware supports explicit mechanisms for passing messages between one node and another. Implementing high-performance multicomputers is challenging, because it is hard to avoid inordinate software overhead when sending and receiving each message.

Parallel computing has had a significant impact on computing. Furthermore, we expect it to be even more important in the future. Traditionally, it has been a way to speed high-end applications at any cost. Today, we recognize that it can also be cost effective [41]. A p-processor system is cost effective relative to a uniprocessor if its speed improvement in executing a workload exceeds its cost premium (versus the uniprocessor). In many cases, the cost premium for adding additional processors is low, because substantial costs go into the memory and I/O systems. In 1995, for example, an eight-processor Silicon Graphics Challenge XL with 1 GByte memory cost 2.5 times a comparable uniprocessor [41]. Thus, the eight-processor XL was cost effective for all workloads it could speed up by more than 2.5 times.

The next sections discuss parallel computer software, shared memory multiprocessors, and multicomputers. More background on parallel software and hardware can be found in Almasi and Gottlieb [3] and Culler, Singh, and Gupta [11]. Both books significantly influenced the ideas presented here.

9.2 Parallel Computer Software

Modern parallel systems have three interface levels: *user programming model, application binary interface* (ABI), and the *hardware.* Compilers and libraries work to map applications to an ABI. ABIs are implemented on hardware via operating system services and device drivers. To design parallel hardware, we must understand some about these interfaces and the software that converts between them.

9.2.1 Programming Models

For uniprocessors, programming discussions sometimes consider the relative merits of alternative programming languages, such as Fortran, C, C++, or Java. These languages are actually very similar and make similar demands on hardware. When programming parallel computers, however, a debate on Fortran versus C is secondary to more fundamental issues such as whether data sharing is done by writing a variable or sending a message. These issues determine the *programming model* used.

The four most popular programming models are sequential, data parallel, shared memory, and message passing. With the *sequential* model, programmers write regular uniprocessor programs and rely on system software (mostly compilers) to parallelize their code and data. This approach relieves programmers of the burden of parallelization and is successful in some cases but is not robust enough for general use despite decades of work.

With the *data-parallel* model, programmers write code that is sequential in control flow but parallel in data operations (e.g., in High Performance Fortran). Assume that all the following variables represent matrices:

```
A = B + C
E = A * D.
```

With data parallel, all processors would appear to execute the many additions in the matrix add before any began the multiplies and adds of the matrix multiply. In many ways, data-parallel programming is an abstraction of single instruction multiple data (SIMD) processing. It can be wildly successful, but many other important programs work poorly with it or cannot be easily expressed.

The *shared-memory* model is based on multiple sequential threads sharing data through shared variables. It provides the same model as a multitasking uniprocessor. It has achieved great success in small- to medium-sized systems (less than 30 processors) for applications such as online transaction processing and scientific simulation. The greatest challenge of shared-memory programming is to include sufficient synchronization so that data communication is meaningful (e.g., a load does not read data before the store that writes it executes).

Finally, the *message-passing* model allows programming with conventional uniprocessor languages augmented with explicit calls for communication. In most cases, communication is initiated with a send call that copies data from a buffer and sends it to a destination. An application usually obtains the communicated data with a receive call that copies data into a specified buffer. If the data are not yet available, the receive call can block or return a not-ready flag. The message-passing model closely resembles the model used in network computing. Message passing has had many successes but can make it difficult to correctly implement complex, pointer-based data structures.

9.2.2 Application Binary Interfaces (ABIs)

Over most of the history of parallel computing, there has been no separation between programming model and hardware. Rather, machines were characterized by the programming model that they supported. Data parallel or SIMD machines include the Illinois ILLIAC IV and Thinking Machines CM-1. Message-passing machines include the Caltech Cosmic Cube, Intel Hypercube, and Intel Paragon. Shared-memory machines include CMU C.mmp, Sequent Balance, and SGI 2000.

Today we understand that programming models and hardware are different. Any hardware can support any programming model. Modern systems use a compiler and libraries to map an application to an ABI. They then use operating-system services and device drivers to implement an ABI on hardware. The challenge then is to identify ABIs and hardware mechanisms that work well.

Today's parallel systems have evolved into two

classes of ABIs: shared memory and messaging. The *shared-memory ABI* presents applications with an interface similar to a multitasking uniprocessor. Compilers and libraries map applications written in user programming models to the shared-memory ABI. Mapping the sequential programming and data-parallel programming models to a shared-memory ABI requires extensive compiler support. Supporting shared memory is straightforward. Implementing message passing requires only a library that implements send and receive calls in shared memory.

The *messaging ABI* presents applications with an interface similar to communicating on a network. Nodes have separate memory and separate I/O spaces but can exchange data through messages. Mapping user programming models to the message-passing ABI is challenging. Implementing sequential and data-parallel programming models on a message-passing ABI requires even better compiler support than on a shared-memory ABI, because the cost of unnecessary messages is usually higher than the cost of unnecessary memory references. Implementing the shared-memory programming model on a message-passing ABI is also hard when good performance is required. Supporting a message-passing program on a message-passing ABI, however, requires only a straightforward library. The most popular such library for scientific programming is *Message Passing Interface* (MPI) [16, 35].

9.2.3 Hardware

Finally, one must implement the two ABIs, shared memory and messaging, on the two classes of hardware platforms—multiprocessors and multicomputers.

- *Shared-memory ABI on a shared-memory multiprocessor.* The most significant challenge is developing an operating system that runs well on many processors.
- *Messaging ABI on a shared-memory multiprocessor.* Communication can be done with standard operating system mechanisms provided they perform well enough.
- *Shared-memory ABI on a multicomputer.* This is hard. Li and Hudak [26], discussed later, give some answers for sharing memory, but sharing I/O must also be implemented.
- *Messaging ABI on a multicomputer.* This can be implemented with a standard operating system with standard networking. The challenge is to obtain good messaging performance, especially if the operating system is involved with every message.

The relationships between programming model, ABI, and hardware can be confusing, but making these distinctions can be important. There are results, for example, that show that (1) message-passing programming on a shared-memory ABI on a multiprocessor can lead to higher performance than either (2) shared-memory programming on a shared-memory ABI on a multiprocessor or (3) message-passing programming on a messaging ABI on a multicomputer.

Now for a quiz: What is the difference between (1) a shared-memory program on a messaging ABI on a multicomputer and (2) a shared-memory program on a shared-memory ABI on a multicomputer? Answer: In (1), compilers or libraries would convert accesses to shared variables into messages (e.g., Berkeley Split-C [10]). In (2), the application actually uses load and store instructions and the system makes things work correctly (e.g,. Li and Hudak's Ivy [26]).

9.3 Shared-Memory Multiprocessors

This section examines the evolution of shared-memory multiprocessors. In these machines, a processor can use normal memory-referencing instructions (e.g., loads and stores) to access all memory, and all processors can access the same memory location with the same address.

Most shared-memory multiprocessors allow processors to have caches. Caches work by making a copy of data that are still associated with the data's original address. Ensuring that processors (and devices) obtain and update the most recent copy of data is the *cache coherence problem* and is usually solved by a *cache coherence protocol* (e.g., Goodman's write-once described in Chapter 6). Multiprocessors that use cache coherence often get the designation *CC*, whereas those that do not are *NCC*.

Multiprocessors also differ in whether all accesses to memory encounter a similar delay (*uniform memory access* or *UMA*) or not (*non-UMA* or *NUMA*). This leads to four basic categories of multiprocessors: NCC-UMA, NCC-NUMA, CC-UMA, and CC-NUMA.[1] CC-UMAs are also called *symmetric multiprocessors* (SMPs).

9.3.1 Wulf and Harbison's "Reflections in a Pool of Processors/An Experience Report on C.mmp/Hydra" [42]

Wulf and Harbison summarize a seminal 1970s research project on multiprocessor hardware and operating systems. This project, begun at Carnegie Mellon University in 1972, developed the *C.mmp* hardware and the *Hydra* operating system. C.mmp provided uniform-delay access from all 16 DEC PDP-11 processors to 16 interleaved memory modules using a crossbar switch but no caches. It pioneered a NCC-UMA architecture using off-the-shelf components. Hydra was a symmetric operating system (no master-slave relationships) that also separated policy from kernel mechanisms and used capabilities.

Wulf and Harbison's paper is also notable as one of the most thorough and balanced research-project retrospectives we have ever seen. If all research projects were as forthcoming about their technical and nontechnical successes and failures as C.mmp, we could all learn much more from one another. Readers wishing to probe further into this era should also read about C.mmp's successor CMU CM* [36].

9.3.2 Lamport's "How to Make a Multiprocessor Computer That Correctly Executes Multiprocess Programs" [22]

As architects began to consider performance optimization for shared-memory systems—such as write buffers and caches—it became useful to define exactly what correct shared memory should do. In a uniprocessor, a load to memory should return the value of the *last* store to the same address. In a multitasking uniprocessor, a load should return the value of the last store to the same address, but now this store could be from the load's thread or from another thread that was multiplexed onto the processor since the load's thread last stored this address.

Lamport uses this sort of reasoning to define *sequential consistency* (SC). Informally, a multiprocessor implements SC if it always behaves like a multitasking uniprocessor. Lamport formalizes this with a total order of all memory operations that respects the program order at each processor. Implementations of SC must keep performance optimizations—such as write buffers and caches—hidden from programmers.

To improve performance, other *memory consistency models* have been proposed and deployed. Some models expose first-in-first-out write buffers to programmers: *processor consistency, SPARC TSO,* and *Intel IA-32*. Other models allow some memory operations to be completely out of order: *weak consistency, release consistency, DEC/Compaq Alpha, IBM PowerPC,* and *Sun RMO*. Adve and Gharachorloo [1] provide a

---

[1]NCC-UMA and NCC-NUMA machines are often called UMAs and NUMAs, respectively. We include the prefix NCC to avoid ambiguity.

contemporary tutorial on alternative models, and Hill [19] argues that speculative execution should drive shared-memory multiprocessors back to sequential consistency.

9.3.3 Snooping Cache Coherence

Goodman's "Using Cache Memory to Reduce Processor-Memory Traffic" [15] appears in Chapter 6 and is described more fully there. What is important for this chapter is Goodman's definition of the *write-once* protocol, the first snooping cache coherence protocol. On the first write to a block, the write-once protocol performs a write-through that also invalidates other cached copies. On subsequent writes, write-back is used. Write-once spawned a series of alternative snooping protocols that were then unified with the MOESI framework [37].

More importantly, snooping protocols have led to the most successful class of commercial multiprocessors: CC-UMAs or *symmetric multiprocessors* (SMPs). An early commercial SMP is the Sequent Balance [39]. An example of the state of the art is Sun UltraEnterprise 5000 [34]. Its bus supports up to 112 simultaneous transactions from up to 30 CPUs and updates coherence state immediately after a transaction begins and regardless of the order of data transfers.

9.3.4 Censier and Feautrier's "A New Solution to Coherence Problems in Multicache Systems" [8]

Censier and Feautrier present the first *directory* cache coherence protocol approach suitable for scaling to a large number of processors. This paper predates the invention of snooping but is only now becoming important in commercial systems. Each block in memory has a directory entry that provides information on the block's caching status. The directory entry is at a known location, regardless of where the block is cached. Censier and Feautrier's directory entry has a bit to identify which processor caches a block. This scheme was later classified as Dir_nNB by Agarwal et al. [2]. In each cache, two state bits identify whether a block is modified (and therefore exclusive), valid (but unmodified and potentially shared), or invalid. On a processor read of an invalid block or a processor write of an unmodified block, a request is sent to the directory, which may in turn send messages to obtain the block or invalidate soon-to-be-stale copies.

Prior to Censier and Feautrier, Tang [38] developed a coherence protocol more suitable for a small number of processors, because it duplicated cache tags for all processors at the memory controller.

9.3.5 Lenoski et al.'s "The Stanford DASH Multiprocessor" [25]

A decade after Censier and Feautrier's directory proposal, Stanford University implemented a refinement of the idea in the DASH shared-memory multiprocessor prototype. Stanford DASH connected up to 16 SGI four-way SMPs using two two-dimensional mesh networks. It implemented shared memory with a CC-NUMA architecture using a distributed directory protocol. The project is notable for many research ideas on coherence protocols, memory consistency models, benchmarking, and so forth. Equally important, DASH "put it all together" to explore race-condition, deadlock, and other implementation issues. This exploration cleared the way for commercial follow-ons, such as the SGI Origin 2000 [23].

9.3.6 Hagersten, Landin, and Haridi's "DDM—A Cache-Only Memory Architecture" [17]

Hagersten et al. observe that CC-NUMA machines pay substantial memory cost to keep locally cached copies of data from more distant memory modules. To counter this waste, they propose to turn all memory into cache so that data used at one node need not also exist at a remote node where it is not used. This architecture was dubbed *cache-only memory architecture* (COMA). Key challenges for implementing COMA include finding data that has no permanent home and replacing data from a cache when it does not currently exist elsewhere in the system. These ideas were independently developed for the KSR-1, a commercial machine from Kendall Square Research [31]. To date, there have been no commercially successful COMA machines, but researchers are still looking at ways to modify the idea to make it less complex to implement.

9.3.7 Multiprocessors Today and Tomorrow

Shared-memory multiprocessors are now commonly used for servers and larger computers. Most of these are symmetric multiprocessors—CC-UMAs that use a bus. A few large machines, such as the Silicon Graphics Origin 2000, employ the CC-NUMA design. The Cray T3E is a NCC-NUMA [32]. We are not aware of any current NCC-UMAs.

For the cost-effectiveness arguments given, we expect more desktop machines to become SMPs (CC-UMAs). SMPs will continue to flourish for low-end servers, whereas directory-based CC-NUMAs become more widely deployed at the high end. Exactly what size will divide SMPs from CC-NUMA will depend on the relative ingenuity of the engineers designing these systems. We expect NCC-NUMAs and NCC-UMAs to die out, because coherent caching is important for obtaining good performance on general-purpose user and system software.

9.4 Multicomputing

This section concentrates on systems that do not globally share memory. Instead, nodes contain one or more processors, locally shared memory, optional I/O devices, and an interconnection network interface. Processors use normal memory-referencing instructions to obtain data within a node, but obtain remote data with other mechanisms. At the extreme, a collection of hosts on the Internet meets the above definition. We, however, will concentrate on systems that are more strongly coupled. These systems are sometimes called *multicomputers* or *NORMAs* (NO Remote Memory Access).

9.4.1 Seitz's "The Cosmic Cube" [33]

Seitz describes the Caltech Cosmic Cube. The Cosmic Cube pioneered the multicomputer hardware architecture and message-passing programming model. It included 64 nodes connected by a hypercube network. Each node contained an Intel 8086/8087 processor and 128 Kbytes of memory. It was programmed with message passing. With message passing, per-node programs are augmented with explicit send() and receive() calls to perform internode communication.

9.4.2 Multicomputer Follow-Ons

The Caltech Cosmic Cube led to a series of Intel multicomputers, including the iPSC/1, iPSC/2 and Paragon, and influenced all other multicomputers vendors. These machines were employed by scientists at research labs and universities, but they did not enjoy broad commercial success. One problem is that message-passing overheads have been large (> 1 ms). A second problem is that these machines targeted message passing exclusively, and this programming model is too limiting for many applications.

Many efforts have sought to reduce message-passing overhead. We mention four here. The Thinking Machines CM-5 [24] was a commercial multicomputer that moved its network interface (NI) from the I/O to the memory bus. Furthermore, it mapped the NI into user-space so that user-level software could send and receive messages with uncached loads and stores.

Protection was still maintained with a partitionable network and special context switch mechanisms. A special network supported rapid global reductions for many associative operations (e.g., the sum of integers where each node contributes one number).

Berkeley active messages [40] was a software-only idea that sought to move the message abstraction down to something close to what hardware could actually implement. An active message contains a handler address and zero or more arguments. Messages arriving at their destination spawn a thread that begins execution at the handler address. There is no explicit receive() call.

The MIT J-Machine [27] explored connecting many small nodes (e.g., 1024). Each node contains 1 Mbyte of memory and a custom "message-driven processor." Particularly interesting is the processor's custom support for communication (message-send instructions and a hardware receive/dispatch queue), synchronization (through tags), and naming (with instructions for loading and querying an associative table).

A final way multicomputers are evolving is toward greater exploitation of standard hardware and software. The IBM SP/2 uses workstation boards running IBM's standard Unix, but it adds a custom NI and custom network and wraps everything in a custom box. Other systems use conventional workstations placed close together and connected with a custom local area network, such as Myricom Myrinet. Finally, one can run systems like Oak Ridge Parallel Virtual Machine (PVM) [13] to harness idle workstations from across your organization's desktops.

9.4.3 Li and Hudak's "Memory Coherence in Shared Virtual Memory Systems" [26]

Li and Hudak do not present a new multicomputer. Instead, they present Ivy—the first implementation of the shared memory ABI on a multicomputer (actually a network of workstations). This kind of a system—now called a *software-distributed shared-memory* system[2]—allows shared-memory application binaries to issue loads and stores and transparently ensures that shared memory behaves correctly (e.g., sequentially consistent) across the system. The key is using standard virtual-memory page protection—valid and writable—to simulate caching state. On a load or store to an inappropriate page, hardware generates a page fault that gets forwarded to Ivy so that it can send

---

[2] Machines like the SGI Origin 2000 are called *hardware-distributed shared-memory* machines. Some use *DSM* to refer to both software- and hardware-distributed shared-memory machines, whereas others reserve DSM for software-distributed shared-memory machines only.

messages (following a directory protocol) to obtain the data and resume the application.

Substantial subsequent work [4, 29] seeks to ameliorate two key problems with Ivy: (1) false sharing from maintaining coherence on whole pages and (2) long message delays between loosely coupled machines. Some solutions blur the distinction between software-distributed shared memory and COMA by maintaining coherence on cache blocks but naming locally cached remote data with virtual-memory hardware [18, 20]. Like COMA, DSM ideas cannot yet claim any substantial commercial successes.

9.4.4 Multicomputers Today and Tomorrow

Today the most successful multicomputers have nodes that are (or are similar to) workstations. The most successful product is the IBM SP/2. More widely deployed are hundreds of sites that employ "networks of workstations" [5]. These are not optimal computing systems, but the marginal cost for employing them can be nearly zero, as the workstations are already deployed on people's desks. In our opinion, however, multicomputers will become less important than multiprocessors for large-scale computation, because the overheads of messages bleed away too much performance.

Multicomputers, however, are and will continue to flourish in *high-availability* computing. *Availability* is the probability at a given time that enough of the system is up to performing a given task. High availability is important for Web servers and critical for data bases. Multicomputers are a natural fit for high availability, because it is relatively straightforward to isolate multicomputer nodes when a node crashes. This allows an *n*-node system to continue to be available at *(n – 1)/n* throughput while another node is rebooting.

Highly available multicomputers will continue to evolve. Today, most multicomputers are connected with standard local area networks (e.g., 100 Mbits/s Ethernet), but some use custom local area networks such as Myricom Myrinet. Some people argue that custom local area networks will evolve into a new class of networks—called *system area networks*—that provide better bandwidth and latency than local area networks do [21].

Finally, it is possible that there will be a blurring of the line between multicomputers and multiprocessors. One thrust toward making this happen is an effort to allow multicomputers to shared information without the operating system being involved with every message.

Efforts, such as DEC Memory Channel [14] and Compaq/Intel/Microsoft's Virtual Interface Architecture [12], can move multicomputer communication bandwidths and latencies closer to those of multiprocessors. Alternatively, multiprocessors could be made more like multicomputers if parts of the system can continue to be available, even as other parts crash. Techniques like those used in Stanford HIVE [9] and DISCO [7] are steps in this direction.

9.5 References

[1]   S. V. Adve and K. Gharachorloo, "Shared memory consistency models: A tutorial," *IEEE Computer*, 29(12):66–76, Dec. 1996.

[2]   A. Agarwal, R. Simoni, M. Horowitz, and J. Hennessy, "An evaluation of directory schemes for cache coherence," *Proceedings of the 15th Annual International Symposium on Computer Architecture*, pp. 280–289, 1988.

[3]   G. S. Almasi and A. Gottlieb, *Highly Parallel Computing*. Menlo Park, CA: Benjamin/Cummings, 1994.

[4]   C. Amza, A. L. Cox, S. Dwarkadas, P. Keleher, H. Lu, R. Rajamony, W. Yu, and W. Zwanepoel, "TreadMarks: Shared memory computing on networks of workstations," *IEEE Computer*, 29(2):18–28, 1996.

[5]   T. E. Anderson, D. E. Culler, D. A. Patterson, and the NOW team, "A case for NOW (networks of workstations)," *IEEE Micro*, 15(1):54–64, 1995.

[6]   N. J. Boden, D. Cohen, R. E. Felderman, A. E. Kulawik, C. L. Seitz, J. N. Seizovic, and W.-K. Su, "Myrinet: A gigabit-per-second local area network," *IEEE Micro*, 15(1):29–36, 1995.

[7]   E. Bugnion, S. Devine, K. Govil, and M. Rosenblum, "Disco: Running commodity operating systems on scalable multiprocessors," *ACM Transactions on Computer Systems*, 15(4):412–447, 1997.

[8]   L. M. Censier and P. Feautrier, "A new solution to coherence problems in multicache systems," *IEEE Transactions on Computers*, C-27(12):1112–1118, 1978.

[9]   J. Chapin, M. Rosenblum, S. Devine, T. Lahiri, D. Teeodosiu, and A. Gupta "Hive: Fault containment for shared-memory multiprocessors," *Proceedings of the 15th ACM Symposium on Operating System Principles (SOSP)*, pp. 12–25, Dec. 1995.

[10]   D. E. Culler, A. Dusseau, S. C. Goldstein, A. Krishnamurthy, S. Lumetta, T. von Eicken, and K. Yelick, "Parallel programming in Split-C," *Proceedings of Supercomputing '93*, pp. 262–273, Nov. 1993.

[11] D. Culler, J. P. Singh, and A. Gupta, *Parallel Computer Architecture: A Hardware/Software Approach*. San Francisco, CA: Morgan Kaufmann, 1998.

[12] D. Dunning, G. Regnier, G. McAlpine, D. Cameron, B. Shubert, F. Berry, A. M. Merritt, E. Gronke, and C. Dodd, "The virtual interface architecture," *IEEE Micro*, 18(2):66–76, 1998.

[13] A. Geist, A. Beguelin, J. Dongarra, W. Jiang, R. Manchek, and V. Sunderam, in *PVM: A users' guide and tutorial for networked parallel computing*. Cambridge, MA: MIT Press, 1994. Available electronically at *ftp://www.netlib.org/pvm3/book/pvm-book.ps*

[14] R. B. Gillett, "Memory channel network for PCI," *IEEE Micro*, 16(1):12–18, 1996.

[15] J. R. Goodman, "Using cache memory to reduce processor-memory traffic," *Proceedings of the Tenth International Symposium on Computer Architecture*, pp. 124–131, June 1983.

[16] W. Gropp, S. Huss-Lederman, A. Lumsdaine, E. Lusk, B. Nitzberg, W. Saphir, and M. Snir, *MPI—The Complete Reference: Vol. 2, The MPI-2 Extensions*. Cambridge, MA: MIT Press, 1998.

[17] E. Hagersten, A. Landin, and S. Haridi, "DDM-A cache-only memory architecture," *IEEE Computer*, 25(9):44–54, 1992.

[18] E. Hagersten, A. Saulsbury, and A. Landin, "Simple COMA node implementations," *Proceedings of the 27th Hawaii International Conference on System Sciences*, Jan. 1994.

[19] M. D. Hill, "Multiprocessors should support simple memory consistency models," *IEEE Computer*, 31(8):28–34, 1998.

[20] M. D. Hill, J. R. Larus, and D. A. Wood, "Tempest: A substrate for portable parallel programs," *Proceedings of COMPCON '95*, pp. 327–332, San Francisco, CA, Mar. 1995.

[21] R. W. Horst, "TNet: A reliable system area network," *IEEE Micro*, 15(1):37–45, 1995.

[22] L. Lamport, "How to make a multiprocessor computer that correctly executes multiprocess programs," *IEEE Transactions on Computers*, C-28(9):690–691, 1979.

[23] J. Laudon and D. Lenoski, "The SGI origin: A ccNUMA highly scalable server," *Proceedings of the 24th Annual International Symposium on Computer Architecture*, pp. 241–251, June 1997.

[24] C. E. Leiserson, Z. S. Abuhamdeh, D. C. Douglas, C. R. Feynman, M. N. Ganmukhi, J. V. Hill, W. D. Hillis, B. C. Kuszmaul, M. A. St. Pierre, D. S. Wells, M. C. Wong, S.-W. Yang, and R. Zak, "The network architecture of the connection machine CM-5," *Proceedings of the Fifth ACM Symposium on Parallel Algorithms and Architectures (SPAA)*, July 1993.

[25] D. Lenoski, J. Laudon, K. Gharachorloo, W.-D. Weber, A. Gupta, J. Hennessy, M. Horowitz, and M. Lam, "The Stanford DASH multiprocessor," *IEEE Computer*, 25(3):63–79, 1992.

[26] K. Li and P. Hudak, "Memory coherence in shared virtual memory systems," *ACM Transactions on Computer Systems*, 7(4):321–359, 1989.

[27] M. D. Noakes, D. A. Wallach, and W. J. Dally, "The J-machine multicomputer: An architectural evaluation," *Proceedings of the 20th Annual International Symposium on Computer Architecture*, pp. 224–235, May 1993.

[28] L. L. Peterson and B. S. Davie, *Computer Networks: A Systems Approach*. San Francisco, CA: Morgan Kaufmann, 1996.

[29] J. Protic, M. Tomasevic, and V. Milutinovic, "Distributed shared memory: Concepts and systems," *IEEE Parallel & Distributed Technology, Systems, & Applications*, 4(2):63–79, 1996.

[30] R. M. Russell, "The Cray-1 computer system" *Communications of the ACM*, 21(1):63–72, 1978.

[31] R. H. Saavedra, R. S. Gaines, and M. J. Carlton, "Micro benchmark analysis of the KSR1," *Proceedings of Supercomputing '93*, pp. 202–213, Nov. 1993.

[32] S. L. Scott, "Synchronization and communication in the T3E multiprocessor," *Proceedings of the 7th International Conference on Architectural Support for Programming Languages and Operating Systems*, pp. 26–36, Oct. 1996.

[33] C. L. Seitz, "The cosmic cube," *Communications of the ACM*, pp. 22–33, Jan. 1985.

[34] A. Singhal, D. Broniarczyk, F. Cerauskis, J. Price, L. Yaun, C. Cheng, D. Doblar, S. Fosth, N. Agarwal, K. Harvery, E. Hagersten, and B. Liencres, "Gigaplane: A high performance bus of large SMPs," *Proceedings of the IEEE Hot Interconnects*, pp. 41–52, Aug. 1996.

[35] M. Snir, S. Otto, S. Huss-Lederman, D. Walker, and J. Dongarra, *MPI—The Complete Reference: Vol. 1, The MPI Core*. Cambridge, MA: MIT Press, 1998.

[36] R. J. Swan, S. H. Fuller, and D. P. Siewiorek, "Cm* — A modular, multi-microprocessor," *Proceedings of the AFIPS National Computer Conference*, pp. 637–644, 1977.

[37] P. Sweazey and A. J. Smith, "A class of compatible cache consistency protocols and their support by the

IEEE Futurebus," *Proceedings of the 13th Annual International Symposium on Computer Architecture*, pp. 414–423, June 1986.

[38] C. K. Tang, "Cache system design in the tightly compled multiprocessor system," *Proceedings of the AFIPS National Computing Conference*, pp. 749–753, June 1976.

[39] S. Thakkar, P. Gifford, and G. Fielland, "Balance: A shared memory multiprocessor system," *Proceedings of the 2nd International Conference on Supercomputing*, pp. 93–101, 1987.

[40] T. von Eicken, D. E. Culler, S. C. Goldstein, and K. E. Schauser, "Active messages: A mechanism for integrating communication and computation," *Proceedings of the 19th Annual International Symposium on Computer Architecture*, pp. 256–266, May 1992.

[41] D. A. Wood and M. D. Hill, "Cost-effective parallel computing," *IEEE Computer*, 28(2):69–72, 1995.

[42] W. A. Wulf and S. P. Harbison, "Reflections in a pool of processors/An experience report on C.m mp/Hydra," *Proceedings of the National Computer Conference (AFIPS)*. pp. 939–951, June 1978.

Reflections in a pool of processors—
An experience report on C.mmp/Hydra*

by WILLIAM A. WULF and SAMUEL P. HARBISON

Carnegie-Mellon University
Pittsburgh, Pennsylvania

INTRODUCTION

This paper is a frankly subjective reflection upon the successes and failures in a large research project—the construction of a multiprocessor computer, C.mmp, and its operating system, Hydra—by those most intimately involved in its design, construction, and use.

C.mmp and Hydra have now reached a sufficient level of maturity to establish themselves as useful and reliable computing resources at Carnegie-Mellon University. The user community has grown from primarily operating system implementors to include researchers in other operating systems and multiprocessors and casual or curious users interested in using the unique features of the system (e.g., the Algol 68 language, whose first implementation at CMU was on C.mmp.).

Some of the scientific results we originally hoped for have been published and are listed in the bibliography at the end of the paper. Other results will be published in the future as we observe the system under varied loads and over longer periods of time. In addition to these factual results, however, we have learned a number of things of a more subjective nature—things that we did right and, perhaps more importantly, things that we did wrong. We believe that many of these lessons are not unique to our project, and their presentation here will be valuable to the larger computer science community.

For those people unfamiliar with C.mmp and Hydra, we shall provide a brief overview of multiprocessor research at CMU, and some details about C.mmp, Hydra, and the goals we originally set for the research project. This information should serve as a general background against which our evaluation of the project can be cast. The interested reader will find more details in the bibliography.

Multiprocessor research at CMU

In late 1971 we at CMU decided to embark on a research program to explore multicomputer structures—especially those structures in which the several computers share a common address space. At the time it appeared to us that the economics of LSI technology would make multi-mini or multi-micro structures the architecture of choice for many medium- to large-scale applications. In addition to the economic arguments, there appeared to be many other advantages to such structures, including high availability, expansability, and so on.

Despite the fact that a number of multiprocessor computers had been built prior to 1971, relatively little of a scientific nature was known about them. Our goal was to explore a number of alternative multiprocessor designs, examining both the hardware and software issues, and to report on these explorations. To that end we undertook the design and construction of two multiprocessor systems, C.mmp and Cm*, and their associated software.

C.mmp, the subject of this paper, is a relatively straightforward multiprocessor. Begun in 1972, it connects 16 processors to a large shared memory (up to 32 megabytes) through a central crosspoint switch. The access time from any processor to any word of memory is identical. Cm*, started in 1975, replaces the crosspoint switch with a distributed, bus-oriented interconnection scheme between processor-memory pairs. In contrast to C.mmp, the access time from a Cm* processor to a word of memory can vary by an order of magnitude depending upon the particular processor and memory module involved. These two machines have quite different implications on the software which runs on them; between them we are able to explore many of the interesting issues of distributed processing.

C.mmp

C.mmp is a multiprocessor composed of 16 PDP-11's, 16 independent memory banks, a crosspoint switch which permits any processor to access any memory, and a typical complement of I/O equipment. A path through the switch is independently established for each memory request and up to 16 paths may exist simultaneously. An independent bus, the IP-bus, carries control signals from one processor to another; no data is carried by this bus. Collectively the 16 processors execute about 6 million instructions per second;

* The research described here was supported by the Defense Advanced Research Projects Agency (Contract: F44620-73-C-0074, monitored by the Air Force Office of Scientific Research). The views expressed are those of the authors.

the total memory bandwidth is about 500 million bits per second. In short, despite the fact that it is built from mini-computers, C.mmp is a large-scale machine.

The current configuration of C.mmp includes 5 PDP-11/20 processors (5 usec/instruction), 11 PDP-11/40 processors (2.5 usec/instruction), and 3 megabytes of shared memory (650 nsec core and 300 nsec semiconductor). All of the 11/40 processors have been modified to include writable microstores; thus we are able to tailor their instruction sets to specific applications. The cost of this configuration is roughly $600,000, of which $300,000 is the cost of processors, $200,000 is memory, and $100,000 is the switch, IP-bus and other special equipment. Of course, there is an additional cost associated with I/O devices.

Hydra

Hydra is the "kernel" of the operating system for C.mmp; it is not intended to provide most of the familiar features of an operating system (e.g., it does not provide files, a command language, or even a scheduler). Rather, Hydra provides an environment in which it is (intended to be) easy to write user-level programs that supply these familiar facilities. Hydra was designed in this kernal fashion in order to permit (and encourage) experimentation with features and policies appropriate to multiprocessors.

Hydra, which was a research project in its own right, uses a capability-based protection structure, a scheme in which only the possession of the appropriate kind of reference to an object (e.g., a file) grants access to that object. In order to allow user-level definition of operating system facilities, Hydra extends the basic capability scheme with the ability to define new types of objects and (protected) operations on these object types. Thus it is possible for a user to define new types of files, processes, message buffers, or whatever. These newly defined types share an equal status with those that already exist—which is another way of saying that Hydra attempts to preempt as few decisions as possible, thus allowing the users to tailor the system to their needs.

Software already built on top of Hydra in this manner includes file systems, directory systems, schedulers, and language processors (for Algol 68, L*, and a flexible command language).

Project goals

Two general goals influenced both the hardware and the software design from the outset. The C.mmp/Hydra system was envisioned as both *symmetric* and *general purpose*. By *symmetric* we mean that replicated components, such as processors, are treated as an anonymous pool; no one of them is special in any sense. By *general purpose* we simply mean that we did not intend to cater to *only* those programs which need a multiprocessor; the multiprocessor character of the machine is used to improve throughput across a set of independent jobs as well as to multiprocess single jobs. Both the hardware and software were designed with these goals in mind.

The *symmetry* goal is manifest in a number of ways. At the hardware level, for example, an interprocessor interrupt mechanism was designed so that every processor could interrupt every other processor (including itself) with equal ease. At the software level there is no "master-slave" relation among the processors—any processor may execute any part of the operating system at any time (subject, of course, to mutual exclusion in accessing shared data structures). At the user level, a job may execute on any processor, and indeed may switch from one processor to another many times during its execution.

The impact of the *general purpose* assumption is more subtle; it implies that we have to provide a broader range of software than would be expected if our focus had been more narrow. It also implies that optimizations to a specialized problem domain should not be made in the operating system. Some of the specific effects of this goal will be found later in the evaluations.

Performance evaluation tools

Many of our evaluations of C.mmp are based on data obtained from a number of tools designed to measure system performance. Although not one of our greatest successes, we think these tools are important enough to present here. We have three measurement tools: a script driver, a hardware monitor, and a kernel tracer.

The Script Driver is a program which can place a measured load on the system by simulating a number of users at terminals performing various tasks. This known load can make the interpretation of performance measurements much easier.

The Hardware Monitor is a device built at CMU which can monitor in real time the signals on a PDP-11's bus. The Monitor is very useful in measuring the activity of a single C.mmp processor, and for recording the activity of small portions of the operating system. It is less effective in measuring total system performance.

The Kernel Tracer, the most commonly used tool, is built into the Hydra kernel. It allows selected operating system events (e.g., blocking on semaphores, context swaps) to be recorded while applications are running. The accumulated data can be processed off-line to give a detailed record of what was happening on each processor. Naturally, the use of the tracer slows down the entire system, but this obvious point doesn't really seem to matter in practice.

The importance of these tools should not be underestimated. In any system as complex as an operating system, design decisions are often based on intuitive assumptions of performance tradeoffs. Without accurate measurements, these design assumptions cannot be verified. Certainly we found that some of our assumptions were wrong, causing us to redesign several parts of Hydra.

Format of the paper

The body of this paper is a highly edited report of a meeting called specifically to evaluate the C.mmp/Hydra project. The attendees were representatives of the various groups involved in the design, implementation, and use of C.mmp and Hydra; hardware designers, operating system implementors, those doing performance evaluation, and four major users. In all, sixteen persons attended, the maximum number we felt could interact productively.

The purpose of the meeting was to solicit the opinions of the participants concerning the nature of our successes and failures. We had also solicited written opinions from a wider group—in fact, just about everyone who has had anything to do with C.mmp and Hydra. The participants knew, of course, that the results would be reported in this paper.

The meeting and written responses produced over a hundred distinct comments. To organize these in a coherent fashion we asked the participants to decide upon our five greatest successes and five greatest failures. With some exceptions the comments have been organized under these headings; the participants' comments have been indented to separate them from background information and summary comments.

Any paper that sets out to reflect upon the successes and failures of a research project is potentially self-serving. We were extremely conscious of that danger and have attempted, through the format of the meeting and the editing of its transcript, to construct the paper in a manner which minimizes this effect. Either our initial fear of being self-serving was groundless, or the format chosen worked extremely well. We shall let the readers judge for themselves, but we feel that the result has been a reasonably objective, well-balanced view of the C.mmp/Hydra project.

OUR GREATEST SUCCESSES AND FAILURES

We shall begin this report with what, in fact, happened last at the meeting—a listing of our most notable accomplishments and mistakes. This list was created after all opinions had been expressed, thus the participants had the opportunity to hear the opinions of the others before deciding upon the content of the list. To keep the discussion crisp we arbitrarily chose to limit each list to five items. Surprisingly (to the editors at least), despite the differing interests of the participants there was essentially complete agreement on the items to be included on each list.

Our notable accomplishments:

We constructed a cost-effective, symmetric multiprocessor.

We provided, in Hydra, a capability-based protection system which allows the construction of operating system facilities as normal user programs.

We were able to distribute the Hydra kernel symmetrically over all processors.

We provided successful mechanisms for the detection of, and recovery from, software and hardware errors.

We used an effective methodology for constructing the Hydra kernel.

Our notable disappointments:

The hardware is less reliable than we would like.

The small address of the PDP-11 has a large negative impact on program structure and performance.

We are unable to partition C.mmp into disjoint systems.

We did not put enough human-engineering into the software interface to the user.

We did not give enough attention to project management.

Neither our successes nor failures are, of course, unqualified, and the story behind each is littered with smaller successes and mistakes. Moreover, there are dependencies between the things that went well and those that didn't; the fact that we have a running 16-processor system must be tempered, for example, by a poorer-than-expected reliability record. The reliability record, on the other hand, led us to greater concern for software structures that detect and survive hardware malfunction—and we count those structures among our most important accomplishments. For all these reasons, while we have used the success/failure list to organize the paper, one should not expect all the points listed under a "success" to be positive in nature. On the contrary, we believe it important to expose the contributing events, both positive and negative, as well as the major points listed here.

With that introduction then, here is the report of the meeting.

THE SUCCESSES

A cost-effective multiprocessor

C.mmp's design goals included speed, simplicity, and the use of as many commercially-available components as possible. Because C.mmp is a unique computer some critical parts had to be designed and built especially for the project. While this was a burden, it did give us maximum freedom in the design of these critical components, including the crosspoint switch, the IP-bus, and the processor modifications for memory relocation. These were all built by the CMU Computer Science Department Engineering Laboratory.

The basic design goals have been justified by experience, with speed having been the least important emphasis.

CMU-built hardware is not a large proportion of the total system cost.

The crosspoint switch is very reliable, and fast enough.

The use of immediately available components was a major factor in getting C.mmp built as fast as we did, but it limited us in taking advantage of technology which developed in succeeding years.

We were especially happy about the evaluation of the crosspoint switch, which many people thought would be C.mmp's Achilles' heel. In retrospect we think we were too concerned about raw speed in the design of the switch and memory; as it turns out, most applications are sped up by decomposing their algorithms to use the multiprocessor structure, not by executing on a processor with short memory access times.

The comments at the meeting did reflect some specific complaints about the hardware, several of which we later decided were significant enough to be listed as some of our major disappointments. Many of these stemmed from our choice of a processor for C.mmp. In 1971, only the PDP-11/20 minicomputer met our requirements. In 1974 we decided to take advantage of technology advances and use the new, faster PDP-11/40 processors to complete C.mmp. One feature of the PDP-11 architecture which might be expected to impact the goal of symmetry for C.mmp is the close association of an I/O device with exactly one processor.

The PDP-11 processors required more modifications than we expected to ensure the security of the operating system.

The PDP-11's 16-bit address is too small for many interesting applications.

Having to supporting two PDP-11 models complicated the development of the processor modifications and the operating system. It would have been better to have had a single processor model, regardless of its speed.

Having I/O devices bound to particular processors made it difficult to move a device from a malfunctioning processor to a good one, but device utilization was not otherwise sacrificed.

Perhaps more than anything else, our experience with the PDP-11 has given us a much clearer idea about what features are really important in choosing a processor, and which are not. Our consensus is that speed is not very important, for reasons already cited in conjunction with the crosspoint switch. Reliability is very important, but we found that much can be done in software to increase the overall system reliability, as long as the hardware has some basic error-detection mechanisms. (Our own approach to this is described later.) The address size is important because if it is too small for the expected applications, the ensuing problems cannot be completely overcome by software. The PDP-11 I/O architecture is an example of a feature that turned out to be unimportant because it could be completely hidden from users by software.

At a higher level, users of C.mmp seemed satisfied with the overall system performance.

Our ability to support multiprocess algorithms is well established by the performance of the many applications on C.mmp.

We have successfully supported user processes that require real-time response, although this was not one of our major goals.

At the end of the paper we will give some performance figures for an application which runs on several CMU computers, including C.mmp.

Most often cited criticisms of the system were:

Interaction with operating system facilities, in or out of the kernel, is accompanied by a high overhead.

The most serious obstacle to rapid execution of large systems is the limitation imposed on programming by the small PDP-11 address.

Memory contention significantly degrades performance when many processes are accessing the same memory page. This is usually caused by the processes sharing the same code pages.

Memory contention is very serious when using high-performance I/O devices which depend on rapid access to memory during transfers.

The performance bottlenecks are due to a combination of avoidable and unavoidable factors. We were initially distressed at the high operating system overhead (it takes about 500 microseconds to enter and exit the kernel), but we attribute most of it to a lack of experience with the fairly complex features we wished to implement. We are confident that the overhead is not an inevitable result of our protection mechanisms, nor is it due to the hardware design.

Memory contention, caused by several processors trying to access the same memory simultaneously, was a performance concern from the outset of the project. Our simulation studies indicated that its effect would be minimal, but in practice several circumstances conspired to make the problem significant. First, typical large multiprocess applications tend to share the same code among all processes, and this greatly increases the probability of accesses to the same memory. Second, the installation of per-processor caches, which were to handle this code-reference problem, has been delayed due to various resource shortages. Finally, we found that devices such as our disks and drums could not tolerate the long memory access times characteristic of periods of high contention. A software solution to this problem had to be implemented.

The small address problem is serious for large applications which cannot fit within the 64K address space on the PDP-11. Although we could not have avoided this problem, we were guilty of underestimating its significance for the applications which were to run on C.mmp. The problem is considered in more detail later in this paper.

Protected subsystems

In Hydra, the construction of operating system facilities outside the kernel is centered around an abstraction called a *protected subsystem*. A subsystem is, in its basic form, a new object type combined with a set of procedures which operate on objects of that type.

Our experience derives from over twenty working subsystems implementing schedulers (*Policy Modules* in Hydra terminology), files, directories, an I/O device allocator, and a host of other traditional operating system facilities. As software development continued by diverse users, we were curious to see whether all the required software could be built within the subsystem abstraction, whether such development could be done easily and quickly, and whether the resulting facilities could be easily merged into the user environment.

The protected subsystems abstraction is very powerful in designing operating system software in a capability environment.

It is easy to design subsystems which are easy to use and which are protected from any interference from software outside the subsystem.

The subsystem structure makes it easy to provide several coexisting and competing facilities.

The subsystem structure is useful for isolating facilities under development or being debugged.

New subsystems are easily incorporated into the standard system.

We think the subsystem concept in Hydra is as useful as the closely-related notion of extended data types has been in the field of programming languages. Part of the original motivation for the subsystem concept was our desire to allow alternate solutions to problems which we could not foresee in a multiprocessor environment. However, we found that subsystems are also very useful in debugging versions of "standard" systems without interfering with users.

Many people at the meeting were critical of the failure to follow up the subsystem design with the software tools which would encourage building subsystems in this new environment.

Subsystem construction still suffers from being ad hoc, there being inadequate software support for managing the programs, data structures, and documentation which comprise the subsystem.

The development of system software (subsystems) by many different people makes it more difficult to impose any standardization.

Subsystems are less likely to be successful when they attempt to implement traditional (non-capability) systems in traditional ways.

These problems are the result of our not giving the user environment outside the kernel as much attention as we gave the Hydra kernel itself. We consider it one of our worst mistakes and will discuss it more later in the paper.

Scheduling is an example of a traditional operating system function which, in Hydra, is partially implemented outside the kernel by a subsystem called the Policy Module (PM). We thought that providing scheduling policy outside the kernel would allow us to experiment with different specialized strategies for scheduling cooperating processes.

The first Policy Module is a distinguished subsystem for several reasons. First, it was one of the first subsystems built outside the kernel and exhibits many of the mistakes of any first attempt. Second, it is a particularly nice example of our ability to build operating system facilities outside the kernel. Finally, it interacts very closely with the kernel, so the efficiency of the kernel interface is emphasized.

The first Policy Module was operational from 1974 through May, 1977. Our basic evaluation at the meeting was that

The first Policy Module adequately demonstrated that traditional policy decisions could be made outside the kernel.

In spite of this, many people noted flaws in the implementation which were glossed over in our rush to see if the PM would work.

Insufficient attention was paid to reliability and throughput in the Policy Module.

The PM-kernel interface turned out to be more complex than we had anticipated.

We included things in the kernel facilities which logically belonged outside; this acted to complicate the kernel interface. [*For efficiency reasons, we implemented in the kernel some facilities which should have been outside according to our philosophy.*

Hence,

The construction of Policy Modules was not as easy as we had imagined before we actually tried it.

Because we expected a PM to incorporate specific knowledge about the processes it was scheduling, we anticipated having many PM's simultaneously scheduling different sets of processes. Indeed, having several PM's run at the same time was no problem, but again the performance left something to be desired.

To support multiple Policy Modules, more facilities are needed in the kernel to ensure a fair allocation of processor and memory resources to each Policy Module.

We began to build a second version of the Policy Module almost as soon as the deficiencies in the first were recognized. This design proceeded in parallel with performance improvements to the first PM, and in fact we were running both PM's simultaneously for a short time.

The distributed operating system

Hydra was designed with no master-slave relationship among processors. With the exception of the lowest level of I/O device support, all system tasks may run on any and all processors. An immediate result of this is that we expected a high degree of parallelism in Hydra and the corresponding need for effective synchronization methods.

There are two notable aspects to our approach to synchronization. First, we decided to synchronize on data rather than code. Every data structure which can be accessed by more than one processor is provided with a lock or semaphore which is used to ensure mutual exclusion.

Second, we provided a range of synchronization primitives, from very fast "locks" to much slower "semaphores." The tradeoff here is the overhead needed to P or V the lock or semaphore against the resources which will be tied up by a process waiting to pass the lock or semaphore. Small data structures which are locked for short periods of time (order 300 microseconds) use locks, which involve a very small overhead (approximately four instructions) when the process does not block. Large data structures, or data structures whose processing may be interrupted for long periods of time (as when waiting for I/O) use semaphores, which tie up fewer resources when blocking is necessary.

The simple, symmetric hardware has permitted a much simpler operating system design.

Hydra hides the processor-device correspondence so well that most of Hydra, and all the software at the user level, is unaware of the actual location of I/O devices.

The symmetric distribution of the operating system has been an unqualified success. We are able to achieve a high degree of parallelism within Hydra, and the system is insensitive about the number of processors available.

The use of asynchronous processes ("demons") to implement system functions resulted in simpler designs and improved performance.

In providing synchronization within the kernel, we believe we profited by locking data structures rather than code.

Our decision to provide several types of synchronization mechanisms gave us much design flexibility.

The natural synchronization primitives and our conscious and constant commitment to a high degree of parallelism has resulted in our encountering few software bugs caused by inadequate synchronization.

We have found that the use of demons to absorb much of the system work load outside the normal computational stream has simplified much of Hydra's design. We might not have used this technique if we did not have so much confidence in our synchronization techniques and our ability to achieve a high degree of parallelism.

Coverage of hardware and software errors

There are times when clouds do have silver linings. From the earliest days of the project we had to contend with unreliable hardware and our own software mistakes; moreover, we could not afford a 24 hour/day operator to reload the system after each crash. Thus we were forced to consider the general problems of software detection and recovery from errors—whether they be hardware or software induced.

When an error is detected by Hydra, we try to answer a number of questions. What was the exact error? Can we tell if it is due to a hardware or software malfunction? If hardware, is the problem repeatable or transient? Have any critical data structures been damaged? If so, can the damage be repaired? Can we eliminate a piece of malfunctioning (or just suspicious) hardware and still run? In all cases, our aim is to keep the system running with as much functionality as possible.

Our probability of detecting an error soon after it has occurred is increased by building error-detection mechanisms into the hardware and software. The CMU-built memory relocation units implement parity checking on every memory byte and on the address bus through the crosspoint switch. Software modules employ redundant representation and other techniques to try to limit the propagation of errors not detected by the hardware.

Recovery mechanisms invoked by the detection of any error employ a "suspect-monitor" paradigm to ensure that a failure in the recovery processor may be detected cleanly. Two processors are always involved; one, the *suspect*, attempts to record the system state at the time of the error; the other, the *monitor*, watches the suspect and assumes control if the suspect is unable to finish. The suspect is always the processor on which the error occurred. The monitor is selected at random from all other processors. There are a number of steps which can be taken during a recovery action depending on the type of error, including removing processors or memories from the system and producing extensive crash dumps for later off-line analysis.

The fault tolerance built into some kernel modules resulted in making them among the most reliable in the system—more reliable than other modules coded by the same programmer without using such techniques.

The software facilities for detecting software and hardware errors and restarting the system automatically have been a big success.

Similar facilities in user software are beginning to be developed and show much promise in improving overall system reliability.

Even though we are proud of our current error-handling mechanisms, we know that system needs more work in this area, particularly in the area of supplying policies to determine which mechanisms should be invoked for different types of errors. While it is true that we can recover from virtually any error by initiating an automatic reloading of the operating system, this is a drastic action we would like to use only in the case of truly catastrophic errors. Unfortunately, the difficulty in pinpointing the exact location of some hardware errors and the difficulty in verifying the consistency of the complex capability data structure has resulted in our classifying almost all errors as "catastrophic'' in this sense. We are in the midst of redesigning both hardware and software to correct these deficiencies.

Software development methodology

Our initial goals for the Hydra implementation did not explicitly include the notion of exploring a software engineering methodology. Nevertheless, we used a method based on Parnas' ''modular decomposition''* and it worked quite well; indeed many of us believe that without it the project would not have succeeded.

The methodology used caused us to divide the units of work (programming tasks) along the lines of the major data structures in the system. A module (and hence a programmer) was responsible for the representation of, and all operations on, a data structure. No one other than the responsible programmer had access to knowledge concerning the implementation details.

Because methodology *per se* was not our major goal we were not fanatical about enforcing the methodology, and were often less precise about the specifications than we might have been. Both the positive and negative aspects of this informal approach are reflected in the following remarks:

We believe that it is a measure of the success of the modular implementation of the kernel that one full-time programmer can maintain this program which comprises 2000 (listing) pages of source code.

The independent implementation of the modules in Hydra resulted in a lack of any uniform coding style and in some duplicated effort in interfacing to the underlying hardware. The effect was not very serious since all the implementors were highly talented, exhibiting differences in style rather than quality.

Because modules were implemented independently, no one initially had a detailed knowledge of the entire system. This made debugging more difficult and resulted in a difficult transition when Hydra began to be maintained by a single programmer who was not part of the original implementation team.

Coding of the kernel began quickly after the initial design. Some think too quickly.

Loose management coupled with the modularization technique worked well except in promoting a standardization of coding styles.

Information hiding as a modularization technique resulted in coding situations in which information necessary to make a decision was not available.

As Hydra developed and was modified, the original, clean modularization began to break down as new features were added and performance bottlenecks removed.

---

* Parnas, ''On the Criteria to be Used in Decomposing Systems into Modules,'' *CACM*, 15, 12, pp. 1053-1058, 1972.

We still think the modular decomposition methodology is extremely good for structuring large systems. In our experience, breakdown of the modular structure occurs mainly when programmers in the midst of debugging adapt ''quick and dirty'' solutions which do not preserve modularity.

All but a very small part of Hydra is written in a high-level implementation language, Bliss-11. There seems to be no question that it was possible, indeed advantageous, to write the kernel in Bliss, but there were problems. The Bliss-11 compiler was developed only shortly before the kernel was begun and was an independent research project (investigating compiler optimization techniques). There was some initial friction between the two groups, but both appear to have benefited in the long run.

The Bliss-11 compiler was designed to compile a slightly modified version of the Bliss-10 language into very compact PDP-11 code. This it does.

The implementors of the Hydra kernel were, and continue to be, a major influence on the addition of new features to Bliss-11.

The facilities of the Bliss-11 language and compiler had a significant influence on the coding of Hydra.

Some of us believe that Hydra could not have been written in this environment without a language of Bliss's caliber.

Bliss-11 preceded Hydra by too short a time. The unreliability of the compiler during its first year of use hindered kernel development.

Compatibility between Bliss-11 and Hydra was a problem. Changes in Bliss-11 sometimes had unfortunate consequences on Hydra code.

We think these comments reflect the close interdependence between a large programming project (Hydra) and the software engineering tools it uses (Bliss-11). Bliss was in a real sense critical to Hydra's development. The need to debug both Bliss and Hydra simultaneously was a necessary burden.

A common measure, albeit a crude one, of a methodology is the productivity of the programmers which used the methodology. By that measure our development strategy worked very well; the average productivity has been about 20 instructions per man-day for kernel code (the typical industrial average for similar code is 5-7 instructions per man-day).

THE FAILURES

Hardware reliability

Hardware (un)reliability was our largest day-to-day disappointment at the time the evaluation meeting took place. The aggregate mean-time-between-failure (MTBF) of C.mmp/Hydra fluctuated between two to six hours, where a failure is defined to be any situation which triggers the recovery actions described earlier. About two-thirds of the failures were directly attributable to hardware problems.

There is insufficient fault detection built into the hardware.

We found the PDP-11 UNIBUS to be especially noisy and error-prone.

Our paging drums were chosen for their predicted performance, but their reliability was so poor that performance was often a moot point.

The crosspoint switch design is too trusting of other components; it can be hung by malfunctioning memories or processors. [*This almost never happens, but when it does automatic recovery is impossible.*]

We made a serious error in not writing good diagnostics for the hardware. The software developers should have written such programs for the hardware.

In our experience, diagnostics written by the hardware group often did not test components under the type of load generated by Hydra, resulting in much finger-pointing between groups. Faulty hardware is often kept in the user system because only Hydra can provoke and pinpoint errors.

Several components of the system have gone through several development cycles, mostly to improve the handling of exceptional conditions, but we are basically limited by the capabilities of the PDP-11 and its UNIBUS. There appear to be two flaws in many of the off-the-shelf components. One of these was mentioned during the meeting: the lack of mutual suspicion. There are a number of ways in which the entire system can be made to fail if one inessential component does not operate according to specifications. The other flaw was not mentioned: the failure to *contain* errors. Once an error has been detected the goal should be to make absolutely sure that the damage won't spread. Many of the standard components, unfortunately, will ''complete'' an operation even when an error is known to exist; in completing the operation they destroy data, thus making the error unrecoverable.

There is some good news to report, however. Following the meeting, increased emphasis was given to hardware maintenance. As this paper is written (January 1978) our MTBF has increased to about ten hours and many of the hardware problems seem to be settling out.

The small address space problem

The PDP-11 is a 16-bit minicomputer; of particular interest is the fact that this restricts all addresses generated by a user program to be 16 bits long. These 16 bits can be used to address no more than 64K bytes of memory. We refer to this limitation as the ''small address problem'', or SAP.

Although we were initially aware that the operating system would have to provide some sort of facility for allowing a user to address more than this amount of memory, we did not appreciate how restrictive the 16-bit limitation would be or to what extent circumventing it would affect performance.

Our initial impression was that the 16-bit limitation would be offset by the ability to create multiprocess programs—that the typical program organization would be a larger number of processes, each addressing a smaller amount of memory. That impression turned out to be false, as is reflected in some of the comments made at the meeting:

> Our initial prediction that programs would be implemented as small subsystems using less than 64K was wrong.

> Multiprocess algorithms do not always produce small programs.

> Even though programmers are writing programs which execute on PDP-11's, their tasks are CDC 6600-size.

> There is nothing good to say about this problem other than that we were pretty much forced into it.

To circumvent this problem, Hydra provides a facility, supported by the hardware, to divide the address space into 8 pieces, each of which is called a ''page.'' The user is permitted to have an indefinitely large number of pages, but to address only 8 of them at any instant. Operating system facilities are provided to allow the user to dynamically designate which of his pages are to be addressable; he does this by associating a page with one of the 8 ''relocation registers'' maintained by the hardware. Thus, except that the cost of loading is larger, the addressing scheme is very similar to the use of ''base registers'' on 360-370 style machines. We have found this facility, however, to be less than ideal.

> Page boundaries are absolute, and the programmer must always be aware of them.

> The problem is in addressing data. There are easy solutions to addressing code segments.

> More relocation registers and a smaller page size would reduce but not eliminate the problem.

> We believe the problem would exist even if making pages addressable required no overhead.

Because of the performance penalties associated with managing the address space, the inconvenience cannot be hidden from the user through a high-level language:

> L*'s ability to allow access to large amounts of memory has been hindered by the short PDP-11 address. [*L* is a list processing language used for the implementation of large systems.*]

It must be emphasized that not *all* programs are affected by the small address space problem:

> In practice, most subsystems have no problem fitting into 64K.

Our failure on the small address problem was really one of misappreciating the way in which the machine would actually be used. The remark above to the effect that many tasks are 6600-size is a telling one. The machine is comparable in size to a 6600 and people want to use it that way. Big problems often imply big data and we failed to appreciate that during the initial design.

The partitionable system

When we first considered the possibility of building a multiprocessor in 1971, the ability to partition it into several disjoint subsystems was on our list of advantages for such architectures. While we are able to partition processors and memory, we are not able to run Hydra in more than one partition.

C.mmp can be partitioned in such a way that some processors and memories can undergo maintenance and run stand-alone diagnostics without interfering with the larger partition running the operating system.

The primary obstacle to running the operating system in two partitions is the money required to provide each partition with an adequate complement of I/O devices and memory.

We do not know how to provide meaningful communication between the capability structures of the two operating systems.

The principal effect of the failure to meet this goal has been that we must allocate disjoint time for users, hardware maintenance, and operating system testing. At present 28 hours each week are reserved for maintenance. This partitioning has been very inconvenient for all concerned, and has certainly impeded progress on several occasions. Yet it seems clear that we have been unwilling to spend the money necessary to solve the problem—thus it seems safe to conclude that the inconvenience has not been debilitating.

(The lack of) human engineering

As we have mentioned in several contexts previously, the human interface to the C.mmp/Hydra system is not well designed. To some extent this resulted from the novelty of the underlying system structure (we couldn't anticipate some of the kinds of facilities that would be needed by users of either a capability-based or a multiprocessor system). To a large extent, however, the failure seems to have been one of having concentrated on the new, innovative aspects of the system and ignoring more mundane issues.

There is a lack of human engineering in the operating system software which interacts directly with a user sitting at a terminal.

It is difficult to pick up the minimal knowledge needed to know how to do useful things at a terminal.

New users tend to have bad first impressions of the system.

We did not realize how much work was required to make a smooth user interface and so did not allocate enough resources for it.

We suspect the user environment would have received more work had the kernel implementors had to use it during their software development. (All kernel development and maintenance has been done on the PDP-10 computer, which has the Bliss-11 compiler and a linker for C.mmp.)

One particular aspect of the human interface is especially interesting—the command language. It seems to be an almost universal phenomenon that people don't like whatever command language they have used in the past. We were no exception. Thus, rather than modeling our command language on any existing one, we chose to strike out in another direction. In particular, we chose to make the command language a (modest) interactive programming language—with declarations of variables, assignments, conditional and looping control constructs, macros, and so on. The power of this approach seems unquestionable, as is reflected by the following remarks. The remarkable thing (to the editors) is the lack of negative remarks during the meeting; the command language usually comes under heavy attack on other occasions.

The Command Language is much more flexible and powerful than the command scanners found on most systems.

The concept of the Command Language as a programming language was good.

The Command Language user on C.mmp is unique in having complete access to the Hydra environment. Subsystems can almost be implemented directly in the Command Language.

Error reporting by the Command Language is poor.

Another aspect of the human interface is the (lack of a) spectrum of programming languages:

C.mmp lacks the wide range of languages available on conventional systems.

The L* system provides its users with a complete environment compatible with that provided on the PDP-10 by its version of L*.

The L* environment does not seem conducive to the construction of subsystems.

The Algol 68 implementation on C.mmp gives users access to the multiprocess capabilities of C.mmp, but does not yet provide access to capabilities or the Hydra protection environment.

The fact that most subsystem development takes place partially on C.mmp and partially on the PDP-10's (which have Bliss-11 compilers) is not a severe hindrance now that smooth communication facilities exist between the machines.

It is interesting (to the editors) that the word "baroque" was not used during the meeting; in other contexts it often is. Several features of Hydra and its subsystems do exhibit "second-system-itis". There are things which are more general, and more complicated, than necessary.

Project management

The C.mmp/Hydra project was not a large project by most standards; there were never more than about 15 people, mostly students, working on the project at any one time. Nevertheless we made a number of errors which can only be classified as failures in the management of the project; taken together, these errors constitute one of our largest failures.

Among our errors is a classic! Because the hardware and Hydra structures were new and exciting, we tended to focus on them to the exclusion of the more mundane things which also determine the ultimate utility of any system. This point recurred in many of the points raised at the meeting:

The manpower allocated to the Policy Module was inadequate. In fact this was true of all software outside the kernel.

The failure to stress reliability and performance in the first PM was a mistake.

The user environment was ignored at first because of our natural preoccupation with the Hydra kernel and the research problems it embodied.

We underestimated how much work would be involved in constructing the user environment.

We have a much better idea now about the proper structure (or at least an adequate one) of the user environment than we did when we began building the first subsystems. Implementing basic concepts such as "jobs" and "terminals" in nonpriviledged software has subtle design and reliability implications which we are just now appreciating.

The management style used throughout the project was informal. There were very few memos, formal design reviews, or the other mechanisms of tight management control. In most ways this felt appropriate to the academic environment and the high caliber of the individuals involved. It led to a number of problems, however, and the consensus of the meeting was that the management had been too loose. This is especially evident in the comments relating to a lack of formal specifications and the lack of uniform documentation and coding standards.

The fact that the Hydra implementors did not have to use C.mmp for software development contributed to the neglect of the user environment.

The lack of detailed hardware specifications hindered the parallel development of hardware and software but not the end result.

Software was occasionally developed which took advantage of unspecified "features" of the hardware, making them difficult to change.

Loose management coupled with the modularization technique worked well except in forcing standardization of coding styles.

We should not have depended on graduate students for complete software development for so long. Graduate students cannot keep deadlines reliably and are not tied to the project. [*Furthermore, we feel that Ph.D. students should not spend an inordinate amount of time doing the standard programming chores which characterize any attempt to bring up a complete operating system.*]

Another class of management errors relates to what might be termed "public relations." Being academics, we instinctively react somewhat negatively to the "attention-getting" aspect of PR, forgetting that its "information-providing" function is absolutely necessary. In a number of ways we failed to make information available publicly.

Our problem is basically public relations—performance measurements indicate we have a winner on our hands.

The lack of a smooth user environment was a deterrent to new users which could form the foundation of a happy and vocal user community.

Since Hydra was not easily accessible to people outside the department, we could not adopt a "try it and see" attitude.

Documentation is needed to encourage use internally and generate credibility externally.

A DATA SAMPLER

The previous section concludes our report of the meeting. Since the body of the report contains many subjective and unsubstantiated comments, we decided to include a few examples of the kinds of data on which these comments are based. We have chosen two examples: (1) a study of the effect of the small address problem on a specific user program, and (2) a study of the contention for locks in the Hydra kernel.

A study of the small address problem

The program used in this study of the SAP is HARPY. HARPY is a speech-understanding system which has been implemented on all of the departments major computers: C.mmp, a stand-alone PDP-11 running under UNIX, and the PDP-10 (both KA10, circa 1967, and KL10, circa 1976, processors are available in the department). Since HARPY ex-

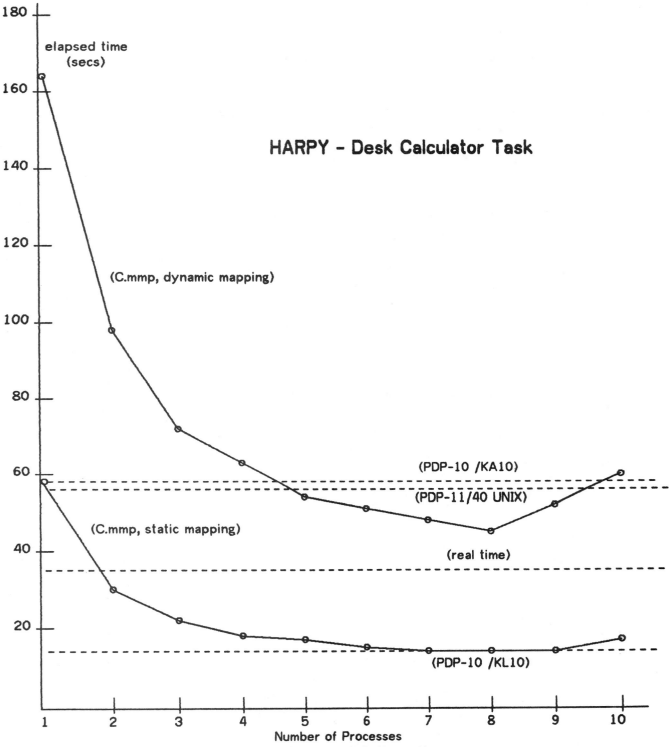

Figure 1—A look at the small address problem

ists on all these machines, it makes a convenient benchmark. (We should point out that HARPY is not necessarily the best application for C.mmp, nor are the HARPY implementations on C.mmp known to be optimal.)

Figure 1 summarizes the data obtained from a series of experiments with HARPY working on a rather small task, namely a voice-input desk calculator that has a 37 word vocabulary.

The horizontal dashed lines represent the performance of single-process implementations of HARPY on the departments uniprocessors. The solid curves represent the performance of two implementations on C.mmp, both of which can utilize any number of processes.

The two HARPY versions on C.mmp differ in their assumptions about the addressability of data. The "static mapping" version knows that all of its data is always addressable, while the "dynamic mapping" version expects to have to do some mapping of relocation registers in order to address the data. In this second version, it must be realized that, in fact, all the data is addressable, and thus no operating system overhead is involved. (The overhead is HARPY checking to see if relocation is necessary—it never is.)

This type of data dramatically illustrates the effect of the SAP on performance—it costs nearly a factor of three in this example. The effect on programming difficulty is at least as great, but is not so easy to illustrate.

Note that the one-process, static mapping version of HARPY runs very nearly as fast as the version running under UNIX, even though the C.mmp version has all the necessary mechanisms for multiprocessing. We think this indicates that the synchronization primitives (spinlocks in shared memory) do not contribute much overhead in this application.

Also note that little improvement in performance is seen beyond three or four processes. This is simply due to a lack of work to do—the small vocabulary simply isn't complicated enough to keep the processors busy. On larger vocabularies we typically see noticeable improvement out to eight processes. The upturn in the curves towards the end is due to the fact that all the faster PDP-11/40 processors are in use. As soon as one PDP-11/20 is used, the whole assemblage of processes slows down. This is because the particular decomposition of the algorithm limits the speed to that of the slowest process.

A study of kernel lock contention

One of the largest potential bottlenecks in a distributed operating system is contention for locks on shared data structures. The hardware monitor has been used to study this; the types of results obtained are shown in Figure 2.

In this study, three programs with seemingly different demands on the system were run while the hardware monitor measured the activity on one processor. The data is illustrative only, since no claim is made that the programs in any way represented a "typical" system load.

The principle result is that it seems we spend consistently less than 1 percent of the time blocked on locks. We do not

Static	Program 1	Program 2	Program 3
Total time of measurement (millis)	17393	32924	20255
Number of different locks detected	53	79	181
Average time inside a critical section (micros)	279	378	279
Total number of lock operations	2955	504	4360
Percent of locks which blocked	5.5	11.7	6.1
Percent of time spent in kernel code	61.8	16.9	37.7
Percent of time spent in blocked state	.29	.83	.74

Figure 2—A study of kernel lock contention

yet have any measurement of the time lost due to blocking on semaphores.

CONCLUSIONS

The C.mmp/Hydra project has reached the point at which many of its most interesting and important results will emerge. With a growing user community, increasing reliability and a smoother user interface, we are in a position to gether data on various aspects of system performance under real loads. This data will augment that already collected on isolated algorithms to provide a comprehensive picture of C.mmp/Hydra performance. Along the way to constructing the current system we managed, in our opinion, to do some things well and some things not so well. This paper has been our attempt to report those opinions in the hope that others may benefit from our experiences.

ACKNOWLEDGMENTS

A large fraction of the faculty and staff of the Computer Science Department at CMU have been involved with C.mmp and Hydra over the past five years—as designer/implementors, as users, or as constructive critics. We are deeply indebted to all of them. We are especially indebted, however, to those who participated in the meeting that is reported here:

Hardware:	Bill Broadley, Jim Teter
Hydra:	Sam Harbison, Dave Jefferson, Roy Levin, Hank Mashburn, Fred Pollack
Non-kernel OS:	Bill Corwin, Rick Gumpertz
Performance Evaluation:	Sam Fuller
Major Users:	Anita Jones, Bruce Leverett, Pete Oleinick, George Robertson
Others:	Joe Newcomer, Bill Wulf

We would also like to thank Guy Almes, Peter Schwarz, and the NCC '78 referees for their helpful suggestions for this paper.

C.mmp/Hydra BIBLIOGRAPHY

This bibliography includes references to papers, articles, and theses related to the design, development, and measurement of C.mmp and Hydra. There are numerous internal documents and memos which are not included.

1. Almes, G. and G. Robertson, "An Extensible File System for Hydra," Department of Computer Science Technical Report, Carnegie-Mellon University, Pittsburgh, Pa. 1978. (This paper will appear in the *Proceedings of the Third International Conference on Software Engineering*, 1978.)
2. Bell, C. G., W. Broadley, W. A. Wulf, and A. Newell, "C.mmp: The CMU Multiminiprocessor Computer: Requirements and Overview of the Initial Design," Department of Computer Science Technical Report, Carnegie-Mellon University, Pittsburgh, Pa., August 1971.
3. Bhandarkar, D. P., "Analytic Models for Memory Interference in Multiprocessor Computer Systems," Ph.D. Dissertation, Department of Computer Science, Carnegie-Mellon University, Pittsburgh, Pa., September 1973.
4. Bhandarkar, D. P. and S. Fuller, "Markov Chain Models for Analyzing Memory Interference in Multiprocessors," *ACM/IEEE First Annual Symposium on Computer Architecture*, Dec. 1973, pp. 231-239.
5. Cohen, E., "Problems, Mechanisms and Solutions," Ph.D. Dissertation, Department of Computer Science, Carnegie-Mellon University, Pittsburgh, Pa., August 1976.
6. Cohen, E. and D. Jefferson, "Protection in the Hydra Operating System," *Proceedings of the 5th Symposium on Operating System Principles*, Austin, Texas, Nov. 1975, pp. 141-160.
7. Fuller, S. and P. Oleinick, "Initial Measurements of Parallel Programs on a Multi-miniprocessor," *IEEE CompCon'76*, September 1976, pp. 358-363.
8. Fuller, S., "A Cost/Performance Comparison of C.mmp and the PDP-10," ACM/IEEE Symposium on Computer Architecture, Jan. 1976.
9. Fuller, S., Swan, R. and W. A. Wulf, "The Instrumentation of C.mmp: A multi-(mini)-processor," *IEEE CompCon'73*, 1973, pp. 177-180.
10. Fuller, S. H., and D. K. Stevenson, "The Performance Monitor for C.mmp," *11th Annual Allerton Conference*, Urbana, Illinois, October 1973.
11. Fuller, S. H., "Recent Developments in Multiprocessor Computer Systems," *CALCOLO*, Vol. XII, No. 1, June 1975, pp. 35-58.
12. Jones, A. K. and W. A. Wulf, "Toward the Design of Secure Systems," *Software—Practice and Experience*, Vol. 5, 1975, pp. 321-333.
13. Levin, R., E. Cohen, W. Corwin, F. Pollack, and W. A. Wulf, "Policy/Mechanism Separation in Hydra," *Proceedings of the 5th Symposium on Operating System Principles*, Austin, Texas, Nov. 1975, pp. 132-140.
14. Marathe, M., and S. H. Fuller, "A Study of Multiprocessor Contention for Shared Data in C.mmp," *ACM SIGMETRICS Conference*, Washington, D.C., December 1977.
15. Newcomer, J., E. Cohen, W. Corwin, D. Jefferson, T. Lane, R. Levin, F. Pollack, and W. Wulf, "Hydra: Basic Kernel Reference Manual," Department of Computer Science Technical Report, Carnegie-Mellon University, Pittsburgh, Pa., 1976.
16. Newell, A., P. Freeman, D. McCracken, and G. Robertson, "The Kernel Approach to Building Software Systems," Computer Science Research Review 1970-71, Computer Science Department, Carnegie-Mellon University, Pittsburgh, Pa., 1971.
17. Newell, A., D. McCracken, and G. Robertson, "L*: An Interactive, Symbolic Implementation System," Department of Computer Science Technical Report, Carnegie-Mellon University, October 1977.
18. Newell, A. and G. Robertson, "Some Issues in Programming Multi-Mini-Processors," in *Behavior Research Methods and Instrumentation*, Vol. 7, No. 2, March 1975, pp. 75-86.
19. Oleinick, P. H., and S. H. Fuller, "The Implementation and Evaluation of a Parallel Algorithm on C.mmp," Department of Computer Science Technical Report, Carnegie-Mellon University, December 1978.
20. Reid, B. K. and J. Newcomer, ed., "The Hydra Songbook—A Vigilante User's Manual," Department of Computer Science Technical Report, Carnegie-Mellon University, Pittsburgh, Pa., October 1975.
21. Reiner, A., and J. Newcomer, ed., "Hydra User's Manual," Department of Computer Science Technical Report, Carnegie-Mellon University, Pittsburgh, Pa., August 1977.
22. Strecker, W. D., "An Analysis of the Instruction Execution Rate in Certain Computing Structures," Ph.D. Dissertation, Carnegie-Mellon University, 1971.
23. Wulf, W. A. and C. G. Bell, "C.mmp—A Multi-mini-processor," *Proceedings of the Fall Joint Computer Conference*, 1972, pp. 765-777.
24. Wulf, W. A. and R. Levin, "A Local Network," *Datamation*, February 1975.
25. Wulf, W. A., "Reliable Hardware-Software Architecture," *Proceedings of the International Conference on Reliable Software*, Los Angeles, 1975.
26. Wulf, W. A., E. Cohen, W. Corwin, A. Jones, R. Levin, C. Pierson, and F. Pollack, "Hydra: The Kernel of a Multiprocessor Operating System," *CACM* 17, 6, June 1974, pp. 337-345.
27. Wulf, W. A., R. Levin, and C. Pierson, "Overview of the Hydra Operating System," *Proceedings of the 5th Symposium on Operating System Principles*, Austin, Texas, Nov. 1975, pp. 122-131.

How to Make a Multiprocessor Computer That Correctly Executes Multiprocess Programs

LESLIE LAMPORT

Abstract—Many large sequential computers execute operations in a different order than is specified by the program. A correct execution is achieved if the results produced are the same as would be produced by executing the program steps in order. For a multiprocessor computer, such a correct execution by each processor does not guarantee the correct execution of the entire program. Additional conditions are given which do guarantee that a computer correctly executes multiprocess programs.

Index Terms—Computer design, concurrent computing, hardware correctness, multiprocessing, parallel processing.

A high-speed processor may execute operations in a different order than is specified by the program. The correctness of the execution is guaranteed if the processor satisfies the following condition: the result of an execution is the same as if the operations had been executed in the order specified by the program. A processor satisfying this condition will be called *sequential*. Consider a computer composed of several such processors accessing a common memory. The customary approach to designing and proving the correctness of multiprocess algorithms [1]–[3] for such a computer assumes that the following condition is satisfied: the result of any execution is the same as if the operations of all the processors were executed in some sequential order, and the operations of each individual processor appear in this sequence in the order specified by its program. A multiprocessor satisfying this condition will be called *sequentially consistent*. The sequentiality of each individual processor does not guarantee that the multiprocessor computer is sequentially consistent. In this brief note, we describe a method of interconnecting sequential processors with memory modules that insures the sequential consistency of the resulting multiprocessor.

We assume that the computer consists of a collection of processors and memory modules, and that the processors communicate with one another only through the memory modules. (Any special communication registers may be regarded as separate memory modules.) The only processor operations that concern us are the operations of sending fetch and store requests to memory modules. We assume that each processor issues a sequence of such requests. (It must sometimes wait for requests to be executed, but that does not concern us.)

Manuscript received September 28, 1977; revised May 8, 1979.
The author is with the Computer Science Laboratory, SRI International, Menlo Park, CA 94025.

We illustrate the problem by considering a simple two-process mutual exclusion protocol. Each process contains a *critical section*, and the purpose of the protocol is to insure that only one process may be executing its critical section at any time. The protocol is as follows.

process 1

   a := 1;

   if b = 0 then critical section;

            a := 0

        else   ···   fi

process 2

   b := 1;

   if a = 0 then critical section;

            b := 0

        else   ···   fi

The else clauses contain some mechanism for guaranteeing eventual access to the critical section, but that is irrelevant to the discussion. It is easy to prove that this protocol guarantees mutually exclusive access to the critical sections. (Devising a proof provides a nice exercise in using the assertional techniques of [2] and [3], and is left to the reader.) Hence, when this two-process program is executed by a sequentially consistent multiprocessor computer, the two processors cannot both be executing their critical sections at the same time.

We first observe that a sequential processor could execute the "b := 1" and "fetch b" operations of process 1 in either order. (When process 1's program is considered by itself, it does not matter in which order these two operations are performed.) However, it is easy to see that executing the "fetch b" operation first can lead to an error—both processes could then execute their critical sections at the same time. This immediately suggests our first requirement for a multiprocessor computer.

Requirement R1: Each processor issues memory requests in the order specified by its program.

Satisfying Requirement R1 is complicated by the fact that storing a value is possible only after the value has been computed. A processor will often be ready to issue a memory fetch request before it knows the value to be stored by a preceding store request. To minimize waiting, the processor can issue the store request to the memory module without specifying the value to be stored. Of course, the store request cannot actually be executed by the memory module until it receives the value to be stored.

Requirement R1 is not sufficient to guarantee correct execution. To see this, suppose that each memory module has several ports, and each port services one processor (or I/O channel). Let the values of "a" and "b" be stored in separate memory modules, and consider the following sequence of events.

1) Processor 1 sends the "a := 1" request to its port in memory module 1. The module is currently busy executing an operation for some other processor (or I/O channel).
2) Processor 1 sends the "fetch b" request to its port in memory module 2. The module is free, and execution is begun.
3) Processor 2 sends its "b := 1" request to memory module 2. This request will be executed after processor 1's "fetch b" request is completed.
4) Processor 2 sends its "fetch a" request to its port in memory module 1. The module is still busy.

There are now two operations waiting to be performed by memory module 1. If processor 2's "fetch a" operation is performed first, then both processes can enter their critical sections at the same time, and the protocol fails. This could happen if the memory module uses a round robin scheduling discipline in servicing its ports.

In this situation, an error occurs only if the two requests to memory module 1 are not executed in the same order in which they were received. This suggests the following requirement.

Requirement R2: Memory requests from all processors issued to an individual memory module are serviced from a single FIFO queue. Issuing a memory request consists of entering the request on this queue.

Condition R1 implies that a processor may not issue any further memory requests until after its current request has been entered on the queue. Hence, it must wait if the queue is full. If two or more processors are trying to enter requests in the queue at the same time, then it does not matter in which order they are serviced.

Note. If a fetch requests the contents of a memory location for which there is already a write request on the queue, then the fetch need not be entered on the queue. It may simply return the value from the last such write request on the queue. ☐

Requirements R1 and R2 insure that if the individual processors are sequential, then the entire multiprocessor computer is sequentially consistent. To demonstrate this, one first introduces a relation → on memory requests as follows. Define A → B if and only if 1) A and B are issued by the same processor and A is issued before B, or 2) A and B are issued to the same memory module, and A is entered in the queue before B (and is thus executed before B). It is easy to see that R1 and R2 imply that → is a partial ordering on the set of memory requests. Using the sequentiality of each processor, one can then prove the following result: each fetch and store operation fetches or stores the same value as if all the operations were executed sequentially in any order such that A → B implies that A is executed before B. This in turn proves the sequential consistency of the multiprocessor computer.

Requirement R2 states that a memory module's request queue must be serviced in a FIFO order. This implies that the memory module must remain idle if the request at the head of its queue is a store request for which the value to be stored has not yet been received. Condition R2 can be weakened to allow the memory module to service other requests in this situation. We need only require that all requests *to the same memory cell* be serviced in the order that they appear in the queue. Requests to different memory cells may be serviced out of order. Sequential consistency is preserved because such a service policy is logically equivalent to considering each memory cell to be a separate memory module with its own request queue. (The fact that these modules may share some hardware affects the rate at which they service requests and the capacity of their queues, but it does not affect the logical property of sequential consistency.)

The requirements needed to guarantee sequential consistency rule out some techniques which can be used to speed up individual sequential processors. For some applications, achieving sequential consistency may not be worth the price of slowing down the processors. In this case, one must be aware that conventional methods for designing multiprocess algorithms cannot be relied upon to produce correctly executing programs. Protocols for synchronizing the processors must be designed at the lowest level of the machine instruction code, and verifying their correctness becomes a monumental task.

REFERENCES

[1] E. W. Dijkstra, "Hierarchical ordering of sequential processes," *Acta Informatica*, vol. 1, pp. 115–138, 1971.
[2] L. Lamport, "Proving the correctness of multiprocess programs," *IEEE Trans. Software Eng.*, vol. SE-3, pp. 125–143, Mar. 1977.
[3] S. Owicki and D. Gries, "Verifying properties of parallel programs: an axiomatic approach," *Commun. Assoc. Comput. Mach.*, vol. 19, pp. 279–285, May 1976.

A New Solution to Coherence Problems in Multicache Systems

LUCIEN M. CENSIER AND PAUL FEAUTRIER

Abstract—A memory hierarchy has coherence problems as soon as one of its levels is split in several independent units which are not equally accessible from faster levels or processors. The classical solution to these problems, as found for instance in multiprocessor, multicache systems, is to restore a degree of interdependence between such units through a set of high speed interconnecting buses. This solution is not entirely satisfactory, as it tends to reduce the throughput of the memory hierarchy and to increase its cost.

A new solution is presented and discussed here: the presence flag solution. It has both a lower cost and a lower overhead than the classical solution. A very important feature of this solution is that it is possible, in a cache-main memory subsystem, to delay updating the main memory until a block is needed in the cache (nonstore-through mode of operation).

Index Terms—Caches, coherence, memory hierarchy, multiprocessor systems, nonstore-through.

I. INTRODUCTION

THE IDEA that a computer should use a memory hierarchy dates back to the early days of the field. There is for instance, a suggestion to this effect in the classical paper of von Neumann *et al.* [11]. A hierarchy is useful because the access time of main memory increases with its size. As soon as a certain capacity is required, the memory is inherently slower than the processor and becomes the bottleneck in the system. By adding a small memory which fits the processor speed, one may expect a considerable increase in performance if this memory is cleverly used.

The first system in which this process was automated was the ATLAS demand paging supervisor (Fotheringham [5]). The ATLAS hierarchy had two levels: a core memory and a drum. As the drum latency time is of the order of several milliseconds, it was possible to implement the supervisor as software modules.

The first proposal to apply similar techniques to fast levels was by Bloom *et al.* [2]. After a variety of theoretical studies of which Wilkes [12] and Opler [9] are examples, the first implementation of the idea was the IBM 360/85 (Gibson [6], Conti *et al.* [4], Liptay [7], Conti [4]). The resulting device, the cache memory, is now a component of most computers in the medium to high performance range.

In such a system, all data are referenced by their main memory address. At any given time, a certain subset of the

Manuscript received April 27, 1976; revised April 11, 1978. This work was supported in part by the Institut de Recherche en Informatique et Automatique under Contract 74/185.

L. M. Censier is with CII-Honeywell Bull, Les Clayes-sous-Bois, France.

P. Feautrier is with Université Pierre et Marie Curie, Paris, France.

contents of the main memory is copied in the cache. One says that such a datum is present in the cache. If a processor reads a datum in this subset, then the corresponding value is returned without referencing the main memory, after a delay which is of the order of one processor cycle time. This event is called a "hit." A directory records the addresses of all data which are present in the cache. To reduce the size of this directory, the main memory and the cache are divided in equal sized "blocks," all bits of a block being simultaneously all present or all absent from the cache. The block is then the allocation unit in the cache and also the minimum amount of data which may be transmitted between the cache and main memory. A combination of hash-coding and associative technique is used to implement a very fast search algorithm in the directory (see for instance the discussion in Bell *et al.* [1]).

In addition to the main memory address, the directory may include several flags per cache block. The VALID flag, when set, indicates that the corresponding block does hold the latest information associated to its main memory address. It is reset when the contents of the cache are undefined (for instance, at Initial Program Loading Time). Some designs include a MODIFIED flag. When set, it indicates that the block has been modified by the attached instruction processor.

The effective access time of a cache system depends critically on the hit ratio, i.e., on the probability that a requested datum is present in the cache. This in turn depends on the proper selection, by a replacement algorithm, of the cache content. A block is copied in the cache only when found absent after an access from the processor (a "miss"). This means that another block must be expelled. The usual choice is the Least Recently Used block (among a group of blocks with the same hash-code). Obviously, when the cache contains blocks with their VALID bit reset, these are used up before any valid block is expelled.

Two quite different modes of operation have been proposed for the processing of STORE accesses. In the store-through mode, a modified datum is always written in main memory and is written in the cache only if it is already present there. This mode is used in most systems (IBM 370/168, etc. ···). In the nonstore-through mode, LOAD and STORE accesses are treated alike: if the block to be written into is absent from the cache, then it is copied from main memory. All subsequent accesses to this block, whether read or write, are processed by the cache, until such time as it is selected by the replacement algorithm. At this time, it is written back to main memory. This step may be bypassed for blocks which were not written into while in the cache, if a MODIFIED bit is implemented. The net result is that a single memory access by a processor may induce zero, one or two accesses to main memory, thereby complicating the timing of the data access algorithm.

The advantage of the nonstore-through mode is that, at least in theory, the access rate to the main store may be reduced to any desired value by a sufficient increase of the size of the cache. In contrast to this, in the store-through mode, the access rate to main memory cannot be lower than the write access rate of the processor. Examination of instruction mixes shows that, depending on the processor architecture, from one tenth to one third of all accesses are STORE accesses. This figure is then a lower limit for the miss ratio of a cache in the store through mode. A simulation analysis which supports these views is reported in Bell *et al.* [1].

Both modes of operation run into coherence problems when applied to multiprocessor systems. A memory scheme is coherent if the value returned on a LOAD instruction is always the value given by the latest STORE instruction with the same address. There is obviously no coherence problems in a memory hierarchy with only one access path between each level. This however causes technical problems in high performance systems. The unique access mechanism would have to be prohibitively fast. Furthermore, a cache must be closely integrated to its processor to avoid transmission delays. I/O processors, on the other hand, have data rates substantially lower than instruction processors. There is no element of locality in the data addresses they issue and therefore no performance advantage in connecting them to a cache. This induces new coherence problems.

To take a specific example, let us consider the simple case of a biprocessor system with two caches in the nonstore-through mode, the main memory being shared by both processors. Let T_1 and T_2 be two tasks running on processors P_1 and P_2 with caches K_1 and K_2. Let a be the main memory address of a block which is read and modified by both tasks. One may assume that T_1 and T_2 are correctly programmed: for instance, that all modifications of the contents of a are protected in critical sections. A modification of the contents of a by T_1 is done in K_1 but is not transmitted to main memory; in consequence, a subsequent LOAD by T_2 will find an obsolete value of a.

Another difficulty arises when one task T may be executed by P_1 or P_2 depending, for instance, on the time of arrival of external interrupt signals. It may happen that a has a copy in both caches; in this situation a modification to a executed in K_1 is not reflected to K_2. After a processor switch to P_2, T will obtain an obsolete value of a. This example shows that there may be coherence problems even if no datum is shared between tasks.

It is clear that the store-through mode is not sufficient in itself to insure coherence. In the example above, on a LOAD instruction, neither processor will access main memory and modifications to the contents of a by P_1 and P_2 will be entirely uncoupled.

Evidently, a solution to the coherence problem implies the invalidation of blocks when there is a risk that their contents have been modified elsewhere in the system. One may use total preventive invalidation on carefully selected events: task switches, exit from critical sections, etc. ⋯. One may prove that this suffices to insure coherence in the absence of programming errors. This solution, however, will greatly decrease the hit ratio of the cache, and is not suited to high performance systems.

In another solution, addresses of modified blocks are broadcast throughout the system for invalidation. This is the classical solution and will be studied in the next paragraph. We will then describe a new solution in which the frequency of invalidation order is reduced by keeping tabs on the whereabout of block copies.

II. THE CLASSICAL SOLUTION

This solution is found in biprocessor systems or in monoprocessors with an independent I/O processor. These systems use the store-through mode.

To insure coherence, every cache is connected to an auxiliary data path over which all other active units send the addresses of blocks to be modified. Each cache permanently monitors this path and executes the search algorithm on all addresses thus received. In case of a hit, the VALID bit of the affected block is turned off.

The drawbacks of this solution are the following.

1) The invalidation data path must accommodate a very high traffic. The mean write rate for most processor architectures is between 10 and 30 percent. For some instructions, the peak rate is much higher: 50 percent for a long move and 100 percent for a move immediate. If the number of processors is higher than two, the productive traffic between a cache and its associated processor may be lower than the parasitic traffic between the cache and all other processors. This explains why the classical solution has been confined to systems with at most two caches.

2) Unless special precautions are taken, the cache will spend most of its time monitoring the parasitic traffic. The usual way out of this problem is to duplicate the cache directory. There is no need to interlock accesses to the two copies unless a modification of the directory is required: this is a comparatively rare event.

3) To accommodate the peak invalidation traffic, one may have to insert a small buffer to queue up addresses of modified blocks. There is a small probability of noncoherence if a read request by processor P_1 is executed between a modification by the other processor and the actual invalidation in P_1 cache. This phenomenon may or may not occur depending on such parameters as the relative timing of the cache and main store, priority schemes, etc. The resulting very low frequency inconsistencies are probably ascribed to nonreproducible hardware errors.

III. THE PRESENCE FLAG TECHNIQUE

The objective of this method is to reduce the coherence overhead by filtering out all or almost all uneffective invalidation requests.

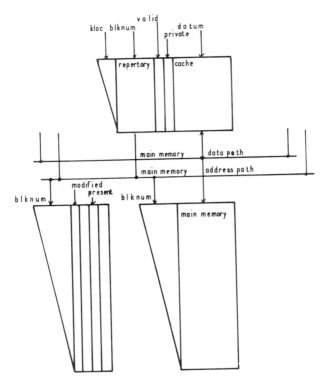

Fig. 1.   Conceptual design of a multicache system.

A first filter is implemented by associating a PRIVATE flag to each cache block. When this flag is set in a cache, this cache is the only one to have a valid copy of the block. Hence, all invalidation requests on subsequent STORE accesses may be suppressed (see Fig. 1).

A second filter may be implemented in the main memory control. In the basic design, one associates as much PRESENT flags per main memory block as there are caches in the system; the setting of the PRESENT flag for block a and cache k indicates that a has a valid copy in k. This copy may or may not be identical to its main memory counterpart. When a cache interrogates main memory, invalidation or update requests need be sent only to those cache for which PRESENT is set.

A last filter is obtained by associating a MODIFIED flag to each block in main memory, this flag being reset if the content of a main memory block is identical to all its cache copies. This allows suppression of all update requests on read-only data (e.g., instructions).

The MODIFIED and PRESENT flags are invisible from the processor point of view. They may be stored in a small auxiliary memory which is part of the main memory control. This table is addressed by the high order bits (or block number) of the address, in parallel with the main memory data stacks.

The bit overhead of this scheme is not prohibitive: for moderately sized blocks, it is much lower than the overhead of most error detection/correction designs. If this is felt to be too much, one may divide main memory in fixed size pages and effectively OR together the PRESENT flags of all blocks in a page, at the cost of a slight increase in the number of invalidation requests.

The following properties of the PRIVATE, PRESENT, and MODIFIED flags are essential to the correctness of the coherence algorithm:

1) If PRESENT is set in main memory for block a and cache k, then a has a valid copy in k.

2) If MODIFIED is set in main memory for block a, then a has a valid copy in some cache and has been modified in it since the latest update of main memory.

3) If PRIVATE is set in cache k for a VALID block a, then there is no copy of a in other caches. This implies that there is exactly one PRESENT flag set for a in main memory.

4) If PRIVATE is reset in cache k for a VALID block a, then the contents of a are identical to its counterpart in main memory. This implies that MODIFIED is reset for a.

The data access algorithms must be defined in such a way that these properties are always true, transition times being excepted.

These algorithms are divided in two processes running asynchronously in the cache controllers and in the main memory logic. These two processes exchange commands and synchronization signals. A list of these commands with a short description is given below. The precise description of each command is given in the Appendix as an Algol procedure. Integer arrays are used to represent the main memory, cache memory, and directory. Boolean arrays represent the various flags (Fig. 2).

In this mode of representation, there is no possibility to exhibit the parallelism between the different steps of the

cache

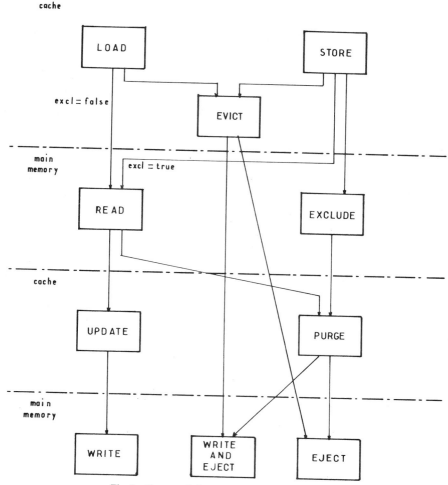

Fig. 2.   Structural chart of the coherence algorithm.

algorithms. One may say that each Algol procedure call will be replaced in the real system by the emission of a command, followed by a wait for a DONE signal. To avoid deadlocks, some priority scheme must be devised. Our proposal is to have the cache controllers always obeying the main memory commands, even while waiting for a completion signal. The responsibility for avoiding deadlocks then falls to the main memory control.

A. Instruction Processor Commands

1) LOAD requests the contents of a specified memory location.

2) STORE requests a modification to the contents of a specified memory location.

These commands are executed by the cache controller. For simplicity it will be supposed that LOAD and STORE always act on a full cache block. The modifications for implementing partial LOAD and STORE are self-evident.

B. Cache Commands

1) READ requests the contents of a specified main memory location.

2) WRITE requests a modification to the contents of a specified main memory location.

3) EJECT indicates that a non PRIVATE block has been invalidated in a cache.

4) WRITE AND EJECT combines the effects of WRITE and EJECT.

5) EXCLUDE indicates that a VALID block is going to be modified and that all copies must be PURGED.

READ may be executed in two modes:

a) The standard mode is used following a LOAD. Caches having a copy of the addressed block will be requested to send its contents back to main memory.

b) The exclusive mode is used following a STORE. Caches having a copy of the addressed block will be requested to invalidate it.

In the Algol procedure given below, these two modes are distinguished by a Boolean argument.

These commands are emitted by the cache controller and executed by the main memory controller.

C. Main Memory Commands

1) UPDATE requests that the contents of the addressed block should be copied back to main memory.

2) PURGE is similar to UPDATE, but the addressed block must be invalidated.

These commands are emitted by the main memory controller and executed by the cache controller.

D. Variations on the Presence Flag Technique

It may be felt that associating several presence flags to each block in main memory is too much of an overhead. A solution is then to divide the main memory in pages (which may or may not be the same as the pages used for a demand paging algorithm, if any), and to associate a presence flag to a page. The setting of such a flag will indicate that at least one block was copied from the page into the cache. To help in the setting of these flags, one must implement block counts, which are conveniently located in each cache in an auxiliary low speed associative memory. The block count for a page is incremented at each READ and decremented after a replacement or a successful EXCLUDE. When it steps down to zero, WRITE is replaced by WRITE AND EJECT, thus resetting the corresponding presence flag in main memory.

There are other interesting variations on the basic technique. For instance, when it is found after a LOAD or STORE that the latest version of a block is not in main memory but in a cache, it is possible to transmit directly its contents from cache to cache. The main memory may be updated in parallel with this transmission. It is also possible to postpone this operation until the block is evicted from all caches.

Other variations aim at a reduction of the miss ratio and are beyond the scope of this paper. Examples of those will be found in Bell et al. [1]. Another example is the "partial store through" mode in which a STORE is executed in the cache if the block is present and in main memory if absent. The reader will easily convince himself that these variations have no effect on coherence.

E. Performance Estimates

A rough comparison of different coherence schemes may be given under simplifying hypotheses on the data access behavior of the system. As a performance index, we will use the ratio of overhead cycles (execution of PURGE and UPDATE) to useful cycles (LOAD and STORE).

The number of caches in the system will be n. Each will contain k blocks, while the main memory will contain m blocks. α, β, and γ will designate, respectively, the proportion of instruction and constant fetches, of variable fetches, and of modifications. Obviously,

$$\alpha + \beta + \gamma = 1.$$

We will suppose that the contents of each cache are a random selection of the contents of main memory. Hence, the probability for a given block to be in a given cache will be k/m. The data accesses of a processor will not be equally distributed in memory. A proportion $(1 - \varepsilon)$ will be found in the associated cache, while the remaining accesses will be randomly distributed in memory. For the sake of simplicity, we will assume that the hit ratio is the same for LOAD and STORE accesses. This is not exactly true in reality.

The overhead ratio of the classical solution is simply

$$\rho_1 = (n - 1)\gamma$$

(each data modification will induce a PURGE in all other caches).

In the presence flag solution, a first cause of overhead will be the necessity to execute the EXCLUDE command when attempting to modify a block for which PRIVATE has been reset. Let K be a cache which receives a STORE command for block a which is present. EXCLUDE will be executed in two cases:

1) When another cache K' has executed a LOAD on a since the last STORE to a in K;
2) When a is present in K as the result of a LOAD, and no STORE has been executed on a.

As to the first cause of overhead, it is easy to see that, under our hypothesis, the mean number of cache cycles between two accesses to a in K will be of the order of k. The probability of a LOAD of a by another cache in this time interval will be $(n - 1)(\varepsilon/m)$ and the number of exclude per STORE will be of the order of $(n - 1)\varepsilon(k/m)$. As k/m is small, this is negligible with respect to $\gamma\varepsilon$ which is the number of exclusive READ induced by STORE in case of a miss.

As to the second cause of additional overhead, an upper bound may be obtained by assuming that each variable block which is brought in the cache will subsequently be modified by a STORE (this is a pessimistic assumption). Let π be the mean number of presence flags which are set for a given block, excluding the one for the cache under observation. The mean number of overhead cycles induced by LOAD on variables (in case of a miss) and STORE (in case of a hit) will be bounded by $2\varepsilon\beta\pi$. The overhead induced by STORE in case of miss will be $\varepsilon\gamma\pi$. Finally, a constant or instruction LOAD will induce no overhead, as the MODIFIED flag will always be reset in this case.

The probability of a block to be present in p caches out of $(n - 1)$ will be

$$\binom{n - 1}{p}\left(\frac{k}{m}\right)^p \left(1 - \frac{k}{m}\right)^{n - 1 - p}$$

Hence π is given by

$$\pi = \sum_{p=1}^{n-1} p \binom{n - 1}{p}\left(\frac{k}{m}\right)^p \left(1 - \frac{k}{m}\right)^{n - 1 - p} = (n - 1)\frac{k}{m}.$$

The total overhead is then less than

$$\rho_2 \leq \varepsilon(2\beta + \gamma)(n - 1)\frac{k}{m},$$

and the ratio ρ_2/ρ_1 is bounded by

$$\frac{\rho_2}{\rho_1} \leq \varepsilon \frac{2\beta + \gamma}{\gamma}\frac{k}{m}.$$

Typical values are $\beta = 0.3$, $\gamma = 0.2$, $\varepsilon = 0.1$, $k/m = 32 \cdot 10^3/4 \cdot 10^6 = 8 \cdot 10^{-3}$. This gives $\rho_2/\rho_1 \leq 3 \cdot 10^{-3}$, an improvement of nearly three orders of magnitude.

IV. CONCLUSION

While the work reported here was done without knowledge of Tang [10] the resulting design is seen to be very similar. In particular, allowing for differences in vocabulary, the set of commands exchanged between cache and main memory are nearly identical. However, Tang clearly believes that the implementation of his scheme requires duplication of all cache directories in the main memory controller: Our main contribution is to show that this is not necessary. One needs only a few bits per block in main memory (or even less if the suggestion in Section III-D is followed). It is likely that the main extra hardware in our design will be needed in the memory data path which must now be able to accommodate a bidirectional control flow.

The presence flag technique was described in the familiar context of a multicache, multiprocessor configuration. It is, however, applicable in a whole range of different situations.

A first case is that of I/O processors. It is possible to connect them directly to a main memory as long as they conform to the rules set in the preceding paragraphs, in particular as to the use of EXCLUDE and EJECT commands. The technique is specially well adapted for the exchange of orders and status information between the I/O and instruction processors.

The LOAD AND SET instruction will be implemented as an indivisible LOAD-STORE cycle from the processor to the cache; there will be no need to interlock access to the main memory. The reader may wish to convince himself that a processor executing a "busy waiting" loop (LOAD AND SET followed by a test) will not access the main memory unless another processor modifies the block addressed by the LOAD and SET instruction.

Another case is that of extracts from pages and segment tables which are held in a fast associative memory to expedite the conversion between virtual and real addresses. This memory may be considered as a kind of cache. Use of presence flags will obviate the need for systematic invalidation of the associative memory at task switching time.

Last but not least, these mechanisms may be used at all levels of a storage hierarchy, as long as a level is split in separate units which are not equally accessible from all processors.

APPENDIX

PROGRAM GLOSSARY

search — an unspecified Boolean procedure that inspects the repertory for a given block address. In case of a hit, "search" returns the cache location of the block and has the value "true."

select — an unspecified integer procedure that selects the cache block to be evicted to make room for a requested block after a miss.

blknum — a main memory block address.

knum — a cache identifier.

kloc — a cache block address.

nk — the number of caches in the system.

CACHE REPRESENTATION

cache [i, j] — an integer array representing the data part of cache j.

directory [i, j] — an integer array representing the main memory address of the block whose contents are in cache [i, j].

valid [i, j] — Boolean arrays representing the VALID.

private [i, j] — and PRIVATE flags.

MAIN MEMORY REPRESENTATION

mainmemory [i] — an integer array representing the data part of main memory.

present [i, j] — Boolean arrays representing the PRE-

modified [i] — SENT and MODIFIED flags.

```
Integer procedure load (blknum, knum);
        integer blknum, knum;
comment this procedure is executed by the cache in answer
        to a data request by an instruction processor;
begin integer kloc; boolean t;
    t := search (blknum, knum, kloc);
    if t then t := valid [kloc, knum];
    if not t then
    begin kloc := evict (blknum, knum);
        cache [kloc, knum] := read (blknum, knum,
        false);
        valid [kloc, knum] := true;
        private [kloc, knum] := false;
        directory [kloc, knum] := blknum;
    end;
    load := cache [kloc, knum];
end load;
procedure store (blknum, knum, datum);
        integer blknum, knum, datum;
comment this procedure is executed by the cache in answer
        to a data modification request by an instruction
        processor;
begin integer kloc; boolean t;
    t := search (blknum, knum, kloc);
    if t then t := valid [kloc, knum];
    if not t then begin kloc := evict (blknum, knum);
            cache [kloc, knum] := read (blknum,
            knum, true);
            valid [kloc, knum] := true;
            directory [kloc, knum] := blknum;
            end;
        else if not private [kloc, knum]
            then exclude (blknum, knum);
    private [kloc, knum] := true;
    cache [kloc, knum] := datum;
end store;
integer procedure read (blknum, knum, excl);
        integer blknum, knum; boolean excl;
comment this command is executed by main memory in
        answer to a data request by a cache;
begin integer i;
    for i := 1 step 1 until nk do
        if i ≠ knum and present [blknum, i]
        then begin if excl then purge (blknum, i);
                else if modified [blknum] then
                update (blknum, i);
            end;
    present [blknum, knum] := true;
    read := mainmemory [blknum];
    modified [blknum] := excl;
end read;
procedure exclude (blknum, knum);
        integer blknum, knum;
```

comment this procedure is executed by main memory in answer to a privacy request by a cache;

begin integer i;

    for i := 1 **step** 1 **until** nk **do**

        if i ≠ knum **and** present [blknum, i] **then**

        purge (blknum, i);

    modified [blknum] := **true**;

end exclude;

procedure update (blknum, knum);

    integer blknum, knum;

comment this procedure is executed by a cache in order to return the latest contents of a block to main memory;

begin integer kloc; **boolean** t;

    t := search (blknum, knum, kloc);

    if t **then** t := valid [kloc, knum] **and** private [kloc, knum];

    if t **then**

begin write (blknum, knum, cache [kloc, knum]);

    private [kloc, knum] := **false**;

    end;

end update;

procedure purge (blknum, knum);

    integer blknum, knum;

comment this procedure invalidates a bloc in a cache;

begin integer kloc; **boolean** t;

    t := search (blknum, knum, kloc);

    if t **then** t := valid [kloc, knum];

    if t **then**

    begin if private [kloc, knum]

        then write and eject (blknum, knum, cache [kloc, knum])

        else eject (blknum, knum);

        valid [kloc, knum] := **false**;

    end;

end purge;

integer procedure evict (blknum, knum);

    integer blknum, knum;

comment this procedure is not a command, but a common part of the LOAD and STORE commands;

begin integer kloc, addr;

    kloc := select (blknum, knum);

    if valid [kloc, knum] **then begin**

    addr := directory [kloc, knum];

    if private [kloc, knum]

        then write and eject (addr, knum, cache [kloc, knum]);

        else eject (addr, knum);

    end;

    evict := kloc;

end evict;

procedure write (blknum, knum, datum);

    integer blknum, knum, datum;

comment a procedure used to update main memory; mainmemory [blknum] := datum;

procedure eject (blknum, knum);

    integer blknum, knum;

comment a procedure used to reset a presence flag; present [blknum, knum] := **false**;

procedure writeandeject (blknum, knum, datum);

    integer blknum, knum, datum;

comment a combination of write and eject;

begin mainmemory [blknum] := datum;

     present [blknum, knum] := **false**;

    modified [blknum] := **false**

end write and eject;

ACKNOWLEDGMENT

The authors wish to thank A. Recoque and other colleagues at CII-Honeywell Bull for their constructive criticisms. The presence Flag Solution is covered by a French Patent 75.12014 assigned to CII-Honeywell Bull.

REFERENCES

[1] J. Bell, D. Casasent, and C. G. Bell, "An investigation of alternative cache organization," *IEEE Trans. Comput.*, vol. C-23, p. 346, Mar. 1974.

[2] L. Bloom, M. Cohen, and S. Porter, "Consideration in the design of a computer with a high logic-to-memory speed ratio," in *Proc. Gigacycles Computing Systems, AIEE, Winter Meeting*, Jan. 1962.

[3] C. J. Conti, D. H. Gibson, and S. H. Pitkowski, "Structural aspects of the system 360/85—General organization," *IBM Syst. J.*, vol. 7, p. 2, 1968.

[4] C. J. Conti, "Concepts for buffer storage," *IEEE Computer Group News*, vol. 2, p. 9, 1969.

[5] J. Fotheringhan, "Dynamic storage allocation in the ATLAS computer, including an automatic use of a backing store," *Comm. ACM*, vol. 4, p. 435, 1961.

[6] D. H. Gibson, "Considerations in block oriented system design," in *AFIPS Proc. SJCC*, vol. 30, p. 75, 1967.

[7] J. S. Liptay, "Structural Aspects of the System 360/85. II The cache," *IBM Syst. J.*, vol. 7, p. 15, 1968.

[8] R. M. Meade, "On memory system design," in *AFIPS FJCC*, vol. 37, p. 33, 1970.

[9] A. Opler, "Dynamic flow of programs and data through hierarchical storage," in *Proc. IFIPS Congress*, vol. 1, p. 273, 1965.

[10] C. K. Tang, "Cache system design in the tightly coupled multiprocessor system," in *AFIPS Proc.*, vol. 45, p. 749, 1976.

[11] J. Von Neumann, A. W. Burks, and H. Goldstine, "Preliminary discussion of the logical design of an electronic computing instrument," in J. Von Neumann, *Collected Works, Vol. V*. Oxford: Pergamon Press, 1963.

[12] M. V. Wilkes, "Slave memories and dynamical storage Allocation," Project MAC-M-164. Cambridge, MA: MIT, 1964.

Lucien M. Censier was born in Paris, France, in 1932. He received the Diplome d'Ingenieur from the Ecole Supérieure d'Electricité, Paris, France, in 1956.

Until 1970, his activity was oriented in research and development in the application of advanced technologies to different memory levels. Between 1970 and 1974, he participated in the design and the realization of a new minicomputer. Since 1974 his activity has been devoted towards computer architecture, memory hierarchies, and intersystem communications. He is currently with CII-Honeywell Bull, Les Clayes-sous-Bois, France.

Paul Feautrier was born in Marseille, France, in 1940. He received the Doctorate degree from Ecole Normale Supérieure, Paris, in 1968.

From 1962 to 1968, he was with the Paris Observatory, where he did research in theoretical astrophysics. Since 1968, he has been Professor at the University Pierre et Marie Curie, Paris, where he is Manager of the campus computing facility. He is currently doing research in theoretical computer science and computer architecture.

The Stanford Dash Multiprocessor

Daniel Lenoski, James Laudon, Kourosh Gharachorloo,
Wolf-Dietrich Weber, Anoop Gupta, John Hennessy,
Mark Horowitz, and Monica S. Lam
Stanford University

Directory-based cache coherence gives Dash the ease-of-use of shared-memory architectures while maintaining the scalability of message-passing machines.

The Computer Systems Laboratory at Stanford University is developing a shared-memory multiprocessor called Dash (an abbreviation for Directory Architecture for Shared Memory). The fundamental premise behind the architecture is that it is possible to build a scalable high-performance machine with a single address space and coherent caches.

The Dash architecture is scalable in that it achieves linear or near-linear performance growth as the number of processors increases from a few to a few thousand. This performance results from distributing the memory among processing nodes and using a network with scalable bandwidth to connect the nodes. The architecture allows shared data to be cached, thereby significantly reducing the latency of memory accesses and yielding higher processor utilization and higher overall performance. A distributed directory-based protocol provides cache coherence without compromising scalability.

The Dash prototype system is the first operational machine to include a scalable cache-coherence mechanism. The prototype incorporates up to 64 high-performance RISC microprocessors to yield performance up to 1.6 billion instructions per second and 600 million scalar floating point operations per second. The design of the prototype has provided deeper insight into the architectural and implementation challenges that arise in a large-scale machine with a single address space. The prototype will also serve as a platform for studying real applications and software on a large parallel system.

This article begins by describing the overall goals for Dash, the major features of the architecture, and the methods for achieving scalability. Next, we describe the directory-based coherence protocol in detail. We then provide an overview of the prototype machine and the corresponding software support, followed by some preliminary performance numbers. The article concludes with a discussion of related work and the current status of the Dash hardware and software.

Dash project overview

The overall goal of the Dash project is to investigate highly parallel architectures. For these architectures to achieve widespread use, they must run a variety of applications efficiently without imposing excessive programming difficulty. To achieve both high performance and wide applicability, we believe a parallel architecture must provide scalability to support hundreds to thousands of processors, high-performance individual processors, and a single shared address space.

The gap between the computing power of microprocessors and that of the largest supercomputers is shrinking, while the price/performance advantage of microprocessors is increasing. This clearly points to using microprocessors as the compute engines in a multiprocessor. The challenge lies in building a machine that can scale up its performance while maintaining the initial price/performance advantage of the individual processors. Scalability allows a parallel architecture to leverage commodity microprocessors and small-scale multiprocessors to build larger scale machines. These larger machines offer substantially higher performance, which provides the impetus for programmers to port their sequential applications to parallel architectures instead of waiting for the next higher performance uniprocessor.

High-performance processors are important to achieve both high total system performance and general applicability. Using the fastest microprocessors reduces the impact of limited or uneven parallelism inherent in some applications. It also allows a wider set of applications to exhibit acceptable performance with less effort from the programmer.

A single address space enhances the programmability of a parallel machine by reducing the problems of data partitioning and dynamic load distribution, two of the toughest problems in programming parallel machines. The shared address space also improves support for automatically parallelizing compilers, standard operating systems, multipro-

The Dash team

Many graduate students and faculty members contributed to the Dash project. The PhD students are Daniel Lenoski and James Laudon (Dash architecture and hardware design); Kourosh Gharachorloo (Dash architecture and consistency models); Wolf-Dietrich Weber (Dash simulator and scalable directories); Truman Joe (Dash hardware and protocol verification tools); Luis Stevens (operating system); Helen Davis and Stephen Goldschmidt (trace generation tools, synchronization patterns, locality studies); Todd Mowry (evaluation of prefetch operations); Aaron Goldberg and Margaret Martonosi (performance debugging tools); Tom Chanak (mesh routing chip design); Richard Simoni (synthetic load generator and directory studies); Josep Torrellas (sharing patterns in applications); Edward Rothberg, Jaswinder Pal Singh, and Larry Soule (applications and algorithm development). Staff research engineer David Nakahira contributed to the hardware design.

The faculty associated with the project are Anoop Gupta, John Hennessy, Mark Horowitz, and Monica Lam.

gramming, and incremental tuning of parallel applications — features that make a single-address-space machine much easier to use than a message-passing machine.

Caching of memory, including shared writable data, allows multiprocessors with a single address space to achieve high performance through reduced memory latency. Unfortunately, caching shared data introduces the problem of cache coherence (see the sidebar and accompanying figure).

While hardware support for cache coherence has its costs, it also offers many benefits. Without hardware support, the responsibility for coherence falls to the user or the compiler. Exposing the issue of coherence to the user would lead to a complex programming model, where users might well avoid caching to ease the programming bur-

den. Handling the coherence problem in the compiler is attractive, but currently cannot be done in a way that is competitive with hardware. With hardware-supported cache coherence, the compiler can aggressively optimize programs to reduce latency without having to rely purely on a conservative static dependence analysis.

The major problem with existing cache-coherent shared-address machines is that they have not demonstrated the ability to scale effectively beyond a few high-performance processors. To date, only message-passing machines have shown this ability. We believe that using a directory-based coherence mechanism will permit single-address-space machines to scale as well as message-passing machines, while providing a more flexible and general programming model.

Dash system organization

Most existing multiprocessors with cache coherence rely on snooping to maintain coherence. Unfortunately, snooping schemes distribute the information about which processors are caching which data items among the caches. Thus, straightforward snooping schemes require that all caches see every memory request from every processor. This inherently limits the scalability of these machines because the common bus and the individual processor caches eventually saturate. With today's high-performance RISC processors this saturation can occur with just a few processors.

Directory structures avoid the scalability problems of snoopy schemes by removing the need to broadcast every memory request to all processor caches. The directory maintains pointers to the processor caches holding a copy of each memory block. Only the caches with copies can be affected by an access to the memory block, and only those caches need be notified of the access. Thus, the processor caches and interconnect will not saturate due to coherence requests. Furthermore, directory-based coherence is not dependent on any specific interconnection network like the bus used by most snooping schemes. The same scalable, low-latency networks such as Omega networks or k-nary n-cubes used by non-cache-coherent and

Cache coherence

Cache-coherence problems can arise in shared-memory multiprocessors when more than one processor cache holds a copy of a data item (a). Upon a write, these copies must be updated or invalidated (b). Most systems use invalidation since this allows the writing processor to gain exclusive access to the cache line and complete further writes into the cache line without generating external traffic (c). This further complicates coherence since this dirty cache must respond instead of memory on subsequent accesses by other processors (d).

Small-scale multiprocessors frequently use a snoopy cache-coherence protocol,[1] which relies on all caches monitoring the common bus that connects the processors to memory. This monitoring allows caches to independently determine when to invalidate cache lines (b), and when to intervene because they contain the most up-to-date copy of a given location (d). Snoopy schemes do not scale to a large number of processors because the common bus or individual processor caches eventually saturate, since they must process every memory request from every processor.

The directory relieves the processor caches from snooping on memory requests by keeping track of which caches hold each memory block. A simple directory structure first proposed by Censier and Feautrier[2] has one directory entry per block of memory (e). Each entry contains one presence bit per processor cache. In addition, a state bit indicates whether the block is uncached, shared in multiple caches, or held exclusively by one cache (that is, whether the block is dirty). Using the state and presence bits, the memory can tell which caches need to be invalidated when a location is written (b). Likewise, the directory indicates whether memory's copy of the block is up to date or which cache holds the most recent copy (d). If the memory and directory are partitioned into independent units and connected to the processors by a scalable interconnect, the memory system can provide scalable memory bandwidth.

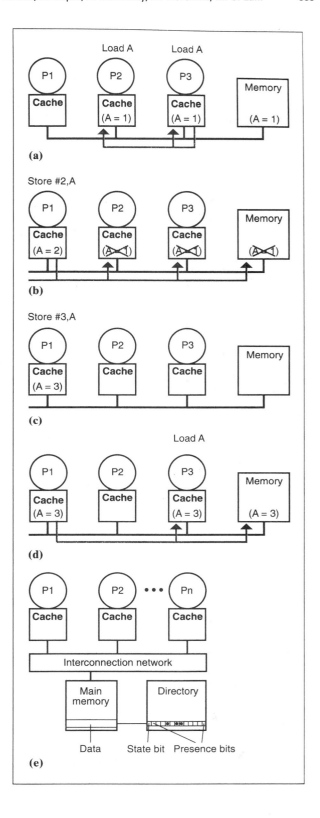

References

1. J. Archibald and J.-L. Baer, "Cache Coherence Protocols: Evaluation Using a Multiprocessor Simulation Model," *ACM Trans. Computer Systems*, Vol. 4, No. 4, Nov. 1986, pp. 273-298.

2. L. Censier and P. Feautrier, "A New Solution to Coherence Problems in Multicache Systems," *IEEE Trans. Computers*, Vol. C-27, No. 12, Dec. 1978, pp. 1,112-1,118.

message-passing machines can be employed.

The concept of directory-based cache coherence is not new. It was first proposed in the late 1970s. However, the original directory structures were not scalable because they used a centralized directory that quickly became a bottleneck. The Dash architecture overcomes this limitation by partitioning and distributing the directory and main memory, and by using a new coherence protocol that can suitably exploit distributed directories. In addition, Dash provides several other mechanisms to reduce and hide the latency of memory operations.

Figure 1 shows Dash's high-level organization. The architecture consists of a number of processing nodes connected through directory controllers to a low-latency interconnection network. Each processing node, or *cluster*, consists of a small number of high-performance processors and a portion of the shared memory interconnected by a bus. Multiprocessing within the cluster can be viewed either as increasing the power of each processing node or as reducing the cost of the directory and network interface by amortizing it over a larger number of processors.

Distributing memory with the processors is essential because it allows the system to exploit locality. All private data and code references, along with some of the shared references, can be made local to the cluster. These references avoid the longer latency of remote references and reduce the bandwidth demands on the global interconnect. Except for the directory memory, the resulting system

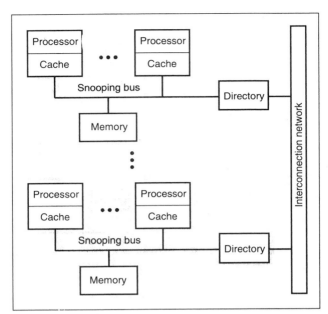

Figure 1. The Dash architecture consists of a set of clusters connected by a general interconnection network. Directory memory contains pointers to the clusters currently caching each memory line.

architecture is similar to many scalable message-passing machines. While not optimized to do so, Dash could emulate such machines with reasonable efficiency.

Scalability of the Dash approach

We have outlined why we believe a single-address-space machine with cache coherence holds the most promise for delivering scalable performance to a wide range of applications. Here, we address the more detailed issues in scaling such a directory-based system. The three primary issues are ensuring that the system provides scalable memory bandwidth, that the costs scale reasonably, and that mechanisms are provided to deal with large memory latencies.

Scalability in a multiprocessor requires the total memory bandwidth to scale linearly with the number of processors. Dash provides scalable bandwidth to data objects residing in local memory by distributing the physical memory among the clusters. For data accesses that must be serviced remotely, Dash uses a scalable interconnection network. Support

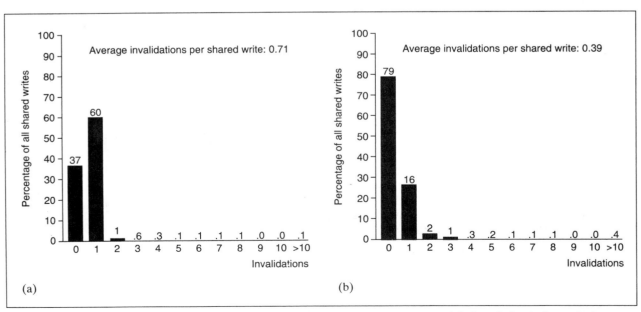

Figure 2. Cache invalidation patterns for MP3D (a) and PThor (b). MP3D uses a particle-based simulation technique to determine the structure of shock waves caused by objects flying at high speed in the upper atmosphere. PThor is a parallel logic simulator based on the Chandy-Misra algorithm.

of coherent caches could potentially compromise the scalability of the network by requiring frequent broadcast messages. The use of directories, however, removes the need for such broadcasts and the coherence traffic consists only of point-to-point messages to clusters that are caching that location. Since these clusters must have originally fetched the data, the coherence traffic will be within some small constant factor of the original data traffic. In fact, since each cached block is usually referenced several times before being invalidated, caching normally reduces overall global traffic significantly.

This discussion of scalability assumes that the accesses are uniformly distributed across the machine. Unfortunately, the uniform access assumption does not always hold for highly contended synchronization objects and for heavily shared data objects. The resulting *hot spots* — concentrated accesses to data from the memory of a single cluster over a short duration of time — can significantly reduce the memory and network throughput. The reduction occurs because the distribution of resources is not exploited as it is under uniform access patterns.

To address hot spots, Dash relies on a combination of hardware and software techniques. For example, Dash provides special extensions to the directory-based protocol to handle synchronization references such as queue-based locks (discussed further in the section, "Support for synchronization"). Furthermore, since Dash allows caching of shared writable data, it avoids many of the data hot spots that occur in other parallel machines that do not permit such caching. For hot spots that cannot be mitigated by caching, some can be removed by the coherence protocol extensions discussed in the section, "Update and deliver operations," while others can only be removed by restructuring at the software level. For example, when using a primitive such as a barrier, it is possible for software to avoid hot spots by gathering and releasing processors through a tree of memory locations.

Regarding system costs, a major scalability concern unique to Dash-like machines is the amount of directory memory required. If the physical memory in the machine grows proportionally with the number of processing nodes, then using a bit-vector to keep track of all

clusters caching a memory block does not scale well. The total amount of directory memory needed is $P^2 \times M/L$ megabits, where P is the number of clusters, M is the megabits of memory per cluster, and L is the cache-line size in bits. Thus, the fraction of memory devoted to keeping directory information grows as P/L. Depending on the machine size, this growth may or may not be tolerable. For example, consider a machine that contains up to 32 clusters of eight processors each and has a cache (memory) line size of 32 bytes. For this machine, the overhead for directory memory is only 12.5 percent of physical memory as the system scales from eight to 256 processors. This is comparable with the overhead of supporting an error-correcting code on memory.

For larger machines, where the overhead would become intolerable, several alternatives exist. First, we can take advantage of the fact that at any given time a memory block is usually cached by a very small number of processors. For example, Figure 2 shows the number of invalidations generated by two applications run on a simulated 32-processor machine. These graphs show that most writes cause invalidations to only a few caches. (We have obtained similar results for a large number of applications.) Consequently, it is possible to replace the complete directory bit-vector by a small number of pointers and to use a limited broadcast of invalidations in the unusual case when the number of pointers is too small. Second, we can take advantage of the fact that most main memory blocks will not be present in any processor's cache, and thus there is no need to provide a dedicated directory entry for every memory block. Studies[1,2] have shown that a small directory cache performs almost as well as a full directory. These two techniques can be combined to support machines with thousands of processors without undue overhead from directory memory.

The issue of memory access latency also becomes more prominent as an architecture is scaled to a larger number of nodes. There are two complementary approaches for managing latency: methods that reduce latency and mechanisms that help tolerate it. Dash uses both approaches, though our main focus has been to reduce latency as much as possible. Although latency tolerating techniques are important, they often

require additional application parallelism to be effective.

Hardware-coherent caches provide the primary latency reduction mechanism in Dash. Caching shared data significantly reduces the average latency for remote accesses because of the spatial and temporal locality of memory accesses. For references not satisfied by the cache, the coherence protocol attempts to minimize latency, as shown in the next section. Furthermore, as previously mentioned, we can reduce latency by allocating data to memory close to the processors that use it. While average memory latency is reduced, references that correspond to interprocessor communication cannot avoid the inherent latencies of a large machine. In Dash, the latency for these accesses is addressed by a variety of latency hiding mechanisms. These mechanisms range from support of a relaxed memory consistency model to support of nonblocking prefetch operations. These operations are detailed in the sections on "Memory consistency" and "Prefetch operations."

We also expect software to play a critical role in achieving good performance on a highly parallel machine. Obviously, applications need to exhibit good parallelism to exploit the rich computational resources of a large machine. In addition, applications, compilers, and operating systems need to exploit cache and memory locality together with latency hiding techniques to achieve high processor utilization. Applications still benefit from the single address space, however, because only performance-critical code needs to be tuned to the system. Other code can assume a simple uniform memory model.

The Dash cache-coherence protocol

Within the Dash system organization, there is still a great deal of freedom in selecting the specific cache-coherence protocol. This section explains the basic coherence protocol that Dash uses for normal read and write operations, then outlines the resulting memory consistency model visible to the programmer and compiler. Finally, it details extensions to the protocol that support latency hiding and efficient synchronization.

Memory hierarchy. Dash implements an invalidation-based cache-coherence protocol. A memory location may be in one of three states:

- *uncached* — not cached by any cluster;
- *shared* — in an unmodified state in the caches of one or more clusters; or
- *dirty* — modified in a single cache of some cluster.

The directory keeps the summary information for each memory block, specifying its state and the clusters that are caching it.

The Dash memory system can be logically broken into four levels of hierarchy, as illustrated in Figure 3. The first level is the processor's cache. This cache is designed to match the processor speed and support snooping from the bus. A request that cannot be serviced by the processor's cache is sent to the second level in the hierarchy, the *local cluster*. This level includes the other processors' caches within the requesting processor's cluster. If the data is locally cached, the request can be serviced within the cluster. Otherwise, the request is sent to the *home cluster* level. The home level consists of the cluster that contains the directory and physical memory for a given memory address. For many accesses (for example, most private data references), the local and home cluster are the same, and the hierarchy collapses to three levels. In general, however, a request will travel through the interconnection network to the home cluster. The home cluster can usually satisfy the request immediately, but if the directory entry is in a dirty state, or in shared state when the requesting processor requests exclusive access, the fourth level must also be accessed. The *remote cluster* level for a memory block consists of the clusters marked by the directory as holding a copy of the block.

To illustrate the directory protocol, first consider how a processor read traverses the memory hierarchy:

- *Processor level* — If the requested location is present in the processor's cache, the cache simply supplies the data. Otherwise, the request goes to the local cluster level.
- *Local cluster level* — If the data resides within one of the other caches within the local cluster, the data is sup-

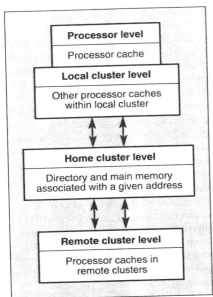

Figure 3. Memory hierarchy of Dash.

plied by that cache and no state change is required at the directory level. If the request must be sent beyond the local cluster level, it goes first to the home cluster corresponding to that address.

- *Home cluster level* — The home cluster examines the directory state of the memory location while simultaneously fetching the block from main memory. If the block is clean, the data is sent to the requester and the directory is updated to show sharing by the requester. If the location is dirty, the request is forwarded to the remote cluster indicated by the directory.
- *Remote cluster level* — The dirty cluster replies with a shared copy of the data, which is sent directly to the requester. In addition, a sharing write-back message is sent to the home level to update main memory and change the directory state to indicate that the requesting and remote cluster now have shared copies of the data. Having the dirty cluster respond directly to the requester, as opposed to routing it through the home, reduces the latency seen by the requesting processor.

Now consider the sequence of operations that occurs when a location is written:

- *Processor level* — If the location is dirty in the writing processor's cache, the write can complete immediately. Otherwise, a read-exclusive request is

issued on the local cluster's bus to obtain exclusive ownership of the line and retrieve the remaining portion of the cache line.

- *Local cluster level* — If one of the caches within the cluster already owns the cache line, then the read-exclusive request is serviced at the local level by a cache-to-cache transfer. This allows processors within a cluster to alternately modify the same memory block without any intercluster interaction. If no local cache owns the block, then a read-exclusive request is sent to the home cluster.
- *Home cluster level* — The home cluster can immediately satisfy an ownership request for a location that is in the uncached or shared state. In addition, if a block is in the shared state, then all cached copies must be invalidated. The directory indicates the clusters that have the block cached. Invalidation requests are sent to these clusters while the home concurrently sends an exclusive data reply to the requesting cluster. If the directory indicates that the block is dirty, then the read-exclusive request must be forwarded to the dirty cluster, as in the case of a read.
- *Remote cluster level* — If the directory had indicated that the memory block was shared, then the remote clusters receive an invalidation request to eliminate their shared copy. Upon receiving the invalidation, the remote clusters send an acknowledgment to the requesting cluster. If the directory had indicated a dirty state, then the dirty cluster receives a read-exclusive request. As in the case of the read, the remote cluster responds directly to the requesting cluster and sends a dirty-transfer message to the home indicating that the requesting cluster now holds the block exclusively.

When the writing cluster receives all the invalidation acknowledgments or the reply from the home or dirty cluster, it is guaranteed that all copies of the old data have been purged from the system. If the processor delays completing the write until all acknowledgments are received, then the new write value will become available to all other processors at the same time. However, invalidations involve round-trip messages to multiple clusters, resulting in potentially long delays. Higher processor utilization can be obtained by allowing the write to proceed immediately after the ownership reply is received from the home. Unfortunately, this may lead to inconsistencies with the memory model assumed by the programmer. The next section describes how Dash relaxes the constraints on memory request ordering, while still providing a reasonable programming model to the user.

Memory consistency. The memory consistency model supported by an architecture directly affects the amount of buffering and pipelining that can take place among memory requests. In addition, it has a direct effect on the complexity of the programming model presented to the user. The goal in Dash is to provide substantial freedom in the ordering among memory requests, while still providing a reasonable programming model to the user.

At one end of the consistency spectrum is the *sequential consistency* model,[3] which requires execution of the parallel program to appear as an interleaving of the execution of the parallel processes on a sequential machine. Sequential consistency can be guaranteed by requiring a processor to complete one memory request before it issues the next request.[4] Sequential consistency, while conceptually appealing, imposes a large performance penalty on memory accesses. For many applications, such a model is too strict, and one can make do with a weaker notion of consistency.

As an example, consider the case of a processor updating a data structure within a critical section. If updating the structure requires several writes, each write in a sequentially consistent system will stall the processor until all other cached copies of that location have been invalidated. But these stalls are unnecessary as the programmer has already made sure that no other process can rely on the consistency of that data structure until the critical section is exited. If the synchronization points can be identified, then the memory need only be consistent at those points. In particular, Dash supports the use of the *release consistency* model,[5] which only requires the operations to have completed before a critical section is released (that is, a lock is unlocked).

Such a scheme has two advantages. First, it provides the user with a reasonable programming model, since the programmer is assured that when the critical section is exited, all other processors will have a consistent view of the mod-

> **Release consistency provides a 10- to 40-percent increase in performance over sequential consistency.**

ified data structure. Second, it permits reads to bypass writes and the invalidations of different write operations to overlap, resulting in lower latencies for accesses and higher overall performance. Detailed simulation studies for processors with blocking reads have shown that release consistency provides a 10- to 40-percent increase in performance over sequential consistency.[5] The disadvantage of the model is that the programmer or compiler must identify all synchronization accesses.

The Dash prototype supports the release consistency model in hardware. Since we use commercial microprocessors, the processor stalls on read operations until the read data is returned from the cache or lower levels of the memory hierarchy. Write operations, however, are nonblocking. There is a write buffer between the first- and second-level caches. The write buffer queues up the write requests and issues them in order. Furthermore, the servicing of write requests is overlapped. As soon as the cache receives the ownership and data for the requested cache line, the write data is removed from the write buffer and written into the cache line. The next write request can be serviced while the invalidation acknowledgments for the previous write operations filter in. Thus, parallelism exists at two levels: the processor executes other instructions and accesses its first-level cache while write operations are pending, and invalidations of multiple write operations are overlapped.

The Dash prototype also provides fence operations that stall the processor or write-buffer until previous operations complete. These fence operations allow software to emulate more stringent consistency models.

Memory access optimizations. The use of release consistency helps hide the latency of write operations. However,

since the processor stalls on read operations, it sees the entire duration of all read accesses. For applications that exhibit poor cache behavior or extensive read/write sharing, this can lead to significant delays while the processor waits for remote cache misses to be filled. To help with these problems Dash provides a variety of prefetch and pipelining operations.

Prefetch operations. A prefetch operation is an explicit nonblocking request to fetch data before the actual memory operation is issued. Hopefully, by the time the process needs the data, its value has been brought closer to the processor, hiding the latency of the regular blocking read. In addition, nonblocking prefetch allows the pipelining of read misses when multiple cache blocks are prefetched. As a simple example of its use, a process wanting to access a row of a matrix stored in another cluster's memory can do so efficiently by first issuing prefetch reads for all cache blocks corresponding to that row.

Dash's prefetch operations are nonbinding and software controlled. The processor issues explicit prefetch operations that bring a shared or exclusive copy of the memory block into the processor's cache. Not binding the value at the time of the prefetch is important in that issuing the prefetch does not affect the consistency model or force the compiler to do a conservative static dependency analysis. The coherence protocol keeps the prefetched cache line coherent. If another processor happens to write to the location before the prefetching processor accesses the data, the data will simply be invalidated. The prefetch will be rendered ineffective, but the program will execute correctly. Support for an exclusive prefetch operation aids cases where the block is first read and then updated. By first issuing the exclusive prefetch, the processor avoids first obtaining a shared copy and then having to rerequest an exclusive copy of the block. Studies have shown that, for certain applications, the addition of a small number of prefetch instructions can increase processor utilization by more than a factor of two.[6]

Update and deliver operations. In some applications, it may not be possible for the consumer process to issue a prefetch early enough to effectively hide the latency of memory. Likewise, if multiple consumers need the same item of data, the communication traffic can be reduced if data is multicast to all the consumers simultaneously. Therefore, Dash provides operations that allow the producer to send data directly to consumers. There are two ways for the producing processor to specify the consuming processors. The *update-write* operation sends the new data directly to all processors that have cached the data, while the *deliver* operation sends the data to specified clusters.

The *update-write* primitive updates the value of all existing copies of a data word. Using this primitive, a processor does not need to first acquire an exclusive copy of the cache line, which would result in invalidating all other copies. Rather, data is directly written into the home memory and all other caches holding a copy of the line. These semantics are particularly useful for event synchronization, such as the release event for a barrier.

The *deliver* instruction explicitly specifies the destination clusters of the transfer. To use this primitive, the producer first writes into its cache using normal, invalidating write operations. The producer then issues a deliver instruction, giving the destination clusters as a bit vector. A copy of the cache line is then sent to the specified clusters, and the directory is updated to indicate that the various clusters now share the data. This operation is useful in cases when the producer makes multiple writes to a block before the consumers will want it or when the consumers are unlikely to be caching the item at the time of the write.

Support for synchronization. The access patterns to locations used for synchronization are often different from those for other shared data. For example, whenever a highly contended lock is released, waiting nodes rush to grab the lock. In the case of barriers, many processors must be synchronized and then released. Such activity often causes hot spots in the memory system. Consequently, synchronization variables often warrant special treatment. In addition to update writes, Dash provides two extensions to the coherence protocol that directly support synchronization objects. The first is queue-based locks, and the second is fetch-and-increment operations.

Most cache-coherent architectures handle locks by providing an atomic

test&set instruction and a cached test-and-test&set scheme for spin waiting. Ideally, these spin locks should meet the following criteria:

- minimum amount of traffic generated while waiting,
- low latency release of a waiting processor, and
- low latency acquisition of a free lock.

Cached test&set schemes are moderately successful in satisfying these criteria for low-contention locks, but fail for high-contention locks. For example, assume there are N processors spinning on a lock value in their caches. When the lock is released, all N cache values are invalidated, and N reads are generated to the memory system. Depending on the timing, it is possible that all N processors come back to do the test&set on the location once they realize the lock is free, resulting in further invalidations and rereads. Such a scenario produces unnecessary traffic and increases the latency in acquiring and releasing a lock.

The *queue-based locks* in Dash address this problem by using the directory to indicate which processors are spinning on the lock. When the lock is released, one of the waiting clusters is chosen at random and is granted the lock. The grant request invalidates only that cluster's caches and allows one processor within that cluster to acquire the lock with a local operation. This scheme lowers both the traffic and the latency involved in releasing a processor waiting on a lock. Informing only one cluster of the release also eliminates unnecessary traffic and latency that would be incurred if all waiting processors were allowed to contend. A time-out mechanism on the lock grant allows the grant to be sent to another cluster if the spinning process has been swapped out or migrated. The queued-on-lock-bit primitive described in Goodman et al.[7] is similar to Dash's queue-based locks, but uses pointers in the processor caches to maintain the list of the waiting processors.

The *fetch-and-increment* and *fetch-and-decrement* primitives provide atomic increment and decrement operations on uncached memory locations. The value returned by the operations is the value before the increment or decrement. These operations have low serialization and are useful for implementing several

synchronization primitives such as barriers, distributed loops, and work queues. The serialization of these operations is small because they are done directly at the memory site. The low serialization provided by the fetch-and-increment operation is especially important when many processors want to increment a location, as happens when getting the next index in a distributed loop. The benefits of the proposed operations become apparent when contrasted with the alternative of using a normal variable protected by a lock to achieve the atomic increment and decrement. The alternative results in significantly more traffic, longer latency, and increased serialization.

The Dash implementation

A hardware prototype of the Dash architecture is currently under construction. While we have developed a detailed software simulator of the system, we feel that a hardware implementation is needed to fully understand the issues in the design of scalable cache-coherent machines, to verify the feasibility of such designs, and to provide a platform for studying real applications and software running on a large ensemble of processors.

To focus our effort on the novel aspects of the design and to speed the completion of a usable system, the base cluster hardware used in the prototype is a commercially available bus-based multiprocessor. While there are some constraints imposed by the given hardware, the prototype satisfies our primary goals of scalable memory bandwidth and high performance. The prototype includes most of Dash's architectural features since many of them can only be fully evaluated on the actual hardware. The system also includes dedicated performance monitoring logic to aid in the evaluation.

Dash prototype cluster. The prototype system uses a Silicon Graphics Power Station 4D/340 as the base cluster. The 4D/340 system consists of four Mips R3000 processors and R3010 floating-point coprocessors running at 33 megahertz. Each R3000/R3010 combination can reach execution rates up to 25 VAX MIPS and 10 Mflops. Each

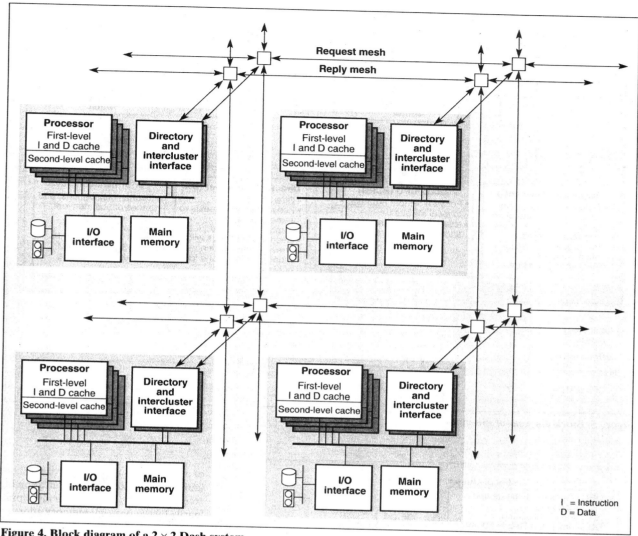

Figure 4. Block diagram of a 2 × 2 Dash system.

CPU contains a 64-kilobyte instruction cache and a 64-Kbyte write-through data cache. The 64-Kbyte data cache interfaces to a 256-Kbyte second-level write-back cache. The interface consists of a read buffer and a four-word-deep write buffer. Both the first- and second-level caches are direct-mapped and support 16-byte lines. The first level caches run synchronously to their associated 33-MHz processors while the second level caches run synchronous to the 16-MHz memory bus.

The second-level processor caches are responsible for bus snooping and maintaining coherence among the caches in the cluster. Coherence is maintained using an Illinois, or MESI (modified, exclusive, shared, invalid), protocol. The main advantage of using the Illinois protocol in Dash is the cache-to-cache transfers specified in it. While they do little

to reduce the latency for misses serviced by local memory, local cache-to-cache transfers can greatly reduce the penalty for remote memory misses. The set of processor caches acts as a cluster cache for remote memory. The memory bus (MPbus) of the 4D/340 is a synchronous bus and consists of separate 32-bit address and 64-bit data buses. The MP-bus is pipelined and supports memory-to-cache and cache-to-cache transfers of 16 bytes every four bus clocks with a latency of six bus clocks. This results in a maximum bandwidth of 64 Mbytes per second. While the MPbus is pipelined, it is not a split-transaction bus.

To use the 4D/340 in Dash, we have had to make minor modifications to the existing system boards and design a pair of new boards to support the directory memory and intercluster interface. The main modification to the existing boards

is to add a bus retry signal that is used when a request requires service from a remote cluster. The central bus arbiter has also been modified to accept a mask from the directory. The mask holds off a processor's retry until the remote request has been serviced. This effectively creates a split-transaction bus protocol for requests requiring remote service. The new directory controller boards contain the directory memory, the intercluster coherence state machines and buffers, and a local section of the global interconnection network. The interconnection network consists of a pair of wormhole routed meshes, each with 16-bit wide channels. One mesh is dedicated to the request messages while the other handles replies. Figure 4 shows a block diagram of four clusters connected to form a 2 × 2 Dash system. Such a system could scale to support hundreds

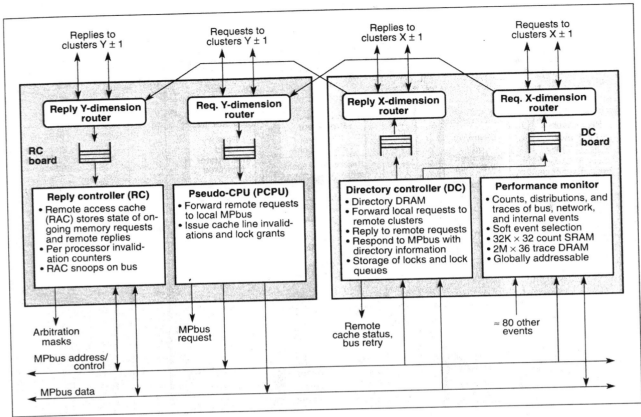

Figure 5. Block diagram of directory boards.

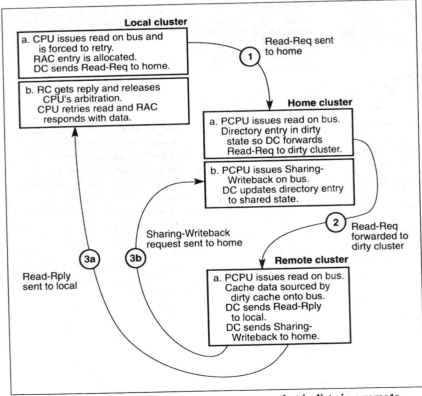

Figure 6. Flow of a read request to remote memory that is dirty in a remote cluster.

of processors, but the prototype will be limited to a maximum configuration of 16 clusters. This limit was dictated primarily by the physical memory addressability (256 Mbytes) of the 4D/340 system, but still allows for systems up to 64 processors that are capable of 1.6 GIPS and 600 scalar Mflops.

Dash directory logic. The directory logic implements the directory-based coherence protocol and connects the clusters within the system. Figure 5 shows a block diagram of the directory boards. The directory logic is split between the two logic boards along the lines of the logic used for outbound and inbound portions of intercluster transactions.

The directory controller (DC) board contains three major sections. The first is the directory controller itself, which includes the directory memory associated with the cachable main memory contained within the cluster. The DC logic initiates all outbound network requests and replies. The second section is the performance monitor, which can count and trace a variety of intra- and intercluster events. The third major section is the request and reply outbound network logic together with the X-dimension of the network itself.

Each bus transaction accesses directory memory. The directory information is combined with the type of bus operation, the address, and the result of snooping on the caches to determine what network messages and bus controls the DC will generate. The directory memory itself is implemented as a bit vector with one bit for each of the 16 clusters. While a full-bit vector has limited scalability, it was chosen because it requires roughly the same amount of memory as a limited pointer directory given the size of the prototype, and it allows for more direct measurements of the machine's caching behavior. Each directory entry contains a single state bit that indicates whether the clusters have a shared or dirty copy of the data. The directory is implemented using dynamic RAM technology, but performs all necessary actions within a single bus transaction.

The second board is the reply controller (RC) board, which also contains three major sections. The first section is the reply controller, which tracks outstanding requests made by the local processors and receives and buffers replies from remote clusters using the remote access cache (RAC). The second section is the pseudo-CPU (PCPU), which buffers incoming requests and issues them to the cluster bus. The PCPU mimics a CPU on this bus on behalf of remote processors except that responses from the bus are sent out by the directory controller. The final section is the inbound network logic and the Y-dimension of the mesh routing networks.

The reply controller stores the state of ongoing requests in the remote access cache. The RAC's primary role is the coordination of replies to intercluster transactions. This ranges from the simple buffering of reply data between the network and bus to the accumulation of invalidation acknowledgments and the enforcement of release consistency. The RAC is organized as a 128-Kbyte direct-mapped snoopy cache with 16-byte cache lines.

One port of the RAC services the inbound reply network while the other snoops on bus transactions. The RAC is lockup-free in that it can handle several outstanding remote requests from each of the local processors. RAC entries are allocated when a local processor initiates a remote request, and they persist until all intercluster transactions relative to that request have completed. The snoopy nature of the RAC naturally lends itself to merging requests made to the same cache block by different processors and takes advantage of the cache-to-cache transfer protocol supported between the local processors. The snoopy structure also allows the RAC to supplement the function of the processor caches. This includes support for a dirty-sharing state for a cluster (normally the Illinois protocol would force a write-back) and operations such as prefetch.

Interconnection network. As stated in the architecture section, the Dash coherence protocol does not rely on a particular interconnection network topology. However, for the architecture to be scalable, the network itself must provide scalable bandwidth. It should also provide low-latency communication. The prototype system uses a pair of *wormhole* routed meshes to implement the interconnection network. One mesh handles request messages while the other is dedicated to replies. The networks are based on variants of the mesh routing chips developed at the California Institute of Technology, where the data paths have been extended from 8 to 16 bits. Wormhole routing allows a cluster to forward a message after receiving only the first flit (flow unit) of the packet, greatly reducing the latency through each node. The average latency for each hop in the network is approximately 50 nanoseconds. The networks are asynchronous and self-timed. The bandwidth of each link is limited by the round-trip delay of the request-acknowledge signals. The prototype transfers flits at approximately 30 MHz, resulting in a total bandwidth of 120 Mbytes/second in and out of each cluster.

An important constraint on the network is that it must deliver request and reply messages without deadlocking. Most networks, including the meshes used in Dash, are guaranteed to be deadlock-free if messages are consumed at the receiving cluster. Unfortunately, the Dash prototype cannot guarantee this due, first, to the limited buffering on the directory boards and also to the fact that a cluster may need to generate an outgoing message before it can consume an incoming message. For example, to service a read request, the home cluster must generate a reply message containing the data. Similarly, to process a request for a dirty location in a remote cluster, the home cluster needs to generate a forwarding request to that cluster. This requirement adds the potential for deadlocks that consist of a sequence of messages having circular dependencies through a node.

Dash avoids these deadlocks through three mechanisms. First, reply messages can always be consumed because they are allocated a dedicated reply buffer in the RAC. Second, the independent request and reply meshes eliminate request-reply deadlocks. Finally, a back-off mechanism breaks potential deadlocks due to request-request dependencies. If inbound requests cannot be forwarded because of blockages on the outbound request port, the requests are rejected by sending negative acknowledgment reply messages. Rejected requests are then retried by the issuing processor.

Coherence examples. The following examples illustrate how the various structures described in the previous sections interact to carry out the coherence protocol. For a more detailed discussion of the protocol, see Lenoski et al.[8]

Figure 6 shows a simple read of a memory location whose home is in a remote cluster and whose directory state is dirty in another cluster. The read request is not satisfied on the local cluster bus, so a Read-Req (message 1) is sent to the home. At this time the processor is told to retry, and its arbitration is masked. A RAC entry is allocated to track this message and assign ownership of the reply. The PCPU at the home receives the Read-Req and issues a cache read on the bus. The directory memory is accessed and indicates that the cache block is dirty in another cluster. The directory controller in the home forwards the Read-Req (message 2) to the dirty remote cluster. The PCPU in the dirty cluster issues the read on the dirty cluster's bus and the dirty processor's cache responds. The DC in the dirty cluster sends a Read-Rply (message 3a) to the local cluster and a Sharing-Write-back (message 3b) request to the home to update the directory and main memory. The RC in the local cluster receives the reply into the RAC, releases the requesting CPU for arbitration, and then sources the data onto the bus when the processor retries the read. In parallel,

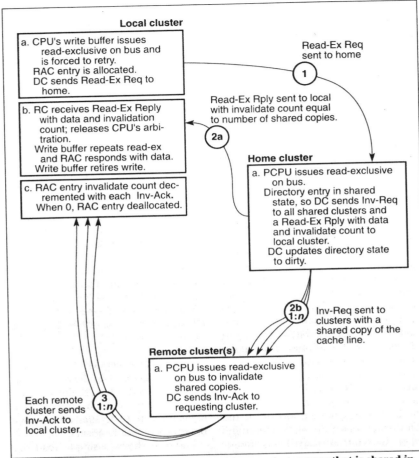

Figure 7. Flow of a read-exclusive request to remote memory that is shared in remote clusters.

the Sharing-Writeback request is received by the home PCPU, which issues it onto the bus. The sharing writeback updates the directory to a shared state indicating that the local and dirty clusters now have a read-only copy of the memory block.

Figure 7 shows the corresponding sequence for a store operation that requires remote service. The invalidation-based protocol requires the processor (actually the write buffer) to acquire exclusive ownership of the cache block before completing the store. Thus, if a store is made to a block that the processor does not have cached, or only has cached in a shared state, the processor issues a read-exclusive request on the local bus. In this case, no other cache holds the block dirty in the local cluster so a Read-Ex Req (message 1) is sent to the home cluster. As before, a RAC entry is allocated in the local cluster. At the home, the PCPU issues the read-exclusive request to the bus. The directory indicates that the line is in the shared state. This results in the DC sending a Read-Ex Rply (message 2a) to the local cluster and invalidation requests (Inv-Req, messages 2b) to the sharing clusters. The home cluster owns the block, so it can immediately update the directory to the dirty state indicating that the local cluster now holds an exclusive copy of the memory line. The

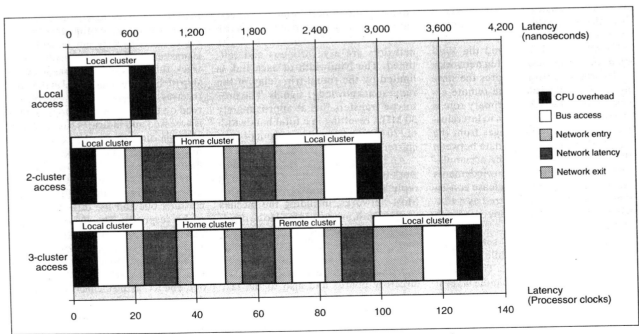

Figure 8. Latency of read requests on a 64-processor Dash prototype without contention.

Read-Ex Rply message is received in the local cluster by the RC, which can then satisfy the read-exclusive request. To assure consistency at release points, however, the RAC entry persists even after the write-buffer's request is satisfied. The RAC entry is only deallocated when it receives the number of invalidate acknowledgments (Inv-Ack, message 3) equal to an invalidation count sent in the original reply message. The RC maintains per-processor RAC allocation counters to allow the hardware to stall releasing synchronization operations until all earlier writes issued by the given processor have completed systemwide.

An important feature of the coherence protocol is its forwarding strategy. If a cluster cannot reply directly to a given request, it forwards responsibility for the request to a cluster that should be able to respond. This technique minimizes the latency for a request, as it always forwards the request to where the data is thought to be and allows a reply to be sent directly to the requesting cluster. This technique also minimizes the serialization of requests since no cluster resources are blocked while intercluster messages are being sent. Forwarding allows the directory controller to work on multiple requests concurrently (that is, makes it multithreaded) without having to retain any additional state about forwarded requests.

Software support

A comprehensive software development environment is essential to make effective use of large-scale multiprocessors. For Dash, our efforts have focused on four major areas: operating systems, compilers, programming languages, and performance debugging tools.

Dash supports a full-function Unix operating system. In contrast, many other highly parallel machines (for example, Intel iPSC2, Ncube, iWarp) support only a primitive kernel on the node processors and rely on a separate host system for program development. Dash avoids the complications and inefficiencies of a host system. Furthermore, the resident operating system can efficiently support multiprogramming and multiple users on the system. Developed in cooperation with Silicon Graphics, the Dash OS is a modified version of the existing operating system on the 4D/340 (Irix, a variation of Unix System V.3). Since Irix was already multithreaded and worked with multiple processors, many of our changes have been made to accommodate the hierarchical nature of Dash, where processors, main memory, and I/O devices are all partitioned across the clusters. We have also adapted the Irix kernel to provide access to the special hardware features of Dash such as prefetch, update write, and queue-based locks. Currently, the modified OS is running on a four-cluster Dash system, and we are exploring several new algorithms for process scheduling and memory allocation that will exploit the Dash memory hierarchy.

At the user level, we are working on several tools to aid the development of parallel programs for Dash. At the most primitive level, a parallel macro library provides structured access to the underlying hardware and operating-system functions. This library permits the development and porting of parallel applications to Dash using standard languages and tools. We are also developing a parallelizing compiler that extracts parallelism from programs written for sequential machines and tries to improve data locality. Locality is enhanced by increasing cache utilization through *blocking* and by reducing remote accesses through *static partitioning* of computation and data. Finally, *prefetching* is used to hide latency for remote accesses that are unavoidable.

Because we are interested in using Dash for a wide variety of applications, we must also find parallelism beyond the loop level. To attack this problem we have developed a new parallel language called Jade, which allows a programmer to easily express dynamic coarse-grain parallelism. Starting with a sequential program, a programmer simply augments those sections of code to be parallelized with side-effect information. The compiler and runtime system use this information to execute the program concurrently while respecting the program's data dependence constraints. Using Jade can significantly reduce the time and effort required to develop a parallel version of a serial application. A prototype of Jade is operational, and applications developed with Jade include sparse-matrix Cholesky factorization, Locus Route (a printed-circuit-board routing algorithm), and MDG (a water simulation code).

To complement our compiler and language efforts, we are developing a suite of performance monitoring and analysis tools. Our high-level tools can identify portions of code where the concurrency is smallest or where the most execution time is spent. The high-level tools also provide information about synchronization bottlenecks and load-balancing problems. Our low-level tools will couple with the built-in hardware monitors in Dash. As an example, they will be able to identify portions of code where most cache misses are occurring and will frequently provide the reasons for such misses. We expect such noninvasive monitoring and profiling tools to be invaluable in pinpointing critical regions for optimization to the programmer.

Dash performance

This section presents performance data from the Dash prototype system. First, we summarize the latency for memory accesses serviced by the three lower levels of the memory hierarchy. Second, we present speedup for three parallel applications running on a simulation of the prototype using one to 64 processors. Finally, we present the actual speedups for these applications measured on the initial 16-processor Dash system.

While caches reduce the effective access time of memory, the latency of main memory determines the sensitivity of processor utilization to cache and cluster locality and indicates the costs of interprocessor communication. Figure 8 shows the unloaded latencies for read misses that are satisfied within the local cluster, within the home cluster, and by a remote (that is, dirty) cluster. Latencies for read-exclusive requests issued by the write buffer are similar. A read miss to the local cluster takes 29 processor clocks (870 ns), while a remote miss takes roughly 3.5 times as long. The delays arise primarily from the relatively slow bus in the 3D/340 and from our implementation's conservative technology and packaging. Detailed simulation has shown that queuing delays can add 20 to 120 percent to these delays. While higher levels of integration could reduce the absolute time of the prototype latencies, we believe

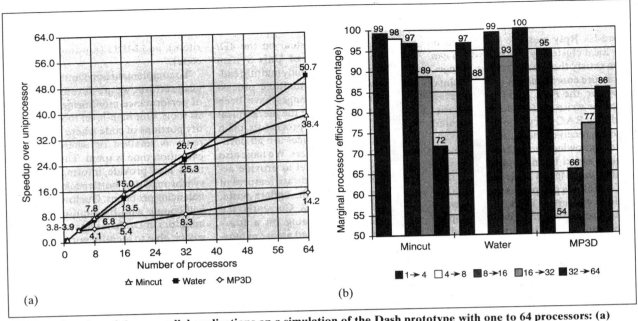

Figure 9. Speedup of three parallel applications on a simulation of the Dash prototype with one to 64 processors: (a) overall application speedup; (b) marginal efficiency of additional clusters.

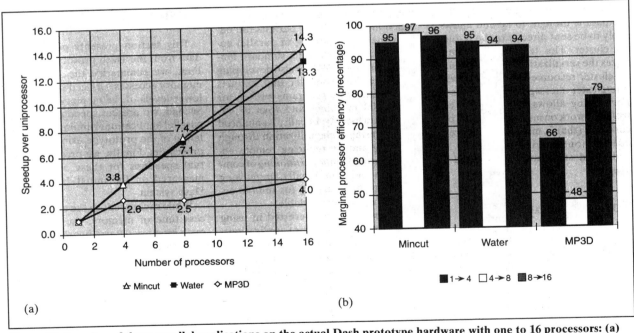

Figure 10. Speedup of three parallel applications on the actual Dash prototype hardware with one to 16 processors: (a) overall application speedup; (b) marginal efficiency of additional clusters.

the increasing clock rate of microprocessors implies that the latencies measured in processor clocks will remain similar.

Applications for large-scale multiprocessors must utilize locality to realize good cache hit rates, minimize remote accesses, and achieve high processor utilization. Figure 9 shows the speedup and processor efficiency for three appli-

cations on simulated Dash systems consisting of one to 64 processors (that is, one to 16 clusters). The line graph shows overall application speedup, while the bar chart shows the marginal efficiency of additional clusters. The marginal efficiency is defined as the average processor utilization, assuming processors were 100 percent utilized at the previous data point. The three applications

simulated are Water, Mincut, and MP3D. Water is a molecular-dynamics code that computes the energy of a system of water molecules. Mincut uses parallel simulated annealing to solve a graph-partitioning problem. MP3D models a wind tunnel in the upper atmosphere, using a discrete particle-based simulation.

The applications were simulated using a combination of the Tango multiprocessor simulator and a detailed memory simulator for the Dash prototype. Tango allows a parallel application to run on a uniprocessor and generates a parallel memory-reference stream. The detailed memory simulator is tightly coupled with Tango and provides feedback on the latency of individual memory operations.

On the Dash simulator, Water and Mincut achieve reasonable speedup through 64 processors. For Water, the reason is that the application exhibits good locality. As the number of clusters increases from two to 16, cache hit rates are relatively constant, and the percent of cache misses handled by the local cluster only decreases from 69 to 64 percent. Thus, miss penalties increase only slightly with system size and do not adversely affect processor utilizations. For Mincut, good speedup results from very good cache hit rates (98 percent for shared references). The speedup falls off for 64 processors due to lock contention in the application.

MP3D obviously does not exhibit good speedup on the Dash prototype. This particular encoding of the MP3D application requires frequent interprocessor communication, thus resulting in frequent cache misses. On average, about 4 percent of the instructions executed in MP3D generate a read miss for a shared data item. When only one cluster is being used, all these misses are serviced locally. However, when we go to two clusters, a large fraction of the cache misses are serviced remotely. This more than doubles the average miss latency, thus nullifying the potential gain from the added processors. Likewise, when four clusters are used, the full benefit is not realized because most misses are now serviced by a remote dirty cache, requiring a three-hop access.

Reasonable speedup is finally achieved when going from 16 to 32 and 64 processors (77 percent and 86 percent marginal efficiency, respectively), but overall speedup is limited to 14.2. Even on MP3D, however, caching is beneficial. A 64-processor system with the timing of Dash, but without the caching of shared data, achieves only a 4.1 speedup over the cached uniprocessor. For Water and Mincut the improvements from caching are even larger.

Figure 10 shows the speedup for the three applications on the real Dash hardware using one to 16 processors. The applications were run under an early

version of the Dash OS. The results for Water and Mincut correlate well with the simulation results, but the MP3D speedups are somewhat lower. The problem with MP3D appears to be that simulation results did not include private data references. Since MP3D puts a heavy load on the memory system, the extra load of private misses adds to the queuing delays and reduces the multiprocessor speedups.

We have run several other applications on our 16-processor prototype. These include two hierarchical *n*-body applications (using Barnes-Hut and Greengard-Rokhlin algorithms), a radiosity application from computer graphics, a standard-cell routing application from very large scale integration computer-aided design, and several matrix-oriented applications, including one performing sparse Cholesky factorization. There is also an improved version of the MP3D application that exhibits better locality and achieves almost linear speedup on the prototype.

Over this initial set of 10 parallel applications, the harmonic mean of the speedup on 16 processors in 10.5 Furthermore, if old MP3D is left out, the harmonic mean rises to over 12.8. Overall, our experience with the 16-processor machine has been very promising and indicates that many applications should be able to achieve over 40 times speedup on the 64-processor system.

Related work

There are other proposed scalable architectures that support a single address space with coherent caches. A comprehensive comparison of these machines with Dash is not possible at this time, because of the limited experience with this class of machines and the lack of details on many of the critical machine parameters. Nevertheless, a general comparison illustrates some of the design trade-offs that are possible.

Encore GigaMax and Stanford Paradigm. The Encore GigaMax architecture[9] and the Stanford Paradigm project[10] both use a hierarchy-of-buses approach to achieve scalability. At the top level, the Encore GigaMax is composed of several clusters on a global bus. Each cluster consists of several processor modules, main memory, and a cluster cache. The cluster cache holds a copy of

all remote locations cached locally and also all local locations cached remotely. Each processing module consists of several processors with private caches and a large, shared, second-level cache. A hierarchical snoopy protocol keeps the processor and cluster caches coherent.

The Paradigm machine is similar to the GigaMax in its hierarchy of processors, caches, and buses. It is different, however, in that the physical memory is all located at the global level, and it uses a hierarchical directory-based coherence protocol. The clusters containing cached data are identified by a bit-vector directory at every level, instead of using snooping cluster caches. Paradigm also provides a lock bit per memory block that enhances performance for synchronization and explicit communication.

The hierarchical structure of these machines is appealing in that they can theoretically be extended indefinitely by increasing the depth of the hierarchy. Unfortunately, the higher levels of the tree cannot grow indefinitely in bandwidth. If a single global bus is used, it becomes a critical link. If multiple buses are used at the top, the protocols become significantly more complex. Unless an application's communication requirements match the bus hierarchy or its traffic-sharing requirements are small, the global bus will be a bottleneck. Both requirements are restrictive and limit the classes of applications that can be efficiently run on these machines.

IEEE Scalable Coherent Interface. The IEEE P1596 Scalable Coherent Interface (SCI) is an interface standard that also strives to provide a scalable system model based on distributed directory-based cache coherence.[11] It differs from Dash in that it is an interface standard, not a complete system design. SCI only specifies the interfaces that each processing node should implement, leaving open the actual node design and exact interconnection network. SCI's role as an interface standard gives it somewhat different goals from those of Dash, but systems based on SCI are likely to have a system organization similar to Dash.

The major difference between SCI and Dash lies in how and where the directory information is maintained. In SCI, the directory is a distributed sharing list maintained by the processor caches themselves. For example, if processors A, B, and C are caching some location, then the cache entries storing this location include pointers that form a doubly linked list. At main memory, only a pointer to the processor at the head of the linked list is maintained. In contrast, Dash places all the directory information with main memory.

The main advantage of the SCI scheme is that the amount of directory pointer storage grows naturally as new processing nodes are added to the system. Dash-type systems generally require more directory memory than SCI systems and must use a limited directory scheme to scale to a large configuration. On the other hand, SCI directories would typically use the same static RAM technology as the processor caches while the Dash directories are implemented in main memory DRAM technology. This difference tends to offset the potential storage efficiency gains of the SCI scheme.

The primary disadvantage of the SCI scheme is that the distribution of individual directory entries increases the latency and complexity of the memory references, since additional directory-update messages must be sent between processor caches. For example, on a write to a shared block cached by N processors (including the writing processor), the writer must perform the following actions:

- detach itself from the sharing list,
- interrogate memory to determine the head of the sharing list,
- acquire head status from the current head, and
- serially purge the other processor caches by issuing invalidation requests and receiving replies that indicate the next processor in the list.

Altogether, this amounts to $2N + 6$ messages and, more importantly, $N + 1$ serial directory lookups. In contrast, Dash can locate all sharing processors in a single directory lookup, and invalidation messages are serialized only by the network transmission rate.

The SCI working committee has proposed several extensions to the base protocol to reduce latency and support additional functions. In particular, the committee has proposed the addition of directory pointers that allow sharing lists to become sharing trees, support for request forwarding, use of a clean cached state, and support for queue-based locks. While these extensions reduce the differences between the two protocols, they also significantly increase the complexity of SCI.

MIT Alewife. The Alewife machine[12] is similar to Dash in that it uses main memory directories and connects the processing nodes with mesh network. There are three main differences between the two machines:

- Alewife does not have a notion of clusters — each node is a single processor.
- Alewife uses software to handle directory pointer overflow.
- Alewife uses multicontext processors as its primary latency-hiding mechanism.

The size of clusters (one processor, four processors, or more) is dictated primarily by the engineering trade-offs between the overhead of hardware for each node (memory, network interface, and directory) and the bandwidth available within and between clusters. Techniques for scaling directories efficiently are a more critical issue. Whether hardware techniques, such as proposed in O'Krafka and Newton[2] and Gupta et al.,[1] or the software techniques of Alewife will be more effective remains an open question, though we expect the practical differences to be small. Multiple contexts constitute a mechanism that helps hide memory latency, but one that clearly requires additional application parallelism to be effective. Overall, while we believe that support for multiple contexts is useful and can complement other techniques, we do not feel that its role will be larger than other latency-hiding mechanisms such as release consistency and nonbinding prefetch.[13]

W e have described the design and implementation decisions for Dash, a multiprocessor that combines the programmability of single-address-space machines with the scalability of message-passing machines. The key means to this scalability are a directory-based cache-coherence protocol, distributed memories and directories, and a scalable interconnection network. The design focuses on reducing memory latency to keep processor performance high, though it also provides latency-hiding techniques such as prefetch and release consistency to mit-igate the effects of unavoidable system delays.

At the time of this writing, the 2×2 Dash prototype is stable. It is accessible on the Internet and used daily for research into parallel applications, tools, operating systems, and directory-based architectures. As indicated in the performance section, results from this initial configuration are very promising. Work on extending the 2×2 cluster system to the larger 4×4 (64-processor) system is ongoing. All major hardware components are on hand and being debugged. By the time this article is in print, we expect to have an initial version of the Unix kernel and parallel applications running on the larger machine. ∎

Acknowledgments

This research was supported by DARPA contracts N00014-87-K-0828 and N00039-91-C-0138. In addition, Daniel Lenoski is supported by Tandem Computers, James Laudon and Wolf-Dietrich Weber are supported by IBM, and Kourosh Gharachorloo is supported by Texas Instruments. Anoop Gupta is partly supported by a National Science Foundation Presidential Young Investigator Award.

We also thank Silicon Graphics for their technical and logistical support and Valid Logic Systems for their grant of computer-aided engineering tools.

References

1. A. Gupta, W.-D. Weber, and T. Mowry, "Reducing Memory and Traffic Requirements for Scalable Directory-Based Cache Coherence Schemes," *Proc. 1990 Int'l Conf. Parallel Processing*, IEEE Computer Society Press, Los Alamitos, Calif., Order No. 2101, pp. 312-321.

2. B.W. O'Krafka and A.R. Newton, "An Empirical Evaluation of Two Memory-Efficient Directory Methods," *Proc. 17th Int'l Symp. Computer Architecture*, IEEE CS Press, Los Alamitos, Calif., Order No. 2047, 1990, pp. 138-147.

3. L. Lamport, "How to Make a Multiprocessor Computer That Correctly Executes Multiprocess Programs," *IEEE Trans. Computers*, Sept. 1979, Vol. C-28, No. 9, pp. 241-248.

4. C. Scheurich and M. Dubois, "Dependency and Hazard Resolution in Multiprocessors," *Proc. 14th Int'l Symp. Computer Architecture*, IEEE CS Press, Los Alamitos, Calif., Order No. 776, 1987, pp. 234-243.

5. K. Gharachorloo, A. Gupta, and J. Hennessy, "Performance Evaluation of Memory Consistency Models for Shared-Memory Multiprocessors," *Proc. Fourth Int'l Conf. Architectural Support for Programming Languages and Operating Systems,* ACM, New York, 1991, pp. 245-257.

6. T. Mowry and A. Gupta, "Tolerating Latency Through Software in Shared-Memory Multiprocessors," *J. Parallel and Distributed Computing,* Vol. 12, No. 6, June 1991, pp. 87-106.

7. J.R. Goodman, M.K. Vernon, and P.J. Woest, "Efficient Synchronization Primitives for Large-Scale Cache-Coherent Multiprocessors," *Proc. Third Int'l Conf. Architectural Support for Programming Languages and Operating Systems,* IEEE CS Press, Los Alamitos, Calif., Order No. 1936, 1989, pp. 64-73.

8. D. Lenoski et al., "The Directory-Based Cache Coherence Protocol for the Dash Multiprocessor," *Proc. 17th Int'l Symp. Computer Architecture,* IEEE CS Press, Los Alamitos, Calif., Order No. 2047, 1990, pp. 148-159.

9. A.W. Wilson, Jr., "Hierarchical Cache/Bus Architecture for Shared Memory Multiprocessors," *Proc. 14th Int'l Symp. Computer Architecture,* IEEE CS Press, Los Alamitos, Calif., Order No. 776, 1987, pp. 244-252.

10. D.R. Cheriton, H.A. Goosen, and P.D. Boyle, "Paradigm: A Highly Scalable Shared-Memory Multicomputer Architecture," *Computer,* Vol. 24, No. 2, Feb. 1991, pp. 33-46.

11. D.V. James et al., "Distributed-Directory Scheme: Scalable Coherent Interface," *Computer,* Vol. 23, No. 6, June 1990, pp. 74-77.

12. A. Agarwal et al., "Limitless Directories: A Scalable Cache Coherence Scheme," *Proc. Fourth Int'l Conf. Architectural Support for Programming Languages and Operating Systems,* ACM, New York, 1991, pp. 224-234.

13. A. Gupta et al., "Comparative Evaluation of Latency Reducing and Tolerating Techniques," *Proc. 18th Int'l Symp. Computer Architecture,* IEEE CS Press, Los Alamitos, Calif., Order No. 2146, 1991, pp. 254-263.

Daniel Lenoski is a research scientist in the Processor and Memory Group of Tandem Computers. He recently completed his PhD in electrical engineering in the Computer Systems Laboratory at Stanford University. His research efforts concentrated on the design and implementation of Dash and other issues related to scalable multiprocessors. His prior work includes the architecture definition of Tandem's CLX 600, 700, and 800 series processors.

Lenoski received a BSEE from the California Institute of Technology in 1983 and an MSEE from Stanford in 1985.

James Laudon is a PhD candidate in the Department of Electrical Engineering at Stanford University. His research interests include multiprocessor architectures and algorithms.

Laudon received a BS in electrical engineering from the University of Wisconsin-Madison in 1987 and an MS in electrical engineering from Stanford University in 1988. He is a member of the IEEE Computer Society and ACM.

Kourosh Gharachorloo is a PhD candidate in the Computer Systems Laboratory at Stanford University. His research interests focus on techniques to reduce and tolerate memory latency in large-scale shared-memory multiprocessors.

Gharachorloo received the BS and BA degrees in electrical engineering and economics, respectively, in 1985 and the MS degree in electrical engineering in 1986, all from Stanford University.

Wolf-Dietrich Weber is a PhD candidate in the Computer Systems Laboratory at Stanford University. His research interests focus on directory-based cache coherence for scalable shared-memory multiprocessors.

Weber received the BA and BE degrees from Dartmouth College in 1986. He received an MS degree in electrical engineering from Stanford University in 1987.

Anoop Gupta is an assistant professor of computer science at Stanford University. His primary interests are in the design of hardware and software for large-scale multiprocessors.

Prior to joining Stanford, Gupta was on the research faculty of Carnegie Mellon University, where he received his PhD in 1986. Gupta was the recipient of a DEC faculty development award from 1987-1989, and he received the NSF Presidential Young Investigator Award in 1990.

John Hennessy is a professor of electrical engineering and computer science at Stanford University. His research interests are in exploiting parallelism at all levels to build higher performance computer systems.

Hennessy is the recipient of a 1984 Presidential Young Investigator Award. In 1987, he was named the Willard and Inez K. Bell Professor of Electrical Engineering and Computer Science. In 1991, he was elected an IEEE fellow. During a leave from Stanford in 1984-85, he cofounded Mips Computer Systems where he continues to participate in industrializing the RISC concept as chief scientist.

Mark Horowitz is an associate professor of electrical engineering at Stanford University. His research interests include high-speed digital integrated circuit designs, CAD tools for IC design, and processor architecture. He is a recipient of a 1985 Presidential Young Investigator Award. During a leave from Stanford in 1989-90, he cofounded Rambus, a company that is working on improving memory bandwidth to and from DRAMs.

Horowitz received the BS and SM degrees in electrical engineering and computer science from the Massachusetts Institute of Technology and his PhD in electrical engineering from Stanford University.

Monica S. Lam has been an assistant professor in the Computer Science Department at Stanford University since 1988. Her current research project is to develop a compiler system that optimizes data locality and exploits parallelism at task, loop, and instruction granularities. She was one of the chief architects and compiler designers for the CMU Warp machine and the CMU-Intel's iWarp.

Lam received her BS from University of British Columbia in 1980 and a PhD in computer science from Carnegie Mellon University in 1987.

Readers may contact Daniel Lenoski at Tandem Computers, 19333 Vallco Parkway, MS 3-03, Cupertino, CA 95014; e-mail lenoski_dan @tandem.com. Anoop Gupta can be reached at Stanford Univ., CIS-212, Stanford, CA 94305; e-mail ag@pepper.stanford.edu.

DDM — A Cache-Only Memory Architecture

Erik Hagersten, Anders Landin, and Seif Haridi
Swedish Institute of Computer Science

A new architecture has the programming paradigm of shared-memory architectures but no physically shared memory. Caches attached to the processors contain all the system memory.

Multiprocessors providing a shared memory view to the programmer are typically implemented as such — with a shared memory. We introduce an architecture with large caches to reduce latency and network load. Because all system memory resides in the caches, a minimum number of network accesses are needed. Still, it presents a shared-memory view to the programmer.

Single bus. Shared-memory systems based on a single bus have some tens of processors, each one with a local cache, and typically suffer from bus saturation. A cache-coherence protocol in each cache snoops the traffic on the common bus and prevents inconsistencies in cache contents.[1] Computers manufactured by Sequent and Encore use this kind of architecture. Because it provides a uniform access time to the whole shared memory, it is called a uniform memory architecture (UMA). The contention for the common memory and the common bus limits the scalability of UMAs.

Distributed. Computers such as the BBN Butterfly and the IBM RP3 use an architecture with distributed shared memory, known as a nonuniform memory architecture (NUMA). Each processor node contains a portion of the shared memory, so access times to different parts of the shared address space can vary. NUMAs often have networks other than a single bus, and the network delay can vary to different nodes. The earlier NUMAs did not have coherent caches and left the problem of maintaining coherence to the programmer. Today, researchers are striving toward coherent NUMAs with directory-based cache-coherence protocols.[2] By statically partitioning the work and data, programmers can optimize programs for NUMAs. A partitioning that enables processors to make most of their accesses to their part of the shared memory achieves a better scalability than is possible in UMAs.

Cache-only. In a cache-only memory architecture (COMA), the memory organization is similar to that of a NUMA in that each processor holds a portion of the address space. However, the partitioning of data among the memories does not have to be static, since all distributed memories are organized like large (second-level) caches. The task of such a memory is twofold. Besides being a large cache for the processor, it may also contain some data from the shared address space that the processor never has accessed — in other words, it is a cache and a virtual part of the shared memory. We call this intermediate form of memory *attraction memory*. A coherence protocol attracts the data used by a processor to its attraction memory. Comparable to a cache line, the coherence unit moved around by the protocol is called an *item*. On a memory reference, a virtual address is translated into an item identifier. The item identifier space is logically the same as the physical address space of typical machines, but there is no permanent mapping between an item identifier and a physical memory location. Instead, an item identifier corresponds to a location in an attraction memory, whose tag matches the item identifier. Actually, there are cases where multiple locations of different attraction memories could match.

A COMA provides a programming model identical to that of shared-memory architectures, but it does not require static distribution of execution and memory usage to run efficiently. Running an optimized NUMA program on a COMA results in a NUMA-like behavior, since the work spaces of the different processors migrate to their attraction memories. However, a UMA version of the same program would have a similar behavior, because the data are attracted to the using processor regardless of the address. A COMA also adapts to and performs well for programs with a more dynamic or semidynamic scheduling. The work space migrates according to its usage throughout the computation. Programs can be optimized for a COMA to take this property into account to achieve a better locality.

A COMA allows for dynamic data use without duplicating much memory, compared with an architecture in which a cached datum also occupies space in the shared memory. To avoid increasing the memory cost, the attraction memories should be implemented with ordinary memory components. Therefore, we view the COMA approach as a second-level, or higher level, cache technique. The accessing time to the attraction memory of a COMA is comparable to that to the memory of a cache-coherent NUMA. Figure 1 compares COMAs to other shared-memory architectures.

A new COMA. This article describes the basic ideas behind a new COMA. The architecture, called the Data Diffusion Machine (DDM),[3] relies on a hier-

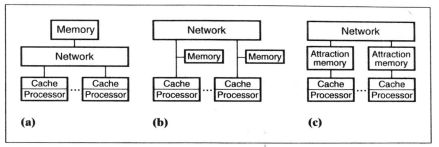

Figure 1. Shared-memory architectures compared with COMAs: (a) uniform memory architecture (UMA), (b) nonuniform memory architecture (NUMA), and (c) cache-only memory architecture (COMA).

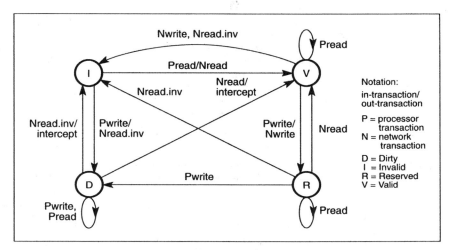

Figure 2. An example of a protocol similar to the write-once protocol.

archical network structure. We introduce the key ideas behind DDM by describing a small machine and its protocol. We also describe a large machine with hundreds of processors, overview the ongoing prototype project, and provide simulated performance figures.

Cache-coherence strategies

The problem of maintaining coherence among read-write data shared by different caches has been studied extensively. Either software or hardware can maintain coherence. We believe hardware coherence is needed in a COMA for efficiency, since the item must be small to prevent performance degradation by false sharing. (In false sharing, two processors accessing different parts of the same item conflict with each other, even though they do

not share any data.) We measured a speedup of 50 percent when false sharing was removed from the wind tunnel application, MP3D-Diff, reported in the "Simulated performance" section. Hardware-based schemes maintain coherence without involving software and can be implemented more efficiently. Examples of hardware-based protocols are snooping-cache protocols and directory-based protocols.

Snooping-cache protocols have a distributed implementation. Each cache is responsible for snooping traffic on the bus and taking actions to avoid an incoherence. An example of such a protocol is the write-once protocol introduced by Goodman and discussed by Stenström.[1] As Figure 2 shows, in that protocol, each cache line can be in one of four states: Invalid, Valid, Reserved, or Dirty. Many caches can have the same cache line in the state Valid at the same time, and may read it locally. When writing to a cache line in Valid, the line changes state to Reserved, and a write is sent on the common bus to the common memory. All other caches with lines in Valid snoop the write and invalidate their copies. At this point there is only one cached copy of the cache line containing the newly written value. The common memory now also contains the new value. If a cache already has the cache line in Reserved, it can perform a write locally without any transactions on the common bus. Its value now differs from that in the memory, and its state is therefore changed to Dirty. Any read requests from other caches to that cache line must now be intercepted to provide the new value (marked by "intercept" in Figure 2).

Snooping caches rely on broadcasting and are not suited for general interconnection networks: Unrestricted broadcasting would drastically reduce the available bandwidth, thereby obviating the advantage of general networks. Instead, directory-based schemes send messages directly between nodes.[1] A read request is sent to main memory, without any snooping. The main memory knows if the cache line is cached — and in which cache or caches — and whether it has been modified. If the line has been modified, the read request is passed on to the cache with a copy, which provides a copy for the requesting cache. On a write to a shared cache line, a write request sent to the main memory causes invalidation messages to all caches with copies to be sent. The caches respond with acknowledge messages. To achieve sequential consistency, all acknowledgments must be received before the write is performed.

The cache-coherence protocol for a COMA can adopt techniques used in other cache-coherence protocols and extend them with the functionality for finding a datum on a cache read miss and for handling replacement. A directory-based protocol could have a part of the directory information, the *directory home*, statically distributed in a NUMA fashion, while the data would be allowed to move freely. Retrieving the data on a read miss would then require one extra indirect access to the directory home to find where the item currently resides. The access time, including this extra indirection, would be identical to that required for reading a dirty cache line not in a NUMA's home node. The directory home can also make sure that the last copy of an item is not lost.

Instead of the above strategy, DDM is based on a hierarchical snooping bus architecture and uses a hierarchical search algorithm for finding an item. The directory information in DDM is dynamically distributed in the hierarchy.

A minimal COMA

We introduce DDM by looking at the smallest instance of the architecture, which could be a COMA on its own or a subsystem of a larger COMA. A single bus connects the attraction memories of the minimal DDM. The distribution and coherence of data among the attraction memories are controlled by the snooping protocol *memory above*, and the interface between the processor and the attraction memory is defined by the protocol *memory below*. The protocol views a cache line of an attraction memory, here called an item, as one unit. The attraction memory stores one small state field per item. Figure 3 shows the node architecture in the single-bus DDM.

DDM uses an asynchronous split-transaction bus: The bus is released between a requesting transaction and its reply, for example, between a read re-

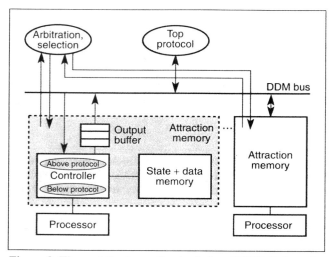

Figure 3. The architecture of a single-bus DDM. Below the attraction memories are the processors. On top of the bus are arbitration and selection.

quest and its data reply. The delay between the request and its reply can be of arbitrary length, and there might be a large number of outstanding requests. The reply transaction will eventually appear on the bus as a different transaction. Unlike other buses, the DDM bus has a selection mechanism to make sure that at most one node is selected to service a request. This guarantees that each transaction on the bus does not produce more than one new transaction for the bus, a requirement necessary for deadlock avoidance.

Single-bus DDM protocol. We developed a new protocol, similar in many ways to the snooping-cache protocol, limiting broadcast requirements to a smaller subsystem and adding support for replacement.[4] The write coherence part of the protocol is the write-invalidate type: To keep data coherent, all copies of the item except the one to be updated are erased on a write. In a COMA with a small item size, the alternative approach, write update, could also be attractive: On a write, the new value is multicast to all "caches" with a shared copy of the item.

The protocol also handles the attraction of data (read) and replacement when a set in an attraction memory gets full. The snooping protocol defines a new state and a new transaction to send as a function of the transaction appearing on the bus, and the present state of the item in the attraction memory:

Protocol: old state × transaction → new state × new transaction

An item can be in one of seven states (the subsystem is the attraction memory):

- *Invalid.* This subsystem does not contain the item.
- *Exclusive.* This subsystem and no other contains the item.
- *Shared.* This subsystem and possibly other subsystems contain the item.
- *Reading.* This subsystem is waiting for a data value after having issued a read.

- *Waiting.* This subsystem is waiting to become Exclusive after having issued an erase.
- *Reading-and-Waiting.* This subsystem is waiting for a data value, later to become Exclusive.
- *Answering.* This subsystem has promised to answer a read request.

The first three states — Invalid, Exclusive, and Shared — correspond to the states Invalid, Reserved, and Valid in Goodman's write-once protocol. The state Dirty in that protocol — with the meaning that this is the only cached copy and its value differs from that in the memory — has no correspondence in a COMA. New states in the protocol are the transient states Reading, Waiting, Reading-and-Waiting, and Answering. Transient states are required because of the split-transaction bus and the need to remember outstanding requests.

The bus carries the following transactions:

- *Erase.* Erase all copies of this item.
- *Exclusive.* Acknowledge an erase request.
- *Read.* Read a copy of the item.
- *Data.* Carry the data in reply to an earlier read request.
- *Inject.* Carry the only copy of an item and look for a subsystem to move into — caused by a replacement.
- *Out.* Carry the item on its way out of the subsystem — caused by a replacement. It will terminate when another copy of the item is found.

A processor writing an item in Exclusive state or reading an item in Exclusive or Shared state proceeds without interruption. As Figure 4 shows, a read attempt of an item in Invalid will result in a Read request and a new state, Reading. The bus selection mechanism will select one attraction memory to service the request, eventually putting a Data transaction on the bus. The requesting attraction memory, now in Reading, will grab the Data transaction, change to Shared, and continue.

Processors are allowed to write only to items in Exclusive state. If the item is in Shared, all other copies have to be erased and an acknowledgment received before the writing is allowed. The attraction memory sends an Erase transaction and waits for the Exclusive ac-

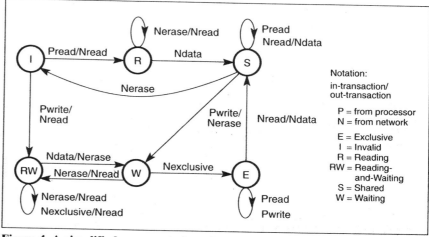

Figure 4. A simplified representation of the attraction memory protocol not including replacement.

knowledgment in the new state, Waiting. Many simultaneous attempts to write the same item will result in many attraction memories in Waiting, all with an outstanding Erase transaction in their output buffers. The first Erase to reach the bus is the winner of the write race.

All other transactions bound for the same item are removed from the small output buffers. Therefore, the buffers also have to snoop transactions. The output buffers can be limited to a depth of three, and deadlock can still be avoided with a special arbitration algorithm. The losing attraction memories in Waiting change state to Reading-and-Waiting, while one of them puts a read request in its output buffer. Eventually the top protocol of the bus replies with an Exclusive acknowledgment, telling the only attraction memory left in Waiting that it may now proceed. Writing to an item in the Invalid state results in a Read request and a new state, Reading-and-Waiting. Upon the Data reply, the state changes to Waiting and an Erase request is sent.

Replacement. Like ordinary caches, the attraction memory will run out of space, forcing some items to make room for more recently accessed ones. If the set where an item is supposed to reside is full, one item in the set is selected to be replaced. For example, the oldest item in Shared, of which there might be other copies, may be selected. Replacing an item in Shared generates an Out transaction. The space used by the item can now be reclaimed. If an Out transaction sees an attraction memory in

Shared, Reading, Waiting, or Reading-and-Waiting, it does nothing; otherwise it is converted to an Inject transaction by the top protocol. An Inject transaction can also be produced by replacing an item in Exclusive. The inject transaction is the last copy of an item trying to find a new home in a new attraction memory. In the single-bus implementation, it will do so first by choosing an empty space (Invalid state), and second by replacing an item in Shared state — in other words, it will decrease the amount of sharing. If the item identifier space, which corresponds to the physical address space of conventional architectures, is not made larger than the sum of the attraction memory sizes, it is possible to devise a simple scheme that guarantees a physical location for each item.

Often a program uses only a portion of a computer's physical address space. This is especially true of operating systems with a facility for eager reclaiming of unused work space. In DDM, the unused item space can be used to increase the degree of sharing by purging the unused items. The operating system might even change the degree of sharing dynamically.

The hierarchical DDM

So far, we have presented a cache-coherent single-bus multiprocessor without physically shared memory. Instead, the resources form huge second-level caches called attraction memories, minimizing the number of accesses to the

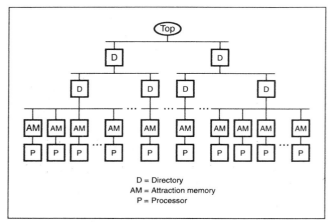

Figure 5. A hierarchical DDM with three levels.

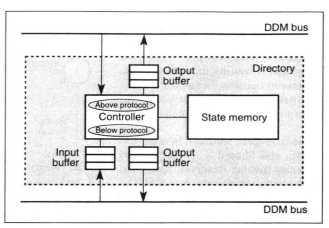

Figure 6. The architecture of a directory.

only shared resource left: the shared bus. Data can reside in any or many of the attraction memories. Data are automatically moved where needed.

To make the single-bus DDM a subsystem of a large hierarchical DDM, we replace the top with a directory, which interfaces between the bus and a higher level bus of the same type. Figure 5 shows the hierarchy.

The directory is a set-associative state memory that keeps information for all the items in the attraction memories below it, but contains no data. The directory can answer these questions: "Is this item below me?" and "Does this item exist outside my subsystem?" From the bus above, the directory's snooping protocol *directory above* behaves very much like the *memory above* protocol. From the bus below, its *directory below* protocol behaves like the *top protocol* for items in the Exclusive state. This makes operations on items local to a bus identical to those of the single-bus DDM. The directory passes through only transactions from below that cannot be completed inside its subsystem or transactions from above that need to be serviced by its subsystem. In that sense, the directory acts as a filter.

As Figure 6 shows, the directory has a small output buffer above it to store transactions waiting to be sent on the higher bus. Transactions for the lower bus are stored in another output buffer below, and transactions from the lower bus are stored in an input buffer. A directory reads from the input buffer when it has the time and space to do a lookup in its status memory. This is not part of the atomic snooping action of the bus.

The hierarchical DDM and its protocol have several similarities with architectures proposed by Wilson[5] and Goodman and Woest.[6] DDM is, however, different in its use of transient states in the protocol, its lack of physically shared memory, and its network (higher level caches) that stores only state information and no data.

Multilevel read. If the subsystems connected to the bus cannot satisfy a read request, the next higher directory retransmits the request on the next higher bus. The directory also changes the item's state to Reading, marking the outstanding request. Eventually, the request reaches a level in the hierarchy where a directory containing a copy of the item is selected to answer the request. The selected directory changes the item's state to Answering, marking an outstanding request from above, and retransmits the Read request on its lower bus. As Figure 7 shows, the transient states Reading and Answering in the directories mark the request's path through the hierarchy, like an unwound red read thread that shows the way through a maze, appearing in red in Figure 7.

A flow-control mechanism in the protocol prevents deadlock if too many processors try to unwind a read thread to the same set in a directory. When the request finally reaches an attraction memory with a copy of the item, its data reply simply follows the read thread back to the requesting node, changing all the states along the path to Shared.

Combined reads and broadcasts are simple to implement in DDM. If a Read request finds the read thread unwound

for the requested item (Reading or Answering state), it simply terminates and waits for the Data reply that eventually will follow that path on its way back.

Multilevel write. An Erase from below to a directory with the item in Exclusive state results in an Exclusive acknowledgment being sent below. An Erase that cannot get its acknowledgment from the directory will work its way up the hierarchy, changing the directories' states to Waiting to mark the outstanding request. All subsystems of a bus carrying an Erase transaction will get their copies erased. The propagation of the Erase ends when it reaches a directory in Exclusive (or the top), and the acknowledgment is sent back along the path marked Waiting, changing the states to Exclusive.

A write race between any two processors in the hierarchical DDM has a solution similar to that of a single-bus DDM. The two Erase requests are propagated up the hierarchy. The first Erase transaction to reach the lowest bus common to both processors is the winner, as shown in Figure 8. The losing attraction memory (in Reading-and-Waiting) will restart a new write action automatically upon receipt of the erase.

Replacement in the hierarchical DDM. Replacement of a Shared item in the hierarchical DDM results in an Out transaction propagating up the hierarchy and terminating when it finds a subsystem in any of the following states: Shared, Reading, Waiting, or Answering. If the last copy of an item marked Shared is replaced, an Out transaction

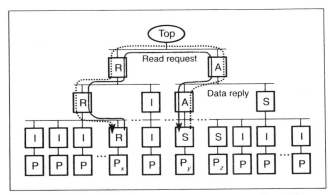

Figure 7. A read request from processor P_x has found its way to a copy of the item in the attraction memory of processor P_y. Its path is marked with states Reading (R) and Answering (A), which will guide the data reply back to P_x. (I indicates processors in the Invalid state, S processors in the Shared state.)

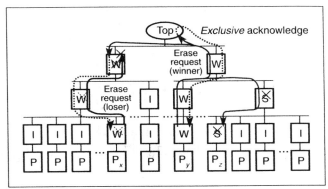

Figure 8. A write race between two processors P_x and P_y is resolved when the request originating from P_y reaches the top bus (the lowest bus common to both processors). The top can now send the acknowledgment, Exclusive, which follows the path marked with W's (processors in the Waiting state) back to the winning processor P_y. The Waiting states are changed to Exclusive by the acknowledgment. The Erase transaction will erase the data in P_x and P_z, forcing P_x to redo its write attempt.

that fails to terminate will reach a directory in Exclusive and turn into an Inject transaction. Replacing an item in Exclusive generates an Inject transaction that tries to find an empty space in a neighboring attraction memory. Inject transactions first try to find an empty space in the attraction memories of the local DDM bus, as in the single-bus DDM. Unlike in a single-bus DDM, an Inject failing to find an empty space on the local DDM bus will turn to a special bus, its home bus, determined by the item identifier. On the home bus, the Inject will force itself into an attraction memory, possibly by throwing out a foreigner or a Shared item. The item home space is equally divided between the bottommost buses, and therefore space is guaranteed on the home bus.

The preferred location in DDM is different from memory location in NUMAs in that an item seeks a home only at replacement after failing to find space elsewhere. When the item is not in its home place, other items can use its place. The home also differs from the NUMA approach in being a bus: Any attraction memory on that bus will do. The details of the directory protocols are available elsewhere.[4]

Replacement in a directory. Baer and Wang studied the multilevel inclusion property,[7] which has the following implications for our system: A directory at level $i + 1$ has to be a superset of the

directories, or attraction memories, at level i. In other words, the size of a directory and its associativity (number of ways) must be B_i times that of the underlying level i, where B_i is the branch factor of the underlying level i, and size means the number of items:

Size: $Dir_{i+1} = B_i * Dir_i$
Associativity: $Dir_{i+1} = B_i * Dir_i$

Even if implementable, higher level memories would become expensive and slow if those properties were fulfilled for a large hierarchical system. However, the effects of the multilevel inclusion property are limited in DDM. It stores only state information in its directories and does not replicate data in the higher levels. Yet another way to limit the effect is to use "imperfect directories" with smaller sets (lower number of ways) than what is required for multilevel inclusion and to give the directories the ability to perform replacement, that is, to move all copies of an item out of their subsystem. We can keep the probability of replacement at a reasonable level by increasing the associativity moderately higher up in the hierarchy. A higher degree of sharing also helps to keep that probability low. A shared item occupies space in many attraction memories, but only one space in the directories above them. The implementation of directory replacement requires one extra state and two extra transactions.[4]

Other protocols. Our protocol gives the programmer a *sequentially consistent* system. It fulfills the strongest memory access model, but performance is degraded because the processor has to wait for the acknowledgment before it can perform the write. However, the acknowledgment is sent by the topmost node of the subsystem in which all copies of the item reside, instead of by each individual attraction memory with a copy. This not only reduces the remote delay, it also cuts down the number of system transactions. The writer might actually receive the acknowledgment before all copies are erased. Nevertheless, sequential consistency can be guaranteed.[8] The hierarchical structure can also efficiently support looser forms of consistency providing higher performance. We have designed a processor-consistent protocol[8] and a protocol combining processor consistency with an adaptive write update strategy.

Increasing the bandwidth

Although most memory accesses tend to be localized in the machine, the hierarchy's higher levels may nevertheless demand a higher bandwidth than the lower systems, creating a bottleneck. To take the load off the higher levels, we can use a smaller branch factor at the

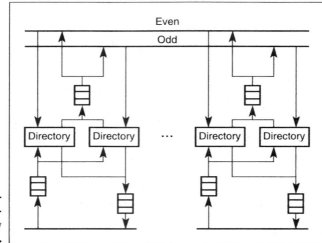

Figure 9. Increasing the bandwidth of a bus by splitting buses.

top of the hierarchy than lower down. This solution, however, increases the levels in the hierarchy, resulting in a longer remote access delay and an increased memory overhead. Instead, we can widen the higher levels of the hierarchy to produce a fat tree.[9] We split a directory into two directories half the original directory's size. The two directories deal with different address domains (even and odd). The communication with other directories is also split, which doubles the bandwidth. We can perform a split any number of times and at any level of the hierarchy. Figure 9 shows that regardless of the number of splits, the architecture is still hierarchical to each specific address.

Yet another solution is a heterogeneous network: We use the hierarchy with its advantages as far as possible and tie several hierarchies together at their tops by a general network with a directory-based protocol. This scheme requires some changes in the protocol to achieve the same consistency model.

The DDM prototype project

A prototype DDM design is near completion at the Swedish Institute of Computer Science. The hardware implementation of the processor and attraction memory is based on the system TP881V by Tadpole Technology, UK. Each such system has up to four Motorola MC88100 20-MHz processors, each one with two MC88200 16-Kbyte caches and memory management units; 8 or 32 Mbytes of DRAM; and interfaces for the SCSI bus, Ethernet, and terminals, all connected by the Motorola Mbus as shown in Figure 10.

We are developing a DDM node controller board to host a single-ported state memory. As Figure 10 shows, it will interface the TP881V node with the first-level DDM bus. The node controller snoops accesses between the processor caches and the memory of the TP881V according to the memory-below protocol, and also snoops the DDM bus according to the memory-above protocol. We have integrated the copy-back protocol of multiple processor caches into the protocol mechanisms. The node controller thus changes the memory's behavior into that of an attraction memory. Read accesses to the attraction memory take eight cycles per cache line, which is one more than in the original TP881V system. Write accesses to the attraction memory take 12 cycles compared with 10 cycles for the original system. A read/write mix of 3/1 to the attraction memory results in an access time to the attraction memory on the average 16 percent slower than that to the original TP881V memory.

As Table 1 shows, a remote read to a node on the same DDM bus takes 55 cycles at best, most of which are spent making Mbus transactions (a total of four accesses). Read accesses climbing one step up and down the hierarchy add about 45 extra cycles. Write accesses to shared state take at best 40 cycles for one level and 50 cycles for two levels.

The DDM bus is pipelined in four phases: transaction code, snoop, selection, and data. We designed our initial

Related activities

At the Swedish Institute of Computer Science, we are developing an operating system for the DDM prototype. This work is based on the Mach operating system from Carnegie Mellon University, which we modified to support DDM efficiently. Related activities involve a hardware prefetching scheme that dynamically prefetches items to the attraction memory; this is especially useful when a process is started or migrated. We are also experimenting with alternative protocols.[1]

A DDM emulator is currently under development at the University of Bristol.[2] The emulator runs on the Meiko transputer platform and models an architecture with a tree-shaped link-based structure, with transputers as directories. The transputers' four links permit a branch factor of three at each level. The transputers at the leaves execute the application. All references to global data are intercepted and handled in a DDM manner by software. The emulator's DDM protocol has a different representation suited for a link-based architecture structured like a tree, rather than for a bus-based architecture. The implementation has certain similarities to directory-based systems.

References

1. E. Hagersten, *Towards a Scalable Cache-Only Memory Architecture,* PhD thesis, SICS Dissertation Series 08, Swedish Institute of Computer Science, Kista, Sweden, 1992.

2. S. Raina and D.H.D. Warren, "Traffic Patterns in a Scalable Multiprocessor Through Transputer Emulation," *Proc. Hawaii Int'l Conf. System Sciences,* Vol. I, IEEE-CS Press, Los Alamitos, Calif., Order No. 2420, 1992, pp. 267-276.

bus conservatively, since pushing the bus speed is not a primary goal of this research. The prototype DDM bus operates at 20 MHz, with a 32-bit data bus and a 32-bit address bus. It provides a moderate bandwidth of about 80 Mbytes per second, which is enough for connecting up to eight nodes — that is, 32 processors. Still, the bandwidth has not been the limiting factor in our simulation studies. We can increase bus bandwidth many times by using other structures. The slotted ring bus proposed by Barosso and Dubois[10] has a bandwidth one order of magnitude higher.

For translations to item identifiers, DDM uses the normal procedures for translating virtual addresses to physical addresses, as implemented in standard memory management units. This means that an operating system has knowledge of physical pages.

Any attraction memory node can have a connected disk. Upon a page-in, the node first attracts all the data of an item page as being temporarily locked to its attraction memory. If the items of that page were not present in the machine earlier, they are "born" at this time through the protocol. Then the node copies (by direct memory access) the page from the disk to the attraction memory, unlocking the data at the same time. Page-out reverses the process, copying a dirty page back to the disk. The operating system can purge the items of unused pages for more sharing.

Memory overhead

It might seem that an implementation of DDM would require far more memory than alternative architectures. Extra memory is required for storing state bits and address keys for the set-associative attraction memories, as well as for the directories. We have calculated the extra bits needed if all items reside in only one copy (worst case). We assume an item size of 16 bytes — the cache line size of the Motorola MC88200.

A 32-processor DDM — that is, a one-level DDM with a maximum of eight two-way set-associative attraction memories — needs four bits of address tag per item, regardless of the attraction memory size. As we said earlier, the item space is not larger than the sum of the sizes of the attraction memories, so the size of each attraction memory is

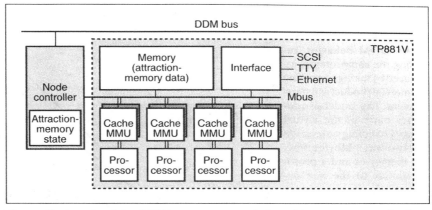

Figure 10. A node of the DDM prototype consisting of four processors sharing one attraction memory.

one eighth of the item space. Because each set in the attraction memory is divided two ways, 16 items can reside in the same set. In addition to the four bits needed to tell items apart, each item needs four bits of state. Thus, an item size of 128 bits gives an overhead of (4+4)/128 = 6 percent.

Adding another layer with eight eight-way set-associative directories brings the maximum number of processors to 256. The size of the directories is the sum of the sizes of the attraction memories in their subsystems. A directory entry consists of six bits for the address tag and four bits of state per item, using a calculation similar to the one above. The overhead in the attraction memories is larger than in the previous example because of the larger item space: seven bits of address tag and four bits of state. The total overhead per item is (6+4+7+4)/128 = 16 percent. A larger item size would, of course, decrease these overheads.

To minimize the memory overhead, we can use a different interpretation of the implicit state for different parts of the item space. In our initial implementation of DDM, the absence of an entry in a directory is interpreted as Invalid. The replacement algorithm introduces a home bus for an item. If an item is most often found in its home bus and nowhere else, the absence of an entry in a directory could instead be interpreted

Table 1. Remote delay in a two-level DDM (best cases).

CPU Access	State in Attraction Memory	Delay, One Level (cycles)	Delay, Two Levels (cycles)
Read	Invalid	55	100
Write	Shared	40	50
Write	Invalid	80	130

as Exclusive for items in its home subsystem, and as Invalid for items from outside. This would drastically reduce a directory's size. The technique would be practical only to a limited extent. Too small directories restrict the number of items moving out of their subsystems and thus limit sharing and migration, resulting in drawbacks similar to those of NUMAs.

Item space is slightly smaller than the sum of the attraction memories because of sharing in the system. This introduces a memory overhead not taken into account in the above calculations. However, in a COMA a "cached" item occupies only one space, while in other shared-memory architectures it requires two spaces: one in the cache and one in the shared memory.

Simulated performance

We used an execution-driven simulation environment that lets us study large programs running on many processors in a reasonable amount of time. We parameterized the DDM simulation model with data from our ongoing prototype project. The model accurately describes DDM behavior, including the compromises introduced by taking an existing commercial product as a starting point. The model also describes parts of the virtual memory handling system. We used two-way 1-Mbyte attraction memories and a protocol similar to the one described here, providing sequential consistency.

For a representation of applications from engineering and symbolic computing, we studied parallel execution of the Stanford Parallel Applications for Shared Memory (Splash),[11] the OR-parallel Prolog system Muse, and a matrix multiplication program. All programs were originally written for UMA architectures (Sequent Symmetry or Encore Multimax computers) and use static or dynamic scheduler algorithms. They adapt well to a COMA without any changes. All programs take on the order of one CPU minute to run sequentially, without any simulations,

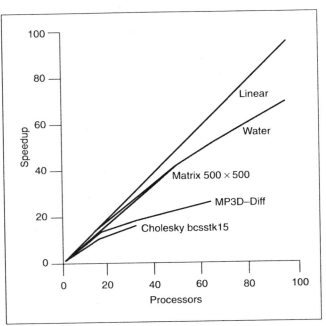

Figure 11. Speedup curves for some of the reported programs.

on a Sun Sparcstation. The speedups reported in Figure 11 and Table 2 are relative to the execution of a single DDM node with one processor, assuming a 100 percent hit rate in the attraction memory.

The Splash-Water program simulates the movements of water molecules. Its execution time is $O(m^2)$, where m is the number of molecules. Therefore, it is often simulated with a small working set. We used 192 molecules and a working set of 320 Kbytes. Each of the 96 processors in Figure 11 handles only two molecules. Most of the locality in the small working set can be exploited on the processor cache, and only about 44 percent of the transactions reaching the attraction memory will hit. A real-size working set would still have the same good locality and would benefit more from the large attraction memories to maintain the speedup. We tested this hypothesis with a single run with 384 molecules, as shown in Table 2.

The Splash-MP3D program is a wind tunnel simulator with which a good speedup is harder to achieve because of a high invalidation frequency resulting in a poor hit rate. The program is often run with the memory filled with data

Table 2. Statistics from DDM simulations. Hit rate statistics are for data only, except with Muse, where we used a unified I + D cache. The remote access rate is the percentage of the data accesses issued by a processor that create remote coherence traffic. An increased working set results in less load on the buses for Water and Cholesky.

	Water		MP3D	MP3D-Diff	Cholesky		Matrix	Muse
Input data	192 molecules	384 molecules	75,000 particles	75,000 particles	m14 (small)	m15 (large)	500×500	Pundit
Cold start included?	yes	yes	no	no	yes	yes	yes	no
DDM topology	2×8×4	2×8×4	2×8×2	2×8×2	2×8×2	2×8×2	8×4	4×4
Hit rate (data) percent								
D cache	99	99	86	92	96	89	92	98.5
Attraction memory	44	65	40	88	6	74	98	91
Remote access rate	0.6	0.4	8.4	1.0	3.8	2.8	0.16	0.20
Bus utilization percent								
Mbus	31	26	86	54	70	60	55	—
Lower DDM bus	39	30	88	24	80	66	—	—
Top DDM bus	25	20	66	13	70	49	4	—
Speedup per number of processors	52/64	53/64	6/32	19/32	10/32	17/32	29/32	—/16

structures representing particles, divided equally among the processors. The three-dimensional space is divided into space cells represented by data structures. MP3D runs in time phases and moves each particle once each phase. Moving a particle involves updating its state and also the state of the space cell where the molecule currently resides. All processors must write to all the space cells, resulting in a poor locality. In fact, 95 percent of the misses we found in DDM were due to this write-invalidate effect. We simulated 75,000 particles, a working set of 4 Mbytes.

MP3D-Diff is a rewritten version of the program that achieves a better hit rate. Particle distribution over processors is based on their current location in space. In other words, all particles in the same space cells are handled by the same processor. Updating of both particle state and space cell state is local to the processor. When a particle moves across a processor border, a new processor handles its data — the particle data diffuse to the new processor's attraction memory. The rewritten program has some 30 extra lines and requires a COMA to run well. In a COMA the particle data that occupy the major part of the physical memory are allowed to move freely among the attraction memories.

Splash-Cholesky factorizes a sparsely positive definite matrix. The matrix is divided into supernodes in a global task queue to be picked up by any worker — the scheduling is dynamic. We used the large input matrix bcsstk15 (m15), which occupies 800 Kbytes unfactored and 7.7 Mbytes factored. The nature of the Cholesky algorithm limits the available parallelism, which depends on the size of the input matrix. For comparison, Table 2 presents a run with the smaller matrix bcsstk14 (m14) of 420 Kbytes unfactored and 1.4 Mbytes factored.

The matrix multiplication program performs plain matrix multiplication on a 500×500 matrix using a blocked algorithm. The working set is about 3 Mbytes.

Muse is an OR-parallel Prolog system implemented in C at the Swedish Institute of Computer Science. Its input is the large natural language system Pundit from Unisys Paoli Research Center. An active working set of 2 Mbytes is touched during the execution. Muse distributes work dynamically and shows a good locality on a COMA. Because we ran Muse on an earlier version of the

simulator, some of the statistics are not reported in Table 2.

Simulation shows that the COMA principle works well for programs originally written for UMA architectures and that the slow buses of our prototype can accommodate many processors. The overhead of the COMA explored in our hardware prototype is limited to 16 percent in the access time between the processor caches and the attraction memory. Memory overhead is 6 to 16 percent for 32 to 256 processors. ■

Acknowledgments

The Swedish Institute of Computer Science is a nonprofit research foundation sponsored by the Swedish National Board for Technical Development (NUTEK), Swedish Telecom, Ericsson Group, ASEA Brown Boveri, IBM Sweden, Nobel Tech System AB, and the Swedish Defence Materiel administration (FMV). Part of the work on DDM is being carried out within the ESPRIT project 2741 PEPMA.

We thank our many colleagues involved in or associated with the project, especially David H.D. Warren of the University of Bristol, who is a coinventor of DDM. Mikael Löfgren of the Swedish Institute of Computer Science wrote the DDM simulator, basing his work on "Abstract Execution," which was provided to us by James Larus of the University of Wisconsin.

References

1. P. Stenström, "A Survey of Cache Coherence for Multiprocessors," *Computer*, Vol. 23, No. 6, June 1990, pp. 12-24.

2. D. Lenoski et al., "The Directory-Based Cache Coherence Protocol for the DASH Multiprocessor," *Proc. 17th Ann. Int'l Symp. Computer Architecture*, IEEE-CS Press, Los Alamitos, Calif., Order No. 2047, 1990, pp. 148-159.

3. D.H.D. Warren and S. Haridi, "Data Diffusion Machine—A Scalable Shared Virtual Memory Multiprocessor," *Int'l Conf. Fifth Generation Computer Systems*, ICOT, Ohmsha, Ltd., Tokyo, 1988, pp. 943-952.

4. E. Hagersten, S. Haridi, and D.H.D. Warren, "The Cache-Coherence Protocol of the Data Diffusion Machine," in *Cache and Interconnect Architectures in Multiprocessors*, M. Dubois and S.

Thakkar, eds., Kluwer Academic, Norwell, Mass., 1990, pp. 165-188.

5. A. Wilson, "Hierarchical Cache/Bus Architecture for Shared Memory Multiprocessor," Tech. Report ETR 86-006, Encore Computer Corp., Marlborough, Mass., 1986.

6. J.R. Goodman and P.J. Woest, "The Wisconsin Multicube: A New Large-Scale Cache-Coherent Multiprocessor," *Proc. 15th Ann. Int'l Symp. Computer Architecture*, IEEE-CS Press, Los Alamitos, Calif., Order No. 861, 1988, pp. 422-431.

7. J.-L. Baer and W.-H. Wang, "On the Inclusion Properties for Multi-Level Cache Hierarchies," *Proc. 15th Ann. Int'l Symp. Computer Architecture*, IEEE-CS Press, Los Alamitos, Calif., Order No. 861, 1988, pp. 73-80.

8. A. Landin, E. Hagersten, and S. Haridi. "Race-Free Interconnection Networks and Multiprocessor Consistency," *Proc. 18th Ann. Int'l Symp. Computer Architecture*, IEEE-CS Press, Los Alamitos, Calif., Order No. 2146, 1991, pp. 106-115.

9. C.E. Leiserson, "Fat Trees: Universal Networks for Hardware-Efficient Supercomputing," *IEEE Trans. Computers*, Vol. 34, No. 10, Oct. 1985, pp. 892-901.

10. L. Barroso and M. Dubois, "Cache Coherence on a Slotted Ring," *Proc. Int'l Conf. Parallel Processing*, IEEE-CS Press, Los Alamitos, Calif., Order No. 2355, 1991, pp. 230-237.

11. J.S. Singh, W.-D. Weber, and A. Gupta, *Splash: Stanford Parallel Applications for Shared Memory*, Tech. Report, CSL-TR-91-469, Computer Systems Laboratory, Stanford Univ., Stanford, Calif., 1991.

Erik Hagersten has led the Data Diffusion Machine Project at the Swedish Institute of Computer Science since 1988. He is a coinventor of the Data Diffusion Machine. His research interests include computer architectures, parallel processing, and simulation methods. From 1982 to 1988, he worked at the Ericsson Computer Science Lab on new architectures and at Ericsson Telecom on high-performance fault-tolerant processors.

From 1984 to 1985, he was a visiting research engineer in the Dataflow Group at MIT.

Hagersten received his MS in electrical engineering in 1982 from the Royal Institute of Technology, Stockholm, where he is currently finishing off his PhD degree.

Anders Landin is a research staff member at the Swedish Institute of Computer Science, where he has been working with the DDM project since 1989. His research interests include computer architecture, parallel processing, memory systems for shared-memory multiprocessors, and VLSI systems and simulation.

Landin received his MS in computer science and engineering from Lund University, Sweden, in 1989. He is a PhD student at the Royal Institute of Technology, Stockholm.

Seif Haridi is leader of the Logic Programming and Parallel Systems Lab at the Swedish Institute of Computer Science. He is also an adjunct professor at the Royal Institute of Technology, Stockholm. His research interests include combining parallel logic programming, concurrent objects, and constraints, and multiprocessor architectures suitable for such programming paradigms. He is a coinventor of DDM. Before joining the Swedish Institute of Computer Science, he was at the IBM T.J. Watson Research Center.

Haridi received his BS from Cairo University and his PhD from the Royal Institute of Technology.

THE COSMIC CUBE

Sixty-four small computers are connected by a network of point-to-point communication channels in the plan of a binary 6-cube. This "Cosmic Cube" computer is a hardware simulation of a future VLSI implementation that will consist of single-chip nodes. The machine offers high degrees of concurrency in applications and suggests that future machines with thousands of nodes are both feasible and attractive.

CHARLES L. SEITZ

The Cosmic Cube is an experimental computer for exploring the practice of highly concurrent computing. The largest of several Cosmic Cubes currently in use at Caltech consists of 64 small computers that work concurrently on parts of a larger problem and coordinate their computations by sending messages to each other. We refer to these individual small computers as *nodes*. Each node is connected through bidirectional, asynchronous, point-to-point communication channels to six other nodes, to form a communication network that follows the plan of a six-dimensional hypercube, what we call a *binary 6-cube* (see Figure 1). An operating system kernel in each node schedules and runs processes within that node, provides system calls for processes to send and receive messages, and routes the messages that flow through the node.

The excellent performance of the Cosmic Cube on a variety of complex and demanding applications and its modest cost and open-ended expandability suggest that

The research described in this paper was sponsored by the Defense Advanced Research Projects Agency, ARPA order number 3771, and monitored by the Office of Naval Research under contract number N00014-79-C-0597.

highly concurrent systems of this type are an effective means of achieving faster and less expensive computing in the near future. The Cosmic Cube nodes were designed as a hardware simulation of what we expect to be able to integrate onto one or two chips in about five years. Future machines with thousands of nodes are feasible, and for many demanding computing problems, these machines should be able to outperform the fastest uniprocessor systems. Even with current microelectronic technology, the 64-node machine is quite powerful for its cost and size: It can handle a variety of demanding scientific and engineering computations five to ten times faster than a VAX11/780.

THE MESSAGE-PASSING ARCHITECTURE

A significant difference between the Cosmic Cube and most other parallel processors is that this multiple-instruction multiple-data machine uses *message passing* instead of shared variables for communication between concurrent processes. This computational model is reflected in the hardware structure and operating system, and is also the explicit communication and synchronization primitive seen by the programmer.

The hardware structure of a message-passing machine like the Cosmic Cube differs from a shared-storage multiprocessor in that it employs no switching network between processors and storage (see Figure 2). The advantage of this architecture is in the separation of engineering concerns into processor-storage communication and the interprocess communication. The critical path in the communication between an instruction processor and its random-access storage, the so-called von Neumann bottleneck, can be engineered to exhibit a much smaller latency when the processor and storage are physically localized. The processor and storage might occupy a single chip, hybrid package, or circuit board, depending on the technology and complexity of the node.

It was a premise of the Cosmic Cube experiment that the internode communication should scale well to very large numbers of nodes. A *direct* network like the hypercube satisfies this requirement, with respect to both the aggregate bandwidth achieved across the many concurrent communication channels and the feasibility of the implementation. The hypercube is actually a distributed variant of an *indirect* logarithmic switching network like the Omega or banyan networks: the kind that might be used in shared-storage organizations. With the hypercube, however, communication paths traverse different numbers of channels and so exhibit

different latencies. It is possible, therefore, to take advantage of communication locality in placing processes in nodes.

Message-passing machines are simpler and more economical than shared-storage machines; the greater the number of processors, the greater this advantage. However, the more tightly coupled shared-storage machine is more versatile, since it is able to support code and data sharing. Indeed, shared-storage machines can easily simulate message-passing primitives, whereas message-passing machines do not efficiently support code and data sharing.

Figure 2 emphasizes the differences between shared-storage and message-passing organizations by representing the extreme cases. We conjecture that shared-storage organizations will be preferred for systems with tens of processors, and message-passing organizations for systems with hundreds or thousands of processing nodes. Hybrid forms employing local or cache storage with each processor, with a message-passing approach to nonlocal storage references and cache coherence, may well prove to be the most attractive option for systems having intermediate numbers of processors.

PROCESS PROGRAMMING

The hardware structure of the Cosmic Cube, when viewed at the level of nodes and channels, is a difficult target for programming any but the most highly regular computing problems. The resident operating system of the Cosmic Cube creates a more flexible and machine-independent environment for concurrent computations. This process model of computation is quite similar to the hardware structure of the Cosmic Cube but is usefully abstracted from it. Instead of formulating a problem to fit on nodes and on the physical communication channels that exist only between certain pairs of nodes, the programmer can formulate problems in terms of processes and "virtual" communication channels between processes.

The basic unit of these computations is the *process*, which for our purposes is a sequential program that sends and receives messages. A single node may contain many processes. All processes execute concurrently, whether by virtue of being in different nodes or by being interleaved in execution within a single node. Each process has a unique (global) ID that serves as an address for messages. All messages have headers containing the destination and the sender ID, and a message type and length. Messages are queued in transit, but message order is preserved between any pair of processes. The semantics of the message-passing operations are independent of the placement of processes in nodes.

Process programming environments with interprocess communication by messages are common to many multiprogramming operating systems. A copy of the resident operating system of the Cosmic Cube, called the "kernel," resides in each node. All of these copies are concurrently executable. The kernel can spawn and

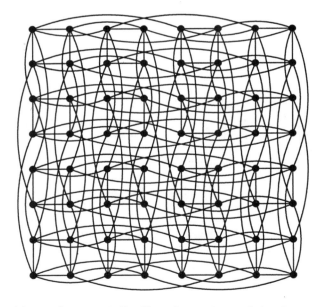

A hypercube connects $N = 2^n$ small computers, called nodes, through point-to-point communication channels in the Cosmic Cube. Shown here is a two-dimensional projection of a six-dimensional hypercube, or binary 6-cube, which corresponds to a 64-node machine.

FIGURE 1.   A Hypercube (also known as a binary cube or a Boolean *n*-cube)

kill processes within its own node, schedule their execution, spy on them through a debug process, manage storage, and deal with error conditions. The kernel also handles the queuing and routing of messages for processes in its node, as well as for messages that may pass through its node. Many of the functions that we would expect to be done in hardware in a future integrated node, such as message routing, are done in the kernel in the Cosmic Cube. We are thus able to experiment with different algorithms and implementations of low-level node functions in the kernel.

The Cosmic Cube has no special programming notation. Process code is written in ordinary sequential programming languages (e.g., Pascal or C) extended with statements or external procedures to control the sending and receiving of messages. These programs are compiled on other computers and loaded into and relocated within a node as binary code, data, and stack segments.

PROCESS DISTRIBUTION

It was a deliberate decision in the design of the kernel that once a process was instantiated in a node, the kernel would not relocate it to another node. One consequence of this restriction is that the physical node number can be included in the ID for a process. This eliminates the awkward way in which a distributed map from processes to nodes would otherwise scale with the number of nodes. Messages are routed according to the physical address part of the destination process ID in the message header.

This decision was also consistent with the notion that programmers should be able to control the distribution of processes onto the nodes on the basis of an understanding of the structure of the concurrent computation being performed. Alternatively, since it is only the efficiency of a multiple-process program that is influenced by process placement, the choice of the node in which

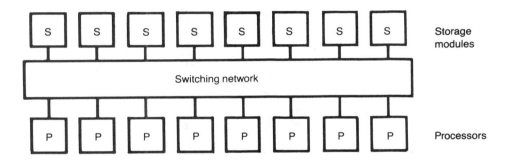

(a) Most multiprocessors are structured with a switching network, either a crossbar connection of buses or a multi-stage routing network, between the processors and storage. The switching network introduces a latency in the communication between processors and storage, and does not scale well to large sizes. Communication between processes running concurrently in different processors occurs through shared variables and common access to one large address space.

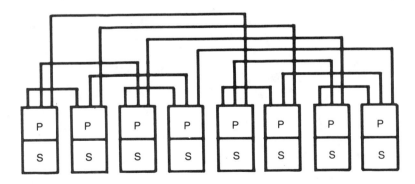

(b) Message-passing multicomputer systems retain a physically close and fast connection between processors and their associated storage. The concurrent computers (nodes) can send messages through a network of communication channels. The network shown here is a three-dimensional cube, which is a small version of the communication plan used in six dimensions in the 64-node Cosmic Cube.

NOTE: Actual machines need not follow one model or the other absolutely: Various hybrids are possible.

FIGURE 2. A Comparison of Shared-Storage Multiprocessors and Message-Passing Machines

a process is to be spawned can be deferred to a library process that makes this assignment after inquiring about processing load and storage utilization in nearby nodes.

A careful distribution of processes to nodes generally involves some trade-offs between load balancing and message locality. We use the term *process structure* to describe a set of processes and their references to other processes. A static process structure, or a snapshot of a dynamic process structure, can be represented as a graph of process vertices connected by arcs that represent reference (see Figure 3). One can also think of the arcs as virtual communication channels, in that process A having reference to process B is what makes a message from A to B possible.

The hardware communication structure of this class of message-passing machines can be represented similarly as a graph of vertices for nodes and (undirected) edges for the bidirectional communication channels.

The mapping of a process structure onto a machine is an embedding of the process structure graph into the machine graph (see Figure 4). In general, the arcs map not only to internal communication and single edges, but also to paths representing the routing of messages in intermediate nodes. It is this embedding that determines both the locality of communication achieved and the load-balancing properties of the mapping.

CONCURRENCY APPROACH

Most sequential processors, including microprocessors like the RISC chips described elsewhere in this issue,[1] are *covertly* concurrent machines that speed up the interpretation of a single instruction stream by techniques such as instruction prefetching and execution pipelining. Compilers can assist this speedup by recovering the concurrency in expression evaluations and

---

[1] See David A. Patterson's article, "Reduced Instruction Set Computers" (*Commun. ACM 28*, 1 (Jan. 1985)), on pages 8–21 of this issue.

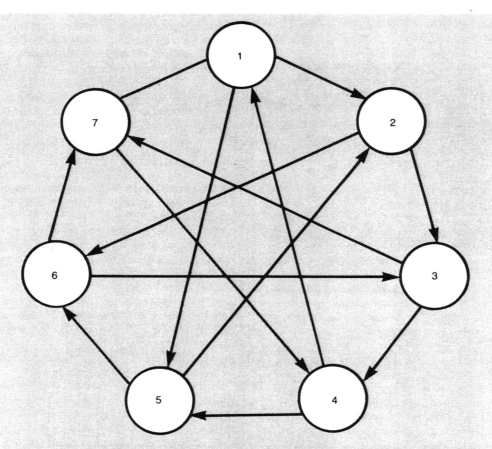

In this example, the processes are computing the time evolution, or orbital positions, of seven bodies interacting by a symmetrical force, such as gravity. Messages containing the position and mass of each particle are sent from each process $(N - 1)/2$ steps around the ring, accumulating the forces due to each interaction along the way, while the process that is host to that body accumulates the other $(N - 1)/2$ forces. The messages are then returned over the chordal paths to the host process, where the forces are summed and the position and velocity of the body are updated. This example is representative of many computations that are demanding simply because of the number of interacting parts, and not because the force law that each part obeys is complex. However, this is not the formulation one would use for very many bodies.

FIGURE 3. The Process Structure for a Concurrent Formulation of the *N*-Body Problem

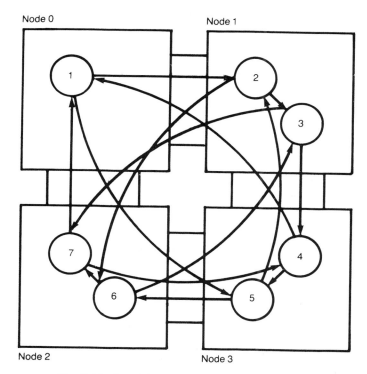

Node 0   Node 1

Node 2   Node 3

The distribution of the processes does not influence the computed results, but it does, through load balancing and message locality, influence the speedup achieved by using four computers for this task instead of one.

FIGURE 4.   The Process Structure for the 7-Body Example Embedded into a 4-Node Machine

in the innermost iterations of a program, and then generating code that is "vectorized" or in some other way allows the processor to interpret the sequential program with some concurrency. These techniques, together with caching, allow about a ten-fold concurrency and speedup over naive sequential interpretation.

We can use such techniques within nodes, where we are tied to sequential program representations of the processes. In addition, we want to have at least as many concurrent processes as nodes. Where are such large degrees of concurrency to be discovered in a computation? One quick but not quite accurate way of describing the approach used in the Cosmic Cube is that we *overtly* exploit the concurrency found in the outermost, rather than innermost, program constructs of certain demanding computations. It appears that many highly demanding computing problems can be expressed in terms of concurrent processes with either sparse or predictable interaction. Also, the degree of concurrency inherent in such problems tends to grow with the size and computing demands of the problem.

It is important to understand that the compilers used to generate process code for the Cosmic Cube do not "automatically" find a way to run sequential programs

concurrently. We do not know how to write a program that translates application programs represented by old, dusty FORTRAN decks into programs that exploit concurrency between nodes. In fact, because efficient concurrent algorithms may be quite different from their sequential counterparts, we regard such a translation as implausible, and instead try to formulate and express a computation explicitly in terms of a collection of communicating concurrent processes.

Dataflow graphs, like those discussed in this issue in the article on the Manchester dataflow machine,[2] also allow an explicit representation of concurrency in a computation. Although we have not yet tried to do so, dataflow computations can be executed on machines like the Cosmic Cube. One of the reasons we have not done so is that many of the computations that show excellent performance on the Cosmic Cube or on other parallel machines, and are very naturally expressed in terms of processes (or objects), are simulations of physical systems. With such simulations, the state of a system is repeatedly evaluated and assigned to state variables. The functional (side-effect free) semantics of dataflow, in pure form, appears to get in the way of a straightforward expression of this type of computation. The process model that we use for programming the Cosmic Cube is relatively less restrictive than dataflow and, in our implementation, is relatively more demanding of attention to process placement and other details.

CONCURRENT FORMULATIONS

The crucial step in developing an application program for the Cosmic Cube is the concurrent formulation: It is here that both the correctness and efficiency of the program are determined. It is often intriguing, and even amusing, to devise strategies for coordinating a myriad of concurrent computing activities in an orderly way.

For many of the demanding computations encountered in science and engineering, this formulation task has not proved to be very much more difficult than it is on sequential machines. These applications are often based on concurrent adaptations of well-known sequential algorithms or are similar to the systolic algorithms that have been developed for regular VLSI computational arrays. The process structure remains static for the duration of a computation.

At the risk of creating the impression that all of the application programs for the Cosmic Cube are as simple, let us offer one concrete example of a formulation and its process code. The problem is to compute the time evolution of a system of N bodies that interact by gravitational attraction or some other symmetrical force. Because each of the N bodies interacts with all of the other $N - 1$ bodies, this problem might not seem to be as appropriate for the Cosmic Cube as matrix, gridpoint, finite-difference, and other problems based solely

---

[2] See J.R. Gurd, C.C. Kirkham, and I. Watson's article, "The Manchester Prototype Dataflow Computer" (*Commun. ACM 28*, 1 (Jan. 1985)), on pages 34–52 of this issue.

on local interaction. Actually, universal interaction is easy because it maps beautifully onto the ring process structure shown for $N = 7$ in Figure 3.

Each of N identical processes is "host" to one body and is responsible for computing the forces due to $(N - 1)/2$ other bodies. With a symmetrical force, it is left to other processes to compute the other $(N - 1)/2$ forces.

The process also accumulates the forces and integrates the position of the body it hosts. As can be seen in the C process code in Figure 5, the process that is host to body 1 successively receives guests 7, 6, and 5, and accumulates forces due to these interactions. Meanwhile, a message containing the position, mass, accumulated force, and host process ID of body 1 is con-

```
/* process for an n-body computation, n odd, with symmetrical forces */
#include "cubedef.h"          /* cube definitions */
#include "force.h"            /* procedures for computing forces and positions */

struct body      {    double pos[3];      /* body position x,y,z         */
                      double vel[3];      /* velocity vector x,y,z       */
                      double force[3];    /* to accumulate forces        */
                      double mass;        /* body mass                   */
                      int    home_id;     /* id of body's home process   */
                 } host, guest;

struct startup {    int n;              /* number of bodies            */
                    int next_id;        /* ID of next process on ring  */
                    int steps;          /* number of integration steps */
               } s;

struct desc my_body_in, my_body_out, startup_in;  /* IH channels            */
struct desc body_in, body_out, body_bak;          /* inter-process channels */

cycle() /* read initial state, compute, and send back final state */
{
    int i; double FORCE[3];

    /* initialize channel descriptors */
    /* init(*desc, id, type, buffer_len, buffer_address); */
    init(&my_body_in ,0,0,sizeof(struct body)/2,&host); recv_wait(&my_body_in);
    init(&startup_in ,0,1,sizeof(struct startup)/2,&s); recv_wait(&startup_in);
    init(&my_body_out,      IH_ID, 2, sizeof(struct body)/2, &host);
    init(&body_in    ,          0, 3, sizeof(struct body)/2, &guest);
    init(&body_out   , s.next_id, 3, sizeof(struct body)/2, &guest);
    init(&body_bak   ,          0, 4, sizeof(struct body)/2, &guest);

    while(s.steps--) /* repeat s.steps computation cycles */
    {
        body_out.buf = &host;                    /* first time send out host body */

        for(i = (s.n-1)/2; i--;)                  /* repeat (s.n-1)/2 times      */
        {
            send_wait(&body_out);                 /* send out the host|guest     */
            recv_wait(&body_in);                  /* receive the next guest      */
            COMPUTE_FORCE(&host,&guest,FORCE);    /* calculate force             */
            ADD_FORCE_TO_HOST(&host,FORCE);       /* may the force be with you   */
            ADD_FORCE_TO_GUEST(&guest,FORCE);     /* and with the guest, also    */
            body_out.buf = &guest;                /* prepare to pass the guest   */
        }
        body_bak.id = guest.home_id;                      /* send guest back     */
        send_wait(&body_bak); recv_wait(&body_bak);       /* the envoy returns   */
        ADD_GUEST_FORCE_TO_HOST(&host,&guest);
        UPDATE(&host);                                    /* integrate position  */
    }
    send_wait(&my_body_out);  /* send body back to host, complete one cycle */
}

main() { while(1) cycle(); }   /* main execute cycle repeatedly */
```

FIGURE 5. Process Code for the *N*-Body Example in the C Language

veyed through the processes that are host to bodies 2, 3, and 4 with the forces due to these interactions accumulated. After $(N-1)/2$ visits, the representations of the bodies are returned in a message to the process that is host to the body, the forces are combined, and the positions are updated.

A detail that is not shown in Figure 5 is the process that runs in the Cosmic Cube intermediate host (IH), or on another network-connected machine. This process spawns the processes in the cube and sends messages to the cube processes that provide the initial state, the ID of the next process in the ring, and an integer specifying the number of integration steps to be performed. The computation in the Cosmic Cube can run autonomously for long periods between interactions with the IH process. If some exceptional condition were to occur in the simulation, such as a collision or close encounter, the procedure that computes the forces could report this event via a message back to the IH process.

This ring of processes can, in turn, be embedded systematically into the machine structure (see Figure 4). In mapping seven identical processes, each with the same amount of work to do, onto 4 nodes, the load obviously cannot be balanced perfectly. Using a simple performance model originally suggested by Willis Ware, "speedup"—S—can be defined as

$$S = \frac{\text{time on 1 node}}{\text{time on } N \text{ nodes}}.$$

For this 7-body example on a 4-node machine, neglecting the time required for the communication between nodes, the speedup is clearly 7/2. Since computation proceeds 3.5 times faster using 4 nodes than it would on a single node, one can also say that the efficiency $e = S/N$ is 0.875, which is the fraction of the available cycles that are actually used.

More generally, if k is taken as the fraction of the steps in a computation that, because of dependencies, must be sequential, the time on N nodes is $\max(k, 1/N)$, so that the speedup cannot exceed $\min(1/k, N)$. This expression reduces to "Amdahl's argument," that $1/k$, the reciprocal of the fraction of the computation that must be done sequentially, limits the number of nodes that can usefully be put to work concurrently on a given problem. For example, nothing is gained in *this* formulation of an N-body problem by using more than N nodes.

Thus we are primarily interested in computations for which $1/k \gg N$: in effect, in computations in which the concurrency opportunities exceed the concurrent resources. Here the speedup obtained by using N nodes concurrently is limited by (1) the idle time that results from imperfect load balancing, (2) the waiting time caused by communication latencies in the channels and in the message forwarding, and (3) the processor time dedicated to processing and forwarding messages, a consideration that can be effectively eliminated by architectural improvements in the nodes. These factors are rather complex functions of the formulation, its

mapping onto N nodes, the communication latency, and the communication and computing speed of the nodes. We lump these factors into an "overhead" measure, σ, defined by the computation exhibiting a speedup of $S = N/(1 + \sigma)$. A small σ indicates that the Cosmic Cube is operating with high efficiency, that is, with nodes that are seldom idle, or seldom doing work they would not be doing in the single-node version of the computation.

COSMIC CUBE HARDWARE
Having introduced the architecture, computational model, and concurrent formulations, let us turn now to some experimental results.

Figure 6 is a photograph of the 64-node Cosmic Cube. For such a small machine, only 5 feet long, a one-dimensional projection of the six-dimensional hypercube is satisfactory. The channels are wired on a backplane beneath the long box in a pattern similar to that shown in Figure 2b. Larger machines would have nodes arrayed in two or three dimensions like the two-dimensional projection of the channels shown in Figure 1. The volume of the system is 6 cubic feet, the power consumption is 700 watts, and the manufacturing cost was $80,000. We also operate a 3-cube machine to support software development, since the 6-cube cannot readily be shared.

Most of the choices made in this design are fairly easy to explain. First of all, a binary n-cube communication plan was used because this network was shown by simulation to provide very good message-flow properties in irregular computations. It also contains all meshes of lower dimension, which is useful for regular mesh-connected problems. The binary n-cube can be viewed recursively. As one can see from studying Figure 1, the n-cube that is used to connect $2^n = N$ nodes is assembled from two $(n-1)$-cubes, with corresponding nodes connected by an additional channel. This property simplifies the packaging of machines of varying size. It also explains some of the excellent message-flow properties of the binary n-cube on irregular problems. The number of channels connecting the pairs of subcubes is proportional to the number of nodes and hence on average to the amount of message traffic they can generate.

With this rich connection scheme, simulation showed that we could use channels that are fairly slow (about 2 Mbit/sec) compared with the instruction rate. The communication latency is, in fact, deliberately large to make this node more nearly a hardware simulation of the situation anticipated for a single-chip node. The processor overhead for dealing with each 64-bit packet is comparable to its latency. The communication channels are asynchronous, full duplex, and include queues for a 64-bit "hardware packet" in the sender and in the receiver in each direction. These queues are a basic minimum necessary for decoupling the sending and receiving processes.

The Intel 8086 was selected as the instruction processor because it was the only single-chip instruction proc-

The nodes are packaged as one circuit board per node in the long card frame on the bench top. The six communication channels from each node are wired in a binary 6-cube on the backplane on the underside of the card frame. The separate units on the shelf above the long 6-cube box are the power supply and an "intermediate host" (IH) that connects through a communication channel to node 0 in the cube.

FIGURE 6.   The 64-Node Cosmic Cube in Operation

essor available with a floating-point coprocessor, the Intel 8087. Reasonable floating-point performance was necessary for many of the applications that our colleagues at Caltech wished to attempt. The system currently operates at a 5 MHz clock rate, limited by the 8087, although it is designed to be able to run at 8 MHz when faster 8087 chips become available. After our first prototypes, Intel Corporation generously donated chips for the 64-node Cosmic Cube.

The storage size of 128K bytes was decided upon after a great deal of internal discussion about "balance" in the design. It was argued that the cost incurred in doubling the storage size would better be spent on more nodes. In fact, this choice is clearly very dependent on target applications and programming style. The dynamic RAM includes parity checking but not error correction. Each node also includes 8 Kbytes of read-only

storage for initialization, a bootstrap loader, dynamic RAM refresh, and diagnostic testing programs.

Since building a machine is not a very common enterprise in a university, an account of the chronology of the hardware phase of the project may be of interest. A prototype 4-node (2-cube) system on wirewrap boards was designed, assembled, and tested in the winter of 1981–1982, and was used for software development and application programs until it was recently disassembled. The homogeneous structure of these machines was nicely exploited in the project when a small hardware prototype, similar to scaled-up machines, was used to accelerate software development. Encouraged by our experience with the 2-cube prototype, we had printed circuit boards designed and went through the other packaging logistics of assembling a machine of useful size. The Cosmic Cube grew from an 8-node to a

64-node machine over the summer of 1983 and has been in use since October 1983.

In its first year of operation (560,000 node-hours), the Cosmic Cube has experienced two hard failures, both quickly repaired; a soft error in the RAM is detected by a parity error on average once every several days.

COSMIC CUBE SOFTWARE

As is the case in many "hardware" projects, most of the work on the Cosmic Cube has been on the software. This effort has been considerably simplified by the availability of cross-compilers for the Intel 8086/8087 chips and because most of the software development is done on conventional computers. Programs are written and compiled in familiar computing environments, and their concurrent execution is then simulated on a small scale. Programs are downloaded into the cube through a connection managed by the intermediate host. In the interest of revealing all of the operational details of this unconventional machine, we begin with the start-up procedures.

The lowest level of software is part of what we call the *machine intrinsic* environment. This includes the instruction set of the node processor, its I/O communication with channels, and a small initialization and bootstrap loader program stored along with diagnostic programs in read-only storage in each processor. A start-up packet specifies the size of the cube to be initialized and may specify that the built-in RAM tests be run (concurrently) in the nodes. As part of the initialization process, each of the identical nodes discovers its position in whatever size cube was specified in the start-up packet sent from the intermediate host by sending messages to the other nodes. The initialization, illustrated in Figure 7, also involves messages that check the function of all of the communication channels to be used. Program loading following initialization typically loads the kernel.

A *crystalline* applications environment is characterized by programs written in C in which there is a single process per node and in which messages are sent by direct I/O operations to a specified channel. This system was developed by physics users for producing very efficient application programs for computations so regular they do not require message routing.

The operating system kernel, already described in outline, supports a *distributed process* environment with a copy of the kernel running in each node. The kernel is 9 Kbytes of code and 4 Kbytes of tables, and is divided into an "inner" and an "outer" kernel. Any storage in a node that is not used for the kernel or for processes is allocated as a kernel message buffer for queuing messages.

The inner kernel, written in 8086 assembly language, sends and receives messages in response to system calls from user processes. These calls pass the address of a message descriptor, which is shared between the kernel and user process. There is one uniform message format that hides all hardware characteristics, such as packet

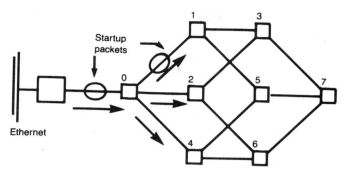

In the initialization, each of the identical nodes discovers its identity and checks all the communication channels with a message wave that traverses the 3-cube from node 0 to node 7, and then from node 7 to node 0. If node 3, for instance, did not respond to messages, then nodes 1, 2, and 7 would report this failure back to the host over other channels.

FIGURE 7. The Initialization of the Cosmic Cube

size. The kernel performs the construction and interpretation of message headers from the descriptor information. The hardware communication channels allow very fast and efficient "one-trip" message protocols; long messages are automatically fragmented. Messages being sent are queued in the sending process instead of being copied into the kernel message buffer, unless the message is local to the node. Local messages are either copied to the destination if the matching receive call has already been executed, or copied into the message buffer to assure a consistency in the semantics of local and nonlocal send operations.

Processes are often required to manage several concurrent message activities. Thus the send and receive calls do not "block." The calls return after creating a request that remains *pending* until the operation is completed. The completion of the message operation is tested by a lock variable in the message descriptor. Program execution can continue concurrently with many concurrently pending communication activities. A process can also use a *probe* call that determines whether a message of a specified type has been received and is queued in the kernel message buffer. A process that is in a situation where no progress can be made until some set of message areas is filled or emptied may elect to defer execution to another process. The inner kernel schedules user processes by a simple round robin scheme, with processes running for a fixed period of time or until they perform the system call that defers to the next process. The storage management and response to error conditions are conventional.

The outer kernel is structured as a set of privileged processes that user processes communicate with by messages rather than by system calls. One of these outer kernel processes spawns and kills processes: A process can be spawned either as a copy of a process already present in the node, in which case the code segment is shared, or from a file that is accessed by system messages between the spawn process and the intermediate host. Because process spawning is invoked by messages, it is equally possible to build process structures from processes running in the cube, in the intermediate host, or in network-connected machines. One other essential outer kernel process is known as the *spy* process and permits a process in the intermediate host to examine and modify the kernel's tables, queued messages, and process segments.

Our current efforts are focused on intermediate host software that will allow both time- and space-sharing of the cube.

APPLICATIONS AND BENCHMARKS

Caltech scientists in high-energy physics, astrophysics, quantum chemistry, fluid mechanics, structural mechanics, seismology, and computer science are developing concurrent application programs to run on Cosmic Cubes. Several research papers on scientific results have already been published, and other applications are developing rapidly. Several of us in the Caltech computer science department are involved in this research both as system builders and also through interests in concurrent computing and applications to VLSI analysis tools and graphics.

Application programs on the 64-node Cosmic Cube execute up to 3 million floating-point operations per second. The more interesting and revealing benchmarks are those for problems that utilize the machine at less than peak speeds. A single Cosmic Cube node at a 5 MHz clock rate runs at one-sixth the speed of the same program compiled and run on a VAX11/780. Thus we should expect the 64-node Cosmic Cube to run at best $(1/6)(64) \approx 10$ times faster than the VAX11/780. Quite remarkably, many programs reach this performance, with measured values of σ ranging from about 0.025 to 0.500. For example, a typical computation with $\sigma = 0.2$ exhibits a speedup $S = (64)/(1.2) \approx 50$. One should not conclude that applications with larger σ are unreasonable; indeed, given the economy of these machines, it is still attractive to run production programs with $\sigma > 1$.

A lattice computation programmed by physics postdoc Steve Otto at Caltech has run for an accumulated 2500 hours on the 6-cube. This program is a Monte Carlo simulation on a $12 \times 12 \times 12 \times 16$ lattice, an investigation of the predictions of quantum chromodynamics, which is a theory that explains the substructure of particles such as protons in terms of quarks and the glue field that holds them bound. Otto has shown for the first time in a single computation both the short-range Coulombic force and the constant long-range force between quarks. The communication overhead in this naturally load balanced computation varies from $\sigma = 0.025$ in the phase of computing the gauge field to $\sigma = 0.050$ in computing observables by a contour integration in the lattice.

Among the most interesting and ambitious programs

currently in development is a concurrent MOS-VLSI circuit simulator, called CONCISE, formulated and written by computer science graduate student Sven Mattisson. This program has been useful for developing techniques for less regular computations and promises very good performance for a computation that consumes large fractions of the computing cycles on many high-performance computers.

The simulation of an electrical circuit involves repeated solution of a set of simultaneous nonlinear equations. The usual approach, illustrated in Figure 8, is to compute piecewise linear admittances from the circuit models and then to use linear equation solution techniques. CONCISE uses a nodal admittance matrix formulation for the electrical network. The admittance matrix is sparse but, because electrical networks have arbitrary topology, does not have the crystalline regularity of the physics computations. At best the matrix is "clumped" because of the locality properties of the electrical network.

This program is mapped onto the cube by partitioning the admittance matrix by rows into concurrent processes. The linear equation solution phase of the computation, a Jacobi iteration, involves considerable communication, but the linearization that requires about 80 percent of the execution time on sequential computers is completely uncoupled. Integration and output in computing transient solutions are small components of the whole computation. The computation is actually much more complex than we can describe here; for example, the integration step is determined adaptively from the convergence of previous solutions.

Among the many unknowns in experimenting with circuit simulation is the interaction between communication cost and load balancing in the mapping of processes to nodes. Although "clumping" can be exploited in this mapping to localize communication, it may also concentrate many of the longer iterations occurring during a signal transient into a single node, thus creating a "dynamic" load imbalance in the computation.

FUTURE PERFECT CUBES

Today's system is never as perfect as tomorrow's. Although software can be polished and fixed on a daily basis, the learning cycle on the architecture and hardware is much longer. Let us then summarize briefly what this experiment has taught us so far and speculate about future systems of this same general class.

Although programming has not turned out to be as difficult as we should have expected, we do have a long agenda of possible improvements for the programming tools. Most of the deficiencies are in the representation and compilation of process code. There is nothing in the definition of the message-passing primitives that we would want to change, but because we have tacked these primitives onto programming languages simply as external functions, the process code is unnecessarily baroque.

The way the descriptors for "virtual channels" are

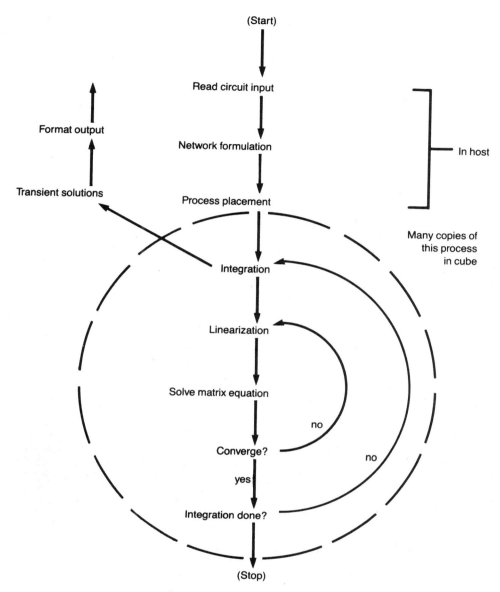

(Start)

Read circuit input

Network formulation

Format output

Transient solutions

Process placement

In host

Many copies of
this process
in cube

Integration

Linearization

Solve matrix equation

no

no

Converge?

yes

Integration done?

(Stop)

The sequential and concurrent versions of this program differ in that the concurrent program employs many copies of the process depicted inside the dashed circle.

FIGURE 8.   The Organization of the CONCISE Circuit Simulator

declared, initialized, and manipulated (see Figure 5), for instance, is not disguised by a pretty syntax. More fundamentally, the attention the programmer must give to blocking on lock variables is tedious and can create incorrect or unnecessary constraints on message and program sequencing. Such tests are better inserted into the process code automatically, on the basis of a data-flow analysis similar to that used by optimizing compilers for register allocation. These improvements may be only aesthetic, but they are a necessary preliminary for making these systems less intimidating for the beginning user.

The cost/performance ratio of this class of architectures is quite good even with today's technologies, and progress in microelectronics will translate into either increased performance or decreased cost. The present Cosmic Cube node is not a large increment in complexity over the million-bit storage chips that are expected in a few years. Systems of 64 single-chip node elements could fit in workstations, and systems of thousands of nodes would make interesting supercomputers. Although this approach to high-performance computation is limited to applications that have highly concurrent formulations, the applications developed on the Cosmic

Cube have shown us that many, perhaps even a majority, of the large and demanding computations in science and engineering are of this type.

It is also reasonable to consider systems with nodes that are either larger or smaller than the present Cosmic Cube nodes. We have developed at Caltech a single-chip "Mosaic" node with the same basic structure as the Cosmic Cube node, but with less storage, for experimenting with the engineering of systems of single-chip nodes and with the programming and application of finer grain machines. Such machines offer a cost/performance ratio superior even to that of the Cosmic Cube. However, we expect them to be useful for a somewhat smaller class of problems. Similarly, the use of better, faster instruction processors, higher capacity storage chips, and integrated communication channels suggests machines with nodes that will be an order of magnitude beyond the Cosmic Cube in performance and storage capacity, but at the same physical size.

The present applications of the Cosmic Cube are all compute- rather than I/O-intensive. It is possible, however, to include I/O channels with each node and so to create sufficient I/O band width for almost any purpose. Such machines could be used, for example, with many sensors, such as the microphone arrays towed behind seismic exploration ships. The computing could be done in real time instead of through hundreds of tapes sent on to a supercomputer. It is also possible to attach disks for secondary storage to a subset of the nodes.

APPENDIX—HISTORY AND ACKNOWLEDGMENTS

The origins of the Cosmic Cube project can be traced to research performed at Caltech during 1978–1980 by graduate students Sally Browning and Bart Locanthi [1, 8]. These ideas were in turn very much influenced by several other researchers. We sometimes refer to the Cosmic Cube as a *homogeneous machine*, from a term used in a 1977 paper by Herbert Sullivan and T.L. Brashkow [13]. They define their homogeneous machine as a machine "of uniform structure." C.A.R. Hoare's communicating sequential processes notation, the actor paradigm developed by Carl Hewitt, the processing surface experiments of Alain Martin, and the systolic algorithms described by H.T. Kung, Charles Leiserson, and Clark Thompson encouraged us to consider message passing as an explicit computational primitive [2, 4, 6, 10].

The Cosmic Cube design is based in largest part on extensive program modeling and simulations carried out during 1980–1982 by Charles R. Lang [7]. It was from this work that the communication plan of a binary *n*-cube, the bit rates of the communication channels, and the organization of the operating system primitives were chosen. Together with early simulation results, a workshop on "homogeneous machines" organized by Carl Hewitt during the summer of 1981 helped give us the confidence to start building an experimental machine.

The logical design of the Cosmic Cube is the work of computer science graduate students Erik DeBenedictis and Bill Athas. The early crystalline software tools were developed by physics graduate students Eugene Brooks and Mark Johnson. The machine intrinsic and kernel code was written by Bill Athas, Reese Faucette, and Mike Newton, with Alain Martin, Craig Steele, Jan van de Snepscheut, and Wen-King Su contributing valuable critical reviews of the design and implementation of the distributed process environment.

The ongoing work described in part in this article is sponsored through the VLSI program of the Information Processing Techniques Office of DARPA. We thank Bob Kahn, Duane Adams, and Paul Losleben for their support and interest.

REFERENCES
1. Browning, S.A. The tree machine: A highly concurrent computing environment. Tech. Rep. 3760:TR:80, Computer Science Dept., California Institute of Technology, Pasadena, 1980.
2. Clinger, W.D. Foundations of actor semantics. Ph.D. thesis, Dept. of Electrical Engineering and Computer Science, Massachusetts Institute of Technology, Cambridge, May 1981.
3. Fox, G.C., and Otto, S.W. Algorithms for concurrent processors. *Phys. Today* 37, 5 (May 1984), 50–59.
4. Hoare, C.A.R. Communicating sequential processes. *Commun. ACM* 21, 8 (Aug. 1978), 666–677.
5. Hockney, R.W., and Jesshope, C.R. *Parallel Computers*. Adam Hilger, Bristol, United Kingdom, 1981.
6. Kung, H.T. The Structure of Parallel Algorithms. In *Advances in Computers*, vol 19. Academic Press, New York, 1980.
7. Lang, C.R. The extension of object-oriented languages to a homogeneous, concurrent architecture. Tech. Rep. 5014:TR:82, Computer Science Dept., California Institute of Technology, Pasadena, 1982.
8. Locanthi, B.N. The homogeneous machine, Tech. Rep. 3759:TR:80, Computer Science Dept., California Institute of Technology, Pasadena, 1980.
9. Lutz, C., Rabin, S., Seitz, C., and Speck, D. Design of the Mosaic Element. In *Proceedings of the Conference on Advanced Research in VLSI* (MIT), P. Penfield, Ed, Artech House, Dedham, Mass., 1984, pp. 1–10.
10. Martin, A.J. A distributed implementation method for parallel programming. *Inf. Process. 80* (1980), 309–314.
11. Schwartz, J.T. Ultracomputers. *ACM Trans. Program. Lang. Syst.* 2, 4 (Oct. 1980), 484–521.
12. Seitz, C.L. Experiments with VLSI ensemble machines. *J. VLSI Comput. Syst.* 1, 3 (1984).
13. Sullivan, H., and Brashkow, T.R. A large scale homogeneous machine I & II. In *Proceedings of the 4th Annual Symposium on Computer Architecture*, 1977, pp. 105–124.
14. Ware, W.H. The ultimate computer. *IEEE Spectrum* (Mar. 1972), 84–91.

CR Categories and Subject Descriptors: C.1.2 [**Processor Architectures**]: Multiple Data Stream Architectures (Multiprocessors); C.5.4 [**Computer System Implementation**]: VLSI Systems; D.1.3 [**Programming Techniques**]: Concurrent Programming; D.4.1 [**Operating Systems**]: Process Management
General Terms: Algorithms, Design, Experimentation
Additional Key Words and Phrases: highly concurrent computing, message-passing architectures, message-based operating systems, process programming, object-oriented programming, VLSI systems

Memory Coherence in Shared Virtual Memory Systems

KAI LI
Princeton University
and
PAUL HUDAK
Yale University

The memory coherence problem in designing and implementing a shared virtual memory on loosely coupled multiprocessors is studied in depth. Two classes of algorithms, centralized and distributed, for solving the problem are presented. A prototype shared virtual memory on an Apollo ring based on these algorithms has been implemented. Both theoretical and practical results show that the memory coherence problem can indeed be solved efficiently on a loosely coupled multiprocessor.

Categories and Subject Descriptors: C.2.1 [**Computer-Communication Networks**]: Network Architecture and Design—*network communications*; C.2.4 [**Computer-Communication Networks**]: Distributed Systems—*network operating systems*; D.4.2 [**Operating Systems**]: Storage Management—*distributed memories; virtual memory*; D.4.7 [**Operating Systems**]: Organization and Design—*distributed systems*

General Terms: Algorithms, Design, Experimentation, Measurement, Performance

Additional Key Words and Phrases: Loosely coupled multiprocessors, memory coherence, parallel programming, shared virtual memory

1. INTRODUCTION

The benefits of a virtual memory go without saying; almost every high performance sequential computer in existence today has one. In fact, it is hard to believe that loosely coupled multiprocessors would not also benefit from virtual memory. One can easily imagine how virtual memory would be incorporated into a *shared*-memory parallel machine because the memory hierarchy need not be much different from that of a sequential machine. On a multiprocessor in which the physical memory is *distributed*, however, the implementation is not obvious.

The *shared virtual memory* described in this paper provides a virtual address space that is shared among all processors in a loosely coupled distributed-memory multiprocessor system. Application programs can use the shared virtual memory just as they do a traditional virtual memory, except, of course, that processes can run on different processors in parallel. The shared virtual memory not only "pages" data between physical memories and disks, as in a conventional virtual memory system, but it also "pages" data between the physical memories of the individual processors. Thus data can naturally *migrate* between processors on demand. Furthermore, just as a conventional virtual memory swaps *processes*, so does the shared virtual memory. Thus the shared virtual memory provides a natural and efficient form of *process migration* between processors in a distributed system. This is quite a gain because process migration is usually very difficult to implement. In effect, process migration subsumes *remote procedure calls*.

The main difficulty in building a shared virtual memory is solving the *memory coherence problem*. This problem is similar to that which arises with *multicache* schemes for shared memory multiprocessors, but they are different in many ways. In this paper we concentrate on the memory coherence problem for a shared virtual memory. A number of algorithms are presented, analyzed, and compared. A prototype system called IVY has been implemented on a local area network of Apollo workstations. The experimental results of nontrivial parallel programs run on the prototype show the viability of a shared virtual memory. The success of this implementation suggests an operating mode for such architectures in which parallel programs can exploit the total processing power and memory capabilities in a far more unified way than the traditional "message-passing" approach.

2. SHARED VIRTUAL MEMORY

A *shared virtual memory* is a single address space shared by a number of processors (Figure 1). Any processor can access any memory location in the address space directly. *Memory mapping managers* implement the mapping between local memories and the shared virtual memory address space. Other than mapping, their chief responsibility is to keep the address space *coherent* at all times; that is, the value returned by a read operation is always the same as the value written by the most recent write operation to the same address.

A shared virtual memory address space is partitioned into *pages*. Pages that are marked *read-only* can have copies residing in the physical memories of many processors at the same time. But a page marked *write* can reside in only one processor's physical memory. The memory mapping manager views its local memory as a large cache of the shared virtual memory address space for its associated processor. Like the traditional virtual memory [17], the shared memory itself exists only *virtually*. A memory reference causes a page fault when the page containing the memory location is not in a processor's current physical memory. When this happens, the memory mapping manager retrieves the page from either disk or the memory of another processor. If the page of the faulting memory reference has copies on other processors, then the memory mapping manager must do some work to keep the memory coherent and then continue the faulting instruction. This paper discusses both centralized manager algorithms and

This research was supported in part by National Science Foundation grants MCS-8302018, DCR-8106181, and CCR-8814265. A preliminary version of this paper appeared in the *Proceedings of the 5th Annual ACM Symposium on Principles of Distributed Computing* [36].

focused on the design of virtual memory systems for uniprocessors. A number of the early systems used memory mapping to provide access to different address spaces. The representative systems are Tenex and Multics [5, 13]. In these systems, processes in different address spaces can share data structures in mapped memory pages. But the memory mapping design was exclusively for uniprocessors.

Spector proposed a remote reference/remote operation model [42] in which a master process on a processor performs remote references and a slave process on another processor performs remote operations. Using processor names as part of the address in remote reference primitives, this model allows a loosely coupled multiprocessor to behave in a way similar to CM* [24, 29] or Butterfly [6] in which a shared memory is built from local physical memories in a static manner. Although implementing remote memory reference primitives in microcode can greatly improve efficiency, the cost of accessing a remote memory location is still several orders of magnitude more expensive than a local memory reference. The model is useful for data transfer in distributed computing, but it is unsuitable for parallel computing.

Among the distributed operating systems for loosely coupled multiprocessors, Apollo Aegis [2, 32, 33] and Accent [20, 38] have had a strong influence on the integration of virtual memory and interprocess communication. Both Aegis and Accent permit mapped access to data objects that can be located anywhere in a distributed system. Both of them view physical memory as a cache of virtual storage. Aegis uses mapped read and write memory as its fundamental communication paradigm. Accent has a similar facility called *copy-on-write* and a mechanism that allows processes to pass data *by value*. The data sharing between processes in these systems is limited at the object level; the system designs are for distributed computing rather than parallel computing.

Realistic parallel computing work on loosely coupled multiprocessors has been limited. Much work has focused on message passing [11, 19, 39]. It is possible to gain large speedups over a uniprocessor by message passing, but programming applications are difficult [11]. Furthermore, as mentioned above, message passing has difficulties in passing complicated data structures.

Another direction has been to use a set of primitives, available to the programmer in the source language, to access a global data space for storing shared data structures [8, 11]. The chief problem with such an approach is the user's need to control the global data space explicitly, which can become especially complex when passing large data structures or when attempting process migration. In a shared virtual memory such as we propose, no explicit data movement is required (it happens implicitly upon memory reference), and complex data is moved as easily as simple data. Another serious problem with the explicit global data space approach is that efficiency is impaired even for local data since use of a primitive implies at least the overhead of a procedure call. This problem becomes especially acute if one of the primitive operations occurs in an inner loop, in which case execution on one processor is much slower than that of the best sequential program, that is, one in which the operation is replaced with a standard memory reference. In contrast, when using our shared virtual memory, the inner loop would look just the same as its sequential version, and thus the overhead for accessing local data would be exactly the cost of a standard memory reference.

distributed manager algorithms, and in particular shows that a class of distributed manager algorithms can retrieve pages efficiently while keeping the memory coherent.

Our model of a parallel program is a set of *processes* (or threads) that share a single virtual address space. These processes are "lightweight"—they share the same address space, and thus the cost of a context switch, process creation, or process termination is small, say, on the order of a few procedure calls (Roy Levin, personal communication, 1986). One of the key goals of the shared virtual memory, of course, is to allow processes of a program to execute on different processors in parallel. To do so, the appropriate process manager and memory allocation manager must be integrated properly with the memory mapping manager. The process manager and the memory allocation manager are described elsewhere [34]. We refer to the whole system as a *shared virtual memory system*.

The performance of parallel programs on a shared virtual memory system depends primarily on two things: the number of parallel processes and the degree of updating of shared data (which creates contention on the communication channels). Since any processor can reference any page in the shared virtual memory address space and memory pages are moved and copied on demand, the shared virtual memory system does not exhibit pathological thrashing for unshared data or shared data that is read-only. Furthermore, updating shared data does not necessarily cause thrashing if a program exhibits *locality of reference*. One of the main justifications for traditional virtual memory is that memory references in sequential programs generally exhibit a high degree of locality [16, 17]. Although memory references in parallel programs may behave differently from those in sequential ones, a single process is still a sequential program and should exhibit a high degree of locality. Contention among parallel processes for the same piece of data depends on the algorithm, of course, but a common goal in designing parallel algorithms is to minimize such contention for optimal performance.

There is a large body of literature related to the research of shared virtual memory. The closest areas are virtual memory and parallel computing on loosely coupled multiprocessors.

Research on virtual memory management began in the 1960s [15] and has been an important topic in operating system design ever since. **The research**

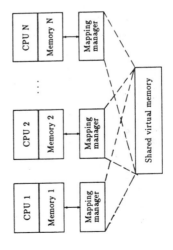

Fig. 1. Shared virtual memory mapping.

The point being that, once the pages holding a global data structure are paged in, the mechanism for accessing the data structure is precisely the same as on a uniprocessor.

The concept of a shared virtual memory for loosely coupled multiprocessors was first proposed in [36] and elaborated in the Ph.D. dissertation [34]. Details of the first implementation, IVY, on a network of workstations was reported in [34] and [35]. On the basis of this early work, a shared virtual memory system was later designed for the Lotus operating system kernel [21]. Most recently, the concept has been applied to a large-scale interconnection network based shared-memory multiprocessor [12] and a large-scale hypercube multiprocessor [37].

Other related work includes software caches and analysis of memory references. The VMP project at Stanford implements a software virtual addressed cache [10] to provide multicomputers with a coherent shared memory space. Their initial experience shows that a cache line size can be as large as 128 or 256 bytes without performance degradation. The cache consistency protocol is similar to the dynamic distributed manager algorithm for shared virtual memory in this paper and its preliminary version [34]. Finally, techniques for analyzing memory references of parallel programs [18, 45] may be applicable to analyzing the behaviors of parallel programs using a shared virtual memory system.

3. MEMORY COHERENCE PROBLEM

A memory is *coherent* if the value returned by a read operation is always the same as the value written by the most recent write operation to the same address. An architecture with one memory access path should have no coherence problem. A single access path, however, may not satisfy today's demand for high performance. The memory coherence problem was first encountered when caches appeared in uniprocessors (see [40] for a survey) and has become more complicated with the introduction of "multicaches" for shared memories on multiprocessors [9, 23, 25, 31, 43, 46 and Chuck Thacher, personal communication, 1984].

The memory coherence problem in a shared virtual memory system differs, however, from that in multicache systems. A multicache multiprocessor usually has a number of processors sharing a physical memory through their private caches. Since the size of a cache is relatively small and the bus connecting it to the shared memory is relatively fast, a sophisticated coherence protocol is usually implemented in the multicache hardware such that the time delay of conflicting writes to a memory location is small. On the other hand, a shared virtual memory on a loosely coupled multiprocessor has no physically shared memory, and the communication cost between processors is nontrivial. Thus conflicts are not likely to be solved with negligible delay, and they resemble much more a "page fault" in a traditional virtual memory system.

There are two design choices that greatly influence the implementation of a shared virtual memory: the granularity of the memory units (i.e., the "page size") and the strategy for maintaining coherence. These two design issues are studied in the next two subsections.

3.1 Granularity

In a typical loosely coupled multiprocessor, sending large packets of data (say one thousand bytes) is not much more expensive than sending small ones (say less than ten bytes) [41]. This similarity in cost is usually due to the software protocols and overhead of the virtual memory layer of the operating system. If these overheads are acceptable, relatively large memory units are possible in a shared virtual memory. On the other hand, the larger the memory unit, the greater the chance for contention. Detailed knowledge of a particular implementation might allow the clients' programmer to minimize contention by arranging concurrent memory accesses to locations in different memory units. Either clients or the shared virtual memory storage allocator may try to employ such strategies, but this may introduce inefficient use of memory. So, the possibility of contention indicates the need for relatively small memory units.

A suitable compromise in granularity is the typical *page* as used in conventional virtual memory implementations, which vary in size on today's computers from 256 bytes to 8K bytes. Our experience indicates that a page size of about 1K bytes is suitable with respect to contention, and as mentioned above should not impose undue communications overhead. We expect that smaller page sizes (perhaps as low as 256 bytes) work well also, but we are not as confident about larger page sizes, due to the contention problem. The right size is clearly application dependent, however, and we simply do not have the implementation experience to say what size is best for a sufficiently broad range of parallel programs. In any case, choosing a page size consistent with that used in conventional virtual memory implementations has the advantage of allowing one to use existing page fault schemes. In particular, one can use the protection mechanisms in a hardware Memory Management Unit (MMU) that allow single instructions to trigger page faults and to trap appropriate fault handlers. A program can set the access rights to the pages in such a way that memory accesses that could violate memory coherence cause a page fault; thus the memory coherence problem can be solved in a modular way in the page fault handlers and their servers.

3.2 Memory Coherence Strategies

It is helpful to first consider the spectrum of choices one has for solving the memory coherence problem. These choices can be classified by the way in which one deals with *page synchronization* and *page ownership*, as shown in Table I.

Page Synchronization. There are two basic approaches to page synchronization: *invalidation* and *write-broadcast*. In the *invalidation* approach, there is only one owner processor for each page. This processor has either write or read access to the page. If a processor Q has a write fault to a page p, its fault handler then

—invalidates all copies of p,
—changes the access of p to write,
—moves a copy of p to Q if Q does not have one already, and
—returns to the faulting instruction.

After returning, processor Q "owns" page p and can proceed with the write operation and other read or write operations until the page ownership is relinquished to some other processor. Processor Q, of course, does not need to move the copy of the page if it owns the page for reading. If a processor Q has a read

is an expensive solution for existing loosely coupled multiprocessors. Furthermore, it constrains desired modes of parallel computation. Thus we only consider dynamic page ownership strategies, as indicated in Table I.

The strategies for maintaining dynamic page ownership can be subdivided into two classes: *centralized* and *distributed*. Distributed managers can be further classified as either *fixed* or *dynamic*, referring to the distribution of ownership data.

The resulting combinations of strategies are shown in Table I, where we have marked as "very expensive" or "not allowed" all combinations involving write-broadcast synchronization or fixed page ownership. This paper only considers the remaining choices: algorithms based on invalidation using either a centralized manager, a fixed distributed manager, or a dynamic distributed manager.

Table I. Spectrum of Solutions to the Memory Coherence Problem

Page synchronization method	Page ownership strategy			
	Fixed	Dynamic		
		Centralized manager	Distributed manager	
			Fixed	Dynamic
Invalidation	Not allowed	Okay	Good	Good
Write-broadcast	Very expensive	Very expensive	Very expensive	Very expensive

fault to a page p, the fault handler then

—changes the access of p to read on the processor that has write access to p,
—moves a copy of p to Q and sets the access of p to read, and
—returns to the faulting instruction.

After returning, processor Q can proceed with the read operation and other read operations to this page in the same way that normal local memory does until p is relinquished to someone else.

In the *write-broadcast* approach, a processor treats a read fault just as it does in the *invalidation* approach. However, if a processor has a write fault, the fault handler then

—writes to all copies of the page, and
—returns to the faulting instruction.

The main problems with this approach is that it requires special hardware support. *Every* write to a shared page needs to generate a fault on the writing processor and update all copies because the philosophy of a shared virtual memory requires that pages be shared freely. To prevent the processor from having the same page fault again when returning to the faulting instruction, the hardware must be able to skip the faulted write cycle. We do not know of any existing hardware with this functionality.

The theoretical analysis on "snoopy cache" coherence [30] suggests that combining the invalidation approach with the write-broadcast approach may be a better solution. However, whether this approach can apply to the shared virtual memory is an open problem because the overhead of a write fault is much more than a write on a snoopy cache bus. Since the algorithms using write-broadcast do not seem practical for loosely coupled multiprocessors, they are not considered further in this paper.

Page Ownership. The ownership of a page can be *fixed* or *dynamic*. In the fixed ownership approach, a page is always owned by the same processor. Other processors are never given full write access to the page; rather they must negotiate with the owning processor and must generate a write fault every time they need to update the page. As with the write-broadcast approach, fixed page ownership

3.3 Page Table, Locking, and Invalidation

All of the algorithms for solving the memory coherence problem in this paper are described by using page fault handlers, their servers, and the data structure on which they operate. The data structures in different algorithms may be different, but they have at least the following information about each page:

—*access*: indicates the accessibility to the page,
—*copy set*: contains the processor numbers that have read copies of the page, and
—*lock*: synchronizes multiple page faults by different processes on the same processor and synchronizes remote page requests.

Following uniprocessor virtual memory convention, this data structure is called a *page table*. Every processor usually has a page table on it, but the same page entry in different page tables may be different.

There are two primitives operating on the lock field in the page table:

```
lock(PTable[p].lock):
    LOOP
        IF test-and-set the lock bit THEN EXIT;
        IF fail THEN queue this process;

unlock(PTable[p].lock):
    clear the lock bit;
    IF a process is waiting on the lock THEN
        resume the process;
```

These two primitives are used to synchronize multiple page fault requests on the same processor or different processors.

Another primitive that we use in memory coherence algorithms is *invalidate*. There are at least three ways to invalidate the copies of a page: *individual*, *broadcast*, and *multicast*. The individual invalidation is just a simple loop:

```
Invalidate:
    Invalidate(p, copy_set)
        FOR i in copy_set DO
            send an invalidation request to processor i;
```

Broadcast or multicast invalidation does not need a copy set; each just requires a simple broadcast message.

The server of the invalidation operation is simple:

Invalidate server:
    PTable[p].access := nil;

Although there are many ways to implement remote operations, it is reasonable to assume that any remote operation requires two messages, a request and a reply, and that a reliable communication protocol is used so that once a processor sends a request (no matter whether it is a point-to-point message, broadcast, or multicast), it eventually receives a reply. With such an assumption, for m copies on an N processor system, an individual invalidation requires $2m$ messages, m for requests, and m for replies. A broadcast invalidation sends $m + 1$ messages and receives $N + m - 1$ messages of which $N - 1$ messages are received in parallel. A multicast invalidation needs to send $m + 1$ messages and receive $2m$ messages of which m messages are received in parallel.

The cost of receiving k messages in parallel is greater than or equal to that of receiving one message and less than or equal to that of receiving k messages sequentially. If all k processors are idle, receipt of these messages in parallel costs *nothing* since the idle time would otherwise be wasted. On the other hand, if all k processors are busy, receipt of the messages would cost more since all k processors would need to be interrupted in order to process the messages. Clearly, multicast invalidation has the best performance, although most loosely coupled systems do not have a multicast facility that can use the page table information. Broadcast invalidation is expensive when N is large.

A copy set can be represented by a bit vector [1] when N is small (e.g., less than 64). When N is large, we may need to compact the copy set field. Three simple compaction methods are considered:

—*linked bit vector:* represents a copy set as a linked list that only links meaningful bit-vectors together to save space.

—*neighbor bit vector:* uses a bit vector as its copy set for neighbor processors (directly connected processors). This method requires processors to propagate invalidation requests.

—*vaguely defined set:* uses a tag to indicate whether there is a valid copy set. This allows the shared virtual memory to dynamically allocate memory for copy sets.

More detailed discussion on page table compaction can be found in [34].

4. CENTRALIZED MANAGER ALGORITHMS

4.1 A Monitor-Like Centralized Manager Algorithm

Our centralized manager is similar to a *monitor* [7, 27] consisting of a data structure and some procedures that provide mutually exclusive access to the data structure. The coherence problem in multicache systems has a similar solution [9]. The centralized manager resides on a single processor and maintains a table called Info which has one entry for each page, each entry having three fields:

(1) The *owner* field contains the single processor that owns that page, namely, the most recent processor to have write access to it.

Algorithm 1 *MonitorCentralManager*

Read fault handler:
```
Lock( PTable[ p ].lock );
IF I am manager THEN BEGIN
    Lock( Info[ p ].lock );
    Info[ p ].copyset
        := Info[ p ].copyset ∪ {ManagerNode};
    receive page p from Info[ p ].owner;
    Unlock( Info[ p ].lock );
END;
ELSE BEGIN
    ask manager for read access to p and a copy of p;
    receive p;
    send confirmation to manager;
END;
PTable[ p ].access := read;
Unlock( PTable[ p ].lock );
```

Read server:
```
Lock( PTable[ p ].lock );
IF I am owner THEN BEGIN
    PTable[ p ].access := read;
    send copy of p;
END;
Unlock( PTable[ p ].lock );
IF I am manager THEN BEGIN
    Lock( Info[ p ].lock );
    Info[ p ].copyset
        := Info[ p ].copyset ∪ {RequestNode};
    ask Info[ p ].owner to send copy of p to RequestNode;
    receive confirmation from RequestNode;
    Unlock( Info[ p ].lock );
END;
```

Write fault handler:
```
Lock( PTable[ p ].lock );
IF I am manager THEN BEGIN
    Lock( Info[ p ].lock );
    Invalidate( p, Info[ p ].copyset );
    Info[ p ].copyset := {};
    Unlock( Info[ p ].lock );
END;
ELSE BEGIN
    ask manager for write access to p;
    receive p;
    send confirmation to manager;
END;
```

Figure 2

mechanism in the data structure, the manager synchronizes the multiple requests from different processors.

A read-page fault on the manager processor needs two messages, one to the owner of the page, another from the owner. A read-page fault on a nonmanager processor needs four messages, one to the manager, one from the owner, and one for confirmation. A write-page fault costs the same as a read-page fault except that it includes the cost of an invalidation.

Since the centralized manager plays the role of helping other processors locate where a page is, a traffic bottleneck at the manager may occur as N becomes large and there are many page faults. The number of messages for locating a page is a measure of the complexity of the algorithm. When a nonmanager processor has a page fault, it sends a message to the manager and gets a reply message from the manager, so the algorithm has the following property:

PROPOSITION 1. *The worst-case number of messages to locate a page in the centralized manager algorithm is two.*

Although this algorithm uses only two messages in locating a page, it requires a confirmation message whenever a fault appears on a nonmanager processor. Eliminating the *confirmation* operation is the motivation for the following improvement to this algorithm.

4.2 An Improved Centralized Manager Algorithm

The primary difference between the improved centralized manager algorithm and the previous one is that the synchronization of page ownership has been moved to the individual owners, thus eliminating the *confirmation* operation to the manager. The locking mechanism on each processor now deals not only with multiple local requests, but also with remote requests. The manager still answers the question of where a page owner is, but it no longer synchronizes requests.

To accommodate these changes, the data structure of the manager must change. Specifically, the manager no longer maintains the copy set information, and a page-based lock is no longer needed. The information about the ownership of each page is still in a table called Owner kept on the manager, but an entry in the PTable on each processor now has three fields: *access*, *lock*, and *copy set*. The copy set field is *valid* if and only if the processor that holds the page table is the owner of the page. The fault handlers and servers for this algorithm can be found in Appendix A.

Although the synchronization responsibility of the original manager has moved to individual processors, the functionality of the synchronization remains the same. For example, consider a scenario in which two processors P_1 and P_2 are trying to write into the same page owned by a third processor P_3. If the request from P_1 arrives at the manager first, the request is forwarded to P_3. Before the paging is complete, suppose the manager receives a request from P_2, then forwards it to P_1. Since P_1 has not received ownership of the page yet, the request from P_2 is queued until P_1 finishes paging. Therefore, both P_1 and P_2 receive access to the page in turn.

Compared with the cost of a read-page fault in the monitor-like algorithm, this algorithm saves one send and one receive per page fault on all processors, an

```
PTable[ p ].access := write;
Unlock( PTable[ p ].lock );

Write server:
    Lock( PTable[ p ].lock );
    IF I am owner THEN BEGIN
        send copy of p;
        PTable[ p ].access := nil;
    END;
    Unlock( PTable[ p ].lock );
    IF I am manager THEN BEGIN
        Lock( Info[ p ].lock );
        Invalidate( p, Info[ p ].copyset );
        Info[ p ].copyset := {};
        ask Info[ p ].owner to send p to RequestNode;
        receive confirmation from RequestNode;
        Unlock( Info[ p ].lock );
    END;
```

Figure 2. (continued)

(2) The *copy set* field lists all processors that have copies of the page. This allows an invalidation operation to be performed without using broadcast.

(3) The *lock* field is used for synchronizing requests to the page, as we describe shortly.

Each processor also has a page table called PTable that has two fields: *access* and *lock*. This table keeps information about the accessibility of pages on the local processor.

In this algorithm, a page does not have a fixed owner, and there is only one manager that knows who the owner is. The owner of a page sends a copy to processors requesting a read copy. As long as a read copy exists, the page is not writeable without an *invalidation* operation, which causes invalidation messages to be sent to all processors containing read copies. Since this is a monitor-style algorithm, it is easy to see that the successful writer to a page always has ownership of the page. When a processor finishes a read or write request, a *confirmation* message is sent to the manager to indicate completion of the request.

Both Info table and PTable have page-based locks. They are used to synchronize the local page faults (i.e., fault handler operations) and remote fault requests (i.e., server operations). When there is more than one process on a processor waiting for the same page, the locking mechanism prevents the processor from sending more than one request. Also, if a remote request for a page arrives and the processor is accessing the page table entry, the locking mechanism queues the request until the entry is released.

As for all manager algorithms in this paper, the centralized manager algorithm in Figure 2 is characterized by the fault handlers and their servers.

The *confirmation* message indicates the completion of a request to the manager so that the manager can give the page to someone else. Together with the locking

obvious improvement. Decentralizing the synchronization improves the overall performance of the shared virtual memory, but for large N there still might be a bottleneck at the manager processor because it must respond to every page fault.

5. DISTRIBUTED MANAGER ALGORITHMS

In the centralized manager algorithms described in the previous section, there is only one manager for the whole shared virtual memory. Clearly such a centralized manager can be a potential bottleneck. This section discusses several ways of distributing the managerial task among the individual processors.

5.1 A Fixed Distributed Manager Algorithm

In a *fixed* distributed manager scheme, every processor is given a predetermined subset of the pages to manage. The primary difficulty in such a scheme is choosing an appropriate mapping from pages to processors. The most straightforward approach is to distribute pages evenly in a fixed manner to all processors. The distributed directory map solution to the multicache coherence problem [3] is similar. For example, suppose there are M pages in the shared virtual memory and that $I = \{1, \ldots, M\}$. An appropriate hashing function H could then be defined by

$$H(p) = p \bmod N \qquad (1)$$

where $p \in I$ and N is the number of processors. A more general definition is

$$H(p) = \left(\frac{p}{s}\right) \bmod N \qquad (2)$$

where s is the number of pages per *segment*. Thus defined, this function distributes manager work by segments.

Other variations include using a suitable hashing function or providing a default mapping function that clients may override by supplying their own mapping. In the latter case, the map could be tailored to a particular application and its expected behavior with respect to concurrent memory references.

With this approach there is one manager per processor, each responsible for the pages specified by the fixed mapping function H. When a fault occurs on page p, the faulting processor asks processor $H(p)$ where the true page owner is, and then proceeds as in the centralized manager algorithm.

Our experiments have shown that the fixed distributed manager algorithm is superior to the centralized manager algorithms when a parallel program exhibits a high rate of page faults. However, it is difficult to find a good fixed distribution function that fits all applications well. Thus we would like to investigate the possibility of distributing the work of managers *dynamically*.

5.2 A Broadcast Distributed Manager Algorithm

An obvious way to eliminate the centralized manager is to use a *broadcast* mechanism. With this strategy, each processor manages precisely those pages that it owns, and faulting processors send broadcasts into the network to find the true owner of a page. Thus the Owner table is eliminated completely, and the information of ownership is stored in each processor's PTable, which, in addition to *access*, *copy set*, and *lock* fields, has an *owner* field.

More precisely, when a read fault occurs, the faulting processor P sends a *broadcast read request*, and the true owner of the page responds by adding P to the page's *copy set* field and sending a copy of the page to P. Similarly, when a write fault occurs, the faulting processor sends a *broadcast write request*, and the true owner of the page gives up ownership and sends back the page and its *copy set*. When the requesting processor receives the page and the *copy set*, it invalidates all copies. All broadcast operations are atomic. The fault handlers and servers for such a naive algorithm are given in Appendix B.

The simplicity of this approach is appealing. Yet, the correctness of the algorithm is not obvious at first. Consider the case in which two write faults to the same page happen simultaneously on two processors P_1 and P_2, and consider the instant when the owner of the page, P_3, receives a broadcast request from P_1 and gives up its ownership but P_1 has not yet received the message granting ownership. At this point, P_2 sends its broadcast request, but there is no owner. However, this is not a problem because P_2's message is queued on P_1 waiting for the lock on the page table entry; after P_1 receives ownership, the lock is released, and P_2's message is then processed by P_1 (recall the definition of the *lock* and *unlock* primitives given in Section 3.3).

A read-page fault causes a broadcast request that is received by $N-1$ processors but is replied to by only one of them. The cost for a write-page fault is the same, plus the overhead of an invalidation. Although the algorithm is simple, for a large N, performance is poor because all processors have to process each broadcast request, slowing down the computation on all processors. Our experiments show that the cost introduced by the broadcast requests is substantial when $N \geq 4$. A parallel program with many read- and write-page faults does not perform well on a shared virtual memory system based on a broadcast distributed manager algorithm.

5.3 A Dynamic Distributed Manager Algorithm

The heart of a dynamic distributed manager algorithm is keeping track of the ownership of all pages in each processor's local PTable. To do this, the *owner* field is replaced with another field, *probOwner*, whose value can be either the true owner or the "probable" owner of the page. The information that it contains is just a hint; it is not necessarily correct at all times, but if incorrect it at least provides the beginning of a sequence of processors through which the true owner can be found. Initially, the *probOwner* field of every entry on all processors is set to some default processor that can be considered the initial owner of all pages. It is the job of the page fault handlers and their servers to maintain this field as the program runs.

In this algorithm a page does not have a fixed owner or manager. When a processor has a page fault, it sends a request to the processor indicated by the *probOwner* field for that page. If that processor is the true owner, it proceeds as in the centralized manager algorithm. If it is not, it forwards the request to the processor indicated by its *probOwner* field. When a processor forwards a request, it need not send a reply to the requesting processor.

The *probOwner* field changes on a write-page fault as well as a read-page fault. As with the centralized manager algorithms, a read fault results in making a copy of the page, and a write fault results in making a copy of the page. The *probOwner* field is updated whenever a processor receives an invalidation request, a processor relinquishes ownership of the page, which can happen on a read- or write-page fault, or a processor forwards a page-fault request.

In the first two cases, the *probOwner* field is changed to the new owner of the page. Changing ownership of the page on a read-page fault makes analysis simpler. Later, we modify the algorithm so that a read-page fault no longer changes ownership. In the last case, the *probOwner* is changed to the original requesting processor, which becomes the true owner in the near future. The algorithm is shown in Figure 3.

The two critical questions about this algorithm are whether forwarding requests eventually arrive at the true owner and how many forwarding requests are needed. In order to answer these questions, it is convenient to view all the *probOwners* of a page p as a directed graph $G_p = (V, E_p)$ where V is the set of processor numbers $1, \ldots, N$, $|E_p| = N$ and an edge $(i, j) \in E_p$ if and only if the *probOwner* for page p on processor i is j. Using this approach, we can show

THEOREM 1. *Using Algorithm 2, a page fault on any processor reaches the true owner of the page using at most $N - 1$ forwarding request messages.*

PROOF. See Appendix C. □

THEOREM 2. *Using Algorithm 2, the worst-case number of messages for locating the owner of a single page K times is $O(N + K \log N)$.*

PROOF. See Appendix C. □

COROLLARY 1. *Using the dynamic distributed manager algorithm, if q processors have used a page, an upper bound on the total number of messages for locating the owner of the page K times is $O(p + K \log q)$ if all contending processors are in the q processor set.*

This is an important corollary since it says that the algorithm does not degrade as more processors are *added to the system* but rather degrades (logarithmically) only as more processors *contend for the same page*. Our experiments show that usually few processors are using the same page at the same time. Normally, $p = 2$. Furthermore, an invalidation operation can collapse all the read-copy paths in the graph. These facts suggest that the dynamic distributed manager algorithm has the potential to implement a shared virtual memory system on a large-scale multiprocessor system.

Note that in Algorithm 2, the read-fault handler and its server change the *probOwner* graph in the same way as the write-fault handler and its server, except that the write-fault handler does invalidation according to the copy set field. This was done primarily to make the cost analysis easier; for a real implementation, the read-fault handler and its server should be slightly modified to get

Algorithm 2 *DynamicDistributedManager*

Read fault handler:
```
Lock( PTable[ p ].lock );
ask PTable[ p ].probOwner for read access to p;
PTable[ p ].probOwner := self;
PTable[ p ].access := read;
Unlock( PTable[ p ].lock );
```

Read server:
```
Lock( PTable[ p ].lock );
IF I am owner THEN BEGIN
    PTable[ p ].copyset
        := PTable[ p ].copyset U {Self};
    PTable[ p ].access := read;
    send p and PTable[ p ].copyset;
    PTable[ p ].probOwner := RequestNode;
    END
ELSE BEGIN
    forward request to PTable[ p ].probOwner;
    PTable[ p ].probOwner := RequestNode;
    END;
Unlock( PTable[ p ].lock );
```

Write fault handler:
```
Lock( PTable[ p ].lock );
ask PTable[ p ].probOwner for write access to page p;
Invalidate( p, PTable[ p ].copyset );
PTable[ p ].probOwner := self;
PTable[ p ].access := write;
PTable[ p ].copyset := {};
Unlock( PTable[ p ].lock );
```

Write server:
```
Lock( PTable[ p ].lock );
IF I am owner THEN BEGIN
    PTable[ p ].access := nil;
    send p and PTable[ p ].copyset;
    PTable[ p ].probOwner := RequestNode;
    END
ELSE BEGIN
    forward request to PTable[ p ].probOwner;
    PTable[ p ].probOwner := RequestNode;
    END;
Unlock( PTable[ p ].lock );
```

Invalidate server:
```
PTable[ p ].access := nil;
PTable[ p ].probOwner := RequestNode;
```

Figure 3

better performance:

```
Read-fault handler:
    Lock(PTable[p].lock);
    ask PTable[p].probOwner for read access to p;
    PTable[p].probOwner := ReplyNode;
    PTable[p].access := read;
    Unlock(PTable[p].lock);

Read server:
    Lock(PTable[p].lock);
    IF I am owner THEN BEGIN
        PTable[p].copyset
            := PTable[p].copyset ∪ {RequestNode};
        PTable[p].access := read;
        send p to RequestNode;
    END
    ELSE BEGIN
        forward request to PTable[p].probOwner;
        PTable[p].probOwner := RequestNode;
    END;
    Unlock(PTable[p].lock);
```

Table II. Longest Path First Finds

Number of nodes	Average number of messages/find			
n	$M = N/4$	$M = N/2$	$M = 3N/4$	$M = N$
4	1.00	1.50	1.30	1.75
8	1.50	1.75	2.00	2.13
16	1.75	2.13	2.42	2.63
32	2.13	2.63	2.83	3.00
64	2.63	3.00	3.25	3.45
128	3.00	3.45	3.71	3.88
256	3.45	3.88	4.14	4.35
512	3.88	4.35	4.62	4.80
1,024	4.35	4.80	5.05	5.26

The modified read-fault handler and its server still compress the access path from the faulting processor to the owner, but they do not change the ownership of a page; rather, they change its *probOwner* field. The modified algorithm reduces one message for each read-page fault, an obvious improvement. For the modified algorithm, the worst case number of messages for locating K owners of a single page is difficult to define cleanly because the read-fault handler and its server behave as a pure forwarding address scheme, which can be reduced to the set union find problem of a compressing path with naive linking [22], while the write-fault handler and its server behave differently.

The algorithm proposed in this section needs a broadcast or multicast facility only for the invalidation operation. If the invalidation is done by sending individual messages to the copy holders, there is no need to use the broadcast facility at all, and the benefits of the general approach can still be gained.

5.4 An Improvement by Using Fewer Broadcasts

In the previous algorithm, at initialization or after a broadcast, all processors know the true owner of a page. The following theorem gives the performance for K page faults on different processors in this case:

THEOREM 3.   *After a broadcast request or a broadcast invalidation, the total number of messages for locating the owner of a page for K page faults on different processors is $2K - 1$.*

PROOF.   This can be shown by the transition of a *probOwner* graph after a broadcast. The first fault uses 1 message to locate a page and every fault after that uses 2 messages. □

This theorem suggests the possibility of further improving the algorithm by enforcing a broadcast message (announcing the true owner of a page) after every M page faults to a page. In this case, a counter is needed in each entry of the page table and is maintained by its owner. The necessary changes to Algorithm 2 are fairly straightforward, and we leave the details to the reader. It is interesting to note that when $M = 0$, this algorithm is functionally equivalent to the broadcast distributed manager algorithm, and when $M = N - 1$, it is equivalent to the unmodified dynamic distributed manager algorithm.

In order to choose the value of M, it is necessary to consider the general case in which the same processor may have any number of page faults because Theorem 3 only shows the performance for page faults on *distinct* processors. In the last section we showed that the worst-case number of messages for locating K owners for a single page is $O(N + K \log N)$, but our intuition says that the performance of K page faults right after a broadcast message should be better because in the starting *probOwner* graph, all the processors know the true owner.

Since it is difficult to find a function describing the relationship between M and N for the general case, two simulation programs were run for two different situations: approximated worst-case and approximated random-case behavior. The initial *probOwner* graph used in both programs is the graph after a broadcast in which all the processors know the true owner. The programs record the number of messages used for each find (locating an owner) operation.

The first program approximates the worst case by choosing at each iteration a node with the longest path to the owner. Table II shows the average number of messages for each find operation for $M = N/4$, $M = N/2$, $M = 3N/4$, and $M = N$. The table shows that the average number of messages steadily increases as N gets large. Although picking the node with the longest path does not always generate the worst-case *probOwner* graph, our experiments show that the program actually converges when M is very large. For example, the average number of messages becomes stable when $N = 64$ and $M > 1024$ from our experiments. Whether the case in which the average number of messages becomes stable is the worst case is an open problem.

The second program approximates random behavior by choosing a node randomly at each iteration. The average number of messages for each find operation is shown in Table III. The table was produced by running the program four times and computing the average values among all the executions. In

Algorithm 3 *DynamicDistributedCopySet*

Read fault handler:
```
Lock( PTable[ p ].lock );
ask PTable[ p ].probOwner for read access to p;
PTable[ p ].probOwner := ReplyNode;
PTable[ p ].access := read;
Unlock( PTable[ p ].lock );
```

Read server:
```
Lock( PTable[ p ].lock );
IF PTable[ p ].access ≠ nil THEN BEGIN
    PTable[ p ].copyset
        := PTable[ p ].copyset ∪ {RequestNode};
    PTable[ p ].access := read;
    send p;
    END
ELSE BEGIN
    forward request to PTable[ p ].probOwner;
    PTable[ p ].probOwner := RequestNode;
    END;
Unlock( PTable[ p ].lock );
```

Write fault handler:
```
Lock( PTable[ p ].lock );
ask PTable[ p ].probOwner for write access to p;
Invalidate( p, PTable[ p ].copyset );
PTable[ p ].probOwner := self;

PTable[ p ].access := write;
PTable[ p ].copyset := {};
Unlock( PTable[ p ].lock );
```

Write server:
```
Lock( PTable[ p ].lock );
IF I am owner THEN BEGIN
    PTable[ p ].access := nil;
    send p and PTable[ p ].copyset;
    PTable[ p ].probOwner := RequestNode;
    END
ELSE BEGIN
    forward request to PTable[ p ].probOwner;
    PTable[ p ].probOwner := RequestNode;
    END;
Unlock( PTable[ p ].lock );
```

Figure 4

Table III. Random Finds

Number of nodes N	Average number of messages/find			
	$M = N/4$	$M = N/2$	$M = 3N/4$	$M = N$
4	1.00	1.50	1.67	1.75
8	1.50	1.75	1.99	2.08
16	1.75	1.96	2.22	2.53
32	1.93	2.39	2.79	2.90
64	2.09	2.78	2.90	3.12
128	2.06	2.68	2.80	3.16
256	2.20	2.77	3.18	3.39
512	2.46	3.09	3.32	3.56
1,024	2.34	3.08	3.34	3.64

comparing Table II with Table III, note that, on average, random finds use fewer numbers of messages.

To choose an appropriate value of M, the two tables should be used together with the information about the expected number of contending processors because the performance of the dynamic distributed manager algorithm is only related to such a number rather than the number of processors in the system (Corollary 1).

5.5 Distribution of Copy Sets

Note that in the previous algorithm, the *copy set* of a page is used only for the invalidation operation induced by a write fault. The *location* of the set is unimportant as long as the algorithm can invalidate the read copies of a page correctly. Further note that the *copy set* field of processor i contains j if processor j copied the page from processor i, and thus the *copy set* fields for a page are subsets of the real *copy set*.

These facts suggest an alternative to the previous algorithms in which the *copy set* data associated with a page is stored as a *tree* of processors rooted at the owner. In fact, the tree is bidirectional, with the edges directed from the root formed by the *copy set* fields and the edges directed from the leaves formed by *probOwner* fields. The tree is used during faults as follows: A *read* fault collapses the path up the tree through the *probOwner* fields to the owner. A *write* fault invalidates all copies in the tree by inducing a wave of invalidation operations starting at the owner and propagating to the processors in its *copy set*, which, in turn, send invalidation requests to the processors in their *copy sets*, and so on.

The algorithm in Figure 4 is a modified version of the original dynamic distributed manager algorithm.

Since a write-page fault needs to find the owner of the page, the lock at the owner synchronizes concurrent write-page fault requests to the page. If read faults on some processors occur concurrently, the locks on the processors from which those faulting processors are copying synchronize the possible conflicts of

```
Invalidate server:
    IF PTable[ p ].access ≠ nil THEN BEGIN
        Invalidate( p, PTable[ p ].copyset );
        PTable[ p ].access := nil;
        PTable[ p ].probOwner := RequestNode;
        PTable[ p ].copyset := {};
    END;
```

Figure 4. (continued)

the write-fault requests and read-fault requests. In this sense, the algorithm is equivalent to the original one.

Distributing *copy sets* in this manner improves system performance for the architectures that do not have a broadcast facility in two important ways. First, the propagation of invalidation messages is usually faster because of its "divide and conquer" effect. If the *copy set* tree is perfectly balanced, the invalidation process takes time proportional to $\log m$ for m read copies. This faster invalidation response shortens the time for a write fault.

Second, and perhaps more important, a read fault now only needs to find a single processor (not necessarily the owner) that holds a copy of the page. To make this work, recall that a lock at the owner of each page synchronizes concurrent write faults to the page. A similar lock is now needed on processors having read copies of the page to synchronize sending copies of the page in the presence of other read or write faults.

Overall this refinement can be applied to any of the foregoing distributed manager algorithms, but it is particularly useful on a multiprocessor lacking a broadcast facility.

6. EXPERIMENTS

Since parallel programs are complex and the interactions between parallel processes are often unpredictable, the only convincing way to justify a shared virtual memory on loosely coupled multiprocessors is to implement a prototype system and run some realistic experiments on it. We have implemented a prototype shared virtual memory system called IVY (Integrated shared Virtual memory at Yale). It is implemented on top of a modified Aegis operating system of the Apollo DOMAIN computer system [2, 33]. IVY can be used to run parallel programs on any number of processors on an Apollo ring network.

We have tested a number of memory coherence algorithms, including the improved centralized manager, the dynamic distributed manager, and the fixed distributed manager. To exercise the system we selected a set of benchmark programs that represent a spectrum of likely practical parallel programs that have a reasonably fine granularity of parallelism and side effects to shared data structures. Our goal in using these criteria was to avoid weighing the experiments in favor of the shared virtual memory system by picking problems that suit the system well.

In this paper we present the results of running four parallel programs. All of them are written in Pascal and transformed manually from sequential ones in a straightforward way. In order to measure performance, each processor at run time records statistical information into a file, including the number of read page faults, the number of write page faults, process migration data, and memory page distribution data. Information about disk paging and network traffic is obtained from the Aegis operating system.

6.1 Four Parallel Programs

The first is a parallel Jacobi program for solving three dimensional partial differential equations (PDEs). It solves a linear equation $Ax = b$ where A is an n-by-n sparse matrix. In each iteration, $x^{(k+1)}$ is obtained by

$$x_i^{(k+1)} = \left(\frac{b_i - \sum_{j=1}^{i-1} a_{ij} x_j^{(k)} - \sum_{j=i+1}^{n} a_{ij} x_j^{(k)}}{a_{ii}} \right).$$

The parallel algorithm creates a number of processes to partition the problem by the number of rows of matrix A. All the processes are synchronized at each iteration by using an event count. Since matrix A is a sparse matrix and it is never updated, we adopt the standard technique in scientific computing of encoding its contents in-line (William Gropp, personal communication, 1985). The vectors x and b are stored in the shared virtual memory, and thus the processes access them freely without regard to their location. Such a program is much simpler than that which results from the usual message-passing paradigm because the programmer does not have to perform data movement explicitly at each iteration. The program is written in Pascal and transformed manually from the sequential algorithm into a parallel one in a straightforward way.

The second program is parallel sorting; more specifically, a variation of the block odd-even based merge-split algorithm described in [4]. The sorted data is a vector of records that contain random strings. At the beginning, the program divides the vector into $2N$ blocks for N processors, and creates N processes, one for each processor. Each process sorts two blocks by using a quicksort algorithm [26]. This internal sorting is naturally done in parallel. Each process then does an odd-even block merge-split sort $2N - 1$ times. The vector is stored in the shared virtual memory, and the spawned processes access it freely. Because the data movement is implicit, the parallel transformation is straightforward.

The third program is a parallel matrix multiply that computes $C = AB$ where A, B, and C are square matrices. A number of processes are created to partition the problem by the number of rows of matrix C. All the matrices are stored in the shared virtual memory. The program assumes that matrix A and B are on one processor at the beginning and that they are paged to other processors on demand.

The last program is a parallel dot-product program that computes

$$S = \sum_{i=1}^{n} x_i y_i.$$

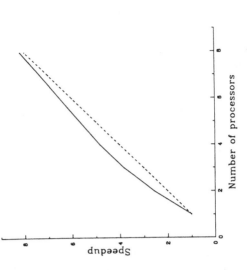

Fig. 5.   Speedups of a 3-D PDE where $n = 50^3$.

A number of processes are created to partition the problem. Process i computes the sum

$$S_i = \sum_{j=l_i}^{u_i} x_j y_j.$$

S is obtained by summing up the sums produced by the individual processes

$$S = \sum_{i=1}^{m} S_i,$$

where m is the number of processes. Both vectors x and y are stored in the shared virtual memory in a random manner, under the assumption that x and y are not fully distributed before doing the computation. The main reason for choosing this example is to show the weak side of the shared virtual memory system; dot-product does little computation but requires a lot of data movement.

6.2 Speedups

The speedup of a program is the ratio of the execution time of the program on a single processor to that on the shared virtual memory system. The execution time of a program is the elapsed time from program start to program end, which is measured by the clock in the system. The execution time does not include the time of initializing data structures in the program because the initialization has little to do with the algorithm itself. For instance, the initialization of the merge-split sort program initializes an unsorted vector of records with random strings in their key fields. The time spent on the initialization depends on the generation of random strings; a complicated random string generating algorithm can well consume a lot of time. Indeed, if this initialization is included in the execution time of the program, and such an initialization is performed in parallel, it is possible to get a better speedup than the ideal speedup since ideally this parallel algorithm does not yield a linear speedup.

In order to obtain a fair speedup measurement, all the programs in the experiments partition their problems by creating a certain number of processes according to the number of processors used. As a result of such a parameterized partitioning, each program does its best for a given number of processors. If a fixed partitioning strategy were used, one could demonstrate better (or worse) speedups, but such an approach is unreasonable. To help assess overall system performance, all the speedups are compared against the ideal.

The results for the parallel 3-D PDE solver are shown in Figure 5, where $n = 50^3$. The dashed line in the figure is the ideal (linear) speedup curve. Note that the program experiences *super-linear speedup*.

At first glance this result seems impossible because the fundamental law of parallel computation says that a parallel solution utilizing p processors can improve the best sequential solution by at most a factor of p. Something must be interacting in either the program or the shared virtual memory implementation. Since the algorithm in the program is a straightforward transformation from the sequential Jacobi algorithm and all the processes are synchronized at each

iteration, the algorithm cannot yield super-linear speedup. So, the speedup must be in the shared virtual memory implementation.

The shared virtual memory system can indeed provide super-linear speedups because the fundamental law of parallel computation assumes that every processor has an infinitely large memory, which is not true in practice. In the parallel 3-D PDE example above, the data structure for the problem is greater than the size of physical memory on a single processor, so when the program is run on one processor there is a large amount of paging between the physical memory and disk.

Figure 6 shows the disk paging performance on one and two processors. The solid line in the figure shows the number of disk I/O pages when the program runs on one processor. The dashed and dotted lines show the numbers of disk I/O pages when the program runs on two processors—the dashed line for the processor with initialized data (processor 1) and the dotted line (which can hardly be seen) for the processor without initialized data (processor 2). The two curves are very different because the program initializes its data structures only on one processor. Since the virtual memory paging in the Aegis operating system performs an approximated LRU strategy, and the pages that move to processor 2 are recently used on processor 1, processor 1 had to page out some pages that it needs later, causing more disk I/O page movement. This explains why the number of disk I/O pages on processor 1 decreases after the first few iterations.

The shared virtual memory, on the other hand, distributes the data structure into individual physical memories whose cumulative size is large enough to inhibit disk paging. It is clear from this example alone that the shared virtual memory can indeed exploit the combined physical memories of a multiprocessor system.

Figure 7 shows another speedup curve for the 3-D PDE program, but now with $n = 40^3$, in which case the data structure of the problem is not larger than the

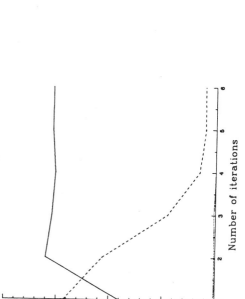

Fig. 8. Speedup of the merge-split sort.

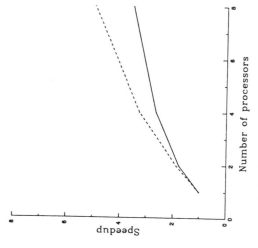

Fig. 6. Disk paging on one processor and two processors.

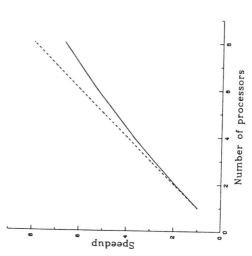

Fig. 7. Speedups of a 3-D PDE where $n = 40^3$.

on each processor. The main reason that the performance of this program is so good in the shared virtual memory system is that the program exhibits a high degree of locality on each execution path. While the shared virtual memory system pays the cost of local memory references, CM* pays the cost of remote memory references across its K maps.

Parallel sorting on a loosely coupled multiprocessor is generally difficult. The speedup curve of the parallel merge-split sort of 200K elements shown in Figure 8 is not very good. In theory, even with no communication costs, this algorithm does not yield linear speedup. Thus, to provide a better comparison of performance we added the dashed line in the figure to show the speedup when the costs of all memory references are the same. Also recall that our program uses the best strategy for a given number of processors. For example, one merge-split sorting is performed when running the program on one processor, four when running on two processors, and n^2 when running on an n processor. Using a fixed number of blocks for any number of processors would result in a better speedup, but such a comparison would be unfair.

Figure 9 shows the speedup curve of the parallel dot-product program in which each vector has 128K elements. It is included here so as not to paint too bright a picture. To be fair, the program assumes that the two vectors have a random distribution on each processor. Even with such an assumption, the speedup curve is not good, as indicated by the solid line in Figure 9. If the two vectors are located on one processor, there is no speedup at all, as indicated by the dotted curve in Figure 9, because the ratio of the communication cost to the computation cost in this program is large. For programs like dot-product, a shared virtual memory system is not likely to provide significant speedup.

physical memory on a processor. This curve is what we see in most parallel computation papers. The curve is quite similar in fact to that generated by similar experiments on CM*, a pioneer shared memory multiprocessor [14, 24, 28]. Indeed, the shared virtual memory system is as good as the best curve in the published experiments on CM* for the same program, but the efforts and costs of the two approaches are dramatically different. In fact, the best curve in CM* was obtained by keeping the private program code and stack in the local memory

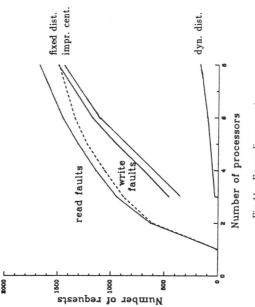

Fig. 11. Forwarding requests.

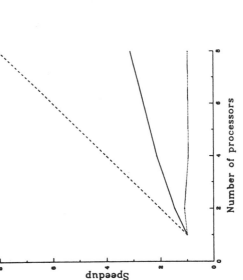

Fig. 9.   Speedup of the dot-product program.

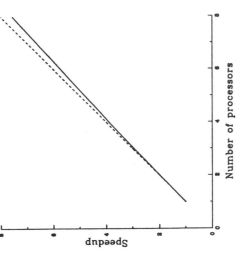

Fig. 10.   Speedup of the matrix multiplication program.

In general, the experimental results show that a shared virtual memory implementation is indeed practical even on a very loosely coupled architecture such as the Apollo ring.

6.3 Memory Coherence Algorithms

Our experiments indicate that all three memory coherence algorithms have similar numbers of page faults. Due to the limitation on the number of processors, we could not show explicit differences among the three algorithms by comparing their system performance. The alternative approach we took was to measure the total number of messages used in an algorithm. In fact, the number of forwarding requests was used as a criterion for comparing algorithms.

Figure 11 shows the number of forwarding requests for locating true pages during the first six iterations of the 3D PDE program using the improved centralized manager algorithm, the fixed distributed manager algorithm, and the dynamic distributed manager algorithm.

In the fixed distributed manager algorithm, the manager mapping function is $H(p) = p$ mod N, where p is a page number and N is the number of processors. The curve of the forwarding requests of the fixed distributed manager algorithm is similar to that of the improved centralized manager algorithm because both algorithms need a forwarding request to locate the owner of the page for almost every page fault that occurs on a nonmanager processor. Since the workload of the fixed distributed manager algorithm is a little better than that of the improved centralized manager algorithm, the performance of the former is a little better than the latter as the number of processors increases.

The figures show that the overhead of the dynamic distributed manager algorithm is much less than that of the other two algorithms. This confirms the

Figure 10 shows the speedup curve of the matrix multiplication program for $C = AB$ where both A and B are 128-by-128 square matrices. This example shows the good side of the shared virtual memory system. The speedup curve is close to linear because the program exhibits a high degree of localized computation, even though the input matrices are shared heavily.

7. CONCLUSIONS

This paper has studied two general classes of algorithms (centralized manager and distributed manager) for solving the memory coherence problem, and both of them have many variations. The centralized manager algorithm is straightforward and easy to implement, but it may have a traffic bottleneck at the central manager when there are many page faults. The fixed distributed manager algorithm alleviates the bottleneck, but, on average, a processor still needs to spend about two messages to locate an owner. The dynamic distributed manager algorithm and its variations seem to have the most desirable overall features. As mentioned earlier, the dynamic distributed manager algorithm may need as little as one message to locate an owner. Furthermore, Theorem 3 shows that by using fewer broadcasts the average number of messages for locating a page is a little less than two for typical cases. Further refinement can also be done by distributing copy sets.

In general, dynamic distributed manager algorithms perform better than other methods when the number of processors sharing the same page for a short period of time is small, which is the normal case. The good performance of the dynamic distributed manager algorithms shows that it is possible to apply it to an implementation on a large-scale multiprocessor.

Our experiments with the prototype system indicate that many parallel programs exhibit good speedups on loosely coupled multiprocessors using a shared virtual memory. Performance is generally good even for parallel programs that share data in a fine-grained way, as long as most of the references are read-only. We conjecture that the main class of parallel programs that would perform poorly are those with frequent updates to shared data or those with excessively large data sets that are only read once (such as the dot-product example).

Because of resource limitations we could not run our experiments on more than eight processors. Thus we do not know for sure how well the shared virtual memory system will scale. On the other hand, the data we have gathered on the distributed manager algorithms gives us every reason to believe that it will scale well, as argued earlier. A more difficult question is what the best page size should be. Currently we only have experience with two sizes: 1K byte and 32K bytes. Since this parameter is not only system dependent but also applications dependent, much more experience with a real implementation is necessary before all of the trade-offs are fully understood.

The memory coherence algorithms proposed in this paper and the success of our experiments on our prototype system suggest the possibility of using a shared virtual memory system to construct a large-scale shared memory multiprocessor system. Such a project is, in fact, underway at Princeton in collaboration with the DEC Systems Research Center. Through this project we intend to address many of the unanswered questions raised by this research.

APPENDIX A
IMPROVED CENTRALIZED MANAGER ALGORITHM

CentralManager

Read fault handler:
```
Lock( PTable[ p ].lock );
IF I am manager THEN
    receive page p from owner[ p ];
ELSE
    ask manager for read access to p and a copy of p;
PTable[ p ].access := read;
Unlock( PTable[ p ].lock );
```

Read server:
```
Lock( PTable[ p ].lock );
IF I am owner THEN BEGIN
    PTable[ p ].copyset
        := PTable[ p ].copyset ∪ {RequestNode};
    PTable[ p ].access := read;
    send p;
    END
ELSE IF I am manager THEN BEGIN
    Lock( ManagerLock );
    forward request to owner[ p ];
    Unlock( ManagerLock );
    END;
Unlock( PTable[ p ].lock );
```

Write fault handler:
```
Lock( PTable[ p ].lock );
IF I am manager THEN
    receive page p from owner[ p ];
ELSE
    ask manager for write access to p and p's copyset;
Invalidate( p, PTable[ p ].copyset );
PTable[ p ].access := write;
PTable[ p ].copyset := {};
Unlock( PTable[ p ].lock );
```

Write server:
```
Lock( PTable[ p ].lock );
IF I am owner THEN BEGIN
    send p and PTable[ p ].copyset;
    PTable[ p ].access := nil;
    END
```

analysis on the dynamic distributed manager algorithm. The main reason it is better is that the *prob-owner* fields usually give correct hints (thus the number of forward requests is very small) and within a short period of time the number of processors sharing a page is small.

APPENDIX C
PROPERTIES OF DYNAMIC DISTRIBUTED MANAGER ALGORITHMS

In the following, we first show some properties of the *probOwner* graph by assuming that page faults are generated and processed sequentially. In other words, it is assumed that if processor i has a fault on page p, then no other processor has a fault on page p until processing the page fault on processor i is complete. We then show the correctness of the concurrent page fault case by reducing it to a sequential case.

LEMMA 1. *If page faults of page p occur sequentially, every probOwner graph* $G_p = (V, E_p)$ *has the following properties:*

(1) *there is exactly one node i such that $(i, i) \in E_p$;*
(2) *graph $G'_p = (V, E_p - (i, i))$ is acyclic; and*
(3) *for any node x, there is exactly one path from x to i.*

PROOF. By induction on the number of page faults on page p. Initially, all the *probOwners* of the processors in V are initialized to a default processor. Obviously, all three properties are satisfied.

After k page faults, the *probOwner* graph G_p satisfies the three properties as shown in Figure 12(a). There are two cases when a page fault occurs on processor j.

(1) If it is a read-page fault, the path from j to i is collapsed by the read-fault handler and its server in the algorithm such that all the nodes on the path now point to j (Figure 12(b)). The resulting graph satisfies 1 since (i, i) is deleted from E_p and (j, j) is added to E_p. It satisfies 2 because the subgraphs $g_j, g_u, \ldots, g_v, g_i$ (g_x is a subgraph of G_p rooted at node x) are acyclic and they are not changed. For any node $x \in V$, there is exactly one path to i. Suppose the first node in the path (in the node set $\{j, u, \ldots, v, i\}$) is y. The edge from y is changed to (y, j), so there is no other path from y to j.

(2) If it is a write-page fault and there is no read-only copy of page p, then the resulting graph is the same as the read-page fault case. If it is a write-page fault and there are r read-only copies on processors $v_1, \ldots, v_r$, then in addition to collapsing the path from j to i, the invalidation procedure makes nodes $v_1, \ldots, v_r$ point to j (Figure 12(c)). The resulting graph satisfies 1 since (i, i) is deleted from the graph and (j, j) is added. A subgraph g_x is not equal to g'_x only if there is a node w in g_x such that $w \in \{v_1, \ldots, v_r\}$. However, g'_x is acyclic because making w point to j does not isolate the subgraph g_w from g_x. Hence, the subgraphs $g_j, g'_u, \ldots, g_v, g'_i$ and $g_{v_1}, \ldots, g_{v_r}$ are acyclic, and the resulting graph satisfies 2. Similar to the read fault case, any node $x \in V$ has exactly one path to i. Suppose that the first node in the path (in the node set $\{j, u, \ldots, v, i, v_1, \ldots, v_r\}$) is y. The edge from y is changed to (y, j), so there is no other path from y to j. $\square$

Lemma 1 demonstrates that any page fault can find the true owner of the page if the page faults to the same page are processed sequentially. This shows the correctness of the algorithm in the sequential case.

```
ELSE IF I am manager THEN BEGIN
    Lock( ManagerLock );
    forward request to owner[ p ];
    owner[ p ] := RequestNode;
    Unlock( ManagerLock );
    END;
Unlock( PTable[ p ].lock );
```

APPENDIX B
BROADCAST DISTRIBUTED MANAGER ALGORITHM

BroadcastManager

Read fault handler:
```
Lock( PTable[ p ].lock );
broadcast to get p for read;
PTable[ p ].access := read;
Unlock( PTable[ p ].lock );
```

Read server:
```
Lock( PTable[ p ].lock );
IF I am owner THEN BEGIN
    PTable[ p ].copyset :=
        PTable[ p ].copyset ∪ [ RequestNode ];
    PTable[ p ].access := read;
    send p;
    END;
Unlock( PTable[ p ].lock );
```

Write fault handler:
```
Lock( PTable[ p ].lock );
broadcast to get p for write;
Invalidate( p, PTable[ p ].copyset );
PTable[ p ].access := write;
PTable[ p ].copyset := {};
PTable[ p ].owner := self;
Unlock( PTable[ p ].lock );
```

Write server:
```
Lock( PTable[ p ].lock );
IF I am owner THEN BEGIN
    send p and PTable[ p ].copyset;
    PTable[ p ].access := nil;
    END;
Unlock( PTable[ p ].lock );
```

PROOF. By Lemma 1, there is only one path to the true owner and there is no cycle in the *probOwner* graph. So, the worst case occurs when the *probOwner* graph is a linear chain

$$E_p = \{(v_1, v_2), (v_2, v_3), \ldots, (v_{N-1}, v_N), (v_N, v_N)\}$$

in which case a fault on processor v_1 generates $N-1$ forwarding messages in finding the true owner v_N. □

At the other extreme, we can state the following best-case performance (which is better than any of the previous algorithms):

LEMMA 2.   *There exists a probOwner graph and page-fault sequence such that the total number of messages for locating N different owners of the same page is N.*

PROOF. Such a situation exists when the a *prob-owner* graph is the same chain that caused the worst-case performance in Corollary 2 in which page faults occur on processors $v_N, v_{N-1}, \ldots, v_1$ sequentially. □

It is interesting that the worst-case single-fault situation is coincident with the best-case *N*-fault situation. Also, once the worst-case situation occurs, *all* processors know the true owner. The immediate question that now arises is what is the *worst-case* performance for *K* faults to the same page in the sequential case. The following lemma answers the question:

LEMMA 3.   *For an N-processor shared virtual memory, using Algorithm 2, the worst-case number of messages for locating the owner of a single page K times as a result of K sequential page faults is $O(N + K \log N)$.*

PROOF.   The algorithm reduces to the *type-0 reversal find operation* for solving the set union-find problem [44].[1] For a *probOwner* graph $G_p = (V, E_p)$, define the node set V to be the set in the set union-find problem and define the node $i \in V$ such that $(i, i) \in E_p$ to be the canonical element of the set. A read-page fault of page p on processor j is then a type-0 reversal find operation $Find(j, V)$ in which the canonical element of the set is changed to j. A write-page fault of page p on processor j is a type-0 reversal find operation plus the collapsing (by an invalidation) of the elements in the copy set of the page. Although the collapsing changes the shape of the graph, it does not increase the number in the find operation. Then, according to the proof by Tarjan and Van Leeuwen [44], the worst-case number of messages for locating K owners of a page is $O(N + K \log N)$. □

Note that without changing the ownership on a read-page fault, the algorithm still works correctly, but the worst-case bound increases when N is large. In that case, the total number of messages for locating K owners depends on the configuration of the *probOwner* graph. If the graph is a chain, then it can be as bad as $O(K N)$. On the other hand, if the graph is a balanced binary true it is

---

[1] The reduction to set-union find was motivated by Fowler's analysis on finding objects [22], though the reduction methods are different.

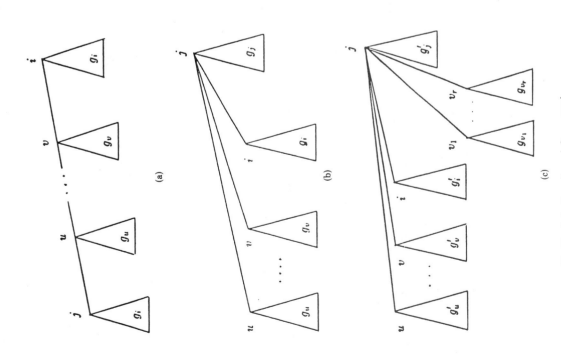

Fig. 12.   Induction of a *probOwner* graph.

The worst-case number of forwarding messages for the sequential case is given by the following corollary:

COROLLARY 2.   *In the N-processor shared virtual memory system, it takes at most N − 1 messages to locate a page if page faults are processed sequentially.*

$O(K \log N)$, and if the graph is at a state in which every processor knows the owner, it is $O(K)$.

All the lemmas and corollaries above are for the sequential page-fault case. In practice, however, the sequential page-fault case is unlikely to happen often, so it is necessary to study the concurrent page-fault case. An important property of the algorithm is the atomicity of each fault handler and its server, provided by the locking and unlocking mechanism. For convenience, we state it in the following lemma:

LEMMA 4. *If a page fault for page p traverses a processor q, then other faults for p that need to traverse processor q, but have yet to, cannot be completed until the first fault completes.*

PROOF. Suppose processing a page fault that occurred on processor i has traversed processor u. The server of the fault handler atomically sets the *prob-Owner* field in the page table entry on processor u to i. The requests for processing other page faults are forwarded to processor i. Since the page table entry on processor i is locked, these requests are queued on processor i until processing the page for processor i is complete. □

Our intention is to show that there exists a sequential page fault processing sequence that matches any given concurrent page fault processing so that the results for the sequential case apply to the concurrent case. Processing concurrent page faults that occur on processors $v_1, \ldots, v_k$ (it is possible that $v_i = v_j$ when $i \neq j$) is said to be *matched* by a sequential processing of a K page fault sequence $(v_1, \ldots, v_k)$ if processing the page fault on processor v_i in the concurrent case traverses the same processors in the same order as in the sequential processing case.

Consider an example in which the owner of a page is v and page faults occur on processor i and processor j concurrently. Suppose that the first common node in the *probOwner* graph that the requests for processing both page faults need to traverse is u (Figure 13(a)). If the request from processor i traverses u first, the algorithm sets the *probOwner* field in the page table entry on processor u to i. When the request from processor j arrives at processor u, it is forwarded to processor i, but the page table entry on processor i is locked until processing the page fault for processor i is complete. So, the request from processor j is queued at the page table entry of processor i, while the request from processor i is traversing the rest of the path from u to v. The *probOwner graph* when the processing is complete is shown in Figure 13(b). When the lock on processor i is released, the request from processor j continues. The resulting graph is shown in Figure 13(c). Thus, the request from processor i traversed the path $i, \ldots, u, \ldots, v$ and the request from processor j traversed the path $j, \ldots, u, i$. This is equivalent to the case in which the following events occur sequentially:

—a page fault occurs on processor i;
—the system processes the page fault;
—a page fault occurs on processor j; and
—the system processes the page fault.

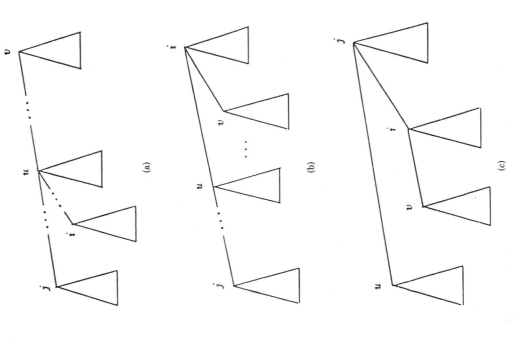

(a)

(b)

(c)

Fig. 13.   Two concurrent page faults.

The matched sequential page-fault processing sequence is therefore (i, j). Obviously, if the request from processor j traverses processor u first, then the matched sequential page-fault processing sequence is (j, i).

LEMMA 5. *For any concurrent page-fault processing, there exists a matched sequential page-fault processing sequence.*

PROOF. By induction on the number of page faults. For one page fault, it is obviously true. For $k + 1$ page fault processing, we look at a page fault on processor i. By Lemma 4, the following is true:

(1) k_1 page fault processing activities are done before processing the page fault for processor i is complete;

(2) there are k_2 page fault processing activities after processing the page fault for processor i is complete; and

(3) $k_1 + k_2 = k$.

According to the assumption, there is a matched sequential page-fault sequence $(u_1, \ldots, u_{k_1})$ for the k_1 concurrent page-fault processings and there is a matched sequential page-fault sequence $(v_1, \ldots, v_{k_2})$ for the k_2 concurrent page-fault processings. The matched page-fault processing sequence is therefore $(u_1, \ldots, u_{k_1}, i, v_1, \ldots, v_{k_2})$. □

PROOF OF THEOREMS 1 AND 2. This lemma not only enables us to apply all the results for the sequential case to the general case but also shows that the find operations in the set-union problem can be done in parallel if each find can be broken into small atomic operations in the same manner as this algorithm. We can therefore prove the two theorems, one for the correctness (Theorem 1 by Lemma 5 and Corollary 2) and one for the worst-case performance of the algorithm (Theorem 2 by Lemma 5 and Lemma 3). □

ACKNOWLEDGMENTS

We wish to thank John Ellis for his invaluable suggestions and helpful discussions in the early stages of this research. We also wish to thank Professor Alan Perlis for his continual help and inspiration.

REFERENCES

1. AHO, A. V., HOPCROFT, J. E., AND ULLMAN, J. D. *The Design and Analysis of Computer Algorithms.* Addison-Wesley, Reading, Mass. 1974.
2. APOLLO COMPUTER. *Apollo DOMAIN Architecture.* Apollo Computer, Inc., Chelmsford, Mass., 1981.
3. ARCHIBALD, J., AND BAER, J. An economical solution to the cache coherence problem. In *Proceedings of the 11th Annual Symposium on Computer Architecture* (Ann Arbor, Mich., June 1984). pp. 355–363.
4. BITTON, D., DEWITT, D. J., HSIAO, D. K., AND MENON, J. A taxonomy of parallel sorting. *ACM Comput. Surv. 16,* 3 (Sept. 1984), 287–318.
5. BOBROW, D. G., BURCHFIEL, J. D., MURPHY, D. L., AND TOMLINSON, R. S. TENEX: A paged time-sharing system for the PDP-10. *Commun. ACM 15,* 3 (Mar. 1972), 135–143.
6. BOLT, BERANEK, AND NEWMAN. *Butterfly Parallel Processor Overview.* Bolt, Beranek, and Newman, Advanced Computers Inc., Cambridge, Mass., 1985.
7. BRINCH, H. *Operating System Principles.* Prentice-Hall, Englewood Cliffs, N.J., 1973.
8. CARRIERO, N., AND GELERNTER, D. The S/Net's Linda kernel. *ACM Trans. Comput. Syst. 4,* 2 (May 1986), 110–129.
9. CENSIER, L. M., AND FEAUTRIER, P. A new solution to coherence problems in multicache systems. *IEEE Trans. Comput. C-27,* 12 (Dec. 1978), 1112–1118.
10. CHERITON, D. R. The VMP multiprocessor: Initial experience, refinements and performance evaluation. In *Proceedings of the 14th Annual Symposium on Computer Architecture* (Pittsburgh, Pa., June 1987).
11. CHERITON, D. R., AND STUMM, M. The multi-satellite star: Structuring parallel computations for a workstation cluster. *J. Distributed Comput.* To appear.
12. COX, A. L., AND FOWLER, R. J. The implementation of a coherent memory abstraction on a NUMA multiprocessor: Experiences with PLATINUM. Tech. Rep. 263, Dept. of Computer Science, University of Rochester, Rochester, N.Y., Mar. 1989.
13. DALEY, R. C., AND DENNIS, J. B. Virtual memory, processes, and sharing in MULTICS. *Commun. ACM 11,* 5 (May 1968), 306–312.
14. DEMINET, J. Experience with multiprocessor algorithms. *IEEE Trans. Comput. C-31,* 4 (Apr. 1982).
15. DENNING, P. J. Virtual memory. *ACM Comput. Surv. 2,* 3 (Sept. 1970), 153–189.
16. DENNING, P. J. On modeling program behavior. In *Proceedings on the Spring Joint Computer Conference* (Atlantic City, N.J., May 16–18, 1972). AFIPS Press, Montudle, N.J., 1972, pp. 937–944.
17. DENNING, P. J. Working sets past and present. *IEEE Trans. Softw. Eng. SE-6,* 1 (Jan. 1980), 64–84.
18. EGGERS, S. J., AND KATZ, R. H. A characterization of sharing in parallel programs and its applications to coherence protocol evaluation. In *Proceedings of the 15th Annual International Symposium on Computer Architecture* (Honolulu, June 1988).
19. FINKEL, R., AND MANBER, U. BIB—A distributed implementation of backtracking. In *The 5th International Conference on Distributed Computing Systems* (Denver, Colo., May 1985).
20. FITZGERALD, R., AND RASHID, R. F. The integration of virtual memory management and interprocess communication in Accent. *ACM Trans. Comput. Syst. 4,* 2 (May 1986) 147–177.
21. FLEISCH, B. D. Distributed shared memory in a loosely coupled distributed system. In *Proceedings of the ACM SIGCOMM 87 Workshop, Frontiers in Computer Communications Technology* (Stowe, Vt., Aug. 11–13, 1987). ACM, New York, 1987, pp. 317–327.
22. FOWLER, R. J. Decentralized object finding using forwarding addresses. Ph.D. dissertation, Dept. of Computer Science, Univ. of Washington, Seattle, 1986.
23. FRANK, S. J. Tightly coupled multiprocessor system speeds memory-access times. *Electronics 57,* 1 (Jan. 1984), 164–169.
24. FULLER, S., OUSTERHOUT, J., RASKIN, L., RUBINFELD, P., SINDHU, P., AND SWAN, R. Multimicroprocessors: An overview and working example. In *Proceedings of the IEEE 66,* 2 (Feb. 1978) pp. 214–228.
25. GOODMAN, J. R. Using cache memory to reduce processor-memory traffic. In *Proceedings of the 10th Annual Symposium on Computer Architecture* (Stockholm, June 1983), pp. 124–131.
26. HOARE, C. A. R. Quicksort. *Comput. J. 5,* 1 (1962), 10–15.
27. HOARE, C. A. R. Monitors: An operating system structuring concept. *Commun. ACM 17,* 10 (Oct. 1974), 549–557.
28. JONES, A. K., AND SCHWARZ, P. Experience using multiprocessor systems—A status report. *ACM Comput. Surv. 12,* 2 (June 1980), 121–166.
29. JONES, A. K., CHANSLER, R. J., DURHAM, I. E., SCHWANS, K., AND VEGDAHL, S. StarOS, a multiprocessor operating system for the support of task forces. In *Proceedings of the 7th Symposium on Operating Systems Principles* (Pacific Grove, Calif., Dec. 10–12, 1979). ACM, New York, 1979, pp. 117–127.
30. KARLIN, A. R., MANASSE, M. S., RUDOLPH, L., AND SLEATOR, D. D. Competitive snoopy caching. In *Proceedings of the 27th Symposium on Foundation of Computer Science* (Toronto, 1986). pp. 244–254.
31. KATZ, R. H., EGGERS, S. J., WOOD, D. A., PERKINS, C. L., AND SHELDON, R. G. Implementing a cache consistency protocol. In *Proceedings of the 12th Annual Symposium on Computer Architecture* (Boston, Mass., June 1985). pp. 276–283.
32. LEACH, P. J., STUMPF, B. L., HAMILTON, J. A., AND LEVINE, P. H. UIDs as internal names in a distributed file system. In *Proceedings of the ACM SIGACT-SIGOPS Symposium on Principles of Distributed Computing* (Ottawa, Ontario, Canada, Aug. 18–20, 1982). ACM, New York, 1982, pp. 34–41.
33. LEACH, P. J., LEVINE, P. H., DOUROS, B. P., HAMILTON, J. A., NELSON, D. L., AND STUMPF, B. L. The architecture of an integrated local network. *IEEE J. Selected Areas in Commun. SAC-1,* 5 (1983).
34. LI, K. Shared virtual memory on loosely coupled multiprocessors. Ph.D. dissertation, Dept. of Computer Science, Yale University, New Haven, Conn. Oct. 1986. Also Tech. Rep. YALEU-RR-492.

35. LI, K. *IVY: A shared virtual memory system for parallel computing.* In *Proceedings of the 1988 International Conference on Parallel Processing* (Aug. 1988). Pennsylvania State University Press, 1988, pp. 94–101.

36. LI, K., AND HUDAK, P. Memory coherence in shared virtual memory systems. In *Proceedings of the 5th Annual ACM Symposium on Principles of Distributed Computing* (Calgary, Alberta, Aug. 11–13, 1986). ACM, New York, 1986, pp. 229–239.

37. LI, K., AND SCHAEFER, R. A hypercube shared virtual memory. In *Proceedings of the 1989 International Parallel Processing Conference* (Dufage, Ill., Aug. 1989).

38. RASHID, R. F., AND ROBERTSON, G. G. Accent: A communication oriented network operating system kernel. In *Proceedings of the 8th Symposium on Operating Systems Principles* (Pacific Grove Calif., Dec. 14–16). ACM, New York, 1981, pp. 64–75.

39. SEITZ, C. L. The cosmic cube. *Commun. ACM 28*, 1 (Jan. 1985), 22–33.

40. SMITH, A. J. Cache memories. *ACM Comput. Surv. 14*, 3 (Sept. 1982), 473–530.

41. SPECTOR, A. Z. Multiprocessing Architectures for Local Computer Networks. Ph.D. dissertation, STAN-CS-81-874, Stanford University, Dept. of Computer Science, Stanford, Calif., Aug. 1981.

42. SPECTOR, A. Z. Performing remote operations efficiently on a local computer network. *Commun. ACM 25*, 4 (Apr. 1982), 260–273.

43. TANG, C. K. Cache system design in the tightly coupled multiprocessor system. In *Proceedings of AFIPS National Computer Conference* (New York, N.Y., June 7–10, 1976). AFIPS Press, Montvale, N.J. 1976, pp. 749–753.

44. TARJAN, R. E., AND VAN LEEUWEN, J. Worst-case analysis of set union algorithms. *J. ACM 31*, 2 (Apr. 1984), 245–281.

45. THOMPSON, J. Efficient analysis of caching systems. Ph.D. dissertation, University of California at Berkeley, Dept. of Computer Science, Oct. 1987. Also Tech Rep. UCB/CSD 87/374.

46. YEN, W. C., YEN, D. W. L., AND FU, K. Data coherence problem in a multicache system. *IEEE Trans. Comput. C-34*, 1 (Jan. 1985), 56–65.

Received February 1987; revised December 1987; October 1988, and May 1989; accepted May 1989

Recent Implementations and Future Prospects

10.1 Introduction

In this section, we continue to look at improvements in base technology that have enabled recent architectural improvements in computers (we define "recent" to mean occurring in the last ten years). We also examine implementation aspects of different types of computers and cost issues. Without a good understanding of cost, implementations will not be economically successful. In the extreme, this can mean the cancellation of projects or even the failure of the business. Without a good understanding of implementation issues, architectural evaluations risk irrelevance. The lack of understanding of the marketplace, business issues, costs, and implementation issues results in many more project failures than architectural naïveté. Unfortunately, marketing, business, and economics are largely beyond the scope of this reader; this section attempts to give merely a flavor of these subjects. We believe all engineering students should take courses to gain an overview of economics, business accounting and finance, marketing, and business organization. Those who have already graduated are well advised to study these subjects on their own time. A quick overview of many important concepts can be found in *The Ten-Day MBA* by Steven Spilbiger [21].

10.2 Recent Microprocessor Design

For our discussion, we break the microprocessor design space into three segments: high-performance microprocessors, embedded volume microprocessors, and embedded high-performance microprocessors.

10.2.1 High-Performance Microprocessors

There have been a number of good papers published in the last decade covering the implementation of various high-performance microprocessors. We have selected one paper on the Pentium and one on the Pentium Pro as examples of in-order and out-of-order superscalar processors. Because they both implement a CISC instruction set, they generally have to deal with most of the issues of a RISC microprocessor design plus more. Also, by choosing two papers on very different microprocessors implementing the same instruction set, the contrast between the two implementations becomes more apparent. Other interesting recent CISC implementations include the IBM S/390 G5 Microprocessor [20] and x86 microprocessors from AMD [15]. There are currently many different RISC architectures, all with good implementations. We refer the reader interested in implementations of specific architectures to these papers on the Compaq Alpha [4, 9], Sun UltraSparc [14, 22], HP PA-RISC [10], and MIPS [24] microprocessors, as well as a book on the IBM/Apple/Motorola Power PC [23].

10.2.2 Embedded Volume Microprocessors

High-volume embedded processors are a very cost-sensitive segment of microprocessor design. The key principle in embedded design dates to the eighteenth century:

> A penny saved is a penny earned.
> —Benjamin Franklin

Embedded microprocessors only need to implement enough computing power to run their particular application; any more functionality is wasted silicon, power, and money. This leads to the 8-bit microprocessor (with 4-bit external bus) still being the highest volume microprocessor in the embedded marketplace [18]. Ben Franklin's maxim also applies at the embedded system level—this pushes system functionality such as EPROM, counters and timers, serial interfaces, and so forth, onto the embedded microprocessor itself to reduce the system part count and hence cost. (There is lots of room left over for system components when you are implementing a single-issue 8-bit microprocessor.)

10.2.3 Embedded High-Performance Microprocessors

High-performance embedded microprocessors often perform long and repetitive numeric computations. This means that complex mainstream techniques, such as sophisticated branch prediction and dynamic scheduling, are not as important in the embedded space. It also means that DSPs are more amenable to architectures such as very long instruction word (VLIW) or vector. One of the more well-known DSPs is the Phillips Trimedia VLIW media processor [19]. Other more-conventional high-performance embedded microprocessors include those in the StrongARM family [11].

10.3 Discussion of Papers on Microprocessor Design

In this section, we present two examples of recent high-performance microprocessor design.

10.3.1 Alpert and Avnon's "Architecture of the Pentium Microprocessor" [1]

This paper describes the architecture and implementation of the Pentium microprocessor as well as some of its design tradeoffs. Although the Pentium originally shipped at 60 MHz in a 0.8-μm BiCMOS technology, shrinks and modifications have enabled it to run at almost 4X that clock rate in 0.35-μm processes. This is a very wide range of performance, thanks to Moore's Law and some redesign.

Like some contemporaneous RISC processors, the Pentium is a dual-issue superscalar with an on-chip FPU, branch prediction, and write-back caches. However, the Pentium also had to maintain backward compatibility with the x86 architecture. This affected the architecture in several ways. For example, it needed a dual port data cache, because the x86 architecture has very few registers, and many instructions have an operand in memory. Besides handling all the x86 CISC instructions (including transcendental functions in hardware), it also had to correctly execute self-modifying code. The Pentium had a transistor budget almost 700 times larger than the 8080. It achieved a 2X speedup for integer code and a 5X speedup for floating-point vector code over the previous i486 design when running at the same clock frequency.

10.3.2 Papworth's "Tuning the Pentium Pro Microarchitecture" [17]

As we discussed earlier, computer instruction-set architecture evolution tends to make the surviving architecture one of the "least fit." However, because the architecture is the most successful, it will be manufactured in volumes that dwarf any other high-performance microprocessor. (Very low cost microprocessors, such as those that play music in some greeting cards, are manufactured in much higher volumes than high-performance microprocessors. However, because of their low cost—sometimes less than one dollar—and the higher prices for high-performance microprocessors, the high-performance microprocessors still result in more total revenue.) Because the processor is manufactured in volumes that dwarf all other high-performance microprocessors combined, much larger amounts of money can be made available for development of that microprocessor family. This can be used to overcome the shortcomings that will be inherent in the most successful high-performance instruction-set architecture. Combined with the enormous manufacturing economies of scale, this allows the most successful microprocessor to still be a price/performance leader even with a very complex design.

A case in point is the P6 design core that first appeared in the Pentium Pro and later in the Pentium II, Celeron, and Xeon processors. This core is the most successful machine with full out-of-order issue (including register renaming) ever built. One of the difficulties in implementing a dynamically scheduled machine is that it is very difficult to design and to verify. Thus, although it can result in significant performance improvements in dealing with unpredictable memory latency because of cache misses, the potential delays to project completion, and the increase in design expense are often not justifiable unless the design is produced in very large quantities.

This paper is interesting because it primarily describes the architecture design process for the Pentium Pro instead of describing just the final implementation. The design process included examining the tradeoffs in using a higher clock frequency with less work done each cycle and a resulting larger CPI. Like the designers of the DEC Alpha (and Seymour Cray before them), they found that raw clock speed is a powerful lever, so they chose a more heavily pipelined design than they had originally expected to. Not mentioned in the paper is that for people who know very little about computers (such as consumers and the management of some corporations), clock speed also serves as an even more meaningless indicator of processor speed than MIPS or MFLOPS. Thus, a highly pipelined design may be easier to sell to both corporate management and the public than a higher performance design with a lower clock frequency.

Another interesting feature of the Pentium Pro is that it combined two chips in a larger package. This allowed its manufacturing cost to be much less than if it consisted of a single chip, and this enabled it to be launched into the marketplace sooner. Although the two chips were more expensive than a simpler one-chip design (like the Pentium), it was initially targeted at server CPU applications where a more-expensive CPU was still a reasonable fraction of the system cost. Combined with the Pentium in the same process, this enabled coverage of a greater range of the product space. The Pentium Pro design was introduced in 0.6-μm technology at 150 MHz; derivatives of this design (the Pentium III) are already available at 550 MHz in 0.25-μm technologies.

10.4 Current Trends and Future Prospects

As we have seen in earlier chapters, the primary driver of progress in computing technology is lithographic scaling of devices according to Moore's Law. This raises the question of how much longer Moore's Law will hold and what will eventually break it. There are at least four potential limits to Moore's Law: device characteristics, lithography, design complexity, and fabrication cost.

10.4.1 Device Characteristics—A Physical Limit
Studies of extremely small transistors in laboratories

have shown that it can be beneficial to scale CMOS transistors down to gate lengths of 0.025 μm [8]. However, starting around the 0.1-μm generation, if improved device performance is to be obtained with scaling, the gate oxide thickness must become so thin that electrons can tunnel through it. This results in a gate leakage current. Obviously, for some applications, such as DRAMs, this is not acceptable, but these applications can often live with lower performance devices. For logic applications, small gate currents can be taken into account in the circuit and logic design process. In this sense, MOS transistors will become more like bipolar devices, which have a base current when they are conducting!

The other important "device" in an integrated circuit are the wires [2]. Scaling of wires results in wires with more resistance and higher capacitance. Thus the inherent RC time constant of a wire itself will become a bigger and bigger factor of an integrated circuit's speed. Changes to copper metalization (for lower resistance wires) and low-K dielectrics (for lower capacitance wires) provide one-time gains on the order of a factor of two each. Because the resistance of copper is quite low and the dielectric constant of low-K dielectrics are near physical limits, further gains of this type should not be expected. The net result of increased wire time constants is somewhat slower performance and increased design complexity. Architectural techniques (such as [16]) that can mitigate long on-chip wire delays are important areas for future research.

10.4.2 Lithography—A Technological Limit
The Rayleigh limit states that the minimum feature size patternable by light is proportional to its wavelength. To pattern features smaller than 0.1 μm, very short wavelengths of light will be required. Unfortunately, most materials absorb these wavelengths, so conventional optical reduction and focusing systems using lenses are not possible. Three lithography options are possible: soft X-rays (about 1-nm wavelength), extreme ultraviolet light (at 13 nm, roughly halfway in logarithmic terms between the deep UV in use today and soft X-rays), and electron beams. Although all of these approaches are quite different from techniques in use today, the extreme-UV approach is the closest to what we are doing today and also potentially has throughputs that could be economically viable. An excellent reference on the future of lithography is Geppert's "Semiconductor Lithography for the Next Decade" [6]. More recently

three National Labs, several companies, and Gordon Moore have announced a new "Limited Liability Extreme-UV Lithography Venture." The announcement of and information on this organization can be found via the online companion to this reader.

10.4.3 Design Complexity—An Implementation Limit

Both design-team size and the verification complexity of large designs can be examples of design complexity limits.

The 8008 was designed in a 10-μm process by two designers [12] and an architect. Recent flagship microprocessor designs have required some 200 designers. Thus, the number of people needed to implement a microprocessor has been increasing in rough inverse proportion to the feature size of the process. Managing such a large team of people to design anything is an enormous design challenge. It also requires large amounts of structure in a design so that aspects of the design can be managed by leaders of smaller teams. For example, in the Pentium paper [1], the authors state that the two parallel execution pipes were given the names U and V, because these were the first two adjacent letters of the alphabet that had not already been used as a box (design subunit) name. This means that there were at least ten boxes in the design, and probably more. One result of adding large amounts of structure is that optimizations between boxes of a design may not be obvious to many people. Also, because the interfaces between boxes must be frozen early in the design, later changes in the machine structure may not be possible without unacceptable delays in the project. Besides having many small teams operate in parallel, such large designs are often pipelined into design stages. These stages consist of overall architecture, microarchitecture, logic design, circuit design, and layout (as well as verification at each stage sometimes done by a separate parallel team). In this kind of design pipeline, negative effects at later stages (e.g., a failure to meet design cycle time goals on a particular unit) are very hard to fix by backing up the pipeline without unacceptable delays in the project. It is even more unlikely that new better ideas at any stage can be implemented once that phase is complete—this would also delay the project.

Today's microprocessor designs are much more complex than were early designs. This is particularly true in the case of out-of-order issue multiprocessors. Verification of simple in-order issue uniprocessors can be done to acceptable quality by the brute force approach of trying to simulate all possibilities.

However, with out-of-order issue multiprocessors, the state space is just too large to cover in total by simulation. Formal verification methods can help, but verification of the design is still in itself an enormous task. If future microprocessors were constructed out of a number of simpler multiprocessor-capable cores or already-verified out-of-order issue processors, the design verification problem would also be simplified [7].

As the number of people required for the design and verification of a microprocessor increases, the development cost increases. This raises the volumes necessary for profitable development of microprocessors and hence leads to further consolidation in the industry.

10.4.4 Fabrication Cost—An Economic Limit

Gordon Moore has stated on several occasions [13] that the capital cost of building a fab is increasing at a rate that is roughly inversely proportional to the feature size. The cost of building a 0.25-μm fab capable of starting 5,000 wafers per week is now about $1.3 billion. If this trend continues, the cost of a 0.03-μm fab a decade from now would be over $10 billion. Very few companies could justify this scale of investment (most semiconductor company *revenues* are less than $10 billion per year!) Thus fewer and fewer companies will be able to build fabs with the necessary economies of scale to be competitive. This will lead to further consolidation in the number of semiconductor companies and products.

The high cost of semiconductor fabrication equipment also leads to increased process development cost. This is because process development must be done with some of the same equipment that will eventually be used for production, and developing a process takes time (e.g., two years). The very-expensive equipment depreciates while it is being used for process development, and this expense alone can make developing a different process prohibitively expensive (e.g., $100 million). This puts an emphasis on evolutionary versus revolutionary process development and leads to a smaller number of processes in the world (e.g., only a basic CMOS, which would have the highest volume versus a BiCMOS or GaAs process).

10.4.5 Prognosis

Moore's Law should continue to hold through the year 2007 [8]. But eventually the scaling curve will saturate, and improvements will occur less frequently, such as doubling instead of quadrupling every three years. But before then, the implications of increasing fabrication cost and design complexity will result in many fewer fabrication lines than we have today (each with higher capacity and much more expensive) controlled by fewer semiconductor companies producing a smaller number of more powerful parts on a smaller number of more powerful fabrication processes. In other words, there will be a loss of diversity in designs (e.g., fewer microprocessors developed each year) and in processes (e.g., convergence on a standard high-performance CMOS process) resulting from economic necessities.

10.5 Discussion of Papers on Current Trends and Future Prospects

In this section we introduce two papers that describe current trends and future prospects in microprocessor engineering.

10.5.1 Slater's "The Microprocessor Today" [18]

Michael Slater is the founder and editorial director of Microprocessor Reports. In those reports and in this article, he tries to consider all the factors that lead to success or failure of various industry approaches.

One of the more important considerations is manufacturing cost versus selling price. This paper contains estimates of various microprocessors' manufacturing costs as well as their selling prices. In one table, he estimates that Intel microprocessors typically cost less to manufacture but sell for more than the AMD or Cyrix parts. This goes a long way toward explaining Intel's dominance of that market and also explains how it can fund investments in many billion-dollar fabs at the same time. RISC processors have much higher ratios of sales prices to manufacturing cost, but this does not include design costs which, because of the RISC processor's much smaller volumes, are much larger per microprocessor. Unfortunately for computer architects, issues like these (and object code compatibility) are more important in the marketplace than architectural strength and purity are.

Although architectural compatibility is very important in the desktop and large system markets, the embedded marketplace has different constraints. Here the primary focus is reducing the cost as much as possible, often by integration of other system functions on the microcontroller. Because object-code compatibility is not such a large issue in this market, "embedded MIPS" are much more of a commodity market, with correspondingly lower prices and margins.

10.5.2 Yu's "The Future of Microprocessors" [25]

This article examines the impact of continued scaling and Moore's Law on future microprocessor performance.

In a related article in 1989 [5], performance projections were made for the coming decade. These previous projections underestimated microprocessor performance circa 1995 by a factor of four by underestimating improvements in cycle time and in IPC. Because the fabrication cost, design cost, and design verification tasks are all increasing in proportion to feature size reductions, these factors may pose the most significant barriers to continued microprocessor evolution in the future.

10.6 References

A large number of interesting papers on future directions for microprocessor architecture appeared in a special issue of *IEEE Computer* "Billion-Transistor Architectures," edited by Burger and Goodman [3]. Please also see the Web companion to this reader for additional Web references.

[1]   D. Alpert and D. Avnon, "Architecture of the Pentium microprocessor," *IEEE Micro*, 13(3):11–21, 1993.

[2]   M. T. Bohr, "Interconnect scaling—the real limiter to high-performance ULSI," *International Electron Devices Meeting Technical Digest*, pp. 241–244, 1995.

[3]   D. Burger and J. R. Goodman, "Billion-transistor architectures," *IEEE Computer*, 30(9):46–48, 1997.

[4]   J. H. Edmondson, P. Rubinfeld, and R. Preston, "Superscalar instruction execution in the 21164 Alpha microprocessor," *IEEE Micro*, 15(3):33–43, 1995.

[5]   P. P. Gelsinger, P. A. Gargini, G. H. Parker, and A. Y. C. Yu, "Microprocessors circa 2000," *IEEE Spectrum*, 26(10):43–47, Oct. 1989.

[6]   L. Geppert, "Semiconductor lithography for the next decade," *IEEE Spectrum*, 33(4):33–38, Apr. 1996.

[7]   L. Hammond, B. A. Nayfeh, and K. Oluktun, "A single-chip multiprocessor," *IEEE Computer*, 30(9):79–85, 1997.

[8]   H. Iwai, "CMOS technology-Year 2010 and beyond," *IEEE Journal of Solid-State Circuits*, 34(3):357–366, 1999.

[9]   R. Kessler, "The Alpha 21264 microprocessor," *IEEE Micro*, 19(2):24–36, 1999.

[10]   A. Kumar, "The HP PA-8000 RISC CPU," *IEEE Micro*, 17(2):27–32, 1997.

[11]   T. Litch and J. Slaton, "StrongARMing portable communications," *IEEE Micro*, 18(2):48–55, 1998.

[12]   S. Mazor, "The history of the microcomputer—Invention and evolution," *Proceedings of the IEEE*, 83(12):1601–1608, 1995.

[13]   G. Moore, "Nanometers and gigabucks," *Proceedings of Hot Chips VII*, Aug. 1995.

[14] K. B. Normoyle et al., "UltraSparc IIi: Expanding the boundaries of system on a chip," *IEEE Micro*, 18(2):14–24, 1998.

[15] S. Oberman, G. Favor, and F. Weber, "AMD 3D Now! technology: Architecture and implementations," *IEEE Micro*, 19(2):37–48, 1999.

[16] S. Palacharla, N. P. Jouppi, and J. E. Smith, "Complexity-effective superscalar processors," *Proceedings of the 24th International Symposium on Computer Architecture*, pp. 206–218, 1997.

[17] D. B. Papworth, "Tuning the Pentium Pro microarchitecture," *IEEE Micro*, 16(2):8–15, 1996.

[18] M. Slater, "The microprocessor today," *IEEE Micro*, 16(6):32–44, 1996.

[19] G. A. Slavenburg, S. Rathnam, and H. Dijkstra, "The Trimedia TM-1 PCI VLIW mediaprocessor," *Proceedings of Hot Chips VIII*, Aug. 1996.

[20] T. J. Slegel et al., "IBM's S/390 G5 microprocessor," *IEEE Micro*, 19(2):12–23, 1999.

[21] S. Spilbiger, *The Ten-Day MBA*. New York: William Morrow, 1993.

[22] M. Tremblay and J. M. O'Connor, "UltraSparc I: A four-issue processor supporting multimedia," *IEEE Micro*, 16(2):42–50, 1996.

[23] S. Weiss and J. E. Smith, *POWER and PowerPC: Principles, Architecture, and Implementation*, San Francisco, CA: Morgan Kaufmann, 1994.

[24] K. C. Yeager, "The Mips R10000 Superscalar microprocessor," *IEEE Micro*, 16(2):28–40, 1996.

[25] A. Yu, "The future of microprocessors," *IEEE Micro*, 16(6):46–53, 1996.

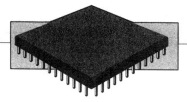

Architecture of the Pentium Microprocessor

The Pentium CPU is the latest in Intel's family of compatible microprocessors. It integrates 3.1 million transistors in 0.8-μm BiCMOS technology. We describe the techniques of pipelining, superscalar execution, and branch prediction used in the microprocessor's design.

Donald Alpert

Dror Avnon

Intel Corporation

The Pentium processor is Intel's next generation of compatible microprocessors following the popular i486 CPU family. The design started in early 1989 with the primary goal of maximizing performance while preserving software compatibility within the practical constraints of available technology. The Pentium processor integrates 3.1 million transistors in 0.8-μm BiCMOS technology and carries the Intel trademark. We describe the architecture and development process employed to achieve this goal.

Technology

The continual advancement of semiconductor technology promotes innovation in microprocessor design. Higher levels of integration, made possible by reduced feature sizes and increased interconnection layers, enable designers to deploy additional hardware resources for more parallel computation and deeper pipelining. Faster device speeds lead to higher clock rates and consequently to requirements for larger and more specialized on-chip memory buffers.

Table 1 (next page) summarizes the technology improvements associated with our three most recent microprocessor generations. The 0.8-μm BiCMOS technology of the Pentium microprocessor enables 2.5 times the number of transistors and twice the clock frequency of the original i486 CPU, which was implemented in 1.0-μm CMOS.

Compatibility

Since introduction of the 8086 microprocessor in 1978, the X86 architecture has evolved through several generations of substantial functional enhancements and technology improvements, including the 80286 and i386 CPUs. Each of these CPUs was supported by a corresponding floating-point unit. The i486 CPU,[1] introduced in 1989, integrates the complete functionality of an integer processor, floating-point unit, and cache memory into a single circuit.

The X86 architecture greatly appealed to software developers because of its widespread application as the central processor of IBM-compatible personal computers. The success of the architecture in PCs has in turn made the X86 popular for commercial server applications as well. Figure 1 shows some of the well-known software environments that are hosted on the architecture.

The common software environments allow the X86 architecture to exercise several operating modes. Applications developed for DOS use 16-bit real mode (or virtual 8086 mode) and MS Windows. Early versions of OS/2 use 16-bit protected mode, and applications for other popular environments use 32-bit flat (unsegmented) mode. The Pentium microprocessor employs general techniques for improving performance in all operating modes, as well as certain techniques for improving performance in specific operating

Table 1. Technology for microprocessor development.

Microprocessor	Year	Technology	No. of transistors	Frequency (MHz)
i386 CPU	1986	1.5-μm CMOS, two-layer metal	275K	16
i486 CPU	1989	1.0-μm CMOS, two-layer metal	1.2M	33
Pentium CPU	1993	0.8-μm BiCMOS, three-layer metal	3.1M	66

16-bit generation	32-bit generation
	Unix SVR4
	SCO
DOS	OSF/1
MS-Windows	Netware 3.11
OS/2 1.x	Next Step
	32-bit OS/2
	Solaris
	Windows NT
	Univel
	Taligent
1980s	1991 199x

Figure 1. Software environments. *(All figures, tables, and photographs published in this article are the property of Intel Corporation.)*

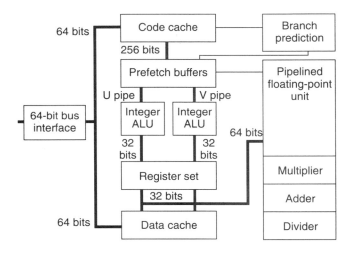

Figure 2. Pentium processor block diagram.

modes. We focus on the 32-bit flat mode here, since this is the most appropriate mode for comparison with the other high-performance microprocessors described at the Hot Chips IV Conference.

The X86 architecture supports the IEEE-754 standard for floating-point arithmetic.[2] In addition to required operations on single-precision and double-precision formats, the X86 floating-point architecture includes operations on 80-bit, extended-precision format and a set of basic transcendental functions.

Pentium CPU designers found numerous exciting technical challenges in developing a microarchitecture that maintained compatibility with such a diverse software base. Later in this article we present examples of techniques for supporting self-modifying code and the stack-oriented, floating-point register file.

Performance

A microprocessor's performance is a complex function of many parameters that vary between applications, compilers, and hardware systems. In developing the Pentium microprocessor, the design team addressed these aspects for each of the popular software environments. As a result, Pentium CPU features tuned compilers and cache memory.

We focus on the performance of SPEC benchmarks for both the Pentium microprocessor and i486 CPU in systems with well-tuned compilers and cache memory. More specifically, the Pentium CPU achieves roughly two times the speedup on integer code and up to five times the speedup on floating-point vector code when compared with an i486 CPU of identical clock frequency.

Organization

Figure 2 shows the overall organization of the Pentium microprocessor. The core execution units are two integer pipelines and a floating-point pipeline with dedicated adder, multiplier, and divider. Separate on-chip instruction code and data caches supply the memory demands of the execution units, with a branch target buffer augmenting the instruction cache for dynamic branch prediction. The external interface includes separate address and 64-bit data buses.

Integer pipeline

The Pentium processor's integer pipeline is similar to that of the i486 CPU.[3] The pipeline has five stages (see Figure 3) with the following functions:

- *Prefetch.* During the PF stage the CPU prefetches code from the instruction cache and aligns the code to the

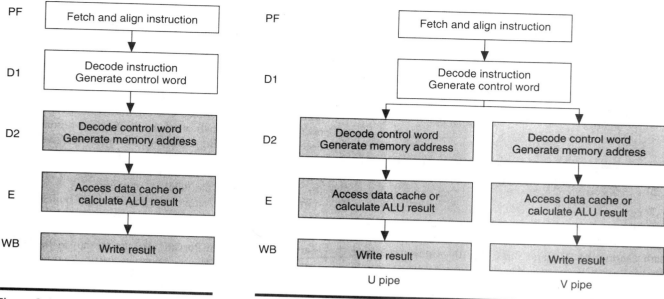

PF	Fetch and align instruction
D1	Decode instruction Generate control word
D2	Decode control word Generate memory address
E	Access data cache or calculate ALU result
WB	Write result

Figure 3. Integer pipeline.

Figure 4. Superscalar execution.

initial byte of the next instruction to be decoded. Because instructions are of variable length, this stage includes buffers to hold both the line containing the instruction being decoded and the next consecutive line.

- *First decode.* In the D1 stage the CPU decodes the instruction to generate a control word. A single control word executes instructions directly; more complex instructions require microcoded control sequencing in D1.
- *Second decode.* In the D2 stage the CPU decodes the control word from D1 for use in the E stage. In addition, the CPU generates addresses for data memory references.
- *Execute.* In the E stage the CPU either accesses the data cache or calculates results in the ALU (arithmetic logic unit), barrel shifter, or other functional units in the data path.
- *Write back.* In the WB stage the CPU updates the registers and flags with the instruction's results. All exceptional conditions must be resolved before an instruction can advance to WB.

Compared to the integer pipeline of the i486 CPU, the Pentium microprocessor integrates additional hardware in several stages to speed instruction execution. For example, the i486 CPU requires two clocks to decode several instruction formats, but the Pentium CPU takes one clock and executes shift and multiply instructions faster. More significantly, the Pentium processor substantially enhances superscalar execution, branch prediction, and cache organization.

Superscalar execution. The Pentium CPU has a superscalar organization that enables two instructions to execute

in parallel. Figure 4 shows that the resources for address generation and ALU functions have been replicated in independent integer pipelines, called U and V. (The pipeline names were selected because U and V were the first two consecutive letters of the alphabet neither of which was the initial of a functional unit in the design partitioning.) In the PF and D1 stages the CPU can fetch and decode two simple instructions in parallel and issue them to the U and V pipelines. Additionally, for complex instructions the CPU in D1 can generate microcode sequences that control both U and V pipelines.

Several techniques are used to resolve dependencies between instructions that might be executed in parallel. Most of the logic is contained in the instruction issue algorithm (see Figure 5) of D1.

```
Decode two consecutive instructions: I1 and I2
If the following are all true
        I1 is a "simple" instruction
        I2 is a "simple" instruction
        I1 is not a jump instruction
        Destination of I1 ≠ source of I2
        Destination of I1 ≠ destination of I2
Then issue I1 to U pipe and I2 to V pipe
Else issue I1 to U pipe
```

Figure 5. Instruction issue algorithm.

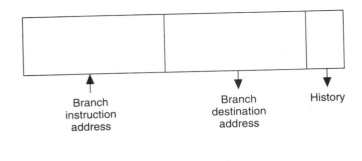

Branch instruction address   Branch destination address   History

Figure 6. Branch target buffer.

Resource dependencies. A resource dependency occurs when two instructions require a single functional unit or data path. During the D1 stage, the CPU only issues two instructions for parallel execution if both are from a class of "simple" instructions, thereby eliminating most resource dependencies. The instructions must be directly executed, that is, not require microcode sequencing. The instruction being issued to the V pipe can be an ALU operation, memory reference, or jump. The instruction being issued to the U pipe can be from the same categories or from an additional set that uses a functional unit available only in the U pipe, such as the barrel shifter. Although the set of instructions identified as "simple" might seem restrictive, more than 90 percent of instructions executed in the Integer SPEC benchmark suite are simple.

Data dependencies. A data dependency occurs when one instruction writes a result that is read or written by another instruction. Logic in D1 ensures that the source and destination registers of the instruction issued to the V pipe differ from the destination register of the instruction issued to the U pipe. This arrangement eliminates read-after-write (RAW) and write-after-write (WAW) dependencies. Write-after-read (WAR) dependencies need not be checked because reads occur in an earlier stage of the pipelines than writes.

The design includes logic that enables instructions with certain special types of data dependency to be executed in parallel. For example, a conditional branch instruction that tests the flag results can be executed in parallel with a compare instruction that sets the flags.

Control dependencies. A control dependency occurs when the result of one instruction determines whether another instruction will be executed. When a jump instruction is issued to the U pipe, the CPU in D1 never issues an instruction to the V pipe, thereby eliminating control dependencies.

Note that resource dependencies and data dependencies between memory references are not resolved in D1. Dependent memory references can be issued to the two pipelines; we explain their resolution in the description of the data cache.

Branch prediction. The i486 CPU has a simple technique for handling branches. When a branch instruction is executed, the pipeline continues to fetch and decode instructions along the sequential path until the branch reaches the E stage. In E, the CPU fetches the branch destination, and the pipeline resolves whether or not a conditional branch is taken. If the branch is not taken, the CPU discards the fetched destination, and execution proceeds along the sequential path with no delay. If the branch is taken, the fetched destination is used to begin decoding along the target path with two clocks of delay. Taken branches are found to be 15 percent to 20 percent of instructions executed, representing an obvious area for improvement by the Pentium processor.

The Pentium CPU employs a branch target buffer (BTB), which is an associative memory used to improve performance of taken branch instructions (see Figure 6). When a branch instruction is first taken, the CPU allocates an entry in the branch target buffer to associate the branch instruction's address with its destination address and to initialize the history used in the prediction algorithm. As instructions are decoded, the CPU searches the branch target buffer to determine whether it holds an entry for a corresponding branch instruction. When there is a hit, the CPU uses the history to determine whether the branch should be taken. If it should, the microprocessor uses the target address to begin fetching and decoding instructions from the target path. The branch is resolved early in the WB stage, and if the prediction was incorrect, the CPU flushes the pipeline and resumes fetching along the correct path. The CPU updates the dual-ported history in the WB stage. The branch target buffer holds entries for predicting 256 branches in a four-way associative organization.

Using these techniques, the Pentium CPU executes correctly predicted branches with no delay. In addition, conditional branches can be executed in the V pipe paired with a compare or other instruction that sets the flags in the U pipe. Branching executes with full compatibility and no modification to existing software. (We explain aspects of interactions between branch prediction and self-modifying code later.)

Cache organization. The i486 CPU employs a single on-chip cache that is unified for code and data. The single-ported cache is multiplexed on a demand basis between sequential code prefetches of complete lines and data references to individual locations. As just explained, branch targets are prefetched in the E stage, effectively using the same hardware as data memory references. There are potential advantages for such an organization over one that separates code and data.

1) For a given size of cache memory, a unified cache has a higher hit rate than separate caches because it balances the total allocation of code and data lines automatically.
2) Only one cache needs to be designed.
3) Handling self-modifying code can be simpler.

Despite these potential advantages of a unified cache, all of which apply to the i486 CPU, the Pentium microprocessor uses separate code and data caches. The reason is that the superscalar design and branch prediction demand more bandwidth than a unified cache similar to that of the i486 CPU can provide. First, efficient branch prediction requires that the destination of a branch be accessed simultaneously with data references of previous instructions executing in the pipeline. Second, the parallel execution of data memory references requires simultaneous accesses for loads and stores. Third, in the context of the overall Pentium microprocessor design, handling self-modifying code for separate code and data caches is only marginally more complex than for a unified cache.

The instruction cache and data cache are each 8-Kbyte, two-way associative designs with 32-byte lines.

Programs executing on the i486 CPU typically generate more data memory references than when executing on RISC microprocessors. Measurements on Integer SPEC benchmarks show 0.5 to 0.6 data references per instruction for the i486 CPU[4] and only 0.17 to 0.33 for the Mips processor.[5] This difference results directly from the limited number (eight) of registers for the X86 architecture, as well as procedure-calling conventions that require passing all parameters in memory. A small data cache is adequate to capture the locality of the additional references. (After all, the additional references have sufficient locality to fit in the register file of the RISC microprocessors.) The Pentium microprocessor implements a data cache that supports dual accesses by the U pipe and V pipe to provide additional bandwidth and simplify compiler instruction scheduling algorithms.

Figure 7 shows that the address path to the translation look-aside buffer and data cache tags is a fully dual-ported structure. The data path, however, is single ported with eight-way interleaving of 32-bit-wide banks. When a bank conflict occurs, the U pipe assumes priority, and the V pipe stalls for a clock cycle. The bank conflict logic also serves to eliminate data dependencies between parallel memory references to a single location. For memory references to double-precision floating-point data, the CPU accesses consecutive banks in parallel, forming a single 64-bit path.

The design team considered a fully dual-ported structure for the data cache, but feasibility studies and performance simulations showed the interleaved structure to be more effective. The dual-ported structure eliminated bank conflicts, but the SRAM cell would have been larger than the cell used in the interleaved scheme, resulting in a smaller cache and lower hit ratio for the allocated area. Additionally, the handling of data dependencies would have been more complex.

With a write-through cache-consistency protocol and 32-bit data bus, the i486DX2 CPU uses buses 80 percent of the time; 85 percent of all bus cycles are writes. (The i486DX2 CPU has a core pipeline that operates at twice the bus clock's

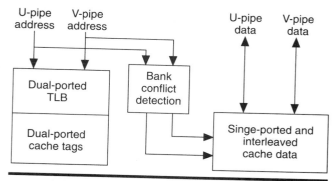

Figure 7. Dual-access data cache.

frequency.) For the Pentium microprocessor, with its higher performance core pipelines and 64-bit data bus, using a write-back protocol for cache consistency was an obvious enhancement. The write-back protocol uses four states: modified, exclusive, shared, and invalid (MESI).

Self-modifying code. One challenging aspect of the Pentium microprocessor's design was supporting self-modifying code compatibly. Compatibility requires that when an instruction is modified followed by execution of a taken branch instruction, subsequent executions of the modified instruction must use the updated value. This is a special form of dependency between data stores and instruction fetches.

The interaction between branch predictions and self-modifying code requires the most attention. The Pentium CPU fetches the target of a taken branch before previous instructions have completed stores, so dedicated logic checks for such conditions in the pipeline and flushes incorrectly fetched instructions when necessary. The CPU thoroughly verifies predicted branches to handle cases in which an instruction entered in the branch target buffer might be modified. The same mechanisms used for consistency with external memory maintain consistency between the code cache and data cache.

Floating-point pipeline

The i486 CPU integrated the floating-point unit (FPU) on chip, thus eliminating overhead of the communication protocol that resulted from using a coprocessor. Bringing the FPU on chip substantially boosted performance in the i486 CPU. Nevertheless, due to limited devices available for the FPU, its microarchitecture was based on a partial multiplier array and a shift-and-add data path controlled by microcode. Floating-point operations could not be pipelined with any other floating-point operations; that is, once a floating-point instruction is invoked, all other floating-point instructions stall until its completion.

The larger transistor budget available for the Pentium microprocessor permits a completely new approach in the design of the floating-point microarchitecture. The aggressive

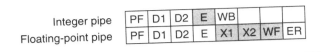

Figure 8. Floating-point pipeline.

performance goals for the FPU presented an exciting challenge for the designers, even with more silicon resources available. Furthermore, maintaining full compatibility with previous products and with the IEEE standard for floating-point arithmetic was an uncompromising requirement.

Floating-point pipeline stages. Pentium's floating-point pipeline consists of eight stages. The first two stages are processed by the common (integer pipeline) resources for prefetch and decode. In the third stage the floating-point hardware begins activating logic for instruction execution. All of the first five stages are matched with their counterpart integer pipeline stages for pipeline sequencing and synchronization (see Figure 8).

- *Prefetch.* The PF stage is the same as in the integer pipeline.
- *First decode.* The D1 stage is the same as in the integer pipeline.
- Second decode. The D2 stage is the same as in the integer pipeline.
- *Operand fetch.* In this E stage the FPU accesses both the data cache and the floating-point register file to fetch the operands necessary for the operation. When floating-point data is to be written to the data cache, the FPU converts internal data format into the appropriate memory representation. This stage matches the E stage of the integer pipeline.
- *First execute.* In the X1 stage the FPU executes the first steps of the floating-point computation. When floating-point data is read from the data cache, the FPU writes the incoming data into the floating-point register file.
- *Second execute.* In the X2 stage the FPU continues to execute the floating-point computation.
- *Write float.* In the WF stage the FPU completes the execution of the floating-point computation and writes the result into the floating-point register file.
- *Error reporting.* In the ER stage the FPU reports internal special situations that might require additional processing to complete execution and updates the floating-point status word.

The eight-stage pipeline in the FPU allows a single cycle throughput for most of the "basic" floating-point instructions such as floating-point add, subtract, multiply, and compare. This means that a sequence of basic floating-point instructions free from data dependencies would execute at a rate of one instruction per cycle, assuming instruction cache and data cache hits.

Data dependencies exist between floating-point instructions when a subsequent instruction uses the result of a preceding instruction. Since the actual computation of floating-point results takes place during X1, X2, and WF stages, special paths in the hardware allow other stages to be bypassed and present the result to the subsequent instruction upon generation. Consequently, the latency of the basic floating-point instructions is three cycles.

The X86 floating-point architecture supports single-precision (32-bit), double-precision (64-bit), and extended-precision (80-bit) floating-point operations. We chose to support all computation for the three precisions directly, by extending the data path width to support extended precision. Although this entailed using more devices for the implementation, it greatly simplified the microarchitecture while improving the performance. If smaller data paths were designed, special rerouting of the data within the FPU and several state machines or microcode sequencing would have been required for calculating the higher precision data.

Floating-point instructions execute in the U pipe and generally cannot be paired with any other integer or floating-point instructions (the one exception will be explained later). The design was tuned for instructions that use one 64-bit operand in memory with the other operand residing in the floating-point register file. Thus, these operations may execute at the maximum throughput rate, since a full stage (E stage) in the pipeline is dedicated to operand fetching. Although floating-point instructions use the U pipe during the E stage, the two ports to the data cache (which are used by the U pipe and the V pipe for integer operations) are used to bring 64-bit data to the FPU. Consequently, during intensive floating-point computation programs, the data cache access ports of the U pipe and V pipe operate concurrently with the floating-point computation. This behavior is similar to superscalar load-store RISC designs where load instructions execute in parallel with floating-point operations, and therefore deliver equivalent throughput of floating-point operations per cycle.

Microarchitecture overview. The floating-point unit of the Pentium microprocessor consists of six functional sections (see Figure 9).

The floating-point interface, register file, and control (FIRC) section is the only interface between the FPU and the rest of the CPU. Since the function of floating-point operations is usually self-contained within the floating-point computation core, concentrating all the interface logic in one section helped to create a modular design of the other sections. The FIRC section also contains most of the common floating-point resources: register file, centralized control logic, and safe instruction recognition logic (described later). FIRC can complete execution of instructions that do not need arithmetic computation. It dispatches the instructions requiring arithmetic computation to the arithmetic sections.

The floating-point exponent section (FEXP) calculates the exponent and the sign results for all the floating-point arithmetic operations. It interfaces with all the other arithmetic sections for all the necessary adjustments between the mantissa and the sign-and-exponent fields in the computation of floating-point results.

The floating-point multiplier section (FMUL) includes a full multiplier array to support single-precision (24-bit mantissa), double-precision (53-bit mantissa), and extended-precision (64-bit mantissa) multiplication and rounding within three cycles. FMUL executes all the floating-point multiplication operations. It is also used for integer multiplication, which is implemented through microcode control.

The floating-point adder section (FADD) executes all the "add" floating-point instructions, such as floating-point add, subtract, and compare. FADD also executes a large set of micro-operations that are used by microcode sequences in the calculation of complex instructions, such as binary coded decimal (BCD) operations, format conversions, and transcendental functions. The FADD section operates during the X1 and X2 stages of the floating-point pipeline and employs several wide adders and shifters to support high-speed arithmetic algorithms while maintaining maximum performance for all data precisions. The CPU achieves a latency of three cycles with a throughput of one cycle for all the operations directly executed by the FADD section for single-precision, double-precision, and extended-precision data.

The floating-point divider (FDIV) section executes the floating-point divide, remainder, and square-root instructions. It operates during the X1 and X2 pipeline stages and calculates two bits of the divide quotient every cycle. The overall instruction latency depends on the precision of the operation. FDIV uses its own sequencer for iterative computation during the X1 stage. The results are fully accurate in accordance with IEEE standard 754 and ready for rounding at the end of the X2 stage.

The floating-point rounder (FRND) section rounds the results delivered from the FADD and FDIV sections. It operates during the WF stage of the floating-point pipeline and delivers a rounded result according to the precision control and the rounding control, which are specified in the floating-point control word.

Safe instruction recognition. Floating-point computation requires longer execution times than integer computation. Pentium's floating-point pipeline uses eight stages, while the integer pipeline uses only five stages. Compatibility requires in-order instruction execution as well as precise exception reporting. To meet these requirements in the Pentium processor, floating-point instructions should not proceed beyond the X1 stage, that is, allow subsequent instructions to proceed beyond the E stage, unless the floating-point instruction is guaranteed to complete without causing an ex-

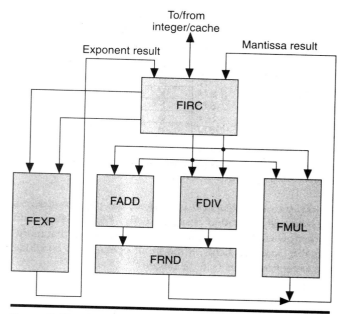

Figure 9. Floating-point unit block diagram.

ception. Otherwise, an instruction may change the state of the CPU, while an earlier floating-point instruction (which has not yet completed) might cause an exception that requires a trap to a software exception handler.

To avoid a substantial performance loss due to stalling instructions until the exception status of a previous floating-point instruction is known, Pentium's floating-point unit employs a mechanism called safe instruction recognition (SIR). This logic determines whether a floating-point instruction is guaranteed to complete without creating an exception and therefore is considered "safe." If an instruction is safe, there is no need to stall the pipeline, and the maximum throughput can be obtained. If, however, the instruction is not safe, the pipeline stalls for three cycles until the unsafe instruction reaches the ER stage and a final determination of the exception status is made.

Six possible exceptions can occur on the Pentium microprocessor's floating-point operations: invalid operation, divide by zero, denormal operand, overflow, underflow, and inexact. The SIR logic needs to determine early in the floating pipeline—in the X1 stage—before any computation takes place whether the instruction is guaranteed to be exception free (safe) or not (unsafe). The first three of the six exceptions can be detected without any floating-point calculation. From the latter three exceptions, the inexact exception is usually "masked" by the operating system or the software application (using the precision mask, or PM, bit in the floating-point control word). Otherwise, a trap will occur whenever rounding of the result is necessary. When the pre-

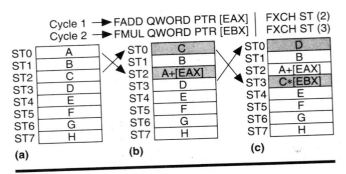

Figure 10. FXCH code example.

cision (inexact) exception is masked, the pipeline delivers the correctly rounded result directly. For overflow and underflow exceptions SIR logic uses an algorithm that monitors the exponent fields of the input operands to conclude the exception status (safe or unsafe).

In the X86 architecture the CPU stores floating-point operands in the floating-point register file with an extended-precision exponent, regardless of the precision control in the floating-point control word. The extended-precision exponent supports much greater range than the double-precision format. Overflow and underflow exceptions caused by converting the data into double-precision or single-precision formats occur only when storing the data into external memory. These characteristics of the X86 floating-point architecture give a unique advantage to the effectiveness of the SIR mechanism in the Pentium CPU, since the SIR algorithm can use the internal (extended-precision) exponent range. Thus, the occurrence of unsafe operations is extremely rare. Our evaluation of the SIR algorithm for the FPU design found no unsafe instructions in simulated execution of the SPEC89 floating-point benchmarks.

Register stack manipulation. The X86 floating-point instruction set uses the register file as a stack of eight registers in which the top of stack (TOS) acts as an accumulator of the results. Therefore, the top of the stack is used for the majority of the instructions as one of the source operands and, usually, as the destination register.

To improve the floating-point pipeline performance by optimizing the use of the floating-point register file, Pentium's FPU can execute the FXCH instruction in parallel with any basic floating-point operation. The FXCH instruction "swaps" the contents of the TOS register with another register in the floating-point register file. All the basic floating-point instructions may be paired with FXCH in the V pipe. The pair execute in parallel, even when data dependency between the two instructions in the pair exists. The use of parallel FXCH redirects the result of a floating-point operation to any selected register in the register file, while bringing a new operand to the top of the stack for immediate use by the next floating-point operation.

The example shown in Figure 10 illustrates the use of parallel FXCH. The code in the example generates the results of two independent floating-point calculations. The floating-point register file contains initial values prior to code execution: register ST0 (TOS) contains the value A, register ST1 contains value B, register ST2 contains value C, and so on. The two operations are

1) floating-point addition of value A with the 64-bit floating-point operand addressed by the general register EAX, and

2) floating-point multiplication of value C by the 64-bit floating-point operand addressed by the general register EBX.

When the floating-point pipeline is fully loaded and these two operations are part of the code sequence, the parallel FXCH allows the calculation to maintain the maximum throughput of one cycle per operation. Within one cycle the Pentium CPU writes the result of the addition to ST2, while the operand for the next operation moves to the top of the stack. On the next cycle, the processor writes the result of the multiplication to ST3, while the top of the stack contains value D, which may be used for a subsequent operation.

Transcendental instructions. The CPU supports all eight transcendental instructions that are defined in the instruction set through direct execution of microcode sequences. The transcendental instructions are

1) FSIN   sine,
2) FCOS   cosine,
3) FSINCOS   sine and cosine,
4) FPTAN   tangent,
5) FPATAN   arctangent,
6) F2XM1 $2**X - 1$,
7) FYL2X   Y * Log2(X), and
8) FYL2XP   1 Y * Log2(X+1)

We developed new, table-driven algorithms for the transcendental functions using polynomial approximation techniques. These algorithms substantially improved performance and accuracy over the i486 CPU implementation, which used the more traditional Cordic algorithms. The approximation tables reside in an on-chip ROM along with the other special constants that are used for floating-point computation.

The performance improvement of the transcendental instructions on the Pentium processor ranges from two to three times over the same instructions on the i486 CPU at the same frequency. The worst-case error for all the transcendental instructions is less than 1 ulp (unit in the last place) when rounding to nearest even and less than 1.5 ulps when rounding in other modes. The functions are guaranteed to be monotonic, with respect to the input operands, throughout the domain supported by the instruction.

Development process

Developing a highly integrated microprocessor involves collaboration between numerous teams having diverse technical specialties and working under the discipline of well-defined methodologies. A small team of architects and VLSI designers developed the initial concepts of the design. This group conducted feasibility studies of parallel instruction decoding and options for branch prediction techniques. Simultaneously, it evaluated performance by hand for short benchmarks and compiler optimizations. As initial directions were established, additional engineers participated, and subteams focused on the following areas:

1) behavioral modeling of the microarchitecture;
2) circuit feasibility design for caches, decoding PLAs (programmable logic arrays), floating-point data path, and other critical functions;
3) a flexible, trace-driven simulator of instruction timing for performance evaluation;
4) a prototype compiler; and
5) enhancements to existing instruction-tracing tools.

Throughout the design we refined the Pentium microprocessor using both top-down and bottom-up methods. Top-down refinement was accomplished through comprehensive characterization of executing benchmark work loads on the i486 CPU[4] and trace-driven experiments concerning alternative machine organizations conducted by architects using the performance simulator.

VLSI design engineers evaluating features critical to the targeted area and frequency refined the design from the bottom up. On two occasions in the design the accumulation of changes from bottom-up refinement caused the need for substantial restructuring of the microprocessor's global chip plan, or "die diets." On those occasions, interdisciplinary teams of specialists collaborated to brainstorm and evaluate ideas that could satisfy the global or local design constraints. In one instance, we found it necessary to refine the set of instructions that could be executed in parallel. Constraints had been assigned to the area and speed of the decoder PLAs. The VLSI designers identified combinations of instruction formats that would feasibly decode in parallel, and the compiler writers determined the optimal selection.

In the end, the measured performance of the Pentium microprocessor in production systems is within 2 percent of that predicted before the design was completed.

The logic validation of the Pentium processor design presented a major challenge to the design team. A comprehensive test base from the validation of previous X86 microprocessors was available. However, the Pentium processor microarchitecture introduced several new fundamental techniques, such as superscalar, write-back cache, and floating-point algorithms, that required a more rigorous veri-

Naming the Pentium processor

In naming the fifth generation of its compatible microprocessor line the Pentium processor, Intel departed from tradition. Pentium breaks a string of CPU products dating back to the late 1970s that used numerics (8086, 286, 386, 486).

"The natural course would be to call this chip the 586," said Andrew S. Grove, president and chief executive officer. "Unfortunately, we cannot trademark those numbers, which means that any company might call any chip a 586, even if it doesn't measure up to the real thing."

Pentium uses the Greek word for five, "pente," as its root to associate with the fifth-generation product and adds "-ium," a common ending from the periodic table of elements. Thus, the Pentium microprocessor is the fifth generation, a key element for future computing.

fication methodology.

We used different validation approaches in pre-silicon testing of the Pentium microprocessor:

1) Architecture verification looked at the "black box" functionality from the programmer's point of view. We designed comprehensive tests to cover all possible aspects of the programming model and all the Pentium processor user-visible features.

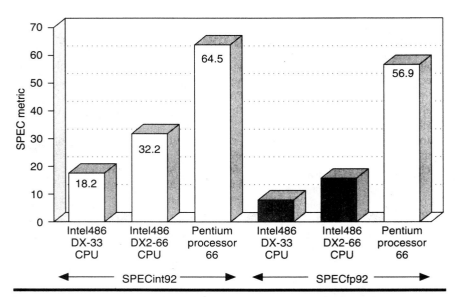

Figure 11. Pentium processor and i486 CPU performance for SPEC benchmarks.

floating-point transcendental functions required an extensive test strategy that verified the accuracy and monotonicity of the results throughout the development process, comparing the results to a "super accurate" software model. Eventually, when the first silicon of the Pentium processor was available for testing, we used automatic testing techniques to assure the correctness of the transcendental instructions.

Compiler optimizations

The compiler technology developed with the Pentium microprocessor includes machine-independent optimizations common to current high-performance compilers, such as inlining, unrolling, and other loop transformations. In addition, we used techniques specifically developed for the X86 architecture and tuned them for the Pentium processor's microarchitecture.

The X86 architecture has certain characteristics that require specialized optimization techniques different from those for RISC architectures. The architecture supports a variety of instruction formats for equivalent operations. Consequently, it is critical to select instruction formats that are decoded most efficiently by the processor. The X86 register set includes only eight integer and eight floating-point registers. We have found that common global register allocation techniques that assign variables to registers for the entire scope of a procedure are ineffective with such a limited number of registers. Registers must be allocated within a narrower scope and together with instruction scheduling.

The compiler schedules instructions to minimize interlocks and to maximize parallel execution for the Pentium processor's superscalar pipelines. These techniques also benefit performance on the i486 CPU (though to a lesser extent) because the processors' pipeline organizations are similar. The instruction-scheduling techniques have minimal impact on performance for the i386 CPU since that processor uses little pipelining. As explained in the description of the floating-point pipeline, the compiler schedules FXCH instructions to avoid floating-point register-stack dependencies.

2) Design verification checked the internal functionality from the point of view of a logic designer who would understand the behavior of every internal signal. This testing approach is considered a "white box" technique, in which tests are written to exercise all the internal logic and verify its correct behavior.

3) Random instruction testing was a valuable tool to cover all those situations that are rarely covered by the more traditional, handwritten tests. Running finely tuned random tests let us verify correct functionality by comparing the results generated by a logic design description of the Pentium processor to the results generated by a software-emulated model.

4) A logic-design hardware model (QuickTurn) enabled increased testing coverage capacity by allowing a much larger software base to run on the processor model before the first silicon was available. We ported the logic model of the Pentium processor onto a QuickTurn setup, which was capable of handling the complete design, and tested major operating systems and application programs before finalizing the design.

In addition to the general validation approach, we dedicated a special effort to verify the new algorithms employed by the FPU. We developed a high-level software simulator to evaluate the intricacies of the specific add, multiply, and divide algorithms used in the design. This simulator then evolved into a testing environment, allowing the verification of the FPU logic design model independently from the rest of the Pentium processor. Also, the new algorithms used for the

THE PENTIUM MICROPROCESSOR employs superscalar integer pipelines, branch prediction, and a highly pipelined FPU to achieve the highest X86 performance levels available elsewhere while preserving binary compatibility with the X86 architecture. Figure 11 summarizes the performance of the Pentium microprocessor and the highest performance i486

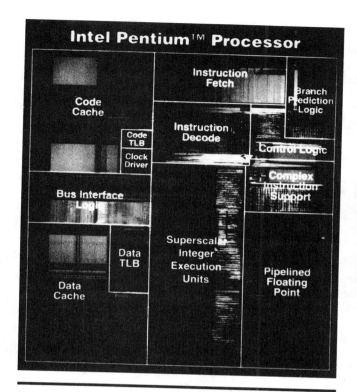

Intel Pentium™ Processor

Code Cache

Code TLB

Clock Driver

Bus Interface Logic

Data TLB

Data Cache

Instruction Fetch

Branch Prediction Logic

Instruction Decode

Control Logic

Complex Instruction Support

Superscalar Integer Execution Units

Pipelined Floating Point

Figure 12. Die photograph.

CPU for the SPEC benchmarks in well-tuned systems. Figure 12 reproduces a photograph of the packaged circuit that integrates 3.1 million transistors. ▣

Acknowledgments

The individuals who made substantial contributions to the Pentium processor's design are too numerous to list here, so instead we acknowledge groups of contributors. The VLSI design team applied their creativity and determined effort throughout the project. The compiler team developed and implemented novel optimization techniques. Software engineers in several groups developed instruction-tracing and performance simulation tools. Hardware engineers and technicians instrumented measurement and tracing systems. Architects facilitated and integrated efforts of these other teams. The efforts in architecture, optimizing compiler, and performance simulation involved collaboration between teams in Santa Clara and Israel.

References

1. *i486 Processor Programmer's Reference Manual,* Intel Corporation, Santa Clara, Calif., 1990.
2. *ANSI/IEEE Standard 754-1985 for Binary Floating-Point Arithmetic,* IEEE Computer Society Press, Los Alamitos, Calif., 1985.
3. John H. Crawford, "The i486 CPU: Executing Instructions in One Clock Cycle," *IEEE Micro,* Vol. 10, No. 1, Feb., 1990, pp. 27-36.
4. Tejpal Chadha and Partha Srinivasan, "The Intel 386 CPU Family—Architecture & Performance Analysis," *Digest of Papers Compcon Spring 1992,* CS Press, Feb. 1992, pp. 332-337.
5. Robert F. Cmelik et al., "An Analysis of Mips and Sparc Instruction Set Utilization on the SPEC Benchmarks," *Proc. ASPLOS-IV Conf., Computer Architecture News,* Vol. 19, No. 2, Apr., 1991, pp. 290-302.

Donald Alpert is an architecture manager in Intel Corporation's Microprocessor Division. He holds responsibility for managing the architecture team that developed specifications and modeling and evaluating performance of the Pentium processor. Previously, he held various microprocessor development positions at National Semiconductor Corporation and Zilog.

Alpert received a BS degree from MIT and MS and PhD degrees from Stanford University, all in electrical engineering. He is a member of the IEEE Computer Society and the Association of Computing Machinery.

Dror Avnon is design manager of the floating-point unit of the Pentium processor. He holds responsibility for the microarchitecture, design, performance analysis, and verification for the FPU logic and microcode. He previously held design engineering positions at National Semiconductor Corporation, Computer Consoles, and Elscint.

Avnon received a BSc degree in electronic engineering from Technion-Israel Institute of Technology in Haifa. He is a member of the IEEE Computer Society.

TUNING THE PENTIUM PRO MICROARCHITECTURE

David B. Papworth

Intel Corporation

This inside look at a large microprocessor development project reveals some of the reasoning (for goals, changes, trade-offs, and performance simulation) that lay behind its final form.

Designing a wholly new microprocessor is difficult and expensive. To justify this effort, a major new microarchitecture must improve performance one and a half or two times over the previous-generation microarchitecture, when evaluated on equivalent process technology. In addition, semiconductor process technology continues to evolve while the processor design is in progress. The previous-generation microarchitecture increases in clock speed and performance due to compactions and conversion to newer technology. A new microarchitecture must "intercept" the process technology to achieve a compounding of process and microarchitectural speedups.

The process technology, degree of pipelining, and amount of effort a team is willing to spend on circuit and layout issues determine the clock speed of a microarchitecture. Typically, a microarchitecture will start with the same clock speed as a prior microarchitecture (adjusted for process technology scaling). This enables the maximum reuse of past designs and circuits, and fits the new design to the existing product development tools and methodology. Performance enhancements should come primarily from the microarchitecture and not from clock speed enhancements per se.

Often, a new processor's die area is close to the maximum that can be manufactured. This design choice stems from marketplace competitiveness and efforts to get as much performance as possible in the new microarchitecture. While making the die smaller and cheaper and improving performance are desirable, it is generally not possible to achieve a 1.5-to-2-times-better performance goal without using at least 1.5 to 2 times a prior design's transistors.

Finally, new processor designs often incorporate new features. As the performance of the core logic improves, designs must continue to enhance the bus and cache architecture to keep pace with the core. Further, as other technologies (such as multiprocessing) mature, there is a natural tendency to draw them into the processor design as a way of providing additional features and value for the end user.

Mass-market designs

The large installed base and broad range of applications for the Intel architecture place additional constraints on the design, constraints beyond the purely academic ones of performance and clock frequency. We do not have the flexibility to control software applications, compilers, or operating systems in the same way system vendors can. We cannot remove obsolete features and must cater to a wide variety of coding styles. The processor must run thousands of shrink-wrapped applications, rather than only those compiled by a vendor-provided compiler running on a vendor-provided operating system on a vendor-provided platform. These limitations leave fewer avenues for workarounds and the processor exposed to a much greater variety of instruction sequences and boundary conditions.

Intel's architecture has accumulated a great deal of history and features in 15 years. The product must deliver world-class performance and also successfully identify and resolve compatibility issues. The microprocessor may be an assemblage of pieces from many different vendors, yet must function reliably and be easy for the general public to use.

Since a new design needs to be manufacturable in high volume from the very beginning, designers cannot allow the design to expand to the limits of the technology. It also must meet stringent environmental and design-life limits. It must deliver high performance using a set of motherboard components costing less than a few hundred dollars.

Meeting these additional design constraints is critical for business success. They add to the complexity of the project and the total effort required, compared to a brand-new instruction set architecture. The additional complexity results in extra staffing and longer schedules. A vital ingredient in long-term success is proper planning and management of the demands of extra complexity; management must ensure that the complexity does not impact the product's long-term performance and availability.

Our first effort

After due consideration of the performance, area, and mass-market constraints, we knew we would have to implement out-of-order execution and register renaming to wring more instruction level parallelism out of existing code. Further, the modest register file of the Intel architecture constrains any compiler. That is, it limits the amount of instruction reordering that a compiler can do to increase superscalar parallelism and basic block size. Clearly, a new microarchitecture would have to provide some way to escape the constraints of false dependencies and provide a form of dynamic code motion in hardware.

To conform to projected Pentium processor goals, we initially targeted a 100-MHz clock speed using 0.6-micron technology. Such a clock speed would have resulted in roughly a 10-stage pipeline. It would have much the same structure as the Pentium processor with an extra decode stage added for more instruction decode bandwidth. It would also require extra stages to implement register renaming, runtime scheduling, and in-order retirement functions.

We expected a two-clock data cache access time (like the Pentium processor) and other core execution units that would strongly resemble the Pentium processor. The straw-man microarchitecture would have had the following components:

- a 100-MHz clock using 0.6-micron technology,
- a 10-stage pipeline,
- four-instruction decoding per clock cycle,
- four-micro-operation renaming and retiring per clock cycle,
- a 32-Kbyte level-1 instruction cache,
- a separate 32-Kbyte L1 data cache,
- two general load/store ports, and
- a total of 10 million transistors.

From the outset we planned to include a full-frequency, dedicated L2 cache, with some flavor of advanced packaging connecting the cache to the processor. Our intent was to enable effective shared-memory multiprocessing by removing the processor-to-L2 transactions from the traditional global interconnect, or front-side, bus, and to facilitate board and platform designs that could keep up with the high-speed processor. Remember that in 1990/1991 when we began the project, it was quite a struggle to build 50- and 66-MHz systems. It seemed prudent to provide for a package-level solution to this problem.

Terminology

This article uses "performance" to mean work done per unit time. We termed a time reduction of 1/3 (100 seconds to 67 seconds) to be a performance improvement of 50 percent. A clock-per-instruction degradation of 20 percent results in a program taking 20 percent longer at a constant clock rate, which amounts to a performance degradation of 20 percent over the baseline.

What we actually built

The actual Pentium Pro processor looks much different from our first straw man:

- a 150-MHz clock using 0.6-micron technology,
- a 14-stage pipeline,
- three-instruction decoding per clock cycle,
- three micro-operations (micro-ops) renamed and retired per clock cycle,
- an 8-Kbyte L1 instruction cache,
- an 8-Kbyte L1 data cache,
- one dedicated load port and one store port, and
- 5.5 million transistors.

The evolution process

Our first efforts centered on designing and simulating a high-performance dynamic-execution engine. We attacked the problems of renaming, scheduling, and dispatching, and designed core structures that implemented the desired functionality.

Circuit and layout studies overlapped this effort. We discovered that the basic out-of-order core and the functional units could run at a higher clock frequency than 100 MHz. In addition, instruction fetching and decoding in two pipeline stages and data cache access in two clock cycles were the main frequency limiters.

One of our first activities was to create a microarchitect's workbench. Basically, this was a performance simulator capable of modeling the general class of dynamic execution microarchitectures. We didn't base this simulator on silicon structures or detailed modeling of any particular implementation. Instead, it took an execution trace as input and applied various constraints to each instruction, modeling the functions of decoding, renaming, scheduling, dispatching, and retirement. It processed one micro-operation at a time, from decoding until retirement, and at each stage applied the limitations extant in the design being modeled.

This simulator was very flexible in allowing us to model any number of possible architectures. Modifying it was much faster than modifying a detailed, low-level implementation, since there was no need for functional correctness or routing signals from one block to another. We set up this simulator to model our initial straw-man microarchitecture and then performed a sensitivity analysis of the major microarchitectural areas that affect performance, clock speed, and die area.

We simulated each change or potential change against at least 2 billion instructions from more than 200 programs. We

Pentium Pro structure and features

The Pentium Pro processor is a 32-bit Intel architecture microprocessor. It implements a dynamic-execution microarchitecture, incorporating speculative and out-of-order execution. A micro-dataflow approach identifies instruction level parallelism and controls the dispatch of operations to a superscalar, superpipelined core.

The processor incorporates an 8-Kbyte instruction cache and an 8-Kbyte data cache. These nonblocking caches let multiple cache misses proceed in parallel; cache hits proceed during outstanding cache misses to other addresses.

We packaged the processor, along with a separate 256-Kbyte L2 cache, in a dual-cavity, ceramic pin grid array (Figure A). This pipelined and nonblocking cache connects to the processor via a 64-bit, full-frequency bus. The four-way set associative L2 cache employs 32-byte cache lines and contains 8 bits of error-correcting code for each 64 bits of data.

The processor connects to input/output and memory via a 64-bit bus operating at up to 66 MHz. The bus implements shared-memory multiprocessing and supports high bandwidth via deep pipelining and split address and data cycles.

Figure B is a simplified block diagram. The instruction fetch unit (IFU) fetches 16 bytes every clock cycle and delivers them to the instruction decoder (ID). The ID buffers multiple 16-byte fetches, rotates these bytes to the starting point of the next instruction, and decodes up to three instructions per clock. The decoder converts instructions into dataflow nodes (called micro-ops), buffering them in a six-entry micro-op queue.

The micro-ops then pass through a register-renaming stage (the register alias table, or RAT) for remapping of the architectural registers to a set of 40 physical registers. This stage removes false dependencies caused by a limited number of architectural registers while preserving the true data dependencies (reads after writes).

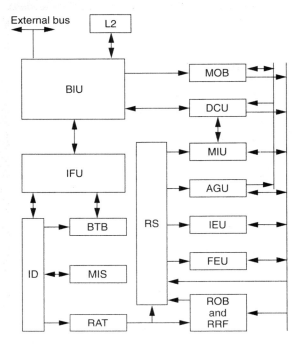

Figure A. Pentium Pro processor and L2 cache in a dual-cavity package.

AGU	Address generation unit
BIU	Bus interface unit
BTB	Branch target buffer
DCU	Data cache unit
FEU	Floating-point execution unit
ID	Instruction decoder
IEU	Integer execution unit
IFU	Instruction fetch unit (includes I-cache)
L2	Level-2 cache
MIS	Microinstruction sequencer
MIU	Memory interface unit
MOB	Memory reorder buffer
RAT	Register alias table
ROB	Reorder buffer
RRF	Retirement register file
RS	Reservation station

Figure B. Basic processor block diagram.

studied the effects of L1 cache size, pipeline depth, branch prediction effectiveness, renaming width, reservation station depth and organization, and reorder buffer depth. Quite often, we found that our initial intuition was wrong and that every assumption had to be tested and tuned to what was proven to work.

The trade-off

Based on our circuit studies, we explored what would happen if we boosted the core frequency by 1.5 times over our initial straw man. This required a few simple changes to the reservation station, but clearly we could build the basic core to operate at this frequency. It would allow us to retain

Pentium Pro (continued)

Following renaming, the operations wait in a 20-entry reservation station (RS) until all of their operands are data ready and a functional unit is available. As many as 5 micro-ops per clock can pass from the reservation station to the various execution units. These units perform the desired computation and send the result data back to data-dependent micro-ops in the reservation stations, as well as storing the result in the reorder buffer (ROB).

The reorder buffer stores the individual micro-ops in the original program order and retires as many as three per clock in the retirement register file (RRF). This file examines each completed micro-op for the presence of faults or branch mispredictions, and aborts further retirement upon detecting such a discontinuity. This reimposes the sequential fault model and the illusion of a microarchitecture that executes each instruction in strict sequential order.

The L1 data cache unit (DCU) acts as one of the execution units. It can accept a new load or store operation every clock and has a data latency of three clocks for loads. It contains an 8-Kbyte, two-way associative cache array plus fill buffers to buffer data and track the status of as many as four simultaneously outstanding data cache misses.

The bus interface unit (BIU) processes cache misses. This unit manages the L2 cache and its associated 64-bit, full-frequency bus, as well as the front-side system bus, which typically operates at a fraction of the core frequency, such as 66-MHz on a 200-MHz processor. Transactions on the front-side and dedicated buses are organized as 32-byte cache line transfers. The overall bus architecture permits multiple Pentium Pro processors to be interconnected on the front-side bus to form a glueless, symmetric, shared-memory multiprocessing system.

For a detailed discussion of the microarchitecture, see Colwell and Steck,[1] the Intel Web site,[2] and Gwennap.[3]

References

1. R. Colwell and R. Steck, "A 0.6-µm BiCMOS Microprocessor with Dynamic Execution," *Proc. Int'l Solid-State Circuits Conf.*, IEEE, Piscataway, N.J., 1995, pp. 176-177.

2. http://www.intel.com/procs/p6/p6white/index.html (Intel's World Wide Web site).

3. L. Gwennap, "Intel's P6 Uses Decoupled Superscalar Design," *Microprocessor Report*, Vol. 9, No. 2, Feb. 16, 1995, pp. 9-15.

single-cycle execution of basic arithmetic operations at a 50 percent higher frequency. The rest of the pipeline would then have to be retuned to use one-third fewer gates per clock than a comparable Pentium microarchitecture.

We first added a clock cycle to data cache lookup, changing it from two to three cycles. We used the performance

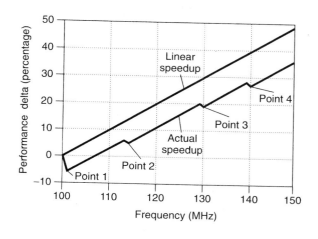

Figure 1. Delivered performance versus clock frequency.

simulator to model this change and discovered that it resulted in a 7 percent degradation (increase) in clock cycles per instruction.

The next change was to rework the instruction fetch/decode/rename pipeline, resulting in an additional two stages in the in-order fetch pipeline. Retirement also required one additional pipe stage. This lengthening resulted in a further clock-per-instruction (CPI) degradation of about 3 percent.

Finally, we pursued a series of logic simplifications to shorten critical speed paths. We applied less aggressive organizations to several microarchitecture areas and experienced another 1 percent in CPI loss.

The high-frequency microarchitecture completes instructions at a 50 percent higher rate than the lower frequency microarchitecture, but requires 11 percent more of the now-faster clocks per 100 instructions to enable this higher frequency. The net performance is $(1.5/1.0) * (1.0/1.11) = 1.35$, or a 35 percent performance improvement—a very significant gain compared to most microarchitecture enhancements.

In Figure 1 we see that performance generally improves as clock frequency increases. The improvement is not linear or monotonic, however. Designers must make a series of microarchitectural changes or trade-offs to enable the higher frequency. This in turn results in "jaggies" or a CPI degradation and performance loss at the point at which we make a change. The major drop shown at point 1 represents the 7 percent CPI loss due to the added data cache pipe stage. The series of minor deflections at points 2, 3, and 4 shows the effect of added front-end pipe stages. The overall trend does not continue indefinitely, as the CPI starts to roll off dramatically once the central core no longer maintains one-clock latency for simple operations.

The right of this graph shows a fairly clear performance win, assuming that one picks a point that is not in the valley of one of the CPI dips, and assuming that the project can absorb the additional effort and complexity required to hit higher clock speeds.

When we first laid out the straw man, we did not expect the CPI-clock frequency curve to have this shape. Our ini-

Our initial intuition suggested that the cost of an extra clock of latency on loads would be more severe than it actually is.

tial intuition suggested that the cost of an extra clock of latency on loads would be more severe than it actually is. Further, past industry experience suggests that high frequency at the expense of deep pipelines often results in a relative standstill in performance for general-purpose integer code. However, our performance simulator showed the graphed behavior and the performance win possible from higher clock speeds. Since we had carefully validated the simulator with micro-benchmarks (to ensure that it really modeled the effect in question), we were inclined to believe its results over our own intuition and went ahead with the modified design. We did, however, work to come up with qualitative explanations of the results, which follow.

Consider a program segment that takes 100 clock cycles at 100 MHz. The baseline microarchitecture takes 1 microsecond to execute this segment. We modify this baseline by adding an extra pipe stage to loads. If 30 percent of all operations are loads, this would add 30 clocks to the segment, and take 130 clocks to execute. If the extra pipe stage enables a 50 percent higher frequency, the total execution time becomes 130/150 or 0.867 microseconds. This amounts to a 15 percent performance improvement (1/0.867). This is certainly a higher performance microarchitecture but hardly the 50 percent improvement one might naively expect from clock rate alone. Such a result is typical of past experience with in-order pipelines when we seek the CPI-frequency balance.

The Pentium Pro microarchitecture does not suffer this amount of CPI degradation from increased load latency because it buffers multiple loads, dispatches them out of order, and completes them out of order. About 50 percent of loads are not critical from a dataflow perspective. These loads (typically from the stack or from global data) have their address operands available early. The 20-entry reservation station in the Pentium Pro processor can buffer a large pool of micro-ops, and these "data-ready" load micro-ops can bubble up and issue well ahead of the critical-path operations that need their results. For this class of loads, an extra clock of load latency does not impact performance.

The remaining 50 percent of the loads have a frequent overlap of multiple critical-path loads. For example, the code fragment a = b + c might compile into the sequence

```
load b => r1
load c => r2
r1 plus r2 => r3
```

Both b and c are critical-path loads, but even if each takes an extra clock of latency, only one extra clock is added for both, assuming loads are pipelined and nonblocking. This blocking-factor effect varies, depending upon the program mix. But a rule of thumb for the Pentium Pro processor is that additional clocks of load latency cost approximately half of what they do in a strict in-order architecture.

Thus the 15 percent of micro-ops that are critical-path loads take an extra clock, but the overlap factor results in one half of the equivalent in-order penalty, or about 7.5 percent. This is close to what we measured in the detailed simulation of actual code.

Now let's look at the effect of additional fetch pipeline stages. If branches are perfectly predicted, the fetch pipeline can be arbitrarily long, at no performance cost. The cost of extra pipe stages comes only on branch mispredictions. If 20 percent of the micro-ops are branches, and branch prediction is 90 percent accurate, then two micro-ops in 100 are mispredictions. Each additional clock in the fetch pipeline will add one clock per misprediction. If the base CPI is about 1, we'll see about two extra clocks per 100 micro-ops or and additional 2 percent per pipe stage. The actual penalty is somewhat less, because branch prediction is typically better than 90 percent, and there is a compound-interest effect. As the pipeline gets longer, the CPI degrades and the cost of yet another pipe stage diminishes.

Clock frequency versus effort

This all sounds like a fine theoretical basis for building a faster processor, but it comes at a nontrivial cost. Using a higher clock frequency reduces the margin for error in any one pipe stage. The consequence of needing one too many gates to get the required functionality into a given pipe stage is a 9 to 10 percent performance loss, rather than a 4 to 5 percent loss. So the design team must make a number of small microarchitecture changes as the design matures, since it is impossible to perfectly anticipate every critical path and design an ideal pipeline. This results in rework and a longer project schedule. Further, with short pipe stages, many paths cannot absorb the overhead of logic synthesis, increasing the proportion of the chip for which we must hand-design circuits.

Higher clock speeds require much more hand layout and careful routing. The densities achievable by automatic placement and routing are often inadequate to keep parasitic delays within what will fit in a clock cycle. Beyond that, the processor spends a bigger fraction of each clock period on latched delay, set-up time, clock skew, and parasitics than with a slower, wider pipeline. This puts even more pressure on designers to limit the number of gates per pipe stage.

The higher performance that results from higher clock speeds places more pressure on the clock and power distribution budget. The shorter clock period is less able to absorb clock jitter and localized voltage sags, requiring very careful and detailed speed path simulations.

As long as a design team expects, manages, and supports this extra effort, clock speedups provide an excellent path to higher performance. Even if this comes at some CPI degradation, the end result is both a higher performance product and one that hits production earlier than one that attempts to retrofit higher clock frequency into a pipeline not designed for it.

The terms "architectural efficiency" or "performance at the same clock" are sometimes taken as metrics of goodness in and of themselves. Perhaps this is one way of apologizing for low clock rates or a way to imply higher performance when the microarchitecture "someday" reaches a clock rate that is in fact unobtainable for that design with that process technology. Performance at the same clock is not a good microarchitectural goal, if it means building bottlenecks into the pipeline that will forever impact clock frequency. Similarly, low latency by itself is not an important goal. Designers must consider the balance between latency, available parallelism in the application, and the impact on clock speed of forcing a lot of functionality into a short clock period.

It is equally meaningless to brag about high clock frequency without considering the CPI and other significant performance trade-offs made to achieve it. In designing the Pentium Pro microarchitecture, we balanced our efforts on increasing frequency and reducing CPI. As architects, we spent the same time working on clock frequency and layout issues as on refining parallel-execution techniques. The true measure of an architecture is delivered performance, which is clock speed/CPI and not optimal CPI with low clock speed or great clock speed but poor CPI.

One final interesting result was that the dynamic-execution microarchitecture was actually a major enabler of higher clock frequency. In 1990, many pundits claimed that the complexity of out-of-order techniques would ultimately lead to a clock speed degradation, due to the second-order effects of larger die size and bigger projects with more players. In the case of the Pentium Pro processor, we often found that dynamic execution enabled us to add pipe stages to reduce the number of critical paths. We did not pay the kind of CPI penalty that an in-order microarchitecture would have suffered for the same change. By alleviating some of the data-path barriers to higher clock frequency, we could focus our efforts on the second-order effects that remained.

Tuning area and performance

Another critical tuning parameter is the trade-off between silicon area and CPU performance. As designers of a new microarchitecture, we are always tempted to add more capability and more features to try to hit as high a performance as possible. We try to guesstimate what will fit in a given level of silicon technology, but our early estimates are generally optimistic and the process is not particularly accurate.

As we continued to refine the Pentium Pro microarchitecture, we discovered that, by and large, most applications do not perform as well as possible, being unable to keep all of the functional units busy all of the time. At the same time, better understanding of layout issues revealed that the die size of the original microarchitecture was uncomfortably large for high-volume manufacturing.

We found that the deep buffering provided by the large, uniform reservation station allowed a time-averaging of functional-unit demand. Most program parallelism is somewhat bursty (that is, it occurs in nonuniform clumps spread through the application). The dynamic-execution architecture can average out bursty demands for functional units; it draws micro-ops from a large range of the program and dis-

It is equally meaningless to brag about high clock frequency without considering the CPI and other significant performance trade-offs made to achieve it.

patches them whenever they and a functional unit become ready. No particular harm comes from delaying any one micro-op, since a micro-op can execute in several different clocks without affecting the critical path through the flow graph. This contrasts with in-order superscalar approaches, which offer only one opportunity to execute an operation that will not result in adding a clock or more to the execution time. The in-order architecture runs in feast-or-famine mode, its multiple functional units idle much of the time and only coming into play when parallelism is instantaneously available to fit its available templates.

The same phenomenon occurs in the instruction decoder. A decoder for a complex instruction set will typically have restrictions (termed "templates" here) placed upon it. This refers to the number and type of instructions that can be decoded in any one clock period. The Pentium Pro's decoder operates to a 4-1-1 template. It decodes up to three instructions each clock, with the first decoder able to handle most instructions and the other two restricted to single dataflow nodes (micro-ops) such as loads and register-to-register. A hypothetical 4-2 template could decode up to two instructions per clock, with the second decoder processing stores and memory-to-register instructions as well as single micro-op instructions.

The Pentium Pro's instruction decoder has a six-micro-op queue on its output, and the reservation station provides a substantial amount of additional buffering. If a template restriction forces a realignment, and only two micro-ops are decoded in a clock, opportunities exist to catch up in subsequent clocks. At an average CPI of about 1, there is no long-term need to sustain a decode rate of three instructions per clock. Given adequate buffering and some overcapacity, the decoder can stay well ahead of the execution dataflow. The disparity between CPI and the maximum decode rate reduce the template restrictions to a negligible impact.

After observing these generic effects, we performed sensitivity studies on other microarchitecture aspects. We trimmed each area of the preliminary microarchitecture until we noted a small performance loss.

For example, we observed that each of the two load/store ports were used about 20 percent of the time. We surmised that changing to one dedicated load port and one dedicated store port should not have a large effect on performance.

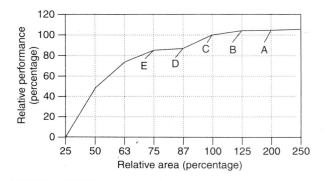

Figure 2. Performance versus die area for different decoder designs.

The load port would operate about 30 percent of the time and the store port at about 10 percent of the time. This proved to be the case, with less than a 1 percent performance loss for this change.

Changing from a 4-2-2-2 decode template (four instructions per clock) to a 4-2-2 template (three instructions per clock) also was a no-brainer, with no detectable performance change on 95 percent of programs examined.

We also changed the renaming and retirement ports from four micro-ops per clock to three, which resulted in a slightly larger, but still manageable 2 percent performance loss.

Finally, we reduced the L1 cache size from 16 to 8 Kbytes. In doing this, we took advantage of the full-frequency dedicated bus we had already chosen. Since the L1 cache is backstopped by a full bandwidth, three-clock L2 cache, the extra L1 misses that result from cutting the L1 cache size cause a relatively minor 1.5 percent performance loss.

The reduction from four- to three-way superscalar operation and the reduction in L1 cache size had some negative impact on chest-thumping bragging rights, but we could not justify the extra capacity by the delivered performance. Further, tenaciously holding on to extra logic would have resulted in significant negative consequences in die area, clock speed, and project schedule.

As the design progressed, we eventually found that even the first round of trimming was not enough. We had to make further reductions to keep die size in a comfortable range, and, as it turned out later, maintain clock frequency. This required making further cuts, which resulted in detectable performance loss, rather than the truly negligible losses from the earlier changes.

We made two major changes. We cut back the decoder to a 4-1-1 template from a 4-2-2 template. This amounted to about a 3 percent performance loss. We also cut back the branch target buffer from 1,024 to 512 entries, which barely affected SPECint92 results (1 percent) but did hurt transaction processing (5 percent). It was emotionally difficult (at the time) for the microarchitecture team to accept the resulting performance losses, but these results turned out to be critical to keeping the die area reasonable and obtaining a high clock frequency. This kind of careful tuning and flexibility in product goals was essential to the ultimate success of the program.

It is important to consider the actual shape of the area-performance curve. Most high-end CPU designs operate well past the knee of this curve. Efficiency is not a particularly critical goal. For example, the market demands as much performance as possible from a given technology, even when that means using a great deal of silicon area for relatively modest incremental gains

Figure 2 illustrates this effect. This graph charts the performance of various instruction decoder schemes coupled to a fixed execution core. All of the architectures discussed earlier are clearly well past the knee of the performance curve. Moving from point A (a 4-2-2-2 template) to point B (4-2-2) is clearly the right choice, since the performance curve is almost flat. Moving down to point C (4-1-1) shows a detectable performance loss, but it is hardly disastrous in the grand scheme of things. Point D (4-2—one we actually considered at one time) occupies an awkward valley in this curve, barely improved over point E (4-1) for significantly more area and noticeably lower performance than point C.

As we converted the microarchitecture to transistors and then to layout, execution quality became critical. All members of the project team participated in holding the line on clock frequency and area. Some acted as firefighters, handling the hundreds of minor emergencies that arose.

This phase is very critical in any major project. If a project takes shortcuts and slips clock frequency or validation to achieve earlier silicon, the design often contains bugs and suffers unrecoverable performance losses. This design phase determines a project's ultimate success. The best planned and most elegant microarchitecture will fail if the design team does not execute implementations well. As CPU architects, we were very fortunate to work with a strong design and layout team that could realize our shared vision in the resulting silicon.

THE PENTIUM PRO PROCESSOR ran DOS, Windows, and Unix within one week of receiving first silicon. We had most major operating systems running within one month. We made a series of small metal fixes to correct minor bugs and speed paths. The A2 material, manufactured using a 0.6-micron process, ran at 133 MHz with a production-quality test program, including 85 degree case temperature and 5 percent voltage margins).

The B0 stepping incorporated several microcode bug and speed path fixes for problems discovered on the A-step silicon, and added frequency ratios to the front-side bus. Our success with early Pentium Pro processor silicon, plus positive early data on the 0.35-micron process, encouraged us to retune the L2 access pipeline. Retuning allowed for dedicated bus frequencies in excess of 200 MHz. We added one clock to the L2 pipeline, splitting the extra time between address delivery and path while retaining the full-core clock frequency and the pipelined/nonblocking data access capability. The 0.6-micron B0 silicon became a 150-MHz, production-worthy part and met our goals for performance and frequency using 0.6-micron Pentium processor technology.

We optically shrank the design to the newly available 0.35-

Table 1. Pentium Pro performance.	
Processor (0.6 micron, 150 MHz, 256-Kbyte L2 cache)	Processor (0.35 micron, 200 MHz, 256-Kbyte L2 cache)
6.08 SPECint95 5.42 SPECfp95	8.09 SPECint95 6.75 SPECfp95

micron process, which allowed Intel to add a 200-MHz processor to the product line. Table 1 shows the delivered performance on some industry-standard benchmarks.

These results are competitive with every processor built today on any instruction set architecture.

The Pentium Pro processor was formally unveiled on November 1, 1995, 10 months after first silicon. Since then, more than 40 systems vendors have announced the availability of computer systems based on the processor. In the future, we will enhance the basic microarchitecture with multimedia features and ever higher clock speeds that will become available as the microarchitecture moves to 0.25-micron process technology and beyond. ▣

David B. Papworth is a principal processor architect for Intel Corporation and one of the senior architects of the Pentium Pro processor. Earlier, he was director of engineering for Multiflow Computer, Inc., and one of the architects of the first commercial VLIW processor. He holds a BSE degree from the University of Michigan.

THE MICROPROCESSOR TODAY

Michael Slater

MicroDesign Resources

Microprocessor

Report*'s publisher*

outlines technology

and business issues in

today's

microprocessor

industry.

From their humble beginnings 25 years ago, microprocessors have proliferated into an astounding range of chips, powering devices ranging from telephones to supercomputers. Today, microprocessors for personal computers get widespread attention—and have enabled Intel to become the world's largest semiconductor maker. In addition, embedded microprocessors are at the heart of a diverse range of devices that have become staples of consumers worldwide.

Microprocessors have become specialized in many ways. Those for desktop computers fall into classes based on their instruction set architectures: either x86, the primary surviving complex instruction set computing (CISC) architecture, or one of the five major reduced instruction set computing (RISC) architectures—PA-RISC, Mips, Sparc, Alpha, and PowerPC. Such chips typically integrate few functions other than cache memory and bus interfaces with the processor but usually include a floating-point unit and memory management unit.

Embedded microprocessors, on the other hand, typically do not have floating-point or memory management units but often integrate various peripheral functions with the processor to reduce system cost. This makes them more application specific, leading to a massive proliferation of devices characterized not only by their processor's instruction set and core CPU performance but also by their on-chip peripherals.

Digital signal processors (DSPs) are the most specialized embedded microprocessors. Designed for real-time processing of digitized analog signals, these processors have unique instruction sets and other architectural features that give them high performance for a relatively narrow range of tasks. Recently, a new class of DSPs, called media processors, has emerged to handle audio, video, graphics, and communication tasks in multimedia PCs.

Although the desktop computer market tends to discard old processors in just a few years, many processors survive for an amazingly long time in the embedded market. Personal computers have moved from 8- to 16-bit and now to 32-bit processors, and many workstations and servers are already using 64-bit microprocessors. In the embedded market, however, even 4-bit microprocessors continue to sell well, and 8-bit devices lead in volume.

Figure 1 shows the changes in market share for 32- and 64-bit microprocessors over the past five years. Driven by the success of the PC, the x86 architecture has dominated. Motorola's 68000 has held a strong second-place position in units (though not in dollars), with the embedded market as its stronghold. Hitachi's SuperH has come from nowhere to take third place, while other architectures have much more modest positions. As the dramatic changes during this period show, market share can be quite turbulent among these second-tier embedded processors.

There are far more microprocessors available for sale today than it would be possible to describe, even briefly, in an article such as this. The current market includes more than 50 surviving instruction set architectures, hundreds of different implementations, and thousands of minor variations. Rather than attempting to be comprehensive, I will focus on a selection of the leading-edge microprocessors and issues in each market segment.

Dividing up the market

Microprocessors for personal computers get the most public attention because the performance and compatibility of PCs depend on the microprocessors at their cores. In recent years, PC microprocessors have become so high profile that a bug of minor significance in Intel's Pentium processor captured headlines in the mainstream press for months. Microprocessor commercials even appear on prime-time television. Embedded applications, on the other hand, have a fixed complement of software, so the microprocessor inside is of relatively little interest to the consumer.

PC microprocessors are also a major profit area in the microprocessor business. PCs are the only application so far that uses expensive microprocessors—typically costing $75 to $500—in volumes of tens of millions per year. Embedded applications use far more processors—literally billions per year—but most of them are very low cost devices, selling for under $5, with thin profit margins. Some embedded applications use processors in the same price range as PCs, but they are very low volume—often only thousands of units per year. Today, even among 32-bit embedded processors, more than 60 chips sell for less than $40 and some for less than $10.

Microprocessors for PCs generate far more profit than embedded processors for two reasons. First, because the PC is the most expensive device to use a microprocessor in high volume, PC makers can afford more expensive processors. When coupled with large amounts of DRAM, disk drives, and CRT displays that cost hundreds of dollars each, even a relatively expensive microprocessor does not dominate system cost. Second, the overwhelming importance of software compatibility in the PC market has enabled Intel to achieve tremendous control over the PC microprocessor market. With no close competitors, Intel can enforce much higher profit margins than makers of embedded microprocessors, which must compete in a field where instruction set compatibility commands less value.

Unix workstations constitute the high-performance segment of the desktop computer market. (I use the term desktop computer as a shorthand for a single-user, general-purpose computer; in this context, it includes deskside and portable systems as well as true desktops, workstations as well as PCs, and even many servers.) The workstation market has some of the same attributes as the PC market, in that application software compatibility with previous-generation systems is of great importance. There are two big differences, however. First, the total Unix workstation market, in units, is less than 1% of the PC market, and second, performance is more important than price. As a result, microprocessors for workstations are typically designed with performance as a higher priority than price.

This digression into business issues is necessary for any comprehensive discussion of the microprocessor industry, because these issues have a pervasive effect on microprocessor design and manufacturing. Companies such as Intel and Motorola fund leading-edge manufacturing plants for logic devices with the high profits they make (or hope to make) supplying microprocessors for desktop computers. In contrast, makers of embedded processors generally get by with lower cost manufacturing processes and depreciated fabrication plants. The divergent characters of the embedded and PC microprocessor markets also drives the evolution of instruction set architectures: New architectures find relatively easy entry into the embedded market, while desktop processor makers go to great lengths to stick with dominant architectures.

Economics have had a huge effect on microprocessors

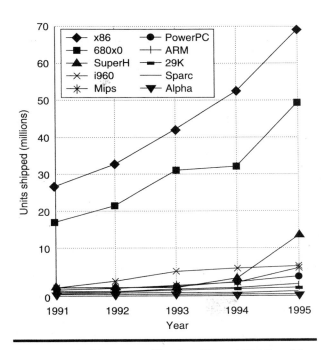

Figure 1. Unit shipments of leading 32- and 64-bit architectures.

designed for workstations. Because they are built in much lower volumes than PC microprocessors, their amortized design cost per unit is much greater. Such processors have survived primarily because they enable system businesses that produce far more revenue (and profit) than would the sale of a comparable number of microprocessors. This economic reality has led to large workstation makers designing nearly all of today's workstation-specific microprocessors, with chip companies playing little more than a foundry role.

As microprocessors for PCs have increased in speed, they have reached a performance level that makes them suitable for much of the workstation market. This factor, combined with the emergence of Microsoft's Windows NT as a viable alternative to Unix as a workstation operating system, is leading to a convergence of the technology for PCs with that for workstations. Ultimately, this convergence will threaten the survival of some of the workstation processor architectures.

The battle for the desktop

Two operating systems account for the vast majority of desktop computer use today: Microsoft Windows (in its various versions) and Macintosh. IBM's OS/2 is in third place, and Unix is a distant fourth. Windows' popularity has given Intel's x86 architecture a preeminent position, while the Macintosh has established PowerPC as the only RISC architecture with a significant share of the desktop market. Even so, the Mac's share is modest—around 8%—and shows no signs of increasing.

Nearly every maker of RISC microprocessors has dreamed of capturing part of the x86 architecture's high-volume market. The first to try was Sun, which hoped to repeat the PC industry phenomenon by making its Sparc-based workstations, running Sun's version of Unix, an openly licensed stan-

Table 1. Originators and licensees for leading desktop architectures.		
Architecture	Originator	Licensees
Alpha	Digital Semiconductor	Mitsubishi, Samsung
Mips	Mips Technologies	IDT, NEC, Toshiba
PA-RISC	Hewlett-Packard	Hitachi, Samsung
PowerPC	Apple, IBM, Motorola	Groupe Bull, Exponential
Sparc	Sun Microelectronics	Fujitsu (includes HaL, ICL, and Ross)

dard. This effort failed miserably for at least two reasons. First, Unix was, and is, unsuitable for a mass-market operating system because of its complexity, its resource requirements, and its lack of personal productivity applications. Second, Sun was never willing to let Sun-compatible system makers operate unrestrained, for fear of the effect that might have on Sun's own hardware business.

Next up was Mips, then an independent company (Mips Computer Systems). Microsoft chose Mips as the first RISC architecture that the emerging high-end version of Windows, Windows NT, would support. Mips engineered the ACE initiative, and at one point had both Digital Equipment Corporation and Compaq planning to build Mips-based systems to run Windows NT. But the timing was bad; Compaq fell on hard times as lower cost PC clones eroded its business, and Digital decided to create its own architecture and abandon Mips.

Mips made its own contribution to the failure of ACE by trying to collect large license fees for reference system designs. Silicon Graphics (SGI) soon thereafter swallowed Mips Computer Systems, which became SGI's Mips Technologies subsidiary. SGI has shown no interest in either Windows NT or the high-volume desktop market, and Microsoft is dropping Mips support in Windows NT.

Then came PowerPC, backed by IBM, Motorola, and Apple. Apple has successfully converted the Macintosh line to PowerPC, giving PowerPC the biggest desktop market of any RISC processor. Because Apple and the Macintosh platform itself are struggling to maintain their modest position, however, this doesn't represent much of a growth opportunity. Efforts to go beyond Macintosh on the mainstream desktop have largely failed: IBM's OS/2 for PowerPC was stillborn, Taligent folded its tent, and PowerPC's position in the Windows NT market is weak.

The most recent architecture to aim at the desktop market is Alpha, Digital's home-brewed replacement for the Mips architecture. Digital wholeheartedly embraced Windows NT and has the benefit of owning its own systems business, including a PC business. But Windows NT is only now approaching the maturity that will enable it to become a mainstream operating system; and DRAM prices are only now becoming low enough to render Windows NT's additional memory requirement insignificant.

Until now, Digital has used Alpha's outstanding performance to sell very fast systems at premium prices—a nice niche business, but hardly a factor in the PC market. Next year,

Digital plans to begin moving down into high-end PCs, setting the stage for an eventual attack on the mainstream PC market. It is a long shot for Alpha to capture a significant mainstream role, but at least it can't be counted out yet.

It is in this light that PowerPC's position in the Windows NT market appears so weak. PowerPC processors are not nearly as fast as the Alpha chips and don't offer a significant performance advantage over Intel processors, leaving them between a rock and a hard place. Customers looking for safety and compatibility choose Intel; those seeking maximum performance on a small set of applications are drawn to Alpha. This leaves few for whom PowerPC would be a compelling choice.

The staying power of the PowerPC backers is the architecture's key strength. If a future generation of chips is much stronger than today's, the architecture could end up head to head with Alpha in an attempt to capture the number two position in the Windows NT market.

This leaves Hewlett-Packard's PA-RISC as the only RISC architecture whose owner never attempted to use it in an attack on Intel's market share. This may have been an excellent decision, considering the fate of companies that have tried. HP is now engaged with Intel in a joint development project that will lead to a new architecture around 1998. The architecture, called IA-64 and to be first implemented in a chip code-named Merced, will provide backward compatibility with both x86 and PA-RISC programs. Having built a large computer business around its architecture, HP has found no compelling reason to spend billions of dollars on fabrication facilities and chip designs to provide processors for these systems. Thus, it has joined future paths with Intel.

Table 1 shows the companies backing each of the architectures for general-purpose computers. (Not shown are licensed implementations; for example, Cyrix has licensed its x86 processor designs to IBM Microelectronics and SGS-Thomson.) Although there has been a mad rush to sign up licensees, it has turned out to be relatively insignificant; the owners and primary backers of each architecture determine its fate.

Pentium dominates computing today

Intel's Pentium processor series dominates today's desktop computer market. Depending on clock speed, this chip spans a price range (in quantities of 1,000) from about $75 to just over $500, putting it at the appropriate price points for most PCs. Although early Pentium processors provided little advantage over 486 chips, Intel's aggressive promotion of Pentium and rapid increase in the chip's clock speed enabled it to sweep the desktop market by the end of 1995 and the notebook market in the first half of 1996.

Following a familiar pattern in the microprocessor industry—but at an accelerated pace—Intel has twice moved Pentium to a new process technology. The initial chips, code-named P5, were built in 0.8-micron BiCMOS and ran at 60 and 66 MHz. These chips were power hungry, and Intel phased them out before Pentium began its move into the mainstream PC market. The next version, the P54C, shrank the design to 0.6-micron BiCMOS and enabled clock rates of 75 to 120 MHz. This version also cut the supply voltage to 3.3 V and added dynamic power management circuitry.

This feature shuts down portions of the chip not in use on a cycle-by-cycle basis, slashing typical power consumption. Then Intel shrank the design once again to 0.35-micron BiCMOS, enabling clock speeds up to 166 MHz. A minor revision of this design pushes the clock speed to 200 MHz—more than three times that of the original Pentium.

To keep system design relatively easy, however, Intel has held the system bus speed at 60 or 66 MHz. Because of this, there is a huge gap between increasing core CPU speeds and the bandwidth of the external bus, which provides access to the level-two cache as well as to main memory. This reduces the benefit of faster core speeds; the 200-MHz Pentium has a typical performance gain of less than 10% over the 166-MHz chip. Power consumption has also crept up to uncomfortable levels as the clock speed has increased, keeping the 166-MHz and faster chips out of portable systems.

Intel will mitigate these problems early next year with a new version of Pentium, code-named the P55C and implemented in 0.28-micron CMOS. By doubling the size of the on-chip cache, Intel estimates that the miss rate will decrease 20 to 40% on typical Windows applications, mitigating the performance loss from the relatively slow external bus. The P55C will also include pipeline enhancements to boost its per-clock performance, as well as the MMX instruction set extensions for multimedia (described later).

The P55C will mark Intel's shift away from the BiCMOS process technology of earlier Pentiums. The 0.28-micron (drawn gate size) process enables Intel to reduce the supply voltage from 3.3 to 2.8 V, which significantly reduces power consumption. At this low voltage, however, bipolar transistors offer little benefit, making the extra process steps of BiCMOS unjustified. The supply voltage reduction will make higher clock rates practical for portable systems and will simplify cooling in desktop systems.

Intel's new frontier: Pentium Pro

The Pentium design uses a simple, restrictive approach to superscalar operation. Its two pipelines do not operate entirely independently; when one stalls, the other must stop as well, so no out-of-order execution is allowed. Furthermore, the floating-point unit is not autonomous but relies on the integer pipelines, so integer and floating-point instructions cannot execute in parallel.

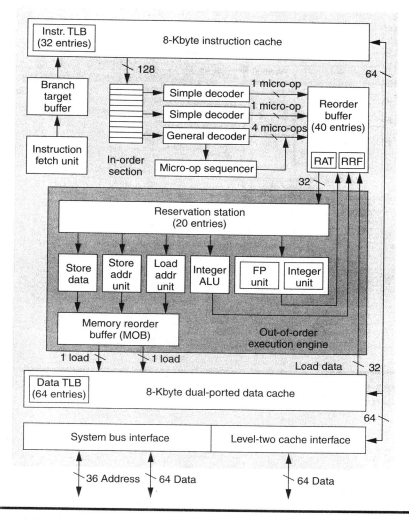

Figure 2. Pentium Pro microprocessor block diagram. TLB: translation look-aside buffer.

Intel's most recent microprocessor design, Pentium Pro (P6), takes a far more aggressive approach to deliver more performance per clock cycle while also enabling higher clock speeds. Figure 2 shows the processor's block diagram.

The Pentium Pro design completely decouples instruction dispatch and execution, translating x86 instructions into internal micro-operations, not unlike traditional microcode instructions. These micro-ops then pass to a 40-entry reorder buffer, where they are stored until any required operands are available. From there, they are issued to a 20-entry reservation station, which queues them until the needed execution unit is free. This design allows micro-ops to execute out of order, making it easier to keep parallel execution resources busy. At the same time, the fixed-length micro-ops are easier to handle in the speculative, out-of-order core than complex, variable-length x86 instructions.

To enable high clock speeds, Pentium Pro is very deeply pipelined (also called superpipelined). Because the reservation station represents an elastic element, the pipeline does

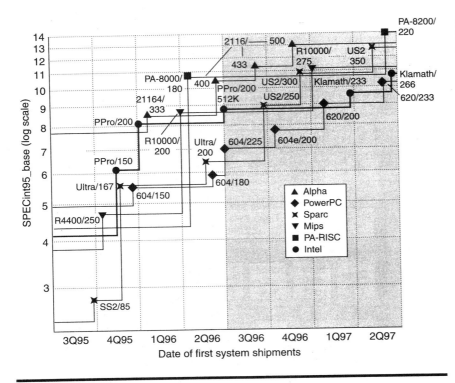

Figure 3. SPECint95 (base) performance versus time for x86 and RISC architectures. Numbers following processor names are clock speeds in MHz.

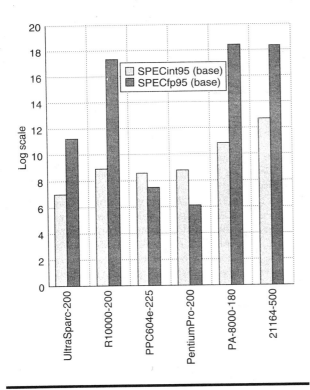

Figure 4. SPEC (base) microprocessor performance for high-end microprocessors shipping today.

not have a fixed number of stages, but the minimum number of clock cycles for an instruction to complete is 12. Cache access and instruction decoding are each split across two and one-half clock cycles.

To push Pentium Pro performance as high as possible, Intel designed a special level-two cache chip that is mounted in the same package with the CPU chip. The connections between the CPU and the cache chip are point to point and don't leave the package, which enables Intel to use nonstandard voltage levels and achieve high data rates. The level-two cache chip, which Intel makes in both 256- and 512-Kbyte versions, delivers 64 bits per clock cycle, even with CPU clock speeds up to 200 MHz.

This cache strategy was effective in bringing Pentium Pro to market with performance numbers that sent shock waves through the planning departments of most RISC microprocessors makers. As Figure 3 shows, at its introduction Pentium Pro exceeded the SPECint95 performance of all shipping RISC microprocessors. This position didn't last long, however, as Intel has gone more than a year without either increasing clock speed or introducing a new microarchitecture. Each of Intel's RISC competitors has done one or both. As Figure 4 shows, Pentium Pro is even further behind the RISCs when it comes to floating-point performance.

In the long run, however, Intel doesn't want to devote half its fab capacity to relatively low-margin SRAMs; it has been working with SRAM makers to provide industry-standard memory chips for future versions of the P6. In particular, Intel has disclosed plans for the P6 series' second member, code-named Klamath, which will use external SRAMs running at half the processor's clock speed for the level-two cache and will implement the MMX instruction set extensions. Intel intends Klamath, due in the first half of 1997, to be the P6 chip that drives that architecture into mainstream systems.

Going after Intel directly

RISC microprocessor makers have tried to take some of Intel's market share by leveraging their superior instruction sets to produce faster and less expensive processors. This has proven a very difficult game, however, due primarily to the enormous software barriers that new architectures in the desktop market face.

Other companies have challenged Intel on its own turf, building microprocessors that run the same software as Intel's chips. Today, the primary players are Advanced Micro Devices (AMD) and Cyrix Corporation, along with Cyrix licensees IBM Microelectronics and SGS-Thomson. Texas Instruments also serves the low end of the market with 486

Table 2. Key features of selected x86 microprocessors.

Feature	Intel Pentium P54C	Pentium P54CS	Pentium P55C	Pentium Pro P6	Pentium Pro P6S	Klamath	AMD K5	K6	Cyrix 6x86 M1	M2
Maximum clock rate (MHz)	120	200	200	150	200	233-266†	100	>180	150	225
Pinout	P54C	P54C	P54C	PPro	PPro	Klamath	P54C	P55C	P54C	P55C
Cache (data/ instr., Kbytes)	8/8	8/8	16/16	8/8	8/8	N.A.	8/16	32/32	16/16	64 (unified)
MMX	No	No	Yes	No	No	Yes	No	Yes	No	Yes
Decode rate (instr./clock cycle)	2	2	2	3	3	3	1-4	2	2	2
Issue rate per clock cycle	2 instr.*	2 instr.	2 instr.	5 micro-ops	5 micro-ops	5 micro-ops	4 micro-ops	4 micro-ops	2 instr.	2 instr.
Out-of-order execution	No	No	No	Yes	Yes	Yes	Yes	Yes	Limited	Limited
Die size (mm²)	148	90	140	308	196	N.A.**	181	~180	167	<200
Transistors (millions)	3.3	3.3	4.5	5.5	5.5	N.A.	4.0	8.8	3.3	6.0
Process (μm/layers)	0.5/4 BiCMOS	0.35/4 BiCMOS	0.28/4 CMOS	0.5/4 BiCMOS	0.35/4 BiCMOS	0.28/4 CMOS	0.35/3 CMOS	0.35/5 CMOS	0.44/5 CMOS	0.35/5 CMOS
Mfg. cost††	$50	$40	$60	$180††	$145††	N.A.	$70	$85	$70	$95
Production	Now	Now	1Q97	Now	Now	1H97	Now	1H97	Now	1H97
List price***	$106-134	$204-509	N.A.	$534	$428-1,035	N.A.	$60-134	N.A.	$98-299	N.A

* Indicates x86 instructions
** Not available
*** As of 4Q96, quantities of 1,000

† MicroDesign Resources estimates
†† Includes 256-Kbyte level-two cache

microprocessors. Table 2 summarizes the key features of today's most important x86 microprocessors.

AMD has a long history as an alternative supplier of x86 microprocessors. The company was a licensed alternate source of Intel's 8086 and 286 microprocessors, but the technology exchange agreement between the two companies broke down into a bitter and drawn-out arbitration. As a result, Intel never transferred its 386 or later technology to AMD. Instead, AMD entered the 386 and 486 markets by reverse-engineering Intel's chips. This involved extracting the circuit designs, making minor modifications (such as for static rather than dynamic operation), and producing new physical layouts tuned for AMD's process technology.

This path proved successful in that it enabled AMD to continue supplying microprocessors to the PC industry. However, it offered AMD little opportunity for differentiation and no chance of catching up with Intel's performance level. AMD couldn't even begin its reverse-engineering and reimplementation process until Intel shipped a product.

AMD therefore decided to create an entirely independent design, taking from the Intel chips only the instruction set (for software compatibility) and the bus interface and pinout (for system interface compatibility). After several delays, the K5 reached the market, but without delivering the anticipated performance level. The chip was supposed to deliver performance 30% higher than an Intel Pentium processor at the same clock rate. Instead, it barely matched Intel's per-clock performance on Windows application benchmarks, despite a much

more complex design and a 30% greater transistor count.

As of October 1996, AMD had been unable to make the chip run faster than 100 MHz, while Intel was shipping Pentiums at up to 200 MHz. This failing relegated AMD to the low end of the PC microprocessor business, leaving little profit for a chip as large as the K5 (see Table 2). At the same time, the 486 market had largely dried up, and what remained was priced in the $20-30 range, leaving AMD no significant older products to fall back on.

AMD recently released an improved version of the K5 design that eliminates bottlenecks and reaches the originally targeted performance levels. At 100 MHz, it delivers performance equivalent to a 133-MHz Pentium, moving AMD into the midrange Pentium market.

AMD's big opportunity, however, depends on the K6—a design that started life as the NexGen 686, which AMD bought NexGen to obtain. Like the Pentium Pro and K5, the K6 uses a decoupled decode/execute design in which x86 instructions are first decoded into internal, RISC-like operations. AMD also is adding the MMX instruction set extensions. As the K5 design has shown, though, the devil is in the details: A design's effectiveness depends on a multitude of subtle design issues, any one of which can become a performance-limiting bottleneck. On paper, the K6 looks good, but until AMD ships its first K6 samples, due by the end of 1996, how well it performs will remain an unknown.

Unlike AMD, Cyrix designed its own x86 cores from the start. The company started with a low-end 486-class core,

Table 3. Key features of selected high-performance microprocessors. (Source: Vendors except where noted)

Feature	Digital 21164	PowerPC 620	PowerPC 604e	Sun UltraSparc	Micro Sparc-2	HP PA-8000	HP PA-7300LC	Mips R10000	Mips R5000	Pentium Pro
Clock rate (MHz)	500	200	225	250	110	180	160*	200	180	200
Cache size (Kbytes)	8/8/96	32/32	32/32	16/16	16/8	None	64/64	32/32	32/32	8/8
Issue rate (instr./cycle)	4	4	4	4	2	4	2	4	2	3
Pipeline stages	7	5	6	6/9	5	7-9	5	5-7	5	12-14
Out-of-order execution	6 loads	16 instr.	16 instr.	None	None	56 instr.	None	32 instr.	None	40 ROPs
Rename registers	None	8 int/ 8 FP	12 int/ 8 FP	None	None	56 total	None	32int/ 32FP	None	40 total
Memory bandwidth (Mbytes/s)	~400	1,200	~180	1,300	~100	768	213	539	~160	528
Package, pins	CPGA-499	CBGA-625	CBGA-255	PBGA-521	CPGA-321	LGA-1,085	CPGA-464	CPGA-527	SBGA-272	MCM-387
Process (µm/layers)	0.35/4	0.35/4	0.35/4	0.29/5	0.4/3	0.5/4	0.5/4	0.35/4	0.35/3	0.35/4
Die size (mm²)	209	240*	148	149	233	345	259	298	84	196
Transistors (millions)	9.3	6.9	5.1	3.8	2.3	3.9	9.2	5.9	3.6	5.5
Estimated mfg. cost*	$150	$210	$60	$90	$80	$290	$95	$160	$25	$175**
Maximum power (W)	25	30	20*	30	9	>40	15	30	10	35**
SPEC95 baseline performance (integer/FP)	12.6/18.3	9.0/9.0*	8.5/7.0	8.5/15	1.4/1.9	10.8/18.3	5.5/7.3	8.9/17.2	4.0/3.7	8.7/6.0
Availability	Now	1H97	Now	Now	Now	Now	Now	Now	Now	Now
List price (1,000)	N.A.	N.A.	$594	$1,995	$379	N.A.	N.A.	$3,000	$365	$1,035

* MicroDesign Resources estimate   ** Includes 512-Kbyte level-two cache

which it leveraged into a range of products from the 386SX-pin-compatible 486SLC to a 486DX2. Cyrix abandoned these products at the end of 1995, however, as it began the switch to its Pentium-class core, code-named the M1 and officially called the 6x86. This chip delivers impressive performance per clock cycle: At 133 MHz, for example, it outperforms a 166-MHz Pentium on common Windows application benchmarks. Rather than using the complex decoupled decode/execute approach of Pentium Pro and the K5, the 6x86 extends Pentium's relatively straightforward dual-pipeline approach with additional features that enable both pipelines to run concurrently more often.

If Cyrix had access to Intel's leading-edge process technology, its chips might match Intel's Pentium clock rates. But as things stand, Cyrix uses 0.44-micron CMOS technology to compete against Intel's 0.35-micron chips. That Cyrix can beat Intel's Pentium performance even with this handicap is a testament to the efficiency of its design.

Like AMD, Cyrix will move to a next-generation design in early 1997 that will be key to its future success. Code-named the M2, this chip is based on the 6x86 core but adds a much larger 64-Kbyte cache and other performance enhancements, as well as the MMX instruction set extensions.

In 1997, makers of leading-edge PCs will be able to use Intel's P55C or P6-series chips, AMD's K6, or Cyrix's M2. Intel is all but guaranteed the lion's share of the market, but AMD and Cyrix have the opportunity to gain a minority share big enough to be quite significant for them—if they execute well.

By the end of 1997, however, there may be other competitors to contend with. Texas Instruments has a long-pending effort to develop its own x86 CPU core; at least four start-ups in the United States are working on x86 microprocessors; and semiconductor makers in Korea and Japan are probably considering similar efforts as well.

The pursuit of speed

In the never-ending pursuit of maximum performance, microprocessor makers have followed a variety of strategies. In each case, designers must make countless judgment calls—generally backed by simulations—on myriad design options, hoping to make the best use of transistor budgets. Table 3 summarizes the key characteristics of today's highest performance microprocessors.

Perhaps the most fundamental trade-off is between doing lots of work in each clock cycle—which tends to generate complex designs with limited clock rates—or streamlining the design as much as possible in pursuit of maximum clock speed. Sun's SuperSparc is a notable example of a chip that pushed complexity too far, giving up too much in clock rate to justify the per-clock efficiency. Sun remedied this in its next design, UltraSparc.

Digital has been the most successful proponent of the maximum clock speed approach. The company plans to ship 500-MHz processors this year, while most other vendors' chips will be at 200 to 250 MHz. Digital's Alpha 21164 does deliver the industry's best performance, but not by as big a margin as the high clock speed would indicate. As part of the speed/complexity trade-off, it has among the industry's worst performance per clock cycle. Figure 5 shows a block diagram of the 21164.

Cache strategy is another area where many approaches are possible. Here again, Digital stands out from the pack, with the only microprocessor with a two-level cache on chip. Separate 8-Kbyte first-level instruction and data caches enable single-cycle access even at high clock rates. A slower 96-Kbyte second-level cache provides faster access than could an external cache. Typical 21164 system designs have an external level-three cache.

Intel's Pentium Pro has the smallest on-chip caches of any high-performance processor: a mere 8 Kbytes each for instructions and data. This is because the custom-designed level-two cache chip (described earlier) is mounted in the same package as the processor and can deliver near on-chip speeds. Most other high-performance processors have on-chip level-one caches of either 16 or 32 Kbytes each for instructions and data. HP's 7300LC has the largest caches, at 64 Kbytes each.

All of today's high-performance microprocessors are superscalar; most issue four instructions per clock cycle. One exception is Intel's Pentium Pro. Its x86 instruction set encodes more functions into each instruction, so it reaches comparable performance levels (on integer code) decoding only three instructions per clock cycle. Pentium Pro must deal with the additional complexity of the x86's variable-length instructions, which make parallel decoding considerably more challenging. It also has an additional block of logic to convert complex x86 instructions into multiple internal instructions. RISC architectures make no such distinction between external and internal instructions.

Most high-performance microprocessors support some degree of out-of-order execution to keep the entire machine from stalling when one instruction stalls. Digital's 21164 designers, in pursuit of high clock speed, provided minimal

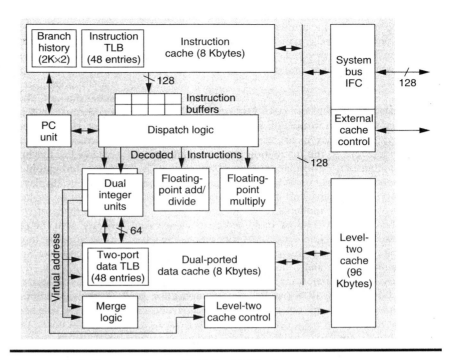

Figure 5. Block diagram of Digital's Alpha 21164 microprocessor.

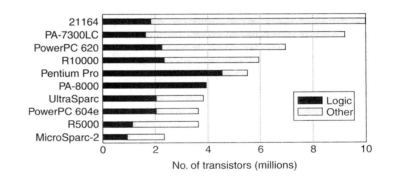

Figure 6. Allocation of transistors in high-end microprocessors.

out-of-order support, allowing reordering of load operations only. Sun likewise avoided the complexity of out-of-order operation. Others allow from 16 to 56 instructions to execute out of order.

Other microarchitectural features for which designers have chosen different strategies include the size of translation look-aside buffers, the complexity of the branch prediction algorithm, and the size of the branch history table. As for external interfaces, 64- or 128-bit-wide data buses are universal, and the fastest devices tend to provide a dedicated bus connected to an external level-two cache.

Figure 6 shows how today's leading high-performance microprocessors allocate transistors. Digital's 21164, with nearly 10 million transistors, is the biggest chip overall, but Pentium Pro, with its more complex instruction set, has more than twice as many logic transistors. The figure shows that high-end processors today typically have CPU cores with 2 to 4 million transistors devoted to logic. The number of transistors devoted to memory ranges from less than 1 million to more than 6 million.

Extending instruction sets for multimedia

Although the gulf in instruction set design style between the x86 and RISC camps remains, they do agree on one point: Modest extensions to the instruction set can significantly improve multimedia performance. A small increase in die area delivers a significant boost in performance for functions such as MPEG encoding and decoding, audio synthesis, image processing, and modems.

At the heart of most vendors' multimedia extensions are single-instruction, multiple-data (SIMD) operations. By taking a 64-bit ALU and allowing the carry chain to be broken at various points, essentially the same amount of logic can perform two 32-bit operations, four 16-bit operations, or eight 8-bit operations, all in parallel. One complication is that multiple carry bits are not available. Fortunately, however, most signal-processing operations benefit from saturation arithmetic. Instead of rolling over and setting the carry bit, saturation arithmetic sets the result at the minimum or maximum value. Most multimedia extensions add saturation arithmetic as an option. Other common additions are instructions for multiply-add and data element packing and unpacking.

HP was the first to add such extensions to its RISC architecture, but HP's instructions are quite simple. Sun offers the most comprehensive set of extensions in its VIS (Visual Instruction Set), implemented in UltraSparc. Sun's extensions include some relatively complex instructions, such as pixel distance, in addition to the simpler SIMD operations.

The most widely discussed, though not yet shipped, set of extensions is Intel's MMX, which will appear next year in the P55C and Klamath processors. Both AMD and Cyrix will offer MMX-compatible extensions next year as well. Intel estimates that the performance of MMX-enhanced code will be from 1.4 times better for MPEG video decoding to more than 4 times better for still-image processing (such as Adobe Photoshop filtering). Of course, most programs won't benefit at all, and compilers don't use MMX—programmers must handcraft the code to realize the benefits.

The Mips and Alpha camps recently announced their own multimedia extensions, leaving PowerPC as the only popular architecture not to follow suit. This is ironic, since PowerPC's primary user—Apple—focuses on multimedia, and one of the PowerPC's predecessors—Motorola's ill-fated 88110—had a set of graphics instruction set extensions.

Media processors enter the fray

General-purpose microprocessors can improve their handling of multimedia data types through instruction set extensions, but there are compelling reasons to use a separate processor for these tasks. DSP-like architectures provide multiple operand data paths, very-long-instruction-word-like arrangements, and other special features that make them fast but often hard to program. With these characteristics, a given

silicon area can deliver much greater performance on signal-processing applications than could an equal area in an extended general-purpose architecture.

DSP chips are not new; indeed, they are at the heart of most modems, cellular phones, disk drives, and countless other devices. They have had little success in PCs, however, because they aren't well optimized for the PC environment. However, several companies are now making media processors carefully designed for PCs. These chips typically have PCI bus interfaces, integrated codecs or codec interfaces, and graphics engines that provide compatibility with legacy PC display controller standards (such as VGA). Most importantly, makers of these PC media processors also provide driver software that enables applications to communicate with the chips via Microsoft's DirectX application programming interfaces (APIs). Thus, programmers need not customize application programs for each hardware design.

Today, a start-up company called Chromatic Research (Sunnyvale, Calif.) is the closest to shipping such a media processor. Like many pioneering microprocessor companies of recent times, Chromatic Research is fabless. LG Semicon and Toshiba manufacture and sell the chips, while Chromatic sells the software that makes them work. Chromatic's Mpact media processor can perform not only 2D and 3D graphics rendering but also MPEG-1 and MPEG-2 decompression, MPEG-1 compression, teleconferencing, 33-Kbps fax/modem, and audio synthesis. Philips has its own media processor, TriMedia; Samsung, Mitsubishi, IBM, and others have media processors in the works.

Whether these media processors have a long-term role in PCs remains a subject of controversy. From Intel's perspective, there is room for only one programmable processor in a system. In this view, functions that require hardware acceleration—such as 3D rendering—are best performed by fixed-function accelerators. In time, as the PC's central processor becomes faster, less opportunity will remain for media processors. In the near term, though, there appears to be a clear opportunity for such processors to boost PC capabilities for a modest incremental cost.

Embedded processors enable digital consumer electronics

Embedded microprocessors rarely bask in public attention or earn huge profits, but manufacturers produce them in enormous volume and in great diversity. Because software compatibility is not as driving a force as in the desktop market, the embedded market allows more architectures to survive.

Early embedded microprocessor applications were control oriented: Traffic-light and elevator controllers are the classic examples. As microprocessor performance increased, the range of tasks that processors can handle broadened. The vast majority of embedded applications don't demand any more performance than low-cost 8-bit—or even 4-bit—processors offer. Figure 7 shows that, as a result, the bulk of the volume remains with these older devices, which continue to evolve by adding more on-chip peripherals and memory. Ancient 4-bit processors have remained surprisingly popular, but new designs rarely use them because low-end 8-bit devices have dropped to very low prices and are easier to program. Even so, 4-bit chips—long considered obsolete by most observers—are only now beginning to fade away and will continue shipping more than a billion units per year through the end of the decade.

Some automotive engine controllers, as well as disk and network cards for PCs, use 16-bit embedded processors. (Note that Figure 7 defines 16-bit processors by their external bus width, so it includes in this category many chips with 32-bit internal designs.) Many of these applications are moving to the 32-bit level as application demands increase and 32-bit processor prices drop. In the long run, 8-bit embedded processors will continue to serve the most cost-sensitive applications, while most others gravitate toward 32-bit processors, leaving little room for other sizes.

The most exciting application area for embedded processors is digital consumer electronics. Digital control came to hi-fi equipment years ago, replacing knobs and dials with push buttons and displays. Video cassette recorders gave the microprocessor more sophisticated control functions, but poor user interfaces left most users unwilling to invest the time to learn the new functions. Digital answering machines and compact disc players put the microprocessor in the signal path, marking the beginning of the end of tape for audio storage. Later this year, DVD technology will move video into the digital domain as well.

Video games—which are actually limited-function computers—are the highest volume non-PC applications for 32-bit processors today. Sega's success with its Saturn and Genesis video games, which use Hitachi's SH series processors, has catapulted this relatively recent RISC processor to the third highest volume 32-bit architecture, behind only the venerable x86 and 68000. Sony's PlayStation uses a 32-bit Mips processor, and one video game—the Nintendo 64—uses a 64-bit Mips processor.

Electronic organizers and personal digital assistants (PDAs) are promising application categories for 32-bit embedded processors. Figure 8 (next page) shows one example of a processor designed for such applications. Today's organizers are truly embedded applications; little or no third-party software is available for them. PDAs such as Apple's Newton, on the other hand, are new computing platforms and do depend on third-party software. So far, the success of organizers has been limited to low-cost, limited-function devices, while more-capable PDAs have been successful only in vertical markets. As the technology develops, however, hand-held computing devices could become an even bigger industry (in units) than personal computers. Microsoft's new Windows CE will give this application category a big boost.

Internet opens new opportunities

The Internet—in particular the World Wide Web—is creating new classes of consumer computing devices. In fact, it could make PDAs far more compelling, once devices with larger, more readable screens are available. The Web makes vast amounts of information available, significantly increasing the value of a computing device to the average consumer. Early PDA makers hoped to build their own networks and services to offer information such as city guides and restaurant reviews; the Web will do a far better job of providing this

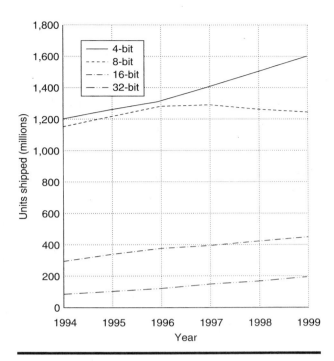

Figure 7. Embedded microprocessor and microcontroller shipments by word size. (*Source: The Information Architects, Mountain View, Calif., 1996*)

content with virtually no investment by the device makers.

While a large-screen PDA might make a great Web access device, it won't be cost-effective until there are major price/performance advances in color flat-panel displays. In the near term, many companies are building Web terminals that connect to televisions for display. WebTV is one company leading the pack in this arena. Its device, built by licensees, uses a Mips R4000-derivative processor created by design-house-turned-fabless-chip-maker Quantum Effect Design (Santa Clara, Calif.). The Web is becoming a central information resource that could eliminate printed phone books and newspaper classified ads; provide customer service and order-processing links to businesses of all kinds; and eventually become a primary delivery mechanism for news and entertainment. As this happens, Web access devices could become a major new class of embedded microprocessor applications.

Advocates of PCs have reacted to Web terminals, not surprisingly, with scorn and derision. After all, they represent a potentially major threat to future PC market growth. If the Web achieves its potential, however, the reality is that easy-to-use, minimum-cost devices that focus on Web access will be successful.

This trend is significant for microprocessor makers, because it breaks the application-software stranglehold the x86 architecture has had on the PC market. A Web browser can run on nearly any architecture. Even applications loaded over the Web can be processor independent if they are written in Java. The Internet, which has already created major markets for 32-bit embedded processors in routers and other network

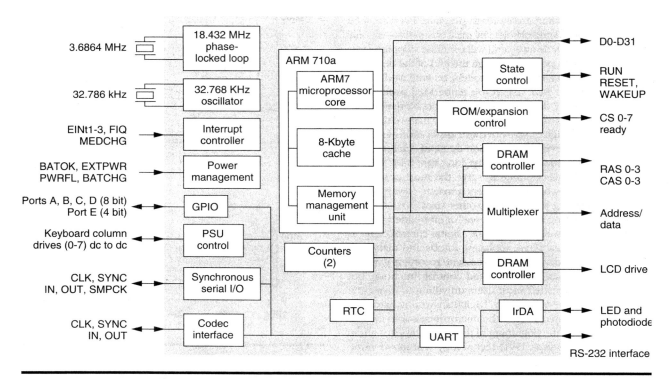

Figure 8. Block diagram of Cirrus Logic's CL-PS7110 integrated processor with ARM7 core.

infrastructure elements, could be a significant enabler of broader competition in the microprocessor business.

Embedded processors proliferate

Table 4 summarizes the key features of a few of the more than one hundred 32- and 64-bit embedded processors now available. As application demands and the competitive environment have changed, architectures have evolved. Digital's StrongARM is a stunningly fast derivative of the power-miserly but not especially fast ARM architecture. Hitachi's new SuperH series has a wide range of devices, of which the table lists only one. Similarly, Motorola and IBM are each producing numerous PowerPC variations for embedded control applications.

Motorola is the champion of embedded processor proliferations, with uncounted 68000 variations. Now it has even modified the base instruction set architecture to produce the RISC-like ColdFire subset. NEC, along with IDT and LSI Logic, is pushing the Mips architecture into embedded applications; Table 4 shows only one of many options. Intel continues to develop its 960 series, which is successful in some markets but shows little sign of progress in the expanding market for low-cost 32-bit processors. (The PC market is a formidable distraction for Intel.)

As high-performance embedded processors move into consumer electronics, low power consumption becomes as important as low price. In portable applications, the value of low power is obvious: longer battery life or smaller, lighter batteries. Even in nonportable consumer applications, however, low power consumption is important, because it reduces the cost of power supplies and eliminates the need for a fan.

These changes in the embedded market have led to major shifts in market share. As Figure 1 shows, Hitachi's SH series has come from nowhere to lead 32-bit RISC processor shipments on the strength of Sega's video games and other consumer applications. Meanwhile, Intel's more traditional 960 series, once the industry leader, has stagnated. AMD has entirely stopped future development of its 29000 family, once the 960's top competitor.

Customization for embedded applications

As transistor counts in chips selling for under $100 (and eventually under $30) skyrocket to millions—and soon to tens of millions—processors for PCs will continue to use most of these transistors to increase performance. For most embedded applications, however, the demands for ever-higher performance just aren't there. Instead, embedded-application designers would like to reduce system costs by integrating more functions on the same chip with the microprocessor. The logical end point of this evolution is a complete system on a chip. Technology is reaching a point where chips can integrate even significant amounts of memory. For example, eliminating half the DRAM array from a 64-Mbit DRAM still leaves 4 Mbytes of memory and room for millions of logic transistors.

As embedded microprocessors evolve toward systems on a chip, they inevitably become more specialized. Different applications have different needs for memory, peripheral controllers, and interfaces to the external world. The desire for

Table 4. Key features of selected embedded microprocessors. *(Source: Vendors except where noted)*

Feature	Digital SA-110	VLSI ARM710	NEC R4300	Hitachi SH7604	IBM PPC 403GA	Motorola 860DC	Motorola 68EC040	Motorola CF5102	Intel 960JA	Intel 960HT
Architecture	ARM	StrongARM	Mips	SuperH	PowerPC	PowerPC	68000	ColdFire	i960	i960
Clock rate (MHz)	200	40	133	20	33	40	40	25	33	60
Instr./data cache size (Kbytes)	16/16	8/8	16/8	4/4	2/1	4/4	4/4	2/1	2/1	16/8
FPU	No	No	Yes	No	No	No	Yes	No	No	No
MMU	Yes	Yes	Yes	No	No	Yes	Yes	No	No	No
Bus frequency (MHz)	66	40	66	20	33	40	40	25	33	20
MIPS†	230	36	160*	20	41	52	44	27	28	100*
Voltage	2.0/3.3**	5	3.3	3.3	3.3	3.3	5	3.3	3.3	3.3
Power (typical, mW)	900	424	2,200	200	265	900	4,500	900	500	4,500
MIPS/watt	239	85	73	100	155	58	10	30	56	22
MIPS/price	4.30	1.04	5.00	0.24	1.05	0.51	0.59	N.A.	0.76	0.79
Transistors (millions)	2.1	0.6	1.7	0.45	0.58	1.8	1.2	N.A.	0.75	2.3
Process (μm/layers)	0.35/3	0.6/2	0.35/3	0.8/2	0.5/3	0.5/3	0.65/3	0.6/3	0.8/3	0.6/4
Die size (mm²)	50	34	45	82	39	25	163	N.A.	64	100
Estimated mfg. cost*	$18	$9	$11	$7	$14	$20	$30	$9	$8	$34
Availability	Now	Now	Now	Now	Now	Now	Now	Now	Now	Now
List price (10,000s)	$49	$28	$32	$27	$28	$102	$75	$25	$37	$126

* MicroDesign Resources estimate   ** Core/bus voltage   † MIPS rating as supplied by vendor, based on Dhrystone 2.1

highly integrated system chips is increasing the demand for building-block microprocessors that can function as parts of application-specific integrated circuits (ASICs). Many of the leading microprocessor vendors are not major ASIC suppliers, however, nor are they set up to customize chips for every customer. Indeed, eliminating the need to do so was a key benefit of the microprocessor in the first place.

LSI Logic is one company that has pioneered the design of ASICs with microprocessor cores. Many other companies, including Texas Instruments, IBM Microelectronics, VLSI Technology, and NEC, are also aggressively developing this technology. Not only must these companies have a range of microprocessor cores available, but they must provide a variety of other complex building blocks, such as MPEG decoders and graphics engines, as well as the software tools to design, debug, verify, and test the chips. In the future embedded-processor market, these factors may be more important than the processor cores themselves.

In this world of core-based ASICs, some microprocessor cores are becoming near commodities. Advanced RISC Machines (ARM) in the UK has licensed its core designs widely, and many companies offer ARM cores as part of their ASIC libraries. Mips has also licensed its cores widely, though not as widely as ARM, and Sparc cores have a few licensees.

Table 5. Originators and licensees of RISC processors for embedded applications.

Architecture	Originator	Licensees
ARM	ARM Ltd.	Asahi Kasei Microsystems (AKM), Alcatel, Atmel, Cirrus Logic, Digital, GEC Plessey, LG Semicon, NEC, Oki, Samsung, Sharp, Symbios Logic, Texas Instruments, VLSI Technology, Yamaha
ColdFire	Motorola	Mitsubishi
Mips	Mips Technologies	Integrated Device Technology, LSI Logic, NEC, NKK, Philips, QED, Sony, Toshiba
PowerPC	IBM Microelectronics	Mitsubishi
SuperH	Hitachi	VLSI Technology
Sparc	Sun Microelectronics	C-Cube, Fujitsu, Hyundai, Matra MHS, Scientific Atlanta, TGI

Table 5 shows CPU architectures that companies have licensed to chip and equipment makers for embedded applications. Motorola continues to keep most of its cores proprietary and is gradually allowing more and more customer involvement in the design process.

Packaging is another key area that needs improvement. As designers put more functions on a chip, the chips need more input/output pins. Today's common plastic quad flat packs offer a cost per pin around 2 cents, but can't provide pin counts much beyond 200. High-pin-count pin grid arrays typically have costs around 10 cents per pin—leading to a $50 package for a 500-pin device. New packaging technologies, such as plastic ball grid arrays and various chip-scale packages, promise high-pin-count packages with costs approaching a penny per

---

Web resources on microprocessors

Independent sites

Hitex Software's numerical chip directory:
    www.hitex.com/chipdir
IEEE Micro: www.computer.org/pubs/micro/micro.htm
John Bayko's "Great Microprocessors of the Past and
    Present": www.cs.uregina.ca:80/~bayko/cpu.html
Ken Polsson's Timeline of Microcomputers: www.
    islandnet.com/~kpolsson/comphist.htm
MicroDesign Resources: www.chipanalyst.com
SPEC benchmark results: www.specbench.org
The Actual Size Processor Page:
    www.gulf.net/~stone/processor
UC Berkeley CPU Info Center:
    infopad.eecs.berkeley.edu/CIC

Microprocessor manufacturers

AMD: www.amd.com
ARM: www.arm.com
Cyrix: www.cyrix.com
Chromatic Research: www.chromatic.com
Digital: www.digital.com

Fujitsu: www.fujitsu.com
Hewlett-Packard (PA-RISC): www.hp.com/wsg/strategies/
    strategy.html
Hitachi: www.hitachi.com
IBM Microelectronics: www.chips.ibm.com
Integrated Device Technology: www.idt.com
Intel: www.intel.com
LSI Logic: www.lsilogic.com
Microchip: www.microchip.com
Mips: www.mips.com
Motorola: www.mot.com/SPS/General
National Semiconductor: www.nsc.com
NEC: www.nec.com
Oki: www.oki.com
Philips: www.semiconductors.philips.com
QED: www.qedinc.com
Ross Technology: www.ross.com
Siemens Semiconductor: www.sci.siemens.com
Texas Instruments: www.ti.com
VLSI Technology: www.vlsi.com
Zilog: www.zilog.com

---

pin in the next few years. If this comes to pass, it would be a significant enabling technology for highly integrated, low-cost chips. Sometimes the silicon seems like the easy part!

WHERE NEXT? After 25 years of development, advancements in microprocessor technology show no signs of slowing down. The pace of new architecture introductions has slowed, especially in the desktop market, but new implementations are coming out at record rates. Rapidly increasing transistor counts and clock speeds are challenging designers to innovate continually to deliver the most value from the technology. And as the Web has so vividly demonstrated, major new applications may be just around the corner—but are extraordinarily difficult to forecast.

PCs are becoming potent communication and entertainment devices and are moving into homes in a big way. At the same time, many new consumer electronics devices—from Web terminals to DVD players—are becoming available. It is hard to predict just which devices will succeed. But it is a sure bet that ever-advancing microprocessor technology will be crucial to the products enabling the much-discussed convergence of computing, communication, and entertainment. This ensures the microprocessor's role at the heart of the electronics industry for the next 25 years or longer.

Acknowledgments

This article would not have been possible without the combined efforts of the MicroDesign Resources analyst team. In particular, I'd like to thank Linley Gwennap, who is both our expert on high-performance microprocessor design and the leader of the team; Jim Turley, who tracks embedded microprocessors and their applications; and Yong Yao, Peter Glaskowsky, and Steve Hammond, who track a range of PC hardware technologies.

Michael Slater is the founder and editorial director of MicroDesign Resources and publisher of *Microprocessor Report,* an industry newsletter. He also organizes the Microprocessor Forum and PC Tech Forum conferences and consults for leading microprocessor and computer companies on new product strategies. A well-known speaker on microprocessor technology and system trends, Slater is also a columnist for *Electronic Engineering Times, Nikkei Electronics Asia,* and *Computer Shopper.*

THE FUTURE OF MICROPROCESSORS

Albert Yu

Intel Corporation

Intel's head of

microprocessor

products looks 10

years ahead to 2006.

In my role as head of Intel's microprocessor products, I am often asked to paint a picture of the microprocessor of the future. Even if our newest processor has just hit the streets and has not even come close to full use, people naturally crave information about where they're going rather than where they've been.

My colleagues and I have been trying for about 10 years now to identify trends about the microprocessor of the future. While these are based on a wide variety of unknown factors inherent in developing new technology, for the most part, we have been close to the mark. However, before making statements about microprocessor trends 10 years out—Micro 2006—it might be useful to revisit our past statements[1,2] about the microprocessor of today and the microprocessor of 2000. Then we can see where we have been right and where wrong. This retrospective will reveal important trends that promise to give some insight into the microprocessor of the next decade.

Performance, capital costs

Over the last 10 years, evolving microprocessor performance increased at a higher than envisioned rate; unfortunately, so did manufacturing capital costs. Table 1 lists our 1989 predictions for today's microprocessor performance at speeds of 100 MIPS (millions of instructions per second), which is equivalent to an ISPEC95 rating of 2.5 and clock rates of 150 MHz. Surprisingly, today's performance dramatically exceeds this. The Intel Pentium Pro processor runs at 400 MIPS, with an ISPEC95 rating of about 10 and a 200-MHz clock rate. This great performance boost has stimulated a huge range of applications for business, home, and entertainment, from mobile computers to servers. As a result, the PC market segment is a lot larger today than we anticipated years ago.

The bad news is that producing advanced microprocessors involves much higher capital cost than anyone ever expected. At Intel, we've augmented Moore's law (the number of transistors on a processor doubles approximately every 18 months) with Moore's law 2. Law 2 says that as the sophistication of chips increases, the cost of fabrication rises exponentially (see Figures 1 and 2). In 1986, we manufactured our 386 containing 250,000 transistors in fabs costing $200 million. Today, the Pentium Pro processor contains 6 million transistors but requires a $2 billion facility to produce.

Looking ahead, the important technological fact that emerges is that Moore's law continues to reign, with the number of transistors per chip increasing exponentially. Today's performance trend can continue, thanks to microarchitecture and design innovations beyond raw transistor count. The personal computer market, by far the biggest market for microprocessors, continues to grow at a healthy rate. It can provide the volume markets needed to absorb the huge manufacturing capital costs. To be sure, we have a number of key technology barriers to overcome as device geometry migrates well below the submicron range. However, all indications are that the microprocessor of 2006—and beyond—will be well worth the wait.

Micro 2000 revisited

As Table 1 shows, we anticipated in 1989 that in 2000 a processor would carry 50 million transistors in a 1.2-in. (square) die. The industry is mostly on track to deliver a 40-million-transistor chip on a 1.1-in. die in 2000. This 20 percent offset is not a technology limitation but an economic one, necessitated by creating a reasonable die cost (see Figure 1).

Silicon technology. Our visions about

silicon process line width were right on the money, as Intel is currently in production with 0.35-micron technology for the Pentium and Pentium Pro. I believe that line width will continue to drop to 0.2 micron in 2000 and to 0.1 micron in 2006 (see Figure 3). Also, the dielectric thickness and the voltage supply will have decreased correspondingly. This incredible shrinkage will continue unabated for the forseeable future. The number of metal interconnects has increased from two to five over the last 10 years and will increase further as we need more interconnects to hook up all the devices.[3] In fact, this is one of the biggest performance-limiting factors we contend with (see later discussion).

In addition, the problem of interconnects from the chip to the package and eventually to the system board is another major limiting factor for performance. Actually, we want to build single chips to avoid performance loss when sending signals off chip. We added cache and floating-point units on the 486 processor mostly for that reason. For the Pentium Pro processor, we placed the second-level cache and the processor in the same package to achieve the bandwidth needed between the two. The future trend will be to incorporate more performance and bandwidth-sensitive elements on chip and to continuously improve the package interconnect performance. Several companies are investigating MCM (multichip module) technology to eliminate chip packaging altogether, and I believe this will be an important trend for future high-performance processors.

Performance. It is amazing that the actual performance of microprocessors exceeds our 1989 vision by quite a lot. There are several reasons for this. Although the silicon process advances were pretty much on target, we have achieved higher frequency out of these advances with novel microarchitecture and circuit techniques. In addition, the number of instructions per clock has increased faster, and we have exploited superscalar architectures and greater degrees of parallelism. There have also been significant innovations in compiler technology that boost performance even higher. I see these trends continuing.[4,5]

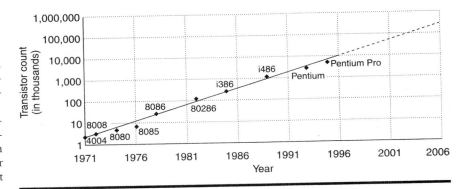

Table 1. Visualizing trends for the microprocessor of the future.

Characteristic	1989 predictions for 1996	1996 actuals	1989 predictions for 2000	1996 predictions for 2000	1996 predictions for 2006
Transistors (millions)	8	6	50	40	350
Die size* (inches)	0.800	0.700	1.2	1.1	1.4
Line width (microns)	0.35	0.35	0.2	0.2	0.1
Performance:					
MIPS	100	400	700	2,400	20,000
ISPEC95	2.5	10	17.5	60	500
Clock speed (MHz)	150	200	250	900	4,000

*Length of single side of square die.

Figure 1. Chart showing Moore's law.

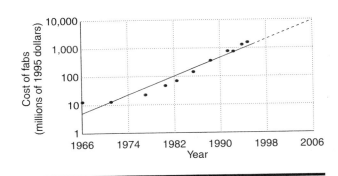

Figure 2. Chart showing Moore's law 2.

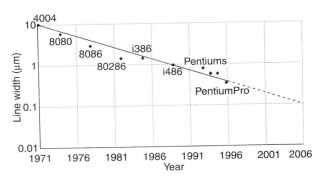

Figure 3. Chart showing line width versus time.

Scaling of MOS technology

Carver A. Mead, California Institute of Technology

The MOS transistor is the workhorse of modern micro-electronics. Reducing the feature size of CMOS fabrication processes has been the primary method by which ever-increasing computation could proceed at ever-decreasing cost and power consumption. How does this scaling affect device performance? Are there fundamental physical limits to how small the MOS device, as we know it today, can be scaled?

Transistor current is the flow of mobile channel charge induced by an equal charge on the gate. For a logic circuit, the supply voltage induces the channel charge, creates an electric field in the channel, and is the difference between output logic levels.

In long-channel devices, the charge velocity is proportional to the electric field in the channel. The channel current is the product of the channel charge and velocity. Therefore, the device current has a quadratic dependence on the supply voltage. This current must charge the load capacitance to approximately one-half of the supply voltage to achieve a logic transition. Thus, circuit speed is linear in the supply voltage—a dependence that kept power-supply voltages artificially high until a few years ago.

For device dimensions below 1 micron, the old scaling dependence no longer holds—charge velocity becomes independent of electric field. Decreasing the supply voltage no longer decreases the channel current. The same factor decreases both the output current and output voltage. In this regime, the only effect of decreased supply voltage is a decrease in the switching energy, with virtually no decrease in performance.

It is imperative to reduce the supply voltage for reasons other than reducing power consumption. To induce sufficient charge in the channel with a lower operating voltage, we must further thin the gate oxide. The sum of the source and drain depletion-layer thicknesses must be less than the channel length. It is inevitable that, as "minification" continues, these dimensions will become sufficiently small that electron tunneling through them will become comparable to other device currents. These parasitic currents are exponential functions of the supply voltage.

I have presented these considerations earlier.[1] The most remarkable conclusion of my work is that transistors with 0.03-micron channel lengths will operate on a 0.4-volt power supply about three times faster than do today's best devices. Only below this scale do parasitic currents overwhelm the energy consumed in the performance of real computation.

The enormous effect of device scaling on computational capability becomes apparent only when viewed from the system level. We'll see systems integrated to upward of 10^9 devices per square centimeter. Interconnects—both within a single chip and across chip boundaries—determine the dominant signal latency. Even today, it has become more economical to break each chip into several processors that can operate in parallel than to build larger "dinosaur" processors.

Massive parallelism is possible in present-day technology; it will become mandatory if we are to realize even a fraction of the potential of more highly evolved technology. Each processor can operate with its own local synchronous timing, with self-timed signaling between processors.

We have never been able to see more than about two technology generations ahead. In spite of our myopia, *the technology will continue to evolve.* It will evolve because that evolution is possible; because we gain so much at the system level by that evolution; and because the same energy and will on the part of bright, energetic, devoted people that have overcome enormous obstacles in the past will overcome those that lie ahead.

Carver A. Mead *is the Gordon and Betty Moore professor of engineering and applied science at the California Institute of Technology in Pasadena, California. He works on VLSI design, neuromorphic systems, and the physics of computation.*

Reference

1. C. Mead, "Scaling of MOS Technology to Submicrometer Feature Sizes," J. *VLSI Signal Processing,* Vol. 8, 1994, pp. 9-25.

We will see clock speeds of about 900 MHz with a 60 ISPEC95 rating in 2000. Such tremendous clock rates place great demands on the resistance and capacitance of the chip's metal interconnects for power and clock distribution. These multimillion-transistor devices also face new hurdles in packaging and power management.

Architecture. In the late 1980s, there was much debate about which microprocessor architecture held the key to fastest performance. RISC (reduced instruction set computing) advocates boasted faster speeds, cheaper manufacturing costs, and easiest implementation. CISC (complex instruction set computing) defenders argued that their technology provided software compatibility, compact code size, and future RISC-matching performance.

Today, the architecture debate has pretty much become a nonissue. Both the debate and the competition have been good for the industry, as both sides learned a great deal from the other, which stimulated faster innovation. There is really no perceptible difference between the two in either performance or cost. Pure RISC chips like the IBM ROMP, Intel 80860, and early Sun Sparc, as well as pure CISC chips like the DEC VAX, Intel 80286, and Motorola 6800, are gone. Smart chip architects and designers have incorporated the best ideas from both camps into today's designs, obliterating the differences between architecture-specific implementations. What counts most in designing the highest performance, lowest cost chip today is the quality of implementation.

Seven years ago in *IEEE Spectrum,*[1] our vision was that the microprocessor of 2000 would have multiple general-purpose CPUs working in parallel. What has instead happened is not separate CPUs on the same chip but a greater degree of parallelism within a single chip. The Pentium processor employs a superscalar architecture with two integer pipes, and the Pentium Pro processor design expanded that to three. Other processors such as the HP PA and IBM PowerPC have used similar superscalar architectures. I see the trend to exploit more parallelism continuing well into the future.

Human interface. The number of transistors devoted to the human interface is increasing too. Human interface functions are those that contribute to making a PC or other device more attractive and easier to use—three-dimensional graphics, full-motion video, voice generation and recognition, and image recognition. Even though we have no way of knowing precisely how future microprocessors will be used, I firmly believe that graphics, sound, and 3D images will play a huge role. We live in a 3D color world, and we naturally want our computers to mirror that. Once the computing power is available to create these kinds of features, application developers will have a huge opportunity to push computing into new realms. Therefore, we'll see a higher percentage of the microprocessor chip allocated to these purposes.

In 1989, we set aside 4 to 8 million transistors—roughly 10 percent of our estimate for 2000—for human interface and graphics functions. Our new MMX technology for the Pentium processor and Sun UltraSparc's VIS (visual instruction set) are examples of general-purpose instructions for accelerating graphics, multimedia, and communication applications.

Bandwidth. What becomes very apparent in moving into the future with complex chips is that microprocessor design is becoming system design. The microprocessor designer must consider everything that touches the chip, which includes the system bus and I/O, among others. As raw processor speed increases, system bandwidth becomes more critical in preventing bottlenecks. We will need very high bandwidth between the CPU and memory and between other system components to deliver the kinds of real speed gains of which the silicon is capable. Toward that end, microprocessor buses continue to increase in throughput. PCI is one of the major standards that allows PCs to increase the I/O bandwidth significantly.

Today, Intel is working with the PC community to spearhead the development of the accelerated graphics port (AGP). This vehicle increases bandwidth between the graphics accelerator and the rest of the system. The AGP will be critical for the full fruition of applications involving 3D and other high-resolution graphics. As communications become even more important for PCs and Internet applications expand, we will need more communications bandwidth.

Design. We saw that our dependence on advanced computer-aided design tools would soar, and it has. Today, we're simulating an entire chip, rather than just portions of it, from behavior to the register-transfer level. CAD tools assist in the entry of various circuit-logic data, verify the global chip timing, and extract the actual layout statistics and verify them against the original simulation assumptions. One of the rapidly developing areas is synthesis, first in logic synthesis but progressing to data path synthesis. These capabilities have improved design productivity enormously.

Future advances will improve the layout density (to reduce product cost) and raise performance (to enable new applications). This is particularly challenging as interconnects are becoming greater performance limiters than are transistors. In addition to electrical simulation, thermal and package simulation will be the norm by 2000. Beyond the chips, the trend is to expand simulation to encompass the whole system, including processor, chip sets, graphics controller, I/O, and memory.

Though the dependency on and rapid innovations in CAD have been pretty much on target, the design complexity and design team size have grown greater than expected. Two engineers developed the first microprocessor in nine months. Modern microprocessor design requires hundreds of people working together as a team.

Though design productivity has improved enormously, it is just barely keeping up with the increased complexity and performance. Looking forward, I see that one of our most challenging areas is how to achieve quantum leaps in design productivity. An obvious help would be for CAD tools to be truly standards-based and fully interoperable. This is not the case today, causing the industry to waste valuable resources struggling with conflicting and proprietary interfaces.

Testing. Testing complex microprocessors has become a huge issue. Though the capital associated with testing microprocessors is still smaller than that associated with wafer testing, it has been escalating beyond our anticipations. Why? First, the tester is more expensive due to increased frequencies and the large number of pins (the Pentium Pro processor runs at 200 MHz and has 387 pins). Second, testers that previously cost $50,000 cost well over $5 million today. Lastly, because of chip complexity and quality requirements of less than 500 DPM (defects per million), test time continues to increase. As a result, the total factory space and capital costs devoted to test have skyrocketed.

In 1989 we envisioned that a larger share of transistors in 2000 would be devoted to self-test—approximately 3 million transistors (6%) out of the total 50 million. A great deal of innovation has happened in this area. Today, roughly 5 percent of the Pentium Pro processor's total transistor count supports built-in self-test. Therefore, our prediction for 2000 stands: About 6 percent or so will be devoted to testing; this number may increase in 2006.

Compatibility. We posited in 1989 that binary compatibility was absolutely critical for investment protection and continuity. There are vast software bases in use today that each year become more valuable assets to businesses. Companies do not want to abandon these, even in favor of faster computers. Thus, even with fairly radical architectural departures such as massively parallel processing, we must maintain compatibility between future microprocessors and today's microprocessors. Only a twofold or greater improvement in system performance makes a switch to incompatible hardware worthwhile. This is more true today than ever

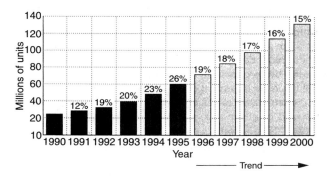

Figure 4. PC shipment trend. *(Source: Dataquest, Apr. 1996)*

and will continue to be one of the most important business and user requirements for future microprocessors. Of course, software is becoming more portable, but no one will devote the resources to recompile and maintain another binary version without major added benefits.

At the same time, the task to ensure compatibility has grown enormously. The number of different operating systems, applications, and system configurations has skyrocketed beyond earlier estimations. Of course, this job of compatibility validation is much harder after the silicon stage than before it, but accomplishing the technical problems with sufficient speed on software models or hardware emulators is an enormous task.

Market segment size. When we had the Pentium processor on the drawing board, we were anticipating sales of only about three million units in 1995. According to IDC reports, Pentium processor shipments in 1995 were close to 60 million. This twentyfold jump has been great for the whole industry. For example, Figure 4 shows Dataquest's estimation of PC shipments through 2000 predicting steady growth of 15 to 19 percent. Lucky for all of us, this market segment growth will allow more R&D dollars and capital investments to drive the microprocessor evolution at the exponential pace of Moore's law.

What about 2006?

Once we understand where we are versus our earlier vision, it is easier for us to look 10 years ahead to 2006.

Transistor and die size. Table 1 and Moore's law show that the number of transistors could jump to about 350 million in 10 years. Remember that plenty of previous-generation processors will continue to ship in huge volumes.

Die size will push toward 1.4 inches to accommodate the tremendous number of transistors and interconnects. Line width will have shrunk to a mere 0.1 micron, stretching today's optical systems to the physical limits. We may well have to look for other alternatives. Silicon technology will continue to advance at a rapid rate, as predicted by Moore's law, and voltage will continue to shrink to well below 1 V.

Performance and architecture. By 2006, performance will have jumped to an incredible 4 GHz or a 500 ISPEC95 rating.[6] All indications are that more opportunities exist for

innovation in performance than ever before. The two trends driving increased performance will continue to be more parallelism and higher frequencies. To exploit more parallelism, we will increasingly focus on compiler and library optimization. To push to higher frequencies, we will need advances in microarchitecture, circuit design, accurate simulation, and interconnects.

I see a great many good ideas that can be implemented for years to come. The performance drive is clearly not bound to the microprocessor but derives from the whole system, as one must build balanced systems to deliver power to users. Interestingly, earlier microprocessors borrowed lots of good architectural ideas from mainframes. From here on out, we are going way beyond the performance any mainframe has ever provided. Therefore, it is also important that the industry devotes more resources to long-term research and forges stronger cooperation with universities.

Barriers. Before we can realize a microprocessor of this complexity, we'll need to meet and resolve several technological and logistical barriers. One of the most basic is grappling with design complexity and the burgeoning size of the design team. Larger design teams are harder to coordinate and ensure communication within. Designing for correctness from the beginning remains a necessity, but becomes far more difficult as designs become exponentially more complex.

Compatibility validation becomes unbelievably difficult in designs as complex as the one we are contemplating for 2006. The task of exhaustively testing all possible computational and compatibility combinations is huge. We need a breakthrough in our validation technology before we can enter the 350-million-transistor realm.

Another area crying out for breakthrough thinking is power. Faster microprocessors obviously need more power, but we also need a way to dissipate the power from the chip through the package and the system. To lower on-chip power, we need breakthroughs to drive voltage requirements way below 1 V. We need innovations in low-power microarchitectures, design, and software to contain the power rise. For mobile applications, the whole electronics complex needs to stay below 20 W. Power poses big challenges not only to microprocessors but to other components in the system such as graphics controllers and disk drives.

As mentioned earlier, interconnects are the major performance limiter and will remain so until scientists discover lower resistance, lower capacitance materials. Today's Pentium Pro processor has five metal layers; future generations will need more. Metallization technologies historically take years to develop, so we urgently need research in this area to create the microprocessor of 2006.

Market segment. We have historically erred on the side of underestimating microprocessor demand. Although I cannot estimate the exact volumes, I do foresee strong continued growth for the PC and microprocessor market segments into the next decade. Although the PC market segment in the United States is maturing, it is just beginning in emerging markets, notably Southeast Asia, South America, and Eastern Europe.

In addition to openings of new geographical markets, new

Mediaprocessors
John Moussouris, MicroUnity Systems Engineering, Inc.

Microprocessors have evolved over the last quarter century as self-contained devices for calculating and controlling things. Growth in electronics is now shifting toward interconnected devices whose primary function is to communicate. The goal of delivering the content and services of the entire global network with an ease and affordability more like TV, radio, and telephone than personal computers will impact processor evolution enough to merit a distinct category: the mediaprocessor.

How do communication algorithms differ from classical embedded and desktop applications? Classical applications typically perform arithmetic, Boolean, and shift operations on a few different data sizes (for example, 32-bit integers; 64-bit floating point). Communication processes, on the other hand, operate on a much wider range of data widths and mathematical domains (such as Galois fields used to compute generalized parity or "syndromes").

Encryption and error-correction codes require bit-level and Galois processing. Video, RF, and modem processing need 2 to 12 bits to represent their samples; audio commonly uses 8 to 24 bits; and packet protocols need thousands of bits. A single sample may require hundreds or thousands of operations in the course of filtering, compression, encryption, modulation, transmission, equalization, demodulation, and error correction. Such high broadband rates strain both computational throughput and bandwidth of the memory system. On the other hand, the total memory required is often small—typically dominated by a few megabytes of frame storage.

Legacy microprocessor architectures have had to respond to these needs. Most have defined multimedia extensions that improve support for audio, video, and graphics. They also are incorporating interfaces for faster memory and real-time I/O. Backward compatibility with legacy code and interfaces, however, adds complexity and cost to these designs.

New mediaprocessor technologies aim to reduce this cost. One area of innovation is execution units that systematically and efficiently implement subinstruction level parallelism such as SIGD (single instruction on groups of data) over all multiprecision data types. Another area is programming models that eliminate redundant register files, condition codes, and mode bits. These models simplify code generation and streamline interlocks, bypass, and exceptions in pipelined and instruction level parallel machines (VLIW, superscalar, and decoupled access execution designs). A third is efficient protection and synchronization mechanisms for the sharing of memory and data path resources among many user level and secure-kernel threads of execution, enabling thread level parallelism. A fourth is packet-oriented interfaces compatible with multiple streams of broadband traffic across few packages at low pin count.

Most of these innovations harness parallelism inherent in communications. The winning approach is modest use of each of these bandwidth-enhancing mechanisms in a mathematically pure and concise architecture. For example, a mediaprocessor with 128-bit, SIGD, 4-operand instructions, four-way issue, and five threads would achieve about 10,000 bits of operand throughput per cycle. This is compatible with very low voltage or the small driver operation needed to save power and silicon area. Efficient uses of these degrees of parallelism, moreover, are within reach of current vectorization and instruction- and thread-scheduling software technology.

Ultimately, the dominant cost in broadband evolution will be the development and maintenance of an enormous body of software. Current microprocessor hardware and software is stretching to accomplish the audio, video, graphics, and GUI processing needed at the presentation and application layers of the communications protocol stack.

Far greater challenges remain at the lower transport to physical layers, where algorithms are evolving to enable broadband and wireless links in the network. The high standards of code robustness needed for these lower layers are inspiring new CASE methodologies, such as symbolic verification. The greatest economy in media processing will derive from amassing rich software development tools around a general and unified programming model that supports the entire communications protocol suite.

John Moussouris is chair and CEO of MicroUnity Systems Engineering, Inc., in Sunnyvale, California, a developer of mediaprocessor architecture and software. Previously, he cofounded and served as vice president of VLSI Development at Mips, where he led the architecture and initial implementation of the Mips microprocessor line. He began his career as a research staff member in VLSI and RISC design at the IBM T.J. Watson Research Center.

functional markets will continue to unfold. Although it is the futurist's job to imagine how computing power will be used in the next century, history shows that incredible innovations will occur only when sufficient computing capability is present. For example, no one predicted the first spreadsheet, and until the first PC appeared on the scene, there was no framework in which such an innovation could come about. Our job is to create the microprocessor and PC platform infra-structure with ever-increasing power and capability; innovative ideas for using them will follow.

As mentioned earlier, one area that I believe will require huge numbers of MIPS (not to mention bandwidth) is human interface enrichment: 3D, rich multimedia, sight, sound, and motion. Tomorrow's applications will increasingly incorporate video, sound, animation, color, 3D images, and other visualization techniques to make PCs and applications easier to use.

The system-on-a-chip, microsystems computer industry
Gordon Bell, Microsoft Corp.

The inevitability of complete computer systems on a chip will create a microsystems industry. In addition, forecasters predict 32-Mbyte memory chips by 1999. So by 2002 we would expect a personal computer on a chip with at least 32 Mbytes, video and audio I/O, built-in speech recognition, and industry-standard buses for mass storage, local area network, and communications.

Technology will stimulate a new computer industry for building application-specific computers that require partnerships among system customers, chip fabricators, ECAD suppliers, intellectual property (IP) owners, and systems builders.

The volume of this new microsystems industry will be huge—at least two orders of magnitude more units than the PC industry. For every PC, there will be thousands of other kinds of systems built around a single-chip computer architecture with on-chip interconnection bus. This architecture will be complete with processor, memory hierarchy, I/O (including speech), firmware, and platform software. Powerful processors will enable firmware to replace hardware.

Silicon Graphics (Mips) supplies the key technology for Nintendo and Sony to build games, and WebTV to build an Internet access set-top. Netscape's Navio licenses software to build Internet consumer access devices including phones, games, and television sets that attempt to replace PCs. (Partners included IBM, NEC, Nintendo, Oracle, Sega, and Sony.) Sun's Microelectronics Division is designing and licensing special processors for the Java language and environment. Acorn licenses its ARM processor. Oracle is licensing its network computer to sell server software. Microsoft has various alliances for designing pocket and set-top computers.

The emerging microsystems industry will encompass

- customers building microsystems for embedded applications like automobiles, room and person monitoring, PC radios, PDAs, telephones, set-top boxes, videophones, and smart refrigerators;
- about a dozen foundries that fabricate microsystems—many in Japan and Korea;
- custom companies such as VLSI Technology and LSI Logic that supply "core" IP and take the systems responsibility;
- existing computer system companies like Digital Equipment Corporation, Hewlett-Packard, IBM, Silicon Graphics, and Sun that have large software invest-

ments tied to particular architectures and software;
- fab-less and chipless IP companies that supply designs for royalty;
- ECAD companies that synthesize logic and provide design services (Cadence and Synopsys);
- circuit wizards who design fast or low-power memories (VLSI libraries), analog for audio (which is also a DSP application), radio and TV tuners, cellular radios, GPSs, and micromechanical structures;
- varieties of processors from traditional CISC and RISC to DSP and multimedia;
- computer-related applications that require designers to understand a great deal of software and algorithms (communications protocols and MPEG); and
- proprietary interface companies like Rambus developing proprietary circuits and signaling standards (traditional IP).

Like previous computer generations stemming from Moore's law, a microsystem will most likely have a common architecture. It will consist of an instruction set architecture such as that of the 8088, Mips, or ARM; a physical or bus interconnect that is wholly on the chip and used to interconnect processor memory and a variety of I/O interfaces (disk, Ethernet, audio); and software to support realtime and end-use applications. As in the past, common architectures are essential to support the myriad of new chips economically.

Will this new industry just be an evolution of custom microcontroller and microprocessor suppliers, or a new structure like the one that created the minicomputer, PC, and workstation industries? Will computer companies make the transition to microsystems companies, or will they just be IP players? Who will be the microsystems companies? What's the role for software companies?

Thirty-six ECAD, computer, and semiconductor firms announced an "alliance" for this purpose on September 4, 1996. [See IEEE Micro, Oct. 1996, p. 2.—Ed.]

Gordon Bell is a computer industry consultant-at-large and senior researcher at Microsoft Corp. in Washington, and former head of R&D at Digital. He is a member of various boards, has participated in several start-ups (including the Computer Museum), authored High Tech Ventures, *and won various awards including the 1991 National Medal of Technology and the IEEE von Neumann Medal. http://www.research.microsoft.com/research/barc/gbell.*

The consumer market segment, rather than the business market segment, is driving PC development in this area. Although the business market struggles with how to interpret and present enormous amounts of information more clearly, home users are leading business people in discovering creative ways to solve problems graphically. There are huge opportunities for enterprising application designers to incorporate 3D visualization in clarifying complex business information. More powerful processors with powerful graphics make it easy to display information visually rather than numerically and therefore easier to interpret the information. PCs with smart user interfaces will enable their users to become active seekers of information rather than passive absorbers.

Some argue that, in the face of the runaway success of the Internet, less rather than more processing power is needed on the desktop. So-called network computers on the drawing board today allow users to download necessary "applets" and data for temporary use. These devices may find a niche, but the amount of processing power on the desktop (or in the living room) will depend on the kind of Internet experience users wish to have. If they simply want to browse through traditional data types, a less powerful processor may suffice. However, if they want a rich multimedia experience, viewing information with 3D images and sound will require considerable MIPS.

Another area that urgently needs attention is the historic lag between hardware and software development. Software has always lagged behind available hardware; just as an application takes advantage of new hardware capabilities, vendors release the next generation of hardware. Widespread object-oriented design may help close this gap, but we need breakthroughs in software development to help software keep pace with hardware developments. I believe this is an area of enormous opportunity. Whoever is first to fully take advantage of the coming microprocessor power to offer innovative applications will be the unquestioned leader.

THE MICROPROCESSOR DEVELOPMENT path we've been on for the past 25 years can easily continue into the next 10. Performance can continue to advance until we reach close to a stunning 400 million transistors on a 1.7-inch chip in the year 2006. However, manufacturing capital costs will be in the multibillion-dollar range, necessitating huge volumes to drive down unit price. Besides the huge cost of manufacturing, we have big technological hurdles to overcome before we realize such a chip. We need to know how to test and validate 400 million transistors, how to connect them, power them, and cool them.

Once in hand, however, computing power of such magnitude will set the stage for huge innovations and market segment opportunities in everything from business computing to "edu-tainment" products for kids. One thing I can predict with certainty: Micro 2006 will surprise us all with applications and devices that will dramatically change our world. 📖

Acknowledgments

I thank fellow Intel employees Richard Wirt and Wen-Hann Wang for assistance in gathering and formulating prediction data.

References

1. P.P. Gelsinger et al., "Microprocessors Circa 2000," *IEEE Spectrum*, Oct. 1989, pp. 43-47.
2. P.P. Gelsinger et al., "2001: A Microprocessor Odyssey," *Technology 2001, The Future of Computing and Communications*, D. Leebaert, ed., The MIT Press, Cambridge, Mass., 1991, pp. 95-113.
3. *The National Technology Roadmap for Semiconductors*, Semiconductor Industry Assoc., San Jose, Calif., 1995.
4. R.P. Colwell and R.L. Steck, "A 0.6 μm BiCMOS Processor With Dynamic Execution," *Proc. Int'l Solid-State Circuits Conf.*, IEEE, Piscataway, N.J., 1995, p. 136.
5. U. Weiser, "Intel MMX Technology—An Overview," *Proc. Hot Chips Symp.*, Aug. 1996, p. 142.
6. "Special Issue: Celebrating the 25th Anniversary of the Microprocessor," *Microprocessor Report*, Aug. 5, 1996.

Albert Y.C. Yu is senior vice president and general manager of the Microprocessor Products Group at Intel Corporation. He has responsibility over Intel Architecture Processor products such as the Pentium, Pentium Pro, and future microprocessors. He also oversees platform architecture, design technology, microprocessor software products, and microcomputer research labs.

Yu received his PhD and MS from Stanford University and his BS from the California Institute of Technology, all in electrical engineering. He is a senior member of the IEEE and the Computer Society.

Author Index

Subject Index